THE
BILL JAMES
BASEBALL
ABSTRACT
1986

Also by Bill James
The Bill James Historical Abstract

THE BILL JAMES BASEBALL ABSTRACT 1986

Bill James

Ballantine Books • New York

Library of Congress Catalog Card Number: 85-90905
ISBN 345-33178-8

Manufactured in the United States of America

First Edition: April 1986

10 9 8 7 6 5 4 3 2 1

This book is dedicated to John and Sue Dewan.

CONTENTS

ACKNOWLEDGMENTS

I have nobody much to thank this year, nobody but Susie, who has (as is her wont) invested a few months of her life in this book and a few more in me. I've got nobody to thank except a few thousand readers, a few dozen people who work for Random House, a few hundred especially hard core baseball fans, some people who helped me in earlier years, a few miscellaneous friends and supporters. Maybe I should run them in alphabetical order:

Geoff Beckman is a Cleveland Indians fan who supports *Project Scoresheet,* and has written a comment inside these pages, which is appreciated.

Steven Copley is a displaced Astros fan, lives in the San Jose area, who has done some bits and pieces of research for me over the last two or three years. Thanks, and say hi to Kathy.

Liz Dahransoff is a super agent.

John Dewan will be explained more later.

Sue Dewan is John Dewan's wife. You probably could have guessed that. She, too, is one of the people who makes it possible for this book to be what it is.

David Driscoll is working real hard at studying the Toronto Blue Jays, and doing a good job of it. This is a very worthwhile thing to do, and I thank him for it.

Peter Gethers is my editor; at the moment, my long-suffering editor. His suffering is appreciated.

Laura Godfrey suffers along with Peter. Thanks, Laura.

Mike Kopf is a unique and remarkable man who lives in Lawrence, Kansas, runs a bookshop and the local effort of *Project Scoresheet*. His friendship is much valued.

Tim Marcou put a lot of his life into an article for Section IV. One could never ask for as much.

Susan McCarthy is my wife. Heckuva good wife.

Dan Okrent is still appreciated for the role that he played several years ago in bringing this book to the attention of the nation.

Pete Palmer is my esteemed colleague and occasional competitor, without whose assistance it would be a lot tougher to put together much of the information in this book.

Mark Podrazik is one of the workhorses of *Project Scoresheet*. Thanks, Mark.

Chuck Waseleski is a well regarded analyst of the game, who also worked on this book. I guess you know Chuck.

Jeff Welch is doing some similar stuff for the Seattle Mariners.

Craig Wright is a treasured friend and compatriot, also familiar to those of you who read this book annually. Thanks again for all you have done, Craig.

This only scratches the surface of the people who have made contributions of one type or another to the book. Many more will be mentioned here and there. Next year we'll have a new one to mention, should be about ten months old by then. I wanted to thank Willie Mays for being Willie Mays, George Brett for being George

Brett and Frank White for being Frank White. They don't give a hoot for the book, but what the heck, it wouldn't be the same without them, would it? Since the Royals won the World Championship, I'll even thank John Schuerholz for being John Schuerholz. Thanks to D,T,B,TBs,C, the S and LF, LC, I, Stokely and Isadora. As a body cannot be whole and a heart cannot beat without every artery, vein and vessel that brings it blood, so too a writer cannot be whole and a book cannot give off a pulse, unless it draw life from all that lives around it.

INTRODUCTION AND METHODS

Let's take the statement that baseball is 75% pitching. First, it is nearly impossible to know what is meant by this. "Baseball" is a lot of things—you got your games, you got your pennant races, your individual accomplishments, your personalities, your box scores, your anecdotes, your hot dogs; you got your Hot Stove league and your televised games, your All-Star game and your World Series. Does this mean that 75% of all ballgames are determined by who the pitcher is? Does it mean that 75% of ballgames are determined by what the pitcher does? Does it refer to 75% of pennant races? Seventy-five percent of short series? Seventy-five percent of batter/pitcher confrontations? Does it mean that 75% of all tall tales are about pitchers? Does it mean that 75% of all hot dogs are eaten while the pitcher has the ball? What?

It doesn't mean any of those things; it's just a number picked out of mid-air and plunked down in the middle of a bunch of words in a way that seems to make sense, provided you don't think too hard about it—quite a bit like saying that "Philosophy is 75% God," "Movies are 75% acting," or "Sex is 75% mental, 25% physical." Or "The statement that baseball is 75% pitching is 90% nonsense."

However, to the extent that it is meaningful, it's false. We don't know what it *does* mean, but there are many things that it *might* mean. If pitching were the dominant part of the game, then there are many other, more specific statements which we would expect to be true. None of them are true. For example:

The teams which have the best pitching staffs would win the pennants 75% of the time. Doesn't happen. The team which has the best earned run average in the league wins the pennant just as often as the team which scores the most runs— but no more often. The correlation of team wins to runs allowed is virtually the same as the correlation of team wins to runs scored.

In a game, the team which has the better pitcher starting would win 75% of the time. Doesn't happen. On a very rare occasion, you might have a pitcher, like Dwight Gooden in 1985, who wins 75% of his starts—but it is a very rare occasion, indeed. If you're saying that "Pitching is 75% of baseball when Dwight Gooden is on the mound, so long as Babe Ruth isn't hitting," I might buy it.

In a free market economy, pitchers would make the most money, since they would be the most sought after players. Hasn't happened. In fact, on the average pitchers make *less* money than players at almost any other position.

Teams would never trade a regular pitcher for a regular player. Think about it—if you've got a 25-man roster with nine pitchers, who have 75% of the value, and 16 other players, who represent 25% of the value of the roster, are you going to trade one pitcher for one hitter? Of course not—but teams do trade pitchers for hitters every winter.

The standard deviation of runs allowed would be larger than the standard deviation of runs scored. If pitching were 75% of the game, then one would expect the differences between teams created by pitching to be larger than those created by hitting. But they aren't; the standard deviations of runs scored and runs allowed are almost the same.

Pitchers would monopolize the award voting. If people really believed that baseball was 75% pitching, then one might expect 75% of the players in the Hall of Fame to be pitchers. They aren't. One might expect 75% of Most Valuable Players to be pitchers. They aren't. Even in the era before the Cy Young Award began to split the vote, pitchers won less than 40% of Most Valuable Player Awards. Pitchers don't win 75% of Rookie of the Year Awards.

The most accurate formulas for predicting wins and losses from runs scored and runs allowed would have to give more weight to runs allowed—representing the team's pitching—than to runs scored. Again, it doesn't happen that way; in fact, the most accurate methods for predicting wins and losses from runs scored and runs allowed weight the two elements evenly— and no formula can be developed which retains a similar degree of accuracy while emphasizing one element over the other.

Teams would put most of their effort into developing strong pitching staffs. Managers would spend most of their time working with their pitchers. Clubs would employ more pitching coaches than hitting coaches or any other kind of coaches. Indeed, if baseball were 75% pitching, then one would expect that most managers and most coaches would be former pitchers, since they would be best qualified to deal with the most important part of the game.

Doesn't happen. Managers spend as much time working with hitters as they do with pitchers. Teams employ as many hitting coaches as pitching coaches. Ex-pitchers are rarely hired as managers; most managers were infielders or catchers.

Almost all first-round draft picks would be pitchers. Less than half of first-round draft picks are pitchers.

Pitchers would be the dominant force in determining where and when each offensive event occurs. In fact, the identity of the pitcher is the recessive element of any such determination; the identity of the hitter is the dominant element.

What I mean by that is that the "spread of occurrence" for any offensive incident is greater for hitters than it is for pitchers:

No pitcher allows home runs as often as Dale Murphy hits home runs. No pitcher allows home runs as seldom as Bob Dernier hits home runs.

No pitcher allows hits as often as Wade Boggs gets hits. No pitcher, not even Dwight Gooden, allows hits as infrequently as Steve Lake will get a hit.

No pitcher strikes out hitters as often as Rob Deer strikes out. No pitcher strikes out hitters as rarely as Bill Buckner strikes out.

This is true of every significant area of performance, including those things like walks and hit batsmen, which are usually considered to be controlled by the pitcher.

And what does that mean? It means that in order to create a working model or simulation of a baseball game, you must allow the hitters to be the dominant, shaping force in the game.

And *if* baseball were 75% pitching, one would not expect that to be true.

In short, none of it is true. We cannot say for certain that baseball is not 75% pitching, but we can say these two things: 1) that the statistical patterns which one would expect to manifest themselves in such an event do not occur, and 2) that while people may *say* that baseball is 75% pitching, no one acts in a manner consistent with this belief. The general manager who says that baseball is 75% pitching will turn around and trade his number-two starting pitcher to get an outfielder. The owner who says that baseball is 75% pitching will still pay out more money to keep the Gold Glove shortstop than he will to keep the relief ace. The manager who says that baseball is 75% pitching will spend an hour a day figuring out batting orders and an hour a week lining out his pitching plans. The reporter who says that baseball is 75% pitching will still vote for Willie McGee over Dwight Gooden as the Most Valuable Player. *No one in baseball acts as if he really believes that baseball is 75% pitching.*

And we are left to conclude that it is probably false.

I have to start the book somewhere, right? Hi. I'm Bill James. Let's assume that you're standing in your local bookstore flipping through the pages and trying to decide whether to buy this book or save the money for a down payment on a pair of nylon underpants for grandpa's birthday. What you have been reading there is a basic sample of what I do for a living. I pick up something that somebody in baseball has said, and I ask "If this were true, what specific consequences would flow from that truth? If this were true, what else would also be true?" In this year's book, I looked into questions like whether artificial turf shortens a player's career, whether teams which finish the season playing well play better in following seasons than teams of equal ability which finish the season poorly, whether college-educated players show more career growth than comparable players who didn't go to college, how often teams change managers after good seasons and after bad seasons, what the *de facto* standards for the Hall of Fame are, whether power pitchers are particularly effective early in the season, whether the types of teams that we think of as doing well on artificial turf actually do . . .

He could go on and does, as a reviewer once wrote about me. I also get into a lot of issues relating to only one team or one individual, like how Gene Mauch's teams have done late in the season and how they have done in one-run games (over the course of his career), what have been the characteristics of successful teams which play in Fenway Park, what a player's chances are of getting 3000 hits . . . sometimes these questions become rather theoretical, like "How many runs would the St. Louis Cardinals score if they didn't steal bases all the time?" If you enjoy thinking about questions like these, and you have a certain amount of patience with statistical information that relates to them, then you'll enjoy this book; if you're not interested, you won't.

I also get side-tracked into a number of issues regarding the decisions of managers and organizations, plus the inevitable arguments about who is better than who and why. That's not what the book is *about*, really, but unlike most people who write about baseball, I don't go hide in the closet when those questions are asked; I don't mind explaining that Steve Garvey is washed up or that Rafael Ramirez is lousy no matter how many people try to tell you that he isn't. I do go hide in the closet when it comes to predictions. I don't try to pick the pennant races.

In the course of studying these things, I uncover a great many more facts and relationships than I can possibly present, and I string these along whenever the spirit moves me. Hitters fac-

ing Dave Stieb last season hit .260 with nobody out in the inning, .208 with one out and .179 with two out. The New York Mets last year had 63 games in which by the end of the fifth inning they had established a lead which they would never relinquish. The St. Louis Cardinals were 55–5 in games in which they scored more than five runs. The Baltimore Orioles scored 397 runs last year in innings of three or more runs—far more than any other major league team.

Whether you want to know any of this stuff is something that only you can decide. All of this info bears some relationship to some question, or it wouldn't have been studied; for example, the belief that the difference between the good teams and the bad teams in baseball is in what they do when the game is on the line is clearly disproven by the simple fact that the differences between teams are just as large in the first three innings as they are in the last three. If all of the games had ended after four innings, the 1985 St. Louis Cardinals would have finished 77–54 (with 31 ties) and the Blue Jays would have been 78–52, whereas the Texas Rangers would have been 48–75 and the San Francisco Giants 55–73.

You can credit that information to Jeffrey Eby of San Diego, by the way. In the ten years that I have been studying questions like these, people have gotten in the habit of doing their own studies and sending them to me. Some of these studies are fascinating (to me, that's who), and I pass them on to you. I wish I could pass *all* of them on to you, but I can't, so I have to try to decide what is interesting and what isn't, and pass along the most interesting stuff, along with the names and addresses of the most interesting people. The *Baseball Abstract,* in this way, has become the focal point of the discussion of a certain range of questions about baseball. We have imitators, but they essentially fail to understand this—they think what we're writing about is *statistics,* rather than *questions*—and thus the book continues to occupy a unique position in the baseball marketplace. These on-going discussions, often carried from year to year, are one of the things that will make up this book.

Another thing that gets carried along from year to year is a collection of methods or analytical "tools" which are used every year to analyze different questions. These are discussed, which is not to say explained, in the next article, *Here We Go Again*.

In the course of each year, I develop some

new methods and refine some old ones. This year's developments are discussed in the three articles which follow that.

Then, after some charts and stuff, we'll get into the main sections of the book, which are the team comments and the player ratings and comments. Then I'll enclose a few articles and things which don't exactly fit in anywhere else, and then I'll close for the year. This, along with a few gratuitous and unnecessary comments about my dogs, my wife, my childhood, jazz music, talk show hosts, sharks, monkeys, teddy bears and the nature of man and space, constitutes *The Baseball Abstract*.

HERE WE GO AGAIN

The search for new knowledge about baseball is called sabermetrics. Sabermetrics is the systematic, scientific (if you will) study of baseball-related questions.

There are hundreds of established principles of sabermetrics, the results of studies which have been made over the past fifteen or twenty years. Most studies are failures; they identify no effect. When a study is successful, it does one of two things: it yields a specific piece of information, or it develops a method which can be used repeatedly to analyze some specific type of problem. Most of the new pieces of information which are generated in a year are too small to repeat from year to year. Most of the methods which are developed are of use only to a specific question. This section explains the major principles and methods which are used and/or referred to repeatedly in sabermetrics.

We'll start with the runs created method. We are all in the habit of looking at a player's offensive statistics, and summing these up in an informal way. We look first at a player's batting average, and we place a certain weight on that. We look at the home runs, the doubles, the triples, the stolen bases, and we put a certain weight on each of those. We look at the runs scored and RBI. Some people put a very heavy weight on those; some people don't trust them. Some people like to look at strikeouts and walks, but data on that is not so easy to come by. At least it wasn't before the weekly lists in *USA Today*.

The problem is that the weight that one person places on each element of the offensive construct is different from the weight that the next person places on each. One guy thinks that batting average is the main thing to look at; the next guy thinks that power is the key element. How does one determine what the proper relationship is?

The proper relationship is the relationship to runs. A hitter at the plate is attempting to produce runs for his team. But individual "run" and "RBI" counts are so heavily polluted by team context that they are of questionable value in assessing the contribution of the individual. Hubie Brooks drove in 100 runs in 1985 because he had the good fortune to bat third and fourth (not at the same time) behind Tim Raines, the National League's best leadoff man, while Kevin Bass drove in only 68 runs despite hitting for the same average with more power. No sensible person would conclude from this that Brooks' RBI count proves him to be a better hitter than Kevin Bass, inasmuch as it is obvious that he benefits greatly from his position in the Montreal batting order.

We can't directly see how many runs each player creates—but we can see how many runs each team creates. By studying the relationships of singles, doubles, triples, etc. to runs resulting on the *team* level, we can apply those relationships to the performance of individuals, and thus distinguish *individual* contributions from *team* context. If a combination of 173 hits, 31 homers, 84 walks and 5 stolen bases in 677 plate appearances would cause a team to score 122 runs, then we figure that a player who has 173 hits, 31 homers, 84 walks and 5 stolen bases in 677 plate appearances has created 122 runs. We'll call him Eddie Murray.

At this point, I usually launch into an explanation of what those relationships are, what the formulas are which predict them; the full show comes replete with charts, diagrams and occasionally graphs. This time I'm not going to do that. It is not terribly important that you understand what those formulas are. If you want to know, they are explained briefly in the appendix.

What is more important is that you understand that they do work. So far as I know, there is no case in the recorded history of baseball in which a team should have scored a large number of runs—let us say 820—but actually scored a small number of runs—let us say 650. The formulas are imperfect, of course; there are many factors of a real-world baseball economy which we cannot measure, or which we can measure only very imperfectly. Base-running is one of those. The ability to move baserunners by making outs—that legendary little thing which doesn't show up in the box score—is another one. The ability to create extra runs by producing at key moments, if such an ability exists, is poorly measured, and not really accounted for in the current formulas.

These unmeasured areas occasionally might cause a very significant error in the estimate of the runs created by each player. They might occasionally cause a team which should lead the league in runs scored to finish, let us say, fourth in the league in runs scored. Maybe fifth. On rare occasions.

But the fact that the formulas work with the accuracy that they do have is a way of saying that there are essentially stable relationships between batting average, home runs, walks, other offensive elements—and runs. The relationship is not random or arbitrary. If a team hits .252 but leads the league in runs scored, there is a reason for it, and the reason for it can always be found in looking at the other offensive statistics. The formulas *do* illustrate for us the relative values of the various offensive elements.

Those relative values have been studied at great length over the past few decades by men such as Pete Palmer, Paul Johnson, Craig Wright and myself. Three essential conclusions can sum up those studies:

1) The old idea that a high-average hitter is the man who makes an offense go, and that low-average power hitters don't really do much for the team, is nonsense. Tony Gwynn hit .317 last year, and he created about 88 runs for his team, which is a good total. But Dwight Evans created many more than that (about 112, or 24 more than Gwynn), and he hit only .263. Power is an extremely important element in the production of runs.

2) Don't ignore the number of walks that a player draws. The number of walks drawn by a player is far more important than many of the more commonly seen statistics, such as how many doubles and triples he hits.

3) On balance, stolen bases have very little to do with runs scored.

These are not arguments, theories or opinions; they are inevitable conclusions which are forced upon us by the stable relationships within offensive statistics. Those relationships can be stated in many different formulas, with slightly different results—but the broad outline of the relationships is clear and consistent, no matter how it is stated.

The major league players creating the most runs in 1985 were George Brett (146), Wade Boggs (143), Rickey Henderson (138), Don Mattingly (136), Dale Murphy (131), Willie McGee (123), Eddie Murray (122), Pedro Guerrero (121), Tim Raines (119), and Kirk Gibson (118). Twelve other players created over a hundred runs for their teams. Runs created counts can be considered equivalent to runs scored or RBI on a one-to-one basis, except that they focus on the individual accomplishments of one player, rather than being so heavily influenced by the players surrounding in the batting order.

There are two statistics which, by themselves and without the aid of any considerations about base running, base stealing, clutch hitting or gravity waves, will predict the number of runs scored by a team. Those two statistics are also available for individual players.

Those two statistics are on-base percentage and slugging percentage.

A team which does well in those two areas will always do well in runs scored, no matter what else they don't do. They can be slow as the devil, they can be terrible bunters, bad clutch hitters, stupid baserunners and completely inept at hitting behind the runner. They will still score runs.

A team which does poorly in those two areas

will always do poorly in runs scored, no matter how well they do anything else.

In analyzing baseball teams, in analyzing offenses and evaluating players, we will use this knowledge repeatedly. An estimate of the number of runs created by each major league player will be presented in the team comments, with the official statistics.

Another relationship which will be referred to repeatedly, though less often, is that known as the Pythagorean theorem: the ratio between a team's wins and losses will be about the same as the ratio between the square of their runs scored and the square of their runs allowed. Again, this relationship can be stated in a number of different ways, but what it always comes down to is that if you score 10% more runs than you allow, you're going to win about 21% more games than you lose. In analyzing teams, this knowledge is very useful because it allows differences in terms of runs to be stated as wins, and vice versa. *Singles, doubles and triples are the bits and pieces of runs; their relationship is stated in the runs created formulas. Runs and runs allowed are the bits and pieces of wins; their relationship is stated in the Pythagorean formula.*

It is by their relationship to wins that runs acquire their significance. The next major point of sabermetrics which needs to be repeated annually is this: that all baseball statistics are circular. Every success in baseball is also a failure. Every win is also a loss. Every strikeout by a pitcher is a strikeout against a hitter. Every home run hit is a home run allowed. Every run scored by an offense is a run allowed by a defense. *The sum total of all baseball statistics is the same in every decade, the same in every season, the same in every game and in every inning and on every pitch. It is always .500.* The players in some games will hit over .400; in other games they will hit near .100—but the sum total of measured successes and measured failures is exactly the same whether the score of a game is 12–11, 1–0 or 12–0.

It is, for this reason, of paramount importance to try to understand the meaning of what the player has done in its own context. Missing this essential point, one would wind up with the conclusion that almost everybody who played in 1930 was a great hitter, while almost no one who played in the 1960s was of the same level. One way to put it would be that if a suit cost a dollar in 1900 and a gallon of milk cost $1.45 in 1986,

that doesn't mean that the suits of 1900 were poorly made or the milk of 1986 is especially delicious. It just means that the cost of things has changed. Similarly, if a utility infielder hits .320 in 1930 and a batting champion hits .301 in 1968, this doesn't mean that the utility infielders of 1930 were better hitters than the batting champions of 1968. It just means that the cost of a win in terms of hits has dropped sharply in the intervening years. *To understand the value of any accomplishment in baseball, we must constantly relate the accomplishment to the context.*

Offensive winning percentage is one of the methods which does this; it states the relationship between offensive productivity and offensive context. The Pythagorean formula is used to translate the player's runs created into a won/lost equivalent. If a team scores five runs a game and allows four, they will win about 61.0% of their games (five squared divided by five squared plus four squared). If a player creates five runs a game in a prevailing context of four runs a game, then his offensive winning percentage would be the same .610—his offense, placed up against the context.

This method has severe limitations; there are many things you can't do with it. But it is useful for comparing players between eras or between conditions in which run levels vary greatly. A player who created 4.00 runs per 27 outs in 1968 might be as valuable as a player who creates 6.00 runs per game now, when runs are more plentiful. A player who creates 80 runs with only 300 outs used might be more valuable than one who creates 100 runs with 450 outs.

The major league players with the highest offensive winning percentages in 1985 were George Brett (.861), Pedro Guerrero (.851), Rickey Henderson (.802), Darryl Strawberry (.793), Willie McGee (.791), Tim Raines (.788), Wade Boggs (.781), Dale Murphy (.762), Mike Schmidt (.757), and Jack Clark (.755). What George Brett's .861 offensive winning percentage literally means is that a team of hitters who all hit like George Brett, with an average combination of pitching and defense, would win 86.1% of its games.

There are two major variables which define context: time and place. The level of run production has changed dramatically over time, and adjustments must always be made for this when comparing players of different eras. The ways in which runs are produced also change over time, although less dramatically; some adaptations in the runs created formulas must be made. The levels of run production also change dramatically from place to place. In 1985 there were 822 runs scored in Wrigley Field (ten per game) whereas there were only 568 runs scored in Dodger Stadium (seven per game). This difference is not created by the personnel on the teams; in fact, when those teams were on the road there were 100 more runs scored in Dodger games than in Cub games (693–593).

Or, to put it another way, ballparks create gigantic illusions in player statistics. It is probably about ten times more difficult to hit .300 in Dodger Stadium than it is in Wrigley Field. Baseball men have known for many years—actually, one might well say that they have always known—that park characteristics can influence the statistics of those who play there. They have always known this, but until the last ten years there was very little systematic evidence available about the subject. There is a great deal of such evidence available now, and it shows beyond any question that those park illusions are of a fairly massive nature. Pedro Guerrero in 1985 hit .320 with 33 home runs in Dodger Stadium. It is very likely that, had he played in Wrigley Field, he would have hit closer to .340 with 45 to 50 home runs. His tremendous offensive productivity, in the very difficult hitter's park, is the reason his offensive winning percentage is so high (.851, highest in the National League). Conversely, if Orel Hershiser pitched in Wrigley Field, it is unlikely that his earned run average would be below 3.00.

It is not possible to make accurate evaluations of any player's accomplishments without adjusting for this bias. The effect of the park in which the man plays must constantly be kept in mind when evaluating his accomplishments. The great majority of batting championships are won by players who play in parks which are conducive to high batting averages. Most home run champions play in home run hitters' parks. Almost all ERA champions play in pitchers' parks. Almost all strikeout champions play in parks which have poor visibility for the hitter.

I used to allow for this by making "park adjustments"—that is, since Dodger Stadium reduces offense by about 15 to 18%, I would increase the runs created by the hitters who play there by 7 and a half to 9 percent. Now I make the adjustment by placing the offensive produc-

tion of the player directly in the context of his team, which accomplishes the same essential goal and is much simpler. If you are not thoroughly familiar with the characteristics of all the parks, you might want to pay careful attention to the information which goes right below the team headings this year, which gives the number of runs scored by the team at home and on the road over a period of ten years, along with a great deal of related information.

There are six other established methods which will be referred to from time to time throughout the second and third sections of this book. Those are:

1) The Value Approximation Method. The Value Approximation Method is a quick, rough way of assessing the total offensive and defensive contribution of a player in a simple integer, such as "9" or "14." The method is not intended to provide the basis of player-to-player comparisons, but is very useful when comparing groups of seasons.

2) The Defensive Spectrum. The Defensive Spectrum is an arrangement of defensive positions, reading from left to right designated hitter, first base, left field, right field, third base, center field, second base, shortstop. The defensive spectrum has many ramifications in the construction of a ballclub, deriving from the essential facts that a) the right-most positions make the largest defensive demands in terms of raw skills, b) capable players are much more scarce at the right end of the defensive spectrum than at the left and c) the differences among players tend to be larger at the right end of the spectrum than at the left.

3) The Brock6 System. The Brock6 system, an evolution of the Brock2 system explained a year ago, is a set of several hundred interlocking formulas which are used to project final career totals for active players. The system makes no claims to accuracy, being merely an objective system which probably is not a lot less accurate than just making a wild guess.

4) Range Factor. A player's range factor is the number of plays per game that he has made in the field—or, in the case of adjusted range factor, introduced and explained by Tim Marcou in section four, the number of plays made per inning. While range factor, *like every other statistic,* is subject to a number of biases and extraneous influences, it is nonetheless apparent that the players who cover the most ground in the

field also wind up making the most plays per game, and thus that their ability to cover ground is measured in most cases in this category.

5) The minors to majors projection system. What a player will hit in the major leagues can be projected with a very high degree of accuracy from what he has hit in the minors. It is not dead simple; it is not unusual for a player to hit .320 with 18 home runs in the minor leagues, and still not be able to hit in the majors. There are illusions which have to be adjusted for. But when those illusions are removed, there is an extremely strong degree of similarity between what players hit as minor leaguers, and what they will hit in the majors.

6) The Favorite Toy. The Favorite Toy is a simple system which is used to estimate the chance that a player will reach some particular, very difficult goal. What is Wade Boggs' chance to get 3000 hits? This method would make an estimate of that (30%). The method is based on the combination of time, momentum and distance; a player's chance of reaching the goal depends upon his age (thus how much time he has left), his momentum (how fast he is approaching the goal) and the distance (how far he needs to travel to reach the goal).

There are many other standard methods which are used in sabermetrics. I'll explain them as they come up, or maybe I won't and will just let you wonder. It's a continual battle trying to make sure that each edition of this book is cross-indexed so as to be self-explanatory, but I usually manage to get things explained somewhere; if you don't understand something you can refer to a) the appendix, or b) earlier editions of the *Abstract*. Every year it gets worse, and the next thing I've got to do here is make next year's problem worse by introducing this year's new methods.

BASEBALL'S BIG HONOR

Which active players will go into the Hall of Fame? What kind of combination of accomplishments does it take to assure a berth in the Hall? What are Lou Whitaker's chances of making it into the Hall of Fame?

Several years ago, I developed a method to look into those questions. This is, depending on how you take it, either a development of or a retreat from that method. That method had a good many problems, but rather than explaining them all and explaining how this method differs from that one, I'm just going to explain this as if it were a brand-new method, and then later make a few remarks about how and why it differs from the original.

What we are trying to do here is not to decide who *should* go into the Hall of Fame. What we are looking at is who *will,* who is likely to and who is not likely to. This is a "point award" system, so many points for hitting .300, so many points for driving in 100 runs, etc. The more points you have, the better chance you have to get into the Hall of Fame. The system is structured so that a player with more than 100 points can be considered a likely Hall of Famer. The area from 70 to 130 is a gray area; some players who are in there will go in, others will not. Players who fail to reach 70, in general, have very little chance to reach the Hall of Fame, while those who clear 130 can be considered virtually automatic selections. There are exceptions.

I constructed this method by an after-the-fact analysis of voting patterns, combined with a limited amount of intuition to cover things that can't be entirely cleared up by the voting. I wrote down a list of ten players at each position, shading gradually from the certain, over-poweringly qualified Hall of Famers, down through the marginal Hall of Famers, the not-quite-Hall of Famers and the not-even-close Hall of Famers. Among catchers, for example, I started with Johnny Bench and Yogi Berra, and worked down through Rick Ferrell and Ray Schalk, then shifted to Bill Freehan, Johnny Edwards and finally came out at Joe Glenn (a part-time player from the thirties). At shortstop I started with Honus Wagner and worked through Joe Cronin and Phil Rizzuto, ending with Woodie Held.

For each player listed, I summarized his accomplishments in a single column, showing how many times he had hit .300, how many All-Star games he had played in, how many MVP awards he had won, how many division, league or World Championship teams he had played on, how many times he had led the league in hits, doubles, batting average . . . about 60 such pieces of information, all together. A few of those seemed to bear little relationship to Hall of Fame selection, or else merely re-stated something which was better measured somewhere else, and were eliminated from the method. Others seemed to bear a very close relationship to Hall of Fame selection, and were given particular significance. For example, among players who play a key defensive position (up the middle, you know), playing on championship teams is clearly very important to Hall of Fame voters. Almost all of the marginal selections there, like Joe Tinker, Earle Combs and Pee Wee Reese, were players who were prominent or perennial champions. Since much of the contribution of defensive players misses the standard statistical assessments, it tends to be free-floating, and easily colored by other influences. Players who play on winning teams automatically negate many of the criticisms which befall other players; all of their peripheral accomplishments tend to be interpreted in light of the success of their teams. Players who have very long careers at key defensive positions usually go into the Hall of Fame, regardless of how well they hit.

On the other hand, I found that playing on championship teams was not particularly important at the left-end defensive positions, where players are usually evaluated almost exclusively on the basis of their hitting. Another unmistakeable bias in the voting is that high-average hitters do much better than low-average power hitters who might actually be better players. Many outstanding power hitters, like Rocky Colavito, Del Ennis, Bob Johnson and Frank Howard, have received hardly a wink in the voting, although there are any number of players in the Hall who are no better qualified, players who didn't play a key defensive position or drive in or score as many runs.

Using observations such as this, I played around with different combinations of point awards, trial and error, until I arrived at a set of values which put most of the players who were in the Hall of Fame over 100, and most of those out of the Hall of Fame under 100.

There are two assumptions here, which are not necessarily false but you wouldn't want to bet your daughter on 'em, either. One is that the types of players who have been chosen to the Hall of Fame in the past will continue to be chosen to the Hall of Fame in the future. Of course, the standards for Hall of Fame selection and the tastes of Hall of Fame voters do evolve over time, somewhat. The other is that we can imitate in a series of charts the way in which a number of diverse groups of people will be influenced by statistical information. As is always true, the model is much simpler than the thing which it is supposed to predict, and many things are left out. Yet obviously, Hall of Fame voters *are* influenced by things like hitting .300, leading the league in RBI and playing on championship

teams. Obviously, they are influenced by some of those accomplishments more heavily than by others. There is no reason we shouldn't be able to imitate those influences in a mathematical form—as, in fact, I have.

The system isn't real easy. I'll list all the point awards here; you can skip them if you're not into calculations. If you want to figure the status of other players, the easiest way to do it is to place all the categories and point awards on a chart, kind of like an IRS 1040 Form, and photocopy the form. Use one form for pitchers, one for other players. Managers would require just a real short form. These are the rules:

Award 2½ points for each season the player hits .300 in 100 or more games, 5 points for each season hitting .350, and 15 points for each season hitting .400. (Seasons are never double-counted; the player cannot count a .400 season as a .350 as well.)

Award 5 points for each season of 200 or more hits.

Award 3 points for each season of 100 RBI or 100 runs scored.

Award 2 points for each season the player hits 30 home runs, 4 points for a season of 40 homers, and 10 points for a season of 50 or more homers.

Award 1 point for hitting 35 doubles in a season, 2 points for hitting 45 doubles.

Award ½ of 1 point for each season drawing 100 or more walks.

Award additional points for leading the league: in Batting Average, 6 points, in Home Runs or RBI, 4 points, in Runs scored, 3 points, in Hits or Stolen Bases, 2 points, in Doubles or Triples, 1 point. (Here accomplishments can be double-counted; a player can receive both the 3 points for 100 RBI and the 4 for leading the league in RBI.)

Award 4 points if the player has 2000 career hits, 15 points if he has 2500 hits, 40 points if he has 3000 hits, and 50 points if he has 3500. Again, no double-counting.

Award 3 points if the player has hit 300 career home runs, 10 points for hitting 400 home runs, 20 points for hitting 500 home runs, and 30 points for hitting 600 home runs.

Award 8 points if the player has a career batting average of .300 (in 1500 or more games), 16 points if his career average is .315, 24 points if his career average is .330.

Award 15 points if the player has played 1200

games as a catcher, 30 points if 1400 games at catcher, 45 points if 1600 games at catcher, 60 points if 1800 games at catcher.

Award 15 points if the player has played 1900 games at second base or shortstop, 30 points if 2200 games at second base or shortstop.

Award 15 points if the player has played 2000 games at third base.

Award *an additional* 15 points if the player's total games at shortstop, second base and third base are 2500 or more.

Award 15 points if the player has a career batting average of .275 or better *and* has played 1500 games at second base, shortstop or catcher.

Award 8 points for each Most Valuable Player Award won (Award awards are the same for pitchers as for other players).

Award 5 points for winning the Cy Young Award.

Award 3 points for each All-Star game participated in.

Award 1 point for each Gold Glove the player has won.

Award 1 point if the player was Rookie of the Year.

If the player played *regularly* on a World Championship team, award 6 points (per season) if he was the catcher or shortstop, 5 points if he was the second baseman or center fielder, 3 points if he was the third baseman, 2 points if he was the left fielder or right fielder, 1 point if he was the first baseman or designated hitter.

If the player played regularly on a league champion team (not a World Champion), award 5 points if he was the shortstop or catcher, 3 points if he was the second baseman or center fielder, 1 point if he was the third baseman.

If the player played regularly on a division champion team (not a league champion) award 2 points if he was the shortstop or catcher, 1 point if he was the second baseman, center fielder or third baseman.

For pitchers, award 2 points for each season of 15–17 wins, 4 points for 18–19 wins, 6 points for 20–22 wins, 8 points for 23 or 24 wins, 10 points for 25–29 wins, and 15 points for 30 or more wins.

Award 2 points for each season of 200 strikeouts, 3 points for 250 strikeouts, 6 points for 300 strikeouts.

Award 2 points for each season with a .700 winning percentage (14 or more wins).

Award 1 point for each season with an ERA below 3.00 (50 games or 150 innings). Award 4 points for an ERA below 2.00.

Award 2 points for a season of 20 or more saves, 5 points for 30 or more saves.

Award 1 point for pitching a no-hitter.

Award 2 points for leading the league in ERA. Award 1 point for leading the league in games, wins, innings, winning percentage, strikeouts, saves or shutouts. Award ½ of 1 point for leading the league in complete games.

Award 5 points for 150 career wins. Award 8 points for 175 career wins. Award 10 points for 200 career wins. Award 15 points for 225 career wins. Award 20 points for 250 career wins. Award 25 points for 275 career wins. Award 35 points for 300 career wins.

Award 1 point for a career winning percentage over .550 (200 or more decisions). Award 3 points for a career winning percentage over .575, 5 points for a winning percentage over .600, 8 points for a winning percentage over .625.

Award 10 points if the pitcher has a career earned run average below 3.00.

Award 10 points if the pitcher has 200 career saves. Award 20 points if the pitcher has 300 career saves.

Award 10 points if the pitcher has pitched in 700 career games. Award 20 points if he has pitched in 850 career games. Award 30 points if he has pitched in 1000 career games.

Award 10 points for 3000 career strikeouts. Award 20 points for 4000 career strikeouts.

Award 2 points for each World Series start, and 2 for each World Series win. Award 1 point for each relief appearance in a World Series game.

Award 1 point for each win in league play-offs.

Total points awarded to pitchers for post-season play are limited to 20.

For managers, award 2 points for each season managed (100 or more games in the season).

Award 8 points for each World Championship team managed.

Award 5 points for managing a league champion.

Award 3 points for managing a division champion.

Award 1 point for each 200 career wins.

Award 1 point for each team managed to 100 or more wins (in a season).

That's all. The essential difference between this method and the earlier one is that the earlier method attempted to draw an absolute line at 100 points; 100 you're in, 99 you're out. With regard to retrospective selections, the method was accurate in doing this; the players who were above 100 were almost all in, and those who were under 100 were almost all out.

But in order to do so, the method had to focus on and exaggerate those features which distinguished the marginally qualified Hall of Famers who were in from the marginally qualified Hall of Famers who were out. This tended to distort the values of accomplishments in the more ordinary case. This made the method more accurate when looking backward, but probably less accurate when looking forward.

Further, since I was attempting *only* to make an in/out selection—there were, as I wrote then, no partial or percentage qualifications—the method had to remain silent on the value of many accomplishments. The system could make judgments only on those features which distinguish Hall of Famers from non-Hall of Famers in a specific case. Since there was no specific case in which one could see that winning Gold Gloves led to a player's being selected to the Hall of Fame, I couldn't make use of Gold Glove Awards. Since there was no specific case in which a player got into the Hall of Fame by hitting doubles, I had to ignore the doubles category.

I decided to revamp the system on the basis of a different assumption, that being that there was an actual gray area. True, every player is either in the Hall of Fame or he's not; there are no half-steps. But it is also true that there are some players who are in the Hall of Fame while others of essentially comparable accomplishments are not. *That* is the gray area, the area of statistical accomplishments from which some players are selected and others not. I had eliminated the gray area; I had found ways to project some players forward from it and hold others back—but to some extent those methods focused not on the valid distinctions which were meaningful to Hall of Fame voters, but on the happenstance characteristics of those who were fortunate enough to be selected. This also made the method so complex that it would only apply to players at a few positions; there was no way to make a guess about a shortstop or a catcher, since they had totally different "biases" or "idiosyncrasies" than those which worked in distinguishing among outfielders.

Why I didn't see this earlier, I don't know. Anyway, the modification of the goal of having players who were "in" at exactly 100 points—a tactical retreat, we'll call it—left me free to deal with a lot more information, reducing the weight given to a few major accomplishments and constructing a much more broad-based system. There is little specific evidence about the value of the Gold Glove award because the award only started in the late fifties, and the great majority of Hall of Famers were retired before then. Nonetheless, there is very clear evidence that defensive ability is an extremely important consideration, and it only makes sense that the Gold Glove selections can be helpful in getting a view of defensive reputations. There may be no specific evidence that scoring 100 runs a year will get you in the Hall of Fame, but there is also no evidence that shows that it doesn't make any contribution, and common sense tells you that it does. If playing on World Championship teams is a key factor for some positions, then it only makes sense that playing on a division champion team is going to turn out to be of some significance, although less.

So we've got a lot more rules here, a lot more information considered. The system is intended *to help the baseball fan monitor the progress of a player toward the Hall of Fame*. It is *not* intended to say who should or should not be selected. I'll give you the point totals of about a hundred players from the past (remember in some cases that these include points as a manager):

Hank Aaron, 405; Dick Allen, 96; Cap Anson, 212; Luis Aparicio, 126; Luke Appling, 142; Earl Averill, 126; Home Run Baker, 81; Dave Bancroft, 78; Ernie Banks, 157; Jake Beckley, 86; Wally Berger, 57; Johnny Bench, 199; Yogi Berra, 255; Walt Bond, 0; Jim Bottomley, 97; Lou Boudreau, 125; Jim Bouton, 16; Roger Bresnahan, 26; Lou Brock, 148; Dan Brouthers, 168; Bobby Brown, 9; Guy Bush, 40; Jim Bunning, 97; Jesse Burkett, 203; Roy Campanella, 105; Campy Campaneris, 71; Max Carey, 83; Orlando Cepeda, 108; Frank Chance, 74; Fred Clarke, 162; Roberto Clemente, 197; Ty Cobb, 463; Mickey Cochrane, 159; Eddie Collins, 257; Earle Combs, 100; Roger Connor, 110; Sam Crawford, 125; Joe Cronin, 175; Mike Cuellar, 71; Kiki Cuyler, 115; Bill Dahlen, 103; Bill Dickey, 180; Bobby Doerr, 78; Hugh Duffy, 169;

Duffy Dyer, 0; Johnny Edwards, 28; Bob Elliott, 58; Ron Fairly, 9; Rick Ferrell, 91; Nellie Fox, 148; Bill Freehan, 70; Frankie Frisch, 223; Charlie Gehringer, 278; Joe Glenn, 0; Goose Goslin, 152; Mule Haas, 16; Stan Hack, 79; Jeff Heath, 23; Woodie Held, 0; Tommy Henrich, 46; Babe Herman, 74; Rogers Hornsby, 387; Carl Hubbell, 140; Catfish Hunter, 106; Joe Jackson, 116; Walter Johnson, 363; Al Kaline, 142; Sandy Koufax, 188; Napoleon Lajoie, 236; Jerry Lumpe, 4; Rabbit Maranville, 74; Eddie Mathews, 151; Willie Mays, 368; Bill Mazeroski, 48; Don Mincher, 6; Stan Musial, 441; Vada Pinson, 89; Pee Wee Reese, 95; Sam Rice, 124; Phil Rizzuto, 84; Brooks Robinson, 143; Frank Robinson, 225; Babe Ruth, 465; Ron Santo, 85; Red Schoendienst, 123; Roy Sievers, 45; Duke Snider, 149; Tris Speaker, 284; Riggs Stephenson, 50; Pie Traynor, 108; Hal Trosky, 77; Honus Wagner, 329; Paul Waner, 252; Hoyt Wilhelm, 100; Ken Williams, 65; Ted Williams, 354; Carl Yastrzemski, 204; Cy Young, 338.

In that list there are 40 eligible Hall of Famers with totals over 130. All of those except one (Nellie Fox) are in the Hall of Fame (and Fox will go as soon as he gets to the Veteran's Committee). There are 16 players in the range 100–129; eleven of the 16 are in the Hall. There are 21 players in the range 70–99, nine are in the Hall, but twelve aren't. There are 21 players listed with totals below 70, of whom only one (Roger Bresnahan) is in the Hall of Fame.

Before I get into the discussions about specific players, I need to say something about how many players get into the Hall of Fame. I will deal here with four "teams" of players (a team selected from each age group), making a total of 48 players. I will say about most of those players that they have at least a pretty good shot at going into the Hall of Fame. You may think that is too many Hall of Famers from one era, but it isn't. There were about 60 players active in the 1925–1930 era who are in the Hall of Fame. Going back just twenty years, there are already 23 players who were active in 1965 who are in the Hall of Fame—and there will probably be at least twice that many in eventually. Those 23 don't include the still-active and recently retired players like Pete Rose, Joe Morgan and Jim Palmer, obvious Hall of Famers. There are many from that era who remain strong candidates in the BBWAA vote, like Billy Williams, Jim Bunning, Catfish

Hunter and Roger Maris. And in the long run, it is not the BBWAA, but the Veteran's Committee, which selects the most players. Although it is the Baseball Writer's Association of America vote which gets the attention, *most* of the players in the Hall of Fame are not there by the BBWAA vote, but by the Veteran's Committee and the other special committees which are set up to cover those missed in the initial go-round.

We don't know for sure that that will continue to be true over a long period of time. But if it is, if the Veteran's Committee continues to come along selecting generously from the left-overs, then eventually it is very likely that players like Tony Oliva, Dick Allen, Elroy Face, Bill Mazeroski and many, many more will be included. We don't know that this will happen, but that's the structure that exists right now, so that's the assumption that we have to go on.

There are probably 150 active players who have *some* chance to make it to the Hall of Fame; I can't deal with all 150 in this article. I don't want to deal with only the best qualified, as this would be repetitious, so I'll select from among the candidates in four groups. The groups are those born in 1947 or before (the old guys), those born 1948–1951 (getting along in years), those born 1952–1956 (still going strong) and those born 1956–1960 (still in their prime). I could consider a few players born after 1960— Gooden, Mattingly, Saberhagen—but that would be very speculative; all I could tell you is that they're going to go if they keep doing the things they've started doing, and they're not if they don't. If you want to know how other players are doing, you have the system.

PLAYERS BORN 1947 OR BEFORE

A player born in 1947 would be, at a minimum, 38 years old for the 1986 baseball season. There are still a good many active players around who fall into this class, due to a remarkable upsurge in career length in the last decade. If these people are going to go into the Hall of Fame, they'd better have done the work by now, because they can't be expected to do too much more. The Hall of Fame candidates include:
Pete Rose, First Base (308 points, born 1941)
Pete Rose is the most overwhelmingly qualified Hall of Fame candidate among active play-

16

ers. He will probably be the first player to be unanimously elected by the Baseball Writer's Association.

Rod Carew, Second Base (235 points, born 1945)

There would be no precedent for denying a Hall of Fame position to any hitter of credentials comparable to Rod Carew's. He is certain to be elected, probably on the first vote.

Tom Seaver, Starting Pitcher (192 points, born 1944)

Obviously, Tom Seaver has long since been certain to go into the Hall of Fame. That he remains an effective pitcher having passed 300 career wins and 3500 strikeouts simply moves him into the Hall of Fame's inner circle. First ballot, automatic.

Reggie Jackson, Right Field (143 points, born 1946)

When Reggie hit his 500th home run, it was widely felt that this removed the final doubt about whether or not he would go into the Hall. The Hall of Fame Assessment system saw it the same way; he was close to being a lock before that, and is now a certain Hall of Famer. A controversial but inevitable selection, with the odds favoring his entry in the first year of eligibility.

Nolan Ryan, Starting Pitcher (136 points, born 1947)

Another controversial Hall of Fame candidate—much like Reggie, in some ways—is Nolan Ryan. While Ryan has been a fine pitcher and is in many ways one of the most singular, most remarkable athletes in the game, I personally would not vote for him. However, Hall of Fame voters have always been kind to two types of pitchers, strikeout pitchers and pitchers who have long careers with records near .500. Ryan is both; he picks up 65 points in the system just for strikeouts. I feel that's a realistic assessment of what those Ks will mean, and the 4000 strikeouts make him a certain Hall of Fame selection.

Rollie Fingers, Relief Pitcher (126 points, born 1946)

The system for evaluating relief pitchers is largely based on an intuitive feel for what things should mean. Because there is only one relief pitcher (Wilhelm) in the Hall of Fame, it is not possible to do the same type of study, comparing from the most qualified through the marginally qualified, that the analysis at the other positions was based on. Some values are pretty obvious—the World Series appearances will help Rollie,

the Most Valuable Player season will help him the same as these things would help a player at any other position. Long granted an almost mythic status for his consistent excellence in a demanding role, I would assume, and the system reflects, that he is very near to being an automatic selection.

Al Oliver, Center Field (117 points, born 1946)

Although he will not be a first-ballot selection (unless he gets a third life and makes it to 3000 hits) Al Oliver is very likely to make it into the Hall of Fame in time. He has 2,743 hits; the only players to be overlooked with a similar number are Vada Pinson (so far), Doc Cramer and George Davis. Just a few more hits would give him more than any player who has been passed over by the Hall of Fame.

Don Sutton, Starting Pitcher (103 points, born 1945)

One of the nation's finest Sports Talk hosts is Chuck Wilson of WEAN-AM in Providence, Rhode Island. Chuck likes to talk about the Hall of Fame; he has a passion for fan's issues, and prefers a good, logical argument to conducting an interview with somebody who's trying to sell some tickets, which I think is what makes his show so good. That's my perspective as a guest, of course . . . anyway, we've gotten into discussions over the air a couple of times about the Cooperstown qualifications of Don Sutton, among others. I've never been able to explain exactly what I was trying to say there, and I hope he doesn't mind if I try to straighten it out here, even though that may require that I paraphrase his position.

The discussion starts out with Chuck asking if I think Don Sutton should go into the Hall of Fame, and I say yes and he says why and I say because he has almost 300 wins and the other pitchers who have similar won/lost records are in the Hall of Fame. This is where we begin to lose it. The Hall of Fame is a self-defining institution; there are no clear guidelines for what is and is not a Hall of Famer, so we are left to define a Hall of Famer in terms of who is in and who is out.

Mr. Wilson says, embarking now upon the liberty of the inexact quote, that that is the lowest common denominator argument, which is dangerous inasmuch as it leads to an inevitable downward spiral in the selections, setting as the standard for future selections the worst mistake that has been made in the past. I agree that the lowest common denominator argument is invalid, for that exact reason; mistakes have been made in the voting, and we can't follow through on them and start putting everybody as good as Freddie Lindstrom or Chick Hafey in the Hall of Fame.

But that is not what I'm saying here. The lowest common denominator argument is, I think, that A should go into the Hall of Fame because B is in the Hall of Fame and A was better than B. You hear that every week—Enos Slaughter should go in because Ralph Kiner is in and Enos Slaughter was better than Ralph Kiner. (Actually, Ralph Kiner was a great player, but most people don't realize this, so he gets used this way a lot.) The lowest common denominator argument in the case of Don Sutton would be that Don Sutton should go in because Jesse Haines is in and Sutton is better than Jesse Haines (a ridiculous 1970 selection). But the argument ends ultimately with everybody in the Hall of Fame who is better than Ralph Kiner, who isn't very good. This is not necessarily a desirable goal.

But I'm not saying that *there is a player* who is comparable to Don Sutton who is in the Hall of Fame. I am saying that there is NO player comparable to Don Sutton who is NOT in the Hall of Fame. *Every* eligible pitcher with a career record comparable to Don Sutton's is in the Hall of Fame; there isn't anybody with anything like 300 wins (in this century) who has been turned down by the Hall of Fame. And it isn't that the Hall of Fame includes *one* pitcher who is *somewhat* less qualified, but rather that it includes *many* pitchers who are *nowhere near* as well qualified.

So Don Sutton is qualified not using the *lowest* common denominator, but using the *highest* common denominator. Every eligible pitcher from this century is in the Hall of Fame if he has more than 250 wins, and that includes Eppa Rixey (266–251), Ted Lyons (260–230), Red Faber (254–212), and Red Ruffing (273–225 with great teams). Sutton is now 295–228. We won't even talk about Waite Hoyt and Herb Pennock.

It is not that there is *a* precedent for putting Don Sutton in the Hall of Fame, but that there is *no* precedent for keeping him out. If you look at the Hall of Fame selections *as a group,* at who is in and who is not, there is a clearly defined line in terms of career won/lost record. Don Sutton is far above that line. He has done what

Hall of Famers have always been expected to do.

There are things that can be pointed out on the other side. You can point out that he has had only one 20-victory season, and that every starting pitcher now in the Hall of Fame had at least two. A real big reason for this is that the Dodgers went to a five-man rotation several years ahead of most of baseball, so Sutton was winning 18 out of 33 starts, but it's still a valid point. You can point out that in this generation there have been an unusual number of pitchers who have had long, successful careers; if we put all of them in the Hall of Fame it's going to be pretty crowded. Chuck Wilson argues that with all of the long careers, there is a need for the standards to adjust in accordance with performance norms, and I think I agree with that. I agree with it up to a point. Without any change, we would have to take in Tommy John, whose 259–207 career record is above the clearly defined line. OK, we need to move the line; if it's tough on Tommy, sorry. MAYBE the line needs to move so far as to exclude Ferguson Jenkins (284–226). Maybe. Maybe it has to move far enough to exclude Jim Kaat (283–237). But jacking the standards up all the way to where we exclude a 300-game winner? No way. Absolutely no way; that's just completely unfair to this generation of pitchers, when there are . . . what, a dozen or so pitchers who don't even have *two hundred* wins, and more with 220 or 230 wins and winning percentages not as good as Sutton's.

But the basic argument against Don Sutton seems to be that he lacks a mystique; despite his imminent 300th victory, nobody ever much thought of him as a great pitcher, like Palmer or Seaver or Carlton. I just happened to notice, though, a comparison between Don Sutton and the man who took his job when he left Los Angeles in 1981. Fernando Valenzuela has a terrific mystique; he's one of the game's biggest stars and most highly regarded pitchers. If you compare the two of them, you'll see that they're quite close in both of the basic ratios of pitcher performance, career winning percentage (Sutton's is .564, Valenzuela's .577) and career ERA (Sutton's is 3.18, Valenzuela's 2.90). The big difference, of course, is that Valenzuela has done this for five years, and Sutton has done it for twenty—and Fernando has never won twenty games in a season. Yet, because of the way he arrived in the major leagues, because of his popularity, because of the way Lasorda uses him,

Valenzuela's a big star. That's great, but if we're going to turn a 300-game winner away from Cooperstown, I think he's entitled to a better explanation than "Gee, Don, you're just not the kind of guy that I always thought of as being a Hall of Famer."

Bob Boone, Catcher (74 points, born 1947)

Though he will take some time to draw attention in the voting, and he will probably not be selected by the BBWAA, Bob Boone has entered the gray area, and has at this point a slight chance of eventually being selected to the Hall of Fame. Catchers with long careers have done very, very well in the voting, even when they were mighty short of supporting credentials. With 1,664 games played at catcher, Bob Boone is now ninth on the all-time list. All eight players ahead of him are either in the Hall of Fame or likely to be (six are in; the other two are Johnny Bench and Ted Simmons). Though his position at this moment is not strong, if Boone lasts for two more seasons as a regular he will claim the record for games caught, and could well prove to be a very serious Hall of Fame candidate.

Larry Bowa, Shortstop (69 points, born 1944)

The system shows Larry Bowa at this moment as being just off the gray area, which begins at 70. This result could very easily be misleading, inasmuch as Bowa's career abounds in accomplishments which cannot be evaluated very well, such as winning the Gold Glove at a key defensive position, playing regularly on many division champion teams and holding the record for fielding percentage at the position. Larry Bowa could well prove to be a strong Hall of Fame candidate.

Graig Nettles, Third Base (56 points, born 1944)

Graig Nettles will not be selected to the Hall of Fame unless 1) his defensive accomplishments count for far more than is estimated here, or 2) he continues to defy the laws of gerontology. Either is possible and neither is likely.

José Cruz, Left Field (24 points; born 1947)

Despite my admiration for him, José Cruz has almost no chance of going into the Hall of Fame based on his accomplishments to this point. He is still playing well.

PLAYERS BORN 1948–1951

A player born in 1951 would be 34 or 35 years old in 1986; a player born in 1948 would be 37 or 38. Although ordinary players usually are finished by age 34—and, in fact, the great majority of players born in the years 1948–1951 are retired by now—Hall of Fame candidates are not ordinary players, and it should be assumed that most of these players will still do *something* to improve their position, by passing career milestones if nothing else. The Hall of Fame candidates include:

Mike Schmidt, Third Base (183 points, born 1949)

Among players still in the productive part of their careers, Mike Schmidt is the most certain go to into the Hall of Fame. He has driven in 100 runs in a season seven times, scored 100 runs seven times; that alone gives him 42 points of the 100 needed. He has had eight 30-homer seasons plus three 40-homer seasons; that's another 28 points. He has won 2 MVP awards, played in 8 All-Star games and won 9 Gold Gloves; that makes another 49. As he nears the 500-homer plateau, there can be no question about his immediate selection for the Hall of Fame.

Ted Simmons, Catcher (117 points, born 1949)

Ted Simmons is very likely, although not certain, to achieve eventual recognition by the Hall of Fame. He is certainly one of the six or eight best-hitting catchers in the history of baseball. Although he has had his defensive problems, starting with the fact that the man was not born to catch, his career totals of 2,370 hits, 238 homers and counting are strong Hall of Fame credentials for the position.

Cecil Cooper, First Base (97 points, born 1949)

Unless his productivity ends now and his career batting average slides below .300, Cecil Cooper has an excellent chance of going into the Hall of Fame in time. He will not be a strong early candidate in the voting, but as time passes the evaluation of a candidate comes to rest more and more upon his batting accomplishments. Cooper has done the front-line things that are easy to summarize in a letter to *The Sporting News*—he has hit .300 many times including a high of .352, he has driven in 100 runs four times (three times more than 120), he has hit 30 home runs a couple of times, he has had 200 hits three times with a high of 219. He has exactly the kind of statistics that history loves.

The system shows Cooper with 97 points, giving him about a 50–50 chance to go into the Hall of Fame on the basis of his current credentials. One thing that doesn't show is that Cooper is moving into the range in which his career statistics will start to help him. He is ten away from 2000 career hits, meaning that with some durability he could expect 2500 hits, 300 home runs. If he does last three or four more years as a regular, and particularly if he keeps his career average above .300, Cecil Cooper will be almost certain to go into the Hall of Fame. Even lacking those assumptions, his chances are pretty good.

Ron Guidry, Starting Pitcher (96 points, born 1950)

Ron Guidry's performance over the last three seasons (21–9 in 1983 and 22–6 in 1985) has made him a very strong Hall of Fame candidate. Now 35, Guidry's record is in many respects similar to those of two other great Yankee lefthanders, Whitey Ford and Lefty Gomez. None had a large *number* of twenty-victory seasons, like Robin Roberts or Warren Spahn or Ferguson Jenkins. Ford won 20 only twice, Guidry three times and Gomez four. But they weren't 21–13 or 22–14 seasons, either; they were 25–4 (Ford), 25–3 (Guidry), 24–7 (Ford and Gomez), 21–9 (Gomez and Guidry), 26–5 (Gomez), 22–6 (Guidry) and 21–11 (Gomez)—all .700+ winning percentages except the last one. All three featured outstanding career winning percentages and pitched extremely well in the World Series. Like Cooper, Guidry has about a 50–50 chance to go into the Hall of Fame on the basis of current accomplishments, and is just reaching the level at which his career totals start to help him.

Goose Gossage, Relief Pitcher (91 points, born 1951)

Again, the evaluation of relief pitchers is speculative, but one would assume that Gossage is well positioned to gain Hall of Fame support, and could clinch a berth with two or three more outstanding seasons. He has been arguably even more consistent than Fingers, having not had an ERA above 3.00 since 1976. He hasn't led the league in many things and hasn't posted the astronomical save and game appearance totals of Quisenberry, but he has improved his credentials steadily with sub-2.00 ERAs, 20 and 30 saves, pitching in All-Star games and pitching in the World Series. He is likely to pick up additional points for 300 saves (he has 257) and 700 game appearances (he has 680), projecting him at least into the "likely to go" category. Seven hundred games isn't a magic number, but long careers are an important plus, and seven hundred games are a step in that direction.

Dave Concepcion, Shortstop (76 points, born 1948)

Dave Concepcion's current position *vis-à-vis* the Hall of Fame is very similar to that of Larry Bowa, perhaps marginally stronger because his teams were more successful in post-season play. The big difference between them is that Concepcion is four years younger, and has time left to strengthen his hand.

Bert Blyleven, Starting Pitcher (72 points, born 1951)

Bert Blyleven continues to make steady, inexorable progress toward the Hall of Fame. He began picking up qualifications at a very early age, and has marched steadily on, striking out 200 or more batters seven times, pitching a no-hitter, winning twenty games once, pitching in a couple of All-Star games, posting low ERAs, winning a World Series game, his career win total mounting rapidly. It will all help, although he would be very unlikely to go into the Hall of Fame if his arm blew out in spring training, 1986. He is likely to strike out 3000 batters in his career, and might very well win 300 games.

Dave Winfield, Right Field (72 points, born 1951)

With his fourth consecutive 100-RBI season in 1985, Dave Winfield entered the gray area; he would have an outside chance of going into the Hall of Fame if his productive years ended now. He is the youngest player listed in this group, and since he is playing so well it must be said that his eventual selection seems fairly likely.

Cesar Cedeno, Center Field (49 points, born 1951)

At age 25, Cesar Cedeno had one foot in the Hall of Fame. His impressive early accomplishments are still a part of his record, and if it should happen that his late-season renaissance in 1985 were to be sustained in 1986 and for a couple more years, he would still be a legitimate Hall of Fame candidate. As it stands now, he has no chance of being selected.

Bobby Grich, Second Base (36 points, born 1949)

Although he has been a legitimately great player, there is no reason to think that Bobby Grich will go into the Hall of Fame. Slugging second basemen who also play good defense, as a class, have done poorly. Probably the most-similar player was Joe Gordon, but others include Bobby Doerr, Del Pratt and Tony Lazzeri. I'll say this: if Bobby Grich goes into the Hall of

Fame, you're going to have real strong evidence that sabermetrics has made an impact on how talent is evaluated by the broader public. I regard Grich as a much greater player than Cecil Cooper or Ted Simmons, but he is much less likely to receive the recognition due him.

Don Baylor, Left Field (34 points, born 1949)

Don Baylor will not go into the Hall of Fame. As time passes the respect and diffidence with which he is regarded by the press will fade rapidly, and the inevitable fact that his batting accomplishments are not Hall of Fame calibre will come to the fore. His career batting average is below .270 and he has no defensive value; that throws him into the category of sluggers. Sluggers who hit .265 aren't Hall of Fame candidates until they get past 400 home runs.

Charlie Hough, Starting Pitcher (14 points, born 1948)

Although a fine pitcher for several years, Charlie Hough to this point in his career has done almost none of the things which Hall of Famers do.

PLAYERS BORN 1952–1955

The players in this group, aged 30 to 35 in 1986, are for the most part still producing at something near their peak level. It should be assumed that most of them will have a few more years similar to the ones they have already had, and thus that their positions with respect to the Hall of Fame are likely to improve very substantially before the question is considered.

George Brett, Third Base (143 points, born 1953)

George Brett is the only player among those in this age group who has virtually locked up a spot in the Hall of Fame. I know of no player with comparable qualifications—a power hitter with many .300 seasons, an MVP Award, a Gold Glove, a .316 lifetime average, major contributions to successful teams—who has not been selected to the Hall of Fame.

Jim Rice, Left Field (117 points, born 1953)

Although I personally would not regard Rice as being as good a player as Dave Winfield—he is not his equal as a fielder or baserunner, and I doubt that he would be a better hitter in the same park—the fact is that Rice has done the things which impress Hall of Fame voters. He has hit .300 (six times, 15 points), driven in 100 runs (seven times, 21 points), led the league in RBI (twice, 8 points), hit 40 home runs (once, 4 points), had 200 hits (three times, 15 points). Jim Rice on the basis of what he has already done would be likely to go in the Hall of Fame, and his career totals will probably make him an automatic selection within a year or two.

Bruce Sutter, Relief Pitcher (89 points, born 1952)

Again, we're making some assumptions about relief pitchers which can't be researched, but one would have to assume that Bruce Sutter has a very nice corner on immortality.

Gary Carter, Catcher (74 points, born 1954)

Gary Carter has moved into the area within which it is possible that he could be elected to the Hall of Fame on current credentials.

Carter has been badly hurt by the near misses of his teams. Had the Mets pulled out the championship last year, along with one or two of Carter's Montreal teams, then Carter might well have won a Most Valuable Player award, and in any case would quite certainly be in a much stronger position. His knees will catch up with him within a few years, and if that happens this year or next year, those near misses might well cost him dearly in Hall of Fame voting. If he remains productive for two or three more years, he should be a very strong candidate, possibly moving into the first-ballot group.

Robin Yount, Shortstop (58 points, born 1955)

Robin Yount has piled up 30% of a full Hall of Fame qualification in seasonal accomplishments (two .300 years, a 200-hit season, one season of 100 RBI, four seasons of 100 runs scored, one season of 35 doubles and two seasons of 45 doubles). He has added 18% more (18 points) with Awards—an MVP award, three All-Star selections, a Gold Glove. He adds 5 points more for leading the league (one in hits, twice in doubles, once in triples) and 5 for playing shortstop on a league champion.

At this time he has no points for career accomplishments—but. You have to remember that he came to the majors early; he's just 30 now and has 1,856 hits, so that if the shoulder has healed at all he's going to get close to 3000. When he starts adding impressive career totals to his impressive seasonal accomplishments, he's going to have a very solid Hall of Fame case to present. He is definitely not a Hall of Famer on the basis of current accomplishments, but I would expect him to have Hall of Fame credentials before the motion comes up for adoption.

Andre Dawson, Right Field (38 points, born 1954)

After appearing to be on a Hall of Fame course two years ago, Andre Dawson has done little to improve his position over the last two years. Dawson will not make the Hall of Fame unless he is able to overcome the knees and play better than he has the last two years.

Scott McGregor, Starting Pitcher (36 points, born 1954)

Were there any outstanding starting pitchers born in this period? I can't think of any. Scott McGregor has an outside chance of putting together a Hall of Fame record, but at this point he isn't close and he isn't moving very fast. His career totals will not begin to work for him in a major way for several years yet; he really needs two more twenty-victory seasons to have much of a chance. A real longshot.

Tony Armas, Center Field (35 points, born 1953)

Tony Armas has picked up some valuable markers—he's led the league in home runs a couple of times and RBI once, has three 100-RBI years. Barring unforeseen circumstances he has no chance of going into the Hall of Fame.

Frank Tanana, Starting Pitcher (32 points, born 1953)

Frank Tanana looked like he would be the great pitcher of his generation. In his first five years (1974–1978) he did a lot of things that would impress a Hall of Fame voter. Then his arm went, and he has done nothing to help himself since—but he is still in there pitching, and he has pushed himself up to 147 wins, while looking at times very much like a pitcher who was ready to turn it around and win 18 games again. I wouldn't be in the least surprised if he were to do that this season. If he were to have a twenty-win season, he would reemerge as a serious Hall of Fame candidate. Short of that, he has no chance.

Willie Randolph, Second Base (25 points, born 1954)

Willie Randolph's progress toward the Hall of Fame is a little stronger than is reflected in the point count. Willie has done none of the statistical things which impress voters—he has never hit .300, never driven in or scored a hundred runs, never led the league in anything except one time in walks. He has won some awards and played a role on some great teams.

Among players of this type, career length is the key factor. Willie is 31, and he's been playing a long time. He could have one of the longest careers ever at his position. Still, the odds against his election are long at this time.

Dennis Eckersley, Starting Pitcher (23 points, born 1954)

Although an impressive pitcher, a quality pitcher, Dennis Eckersley to this point in his career has not established himself as a Hall of Fame candidate.

Jack Clark, First Base (16 points, born 1955)

Due to his frequent injuries, Jack Clark has been unable to do the things that Hall of Famers do. Sluggers have to reach the 30-homer and 100-RBI levels with good regularity in order to make the Hall of Fame. Clark hasn't been able to do this.

PLAYERS BORN 1956 OR LATER

Players born in 1956 or later are still in their twenties; they have just begun to reach the levels at which career accomplishments can begin to help them. In almost all cases, these players will dramatically improve their records before they are considered for the Hall of Fame.

Dale Murphy, Center Field (93 points, born 1956)

Dale Murphy will go into the Hall of Fame.

Wade Boggs, Third Base (80 points, born 1958)

In just four years in the major leagues, Wade Boggs has registered qualifications which might, in and of themselves, be enough to get him elected to the Hall of Fame. He will go.

Eddie Murray, First Base (74 points, born 1956)

Eddie Murray has now entered the gray area; he would have a chance to enter the Hall of Fame on the basis of current accomplishments, even if he were to stop hitting. With career totals of over 1500 hits and over 250 home runs by the age of 29, he is, given the extremely stable, consistent nature of his performance, almost certain to reach levels of accomplishment which will put him in the Hall of Fame.

Cal Ripken, Shortstop (58 points, born 1960)

Cal Ripken is doing all of the things that mark a Hall of Famer at an early age. In fact, it seems quite possible that Ripken might be one of those rare players, like Aaron, Ruth, Rose and Cobb, who reach totals of three or four hundred—players who are sort of ridiculously over-qualified even for baseball's highest honor. It will be a major upset if Cal Ripken fades so badly that he fails even to make the Hall of Fame.

Jack Morris, Starting Pitcher (43 points, born 1956)

Among the pitchers of his generation, Jack Morris is the one who is making the strongest progress toward the Hall of Fame. It is not that he has done anything spectacular that immediately projects him forward, as Dwight Gooden did last year, but that he is picking up plusses here, there and everywhere, adding something almost every year. He has won 20 games; he wins 15 or more, adding something to his image, every year. He has struck out 200 batters; he has led the league in strikeouts. He has thrown a no-hitter. He has led the league in wins and innings pitched. He pitched two complete-game victories in the World Series. He has pitched in three All-Star games. His career winning percentage is good. His career win total, 123, is excellent at his age. He is NOT qualified for the Hall of Fame at this time, not even close. But if he continues to do the things he has done regularly since 1979, he will make the Hall of Fame.

Lance Parrish, Catcher (29 points, born 1956)

Lance Parrish is making good strides toward the Hall of Fame. Because the careers of catchers are shorter than those of other players, and because both the Hall of Fame Assessment System and the Hall of Fame voting make allowances for this, he is already closing in on the career standards which would rapidly project him forward. While he has a great deal of work to be done, his chances of making the Hall of Fame are good.

Lou Whitaker, Second Base (29 points, born 1957)

Lou Whitaker is making excellent early progress toward the Hall of Fame. The next two or three seasons will tell us a great deal about his destiny.

Dave Stieb, Starting Pitcher (29 points, born 1957)

Dave Stieb has been inches away from a number of accomplishments which would have given him a solid foothold on immortality. He could just as easily have won 20 games once or twice. He didn't. He didn't even reach 18. He could just as easily have had 200 strikeouts a couple of times. He didn't. He could have been voted the Cy Young Award. He wasn't. The Blue Jays could just as easily have gotten into the World Series last year. They didn't. These shortcomings might ultimately cost him the honor. Still, he is compiling a very impressive log of accomplishments, and he well might make the Hall of Fame.

Mario Soto, Starting Pitcher (17 points, born 1956)

Though he was, I felt, the best starting pitcher in baseball from 1981 through 1984, Mario Soto has not compiled much of a list of Hall of Fame type qualifications. His chances are very slim.

Harold Baines, Right Field (14 points, born 1959)

Until 1985, Harold Baines had done very few things which might have helped put him in the Hall of Fame. In 1985 he hit .300, drove in 100 runs and played in the All-Star game, all of which are the type of annual bits and pieces that a player of his type needs to accumulate. He is just at the start of the road, but at least he is moving.

Dave Righetti, Relief Pitcher (13 points, born 1958)

Dave Righetti has done a few things that would help him in the context of a productive career—pitched a no-hitter, pitched in a World Series, won a playoff game, won a Rookie of the Year Award. But he has missed out on the basic accomplishments that drive a man into the Hall of Fame. He hasn't won 15 games in a season, hasn't led any leagues in anything. He's very much a longshot at this time.

Tom Brunansky, Left Field (5 points, born 1960)

Tom Brunansky would not reach the Hall of Fame by doing the things that he has done in his career, no matter how long he kept on doing them (within reason). He would have to move up a notch, maybe up to 35, 40 homers and 100 RBI a season, to have a chance.

SIMILARITY SCORES

The most important new method to be introduced this year is that of similarity scores. Similarity scores are a way of objectively fixing the "degree of resemblance" between two players or between two teams. Among all the methods that I have developed over the years, this method is the most flexible, the most adaptable, the most useful in many different contexts. It has been used many times throughout this book, and will be used many more in the future. Let me explain here the goals, general method and potential uses of the notion.

The similarity scores begin with the assumption that players who are identical in all respects considered will have a similarity score of 1000. For each difference between the two, there is a "penalty," or reduction from the 1000. Similarity scores are designed so that:

Similarity scores in the vicinity of 500 (or lower) indicate players who or teams which would not usually be perceived as being essentially similar.

Similarity scores of 600 or thereabouts indicate players who or teams which possess slight similarities, but major differences.

Similarity scores around 700 indicate players who or teams which have important, easily identifiable similarities, but also significant and obvious differences.

Similarity scores around 800 indicate players who or teams which have very prominent, obvious similarities, but some easily identifiable distinctions.

Similarity scores above 850 indicate players who or teams which can usually be described as substantially similar.

Similarity scores above 900 indicate very similar players or teams.

Similarity scores above 950 are rare, and usually indicate that the true similarities of the two players or teams have been emphasized by chance patterns.

Later on, I'll explain what some of the sets of penalties are by which similarity scores can be derived. First, let me suggest a few of the areas in which similarity scores might be very useful in the analysis of baseball.

1) When discussing whether or not a player should be elected to the Hall of Fame, one of the key questions to focus on—probably the most important question—is who are the "most similar" other players, and are they in the Hall of Fame?

Here we would use career similarity scores. Since the Hall of Fame has no fixed standards, this is as good a definition as we have of what a Hall of Famer is, a player who is like the players who are in the Hall of Fame. Of course, other considerations are also important, but if you identify the ten most similar players to a given man and find that eight of them are in the Hall of Fame, then there is a natural assumption that, unless there is some particular reason why this player is different from the others, then he too should go into the Hall of Fame. If none of the other ten is in the Hall of Fame, then that tends to shift the burden of proof; why should this man go in, when the players who are most similar to him are not in?

To talk specifics for a moment, take Nellie Fox. The one most similar player to Nellie Fox as a hitter was Doc Cramer, the American League center fielder of the thirties and forties. Their career batting records are so extremely similar that even though I include a fairly large penalty for the position difference (one a second baseman, one a center fielder) Cramer remains the most similar man:

	G	AB	Runs	H	2B	3B	HR	RBI	BB	SO	SB	Avg.
Fox	2367	9232	1279	2663	355	112	35	790	719	216	76	.288
Cramer	2239	9140	1357	2705	396	109	37	842	571	345	62	.296

Then the question becomes, why should Fox be in the Hall of Fame when Cramer is not?

Of course, there are several possible answers to that question—Fox as a second baseman was more valuable than Cramer as a center fielder; Cramer is very close to Hall of Fame calibre, and the small differences between them are enough to push Fox over the line; Fox's batting statistics were compiled in the fifties, when runs and hits were more scarce than they were in the thirties, and therefore Fox was more valuable; Fox played for better teams and therefore had more of an impact on the pennant race, particularly in 1959; Fox was the more outstanding defensive player; Cramer actually should be in, too . . . anyway, it is not my purpose to propose one player, however comparable, as the test of Hall of Fame suitability, but to lay the groundwork for identification of the entire field of the most-comparable. The ten most comparable players to Nellie Fox in terms of career performance are:

1.	Doc Cramer	932
2.	Red Schoendienst	918
3.	Luis Aparicio	877
	Rabbit Maranville	877
5.	Luke Appling	875
6.	Richie Ashburn	874
7.	Bobby Wallace	871
8.	Billy Herman	869
	Lave Cross	869
10.	Buddy Myer	867

Five of the ten most-comparable—Aparicio, Maranville, Appling, Wallace and Herman—are in the Hall of Fame. At least two of the others,

Schoendienst and Ashburn, are strong candidates. So that leaves us basically back where we started: many of the players most comparable to Nellie are in the Hall, some of them aren't. You can vote for him if you want to. (The next five men, if you wanted to carry it that far, would be Dick Bartell, Lloyd Waner, Harry Hooper, Dick Groat and Bid McPhee.)

You will also note, of course, that many of the most-similar men are also "similar" in other ways. Mostly they were small men, 5′10″ or under—mostly, in fact, about the same height and weight as Nellie. A couple were contemporaries; all hit near the top of the order, and two were the White Sox' other outstanding middle infielders of the mid-part of the century, Aparicio and Appling.

As telling as the fact that several of the most-similar players are Hall of Famers, though, is the fact that there simply aren't that many players who are highly comparable. In looking at the "most similar players" for Lou Gehrig, we get a list that is almost solid Hall of Famers:

1.	Jimmie Foxx	912
2.	Ted Williams	894
3.	Mel Ott	824
4.	Babe Ruth	796
5.	Al Simmons	780
6.	Goose Goslin	777
7.	Stan Musial	776
8.	Frank Robinson	772
9.	Harry Heilmann	762
10.	Billy Williams	755

But more striking than the fact that they are almost all Hall of Famers is the fact that there are only two players—Jimmie Foxx and Ted Williams—who are truly similar to him as hitters. Gehrig, Foxx and Williams are truly similar:

	G	AB	Runs	H	2B	3B	HR	RBI	BB	SO	SB	Avg.
Foxx	2317	8134	1751	2646	458	125	534	1921	1452	1311	88	.325
GEHRIG	2164	8001	1888	2721	535	162	493	1990	1508	789	102	.340
Teddy	2292	7706	1798	2654	525	71	521	1839	2019	709	24	.344

They are close in the major indicators—career length, home runs, batting average, RBI—and most of the minor ones. They are two first basemen and a left fielder, so there are no major penalties for position. But the other players are there not because they are really similar to him, but merely because they are less "dissimilar" than everybody else. There just aren't very many Lou

Gehrig–types around; uniqueness is one of the fundamental tests of quality. By contrast Gil Hodges, while a fine player in the same essential mold as Gehrig, is not a historically unique type of player:

1.	Norm Cash	951
2.	Boog Powell	927
3.	Lee May	926
4.	Willie Horton	919
	Joe Adcock	919
6.	Roy Sievers	915
7.	Dick Allen	913
8.	George Scott	908
9.	Frank Howard	907
10.	Rocky Colavito	906

Hodges hit .273 with 370 home runs in 2,071 games, while Cash hit .271 with 377 home runs in 2,089 games. Even the number ten man, Colavito, isn't far off those totals, with a .266 average and 374 home runs in 1,841 games. Gil Hodges nearly made it into the Hall of Fame a few years ago, just after his death. But there are ten players who have similarity scores in excess of 900—in other words, they are highly similar to him in terms of career batting records—and none of the ten is in the Hall of Fame. Nellie Fox is not nearly as unique as Gehrig, but he was much more of a unique talent than was Hodges.

Again, that doesn't absolutely mean that Hodges should not be elected; none of the other ten players played in seven World Series or was a successful manager. As always, I'm not trying to *end* the discussion, but merely to *contribute to it,* to help us see things a little bit more clearly.

2) Similarity scores are the solution to a problem that has troubled me for ten years—how to measure a player's consistency from season to season. Exactly what we mean by saying that a player is consistent from year to year is that one of his seasons tends to be similar to the next one. Season similarity scores are the perfect way to address the question. I haven't done it yet, but I don't foresee any problems.

3) Similarity scores can be used to evaluate a wide variety of adjustment and projection methods, such as the Brock series career projections and the minors-to-majors translation system. What we mean when we say that the system projects a player's career accurately is that it produces projections that are "similar" to the actual performance that follows. An obvious question: How similar?

In this way, similarity scores can be very useful to us in refining and improving the career projection systems. What we do to develop these is to define a group of players from the past—Dallas Adams is working with a carefully-balanced group of 200—and run the projections for them. When we make changes in the system, those changes will always improve the accuracy of the system in some cases, but diminish its accuracy in others. We need to know whether, on balance, those changes improve the accuracy of the projections. Without similarity scores, what we have to do is calculate the "standard error" or at least the average error in several key categories such as career games, career hits and career home runs. But a much simpler and better alternative is just to track the similarity of the projections to actual records. If the average similarity score goes up, the change helps the system work better.

When I say that the major league translations of minor league batting records are an accurate reflection of the players' skills, what I am saying is that there is a strong degree of "similarity" between the major league translation, and the actual major league records that follow. Suppose that we were to develop a system to project how a given player is likely to do in another park— how Wade Boggs would hit in Dodger Stadium, for example. The test of such a system, of course, would be whether or not it produced projections which were "similar" to the actual records which followed when players moved from park to park. How many games would Bert Blyleven win if he pitched for the Tigers? Develop a method to answer that question, and similarity scores will be the way to test the method.

4) Similarity scores could also be useful to us in making career projections in another way. One very good way to approach the question of what career statistics a player will likely produce would be to identify the players who had had very similar accomplishments up to the same age. Leon Durham has, to this point in his career (his 1985 age was 28) played in 720 games, collected 717 hits for a .284 average with 96 home runs. I haven't done the background work to be able to do it, but I'm certain that you could find another player who through the age of 28 had hit .283 with 94 home runs in 735 games or something, and another with 101 home runs and a .282 average in 718 games, and several more who weren't far off. What those players did in

the rest of their careers would be an excellent guide to what could be expected of Leon Durham.

If the field of good comparables was large enough, then you could check other similarities—similarity of value pattern, similarity of position, park and defensive record—and make the comparisons even more indicative.

5) Salary negotiations essentially revolve around only one issue: what players are most similar to the man in question. It is not an exaggeration to say that 90% of salary negotiations in baseball are an attempt to define the group of the most similar players. Obviously, similarity scores could be extremely useful in this context.

6) Suppose that you were the General Manager of the New York Mets, and you were considering trading for a player from the American League, but you didn't have any idea how well he would hit in Shea Stadium. In this context, one very interesting thing to know would be who the most similar National League players were, and how well *they* hit in Shea Stadium.

All of those uses are fun and potentially valuable, but taken together they do not make up the major value of the method. The great potential use of similarity scores in sabermetrics comes from the fact that similarity scores can be used to do two things:

1) Define control groups which have the characteristics of the group under study in all areas except the one being investigated, and

2) Construct theoretical models (or "profiles") and identify real teams which are similar to the model.

It is these two purposes to which similarity scores have most often been adapted in this book, and it is these two purposes to which they will most often be bent in the future.

One of the great problems in science is developing control groups which reflect the characteristics of the group under study, but without the biases which create the effect to be studied. When people state a proposition, they tend to state it in an "other things being equal" form. Other things being equal, a child raised in poverty is more likely to commit a crime than a child raised in wealth. The problem with checking that out is that wealth and poverty create so many secondary characteristics with respect to health, education and orthodontia that it is nearly impossible to distinguish groups of children which are

the same in many important respects if they are different in this one respect. Other things being equal, a bird could run faster than a man because the relevant muscles are 28 times as strong, but did you ever try to find a bird that had the body weight and general configuration of a person?

In sabermetrics we have the same problem. We can say that other things being equal, a player who plays the outfield is more likely to develop as a hitter than one who plays the middle infield—but the problem is that outfielders and middle infielders are not alike in many ways, and it is difficult to distinguish the degree to which any subsequent development results from the position, rather than (to pick one) the fact that the outfielders were better hitters to start with.

Using similarity scores, it would be possible to hold the other things constant so that this could be studied. It would be possible to define two groups of players who have essentially identical characteristics as hitters and as to age, but one group of outfielders and one of infielders.

Other things being equal, a catcher's career will be shorter than that of a player at any other position. Using this method, we'll be able to measure for the first time exactly how much catching shortens a player's career on the average.

Other things being equal, a 22-year-old rookie should have somewhat more growth potential as a hitter than a 25-year-old rookie. Using this method, we will be able to define equivalent groups of 22-year-old and 25-year-old rookies, and assess what the differences are.

Those are issues that I haven't gotten into in this year's book. There are many questions of this type that I have looked into, and you may be sick to death of similarity scores by the time you get to Houston. We can identify similar players on good teams and bad teams, similar hitters who have speed and who don't, similar players who are black and white or tall and short or blond and bushy-tailed or . . . Is there a New York bias in Hall of Fame selection? Compare similar players who played in New York and St. Louis.

The other great use of similarity scores is that through them we can construct statistical "models" of players or teams, select real players or teams who are most like the model, and study how they are affected by conditions or events. Suppose that you believe that a certain type of pitcher should do well against the Yankees—let's say that you believe that the ultimate Yankee

Killer should be a pitcher who is 6 foot, 7 inches tall, left-handed, a power pitcher inclined to be wild. You can state that image in a statistical model, and compare each pitcher in the league to the model, identifying the pitchers most similar to the profile. Then you can check their performance against the Yankees, and thus reach a reasonable conclusion as to whether the belief is or is not valid. I have also done these types of things several times in this year's book.

At other times, who are the most similar players is something that it is just kind of fun to know. When you look up an old-time player—say, Jimmy Sheckard—it's just kind of fun to wonder what modern players are most similar to him. Since Minnie Minoso was my favorite opposition player as a kid, it's just kind of fun to consider what active player is most similar to him.

One thing to remember about this method is that it has to be adapted for each study. Generally, in studying any particular feature, one either "blocks out" the penalty for that particular category, or else "reverses the sign," counting the difference in this area to be a plus, rather than a minus. This causes the players or teams selected to be *alike* in all other respects, but *different* in one respect. Also, in many cases one might wish to increase the penalties (or bonuses) for some particular difference—in studying strikeouts, for example, one might wish to increase somewhat the emphasis given to strikeouts so as to cause a separation in strikeouts between control and study groups to occur more rapidly.

If I'm studying the effect of any other category on runs scored, which is another common use of the method—we can use it to distinguish very similar teams which are different in terms of strikeouts or stolen bases or triples, and thus measure the impact of one strikeout or one triple—then obviously you have to block out runs scored as well. You have to block out the "impact" category as well as the "variable" column. The values included are not sacred, is what I am saying; they are more "guidelines" than fixed weights to be used in every study. You do have to have weights on the categories; a difference of 300 home runs is a heck of a lot more important than a difference of 300 at bats. In the extreme case, since the difference between a .300 hitter and a .230 hitter is only .07, then a difference of 7 at bats, without any weights, would be one hundred times more important than

the difference between a .300 and a .230 hitter. Obviously, you have to construct a system of weights to prevent that. But if you changed the penalty for a difference in career at bats from 1 per 75 to 1 per 65 or 1 per 100, it is unlikely that this would change who was identified as most similar to the player.

Also, similarity scores are not *one* set of weights, but a series of sets of weights—one for career records, one for season records, one for team batting, one for batting frequencies (to study most-similar ratios of performance in different numbers of plate appearances), one for overall team performance (offensive and defensive, wins and losses), one for finding similar value patterns, one for pitching seasons, one for pitching careers. Maybe the way I should summarize it is this: that how *similar* two players are depends largely on the context in which you ask that question. Players who have similar statistics can be not at all similar with respect to many questions. For example, these two players:

G	AB	Runs	H	2B	3B	HR	RBI	BB	SO	SB	Avg.
151	585	73	161	31	3	25	105	41	93	1	.275
161	608	89	165	29	8	25	105	49	95	10	.271

The records are undeniably similar—but one of the players was Tony Perez, 1980, and the other was Harold Baines, 1982. They could not be described as similar players—one was old, the other young, one was right-handed and the other left-handed, one played right field and the other first base. If you're studying a strictly offensive question—what happens to the team when a hitter of this calibre is out of the lineup, let's say—then they might be considered very similar. In other contexts, studying anything related to future expectations, obviously they are totally different. For any study, we will have to choose the areas of similarity which are germane to the study.

To figure similarity scores, you start with 1000 points and subtract penalties. These are the penalties for career batting (Column 1), season batting (Column 2), team batting (Column 3) and batting frequency (Column 4). For column 4, expand or compress the stats to 1000 plate appearances and take it from there. Subtract one point for each difference of:

	1 Career	2 Season	3 Team	4 Frequency
G	20	5	1	
AB	75	20	20	
R	10	3	1	2
H	15	5	5	1
2B	5	1.5	1.5	.5
3B	4	.1	1	.33
HR	3	.5	.5	.25
RBI	10	20	2	2
W	25	8	2.5	2
SO	150	20	20	5
SB	20	2	3	1
Avg.	.001	.001	.00025	
Sl Pct	.002	.002	.00050	1

For the sake of clarity, the "Slugging Percentage" in column four is total bases per 1000 plate appearances. In studies of seasons, I usually subtract 12 points for each year of difference in the players' ages, more if it is a study involving growth or durability. In many studies, each position is assigned a "score" or "value," which is 10 for a catcher, 8 for a shortstop, 7 for a second baseman, 5 for a center fielder, 4 for a third baseman, 3 for a right fielder, 2 for a left fielder, and 1 for a first baseman. For each 1 point difference in the position value, I subtract 12 points. Without this position penalty, Gil Hodges when compared to Johnny Bench would have a similarity score of 927, putting Bench in the same group with Cash, Powell, May, Adcock et al. I think you can see that this is not desirable. Without a position adjustment, the most similar player to Johnny Bench is Gil Hodges; with the adjustment, the most similar player to Johnny Bench is Yogi Berra.

For illustration, suppose we compare the career records of Henry Aaron and Babe Ruth:

	AARON	RUTH	Difference	Penalty
Games Played	3298	2503	795	39.75
At Bats	12364	8399	3965	52.87
Hits	3771	2873	898	59.87
Doubles	624	506	118	23.6
Triples	98	136	38	9.5
Home Runs	755	714	41	13.67
Runs Scored	2174	2174	0	0
Runs Batted In	2297	2204	93	6.2
Walks	1402	2056	654	26.16
Strikeouts	1383	1330	53	.35
Stolen Bases	240	123	117	5.85
Batting Average	.305	.342	.037	37
Position Value	3	3	0	0

The sum of the penalties is 275 (274.82), so the similarity of the two careers is 725 (1000−275). If the category might be relevant to what you are studying, and if the information is available, you can include stuff like hit batsmen and grounding into double plays. My set of weights for comparing pitchers is pretty much guesswork, and I don't think I've used it in this book, so I'm not going to run it. You can figure one out for yourself if you've got the need. Value pattern similarities use the value approximation method, and look for players who have had the same sorts of career progressions; they're very relevant to salary negotiations.

As I guess you can tell, I'm pretty excited about the method. I've used it for a bunch of things that didn't work well enough to make it into the book, but will sometime. When I think back about it, the amazing thing is how long it took me to develop this. I remember when I cut my first baseball cards off the back of a box of Post cereal in the spring of 1961, one of the first things I was taken with was who was similar to who. I can remember as clearly as anything sitting at the table one evening trying to explain that I had decided that the most similar cards belonged to Jim Davenport and Elston Howard (1960 season). My brother Bob couldn't figure out what the hell the point was and who cared, a reaction which I have encountered quite a number of times in the quarter-century since.

Another thing—about three years ago I remember sitting next to a guy on a plane who predicted weather for the Air Force, and he was telling me about this system they were working on of predicting weather by putting into a computer a vast amount of information about weather patterns at every six-hour period over the last 100+ years. Coding that information, they found they could make accurate predictions by isolating the one situation most similar to the current one (where the fronts were, etc.) and guessing that the way the situation developed then would tend to repeat itself now. I thought that was fascinating, and I was wondering if there was any way to apply the concept to my own work. Then when I eventually did (the San Francisco comment a year ago) I developed a not-very-good system, and completely failed to see the potential of the method.

Caught up in developing systems to measure *quality,* I failed for 25 years to see the things that you could do if you forgot about quality and focused on finding ways to measure *similarity.* Eventually, I guess that all the ideas that are in you work their way out.

HOW IS PROJECT SCORESHEET DOING?

Very well, thank you.

Accounts of all major league games are now available to the public. Through the Herculean efforts of John and Sue Dewan, to whom this book is dedicated, you can now get access to an account of any major league game played in 1985, unless we missed one or two. This was the essential goal of *Project Scoresheet*. 1985 was a very successful season with respect to that goal.

To fill you in if you're new to this, there are millions of questions relating to baseball which can only be answered by studying gamesheets. Just a couple of examples: How many times does each major league player get thrown out on the base paths, and (since we know how many runners each hitter drives in) how many runners does each hitter leave in scoring position? At one point, in beginning this project, I listed a few dozen possible areas of research; you probably can think up as many more.

When I began to study baseball professionally about ten years ago, I wrote to the leagues and some of the teams requesting copies of game scoresheets (offering, of course, to pay for them). I was told that they were not available. They were private property of an accounting service, and I couldn't have them. I was told this repeatedly over a period of years.

Since it is my place in life to study matters such as these, in time I began to grow somewhat disagreeable on the issue. It seemed to me that to tell the public which supported the game that they couldn't see the scoresheets because somebody was trying to make some money off of them was immoral, stupid and counter-productive. At times I was known to speak less than kindly about the brain dead who were smothering the scoresheets. I also began to realize this: that I could not be the only person who wanted access to the information and couldn't get it. What if, I thought, what if I organized those people?

Organization is not my strong suit, and at first we had some tough sledding. There are still many problems, and there are still many things which we have not been able to do. But the scoresheets are now available. If God and the scorers are willing, the public will never again be told that the accounts of public games have somehow become confidential.

Here's the way the system works. All we're trying to do, initially, is collect scoresheets. Hundreds and hundreds of people regularly score games, right? All we need to do is get enough of those people to send us their scoresheets.

The people who are willing to send scoresheets should contact John Dewan, *Project Scoresheet*, P.O. Box 46074, Chicago, Illinois 60646; a postcard is preferred. John will put them in touch with the local captain for the team that they follow. The local captain takes the responsibility for seeing that every game is scored by somebody. Some of the local captains are people who score almost every game themselves; others coordinate an effort involving 25 or 30 people. Then the scoresheets are sent to the P.O. Box in Chicago; John and Sue collate them and keep track of them. Division captains aid in maintaining and repairing the scoring network and in other ways.

Essentially simple, were it not for the fact that there are 2,106 games in a season.

You can buy the paper output—the scoresheets—from *Project Scoresheet* if you want to: it's a little expensive and the paper forms are pretty tough to deal with, but you get them within a few weeks of when the game is played. I buy them, because it's something I need in my work. From there, John or Sue or some other dedicated baseball fan like Mark Podrazik will take the game accounts and record the sequence of play on a computer disc. The computer will turn this into an annotated account-form box score, and those will be printed, photo-copied and bound into a book about the size of a telephone book for a medium-sized city. After the season, you can buy the account-form box scores for an entire league, which will give you the exact sequence of play for each game, for . . . I don't know, $35 or $45 a league. A little bit more than it costs to get the thing photo-copied and mailed. Or you can buy "team books" which have accounts of the games for each team. Local captains for each team receive copies of the team books, I think.

So far, so good; the system does work. It's a lot of work for John and Sue and some other people, but it does function. We're very proud and pleased about that.

The project has had a great many secondary benefits. Through *Project Scoresheet,* I have come in contact with many people, like—I hate to mention any, because I can't mention all—David Driscoll, Brent MacInnis, Jeff Welch and Tim Marcou who have a serious, deep interest in analyzing baseball. These people have very kindly shared their research with us, and some bits of it are cited in these pages.

The gentlemen who formerly controlled the scoresheets have been forced, in economic self defense, to release to the public some of the information which they have miserly hoarded. This wasn't foreseen, but is a significant benefit to the public, attributable directly to *Project Scoresheet.*

Business contacts have been made through the project, which may benefit the baseball public through the availability of more and better information. *STATS,* a St. Louis company directed by Dick Cramer (I am a minor shareholder in the company) markets some of the information developed through *Project Scoresheet* to organized baseball. (For the sake of clarity, all accounts of the games and all facts developed from them are available to the public. What *STATS* markets is sophisticated information-retrieval software which makes it possible to sort through the mountains of scoresheets and get the information you need quickly.)

Newsletters have been started in some cities to make available the information that is developed about the local team.

Some very interesting studies have been done which would not have been possible without the scoresheets.

Perhaps most importantly, in some cities networks of friendships have coalesced among people who share this intense interest in baseball analysis, but didn't know what to do with it before.

There are many other things that we have not, as of yet, been able to do. There have been frustrations and disappointments. There have been things that we want to do but haven't been able to get done as of yet. Let me discuss some of those here. They break down into four areas:

1) *Accuracy and completeness of scoresheets.*

We do not require the use of any type of scoresheet. There are many types of scoresheets; we have one which we prefer, which we call the Craig Wright scoresheet. It's an excellent form; it has a space for each batter, divided into three parts like this:

What the player does during his at bat is placed in the center space, in a note something like "1B" (Single), "1B7" (Single to left field) or G1B7 (Ground single to left) or "4–3" (Batter out Second-to-First) or "HBP" (Hit by pitch) or GDP 1–6–3 (Pitcher-to-short-to-first double play).

On the line *above* the batter, we place the information about anything that happens while the batter is at the plate, such as a stolen base (SB, 1–2 or SB, 2–3), a balk, a runner caught stealing—that is, anything that happens involving an out or the movement of a baserunner.

On the line *below* the batter, we place the information about what happens after the ball is hit, such as 1–3 (Runner goes from first to third), 2XH 8–2 (Runner from second out at home, center fielder to catcher), or B–1, 1–2, 2–3, 3–H (batter goes to first, runner from first moves to second, etc.).

It's the best scoring system I've seen—clean, clear, thorough. You know exactly where every baserunner is all the time. A copy of the form is reproduced on the next page. You are free to reproduce this form and score games on it; Craig Wright has donated it to the public.

On the other hand, not everybody uses it. We're a volunteer network; we take what we can get. There must be a hundred or more scoresheet forms in use around the country, and many of them, to be honest, are just confusing as billy hell. (One of my father's expressions. Don't know where it comes from.) You've probably seen them . . . you know the one with bunches of little boxes divided into four parts representing the four bases, and if he gets to first base you're supposed to make a note in the first little space about how he gets to first base and if he gets to second base . . . and then there's the one with the little diamond drawn in it in broken lines and a multiple-choice quiz in the corner of each box, and you're supposed to circle the method by which the runner reaches or is retired and trace the line as far as he gets . . . and then there is that dreadful one with the honeycomb pattern all over it in green ink and little numbers printed around. I've never figured out what the hell you were supposed to do with that one. The common bonds are that they all have way too much ink on the page before you start trying to make an account of the game, and they all divide the game up so as to provide a space for every hitter to hit in every inning, thus making the spaces so small that you can't hardly get anything in there. Personal taste, I guess; I'm sure they all make sense if your father taught you to use them.

Anyway, using methods like these, and using volunteer scorers, a certain amount of information gets missed. Some scoresheets don't always tell whether runners go from first to third or stop at second. We need to know. Some scorers do not have a great command of the rulebook, and do not know, for example, that if a runner is picked off at first base and thrown out at second, he is charged with a caught stealing (they are logical enough to assume that you are only caught stealing when you are caught stealing). Sometimes they don't note whether such a play goes 1–3–6 or 1–3–6–4–1. Sometimes people will miss the distinction between a double and a hitter taking second on a throw to another base. We need to know. For some of those things, radio scoring is actually better than being there in person, because at the park they won't always tell you whether a play was ruled passed ball or wild pitch or something.

Every game is being covered from two sides, and if we're lucky one side or the other will catch every play—but this requires that the person putting the game up on computer sit there with two scoresheets, scored in different ways, plus a standard summary-form box score from the game, trying to puzzle out what exactly happened. Even with the same scoresheet, some people will use "D7" to mean "drive to left" (an out) and some will use it to mean "double to left." When the person inputting the game sees "D7," he either has to know the idiosyncrasies of the scorer, or he has to count the outs in the inning.

We need to standardize and improve our scoring. We're working on it.

2) *Timeliness of getting games on disc*.

Once the games are on computer disc, distribution of scoresheets and dissemination of information derived from the scoresheets can begin. It has taken us too long, way into the winter, to accomplish this in the first two years. I haven't been able to do too many direct studies off of the scoresheets, just because they are so difficult to deal with in the raw form and so slow in the finished form.

HERE IS WHERE WE MOST NEED YOUR HELP. *If you have (or have access to) IBM-compatible computer equipment, and if you have a little time to try to help the project, it would be greatly appreciated if you would write John Dewan, or call him at (312)–774–3798 (you'll probably get an answering machine, but you can leave your name and address and he'll get back to you). We need more people to put the games on computer.* It takes about 20–30 minutes a game, and there are over 2000 games a year. John, Mark Podrazik, Bob Levittan, Bob Meyerhoff, Andrew Berman, Pete Crockett, Gary Gillette and Don Zminda are doing yeoman work in this regard, but if we had maybe 20 or 30 people trained and equipped to do the work, we could cut the load of each down to a reason-

				at			Date			Local Time	

Scorer | | Attendance Conditions | | |

Umpires: H: 1b: 2b: 3b:

...	....	.....	1	10	19	28	37	46
...	....	.....						
...	....	.....	2	11	20	29	38	47
...	....	.....						
...	....	.....	3	12	21	30	39	48
...	....	.....						
...	....	.....	4	13	22	31	40	49
...	....	.....						
...	....	.....	5	14	23	32	41	50
...	....	.....						
...	....	.....	6	15	24	33	42	51
...	....	.....						
...	....	.....	7	16	25	34	43	52
...	....	.....						
...	....	.....	8	17	26	35	44	53
...	....	.....						
...	....	.....	9	18	27	36	45	54
...	....	.....						

Pos.   Player   Def.Innings

Pitcher	In	Out	IP

Notes:

Support Project Scoresheet!

able size and get the information in a usable form a lot quicker. So please call or write John if you can help.

3) *We need to make the scorer's network more comprehensive and more stable.*

There are a few cities in which the system needs more help, more scorers. St. Louis, Los Angeles and San Diego head the list.

As I mentioned, some local efforts are drawn from a large number of volunteers, others from a small number or even one. From the standpoint of the local captain, small may be best. He doesn't have to keep track of 20 volunteers and make sure *somebody* has got everything and 20 people have got all of the material they need. He doesn't need to worry about people who might let him down. From the standpoint of the Project, larger is better. Small local organizations make us dependant on a few scorers; if those scorers move, die, get tired or just lose interest, we have to start all over in that town.

We hope to sustain this effort for a long period of time, like forever. We need to have a sufficient base of interest in each community that we can carry on if something happens.

Here I am largely at fault, for there are a good number of people who have contacted me over the last couple of years asking about *Project Scoresheet,* whose cards and letters have been left at the bottom of a bin somewhere. I apologize. In the organizational stages, the system had to depend on funnelling mail through me, which is sort of like launching a new airline, Bermuda Triangle Commuter Service. I do answer hundreds of letters a year, but I'd hate to think how many I don't get to.

To those of you who have written to me asking about *Project Scoresheet,* and always wondered what happened to your card, I am sorry. If any of you are good enough to try again, that would be sincerely appreciated.

Anyway, we do need scorers; we need scoresheets. If you score games, why not share them with the public? A postcard to John Dewan, address above, will put you in contact with your local captain. In a couple of cases, you might even wind up as the local captain.

4) *Making the thing pay for itself.*

We are not, thank God, in this to make money; we're just trying to make the scoresheets available to the public, thus getting out and circulating a lot of information that used to be secret.

But it has cost me a lot of money and a lot of other people a great deal of time and money to get the project going. It can't survive as an ongoing financial drain.

We hope to market the information. We will in time; we have to bring our standards of accuracy, speed and reliability up so that we can do this. If people can make newsletters pay for themselves through this information, that's great. I'll help them when I can.

Eventually, we'll bring out a book that contains information drawn from the project, a book that will contain so much material that it will push all previous statistical compendiums about baseball back into the dark ages. Maybe we'll get that book out this year; we hope to, but can't guarantee it. We had hoped to have it out by the spring, but we're not going to make that goal this time.

John Dewan has one of the key abilities which I am missing: he is well organized. He is also committed to making this thing work. I have a lot of respect for that. You know, one of the frustrating things to me in this line of work has been the difficulty in buying good quality work. The irony of it is that I am bombarded with letters from people who want to work in sabermetrics, but when push comes to shove they don't really want to do it. I don't know how many times I have heard from somebody who is dying to work in sabermetrics, but two or three months later I will call them or write them and try to hire them to take on some project—which, after all, nobody did for me—only to be told that they are too busy right now, or they don't have the resource materials needed to do the project. Sometimes people take on the project but do a half-assed job of it. They want to do it if I will hire them or if a team will hire them or if somebody will back them up. In sabermetrics, that's like saying you don't want to do it at all.

John isn't like that; he wants to do the work, as do several of the other people in the Project. He is going to do the work, come hail or high water. For that reason, I can say with confidence that *Project Scoresheet* will make strong strides in these four areas in the next year.

But not without your help. To keep the scoresheets of major league games in the hands of the public, we have to have the scoresheets. In closing, let me list the names of the local captains who got every game or missed only a few in 1985:

Dennis Bretz   Mark Podrazik   Brent MacInnes   Chuck Waseleski
Craig Christmann   Jim Rogde   Mike Marrero   Craig Wright
Shellie Garret   Steve Russell   Susan Nelson   Don Zminda
Mike Hawkins   Scott Segrin
Mike Kerbel   Wayne Townsend   Thanks.
Mike Kopf   John Ungashick

SECTION
II

TEAM COMMENTS

AMERICAN LEAGUE WEST
DIVISION SHEET

Club	1st	2nd	v RHP	v LHP	Home	Road	Grass	Turf	Day	Night	Total	Pct
Kansas City	44-42	47-29	69-51	22-20	50-32	41-39	32-29	59-42	20-26	71-45	91-71	.562
California	52-35	38-37	61-54	29-18	49-30	41-42	76-57	14-15	33-20	57-52	90-72	.556
Chicago	42-42	43-35	62-53	23-24	45-36	40-41	76-62	9-15	28-23	57-54	85-77	.525
Oakland	46-41	31-44	45-59	32-26	43-36	34-49	67-67	10-18	39-26	38-59	77-85	.475
Minnesota	40-45	37-40	57-57	20-28	49-35	28-50	24-35	53-50	23-25	54-60	77-85	.475
Seattle	42-45	32-43	45-64	29-24	42-41	32-47	24-36	50-52	19-19	55-69	74-88	.457
Texas	32-56	30-43	41-70	21-29	37-43	25-56	55-81	7-18	12-25	50-74	62-99	.385

COME FROM BEHIND WINS

Club	1	2	3	4	5	6	7	Total	Points
Kansas City	15	12	4	1				32	87
California	18	16	5	2	0	1		42	121
Chicago	16	9	5	3	1			34	100
Oakland	23	9	7	0	1			40	107
Minnesota	17	10	4	0	0	1		32	87
Seattle	11	5	6	1	1	3		27	93
Texas	14	6	2	2	1	0	1	26	78

BLOWN LEADS

Club	1	2	3	4	5	6	7	8	Total	Points
Kansas City	20	8	5	1	1	0	1		36	103
California	10	11	3	1	2				27	82
Chicago	16	9	3	1					29	76
Oakland	15	7	2	2	0	1			27	76
Minnesota	14	7	4	3	0	0	0	1	29	89
Seattle	18	4	3	2					27	70
Texas	26	12	6						44	112

RECORDS WHEN AHEAD, TIED, BEHIND AFTER SEVEN

Club	Ahead	Tied	Behind
Kansas City	77-11	8- 9	6-51
California	70- 7	10- 5	10-60
Chicago	68- 5	11-13	6-59
Oakland	56- 3	13-11	8-71
Minnesota	62- 7	7- 8	8-70
Seattle	57- 2	10- 9	7-77
Texas	45- 8	11- 9	6-82

CLUB BATTING

Club	G	AB	R	H	TB	2B	3B	HR	RBI	GW	SH	SF	HB	BB	IB	SO	SB	CS	DP	LOB	SHO	Avg	Slug	OBP
Kansas City	162	5500	687	1384	2205	261	49	154	657	87	44	41	36	473	57	840	128	48	125	1057	4	.252	.401	.313
California	162	5442	732	1364	2100	215	31	153	685	80	99	35	39	648	51	902	106	51	139	1165	10	.251	.386	.333
Chicago	163	5470	720	1386	2145	247	37	146	695	78	59	45	43	471	40	843	108	56	119	1009	7	.253	.392	.315
Oakland	162	5581	757	1475	2238	230	34	155	690	71	63	47	16	508	29	861	116	58	129	1073	5	.264	.401	.325
Minnesota	162	5509	705	1453	2240	282	41	141	678	74	39	47	31	502	36	779	68	44	117	1144	12	.264	.407	.326
Seattle	162	5521	719	1410	2276	277	38	171	686	69	28	41	31	564	36	942	94	35	147	1143	8	.255	.412	.326
Texas	161	5361	617	1359	2041	213	41	129	578	56	34	45	33	530	30	819	130	76	136	1100	9	.253	.381	.322

OPPOSITION BATTING

Club	G	AB	R	H	TB	2B	3B	HR	RBI	GW	SH	SF	HB	BB	IB	SO	SB	CS	DP	LOB	SHO	Avg	Slug	OBP
Kansas City	162	5582	639	1433	2087	253	46	103		60	48	42	28	463	37	846	92	50	152	1135	11	.257	.374	.315
California	162	5531	703	1453	2290	252	36	171		70	48	44	27	514	30	767	79	56	169	1089	8	.263	.414	.326
Chicago	163	5509	711	1411	2290	257	42	161		71	57	47	36	569	35	1023	112	56	152	1154	8	.256	.406	.327
Oakland	162	5609	787	1451	2313	286	30	172		80	39	46	25	607	32	785	104	51	156	1181	6	.259	.412	.331
Minnesota	162	5473	782	1468	2320	262	49	164		82	47	55	30	462	31	767	100	54	137	1006	7	.268	.424	.326
Seattle	162	5496	818	1456	2237	251	34	154		80	38	48	41	637	54	868	105	57	170	1146	8	.265	.407	.343
Texas	161	5503	785	1479	2346	266	41	173		95	28	44	36	501	38	863	119	41	165	1092	5	.269	.426	.331

CLUB PITCHING

Club	W	L	ERA	G	CG	SHO	SV	IP	H	TBF	R	ER	HR	SH	SF	HB	TB	IB	SO	WP	BK
Kansas City	91	71	3.49	162	27	11	41	1461.0	1433	6165	639	566	103	48	42	28	463	37	846	43	9
California	90	72	3.91	162	22	8	41	1457.1	1453	6164	703	633	171	48	44	27	514	30	767	45	4
Chicago	85	77	4.07	163	20	8	39	1451.2	1411	6221	720	656	161	57	47	36	569	35	1023	54	5
Oakland	77	85	4.41	162	10	6	41	1453.0	1451	6327	787	712	172	39	46	25	607	32	785	48	5
Minnesota	77	85	4.48	162	41	7	34	1426.1	1468	6067	782	710	164	47	55	30	462	31	767	51	11
Seattle	74	88	4.68	162	23	8	30	1432.0	1456	6260	818	744	154	38	48	41	637	54	868	61	18
Texas	62	99	4.56	161	18	5	33	1411.2	1479	6112	785	715	173	28	44	36	501	38	863	43	7

OPPOSITION PITCHING

Club	W	L	ERA	G	CG	SHO	SV	IP	H	TBF	R	ER	HR	SH	SF	HB	TB	IB	SO	WP	BK
Kansas City	71	91			32	4	34		1384	6094	687		103	44	41	36	473	57	840	42	
California	72	90			25	10	34		1364	6263	732		171	99	35	39	648	51	902	27	
Chicago	77	85			33	7	36		1386	6088	736		161	59	45	43	471	40	843	48	
Oakland	85	77			22	5	33		1475	6215	757		172	63	47	16	508	29	861	48	
Minnesota	85	77			54	12	39		1453	6128	705		164	39	47	31	502	36	779	59	
Seattle	88	74			23	8	50		1410	6185	719		154	28	41	31	564	36	942	49	
Texas	99	62			28	9	45		1359	6003	617		173	34	45	33	530	30	819	35	

CLUB FIELDING

Club	G	PO	A	E	TC	DP	TP	PB	OSB	OCS	OSB%	OA/SFA	Pct	DER	OR
Kansas City	162	4383	1907	127	6417	160	1	10	92	50	.648	24/42	.980	.699	639
California	162	4372	1841	112	6325	202	0	8	79	56	.585	44/44	.982	.709	703
Chicago	163	4355	1677	111	6143	152	0	11	112	56	.667	29/47	.982	.700	720
Oakland	162	4359	1566	140	6065	135	0	19	104	51	.671	26/46	.977	.708	787
Minnesota	162	4279	1732	120	6131	139	0	13	100	54	.649	43/55	.980	.702	782
Seattle	162	4296	1836	122	6254	156	0	22	105	57	.648	36/48	.980	.696	818
Texas	161	4235	1703	120	6058	145	0	23	119	41	.744	38/44	.980	.694	785

KANSAS CITY ROYALS

BREAKDOWNS FOR THE LAST TEN SEASONS

Won-Lost Record: 860-701, .551 (Best in the Division, 4th Best in the Majors)
Runs Scored: 7,175 (Most in the Division, 4th-Highest in Majors)
Runs Allowed: 6,620 (Fewest in the Division, 12th Lowest total in Majors)
Home Runs Hit: 1,113 (6th in the Division, 17th in the Majors)
Home Runs Allowed: 1,205 (6th in the Division, 13th in the Majors)

RECORD IN:
April: 94-82, .534 (3rd Best in the Division, 7th in Majors)
May: 138-129, .517 (Best in the Division, 8th in Majors)
June: 140-123, .532 (Best in the Division, 6th in Majors)
July: 145-106, .578 (Best in the Division, 3rd Best in the Majors)
August: 171-123, .582 (Best in the Division, 4th Best in the Majors)
September: 156-127, .551 (Best in the Division, 6th in Majors)
October: 16-11, .593 (Best in the Division, 4th Best in the Majors)
    (Records for October are for in-season play only: do not include playoffs
    or World Series. When two teams tie for fourth position, as in this case
    (oddly, Kansas City and Pittsburgh have identical records in both September
    and October) both teams will be listed as being fourth.
Won-Lost Record in Road Games: 391-393, .499 (Best in the Division, 7th in Majors)
Won-Lost Record at Home: 469-308, .604 (Best in the Division, 4th Best in Majors)
Home Field Advantage: 81½ Games
Runs Scored on the Road: 3,430 (2nd-Highest in the Division, 7th in Majors)
Runs Scored at Home: 3,745 (Most in the Division, 3rd-Highest in the Majors)
Runs Allowed on the Road: 3,466 (6th-Highest (2nd lowest) in the Division, 11th-Highest in Majors)
Runs Allowed at Home: 3,154 (Fewest in the Division, 10th-Fewest in Majors)

Home Runs Hit on the Road: 634 (4th-Highest in the Division, 11th-Highest in Majors)
Home Runs Hit at Home: 479 (Fewest in the Division, 5th Lowest in the Majors)
Home Runs Allowed on the Road: 685 (2nd Highest (Most) in the Division, 3rd Highest in Majors)
Home Runs Allowed at Home: 520 (Fewest in the Division, 6th-Fewest in Majors)

RECORD FOR LAST THREE SEASONS: 254-232, .523 (2nd in the Division, 10th in Majors)

A HISTORY OF BEING A KANSAS CITY BASEBALL FAN

I am, and have been for as long as it is possible to remember, a fan of the Kansas City baseball teams. In my youth this required that I support the Kansas City Athletics, the only team in modern history which never had a .500 or better season. Well, that's not exactly true; the Milwaukee Brewers of 1901 and the Seattle Pilots of 1969 had losing records in the only seasons of their existence, but that hardly counts, and the Seattle Mariners have not yet had a winning record, but they will within a year or two.

Under current conditions it would be very difficult, if not impossible, for any baseball team to become as bad as the Kansas City Athletics were. In modern baseball, when a team gets to be bad they acquire the high picks in the draft of high school and college players. Unless they were to do an atrocious job of evaluating the talent, this gives them enough of an edge that, over a period of five to seven years, they will begin to move back toward the center of the league. Just as it takes time to reach the levels of greatness represented by such teams as the 1963 Yankees, the 1953 Dodgers and the 1970 Orioles, it takes time to reach the nadir of performance represented by the A's of the mid-sixties. With the draft, the calendar now is working against such a possibility.

Thirteen straight losing seasons . . . the mind reaches for a yardstick. If you are a fan of the San Francisco Giants, you certainly have encountered some rough sailing in recent years. But the longest span of consecutive losing seasons ever turned in by the Giants, either in San Francisco or New York, either in this century or the last, is four.

If you are a fan of the Detroit Tigers, you certainly can remember some tough times here and there between contenders—but again, the longest string of consecutive losing seasons that you could possibly recall would be four, because that's the most they've ever had.

Not many teams have ever had thirteen.

The Brooklyn Dodgers, da bums who suffered centuries of frustration before developing into a powerhouse in the forties, never exposed their fans to thirteen consecutive losing seasons.

The Pittsburgh Pirates were a joke from the early 1940s until the coming of Danny Murtaugh, a team so bad that computer analyst George Wiley says they should have finished 9th in an 8-team league. But the Pittsburgh Pirates have never had thirteen straight losing seasons.

The Mets of the sixties, the late seventies and early eighties were the most spectacular losers of the expansion era, losing 120 games in one season and becoming a campy favorite while making an annual event of last place. But even the Mets have never suffered thirteen straight losing seasons—nor, indeed, has any expansion team, not the Padres, not the Expos, not even the expansion Senators.

For as long as most of us can remember, the Chicago Cubs have been baseball's lovable losers, the team which went into a coma after World War II and did not emerge until 1984. But even the Chicago Cubs have never suffered through thirteen straight losing seasons.

First in War, First in Peace, Last in the American League . . . remember the original Washington Senators? The Washington Senators never suffered through thirteen consecutive losing seasons.

The White Sox punted the World Series in 1919, and were condemned to a long, dark exile of forty years before they got a chance to redeem themselves. They missed that chance and have waited another quarter-century, to date, for another one. But the White Sox never went through thirteen consecutive losing seasons.

The Boston Braves, in their half-century of going head to head with the Red Sox, rarely came out on top; they were the worst team in the National League in the first decade of this century, and were consistently among the worst teams in baseball in the twenties and thirties. But the Boston Braves never had thirteen consecutive losing seasons.

The Cleveland Indians, in our own time, are hardly a model of a perennial powerhouse; it is tough to remember when the organization fielded a good team. But the Cleveland Indians have never had thirteen consecutive losing seasons. In fact, their longest two streaks added together only amount to thirteen seasons.

And *even the Browns*. Even the St. Louis Browns, the hapless Brownies . . . yes, even the Browns never suffered through thirteen consecutive losing seasons.

This one fact, however depressing, testifies only to the duration of the frustration; there was more to it than that. The A's not only never had a winning record, they never came close to having a winning record. They were never in any *danger* of having a winning record.

They very rarely had a winning *month*. Here; I'll list all the months in A's history when they won as many games as they lost (not including Octobers, and they never won more than two games in October):

1955—None
1956—None
1957—None
1958—April (8–4) and September (14–13)
1959—April (9–7) and July (19–11)
1960—None
1961—May (14–12)
1962—August (16–15)
1963—April (12–7) and May (13–12)
1964—None
1965—None
1966—September (13–9)
1967—None

Let's see . . . that makes nine months in which they played .500-or-better ball, which means they had losing records in 69 months out of 78. The best month that the A's ever had in Kansas City was July of 1959; they started that month 9 games out of first place, and finished 9½ out. By the end of August, one month later, they would be 21 behind.

How bad were the A's? Well, consider this: the recent history of the Texas Rangers is not exactly ablaze in glory. *Over the last thirteen seasons the Rangers' won/lost record is one-hundred and forty and one-half games better than the A's record in Kansas City.* The A's record in Kansas City was 829 wins, 1,224 losses; the Rangers have beaten them by 136 wins, and taken 145 fewer losses. How bad is eleven games a year worse than the Rangers?

How bad can you get? The San Francisco Giants, now . . . there's another prize organization. Over the last thirteen years the Giants have beaten the record of the Kansas City A's by 145 games. Or how about using the Cleveland Indians as a standard? Some people have had the audacity to suggest that the Indians have the most dismal history of any major league franchise. Over the last thirteen years the Indians record is 943-1091, which is only a hundred and twenty-three and a half games better than the A's.

The A's won/lost percentage for their years in Kansas City was .404. Only once in the last thirteen seasons— that being 1985, when the Indians lost 102 games—have the Indians had a winning percentage as low as .404, as low as the *average* winning percentage of the Kansas City A's.

The Cleveland Indians have been around for 85 years. In that time they have had six seasons with winning percentages below .400, three of which happened more than seventy years ago. The KC A's, in existence for only thirteen years, had seven seasons with winning percentages below .400. *The Cleveland Indians, in their long and largely dismal history, have had fewer truly dreadful teams than the Kansas City A's were able to pack into their brief thirteen-year life.*

That was my childhood.

In the A's thirteen years in Kansas City, the only pitcher to win as many as 15 games in a season was a fellow named Bud Daley, who twice won 16. Only five pitchers ever won more than 12 in a season, and most of those still had losing records.

In the A's last three years in Kansas City, the most runs driven in by any player in a season was 66. I would guess that no other team has ever gone three years without having a player drive in more than 66 runs.

In the same three years, the highest batting average by a regular was .270.

There have been worse teams. The thirteen consecutive losing seasons is not a record; the Red Sox and both Philadelphia franchises either matched or worsened it. The situation was not quite the same; the fans of the Red Sox and the Philadelphia Athletics could at least console themselves with the memories of the perennial champions who came just before the losing began, whereas the Kansas City fans, reflecting on the time before they were losers, could remember only the time when they were considered bush league.

But I couldn't remember that. I was only five years old when the A's arrived.

Though unified by the execrable quality of the teams, the A's passed through three distinct periods (three "building phases") between Philadelphia and Oakland, each one creating distinct riddles and emotions for me as a child fan. The first period was the Arnold Johnson years. Arnold Johnson, the first owner of the Kansas City Athletics, was a business associate and close friend of Del Webb, co-owner of the Yankees. Apparently believing that the way to make money in the outlands was as a supplier of talent to the wealthier organizations, Johnson funnelled talent to the Yankees in a long series of three-for-one and five-for-two trades. Among the players acquired by the Yankees from Kansas City were Cletis Boyer, Roger Maris, Ryne Duren and Bobby Shantz. Ralph Terry was traded by the Yankees to the A's in 1957 after pitching ineffectively in trials in 1956 and early 1957; he was 21 at the time. When he got his feet on the ground as a major league pitcher, he was returned to the Yankees. When Enos Slaughter got off to a slow start with the Yankees in 1955 he was exiled to Kansas City; when he established that he could still hit and the Yankees needed him, he was sent back.

There was a bad smell about these trades, but much more irritating than the trades of prospects and the "loans" of other players in the development stage were the exchanges of the A's best players to the Yankees. Art Ditmar, the A's leading pitcher in their first two seasons (he won 12 games each year) was traded to the Yankees, where he pitched fairly well for four years, and was the Yankees best starting pitcher in 1960. Harry (Suitcase) Simpson, after driving in 105 runs and hitting .293 for the A's in 1956, was in pinstripes by late 1957. Bob Cerv, after having the best offensive season that any KC A was ever to have in 1958 (he hit .305 with 38 homers, was elected to the All-Star team and batted cleanup for the American League), was returned to the Yankees in 1960. Bud Daley, after winning 16 games for the Athletics in 1959 and 1960, was traded to the Yankees in 1961. Hector Lopez, who seemed to be developing into a fine hitter, was traded to the Yankees in 1959. After Duke Maas pitched well in 1957 (219 innings with a 3.28 ERA), he was shipped on to New York, where he went 26–12 over the next two and a half seasons. If you look at the 1958 Kansas City team, which was the best A's team in the city (they finished 73–81), you might note that the top three home run and RBI men were Cerv, Maris, and Lopez; the team leader in strikeouts, innings and several other pitching categories was Ralph Terry. By 1960, all were with the Yankees.

Kansas City had been a minor league outpost for the Yankees for many years, and nobody minded too much so long as they weren't theoretically competing. But Kansas City is an extremely self-conscious town—we'll get into that later—and the pinstripe pipeline rubbed the city at a raw spot, the rawest spot Johnson could have found. With every KC/New York trade the protests grew louder, the bitterness in them grew sharper.

To a child, none of this quite made sense. I lived 80 miles from Kansas City, never went into the city and never saw them play in person. We didn't have a television, but I listened to them on the radio and studied the sports section of the Topeka paper. Why did so many people hate the Yankees? Why were so many people angry at the owner, when the radio broadcasters (of course) said that he was such a fine man and that what he was doing was in the best interests of Kansas City in the long run? Why did they root for the team if they didn't like them?

The notion of an inferiority complex is difficult for a child to figure out on his own in the best of circumstances. Having never visited either Kansas City or New York, I could have had no sense of the difference between one city and another. The history of the Yankees' overlording of

baseball meant nothing to me. A child has no way of understanding history because his concept of time is too limited; he can't imagine what is meant by a period of years. I could gather from it only that our team did not win very often, and that some people felt we were being taken advantage of. I rejected the idea that we were being taken advantage of because it seemed to me to be related in some way to self-pity.

In truth, how damaging these trades were is not absolutely clear. The group of players who had played well with the A's—Cerv, Simpson, Daley, etc.—were mostly players of marginal value who had one bright fling with the Athletics, and did very little to help the Yankees (or anybody else) after their trades. As for the trades of younger players like Maris, Boyer and Terry, the A's also *received* some good young players from the Yankees, including their two best players of the early sixties, Norm Siebern and Jerry Lumpe, and two other players that they gave up when they acquired Maris, Vic Power and Woodie Held. Terry was a big winner with the Yankees, but I doubt that he would have been much had he stayed in Kansas City.

The certain facts are that:

1) The A's were a bad team,

2) They traded all of their best players to the Yankees, and

3) After that, they were a worse team.

That's enough to convict Arnold Johnson in almost any court, but it should be noted that the A's farm system in these years produced very little talent—maybe 2 or 3 players of quality. He had to try to come up with young players from somewhere. Unfortunately, what he tried didn't work.

Arnold Johnson died on March 10, 1960; in the fullness of time his estate was able to sell the team to one Charles Oscar Finley. At first Finley's Athletics, perhaps influenced by holdover personnel in the front office, perhaps only by habit, continued to make sweetheart deals with the Yankees. The trade of Bud Daley, the A's most successful pitcher ever, was the last straw; the public was outraged. Finley and his new General Manager, Frank Lane, promised the Kansas City public that there would be no more Yankee trades.

The years beginning in 1961 could be described as the era of false promise. In 1961 and 1962 the A's were committed to youth; in 1963 this commitment wavered and in 1964 it collapsed. I was a full-fledged fanatic by now, rarely missing a game, often pacing a harrowed pattern around the front room as the A's wrestled to preserve their victories, more often sitting doggedly through the last out of a depressing rout. In my youth I believed the things that I was told by the announcers—that the A's were just a run here and a run there away from winning a lot more games, that they were just a player or two short of being a contender, that if they could just catch a break here and there they would get some momentum going and be over the hump. Every year we had different announcers in Kansas City, as Finley fired one after another, but each group reassured me about the banalities of the last. It was not merely that I began each spring full of promise, but that I arrived at the middle of August with the same expectation—that at any moment the breaks would change, the momentum would switch and the river would begin to flow uphill.

What seemed especially puzzling to me was the failure of the young players to develop. Annually the A's would spring upon us three or four unheard of youngsters. As the season evolved these kids would rush to the brink of stardom and retreat, looking for the consistency and gaining the experience which would put them among the best in the league at their positions. Yet, while the other organizations would take young players and develop them, none of the Athletics' young performers would ever progress an inch from the point at which they entered the league. I couldn't understand how this could happen, how the A's could so consistently come up with the non-bloomers; it seemed to me that just by the law of averages, as it is familiarly known, it should be our turn to have one develop sooner or later. A few examples, in alphabetical order:

JIM ARCHER pitched 205 innings with a good 3.20 ERA as a rookie in 1961, but would start only one major league game after that season.

NORM BASS won 11 games as a rookie in 1961, but would win only two more games in his remaining major league career, and within a few seasons would give up baseball to concentrate on his football career.

ED CHARLES hit .288 with 17 home runs, 54 walks and 20 stolen bases as a rookie third baseman in 1962, but never again had as good a season.

DICK HOWSER as a rookie shortstop in 1961 was the best lead-off man in baseball, hitting .280, drawing 92 walks, stealing 37 bases (second highest total in baseball) and scoring 108 runs. The only major league leadoff man to have a comparable season was Maury Wills, who hit .282, scored 105 runs and stole 35 bases. Compared to Wills, Howser was several years younger, drew 33 more walks with 12 less strikeouts, and hit for much more power (38 extra base hits against 23). Yet a year later Wills had developed into one of baseball's biggest stars—while Howser, after fracturing a leg in a collision at second base, never approached the same performance.

MANNY JIMÉNEZ hit .301 in 139 games as a rookie in 1962, but never again played regularly in the majors.

JOSÉ TARTABULL, proclaimed by the announcers as the fastest man in baseball in 1962, hit a solid .277 in 107 games as a rookie—but never had as good a season again.

There were other examples. I was mystified by why this kept happening to us. Over the years, I have noted again this effect, that when a good organization comes up with a young player that young player will develop, but that when a weak organization comes up with a good young player he seems less likely to progress. From this distance, several things are apparent. One is the pressure that the bad organization put on the young players. Dick Howser was a fine young player—but he was expected to carry the ballclub. Any time a young pitcher showed promise he would be given a heavy workload and the high expectations that came with it. That pressure complicated the learning process for each youngster.

Second, the players on the A's had no example to guide them. When the White Sox would come up with a young player, he would have the example of Luis Aparicio

to go by, to see how he handled the daily pressures, what his work habits were and how he conducted himself getting ready for the game. When the Dodgers would come up with a young pitcher he would have the example of Don Drysdale or Koufax; when the Orioles had a young player he could study Brooks Robinson, while the Yankees, of course, were surrounded by such quality. The A's players were on their own.

Third, a few of the A's players—but, I would stress, only a few of them—were not really prospects of any particular quality, but rather were the rejects of other organizations, let go because of defensive skills or personal qualities that would manifest themselves after the player got a chance to play. Ed Charles, one of the rookie "finds" of 1962, had been kicking around the minor leagues for almost a decade before he got a chance to play. It is not surprising that he played well in his rookie season, and not surprising that he played less well after that. Jim Archer, too, was no prospect, a throw-in in a trade with the Orioles who surprised everybody and hurt his arm when he pitched well in 1961. While the radio announcers could fool me by extolling the virtues of young players like Jim Gosger, Roger Repoz, Dan Pfister and Haywood Sullivan, the reality was that they simply did not have quality skills.

But fourth and most importantly, the organization suffered from extreme instability, resulting in a truly remarkable lack of commitment to their best young players. In individual instances perhaps one can make excuses for the organization. Granted, Dick Howser did not play well in the first half of the 1962 season. Granted, he was injured badly and out for the second half of the 1962 season; granted, when he was ready to get back in the lineup Wayne Causey was playing very well at the position.

But that's three "granteds," and it only covers one player. One of the stranger cases was that of Manny Jimenez, the only player of his generation from San Pedro de Macoris. Acquired from the Brave system in exchange for Bob Shaw, the big, strong left-handed hitter was among the league leaders in hitting for the first three months of the 1962 season, until Charlie Finley arranged a private conference with him and told him to stop concentrating on hitting for average and to try to hit more home runs. Finley not only did this, but he immediately went up to the press box and told everybody that he had done it, and why he had done it and how he had done it. Later, he would insist that he hadn't done it at all, and when that didn't work he said that he had done it, but only after his manager and his coaches had tried unsuccessfully to tell Jimenez the same thing.

Anyway, Jimenez went into a slump immediately thereafter, and finished the season at .301, losing almost 30 points in the last two months. Jimenez was not a good outfielder or a good baserunner. Even so, .301's alright; .301 with medium-range power (11 homers, 69 RBI in 479 at bats) for a 23-year-old rookie . . . that's a place to start something from.

When Manny Jimenez went to spring training the next year he found himself without a job. In a search for more power, the left field slot had been given to Chuck Essegian, a 31-year-old veteran who had never before played regularly, but had hit 21 homers in 336 at bats with Cleveland in 1962. Finley felt that, playing regularly, he would hit 35 home runs. He hit five. Jimenez spent a good part of the season in the minor leagues. While on the A's roster he pinch hit and filled in, hit .280 on the road to oblivion.

Why did the A's do this astonishingly stupid thing, to replace a 24-year-old .300 hitter with a 31-year-old nobody? The lack of commitment to the young players with talent reflects the extreme instability of the organization. As well as a different radio announcer every year, the organization had a different manager, usually different coaches, frequently a different general manager. It is my belief that men like Finley are compelled to change those who work for them in highly visible positions because their own low self-esteem and feelings of inadequacy cause them to project their own short-comings and weaknesses onto those around them. When Finley saw his own flaws reflected in those who represented him to the public, he felt that he had been exposed, his carefully hidden failings laid bare. This terrified him, and compelled him to fire anyone around him who was anything less than perfect.

But every new manager, every new general manager and every new coach had new ideas about who could help the organization and how he should be used. The most games played by any A's player in their 13 years in Kansas City was 726, by Ed Charles; in other words, not one player was able to last as long as five seasons as a regular. Emphasizing the instability, Finley was forever farting around with the fences, yanking them in as far as the rules would allow and then pushing them back. A pitcher would learn that he could get by with a particular pitch one year, and the next year the same ball would be in the seats, while a young hitter would learn to jerk the ball into the seats one year, only to see those same seats moved back by 25 or 30 feet the next season.

Yet the changes in personnel do not fully explain the organization's amazing lack of commitment to the young players with whom their fate rested. One of the recurrent themes of Bill James' analysis of baseball: bad organizations will tend to project their weaknesses onto their best players, and ultimately will dwell not on what the player *can* do, but on what he *can't*. And what better example of this can there be but Manny Jimenez? The kid's hitting .330, he's got a little power but *we're still losing*. If we're losing he must not be doing all that well. He's not a great outfielder or any kind of a baserunner, so he's got to hit for more power.

At this vantage there is little doubt that, left alone, Jimenez in time would have developed some power, and would have been a quality major league hitter, the type of player who could help win some games. Another example was José Tartabull, the little center fielder. Here, in 1962, was a 23-year-old kid who could fly, play center field and hit .277. Given a full shot, Tartabull would very likely have developed into a player who could help a team win. Instead, the A's saw him as a player who had no power and didn't throw very well; he too was out of a job in the spring of 1963. Bobby Del Greco, a 30-year-old refugee from the National League with a career average of .229, was in center.

A year later the A's had another young center fielder whom I left off the list above, a guy named Nellie Mathews. If you're inclined to focus on the negatives,

Mathews offered no challenge. He ran OK but not as well as you might want your center fielder to run, he struck out too much (143 times), hit .239, was too aggressive on the bases and didn't throw great. If you were inclined to focus on the positives, you'd see a 22-year-old kid who hit some doubles (27), some triples (5) and some homers (14), drew a few walks (43) and, according to all reports, hustled from the beginning of the game to the end. The average wasn't much, but in 1964 there were a great many regulars who hit less. Even the best teams in baseball at that time had .220 hitters in their lineups.

Finley was like a man who planted a garden every spring with energy and enthusiasm, but who saw by midsummer not the green, fresh produce he had envisioned, but a weedy, over-grown patch of dry vegetation. Embarrassed by this, he ripped out the garden so that no one would see his weeds. Unlike Jimenez and Tartabull, I wouldn't hazard a guess as to whether or not Mathews would have developed into a ballplayer. I know for sure that in the A's situation—they lost 105 games that year— I'd have been happy to take the chance. I'd figure that here's a young kid, if he lifts his batting average 20 or 30 points, maybe improves the strikeout and walk data a little bit as he goes along, maybe edges up from 46 extra base hits to 60 . . . well, he's going to have a job. It is equally likely that his faults might have reached up and swallowed him, that the tendency to strike out might have gotten out of hand and choked off his production, as the weeds will choke a garden. But we will never know. When spring training opened in 1965, center field was patrolled by a 31-year-old defensive specialist named Jim Landis. Career batting average, .247.

In the first four years of the Charlie Finley era of the A's (1960–1963), some progress was being made. The team's records for those four years were 58-96, 61-100, 72-90 and 73-89. Though some traits of the man tended to retard the progress, Finley *did* care about winning— indeed, he may have cared more about winning than any other owner of his time. Losing did not reflect well on him. The 1963 team, still a fairly young team, had a very good infield and three or four decent pitchers, although the outfield had no punch and the catching was bush league.

This progress was too slow for Finley; he was tired of losing. He was tired of having the professionals in his organization tell him that you had to build with youth, that you had to build from within, that it just took time. He was very concerned about the team's lack of power—the same concern that had led to the Jimenez and Essegian debacles of earlier years. At some point in the 1963 season he had a conversation with his manager, Ed Lopat, that was to bring this era of progress to a close, and reset the A's clock to the beginning of another building cycle.

Lopat had been a member of the formidable Yankee teams of the late forties and early fifties, and apparently he was trying to explain to Finley the Yankee formula. The Yankees, according to Lopat by way of Finley, had a simple trick for winning the pennant every year: it all had to do with the short dimensions down the lines—296 to right, 301 to left. With the short lines and deep center field area, all the Yankees had to do was keep around some power hitters to pull the ball in the seats, teach their own pitchers to keep the ball out away from the opponent's power hitters, and they'd have a big home run advantage.

No doubt Lopat did not intend to make it sound so simple; the odds are overwhelming that Ed Lopat at least had a clue that there was more to it than this. No doubt he would have explained this to Finley, had the conversation continued a few minutes longer. But Finley took this confession from the ex-Yankee very much to heart, and set out to replicate the conditions. To acquire one power hitter, Jim Gentile, he traded the best player on his team. To acquire another, Rocky Colavito, he traded the rest of the good players on his team. Then, blundering across the fine line between the stupid and the ridiculous, Finley ordered Municipal Stadium in Kansas City to be re-built to the exact field dimensions of Yankee Stadium.

To begin with, this was not physically possible; he would have had to rent center field from the city street department. Second, it was not permitted by the rules of the game, which, though protecting the existing parks, did not permit new fences to be constructed within 325 feet of home plate. And third, the whole idea was nuts.

Never to be deterred by such details, Finley constructed a pavillion in right field and called it his "Pennant Porch," boldly suggesting that what would win the pennant for New York would also win the pennant for Kansas City. The commissioner's office, which was more up on the rules of the game, insisted that Finley have the seats torn out to at least 325 feet. Finley, complaining bitterly of unequal treatment, eventually complied, after which it became the "one-half pennant porch," although a chalk line was painted across the outfield to show where the fence had been. Whenever a fly ball was hit over the line the public address announcer was instructed to announce that "That ball would have been a home run in Yankee Stadium." (It is said that the practice of making this announcement came to an end in the eleventh inning on May second, when the Minnesota Twins became the only team in baseball history to hit four consecutive home runs. It is said that following the home runs by Oliva, Allison, Hall and Killebrew, Earl Battey drove the ball to the wall in left, and the announcer dutifully intoned "That ball . . . would have been a home run . . . in Yankee Stadium." The announcement was discontinued the next day.)

The number of home runs hit in Kansas City increased from 139 to 239. Of the extra 100 home runs, the A's picked up 55, and their opponents 45. Those 45 were enough to enable the Kansas City team to set an all-time record for home runs allowed in a season, with 220. The record will not be broken in the next ten years.

The 1964 season obliterated the steady progress of the previous years. Not until the rookie draft was instituted in 1965 was there any new evidence that the A's would ever escape the second division.

One should not depart this sub-chapter of Kansas City's bleak baseball youth without a note about its lingering effect in the minds of those of us who witnessed it. You who are regular readers will know that one of the things that I look for in and admire in a good manager is his willingness to commit himself to a young player, and that in particular I have cited Dick Williams, Whitey Herzog and Dick Howser as being strong in this area. All three

of those managers know what it is that they expect a young player to do, and all three are able to avoid being distracted or disoriented in those periods when the player's weaknesses manifest themselves more clearly than his strengths. Those three managers (and several others, as well) played for the Kansas City A's in this period. In the same way as nothing will teach a man self-discipline like an extreme example of profligacy, one wonders if perhaps the need to make a commitment to young players was not impressed deeply upon these gentlemen by this obscene example of their youth, a team with no ability to make a commitment to anything or anyone. I would bet that there was a time, about 1960, when Dick Williams and Whitey Herzog sat in the Kansas City dugout and chatted about why they were in last place, and one of them said to the other (or both said at the same time), "You know, there's a lot of guys here who could play the damn game if they would just leave them alone and let them do it."

I was half grown by the mid-sixties, and I got to see a game occasionally. To the credit of Charles O. Finley, he learned from his mistakes. Following the hard lesson of 1964, he accepted the professionals' wisdom, accepted that it just takes time, that a good team must be built of youth and time, and that only patience could combine the two. The willingness of the organization to let a young player develop improved dramatically after 1964. Finley never again fell for the idea that there was a magic formula that could convert his team into a winner overnight. The A's resumed their torturous crawl forward.

In 1968 the Athletics moved to Oakland. At first many of us were determined to keep rooting for the Athletics; I had no experience in loving any other baseball team, and didn't imagine that I ever could. But in truth, rooting for Charlie Finley was damned hard work when he was right in front of you, and all but impossible from halfway across the continent.

In addition to being ugly and smelling bad, the Kansas City A's had a bad personality. I say this, as Broadway Danny Rose said, with all due respect. Charles O. Finley considered himself to be a master showman, and the team fairly swarmed in cutesy promotions and special events. They had the usual stuff like home run hitting contests, fireworks and special days for players who were retiring—even players who weren't any good—as well as more adventurous stuff like cow milking contests and pregame rodeos. Sheep grazed in the grass beyond the outfield; they were joined later by a mule. One year a cellar-bray-tion (a mule brays, get it?) was planned for the day that the A's got out of last place, but they never did. A mechanical rabbit popped out of the ground to deliver clean baseballs to the umpire. An automatic plate duster was installed. Finley put in a public picnic area (well, anybody can have a good idea once in awhile).

Finley would make a "day" out of anything. He once had a special day for an umpire who had been involved in some controversy, presenting him with a seeing-eye dog.

When Rocky Colavito got close to 300 home runs, he tried to generate public interest in the pursuit of this goal by scheduling an event and lining up a list of prizes to give him, headed by a plaque of 300 silver dollars.

He tried to give a "poison pen" award to KC writers who wrote disdainfully about these antics, but of course nobody would accept it.

He inaugurated the era of colored uniforms, and tried to inaugurate colored bases and colored baseballs as well.

There was a rule in the books requiring the pitcher, with no one on base, to deliver the pitch within 20 seconds of receiving the ball from the catcher. If he didn't do so, a ball could be called. Finley felt that this rule should be enforced, and put a clock on the scoreboard to count down the seconds; when the time elapsed a horn would sound. This, of course, was designed to show up the umpires for not enforcing the rule, and you can imagine how the umpires appreciated this. In addition, a pitcher in the act of delivering a pitch was often not enthusiastic about hearing a horn go off, and Finley was told to shut the thing off. He shut off the horn, but kept the clock. One umpire actually did call the penalty ball, against Kansas City pitcher Diego Segui.

For a time we had a woman broadcaster, for a few games late in the season ("Was that a slow one?" she would inquire of her co-workers). Don't get me wrong, I'm all for having a woman broadcaster, but it would help if she was a baseball fan—my wife, for example.

When the Beatles first toured the country, Charlie tried to get them to schedule a stop at Municipal Stadium on their tour. He tried this, however, after the tour was already booked, and when he was initially rebuffed he began throwing money at them to get them to reschedule so as to accommodate. Eventually he paid them an amount of money to make a one-night Kansas City appearance that was reportedly more than he was paying his entire starting lineup for the season. In the weeks before the show, the game broadcasters hyped this event non-stop; Finley was hoping to fill the park, and thus recoup his investment. When the crowd was disappointing, the announcers sniffed that Kansas City wouldn't support Charlie after he had put out a lot of money to get the Beatles to come to town. His players were not particularly appreciative, either.

Finley would appear on his pre-game show once in awhile, but rather than talking about the outlook for the ballclub, he would entertain us with his opinions about who should be in the Hall of Fame, how the rules should be changed and what a wonderful human being he was.

This junk was not the worst part of having Finley around. He feuded constantly with not only the press, but his players, his staff and the league office as well. Bitter holdouts were the order of the day in spring training. Public criticism of the players was commonplace. At times the team would come close to open revolt about some silly rule or about the mistreatment of a player.

He feuded with the city, which owned the park. But that wasn't the worst part, either.

Finley spent virtually his entire time in Kansas City threatening to move. First he tried to move to Dallas–Fort Worth. The league wouldn't let him. He tried to move to Louisville. He signed a lease on the Louisville park. The league wouldn't let him go. He sued the league. He wanted to move to Denver. He wanted to move to New Orleans. He talked about moving to Phoenix. He talked about moving to Seattle. He talked about moving to places that didn't even have ballparks.

He wanted to change cities for the same reason that he wanted to change managers. Once he had embarrassed himself in front of the city he wanted to wipe the slate clean, start all over with some people who didn't know anything about him.

At one point the league tried to kick him out. They had some sort of clause in their agreement—I never really did understand all this, to tell you the truth—that if you were bad enough they could kick you out of the club. Finley was about as bad as you could be, and they tried to kick him out. Apparently the clause was not enforceable, because he refused to leave and they couldn't make him. Or maybe the attempt to expel him was merely intended to force him to agree to stay in Kansas City.

He was involved in constant lawsuits. He hired and fired Frank Lane within about a year; Lane had to sue him for the balance of his contract.

When the expansion Royals came to town, it was immediately obvious that this organization was different. In their first season they won 69 games, which may not sound like much to you but it would have been a good season for the A's, and it is one of the best figures for a first-year expansion team. But more important than that, in the early years, were the small touches which put the signature of class on the organization. The circus atmosphere was gone; the emphasis was all on the ballteam.

Whereas the A's, for announcers, had subjected us to a long succession of ex-network men on the way down, small-timers on the way nowhere, and local announcers who had been fired by other teams, the Royals took the time and trouble to interview hundreds of people and locate a talented young man, Denny Mathews, who would come to represent the organization to Kansas City the way that Ernie Harwell represented the Tigers to Detroit or Vin Scully represented the Dodgers to LA.

Lou Piniella, after winning the American League Rookie of the Year Award in 1969, actually had a *better* season in 1970. Young players who did not succeed were given a respectable amount of time to be evaluated, before they were dismissed. No promotions were built around snake charmers, rock concerts, barnyard animals or attempts to embarrass the owner's enemies.

Whereas the A's organization was rather a grimy, dirty machine, grotesquely inefficient and with a personality nobody liked, the Royals tended to the other extreme; they seemed antiseptic, colorless, mechanically efficient and with not much personality to like or dislike. This was a very welcome change. We had moved from the slums to the suburbs.

In September, 1967, I moved away from home to attend Kansas University; a few days later the A's played their last game in Kansas City. I wonder sometimes how this sudden separation from my childhood affected the type of baseball fan that I became. From years of listening to the A's announcers, I had acquired the inevitable conviction that they had little idea of what they were talking about. I think, really, that this is one reason that so many intelligent people drift away from baseball at about that age, that if you care about it at all you have to realize, as soon as you acquire a taste for independent thought, that a great portion of the sport's traditional knowledge is ridiculous hokum. When baseball's explanations for things begin to look childish, the sport tends to get pushed back into childhood.

I was now, in addition to this, suddenly cut loose from my adolescent devotion, and forced to follow a new, different, and sharply contrasting team. My affection for the game as a whole was too much a part of me to be just cast aside, but my affection for the Royals was decidedly limited, and in fact it would be years before I would learn again to care blindly about my adopted heroes. It was not until Susie began to get involved in the game, ten years later, that I was able to recapture, through sharing her experience, the creative innocence required to abandon my emotions to the flight of the team.

The Royals seemed to me to be a product created for the public's consumption. This put a distance between me and the sport, and for a period of time, rather than simply following the team through the accepting eyes of a fan, I surveyed the game as coldly as if I had stumbled upon it as a foreigner—although, of course, I retained the enormous background of information about baseball that a fan develops. When Susie began following the game in the late seventies, the distinction between those teams which were manufactured in our own time and those which had simply always *been there* meant nothing to her; to her, as it will seem to our child, the Royals were simply there. Like all the other teams.

The accident of fate was that the period of my psychic separation from the emotional level of the sport corresponded to the period of my education, and so it happened that I began to borrow ways of looking at the game not from sportswriters, announcers and other fans, but from the academic disciplines of history and the social sciences.

The Kansas City community had long regarded Charlie Finley's A's as an embarrassment. Given a new, professional team to represent them, the city rallied around the Royals, determined to avoid a repetition of the petty, unpleasant relationship between team and town. An organization of businessmen, known as the Royal Lancers, was formed with the explicit purpose of helping the team to succeed economically. Specifically, they sell season tickets. And they're *real* good at it. I don't really know a lot of the details, but I gather that a local businessman named Earl Smith was quite instrumental in providing the impetus and leadership for this coalescence of the business community.

The A's had no fair complaint as to the crowds they drew. The Braves were in Milwaukee for thirteen years and had winning records all thirteen years. The Athletics were in Kansas City for thirteen years and had losing records all thirteen years. In spite of this, the Athletics drew 1,500,568 fans in their last two seasons in KC—34,073 more than the Braves drew in their last two seasons in Milwaukee. However, this may be misleading because the Milwaukee fans were boycotting the Braves in their last half-season in Milwaukee, whereas the Kansas City fans were sort of doing the opposite. There was a clause in the contract between Finley and Kansas City that the agreement could be abrogated if attendance was below 850,000. There was always speculation that Finley, in his eagerness to move, was deliberately trying to keep attendance down so as to keep this clause in play. In his last years the KC fans obstinately tried to keep attendance up so as to reduce Finley's bargaining power. Besides that, there's always been a lot of people around here who like baseball.

But if the A's attendance was adequate, the attendance of the Royals was abundant. The team was built with astonishing speed—astonishing, at least, to a young man who had grown up thinking that to have a losing team was the normal way of life. I had been conditioned to believe that for a losing team to right itself and become a winning team was an immortal task, and certainly would not be accomplished in less than seven years.

In three years the Royals were in contention, and since then they have virtually never been out. They have been extraordinarily fortunate. In their fifth season they brought up George Brett. No matter how smart you are, no matter how good your system is, when you find a George Brett you're lucky. If you came up with one every five years, you'd never lose a pennant.

In their first four years, under the direction of Cedric Tallis, the Royals turned in a run of trades that ranks with those made by Frank Lane in Chicago about 1950 as the greatest series of exchanges in history, in every case giving up a player who was to do nothing or virtually nothing in the major leagues in exchange for a player who would play in the major leagues for many years, in most cases finishing high in the balloting for Most Valuable Player. I suppose I have listed them before, but let me refresh your memory:

April 1, 1969: Steve Whitaker and John Gelnar for Lou Piniella

December 3, 1969: Joe Foy for Amos Otis and Bob Johnson

June 13, 1970: Fred Rico for Cookie Rojas

December 2, 1970: Bob Johnson and two minor players for Freddie Patek and two minor players

December 2, 1971: Jim York and Lance Clemons for John Mayberry

November 30, 1972: Roger Nelson and Richie Scheinblum for Hal McRae and Wayne Simpson

The only clinker they pulled off in this period was when they gave up Piniella for Lindy McDaniel, but they paid that one back with interest in 1976 by suckering the Brewers out of Darrell Porter and Jim Colborn for three guys who were about even to Jim Colborn.

Of course, as before, they were extremely fortunate in this era; nobody is *that* smart. An odd thing was that almost all of these trades were, at the time they were made, unpopular. The public's reaction to the Hal McRae trade was "Why are we giving up Roger Nelson for this guy?" Watching this unfold, in stark contrast to the patternless, turbulent experience of my earlier favorites, I was left with almost a superstitious awe of the Royals' organization. Until 1983 I reacted calmly to anything that the Royals could do. When they gave away John Mayberry I didn't second-guess them. When they fired Whitey Herzog I didn't second-guess them. I always said, "You gotta figure those guys know what they are doing."

We will assume that you know the history of the Kansas City team in the late seventies, and will pass over it with only one argument. That has to do with the quality of the team. The good fortune that had blessed the organization in the city, in the farm system and in their trades abandoned them in post season play, and they will forever be remembered as the second-best team in the league in the late seventies. There is no convincing evidence that they were not the best. True, they did lose three of four playoff matchups against the Yankees, but they missed winning three of four by only two innings.

To a baseball fan this may be convincing evidence, but if a coin lands on its head three times in four nobody is convinced that the coin is weighted. They were the type of team, like the 1985 Cardinals, that usually doesn't do well in a short, crucial series—too aggressive on the bases, too dependant on speed, too young and inexperienced. The Royals consistently beat all of the powerhouse teams in the American League East throughout those years; it was rare for any of those teams, including the Yankees, to win the season series against KC.

Having written those words, of course, I am compelled to get out the books and check the facts, and now that I do so I see that this occurrence was not rare; it was nonexistent. In *The Bronx Zoo,* Sparky Lyle wrote that "I hope to hell they realign the Divisions like they're talking about and put Kansas City in with us because it would be the last play-off spot they ever see. If they had been in the East this year, they would have been fourth." In fact, in that season the Royals had won outright their series against all of the tough teams in the Eastern Division, beating the Yankees 6 of 11, Boston, Detroit and Milwaukee 6 out of 10, and Baltimore 8 out of 10.

In their four championship seasons, the Royals never lost the season series to any of those teams, and posted winning percentages against them of .656 in 1976, .627 in 1977, .627 in 1978, and .617 in 1980. In 1976 they beat Boston (9–3), Detroit (8–4), Milwaukee (8–4), and the Yankees (7–5) and split with Baltimore. In 1977 they whupped up on Milwaukee (7–2), Detroit (8–3) and Baltimore (7–4) and split with the Yankees and Red Sox. In 1980 they split with Milwaukee and Baltimore and beat the others, including an 18–6 record against the Yankees and Detroit. Although they did lose the series to some of those teams in 1979, when they had an off year, over the three- or five-year period they won most of their games against any and all of those teams, and that remains true if you count the playoff games.

It is much more likely that if they were to realign the divisions, it would be the last play-off spot that the Yankees would ever see. And more likely than that, the Royals would win their share, and so would the other good teams in that division.

But, of course, who had been a better team during the season was not what was at issue in post-season play. When I look at the great teams of history and try to compare one to another, one question that I like to ask about each is "How many players were there here who were really outstanding players, who were good enough players to play in a thousand or 1500 major league games or win 100 or 150 games, and who were at or near the peak of

their game at this time?" Not "What were their stats in this particular year?", but "How good were they, really, and how many good players did they have?"

The Royals in those years had more than a dozen. Five key members of the 1977 Royals were still playing regularly in 1985, eight years and who knows how many games later; those five are Porter, White, Brett, Cowens, and McRae. Two of the *bench players* on that team are still around, those being Wathan and Buck Martinez. Three other regulars have retired after good careers, those being Otis, Mayberry and Patek. The pitching staff included several men who won over a hundred games, including Splittorff, Leonard, Gura and Pattin. Other members of those teams included Willie Wilson, Cookie Rojas and Dan Quisenberry; Rojas was old but the others weren't. There are others that I haven't mentioned who played a thousand or more games. You check out the great teams of history, and you won't find many who can match that.

Following the World Series in 1980, the performance of the Royals' organization began to waver. In the malignant summer of 1981, the Royals finished under .500 for the first time since 1974. There was no apparent reason for the decline. The Royals had won 97 games in 1980 with a team that was actually *younger* than the champions of 1976–1978, due to the development of Willie Wilson, Clint Hurdle and Dan Quisenberry, as well as U. L. Washington's having taken the shortstop job.

In 1982 the Royals won 90 games, but there were many things about the team that concerned me. By now the team was being run by a different General Manager, John Schuerholz. Running short of proven pitchers, the organization had attempted to patch up the staff with burned-out vets like Vida Blue, Dave Frost, Don Hood and Grant Jackson. Clint Hurdle, after having a fine season as a 22-year-old in 1980, encountered personal and health problems in 1981. The organization dumped him and gave the right field job to Jerry Martin, a 33-year-old player of modest ability. This decision seemed to me to be strongly reminiscent of the A's of my childhood, and to be not at all consistent with the practices which had built the Royals into a fine team. Worse than *pitching* Vida Blue, which was all right, was the fact that the organization had given up three pitching prospects, including Atlee Hammakker, to do so.

In 1983 the team reached another low, finishing 79–83 and with a serious drug scandal. The habit of trying to solve the pitching problems with beat-up veterans had reached self-parody. Trying to plug the gaps as key pitchers like Splittorff, Gura and Leonard got old and injured, the Royals had imported Gaylord Perry, Eric Rasmussen, Steve Renko and Bill Castro—on the same staff with holdovers Blue, Hood, Gura and Splittorff. Oh, it was ugly: I don't think anybody on that team could throw 86 miles an hour except Vida, and he couldn't get it over.

Fairly or unfairly, it seemed to me that the succession of trades that Schuerholz had made defined a philosophy about the sport and how to succeed in it. As a fan, I was aghast. I thought "I've seen this done before, and *it doesn't work.*" The team roster had acquired players like

Joe Simpson, Leon Roberts and Grey Pryor. I had taken pleasure in watching young role players like Frank White, U. L. Washington and Dan Quisenberry earn their spurs and grow into valued performers; I was not thrilled to see those positions on the team being filled by players that I knew had no chance to amount to anything.

At this point, in the *1984 Baseball Abstract,* I abandoned my long-held belief that "those guys probably know what they're doing." John Schuerholz, I wrote, "has yet to try anything that worked." Schuerholz "doesn't want to put Ron Johnson in the lineup and find out why he hits .336 at Omaha; he wants to come up with a 'proven' player. Somebody likes Bruce Bochte."

In view of the success of the Royals over the last two seasons, it is incumbent upon me to consider whether my remarks at that time were unfair to Schuerholz. I don't honestly know. It is clear that since then, while *some* of the importing of declining players has continued (i.e., the trades for Jim Sundberg and Lonnie Smith), there has in general been a return to the practices of earlier years. Like Amos Otis, Freddie Patek and John Mayberry, Steve Balboni was a capable young player trapped in a bad situation; the Royals liberated him in exchange for very little, and he was one of the top home run hitters in baseball last season. In the spring of 1984 a commitment was made to the next generation of young pitchers, and those pitchers have turned out to be better than anyone would have dared hope.

The thing is, I really don't know what happened within the offices of Royals' Stadium. Perhaps I inferred incorrectly what John Schuerholz was trying to do in the period 1981–1983. Perhaps Schuerholz was confronted with a situation in which there simply were no good young players available to him, and he felt that the best thing he could do was to try to stabilize the team by bringing in some experienced players until the young ones were ready. If so, what I wrote then was unfair. Another possibility is that there was a time, about the same time that I wrote that article, that Ewing Kauffman held a meeting and said "Look, John, you're a bright young man, you're a good negotiator and we're glad to have you here, but what you're doing with the team just isn't working. We didn't get where we are by dragging in ballplayers three-quarters of the way through their careers. We got here by giving young men a chance to play, letting them surprise people. Let's go back to that." If that's closer to what happened, then what I wrote was fair.

But John Schuerholz has to be given credit for what he has done. It's a simple game; if you win, you deserve credit for it. John Schuerholz has rebuilt the Royals into one of the best teams in baseball.

By August, it was fairly apparent that the 1985 Royals had a chance to be remembered. I try to recall . . . was there a specific game in there, about the tenth of August perhaps, when I suddenly looked down and realized how brutally resilient this team could be when the situation arose, how strong was their will to survive and how sure their instinct for the kill? Whether or not there was one moment, the hunger of the Royals had manifested itself quite suddenly, and seemed, far from being "intangible," to be as palpable as the August heat.

The 1984 team, though the best of a poor division, was not too much of a ballclub; there was little room for disappointment when the Tigers destroyed them in the Championship Series. If that team had been in the A. L. East, they *would* have finished fourth. At best. The pitching staff was a combination of rookies and reclamation projects, and that was the best part of the team.

In early 1985 the Royals looked a little better, while not winning any more consistently. The pitchers had done what second-year pitchers are supposed to do and reclamation projects are not supposed to be able to do; four of the five starters were throwing harder than they had in 1984. George Brett was playing as well as he has ever played, and not too many have ever played better. The offense was inconsistent.

In late July, the offense clicked and the Royals began methodically churning good opponents into mush. From July 19 through the end of the season the Royals played 32 games against teams who finished the season with winning records. They won 23 of those 32 games, a remarkable .719 winning percentage—against the good teams. Excepting a one-game makeup against the Tigers, they won nine straight series against winning teams, beating the Yankees three straight games, the Tigers two out of three and two out of three, the Blue Jays two out of three and two out of three, the White Sox two out of three and then three straight, and the Angels two out of three and three out of four.

It is fortunate that no one was able to market an "Eau de Mariner" or "Essence of Ranger," or the Royals post-season play would have been short and unmemorable. Through the same period, they played poorly against .500-or-less teams, winning 22 but losing 21. The Red Sox were neither a good team nor a bad team, winning 81 and losing as many; in August the Royals beat them in Fenway Park, but lost to them in Kansas City, where the Red Sox have always played poorly. But they seemed to treat each challenge from a strong opponent as a dress rehearsal for post-season play.

They lost Jim Sundberg for a period, and this slowed them down a little; they lost Willie Wilson for a while, and felt his loss as much. But the pitching was there almost every day, and when they were good, they were very, very good. This ability to rise up and strike down the best of opponents was on my mind in the first days of September, when I was analyzing the things that might happen in post-season play for my newsletter. I recognized the weaknesses of the club, and concluded the newsletter with this paragraph:

But the Royals are hungry for a World Championship ring. Ewing Kauffman, who is selling off the team in stages, desperately wants to have a World Championship before he goes, and is probably applying pressure at the top of the organization to see that no effort is spared to bring it about (although if he is, it doesn't get into the papers.) Frank White, George Brett, Jim Sundberg, Dan Quisenberry—these guys are past 30 and have never won it. They know that they're not going to get many more shots. To Willie Wilson and Lonnie Smith, the World Championship would be the ultimate triumph over their personal problems. For Wilson, another World Series would be an opportunity to remove the stigma of the 1980 series, when he was unjustly and inaccurately portrayed as the Royals' goat. My gut tells me that they're going to do it.

Earlier in the newsletter, I had written that, having seen almost every game between the Blue Jays and Royals either in person or on TV, I found it very difficult to believe that the Blue Jays could beat the Royals. When the playoff started, it didn't take them long to make a believer out of me. The Blue Jay team that I had seen was a superbly talented team, but a team which made exactly the kind of mistakes that lose playoffs, and plenty of them.

But in the first two games of the playoff, it was the veteran Royals who made the mistakes. They made so many mistakes in the first game that they wiped themselves out, losing 6–1. In the second game, they made just enough mistakes to lose, being charged with three errors and blowing the lead twice.

Two notes are in order about Game 3, which, even had it not been a playoff game, would rank among the most memorable contests that I've ever seen. I hope the sense of this came across in the TV version; I didn't see the broadcast, but I gather that Bob Costas did an excellent job:

#1 George Brett that night turned in one of the most brilliant individual performances in the annals of the sport. In the first inning he crushed a low pitch into a gentle breeze from right, the ball landing 30 to 40 feet beyond the fence down the right field line. In the top of the third he turned in a spectacular defensive play, spearing a hard smash down the third base line and looping a perfect throw around Damaso Garcia, who was trying to score on the play; the play was, in essence, two very difficult plays—the stop and the throw—unified by a split-second decision. In the fourth, with the wind now howling in from right, he lined a pitch off the top of the fence in right-center for a double; the ball was hit much harder than the homer in the first. In the sixth, with a runner on first and the Royals down by two, he hit the ball a mile high toward center; it eventually came to earth just over the fence to the center field side of the 385 sign in left-center, tying the score. In the eighth he singled and scored the game-winning run.

For the game Brett hit 1.000, slugged 2.750, scored four runs and drove in three. And yet, you know, the Royals could very easily have lost that game. After George had put them ahead 2–0, the Blue Jays scored five runs in the fifth inning, then had the bases loaded with two out. Steve Farr came into the game and got the out that he had to get to keep the game within reach. Jim Sundberg homered in the bottom on the fifth to cut the margin to two and take some of the wind out of the Blue Jays' sails. Willie Wilson got on to start the sixth, doubling the value of Brett's second homer. After Brett reached in the eighth, McRae bunted him to second and Balboni singled him home.

I think that just shows how false, how truly silly, the idea is that one player "carries" a team, or that one player turns a team around, or that one player is, really, anything except one player. The man put on a one-game show that nobody could sustain, nobody could match, even for a pe-

riod of two or three games—and yet without the key contributions of five other players, his team would have lost that one game.

#2 Also missed in the hugger-mugger surrounding Brett's historic game was the realization that the Blue Jays may have played their best game of the series on that night. Ernie Whitt gunned down Willie Wilson stealing in the first, saving a run. In the second Damaso Garcia made a lightning-quick backhand grab of a ball that Frank White floated in front of second. Following Brett's double in the fourth, Hal McRae drove the ball into the gap in right-center. While I was wondering if Mac had enough oats left to make a triple out of this, Jesse Barfield materialized and caught the ball on the dead run. On the very next pitch, Frank White slashed the ball along the same vector, but harder, farther and flatter than McRae's ball. Barfield added a 9.6 bellyflop to his act, and got to this one, too, a remarkable catch. Then, after making a routine catch for the third out, Jesse hit a two-run home run off the Cy Young winner in the top of the fifth, tying the score. Who's George Brett?

And those plays *almost* wound up taking a back seat. On Steve Balboni's game-winning single in the eighth, Tony Fernandez was that far away (hold up thumb and forefinger) from making the greatest defensive play that I have ever seen. Balboni swung hard and fisted the ball into left-center, I would guess 150 feet over the shortstop's head. The ball was not hit hard, but a ball hit with that trajectory in that direction is *always* a single for a power hitter; nobody had any chance to make the play. Fernandez broke into a full gallop at the crack of the bat, and missed by inches of catching it over his shoulder. You know I'm a great admirer of Ripken and Trammell and Yount—but friends, no other shortstop in the American League would have been within 50 feet of that ball when it landed.

In the fourth game the Royals lost when Al Oliver beat Dan Quisenberry for the second time in the series; in the fifth Danny Jackson pitched out of serious fourth-, fifth- and sixth-inning jams en route to a shutout. In that game the Blue Jays made the first of the baserunning mistakes for which I had been waiting.

In the fourth inning the first two hitters, George Bell and Cliff Johnson, singled, with Johnson's ball landing in front of left fielder Lonnie Smith. Bell decided to challenge . . . let us say, Bell decided to *insult* Lonnie's throwing arm, and Lonnie made a fine throw to third. Brett decoyed as if there was no play, then grabbed the ball and slapped the tag on Bell; he argued, but he was out.

This incident became somewhat celebrated as the playoff wore on, as Bell lost his temper a number of times during the playoff and almost got into a fight after being hit with a pitch while, in general, playing magnificent baseball. The fans were on him.

But missed in the controversy (it was a close call) was what is so often missed about an over-aggressive baserunning decision: the damage that it might have done. Reconstruct for yourself what might have happened without that play:

Bell	singled to right
Johnson	singled to left
Barfield	groundout (1–3), runner advancing

Upshaw	groundout (5–3)
Iorg	flared a single into right
Whitt	doubled into right field corner
Fernandez	groundout (5–3)

Iorg's single and Whitt's double came in the fifth inning, because of the extra out; Iorg didn't score but probably would have with two out. Bell's aggressiveness might, just *might* have cost the Blue Jays three runs. They lost the game, 2–0.

And what was the potential gain? The best estimate that I could make, which comes from page 153 of Pete Palmer's *The Hidden Game of Baseball*, is that the difference between having runners on first and second with no one out and having runners on first and third with no one out is 26 hundredths of a run.

An offense is a chain. The value of the chain depends upon its length, how far it will reach. Imagine that this chain is six feet long, but if you stretch out each link of the chain, maybe you can make the chain seven feet long instead of six. But if you stretch a link too hard and it breaks in the middle, then what?

Then what you've got is two worthless pieces of three-foot chain.

By what he had done in the first three games, Al Oliver had taken Dan Quisenberry out of the series. When they returned to Toronto, Dick Howser figured out a way to take Al Oliver out of the series. For four seasons Bobby Cox had followed a policy of strict platooning; when the opposition manager switched from a left-handed pitcher to a right-hander or vice versa, he would pinch hit for any of several players. This policy served him extremely well. With the complications of their profession cut in half, players like Rance Mulliniks, Garth Iorg, Ernie Whitt, Buck Martinez and others had developed into productive hitters. In addition, Cox was able to get the entire roster involved in the winning effort, contributing greatly to the development of a cohesive atmosphere in the Blue Jay clubhouse, plus the fact that, with about 13 players having regular playing time, his bench was extremely strong and his ability to withstand an injury markedly improved.

With the American League pennant on the line, Dick Howser turned that policy around and pointed it at Bobby Cox's temple. The Blue Jays are much better against right-handed than left-handed pitchers, so Howser had begun the series with Mark Gubicza, a right-hander with a 14–10 record, in the bullpen, and thus starting three left-handers. When Howser would bring in his right-handed relief ace, Cox could empty his bench and apply unrelenting pressure.

If, however, he empties his bench as soon as you switch pitchers, then what happens if you make that change in the middle of the game? Howser decided to find out. Gubicza started the fifth game, and, after allowing single runs in the first and third, cruised through the fourth and fifth. In the sixth he had allowed a single and a walk

with only one out. There were eleven outs left in the game, but Al Oliver was at the plate. Howser brought Bud Black, a left-hander, into the game.

Cox pulled the trigger. Cliff Johnson, a right-handed hitter, was brought in to hit for Oliver. In the seventh inning, Garth Iorg was brought in to hit for Mulliniks, and in the eighth Cecil Fielder hit for Ernie Whitt, with Hearron coming in to catch. By the ninth inning the bench was empty—and Dan Quisenberry was able to get back into the series.

Right-hander Bret Saberhagen started the seventh game; he had not pitched well against Toronto either in the season or in the series. In the first inning Saberhagen took a shot off his hand—the second time in the series that the Blue Jays had pounded a safety off his person. The hand swelled up, and Saberhagen left after three innings.

Again, a left-hander came into the game.

Again, Cox pulled the trigger.

Iorg replaced Mulliniks.

Johnson replaced Oliver.

Jeff Burroughs replaced Ernie Whitt.

The left-handers were gone.

Quisenberry came in to finish up.

When Al Oliver was pulled out of the game, the camera showed him in the dugout. He was furious, slapping the seat and scowling. He knew that when he was out, the Royals would go to the right-hander, and the Blue Jays would have no response move.

His deportment was not what it should have been in the situation, and might well have hurt him when he was looking for a job over the winter. But he was right.

One of the great rules of life is that we all establish "policies," although we call them habits or preferences or beliefs or techniques, which are useful to us, but which we continue to use after the reason for them has evaporated. We have a hard time seeing things as they *are* because we can never get what they *were* out of our heads. There's a saying among military men that each war is fought by the lessons of the last one. Political decisions are made the same way; the political leaders of the late forties saw the Korean problem in terms of World War II. Those of the early sixties treated the Viet Nam dilemma as if it were a rerun of Korea. We acted tentatively and indecisively with respect to Iran because after Viet Nam, every potential involvement was viewed as another Viet Nam, rather than being seen as its own complex problem. Now we look at the situation in the Phillipines, and we wonder if we have another Iran on our hands. In each conflict, we have seen not the problem which existed, but the shadow of the last one.

What Dick Howser did to the Blue Jays, you couldn't do over a period of time. He used four starting pitchers in two nights; you can't do that all year. But Howser reacted to the unique situation, and Cox didn't. Had the series gone on one game longer, Cox would have figured out a response to it. He's a fine manager, and he did (on the whole) a super job in Toronto. But he let Dick Howser get one step ahead of him at exactly the wrong moment.

A WORLD SERIES NOTEBANK

Part 1: Prologue

Overlooking the paranoid protestations of Kansas City fans, hypersensitive after years of put-downs in comparisons with the Yankees, it is difficult to understand why the Cardinals were so heavily favored to win the series. There is no credible basis for the belief that the eastern media would favor St. Louis over Kansas City merely because they are 240 miles to the east.

The superiority of the Cardinals' won/lost record was certainly what started the snowball rolling. The habit of dismissing the American League West probably had something to do with it; it was largely ignored that in 1985 the A.L. West had two teams which won 90 games, three teams over .500 and three teams not very far under .500. The Royals' poor record in post-season play over the last ten years had something to do with it. The fact that the Cardinals had beaten two media darlings, the Mets and Dodgers, might possibly have had something to do with it. National League smugness certainly had a great deal to do with it. The tendency to focus on speed, at the expense of more valuable characteristics such as power and front-line pitching, certainly had much to do with it.

In any case, by the time the series was under way, it had reached the point of the preposterous. To an objective observer—one who had not had the opportunity to witness the Royals daily—the Cardinals should have been a slight favorite, perhaps a 7 to 6 favorite. But 9 to 4? John Nelson, writing for the associated press in the last week of the season, wrote that "The Kansas City ballclub of the American League would be woefully overmatched against St. Louis of the National League, and an I-70 Series might become something of a good, old-fashioned Western barbecue." Hal Bodley of *USA Today* wrote that "Versatility and flexibility should carry St. Louis to a World Series victory against cross-state rival Kansas City." The article was accompanied by a chart showing that St. Louis had an edge at every position except third base. Pete Rose said that the Cardinals would win in four straight.

With respect to the *USA Today* chart, let me raise three points:

1) The Cardinals' team earned run average in 1985 was 3.10, which was 49 points (or 13%) better than the National League average. The Royals staff ERA was 3.49, which was 66 points (or 16%) better than the American League average. In spite of this, Bodley rated the Cardinals superior in starting pitching, relief pitching and defense. Now if you have worse starting pitching, worse relief pitching and worse defense, how can you have a better team earned run average?

2) In addition to the positions compared, *USA Today* gave the Cardinals plusses in all the peripheral areas considered—Team Speed, Defense and Bench. But what was not mentioned here was the fact that the Royals have an enormous advantage in power, hitting 154 home runs to the Cardinals 87. Even with adjustments for park and DH, that's an impressive difference; the Royals, playing in a poor home run park, were the only major league team with two players who hit 30 home runs. They also had other players with 14, 22 and 17 home runs, whereas the Cardinals had only one player with more than 13.

Over any period of time, power has been far, far more important in post season play than has speed. Over any period of years, the team hitting more home runs has won the World Series more often than the team stealing more bases. It makes no sense to ignore power and focus on speed in an analysis of a World Series.

3) In comparing the catchers, St. Louis' Darrell Porter was rated the edge over Kansas City's Jim Sundberg. Darrell Porter was released after the season, and there was no perceptible rush to sign him. Jim Sundberg was *not* released after the season, and had he been so he would have received at least eight offers from other teams. This is the most inexplicable error in the analysis, and is difficult to ascribe to anything other than bias.

The Bodley article, actually, was paired with another; his was "Why the Cardinals will win the Series," and the other was "Why the Royals will win the Series." The problem is that, while the "Cardinal" half of the article gave the Cardinals a 10–1 edge in comparisons, the "Royal" half of it also gave the Cardinals a 6–4 edge with the bench being even, and the accompanying article, rather than saying that the Royals would win, argued that it was not impossible that the Royals might win. It concluded with this ringing endorsement:

Kansas City doesn't awe you; there are no less than six AL teams more difficult to contain.

But, the Royals can win, especially in a one-week series, if they can lull the opposition into a conservative game of baseball chess. Against a team as versatile and well-schooled as the Cardinals, it will not be easy.

To return to a familiar theme, I think that to a large extent these biases were fueled by *statistical* misunderstandings, misinterpretations of the statistics. For example:

1) The failure to recognize that the Royals' pitching was as good as it is was created to a substantial degree by the failure to adjust for the ERA difference between the leagues, because of the designated hitter rule. It's funny—people would say that the Royals' offense would be hurt by the loss of designated hitter Hal McRae, but they would fail to pick up the obvious other half of the equation, that their pitchers would be aided by not having to face the other team's designated hitters. There's a difference of a little more than a half a run a game, but—until the series was played—few people seemed to take in that this meant the Royals were starting three pitchers with ERAs of 2.19, 2.37 and 2.92.

2) Another factor which was almost entirely overlooked due to a dysfunction of the statistical information services was the Royals ability to stop the opposition's running game, particularly with Jim Sundberg catching. Information about a team's ability to steal bases is commonly available; it's in *The Sporting News* and *USA Today* every week, and is referred to often. But it's a two-way street; as important as the ability to *steal* bases is the ability to *prevent* stolen bases. The fact that the Royals were the third most-difficult team in baseball to steal bases against, allowing only 92 opposition steals on the season, was not published anywhere, and so was virtually a trade

secret. The Cardinals, while a much better base-stealing team, were not nearly so strong in the prevention category.

3) With respect to certain head-to-head match-ups, there was a tendency before the series to focus on the *season's statistics*, rather than focusing on the *abilities* which those statistics described. There are several examples, but the clearest is in center field, where the Cardinals were often afforded a huge edge for their MVP center fielder, Willie McGee.

If you look at the two players—McGee and Wilson—there is virtually no difference as to their skills and true level of ability. Both players are extremely fast, and have exceptional range in center field. Both are switch hitters, both hit a great many triples and show occasional home run power. Their strikeout and walk frequencies are virtually the same. Their skills as base stealers are virtually identical. Their throwing arms are about the same, fair to good. McGee won the batting championship in 1985, but Wilson also won the batting championship, in 1982. McGee's career average is .307; Wilson's is .301.

The 1985 season should not have convinced any thinking person that Willie McGee is a *significantly* better ballplayer than Willie Wilson. There was no reasonable basis for an expectation that McGee would out-perform Wilson in the 1985 series.

The same can be said of the second basemen. Tommie Herr had a fine season—but it is very hard for me to see that he is distinctly superior to Frank White, or that there was any reasonable basis for the expectation that he would out-perform him in the World Series.

But people didn't see that, because they focused on 1985 statistics, rather than on abilities. One of the fundamental things that I have tried to say to the baseball world in general is not that we need to look at new and different baseball statistics because baseball statistics are good and perfect ways of looking at baseball, but that we need to consider new and different baseball statistics, and new and different ways of looking at the ones we have, because we have many misconceptions which are based on our faulty impressions of what statistics mean.

Game 1

It was something of a shock to the Cardinals, then, to get into the series and discover that the Royals knew in which direction to run the bases, that indeed they seemed to do this almost by second nature, as if they had long practice in it. The Cardinals were amazed to discover the Royals familiar with such nuances of the game as bunting, turning the double play, hitting curve balls and relaying throws back to the infield; they had not been led to expect that it would be this way, and felt rather betrayed by it. The Cardinals should have remembered that the people who said they couldn't lose in October were the same people who said they couldn't win in April. They didn't know what they were talking about in April, and they didn't know what they were talking about in October.

Before the first series game I went in to do a show on a Kansas City television station. They asked me who would win. I have learned from experience that these gentlemen do not appreciate a straight answer—to wit, how the hell would I know—so I said that if it was a short series the Cardinals would win, but if it was a long series the Royals would win. The logic, worth repeating only

because it worked out so well, was that the Cardinals were a good enough team that they were capable of blowing the Royals away before the Royals got their feet planted, but that if the Royals were to maneuver themselves into a position from which they could win, then they'd pull it out.

Susie and I attended the game with Craig Wright and his friends Sean and Cindy. I had never before been to a World Series game, and was surprised at how different the experience was. On the way in I grumbled about the $30 price of the ticket, but on arriving at the park was struck by the absurdity of this; you pay $45 for tickets to a Broadway show and don't think anything of it, and this is *the World Series*. No one has a divine right to attend the event, and if you're not willing to pay a good price for the ticket you shouldn't be there. The parking lot was abuzz with ticket scalpers (trying to buy, mostly), people hawking souvenirs, people winding up tailgate parties, people carrying signs saying "Came all the way from San Diego—Need Tickets." A few thousand standing-room only ducats had been sold, and in places it seemed that there was less room than this advertised. A small jazz band played at the entrance to the park; a marching band was on the field as we arrived. The bunting, the rows of people standing behind the seats and the special auxiliary press box changed the look of the familiar stadium.

Reba McIntire pitched the Star Spangled banner, and Danny Jackson sang the first inning. I *love* to watch Danny Jackson pitch. The first time I saw Danny pitch in '83—it may have been his first major league outing—I wasn't impressed. We had heard a great deal about him as he shot through the farm system, going 17–3 (7–2 in the Southern League) in his first season in professional ball. My initial reaction to him was "What's with this kid? He doesn't throw very hard, although the fastball has good movement, and he doesn't seem to have a curve ball—uses that slider as his breaking pitch." His motion was awkward and he didn't have any kind of control. I saw him again a few days later and couldn't believe I was seeing the same pitcher. He still had the good movement on his fastball and he still didn't throw a curve, but the fastball now cracked into the mitt, he intimidated right-handed hitters with a slider that exploded on their fists, his motion was extraordinarily fluid—what it was was gorgeous—and his control was excellent.

I've seen him pitch many times since, and there has always been that dichotomy. Sometimes he shows up at the park with nothing; he's awkward, flails around out on the mound, doesn't have a clue as to where home plate is and doesn't throw hard enough to get by with pitching there if he did. When he doesn't have it, he's going to lose. Sometimes he'll struggle through two, three, four innings, and you almost think he's going to turn it around, but I've never seen him do it. On those days he mixes in 60% pitches that are OK with 40% pitches that are trouble—a deadly ratio.

But other times, you know he's going to win the game as soon as he takes the mound. He is basically a two-pitch pitcher, with a fastball and a slider, and the batter can put the bat on either pitch most of the time. But the fastball moves so much, and is thrown so hard, that the hitter rarely makes solid contact with it. The slider snaps in on a right-hander's fist so sharply that a right-handed hitter's best shot is to try to bloop it over the infield, while a left-hander is lucky to avoid turning it into a GB5.

Jackson is very tough to run on and hardly ever allows a home run, so that one basically has to beat him by putting together long strings of singles and walks. He's going to walk a few people because his pitches move so much that they'll jump out of the strike zone, but when he has his stuff, Danny is a steam roller. He'll give up a single here, a walk and a run there without ever giving the sense that he is in any trouble. If he were consistent and had a strikeout pitch (either a curve or a good change-up) he would be the best pitcher in the American League.

Whenever I see Danny pitch I always tell whoever I'm with that I can tell in the first inning whether he's going to win. The fifth game of the AL playoffs was the first time I've ever not been able to form an opinion in the first inning. The first game of the World Series was the first time I've ever formed the opinion, and been wrong. In the playoff game, I didn't know that he was going to win until the second inning. I gather that he must have been nervous or something, but in the first inning that night he threw some very good pitches but looked awkward at other times. I've never seen him do that before—look fluid for a couple of pitches and awkward for a couple of pitches in the same outing. He struck out the side in the second inning, and the steam roller was rolling.

In the first series game, Jackson definitely had his stuff, maybe better stuff than he had when he shut out Toronto. The Cardinals are the best team in the National League, and they managed to beat him anyway. In the second inning the Royals got two singles, two walks and an error, but scored only one run because Buddy Biancalana missed the bunt on a suicide squeeze. Howser's strategy here, though never second guessed, is uncharacteristically conservative and perhaps questionable. Here's the sequence of batters beginning with Frank White, leading off the second:

White	2–3
Sundberg	W
Motley	1B
Balboni	1B + E7
Biancalana	W
Jackson	K
L Smith	1B

Tudor was struggling with his control, and seemed to have very little going for him. He walked Jim Sundberg, threw ball one to Motley and gave up a single on the 1–0 pitch, got behind Balboni and gave up a single on a 3–1 pitch, and had missed the strike zone with two out of three pitches to Biancalana before the abortive bunt attempt. He was 18 pitches into the inning, and had thrown nine balls and two line drives to left.

Howser probably guessed that, trying to find the plate, Tudor would take something off and come in the pitch, since a walk to the weak-hitting Biancalana would have been, no pun intended, a cardinal sin. Instead, Tudor threw a terrible pitch, and Biancalana missed connections on the bunt. The price for this was not *simply* the lost runner from third base, but also that 1) the inning ended before Lonnie Smith's single, which would have scored

two runs, and 2) batting with two out, Jackson did not have the opportunity to attempt a sacrifice. Suppose we assume:

a) that Biancalana would have walked anyway,

b) that Jackson, bunting with only one out, might have been able to execute a sacrifice, and

c) that Smith would have gotten the same hit that he did.

(A) (Biancalana's walk) is extremely likely, (b) is problematic but not impossible, and (c) is entirely unknown but the only assumption for which we have a reasonable basis. If it had happened, the Royals score how many runs in the inning? 1–2–3–4; 4–0, KC, and the game is pretty much over. Even if Jackson strikes out, it's three runs. Dick Howser tried to play for a 2–0 lead; it didn't work out, and I'm not faulting him for it. Incidentally, Howser ordinarily does not like to bunt.

Jackson tied the Cardinals in knots for two innings (K, 6–3, 4–3, PO3, SL4, K) then walked Pendleton leading off the third. Darrell Porter, batting eighth, hit a ground ball just out of the reach of Frank White, Pendleton scooting to third. With no one on base and a slow man at bat, Frank White takes his position out in short right field, and the ball would have been an easy play for him; playing for the double play, he had pulled in and edged toward second base, and the ball got into right field. With one out, Willie McGee got Pendleton home with a GB4, and the game was tied.

Things simply were not breaking the Royals' way. Lonnie Smith singled to lead off the third, then got picked off first (1–3–6–3–4), *again* costing the Royals multiple runs (2) given a normal sequence of events. Look at the sequence of batters beginning with Smith:

L Smith	1B
Wilson	PO4
Brett	1B
White	3 –
Sundberg	2B

White's squib down the first base line would certainly have moved the runners up, and Sundberg's double would obviously have scored them.

Instead, it remained tied at 1–1. With one out, Landrum doubled. On a two-two pitch to Cesar Cedeno, Jackson busted the slider on Cedeno's knuckles and shattered his bat, the head of it helicoptering out to the shortstop position. The ball blooped over Brett's head up the left field line, and the Cardinals had a 2–1 lead. It was all the runs they would need.

All season, whenever Susie and I had gone into games we had been extremely fortunate as to the people seated around us; we made it through almost the entire season without being in earshot of an obnoxious drunk. On this memorable occasion, the law of averages caught up with us. We were seated three rows behind the last human being in the Western hemisphere that I would ever want to marry into my family; she is to this day known in our house only as That Dreadful Woman. That Dreadful Woman combined the virtues of a coquetteish Southern Belle, the kind that during a Tennessee Williams play you always want to rush onstage and strangle to speed up the plot, with those of your ordinary garden-variety obnoxious drunken fan. She had a voice that would remind you of a clarinet with a broken reed, set to the volume of an airhorn, and I suppose that she had been a cheerleader two or three years ago, for she was determined to lead the section in cheers. She was a Cardinals fan, which was not the problem; in fact, the ingrained hospitality with which Midwesterners receive guests is probably all that kept her alive as the game progressed. Whenever anything happened . . . no, that's not right . . . whether anything happened or not she would leap to her feet almost with every pitch and, turning around and gesturing with her arms as if tossing an invisible baby into the air, implore the section to screech along with her and give her some sort of reassurance about how cute she was. After about a half-inning of this, every time she got up she would, naturally, be greeted with a chorus of people yelling encouraging things like "Sit Down," "Shut Up," "Watch the Game," "Lady, Pleeeese" and "Will you get your ass out of the way?" However, being apparently none too swift even when sober, she could not take in that it was not anyone in particular who was yelling these things, but everyone in the entire area taking turns. Having focused on someone who was abusing her, she would fasten onto the luckless soul—several, I am sure, will never go back to a baseball game so long as they live—and begin to whimper accusingly about how she didn't mean to do any wrong and she was just trying to enjoy the game and didn't they want to enjoy the game and didn't Royals fans like to have fun and what had she done except cheer for her team and couldn't they be friends? Eventually she would shake hands with whoever it was; this was, after all, the only way to get her to stop whining in your face. Then she would grab her camera and put her arm around her new friend and have her husband (or boyfriend, or whoever the poor bastard was) take a picture of the event.

She had other uses for the camera—for example, she would try on a funny hat, stand up on her seat, hand off the camera to a stranger and have him take a picture of her. She would do this, mind you, with the inning in progress.

The rest of the fans in the right field bleachers were not exactly a prize aggregation, either. There was an ABC crowd camera near us, and scattered around were several dozen children and nitwits whose attention was entirely focused on it. Whenever this camera panned near us they would leap to their feet and hold up banners, requiring the people sitting behind them, which was all of us except the front row, to jump up and down constantly in an attempt to follow the game. There were several beach balls bouncing around, enough that it took the baseball fans in the area two or three innings to capture each one and neutralize it with a pocket knife. It was easily the worst Kansas City baseball crowd that I've seen.

Also seated around us were a number of die-hard, life-long Cardinal fans who had driven over from St. Louis (five hour drive) to see the game. By the fifth inning, That Dreadful Woman had most of them discussing whether they should continue to support the Cardinals or perhaps should switch to the Royals. Several people offered to buy the Dreadful Woman a beer if she would just go stand in line to buy it. She took one guy up on his offer, apparently

not understanding the purpose of it—she warn't easy to insult, this girl—and as she was leaving a guy about ten rows behind us shouted "Remember where your seat is—section 342." Needless to say, Section 342 was in an entirely different part of the ballpark, but it didn't work. We enjoyed the game for a half-inning until she returned.

John Tudor may be a great pitcher—he looked like a great pitcher in Game 4, and you can't argue with 21–8—but he sure as hell didn't show it that evening. In the fourth inning, after Jim Sundberg's double, Darryl Motley flied to right field deep enough that Sundberg, not exactly a speed merchant, was able to move to third base. Steve Balboni popped softly down the left field line, apparently out of play, but Terry Pendleton made a wondrous effort on the ball, racing top-speed down the line to catch the ball near the seats, over his shoulder, then whirling to throw out Sundberg at the plate. In the sixth inning, Willie Wilson led off with a single, Frank White hit a line drive to the warning track in left field and Jim Sundberg made Tudor throw ten pitches before getting him out for the first time. In the seventh inning Motley drove the ball into the left field corner (caught), Lynn Jones hit a pinch-hit triple and Hal McRae was hit by a pitch before Tudor departed, a winning pitcher by the grace of God and his defense.

Danny Jackson was magnificent. After Cedeno's bloop double he faced the mininum number of batters, eleven. Willie McGee doubled but was thrown out at third by Wilson and White; four of the other ten batters struck out and only Clark was able to get the ball out of the infield, popping out to right.

Todd Worrell relieved Tudor. He walked Smith but got Wilson, leaving the bases loaded and George Brett on deck. In the eighth Brett hit the ball a mile high and nailed Van Slyke to the wall in right field, but it remained 2–1. In the ninth the Cardinals added a run against Quisenberry, to make it 3–1. In the Royals' ninth Sheridan led off with a double. With two out, Dane Iorg made Worrell throw nine pitches and drilled the last one at Andy Van Slyke. The Cardinals won.

After the game Bob Gibson was on the radio. The fact that the Cardinals' victory was little short of a miracle had, apparently, not come across on television. The Cardinals had hit only three balls hard—well, two hard and one reasonably hard—in the game; the three were the doubles by McGee and Clark, both thrown out at third, and the ground single by Herr off of Quisenberry. The Royals had blistered the ball all over the park—in fact, I think they hit the ball harder off Tudor in Game 1 than they did in Game 7, when they beat him 11–0. The Royals had twelve balls that were crunched. Each team had lost two runners on the bases; the walks and hit batsmen were even at four apiece. Dave Nightingale of *The Sporting News* had seen the game much the same way I had:

> You might conclude from such a script that the National League champion Cardinals were getting the living bejabbers kicked out of them by the American League champion Royals.
>
> Conclude differently.

But many other people had completely missed the fact that the Cardinals' victory was a stone fluke, and on the radio Gibson was certain that the Cardinals would win the series in four straight. He spared no details in explaining why.

He acknowledged that Jackson had pitched well—he was quite amazed by this—but even so the Royals had not been able to take the game. So from now on they were going to be easy pickings. We drove home in a dark mood, remembering The Dreadful Woman, and remembering how the season had ended in so many other autumns.

Game Two

In the 1913 World Series, Chief Meyers, the star catcher of the New York Giants, split his hand open making a catch in pre-game drills before the second game of the series. He was not able to play in the rest of the games, but his replacement, Larry McLean, filled in sensationally, hitting .500 (6 for 12), making no errors and even doing a good job containing the Philadelphia running game; he was by far the Giants best player in the series. Still, the Giants lost the series, and the Giants' supporters felt sure that they would have had a better chance had Meyers been healthy. As John Foster wrote in the 1914 Spalding Guide, "How much this turn of misfortune had to do with the ultimate outcome, no one can tell. An opinion would be merely the estimate of a critic who endeavors to analyze the possibilities of chance. If the New York team had been at its best, it might still have been defeated. It certainly was not at its best."

A neighbor had asked me to pick up and take to the second game a man who lives in my town who had a ticket but no way to get to the stadium. He turned out to be a very agreeable older man, about 75 to 80, and a big base-ball fan. We drove through Leavenworth on the way, and he remembered seeing Del Crandall play for Leavenworth in 1948 or 1949, he wasn't sure which. I didn't know that Leavenworth had a minor league team then, and we talked about it. I asked if he had ever seen a World Series game before; he said "Oh, no," and added that it had always been a dream of his to see one. I arrived at the stadium thinking how little the winning and losing mattered. Later I got out a book and checked; Del Crandall hit .304 for Leavenworth in 1948.

As Susie and I were walking down the aisle toward our seats the man in front of us yelled gleefully "I don't think she's here!" We broke out laughing; we were looking for the same thing. We had the same seats for all four games in Kansas City, if there were to be four games in Kansas City, and the thought of spending three more games trying to get HER to shut up had considerably dampened our enthusiasm for the event. We never saw her again, but it was easy to spot the people who had been in the same seats the day before. They were distinguished by the wary looks that they cast around until the offending seat was occupied.

Melba Moore sang the National Anthem, and Coretta Scott King threw out the first pitch. Nothing happened through three innings. The Royals got their leadoff man on in each of the three, but lost two of them to quick double plays, and Cox struck out the side the other time. The Cardinals through four innings had only three balls hit out of the infield, mounting one threat on a walk and Tito Landrum's two-out single.

In the fourth the Royals scored two runs before any-one was out. Wilson led off with a single, and Brett and White followed with doubles to right. Mike Roarke visited the mound, and Cox, who had not made a good pitch since

taking the mound at the start of the inning, immediately stiffened. But the Royals had a 2–0 lead.

For some reason Craig and I got to talking about pitchers' motions. Cox throws across his body; at the moment of release he is not squared away toward home plate, so that he throws his arm across his chest, his forearm slapping hard into his chest at the completion of the delivery. It looks to me like there must be tremendous pressure on the muscles just below the joint in his shoulder. I guess it will probably be a little while before it catches up with him, but I'd say there's about an 80% chance that his productive years as a pitcher will be ended by shoulder trouble within three to five years. Be sure to write and remind me if it doesn't happen.

Anyway, we got to talking about motions in general, and Craig had some intriguing ideas about the subject, related to things he has learned from talking to Ranger pitching coaches, evaluated with his own research. He has become a recent convert to the importance of the pitcher's getting the glove out in front of him while throwing the hard pitches, thus 1) hiding the ball, and 2) facilitating the act of throwing the glove hand back as the ball is released, maximizing the forward thrust of the other hand and balancing the body. I told him he should write a book about this stuff. He said he was thinking about it, which is a step forward from what he said the last time I told him that, which was that he *wasn't* thinking about it.

My theory about motions is that most managers don't have a very good sense of when a pitcher is tired, and that this is probably the one thing in baseball that a fan at home watching the game on TV can see *better,* if he pays attention, than the manager can. The fact that managers don't, in general, have any idea when their pitchers are tired is supported, I feel, by the things they say about it—for example, that the pitcher's readings on the radar gun have not dropped, or that what they look for when a pitcher is tired is when he starts dropping down, not coming over the top. I argued that this is an extremely late and unreliable indicator of when a pitcher is tired, and . . . well, I'll get to that in the pitchers comments, or some place. Craig was unconvinced. I told him to put it in his book.

No one reached in the Cardinal fifth, the Royal fifth or the Cardinal sixth. In the Cardinal innings, Brett made the two best defensive plays of the game, fielding a big hop behind third and gunning down Pendleton, then diving for a ball in the hole, stopping it, getting up and throwing out Tommie Herr. In the sixth the Royals got a single, a stolen base and a walk, but didn't score; Brett again drove the ball to the wall, this time in left, but was short. In the seventh the Royals got a walk from Balboni, a bunt from Leibrandt and a single from Lonnie Smith, but Tito Landrum, emerging as the star of the series, nailed Balboni at the plate.

In the eighth Frank White hit a two-out double off the wall in left. A left-hander, Ken Dayley, was on the mound. In my scorebook I had written in "PH—Motley for Sheridan," but had to scratch it out as Sheridan came to the plate. The switch would have been consistent with what Howser had done late in the year, but on reflection I could see why he had not made it. If he had gone to Motley, Herzog would very likely have switched to a right-hander; then, with his other right fielder out of the game, Motley would have had to stay in, and Howser would have taken his best defensive right fielder out of the game, for no gain, with a 2–0 lead. I decided Howser was right; better to save the pinch hitter in case he was needed in the ninth. Sheridan grounded to second.

We have arrived at The Blunder. It had been a fast game up to this point; the first pitch was thrown at 7:31, and at 9:42 the Cardinals began what seemed, until the following Saturday, as if it would be the pivotal inning of the 1985 World Series. Charlie Leibrandt had retired thirteen consecutive hitters entering the inning, and it required a real pessimist to note that the last two had hit the ball hard.

What is a managerial blunder, to begin with? Is it a decision about the odds in the game that is wrong on the percentages? No, it can't be, because *none of us knows exactly what the true odds are* in any given game situation. None of us knows, and none of us will ever know, not a hundred years from now when they have computers that will fit on your fingernail and spit out the history of the universe at a billion words a second, none of us will know for sure what the odds are because each unique situation contains a thousand variables, at least a hundred of which will not have had enough trials to be evaluated. In short, no one can ever know how this pitcher will pitch this batter under these exact lighting conditions when this pitcher is this tired. We will know much more about it later than we know now, but we will never KNOW.

But we do know what the book says. What we know is how an ordinary manager would handle this situation in an ordinary case, and we know WHY he would do it that way. These are three elements of a managerial blunder:

1) It is a move which goes against the conventional practice,

2) It occurs at a key moment of the game, and

3) It doesn't work.

Those three elements are always present when a manager is accused of blundering, and whenever those three elements are present, the manager will be accused of blundering.

Willie McGee, batting leadoff due to the injury of Vince Coleman, was up first. McGee hacked at a pitch inside, then got around late and fouled a pitch into the Kansas City dugout. It was 0–2. Leibrandt fired, and gestured in excitement as if he had struck out McGee. The replay seemed to show that he had, but the National League umpire called it a ball. McGee doubled into the left field corner on the next pitch.

The first pitch to Ozzie Smith came in tight; Ozzie tried to turn his back into it, so as to get on base, but the ball scooted by him into the catcher's glove. Ozzie fouled off two pitches, took ball two to even the count and then grounded out to third. 2–0, tying run still at the plate.

Tommie Herr took ball one, then swung and missed at two pitches before popping out to right field. Leibrandt had retired 15 of 16. Just for a little excitement Pat Sheridan fired to third base, the throw being completely unnecessary and 15 feet off target. No damage; it was still 2–0.

At 9:48, six minutes into the inning, Gary Blaylock visited the mound.

Just days earlier, Jack Clark had effectively ended the National League season with a monstrous home run on the first pitch from Tom Niedenfuer. With that home run, the message finally began to get through to the American public: Jack Clark is the National League's Eddie Murray. He's not as durable as Eddie, and he's not as low-key and selfless—but his dossier of game-breaking batting accomplishments is hardly any less impressive than is Eddie's. He led the National League in "game-winning hits" twice despite playing for the Giants, and one year I did a breakdown of them and showed that almost all were legitimate, late-inning blockbusters. In 1984, according to Elias, he hit .415 in late-inning pressure situations. In 1985, according to my subjective reading of Cardinal scoresheets, he was wall-to-wall deadly.

"So," asked Craig Wright as Blaylock stood at the mound, "Would you bring in Quiz here?" No, I said, I'd let him have the tying run. What he did with the tying run was not impressive. He threw three straight balls, two of them almost in the dirt, and then gave up an RBI single on the 3–0 pitch.

That was it for me; if it was my game Quisenberry was in. That was the way Dick has played it for years: when the game is on the line, Quiz is on the mound. When he was *really* good, a couple of years ago, Quisenberry became a major factor in the game in the fifth inning. The logic was this: let's say that the Royals were one ahead in the fifth inning, but the other team had a man on and Babe Ruth at the plate. You'd be thinking "Well, if he gets the Babe out here he's got the bottom of the order up in the sixth. That means that Babe and Lou and company don't come up again until the seventh at worst, and if it gets *really* tough in the seventh inning, Quiz can come in and the Royals will still win. So *if he just gets Babe out here in the fifth inning, then the Royals win.*"

It wasn't just the Royals who thought this way, either; managers would use their pinch hitters in the fifth or sixth innings, trying to keep Quisenberry out of the game. In a sense, every Royals game revolved around trying to get to Quisenberry, and it was something that you started thinking about, really, as soon as you got to the park.

Quiz wasn't nearly that sharp last year; even so, one generally regarded having him in the game as preferable to *not* having him in the game. Here's the situation: the Cardinals have the tying run at first and two out, so it takes either a home run or a string of hits/walks for the Cardinals to go ahead. Quisenberry doesn't allow many home runs—fewer than Leibrandt even last year, when Leibrandt was having his best year and Quiz wasn't. That's an indication for Quisenberry. Quiz is a right-hander; the next two hitters were right-handers. That's an indication for Quisenberry. True, Herzog could have pinch-hit Van Slyke, but *after one hitter* he would either have to let the right-hander hit, or substitute a lesser hitter. Van Slyke would have been coming in cold, which is preferable to having a hitter at the plate who has been in the game. Van Slyke is no reason not to bring in Quisenberry. In fact, Quisenberry did face Van Slyke later in the inning, and got him out on one pitch to end the nightmare.

Leibrandt had thrown four straight unsuccessful pitches to Clark; that's an indication for Quisenberry. Leibrandt had thrown 17 pitches in the inning; that's an indication for Quisenberry. Leibrandt had thrown 123 pitches in the game; that's an indication for Quisenberry.

In Leibrandt's last previous start, in the Toronto series, he had pitched eight shutout innings, and entered the ninth with 110 pitches behind him and the top of the order up. He lost that game, 2–1. That's an indication for Quisenberry.

In the 1984 season, according to the *Elias Baseball Analyst,* hitters facing Charlie Liebrandt in his third, fourth and fifth innings of work had hit an overall .258 with virtually no power—a .328 slugging percentage. Hitters facing Leibrandt from his sixth inning on hit .297 and had a slugging percentage of .471. Ouch.

Tito Landrum came to the plate, facing Leibrandt. He fouled off the first two pitches, then refused to bite as Charlie nibbled for a corner; it was 2–2. He popped up the next pitch, a pop up drifting softly down the right field line into fair territory. Pat Sheridan, pulled around to center, couldn't get there.

It was 9:54; the Royals were still ahead. Quisenberry was still warm. The lead run was on second, but the Royals were still ahead. Leibrandt had now thrown 22 pitches in the inning.

Then came the decision that I really, sincerely, seriously can't understand. By this time, we in the right field bleachers were tearing our teeth out, wondering why Quisenberry was not in the game, wondering why, if Howser had lost faith in Quisenberry, Joe Beckwith was not in the game, or if not Beckwith then Gubicza, or if not Gubicza then almost anybody would do. Not only did Howser *not* bring in Quisenberry, but *he walked Cedeno.*

Now think about this, first of all, as if it were a table game—a re-creation of the basic percentages of the situation. If this were a table game, you would never walk the man intentionally to load the bases, because if you do that, then that means that another walk drives in the tying run. Since Pendleton's *on base percentage* is obviously higher than Cedeno's *batting average,* it certainly would not be profitable to walk Cedeno in a table game.

This, however, is not a table game—this is far worse. The real situation has an additional damned good reason not to walk Cedeno. If you walk Cedeno, then the hitter *knows* that you can't afford to walk him, too. He *knows* that if he is patient you have got to come into him. The pressure on the pitcher goes up, and the batting average of the man at the plate goes up.

Leibrandt got behind Pendleton 1–0. After Pendleton took a called strike, he got behind him again, 2–1. Finally Terry Pendleton swung. He lofted the ball into the gap in left-center. Cedeno scored from first. It was 4–2, St. Louis—and at the time, the World Series seemed to be over.

I have great respect and admiration for Dick Howser—but I have run that inning through my head again and again, and I just don't get it. Maybe we overreacted, emotionally, because we all expected Quisenberry to come in after Clark, so that it seemed like not one mistake, but three mistakes. What Howser said was that they had made a decision before the inning that Charlie still had his good stuff—his readings on the radar gun were good—

and that it was his game to win or lose. To me, it sounds like saying that you let the house burn down because you'd made a prior decision to ignore the smoke alarm.

Of all of the reasons to get Dan Quisenberry into that game, the most important was the number of pitches that Leibrandt had thrown. After a pitcher has thrown 15 pitches in an inning—any inning—his effectiveness diminishes. Any time a pitcher throws more than 15 pitches from the seventh inning on, you've got to start thinking about getting him out of there. But the pitch that beat Leibrandt was (not counting the four in the intentional walk) his 26th pitch of the ninth inning, and his 132nd pitch of the game. Twenty-six pitches in the ninth inning of a close game? I don't think I've ever heard of that before.

Dan Quisenberry came into the game at 10:01.

Games 3 Through 5

At the end of Game 2, a delegation of Cardinal fans in the right field bleachers stood and conducted organized cheers for several minutes in the midst of the stunned and dismayed Royals fans. When Leibrandt was rolling along in the seventh and eighth, a chant of "Char-lie, Char-lie, Char-lie" had filled the stadium; afterwards, the men in the Red hats picked up the chant, changing the rhythm just enough to make it recognizable as the derisive, taunting singsong of one child tormenting another. It was an extraordinarily rude, boorish performance, a chorus of men who, guests in our park and in our city, in the thrill of victory had chosen to savor not their own victory, but the anguish of the opponent.

When the series moved to St. Louis, Susie and I went home to watch it on the TV with the rest of you, and so began to be exposed to the World Series as it was being seen through the eyes of the media. We learned then that one of the recurring themes of this coverage was the generally oafish behavior of the Cardinals. In the main I tended to attribute this to the poorly managed crush of the bloated series media, which was no doubt suffocating the Cardinals, making it difficult for them to do what they were trying to accomplish, and impossible to enjoy the doing of it. Still, I wondered about the rudeness reported of the Cardinal players, and the rudeness I had witnessed in their fans. Al Michaels reported Cardinal fans shouting into the press box at the New York writers, "Hey, how about your Mets now?" I wondered whether, after a winter of put-downs and a summer of redemption, vindication had not passed into vindictiveness, and self-justification into self-righteousness. It has been my experience that the Lord rarely wastes much time in punishing those particular transgressions.

The third contest was no contest. Both teams threatened in the first but didn't score. In the fourth, Lonnie Smith slashed a two-run double just out of the reach of Van Slyke. In the fifth, Brett singled and White hit a tremendous home run, knocking Andujar out of the game. Bret Saberhagen, who has probably never blown a 4-run lead in his life, began throwing 90% strikes. In the sixth the Cardinals got a run on three straight singles—the only time after the first inning that they were to get a runner as far as second base, prompting Herzog to remark that the Clydesdales, who got a little out of hand in a pre-game show, had spent more time at second base than his players had. The Royals added two more in the seventh on a walk to Brett, a double by White and a single by Biancalana.

In the fourth game, John Tudor was superb. Through six innings Tudor looked like a pitcher who would never allow a run again. In the seventh inning, the Royals could have won the game as easily as not. Brett led off with a single, and White drove the ball to deep center field, but out. Sundberg singled with one out, but Motley popped out. Balboni walked to load the bases with two out. Hal McRae, strapped to the sidelines by the National League rules, pinch hit for Biancalana. A graphic showed that McRae had ground Tudor into pulp when the two went head-to-head in the American League—but, obviously pressing, Mac lunged at the first pitch, which was inches off the ground. The threat ended. It was the only game of the series in which the Cardinals would out-play the Royals.

Tito Landrum started the scoring for the Cardinals with an opposite-field home run in the second. It was Tito's third extra-base hit of the series—all of them, incidentally, hit to right field. By this time, Tito was becoming a folk hero. Tito, who turned 31 on an off day during the series, was noted before this only for his home run that gave Baltimore the American League championship in 1983. He proved to be a capable outfielder and, apparently, the only player on the Cardinal team that the Royals didn't know how to pitch to. The predictable signs appeared—Tito for President, How about our General Tito, Tito, I don't believe we're in Kansas any more. They were bleak, but they provided a relief from the war of the Fat Lady signs. Cardinal fans had jumped the gun with signs like "The Fat Lady is warming up," "Meet me in St. Louis, Fat Lady" and, on Thursday (of course) "The Fat Lady Sings Tonight." Back in KC, Royals fans responded with "The Fat Lady is Choking," "Fat Lady, Go Home" and "Shove it, Fatso." But I'm getting ahead of my story.

Unspoken but apparent in all this is the somewhat local and fraternal nature of the confrontation. Like many Royals fans, I root for the Cardinals in the National League; it's a habit from long ago, when Cardinal broadcasts came into this area. Susie and I went to St. Louis in September to see the Cardinals play a couple of games, and were delighted to see them again in October. But to the outside media, this tended to create the impression that the story of the World Series was not the story of one team against another, but the story of the region in which all of the games were played.

I live in Kansas. Eastern Kansas is not flat; it rolls gently, much like Massachusetts, so that in driving through the country one has the experience of passing through a series of vistas, each covering a quarter of a mile to three quarters of a mile of road time. It is a very beautiful area, so beautiful that when I am required to drive through it daily I grow to enjoy the experience more and more, watching the subtle and sudden changings of the colors in each landscape. The grainfields leap from dark black to brilliant green in days when the crop first appears, fade day by day into a more muted green, then suddenly turn brown or gold or a mixture of colors when the crop ripens. Then that crop will be gone and a patch of dull grey-black earth may set there for a few days before it begins to become something else. The farms are all small

and much of the land is unworkable, so that a wooded area provides a backdrop for almost every field, and each field is divided by one or another kind of fence and small road for the farming equipment. A hundred kinds of wildflowers grow beside the roads, and the colors of the trees change, and the houses change, and the skies change, and the earth changes, and the cows and the sheep and the horses grow up and move around, and the creeks come up and settle back down so that the landscape each day seems different and more graceful than it did the day before.

In spite of this, by some bizarre trick of fate, this area has been chosen in the nation's consciousness to represent Nowhere—an ugly, barren, empty, square space from which people come but do not return. In movies, people who come from nowhere come from Kansas. This preconception is so strong that people who come here often see nothing except what they have been taught to expect, and learn no more of the area around them than a man driving across an Apache reservation picks up of the Apache language.

When I was starting my newsletter, I had a meeting in New York with a man who was interested in investing money or advice or something. He began the meeting by telling me that he had been to Kansas, several times, and regaled me with a few stories about what an awful place it was. It seems he was quite offended by the fact that we don't have any buildings higher than 28 stories. Another time, just before going on national television, a network sports personality asked me where I was from, and upon learning that I was from near Lawrence, Kansas, informed me that he had once spent an evening in Lawrence and that there was nothing to do there.

Of course, it isn't *every* New Yorker who will do this, but a small number who make a deep impression. I always wonder, when this happens, whether if I was black or Jewish these people would take the same opportunity to make use of a few ethnic slurs, or if I was from Bophutswana if they would tell me how insufferably hot and fly-infested it was in Bophutswana. I know that they would not, and I wonder why I am not entitled to the same courtesy. I reflect upon my own episodes of extreme tactlessness, which are frequent and therefore easy to recall, and let the occasion go forward without incident. Usually.

The impressions that we have of a people or a place stem largely from the images of artists (in all fields); the way that people see Mississippi largely originates in the work of Faulkner, Eudora Welty and a few other creative people. It is an unfortunate fact that this area has not been well or honestly served by the nation's artistic community. To give you just a couple of examples, you might remember a song that was made popular by Art Garfunkel a few years ago . . . I think it was called "My Little Town":

And after it rains, there's a rainbow,
And all of the colors are black,
It's not that the colors aren't there,
It's just imagination they lack . . .

That song was written by Paul Simon, a great artist, an enormously talented and intelligent man, who incidentally was born and raised in Brooklyn, New York, still lives in New York City and frankly knows as much about people who live in small towns as a meadowlark knows about the feast of the epiphany. If, in fact, he were to live in a small town, he would discover that one of the great pleasures of living there is that small-town people have wonderful imaginations, probably because they don't live under the minute-to-minute pressures that city life puts on a body, occupying the mind so fully that it cramps the imagination.

Then, too, you might remember the vivid, and depressing, portrayal of small-town life in the movie *The Last Picture Show*, which won a number of Academy Awards in 1971. The movie presented small-town life as a dismal, frustrating series of misdirected ambitions and failed relationships. This cinematic masterpiece was written and directed by Peter Bogdanovich, another very bright and talented artist—and another Brooklyn boy, who, to be honest about it, doesn't have an eggplant's notion about what small-town people do before and after the basketball game. Through carelessness, callousness, indifference to the truth, these people adopt, repeat and perpetuate a set of images about small-time life that is nothing but a stack of filthy lies.

L. Frank Baum, who wrote *The Wizard of Oz* and used Kansas as the grey, bleak Nowhere from which Dorothy escapes, was, like the others, working from his imagination.

If you're illiterate, don't go to movies and never leave the state, I suppose that all of this doesn't get to you, but if you're an active, reading person the naked prejudice directed at you begins to lose its charm after a while. You encounter it virtually every week; let me give you just two examples of things that I was reading during the World Series. In the *Village Voice* of October 22, there was an article by James Ridgeway detailing a murder which was committed by some white-supremacist nut case not far from where I live. "During the 1920s, the Ku Klux Klan was powerful in Kansas," writes Ridgeway, by way of helping explain this murder which happened in Nebraska in 1985, "running entire counties. And today in this region where life is never easy, the farm depression is taking an especially harsh toll." Well, tell me, Mr. Ridgeway, is life easy in New York City? Does the depression take no harsh toll in the ghettos of the east? The allegation about the Ku Klux Klan running entire counties in Kansas is admirably creative, but let us suppose that this was turned around, and that a small-town Kansas newspaper was doing a special on a murder in the Village. In the course of explaining why Tom shot Ralph, they would drag in by-the-by the power of the mob in Little Italy in the twenties, and throw in a few gratuitous comments about how tough life is in the big cities of the East. Would this not strike you as hopelessly provincial, irrelevant and more than a little stupid? Can you imagine the hysterical laughter that it would provoke in the office of *The Village Voice*? Yet it would be far more fair and relevant, for the KKK, so far as I know, has not existed in Kansas for many years, while the same cannot be said of the mob in New York City.

A few days later, reading a fine biography of W. C. Fields, written in 1949 by Robert Lewis Taylor, I encounter the theme again:

(Fields) pondered the bleak plains of Kansas, the arid habits of its people, the high voltage of its divinity . . .

All of which, and most particularly the latter, are entirely fictitious.

With enough repetition this becomes profoundly irritating, but it is also profoundly trivial; the only real cost of it is that at an impressionable age, young Kansans or young Missourians will sometimes believe the lies that are told about them—just as young black people or young Jewish people will develop negative self-images if the slanders directed at them are not effectively countered.

Anyway, comes a World Series, or a National Convention in town, or what have you. Because of this treatment, Kansas City is somewhat of a self-conscious city. This is to put it mildly. They are . . . well, *anxious* to see how they will be reflected in the press attention. They are *so* anxious about this that they make fools of themselves. It is accutely embarrassing at times; visiting press people are shanghaied into television interviews to reveal their feelings about being in Kansas City. "How do you feel about Kansas City? Tell us that you love us. Tell us why you love us. Tell us what you love most about us. Wouldn't you really rather be here than Los Angeles?"

There is a tendency to attribute the negative image of the area to "the media," which is massively unfair; the media, in general, merely reflects the images which are current in the society, and will bend over backward to avoid reflecting them unfairly. There are a few people who will come out from the east for the series and tell us what an ugly place we have, but this is not common. Yet Kansas Citians are so insecure—so paranoid, really—that Al Michaels came under attack merely because he said a number of nice things about St. Louis.

For the benefit of anybody who is not familiar with the cities, St. Louis is a much nicer city than Kansas City, and I'll tell you why in a moment. Yet at every insurgence of the national media, Kansas City press packets are handed out repeating a number of overworked boasts about the place. "Kansas City has more fountains than Rome." Well, I suppose so; the only problem is that about two-thirds of Kansas City's fountains are just jets of water shooting up in front of a branch bank in the middle of a bunch of Burger Kings and stuff, and have the esthetic impact of large lawn sprinklers. "Kansas City has more miles of boulevards than any city except Paris." This one always conjures up images of the International Board of Boulevard Certification, walking along saying "No, I'm afraid this one is just an 'avenue' unless you widen the curb space by four more inches and plant six more trees per half-mile." Another favorite is "Kansas City is the Christmas Card capital of the Midwest." Can you imagine going into New York City for a World Series and having a press person come out to Shea and tell you how many Christmas cards are printed in New York City?

There are about seven reasons why St. Louis is a much nicer city than Kansas City. Number one, it is older, and has a much richer architectural heritage. Number two, its neighborhoods are much stronger. As Kansas City has grown, it has absorbed and neutralized the small cities around it, none of which retains a distinct flavor to contribute to the city. This hasn't happened in St. Louis. Number three, the downtown area is much more pleasant—you can walk around it, there's shopping there, the ballpark is there. Kansas City's downtown area is basically a business area. Number four, St. Louis has integrated the river into the city, adding a great deal to the city esthetically; Kansas City has buried its river underneath a heap of train tracks, access roads and dirty bridges. Number five, St. Louis probably has more good restaurants. If it doesn't have more of them, they're easier to find. Number six, St. Louis has many more areas that one can walk around and enjoy. Kansas City is all built to accommodate the automobile. And number seven, you can drive around St. Louis without getting lost. Unless you stay on the inter-state system, Kansas City has got to be the most confusing, frustrating city to drive around in the United States, with the possible exception of Atlanta, and Atlanta only because all of the streets are named Peachtree. The Kansas City street department renames their streets about every three blocks, so that it is all but impossible to keep track of where you are and how to get where you want to go. Drive you nuts.

That being said, there are things to like about Kansas City. It's reasonably clean. The best restaurants in Kansas City generally don't have any kind of expectations about dress; requesting a jacket or tie is considered rather pretentious. I like that. I'm more comfortable eating out in KC than I am in New York—but anybody who suggested that the third-best restaurant in KC would crack the top 50 in New York would be out of his skull. The city's image would improve a lot if they would just accept themselves for what they are, and stop handing out malarkey about how many miles of boulevard they have.

Kansas City has a world class inferiority complex, but they also have a world class ballclub. On the evening of October 24, 1985, that ballclub was one game away from being eliminated. Fortunately, the man with the nuclear slider was on the mound for Kansas City. The Royals made Bob Forsch throw 26 pitches in the first inning, scoring a run on two singles and two outs. The Cards tied it in the bottom of the first on doubles by Herr and Clark, both hit very hard. I wasn't worried; 15 of the 17 pitches that Danny Jackson threw in the first were strikes.

The Royals scored three runs in the top of the second, the big hit being a two-run triple by Willie Wilson. Forsch left the game a loser, having thrown 54 pitches and gotten only five men out. The Cards didn't get the ball out of the infield in the second. In the third they loaded the bases with two out, but Jackson got Landrum to pop out on a slider.

With one out in the fifth inning, Willie McGee reached base but was picked off first by Jackson. All season long, Steve Balboni had had a great deal of trouble making the throw to second after this happened; he had thrown the ball into left field God knows how many times. All season long, we (Royals fans) were kind of afraid that the other teams would catch onto it, and begin to exploit it. Late in the year, they did, particularly the Rangers; when a runner was picked off first he would simply head for second, figuring that Balboni would probably throw the ball away.

Against the Cardinals, this was a major concern. But in the fourth game of the series, Bud Black picked off Ozzie Smith, and Balboni did one of the things that he had not been doing all year. Instead of trying to throw over

Ozzie, he chased Smith most of the way to second, then made the short flip over his head.

Now, in the fifth inning of the fifth game, Jackson had picked off McGee, and Balboni did the other thing that he hadn't been doing all summer. Racing two or three steps into the infield, he cut McGee out of his line of fire, squared up toward second base and made a nice throw. Maybe he just happened to make those plays when it counted—but it seems much more likely that someone (Lee May, perhaps?) had worked with him in late September to solve the problem. We never did hear. No one commented on the change.

One of the inexplicable things that happened in the mumbo-jumbo chemistry of the nine million soft-corp sports media at the series was that it was determined, somehow, that Steve Balboni was to be the goat of the event. Balboni had had a rather poor playoffs, and the idea that he was not contributing was preserved by a sort of intuitive logical paradigm which went:

a) Steve Balboni doesn't do anything except hit home runs.

b) Steve Balboni hasn't hit any home runs.

c) Steve Balboni isn't doing anything.

Steve Balboni was, in fact, having a very good series, from the beginning. He hit .320 for the series, had an on base percentage of .433, struck out only four times, handled far more chances than any other player in the series and committed no errors, and made several fine defensive plays. While he had only four hits (all singles) in the first five games, his hits in the first two games had been very important ones at the time they occurred, the first one driving in the first run of the series (and the Royals' only run of the game), and the second hit bringing the tying run to the plate with one out in the ninth inning. Between singles and walks, he had made significant offensive contributions in every contest. While it is true that over a period of time how many hits you have counts more than when you hit them, this is only true over a period of time; in a five-game stretch, two well-timed hits are more valuable than a randomly scattered .300 average.

Jackson was never challenged again. In the seventh inning, Brett slid into the dugout in a spectacular, but unsuccessful, attempt to catch a pop up; that failing it became strike one, and Jackson struck out the side on nine pitches. (I wonder if that's ever happened before in a World Series game? I'd be very surprised if it has.) The Royals added a run in the eighth and one in the ninth, and had their second easy victory of the series.

Game 6

The second game of the 1985 World Series was only the eighth such dramatic ninth-inning reversal in the history of the fall classic—that is, the eighth time that a team had gone into the ninth inning behind and had won the game without extra innings. Most of the first seven games are well remembered. In the first game of the 1908 series, Chicago blew a 5–1 lead and trailed 6–5 entering the ninth, then scored five runs to send the Tigers of Cobb and Crawford down to a 10–6 defeat, triggering a 5-game rout for the Cubs. Twenty-one years later, the Cubs were the victims. In the next game after the fabled contest in which the Athletics scored ten runs in the seventh to over-

come an 8–0 lead (which Fred Lieb called the most excit-ing game he ever saw), the Cubs entered the ninth with a 2–0 lead and got the first man out, only to lose the game on a two-run homer by Mule Haas and a run-scoring double by Bing Miller. (All this happened just days before the stock market crash of 1929, incidentally. Any Cub fan who had invested in the market must have thought we were nearing the end of the world.)

Twelve years later, in the fourth game of the 1941 World Series, came the infamous Mickey Owen passed ball. The Brooklyn catcher failed to catch a third strike which would have ended the ballgame. The Yankees scored four runs before the third out was finally recorded, and turned a 4–3 defeat into a 7–4 victory. Six years later, Brooklyn got even in an even more famous game. Yankee pitcher Floyd Bevens had a no-hitter and a 2–1 lead with two out in the bottom of the ninth, but with a runner on second due to a walk and a stolen base. Yankee manager Bucky Harris then flew in the face of the book, intention-ally walking Pete Reiser to put the potential winning run on second base, and suddenly losing the game, the no-hitter and probably his job (a year later) when Cookie Lavagetto doubled off the right field wall, scoring two for a 3–2 Brooklyn win.

It was 25 years before this would happen again. In the fourth game of the 1972 series, the Cincinnati Reds had a 2–1 lead and a man out, needing two more outs to tie the series at two games apiece. The A's hit five consec-utive singles to score two runs and win the game. Three years later, in the second game of the memorable 1975 series, the Red Sox held a 2–1 lead with two out in the ninth inning, when Dave Concepcion singled to tie the score off of Dick Drago, then scored on a double by Ken Griffey.

Kansas City was the victim of the next two incidents. In the fifth game of the 1980 series, the Phillies entered the ninth trailing 3–2, but rallied on a single by Schmidt, a double by Unser and a single by Trillo. In that game, Philadelphia was looking at Dan Quisenberry for the fifth straight game and for the third inning of that game, and it was widely felt that Jim Frey had let the Phillies see too much of Quisenberry.

Then came the second game of the 1985 series, in which it was widely felt that Dick Howser waited too long to let the Cardinals see Dan Quisenberry. Needless to say, it had never before happened twice in one series.

Through eight innings, the sixth game of the 1985 World Series seemed almost like a rerun, combining used parts from the first two contests. As in the second game, Charlie Leibrandt was pitching . . . well, near perfect. Leibrandt retired the Cardinals in order in the first, sec-ond, third, fourth, fifth and seventh; only three balls, all routine flies, were hit out of the infield in those innings. In the sixth the Cardinals had two singles, but the Royals got out of it with a double play.

As in the first game, the Royals were pounding the ball all over the park, but were denied by the determined Cardinals.

In the first inning Lonnie Smith doubled to lead off and moved to third with nobody out, but failed to score when Danny Cox struck out George Brett.

In the second inning, the Royals got one hit and lost another on a superb play by Ozzie Smith, diving for a ball behind second and flipping it backhand to Herr for an inning-ending forceout.

In the third inning, Willie McGee made a fine over-the-shoulder catch of a liner scorched by Lonnie Smith.

Leading off the fourth, George Brett hit another mam-moth, mile-high drive caught by Cedeno inches from the top of the wall. (If this series had been played in Yankee Stadium, Babe Ruth and Reggie Jackson would have be-come second-class legends by the time it was over.) Frank White then bunted for a single, but was called out at sec-ond base trying to steal. The call at second was question-able, and cost the Royals a run, as Sheridan singled to right two pitches later, but in truth the Royals could blame themselves for that one as much as anybody, for had White simply stayed at first he would have scored, given the same sequence, on a single by Sundberg that was ad-journed into the fifth inning. They didn't try to blame any-body. Balboni plastered the third out on a line right at McGee.

In the fifth inning, Sundberg singled leading off and was sacrificed to second, but died on base.

In the sixth inning, Wilson singled leading off, but Brett hit into an easy 4–6–3 double play.

In the seventh inning, the Royals got a walk from Bal-boni and a single from Biancalana.

At that point, the game began in earnest to repeat the essential points of the painful second game. This was a scoreless game, a complete pitcher's duel, now late in the game. Due up after Biancalana's single was Leibrandt. To allow Leibrandt to hit in this situation was tantamount to abandoning an excellent scoring chance, and for that rea-son it made no sense to me. If the Royals had used a good left-handed pinch hitter here—say, Iorg, Orta or Quirk—their chance of scoring a big run would go from about .030 to about .250. Offsetting this, you had the difference between Charlie Leibrandt on the mound, magnificent but with seven innings already gone, or having Dan Quisen-berry. 22/100 of a run over two innings is a rate of about a run a game, and it seemed to me (and still does) quite unlikely that a tiring Leibrandt was that much better than a fresh Dan Quisenberry. I felt that Howser had punched the wrong button.

Immediately, it began to come back at him. As a hit-ter, Leibrandt struck out. As a pitcher, he suddenly lost it. Pendleton drove the ball to deep center field, although Wilson got there. Tito Landrum singled (to right field, as always). Cesar Cedeno walked, putting two on with one out, but Darrell Porter struck out on three pitches. With two out, runners on first and second and the pitcher com-ing up—the exact same situation that Howser had just faced, except a half-inning later in the game—Herzog used his pinch hitter, a journeyman named Brian Harper.

Harper ripped a two-strike pitch into center field. The Cardinals had the lead.

Quisenberry came in to the game. He was outstand-ing, retiring four of the five hitters he faced (McGee, Herr, Clark—people like that) and allowing a scratch single on a ball tapped in front of the plate. But in their turn between those four outs, the Royals didn't score, and the Cardinals still had the lead going into the bottom of the ninth.

At that point, I almost left the ballpark. I *never* leave the park with a ballgame in progress. The last time I left the park before the last out was on opening day at Yankee Stadium, 1983, when the Tigers beat the Yankees 13–2, and it was cold and raining and we had a dinner appointment. But I almost left this one. I remembered that the Cardinals were 88–0 when they held a lead going into the ninth inning. I remembered that the ninth-inning turnaround in the second game was only the eighth in the history of the series. Most of all, sitting there in a pool of wasted enthusiasm, I remembered the last game we had seen here. I remembered the Cardinal fans jeering "Charlie, Char-lie, Char-lie" after it was over. The air felt as heavy as lead, and I felt almost compelled to run away from it, to escape before the last ray of hope was used, and the gloom that hung over us like a zeppelin would land on our shoulders. Three outs, and the season was over. I didn't want to see those three outs. I did not want to be there when the 1985 Royals, a team of such determination and dogged resourcefulness that they had escaped brushes with death a dozen times, finally bit the dust.

I can't understand what happened then. The Royals mounted another challenge—as they had all game—and the Cardinals this time simply fell apart; there is no other way to put it. Jorge Orta beat out an infield single, and Clark argued briefly about the call, and in the nine and one-half innings remaining in the 1985 World Series the Cardinals did absolutely nothing that would remind one of a contending team. Jack Clark misplayed a pop-up, and Steve Balboni drilled a single, putting the winning run on base. Darrell Porter, finally helping to pay the Royals back for the World Championship he cost them in 1980, let a ball get by him, putting the tying run in scoring position. Whitey Herzog decided that Hal McRae was to be intentionally walked, giving the Royals a chance to tie the game with a walk, and giving Howser two chances to win it with the left-handed pinch hitters he had saved from the seventh inning.

The zeppelin struggled away from our shoulders; hope rose in every throat. Dane Iorg blistered a pitch over first base. As it left the bat there was no doubt that it would end the game. Andy Van Slyke almost managed to create some doubt; Van Slyke made one terrific play to cut the ball off and fire home, but the game was over.

No one in the park was sober.

The sudden emotional surge, from severe communal depression to sudden shared ecstasy, was as intoxicating as rum. It is impossible to describe the feeling of the crowd minutes later, but it is possible to describe briefly their actions, which may give you some clue. People jumped up and down until the stadium shook. Strange men hugged each other and wept with joy. A co-ed a few rows in front of us wet her pants. A continuous roar sailed into the air for nearly twenty minutes, until every pair of lungs in the county was too hoarse to contribute any more to it, and then those in the stadium sat and stared at the empty playing field. A half-hour after the game hardly a seat was empty. I'm told that some people didn't leave the parking lot until almost dawn the next morning.

Game 7

The Cardinals, you see, were the Team of Destiny. By late October we had been hearing this for two solid months. The team was supposed to lose at the start of the season—they were an excellent team, but few people seemed to realize this, so they were supposed to lose— and then one thing broke right for them and then another and another, and when Jack Clark went out in late August and *even this* worked out well for the Cardinals, then the Cardinals had become destined to win the championship. I don't know what the Cardinal *players* were thinking, but the Cardinal *fans* were 100% convinced that the 1985 Cardinals were touched by the hand of God, and could not be dissuaded from adding another World Title to the long St. Louis list.

If the Cardinals were the team of destiny, the Royals were the team of determination. Few people outside their clubhouse believed that they could win—but they obviously did. I say that this is obvious not merely from the fact that they *did* win, but from the things they did on the field. Frank White, who earlier in his career was a terrific bunter but doesn't bunt much anymore, began picking out key moments of the game and dropping down bunt singles—I think he must have done this about six or eight times after September 25. Willie Wilson, never a particularly disciplined hitter and a hitter who for that reason sees a lot of pitches a foot out of the strike zone, began at key moments letting those pitches go by, putting him ahead in the count. Their defensive concentration and execution was tremendous—the best I've ever seen. Their individual defensive skills were good to excellent (four regulars have won Gold Gloves, and any of the four could have won the Award in 1985), but on the defensive plays that require two or three or four players to work together, they were extraordinary—as a team of past-30 stars should expect to be if they're going to win. There were several examples of this in the World Series, but the easiest to remember is the remarkable Wilson-to-White-to-Brett relay which caught Willie McGee at third on what everyone assumed was a triple in the fifth inning of the first game. Combining these skills, they would maneuver themselves into a position from which they had a chance to win—and then they would win. The only team that I ever saw that seemed really similar was the 1980 Phillies, which, with Rose, Boone, Schmidt and Bowa (among others) had the same kind of tenacity.

As the teams arrived at the park for Game 7, the series was literally even. Each team had won three games, and each team had their Cy Young candidate rested and ready to go. The Royals were at home, but that seemed to mean little because of a) the closeness and similarity of the two cities (nobody was really far away from home), b) the extreme similarity of the parks themselves—both turf parks with long power alleys, pretty good visibility, and c) the fact that the *visiting* team had won four of the first six games. The series was as even as it could be.

In the 1975 World Series the Red Sox ace starter was Louis Tiant. By the age of 34, Luis Tiant didn't throw particularly hard or lay claim to a spectacular breaking pitch, but he held his innings together by deception and control and a superior defense. He started the first game of the series, and pitched a 5-hit shutout. Four days later he faced the Reds again, and emerged with a complete-game victory.

But when the Reds saw him the third time, the jig was up. Deception is a limited resource; no con man ever made a living very long in one town. Before Tiant departed his third start he had surrendered 11 hits and six runs.

The series was literally even—but the core element of Cardinal magic had been shattered. Maybe I'm completely wrong, but that's the only way I can understand it: the Cardinals thought that they were *supposed to win,* that this was their destiny and that nothing could derail it. When the Royals scratched and clawed their way back into the series, and then a break or two went against the Cardinals, they were suddenly alarmed, flooded with self-doubt. They reacted angrily, as if "What is this? I thought we were supposed to win this thing? We won more games than they did, didn't we? *Everybody told us we were going to win.*" Whitey Herzog actually pointed out angrily after the seventh game that the Cardinals had won 107 games to the Royals 98—as if teams had not been winning World Series with fewer wins than the opponent for more than 80 years.

For the seventh game of the series, Don Denkinger was behind home plate, and it couldn't have mattered less if it was Ray Charles. John Tudor had nothing. In the first inning George Brett ripped a single to right and Frank White drove the ball to the track. No damage.

In the second inning Steve Balboni had home run depth on a foul ball. Craig and I tried to remember times we had seen a batter hit a foul homer and a fair homer in the same at bat. I've seen Balboni do it a couple of times. He didn't see another pitch anywhere near home plate. Darryl Motley, up next, ripped another foul home run, this one just missing the left field line. And then we saw it. We'll remember this one. Motley put the Royals two runs ahead on the next pitch. The crowd went wild and the ball was gone before Motley was out of the batter's box.

In the third inning, the Royals lined foul shots all over the park. Lonnie Smith saw three balls in the dirt and swung at one of them. Among the 55 pitches John Tudor threw that day, this was the only one a Royal batter swung at and missed. With one out and Brett at the plate, Tudor began to stall. While delivering one pitch to the plate, he threw to first base six times; Brett eventually got an infield single. Then, unaccountably, Tudor seemed to forget about the baserunners, and Brett and Smith pulled a double steal on a 1–2 pitch to Frank White. White fouled off five pitches in the process of drawing a walk. Jim Sundberg also walked, forcing in a run. John Tudor left the game. It was 3–0.

Bill Campbell came into the game. Steve Balboni fouled off his first pitch, took two pitches outside and ripped a single between Smith and Pendleton. It was 5–0.

The first pitch of the Royals' third was thrown at 8:04 PM. The inning ended at 8:29.

St. Louis had the heart of their order up in the fourth. McGee, Herr and Clark. The first pitch of the St. Louis fourth was thrown at 8:31. The last was thrown at 8:35.

The Royals had two singles and a stolen base in the fourth, but lost the inning to a 5–4–3 double play. The game was still alive; it was still 5–0.

The first pitch of the St. Louis fifth was thrown at 8:45. The last was thrown at 8:49.

The Detroit Tigers in 1934 led the series three games to two and were coming home to Bennett Park for the last two games. With Schoolboy Rowe pitching the sixth game, they felt the series was theirs. But after a heart-breaking 4–3 loss on Monday afternoon, the Tigers came to the seventh game having to beat Dizzy Dean, the best pitcher in the league, although Diz was working with only one day of rest.

The Cardinals blew the game open in the third inning, scoring seven runs. Stunned, the Tiger fans were silent for a while, but then began to get surly. In the sixth inning, Tiger third baseman Marv Owen made an unnecessary phantom tag of Joe Medwick after Medwick tripled (the ball had been cut off), and so Medwick slid hard into third, expecting the tag. The two exchanged words, but it came to nothing. But when Medwick tried to take the field in the bottom of the sixth . . .

The Cardinals won the seventh game, 11–0.

The top half of the fifth inning of the seventh game of the 1985 World Series lasted 37 minutes, was one of the wildest half-innings ever played in a World Series, and radically changed the image of the St. Louis Cardinal baseball club throughout the nation. I will give you a decoded version of my notes exactly as I took them down at the time, then we'll discuss it later. This was the inning (X means the ball was put in play):

	5TH Vs. Campbell	
1st Pitch: 8:51		
Sundberg	BX	
	Single in front of Van Slyke	
8:52 Herzog out/Jeff Lahti into game		8:55
Bones	SBBX	
	Ground single between 3rd/short	
	Runner to second	
Motley	SBFFX	
	Single to right-center (opposite field)	
	Sundberg scores, Balboni to second	
Biancalana	ScCBX	
	Strikeout Swinging	
	(Sc means attempted to check swing)	
Saberhagen	X	
	Bad Bunt; 3–6 forceout	
	Saberhagen just beat 3–6–1	
	Double Play	
	Balboni to third (No sac awarded	
Smith	BCScFBF	
	(Smoke appears in stadium . . . where is it from?)	
	X	
	Ground Double up third base line	
	Two Runs Score	
	Batter to Third on Throw	

Wilson	SX
	Grounded up middle; Herr made
	nice effort but Wilson beat 4–3
	play
	Smith scores

9:04 Herzog out/Ricky Horton in game   9:06

Brett	X
	Line single to right-center
	Wilson to third
	NO THROW TO THIRD!
	CARDINALS GIVE UP!

White	BB

9:09 Herzog out/Andujar in game

  Double Switch with Jorgensen entering to play left/
batting ninth, Andujar in seventh spot   9:12
(White still batting with 2–0 count)

	CFFFFFFBX
	Single in front of Jorgensen
	Wilson scores, Brett to third
Sundberg	BBFBFB

  Joacquin argues about call
  Herzog comes out to argue

9:19 Herzog thrown out of game! . . . Herzog now livid
. . . really lights into Denkinger (last night's call?)

9:22   X (Ball four)

  Andujar argues again . . . thrown out of game . . .
charges Denkinger . . . four Cardinals hold him off
(Cedeno leading?) . . . did he bump ump? suspensed?

9:23 Forsch to mound 9:26

Bones	B
	Wild Pitch; all three runners
	advance
	BCX
	Drive to center
	Well hit in right/center but McGee
	got it

9:28/ 6 runs/ 7 hits/ 0 errors/ 2 left/ 11–0 Kansas City
Would you believe?

Not fully described here is the Cardinals' behavior on
the field, for which they were torn apart by the nation's
press. If you ever get the time to walk through these notes
in your mind, visualizing what's happening, what you will
get is a picture of a team falling apart as their chances of
winning evaporate.

There are many questions about exactly what happened here. The first one is, why did Dick Howser let
Motley bat? His normal move would have been to pinch
hit Pat Sheridan. Sheridan is a left-handed batter, and
would ordinarily face the right-handed Lahti. Also, Sheridan is the better defensive outfielder, and with a 5–0 lead,
it seems natural to get the best defensive players in the
game. Why didn't Howser do it? As a reward for the mam-
moth home run in the first? Not likely. It is much more
likely that Howser thought that Lahti didn't have his
stuff—which, in view of what happened to him, he obviously didn't—and figured that if he made the switch it
would bring Horton into the game. Whatever the thinking,
it worked; Motley's single ignited the conclusive rally.

I wrote the words "No throw to third . . . Cardinals
give up!" just minutes before all hell broke loose, and in

view of that I was trying to remember why I had written
this. I think what happened was that the Cardinal defense
did not move into position after Brett's single. With a runner scoring on the play and another runner going to third,
there should have been people scurrying around getting in
position to back up throws, etc. The Cardinals, competing
up to that point, suddenly just stopped doing those things;
they stood and watched the play flat-footed. Which, in
view of the fact that the score was now 8–0, is understandable.

And immediately, Herzog brought Andujar into the
game. Now, this is the decision that is *really* hard to explain. The situation is all but out of hand, teetering pre-
cariously on the brink of chaos. A calm head is needed,
and you're going to bring in . . . Joacquin? I mean, I *like*
Joacquin Andujar; I think he's great. But this is like calling
in Don Rickles to arbitrate a touchy labor dispute. This is
like sending James Watt to deliver a message of condo-
lence. This is like calling Jerry Lewis in to assist in a
tricky brain operation. And apart from that, Andujar
hadn't done anything right in a month.

Herzog used five pitchers in the inning (Campbell,
Lahti, Horton, Andujar and Forsch). I remember one other
time when he used five pitchers in an inning, in the sixth
inning of the third game of the A.L. playoffs in 1976. In
1977 he used six pitchers in the last two innings of the
fifth and deciding game, trying unsuccessfully to protect
a lead.

Most managers won't use five pitchers in an inning
because they believe that the more pitchers you use, the
more chances you have to find one who doesn't have his
stuff on that particular day. Herzog will because he doesn't
put much stock in what you have on a given day; he believes that it's the manager's job to get the best possible
matchup of pitcher's abilities against hitter's abilities. I admire him for that, because I agree with him and because
he is willing to take criticism and do what he thinks is
right.

But I thought this day what I thought the other two
times. Whitey, it sure looks bad when it doesn't work.

Too much has been said about the Cardinals' bad behavior in that inning, but since it is too late to undo this,
let me get in my two cents' worth. Ozzie Smith was
quoted as defending the Cardinals' behavior, saying,
"We're competitors. Any time you feel you've been
cheated, you should react that way." That's the John
McEnroe defense: this doesn't count as making an ass of
myself because I *really believe* that ball was out. Gee, Oz,
I never thought of it that way, but since you mention it, I
kind of wonder if maybe the Cardinals' reactions were too
modest. Who's John Tudor trying to fool, anyway, punch-
ing out an electric fan? If he *really* felt like he was
cheated, I'd be thinking he'd look for bigger game, like
maybe a batting practice machine, a helicopter . . . he
should have been willing to drop-kick an air conditioner,
at the very least. And Andujar, he's pretending to be so
upset . . . why, he took the mound unarmed, didn't he? I
can't understand that. The man had 24 hours to stew about
it, and you know it's not that hard to pick up a piece in
our society, yet he took the mound with murder in his heart
but not a damn thing up his sleeve. Felt cheated, indeed.

No, seriously, the Cardinals' behavior wasn't *all* that

bad. Managers get thrown out of games all year; I don't see what the big deal is if it happens in the seventh game of a World Series. We might remember that while it is, to us, the climax of the show, it is, *to the participants,* like witnessing a death in the family, the death of a dream which they have nurtured for months or years, have fought hard and worked hard to bring to the edge of reality. We've never been through anything like it, most of us, but we must imagine the situation as a firestorm of hope, fear, dismay, pressure, hope against hope and hope against the stark terror of the scoreboard. I imagine it's quite a bit like being gathered around your grandmother's deathbed with 40,000 ecstatic strangers yelling, "CROAK! CROAK! CROAK!"

I am not saying that the Cardinals' behavior was laudable, but that the media might have done well to remember that old saw about walking a mile in a pair of used moccasins, or whatever it is. I would point out to you that the only other team which has ever gone through the same thing, the 1934 Tigers, didn't handle it a whole lot better. Just a week earlier, the Royals had done a similar number on the Blue Jays, beaten them decisively in a game that the Jays never expected to have to play to begin with. The Blue Jays handled it well, but their fans didn't. Objects were thrown on the field, and the game was stopped at least three times by fans running out of the stands, including one unfortunate heavyweight who performed so badly that the Toronto broadcaster designated him an American. Which, by the way, I'm not real crazy about. I mean, the Canadians were quite miffed because a half-dozen jerks were quoted as saying they didn't want the World Series played in Canada, and I'll be happy to say that anybody who feels that way—I personally have never encountered anybody who does—should consider having a brain implant. But how would the Canadians react if an American announcer assumed that because a given fan did something stupid, he must be a Canadian? This is not cute, guys, this is bigotry.

With an 11–0 lead, Bret Saberhagen more or less junked his curveball, change and slider and began throwing fastballs. The Cardinals hit them hard, and drove a number of them to the track. Had they been content to take singles, they likely would have gotten on the board—but had they threatened to get on the board, Bret Saberhagen would likely have started mixing in a few breaking pitches.

It took him six minutes and 17 pitches to retire the Cardinals in the sixth.

It took him four minutes and 8 pitches—8 fastballs—to do the job in the seventh.

It took him three minutes and 9 pitches to retire the Cardinals in the eighth.

He threw his first pitch in the ninth at 10:09.

At 10:10, thirty years of frustration had ended.

The Royals were champions of the world.

Epilogue

It's funny, you know. I've been as big a baseball fan as you can be all my life, but *I never knew a baseball game could make you feel so good*. The celebration at the stadium lasted for twenty or thirty minutes before the Royals, showing the inimical corporate taste for which they have long been noted, began trying to clear the stadium.

"Thank you for your support. We'll see you next year." More cheering, yelling and random running around. "Thank you for coming. Tickets will be on sale for the 1986 season at . . ." Still no cessation. "Thank you all for coming. We're going to start turning off the lights now." Lights go out. More lights go out. More announcements. All right, we can take a hint. I suppose they were worried about paying overtime to the cleanup crew.

It took us another 30 minutes to get back to the car, and 40 to escape the parking lots. Susie and I drove to an area of Kansas City called Westport. Thousands, maybe tens of thousands of people swarmed the streets, in many places packed in so tight that it was difficult to move. It was past midnight on Sunday; the bars were closed in self-defense, and people wandered around the crowd trying to buy beer or sell it. There were many more buyers than sellers, and the area was dry as the Sahara in a half hour. Virtually the entire crowd wore blue, but absurdity is in the eye of the beholder, and there were no eyes there to sense the absurdity of us as we meandered in circles, slapping high fives with passing strangers (including, when street conditions permitted, those riding by in convertibles and dune buggies), grinning and singing and yelling in the air phrases without meaning, spelling or distinguishable syllables, hugging and holding onto loved ones, catching an occasional spray of Budweiser in the face from a colleague in revelry, joining in war chants scarcely more intelligible than the random shouts, climbing fire escapes to hang hastily designed banners from the windows of co-operating samaritans, wandering around and around until the faces of the others became familiar landmarks of the scene, seeing others dance and weep with joy and sharing the feeling with them and wanting for the evening not to end and for sleep not to come and divide us from what had happened that night.

I thought about Charlie Finley and the "cellar-bray-tion" he had planned 21 years earlier. At length we headed home, into streets alive with the singing of horns. Whenever two cars met arms would reach out and wave and horns would sound. We stopped at a fast food place for a burger; a carload of young black men behind us tooted and smiled at us, and we honked and waved and smiled back, and repeated the exercise as we drove out. People tingled for days. One hundred and four percent of the Kansas City population became baseball fans; every one I know called to say how much he had enjoyed the series and how amazed he had been at the afterglow of the series; the phone companies made a fortune from the reunions of old friends. Office workers who didn't even like each other smiled at one another until they became self-conscious and began to giggle. It was two weeks before anyone had a thought about anything else.

The Cardinal fans did not universally accept the fact that their team had been fairly beaten, and to help them gain this acceptance, let me point out a number of facts:

1) The Royals hit .288 in the World Series, the highest batting average by a series team since 1980, when the Phillies hit .294 and the Royals .290.

The Cardinals hit .185 in the series, the lowest batting average by a series team since 1969.

The 103 points by which KC out-hit St. Louie barely misses being the largest difference ever, and is by far the largest ever for a seven-game series. If you look at the batting averages for the two series teams, they are almost always in the same range, whether that range is .213-.195, as in 1983, or .294-.290 as in 1980. In 1984 the averages were .253 and .265; in 1982 the Cardinals outhit Milwaukee .273-.269.

The only gap wider than the 103 points in 1985 was the 106 points by which the Giants out-hit the Yankees in 1922 (.309-.203)—and the Giants swept the Yankees four straight.

Even before the seventh game, the Royals had out-hit the Cardinals by a huge margin, .270-.190. And there is no area of play which a Cardinal fan could point to up against this, since the Royals also bettered the Cardinals as baserunners (7 stolen bases for the Royals, 2 for the Cardinals) and there was no appreciable difference in terms of power or defense. Cardinal pitchers issued 28 walks in the series; Royal pitchers issued only 18.

The Cardinals only argument is that, because of the way things worked out, they deserved to win despite being badly outplayed in most phases of the game. The argument is, giving it every advantage, that the Cardinals are a superior team, but merely disintegrated in the face of a bad call. Hell of a defense.

2) The Royals won three games in the series by five runs or more, winning 6–1, 6–1 and 11–0. They were the first team in 25 years to do that. The 1984 Tigers did not win any game so decisively (they had victory margins of 1, 2, 3 and 4). The 1983 Orioles won one game by five runs, and the 1982 Cardinals won one by more than five (12). The last team to win *two* games by decisive margins was the 1978 Yankees, who routed the Dodgers 12-2 and 7-2 (but also lost one 11–5). The Oakland A's, while winning three straight World Championships, never won a World Series game by more than three runs. The 1927 Yankees outscored the Pirates by five runs only once (8–1, third game). Only three other teams in the history of the sport have won three World Series games by margins of five runs or more, and one of those was the 1919 Reds—in an eight-game series, with the co-operation of the opposition.

I don't want to get too deeply into this, because it is something that I discuss somewhere else in the book (California comment, I guess), but the ability to win games *decisively* is one of the best quick indicators of relative quality. Whereas one-run games involve a lot of luck, a bad team very rarely beats a good team by a decisive margin. If you take the 1986 Guide when it comes out and check the games in which the first-place teams played the last-place teams, (that is, Toronto against Cleveland, Toronto against Texas, etc.) I would guess that you would find that the first-place teams would win about 70% of the time overall, but 85% or more of the time when the game was decided by five runs or more. That's why blowouts are one of the most interesting things to watch in the early season. If the Seattle Mariners, for example, were to win several games by big margins in the first few weeks of the season, then you should look for them to be in contention all the way—whereas if they win all of their close games early, it doesn't really mean that much.

3) The team which scores more runs in the series wins about 80% of the time. The last time the team which scored more runs did not win was 1977, when the Dodgers outscored the Yankees 28–26, but lost the series in six games.

The Royals in 1985 outscored the Cardinals by fifteen runs, 28 to 13. This was the largest run advantage in the series in 25 years, and the largest run advantage for a non-Yankee team since 1919, when the Sox threw the series. (It was matched or exceeded by the Yankees in 1928, 1932, 1936, 1937 and 1960. The only other teams to outscore their opponents by as many runs were the Red Sox in 1903 [the first series] and the 1910 Philadelphia A's.) The 1960 Yankees managed to lose the series despite outscoring their opponents by the largest margin of all time, but the others all won in series that were essentially regarded as mis-matches, as we shall see later.

Of course, the 11–0 blowout in the seventh game made the score more lop-sided, but the other sides of that are that a) several other teams have had 11-run blowouts in the course of a series victory, and still not made the list above, b) all of the other teams which beat their opponents by such a large margin also had big games included in the total, and c) the Royals not only *won* one game by 11 runs, they also didn't lose any by any significant margin. If you throw out the one largest margin of victory—the 11–0 game, in this case—the Royals still outscored the Cardinals 17–13, which is a four-run margin and one must still go back to 1976 to find a larger one. In 1976, the Reds destroyed the Yankees in four straight games. The Reds outscored the Yankees 22–8 (14 runs), which would be 15–6 (+9) if you threw out the largest margin of victory. Here, I'll run them down for the last ten years:

1976 Cincinnati 22, New York 8	+14
1977 New York 26, Los Angeles 28	−2
1978 New York 36, Los Angeles 23	+13
1979 Pittsburgh 32, Baltimore 26	+6
1980 Philadelphia 27, Kansas City 23	+4
1981 Los Angeles 27, New York 22	+5
1982 St. Louis 39, Milwaukee 33	+6
1983 Baltimore 18, Philadelphia 9	+9
1984 Detroit 23, San Diego 15	+8
1985 Kansas City 28, St. Louis 13	+15

Detroit beat San Diego in five games in 1984, but the Series in reality was much more evenly played, and the victory less decisive, than was that of 1985. The Tigers allowed more runs and scored fewer than did the Royals.

Let me list below all of the series in which the runs scored and allowed were similar to those in 1985, and following that some samples of the press reaction to those series. If you read carefully, you might notice that one example is somewhat out of line with the others. First the series:

1910 Philadelphia (A)	35	Chicago (N)	15	2.33 – 1
1911 Philadelphia (A)	27	Giants	13	2.07 – 1
1927 Yankees	23	Pittsburgh	10	2.30 – 1
1937 Yankees	28	Giants	12	2.33 – 1
1938 Yankees	22	Chicago (N)	9	2.44 – 1
1939 Yankees	20	Cincinnati	8	2.50 – 1

1954 Giants	21	Cleveland	9	2.33 – 1
1961 Yankees	27	Cincinnati	13	2.07 – 1
1985 Kansas City	28	St. Louis	13	2.15 – 1

Now the reactions:

1910 Series:

"(The Athletics) fairly overwhelmed the hitherto almost invincible Cubs, and won with such ease as to leave no doubt as to their superiority, and nothing for even the most rabid National League partisan to cavil at. The Athletics outranked the Cubs in every department of the game, batting, fielding, running, pitching . . . to leave absolutely no doubt that as a team, or individually, they are not only superior to their defeated opponents, but that they are by long odds the greatest base ball team in the World today."

Francis Richter, 1911 *Reach Guide*

1911 Series:

"The Athletics as a team excelled the Giants in the mechanical points of pitching, batting and fielding; and also in the matter of resourcefulness, perception, co-operation, and steadiness under stress. They were also more adept in the finer points of the game . . . the Athletics showed superior defense, heavier batting power, more resourcefulness and reserve power than the Giants."

Francis Richter, 1912 *Reach Guide*

1927 Series:

"The Series was over before it began as awed Pirate players sat on the top step of their dugout watching Babe Ruth, Lou Gehrig, Tony Lazzeri, and company, considered baseball's finest team ever, pop dozens of balls over the outfield fences in batting practice.

"The display of power destroyed the Pirates' confidence as they went down easily in four straight games."

Maury Allen, *Baseball's 100 Greatest Players*

1937 Series:

"Not many were betting on the Giants, who were three-to-one underdogs. The wise money was right. The Yankee hitting demolished the Giant pitching with such methodical force that (Giant manager) Terry got a telegram from a Giant fan who informed him, tongue in cheek, to 'change your signals. The Yankees know them.'"

John Devaney and Burt Goldblatt
The World Series: A complete Pictorial History

1938 Series:

"Mightier than ever, the New York Yankees retained their title as the No. 1 baseball team of the majors by scoring a grand slam over the Chicago Cubs, National League pennant winners."

Jimmy Isaminger, 1939 *Reach Guide*

1939 Series:

"Quite all base ball-minded people seemingly had picked the Yankees to win the American League pennant before the 1939 race began. With that task accomplished the fans were inclined to the belief that the Yankees also would win the world series. . . (at the end) many critics considered the club the strongest ever organized in base

ball . . . Like other clubs before them (Cincinnati) found out that the New York team of 1939 had too much offensive power for their kind of base ball."

John B. Foster, *1940 Spalding and Reach Guide*

1954 Series:

"The surprising New York Giants sent the Cleveland Indians down to a stunning defeat in the 1954 blue-ribbon classic. The Indians . . . amazed both friend and foe by failing to win a single game as the relentless Giants rolled on to . . . a one-sided victory.

"The Giants, who arose to every occasion during the league season, played the same aggressive, alert, heads-up ball which enabled them to nose out Brooklyn and Milwaukee."

Fred Lieb, *1955 Official Baseball Guide*

1961 Series:

"This mightiest of all home run teams continued its hard hitting in the World Series against Cincinnati, taking the Reds easily in five games, hitting seven home runs along the way.

"The 1961 New York Yankees had (reached) heights never scaled before, and never equaled since."

Donald Honig, *Baseball's 10 Greatest Teams*

1985 Series:

"(The Cardinals) should have been home in St. Louis, nursing their hangovers and picking confetti out of their hair from the joyous parade downtown. They were not undone by the precocity of 21-year-old Bret Saberhagen or the singing sword of George Brett (but by) American League umpire Don Denkinger."

Bill Conlin in *The Sporting News*

No, Mr. Conlin, I'm afraid not. The truth is that the Kansas City Royals kicked the holy crap out of the overmatched National League representatives. By a run of extremely good fortune in the close games, the Cardinals were able to keep the result in doubt for six games and three innings; they should be quite grateful for this.

Also in *The Sporting News,* Jack Craig wrote that the "Series, in all candor, offered relatively little excitement." While "excitement" is a subjective term, and I wouldn't question Craig's right to see it that way if he wants, I sure can't agree with him, either. In addition to the two dramatic ninth-inning rallies, an unprecedented thing, the first game of the series was extremely tense, and the seventh game, while not close, was certainly exciting. The series offered human interest angles (wonder if it's the first time anybody ever had a baby in the middle of winning the series MVP award?), expected heroes (Brett, Saberhagen, Tudor) and unexpected heroes (Iorg, Landrum). The series had a clearly defined story line, developing from the moment it began, in the regional nature of the combatants and the return of Herzog to Kansas City, along with several other players (Porter, Iorg, Lonnie Smith, Braun) going up against old teammates. The series had controversy with a capital C; it was distinguished by a good deal of classy behavior and a few low-rent antics. The fielding, headed by the play on which a million-dollar athlete heaved his body into the dugout trying to catch a pop up, was excellent throughout, and offered a number of memorable moments. The chess game of the series was a second-guesser's delight, with questionable managerial decisions on both sides. The series featured a team that was the heaviest underdog in several years rallying to win from a position which no team had ever escaped before (losing the first two games at home). There were no see-saw contests, due to the inability of the Cardinals to score runs, but I think, honestly, that it was the best World Series in ten years. And I think the performance of the TV ratings, gaining strength almost every night, will bear that out.

The National League representative in the 1911 World Series, the New York Giants, was the greatest base-stealing team of all time, stealing 347 bases, a record which still stands. The leader of the larcenous brigade was their 23-year-old left fielder and leadoff man, Josh Devore. The pitching staff was headed by two twenty-game winners, one right-handed and one left-handed. The National League partisans felt sure that their running game could break through against their series opponents.

Answering for the American League was the Philadelphia Athletics, a team with a mediocre outfield but an exceptional starting rotation and a fine infield, led by third baseman Frank Baker, who hit .334, led the American League in slugging percentage and drove in 115 runs. The editor of the 1912 Reach Guide, Francis Richter, wrote that the National League manager, John McGraw, "was handicapped by the fact that with but two star pitchers against (Connie) Mack's three stars the latter always had an 'ace in the hole' against him."

The first game was a pitcher's duel, and the Giants pulled ahead in the series with a 2–1 victory. Later the Jints added another one-run victory, rallying from a 3–0 deficit with one in the seventh, two in the ninth and one in the tenth for a 4–3 win. But in time, the batting of the Baker, the star third baseman, and the superior pitching depth of the American League representative began to imbalance the series in the favor of the A.L. club. The Athletics won the final and deciding contest in an 11-run blowout, the score being 13–2.

For the series as a whole, the Athletics outscored the Giants 27 to 13, and limited the N.L. club to a puny .189 batting average. John McGraw was given a public reprimand for abusive language on the field, though, as Richter wrote, this incident "was made far too much of by the newspapers." Richter also reported that "The Athletics throughout the series accepted every decision without question and lived in every way up to their reputation as the most gentlemanly team in the arena."

In later years, the editors of Baseball Guides *would become faceless company men, concerned only with compiling the standard elements of the form and giving no one cause for offense, but at this time* Guides *were still personal, fun and informative; editors would digress into amusing sidelights or challenge the reader with original ideas, as they saw fit. Summarizing the series for the 1912* Reach Guide, *Francis Richter wrote these words:*

There could hardly have been any special excellence manifested in the base-stealing line . . . in view of the fact that for both teams grand masters in the art of pitching, catching, throwing and watching the bases were handling the ball in each and every game. In the six games only eight bases were stolen . . . and the Giants' unquestionable excellence in this department had little or no chance to assert itself, for the reason that they seldom reached first base, owing to light batting, and when they did get there they found it impossible to secure the good start so indispensable to successful base stealing . . .

In nearly all forecasts of the 1911 World's Series the base-stealing ability of the Giants was regarded by the critics as a great factor in their favor. In commenting on this the editor of this guide, in an editorial forecast of the World's Series pointed out the fact that "invariably in World's Series 'straight base ball' was the rule; that all series were settled by the pitchers and batters . . . the matter of superior speed on the base paths cutting little or no ice."

COMPLETE BATTING RECORDS

Player	G	AB	R	H	TB	2B	3B	HR	RBI	GW	SH	SF	HB	BB	IB	SO	SB	CS	GiDP	Avg	Slug	OBP	Runs	Outs Made	Runs/27 Outs	OW%	Appr Value
Sundberg	115	367	38	90	140	12	4	10	35	4	4	2	1	33	3	67	0	2	9	.245	.381	.308	42	294	3.85	.470	7
Balboni	160	600	74	146	286	28	2	36	88	9	0	5	5	52	4	166	1	1	14	.243	.477	.307	86	474	4.90	.589	10
White	149	563	62	140	233	25	1	22	69	9	5	3	1	28	2	86	10	4	8	.249	.414	.284	65	443	3.98	.486	11
*Brett	155	550	108	184	322	38	5	30	112	16	0	9	3	103	31	49	9	1	12	.335	.585	.436	146	388	10.17	.861	17
Concepcion	131	314	32	64	77	5	1	2	20	2	12	1	6	16	0	29	4	4	8	.204	.245	.255	19	275	1.91	.178	3
Smith	120	448	77	115	164	23	4	6	41	6	0	5	4	41	0	69	40	7	2	.257	.366	.321	60	347	4.70	.568	6
†Wilson	141	605	87	168	247	25	21	4	43	7	2	1	5	29	3	94	43	11	6	.278	.408	.316	80	457	4.75	.574	12
Motley	123	383	45	85	158	20	1	17	49	4	0	5	2	18	2	57	6	4	17	.222	.413	.257	35	324	2.89	.333	6
McRae	112	320	41	83	144	19	0	14	70	9	2	2	1	44	3	45	0	1	12	.259	.450	.349	49	254	5.20	.618	5
*Orta	110	300	32	80	115	21	1	4	45	6	2	4	2	22	5	28	2	1	8	.267	.383	.317	36	235	4.10	.501	3
*Sheridan	78	206	18	47	69	9	2	3	17	3	3	1	1	23	2	38	11	3	4	.228	.335	.307	23	170	3.58	.434	2
Jones	110	152	12	32	39	7	0	0	9	1	4	2	3	8	0	15	0	1	6	.211	.257	.261	10	133	1.95	.184	2
Wathan	60	145	11	34	47	8	1	1	9	1	2	0	1	17	0	15	1	1	4	.234	.324	.319	15	118	3.47	.418	2
†Biancalana	81	138	21	26	36	5	1	1	6	1	5	0	0	17	0	34	1	4	1	.188	.261	.277	10	122	2.29	.238	2
*Iorg	64	130	7	29	43	9	1	1	21	4	0	0	0	8	2	16	0	1	6	.223	.331	.268	10	108	2.42	.259	1
Pryor	63	114	8	25	31	3	0	1	3	1	3	0	0	8	0	12	0	1	6	.219	.272	.270	7	99	1.97	.187	1
*Moreno	24	70	9	17	30	1	3	2	12	0	0	1	1	3	0	8	0	1	1	.243	.429	.280	8	56	3.85	.470	1
*Quirk	19	57	3	16	21	3	1	0	4	2	0	0	0	2	0	9	0	0	1	.281	.368	.305	6	42	3.99	.487	1
*Leeper	15	34	1	3	3	0	0	0	4	2	0	0	0	1	0	3	0	0	0	.088	.088	.114	0	31	0.32	.006	0
Scranton	6	4	1	0	0	0	0	0	0	0	0	0	0	0	0	0	0	0	0	.000	.000	.000	0	4	0	.000	0
Hegman	1	0	0	0	0	0	0	0	0	0	0	0	0	0	0	0	0	0	0	.000	.000	.000	0	0	0	.000	0

*left-handed hitter, †switch hitter

DEFENSIVE STATISTICS

FIRST

	G	PO	A	Er	TC	DP	PCT.
Balboni	160	1573	101	12	1686	138	.993
Wathan	6	12	1	0	13	0	1.000
Iorg	2	13	1	0	14	2	1.000
Pryor	1	0	0	0	0	0	.000
Quirk	1	2	0	0	2	0	1.000
TEAM:	170	1600	103	12	1715	140	.993
AVG:	180	1440	123	14	1577	141	.991

SECOND

	G	PO	A	Er	TC	DP	PCT.
White	149	342	490	17	849	101	.980
Pryor	20	35	46	1	82	11	.988
Biancalana	4	3	1	0	4	1	1.000
Concepcion	2	0	3	0	3	0	1.000
Hegman	1	0	0	0	0	0	.000
TEAM:	176	380	540	18	938	113	.981
AVG:	189	347	501	15	863	114	.982

THIRD

	G	PO	A	Er	TC	DP	PCT.
Brett	152	107	339	15	461	33	.967
Pryor	26	5	30	2	37	2	.946
Iorg	1	1	3	0	4	0	1.000
TEAM:	179	113	372	17	502	35	.966
AVG:	192	129	327	23	479	32	.953

SHORTSTOP

	G	PO	A	Er	TC	DP	PCT.
Concepcion	128	127	367	21	515	63	.959
Biancalana	74	80	168	10	258	31	.961
Pryor	13	7	11	2	20	3	.900
Scranton	5	1	8	0	9	1	1.000
TEAM:	220	215	554	33	802	98	.959
AVG:	189	269	474	28	771	104	.964

CATCHER

	G	PO	A	Er	TC	DP	PCT.	PB
Sundberg	112	572	41	5	618	10	.992	6
Wathan	49	247	28	4	279	6	.986	2
Quirk	17	64	8	1	73	1	.986	2
TEAM:	178	883	77	10	970	17	.990	10
AVG:	193	895	74	13	982	13	.987	13

OUTFIELD

	G	PO	A	Er	TC	DP	PCT.
Wilson	140	378	4	2	384	1	.995
Smith	119	195	10	9	214	3	.958
Motley	114	198	4	7	209	1	.967
Jones	100	115	2	2	119	1	.983
Sheridan	69	116	3	2	121	0	.983
Iorg	32	41	0	0	41	0	1.000
Moreno	21	30	1	0	31	1	1.000
Leeper	8	13	0	1	14	0	.929
TEAM:	603	1086	24	23	1133	7	980
AVG:	559	1141	33	21	1196	8	.982

COMPLETE PITCHERS RECORDS

Pitcher	W	L	Pct	ERA	G	GS	CG	GF	SHO	SV	IP	H	TBF	R	ER	HR	SH	SF	HB	BB	IB	SO	WP	BK	Appr Value
								Starters (One-half of Game Appearances)																	
*Leibrandt	17	9	.654	2.69	33	33	8	0	3	0	237.2	223	983	86	71	17	8	5	2	68	3	108	4	3	13
Saberhagen	20	6	.769	2.87	32	32	10	0	1	0	235.1	211	931	79	75	19	9	7	1	38	1	158	1	3	15
*Jackson	14	12	.538	3.42	32	32	4	0	3	0	208.0	209	893	94	79	7	5	4	6	76	2	114	4	2	10
*Black	10	15	.400	4.33	33	33	5	0	2	0	205.2	216	885	111	99	17	8	5	8	59	4	122	9	1	7
Gubicza	14	10	.583	4.06	29	28	0	0	0	0	177.1	160	760	88	80	14	1	6	5	77	0	99	12	0	7
								Relievers																	
Quisenberry	8	9	.471	2.37	84	0	0	76	0	37	129.0	142	532	41	34	8	4	3	1	16	5	54	0	0	16
Beckwith	1	5	.167	4.07	49	0	0	21	0	1	95.0	99	410	45	43	9	4	3	3	32	8	80	6	0	2
*Jones	3	3	.500	4.78	33	1	0	16	0	0	64.0	62	290	40	34	6	4	6	0	39	4	32	1	0	2
LaCoss	1	1	.500	5.09	21	0	0	7	0	1	40.2	49	193	25	23	2	3	0	0	29	6	26	2	0	1
Farr	2	1	.667	3.11	16	3	0	5	0	1	37.2	34	164	15	13	2	1	2	2	20	4	36	3	0	0
Huismann	1	0	1.000	1.93	9	0	0	6	0	0	18.2	14	70	4	4	1	1	2	0	3	0	9	0	0	0
*Ferreira	0	0	.000	7.94	2	0	0	1	0	0	5.2	6	24	5	5	0	0	0	0	2	0	5	0	0	0
*Gura	0	0	.000	12.46	3	0	0	2	0	1	4.1	7	23	6	6	1	0	0	0	4	0	2	1	0	0
Leonard	0	0	.000	.00	2	0	0	1	0	0	2.0	1	7	0	0	0	0	0	0	0	0	1	0	0	0

Jim SUNDBERG, Catcher

	G	AB	Hit	2B	3B	HR	Run	RBI	TBB	SO	SB	CS	Avg
10.02 years		515	130	22	3	7	54	54	59	76	2	4	.253
1985	115	367	90	12	4	10	38	35	33	67	0	2	.245
First Half	73	246	61	7	4	8	28	26	18	39	0	0	.248
Second Half	42	121	29	5	0	2	10	9	15	28	0	2	.240
Vs. RHP		244	61	6	3	3	21	18	25	52	0	1	.250
Vs. LHP		123	29	6	1	7	17	17	8	15	0	1	.236
Home	58	188	47	5	3	2	15	13	11	36	0	2	.250
Road	57	179	43	7	1	8	23	22	22	31	0	0	.240
Grass	41	137	32	7	1	5	17	18	15	25	0	0	.234
Turf	74	230	58	5	3	5	21	17	18	42	0	2	.252

Steve BALBONI, First Base

	G	AB	Hit	2B	3B	HR	Run	RBI	TBB	SO	SB	CS	Avg
2.19 years		565	135	26	3	32	68	86	51	167	0	0	.238
1985	160	600	146	28	2	36	74	88	52	166	1	1	.243
First Half	80	308	78	16	0	14	33	39	23	86	0	0	.253
Second Half	80	292	68	12	2	22	41	49	29	80	1	1	.233
Vs. RHP		428	110	19	2	28	49	73	30	119	1	1	.257
Vs. LHP		172	36	9	0	8	25	15	22	47	0	0	.209
Home	81	304	77	21	1	17	35	45	23	73	1	0	.253
Road	79	296	69	7	1	19	39	43	29	93	0	1	.233
Grass	60	227	57	7	1	16	34	35	23	71	0	1	.251
Turf	100	373	89	21	1	20	40	53	29	95	1	0	.239

Frank WHITE, Second Base

	G	AB	Hit	2B	3B	HR	Run	RBI	TBB	SO	SB	CS	Avg
10.20 years		543	140	27	5	11	65	60	25	70	16	7	.258
1985	149	563	140	25	1	22	62	69	28	86	10	4	.249
First Half	74	279	62	10	1	9	26	32	14	37	3	3	.222
Second Half	75	284	78	15	0	13	36	37	14	49	7	1	.275
Vs. RHP		393	98	18	1	13	40	42	21	65	10	4	.249
Vs. LHP		170	42	7	0	9	22	27	7	21	0	0	.247
Home	78	297	72	13	0	9	25	35	14	41	7	1	.242
Road	71	266	68	12	1	13	37	34	14	45	3	3	.256
Grass	57	223	58	9	1	12	30	33	7	36	2	2	.260
Turf	92	340	82	16	0	10	32	36	21	50	8	2	.241

Darryl MOTLEY, Right Field

	G	AB	Hit	2B	3B	HR	Run	RBI	TBB	SO	SB	CS	Avg
2.04 years		539	136	24	4	18	65	68	27	75	9	9	.253
1985	123	383	85	20	1	17	45	49	18	57	6	4	.222
First Half	59	195	45	9	0	9	25	24	8	25	4	1	.231
Second Half	64	188	40	11	1	8	20	25	10	32	2	3	.213
Vs. RHP		213	44	10	0	9	26	26	9	35	5	3	.207
Vs. LHP		170	41	10	1	8	19	23	9	22	1	1	.241
Home	62	187	43	11	1	6	20	24	9	25	1	3	.230
Road	61	196	42	9	0	11	25	25	9	32	5	1	.214
Grass	47	154	34	8	0	8	20	19	6	24	4	1	.221
Turf	76	229	51	12	1	9	25	30	12	33	2	3	.223

George BRETT, Third Base

	G	AB	Hit	2B	3B	HR	Run	RBI	TBB	SO	SB	CS	Avg
9.98 years		625	197	40	11	19	100	98	62	44	14	7	.316
1985	155	550	184	38	5	30	108	112	103	49	9	1	.335
First Half	75	269	94	19	4	10	48	55	51	17	4	0	.349
Second Half	80	281	90	19	1	20	60	57	52	32	5	1	.320
Vs. RHP		360	121	28	4	20	78	73	79	34	8	1	.336
Vs. LHP		190	63	10	1	10	30	39	24	15	1	0	.332
Home	81	285	105	21	4	15	64	66	59	23	7	0	.368
Road	74	265	79	17	1	15	44	46	44	26	2	1	.298
Grass	57	206	63	10	1	15	38	37	37	22	2	1	.306
Turf	98	344	121	28	4	15	70	75	66	27	7	0	.352

Hal McRAE, Designated Hitter

	G	AB	Hit	2B	3B	HR	Run	RBI	TBB	SO	SB	CS	Avg
12.06 years		573	167	39	5	15	76	87	52	61	9	6	.291
1985	112	320	83	19	0	14	41	70	44	45	0	1	.259
First Half	49	97	21	6	0	5	10	19	17	11	0	1	.216
Second Half	63	223	62	13	0	9	31	51	27	34	0	0	.278
Vs. RHP		168	47	8	0	6	22	39	19	25	0	0	.280
Vs. LHP		152	36	11	0	8	19	31	25	20	0	1	.237
Home	60	165	44	11	0	7	23	37	21	24	0	0	.267
Road	52	155	39	8	0	7	18	33	23	21	0	1	.252
Grass	43	133	32	8	0	4	14	23	17	17	0	1	.241
Turf	69	187	51	11	0	10	27	47	27	28	0	0	.273

Onix CONCEPCION, Shortstop

	G	AB	Hit	2B	3B	HR	Run	RBI	TBB	SO	SB	CS	Avg
2.40 years		433	103	14	3	1	45	33	20	39	10	6	.238
1985	131	314	64	5	1	2	32	20	16	29	4	4	.204
First Half	67	183	33	3	0	1	16	11	9	19	3	2	.180
Second Half	64	131	31	2	1	1	16	9	7	10	1	2	.237
Vs. RHP		204	40	3	0	2	20	13	9	19	3	2	.196
Vs. LHP		110	24	2	1	0	12	7	7	10	1	2	.218
Home	67	144	29	4	1	1	20	10	8	11	2	2	.201
Road	64	170	35	1	0	1	12	10	8	18	2	2	.206
Grass	48	129	31	1	0	0	10	9	5	14	2	1	.240
Turf	83	185	33	4	1	2	22	11	11	15	2	3	.178

Jorge ORTA, Designated Hitter

	G	AB	Hit	2B	3B	HR	Run	RBI	TBB	SO	SB	CS	Avg
10.05 years		542	151	25	6	12	69	69	47	67	8	6	.279
1985	110	300	80	21	1	4	32	45	22	28	2	1	.267
First Half	68	225	63	18	0	2	21	34	14	18	1	0	.280
Second Half	42	75	17	3	1	2	11	11	8	10	1	1	.227
Vs. RHP		285	78	21	1	4	32	45	22	23	2	1	.274
Vs. LHP		15	2	0	0	0	0	0	0	5	0	0	.133
Home	55	142	39	11	0	1	15	17	12	12	2	1	.275
Road	55	158	41	10	1	3	17	28	10	16	0	0	.259
Grass	40	112	33	8	1	1	13	20	8	11	0	0	.295
Turf	70	188	47	13	0	3	19	25	14	17	2	1	.250

Lonnie SMITH, Left Field

	G	AB	Hit	2B	3B	HR	Run	RBI	TBB	SO	SB	CS	Avg
4.78 years		552	161	29	6	7	103	51	47	61	57	17	.291
1985	148	544	140	25	6	6	92	48	0	0	52	0	.257
First Half	75	265	66	10	6	2	47	25		29			.249
Second Half	73	279	74	15	0	4	45	23		23			.265
Vs. RHP		376	92			4	32						.244
Vs. LHP		168	48			2	16						.286
Home	75	274	67	11	6	2	49	27		38			.245
Road	73	270	73	14	0	4	43	21		14			.270
Grass	51	187	52	12	0	3	29	13		11			.278
Turf	97	357	88	13	6	3	63	35		41			.246

Willie WILSON, Center Field

	G	AB	Hit	2B	3B	HR	Run	RBI	TBB	SO	SB	CS	Avg
6.86 years		624	188	23	13	3	102	46	32	82	64	12	.301
1985	141	605	168	25	21	4	87	43	29	94	43	11	.278
First Half	81	345	98	14	13	3	51	21	20	55	22	7	.284
Second Half	60	260	70	11	8	1	36	22	9	39	21	4	.269
Vs. RHP		432	116	15	17	3	63	27	23	66	33	8	.269
Vs. LHP		173	52	10	4	1	24	16	6	28	10	3	.301
Home	71	302	83	12	14	1	46	22	14	52	22	4	.275
Road	70	303	85	13	7	3	41	21	15	42	21	7	.281
Grass	52	232	67	10	6	3	31	16	8	29	15	6	.289
Turf	89	373	101	15	15	1	56	27	21	65	28	5	.271

BUD BLACK

	(W–L)	GS	Run	Avg	DP	Avg	SB	Avg
1984	(17-12)	35	134	3.83	21	.60	11	.31
1985	(10-15)	33	127	3.85	28	.85	17	.52
1982-1985		106	435	4.10	90	.85	46	.43

	G	IP	W	L	Pct	ER	BB	SO	ERA
1984 Home	19	145.7	10	7	.588	43	32	85	2.66
1985 Home	18	109.0	6	7	.462	53	37	50	4.38
1984 Road	16	111.3	7	5	.583	46	32	55	3.72
1985 Road	15	96.7	4	8	.333	46	22	72	4.28
1984 Grass	13	87.7	5	4	.556	38	26	43	3.90
1985 Grass	12	72.7	4	7	.364	38	40	58	4.71
1984 Turf	22	169.3	12	8	.600	51	38	97	2.71
1985 Turf	21	129.0	6	8	.429	61	19	64	4.26
1985 Total	33	201.7	10	15	.400	99	59	122	4.42

CHARLIE LEIBRANDT

	(W–L)	GS	Run	Avg	DP	Avg	SB	Avg
1984	(11-7)	23	95	4.13	23	1.00	15	.65
1985	(17-9)	33	151	4.58	31	.94	21	.64
1980-1985		98	417	4.26	101	1.03	87	.89

	G	IP	W	L	Pct	ER	BB	SO	ERA
1984 Home	10	61.7	3	3	.500	24	15	15	3.50
1985 Home	15	105.3	9	2	.818	30	29	50	2.56
1984 Road	13	82.0	8	4	.667	34	23	38	3.73
1985 Road	18	132.3	8	7	.533	41	39	58	2.79
1984 Grass	8	46.7	5	3	.625	21	16	26	4.05
1985 Grass	13	91.3	5	5	.500	33	25	36	3.25
1984 Turf	15	97.0	6	4	.600	37	22	27	3.43
1985 Turf	20	146.3	12	4	.750	38	43	72	2.34
1985 Total	33	237.7	17	9	.654	71	68	108	2.69

BRET SABERHAGEN

	(W–L)	GS	Run	Avg	DP	Avg	SB	Avg
1984	(10-11)	18	62	3.44	14	.78	12	.67
1985	(20-6)	32	144	4.50	30	.94	14	.44
1984-1985		50	206	4.12	44	.88	26	.52

	G	IP	W	L	Pct	ER	BB	SO	ERA
1984 Home	16	77.7	4	5	.444	19	14	32	2.20
1985 Home	17	128.7	10	3	.769	40	22	80	2.80
1984 Road	22	80.0	6	6	.500	42	22	41	4.72
1985 Road	15	106.7	10	3	.769	35	16	78	2.95
1984 Grass	18	72.0	6	5	.545	37	20	37	4.62
1985 Grass	13	95.3	9	2	.818	27	13	73	2.55
1984 Turf	20	85.7	4	6	.400	24	16	36	2.52
1985 Turf	19	140.0	11	4	.733	48	25	85	3.09
1985 Total	32	235.3	20	6	.769	75	38	158	2.87

DANNY JACKSON

	(W–L)	GS	Run	Avg	DP	Avg	SB	Avg
1984	(2-6)	11	40	3.64	14	1.27	4	.36
1985	(14-12)	32	121	3.78	38	1.19	12	.38
1983-1985		46	176	3.83	54	1.17	18	.39

	G	IP	W	L	Pct	ER	BB	SO	ERA
1984 Home	7	37.0	2	2	.500	17	18	20	4.14
1985 Home	15	98.7	6	5	.545	37	29	46	3.3
1984 Road	8	39.0	0	4	0.000	19	17	20	4.38
1985 Road	17	109.3	8	7	.533	42	47	68	3.46
1984 Grass	6	29.3	0	2	0.000	11	14	15	3.38
1985 Grass	13	83.7	6	5	.545	32	39	51	3.44
1984 Turf	9	46.7	2	4	.333	25	21	25	4.82
1985 Turf	19	124.3	8	7	.533	47	37	63	3.40
1985 Total	32	208.0	14	12	.538	79	76	114	3.42

MARK GUBICZA

	(W–L)	GS	Run	Avg	DP	Avg	SB	Avg
1984	(10-14)	29	115	3.97	29	1.00	24	.83
1985	(14-10)	28	128	4.57	27	.96	23	.82
1984-1985		57	243	4.26	56	.98	47	.82

	G	IP	W	L	Pct	ER	BB	SO	ERA
1984 Home	19	134.3	8	8	.500	45	39	62	3.01
1985 Home	14	85.7	7	5	.583	33	31	49	3.47
1984 Road	10	54.7	2	6	.250	40	42	79	6.59
1985 Road	15	91.7	7	5	.583	47	46	50	4.61
1984 Grass	8	42.3	2	4	.333	29	72	125	6.17
1985 Grass	10	65.0	5	2	.714	24	31	36	3.32
1984 Turf	21	146.7	8	10	.444	56	9	16	3.44
1985 Turf	19	112.3	9	8	.529	56	46	63	4.49
1985 Total	29	177.3	14	10	.583	80	77	99	4.06

OTHERS

	(W–L)	GS	Run	Avg	DP	Avg	SB	Avg
Farr	(2-1)	3	13	4.33	3	1.00	2	.67
Jones	(3-3)	1	3	3.00	0	0.00	1	1.00

CALIFORNIA ANGELS

Gene Mauch in 1985 turned in the archetypical Gene Mauch season. Mauch, the only remaining major league skipper who managed Elmer Valo, took over a team which in the previous two seasons had finished 22 games under .500, and, through his extraordinary short-sightedness, poor judgment and compulsive over-managing, prevented them from winning the Worlds' Championship. That, at least, is the story of the season as it seemed destined to be written before *Sports Illustrated,* in its October 7, 1985 issue, rose to the level of journalistic nobility. In a fine article by Ron Fimrite, *SI* wrote that "once again, as he has so relentlessly in the past, Mauch is flogging an under-manned and over-matched team to exceed itself in a pennant race."

The magazine speaks for no one but Time Inc., but they do occupy a unique position in sports journalism. In so writing, *Sports Illustrated* issued public forgiveness to Gene Mauch for his years of irritation and bitterness, and recognized what seems to me to be the unavoidable fact of his failure to win a pennant: the man has never had the horses. In response to this there were the inevitable letters from Minnesota Twins fans, and others, clinging to the more popular interpretation of the 1977 season: Gene Mauch failed to win the pennant in 1977 even though he had the league's Most Valuable Player, the league's two leading hitters, in Rod Carew (.388) and Lyman Bostock (.336) as well as the league's leading RBI man in Larry Hisle. It hardly seems worth pointing out that before Gene Mauch came to Minnesota, the Minnesota fans had been treated to several years of Rod Carew attempting not very successfully to play second base, in which effort he was frequently injured. Gene Mauch shifted the batting champion to first base, where, able to stay in the lineup and concentrate on his offense, Carew *became* the Most Valuable Player.

It hardly seems worth pointing this out, because anybody who is interested in looking at such facts in their true context probably already knows it. By the by, *Sports Illustrated* erred in saying that the Twins, in strong contention in early September "lost 18 of 27 games to finish fourth, 7½ games behind Kansas City." It was seventeen and a half, not seven and a half; while the Twins were losing 18 of 27, Kansas City was turning in one of the greatest stretch runs in baseball history, winning 23 of 24. The Twins would not have won in 1977 even had they won 70% of their games in September and beaten the Royals in their head-on matchups, a performance which would have been pretty remarkable in view of the fact that they were working with a 4-man pitching rotation of Dave Goltz, Paul Thormodsgaard, Pete Redfern and Geoff Zahn.

Anyway, apart from commending *Sports Illustrated* and Fimrite for showing leadership in a profession which too often puts a premium on followership, I wanted to investigate further a couple of points raised by the article. One has to do with the Angels outstanding 1985 record in one-run games. The Angels were 30–13 in one-run games, which, as discussed in the Cincinnati comment, is one of the most significant won/lost "breakdowns" to occur during the season. *Sports Illustrated* quoted Buzzy Bavasi as quoting Walter Alston as saying (and don't tell this to your neighbor, because if you do he is liable to pass it on, and then he will be quoting you when you were quoting me when I was quoting *Sports Illustrated* when *Sports Illustrated* was quoting Buzzy Bavasi when Buzzy Bavasi was quoting Walter Alston, and I don't think Walter could handle that responsibility, what with being dead and all) that a good manager wins the one-run games. That a good manager won the one-run games in 1985 is agreed upon, but has this been a characteristic of Mauch throughout his career, or was it something that simply happened in 1985?

Before getting into this general discussion, one thing I should point out is that one-run games are *not* an indicator of a team's quality. One thing that baseball men like to say sometimes is that the good teams win the close games. What anyone with a background in statistical analysis would assume, however, is that just the opposite is true: that the smaller the margin of victory, the more likely it is that the better team will lose. And, in fact, that is the way it is; .600 teams do not play .600 ball in one-run games, but rather something more than .540 ball, while .400 teams tend to move up to something like .460. Conversely, if the game is decided by 5 or more runs, the better team is very likely to win; a .600 team will usually play about .600 ball (or better) in lop-sided games, while a .400 team will win only about 25 to 30% of their lopsided games. In 1985, for example, the team with the best record in the major leagues, the St. Louis Cardinals, was 38–15 (.717) in games decided by five runs or more, but just 28–19 (.596) in one-run games. The Toronto Blue Jays, with the best record in the American League, were 30–10 (.750) in lop-sided games, but just 26–21 (.553) in one-run contests. The reason that this happens should be fairly evident if you think about it. Saying that the good teams are those which win the close games is logically equivalent to saying that the *great* teams are those which win the close pennant races. Makes no sense.

While it is clearly not true that good teams are those which win the close games, it could well be true that some other type of teams do. Gene Mauch is, as you may know, a one-run manager. What I mean by this is that Mauch tends to use one-run strategies, and most particularly the sacrifice bunt, more than any other major league manager. Strategies such as the sacrifice bunt and the stolen base are called one-run strategies because they tend to increase the number of times that a team will score one run in an inning, but tend to decrease the number of times that a team will score 3, 4, 5 or more runs in an inning. The Angels in 1985 scored 732 runs, about the same number as the Cleveland Indians (729). But whereas the Indians had 185 one-run innings and 198 multiple-run innings, the Angels had 218 one-run innings (33 more) and 188 multiple-run innings (10 fewer).

Statistical analysts are not in love with one-run strategies, and in particular we are not in love with the sacrifice bunt. The reason for this is that whenever and however we try to calculate the gains and losses on the gamble, we tend to come to the conclusion that, as Earl Weaver, Dick Howser and Bobby Cox (among many others) believe, the gain in one-run innings does not compensate for the loss in big innings.

It would go a long way toward rehabilitating the sacrifice bunt, however, if one could show that one-run teams tend to win one-run games. This does not seem to be an unlikely proposition on the face of it, inasmuch as 1) big innings tend after a point to yield diminishing returns in terms of wins (that is, the seventh run that one scores in any inning has comparatively less value, since it is quite likely that one has already won the game), and 2) all teams often reach game situations in which a single run is of enormous importance, and a team which habitually plays one-run baseball might tend to have a superior ability to produce the run that it needs in those circumstances.

So, you see, if we look up Gene Mauch's record in one-run games, and if we find that he has been very successful in them over a period of years, then, since Mauch is the leading proponent of the sacrifice bunt, that would tend to strengthen the position of the defenders of the strategem.

The first thing we need to do here, as a way of sort of clearing the path, is to check to see whether Mauch has *always* used the sac bunt, or whether he perhaps became enamored of it sometime midway in his career—maybe Elmer Valo convinced him of its use one day in the dugout, something Elmer had learned from Connie Mack. This path is easily enough cleared; Mauch developed his fondness for the bunt very early in his career. His first major league team, the 1960 Philadelphia Futillies, dropped down 66 sac bunts, third highest in the league; his 1961 team, which lost 107 games, sacrificed 108 times, the highest in the majors (yes, that is the year Elmer played for him). The 1964 Phillies, the team that did the famous Greg Louganis act, bunted 97 times, second in the league but highest among the league's contenders (incidentally, Walter Alston's teams bunted as much as or even more than Mauch's). The 1973 Montreal team, an expansion collage which Mauch had in contention until the last week of the season, led the majors in bunts with 115. The 1979 Minnesota Twins bunted 142 times *with the Designated Hitter Rule*. Many other Mauch teams have led the majors in sacrifice bunts used.

How did they do in one-run games? Fair. Good, perhaps, not great. The 1985 team was the first Gene Mauch team to post a truly impressive won-lost record in one-run games. I was not able to obtain records of Mauch's teams in one-run games prior to 1963 (that is, I couldn't get them without going to the microfilm room and scanning months worth of old newspapers). In 1963 *The Sporting News Guide* began carrying day-by-day score lists. Since then we can break down the record of Mauch's teams into four groups:

Philadelphia, 1963–1968. The record of Mauch's Philadelphia teams in one-run games was not particularly good, with a couple of exceptions. The famous 1964 team had a good (27–19) record in one-runs, and the 1968 team, which Mauch left in late May, had already won 13 one-run games; they were 13–7 in one-run games, 13–20 otherwise at the time Mauch left. But the other teams, all of which were better-than-.500-but-not-much outfits, finishing with 82 to 87 wins, were not impressive in one-run contests, finishing 29–31, 27–26, 28–25 and 26–32. In total, Mauch's Philadelphia teams (excluding 1960–1962) were 309–263 (.541) in games decided by more than one run, but 150–140 (.517) in one-run contests.

Montreal, 1969–1975. The Montreal Expos under Gene Mauch were very good one-run teams. The first of those teams, the horrible 52–110 unit of 1969, was 16–29 in one-run games, which is a fairly normal performance. But from 1970 through 1975, while the Expos won 70–

79 games every year (73, 71, 70, 79, 79, 75)—that is, a little under .500—they were almost equally consistent at being a little over .500 in one-run games, going 28–25, 20–21, 28–21, 28–24, 26–23 and 27–24. Combined, the seven Montreal Mauch teams were a dismal 326–460 (.415) when not playing one-run games, but a nudge over .500 (173–167, .509) in one-run games.

Minnesota, 1976–1980. The first Minnesota Mauch team, in 1976, won 24 of 39 one-run games, the best record in the league. *This, so far as I know, is the only Mauch team, other than the 1985 Angels, to lead the league in one-run winning percentage*. After that, the record of the Minnesota teams in one-run games got progressively worse, going to 26–25 in 1977, 21–28 in 1978 and 19–29 in 1979, then up to 29–20 in 1980 before Mauch wauched. On the whole, the Twins winning percentage in one-run games was almost exactly the same as in other contests. They were 109–117 (.482) in one-run games, 269–287 (.484) in other contests.

California, 1980–1982 and 1985. The Angels played poorly in one-run games prior to 1985. The 1981 Angels, 5–11 in one run games (under Mauch), might have been in the fight for a post-season berth if they had not done this; they were 24–23 in other games. The 1982 Angels, division champions by way of a 71–45 edge in other contests, were just 22–24 in one-run games. It is not a distinguished record.

Over the entire 20-year period from 1963 through 1982, Gene Mauch's teams won exactly as many one-run games as they lost; they were 459–459. The 1985 season, and only the 1985 season, lifts him above .500. In view of the fact that his teams have been considerably *under* .500 overall, that's a pretty good record:

	Wins – Losses	Pct.
1963–1985 Total:	1548 – 1599	.492
One-Run Games:	489 – 472	.509
Other Games:	1059 – 1127	.485

Another question about Mauch's teams, which relates more to the criticism of him than the support, has to do with their performance late in the season. His two most famous teams, the 1964 Phillies and the 1977 Twins, both collapsed when the crunch came, and the 1985 Angels, though not falling apart, did not play quite well enough to win.

Surprisingly, I have found that Mauch's teams have, on the whole, played their *best* ball late in the year season. These breakdowns go all the way back to 1960:

MAUCH'S TEAMS:

Record in April:	194 – 198	.495
Record in May:	265 – 339	.439
Record in June:	319 – 334	.489
Record in July:	319 – 331	.491
Record in August:	314 – 360	.466
Record in September:	300 – 302	.498
Record in October:	23 – 16	.590
Total	1734 – 1880	.480

With the exception of the aberrant record in 39 games in October, Mauch's *best* record is in September, and his worst is in May. The size of the difference is 36 full games, which would seem to be fairly significant.

However, of course, most of this September performance has come at times when little was on the line. There are three internal patterns:

The disappointments: The 1964, 1977 and 1985 teams all got off to very fast starts—in my opinion, projecting them into pennant races which they really had little business participating in. These three teams had a combined April record of 36–18, or .667 (respectively 9–2, 13–9, 14–7) and played consistently well through May, June, July and August before having September troubles. They had hardly a sub-.500 month prior to September, but were an aggregate 34–49 (.410) in that month.

The fringe of the race teams: A number of Mauch's teams have played poorly in April and May but then, while not exactly *in* in the race, have played very well in September when they at least knew where the pennant race was. The 1966 Phillies went into September only 8 games out of first place, with a record of 71–64, and played well, going 15–10 in September and 1–1 in October. However, the Phillies were eight games out and in fourth place, and one of the other teams was likely to get hot. The Dodgers did.

The 1974 Expos were almost the same, going into September nine games behind the Pirates, but again in fourth place. Again, they played well, going 19–12 after September first. Again, they gained almost nothing.

The year before, the Expos had gone 16–13 in September (0–1) in October, to project them into a sort of a race with the Mets, Cardinals and Pirates. They finished in fourth place but only 3½ games out—so that team must be given credit for playing well while in a pennant race.

The 1976 Minnesota Twins, apparently out of contention on September 1, went 21–8 after September first to close to within five games of the stumbling Royals. This team was not eliminated until the final days of the season—and they did play extremely well in September.

The out of the race teams: A pretty good number of Mauch teams have played well in September while entirely out of the race. A few examples of September records: 1962, 15–7; 1963, 15–11; 1965, 17–13; 1970, 16–14; 1975, 17–12. Others have played less well in the same circumstances.

Out of this, two points can safely be made:

1) To play well early in the season but collapse late is *not* a valid characteristic of Mauch's teams, but

2) Those very few Mauch teams which have been in pennant races have, unfortunately, not followed this pattern.

COMPLETE BATTING RECORDS

Player	G	AB	R	H	TB	2B	3B	HR	RBI	GW	SH	SF	HB	BB	IB	SO	SB	CS	GI DP	Avg	Slug	OBP	Runs	Outs Made	Runs/ 27 Outs	OW%	Appr Value
Boone	150	460	37	114	146	17	0	5	55	7	16	4	3	37	2	35	1	2	12	.248	.317	.306	45	380	3.19	.342	8
*Carew	127	443	69	124	153	17	3	2	39	4	9	1	1	64	9	47	5	5	8	.280	.345	.371	60	342	4.70	.530	7
Grich	144	479	74	116	178	17	3	13	53	5	8	0	3	81	3	77	3	5	18	.242	.372	.355	63	394	4.35	.491	11
DeCinces	120	427	50	104	188	22	1	20	78	9	5	7	2	47	11	71	1	4	18	.244	.440	.317	55	357	4.15	.468	9
Schofield	147	438	50	96	145	19	3	8	41	4	12	3	8	35	0	70	11	4	8	.219	.331	.287	43	369	3.18	.340	8
Downing	150	520	80	137	222	23	1	20	85	12	5	4	13	78	3	60	5	3	12	.263	.427	.371	87	407	5.75	.627	11
†Pettis	125	443	67	114	143	10	8	1	32	2	9	2	0	62	0	125	56	9	5	.257	.323	.347	61	354	4.64	.524	11
*Jackson	143	460	64	116	224	27	0	27	85	11	0	2	1	78	12	138	1	2	16	.252	.487	.360	79	364	5.90	.639	10
*Jones	125	389	66	90	174	17	2	21	67	9	8	2	0	57	2	82	7	4	5	.231	.447	.328	60	318	5.07	.567	9
Beniquez	132	411	54	125	172	13	5	8	42	5	9	1	5	34	3	47	4	3	16	.304	.418	.364	59	315	5.10	.570	8
*Wilfong	83	217	16	41	56	3	0	4	13	0	8	2	0	16	1	32	4	1	0	.189	.258	.243	15	187	2.24	.203	2
Brown	60	153	23	41	64	9	1	4	20	4	3	0	1	7	0	21	0	1	9	.268	.418	.304	16	125	3.47	.381	2
*Howell	43	137	19	27	46	4	0	5	18	2	4	1	0	16	2	33	1	1	1	.197	.336	.279	14	117	3.16	.337	1
*Narron	67	132	12	29	48	4	0	5	14	2	0	0	0	11	2	17	0	0	2	.220	.364	.280	13	105	3.44	.376	2
*Sconiers	44	98	14	28	42	6	1	2	12	1	0	3	0	15	0	18	2	1	2	.286	.429	.371	17	76	5.94	.643	1
*Gerber	65	91	8	24	29	1	2	0	6	0	3	1	0	2	0	3	0	3	2	.264	.319	.277	7	76	2.43	.231	1
Miller	51	48	8	18	28	2	1	2	7	0	0	0	1	1	0	10	0	1	0	.375	.583	.400	11	31	9.44	.820	1
Linares	18	43	7	11	22	2	0	3	11	3	0	1	0	2	0	5	2	0	1	.256	.512	.283	6	34	4.99	.559	1
Hendrick	16	41	5	5	12	1	0	2	6	0	0	1	0	4	1	8	0	0	4	.122	.293	.196	1	41	0.95	.044	0
†White	21	7	7	1	1	0	0	0	0	0	0	0	0	1	0	3	3	1	0	.143	.143	.333	1	7	2.64	.262	0
Keedy	3	4	1	2	6	1	0	1	1	0	0	0	0	0	0	0	0	0	1	.500	1.500	.500	2	3	13.50	.903	0
Polidor	2	1	1	1	1	0	0	0	0	0	0	0	0	0	0	0	0	0	0	.000	1.000	1.000					0

*left-handed hitter, †switch-hitter

DEFENSIVE STATISTICS

FIRST	G	PO	A	Er	TC	DP	PCT.
Carew	116	1055	65	7	1127	121	.994
Beniquez	46	319	24	4	347	42	.988
Grich	16	98	9	0	107	14	1.000
Sconiers	6	35	1	1	37	2	.973
Narron	1	2	0	0	2	0	1.000
TEAM:	185	1509	99	12	1620	179	.993
AVG:	180	1440	123	14	1577	141	.991

SECOND	G	PO	A	Er	TC	DP	PCT.
Grich	116	224	380	2	606	99	.997
Wilfong	69	124	216	5	345	45	.986
Gerber	1	1	0	0	1	0	1.000
TEAM:	186	349	596	7	952	144	.993
AVG:	189	347	501	15	863	114	.982

THIRD	G	PO	A	Er	TC	DP	PCT.
DeCinces	111	95	202	13	310	27	.958
Howell	42	33	75	8	116	10	.931
Grich	15	9	19	1	29	2	.966
Gerber	9	4	3	0	7	0	1.000
Keedy	2	0	0	0	0	0	.000
Miller	1	0	1	0	1	0	1.000
Beniquez	1	1	0	0	1	0	1.000
TEAM:	181	142	300	22	464	39	.953
AVG:	192	129	327	23	479	32	.953

SHORTSTOP	G	PO	A	Er	TC	DP	PCT.
Schofield	147	261	397	25	683	108	.963
Gerber	53	51	109	5	165	27	.970
Polidor	1	0	2	0	2	0	1.000
Beniquez	1	0	1	0	1	0	1.000
TEAM:	202	312	509	30	851	135	.965
AVG:	189	269	474	28	771	104	.964

CATCHER	G	PO	A	Er	TC	DP	PCT.	PB
Boone	147	670	71	10	751	15	.987	6
Narron	45	144	14	0	158	4	1.000	2
Miller	1	1	0	0	1	0	1.000	0
TEAM:	193	815	85	10	910	19	.989	8
AVG:	193	895	74	13	982	13	.987	13

OUTFIELD	G	PO	A	Er	TC	DP	PCT.
Pettis	122	368	13	4	385	5	.990
Downing	121	244	5	2	251	0	.992
Jackson	81	112	6	7	125	1	.944
Jones	73	179	12	1	192	5	.995
Beniquez	71	119	1	0	120	0	1.000
Brown	48	78	3	0	81	1	1.000
Miller	45	38	2	2	42	0	.952
White	16	10	1	0	11	0	1.000
Hendrick	12	18	1	0	19	0	1.000
Linares	2	1	0	0	1	0	1.000
Keedy	1	1	0	0	1	0	1.000
Polidor	1	0	0	0	0	0	.000
TEAM:	593	1168	44	16	1228	12	.987
AVG:	559	1141	33	21	1196	8	.982

COMPLETE PITCHERS RECORDS

Pitcher	W	L	Pct	ERA	G	GS	CG	GF	SHO	SV	IP	H	TBF	R	ER	HR	SH	SF	HB	BB	IB	SO	WP	BK	Appr Value
							Starters (One-half of Game Appearances)																		
Witt	15	9	.625	3.56	35	35	6	0	1	0	250.0	228	1049	115	99	22	4	5	4	98	6	180	11	1	10
Romanick	14	9	.609	4.11	31	31	6	0	1	0	195.0	210	831	101	89	29	4	10	4	62	1	64	2	3	9
McCaskill	12	12	.500	4.70	30	29	6	0	1	0	189.2	189	807	105	99	23	2	5	4	64	1	102	5	0	6
Slaton	6	10	.375	4.37	29	24	1	3	0	1	148.1	162	645	82	72	22	5	5	2	63	1	60	8	0	4
Lugo	3	4	.429	3.69	20	10	1	5	0	0	83.0	86	351	36	34	10	2	2	4	29	1	42	2	0	2
*Candelaria	7	3	.700	3.80	13	13	1	0	1	0	71.0	70	301	33	30	7	4	3	3	24	1	53	2	0	3
*John	2	4	.333	4.70	12	6	0	2	0	0	38.1	51	176	22	20	3	3	2	1	15	1	17	5	0	0
Zahn	2	2	.500	4.38	7	7	1	0	1	0	37.0	44	164	19	18	5	2	1	0	14	0	14	1	0	0
Sutton	2	2	.500	3.69	5	5	0	0	0	0	31.2	27	124	13	13	6	0	0	0	8	0	16	0	0	0
*Kipper	0	1	.000	21.60	2	1	0	0	0	0	3.1	7	20	8	8	1	0	2	0	3	0	0	0	0	0
Mack	0	1	.000	15.43	1	1	0	0	0	0	2.1	8	14	4	4	0	0	0	0	0	0	0	0	0	0
							Relievers																		
Moore	8	8	.500	1.92	65	0	0	57	0	31	103.0	91	417	28	22	9	10	2	0	21	3	72	2	0	14
Cliburn	9	3	.750	2.09	44	0	0	26	0	6	99.0	87	395	25	23	5	5	2	1	26	6	48	2	0	9
*Clements	5	0	1.000	3.34	41	0	0	12	0	1	62.0	47	247	23	23	4	4	0	2	25	2	19	1	0	4
*Sanchez	2	0	1.000	5.72	26	0	0	16	0	2	61.1	67	268	41	39	9	0	3	1	27	3	34	2	0	2
Corbett	3	3	.500	4.89	30	0	0	11	0	0	46.0	49	203	33	25	7	2	1	1	20	3	24	0	0	2
*Holland	0	1	.000	1.48	15	0	0	6	0	0	24.1	17	99	4	4	4	1	0	0	10	1	14	1	0	0
Fowlkes	0	0	.000	9.00	2	0	0	0	0	0	7.0	8	33	7	7	4	0	0	0	4	0	5	1	0	0
Smith	0	0	.000	7.20	4	0	0	2	0	0	5.0	5	20	4	4	1	0	1	0	1	0	3	0	0	0

Bob BOONE, Catcher

	G	AB	Hit	2B	3B	HR	Run	RBI	TBB	SO	SB	CS	Avg
10.49 years		528	134	23	2	8	48	62	47	45	3	4	.253
1985	150	460	114	17	0	5	37	55	37	35	1	2	.248
First Half	73	227	56	5	0	3	16	26	20	18	0	1	.247
Second Half	77	233	58	12	0	2	21	29	17	17	1	1	.249
Vs. RHP		329	81	12	0	4	23	39	22	26	0	2	.246
Vs. LHP		131	33	5	0	1	14	16	15	9	1	0	.252
Home	74	221	52	5	0	0	18	32	21	22	1	2	.235
Road	76	239	62	12	0	5	19	23	16	13	0	0	.259
Grass	126	391	99	16	0	5	33	51	32	33	1	2	.253
Turf	24	69	15	1	0	0	4	4	5	2	0	0	.217

Doug DeCINCES, Third Base

	G	AB	Hit	2B	3B	HR	Run	RBI	TBB	SO	SB	CS	Avg
8.47 years		571	149	32	3	23	76	85	59	87	6	5	.262
1985	120	427	104	22	1	20	50	78	47	71	1	4	.244
First Half	61	230	57	12	0	8	26	39	27	32	0	4	.248
Second Half	59	197	47	10	1	12	24	39	20	39	1	0	.239
Vs. RHP		304	72	15	0	14	36	49	27	52	0	4	.237
Vs. LHP		123	32	7	1	6	14	29	20	19	1	0	.260
Home	59	208	55	12	1	12	28	43	25	32	1	4	.264
Road	61	219	49	10	0	8	22	35	22	39	0	0	.224
Grass	93	327	83	19	1	18	42	64	41	46	1	4	.254
Turf	27	100	21	3	0	2	8	14	6	25	0	0	.210

Rod CAREW, First Base

	G	AB	Hit	2B	3B	HR	Run	RBI	TBB	SO	SB	CS	Avg
15.24 years		611	200	29	7	6	93	67	67	67	23	12	.328
1985	127	443	124	17	3	2	69	39	64	47	5	5	.280
First Half	53	191	49	6	1	1	33	23	31	19	3	0	.257
Second Half	74	252	75	11	2	1	36	16	33	28	2	5	.298
Vs. RHP		335	97	14	3	2	52	32	46	24	5	3	.290
Vs. LHP		108	27	3	0	0	17	7	18	23	0	2	.250
Home	62	219	61	8	1	1	41	17	34	15	2	1	.279
Road	65	224	63	9	2	1	28	22	30	32	3	4	.281
Grass	99	346	95	11	2	1	57	28	45	36	2	3	.275
Turf	28	97	29	6	1	1	12	11	19	11	3	2	.299

Dick SCHOFIELD, Shortstop

	G	AB	Hit	2B	3B	HR	Run	RBI	TBB	SO	SB	CS	Avg
1.90 years		469	97	16	3	8	49	35	39	83	8	3	.206
1985	147	438	96	19	3	8	50	41	35	70	11	4	.219
First Half	75	224	42	8	1	5	22	21	17	41	4	3	.188
Second Half	72	214	54	11	2	3	28	20	18	29	7	1	.252
Vs. RHP		295	59	13	2	6	31	30	25	53	8	2	.200
Vs. LHP		143	37	6	1	2	19	11	10	17	3	2	.259
Home	72	219	48	8	1	5	27	21	12	41	5	3	.219
Road	75	219	48	11	2	3	23	20	23	29	6	1	.219
Grass	121	367	78	14	2	7	42	34	26	60	9	3	.213
Turf	26	71	18	5	1	1	8	7	9	10	2	1	.254

Bobby GRICH, Second Base

	G	AB	Hit	2B	3B	HR	Run	RBI	TBB	SO	SB	CS	Avg
11.79 years		558	148	26	4	18	84	71	89	104	9	7	.266
1985	144	479	116	17	3	13	74	53	81	77	3	5	.242
First Half	72	241	64	9	2	4	37	25	44	27	2	2	.266
Second Half	72	238	52	8	1	9	37	28	37	50	1	3	.218
Vs. RHP		335	77	9	1	8	56	30	57	53	2	2	.230
Vs. LHP		144	39	8	2	5	18	23	24	24	1	3	.271
Home	74	248	62	7	1	7	39	32	39	38	2	2	.250
Road	70	231	54	10	2	6	35	21	42	39	1	3	.234
Grass	120	401	97	14	2	10	64	44	70	63	3	4	.242
Turf	24	78	19	3	1	3	10	9	11	14	0	1	.244

Brian DOWNING, Left Field

	G	AB	Hit	2B	3B	HR	Run	RBI	TBB	SO	SB	CS	Avg
8.85 years		530	141	23	1	16	76	72	78	72	4	3	.266
1985	150	520	137	23	1	20	80	85	78	60	5	3	.263
First half	74	246	56	11	0	5	35	34	40	28	3	2	.228
Second Half	76	274	81	12	1	15	45	51	38	32	2	1	.296
Vs. RHP		354	93	9	1	13	53	59	55	41	5	3	.263
Vs. LHP		166	44	14	0	7	27	26	23	19	0	0	.265
Home	74	249	60	11	0	10	40	44	43	28	3	3	.241
Road	76	271	77	12	1	10	40	41	35	32	2	0	.284
Grass	123	419	105	19	0	17	68	68	69	50	4	3	.251
Turf	27	101	32	4	1	3	12	17	9	10	1	0	.317

Gary PETTIS, Center Field

	G	AB	Hit	2B	3B	HR	Run	RBI	TBB	SO	SB	CS	Avg
1.83 years		507	125	13	9	4	84	37	70	140	61	15	.247
1985	125	443	114	10	8	1	67	32	62	125	56	9	.257
First Half	64	227	58	5	4	1	36	13	36	74	30	4	.256
Second Half	61	216	56	5	4	0	31	19	26	51	26	5	.259
Vs. RHP		310	75	5	7	1	45	20	41	97	41	8	.242
Vs. LHP		133	39	5	1	0	22	12	21	28	15	1	.293
Home	59	182	42	5	4	0	30	12	31	48	22	4	.231
Road	66	261	72	5	4	1	37	20	31	77	34	5	.276
Grass	101	349	88	6	7	1	52	26	52	97	46	7	.252
Turf	24	94	26	4	1	0	15	6	10	28	10	2	.277

Reggie JACKSON, Right Field

	G	AB	Hit	2B	3B	HR	Run	RBI	TBB	SO	SB	CS	Avg
15.88 years		574	152	28	3	33	91	101	79	150	14	7	.264
1985	143	460	116	27	0	27	64	85	78	138	1	2	.252
First Half	71	225	59	14	0	14	32	43	38	64	1	1	.262
Second Half	72	235	57	13	0	13	32	42	40	74	0	1	.243
Vs. RHP		348	93	19	0	24	53	68	57	94	1	2	.267
Vs. LHP		112	23	8	0	3	11	17	21	44	0	0	.205
Home	70	225	49	10	0	15	30	44	38	70	1	0	.218
Road	73	235	67	17	0	12	34	41	40	68	0	2	.285
Grass	118	383	96	24	0	25	54	78	61	115	1	1	.251
Turf	25	77	20	3	0	2	10	7	17	23	0	1	.260

Juan BENIQUEZ, Outfield

	G	AB	Hit	2B	3B	HR	Run	RBI	TBB	SO	SB	CS	Avg
7.80 years		512	140	21	4	8	68	49	37	59	13	9	.273
1985	132	411	125	13	5	8	54	42	34	47	4	3	.304
First Half	72	245	74	6	3	5	32	26	17	24	3	1	.302
Second Half	60	166	51	7	2	3	22	16	17	23	1	2	.307
Vs. RHP		242	65	7	1	2	23	22	19	37	3	1	.269
Vs. LHP		169	60	6	4	6	31	20	15	10	1	2	.355
Home	70	214	70	6	3	6	31	28	20	21	2	0	.327
Road	62	197	55	7	2	2	23	14	14	26	2	3	.279
Grass	109	342	110	13	5	7	46	38	29	38	3	3	.322
Turf	23	69	15	0	0	1	8	4	5	9	1	0	.217

Ruppert JONES, Designated Hitter

	G	AB	Hit	2B	3B	HR	Run	RBI	TBB	SO	SB	CS	Avg
6.91 years		554	140	27	5	18	79	73	65	100	19	12	.252
1985	125	389	90	17	2	21	66	67	57	82	7	4	.231
First Half	63	186	52	9	0	16	40	41	40	42	5	3	.280
Second Half	62	203	38	8	2	5	26	26	17	40	2	1	.187
Vs. RHP		341	81	16	1	19	59	56	53	70	7	4	.238
Vs. LHP		48	9	1	1	2	7	11	4	12	0	0	.188
Home	62	180	46	8	1	10	34	32	32	38	2	3	.256
Road	63	209	44	9	1	11	32	35	25	44	5	1	.211
Grass	105	319	71	12	1	18	54	51	51	72	5	3	.223
Turf	20	70	19	5	1	3	12	16	6	10	2	1	.271

MIKE WITT

	(W–L)	GS	Run	Avg	DP	Avg	SB	Avg
1984	(15-11)	34	138	4.06	27	.79	17	.50
1985	(15-9)	35	144	4.11	44	1.26	22	.63
1981-1985		135	586	4.34	150	1.11	81	.60

	G	IP	W	L	Pct	ER	BB	SO	ERA
1984 Home	16	120.3	8	5	.615	36	35	98	2.69
1985 Home	17	122.7	8	5	.615	46	51	82	3.38
1984 Road	18	126.3	7	6	.538	59	49	98	4.20
1985 Road	18	127.3	7	4	.636	53	47	98	3.75
1984 Grass	28	204.3	13	10	.565	73	72	166	3.22
1985 Grass	30	214.3	13	8	.619	87	91	152	3.65
1984 Turf	6	42.3	2	1	.667	23	33	59	4.89
1985 Turf	5	35.7	2	1	.667	12	7	28	3.03
1985 Total	35	250.0	15	9	.625	99	98	180	3.56

DON SUTTON

	(W–L)	GS	Run	Avg	DP	Avg	SB	Avg
1984	(14-12)	33	126	3.82	21	.64	25	.76
1985	(15-10)	34	158	4.65	24	.71	21	.62
1976-1985		319	1348	4.23	215	.67	273	.86

	G	IP	W	L	Pct	ER	BB	SO	ERA
1984 Home	19	126.0	7	9	.438	56	26	88	4.00
1985 Home	17	114.3	8	3	.727	42	30	47	3.31
1984 Road	14	86.7	7	3	.700	33	25	55	3.43
1985 Road	17	111.7	7	7	.500	55	29	70	4.43
1984 Grass	26	169.0	10	10	.500	70	44	119	3.73
1985 Grass	27	183.3	13	6	.684	68	44	82	3.34
1984 Turf	7	43.7	4	2	.667	19	7	24	3.92
1985 Turf	7	42.0	2	4	.333	29	15	25	6.21
1985 Total	34	225.3	15	10	.600	97	59	107	3.87

RON ROMANICK

	(W–L)	GS	Run	Avg	DP	Avg	SB	Avg
1984	(12-12)	34	148	4.35	33	.97	25	.74
1985	(14-9)	31	149	4.81	42	1.35	16	.52
1984-1985		65	297	4.57	75	1.15	41	.63

	G	IP	W	L	Pct	ER	BB	SO	ERA
1984 Home	20	141.3	6	7	.462	60	39	52	3.82
1985 Home	16	101.7	8	3	.727	40	33	33	3.54
1984 Road	13	88.3	6	5	.545	36	22	35	3.67
1985 Road	15	93.3	6	6	.500	49	29	31	4.73
1984 Grass	28	194.3	9	10	.474	82	54	74	3.80
1985 Grass	26	167.7	14	5	.737	65	53	49	3.49
1984 Turf	5	35.3	3	2	.600	14	7	13	3.57
1985 Turf	5	27.3	0	4	0.000	24	9	15	7.90
1985 Total	31	195.0	14	9	.609	89	62	64	4.11

KIRK McCASKILL

	(W–L)	GS	Run	Avg	DP	Avg	SB	Avg
1985	(12-12)	29	141	4.86	31	1.07	8	.28

	G	IP	W	L	Pct	ER	BB	SO	ERA
1985 Home	15	96.3	7	4	.636	49	23	52	4.58
1985 Road	15	93.3	5	8	.385	50	41	50	4.82
1985 Grass	27	168.7	11	11	.500	92	58	92	4.91
1985 Turf	3	21.0	1	1	.500	7	6	10	3.00
1985 Total	30	189.7	12	12	.500	99	64	102	4.70

JIM SLATON

	(W–L)	GS	Run	Avg	DP	Avg	SB	Avg
1984	(7-10)	22	98	4.45	25	1.14	2	.09
1985	(6-10)	24	95	3.96	35	1.46	8	.33
1984-1985		211	951	4.51	197	.93	110	.52

	G	IP	W	L	Pct	ER	BB	SO	ERA
1984 Home	16	90.3	5	5	.500	44	21	40	4.38
1985 Home	15	77.3	2	4	.333	34	30	27	3.96
1984 Road	16	72.7	2	5	.286	46	35	27	5.70
1985 Road	14	71.0	4	6	.400	38	33	33	4.82
1984 Grass	29	151.3	6	9	.400	78	48	66	4.64
1985 Grass	23	116.0	3	9	.250	60	54	41	4.66
1984 Turf	3	11.7	1	1	.500	12	8	1	9.26
1985 Turf	6	32.3	3	1	.750	12	9	19	3.34
1985 Total	29	148.3	6	10	.375	72	63	60	4.37

OTHERS

	(W–L)	GS	Run	Avg	DP	Avg	SB	Avg
Candelaria	(7-3)	13	70	5.38	10	.77	4	.31
Lugo	(3-4)	10	43	4.30	15	1.50	6	.60
Zahn	(2-2)	7	35	5.00	9	1.29	1	.14
John	(2-4)	6	21	3.50	8	1.33	3	.50
Kipper	(0-1)	1	9	9.00	2	2.00	5	5.00
Mack	(0-1)	1	3	3.00	1	1.00	1	1.00

CHICAGO WHITE SOX

BREAKDOWNS FOR THE LAST TEN SEASONS:

Won-Lost Record: 767-791, .492 (3rd Best in the Division, 15th in the Majors)
Runs Scored: 6,858 (3rd in the Division, 9th in Majors)
Runs Allowed: 6,956 (4th [highest] in the Division, 8th in Majors)
Home Runs Hit: 1,276 (2nd in the Division, 8th in the Majors)
Home Runs Allowed: 1,189 (Fewest in the Division, 13th lowest in the Majors)

Record In:
April: 89–89, .500 (5th in the Division, 13th in Majors)
May: 140-131, .517 (2nd in the Division, 10th in Majors)
June: 127-133, .488 (3rd in the Division, 16th in Majors)
July: 120-134, .472 (4th in the Division, 18th in the Majors)
August: 132-151, .466 (4th in the Division, 19th in the Majors)
September: 144–142, .504 (3rd in the Division, 12th in Majors)
October: 15-11, .577 (3rd in the Division, 7th in the Majors)

Won-Lost Record in Road Games: 359-428, .456 (3rd in the Division, 14th in Majors)
Won-Lost Record at Home: 408-363, .529 (2nd in the Division, 14th in Majors)
Home Field Advantage: 57 Games
Runs Scored on the Road: 3,369 (3rd in the Division, 8th in Majors)
Runs Scored at Home: 3,489 (4th in the Division, 10th in Majors)
Runs Allowed on the Road: 3,531 (5th highest in the Division, 9th highest in Majors)
Runs Allowed at Home: 3,425 (3rd highest in the Division, 9th in Majors)

Home Runs Hit on the Road: 664 (Most in the Division, 7th in Majors)
Home Runs Hit at Home: 612 (3rd in the Division, 12th in the Majors)
Home Runs Allowed on the Road: 642 (4th highest in the Division, 7th in Majors)
Home Runs Allowed at Home: 547 (2nd-lowest total in the Division, 8th-lowest in Majors)

RECORD FOR LAST THREE SEASONS: 258-228, .531 (Best in the Division, 7th in Baseball)

To say what is good about Ken Harrelson, the man seems to have a clear and coherent idea about what he is trying to do, and about how he is going to do it. His emphasis for the ballclub is apparently going to be on defense, speed, line-drive hitting; this, at least, is what he has indicated, and as much could be inferred from such diverse actions as moving back home plate (making the lines longer), trading for Wayne Tolleson and (apparently) shifting Carlton Fisk to outfield or designated hitter so as to install a catching combination of Joel Skinner and Ron Hassey. His personnel philosophy has been to provide what might be called "incentive pressure" or "constructive insecurity," keeping his manager on a one-year contract with a coach on staff (Doug Rader) of whom he is not enamored, and concentrating on bringing in enough major league players to provide competition for playing time for almost anybody on the roster.

Now, it is a very positive thing to know what it is that you are trying to do and how you are trying to do it. I am writing this about three months after Ken Harrelson has taken over the White Sox job; there are a lot of general managers who have been in their jobs for years and you still can't tell what they're trying to do or how they think they're going to do it. I have some reservations about both elements of the plan. The White Sox roster that Harrelson inherited was slow and not real good defensively (is he really planning to have Ron Kittle in left field?) so I don't know how quickly or smoothly he's going to be able to make the transition to the type of team that he desires. I've got doubts about the proposition that people work best when they are insecure and under pressure; it's kind of an old notion that contains a certain amount of useful truth and is attractive to some people, but has (for the most part) yielded to newer and better ideas about security and incentive.

But my basic theory of baseball is that *any* theory of baseball will work if the talent is good enough. A "theory" or a clear idea of how you're going to win is extremely useful to a baseball team, because it organizes the work, clarifies the needs and goals of the team; it provides focus and direction among a dizzying array of options and alternatives. If you're trying to win a pennant it helps to know whether you're trying to win it by pitching or power in exactly the same way that, if you're trying to make a million dollars, it helps to have a clear idea whether you're trying to make the money in real estate or prostitution. Almost every successful organization displays some such presentiment—but it isn't the theory that wins. It's the players.

So the much more serious question concerning Hawk Harrelson is the question of how good his talent judgment is. To be honest, I ain't crazy about what I've seen. Kid Tolleson is a scrappy, hard-nosed little player, fun to watch. His 1985 season, when he hit .313, was way over his head, and even at that level he's a marginal hitter for a third baseman because of a secondary average that is below .200. Ron Hassey is one of those guys that a year ago you could have had for a song* if you wanted him; he had a fine year for the Yankees and they decided to cash it in. Maybe I'm wrong, but I always figured Joe Cowley to be a modern re-incarnation of one of Casey's Yankees from

*Didn't you always wonder what the song was? "Peg O' My Heart"? "Southern Man"? "Rainy Day Women"? "Sittin' on the Dock of the Bay"? "Does Your Chewing Gum Lose It's Flavor on the Bedpost Overnight"?

the fifties, like Don Larson or Tommy Byrne, who can win with the Yankees if you don't pitch him against the wrong teams.

He'll get a chance to prove that I'm wrong, and so will Harrelson, and I wish them both well.

In the clutch, the 1985 Chicago White Sox were a terrific ballclub. According to John Dewan's newsletter, the *Chicago Baseball Report,* the 1985 White Sox:

1) Hit a remarkable .294 for the season with runners in scoring position.

2) Hit .263 (still ten points over their team average) in the late innings of close games, a situation in which overall averages usually decline because of the use of relief aces, and

3) Hit .297 with a .443 slugging percentage with runners in scoring position in the late innings of close games.

With runners in scoring position, the leaders were Harold Baines (.346, .577 slugging) and Carlton Fisk (.336, .641 slugging). Reid Nichols, Jerry Hairston, Bryan Little, Scott Fletcher and Ozzie Guillen all hit over .300 with runners in scoring position.

"In the clutch," by the definition that John uses (the hitter is batting in the seventh inning or later with his team no more than two runs behind or no more than one run ahead) Ozzie Guillen hit .388, Harold Baines hit .354 with a .608 slugging percentage and 16 RBI in 79 at bats, and Greg Walker hit .282 with 6 homers, 21 RBI. Nichols, Hairston and Little were also over .300 in the late innings of close games.

And when the two situations were combined, Carlton Fisk hit .538 (7/13) with 5 walks, Greg Walker hit .478 (11/23) with 15 RBI, and Harold Baines hit .381 (8/21) with 12 RBI, half of the 8 hits being accounted for by doubles and homers.

Because of these clutch performances, the 1985 White Sox exceeded their expected runs scored (according to the technical runs created formula) by a whopping—a historic, even—62 runs, scoring 736 against an expectation of 674. I believe that this was the largest error for the formula in several years. I also identified the "most similar offenses" (see introductory article on similarity scores and article on St. Louis Cardinals) from the last seven years, and found that the Sox scored more runs than any team with highly similar offensive totals—.253 batting average, 146 homers, 471 walks. Interestingly, the *most* similar offense over that period was the champions of this division, the 1985 Royals, an offense which has no major statistical differences from the White Sox, but scored 49 runs fewer.

The White Sox also won two to three more games than could have been expected by the Pythagorean projection for their runs scored and allowed. In other words, the whole of their performance was markedly greater than the sum of their parts, because they did such a good job of putting the pieces together.

And yet, what were they? They were an 85–77 team that should have been 76–86. The 1985 White Sox are the best illustration I have ever seen of how minor is the role that pressure performance plays in steering the fortunes of a ballclub. Many times when a managerial chance is made in mid-season and a coach takes over, the new guy will talk about how close the team is to being a winner, how

they lost 25 one-run games last year and so you can see if they can just get a key hit here and there, they could easily move up 12 or 15 games in the standings.

The logic is seductive because what the new manager is saying is literally true—if the team could just pick up, let's say, 36 more well-timed hits, leading to 24 more runs, they could change twelve of those one-run losses into one-run wins. But the absurdity of this is apparent if you look at what it would mean in the final record. Let's say that the team hit .250 with runners in scoring position in the late innings of close games, which is the situation in which they would have to pick up the extra hits for those extra hits to lead directly to extra wins. Let's say that .250 average is based on 45 hits in 180 at bats (the stats for the White Sox last year were 55 for 185). If you add 36 hits, what do you have? You've got 81 for 180—a .450 clutch average.

And what does this do to the record in one-run games? If the team went 24–25 in one-run games and was able to turn around 12 of those losses into one-run wins, that would mean that they were 36–13 (.735) in one-run games.

So what that innocuous statement ("We can pick up 12 or 15 extra games by just picking up a few hits here and there") really means is, "We can move way up in the standings if we can just hit .450 when the game is on the line and win three-fourths of our close games." This is literally true, but is it a sound approach to winning pennants?

Which is not to say that, in a close race, clutch performances aren't tremendously important. Clutch performances *can't* make the difference between 70 wins and 90, and they won't very often make the difference between 82 and 90, but sometimes they'll make the difference between 88 and 92, and that can be the difference between first and second.

In many ways, the manager who hopes to win the pennant by getting better performances "in the clutch" is like a man who hopes to get rich by making a few well-timed investments in the stock market. "See," the man says, "in the last two months RCVL stock has gone from 17 to 37 and a quarter. Amalgamated Trench Mouth has gone from 4 and a quarter to 13 in just eighteen days since they released their new computer. Now, if I'd just put a second mortgage on my mother-in-law, bought about 30,000 shares of RCVL in February on the margin and put my IRS refund all into Trench Mouth, well, I'd be on my way to being a wealthy man now." It's literally true; if you can consistently choose exactly the right moment to buy exactly the right stock, you can make a fortune in the stock market—and if you can choose exactly the right moment to get exactly the right hit, you can win a pennant. A few lucky breaks in the stock market can give a young entrepreneur a tremendous impetus; a few investments in the stock market are not unwise. A few well-timed base hits can give a contending team a tremendous lift; everybody needs that now and then.

But millionaires are *not* just guys who got lucky in the stock market, and anybody who thinks they are has got zero chance of joining the club. And good ballteams are *not* just teams that hit in the clutch, and the same goes for any manager who thinks they are.

This begs the question of whether such a thing as clutch ability exists. Clutch *performance* certainly exists, but whether it is a function of ability or random chance is an issue on which there is no definitive or convincing evidence. Two years ago, this same team also over-achieved itself as to runs scored, scoring 800 runs with a team which should have been expected to score only 761. At the time, we had no data on performance in key situations, and I suggested that this was most probably due to the number of errors committed by the opponents. In view of the new evidence, I would suggest that it was at least equally likely that the same players—Baines, Walker and Fisk—or some of the same players may also have hit well in the clutch that year, causing the discrepancy.

A few other random notes from the *Chicago Baseball Report,* which is available from John Dewan (P.O. Box 46074, Chicago, Illinois, 60646):

The White Sox left-handed hitters hit .274 on the season against left-handed pitching, as opposed to .255 against right-handers. In particular, Greg Walker, who previously had had great difficulty against left-handers, hit .250 with good power against them, and Harold Baines ripped along at a .332 pace against southpaws.

Bob James missed most of July with an injury, saving only one game in the month whereas he saved about seven a month otherwise. LaRussa was quoted as saying that without this injury James might have made the difference in several games, possibly enough (six) to have made up the difference between the Sox and the top teams in the division.

This is another example of the same type of self-delusion. The White Sox record in July was 14–12; it was their best month except September. If they had won six more games, they'd have been 20–6 (.769) for the month. Does that seem likely to you?

Only one opposition baserunner was picked off first base by a Sox catcher (Fisk) on the season.

Statistics compiled by Don Zminda (I think) and given in the final report show that the White Sox, when bunting to move the runner from first to second, were successful 78% of the time, their opponents 79% of the time. I assume that what he is measuring here is successful sacrifices against putouts of the lead runner, rather than against foul bunts or something.

Zminda's studies also show that the White Sox succeeded in moving a runner from second to third with no outs on 58 of 93 opportunities, their opponents 45 of 90. If the team tends to be particularly "successful" at moving baserunners with outs, this might also cause its ratio of runs/runs created to rise. And anybody who thinks you can win baseball games by making outs is probably one of those guys who tries to tell you that you can get rich by remembering to write your underwear off on your taxes.

The White Sox did not turn a 3–6–3 double play during the season.

COMPLETE BATTING RECORDS

Player	G	AB	R	H	TB	2B	3B	HR	RBI	GW	SH	SF	HB	BB	IB	SO	SB	CS	GI DP	Avg	Slug	OBP	Runs	Outs Made	Runs/ 27 Outs	OW%	Appr Value
Fisk	153	543	85	129	265	23	1	37	107	13	2	6	17	52	12	81	17	9	9	.238	.488	.320	85	440	5.22	.577	12
*Walker	163	601	77	155	273	38	4	24	92	13	0	3	2	44	6	100	5	2	16	.258	.454	.309	81	467	4.68	.523	9
†Cruz	91	234	28	46	54	2	3	0	15	3	1	1	2	32	0	40	8	5	6	.197	.231	.227	17	201	2.34	.215	2
Hullet	141	395	52	106	148	19	4	5	37	2	4	3	4	30	1	81	6	4	8	.268	.375	.324	48	308	4.20	.470	6
*Guillen	150	491	71	134	176	21	9	1	33	3	8	1	1	12	1	36	7	4	5	.273	.358	.291	50	375	3.63	.398	9
*Law	125	390	62	101	146	21	6	4	36	3	5	1	3	27	0	40	29	6	4	.259	.374	.311	49	305	4.32	.484	6
*Baines	160	640	86	198	299	29	3	22	113	13	0	10	1	42	8	89	1	1	23	.309	.467	.348	98	476	5.57	.609	13
Salazar	122	327	39	80	132	18	2	10	45	5	9	5	0	12	2	60	14	4	5	.245	.404	.267	35	270	3.51	.381	5
Kittle	116	379	51	87	177	12	0	26	58	8	0	2	5	31	1	92	1	4	12	.230	.467	.295	48	310	4.19	.469	6
Fletcher	119	301	38	77	93	8	1	2	31	1	11	1	0	35	0	47	5	5	9	.256	.309	.332	31	250	3.37	.363	5
*Boston	95	232	20	53	77	13	1	3	15	2	1	1	0	14	1	44	8	6	3	.228	.332	.271	20	190	2.84	.289	2
†Little	73	188	35	47	64	9	1	2	27	4	3	3	3	26	0	21	0	1	4	.250	.340	.345	24	152	4.22	.472	3
*Gamble	70	148	20	30	47	5	0	4	20	1	0	1	1	34	3	22	0	0	1	.203	.318	.353	19	120	4.37	.489	1
†Hairston	95	140	9	34	48	8	0	2	20	2	0	4	2	29	3	18	0	0	3	.243	.343	.371	20	113	4.86	.542	2
Paciorek	46	122	14	30	32	2	0	0	9	2	0	2	1	8	0	22	2	0	0	.246	.262	.293	10	97	2.74	.274	0
Nichols	51	118	20	35	47	7	1	1	15	2	2	1	0	15	1	13	5	5	1	.297	.398	.373	18	92	5.20	.576	1
Hill	40	75	5	10	12	2	0	0	4	1	8	0	0	12	0	9	0	0	2	.133	.160	.253	4	75	1.46	.097	1
*De Sa	28	44	5	8	16	2	0	2	7	0	1	0	0	3	1	6	0	0	0	.182	.364	.234	4	37	2.85	.289	0
Skinner	22	44	9	15	24	4	1	1	5	0	1	0	0	5	0	13	0	0	2	.341	.545	.408	9	32	7.84	.755	1
*Ryal	12	33	4	5	8	3	0	0	3	0	1	0	0	3	0	3	0	0	2	.152	.242	.222	2	31	1.31	.080	0
†Gilbert	7	22	3	6	7	1	0	0	3	0	0	0	0	4	0	5	0	0	1	.273	.318	.385	3	17	4.42	.495	0
†Cangelosi	5	2	2	0	0	0	0	0	0	0	0	0	1	0	1	0	0	0	0	.000	.000	.333	0	2	0.00	.000	0
Nelson	47	1	0	0	0	0	0	0	0	0	0	0	0	0	0	1	0	0	0	.000	.000	.000	0	1	0.00	.000	0
Spillner	53	0	0	0	0	0	0	0	0	0	0	0	0	0	1	0	0	0	0	.000	.000	.000	0	0	0.00	.000	0
*Squires	2	0	1	0	0	0	0	0	0	0	0	0	0	0	0	0	0	0	0	.000	.000	.000	0	0	0.00	.000	0

*left-handed hitter, †switch hitter

DEFENSIVE STATISTICS

FIRST

	G	PO	A	Er	TC	DP	PCT.
Walker	151	1217	97	8	1322	116	.994
De Sa	9	70	7	0	77	4	1.000
Paciorek	6	45	5	0	50	3	1.000
Salazar	6	40	2	0	42	6	1.000
TEAM:	172	1372	111	8	1491	129	.995
AVG:	180	1440	123	14	1577	141	.991

SECOND

	G	PO	A	Er	TC	DP	PCT.
Cruz	87	158	220	7	385	59	.982
Little	68	100	164	3	267	33	.989
Fletcher	37	38	55	0	93	11	1.000
Hulett	28	48	46	1	95	19	.989
TEAM:	220	344	485	11	840	122	.987
AVG:	189	347	501	15	863	114	.982

THIRD

	G	PO	A	Er	TC	DP	PCT.
Hulett	115	69	210	23	302	22	.924
Fletcher	55	29	70	7	106	7	.934
Salazar	39	22	52	6	80	5	.925
Little	2	0	0	2	2	0	.000
Hill	1	0	2	0	2	0	1.000
TEAM:	212	120	334	38	492	34	.923
AVG:	192	129	327	23	479	32	.953

SHORTSTOP

	G	PO	A	Er	TC	DP	PCT.
Guillen	150	220	382	12	614	80	.980
Fletcher	44	56	83	1	140	18	.993
Little	1	1	1	0	2	1	1.000
TEAM:	195	277	466	13	756	99	.983
AVG:	189	269	474	28	771	104	.964

CATCHER

	G	PO	A	Er	TC	DP	PCT.	PB
Fisk	130	801	60	10	871	13	.989	10
Hill	37	185	11	3	199	1	.985	1
Skinner	21	94	8	3	105	0	.971	0
TEAM:	188	1080	79	16	1175	14	.986	11
AVG:	193	895	74	13	982	13	.987	13

OUTFIELD

	G	PO	A	Er	TC	DP	PCT.
Baines	159	318	8	2	328	2	.994
Law	120	226	7	3	236	3	.987
Boston	93	179	7	2	188	1	.989
Salazar	84	118	3	4	125	2	.968
Kittle	57	88	2	1	91	1	.989
Nichols	48	70	1	0	71	0	1.000
Paciorek	23	31	1	1	33	0	.970
Ryal	12	21	0	0	21	0	1.000
Gilbert	7	14	0	0	14	0	1.000
Hairston	5	5	0	0	5	0	1.000
Cangelosi	3	1	0	0	1	0	1.000
De Sa	1	0	0	0	0	0	.000
Hulett	1	0	0	0	0	0	.000
TEAM:	613	1071	29	13	1113	9	.989
AVG:	559	1141	33	21	1196	8	.982

COMPLETE PITCHERS RECORDS

Pitcher	W	L	Pct	ERA	G	GS	CG	GF	SHO	SV	IP	H	TBF	R	ER	HR	SH	SF	HB	BB	IB	SO	WP	BK	Appr Value
							Starters (One-half of Game Appearances)																		
Seaver	16	11	.593	3.17	35	33	6	0	1	0	238.2	223	993	103	84	22	7	8	8	69	6	134	10	0	11
*Burns	18	11	.621	3.96	36	34	8	1	4	0	227.0	206	944	105	100	26	6	5	2	79	1	172	2	0	12
*Bannister	10	14	.417	4.87	34	34	4	0	1	0	210.2	211	928	121	114	30	9	8	4	100	5	198	11	0	7
*Lollar	3	5	.375	4.66	18	13	0	3	0	0	83.0	83	378	48	43	10	3	4	1	58	1	61	5	2	1
Davis	3	3	.500	4.16	12	11	1	0	0	0	71.1	71	307	34	33	6	1	2	1	26	0	37	1	0	1
Dotson	3	4	.429	4.47	9	9	0	0	0	0	52.1	53	226	30	26	5	1	2	3	17	1	33	0	0	1
Long	0	1	.000	10.29	4	3	0	1	0	0	14.0	25	71	17	16	4	1	1	0	5	2	13	1	0	0
							Relievers																		
Nelson	10	10	.500	4.26	46	18	1	11	0	2	145.2	144	643	74	69	23	9	2	7	67	4	101	11	1	7
James	8	7	.533	2.13	69	0	0	60	0	32	110.0	90	436	31	26	5	7	5	2	23	4	88	3	2	13
Spillner	4	3	.571	3.44	52	3	0	15	0	1	91.2	83	378	39	35	10	3	3	0	33	2	41	4	0	5
*Agosto	4	3	.571	3.58	54	0	0	21	0	1	60.1	45	246	27	24	3	3	3	3	23	1	39	0	0	4
Wehrmeister	2	2	.500	3.43	23	0	0	4	0	2	39.1	35	159	15	15	4	1	0	3	10	0	32	0	0	2
*Gleaton	1	0	1.000	5.76	31	0	0	9	0	1	29.2	37	135	19	19	3	4	1	0	13	3	22	3	0	1
Tanner	1	2	.333	5.33	10	4	0	3	0	0	27.0	34	128	17	16	1	2	1	2	13	1	9	0	0	0
*Fallon	0	0	.000	6.19	10	0	0	4	0	0	16.0	25	79	11	11	5	0	1	0	9	2	17	1	0	0
Stanton	0	1	.000	9.26	11	0	0	5	0	0	11.2	15	60	14	12	2	0	1	0	8	0	12	1	0	0
Correa	1	0	1.000	6.97	5	1	0	3	0	0	10.1	11	51	9	8	2	0	0	0	11	0	10	1	0	0
Fireovid	0	0	.000	5.14	4	0	0	2	0	0	7.0	17	38	4	4	0	0	0	0	2	0	2	0	0	0
Jones	1	0	1.000	1.50	5	0	0	1	0	0	6.0	3	21	2	1	0	0	0	0	3	0	2	0	0	0

Carlton FISK, Catcher

	G	AB	Hit	2B	3B	HR	Run	RBI	TBB	SO	SB	CS	Avg
10.51 years		577	159	29	4	25	91	87	57	87	11	4	.275
1985	153	543	129	23	1	37	85	107	52	81	17	9	.238
First Half	72	253	61	8	0	21	43	50	22	35	8	6	.241
Second Half	81	290	68	15	1	16	42	57	30	46	9	3	.234
Vs. RHP		359	85	11	1	29	57	76	36	59	10	8	.237
Vs. LHP		184	44	12	0	8	28	31	16	22	7	1	.239
Home	77	271	55	9	1	20	42	51	31	42	5	5	.203
Road	76	272	74	14	0	17	43	56	21	39	12	4	.272
Grass	129	457	103	18	1	36	76	100	49	73	14	7	.225
Turf	24	86	26	5	0	1	9	7	3	8	3	2	.302

Greg WALKER, First Base

	G	AB	Hit	2B	3B	HR	Run	RBI	TBB	SO	SB	CS	Avg
2.64 years		517	142	32	4	23	66	87	41	86	6	3	.274
1985	163	601	155	38	4	24	77	92	44	100	5	2	.258
First Half	79	292	82	21	3	14	43	52	22	46	3	1	.281
Second Half	84	309	73	17	1	10	34	40	22	54	2	1	.236
Vs. RHP		418	113	21	4	20	59	69	37	60	3	1	.270
Vs. LHP		183	42	17	0	4	18	23	7	40	2	1	.230
Home	81	293	78	22	4	11	36	47	21	61	2	0	.266
Road	82	308	77	16	0	13	41	45	23	39	3	2	.250
Grass	139	521	133	34	4	19	64	83	40	92	4	2	.255
Turf	24	80	22	4	0	5	13	9	4	8	1	0	.275

Tim HULLETT, Third Base

	G	AB	Hit	2B	3B	HR	Run	RBI	TBB	SO	SB	CS	Avg
0.96 years		425	112	20	4	5	55	39	32	89	8	4	.263
1985	141	395	106	19	4	5	52	37	30	81	6	4	.268
First Half	68	194	52	9	3	3	24	21	13	39	4	3	.268
Second Half	73	201	54	10	1	2	28	16	17	42	2	1	.269
Vs. RHP		238	60	12	0	3	29	20	15	52	3	2	.252
Vs. LHP		157	46	7	4	2	23	17	15	29	3	2	.293
Home	71	195	49	8	4	2	22	15	17	41	1	2	.251
Road	70	200	57	11	0	3	30	22	13	40	5	2	.285
Grass	121	334	87	18	4	5	47	31	27	70	4	3	.260
Turf	20	61	19	1	0	0	5	6	3	11	2	1	.311

Ozzie GUILLEN, Shortstop

	G	AB	Hit	2B	3B	HR	Run	RBI	TBB	SO	SB	CS	Avg
0.93 years		530	145	23	10	1	77	36	13	39	8	4	.273
1985	150	491	134	21	9	1	71	33	12	36	7	4	.273
First Half	75	240	55	8	2	0	32	13	7	18	3	2	.229
Second Half	75	251	79	13	7	1	39	20	5	18	4	2	.315
Vs. RHP		400	115	20	8	1	65	23	11	26	6	4	.288
Vs. LHP		91	19	1	1	0	6	10	1	10	1	0	.209
Home	73	244	68	7	7	1	40	20	7	17	3	4	.279
Road	77	247	66	14	2	0	31	13	5	19	4	0	.267
Grass	127	425	122	20	9	1	67	31	12	30	5	4	.287
Turf	23	66	12	1	0	0	4	2	0	6	2	0	.182

Rudy LAW, Center Field

	G	AB	Hit	2B	3B	HR	Run	RBI	TBB	SO	SB	CS	Avg
4.09 years		517	141	18	8	4	82	40	38	46	52	14	.272
1985	125	390	101	21	6	4	62	36	27	40	29	6	.259
First Half	70	223	56	15	3	2	34	21	17	24	17	4	.251
Second Half	55	167	45	6	3	2	28	15	10	16	12	2	.269
Vs. RHP		366	92	20	5	4	60	32	27	39	26	5	.251
Vs. LHP		24	9	1	1	0	2	4	0	1	3	1	.375
Home	63	192	52	12	1	4	37	14	14	19	18	4	.271
Road	62	198	49	9	5	0	25	22	13	21	11	2	.247
Grass	106	332	89	19	4	4	57	28	25	36	28	6	.268
Turf	19	58	12	2	2	0	5	8	2	4	1	0	.207

Harold BAINES, Right Field

	G	AB	Hit	2B	3B	HR	Run	RBI	TBB	SO	SB	CS	Avg
5.23 years		609	174	29	7	23	80	96	43	86	5	3	.285
1985	160	640	198	29	3	22	86	113	42	89	1	1	.309
First Half	77	301	88	14	1	7	40	45	27	43	0	1	.292
Second Half	83	339	110	15	2	15	46	68	15	46	1	0	.324
Vs. RHP		420	124	22	2	16	57	84	31	55	1	1	.295
Vs. LHP		220	74	7	1	6	29	29	11	34	0	0	.336
Home	80	315	89	16	1	13	40	60	21	40	1	1	.283
Road	80	325	109	13	2	9	46	53	21	49	0	0	.335
Grass	138	554	177	28	3	18	79	99	40	73	1	1	.319
Turf	22	86	21	1	0	4	7	14	2	16	0	0	.244

Ron KITTLE, Designated Hitter

	G	AB	Hit	2B	3B	HR	Run	RBI	TBB	SO	SB	CS	Avg
2.59 years		538	126	19	1	36	76	92	47	151	5	5	.234
1985	116	379	87	12	0	26	51	58	31	92	1	4	.230
First Half	49	149	29	5	0	8	15	16	13	43	0	3	.195
Second Half	67	230	58	7	0	18	36	42	18	49	1	1	.252
Vs. RHP		231	52	9	0	16	26	34	13	55	0	1	.225
Vs. LHP		148	35	3	0	10	25	24	18	37	1	3	.236
Home	61	199	48	8	0	12	27	27	15	42	1	2	.241
Road	55	180	39	4	0	14	24	31	16	50	0	2	.217
Grass	97	316	72	11	0	19	39	45	28	77	1	3	.228
Turf	19	63	15	1	0	7	12	13	3	15	0	1	.238

Luis SALAZAR, Outfield

	G	AB	Hit	2B	3B	HR	Run	RBI	TBB	SO	SB	CS	Avg
3.99 years		533	141	20	6	10	58	58	21	89	26	10	.265
1985	122	327	80	18	2	10	39	45	12	60	14	4	.245
First Half	62	133	25	4	0	5	14	21	8	26	4	0	.188
Second Half	60	194	55	14	2	5	25	24	4	34	10	4	.284
Vs. RHP		156	39	6	1	7	25	23	6	30	7	2	.250
Vs. LHP		171	41	12	1	3	14	22	6	30	7	2	.240
Home	59	150	39	9	1	4	21	20	9	26	7	1	.260
Road	63	177	41	9	1	6	18	25	3	34	7	3	.232
Grass	103	269	67	15	1	8	33	42	12	52	14	4	.249
Turf	19	58	13	3	1	2	6	3	0	8	0	0	.224

Scott FLETCHER, Infield

	G	AB	Hit	2B	3B	HR	Run	RBI	TBB	SO	SB	CS	Avg
2.54 years		428	105	16	4	3	53	39	46	49	8	4	.245
1985	119	301	77	8	1	2	38	31	35	47	5	5	.256
First Half	58	168	35	4	0	0	11	14	18	30	3	2	.208
Second Half	61	133	42	4	1	2	27	17	17	17	2	3	.316
Vs. RHP		133	27	2	0	0	12	17	14	24	0	2	.203
Vs. LHP		168	50	6	1	2	26	14	21	23	5	3	.298
Home	59	142	32	3	0	0	14	17	22	26	1	2	.225
Road	60	159	45	5	1	2	24	14	13	21	4	3	.283
Grass	100	244	57	6	1	1	28	27	28	41	2	3	.234
Turf	19	57	20	2	0	1	10	4	7	6	3	2	.351

Daryl BOSTON, Center Field

	G	AB	Hit	2B	3B	HR	Run	RBI	TBB	SO	SB	CS	Avg
0.80 years		393	83	20	2	4	35	22	22	80	17	7	.213
1985	95	232	53	13	1	3	20	15	14	44	8	6	.228
First Half	64	163	35	8	1	3	11	11	11	35	6	5	.215
Second Half	31	69	18	5	0	0	9	4	3	9	2	1	.261
Vs. RHP		216	51	13	1	3	19	15	12	40	8	6	.236
Vs. LHP		16	2	0	0	0	1	0	2	4	0	0	.125
Home	43	97	17	3	0	1	5	3	5	21	2	1	.175
Road	52	135	36	10	1	2	15	12	9	23	6	5	.267
Grass	77	189	41	11	1	1	14	11	13	36	6	5	.217
Turf	18	43	12	2	0	2	6	4	1	8	2	1	.279

FLOYD BANNISTER

	(W–L)	GS	Run	Avg	DP	Avg	SB	Avg
1984	(14-11)	33	152	4.61	30	.91	14	.42
1985	(10-14)	34	155	4.56	31	.91	23	.68
1977-1985		257	1103	4.29	199	.77	198	.77

	G	IP	W	L	Pct	ER	BB	SO	ERA
1984 Home	16	104.7	6	4	.600	52	39	76	4.47
1985 Home	14	94.7	5	6	.455	38	45	98	3.61
1984 Road	18	113.3	8	7	.533	65	41	76	5.16
1985 Road	20	116.0	5	8	.385	76	55	100	5.90
1984 Grass	28	182.7	10	10	.500	98	68	131	4.83
1985 Grass	27	168.3	8	12	.400	88	81	161	4.70
1984 Turf	6	35.3	4	1	.800	19	12	21	4.84
1985 Turf	7	42.3	2	2	.500	26	19	37	5.53
1985 Total	34	210.7	10	14	.417	114	100	198	4.87

BRITT BURNS

	(W–L)	GS	Run	Avg	DP	Avg	SB	Avg
1984	(4-12)	16	58	3.62	13	.81	10	.62
1985	(18-11)	34	175	5.15	32	.94	24	.71
1978-1985		162	667	4.12	134	.83	107	.66

	G	IP	W	L	Pct	ER	BB	SO	ERA
1984 Home	18	67.0	3	6	.333	36	27	56	4.84
1985 Home	18	117.3	10	6	.625	49	45	99	3.76
1984 Road	16	50.0	1	6	.143	29	18	29	5.22
1985 Road	18	109.7	8	5	.615	51	34	73	4.19
1984 Grass	27	87.7	4	8	.333	49	31	66	5.03
1985 Grass	32	203.7	16	9	.640	88	71	159	3.89
1984 Turf	7	29.3	0	4	0.000	16	14	19	4.91
1985 Turf	4	23.3	2	2	.500	12	8	13	4.63
1985 Total	36	227.0	18	11	.621	100	79	172	3.96

TOM SEAVER

	(W–L)	GS	Run	Avg	DP	Avg	SB	Avg
1984	(15-11)	33	152	4.61	25	.76	30	.91
1985	(16-11)	33	134	4.06	30	.91	31	.94
1976-1985		305	1280	4.20	238	.78	298	.98

	G	IP	W	L	Pct	ER	BB	SO	ERA
1984 Home	18	126.0	9	4	.692	51	32	66	3.64
1985 Home	15	103.3	5	6	.455	50	40	56	4.35
1984 Road	16	110.7	6	7	.462	53	29	65	4.31
1985 Road	20	135.3	11	5	.688	34	29	78	2.26
1984 Grass	29	194.7	14	8	.636	90	52	105	4.16
1985 Grass	31	209.7	15	8	.652	77	61	124	3.31
1984 Turf	4	36.3	2	1	.667	11	9	26	2.72
1985 Turf	4	29.0	1	3	.250	7	8	10	2.17
1985 Total	35	238.7	16	11	.593	84	69	134	3.17

OTHERS

	(W–L)	GS	Run	Avg	DP	Avg	SB	Avg
Nelson	(10-10)	18	81	4.07	12	.87	7	1.60
Davis	(3-3)	11	54	5.33	11	.78	6	.44
Dotson	(3-4)	9	28	5.71	6	1.43	5	.57
Tanner	(1-2)	4	15	5.75	4	1.25	1	.25
Long	(0-1)	3	16	7.50	2	1.00	6	0.00
Spillner	(4-3)	3	16	5.00	4	2.00	2	0.00
Correa	(1-0)	1	3	6.00	2	0.00	0	2.00

MINNESOTA TWINS

BREAKDOWNS FOR THE LAST TEN SEASONS

Won-Lost Record: 730-835, .466 (5th in the Division, 20th in the Majors)
Runs Scored: 6,832 (4th in the Division, 10th in Majors)
Runs Allowed: 7,191 (2nd-Highest in the Division, 3rd-Highest in Majors)
Home Runs Hit: 1,088 (Fewest in the Division, 21st ([Highest] in the Majors)
Home Runs Allowed: 1,363 (2nd-Highest in the Division. 4th-Highest in the Majors)

Record In:
April: 97-109, .471 (6th in the Division, 20th in Majors)
May: 110-154, .417 (The Worst in Baseball)
June: 106-143, .426 (6th in the Division, 24th in Majors)
July: 138-119, .537 (2nd-Best in the Division, 6th-Best in the Majors)
August: 129-163, .442 (6th in the Division. 23rd in the Majors)
September: 136-137, .498 (4th in the Division, 14th in Majors)
October: 14-10, .583 (2nd-Best in the Division, 6th in the Majors)

Won-Lost Record in Road Games: 323-452, .417 (5th in the Division, 21st in Majors)
Won-Lost Record at Home: 407-383, .515 (4th in the Division, 18th in Majors)
Home Field Advantage: 76½ Games
Runs Scored on the Road: 3,134 (6th in the Division, 19th in Majors)
Runs Scored at Home: 3,698 (2nd in the Division, 5th in the Majors)
Runs Allowed on the Road: 3,558 (4th-Highest in the Division, 8th in Majors)
Runs Allowed at Home: 3,633 (2nd-Highest in the Division, 5th in Majors)

Home Runs Hit on the Road: 535 (6th in the Division, 18th in Majors)
Home Runs Hit at Home: 553 (5th in the Division, 17th in the Majors)
Home Runs Allowed on the Road: 661 (3rd-Highest in the Division, 4th-Highest in Majors)
Home Runs Allowed at Home: 702 (2nd-Highest in the Division, 7th in Majors)

RECORD FOR LAST THREE SEASONS: 228-258, .469 (4th in the Division, 19th in Baseball)

There were two observations made about the Twins in last year's book which need to be revisited. In the Twins comment (pages 100-101) I made an attempt to develop a "leading indicator" of the performance of a team by assessing the amount of young talent on their roster, and comparing that "talent pool" to the 1984 performance of the team.

In retrospect, I find the article to be unrelievedly technical. While I still think that some such method could be valuable as a part of a system of "leading indicators" of team performance, I would hope that, if I were to get into that again, I could develop a way to cut more directly to the center of the matter.

Anyway, the damn thing didn't work. The teams shown as "likely to improve" did not improve (they declined on balance by a few games), and the teams shown as "likely to decline" did not decline, but rather picked up the slack—this despite the fact that listed among the likely declines was Detroit, which suffered the league's largest decline from 1984.

The other comment worked out better, being in retrospect more interesting now than it was at the time it was written. This digression, which appeared in the Montreal team comment (page 214) discussed first in general the way that managers react or do not react to the changing needs of their teams:

An interesting example to watch in 1985 is Billy Gardner, the manager of the Twins for the last three and a half seasons. Gardner, ever since he has been there, has been exactly what the Twins' young players needed. He was patient with them; he allowed them to develop their skills and created an environment in which a player of promise knew that if he fouled up Gardner wasn't going to turn on him.

But suddenly, the needs of the Twins organizations have shifted on Billy Gardner. Having developed all those young players to where the Twins now are contenders, the Twins are no longer in need of a manager who can supervise the development of young players. They need a manager who can direct the conduct of a pennant race. Will Gardner be that manager?

In response to this, Craig Wright put forward a fairly persuasive argument that the Twins should never, in fact, have been expected to be in contention in 1985. The basis of his argument was that, while the Twins do possess as many fine young players as any team in the league, their 1984 success (such as it was) was heavily based on the contributions of three starting pitchers (Viola, Butcher and Smithson) who a) pitched a high number of innings in 1984, and b) performed at a level far above their previous seasons. It was, he argued, not reasonable to expect the three pitchers to have the same success again. Further, the Twins had limited ability to replace any of them should they stumble. Therefore, the pitching probably would not be as good, and the team should not have been expected to improve.

He is probably right about that; nonetheless, the expectations that I had for the team—I thought they were the best bet to win the division—were pretty much consistent with the expectations of the Twins fans and management. The Twins started poorly, and Gardner inherited the ax.

Gardner showed no recognition that the needs of the team had changed. Billy's idea in managing was to keep the lineup rolling and let the players take care of things. Ron Davis was having all kinds of trouble as the relief ace, which left Gardner the options of either trying to do something to make Ron Davis more effective, as Ray Miller did, or trying to find somebody else. Gardner's approach was to grit his teeth and keep calling for Davis.

The Twins opened the season without a shortstop, as they have for several years. Whether or not Gardner had a decent option, and I don't really see that he did, it seems to me that it would have been a better gamble to define some sort of work assignments at the position and stick to them; he never did, playing Roy Smalley for a while, Greg Gagne for a while, Ron Washington for a while. The Twins DH production had been poor in 1984, and in spring training 1985 it appeared that Mike Stenhouse had won the job. But the Twins fell on their faces out of the gate, and Randy Bush had a hot week, and Gardner went back to using Bush as the DH—despite having already given Bush two years to prove that he wasn't a major-league quality DH. Gardner used Roy Smalley as a shortstop/DH. This is a new position on a major league roster.

So Ray Miller got the chance. Miller immediately stated the intention of trying to get the entire roster involved in the act—something which had not been done under Gardner, who used an eight-man lineup except for some inscrutable maneuvering at shortstop and catcher. By the end of the year the Twins seemed to have solved the DH problem, with Mark Funderburk apparently taking the job.

But Billy should get another opportunity. He made a positive contribution for almost four years, and left without many enemies.

On to the general question of firing managers . . . last summer a reader (Ward Larkin) sent me a copy of an article reprinted in the *Cleveland Plain Dealer,* originally written for the *Baltimore Sun,* in which Stanley Eitzen, a sociologist at Colorado State University, reported on some of his own research and some of some other research into the effect that managerial changes have on performance. His article focused this research on the managerial change in Baltimore, concluding that "the odds are the Baltimore fans will be disappointed. Weaver will likely have a short term success, but his team is composed of the same players as Altobelli's.'

I'm not sure I buy any of Mr. Eitzen's reasoning, and at one point in the article he lapses into an embarrassing gaffe, commanding the reader to wonder about his grasp of the material:

Yankee owner George Steinbrenner's lack of patience with managers and the rapid turnover (10 changes in 10 years) may be a major reason for his team's poor performance during those years despite excellent personnel.

The Yankees have, of course, been the most successful team in baseball during the last ten years. He errs almost as glaringly in asserting that "Weaver is famous for his record-keeping on three by five cards, but now all managers have access to computer printouts that offer the same information." Absolutely not so; the growth of computerized information inside baseball has proceeded at a hun-

dredth of the pace which many people imagine, and only a few managers would have access to up-to-date, computerized information. Several organizations have no idea, as the season progresses, of even such basic information as how their players are hitting against right-handed and left-handed pitchers.

Nonetheless, I applaud the principle of researching an idea, and Mr. Eitzen raises several interesting points. He contends that there is an illusion at work which causes managerial changes to be perceived as being more successful than they are. Managers are usually fired at a time when the team is going badly, and, by what he refers to as "regression toward the mean," which I refer to as the law of competitive balance, they tend to play better afterward.

I got to wondering, then, about the exact conditions under which managerial changes are often made. My research focused on all American League teams, 1961–1985, and began by sorting seasons into four classes:

Highly successful seasons (those seasons in which the team won six games or more above the total that could have been expected of them, or won a pennant).

Marginally successful seasons (those seasons in which the team won as many games as could have been expected, but did not exceed that total by a significant amount, or seasons in which the team won a divisional title).

Somewhat disappointing seasons (seasons in which the team fell below the number of wins which could have been expected of it, but by less than six games).

Very disappointing seasons (seasons in which the team missed the number of wins that could have been expected of it by at least six games).

The "expectation" was established by figuring a percentage based on:

two parts the previous season.
one part the season before that.
one part of a .500 season.

That is, since the St. Louis Cardinals won 84 games in 1984 and 101 games in 1985, their expectation for 1986 will be 92 wins.

1984	84–78
1985	202–122
.500	81–81
Total	367–281

367–281 projected into 162 games is 92–70, so that's the expectation for the '86 Cards. To have another highly successful season, they'll have to win 98 or more games, or repeat as league champions. To have a marginally successful season, they have to stay above 92 wins or win the divisional title again. If they win 86–91 games, the season will be considered somewhat disappointing. If they win 85 or fewer, the season will be considered very disappointing—although the same season for the Texas Rangers would be classified as highly successful.

The classifications, really, are reasonably straightforward, and in very, very few cases should there be any argument about them. These are the groupings for the 1985 season:

Very Successful Seasons: Cincinnati, Los Angeles, New York and St. Louis in the National League, California,

Kansas City, New York and Toronto in the American League.

Marginally Successful Seasons: Montreal and Houston in the National League, Chicago and Seattle in the American League.

Somewhat Disappointing Seasons: San Diego in the National League, Baltimore, Boston, Milwaukee, Minnesota and Oakland in the American League.

Very Disappointing Seasons: Atlanta, Chicago, Philadelphia, Pittsburgh and San Francisco in the National League, Cleveland, Detroit and Texas in the American League.

Of course one can always differ with the groupings; the Phillies, who went into the year understanding that they were rebuilding, were not particularly disappointed in their record—but it was still the worst record for the team in twelve years. The Red Sox had talked themselves into believing that they were big bananas before the season started, and they treated their 81–81 finish as a disaster—but it was essentially the same sort of season they have been having since 1979. Basically, I think 99% of the time the term applied to the season (Successful, Disappointing, etc) is the appropriate one.

Anyway, the purpose of the study is not to tell the team's fans whether they should be satisfied with the season or disappointed, but rather to construct a framework in which to study the tendency of teams to change managers in relation to the success of their teams, relative to success in previous seasons. I found the following:

Of the 88 teams which had highly successful seasons, 23 (or 26%) changed managers during or immediately after the season.

Of the 81 teams which had marginally successful seasons, 24 (or 30%) changed managers during or after the season.

Of the 67 teams which had somewhat disappointing seasons, 29 (or 43%) changed managers during or after the season.

Of the 74 teams which had very disappointing years, 43 (or 58%) changed managers during or after the season.

Obviously, then, when a manager will be fired can be predicted with some reliability based just on looking at this one factor—yet I was surprised that the relationship wasn't closer than this. I would have guessed that 80% of teams which had very disappointing years would have changed managers, rather than just 58%.

One thing that I particularly noticed was that when a highly successful season was followed by a very disappointing season, the team would almost never change managers—but that if the team didn't start out well in the season following that, *then* they would make the change. I called this a 4–1 pattern, for the notation I was using during the study. A few examples: when the Orioles won the Worlds Championship in 1966 and collapsed in 1967, they stuck with Hank Bauer—but replaced him with Earl Weaver early in the 1968 season. When the Orioles won the Worlds Championship again in 1983 under Joe Altobelli, but then went Altobelli-up in 1984, they didn't fire him—but when they started poorly in 1985, they called Earl back. When the Royals followed a fine 1973 season

with a disappointing 1974, they stuck with Jack McKeon—but replaced him with Whitey Herzog midway through 1975. When the division champion Twins collapsed in 1971, they stuck with Bill Rigney—but fired him early in 1972, when the team failed to recover. When the Yankee dynasty crashed to earth in 1965, the Yankees did not fire Johnny Keane—but did relieve him when the team started poorly in 1966.

There are about as many instances of managers getting the season following the 4–1 pattern off alright, and keeping their jobs—but there are only a couple of examples of managers being fired during or after the second season of a 4–1 pattern. One of those was in Kansas City in 1981—fellow named Jim Frey. There are two teams which carry the 4–1 pattern into the 1985 season. Yes, the Chicago Cubs stuck with Frey when his Cubs followed their 1984 miracle with a disappointing 1985—but if he wants to keep his job, the Cubs better be over .500 on April 30 and May 15 and May 31. The other one is in Detroit, but the Tigers apparently intend to keep Sparky no matter what happens.

Of the 23 cases in which teams changed managers during or immediately after highly successful seasons, almost all fit into one or more of these categories:

*Managers who decided to get out while the getting was good, generally to take a front-office job (as Bobby Cox did in Toronto last year, as Ralph Houk did in 1963, and Gene Mauch in 1984).

*Cases in which a manager was fired early in the season, and the season *became* highly successful under the new man (this happened six times).

*The Yankees. Counting Stengel, who wasn't actually in the study, the Yankees have changed managers during or after a highly successful season eight times since 1960.

An accidental discovery of the study was that there were more "successful" than "unsuccessful" seasons. What does that mean? What it means is that the losses must be larger than the gains—that is, teams must tend to move backward in fewer, but larger, strides than they move forward. Another thing that I was looking at was the tendency of teams to have particularly good or particularly bad seasons in their first full season under a new manager. There clearly was such an impact; of 116 teams in their first season under a new manager, 40 (or 35%) had highly successful seasons, but 28 (or 24%) had very disappointing seasons. Both percentages, but particularly the former, are larger than the percentages for the entire group. Whereas 35% of managers were highly successful in their first season, only 24% were in their second season, only 27% in their third season, and only 8% (2 of 26) in their fourth seasons.

It was during his fourth season that Billy Gardner was fired. To return briefly to the Eitzen article, let me say this: Eitzen states that "the findings (of many different sociologists) are consistent, regardless of sport, and quite different from the conventional wisdom that a managerial change tends to have a positive effect on team performance." Well, that may be, but the most suspicious finding in research is that A has little effect on B. When a researcher finds that A has little effect on B, it means that either

1) A has little effect on B, or

2) The way in which A and B are related is a hell of a lot more complicated than the way in which the researcher has studied their relationship.

Roughly 99.9% of the time, it's the second.

The most basic, most common error that is made in research is the failure to understand this—the tendency to think that, when you have shown that A is not correlated to B, you have shown that A and B are not related. To prove that A and B are not related is, in fact, something which is almost impossible in most cases, as they may be related in any of a million ways which the researcher did not check.

It is my belief that if you look at the history of baseball organizations over time, you will find that the comings and goings of managers, while meaningless in a great many cases, mark the turning points of organizations in many other cases.

I also believe that most baseball managers are hired and fired for very good reasons. They are hired, as Billy Gardner was hired, because they can bring to the organization at that moment something which the organization needs at that moment.

They are fired, as Billy Gardner was fired, because, once they make the contribution that they are capable of making, the needs of the organization change.

Resuming another discussion from a year ago, I presented then projected career statistics for the Twins regulars. The projections were made by the Brock2 system, which was explained elsewhere in that book. I haven't done much with the system in this year's edition. I started some things to evaluate and improve the system, but didn't carry through on them as well as I should have, so they're sort of in transition at the moment, and I decided to let that slide this year.

In retrospect, what I wish I had said about the career projection systems is this: that we all share certain expectations about players' future performance. We all expect Shawon Dunston to be a better ballplayer three years from now than Ron Washington, or for that matter Greg Gagne. We all recognize that George Brett has a better chance of getting 3000 hits in his career than does Larry Sheets. I would suspect that most of us would agree that George will probably get 3000 hits but almost certainly not 4000. *We all share a sense of what normal expectations are in the absence of individual variations.*

What the projections are intended to do is not to account for individual variations, but to sharpen and refine our sense of normal expectations.

Anyway, the current projection system is Brock6, and I did run Brock6 projections for the same players, plus new Twins Salas, Smalley and Gagne. Here they are:

Player	G	AB	Run	Hit	2B	3B	HR	RBI	BB	Avg
Kent Hrbek	2124	7586	1149	2196	405	29	304	1213	860	.289
Kirby Puckett	1550	6183	754	1829	227	82	26	530	351	.296
Tom Brunansky	2033	7059	999	1744	321	28	374	1152	864	.247
Mark Salas	1703	4873	680	1401	256	48	121	601	310	.288
Roy Smalley	1563	5242	705	1340	212	20	145	645	715	.256
Tim Teufel	1448	4632	608	1208	243	23	106	514	552	.261
Gary Gaetti	1361	4626	558	1160	239	15	134	573	349	.251
Mickey Hatcher	744	2472	257	698	134	14	27	260	114	.282
Dave Engle	870	2539	339	674	125	19	53	284	213	.265
Randy Bush	683	1781	217	426	98	15	66	252	176	.239
Greg Gagne	602	1621	169	380	86	15	12	128	125	.235
Ron Washington	513	1336	157	356	50	22	14	120	61	.266
Tim Laudner	513	1433	152	317	72	3	50	174	121	.221
Houston Jimenez	156	403	33	79	17	2	0	29	21	.197

Brock6 tends to be more conservative than Brock2, particularly with respect to certain types of players— power hitters, slower players playing the positions at the left end of the defensive spectrum (lb, lf, dh). Brock2 clearly tended to over-project the careers of power hitters. One study that I did focused on young players with old players' skills—that is, young players who were slow but hit for power and had good strike-zone judgment. I identified 12 such players from the years 1960–1972 and ran career projections for them. Eleven of the twelve fell short of their projections. At this point, Brock6 may still overproject those players, but not so seriously.

Since Kent Hrbek and Tom Brunansky are those kinds of players, Brock6 would be more conservative in their projections; in addition, neither had as good a season in 1985 as in 1984. So their projections have dropped— Brunansky from 500 homers, 1,402 career RBI to 374 and 1,152, about Rocky Colavito's totals, and Hrbek from 353 homers, 1,369 RBI to 304 and 1,213.

Gary Gaetti, who had an off year in 1984, has the most improved set of projections, from 939 career games to 1,361. Kirby Puckett and Tim Teufel are close to where they were projected off their rookie seasons, Puckett's projection now running one season longer and Teufel's a season and a half shorter. Hatcher and Engle have lost a little bit, not much; Bush, Washington and Jimenez show almost exactly the same projections now as they did a year ago. Tim Laudner, hitting .238 instead of his usual .200, improved his expected longevity by one year.

COMPLETE BATTING RECORDS

Player	G	AB	R	H	TB	2B	3B	HR	RBI	GW	SH	SF	HB	BB	IB	SO	SB	CS	GI DP	Avg	Slug	OBP	Runs	Outs Made	Runs/ 27 Outs	OW%	Appr Value
*Salas	120	360	51	108	165	20	5	9	41	7	0	3	1	18	5	37	0	1	7	.300	.458	.332	53	263	5.44	.584	10
*Hrbek	158	593	78	165	263	31	2	21	93	9	0	4	2	67	12	87	1	1	12	.278	.444	.351	93	445	5.65	.602	12
Teufel	138	434	58	113	173	24	3	10	50	4	7	4	3	48	2	70	4	2	14	.260	.399	.335	58	348	4.48	.488	8
Gaetti	160	560	71	138	229	31	0	20	63	8	3	1	7	37	5	89	13	5	15	.246	.409	.301	66	446	4.01	.433	10
Gagne	114	293	37	66	93	15	3	2	23	4	3	3	3	20	0	57	10	4	5	.225	.317	.279	27	242	2.97	.296	4
Hatcher	116	444	46	125	162	28	0	3	49	5	3	2	2	16	1	23	0	0	15	.282	.365	.308	46	339	3.69	.393	7
Puckett	161	691	80	199	266	29	13	4	74	7	5	3	4	41	0	87	21	12	9	.288	.385	.330	88	521	4.55	.495	13
Brunansky	157	567	71	137	254	28	4	27	90	10	0	13	0	71	7	86	5	3	12	.242	.448	.320	83	458	4.89	.532	11
†Smalley	129	388	57	100	156	20	0	12	45	5	1	2	1	60	3	65	0	2	8	.258	.402	.357	58	301	5.17	.560	9
*Bush	97	234	26	56	105	13	3	10	35	4	0	2	5	24	1	30	3	0	3	.239	.449	.321	36	183	5.24	.566	3
*Stenhouse	81	179	23	40	60	5	0	5	21	3	0	1	0	29	1	18	1	0	3	.223	.335	.330	22	143	4.07	.441	2
Engle	70	172	28	44	77	8	2	7	25	3	0	2	0	21	1	28	2	2	3	.256	.448	.333	26	135	5.19	.561	2
Laudner	72	164	16	39	65	5	0	7	19	2	4	1	1	12	0	45	0	1	2	.238	.396	.292	19	133	3.88	.417	2
Washington	70	135	24	37	54	6	4	1	14	2	3	3	0	8	0	15	5	1	3	.274	.400	.308	17	108	4.25	.462	2
Meier	71	104	15	27	36	6	0	1	8	0	3	0	1	18	0	12	0	6	0	.260	.346	.374	13	86	4.24	.460	1
Funderburk	23	70	7	22	37	7	1	2	13	1	0	2	0	5	0	12	0	1	0	.314	.529	.351	11	55	5.52	.591	1
Espinoza	32	57	5	15	17	2	0	0	9	0	3	0	1	0	9	0	1	2	.263	.298	.288	4	48	2.42	.218	0
Lombardozzi	28	54	10	20	26	4	1	0	6	0	4	1	0	6	0	6	3	2	0	.370	.481	.426	12	41	7.71	.739	1
*Reed	7	10	2	2	2	0	0	0	0	0	0	0	0	0	0	0	0	0	0	.200	.200	.200	0	8	1.35	.080	0

*left-handed hitter, †switch hitter

DEFENSIVE STATISTICS

FIRST

	G	PO	A	Er	TC	DP	PCT.
Hrbek	156	1339	114	8	1461	114	.995
Stenhouse	8	59	8	1	68	4	.985
Hatcher	4	31	1	1	33	2	.970
Bush	1	16	0	0	16	1	1.000
Funderburk	1	8	0	0	8	0	1.000
Gaetti	1	6	0	0	6	0	1.000
Laudner	1	3	0	0	3	0	1.000
Smalley	1	4	1	0	5	0	1.000
Washington	1	1	0	0	1	0	1.000
TEAM:	174	1467	124	10	1601	121	.994
AVG:	180	1440	123	14	1577	141	.991

SECOND

	G	PO	A	Er	TC	DP	PCT.
Teufel	137	237	352	12	601	67	.980
Lombardozzi	26	31	80	2	113	16	.982
Washington	24	31	50	4	85	8	.953
TEAM:	187	299	482	18	799	91	.977
AVG:	189	347	501	15	863	114	.982

THIRD

	G	PO	A	Er	TC	DP	PCT.
Gaetti	156	146	316	18	480	31	.963
Smalley	14	9	41	1	51	2	.980
Washington	7	3	12	0	15	1	1.000
TEAM:	177	158	369	19	546	34	.965
AVG:	192	129	327	23	479	32	.953

SHORTSTOP

	G	PO	A	Er	TC	DP	PCT.
Gagne	106	149	269	14	432	48	.968
Smalley	49	57	91	2	150	16	.987
Washington	31	20	38	3	61	5	.951
Espinoza	31	25	69	5	99	15	.949
TEAM:	217	251	467	24	742	84	.968
AVG:	189	269	474	28	771	104	.964

CATCHER

	G	PO	A	Er	TC	DP	PCT.	PB
Salas	115	529	39	5	573	10	.991	11
Laudner	68	233	19	8	260	3	.969	2
Engle	17	58	3	1	62	1	.984	0
Reed	7	9	3	0	12	0	1.000	0
TEAM:	207	829	64	14	907	14	.985	13
AVG:	193	895	74	13	982	13	.987	13

OUTFIELD

	G	PO	A	Er	TC	DP	PCT.
Puckett	161	465	19	8	492	5	.984
Brunansky	155	300	14	5	319	2	.984
Hatcher	97	215	6	2	223	2	.991
Meier	63	77	1	1	79	1	.987
Bush	41	63	0	2	65	0	.969
Stenhouse	16	24	2	2	28	0	.929
Funderburk	5	7	0	0	7	0	1.000
Gaetti	4	10	0	0	10	0	1.000
Engle	3	8	1	0	9	0	1.000
TEAM:	545	1169	43	20	1232	10	.984
AVG:	559	1141	33	21	1196	8	.982

COMPLETE PITCHERS RECORDS

Pitcher	W	L	Pct	ERA	G	GS	CG	GF	SHO	SV	IP	H	TBF	R	ER	HR	SH	SF	HB	BB	IB	SO	WP	BK	Appr Value
											Starters (One-half of Game Appearances)														
Smithson	15	14	.517	4.34	37	37	8	0	3	0	257.0	264	1088	134	124	25	10	7	15	78	1	127	6	1	10
*Viola	18	14	.563	4.09	36	36	9	0	0	0	250.2	262	1059	136	114	26	5	5	2	68	3	135	6	2	12
Butcher	11	14	.440	4.98	34	33	8	0	2	0	207.2	239	893	125	115	24	6	10	6	43	4	92	5	1	6
Schrom	9	12	.429	4.99	29	26	6	1	0	0	160.2	164	679	95	89	28	9	8	0	59	2	74	2	0	4
Blyleven	8	5	.615	3.00	14	14	9	0	1	0	114.0	101	460	45	38	9	1	4	2	26	0	77	3	0	5
Portugal	1	3	.250	5.55	6	4	0	0	0	0	24.1	24	105	16	15	3	0	2	0	14	0	12	1	1	0
Yett	0	0	.000	27.00	1	1	0	0	0	0	0.1	1	5	1	1	0	0	0	0	2	0	0	1	0	0
											Relievers														
*Filson	4	5	.444	3.67	40	6	1	12	0	2	95.2	93	406	42	39	13	3	2	0	30	4	42	1	1	5
Davis	2	6	.250	3.48	57	0	0	50	0	25	64.2	55	285	28	25	7	3	4	4	35	6	72	8	1	8
Eufemia	4	2	.667	3.79	39	0	0	21	0	2	61.2	56	250	27	26	7	2	3	0	21	7	30	2	2	4
Lysander	0	2	.000	6.05	35	1	0	9	0	3	61.0	72	262	43	41	3	2	2	0	22	2	26	9	0	2
*Wardle	1	3	.250	5.51	35	0	0	13	0	1	49.0	49	218	32	30	9	4	1	1	28	0	47	1	1	2
Burtt	2	2	.500	3.81	5	2	0	0	0	0	28.1	20	109	13	12	2	1	1	0	7	0	9	1	1	0
*Howe	2	3	.400	6.16	13	0	0	5	0	0	19.0	28	94	16	13	1	0	3	0	7	2	10	1	0	0
Brown	0	0	.000	6.89	6	0	0	4	0	0	15.2	21	73	13	12	1	0	3	0	10	0	5	0	0	0
*Klawitter	0	0	.000	6.75	7	2	0	3	0	0	9.1	7	45	7	7	2	1	0	0	13	0	5	3	0	0
*Whitehouse	0	0	.000	11.05	5	0	0	2	0	1	7.1	12	36	9	9	4	0	0	0	2	0	4	1	0	0

Mark SALAS, Catcher

	G	AB	Hit	2B	3B	HR	Run	RBI	TBB	SO	SB	CS	Avg
0.83 years		459	133	25	6	11	63	51	22	48	0	1	.289
1985	120	360	108	20	5	9	51	41	18	37	0	1	.300
First Half	60	178	61	8	3	2	22	19	5	19	0	0	.343
Second Half	60	182	47	12	2	7	29	22	13	18	0	1	.258
Vs. RHP		339	104	19	5	9	49	40	14	33	0	0	.307
Vs. LHP		21	4	1	0	0	2	1	4	4	0	1	.190
Home	66	203	64	11	5	6	33	25	10	23	0	1	.315
Road	54	157	44	9	0	3	18	16	8	14	0	0	.280
Grass	39	123	36	8	0	2	13	12	6	11	0	0	.293
Turf	81	237	72	12	5	7	38	29	12	26	0	1	.304

Mickey HATCHER, Left Field

	G	AB	Hit	2B	3B	HR	Run	RBI	TBB	SO	SB	CS	Avg
3.99 years		558	157	30	3	6	57	60	25	39	2	2	.282
1985	116	444	125	28	0	3	46	49	16	23	0	0	.282
First Half	75	311	92	17	0	2	34	31	11	17	0	0	.296
Second Half	41	133	33	11	0	1	12	18	5	6	0	0	.248
Vs. RHP		312	88	18	0	2	33	36	9	19	0	0	.282
Vs. LHP		132	37	10	0	1	13	13	7	4	0	0	.280
Home	66	244	73	20	0	1	27	32	9	11	0	0	.299
Road	50	200	52	8	0	2	19	17	7	12	0	0	.260
Grass	39	156	37	4	0	2	15	15	6	10	0	0	.237
Turf	77	288	88	24	0	1	31	34	10	13	0	0	.306

Kent HRBEK, First Base

	G	AB	Hit	2B	3B	HR	Run	RBI	TBB	SO	SB	CS	Avg
3.78 years		600	177	34	4	23	85	101	66	88	2	2	.295
1985	158	593	165	31	2	21	78	93	67	87	1	1	.278
First Half	80	314	76	16	1	9	36	42	34	48	0	0	.242
Second Half	78	279	89	15	1	12	42	51	33	39	1	1	.319
Vs. RHP		391	115	22	1	15	55	68	46	49	0	0	.294
Vs. LHP		202	50	9	1	6	23	25	21	38	1	1	.248
Home	83	314	98	21	2	10	47	60	34	45	1	1	.312
Road	75	279	67	10	0	11	31	33	33	42	0	0	.240
Grass	56	208	50	5	0	7	17	23	19	33	0	0	.240
Turf	102	385	115	26	2	14	61	70	48	54	1	1	.299

Kirby PUCKETT, Center Field

	G	AB	Hit	2B	3B	HR	Run	RBI	TBB	SO	SB	CS	Avg
1.78 years		700	204	23	10	2	80	59	32	87	20	11	.292
1985	161	691	199	29	13	4	80	74	41	87	21	12	.288
First Half	80	352	101	11	9	2	40	41	20	36	5	3	.287
Second Half	81	339	98	18	4	2	40	33	21	51	16	9	.289
Vs. RHP		471	121	18	6	0	53	40	31	63	16	4	.257
Vs. LHP		220	78	11	7	4	27	34	10	24	5	8	.355
Home	84	352	114	19	6	2	50	40	26	41	15	6	.324
Road	77	339	85	10	7	2	30	34	15	46	6	6	.251
Grass	58	255	69	8	4	1	24	24	10	39	5	5	.271
Turf	103	436	130	21	9	3	56	50	31	48	16	7	.298

Tim TEUFEL, Second Base

	G	AB	Hit	2B	3B	HR	Run	RBI	TBB	SO	SB	CS	Avg
1.95 years		554	147	31	4	14	74	60	65	77	3	3	.265
1985	138	434	113	24	3	10	58	50	48	70	4	2	.260
First Half	76	261	72	13	1	5	38	31	25	42	2	2	.276
Second Half	62	173	41	11	2	5	20	19	23	28	2	0	.237
Vs. RHP		298	85	17	3	9	43	38	31	50	2	2	.285
Vs. LHP		136	28	7	0	1	15	12	17	20	2	0	.206
Home	72	221	61	12	1	6	38	31	21	37	2	0	.276
Road	66	213	52	12	2	4	20	19	27	33	2	2	.244
Grass	50	163	39	11	2	3	18	14	21	29	2	2	.239
Turf	88	271	74	13	1	7	40	36	27	41	2	0	.273

Tom BRUNANSKY, Right Field

	G	AB	Hit	2B	3B	HR	Run	RBI	TBB	SO	SB	CS	Avg
3.71 years		585	144	28	3	30	81	83	72	104	4	4	.246
1985	157	567	137	28	4	27	71	90	71	86	5	3	.242
First Half	80	294	79	13	2	18	41	53	48	37	0	1	.269
Second Half	77	273	58	15	2	9	30	37	23	49	5	2	.212
Vs. RHP		385	98	17	2	22	52	66	45	64	3	1	.255
Vs. LHP		182	39	11	2	5	19	24	26	22	2	2	.214
Home	81	287	73	13	2	12	32	47	35	38	5	2	.254
Road	76	280	64	15	2	15	39	43	36	48	0	1	.229
Grass	57	205	41	10	1	12	27	30	28	30	0	0	.200
Turf	100	362	96	18	3	15	44	60	43	56	5	3	.265

Gary GAETTI, Third Base

	G	AB	Hit	2B	3B	HR	Run	RBI	TBB	SO	SB	CS	Avg
3.91 years		580	143	29	3	19	69	75	44	103	8	4	.246
1985	160	560	138	31	0	20	71	63	37	89	13	5	.246
First Half	79	285	74	22	0	10	41	39	26	48	7	3	.260
Second Half	81	275	64	9	0	10	30	24	11	41	6	2	.233
Vs. RHP		388	103	24	0	14	53	53	24	57	10	4	.265
Vs. LHP		172	35	7	0	6	18	10	13	32	3	1	.203
Home	82	280	73	16	0	10	44	30	17	48	8	1	.261
Road	78	280	65	15	0	10	27	33	20	41	5	4	.232
Grass	59	217	53	11	0	8	22	28	17	27	4	4	.244
Turf	101	343	85	20	0	12	49	35	20	62	9	1	.248

Roy SMALLEY, Designated Hitter

	G	AB	Hit	2B	3B	HR	Run	RBI	TBB	SO	SB	CS	Avg
8.64 years		566	145	24	2	16	76	70	77	90	3	4	.257
1985	129	388	100	20	0	12	57	45	60	65	0	2	.258
First Half	67	215	63	12	0	5	30	27	35	36	0	2	.293
Second Half	62	173	37	8	0	7	27	18	25	29	0	0	.214
Vs. RHP		315	83	13	0	12	48	37	47	52	0	1	.263
Vs. LHP		73	17	7	0	0	9	8	13	13	0	1	.233
Home	67	201	50	11	0	7	32	30	30	34	0	0	.249
Road	62	187	50	9	0	5	25	15	30	31	0	2	.267
Grass	49	148	39	6	0	4	16	13	25	25	0	2	.264
Turf	80	240	61	14	0	8	41	32	35	40	0	0	.254

Greg GAGNE, Shortstop

	G	AB	Hit	2B	3B	HR	Run	RBI	TBB	SO	SB	CS	Avg
0.78 years		413	89	21	4	3	50	33	26	81	13	5	.215
1985	114	293	66	15	3	2	37	23	20	57	10	4	.225
First Half	61	182	48	14	3	2	25	17	13	33	3	2	.264
Second Half	53	111	18	1	0	0	12	6	7	24	7	2	.162
Vs. RHP		165	35	8	1	1	20	15	16	33	9	2	.212
Vs. LHP		128	31	7	2	1	17	8	4	24	1	2	.242
Home	54	142	33	10	2	0	20	13	12	22	6	1	.232
Road	60	151	33	5	1	2	17	10	8	35	4	3	.219
Grass	43	104	23	4	1	2	16	7	7	24	2	1	.221
Turf	71	189	43	11	2	0	21	16	13	33	8	3	.228

Randy BUSH, Designated Hitter

	G	AB	Hit	2B	3B	HR	Run	RBI	TBB	SO	SB	CS	Avg
2.40 years		432	103	25	3	15	53	61	40	70	2	1	.239
1985	97	234	56	13	3	10	26	35	24	30	3	0	.239
First Half	49	112	24	5	2	6	13	17	7	14	0	0	.214
Second Half	48	122	32	8	1	4	13	18	17	16	3	0	.262
Vs. RHP		222	55	12	3	10	26	35	22	30	3	0	.248
Vs. LHP		12	1	1	0	0	0	0	2	0	0	0	.083
Home	56	136	34	9	2	5	15	21	16	15	1	0	.250
Road	41	98	22	4	1	5	11	14	8	15	2	0	.224
Grass	28	78	20	4	1	5	11	12	7	12	1	0	.256
Turf	69	156	36	9	2	5	15	23	17	18	2	0	.231

MIKE SMITHSON

	(W–L)	GS	Run	Avg	DP	Avg	SB	Avg
1984	(15-13)	36	145	4.03	26	.72	29	.81
1985	(15-14)	37	162	4.38	35	.95	30	.81
1982-1985		114	464	4.07	99	.87	93	.82

	G	IP	W	L	Pct	ER	BB	SO	ERA
1984 Home	16	116.0	7	5	.583	50	23	68	3.88
1985 Home	18	120.3	8	6	.571	58	37	66	4.34
1984 Road	20	136.0	8	8	.500	53	31	76	3.51
1985 Road	19	136.7	7	8	.467	66	41	61	4.35
1984 Grass	14	97.0	7	4	.636	32	20	48	2.97
1985 Grass	14	100.3	5	6	.455	45	33	42	4.04
1984 Turf	22	155.0	8	9	.471	71	16	36	4.12
1985 Turf	23	156.7	10	8	.556	79	45	85	4.54
1985 Total	37	257.0	15	14	.517	124	78	127	4.34

BERT BLYLEVEN

	(W–L)	GS	Run	Avg	DP	Avg	SB	Avg
1984	(19-7)	32	170	5.31	23	.72	19	.59
1985	(17-16)	28	150	5.36	29	1.04	35	1.25
1976-1985		273	1163	4.26	250	.92	231	.85

	G	IP	W	L	Pct	ER	BB	SO	ERA
1984 Home	17	122.7	10	2	.833	44	30	86	3.23
1985 Home	21	169.3	11	9	.550	55	37	126	2.92
1984 Road	16	122.3	9	5	.643	34	44	84	2.50
1985 Road	16	123.7	6	7	.462	48	38	80	3.49
1984 Grass	26	188.3	14	6	.700	64	59	128	3.06
1985 Grass	26	204.3	11	11	.500	72	52	145	3.17
1984 Turf	7	56.7	5	1	.833	14	33	66	2.22
1985 Turf	11	88.7	6	5	.545	31	23	61	3.15
1985 Total	37	293.0	17	16	.515	103	75	206	3.16

FRANK VIOLA

	(W–L)	GS	Run	Avg	DP	Avg	SB	Avg
1984	(18-12)	35	145	4.14	31	.89	13	.37
1985	(18-14)	36	148	4.11	30	.83	12	.33
1982-1985		127	540	4.25	118	.93	54	.43

	G	IP	W	L	Pct	ER	BB	SO	ERA
1984 Home	13	105.0	8	2	.800	28	29	75	2.40
1985 Home	17	124.7	9	6	.600	51	27	62	3.68
1984 Road	22	152.7	10	10	.500	64	44	74	3.77
1985 Road	19	126.0	9	8	.529	63	41	73	4.50
1984 Grass	19	131.7	9	9	.529	54	40	62	3.69
1985 Grass	13	88.7	8	4	.667	40	29	52	4.06
1984 Turf	16	126.0	9	4	.692	38	33	87	2.71
1985 Turf	23	162.0	10	10	.500	74	39	83	4.11
1985 Total	36	250.7	18	14	.562	114	68	135	4.09

KEN SCHROM

	(W–L)	GS	Run	Avg	DP	Avg	SB	Avg
1984	(5-11)	21	81	3.86	14	.67	9	.43
1985	(9-12)	26	104	4.00	25	.96	15	.58
1983-1985		75	307	4.09	60	.80	46	.61

	G	IP	W	L	Pct	ER	BB	SO	ERA
1984 Home	14	74.7	4	6	.400	32	17	23	3.86
1985 Home	19	108.0	7	7	.500	65	35	5	5.42
1984 Road	11	62.3	1	5	.167	36	24	26	5.20
1985 Road	10	52.7	2	5	.286	24	24	18	4.10
1984 Grass	8	51.0	1	4	.200	27	18	21	4.76
1985 Grass	8	40.7	2	4	.333	21	19	17	4.65
1984 Turf	17	86.0	4	7	.364	41	23	28	4.29
1985 Turf	21	120.0	7	8	.467	68	40	57	5.10
1985 Total	29	160.7	9	12	.429	89	59	74	4.99

JOHN BUTCHER

	(W–L)	GS	Run	Avg	DP	Avg	SB	Avg
1984	(13-11)	34	147	4.32	34	1.00	19	.56
1985	(11-14)	33	157	4.76	27	.82	19	.58
1980-1985		95	410	4.32	87	.92	49	.52

	G	IP	W	L	Pct	ER	BB	SO	ERA
1984 Home	21	134.7	8	6	.571	54	31	54	3.61
1985 Home	18	107.7	6	8	.429	67	23	54	5.60
1984 Road	13	90.3	5	5	.500	32	22	29	3.19
1985 Road	16	100.0	5	6	.455	48	20	38	4.32
1984 Grass	11	73.7	3	5	.375	31	19	24	3.79
1985 Grass	14	94.7	5	5	.500	36	19	35	3.42
1984 Turf	23	151.3	10	6	.625	55	34	59	3.27
1985 Turf	20	113.0	6	9	.400	79	24	57	6.29
1985 Total	34	207.7	11	14	.440	115	43	92	4.98

OTHERS

	(W–L)	GS	Run	Avg	DP	Avg	SB	Avg
Filson	(4-5)	6	27	4.50	2	.33	3	.50
Portugal	(1-3)	4	20	5.00	3	.75	2	.50
Burtt	(2-2)	2	10	5.00	1	.50	2	1.00
Klawitter	(0-0)	2	15	7.50	1	.50	0	0.00
Lysander	(0-2)	1	2	2.00	0	0.00	1	1.00
Yett	(0-0)	1	7	7.00	3	3.00	2	2.00

OAKLAND ATHLETICS

I haven't . . . how should I say this . . . I don't exactly have the greatest credibility at the moment with the A's fans. If I do, it's an oversight. My reviews of the A's over the last few seasons have not exactly been favorable, and what's more to the point, they haven't exactly been accurate, either. Last year, in reviewing the shortstop position, I opined that "if the A's make Alfredo Griffin their regular shortstop they will lose 100 games." The A's made Alfredo about as regular as you can be—he played 162 games at short—and didn't lose anywhere near 100 games. This isn't the only time I've been completely off-base in discussing the A's in recent years, but it's the most famous time, and in view of this I suppose I should just state up front that I really don't have any idea what the hell the A's are doing, but as long as it seems to be working, who am I to complain?

With that kind of an introduction, I can hardly launch into a serious lecture on the purposes and patterns of the organization, so I won't. Instead, I'll concentrate on listing various odd facts about the A's-trivia, you might call 'em, except that trivia has a certain focus which enables it to be retained, and nobody could remember this stuff; the cut-off ends of analyses that don't quite work, that is more like it.

Let's start with the A's leadoff men. A year ago the A's traded away the best leadoff man in major league history, and gave his jobs (leadoff man and left-fielder) to Dave Collins, who is . . . well, not the greatest leadoff man in major league history. Collins didn't work out as a leadoff hitter, and about half-way through the year, after some other experiments, the A's switched to Alfredo Griffin at leadoff.

Now whatever his virtues, Alfredo Griffin is *not* a leadoff man. Last year he walked 20 times and had an on-base percentage of .290, and that was considered an exceptional performance for him, seeing's how the previous year he walked four times and had no on-base percentage at all. So I thought I would check to see how the A's had done with various leadoff entrepreneurs:

Player	G	AB	Run	Hit	2B	3B	HR	RBI	BB	Avg
Collins	70	297	42	73	11	3	3	19	25	.246
Griffin	72	310	38	82	11	2	0	18	14	.265
S Henderson	17	60	9	18	3	1	0	5	0	.300
Murphy	6	21	3	4	1	1	1	5	0	.190
Substitutes	15	21	1	5	2	0	0	6	0	.235
Totals		709	93	182	28	7	4	53	39	.257

All of the players hit about as well as leadoff men as they did the rest of the time, so that this part of the exercise is not exceptionally instructive.

The A's benched Collins because they weren't happy with what he was giving them, and stayed with Griffin to the end of the season because the team went on a hot streak shortly after he took over—yet taken as a whole, the A's had a much better record when Collins was their leadoff man than when Griffin was. With Collins leading off, the A's scored 4.7 runs a game (321 in 69 starts) and had a won-lost record of 36–33. With Alfredo, they scored only 4.4 runs a game (320 in 72 starts) and had a record of 30–42, seven and a half games worse.

I happened to be in Oakland for the SABR convention at the time when the A's had decided that they just had to do something other than lead off Dave Collins—I agreed with them, as far as that went—and I was out there one day when the leadoff man was announced as Dwayne Murphy, the first time all season that Murphy had led off. Well, I figured, this makes sense; Murphy isn't hitting but he walks and he's a good baserunner. Maybe this is the role for him. The A's scored nine runs that day and blew away Milwaukee—but the next day, they led off Steve Henderson (scored three runs) and the day after that back to Collins (two runs).

On Sunday, the day the SABR convention went out to the game, Murphy batted leadoff again—and Oakland scored eleven runs. The All-Star break came before they played again, but the first game back Murphy led off, and the A's scored six runs.

Despite this, for the next four games the A's led off Henderson, Collins, Collins, and Henderson—and never scored more than five runs. Then they led off Murphy again; he homered, and the A's scored five runs. Dwayne led off again the next day, and the A's scored eleven runs.

That was the last time all year that Murphy led off. He led off five times, the A's were 4–1 and scored 42 runs in five games—and *I received three letters telling me about this stupid thing that Jackie Moore was doing, leading off Dwayne Murphy.*

Now, I'm just guessing, but if three people took the trouble to tell *me* that Jackie Moore shouldn't be leading off Dwayne Murphy, don't you figure about 300 must have told Jackie Moore this? In fact, to lead off Dwayne Murphy just makes all kind of sense, for, even having an off year, Murphy had a .340 on-base percentage, which is far better than Collins or Griffin, plus he's a good baserunner, plus the A's don't need his power in the middle of the order anyway, plus he's no kind of any RBI man anyhow. Leading off all year (730 Plate Appearances with his 1985 performance ratios) Murphy would have scored 105–110 runs—not great, but not Griffin.

Anyway, that was when the A's offense clicked. It wasn't *Alfredo* who got the A's offense rolling, at all—it was Murphy. So, as I see it:

1) The A's had a leadoff problem,
2) Jackie Moore figured out a possible solution that made perfect sense,
3) He tried it,
4) It couldn't possibly have worked any better, but
5) So many people said it was stupid that he had to stop it anyway.

So strong is the prejudice against using a low-average power hitter as a leadoff man that Moore eventually chose to do something which was *truly* stupid—leading off Alfredo—to doing something which *appeared* to be stupid. Amazing way to make a living, isn't it?

Well, I promised you no interpretations, and there I go again. Let's just start pitching random facts, the sillier the better:

• There were only 29 games in 1985 in which an Oakland leadoff man stole a base (39 stolen bases). In those 29 games, the A's leadoff man had (in addition to the 39 steals) a batting average of .423 (52/123) and 26 runs scored. In spite of this, the A's record in those games was just 16–13.

• There were 48 games in which the A's leadoff man was held hitless, going 0 for 206 in those games. The A's went 19–29 in those 48 contests, and scored 3.5 runs per game.

• There were 64 games in which the A's leadoff man had one hit; the A's went 27–37 and scored 4.5 runs per game in those conflagrations.

• There were 40 games in which the A's leadoff man had exactly two hits, hitting .480 in those emulations. The A's were 25–15, and scored 5.75 runs per game. (I don't know what an "emulation" is, either, but the thesaurus lists it as an alternative to "contest.")

• There were ten games in which the leadoff man had three or four hits. In those ten games, the A's went 6–4 but scored 70 runs.

• There were 89 games in which the A's leadoff man scored no runs (sounds like a bunch, don't it?). In those games, the A's were 28–61 and scored 317 runs, or 3.6 per game.

• In the 77 games that the A's won last year, they scored 516 runs.

• In the 85 games that they lost, they scored 241 runs.

• In the games that they won, Oakland leadoff men hit .286 and scored 68 runs.

• In the games that they lost, Oakland leadoff men hit .227 and scored 26 runs.

Wish I had walk data, but I did all this from the box scores. Dunno what any of it means, anyway, but I figure with a little luck I can get through the summer without being quoted in the Oakland newspapers. Based on recent history, that ought to be an improvement.

• Did you notice that over a ten-year period, the A's have the best record in the entire American League in the month of April—this based on 229 games, mind you—but almost the worst record in the majors in all the other months. Do you understand that?

• Over the last ten seasons the Oakland A's have the largest home-field advantage in the American League, having won 86 games more in Oakland than on the road.

• Over the last ten years, the Oakland A's pitchers have allowed more runs and more home runs, when not in their home park, than any other team.

• The A's in 1985 were a very good late-inning team, but a very poor early-inning team. They won six games in which they trailed entering the ninth, and fourteen games in which they trailed entering the seventh. (By contrast the division-champion Royals won only two games in which they trailed entering the ninth, and only six games in which they trailed entering the seventh.)

• Totals of ninth-inning rallies (leading to victory) for the entire league: Baltimore, 5, Boston, 6, California, 9, Chicago, 5, Cleveland, 3, Detroit, 4, Kansas City, 2, Milwaukee, 3, Minnesota, 5, New York, 8, Oakland, 6, Seattle, 3, Texas, 1, Toronto, 3.

• The A's were behind after one inning in 44 games, ahead in only 26 games (−18). After five innings they were behind in 86 games, ahead in only 64 (−22). On that basis, they did a heck of a job to finish only 8 games under .500.

• The A's were outscored by their opponents in the first inning, 91–65; they were also outscored in the second (90–86), third (86–82), fourth (111–83) and fifth (115–92), but rallied to outscore their opponents in the sixth (103–85), seventh (78–73), eighth (92–67) and ninth (65–53).

COMPLETE BATTING RECORDS

Player	G	AB	R	H	TB	2B	3B	HR	RBI	GW	SH	SF	HB	BB	IB	SO	SB	CS	GI DP	Avg	Slug	OBP	Runs	Outs Made	Runs/ 27 Outs	OW%	Appr Value
Heath	138	436	71	109	178	18	6	13	55	5	10	4	1	41	0	63	7	7	13	.250	.408	.313	53	361	3.98	.411	10
*Bochte	137	424	48	125	186	17	1	14	60	6	0	1	0	49	6	58	3	1	14	.295	.439	.367	67	315	5.73	.591	9
†Hill	123	393	45	112	138	13	2	3	48	2	16	4	0	23	2	33	8	4	8	.285	.351	.321	45	313	3.85	.394	6
Lansford	98	401	51	111	172	18	2	13	46	7	4	5	4	18	1	27	2	3	6	.277	.429	.311	53	308	4.61	.483	7
†Griffin	162	614	75	166	204	18	7	2	64	8	5	7	0	20	1	50	24	9	6	.270	.332	.290	60	475	3.43	.341	9
Baker	111	343	48	92	151	15	1	14	52	4	0	3	0	50	0	47	2	1	12	.268	.440	.359	54	267	5.49	.570	7
*Murphy	152	523	77	122	209	21	3	20	59	7	5	4	3	84	3	123	4	5	14	.233	.400	.340	73	429	4.59	.481	10
*Davis	154	547	92	157	265	34	1	24	82	8	3	2	2	50	8	99	24	10	10	.287	.484	.348	91	415	5.93	.608	11
Kingman	158	592	66	141	247	16	0	30	91	9	2	8	2	62	6	114	3	2	17	.238	.417	.309	75	480	4.22	.440	9
†Collins	112	379	52	95	131	16	4	4	29	6	5	4	1	29	2	37	29	8	6	.251	.346	.303	42	307	3.69	.375	5
†Tettleton	78	211	23	53	74	12	0	3	15	1	5	0	2	28	0	59	2	2	6	.251	.351	.344	26	171	4.11	.427	3
Henderson	85	193	25	58	81	8	3	3	31	4	1	1	0	18	0	34	0	0	10	.301	.420	.358	27	147	4.94	.518	3
†Phillips	42	161	23	45	73	12	2	4	17	2	3	1	0	13	0	34	3	2	1	.280	.453	.331	25	123	5.43	.565	2
Picciolo	71	102	19	28	33	2	0	1	8	0	0	0	0	2	0	17	3	2	1	.275	.324	.288	9	77	3.19	.310	1
Canseco	29	96	16	29	47	3	0	5	13	0	0	0	0	4	0	31	1	1	1	.302	.490	.330	15	69	5.89	.604	2
Gallego	76	77	13	16	26	5	1	1	9	1	2	1	1	12	0	14	1	1	2	.208	.338	.319	9	67	3.54	.356	1
Kiefer	40	66	8	13	19	1	1	1	10	1	2	2	0	1	0	18	0	0	1	.197	.288	.203	4	58	1.82	.127	0
*Meyer	14	12	2	0	0	0	0	0	0	0	0	0	0	0	0	0	0	0	1	.000	.000	.077	0	13	0.00	.000	0
O'Brien	16	11	3	3	4	1	0	0	1	0	0	0	0	3	0	3	0	0	0	.273	.364	.429	2	8	6.91	.678	0

*left-handed hitter, †switch hitter

DEFENSIVE STATISTICS

FIRST

	G	PO	A	Er	TC	DP	PCT.
Bochte	128	942	60	10	1012	83	.990
Baker	58	400	26	3	429	33	.993
Picciolo	13	19	4	0	23	2	1.000
Kingman	9	50	1	0	51	3	1.000
TEAM:	208	1411	91	13	1515	121	.991
AVG:	180	1440	123	14	1577	141	.991

SECOND

	G	PO	A	Er	TC	DP	PCT.
Hill	122	228	320	15	563	56	.973
Gallego	42	46	66	1	113	22	.991
Phillips	24	18	43	1	62	7	.984
Picciolo	17	27	39	2	68	7	.971
TEAM:	205	319	468	19	806	92	.976
AVG:	189	347	501	15	863	114	.982

THIRD

	G	PO	A	Er	TC	DP	PCT.
Lansford	97	85	119	5	209	11	.976
Kiefer	34	15	37	7	59	5	.881
Phillips	31	36	60	2	98	6	.980
Picciolo	19	6	18	3	27	2	.889
Heath	13	7	18	1	26	1	.962
Gallego	12	3	11	0	14	1	1.000
Meyer	1	0	0	0	0	0	.000
TEAM:	207	152	263	18	433	26	.958
AVG:	192	129	327	23	479	32	.953

SHORTSTOP

	G	PO	A	Er	TC	DP	PCT.
Griffin	162	278	440	30	748	87	.960
Gallego	21	8	17	0	25	2	1.000
Picciolo	9	4	5	0	9	1	1.000
TEAM:	192	290	462	30	782	90	.962
AVG:	189	269	474	28	771	104	.964

CATCHER

	G	PO	A	Er	TC	DP	PCT.	PB
Heath	112	483	44	10	537	9	.981	9
Tettleton	76	344	24	4	372	9	.989	10
O'Brien	16	23	0	1	24	0	.958	0
TEAM:	204	850	68	15	933	18	.984	19
AVG:	193	895	74	13	982	13	.987	13

OUTFIELD

	G	PO	A	Er	TC	DP	PCT.
Davis	151	370	6	8	384	1	.979
Murphy	150	432	6	5	443	1	.989
Collins	91	221	1	5	227	0	.978
Henderson	58	79	3	4	86	0	.953
Baker	35	65	3	2	70	0	.971
Heath	35	49	5	1	55	0	.982
Canseco	26	56	2	3	61	0	.951
Picciolo	2	0	0	0	0	0	.000
Meyer	1	1	0	0	1	0	1.000
TEAM:	549	1273	26	28	1327	3	.979
AVG:	559	1141	33	21	1196	8	.982

COMPLETE PITCHERS RECORDS

Pitcher	W	L	Pct	ERA	G	GS	CG	GF	SHO	SV	IP	H	TBF	R	ER	HR	SH	SF	HB	BB	IB	SO	WP	BK	Appr Value
											Starters (One-half of Game Appearances)														
Codiroli	14	14	.500	4.46	37	37	4	0	0	0	226.0	228	975	125	112	23	4	8	3	78	2	111	8	1	8
Sutton	13	8	.619	3.89	29	29	1	1	0	0	194.1	194	819	88	84	19	4	5	0	51	0	91	6	0	8
*Krueger	9	10	.474	4.52	32	23	2	4	0	0	151.1	165	674	95	76	13	1	5	2	69	1	56	6	2	6
*Birtsas	10	6	.625	4.01	29	25	2	4	0	0	141.1	124	624	72	63	18	4	5	3	91	0	94	6	0	6
Rijo	6	4	.600	3.53	12	9	0	1	0	0	63.2	70	272	26	25	6	5	0	1	28	2	65	0	0	3
*John	2	6	.250	6.19	11	11	0	0	0	0	48.0	66	221	37	33	6	2	1	1	13	0	8	2	0	0
											Relievers														
Atherton	4	7	.364	4.30	56	0	0	21	0	3	104.2	89	435	51	50	17	3	4	0	42	8	77	2	0	4
Howell	9	8	.529	2.85	63	0	0	58	0	29	98.0	98	414	32	31	5	3	4	1	31	3	68	4	1	13
McCatty	4	4	.500	5.57	30	9	1	8	0	0	85.2	95	383	56	53	10	3	3	4	41	4	36	1	0	1
Ontiveros	1	3	.250	1.93	39	0	0	18	0	8	74.2	45	284	17	16	4	2	2	2	19	2	36	1	0	5
Langford	3	5	.375	3.51	23	3	0	7	0	0	59.0	60	247	24	23	8	2	0	0	15	2	21	2	0	2
Warren	1	4	.200	6.61	16	6	0	2	0	0	49.0	52	243	42	36	13	0	2	4	38	0	48	3	1	0
Mura	1	1	.500	4.13	23	1	0	10	0	1	48.0	41	209	25	22	3	1	1	0	25	4	29	0	0	1
*Young	0	4	.000	7.24	19	7	0	5	0	0	46.0	57	214	38	37	15	0	1	1	22	0	19	1	0	0
*Conroy	0	1	.000	4.26	16	2	0	7	0	0	25.1	22	110	15	12	3	0	1	1	15	1	8	4	0	0
Tellmann	0	0	.000	5.06	11	0	0	3	0	0	21.1	33	106	12	12	3	0	1	1	9	1	8	0	0	0
*Kaiser	0	0	.000	14.58	15	0	0	4	0	0	16.2	25	97	32	27	6	1	2	1	20	2	10	2	0	0

Mike HEATH, Catcher

	G	AB	Hit	2B	3B	HR	Run	RBI	TBB	SO	SB	CS	Avg
4.67 years		541	135	22	4	10	61	62	35	69	7	5	.250
1985	138	436	109	18	6	13	71	55	41	63	7	7	.250
First Half	73	245	61	6	4	8	33	32	22	35	5	5	.249
Second Half	65	191	48	12	2	5	38	23	19	28	2	2	.251
Vs. RHP		287	66	8	3	8	46	33	27	40	4	7	.230
Vs.LHP		149	43	10	3	5	25	22	14	23	3	0	.289
Home	68	209	51	8	1	8	28	31	17	26	2	2	.244
Road	70	227	58	10	5	5	43	24	24	37	5	5	.256
Grass	112	345	88	12	3	12	55	44	32	47	6	5	.255
Turf	26	91	21	6	3	1	16	11	9	16	1	2	.231

Dusty BAKER, Left Field

	G	AB	Hit	2B	3B	HR	Run	RBI	TBB	SO	SB	CS	Avg
12.07 years		569	159	26	2	20	78	82	61	74	11	6	.280
1985	111	343	92	15	1	14	48	52	50	47	2	1	.268
First Half	52	159	47	5	1	10	26	35	23	23	1	0	.296
Second Half	59	184	45	10	0	4	22	17	27	24	1	1	.245
Vs. RHP		198	55	9	1	9	29	35	26	26	0	1	.278
Vs. LHP		145	37	6	0	5	19	17	24	21	2	0	.255
Home	52	161	40	5	1	5	24	19	22	21	1	0	.248
Road	59	182	52	10	0	9	24	33	28	26	1	1	.286
Grass	94	290	76	12	1	11	39	37	39	42	2	0	.262
Turf	17	53	16	3	0	3	9	15	11	5	0	1	.302

Bruce BOCHTE, First Base

	G	AB	Hit	2B	3B	HR	Run	RBI	TBB	SO	SB	CS	Avg
8.72 years		553	157	27	2	11	67	71	67	68	5	4	.284
1985	137	424	125	17	1	14	48	60	49	58	3	1	.295
First Half	68	190	61	9	0	4	21	24	21	20	1	1	.321
Second Half	69	234	64	8	1	10	27	36	28	38	2	0	.274
Vs. RHP		375	109	16	1	10	38	51	39	48	3	1	.291
Vs. LHP		49	16	1	0	4	10	9	10	10	0	0	.327
Home	68	204	64	13	0	6	25	28	21	26	2	0	.314
Road	69	220	61	4	1	8	23	32	28	32	1	1	.277
Grass	114	350	108	17	1	11	38	49	39	45	3	1	.309
Turf	23	74	17	0	0	3	10	11	10	13	0	0	.230

Dwayne MURPHY, Center Field

	G	AB	Hit	2B	3B	HR	Run	RBI	TBB	SO	SB	CS	Avg
6.38 years		549	136	17	3	21	82	77	91	116	14	8	.247
1985	152	523	122	21	3	20	77	59	84	123	4	5	.233
First Half	79	266	58	11	0	12	44	24	50	59	3	2	.218
Second Half	73	257	64	10	3	8	33	35	34	64	1	3	.249
Vs. RHP		374	90	16	2	13	53	42	64	85	3	4	.241
Vs. LHP		149	32	5	1	7	24	17	20	38	1	1	.215
Home	72	242	52	12	1	5	32	18	39	54	3	3	.215
Road	80	281	70	9	2	15	45	41	45	69	1	2	.249
Grass	125	424	97	15	3	18	61	50	71	100	4	4	.229
Turf	27	99	25	6	0	2	16	9	13	23	0	1	.253

Donnie HILL, Second Base

	G	AB	Hit	2B	3B	HR	Run	RBI	TBB	SO	SB	CS	Avg
1.54 years		472	126	17	1	5	56	51	21	43	7	4	.268
1985	123	393	112	13	2	3	45	48	23	33	8	4	.285
First Half	77	237	57	3	2	2	25	25	14	22	3	2	.241
Second Half	46	156	55	10	0	1	20	23	9	11	5	2	.353
Vs. RHP		309	91	10	2	3	33	39	15	22	7	4	.294
Vs. LHP		84	21	3	0	0	12	9	8	11	1	0	.250
Home	62	190	51	6	2	0	17	18	12	17	5	1	.268
Road	61	203	61	7	0	3	28	30	11	16	3	3	.300
Grass	99	314	84	8	2	0	33	34	20	27	8	1	.268
Turf	24	79	28	5	0	3	12	14	3	6	0	3	.354

Mike DAVIS, Right Field

	G	AB	Hit	2B	3B	HR	Run	RBI	TBB	SO	SB	CS	Avg
3.13 years		499	134	27	3	14	71	66	38	85	24	12	.268
1985	154	547	157	34	1	24	92	82	50	99	24	10	.287
First Half	78	283	85	18	0	14	54	46	31	48	15	5	.300
Second Half	76	264	72	16	1	10	38	36	19	51	9	5	.273
Vs. RHP		392	114	26	0	16	59	54	35	63	17	9	.291
Vs. LHP		155	43	8	1	8	33	28	15	36	7	1	.277
Home	74	246	68	15	1	12	38	39	27	46	9	6	.276
Road	80	301	89	19	0	12	54	43	23	53	15	4	.296
Grass	126	447	128	26	1	19	76	66	44	80	19	9	.286
Turf	28	100	29	8	0	5	16	16	6	19	5	1	.290

Carney LANSFORD, Third Base

	G	AB	Hit	2B	3B	HR	Run	RBI	TBB	SO	SB	CS	Avg
6.10 years		637	187	32	4	15	91	81	46	78	15	8	.293
1985	98	401	111	18	2	13	51	46	18	27	2	3	.277
First Half	80	330	90	15	1	12	44	40	16	21	2	2	.273
Second Half	18	71	21	3	1	1	7	6	2	6	0	1	.296
Vs. RHP		271	80	13	1	10	36	33	12	20	2	3	.295
Vs. LHP		130	31	5	1	3	15	13	6	7	0	0	.238
Home	49	205	62	10	1	7	30	26	6	11	1	3	.302
Road	49	196	49	8	1	6	21	20	12	16	1	0	.250
Grass	82	338	94	13	1	13	50	42	14	21	2	3	.278
Turf	16	63	17	5	1	0	1	4	4	6	0	0	.270

Dave KINGMAN, Designated Hitter

	G	AB	Hit	2B	3B	HR	Run	RBI	TBB	SO	SB	CS	Avg
11.09 years		551	131	20	2	37	75	101	52	152	7	4	.238
1985	158	592	141	16	0	30	66	91	62	114	3	2	.238
First Half	82	314	80	9	0	21	37	53	33	61	3	0	.255
Second Half	76	278	61	7	0	9	29	38	29	53	0	2	.219
Vs. RHP		416	98	12	0	17	46	54	39	82	2	1	.236
Vs. LHP		176	43	4	0	13	20	37	23	32	1	1	.244
Home	77	278	62	10	0	14	32	42	35	58	3	2	.223
Road	81	314	79	6	0	16	34	49	27	56	0	0	.252
Grass	130	481	113	14	0	26	53	81	56	94	3	2	.235
Turf	28	111	28	2	0	4	13	10	6	20	0	0	.252

Alfredo GRIFFIN, Shortstop

	G	AB	Hit	2B	3B	HR	Run	RBI	TBB	SO	SB	CS	Avg
6.58 years		580	146	21	9	2	65	43	24	51	16	13	.253
1985	162	614	166	18	7	2	75	64	20	50	24	9	.270
First Half	82	289	79	7	3	2	32	41	13	25	11	2	.273
Second Half	80	325	87	11	4	0	43	23	7	25	13	7	.268
Vs. RHP		424	104	11	4	1	46	39	16	42	17	6	.245
Vs. LHP		190	62	7	3	1	29	25	4	8	7	3	.326
Home	79	292	75	6	3	0	32	33	10	26	11	2	.257
Road	83	322	91	12	4	2	43	31	10	24	13	7	.283
Grass	134	515	141	16	5	2	61	57	18	45	22	7	.274
Turf	28	99	25	2	2	0	14	7	2	5	2	2	.253

Dave COLLINS, Outfield

	G	AB	Hit	2B	3B	HR	Run	RBI	TBB	SO	SB	CS	Avg
7.68 years		529	146	20	6	4	74	41	49	71	45	16	.275
1985	112	379	95	16	4	4	52	29	29	37	29	8	.251
First Half	68	282	69	11	3	2	41	17	18	26	25	6	.245
Second Half	44	97	26	5	1	2	11	12	11	11	4	2	.268
Vs. RHP		294	76	12	4	3	43	22	24	31	21	7	.259
Vs. LHP		85	19	4	0	1	9	7	5	6	8	1	.224
Home	55	190	44	5	1	1	28	9	18	20	16	4	.232
Road	57	189	51	11	3	3	24	20	11	17	13	4	.270
Grass	95	319	80	13	3	3	48	23	26	35	26	7	.251
Turf	17	60	15	3	1	1	4	6	3	2	3	1	.250

CHRIS CODIROLI

	(W–L)	GS	Run	Avg	DP	Avg	SB	Avg
1984	(6-4)	14	66	4.71	11	.79	7	.50
1985	(14-14)	37	177	4.78	29	.78	19	.51
1982-1985		85	393	4.62	71	.84	43	.51

	G	IP	W	L	Pct	ER	BB	SO	ERA
1984 Home	16	39.0	3	3	.500	29	19	15	6.69
1985 Home	17	110.0	9	4	.692	44	43	52	3.60
1984 Road	12	50.3	3	1	.750	29	15	29	5.19
1985 Road	20	116.0	5	10	.333	68	35	59	5.28
1984 Grass	24	72.0	5	3	.625	47	30	32	5.88
1985 Grass	31	187.7	12	11	.522	92	69	90	4.41
1984 Turf	4	17.3	1	1	.500	11	4	12	5.71
1985 Turf	6	38.3	2	3	.400	20	9	21	4.70
1985 Total	37	226.0	14	14	.500	112	78	111	4.46

BILL KRUEGER

	(W–L)	GS	Run	Avg	DP	Avg	SB	Avg
1984	(10-10)	24	118	4.92	32	1.33	28	1.17
1985	(9-10)	23	127	5.52	25	1.09	18	.78
1983-1985		63	323	5.13	75	1.19	52	.83

	G	IP	W	L	Pct	ER	BB	SO	ERA
1984 Home	12	78.7	7	3	.700	32	38	25	3.66
1985 Home	15	79.0	4	6	.400	40	40	32	4.56
1984 Road	14	63.3	3	7	.300	43	47	36	6.11
1985 Road	17	72.3	5	4	.556	36	29	24	4.48
1984 Grass	23	134.7	10	7	.588	60	81	56	4.01
1985 Grass	26	128.3	9	8	.529	65	61	48	4.56
1984 Turf	3	7.3	0	3	0.000	15	4	5	18.41
1985 Turf	6	23.0	0	2	0.000	11	8	8	4.30
1985 Total	32	151.3	9	10	.474	76	69	56	4.52

TIM BIRTSAS

	(W–L)	GS	Run	Avg	DP	Avg	SB	Avg
1985	(10-6)	25	118	4.72	25	1.00	19	.76

	G	IP	W	L	Pct	ER	BB	SO	ERA
1985 Home	14	68.3	4	2	.667	24	39	46	3.16
1985 Road	15	73.0	6	4	.600	39	52	48	4.81
1985 Grass	25	122.0	8	6	.571	56	80	77	4.13
1985 Turf	4	19.3	2	0	1.000	7	11	17	3.26
1985 Total	29	141.3	10	6	.625	63	91	94	4.01

OTHERS

	(W–L)	GS	Run	Avg	DP	Avg	SB	Avg
John	(2-6)	11	34	3.09	8	.73	7	.64
McCatty	(4-4)	9	55	6.11	4	.44	8	.89
Rijo	(6-4)	9	33	3.67	2	.22	6	.67
Young	(0-4)	7	34	4.86	6	.86	1	.14
Warren	(1-4)	6	25	4.17	8	1.33	4	.67
Langford	(3-5)	3	8	2.67	3	1.00	1	.33
Conroy	(0-1)	2	6	3.00	5	2.50	1	.50
Mura	(1-1)	1	3	3.00	0	0.00	1	1.00

SEATTLE MARINERS

If Dick Williams were managing the Seattle Mariners in 1986, they would win the American League's Western Division. I don't mean this in any sense as a knock at Chuck Cottier, who so far as I know hasn't hurt the team any, but the Mariners in the last few years have gone through a period, such as the Tigers had in 1976–79, the Braves had about the same time and the KC-Oakland A's had in the late sixties, of bringing up a large number of talented players. I've no way to predict how long it will take to turn the collection of talented young kids into a winning team; Dick Williams can do it overnight, and Whitey Herzog, too, has that ability. More often it takes a period of several years. How many are there . . . Calderon, Presley, Davis, Bradley, Owen, Tartabull, Moore, Young, Best, Nunez. Some pretty fair prospects, like Darnell Coles, and some decent ballplayers, like Dave Henderson and possibly Spike Owen, are getting pushed out of the picture. One gets the feeling that somewhere between one and three of these kids is going to turn out to be a Hall of Famer, but who can tell which ones?

Seattle, welcome to the major leagues. Sorry it took so long.

At the end of last season, I received in the mail one of the best, if not the best, detailed report that I have ever seen of a team's performance in various, usually uncharted, categories. The Mariner version of *Project Scoresheet* was accomplished by Steve Russell, Dennis Orr and Jeff Welch with great enthusiasm, and Jeff compiled a magnificent report on the effort. Let me share with you some of his findings here, and some more during the comments re the appropriate players. Without studying his scoresheets and duplicating the results, I have no way of knowing how accurate his material is, except that there are a few notes scattered around which can be checked with other sources which were not available to him, and in those areas I found no errors.

1) Jeff compiled a complete listing of the Mariners' and opponents' baserunning errors during the season, similar to that offered for the Texas Rangers in the 1984 *Abstract*. I will present it here in its entirety:

Seattle

Doubled off base on line drive or fly	11
Thrown out at home from second on single	10
Picked off first by pitcher	10
Thrown out trying to score on fly	6
Thrown out trying to stretch a hit	5
Rounded base too far and tagged out	3
Trying to go first to third on single	2
Out at home on double	2
Out at second trying to advance on throw	2
Hit to outfield and runner forced at second	2*
Picked off 2nd by pitcher	1
Caught off first by cut-off man	1
Thrown out by LF after wild throw by catcher	1
Total	56

*Twice Davis was forced at 2nd on hits to left by Thomas. Jeff listed these as baserunning errors.

Opponents

Picked off first by pitcher	19
Doubled off base on line drive or fly	16
Thrown out trying to stretch a hit	7
Out trying to score from second on single	6
Out trying to advance on a fly	5
Out at second after throw to another base	4
Catcher picked runner off first	4
Catcher picked runner off second	3
Out trying to go 1st/3rd on a single	3
Picked off second by pitcher	2
Thrown out at home on a double	1
Out trying to go 1st/3rd on a groundout	1
Out at plate after 6–3 putout	1
Out going 3rd/Home after single trapped in CF	1
Runner failed to score after being sent back to third on baserunner interference	1
Total	74

Jeff had marked this last occurrence with an asterisk, wondering if it should be scored as a baserunning error. Clearly, it should not according to the definition I offered in the earlier analysis—any occurrence in which a runner voluntarily surrenders a base he has safely occupied, resulting in a lost baserunner without a caught stealing being charged. The Mariners in this instance lost a base and, as it turns out, a run—but they did not lose the baserunner.

Jeff did not follow the definition strictly. The fact that Alvin Davis fell victim of a 7–4 forceout twice is certainly an interesting tidbit of descriptive information, but it seems clear to me that it should not be scored a baserunning error. It doesn't fit the description (Davis never occupied second base), and it wouldn't seem to be the type of thing that is usually suggested by the word "error," which implies a failure of concentration or judgment rather than exceptional slowness of foot. He also included runners picked off base as baserunning errors, although most were actually also charged with being caught stealing. I had not included these in the definition to prevent a kind of statistical double jeopardy.

In the original analysis I found that the Rangers had made 48 baserunning errors during the 1983 season, and suggested that this was almost certainly a below-average total. Apparently, this may not be so. Eliminating the runners picked off/caught stealing and the occurrences discussed above, the Mariners would have 44 baserunning errors on the season, their opponents 45 to 52. I am surprised to learn that the figures are so low, but then that's why we study these things.

I am particularly surprised that so few runners are thrown out during a season attempting to stretch a hit— only 5 for the Mariners, 7 for their opponents and 4 for the Rangers in 1983. In 1977, when Hal McRae had 86 extra base hits, I would bet that he was thrown out stretching about 30 times. Seemed like more than that.

This implies, anyway, that hitters don't try to take second on a hit unless they are . . . what, 98.5% sure of making it. The Mariners hit 277 doubles last year, and (according to Welch) had no more than 5 runners thrown out trying to stretch a single. Doesn't that seem strange? Why

are teams so reluctant to challenge outfielders' arms, when they will try to steal second base with no more than a 60% chance of making it.

2) Jim Presley led the Mariners with 8 baserunning errors. In view of the facts that Presley was in his first full season and grounded into 29 double plays, this is not especially surprising. Al Cowens and Dave Henderson committed the fewest errors among Mariner regulars, three apiece.

3) When a Mariner runner was on first base and a single was hit, the runner went to third 24% of the time (67/279). This figure is quite a bit lower than that for the Rangers in the earlier study (33%), the reasons for which we will discuss in a moment. The most successful at going first-to-third on a single was Calderon, doing so 6 of 10 times, followed by Bradley (11/27, 41%), Owen (6/16, 38%), Thomas (10/32, 31%), Cowens (3/11, 27%), Perconte (6/24, 25%), Henderson (6/30, 20%), Kearney (4/21, 19%), Presley (4/27, 15%) and Alvin Davis (5/35, 14%). Cowens and Presley were the only Mariners thrown out attempting to do this.

The low figure for going first-to-third probably reflects two factors other than the lack of speed on the team. One is the small dimensions of the park (that is, the outfielders, with less room behind them, set up closer to the plate and are better able to prevent a runner from going first-to-third). Also, the Mariners were primarily a right-handed hitting team, and had only 63 singles to right field with a runner on first, whereas the Rangers in 1983 had 98 such singles. This also affects the individual totals— that is, the fact that Gorman Thomas was able to go from first to third 31% of the time, and Jack Perconte only 25% of the time, is almost wholly attributable to the fact that Thomas usually had the only left-handed pull hitter in the lineup (Davis) coming up behind him, and hence had twelve chances to go first-to-third on a single to right field, whereas Perconte had only four.

But the percentages are lower for all three fields. Whereas the Rangers went from first to third on a single to left 18% of the time, the Mariners did so only 10%. Whereas the Rangers (in 1983) went from first to third on a single to center 31% of the time, the Mariners did so 30%. And whereas the Ranger runners went from first to third on singles to right field 50% of the time, the Mariners did so only 37% of the time (24/63).

4) Grounding into a double play is counted as part of the traditional statistics, but the point of a double play is that it has two parts. The other part, being erased as the front man on a DP, is not counted. Welch's study shows that Alvin Davis was erased as the lead man in a DP 25 times, and Phil Bradley 19 times, most on the Mariners. The Davis-Presley combination was the most costly on the team in this respect, with neither runner being fast enough to prevent the play. Jack Perconte, often on base leading off an inning, was the lead man on only 11 double plays, and Bob Kearney, surprisingly, on only 3.

5) Ed VandeBerg received a ground-ball double play behind him once for every 6.1 innings of pitching, best on the Mariner team. Frank Wills received the help of only 8 GIDP on the season, one every 15.4 innings, lowest on the team.

6) There are a variety of facts which show that the

young Mariners did not do a particularly good job of moving along baserunners. There were 486 times during the 1985 season (3 per game) in which a Mariner runner reached base leading off an inning. The Mariners were able to score only 218 of those runners, or 45%. By contrast, Mariners opponents had fewer batters reaching leading off an inning (477) but scored 254 of those runners, or 53%.

This difference was particularly marked among runners reaching first base only. The Mariners had 113 leadoff walks, scoring 42 of those (37%). They had 224 leadoff singles, and scored 82 of those (also 37%). They had 22 runners reaching at the start of an inning by error, hit by pitch or K + WP; 7 of the 22, or 32% scored. All together, that makes 359 reaching first base at the start of an inning, 132 of whom scored, for 37%.

By contrast, their opponents scored 52% of leadoff walks (68/132), 42% of leadoff singles (94/226), and 56% of the miscellaneous leadoff men who reached first base (9/16).

The Mariners also had 411 situations in which they had a runner on second with no one out or on third with less than two out. They scored only 250, or 61%, of those runners. Their opponents scored 322 of 459 in this situation, or 70%.

7) Mariner leadoff men hit a dismal .231 on the season, drew a respectable total of 76 walks but scored only 82 runs. Jack Perconte hit .262 batting leadoff—all of his at bats except one were in the position—but other Mariner leadoff men were 28 for 188—a .149 average. It would be particularly enlightening to know what the thinking was behind giving Domingo Ramos 127 plate appearances in the leadoff spot. Ramos is a career .215 hitter who did not steal a base in 1985 and has no particular tendency to walk.

When batting first and actually leading off the inning, Perconte hit .268 (52/194) and drew 19 walks for a decent .336 on-base percentage; other Mariner rally-starters hit .133 (10/75) and were on base only 22.6% of the time. Other Mariner leadoff men included Harold Reynolds and Spike Owen in limited roles.

There were 27 games during the season when the Mariners scored their leadoff man in the first inning; the team was 19–8 in those 27 games.

8) With Mike Moore starting, the Mariners in 1985 were 9–4 when they scored three to five runs, whereas with other pitchers starting they were 14–35, and no better than 4–7 with any other pitcher. Here, I'll present that entire chart, which I think makes an effective point, that being that within normal ranges of performance the test of a big-league pitcher is his ability to win with 3–5 runs, since nobody wins with less than that and everybody wins with more than that. This chart actually includes the team's record in all of the pitcher's starts, rather than just his own record:

Runs Scored By Mariners

	0–2	3–5	6+	Total
Young	3–8	4–11	8–1	15–20
Moore	0–10	9–4	10–1	19–15
Langston	0–7	4–7	6–0	10–14
Swift	2–7	2–3	7–0	11–10

Runs Scored By Mariners

	0–2	3–5	6+	Total
Wills	1–4	2–6	4–1	7–11
Others	0–7	2–8	10–3	12–18
Total	6–43	23–39	45–6	74–88

9) The Mariners did well in short games. They were 27–24 (.529) in games played in 2 hours, 39 minutes or less, whereas they were 47–64 (.423) in games lasting 2 hours, 40 minutes or more, and 17–40 (.298) in games lasting 2:40 to 2:59.

10) Stats contained in the catcher's section show that the Mariners played their best ball when Donnie Scott was their starting catcher, played less well with Bob Kearney and worst with Dave Valle. More detailed stats compiled by Welch confirm this, but also show that the Mariner pitchers had markedly better control with Valle catching than with the others. With Valle catching, Mariner pitchers walked only 61 men in 179 innings (3.07 per nine innings), as compared to 4.04 with Scott and 4.19 with Kearney. However, with Valle catching Mariner pitchers had slightly fewer strikeouts, allowed markedly more hits (9.75 per nine innings, as opposed to 9.1 for Kearney and 9.0 for Scott) and allowed a horrific rate of runs (120 in 179 innings, 6.03 per nine innings). There have been published reports that the Mariner pitchers are not enthralled with Valle's pitch selection.

11) Two Mariner pitchers allowed about one-half of their runs with two out in the inning; other pitchers allowed many fewer. Matt Young allowed 67 runs to score with two men out in the inning, essentially one-half of his runs (67/135); Mark Langston the same (43/85). On the other hand, Mike Moore allowed only 39% of his runs with two out (39/100), Billy Swift just over 40% and Frank Wills, if this isn't a misprint, only 22 of 85, or 26%.

12) Jeff did a fascinating series of breakdowns of the conditions under which the Mariners issued and received intentional walks. The Mariners in 1985 *received* 36 intentional walks, and *issued* 54. What were the factors which accounted for this difference? Look at these two breakdowns:

Number of Men Out:	0	1	2
Issued	2	18	34
Received	3	22	11

Set Up Platoon Advantage?	Yes	No
Issued	40	14
Received	19	17

While it is of course an over-simplification, it would appear to be true that the essential difference was that Cottier would use the intentional walk to try to get out of an inning with a platoon advantage, whereas his opponents rarely issued an intentional walk for only this advantage. When he was behind in the game:

Team issuing walk	Ahead	Tied	Behind
Issued	2	12	40
Received	3	20	13

Following the intentional walk, batters faced by the Mariners went just 9-for-42 but drove in 25 runs, aided by a large number of RBI-on-outs. Among the 54 occasions, the Mariners got out of the inning without an additional run scoring 32 times, which ain't exactly a great record when you consider that they were issuing a lot of these walks with two out. The other 22 times (when their opponents scored) they scored the rather scary number of 64 runs, including 14 times when the runner who was walked subsequently scored. Those 64 runs are 8% of their total runs allowed on the season.

For the Mariners, hitters up following the intentional walk went just 6-for-27 but drove in 12 runs. In the 36 cases, the Mariners subsequently scored 18 times and did not score 18 times. In the 18 times when they did score, they scored 38 runs, so that the rate of runs scored after an IBB was essentially similar for and against the team (64/54 against the Mariners, 38/36 for them). There were only five Mariners who scored after receiving an intentional walk.

13) Making a few estimates to cover just a handful of missing games, Jeff estimates that Mariner pitchers threw 22,903 pitches in 1985; their opponents threw 23,494. Mark Langston required 18.3 pitches to work the average inning, most on the team. Roy Thomas required only 14.6, fewest on the team.

All of the Mariner pitchers except Mark Langston threw almost exactly the same number of pitches per batter, all between 3.53 and 3.69. Langston threw 4.02 pitches per batter faced.

13) Not counting intentional walks, Alvin Davis had sixty (60) 3–0 counts in 1985. Al Cowens had only 16.

14) The Mariners in 1985 were 5–20 in games umpired by Durwood Merrill, 0–6 when Merrill was the home-plate ump. On the other hand, they were 16–6 when John Shulock was on the umpiring crew, 5–0 with Shulock behind the plate.

COMPLETE BATTING RECORDS

Player	G	AB	R	H	TB	2B	3B	HR	RBI	GW	SH	SF	HB	BB	IB	SO	SB	CS	GI DP	Avg	Slug	OBP	Runs	Outs Made	Runs/ 27 Outs	OW%	Appr Value
Kearney	108	305	24	74	108	14	1	6	27	4	5	1	4	11	1	59	1	1	7	.243	.354	.277	29	245	3.16	.307	5
*Davis	155	578	78	166	255	33	1	18	78	7	0	7	2	90	7	71	1	2	14	.287	.441	.381	101	435	6.24	.634	12
*Perconte	125	485	60	128	165	17	7	2	23	2	2	2	3	50	0	36	31	6	9	.264	.340	.335	62	372	4.48	.472	10
Presley	155	570	71	157	276	33	1	28	84	6	1	9	1	44	9	100	2	2	29	.275	.484	.324	80	454	4.74	.500	11
†Owen	118	352	41	91	131	10	6	6	37	3	5	2	0	34	0	27	11	5	5	.259	.372	.322	44	278	4.24	.444	6
Bradley	159	641	100	192	319	33	8	26	88	12	4	2	12	55	4	129	22	9	14	.300	.498	.365	116	478	6.53	.655	14
Henderson	139	502	70	121	195	28	2	14	68	7	1	2	3	48	2	104	6	1	11	.241	.388	.310	61	396	4.17	.436	8
Cowens	122	452	59	120	204	32	5	14	69	5	0	4	1	30	3	56	0	0	23	.265	.451	.310	56	359	4.22	.441	7
Thomas	135	484	76	104	218	16	1	32	87	10	2	3	1	84	6	126	3	2	11	.215	.450	.330	74	398	5.05	.531	9
Calderon	67	210	37	60	108	16	4	8	28	2	1	1	2	19	1	45	4	2	10	.286	.514	.349	34	164	5.67	.588	4
†Scott	80	185	18	41	66	13	0	4	23	4	1	4	0	15	0	41	1	1	3	.222	.357	.275	19	153	3.27	.322	1
Ramos	75	168	19	33	42	6	0	1	15	2	3	2	0	17	0	23	0	1	4	.196	.250	.267	12	145	2.16	.172	1
*Phelps	61	116	18	24	54	3	0	9	24	3	0	0	0	24	2	33	2	0	1	.207	.466	.343	20	93	5.92	.609	3
Bonnell	48	111	9	27	38	8	0	1	10	1	0	0	0	6	1	19	1	2	1	.243	.342	.282	10	87	3.17	.309	1
†Reynolds	67	104	15	15	20	3	1	0	6	0	1	0	0	17	0	14	3	2	0	.144	.192	.264	7	92	1.91	.140	1
Valle	31	70	2	11	12	1	0	0	4	0	1	0	1	1	0	17	0	0	1	.157	.171	.181	2	61	0.95	.038	0
†Moses	33	62	4	12	12	0	0	0	3	0	1	0	0	2	0	8	5	2	3	.194	.194	.219	2	56	1.04	.046	0
Tartabull	19	61	8	20	32	7	1	1	7	0	0	0	0	8	0	14	1	0	1	.328	.525	.406	14	42	8.70	.771	1
Coles	27	59	8	14	21	4	0	1	5	1	0	2	1	9	0	17	0	1	0	.237	.356	.338	8	48	4.49	.473	1
*Chambers	4	4	0	0	0	0	0	0	0	0	0	0	0	0	0	2	0	0	0	.000	.000	.000	0	4	0.00	.000	0
*Nelson	6	2	2	0	0	0	0	0	0	0	0	0	0	0	0	1	0	0	0	.000	.000	.000	0	2	0.00	.000	0

*left-handed hitter, †switch hitter

DEFENSIVE STATISTICS

FIRST	G	PO	A	Er	TC	DP	PCT.
Davis	154	1438	103	13	1554	131	.992
Ramos	14	15	0	0	15	1	1.000
Phelps	8	31	2	0	33	5	1.000
Bonnell	5	23	0	0	23	3	1.000
Calderon	2	8	0	0	8	1	1.000
TEAM:	183	1515	105	13	1633	141	.992
AVG:	180	1440	123	14	1577	141	.991

SECOND	G	PO	A	Er	TC	DP	PCT.
Perconte	125	244	381	9	634	91	.986
Reynolds	61	69	123	8	200	22	.960
Ramos	20	25	36	3	64	9	.953
TEAM:	206	338	540	20	898	122	.978
AVG:	189	347	501	15	863	114	.982

THIRD	G	PO	A	Er	TC	DP	PCT.
Presley	154	82	335	17	434	24	.961
Coles	7	2	7	1	10	0	.900
Ramos	7	3	10	1	14	1	.929
Tartabull	4	2	6	0	8	0	1.000
TEAM:	172	89	358	19	466	25	.959
AVG:	192	129	327	23	479	32	.953

SHORTSTOP	G	PO	A	Er	TC	DP	PCT.
Owen	117	196	361	14	571	76	.975
Ramos	36	44	73	6	123	15	.951
Tartabull	16	26	37	4	67	11	.940
Coles	15	19	37	5	61	10	.918
TEAM:	184	285	508	29	822	112	.965
AVG:	189	269	474	28	771	104	.964

CATCHER	G	PO	A	Er	TC	DP	PCT.	PB
Kearney	108	529	50	3	582	7	.995	11
Scott	74	277	31	6	314	1	.981	11
Valle	31	117	7	3	127	0	.976	0
TEAM:	213	923	88	12	1023	8	.988	22
AVG:	193	895	74	13	982	13	.987	13

OUTFIELD	G	PO	A	Er	TC	DP	PCT.
Bradley	159	336	10	5	351	3	.986
Henderson	138	335	8	5	348	3	.986
Cowens	110	198	10	7	215	2	.967
Calderon	53	100	5	2	107	2	.981
Moses	29	35	1	0	36	0	1.000
Bonnell	22	38	2	1	41	0	.976
Nelson	3	1	0	0	1	0	1.000
Coles	2	4	0	0	4	0	1.000
TEAM:	516	1047	36	20	1103	10	.982
AVG:	559	1141	33	21	1196	8	.982

COMPLETE PITCHERS RECORDS

Pitcher	W	L	Pct	ERA	G	GS	CG	GF	SHO	SV	IP	H	TBF	R	ER	HR	SH	SF	HB	BB	IB	SO	WP	BK	Appr Value
								Starters (One-half of Game Appearances)																	
Moore	17	10	.630	3.46	35	34	14	1	2	0	247.0	230	1016	100	95	18	2	7	4	70	2	155	10	3	13
*Young	12	19	.387	4.91	37	35	5	2	2	1	218.1	242	951	135	119	23	7	3	7	76	3	136	6	2	7
*Langston	7	14	.333	5.47	24	24	2	0	0	0	126.2	122	577	85	77	22	3	2	2	91	2	72	3	3	1
Wills	5	11	.313	6.00	24	18	1	2	0	0	123.0	122	541	85	82	18	4	8	3	68	3	67	9	1	1
Swift	6	10	.375	4.77	23	21	0	0	0	0	120.2	131	532	71	64	8	6	3	5	48	5	55	5	3	2
Beattie	5	6	.455	7.29	18	15	1	1	1	0	70.1	93	335	61	57	9	0	5	3	33	0	45	2	0	0
Morgan	1	1	.500	12.00	2	2	0	0	0	0	6.0	11	33	8	8	2	0	0	0	5	0	2	1	0	0
*Wilkinson	0	2	.000	13.50	2	2	0	0	0	0	6.0	8	30	9	9	2	0	0	0	6	1	5	0	0	0
Lewis	0	1	.000	7.71	2	1	0	0	0	0	4.2	8	23	4	4	1	1	0	2	1	0	1	0	0	0
								Relievers																	
Thomas	7	0	1.000	3.36	40	0	0	9	0	1	93.2	66	385	37	35	8	2	7	2	48	12	70	4	2	5
Nunez	7	3	.700	3.09	70	0	0	53	0	16	90.1	79	378	36	31	13	4	3	0	34	5	58	2	1	10
Vande Berg	2	1	.667	3.72	76	0	0	22	0	3	67.2	71	296	30	28	4	2	3	1	31	5	34	4	0	4
Barojas	0	5	.000	5.98	17	4	0	3	0	0	52.2	65	250	40	35	6	2	2	0	33	5	27	6	0	1
Long	0	0	.000	3.76	28	0	0	13	0	0	38.1	30	162	17	16	7	0	0	2	17	1	29	2	0	0
*Snyder	1	2	.333	6.37	15	6	0	5	0	1	35.1	44	166	28	25	2	1	1	1	19	2	23	4	2	0
Best	2	1	.667	1.95	15	0	0	7	0	4	32.1	25	128	9	7	1	0	0	1	6	0	32	0	0	2
Stanton	1	2	.333	5.28	24	0	0	11	0	1	29.0	32	140	20	17	4	1	0	3	21	3	17	2	0	0
*Geisel	0	0	.000	6.33	12	0	0	1	0	0	27.0	35	128	21	19	3	0	0	0	15	3	17	0	1	0
Lazorko	0	0	.000	3.54	15	0	0	4	0	1	20.1	23	92	10	8	1	2	0	3	8	1	7	0	0	0
*Mirabella	0	0	.000	1.32	10	0	0	1	0	0	13.2	9	57	4	2	0	1	2	2	4	1	8	0	0	0
Tobik	1	0	1.000	6.00	8	0	0	4	0	1	9.0	10	40	8	6	2	0	2	0	3	0	8	1	0	0

Bob KEARNEY, Catcher

	G	AB	Hit	2B	3B	HR	Run	RBI	TBB	SO	SB	CS	Avg
2.31 years		479	112	23	1	9	45	46	23	79	4	4	.234
1985	108	305	74	14	1	6	24	27	11	59	1	1	.243
First Half	63	167	37	5	1	4	12	18	7	30	1	1	.222
Second Half	45	138	37	9	0	2	12	9	4	29	0	0	.268
Vs. RHP		208	55	11	1	3	19	19	5	48	0	1	.264
Vs. LHP		97	19	3	0	3	5	8	6	11	1	0	.196
Home	58	160	38	9	1	2	11	15	4	31	0	0	.238
Road	50	145	36	5	0	4	13	12	7	28	1	1	.248
Grass	39	115	29	3	0	3	12	10	6	19	0	1	.252
Turf	69	190	45	11	1	3	12	17	5	40	1	0	.237

Jim PRESLEY, Third Base

	G	AB	Hit	2B	3B	HR	Run	RBI	TBB	SO	SB	CS	Avg
1.39 years		591	154	32	1	27	71	86	36	117	2	2	.261
1985	155	570	157	33	1	28	71	84	44	100	2	2	.275
First Half	80	291	81	16	0	18	37	44	28	54	1	1	.278
Second Half	75	279	76	17	1	10	34	40	16	46	1	1	.272
Vs. RHP		419	103	23	0	20	46	58	30	81	2	2	.246
Vs. LHP		151	54	10	1	8	25	26	14	19	0	0	.358
Home	80	296	78	17	1	12	32	34	25	50	0	0	.264
Road	75	274	79	16	0	16	39	50	19	50	2	2	.288
Grass	59	220	58	10	0	13	28	41	13	42	2	2	.264
Turf	96	350	99	23	1	15	43	43	31	58	0	0	.283

Alvin DAVIS, First Base

	G	AB	Hit	2B	3B	HR	Run	RBI	TBB	SO	SB	CS	Avg
1.90 years		604	173	35	2	24	83	102	99	79	3	3	.286
1985	155	578	166	33	1	18	78	78	90	71	1	2	.287
First Half	77	287	76	13	0	6	34	32	45	29	0	1	.265
Second Half	78	291	90	20	1	12	44	46	45	42	1	1	.309
Vs. RHP		402	124	24	1	14	50	54	64	45	0	2	.308
Vs. LHP		176	42	9	0	4	28	24	26	26	1	0	.239
Home	80	297	87	15	1	11	39	41	50	31	0	2	.293
Road	75	281	79	18	0	7	39	37	40	40	1	0	.281
Grass	56	218	61	13	0	7	31	32	24	30	1	0	.280
Turf	99	360	105	20	1	11	47	46	66	41	0	2	.292

Spike OWEN, Shortstop

	G	AB	Hit	2B	3B	HR	Run	RBI	TBB	SO	SB	CS	Avg
2.16 years		550	130	18	8	5	67	47	48	62	17	9	.237
1985	118	352	91	10	6	6	41	37	34	27	11	5	.259
First Half	72	215	53	7	4	3	24	19	24	18	11	3	.247
Second Half	46	137	38	3	2	3	17	18	10	9	0	2	.277
Vs. RHP		262	68	4	6	5	29	26	29	18	9	4	.260
Vs. LHP		90	23	6	0	1	12	11	5	9	2	1	.256
Home	69	201	55	7	3	3	19	19	20	16	6	5	.274
Road	49	151	36	3	3	3	22	18	14	11	5	0	.238
Grass	37	117	25	3	3	2	18	13	11	10	5	0	.214
Turf	81	235	66	7	3	4	23	24	23	17	6	5	.281

Jack PERCONTE, Second Base

	G	AB	Hit	2B	3B	HR	Run	RBI	TBB	SO	SB	CS	Avg
2.52 years		542	148	18	6	1	73	29	55	45	30	5	.273
1985	125	485	128	17	7	2	60	23	50	36	31	2	.264
First Half	67	270	63	11	3	1	28	9	17	18	17	2	.233
Second Half	58	215	65	6	4	1	32	14	33	18	14	0	.302
Vs. RHP		354	96	15	6	2	45	17	35	22	24	1	.271
Vs. LHP		131	32	2	1	0	15	6	15	14	7	1	.244
Home	64	247	62	8	3	2	32	13	22	22	20	2	.251
Road	61	238	66	9	4	0	28	10	28	14	11	0	.277
Grass	45	180	55	7	3	0	21	9	17	11	8	0	.306
Turf	80	305	73	10	4	2	39	14	33	25	23	2	.239

Phil BRADLEY, Left Field

	G	AB	Hit	2B	3B	HR	Run	RBI	TBB	SO	SB	CS	Avg
1.89 years		545	163	25	6	14	83	62	51	103	24	10	.298
1985	159	641	192	33	8	26	100	88	55	129	22	9	.300
First Half	81	326	104	18	5	12	46	43	26	57	10	4	.319
Second Half	78	315	88	15	3	14	54	45	29	72	12	5	.279
Vs. RHP		463	145	26	6	17	66	64	38	88	17	6	.313
Vs. LHP		178	47	7	2	9	34	24	17	41	5	3	.264
Home	81	321	98	18	4	15	50	43	30	58	11	3	.305
Road	78	320	94	15	4	11	50	45	25	71	11	6	.294
Grass	59	244	78	11	3	9	41	37	19	51	9	6	.320
Turf	100	397	114	22	5	17	59	51	36	78	13	3	.287

Dave HENDERSON, Center Field

	G	AB	Hit	2B	3B	HR	Run	RBI	TBB	SO	SB	CS	Avg
3.40 years		525	133	28	2	19	66	67	43	101	7	4	.253
1985	139	502	121	28	2	14	70	68	48	104	6	1	.241
First Half	72	260	65	13	1	7	36	37	22	47	2	1	.250
Second Half	67	242	56	15	1	7	34	31	26	57	4	0	.231
Vs. RHP		375	87	18	1	12	50	52	37	85	6	1	.232
Vs. LHP		127	34	10	1	2	20	16	11	19	0	0	.268
Home	70	253	63	11	2	8	37	37	28	44	3	0	.249
Road	69	249	58	17	0	6	33	31	20	60	3	1	.233
Grass	52	192	39	11	0	4	26	22	16	46	3	1	.203
Turf	87	310	82	17	2	10	44	46	32	58	3	0	.265

Al COWENS, Right Field

	G	AB	Hit	2B	3B	HR	Run	RBI	TBB	SO	SB	CS	Avg
9.60 years		568	154	28	7	11	73	74	40	67	12	8	.271
1985	122	452	120	32	5	14	59	69	30	56	0	0	.265
First Half	58	211	54	13	2	9	29	34	13	30	0	0	.256
Second Half	64	241	66	19	3	5	30	35	17	26	0	0	.274
Vs. RHP		314	83	22	2	9	36	47	15	45	0	0	.264
Vs. LHP		138	37	10	3	5	23	22	15	11	0	0	.268
Home	59	211	60	12	1	8	30	34	19	22	0	0	.284
Road	63	241	60	20	4	6	29	35	11	34	0	0	.249
Grass	48	187	49	17	4	6	25	30	9	24	0	0	.262
Turf	74	265	71	15	1	8	34	39	21	32	0	0	.268

Gorman THOMAS, Designated Hitter

	G	AB	Hit	2B	3B	HR	Run	RBI	TBB	SO	SB	CS	Avg
8.23 years		530	120	25	1	31	77	91	78	150	6	5	.227
1985	135	484	104	16	1	32	76	87	84	126	3	2	.215
First Half	58	194	45	6	0	12	34	33	46	47	1	2	.232
Second Half	77	290	59	10	1	20	42	54	38	79	2	0	.203
Vs. RHP		332	72	12	1	19	49	50	57	84	1	1	.217
Vs. LHP		152	32	4	0	13	27	37	27	42	2	1	.211
Home	72	251	52	7	1	16	37	46	50	65	2	1	.207
Road	63	233	52	9	0	16	39	41	34	61	1	1	.223
Grass	45	162	40	7	0	14	30	33	31	44	1	1	.247
Turf	90	322	64	9	1	18	46	54	53	82	2	1	.199

Ivan CALDERON, Outfield

	G	AB	Hit	2B	3B	HR	Run	RBI	TBB	SO	SB	CS	Avg
0.48 years		486	135	35	8	19	81	60	44	104	10	4	.278
1985	67	210	60	16	4	8	37	28	19	45	4	2	.286
First Half	47	139	40	9	4	6	25	19	17	25	4	2	.288
Second Half	20	71	20	7	0	2	12	9	2	20	0	0	.282
Vs. RHP		139	39	10	3	5	23	17	9	27	4	2	.281
Vs. LHP		71	21	6	1	3	14	11	10	18	0	0	.296
Home	35	111	33	8	1	6	22	16	10	21	3	1	.297
Road	32	99	27	8	3	2	15	12	9	24	1	1	.273
Grass	24	74	20	4	3	1	12	9	8	18	1	1	.270
Turf	43	136	40	12	1	7	25	19	11	27	3	1	.294

MATT YOUNG

	(W–L)	GS	Run	Avg	DP	Avg	SB	Avg
1984	(6-8)	22	122	5.55	22	1.00	13	.59
1985	(12-19)	35	155	4.43	35	1.00	21	.60
1983-1985		88	377	4.28	85	.97	59	.67

	G	IP	W	L	Pct	ER	BB	SO	ERA
1984 Home	12	64.0	5	4	.556	33	30	38	4.64
1985 Home	21	133.3	8	8	.500	57	46	92	3.85
1984 Road	10	49.3	1	4	.200	39	27	25	7.11
1985 Road	16	85.0	4	11	.267	62	30	44	6.56
1984 Grass	8	39.7	1	3	.250	31	22	20	7.03
1985 Grass	11	52.3	3	7	.300	46	23	29	7.91
1984 Turf	14	73.7	5	5	.500	41	35	53	5.01
1985 Turf	26	166.0	9	12	.429	73	53	107	3.96
1985 Total	37	218.3	12	19	.387	119	76	136	4.91

MIKE MOORE

	(W–L)	GS	Run	Avg	DP	Avg	SB	Avg
1984	(7-17)	33	127	3.85	22	.67	25	.76
1985	(17-10)	34	149	4.38	30	.88	12	.35
1982-1985		115	453	3.94	89	.77	84	.73

	G	IP	W	L	Pct	ER	BB	SO	ERA
1984 Home	18	120.7	6	8	.429	61	52	98	4.55
1985 Home	18	133.0	8	5	.615	47	40	83	3.18
1984 Road	16	91.3	1	9	.100	56	33	60	5.52
1985 Road	17	114.0	9	5	.643	48	30	72	3.79
1984 Grass	11	57.7	0	7	0.000	39	22	38	6.09
1985 Grass	13	86.0	7	3	.700	34	21	59	3.56
1984 Turf	23	154.3	7	10	.412	78	32	61	4.55
1985 Turf	22	161.0	10	7	.588	61	49	96	3.41
1985 Total	35	247.0	17	10	.630	95	70	155	3.46

MARK LANGSTON

	(W–L)	GS	Run	Avg	DP	Avg	SB	Avg
1984	(17-10)	33	126	3.82	27	.82	15	.45
1985	(7-14)	24	95	3.96	25	1.04	19	.79
1984-1985		57	221	3.88	52	.91	34	.60

	G	IP	W	L	Pct	ER	BB	SO	ERA
1984 Home	17	121.7	10	3	.769	34	60	123	2.52
1985 Home	10	56.3	4	5	.444	34	31	30	5.43
1984 Road	18	103.3	7	7	.500	51	58	81	4.44
1985 Road	14	70.3	3	9	.250	43	60	42	5.50
1984 Grass	13	74.0	6	5	.545	32	45	61	3.89
1985 Grass	10	49.3	2	7	.222	33	42	29	6.02
1984 Turf	22	151.0	11	5	.688	53	73	143	3.16
1985 Turf	14	77.3	5	7	.417	44	49	43	5.12
1985 Total	24	126.7	7	14	.333	77	91	72	5.47

BILL SWIFT

	(W–L)	GS	Run	Avg	DP	Avg	SB	Avg
1985	(6-10)	21	85	4.05	23	1.10	14	.67

	G	IP	W	L	Pct	ER	BB	SO	ERA
1985 Home	11	60.3	2	6	.250	38	21	25	5.67
1985 Road	12	60.3	4	4	.500	26	27	30	3.88
1985 Grass	9	44.7	3	4	.429	24	22	22	4.84
1985 Turf	14	76.0	3	6	.333	40	26	33	4.74
1985 Total	23	120.7	6	10	.375	64	48	55	4.77

OTHERS

	(W–L)	GS	Run	Avg	DP	Avg	SB	Avg
Wills	(5-11)	18	78	4.33	15	.83	12	.67
Beattie	(5-6)	15	91	6.07	15	1.00	11	.73
Snyder	(1-2)	6	27	4.50	4	.67	3	.50
Barojas	(0-5)	4	7	1.75	5	1.25	6	1.50
Morgan	(1-1)	2	21	10.50	0	0.00	4	2.00
Wilkinson	(0-2)	2	8	4.00	3	1.50	1	.50
Lewis	(0-1)	1	3	3.00	3	3.00	2	2.00

TEXAS RANGERS

BREAKDOWNS FOR THE LAST TEN SEASONS

Won-Lost Record: 745-815, .478 (4th in the Division, 16th in the Majors)
Runs Scored: 6,535 (5th in the Division, 16th in Majors)
Runs Allowed: 6,637 (6th highest in the Division, 14th in Majors)
Home Runs Hit: 1,130 (5th in the Division, 15th in the Majors)
Home Runs Allowed: 1,215 (5th in the Division, 11th in the Majors)

RECORD IN:
April: 93-92, .503 (4th in the Division, 12th in Majors)
May: 124-142, .466 (4th in the Division, 20th in Majors)
June: 141-124, .532 (2nd Best in the Division, 7th in Majors)
July: 102-151, .403 (2nd Worst in the Division and in the Major Leagues)
August: 128-159, .446 (5th in the Division, 21st in the Majors)
September: 144-136, .514 (2nd Best in the Division, 9th in Majors)
October: 13-11, .542 (4th in the Division, 10th in the Majors)

Won-Lost Record in Road Games: 342-435, .440 (4th in the Division, 16th in Majors)
Won-Lost Record at Home: 403-380, .515 (5th in the Division, 19th in Majors)
Home Field Advantage: 63 Games
Runs Scored on the Road: 3,210 (5th in the Division, 16th in Majors)
Runs Scored at Home: 3,325 (5th in the Division, 18th in Majors)
Runs Allowed on the Road: 3,392 (Lowest total in the Division, 14th highest in the Majors)
Runs Allowed at Home: 3,245 (6th highest in the Division, 14th in Majors)

Home Runs Hit on the Road: 599 (5th in the Division, 13th in Majors)
Home Runs Hit at Home: 531 (6th in the Division, 18th in Majors)
Home Runs Allowed on the Road: 616 (Fewest in the Division, 11th highest total in Majors)
Home Runs Allowed at Home: 599 (5th highest in the Division, 14th in Majors)

RECORD FOR LAST THREE SEASONS: 208-276, .430 (6th in the Division, 23rd in the Majors)

TEXAS RANGERS
ESSAY ON THE ORIGINS AND EFFECTS OF MEDIOCRITY

Everybody kicks you while you're down, chapter 117. If you caught the Toronto Blue Jays late in the season, you no doubt heard about the Texas Rangers' latest pitching mistake, which, as it was explained repeatedly, was this: the Rangers signed Cliff Johnson as a free agent, which meant that the Blue Jays got to pick a player from the compensation pool to replace Johnson. The Blue Jays picked Tom Henke, from the Rangers; Henke turned out to be a late-season sensation, and since Johnson was returned to Toronto late in the year what it all adds up to is that the Rangers had in essence given up Tom Henke for four months worth of Cliff Johnson.

Except that, in fact, that's not what it adds up to, at all. The Rangers didn't *give* Cliff Johnson back to Toronto, they *traded* him back for a couple of young pitchers. One of those pitchers was Matt Williams. Henke for the Blue Jays pitched 40 innings late in the year with a 2.03 ERA; Williams for the Rangers pitched 26 innings late in the year with a 2.42 ERA. Williams is not exactly a prize pitching prospect, but the point is that it is, as of now, essentially an even trade.

Nobody cares too much about being fair to the Rangers on details like that, because the Rangers have, by a series of mistakes, misfortunes and misjudgments, become the worst team in the worst division in baseball. The American League's Western Division has been so bad for so long that I thought perhaps we ought to take a look at the division as a whole, how bad they are and whether there is any prospect of things beginning to even up.

Some of you may have the impression that the weak-ness of the A.L. West dates back to the time of the split into divisions, and that the American League East was the superior division even in the early seventies, although Oakland had the one best team in the division. This is simply not so. When the American League expanded in 1969, the Western division got both expansion teams (the Royals and the Seattle Pilots), and for the first two years, the division got creamed in inter-division play (totals given are for inter-division games won, if that isn't obvious):

1969	East	245	.569	West	187	.431
1970	East	243	.565	West	189	.435

But in 1971 one of those two teams (the Royals) jumped into competition, and for the seven years following there was absolute balance between the two divisions:

1971	West	216	.502	East	214	.498
1972	West	215	.500	East	215	.500
1973	East	226	.523	West	206	.477
1974	East	219	.507	West	213	.493
1975	West	221	.518	East	206	.482
1976	East	223	.516	West	209	.484
1977	West	257	.510	East	247	.490

During that period there occurred only small-scale, probably random deviations from even performance. This seven-year period, I think, is a key to the accurate perception of the disparity.

In 1978 this changed abruptly—at the time, I would have assumed, temporarily.

1978 East 281 .561 West 220 .439

However, in view of the pattern of long-term dominance which began at that time, it is worth looking again at the specifics of the 1978 season, and at how the imbalance was created.

There are essentially four factors. In retrospect, we can see the first of those four one year earlier, when the Oakland A's collapsed, going from 87–74 to 63–98 following the mass defection of free agents (Rudi, Baylor, Bando, Fingers, etc.). This transformed an organization which had been one of the strongest in baseball instantly into one of the weakest in baseball—and, in a seven-team division, one switch such as that has an enormous impact. The effect of this was disguised for one year as the rest of the division had a strong year, the Texas Rangers winning 94 games.

In 1978 two very positive things happened to the teams in the A.L. East, which accentuated this. The Detroit Tigers in 1978 had one of the greatest rookie crops of all time (Whitaker, Trammell, Parrish, Jack Morris) which, combined with the maturing of good rookie crops of the previous two years, transformed them from a .400 to a .550 ballclub overnight. The Milwaukee Brewers in the same season made a completely unexpected leap into contention with the arrival of Harry Dalton and George Bamberger, jumping from 67–95 to 93–69 in one season without any subsequent relapse—one of the most sudden and dramatic coalescences of any ballclub ever.

And fourth and finally, a second A.L. West team fell apart. More gradually than the A's but of the same original cause, the Minnesota Twins began to unravel; in 1978 they won but 73 games. Since then, the competitive imbalance has become self-sustaining:

1979	East	327	.558	West	259	.442
1980	East	329	.563	West	255	.437
1981	East	208	.537	West	180	.463
1982	East	323	.549	West	265	.451
1983	East	332	.565	West	256	.435
1984	East	320	.547	West	265	.453
1985	East	304	.518	West	283	.482

Last winter, three of the best players in the American League West moved to the Eastern division—Rickey Henderson to New York, Fred Lynn to Baltimore and Bill Caudill to Toronto. At the time it was widely written that the imbalance between the divisions would be worse than ever in 1985. As you will note, this did not prove to be so; the West had its best year since 1977.

In explaining the disparity between divisions, it has become common to place an emphasis on the fact that the eastern teams are by and large older and more established. In analyzing the issue in a fine article in the February 24, 1985 *Kansas City Star*, Tracy Ringolsby pointed out that only one American League West team (the White Sox) has operated in its present city for more than 25 years, whereas five of the teams in the East have done so. He quoted Roland Hemond, then GM of the White Sox, as

saying that "Clubs which transfer are not doing well where they were. That means they are not acquiring good players, and that means attendance problems. The East is a more-established, long-term division." Well, it seems to me that there is a serious problem with this argument—that is, the seven-year period (1971–1977) in which the American League West was just as strong as the American League East.

It seems to me that, while the distinction between a new team and an established team *might be* important for a few years, it is a distinction which loses significance very rapidly after about 15 years. Now, if you go back to 1971, you can see that the A.L. West at that time was quite raw. The Royals then were just in their third season of existence; the A's were just in their fourth season in Oakland. The Angels and Rangers (who came to the West in 1972) had existed for only a decade, and the Twins had been in Minnesota for only a decade. That is an *extremely* young division, and it would then have been reasonable to expect them to be over-matched—yet for seven years, they played even with the established teams in the East. Seven years is a long time, surely long enough for any underlying difference between the young and old to manifest itself.

But that difference is nothing now, in 1985, compared to what it was then—yet the effect exists now, and it didn't exist then. It is difficult for me to understand how the difference between an 85-year-old organization and a 25-year-old organization can be so meaningful, when the difference between a 70-year-old organization and a 10-year-old organization was so inconsequential.

This is not the only problem with the theory. There simply is not a good correlation between the length of time any organization has been anywhere, and the strength of the organization—either in the American League or the National. One of the oldest organizations in the A.L. East is the Cleveland Indians—but the Indians are the only team in the division which has not participated in the persecution of the West. The Baltimore Orioles, long-term failures in St. Louis, have been one of the great powerhouses of the A.L. East throughout all of this period—yet they are only a few years older in Baltimore than the Twins are in Minnesota. The Orioles have been powerful since 1960, their eighth season in Baltimore, and the Twins were one of the most powerful teams in all of baseball in their first decade in Minnesota. The brand-new organizations in the East—the Brewers and the Blue Jays— have been among the strong teams in the division, the Brewers from 1978–83 and the Blue Jays the last three years. The White Sox, the old established team in the A.L. West, have been just as bad as the rest of the division.

I simply can't see any generalized connection between how long-established an organization is in a city, and how successful their team is. In the National League, of course you've got the enormous counter-example of the Dodgers, but you've also got the San Francisco Giants, who moved to that city in 1958 and were one of the strongest teams in baseball during the following thirteen years, and you've got the Milwaukee Braves, who were contenders from the day they arrived in Milwaukee until the day they left. It seems to me that it would be extremely difficult to conclude that the length of time a team has been where it is is a variable affecting the performance of the team.

So we've got two major problems with that theory—number one, that it does not predict the actual form of the condition (that is, the development of the imbalance only following a seven-year delay), and number two, that it is a specific application of an effect which cannot be shown to exist in general. So, while I might have bought this theory a year ago, I would have to say now that I don't think that the more established nature of the A.L. East has damn-all to do with its dominance.

A year ago, I proposed an argument that the mediocrity of the Western Division was strategically self-perpetuating—that is, that since the teams in the A.L. West felt that they could "win" at a low level of success, they tend to adopt strategies which reach only so far as that level. In the Ringolsby article, Pat Gillick more or less voted for this explanation. "I feel there are more shakers and movers in the East," Gillick said. "George pushes you to do more than you normally would."

Dick Howser hit the same theme. "If you don't keep up in the East or get better, you can be buried," Howser was quoted as saying.

This brings us back to the question of whether the superiority of the East is near to working itself out. I am more encouraged on that issue than I have been for several years. For one thing, I have convinced at least myself that the entrenched nature of the Eastern teams is irrelevant,

and thus that the A.L. West has not suffered because they are working under a true handicap, as much as because of their own failures in judgment. If the superiority of the East is merely self-sustaining, then the odds are that once it is gone it will be gone, and will not reassert itself.

It wasn't gone last year, but it was smaller. The A.L. West seems to me to have more than its share of young talent. The Twins and Mariners probably have more young talent than any team in the A.L. East. The A's, with Canseco, Mike Davis and others, have some young talent mixed with an apparent determination not to relapse into the 100-loss range. The Rangers have a number of young players that I like a great deal. I think that in two or three years Don Slaught will be the best catcher in the American League, and Oddibe McDowell might be one of the best players in baseball. I like O'Brien, and he's young, too. At this time, they don't have as many of them as the Twins and Mariners have.

But at the same time, one must note that the successes of 1985 were not exactly built on quartzite. The Angels, who were 45–39 against the East, are an old, veteran team that squeezed a good year out of their talent, and will be lucky to do it again, whereas the Cleveland Indians of the East, who went 28–56 against the West, have far more talent than is reflected in their won/lost record. If those two teams return to the level of their talent in 1986, and nothing else changes to off-set that, the imbalance between the divisions will return to what it was.

COMPLETE BATTING RECORDS

Player	G	AB	R	H	TB	2B	3B	HR	RBI	GW	SH	SF	HB	BB	IB	SO	SB	CS	GI DP	Avg	Slug	OBP	Runs	Outs Made	Runs/ 27 Outs	OW%	Appr Value
Slaught	102	343	34	96	145	17	4	8	35	4	1	0	6	20	1	41	5	4	8	.280	.423	.331	46	260	4.77	.579	8
*O'Brien	159	573	69	153	259	34	3	22	92	10	3	9	1	69	4	53	5	10	18	.267	.452	.342	85	460	4.98	.567	11
Harrah	126	396	65	107	154	18	1	9	44	6	2	6	4	113	2	60	11	4	4	.270	.389	.432	80	305	7.11	.727	8
Buechele	69	219	22	48	78	6	3	6	21	0	0	1	2	14	2	38	3	2	11	.219	.356	.271	18	185	2.64	.269	3
†Wilkerson	129	360	35	88	111	11	6	0	22	3	6	3	4	22	0	63	14	7	7	.244	.308	.293	33	295	3.01	.323	5
Ward	154	593	77	170	257	28	7	15	70	5	0	5	1	39	3	97	26	7	19	.287	.433	.329	82	454	4.85	.554	12
*McDowell	111	406	63	97	175	14	5	18	42	7	5	2	3	36	2	85	25	7	6	.239	.431	.304	55	329	4.49	.516	6
Parrish	94	346	44	86	150	11	1	17	51	4	0	2	1	33	2	77	0	2	13	.249	.434	.314	44	277	4.27	.490	4
Johnson	82	296	31	76	131	17	1	12	56	2	1	3	3	31	2	44	0	0	3	.257	.443	.330	45	227	5.39	.605	3
†Wright	109	363	21	69	88	13	0	2	18	1	3	2	0	25	5	49	4	7	9	.190	.342	.241	19	315	1.67	.128	2
†Tolleson	123	323	45	101	123	9	5	1	18	6	9	2	0	21	0	46	21	12	6	.313	.381	.353	43	251	4.57	.524	7
Bell	84	313	33	74	105	13	3	4	32	3	0	4	1	33	1	21	3	2	14	.236	.335	.308	31	259	3.20	.351	4
*Jones	83	134	14	30	47	2	0	5	23	1	0	1	1	11	1	30	1	0	1	.224	.350	.284	14	107	3.59	.405	1
*Walker	53	132	14	23	40	2	0	5	11	0	0	0	1	15	0	29	2	1	2	.174	.303	.264	11	112	2.65	.270	2
Bannister	57	122	17	32	41	4	1	1	6	0	1	0	0	14	0	17	8	2	1	.262	.336	.338	15	94	4.45	.510	2
Brummer	49	108	7	30	34	4	0	0	5	0	0	0	2	11	1	22	1	5	2	.278	.315	.355	11	85	3.56	.400	1
*Dunbar	45	104	7	21	28	4	0	1	5	0	0	0	1	12	3	9	0	3	5	.202	.269	.291	7	91	2.02	.177	0
†Petralli	42	100	7	27	29	2	0	0	11	1	3	4	1	8	0	12	1	0	4	.270	.290	.319	10	84	3.15	.343	1
Stein	44	79	5	20	28	3	1	1	12	1	0	0	1	1	1	15	0	0	2	.253	.354	.272	7	61	3.09	.335	1
Valentine	11	38	5	8	15	1	0	2	4	2	0	0	0	2	0	8	0	1	1	.211	.395	.250	3	32	2.62	.266	0
Capra	8	8	1	1	1	0	0	0	0	0	0	0	0	0	0	0	0	0	0	.125	.125	.125	0	7	0.48	.012	0
Kunkel	2	4	1	1	1	0	0	0	0	0	0	0	0	0	0	3	0	0	0	.250	.250	.250	0	3	2.25	.229	0
Pujols	1	1	0	1	1	0	0	0	0	0	0	0	0	0	0	0	0	0	0	1.000	1.000	1.000	0	0	0	0	0

*left-handed hitter, †switch hitter

DEFENSIVE STATISTICS

FIRST	G	PO	A	Er	TC	DP	PCT.
O'Brien	159	1457	98	8	1563	125	.995
Stein	8	40	3	1	44	2	.977
Jones	4	14	0	0	14	1	1.000
Bannister	4	11	1	0	12	2	1.000
TEAM:	175	1522	102	9	1633	130	.994
AVG:	180	1440	123	14	1577	141	.991

SECOND	G	PO	A	Er	TC	DP	PCT.
Harrah	122	212	351	6	569	71	.989
Tolleson	29	44	65	4	113	11	.965
Wilkerson	19	40	54	3	97	15	.969
Bannister	10	16	16	1	33	2	.970
Stein	3	2	2	0	4	1	1.000
Buechele	1	0	1	0	1	0	1.000
TEAM:	184	314	489	14	817	100	.983
AVG:	189	347	501	15	863	114	.982

THIRD	G	PO	A	Er	TC	DP	PCT.
Bell	83	70	192	16	278	22	.942
Buechele	69	52	137	6	195	17	.969
Tolleson	12	9	8	2	19	0	.895
Stein	11	5	15	1	21	1	.952
Bannister	5	0	1	0	1	0	1.000
Parrish	2	0	3	0	3	0	1.000
TEAM:	182	136	356	25	517	40	.952
AVG:	192	129	327	23	479	32	.953

SHORTSTOP	G	PO	A	Er	TC	DP	PCT.
Wilkerson	110	125	274	18	417	50	.957
Tolleson	81	96	182	8	286	37	.972
Harrah	2	0	0	0	0	0	.000
Kunkel	2	2	5	0	7	1	1.000
TEAM:	195	223	461	26	710	88	.963
AVG:	189	269	474	28	771	104	.964

CATCHER	G	PO	A	Er	TC	DP	PCT.	PB
Slaught	102	550	33	6	589	4	.990	13
Brummer	47	182	5	2	189	2	.989	7
Petralli	41	179	16	2	197	6	.990	3
Pujols	1	1	0	0	1	0	1.000	0
TEAM:	191	912	54	10	976	12	.990	23
AVG:	193	895	74	13	982	13	.987	13

OUTFIELD	G	PO	A	Er	TC	DP	PCT.
Ward	153	304	11	10	325	2	.969
McDowell	103	282	9	2	293	2	.993
Wright	102	213	8	2	223	2	.991
Parrish	69	111	4	1	116	0	.991
Walker	32	51	6	0	57	1	1.000
Jones	30	30	0	0	30	0	1.000
Bannister	14	19	0	0	19	0	1.000
Dunbar	14	14	0	1	15	0	.933
Capra	8	11	0	0	11	0	1.000
Valentine	7	7	0	0	7	0	1.000
Stein	3	5	0	0	5	0	1.000
Brummer	1	1	0	0	1	0	1.000
TEAM:	536	1048	38	16	1102	7	.985
AVG:	559	1141	33	21	1196	8	.982

COMPLETE PITCHERS RECORDS

Pitcher	W	L	Pct	ERA	G	GS	CG	GF	SHO	SV	IP	H	TBF	R	ER	HR	SH	SF	HB	BB	IB	SO	WP	BK	Appr Value
								Starters (One-half of Game Appearances)																	
Hough	14	16	.467	3.31	34	34	14	0	1	0	250.1	198	1018	102	92	23	1	7	7	83	1	141	11	3	11
*Mason	8	15	.348	4.83	38	30	1	1	1	0	179.0	212	800	113	96	22	4	10	3	73	4	92	4	1	5
Hooton	5	8	.385	5.23	29	20	2	2	0	0	124.0	149	546	78	72	18	0	5	0	40	2	62	2	0	2
*Tanana	2	7	.222	5.91	13	13	0	0	0	0	77.2	89	340	53	51	15	2	4	1	23	2	52	3	0	0
Russell	3	6	.333	7.55	13	13	0	0	0	0	62.0	85	295	55	52	10	1	3	2	27	1	44	2	0	0
Cook	2	3	.400	9.45	9	7	0	1	0	0	40.0	53	187	42	42	12	0	4	3	18	1	19	1	0	0
Guzman	3	2	.600	2.76	5	5	0	0	0	0	32.2	27	140	13	10	3	0	0	0	14	1	24	1	0	1
Williams	2	1	.667	2.42	6	3	0	1	0	0	26.0	20	106	7	7	3	1	0	0	10	0	22	2	0	1
Sebra	0	2	.000	7.52	7	4	0	0	0	0	20.1	26	102	17	17	4	0	2	1	14	2	13	0	0	0
								Relievers																	
Harris	5	4	.556	2.47	58	0	0	35	0	11	113.0	74	450	35	31	7	3	2	5	43	3	111	2	1	9
Noles	4	8	.333	5.06	28	13	0	3	0	1	110.1	129	488	67	62	11	2	0	6	33	1	59	1	0	2
Rozema	3	7	.300	4.19	34	4	0	16	0	7	88.0	100	374	45	41	10	1	1	2	22	3	42	1	0	4
Schmidt	7	6	.538	3.15	51	4	1	35	1	5	85.2	81	356	36	30	6	3	2	0	22	8	46	2	1	6
Stewart	0	6	.000	5.42	42	5	0	29	0	4	81.1	86	361	53	49	13	5	2	2	37	5	64	5	1	1
*Welsh	2	5	.286	4.13	25	6	0	4	0	0	76.1	101	351	40	35	11	1	1	4	25	3	31	5	0	2
Henry	2	2	.500	2.57	16	0	0	10	0	3	21.0	16	86	7	6	0	2	1	0	7	0	20	1	0	2
Surhoff	0	1	.000	7.56	7	0	0	5	0	0	8.1	12	39	7	7	2	1	0	0	3	0	8	0	0	0
*Wright	0	0	.000	4.70	5	0	0	1	0	0	7.2	5	32	4	4	0	0	0	0	5	1	7	0	0	0
Boggs	0	0	.000	11.57	4	0	0	0	0	0	7.0	13	36	9	9	3	0	0	0	2	0	6	0	0	0
Murray	0	0	.000	18.00	1	0	0	0	0	0	1.0	3	5	2	2	0	1	0	0	0	0	0	0	0	0

Don SLAUGHT, Catcher

	G	AB	Hit	2B	3B	HR	Run	RBI	TBB	SO	SB	CS	Avg
2.17 years		526	148	29	6	7	54	52	28	62	4	2	.282
1985	102	343	96	17	4	8	34	35	20	41	5	4	.280
First Half	67	227	59	10	3	4	23	19	15	24	2	2	.260
Second Half	35	116	37	7	1	4	11	16	5	17	3	2	.319
Vs. RHP		242	67	12	4	5	22	24	13	25	3	1	.277
Vs. LHP		101	29	5	0	3	12	11	7	16	2	3	.287
Home	55	181	53	10	2	4	17	18	12	21	3	2	.293
Road	47	162	43	7	2	4	17	17	8	20	2	2	.265
Grass	85	288	85	15	3	7	25	30	16	34	4	3	.295
Turf	17	55	11	2	1	1	9	5	4	7	1	1	.200

Pete O'BRIEN, First Base

	G	AB	Hit	2B	3B	HR	Run	RBI	TBB	SO	SB	CS	Avg
2.93 years		574	151	30	4	18	65	81	63	59	5	6	.262
1985	159	573	153	34	3	22	69	92	69	53	5	10	.267
First Half	83	294	71	18	1	9	32	41	35	30	2	6	.241
Second Half	76	279	82	16	2	13	37	51	34	23	3	4	.294
Vs. RHP		404	115	28	3	20	54	72	53	28	3	7	.285
Vs. LHP		169	38	6	0	2	15	20	16	25	2	3	.225
Home	79	277	81	18	0	12	41	55	35	26	2	6	.292
Road	80	296	72	16	3	10	28	37	34	27	3	4	.243
Grass	134	477	131	29	0	18	59	77	58	43	4	8	.275
Turf	25	96	22	5	3	4	10	15	11	10	1	2	.229

Toby HARRAH, Second Base

	G	AB	Hit	2B	3B	HR	Run	RBI	TBB	SO	SB	CS	Avg
12.72 years		559	149	23	3	15	85	69	87	64	19	7	.266
1985	126	396	107	18	1	9	65	44	113	60	11	4	.270
First Half	74	226	65	8	1	6	43	24	78	32	7	2	.288
Second Half	52	170	42	10	0	3	22	20	35	28	4	2	.247
Vs. RHP		254	63	11	1	4	37	23	75	38	10	2	.248
Vs. LHP		142	44	7	0	5	28	21	38	22	1	2	.310
Home	60	187	54	9	0	5	41	22	59	24	7	0	.289
Road	66	209	53	9	1	4	24	22	54	36	4	4	.254
Grass	107	331	88	12	0	8	57	33	97	49	10	3	.266
Turf	19	65	19	6	1	1	8	11	16	11	1	1	.292

Larry PARRISH, Right Field

	G	AB	Hit	2B	3B	HR	Run	RBI	TBB	SO	SB	CS	Avg
9.20 years		583	155	33	3	20	73	81	43	107	3	4	.265
1985	94	346	86	11	1	17	44	51	33	77	0	2	.249
First Half	73	269	64	7	1	13	33	37	27	64	0	2	.238
Second Half	21	77	22	4	0	4	11	14	6	13	0	0	.286
Vs. RHP		253	63	8	1	9	28	30	22	56	0	2	.249
Vs. LHP		93	23	3	0	8	16	21	11	21	0	0	.247
Home	52	188	41	4	1	8	24	31	18	43	0	1	.218
Road	42	158	45	7	0	9	20	20	15	34	0	1	.285
Grass	78	285	68	8	1	14	37	44	26	65	0	1	.239
Turf	16	61	18	3	0	3	7	7	7	12	0	1	.295

Steve BUECHELE, Third Base

	G	AB	Hit	2B	3B	HR	Run	RBI	TBB	SO	SB	CS	Avg
0.43 years		514	113	14	7	14	52	49	33	89	7	5	.219
1985	69	219	48	6	3	6	22	21	14	38	3	2	.219
First Half	0	0	0	0	0	0	0	0	0	0	0	0	.000
Second Half	69	219	48	6	3	6	22	21	14	38	3	2	.219
Vs. RHP		144	28	5	2	3	13	14	10	25	2	1	.194
Vs. LHP		75	20	1	1	3	9	7	4	13	1	1	.267
Home	36	110	24	4	1	5	15	14	5	21	1	1	.218
Road	33	109	24	2	2	1	7	7	9	17	2	1	.220
Grass	58	185	40	4	2	6	20	20	12	35	3	1	.216
Turf	11	34	8	2	1	0	2	1	2	3	0	1	.235

George WRIGHT, Left Field

	G	AB	Hit	2B	3B	HR	Run	RBI	TBB	SO	SB	CS	Avg
3.22 years		601	150	25	5	12	65	61	34	82	5	7	.250
1985	109	363	69	13	0	2	21	18	25	49	4	7	.190
First Half	40	129	22	3	0	0	7	4	11	11	2	2	.171
Second Half	69	234	47	10	0	2	14	14	14	38	2	5	.201
Vs. RHP		241	48	7	0	2	19	10	15	30	3	7	.199
Vs. LHP		122	21	6	0	0	2	8	10	19	1	0	.172
Home	52	158	25	3	0	2	9	6	11	25	1	1	.158
Road	57	205	44	10	0	0	12	12	14	24	3	6	.215
Grass	94	313	57	10	0	2	16	16	19	42	4	4	.182
Turf	15	50	12	3	0	0	5	2	6	7	0	3	.240

Curtis WILKERSON, Shortstop

	G	AB	Hit	2B	3B	HR	Run	RBI	TBB	SO	SB	CS	Avg
1.84 years		478	116	13	4	1	48	27	25	76	16	9	.243
1985	129	360	88	11	6	0	35	22	22	63	14	7	.244
First Half	65	190	50	5	4	0	21	11	12	38	8	4	.263
Second Half	64	170	38	6	2	0	14	11	10	25	6	3	.224
Vs. RHP		274	64	5	4	0	23	17	11	54	11	5	.234
Vs. LHP		86	24	6	2	0	12	5	11	9	3	2	.279
Home	58	160	36	4	1	0	14	9	8	26	7	2	.225
Road	71	200	52	7	5	0	21	13	14	37	7	5	.260
Grass	106	294	75	9	5	0	30	18	17	51	13	7	.255
Turf	23	66	13	2	1	0	5	4	5	12	1	0	.197

Wayne TOLLESON, Shortstop

	G	AB	Hit	2B	3B	HR	Run	RBI	TBB	SO	SB	CS	Avg
2.64 years		465	116	12	3	1	59	19	36	68	30	10	.251
1985	123	323	101	9	5	1	45	18	21	46	21	12	.313
First Half	56	123	39	4	0	0	13	4	11	15	10	6	.317
Second Half	67	200	62	5	5	1	32	14	10	31	11	6	.310
Vs. RHP		234	78	4	3	1	36	12	18	35	14	10	.333
Vs. LHP		89	23	5	2	0	9	6	3	11	7	2	.258
Home	63	178	63	4	3	0	27	11	13	24	14	10	.354
Road	60	145	38	5	2	1	18	7	8	22	7	2	.262
Grass	102	275	89	8	4	1	41	17	19	39	19	11	.324
Turf	21	48	12	1	1	0	4	1	2	7	2	1	.250

Gary WARD, Left Field

	G	AB	Hit	2B	3B	HR	Run	RBI	TBB	SO	SB	CS	Avg
4.47 years		613	175	29	8	19	87	82	47	101	13	4	.285
1985	154	593	170	28	7	15	77	70	39	97	26	7	.287
First Half	79	312	89	18	4	5	38	38	21	41	13	3	.285
Second Half	75	281	81	10	3	10	39	32	18	56	13	4	.288
Vs. RHP		413	116	18	4	8	49	41	24	70	18	3	.281
Vs. LHP		180	54	10	3	7	28	29	15	27	8	4	.300
Home	74	282	97	15	5	10	48	50	15	45	15	2	.344
Road	80	311	73	13	2	5	29	20	24	52	11	5	.235
Grass	129	497	141	22	6	14	68	64	29	88	23	5	.284
Turf	25	96	29	6	1	1	9	6	10	9	3	2	.302

Oddibe McDOWELL, Center Field

	G	AB	Hit	2B	3B	HR	Run	RBI	TBB	SO	SB	CS	Avg
0.69 years		593	142	20	7	26	92	61	53	124	36	10	.239
1985	111	406	97	14	5	18	63	42	36	85	25	7	.239
First Half	48	186	38	7	2	3	25	18	11	42	10	4	.204
Second Half	63	220	59	7	3	15	38	24	25	43	15	3	.268
Vs. RHP		283	67	8	1	15	42	33	26	51	18	6	.237
Vs. LHP		123	30	6	4	3	21	9	10	34	7	1	.244
Home	56	203	54	4	3	10	38	23	15	35	16	3	.266
Road	55	203	43	10	2	8	25	19	21	50	9	4	.212
Grass	94	346	82	10	4	15	54	35	31	70	22	6	.237
Turf	17	60	15	4	1	3	9	7	5	15	3	1	.250

CHARLIE HOUGH

	(W–L)	GS	Run	Avg	DP	Avg	SB	Avg
1984	(16-14)	36	157	4.36	33	.92	26	.72
1985	(14-16)	34	123	3.62	28	.82	23	.68
1979-1985		192	683	3.56	135	.70	118	.61

	G	IP	W	L	Pct	ER	BB	SO	ERA
1984 Home	16	128.7	8	5	.615	42	41	75	2.94
1985 Home	16	115.0	8	6	.571	45	36	70	3.52
1984 Road	20	137.3	8	9	.471	69	53	89	4.52
1985 Road	18	135.3	6	10	.375	47	47	71	3.13
1984 Grass	29	216.3	12	12	.500	93	73	135	3.87
1985 Grass	27	196.0	12	12	.500	73	64	117	3.35
1984 Turf	7	49.7	4	2	.667	18	21	28	3.26
1985 Turf	7	54.3	2	4	.333	19	19	24	3.15
1985 Total	34	250.3	14	16	.467	92	83	141	3.31

MIKE MASON

	(W–L)	GS	Run	Avg	DP	Avg	SB	Avg
1984	(9-13)	24	82	3.42	26	1.08	13	.54
1985	(8-15)	30	121	4.03	32	1.07	21	.70
1984-1985		54	203	3.76	58	1.07	34	.63

	G	IP	W	L	Pct	ER	BB	SO	ERA
1984 Home	18	89.0	4	6	.400	40	27	62	4.04
1985 Home	17	83.0	4	6	.400	46	28	46	4.99
1984 Road	18	95.3	5	7	.417	34	24	51	3.21
1985 Road	21	96.0	4	9	.308	50	45	46	4.69
1984 Grass	30	139.0	5	11	.312	64	42	90	4.14
1985 Grass	33	150.7	7	13	.350	82	60	75	4.90
1984 Turf	6	45.3	4	2	.667	10	9	23	1.99
1985 Turf	5	28.3	1	2	.333	14	13	17	4.45
1985 Total	38	179.0	8	15	.348	96	73	92	4.83

BURT HOOTON

	(W–L)	GS	Run	Avg	DP	Avg	SB	Avg
1984	(3-6)	6	19	3.17	6	1.00	8	1.33
1985	(5-8)	20	80	4.00	20	1.00	10	.50
1976-1985		255	1060	4.16	211	.83	223	.87

	G	IP	W	L	Pct	ER	BB	SO	ERA
1984 Home	26	52.0	1	1	.500	19	19	33	3.29
1985 Home	16	66.3	2	3	.400	35	24	37	4.75
1984 Road	28	58.0	2	5	.286	23	24	29	3.57
1985 Road	13	57.7	3	5	.375	37	16	25	5.77
1984 Grass	46	92.3	2	4	.333	36	35	54	3.51
1985 Grass	27	110.0	4	7	.364	66	39	55	5.40
1984 Turf	8	17.7	1	2	.333	6	8	8	3.06
1985 Turf	2	14.0	1	1	.500	6	1	7	3.86
1985 Total	29	124.0	5	8	.385	72	40	62	5.23

OTHERS

	(W–L)	GS	Run	Avg	DP	Avg	SB	Avg
Noles	(4-8)	13	50	3.85	13	1.00	20	1.54
Russell	(3-6)	13	58	4.46	11	.85	15	1.15
Cook	(2-3)	7	35	5.00	7	1.00	4	.57
Welsh	(2-5)	6	20	3.33	3	.50	1	.17
Guzman	(3-2)	5	20	4.00	5	1.00	5	1.00
Stewart	(0-6)	5	12	2.40	2	.40	5	1.00
Rozema	(3-7)	4	12	3.00	3	.75	1	.25
Schmidt	(7-6)	4	21	5.25	1	.25	4	1.00
Sebra	(0-2)	4	9	2.25	3	.75	3	.75
Williams	(2-1)	3	11	3.67	5	1.67	0	0.00

AMERICAN LEAGUE EAST
DIVISION SHEET

Club	1st	2nd	vRHP	vLHP	Home	Road	Grass	Turf	Day	Night	Total	Pct
Toronto	53-35	46-27	75-36	24-26	54-26	45-36	35-28	64-34	34-24	65-38	99-62	.615
New York	49-36	48-28	65-37	32-27	58-22	39-42	84-53	13-11	37-20	60-44	97-64	.602
Detroit	48-37	36-40	58-53	26-24	44-37	40-40	73-63	11-14	27-27	57-50	84-77	.522
Baltimore	44-41	39-37	51-51	32-27	45-36	38-42	72-66	11-12	24-23	59-55	83-78	.516
Boston	45-42	36-39	58-55	23-26	43-37	38-44	67-69	14-12	27-29	54-52	81-81	.500
Milwaukee	37-47	34-43	43-58	28-32	40-40	31-50	64-71	7-19	16-39	55-51	71-90	.441
Cleveland	28-58	32-44	40-74	20-28	38-43	22-59	53-85	7-17	22-35	38-67	60-102	.370

COME FROM BEHIND WINS

Club	1	2	3	4	5	6	7	8	Total	Points
Toronto	20	13	5	2					40	109
New York	19	12	5	2	0	0	0	1	39	113
Detroit	15	7	6	3					31	90
Baltimore	22	14	4	5	2	1			48	146
Boston	17	11	1	4					33	91
Milwaukee	13	15	5	0	1	2			36	111
Cleveland	15	6	3	2	1				27	76

BLOWN LEADS

Club	1	2	3	4	5	6	7	8	Total	Points
Toronto	13	7	6	1	1	1			29	89
New York	18	8	7	2	1				36	104
Detroit	17	11	3	3	1	2			37	114
Baltimore	15	17	1	2	1	1			37	108
Boston	18	12	2	4					36	100
Milwaukee	18	11	8	2	0	1			40	118
Cleveland	17	21	9	3	1	2			53	168

RECORDS WHEN AHEAD, TIED, BEHIND, AFTER SEVEN

Club	Ahead	Tied	Behind
Toronto	82-13	11-99	6-40
New York	79- 4	9-11	9-49
Detroit	65-10	10- 8	9-59
Baltimore	63-11	12- 9	8-58
Boston	70- 7	2-11	9-63
Milwaukee	54- 8	11- 8	6-74
Cleveland	48- 9	5-10	7-83

CLUB BATTING

Club	G	AB	R	H	TB	2B	3B	HR	RBI	GW	SH	SF	HB	BB	IB	SO	SB	CS	DP	LOB	SHO	Avg	Slug	OBP
Toronto	161	5508	759	1482	2343	281	53	158	714	90	21	44	30	503	44	807	143	77	121	1067	5	.269	.425	.331
New York	161	5458	839	1458	2320	272	31	176	793	87	48	60	50	620	50	771	155	53	119	1125	6	.267	.425	.344
Detroit	161	5575	729	1413	2363	254	45	202	703	81	40	53	27	526	56	926	75	41	81	1142	6	.253	.424	.318
Baltimore	161	5517	818	1451	2371	234	22	214	773	80	31	40	19	604	30	908	69	43	132	1124	7	.263	.430	.336
Boston	163	5720	800	1615	2455	292	31	162	760	80	50	57	30	562	39	816	66	27	164	1241	8	.282	.429	.347
Milwaukee	161	5568	690	1467	2108	250	44	101	636	64	54	55	19	462	33	746	69	34	145	1130	10	.263	.379	.319
Cleveland	162	5527	729	1465	2129	254	31	116	689	58	38	48	15	492	26	817	132	72	139	1068	12	.265	.385	.324

OPPOSITION BATTING

Club	G	AB	R	H	TB	2B	3B	HR	RBI	GW	SH	SF	HB	BB	IB	SO	SB	CS	DP	LOB	SHO	Avg	Slug	OBP
Toronto	161	5406	588	1312	2029	220	28	147		60	47	41	26	484	26	823	83	44	157	1080	9	.243	.375	.306
New York	161	5459	660	1373	2132	220	34	157		60	32	42	13	518	20	907	106	45	158	1084	9	.252	.391	.316
Detroit	161	5462	688	1313	2038	226	38	141		73	43	49	23	556	67	943	93	53	107	1079	11	.240	.373	.311
Baltimore	161	5491	764	1480	2283	267	28	160		74	59	41	23	568	57	793	130	38	163	1136	6	.270	.416	.338
Boston	163	5619	720	1487	2228	275	38	130		74	49	38	35	540	54	913	94	63	197	1177	8	.265	.397	.331
Milwaukee	161	5577	802	1510	2366	247	42	175		82	52	51	33	499	31	777	109	54	172	1099	6	.271	.424	.331
Cleveland	162	5540	861	1556	2429	281	41	170		94	61	70	43	547	45	702	133	53	165	1138	7	.281	.438	.346

CLUB PITCHING

Club	W	L	ERA	G	CG	SHO	SV	IP	H	TBF	R	ER	HR	SH	SF	HB	BB	IB	SO	WP	BK
Toronto	99	62	3.31	161	18	9	47	1448.0	1312	6004	588	532	147	47	41	26	484	26	823	36	5
New York	97	64	3.69	161	25	9	49	1440.1	1373	6065	660	590	157	32	42	13	518	20	907	34	5
Detroit	84	77	3.78	161	31	11	40	1456.0	1313	6135	688	612	141	43	49	23	556	67	943	62	6
Baltimore	83	78	4.38	161	32	6	33	1427.1	1480	6182	764	694	160	59	41	23	568	57	793	32	7
Boston	81	81	4.06	163	35	8	29	1461.1	1487	6281	720	659	130	49	38	35	540	54	913	34	13
Milwaukee	71	90	4.39	161	34	6	37	1437.0	1510	6212	802	701	175	52	51	33	499	31	777	51	4
Cleveland	60	102	4.91	162	24	7	28	1421.0	1556	6262	861	776	170	61	70	43	547	45	702	46	7

OPPOSITION PITCHING

Club	W	L	ERA	G	CG	SHO	SV	IP	H	TBF	R	ER	HR	SH	SF	HB	BB	IB	SO	WP
Toronto	62	99			24	5	23		1482	6106	759		147	21	44	30	503	44	807	52
New York	64	97			17	6	29		1458	6236	839		157	48	60	50	620	50	771	51
Detroit	77	84			30	6	30		1413	6221	729		141	40	53	27	526	56	926	45
Baltimore	78	83			23	7	34		1451	6211	818		160	31	40	19	604	30	908	48
Boston	81	81			21	8	45		1615	6419	800		130	50	57	30	562	39	816	53
Milwaukee	90	71			32	10	41		1467	6158	690		175	54	55	19	462	33	746	40
Cleveland	102	60			24	12	51		1465	6120	729		170	38	48	15	492	26	817	43

CLUB FIELDING

Club	G	PO	A	E	TC	DP	TP	PB	OSB	OCS	OSB%	OA/SFA	Pct	DER	OR
Toronto	161	4344	1729	125	6198	164	0	3	83	44	.654	42/41	.980	.723	588
New York	161	4321	1563	126	6010	172	0	18	106	45	.702	35/42	.979	.709	660
Detroit	161	4368	1671	143	6182	152	0	10	93	53	.637	17/49	.977	.715	688
Baltimore	161	4282	1714	129	6125	168	0	4	130	38	.774	34/41	.979	.696	764
Boston	163	4384	1846	145	6375	161	0	14	94	63	.599	25/38	.971	.687	720
Milwaukee	161	4311	1686	142	6139	153	0	12	109	54	.669	27/51	.977	.697	802
Cleveland	162	4263	1703	141	6107	161	0	13	133	53	.715	40/70	.977	.690	861

TORONTO BLUE JAYS

BREAKDOWNS FOR THE LAST TEN SEASONS

Won-Lost Record: 625-774, .447 (Poorest in the Division, 25th in the Majors)
Runs Scored: 5,716 (Poorest in the Division, 19th in Majors)
    As noted re Seattle, Toronto and Seattle have only been in the Majors for
    nine years. Rankings are adjusted for this.
Runs Allowed: 6,398 (2nd Highest in the Division, 4th Highest in Majors)
Home Runs Hit: 1,054 (6th in the Division, 13th in the Majors)
Home Runs Allowed: 1,252 (2nd Highest in the Division, 3rd Highest in the Majors)

RECORD IN:
April: 83-96, .464 (6th in the Division, 21st in Majors)
May: 111-129, .463 (Worst in the Division, 21st in Majors)
June: 98-134, .422 (Worst in the Major Leagues)
July: 101-122, .453 (6th in the Division, 23rd in the Majors)
August: 120-140, .462 (Worst in the Division, 20th in the Majors)
September: 102-141, .420 (Worst in the Major Leagues)
October: 10-12, .455 (6th in the Division, 20th in the Majors)

Won-Lost Record in Road Games: 284-416, .406 (Worst in the Division, 24th in Majors)
Won-Lost Record at Home: 341-358, .488 (Worst in the Division, 23rd in Majors)
Home Field Advantage: 57½ Games
Runs Scored on the Road: 2,684 (Last in the Division, 23rd in Majors)
Runs Scored at Home: 3,032 (Last in the Division, 17th in Majors)
Runs Allowed on the Road: 3,131 (3rd Highest in the Division, 6th in Majors)
Runs Allowed at Home: 3,267 (2nd Highest in the Division, 4th in Majors)

Home Runs Hit on the Road: 522 (6th in the Division, 16th in the Majors)
Home Runs Hit at Home: 532 (6th in the Division, 14th in the Majors)
Home Runs Allowed on the Road: 583 (3rd Highest in the Division, 6th in Majors)
Home Runs Allowed at Home: 669 (2nd Highest in the Division, 4th in Majors)

RECORD FOR LAST THREE SEASONS: 277-208, .571 (2nd Best in the Division, 2nd Best in Baseball)

The Toronto Blue Jay comment in the 1985 *Abstract* was a report by a young man named David Driscoll, who had scored over a hundred Blue Jay games from 1984 and done a number of studies about the performance of players under different ball/strike conditions, focusing particularly on the outcomes of the first pitch. During the 1985 season, Mr. Driscoll scored every game, every pitch of the Toronto Blue Jays' championship season. From this he has compiled an astonishing 171-page collection of studies of the Blue Jay season.

Let me back up for a minute. No two chemists, no two physicists have exactly the same interests, use exactly the same methods or share the same beliefs about the significance of their profession. No two have exactly the same reason for studying in the field. At times, the interests of one may seem far-fetched and bizarre to another, and the beliefs of one may seem wrong and even dangerous to another. In spite of this, they recognize a community of interest among themselves, and share ideas and knowledge.

When I began studying baseball professionally, ten years ago, I initially wanted to study closely the records of games. Because the records of the games were not available to the public at that time—they are now, through Project Scoresheet—I found it impossible to do this, so instead I backed off and studied the game through the records of *teams* and *players*. In essence, I was studying records which were already public, trying to derive from them insights which others had missed. While this was a source of some frustration at the time—I wanted to be able to develop records that were completely new, completely fresh—I feel that in the long run it was serendipitous, for,

in studying the records of teams and players, I was directed to focus on larger, more general and universal questions than one would study through the records of individual games. My greatest interest in sabermetrics has settled into questions relating to why one team or one type of team succeeds, and to the relationships among large elements of the game such as offense and defense, base stealing and power. What I have most often tried to do is to design small studies which would yield bits of specific information which were in some way related to those questions.

In the employ of the Texas Rangers, Craig Wright's interest was more focused on specific issues making an immediate impact on the team's decisions—yet, like me, he has most often studied the records of teams and players, rather than the records of games. But a new generation of sabermetricians is emerging now which is focusing on the things that I originally wanted to study—records of games, records of pitches, records of minute sections of baseball life. This is different—it leads to different types of new knowledge—and many of you no doubt have noticed the difference. But physicists use both microscopes and telescopes; I'm very happy to see the types of information that I wanted to make available ten years ago gradually getting out, through the efforts of people like John Dewan, Chuck Waseleski, Davis Jackson, Jeff Welch and David Driscoll.

One of the problems with this, however, is that one must go through a long period of *assembling* and *presenting* this material before one can begin to *study* it. It is fortunate that some people enjoy this process, because I sure as hell don't. In the Seattle comment, I introduced scatter-shot a sampling of the information that Jeff Welch has developed about the Seattle Mariners. David Driscoll has put together many of the same types of information about the Toronto Blue Jays, many of the same and even more. His study, which is available from David Driscoll, P.O. Box 6493, Station D, London, Ontario, N5W 5S5, contains 30 reports, analyzing the performance of the Blue Jay pitchers and hitters in a bewildering variety of ways. The effect of these reports is initially somewhat overwhelming, but once you stare at the book for a couple of hours so that you can begin to get a handle on what he is doing, many of the studies are fascinating and offer unique insights into the game. I would recommend his book very highly, not only for Blue Jays' fans but for anyone who is interested in a sort of nuts-and-bolts diagram of a successful season.

Anyway, whereas what I did with Seattle was simply to present some random facts gathered from Welch's study of the season, what I wanted to do here was to try to use the material to explore relationships in the game. For instance:

1. How many extra strikes does it take to make a strikeout pitcher? Among the three Toronto regular starters, Jimmy Key was the least likely to strike out or walk a batter, with 85 strikeouts and only 50 walks in 213 innings. Dave Stieb was the most likely, with 167 strikeouts and 96 walks—nearly double Key's figures—in 265 innings. Let's compare their complete strike/ball breakdowns:

	KEY	STIEB
Balls	1139	1413
Called Strikes	460	626
Foul Strikes	535	655
Swinging Strikes	216	327
Put In Play	719	816
TOTAL	3069	3837

If you expand Key's ratio to Stieb's 3,837 pitches for comparison, you'll see that the differences in terms of pitch frequencies are alarmingly small. In fact, although Stieb walked almost twice as many men as Key (with adjustment for innings, Stieb walked men about 50% more often), *Key threw more balls as a percentage of pitches than did Stieb.* Not many more—37.1% as opposed to 36.8%—but still more. The reason that Key walked fewer men was (apparently) that he had a higher percentage of balls put into play—hence escaping the sequence before it culminated in a walk.

Based on 3,837 pitches, Stieb and Key would be almost even in balls thrown (1,413–1,424). Stieb would have more called strikes (626–575) and more swinging strikes (327–270); Key, being easier to hit, would have a few more foul strikes (655–669). Although the difference in strikeouts is about 50%, the difference in strikes thrown is only 7%. Key would have more balls put in play (816–899), a difference that is small as a percentage but enormously significant. Dave Stieb had 90% as many balls in play as Jimmie Key—but Freddie Patek was also 90% as tall as Henry Aaron, and Alan Bannister's career batting average is 90% of Willie Mays'.

2. How does the strike count relate to stolen base at-

tempts? The Blue Jays loved to run on a 2–2 count, and were very successful in so doing, stealing 17 bases in 19 attempts on a 2–2 count. However, surprisingly, Blue Jay opponents showed little inclination to run on this option pitch, attempting only 5 stolen bases (they were 3/5).

Cox liked to start his baserunners on a 3–1 or 3–2 count, and the Blue Jays stolen base percentage was considerably lowered by this. The Blue Jays had 11 stolen base attempts coming on a 3–1 count (they were just 5/11) and 18 stolen base attempts coming on a 3–2 count (they were an unfortunate 6/18, losing two-thirds of their runners). These attempts lowered the Blue Jays' stolen base success rate from 70.0% (133/190) to 65.8% (144/219). By contrast, Blue Jay opponents ran only twice on the 3–1 count, and only five times on a 3–2 count. They also lost most of the runners they sent on these counts, going 2 for 7 in these stolen base attempts.

Of course, this does not prove that Cox lost the gamble. The reason for starting your runners 3–2 is that there is a high probability of the ball being put in play, and if it is the runner will have the advantage of being off with the pitch. However, he certainly lost the gamble when the ball was not put in play.

I've always been a little doubtful about the percentages of this play—as, apparently, are most other American League managers. Some people will tell you that the risk is lowered because, even if the runner doesn't get a good jump, he can be safe at second on the walk; he can only be thrown out if the batter strikes out. What seems obvious to me is that if the risk is lowered, so is the payoff; if he gets a good jump and the pitch is ball four, then there is no benefit to starting the runner, since he winds up at second just the same. The gamble seems to me to be just the same as any other pitch, only reduced in significance. Maybe the payoff is increased because of the increased likelihood of the ball being put in play, I don't know. Sometime I'll try to puzzle out the percentages in it, but not right now.

The Blue Jays were most successful stealing when their hitter was *even* in the count, stealing 29 of 39 tries with the count 1–1 or 2–2 (74%). They were *least* successful in stealing when their hitter was ahead in the count, stealing 41 with 30 runners caught stealing (58%).

3. How does the stolen base attempt affect the hitter at the plate? This one is a real stunner. Mr. Driscoll's study shows that *after a successful steal attempt,* Toronto hitters hit for an average of .198 (21/106). *After an unsuccessful steal attempt,* they were even worse—4 for 40, a .100 average. All taken together, Toronto hitters hit just .171 with very little power (but a good number of walks) during plate appearances in which a stolen base was attempted.

Toronto opponents were about the same, except worse. After a successful steal attempt, Toronto opponents hit .127 (9/71). After an unsuccessful attempt, they hit .154 (4/26).

These outcomes could be influenced by several distorting factors. To name the most obvious, there might be a tendency to steal late in the count, and a tendency to steal when a weak hitter is at the plate. However, the first looks like a red herring, since the Blue Jays attempted many more steals with the batter ahead in the count than with the runner behind in the count, so that this should have weighted the outcome in favor of the hitter, rather than against him. And as to stealing with the weaker hitters at the plate—well, the Blue Jays don't have any .171 hitters in their lineup. In fact, it is extremely difficult to say who their weakest hitters are.

What seems much more likely is that hitters swung at pitches to protect the base stealer, and got behind in the count—hence largely ruining the at bat. I think this could be yet another very damning indictment of the stolen base as an offensive weapon, but we will have to wait until additional studies are made of the issue.

4. How does an offense change at home as opposed to on the road? An intriguing note about this appears on page 132 of Driscoll's study. In their home games, the Blue Jays outscored their opponents by a slim 37–32 margin. In the second inning, it was 40–20. On the road, the Blue Jays outscored their opponents in the first inning 36–35, but lost the second 35–27.

What is the difference between the first and second innings? The difference, of course, is that the good hitters hit in the first, and the bottom of the order hits in the second. Is it possible, I wonder, that poorer hitters are much more affected by being on the road than are good hitters? Seems possible.

I could have done, with Driscoll's study, what I did in the Seattle comment—go rummaging through the report picking out odd and interesting facts and passing them along. I could have pointed out that Rance Mulliniks hit .350 when he was ahead in the count, but .218 when he was behind. I decided not to do that. I could have pointed out that Lloyd Moseby hit .303 when opposition pitchers were working from the stretch, but .226 when they were working from a full windup. I decided not to. I could have pointed out that Tim McClelland called strikes on 32% of the pitches taken by hitters, whereas Dan Morrison called strikes on only 22%. I could have pointed out that the Blue Jays had 88 big innings, while their opponents had only

43. I could have pointed out that Dave Stieb limited opposition leadoff men to a .186 batting average (22/118), while eighth and ninth place hitters did better against him, or I could have pointed to the seemingly related fact that Stieb had a remarkable 1.50 ERA in the first inning, when many runs are usually scored (it was actually his best inning). I could have pointed out that while Doyle Alexander did allow 28 home runs in 1985, this accounted for only 10.2% of the fly balls hit to the outfield against him, actually one of the lowest percentages on the Blue Jay team (Luis Leal surrendered home runs on 16.9% of fly balls to the outfield, and Stieb and Key were both above 10.2). I could have pointed out that Toronto hitters hit .405 and slugged .714 when they hit a 2–0 pitch. I could have pointed out that Tom Henke had a far greater tendency to throw a strike on the first pitch than any other Toronto pitcher, or I could have discussed the obviously related fact that opposition hitters had a greater tendency to swing at Henke's first pitch than for any other pitcher. I could have pointed out that Rance Mulliniks was by far the most successful Blue Jay at advancing baserunners, moving up 49.7% of the runners who were on base when he came to bat (no one else was close; Ernie Whitt was second at 42.1%), or that Al Oliver was the poorest on the team in this respect, advancing only 29 of 95 runners who were on base when he came to the plate.

I didn't get into any of that, so if you're interested in that type of information, you'll just have to get Driscoll's report. I'm not selling him, you see, but I did want to say that I think Driscoll is one of the most talented and exciting young analysts of the game that I've ever run across, and I did want to say that it would be a damn shame if he couldn't make a living doing this, and had to give it up to sell pencils on the corner of 19th and Royal Crescent in London, Ontario. You can help avoid this fate if you'll write to the address I gave you, and inquire about a copy of his fascinating study.

COMPLETE BATTING RECORDS

Player	G	AB	R	H	TB	2B	3B	HR	RBI	GW	SH	SF	HB	BB	IB	SO	SB	CS	GI DP	Avg	Slug	OBP	Runs	Outs Made	Runs/ 27 Outs	OW%	Appr Value
*Whitt	139	412	55	101	183	21	2	19	64	8	3	2	1	47	9	59	3	6	7	.245	.444	.323	58	329	4.74	.562	9
*Upshaw	148	501	79	138	224	31	5	15	65	7	1	3	4	48	7	71	8	8	6	.275	.447	.342	76	381	5.42	.626	11
Garcia	146	600	70	169	226	25	4	8	65	10	5	3	4	15	2	41	28	15	13	.282	.377	.302	64	467	3.68	.436	10
*Mulliniks	129	366	55	108	166	26	1	10	57	11	1	5	0	55	2	54	2	0	10	.295	.454	.383	64	274	6.49	.707	9
†Fernandez	161	564	71	163	220	31	10	2	51	6	7	2	2	43	2	41	13	6	12	.289	.390	.340	75	428	4.71	.559	10
Bell	157	607	87	167	291	28	6	28	95	11	0	8	8	43	6	90	21	6	8	.275	.479	.327	97	462	5.69	.649	12
*Moseby	152	584	92	151	249	30	7	18	70	10	1	5	4	76	4	91	37	15	12	.259	.426	.345	89	466	5.14	.601	12
Barfield	155	539	94	156	289	34	9	27	84	12	0	3	4	66	5	143	22	8	14	.289	.536	.369	106	408	7.03	.739	16
Johnson	24	73	4	20	23	0	0	1	10	0	0	1	0	9	0	15	0	0	1	.274	.315	.349	9	55	4.28	.512	0
Iorg	131	288	33	90	135	22	1	7	37	0	2	1	0	21	3	26	2	6	6	.313	.469	.358	45	213	5.72	.652	6
Burroughs	86	191	19	49	82	9	3	6	28	2	0	2	0	34	1	36	0	1	7	.257	.429	.366	30	152	5.38	.623	3
*Oliver	61	187	20	47	70	6	1	5	23	3	0	0	1	7	2	13	0	0	8	.251	.374	.282	17	148	3.15	.361	2
*Matuszek	62	151	23	32	48	6	2	2	15	0	0	4	0	11	0	24	2	1	5	.212	.318	.259	12	129	2.52	.266	1
Martinez	42	99	11	16	31	3	0	4	14	3	0	3	1	10	0	12	0	0	3	.162	.313	.239	8	89	2.28	.229	1
Fielder	30	74	6	23	39	4	0	4	16	4	0	1	0	6	0	16	0	0	2	.311	.527	.358	14	54	6.85	.728	1
*Thornton	56	72	18	17	23	1	1	1	8	1	0	0	1	2	0	24	1	0	2	.236	.319	.267	6	57	2.76	.304	0
†Lee	64	40	9	8	8	0	0	0	0	0	1	0	0	2	0	9	1	4	2	.200	.200	.238	1	39	0.62	.021	0
*Leach	16	35	2	7	9	0	1	0	1	0	0	0	0	3	1	9	0	0	0	.200	.257	.263	3	28	2.42	.250	0
Shepherd	38	35	7	4	6	2	0	0	1	0	0	0	0	2	0	12	3	0	1	.114	.171	.162	1	32	0.92	.046	0
Allenson	14	34	2	4	5	1	0	0	3	0	0	0	0	0	0	10	0	0	1	.118	.147	.118	0	31	0.38	.008	0
*Aikens	12	20	2	4	8	1	0	1	5	1	0	1	0	3	0	6	0	0	1	.200	.400	.292	2	18	3.49	.410	0
Nicosia	6	15	0	4	4	0	0	0	0	0	0	0	0	0	0	2	0	0	0	.267	.267	.267	1	11	2.68	.295	0
Gruber	5	13	0	3	3	0	0	0	1	1	0	0	0	0	0	3	0	0	0	.231	.231	.231	1	10	1.87	.123	0
Hearron	4	7	0	1	1	0	0	0	0	0	0	0	0	0	0	2	0	0	0	.143	.143	.143	0	6	0.84	.031	0
†Webster	4	1	0	0	0	0	0	0	0	0	0	0	0	0	0	0	0	0	0	.000	.000	.000	0	1	0.00	.000	0
Key	36	0	0	0	0	0	0	0	0	0	0	0	0	0	0	0	0	0	0	.000	.000	.000	0	0	0.00	.000	0

*left-handed hitter, †switch hitter

DEFENSIVE STATISTICS

FIRST	G	PO	A	Er	TC	DP	PCT.
Upshaw	147	1157	104	10	1271	111	.992
Fielder	25	171	17	4	192	21	.979
Leach	10	72	6	1	79	8	.987
Matuszek	5	19	2	0	21	1	1.000
Johnson	3	17	1	1	19	4	.947
Oliver	1	3	0	0	3	0	1.000
TEAM:	191	1439	130	16	1585	145	.990
AVG:	180	1440	123	14	1577	141	.991

SECOND	G	PO	A	Er	TC	DP	PCT.
Garcia	143	302	371	13	686	88	.981
Lee	38	27	40	2	69	8	.971
Iorg	23	32	55	0	87	11	1.000
Gruber	1	0	0	0	0	0	.000
TEAM:	205	361	466	15	842	107	.982
AVG:	189	347	501	15	863	14	.982

THIRD	G	PO	A	Er	TC	DP	PCT.
Mulliniks	119	75	162	7	244	16	.971
Iorg	104	39	137	9	185	13	.951
Gruber	5	2	6	0	8	0	1.000
Lee	5	0	3	0	3	0	1.000
Bell	2	0	1	0	1	0	1.000
TEAM:	235	116	309	16	441	29	.964
AVG:	192	129	327	23	479	32	.953

SHORTSTOP	G	PO	A	Er	TC	DP	PCT.
Fernandez	160	283	478	30	791	109	.962
Lee	8	7	13	1	21	3	.952
TEAM:	168	290	491	31	812	112	.962
AVG:	189	269	474	28	771	104	.964

CATCHER	G	PO	A	Er	TC	DP	PCT.	PB
Whitt	134	649	38	8	695	6	.988	2
Martinez	42	155	16	2	173	5	.988	1
Allenson	14	39	2	0	41	0	1.000	0
Nicosia	6	23	2	0	25	1	1.000	0
Hearron	4	16	1	0	17	0	1.000	0
TEAM:	200	882	59	10	951	12	.989	3
AVG:	193	895	74	13	982	13	.987	13

OUTFIELD	G	PO	A	Er	TC	DP	PCT.
Bell	157	320	13	11	344	3	.968
Barfield	154	349	22	4	375	8	.989
Moseby	152	394	7	8	409	1	.980
Thornton	35	44	0	2	46	0	.957
Shepherd	16	24	0	0	24	0	1.000
Leach	4	6	0	0	6	0	1.000
Webster	2	0	0	0	0	0	.000
TEAM:	520	1137	42	25	1204	12	.979
AVG:	559	1141	33	21	1196	8	.982

COMPLETE PITCHERS RECORDS

Pitcher	W	L	Pct	ERA	G	GS	CG	GF	SHO	SV	IP	H	TBF	R	ER	HR	SH	SF	HB	BB	IB	SO	WP	BK	Appr Value
								Starters (One-half of Game Appearances)																	
Stieb	14	13	.519	2.48	36	36	8	0	2	0	265.0	206	1087	89	73	22	14	2	9	96	3	167	4	1	15
Alexander	17	10	.630	3.45	36	36	6	0	1	0	260.2	268	1090	105	100	28	6	3	6	67	0	142	9	0	13
*Key	14	6	.700	3.00	35	32	3	0	0	0	212.2	188	856	77	71	22	5	5	2	50	1	85	6	1	10
Clancy	9	6	.600	3.78	23	23	1	0	0	0	128.2	117	527	54	54	15	0	5	0	37	0	66	2	0	5
Leal	3	6	.333	5.75	15	14	0	1	0	0	67.1	82	303	46	43	13	1	4	3	24	3	33	3	1	1
Filer	7	0	1.000	3.88	11	9	0	0	0	0	48.2	38	192	21	21	6	2	1	0	18	0	24	0	1	4
*Davis	2	1	.667	3.54	10	5	0	1	0	0	28.0	23	117	14	11	5	0	1	0	13	0	22	0	0	0
								Relievers																	
Lamp	11	0	1.000	3.32	53	1	0	11	0	2	105.2	96	426	42	39	7	5	6	0	27	3	68	5	0	8
Acker	7	2	.778	3.23	61	0	0	26	0	10	86.1	86	370	35	31	7	1	2	3	43	1	42	2	0	7
*Lavelle	5	7	.417	3.10	69	0	0	19	0	8	72.2	54	298	30	25	5	8	2	0	36	5	50	0	1	7
Caudill	4	6	.400	2.99	67	0	0	51	0	14	69.1	53	297	26	23	9	3	4	2	35	6	46	0	0	8
Musselman	3	0	1.000	4.47	25	4	0	9	0	0	52.1	59	236	28	26	2	0	4	0	24	2	29	3	0	2
Henke	3	3	.500	2.03	28	0	0	22	0	13	40.0	29	153	12	9	4	2	2	0	8	2	42	0	0	5
*Cerutti	0	2	.000	5.40	4	1	0	1	0	0	6.2	10	36	7	4	1	0	0	1	4	0	5	2	0	0
*Clarke	0	0	.000	4.50	4	0	0	2	0	0	4.0	3	16	2	2	1	0	0	0	2	0	2	0	0	0

Ernie WHITT, Catcher

	G	AB	Hit	2B	3B	HR	Run	RBI	TBB	SO	SB	CS	Avg
4.35 years		439	107	20	2	16	50	61	49	63	3	4	.244
1985	139	412	101	21	2	19	55	64	47	59	3	6	.245
First Half	68	198	54	14	1	10	31	37	19	23	1	3	.273
Second Half	71	214	47	7	1	9	24	27	28	36	2	3	.220
Vs. RHP		338	85	19	2	17	47	56	36	37	3	5	.251
Vs. LHP		74	16	2	0	2	8	8	11	22	0	1	.216
Home	69	197	44	13	1	7	27	26	27	33	1	5	.223
Road	70	215	57	8	1	12	28	38	20	26	2	1	.265
Grass	56	175	48	6	0	12	26	34	18	22	2	1	.274
Turf	83	237	53	15	2	7	29	30	29	37	1	5	.224

Willie UPSHAW, First Base

	G	AB	Hit	2B	3B	HR	Run	RBI	TBB	SO	SB	CS	Avg
5.00 years		525	143	25	6	18	77	72	51	82	9	7	.272
1985	148	501	138	31	5	15	79	65	48	71	8	8	.275
First Half	83	309	72	18	3	8	46	41	32	45	2	5	.233
Second Half	65	192	66	13	2	7	33	24	16	26	6	3	.344
Vs. RHP		331	92	21	2	10	59	32	40	41	8	5	.278
Vs. LHP		170	46	10	3	5	20	33	8	30	0	3	.271
Home	74	236	70	19	3	6	39	33	26	36	4	4	.297
Road	74	265	68	12	2	9	40	32	22	35	4	4	.257
Grass	56	200	53	10	0	9	31	26	15	29	4	2	.265
Turf	92	301	85	21	5	6	48	39	33	42	4	6	.282

Damaso GARCIA, Second Base

	G	AB	Hit	2B	3B	HR	Run	RBI	TBB	SO	SB	CS	Avg
4.99 years		646	186	30	5	5	81	51	20	52	38	16	.287
1985	146	600	169	25	4	8	70	65	15	41	28	15	.282
First Half	82	352	99	14	4	3	39	43	9	20	22	8	.281
Second Half	64	248	70	11	0	5	31	22	6	21	6	7	.282
Vs RHP		380	114	15	3	6	49	50	8	24	23	10	.300
Vs. LHP		220	55	10	1	2	21	15	7	17	5	5	.250
Home	77	300	91	16	4	4	41	45	12	19	14	9	.303
Road	69	300	78	9	0	4	29	20	3	22	14	6	.260
Grass	52	224	60	5	0	4	22	18	1	18	11	5	.268
Turf	94	376	109	20	4	4	48	47	14	23	17	10	.290

Jesse BARFIELD, Right Field

	G	AB	Hit	2B	3B	HR	Run	RBI	TBB	SO	SB	CS	Avg
3.44 years		505	135	22	5	26	78	78	49	126	11	6	.267
1985	155	539	156	34	9	27	97	84	66	143	22	8	.289
First Half	79	276	70	12	2	12	43	38	31	79	11	1	.254
Second Half	76	263	86	22	7	15	54	46	35	64	11	7	.327
Vs. RHP		332	93	17	2	18	62	56	41	87	14	6	.280
Vs. LHP		207	63	17	2	9	35	28	25	56	8	2	.304
Home	76	255	73	16	5	15	49	49	33	71	16	4	.286
Road	79	284	83	18	4	12	48	35	33	72	6	4	.292
Grass	61	209	59	12	3	10	39	30	30	48	6	3	.282
Turf	94	330	97	22	6	17	58	54	36	95	16	5	.294

Rance MULLINIKS, Third Base

	G	AB	Hit	2B	3B	HR	Run	RBI	TBB	SO	SB	CS	Avg
4.33 years		448	121	30	3	7	57	53	52	65	2	2	.270
1985	126	366	108	26	1	10	55	57	55	54	2	0	.295
First Half	67	186	57	12	0	5	25	32	31	30	2	0	.306
Second Half	59	180	51	14	1	5	30	25	24	24	0	0	.283
Vs. RHP		344	103	24	1	10	51	56	49	50	2	0	.299
Vs. LHP		22	5	2	0	0	4	1	6	4	0	0	.227
Home	58	174	55	15	1	4	33	25	28	25	1	0	.316
Road	68	192	53	11	0	6	22	32	27	29	1	0	.276
Grass	53	168	45	10	0	5	21	29	25	25	1	0	.268
Turf	73	198	63	16	1	5	34	28	30	29	1	0	.318

Cliff JOHNSON, Designated Hitter

	G	AB	Hit	2B	3B	HR	Run	RBI	TBB	SO	SB	CS	Avg
7.79 years		463	120	23	1	23	63	83	66	85	1	1	.258
1985	106	369	96	17	1	13	35	66	40	59	0	0	.260
First Half	54	192	49	11	1	9	23	40	23	25	0	0	.255
Second Half	52	177	47	6	0	4	12	26	17	34	0	0	.266
Vs. RHP		259	60	11	1	11	20	53	23	44	0	0	.232
Vs. LHP		110	36	6	0	2	15	13	17	15	0	0	.327
Home	52	172	43	5	1	9	20	43	23	32	0	0	.250
Road	54	197	53	12	0	4	15	23	17	27	0	0	.269
Grass	80	278	73	12	1	12	29	56	32	45	0	0	.263
Turf	26	91	23	5	0	1	6	10	8	14	0	0	.253

Tony FERNANDEZ, Shortstop

	G	AB	Hit	2B	3B	HR	Run	RBI	TBB	SO	SB	CS	Avg
1.63 years		510	144	23	9	3	64	44	38	36	11	9	.283
1985	161	564	163	31	10	2	71	51	43	41	13	6	.289
First Half	83	284	80	14	5	2	33	29	21	17	8	2	.282
Second Half	78	280	83	17	5	0	38	22	22	24	5	4	.296
Vs. RHP		370	106	18	5	2	48	36	21	27	12	4	.286
Vs. LHP		194	57	13	5	0	23	15	22	14	1	2	.294
Home	80	265	81	22	6	1	40	23	23	16	5	4	.306
Road	81	299	82	9	4	1	31	28	20	25	8	2	.274
Grass	63	236	64	5	2	1	24	20	14	23	6	1	.271
Turf	98	328	99	26	8	1	47	31	29	18	7	5	.302

Garth IORG, Third Base

	G	AB	Hit	2B	3B	HR	Run	RBI	TBB	SO	SB	CS	Avg
4.15 years		437	116	23	4	3	45	40	18	48	4	4	.266
1985	131	288	90	22	1	7	33	37	21	26	2	6	.313
First Half	64	125	41	10	0	2	17	13	11	9	2	3	.328
Second Half	67	163	49	12	1	5	16	24	10	17	0	3	.301
Vs. RHP		87	28	5	0	2	8	14	5	13	0	1	.322
Vs. LHP		201	62	17	1	5	25	23	16	13	2	5	.308
Home	63	119	45	10	0	5	18	19	8	9	1	3	.378
Road	68	169	45	12	1	2	15	18	13	17	1	3	.266
Grass	51	118	31	9	1	1	10	11	9	14	1	3	.263
Turf	80	170	59	13	0	6	23	26	12	12	1	3	.347

George BELL, Left Field

	G	AB	Hit	2B	3B	HR	Run	RBI	TBB	SO	SB	CS	Avg
2.56 years		581	161	29	6	24	77	82	30	86	14	4	.277
1985	157	607	167	28	6	28	87	95	43	90	21	6	.275
First Half	81	317	92	14	4	17	48	54	20	55	12	2	.290
Second Half	76	290	75	14	2	11	39	41	23	35	9	4	.259
Vs. RHP		390	112	20	4	17	56	64	25	61	17	3	.287
Vs. LHP		217	55	8	2	11	31	31	18	29	4	3	.253
Home	78	286	73	16	2	10	40	48	27	46	10	2	.255
Road	79	321	94	12	4	18	47	47	16	44	11	4	.293
Grass	61	243	74	11	2	13	36	38	14	32	9	2	.305
Turf	96	364	93	17	4	15	51	57	29	58	12	4	.255

Lloyd MOSEBY, Center Field

	G	AB	Hit	2B	3B	HR	Run	RBI	TBB	SO	SB	CS	Avg
5.07 years		585	154	29	8	16	84	76	57	113	25	10	.262
1985	152	584	151	30	7	18	92	70	76	91	37	15	.259
First Half	82	314	75	19	4	5	44	28	46	52	23	10	.239
Second Half	70	270	76	11	3	13	48	42	30	39	14	5	.281
Vs. RHP		350	91	19	7	11	55	48	52	43	26	10	.260
Vs. LHP		234	60	11	0	7	37	22	24	48	11	5	.256
Home	75	283	73	16	5	11	50	45	38	43	19	6	.258
Road	77	301	78	14	2	7	42	25	38	48	18	9	.259
Grass	59	225	53	9	2	6	33	18	33	33	13	6	.236
Turf	93	359	98	21	5	12	59	52	43	58	24	9	.273

DOYLE ALEXANDER

	(W–L)	GS	Run	Avg	DP	Avg	SB	Avg
1984	(17-6)	35	165	4.71	30	.86	10	.29
1985	(17-10)	36	153	4.25	32	.89	18	.50
1976-1985		266	1155	4.34	235	.88	169	.64

	G	IP	W	L	Pct	ER	BB	SO	ERA
1984 Home	20	163.7	12	3	.800	47	31	85	2.58
1985 Home	21	162.3	11	5	.688	51	43	92	2.83
1984 Road	16	98.0	5	3	.625	44	28	54	4.04
1985 Road	15	98.3	6	5	.545	49	24	50	4.04
1984 Grass	13	76.0	2	3	.400	38	25	48	4.50
1985 Grass	11	73.7	4	4	.500	38	19	36	4.64
1984 Turf	12	78.7	5	4	.556	38	34	91	4.35
1985 Turf	25	187.0	13	6	.684	62	48	106	2.98
1985 Total	36	260.7	17	10	.630	100	67	142	3.45

DAVE STIEB

	(W–L)	GS	Run	Avg	DP	Avg	SB	Avg
1984	(16-8)	35	156	4.46	37	1.06	13	.37
1985	(14-13)	36	160	4.44	31	.86	14	.39
1979-1985		210	904	4.30	229	1.09	96	.46

	G	IP	W	L	Pct	ER	BB	SO	ERA
1984 Home	15	116.3	9	4	.692	35	35	85	2.71
1985 Home	15	112.3	8	6	.571	37	37	66	2.96
1984 Road	20	150.7	7	4	.636	49	53	113	2.93
1985 Road	21	152.7	6	7	.462	36	59	101	2.12
1984 Grass	15	110.7	4	3	.571	42	44	79	3.42
1985 Grass	16	117.3	5	5	.500	29	51	75	2.22
1984 Turf	20	156.3	12	5	.706	42	44	119	2.42
1985 Turf	20	147.7	9	8	.529	44	45	92	2.68
1985 Total	36	265.0	14	13	.519	73	96	167	2.48

JIM CLANCY

	(W–L)	GS	Run	Avg	DP	Avg	SB	Avg
1984	(13-15)	36	152	4.22	50	1.39	22	.61
1985	(9-6)	23	120	5.22	15	.65	12	.52
1977-1985		243	989	4.07	239	.98	115	.47

	G	IP	W	L	Pct	ER	BB	SO	ERA
1984 Home	15	86.0	6	9	.400	56	36	46	5.86
1985 Home	8	46.3	4	1	.800	13	10	26	2.53
1984 Road	21	133.7	7	6	.538	69	52	72	4.65
1985 Road	15	82.3	5	5	.500	41	40	27	4.48
1984 Grass	17	105.3	7	6	.538	58	43	55	4.96
1985 Grass	12	64.7	3	4	.429	35	22	28	4.87
1984 Turf	21	141.7	11	5	.688	62	45	63	3.94
1985 Turf	11	64.0	6	2	.750	19	15	38	2.67
1985 Total	23	128.7	9	6	.600	54	37	66	3.78

JIMMY KEY

	(W–L)	GS	Run	Avg	DP	Avg	SB	Avg
1985	(14-6)	32	149	4.66	43	134	18	.56

	G	IP	W	L	Pct	ER	BB	SO	ERA
1985 Home	21	128.7	10	3	.769	38	54	27	2.66
1985 Road	14	84.0	4	3	.571	33	23	31	3.54
1985 Grass	12	72.0	4	3	.571	30	21	29	3.75
1985 Turf	23	140.7	10	3	.769	41	29	56	2.62
12985 Total	35	212.7	14	6	.700	71	50	85	3.00

OTHERS

	(W–L)	GS	Run	Avg	DP	Avg	SB	Avg
Noles	(4-8)	13	50	3.85	13	1.00	20	1.54
Russell	(3-6)	13	58	4.46	11	.85	15	1.15
Cook	(2-3)	7	35	5.00	7	1.00	4	.57
Welsh	(2-5)	6	20	3.33	3	.50	1	.17
Guzman	(3-2)	5	20	4.00	5	1.00	5	1.00
Stewart	(0-6)	5	12	2.40	2	.40	5	1.00
Rozema	(3-7)	4	12	3.00	3	.75	1	.25
Schmidt	(7-6)	4	21	5.25	1	.25	4	1.00
Sebra	(0-2)	4	9	2.25	3	.75	3	.75
Williams	(2-1)	3	11	3.67	5	1.67	0	0.00

NEW YORK YANKEES

SECONDARY AVERAGE

One of the new terms I've been using this year is "secondary average." A player's secondary average is *the sum of his extra bases on hits, walks and stolen bases, expressed on a per-at bat basis*. Don Mattingly in 1985 had 211 hits in 652 at bats, a batting average of a fine .324. But he also had 159 extra bases on hits, 56 walks and 2 stolen bases, a total of 217 secondary bases, for a secondary average of a fine .333.

Unlike total average, runs produced, estimated runs produced, runs created, base/out percentage, linear weights and runs *ad infinitum,* secondary average does not attempt to sum up *all* of a player's offensive contributions; rather, it focuses on *the major areas of offensive productivity which are not reflected in the player's batting average*.

Unlike most of the other new methods that I introduce from year to year—similarity scores, minors-to-majors translations, approximate value, etc.—secondary average could not be described as an analytical tool; it is not a method that would be adapted to explore some particular question or some set of questions. It does not constitute new knowledge; rather, it is a new way of expressing a set of values which have already been accepted.

What we have always known, basically, is that a player who has a low batting average can, at times, be a good hitter. A player who hits .240 can be on base more often than another hitter who hits .320, if the .240 hitter is more selective. A .240 hitter can drive in more runs than a .320 hitter, if he spikes his .240 average with enough power. The hitter's value does not depend on his batting average, but on his ability to produce runs. The secondary average is a summation of the strength of the "kickers" to the player's primary average.

This "kicker strength" is something that I and other sabermetricians have to deal with over and over in explaining why we value one player highly and another not so highly. If I'm talking to somebody from Atlanta, he'll want to know why I feel that Rafael Ramirez is such a terrible hitter, when his batting averages are pretty good for a shortstop. It's hard to explain—he doesn't hit for much power, but then there are only a few shortstops who do hit for power, and he doesn't walk very often, but then there are a lot of people who don't walk much and some of them are good hitters despite that, and he's a poor base stealer but then so is Jack Clark. No one of those failings would justify calling him a lousy hitter, and if you cite them one by one it sounds like you're picking out all of his weaknesses and ignoring his strengths. The reason he's a lousy hitter is that the sum of his offensive contributions, apart from batting average, is very small. In other words, he has a low secondary average.

Or if I was talking to a reporter who liked Enos Cabell, and reporters like Enos Cabell, he would want to know why I thought Enos was a bad hitter even though he has hit .300. There are a lot of reasons for it, but a simple way to put them is this: in 1983 Enos Cabell hit .311, but his secondary average was .171. Or if you know any sabermetricians you will know that we all love Andy Van Slyke. But if we try to explain to somebody that we think Andy's an outstanding player and going to be even better, the idea comes across that we think Van Slyke's going to hit .330 one fine year. That's not it; the reason we love

Andy Van Slyke is that last season he hit just .259 but had a secondary average of .370. *That's* the potential that we're excited about, the very real chance that he will have a secondary average of .450—not the off chance that he might hit .330.

I've been looking for several years for better ways to express this central idea. Two or three years ago I tried describing a player who got on base a lot by walks and also hit for power as a "Type AA" player, while a player who was low in both areas was a "Type CC" player—or maybe it was the other way around; who remembers. I couldn't exactly go on the radio and say that Rafael Ramirez was a terrible offensive player because he was a "Type CC" hitter, and the fact that I couldn't do this is a way of saying that the expression wasn't meaningful to anybody who didn't already understand what I was talking about. Then I tried using the term "peripheral statistics"—yes, I know Bill Buckner hits for a good average, I would say, but his peripheral statistics aren't very good. This was rather confusing because "peripheral statistics" has no precise definition ("What do you mean his peripheral statistics aren't very good? He hit 46 doubles, drove in 110 runs and set a major league record for assists, didn't he?"). Besides, "peripheral" is an ugly word, particularly in this era of AIDS, and nobody likes to be told that his favorite player has bad peripherals.

I tried a couple of other things. Sometimes I'd try to say that I liked Darrell Evans because "he's a good percentage player." Sounds like he spends his winters in Las Vegas. Like "peripheral statistics," "percentage player" focuses on the numbers, rather than on the player. At other times I would describe a player I liked as a "Ted Williams-type" offensive player or a "Joe Morgan-type" offensive player, which is a Ted Williams type with less power but more speed. But if you get some six-foot-three inch white guy, plays center field and bats right-handed, how can you describe him as a Joe Morgan-type hitter? Whoever you are talking to will reckon that he must flap his arm before he swings.

Last summer I was looking through my Macmillan one day, and I got out a pen and paper and figured this for one player, and then for another and then another until I was kind of hooked on it, and I figured that if it worked for me it might work for other people to. These are a few of the characteristics of secondary average which make it a handy way of expressing the idea:

Overall secondary averages are almost identical to overall primary batting averages. The American League batting average last year was .261; the secondary average was .260. The National League batting average was .252; the secondary average was .244. This is also often true for individuals, as it is for Don Mattingly; for example, last year Glenn Hubbard had averages of .232 (batting) and .219 (secondary), Thad Bosley was at .328 and .322, Bobby Meacham at .218 and .212, Jim Rice at .291 and .293, Dick Schofield at .219 and .217, and Kent Hrbek at .278 and .280. This is very useful because it eliminates the largest barrier to using a new statistic—the need to educate people about standards. The center is just the same as batting average, so it's easy to understand where a player is.

Secondary average makes use of, and thus can be figured from, the records available in a number of common references, such as the Big Mac and the weekly stats in USA Today. In a sense, other contributions such as sacrifice hits and sac flies are a legitimate part of secondary offensive contributions, but who wants to bother with them? Analytical methods should be as complex as needed to do the job, but descriptive stats should be kept simple. This is descriptive.

The similarity of secondary to primary averages is useful again in combination with this simplicity. Since the two are about the same overall, all you really need to see is how the *secondary* bases compare to the hits. If you look at a line in Macmillan (Sixto Lezcano, 1975):

G	AB	H	2B	3B	HR	R	RBI	BB	SO	SB	BA	SA
134	429	106	19	3	11	55	43	46	93	5	.247	.382

It's pretty easy to total up the extra bases (19, 25, 58), the walks (104) and stolen bases (109), and see how they compare to the hits. If they're about the same, as they are in this case, you can figure that the player's batting average is a valid indicator of his offensive contribution. But if the secondary bases are considerably more or considerably fewer than the base hits, then you can see quickly that the player is a better or a lesser hitter than his average reflects.

Secondary average is more important (a better indicator of hitting ability) than is batting average. The Yankees in 1985 were third in the American League in batting average; the Orioles were eighth. Yet those two teams were 1–2 in the league in runs scored. Why? Because they had the highest secondary averages. The Yankees' secondary average, as a team, was .300; Baltimore's was .289.

I haven't done a systematic study of it, but I'd certainly bet that the team which leads a league in secondary average is much more likely to lead in runs scored than is the team which leads in batting average. The Cardinals, in the National League, led in both batting (.264) and secondary average (.279); naturally, they did lead the league in runs scored. One point of secondary average is clearly *not* as valuable as one point of batting average. If you have a choice between a player who has a batting average of .300 and a secondary average of .250, and a player with the reverse combination, take the player with the higher batting average. A team with a batting average of .270 but a secondary average of .240 will score more runs than a team with a batting average of .240 but a secondary average of .270.

The reason secondary average is more powerful is that the spread is much larger. The Yankees had a secondary average of .300, while the Brewers had a secondary average of .210. That is more important than any difference in batting average because it is much larger than any difference in batting average; no team hits .300, or close to it, and no team hits .210, or close to it.

The same is true for individuals. All regular players, or 97% of them, are going to hit in a 100-point range between .225 and .325. But there are regular players who have secondary averages of .140, and there are regular players who have secondary averages of .400. (In fact, there is even a Hall of Famer who had a secondary average of .140.) I would guess that one point of secondary average is worth about one-half of one point of batting average—but the spread of secondary averages is more than twice as large as the spread of batting averages.

Secondary average is a collection category, like Boswell's total average. It adds together things which are not exactly of equal value, like one walk and one stolen base, without making any attempt to distinguish the values of them. Of course, the same is true of each hit that makes up a batting average—some hits are not equal to other hits—but if it was an analytical tool, rather than a new descriptive stat, I would attempt to make the adjustments.

Like slugging percentage, secondary average is not a true percentage measure. It is theoretically possible to exceed 1.000.

NAMING NAMES—THE BEST AND WORST

Who had the best and worst secondary averages of 1985? The charts below give the lists, using 400 AB or qualification for the batting title as the eligibility standard:

NATIONAL LEAGUE BEST		NATIONAL LEAGUE WORST	
1. Pedro Guerrero	.452	1. Rafael Santana	.102
2. Tim Raines	.417	2. Rafael Ramirez	.123
3. Mike Schmidt	.415	3. Jose Uribe	.158
4. Jack Clark	.412	4. Manny Trillo	.160
5. Dale Murphy	.401	5. Terry Pendleton	.163
6. Ryne Sandberg	.381	6. Terry Kennedy	.169
7. Andy Van Slyke	.370	7. Ron Oester	.173
8. Carmello Martinez	.350	8. Tony Gwynn	.186
9. Jason Thompson	.346	9. Tony Pena	.187
10. Bob Horner	.337	10. Dave Concepcion	.196

AMERICAN LEAGUE BEST		AMERICAN LEAGUE WORST	
1. Rickey Henderson	.528	1. Mickey Hatcher	.119
2. George Brett	.455	2. Ozzie Guillen	.124
3. Darrell Evans	.440	3. Alfredo Griffin	.134
4. Toby Harrah	.432	4. Bob Boone	.152
5. Gorman Thomas	.415	5. Jim Gantner	.157
6. Jesse Barfield	.410	6. Pat Tabler	.163
7. Reggie Jackson	.407	7. Damaso Garcia	.167
8. Kirk Gibson	.404	8. Ernest Riles	.176
9. Dwight Evans	.387	9. George Vukovich	.180
10. Eddie Murray	.379	10. Kirby Puckett	.187

There are three elements of secondary average: those are power, strike zone judgement, and speed. No one element dominates. Power may be the most important of the three, but Dave Kingman's secondary average is not especially high (.289), and there are several among the leaders who are not power hitters. Henderson's .528 secondary average is a remarkable figure, a result of across-the-board excellence in all three categories—110 extra bases on hits, 99 walks, 80 stolen bases. There is no doubt in my mind that Rickey Henderson was the greatest everyday player in baseball in 1985.

It's a remarkable figure for anybody else; it's normal for Rickey. Rickey's secondary average has been over .400 every year of his career except for his half-season in 1979, and his major-league leading .528 in 1985 was the third highest of his career; he had secondary averages of .575 in 1982 and .540 in 1983. But he's a better hitter now, because his batting average is higher and he's not making as many outs as he used to on the bases. Rickey's career secondary average is .474.

I believe (I'm not positive) that Henderson's .575 secondary average in 1982 was the highest posted by any active player. Mike Schmidt has also been over .500 seven times, with a career high .568 in the strike-shortened 1981 season (354 at bats). I'm not aware of any other player who has been over .500.

Among the all-time greats, Henderson's .474 average ranks him sixth, behind Babe Ruth (.607), Ted Williams (.555), Lou Gehrig (.493), Mickey Mantle (.492), and Mike Schmidt (.481); Joe Morgan was a still-powerful .431. Morgan was over .500 for five straight years (1973–1977), and reached peaks of .580 and .625 in his MVP seasons (1975–76). Mantle was over .500 nine times, and reached highs of .582, .641 and .631 in his MVP years (1956, 1957 and 1962), plus a .638 figure in 1961, when Maris won the MVP. Ted Williams was over .500 thirteen times and over .600 five times, with a high of .651, which came in his .400 season. And Babe Ruth—well, Babe's off on his own planet, as usual. Babe was over .500 every year from 1919 to the end of his career except for the year that he had the gastroenteritis (1925); he was even ringing in at .528 in his last hurrah in Boston, when his batting average was .181. He was over .600 nine times, over .700 in his three greatest years (1920, 1921 and 1923) and reached a peak of .825 in 1920, when he had 378 secondary bases in 458 at bats.

Incidentally, there is another major league player around now whose secondary average is comparable to Henderson's. The basic reason for citing secondary average is that it tends to be overlooked; your average is in the paper every week, but the sum of your other contributions can be missed. They can be *so* overlooked that this other player has never been able to latch onto a regular job in the major leagues, although he had a secondary average last year of .537 in half-time play, and has a career mark that is well over .400. His batting average isn't real good, but his secondary offensive skills are comparable to Henderson's; he walks, steals bases and has some pop in his bat—yet he is available for trade as I write this, and is so little thought of that he may have been traded for very little before you read it. Can you figure out who he is? I'll let you stew on it a while.

But hey, I don't mean to make this sound easy. That's the stratosphere; that's for the all-time greats. Even guys like Ty Cobb, Hank Aaron, Jim Rice and Stan Musial never get up there. A few people every year do get over .350—but when you get over .350, you're one of the best in baseball. A .400 secondary average is nothing as rare as a .400 batting average, but it ain't something that Mariano Duncan is going to pick up, either. Even great players are more likely to be in the .300s than the .400s. These are the career secondary averages of a few selected greats, near greats, sort of greats, etc., from history, arranged more or less in chronological form:

19th century:
Notable High: Sliding Billy Hamilton, .426
Notable Low: Monte Ward, .187
Others of note:

Cap Anson, .249; Jim O'Rourke, .200; Dan Brouthers, .337; Roger Connor, .326; Buck Ewing, .288; King Kelly, .276; Jake Beckley, .227; Jesse Burkett, .277; Sam Thompson, .286; Bill Dahlen, .289; Tommy McCarthy, .282; Joe Kelley, .327; Jimmy Collins, .205; Hugh Duffy, .301; Willie Keeler, .194; Ed Delahanty, .318; Honus Wagner, .301; Bobby Wallace, .206; Nap Lajoie, .222; Fred Clarke, .278; Jimmy Sheckard, .315; Roy Thomas, .286; Roger Bresnahan, .306.

Dead Ball Era:
Notable High: Ty Cobb, .334
Notable Low: Rabbit Maranville, .193
Others of note:

Elmer Flick, .315; Sam Crawford, .261; Joe Tinker, .208; Frank Chance, .321; Johnny Evers, .244; Tris Speaker, .333; Home Run Baker, .253; Donie Bush, .267; Eddie Collins, .321; Ray Schalk, .216; Zack Wheat, .227; Shoeless Joe Jackson, .306; Sam Rice, .219; Harry Hooper, .278; Edd Rousch, .225.

Baseball Between the Wars:
Notable High: (other than Ruth and Gehrig) Jimmie Foxx, .473
Notable Low: Lloyd Waner, .140
Others of note:

Dave Bancroft, .215; Ken Williams, .359; George Sisler, .230; Harry Heilmann, .303; Rogers Hornsby, .362; George Kelly, .231; Frankie Frisch, .242; Hack Wilson, .390; Jim Bottomley, .287; Bill Terry, .257; Joe Sewell, .230; Goose Goslin, .314; Gabby Hartnett, .305; Kiki Cuyler, .292; Maxie Bishop, 362; Riggs Stephenson, .259; Al Simmons, .281; Earle Combs, .271; Earl Averill, .348; Travis Jackson, .222; Heine Manush, .230; Max Carey, .291; Ross Youngs, .270; Chick Hafey, .305; Babe Herman, .317; Mickey Cochrane, .336; Charlie Gehringer, .314; Pie Traynor, .199; Paul Waner, .266; Fred Lindstrom, .212; Chuck Klein, .328; Lu Blue, .372; Rick Ferrell, .242; Bob Johnson, .378; Bill Dickey, .287; Joe Cronin, .318; Luke Appling, .255; Mel Ott, .419; Hank Greenberg, .467; Joe Medwick, .244; Stan Hack, .268; Billy Herman, .207; Harlond Clift, .368; Arky Vaughan, .295; Johnny Mize, .387; Joe DiMaggio, .374.

The Post-War Era
Notable High: (other than Mantle and Williams): Ralph Kiner, .468
Notable Low: Nellie Fox, .160
Others of note:

Enos Slaughter, .290; Lou Boudreau, .260; Monte Irvin, .334; Jackie Robinson, .355; Pee Wee Reese, .287; Roy Campanella, .356; Phil Rizzuto, .219; Stan Musial, .381; George Kell, .207; Yogi Berra, .295; Minnie Minoso, .316; Eddie Yost, .347; Richie Ashburn, .246; Duke Snider, .394; Ernie Banks, .312; Willie Mays, .421; Eddie Mathews, .415.

The Expansion Era
Notable High: Harmon Killebrew, .446
Notable Low: Maury Wills, .200
Others of Note:

Luis Aparicio, .202; Hank Aaron, .382; Roberto Clemente, .232; Norm Cash, .379; Al Kaline, .322; Frank Robinson, .405; Brooks Robinson, .217; Willie McCovey, .412; Vada Pinson, .247; Billy Williams, .323; Lou Brock, .282; Carl Yastrzemski, .345; Ron Santo, .328; Richie Allen, .404; Willie Stargell, .367; Jimmy Wynn, .404; Gene Tenace, .420; Johnny Bench, .334; Ken Singleton, .332.

You may notice that while batting averages were in their long decline, from 1930 to 1968, secondary averages did not follow. During that period secondary average wandered up and down, but on balance secondary averages are a little higher now than they were in the big-hitting twenties and thirties. In 1930 the major league batting average was .296, but the secondary average was .242; in 1985 the averages were .257 and .252.

One of the questions that I had to look at in forming this statistic was whether or not stolen bases should be included. A stolen base attempt is a gamble which can increase or decrease the number of runs a team scores; in counting the positive without counting the negative, we run the risk of including in the measurement only the positive outcomes of an essentially break-even gamble—sort of the way an IRS auditor figures your profit and loss. As a result of this, as you may know, stolen bases bear a rather nebulous relationship to runs scored, unlike any of the other offensive statistics which we usually study. A group of teams which draw an average of 505 walks will reliably score more runs than a group of teams which draw an average of 495 walks. A group of teams which hit an average of 155 home runs will rather quickly score noticeably more runs than a group of teams which hit an average of 145, so long as the two groups are not selected to prevent this from happening. But a group of teams which steals an average of 155 bases will not score noticeably more runs than a group of teams which steals 145 bases—nor, indeed, will a group of teams stealing 200 bases score noticeably more runs than a group of teams stealing 50.

For this reason, it is questionable whether the stolen bases should be included in the category. But the purpose of the category is to sum up all of the non-batting average contributions of an offensive player. It's a descriptive stat; I didn't want to be in the position of saying that I don't think Tony Gwynn is too much of an offensive threat, despite his .317 average, because his secondary average is .164, and have somebody come back to me with "Yeah, but you're not counting his base stealing in that." I don't want to give the appearance of unfairness to the base stealers; I'll express my reservations about the gamble in other ways. Also, as I said, it is very useful to have the league batting average and the league secondary average be about the same—and the inclusion of stolen bases helps to accomplish that.

One thing that is easy to see is this: that historically, base stealing responds to the other elements of secondary average. The lower the other elements of secondary average, the more stolen bases there will be:

In 1905, when the other elements would have created a secondary average of .152 for the major leagues as a whole, there were 119 bases stolen per 100 team games.

By 1915, the other elements of secondary average had increased to .169, and stolen bases per 100 team/games had dropped to 111.

By 1920, the other elements of secondary average were up to .176—and stolen bases per 100 games were down to 70.

By 1925, the other elements of secondary average had gone up to .210—and stolen bases had dropped to 56 per 100 team games.

By 1930, the other elements of secondary average were up to a league average of .229—and stolen bases per 100 team games were down to 44.

By 1935—this is the one exception to the pattern that I will cite—the other elements of secondary average had dropped to .209, but stolen bases had continued their descent, to 36 per 100 games.

But by 1945, as the other elements of secondary average continued to drop (they were down to .193), stolen bases began to increase, up to 40 per 100 team games.

By 1950, both trends had reversed; the other elements of secondary average had shot up to .253—and stolen bases had dropped all the way to 26 per 100 team games. In that period, the other elements of secondary average were the highest they have ever been—and stolen bases were the lowest that they have ever been.

By 1955, both trends had reversed again. The other elements of secondary average had edged down to .240, and stolen bases per 100 games had edged up to 28.

By 1960, the other elements of secondary average were down to .232—and stolen bases were up to 37 per 100 team games.

By 1965, the other elements of secondary average were down to .218—and stolen bases were up to 49 per 100 games.

By 1975, the other secondary elements were holding steady at .218, while stolen bases continued to increase, up to 65.

But by 1980, the other elements of secondary average had dropped to .215, while stolen bases continued their increase, to 78 per 100 games.

By 1985, both trends had reversed again. The other elements of secondary average had gone back up to .231—and stolen bases had gone down to 74 per 100 games.

I left out three aberrant data intervals (1910, 1940 and 1970) to simplify the pattern, but to me it seems that there is a clear relationship. Batting average is the most stable element of offense, and the most difficult to alter. Secondary average represents the relatively more fluid elements of offense. Base stealing is the most fluid of those elements, being the only one directly subject to influence by managerial decisions, and responds to changes in the other factors. When offense shrinks due to movements in the other areas, baseball men will try to stretch what they have by using the running game. When the offense is otherwise productive, they will not risk what they have in baserunning gambles. One could argue that this proves that the stolen base is a part of secondary average, because the two are closely related, or one could say that it proves that stolen bases are not a part of secondary average, because the relationship is inverse, with stolen bases always moving in the opposite direction from secondary average. How you would resolve that issue would depend on precisely how you would define secondary average.

I've defined it in. And the Yankees, led by one of the all-time greats, were the 1985 major league leaders in secondary average. And runs scored.

COMPLETE BATTING RECORDS

Player	G	AB	R	H	TB	2B	3B	HR	RBI	GW	SH	SF	HB	BB	IB	SO	SB	CS	GI DP	Avg	Slug	OBP	Runs	Outs Made	Runs/ 27 Outs	OW%	Appr Value
†Wynegar	102	309	27	69	99	15	0	5	32	3	1	1	0	64	2	43	0	0	11	.223	.320	.356	38	253	4.03	.429	7
*Mattingly	159	652	107	211	370	48	3	35	145	21	2	15	2	56	13	41	2	2	15	.324	.567	.371	136	475	7.72	.733	16
Randolph	143	497	75	137	177	21	2	5	40	6	5	6	4	85	3	39	16	9	24	.276	.356	.382	69	404	4.61	.495	12
*Pagliarulo	138	380	55	91	168	16	2	19	62	5	3	3	4	45	4	86	0	0	6	.239	.442	.324	56	301	5.05	.541	8
†Meacham	156	481	70	105	128	16	2	1	47	3	23	3	5	54	1	102	25	7	7	.218	.266	.302	45	416	2.92	.282	9
*Griffey	127	438	68	120	186	28	4	10	69	6	0	8	0	41	4	51	7	7	2	.274	.425	.331	63	335	5.12	.547	6
Henderson	143	547	146	172	282	28	5	24	72	6	0	5	3	99	1	65	80	10	8	.314	.516	.419	138	398	9.36	.802	17
Winfield	155	633	105	174	298	34	6	26	114	19	0	4	0	52	8	96	19	7	17	.275	.471	.328	94	487	5.22	.557	13
Baylor	142	477	70	110	205	24	1	23	91	10	1	10	24	52	6	90	0	4	10	.231	.430	.330	70	392	4.81	.516	8
*Hassey	92	267	31	79	136	16	1	13	42	6	0	0	3	28	4	21	0	0	7	.296	.509	.369	49	195	6.84	.684	5
*Pasqua	60	148	17	31	63	3	1	9	25	1	0	1	1	16	4	38	0	0	1	.209	.426	.289	19	119	4.30	.460	3
Sample	59	139	18	40	48	5	0	1	15	0	2	2	2	9	0	10	2	1	2	.288	.345	.336	17	106	4.29	.459	2
Robertson	50	125	16	41	52	5	0	2	17	0	2	2	1	6	0	24	1	2	3	.328	.416	.358	18	93	5.18	.553	3
Berra	48	109	8	25	35	5	1	1	8	1	2	0	0	7	0	20	1	1	2	.229	.321	.276	9	89	2.86	.274	1
*Moreno	34	66	12	13	22	4	1	1	4	0	1	0	0	1	0	16	1	1	1	.197	.333	.209	4	56	1.98	.154	0
Cotto	34	56	4	17	21	1	0	1	6	0	1	0	0	3	0	12	1	1	1	.304	.375	.339	7	42	4.40	.472	1
Hudler	20	51	4	8	10	0	1	0	1	0	5	0	0	1	0	9	0	1	0	.157	.196	.173	2	49	0.99	.044	0
*Bradley	19	49	4	8	12	2	1	0	1	0	0	0	1	1	0	5	0	0	2	.163	.245	.196	2	43	1.23	.066	0
Bonilla	8	16	0	2	3	1	0	0	2	0	0	0	0	0	0	3	0	0	0	.125	.188	.125	0	14	0.72	.024	0
Espino	9	11	0	4	4	0	0	0	0	0	0	0	0	0	0	0	0	0	0	.364	.364	.364	1	7	5.61	.592	0
Mata	6	7	1	1	1	0	0	0	0	0	0	0	0	0	0	0	0	0	0	.143	.143	.143	0	6	0.64	.019	0
†Smith	4	0	1	0	0	0	0	0	0	0	0	0	0	0	0	0	0	0	0	.000	.000	.000	0	0	0.00	.000	0

*left-handed hitter, †switch hitter

DEFENSIVE STATISTICS

FIRST	G	PO	A	Er	TC	DP	PCT.
Mattingly	159	1318	87	7	1412	154	.995
Hassey	2	18	0	0	18	2	1.000
Hudler	1	6	0	0	6	2	1.000
Griffey	1	5	0	0	5	0	1.000
TEAM:	163	1347	87	7	1441	158	.995
AVG:	180	1440	123	14	1577	141	.991

SECOND	G	PO	A	Er	TC	DP	PCT.
Randolph	143	303	425	11	739	104	.985
Hudler	16	36	50	2	88	12	.977
Bonilla	7	7	14	1	22	3	.955
Robertson	2	5	4	0	9	2	1.000
TEAM:	168	351	493	14	858	121	.984
AVG:	189	347	501	15	863	114	.982

THIRD	G	PO	A	Er	TC	DP	PCT.
Pagliarulo	134	67	187	13	267	15	.951
Berra	41	20	68	8	96	9	.917
Robertson	33	11	41	8	60	6	.867
TEAM:	208	98	296	29	423	30	.931
AVG:	192	129	327	23	479	32	.953

SHORTSTOP	G	PO	A	Er	TC	DP	PCT.
Meacham	155	236	390	24	650	103	.963
Robertson	14	16	22	2	40	8	.950
Berra	6	2	6	1	9	0	.889
Smith	3	0	1	0	1	0	1.000
Hudler	1	0	1	0	1	0	1.000
TEAM:	179	254	420	27	701	111	.961
AVG:	189	269	474	28	771	104	.964

CATCHER	G	PO	A	Er	TC	DP	PCT.	PB
Wynegar	96	547	34	6	587	7	.990	3
Hassey	69	402	20	7	429	2	.984	15
Espino	9	16	4	0	20	0	1.000	0
Bradley	3	12	0	1	13	0	.923	0
TEAM:	177	977	58	14	1049	9	.987	18
AVG:	193	895	74	13	982	13	.987	13

OUTFIELD	G	PO	A	Er	TC	DP	PCT.
Winfield	152	316	13	3	332	3	.991
Henderson	141	439	7	9	455	3	.980
Griffey	110	222	8	7	237	3	.970
Sample	55	89	1	1	91	0	.989
Pasqua	37	72	2	0	74	0	1.000
Cotto	30	41	2	1	44	0	.977
Moreno	26	56	2	0	58	0	1.000
Mata	3	1	0	0	1	0	1.000
TEAM:	554	1236	35	21	1292	9	.984
AVG:	559	1141	33	21	1196	8	.982

COMPLETE PITCHERS RECORDS

Pitcher	W	L	Pct	ERA	G	GS	CG	GF	SHO	SV	IP	H	TBF	R	ER	HR	SH	SF	HB	BB	IB	SO	WP	BK	Appr Value
							Starters (One-half of Game Appearances)																		
*Guidry	22	6	.786	3.27	34	33	11	0	2	0	259.0	243	1033	104	94	28	3	8	0	42	3	143	3	1	15
P. Niekro	16	12	.571	4.09	33	33	7	0	1	0	220.0	203	955	110	100	29	1	3	2	120	1	149	5	2	9
Cowley	12	6	.667	3.95	30	26	1	2	0	0	159.2	132	684	75	70	29	1	4	6	85	2	97	5	1	8
Whitson	10	8	.556	4.88	30	30	2	0	2	0	158.2	201	705	100	86	19	3	7	2	43	0	89	1	0	5
*Shirley	5	5	.500	2.64	48	8	2	9	0	2	109.0	103	446	34	32	5	5	4	0	26	2	55	1	0	6
*Rasmussen	3	5	.375	3.98	22	16	2	1	0	0	101.2	97	429	56	45	10	1	5	1	42	1	63	3	1	3
Bystrom	3	2	.600	5.71	8	8	0	0	0	0	41.0	44	180	29	26	8	2	1	1	19	0	16	0	0	1
J. Niekro	2	1	.667	5.84	3	3	0	0	0	0	12.1	14	58	8	8	3	0	0	0	8	0	4	0	0	0
							Relievers																		
*Righetti	12	7	.632	2.78	74	0	0	60	0	29	107.0	96	452	36	33	5	6	3	0	45	3	92	7	0	13
Fisher	4	4	.500	2.38	55	0	0	23	0	14	98.1	77	391	32	26	4	3	2	0	29	3	85	3	0	9
Bordi	6	8	.429	3.21	51	3	0	16	0	2	98.0	95	415	41	35	5	6	3	1	29	4	64	1	0	6
Allen	1	0	1.000	2.76	17	0	0	10	0	1	29.1	26	124	9	9	1	0	0	0	13	0	16	2	0	0
Armstrong	0	0	.000	3.07	9	0	0	8	0	0	14.2	9	54	5	5	4	0	0	0	2	0	11	1	0	0
*Scurry	1	0	1.000	2.84	5	0	0	2	0	1	12.2	5	51	4	4	2	1	0	0	10	1	17	0	0	0
Cooper	0	0	.000	5.40	7	0	0	2	0	0	10.0	12	44	6	6	2	0	1	0	3	0	4	1	0	0
Montefusco	0	0	.000	10.29	3	1	0	1	0	0	7.0	12	34	8	8	3	0	1	0	2	0	2	0	0	0
Murray	0	0	.000	13.50	3	0	0	2	0	0	2.2	4	10	3	3	0	0	0	0	0	0	0	1	0	0

Butch WYNEGAR, Catcher

	G	AB	Hit	2B	3B	HR	Run	RBI	TBB	SO	SB	CS	Avg
7.30 years		547	141	23	2	8	64	64	79	53	1	2	.258
1985	102	309	69	15	0	5	27	32	64	43	0	0	.223
First Half	61	197	47	8	0	4	18	23	33	24	0	0	.239
Second Half	41	112	22	7	0	1	9	9	31	19	0	0	.196
Vs. RHP		172	40	7	0	3	13	21	33	19	0	0	.233
Vs. LHP		137	29	8	0	2	14	11	31	24	0	0	.212
Home	53	158	31	8	0	2	11	13	33	22	0	0	.196
Road	49	151	38	7	0	3	16	19	31	21	0	0	.252
Grass	89	268	59	13	0	3	22	25	55	39	0	0	.220
Turf	13	41	10	2	0	2	5	7	9	4	0	0	.244

Don MATTINGLY, First Base

	G	AB	Hit	2B	3B	HR	Run	RBI	TBB	SO	SB	CS	Avg
2.53 years		611	197	42	4	24	92	114	47	42	1	1	.323
1985	159	652	211	48	3	35	107	145	56	41	2	2	.324
First Half	78	319	97	23	2	8	38	59	23	19	2	0	.304
Second Half	81	333	114	25	1	27	69	86	33	22	0	2	.342
Vs. RHP		388	135	28	3	17	65	78	38	25	1	2	.348
Vs. LHP		264	76	20	0	18	42	67	18	16	1	0	.288
Home	80	318	107	21	1	22	56	87	24	21	1	1	.336
Road	79	334	104	27	2	13	51	58	32	20	1	1	.311
Grass	135	548	180	40	2	29	92	126	51	33	2	2	.328
Turf	24	104	31	8	1	6	15	19	5	8	0	0	.298

Willie RANDOLPH, Second Base

	G	AB	Hit	2B	3B	HR	Run	RBI	TBB	SO	SB	CS	Avg
8.35 years		601	165	24	6	4	98	48	94	48	26	9	.274
1985	143	497	137	21	2	5	75	40	85	39	16	9	.276
First Half	76	277	79	8	2	1	39	22	44	21	5	6	.285
Second Half	67	220	58	13	0	4	36	18	41	18	11	3	.264
Vs. RHP		312	79	11	1	3	45	29	53	30	8	6	.253
Vs. LHP		185	58	10	1	2	30	11	32	9	8	3	.314
Home	69	221	58	12	1	3	32	21	45	16	7	5	.262
Road	74	276	79	9	1	2	43	19	40	23	9	4	.286
Grass	119	414	111	19	1	5	62	35	72	33	14	7	.268
Turf	24	83	26	2	1	0	13	5	13	6	2	2	.313

Mike PAGLIARULO, Third Base

	G	AB	Hit	2B	3B	HR	Run	RBI	TBB	SO	SB	CS	Avg
1.27 years		459	110	24	4	21	62	76	47	104	0	0	.239
1985	138	380	91	16	2	19	55	62	45	86	0	0	.239
First Half	63	172	38	9	0	6	27	28	24	34	0	0	.221
Second Half	75	208	53	7	2	13	28	34	21	52	0	0	.255
Vs. RHP		327	83	16	2	17	49	55	40	64	0	0	.254
Vs. LHP		53	8	0	0	2	6	7	5	22	0	0	.151
Home	68	178	43	5	1	8	21	29	20	39	0	0	.242
Road	70	202	48	11	1	11	34	33	25	47	0	0	.238
Grass	119	329	78	15	2	15	48	52	35	71	0	0	.237
Turf	19	51	13	1	0	4	7	10	10	15	0	0	.255

Bobby MEACHAM, Shortstop

	G	AB	Hit	2B	3B	HR	Run	RBI	TBB	SO	SB	CS	Avg
1.71 years		522	122	18	4	2	80	44	53	106	25	7	.233
1985	156	481	105	16	2	1	70	47	54	102	25	7	.218
First Half	77	238	54	10	2	0	34	28	36	52	10	4	.227
Second Half	79	243	51	6	0	1	36	19	18	50	15	3	.210
Vs. RHP		300	67	10	2	1	48	31	34	61	17	5	.223
Vs. LHP		181	38	6	0	0	22	16	20	41	8	2	.210
Home	77	231	39	5	1	1	31	15	23	59	13	3	.169
Road	79	250	66	11	1	0	39	32	31	43	12	4	.264
Grass	132	406	87	12	1	1	55	40	46	97	18	6	.214
Turf	24	75	18	4	1	0	15	7	8	5	7	1	.240

Ken GRIFFEY, Left Field

	G	AB	Hit	2B	3B	HR	Run	RBI	TBB	SO	SB	CS	Avg
9.50 years		593	178	31	7	11	96	68	59	72	18	6	.300
1985	127	438	120	28	4	10	68	69	41	51	7	2	.274
First Half	60	211	53	12	3	6	28	35	20	28	4	1	.251
Second Half	67	227	67	16	1	4	40	34	21	23	3	6	.295
Vs. RHP		330	97	23	4	8	58	51	35	40	7	6	.294
Vs. LHP		108	23	5	0	2	10	18	6	11	0	1	.213
Home	57	195	57	12	3	6	36	32	21	26	2	2	.292
Road	70	243	63	16	1	4	32	37	20	25	5	5	.259
Grass	106	367	104	21	4	9	59	59	35	43	6	6	.283
Turf	21	71	16	7	0	1	9	10	6	8	1	1	.225

Rickey HENDERSON, Center Field

	G	AB	Hit	2B	3B	HR	Run	RBI	TBB	SO	SB	CS	Avg
5.77 years		601	177	27	6	13	127	59	107	83	99	26	.295
1985	143	547	172	28	5	24	146	72	99	65	80	10	.314
First Half	67	263	94	13	4	11	70	37	37	24	38	3	.357
Second Half	76	284	78	15	1	13	76	35	62	41	42	7	.275
Vs. RHP		366	107	15	3	12	88	47	54	38	53	4	.292
Vs. LHP		181	65	13	2	12	58	25	45	27	27	6	.359
Home	68	246	75	12	1	8	75	22	46	31	37	7	.305
Road	75	301	97	16	4	16	71	50	53	34	43	3	.322
Grass	119	456	144	25	4	21	130	60	82	52	74	9	.316
Turf	24	91	28	3	1	3	16	12	17	13	6	1	.308

Dave WINFIELD, Right Field

	G	AB	Hit	2B	3B	HR	Run	RBI	TBB	SO	SB	CS	Avg
11.17 years		602	173	29	6	25	94	101	64	84	17	6	.288
1985	155	633	174	34	6	26	105	114	52	96	19	7	.275
First Half	77	315	91	13	2	10	49	49	20	45	8	3	.289
Second Half	78	318	83	21	4	16	56	65	32	51	11	4	.261
Vs. RHP		418	120	23	3	16	69	78	21	68	14	5	.287
Vs. LHP		215	54	11	3	10	36	36	31	28	5	2	.251
Home	77	298	85	19	1	15	56	61	27	42	10	4	.285
Road	78	335	89	15	5	11	49	53	25	54	9	3	.266
Grass	131	529	149	28	4	24	89	100	46	78	17	7	.282
Turf	24	104	25	6	2	2	16	14	6	18	2	0	.240

Don BAYLOR, Designated Hitter

	G	AB	Hit	2B	3B	HR	Run	RBI	TBB	SO	SB	CS	Avg
11.80 years		590	156	28	2	24	89	92	56	72	23	9	.265
1985	142	477	110	24	1	23	70	91	52	90	0	4	.231
First Half	73	258	61	11	1	14	38	55	31	45	0	3	.236
Second Half	69	219	49	13	0	9	32	36	21	45	0	1	.224
Vs. RHP		283	61	11	1	12	36	52	20	60	0	3	.216
Vs. LHP		194	49	13	0	11	34	39	32	30	0	1	.253
Home	72	231	50	14	0	12	32	50	22	44	0	1	.216
Road	70	246	60	10	1	11	38	41	30	46	0	3	.244
Grass	123	413	93	23	0	17	59	75	44	78	0	4	.225
Turf	19	64	17	1	1	6	11	16	8	12	0	0	.266

Ron HASSEY, Catcher

	G	AB	Hit	2B	3B	HR	Run	RBI	TBB	SO	SB	CS	Avg
4.20 years		474	131	23	1	10	49	65	54	50	2	2	.275
1985	92	267	79	16	1	13	31	42	28	21	0	0	.296
First Half	41	99	30	9	1	4	11	12	12	8	0	0	.303
Second Half	51	168	49	7	0	9	20	30	16	13	0	0	.292
Vs. RHP		219	71	15	1	13	31	41	22	16	0	0	.324
Vs. LHP		48	8	1	0	0	0	1	6	5	0	0	.167
Home	45	115	38	7	0	3	13	14	16	10	0	0	.330
Road	47	152	41	9	1	10	18	28	12	11	0	0	.270
Grass	77	225	72	14	1	13	29	39	23	18	0	0	.320
Turf	15	42	7	2	0	0	2	3	5	3	0	0	.167

RON GUIDRY

	(W–L)	GS	Run	Avg	DP	Avg	SB	Avg
1984	(10-11)	28	130	4.64	21	.75	15	.54
1985	(22-6)	33	178	5.39	38	1.15	13	.39
1977-1985		265	1285	4.85	241	.91	107	.40

	G	IP	W	L	Pct	ER	BB	SO	ERA
1984 Home	14	101.3	8	2	.800	33	12	73	2.93
1985 Home	17	137.3	13	2	.867	43	22	78	2.82
1984 Road	15	94.3	2	9	.182	65	32	54	6.20
1985 Road	17	121.7	9	4	.692	51	20	65	3.77
1984 Grass	25	173.7	10	8	.556	79	36	116	4.09
1985 Grass	31	235.0	19	6	.760	86	40	132	3.29
1984 Turf	4	22.0	0	3	0.000	19	8	11	7.77
1985 Turf	3	24.0	3	0	1.000	8	2	11	3.00
1985 Total	34	259.0	22	6	.786	94	42	143	3.27

PHIL NIEKRO

	(W–L)	GS	Run	Avg	DP	Avg	SB	Avg
1984	(16-8)	31	163	5.26	39	1.26	12	.39
1985	(16-12)	33	155	4.70	39	1.18	27	.82
1976-1985		357	1553	4.35	295	.83	322	.90

	G	IP	W	L	Pct	ER	BB	SO	ERA
1984 Home	16	105.7	7	4	.636	41	36	58	3.49
1985 Home	17	110.0	9	5	.643	47	66	73	3.85
1984 Road	16	110.0	9	4	.692	33	40	78	2.70
1985 Road	16	110.0	7	7	.500	53	54	76	4.34
1984 Grass	26	172.0	12	6	.667	63	63	103	3.30
1985 Grass	27	175.0	13	11	.542	85	100	126	4.37
1984 Turf	6	43.7	4	2	.667	11	13	33	2.27
1985 Turf	6	45.0	3	1	.750	15	20	23	3.00
1985 Total	33	220.0	16	12	.571	100	120	149	4.09

JOE COWLEY

	(W–L)	GS	Run	Avg	DP	Avg	SB	Avg
1984	(9-2)	11	76	6.91	5	.45	5	.45
1985	(12-6)	26	134	5.15	20	.77	20	.77
1984-1985		37	210	5.68	25	.68	25	.68

	G	IP	W	L	Pct	ER	BB	SO	ERA
1984 Home	10	62.0	7	1	.875	16	20	55	2.32
1985 Home	13	69.3	4	2	.667	25	35	45	3.25
1984 Road	6	21.3	2	1	.667	17	11	16	7.17
1985 Road	17	90.3	8	4	.667	45	50	52	4.48
1984 Grass	16	83.3	9	2	.818	33	71	128	3.56
1985 Grass	25	135.3	10	3	.769	51	74	89	3.39
1984 Turf	0	0.0	0	0	0.000	0	0	0	0.00
1985 Turf	5	24.3	2	3	.400	19	11	8	7.03
1985 Total	30	159.7	12	6	.667	70	85	97	3.95

ED WHITSON

	(W–L)	GS	Run	Avg	DP	Avg	SB	Avg
1984	(14-8)	31	131	4.23	32	1.03	29	.94
1985	(10-8)	30	178	5.93	33	1.10	16	.53
1977-1985		173	724	4.18	150	.87	148	.86

	G	IP	W	L	Pct	ER	BB	SO	ERA
1984 Home	16	104.0	9	4	.692	34	26	58	2.94
1985 Home	12	68.3	4	2	.667	31	13	39	4.08
1984 Road	15	85.0	5	4	.556	34	16	45	3.60
1985 Road	18	90.3	6	6	.500	55	30	50	5.48
1984 Grass	24	146.0	12	7	.632	50	33	80	3.08
1985 Grass	24	131.3	8	6	.571	68	36	75	4.66
1984 Turf	7	43.0	2	1	.667	18	9	23	3.77
1985 Turf	6	27.3	2	2	.500	18	7	14	5.93
1985 Total	30	158.7	10	8	.556	86	43	89	4.88

OTHERS

	(W–L)	GS	Run	Avg	DP	Avg	SB	Avg
Rasmussen	(3-5)	16	74	4.62	16	1.00	10	.62
Bystrom	(3-2)	8	38	4.75	10	1.25	11	1.38
Shirley	(5-5)	8	32	4.00	9	1.12	4	.50
Bordi	(6-8)	3	15	5.00	4	1.33	3	1.00
J. Niekro	(2-1)	3	19	6.33	1	.33	3	1.00
Montefusco	(0-0)	1	10	10.00	1	1.00	0	0.00

DETROIT TIGERS

WHU' HAPPEN?

In each baseball season, there are a few things which cry out for a fundamental analysis. In the 1985 season, the most obvious one of those was the sudden, unexpected decline of the Detroit Tigers. The team, which in 1984 had seemed perched on the rim of greatness, suddenly tumbled into the bowl of mediocrity, finishing only a few games over .500—and yet many key players on the team, perhaps even most of them, played as well or better in 1985 as in 1984. What happened?

There is no easy answer; there is no one answer. The two answers most often heard during the season were the failure of the bullpen, where Willie Hernandez had been the Most Valuable Player in 1984, and the breakdown of the defense, as the solid Tigers committed 143 errors and had the lowest fielding percentage in the league.

There is a basic problem with both of these explanations, that being that they both focus on the defense, while the largest part of the problem was not defensive, but offensive. The standard form that I follow in doing a fundamental analysis of a radical change begins by asking three questions, the purpose of which is to locate the part of the body which should be examined in more detail. Those three questions are:

1. Is the change more offensive or defensive?
2. Is the change in the won/lost record consistent with the change in the runs scored and runs allowed? and
3. Is the change in runs scored predicted by the runs created formula?

We begin by dividing the decline into its basic parts, offensive and defensive:

	1984	1985	Loss
Runs Scored	829	729	100 runs
Runs Allowed	643	688	45 runs

So the loss was a little more than two-thirds offensive, one-third defensive. Actually, it is more than that; the American League average of runs per game increased in 1985 from 716 to 737, so that the loss *relative to the league* was 121 runs offensively, 24 defensively—or more than 80% a decline of the offense.

The 1984 Tigers were first in the league in runs scored and first in (fewest) runs allowed; the 1985 Tigers were fourth in fewest runs allowed, but tied with Cleveland for eighth in runs scored. And that being the case, most of the analysis which follows will focus on the offense, rather than on the pitching staff.

The purpose of asking the second and third questions is to tell us whether we can get answers by the use of the standard sabermetric measures such as runs created. If a team's runs scored total has declined by 75 runs, but their runs created have declined by only 24 runs, then it would be fruitless to study the patterns of runs created on the team, since they wouldn't tell us where the changes were. That isn't entirely the case here, although it is to a minor extent. The Tigers runs scored declined by 100; their runs created by 78, from 843 to 765. Our subsequent analysis, then, can be expected to come up about 22 runs short of explaining the decline.

Similarly, if a team's decline in wins and losses is not

reflected in runs scored and runs allowed, then there is no point in studying runs scored and runs allowed. To a small extent, again, this is true in this case. The Tigers declined from 104–58 to 84–77, but their expected wins by the Pythagorean method declined only from 101 to 85. What that means is that they did a slightly worse job of putting runs together in a timely fashion in 1985, and that about four games of their decline can be attributed to this. We'll deal with that toward the close of the article.

Since the Tigers declined by 100 to 121 runs offensively, where did the declines come from? Who had a worse season in 1985 than 1984?

The Tigers returned seven regulars from 1984 to 1985; they made a change at third base. Essentially, those seven players showed no decline in terms of runs created. Whitaker and Trammell are often thought of together; Trammell had a worse season with the bat but Whitaker a better one, and the runs created by the two of them totalled 183 in 1984, and 183 in 1985. No change.

The three most-regular outfielders, again, show almost no change. Larry Herndon created 55 runs in 1984, and 50 in 1985; that's −5. Chet Lemon dropped from 86 to 78; that's −8, a total of −13. But Kirk Gibson, who created 106 runs in 1984, most on the Tigers, was up to 118 in 1985; that's +12, and that leaves the outfield only one run short of its 1984 production.

At catcher, Lance Parrish created 71 runs in 1984, and 82 in 1984; that's +11. At first base, Darrell Evans created 58 runs in 1984 and 96 in 1985; that's +38. Net gain for the seven retained players: 48 runs.

Not so fast. Trammell and Whitaker created the same number of runs in 1985 that they had in 1984—but they used 106 more outs to do so, up from 830 to 936. The three outfielders created one fewer run in 1985 than in 1984—but they were responsible for 1,100 outs in 1984, and 1,172 in 1985—up 72. While Lance Parrish was responsible for 41 fewer outs in 1985 than 1984, Darrell Evans was responsible for 70 more—another 29 outs gravitating toward these seven returning regulars.

So, taken as a group, they created 48 extra runs but 217 extra outs. You can play with the stats some more if you want; they increased their runs created by 48, but by only 33 relative to league (adjusting for the extra runs scored in the 1985 season). However, I am not doing an audit here; I'm not attempting to account for every last loose little run. On the whole, I think it is accurate to say that the offensive contribution of these seven players changed very little—but their workload increased significantly.

Be patient with me; this is all going to pull together. There was a change made at the other position, and it didn't work out well. At third base, where Howard Johnson in 1984 had had a decent season, hitting .248 with 12 homers, 50 RBI in 355 at bats, Tom Brookens played regularly in 1985. Brookens was a disaster, hitting for a low average (.237) with little power (7 homers, though he did hit 34 doubles) and very few walks (27; his on base percentage was a ridiculous .277). As a defensive player, he fielded .943, the lowest in the league except for Hulett of Chicago, and showed unexceptional range.

So there was a decline at one regular position, third base. How much did that decline cost them, in runs? John-son created 46 runs but used only 285 outs; Brookens created four more runs but used 393 outs. Valuing an out at about 15/100 of a run (an estimate that I will use in charts that follow), the switch at third base cost the Tigers about 12 runs.

Player	HR	RBI	Avg	Runs Created	Outs
Johnson, 1984	12	50	.248	46	285
Brookens, 1985	7	47	.237	50	393
NET LOSS:				12 Runs	
Relative to League:				13 Runs	

So of an approximate 100-run offensive loss, about 78 of which we expect to find in the statistics of individual players, we are still missing 66 runs at this moment. What happened to them? What haven't we considered? Designated hitter, and the bench. Since Sparky doesn't use a regular, semi-regular, near-semi-regular or quasi-near-semi-regular designated hitter, it seems best to simply consider the Designated Hitter at bats as part of the bench. But you can't lose a hundred runs off the bench, can you?

When we begin to look at the bench, the lost runs jump suddenly into focus. Before the season, the Tigers lost Ruppert Jones via free agency; his playing time was assumed by Nelson Simmons. Although Simmons played well, he didn't replace Jones:

Player	HR	RBI	Avg	Runs Created	Outs
Jones, 1984	12	37	.284	36	164
Simmons, 1985	10	33	.239	32	199
NET LOSS:				9 Runs	
Relative to League:				10 Runs	

Early in the season, the Tigers lost Rusty Kuntz, who had had a fine season in 1984, to an injury. His playing time was taken over by another rookie, Alejandro Sanchez. What the triple crown comparison doesn't show is that whereas Kuntz had drawn 25 walks for a terrific .393 on-base percentage, Sanchez made it through 133 at bats in 1984 without drawing a walk:

Player	HR	RBI	Avg	Runs Created	Outs
Kuntz, 1984	2	22	.286	25	106
Sanchez, 1985	6	12	.248	13	106
NET LOSS:				12 Runs	
Relative to League:				12 Runs	

In 1984, Dave Bergman had had a fine season, hitting .273 with good power, quite a few walks and superb defense. In 1985 he just stopped hitting:

Player	HR	RBI	Avg	Runs Created	Outs
Bergman, 1984	7	44	.273	41	214
Bergman, 1985	3	7	.179	9	124
NET LOSS:				19 Runs	
Relative to League:				20 Runs	

John Grubb didn't drop off quite so dramatically, and his RBI count was up because, with Jones gone, he tended to be used later in the inning (that is, as a rally-finishing, rather than rally-starting, pinch hitter). Still, Grubb declined in batting average, power, and frequency of walks drawn:

Player	HR	RBI	Avg	Runs Created	Outs
Grubb, 1984	8	17	.267	33	132
Grubb, 1985	5	25	.245	22	127
NET LOSS:				10 Runs	
Relative to League:				11 Runs	

Barbaro Garbey, in his second season in the league, lost 30 points off his average—and Barbaro doesn't really do anything *except* hit for average:

Player	HR	RBI	Avg	Runs Created	Outs
Garbey, 1984	5	35	.287	38	250
Garbey, 1985	6	29	.257	27	189
NET LOSS:				2 Runs	
Relative to League:				3 Runs	

The loss was limited here because his playing time was reduced, and he did increase his secondary average, from .174 to .198.

Marty Castillo, the infielder-catcher who had hit a reasonably solid .234 in 1984, managed to wind up the 1985 season hitting 20 points less than the more-noted Chris Bando, and nowhere near the famous Mendoza line:

Player	HR	RBI	Avg	Runs Created	Outs
Castillo, 1984	4	17	.234	15	116
Castillo, 1985	2	5	.119	2	78
NET LOSS:				7 Runs	
Relative to League:				7 Runs	

Dwight Lowry, the Tigers' spare catcher in 1984, was replaced by Bob Melvin. Melvin made almost twice as many outs as Lowry had, and contributed no offense:

Player	HR	RBI	Avg	Runs Created	Outs
Lowrey, 1984	2	7	.244	5	41
Melvin, 1985	0	4	.220	2	78
NET LOSS:				7 Runs	
Relative to League:				7 Runs	

And finally, Tom Brookens, who in 1984 was a productive bench player, creating 27 runs in 186 outs, in 1985 became instead an *unproductive* regular.

If we add this up, we have accounted for a loss of (how many?) exactly 78 runs. Well, that it is exactly 78 runs is a coincidence, but that it is approximately 78 is the key ingredient, so this seems like a good place to leave it, without mentioning names like Doug Bair, Doug Baker and Doug Flynn. Does Sparky have a thing about Dougs?

Return now to the analysis of the Tiger regulars. Remember that we noticed how everybody was picking up a few extra outs, as a consequence of having a few more at bats? The seven regulars picked up 217 outs, which becomes 323 if you include Brookens at third rather than Johnson. The 33 runs in 217 outs essentially soak up the extra outs on the bench represented by Brookens as a bench player in 1984. What happened to the Tiger offense in 1985, in short, is exactly this: the bench, which had been almost phenomenally strong in 1984, became almost phenomenally weak in 1985.

There were two things which happened over the winter of 1984–85 which set this in motion. When the Tigers traded Hojo to New York, they moved a player (Brookens) off of their bench into the lineup, with the intervening comedy of the Chris Pittaro experiments. When Rupe Jones left to join the Angels, another valuable bench performer was lost. The bench was down two.

And from that point on, every damn thing you can imagine went wrong. Rusty Kuntz, a productive player in 1984, was injured and sent to Nashville. The bench was down three. Nelson Simmons got hurt right at the start of the season. Grubb and Castillo didn't play the way it might have been hoped. Bob Melvin was a disappointment. Bergman was a bitter disappointment.

Attempting to cope with this, Sparky asked his regulars to do more and more—and by and large, they did. But they couldn't completely cover the disaster. The bench was a washout.

What I cannot answer is whether there was a "center" to the bench, whether there was one central reason why all of the bench players had poor years. Did they stop producing because Sparky stopped using them? Did he make a mistake in trying to make a regular out of Pittaro, pushing him ahead of a half dozen productive bench players? Did he make a mistake in sending Rusty Kuntz down so that Mike Laga could get in a few swings? Did he lose confidence in Dave Bergman too quickly? Did he make a mistake in making Melvin, rather than Lowry, his backup catcher?

I can't honestly answer those questions. I would caution that there is a tendency in all human beings to perceive a "center" to things, even when no center exists.

I will point out, as I think it has been largely forgotten, that Sparky's first championship team, the 1970 Reds, also fell apart the next season. After winning 102 games in 1970, they dropped off even worse than the Tigers, falling to 79-83 before rebounding to become the powerhouse of the seventies. There are some similarities. Most of his regulars had good years in 1971, and his first baseman (Lee May) hit 39 homers and drove in 98 runs. As he did last year, Sparky tried to force a green kid (George Foster) into the lineup. As happened last year, his bench had a disappointing season. As happened last year, his relief ace (Wayne Granger) fell off badly. Oddly enough, Milt Wilcox got hurt both years. One could make too much of these parallels; Johnny Bench had a terrible year in 1971, and Jim Merritt, a 20-game winner, got hurt.

There are a few other causative factors of the 1985 Tiger disappointment that should be noted to avoid their exclusion. While Willie Hernandez in 1985 remained one of the league's better relievers, the Tigers in '85 did lose ten games in which they held a lead after seven innings, as opposed to three in 1984. However, the number of games in which they *held* a lead through seven innings declined from 90 to 75, and that can't be Willie Hernandez' fault.

In addition to Hernandez being off some, Aurelio Lopez went from the league's best set-up man in 1984 to worthless in 1985. The combined decline of Hernandez and Lopez probably caused the four-game decline relative to performance predicted by the pythagorean projection (that is, because the bullpen had an off year, the ratio of wins and losses to runs scored and runs allowed was less favorable).

The 1985 Tigers were second in the league in errors, and they did lose a few double plays due to Alan Trammell's not throwing as well as before (double plays were down ten). As to the errors, how many runs are we talking about here? The Tigers in 1984 committed 129 errors and fielded .979; in 1985 they committed 143 errors and fielded .977. Their total of unearned runs allowed increased from 75 to 76. It seems a little hasty to attribute too much of a 19 and a half-game decline to one additional unearned run.

And to many of you, it no doubt seems inadequate to allow the bench to absorb the largest share of the credit for such a huge decline. I can't say that I blame you. But I would point out two things: the Tiger bench players, even in 1985, had over a thousand at bats, essentially the number that would be given to two regulars. And the production for those two regulars went from extremely strong to extremely weak. If two of the Tigers' stars—say, Gibson and Whitaker—had had terrible seasons, would you question that this was the basic reason for a large decline? Whether you accept it or not, the essential difference between the Tigers in 1984 and those of 1985 was the offense. And the essential difference in the offense between 1984 and 1985 was the bench.

COMPLETE BATTING RECORDS

Player	G	AB	R	H	TB	2B	3B	HR	RBI	GW	SH	SF	HB	BB	IB	SO	SB	CS	GI DP	Avg	Slug	OBP	Runs	Outs Made	Runs/ 27 Outs	OW%	Appr Value
Parrish	140	549	64	150	263	27	1	28	98	16	3	5	2	41	5	90	2	6	10	.273	.479	.323	82	423	5.24	.586	13
*Evans	151	505	81	125	262	17	0	40	94	10	1	2	1	85	12	85	0	4	5	.248	.519	.356	96	392	6.62	.694	12
*Whitaker	152	609	102	170	278	29	8	21	73	9	5	5	2	80	9	56	6	4	3	.279	.456	.362	107	456	6.32	.673	14
Brookens	156	485	54	115	182	34	6	7	47	5	9	1	0	27	0	78	14	5	8	.237	.375	.277	50	393	3.42	.377	7
Trammell	149	605	79	156	230	21	7	13	57	5	11	9	2	50	4	71	14	5	6	.258	.380	.312	76	480	4.26	.484	9
Herndon	137	442	45	108	170	12	7	12	37	5	1	1	1	33	1	79	2	1	9	.244	.385	.298	50	346	3.89	.439	6
Lemon	145	517	69	137	227	28	4	18	68	9	0	3	10	45	3	93	0	2	5	.265	.439	.334	78	390	5.39	.600	11
*Gibson	154	581	96	167	301	37	5	29	97	8	3	10	5	71	16	137	30	4	5	.287	.518	.364	118	436	7.33	.735	13
†Simmons	75	251	31	60	101	11	0	10	33	4	0	4	0	26	5	41	1	0	4	.239	.402	.306	32	199	4.32	.491	3
Garbey	86	237	27	61	90	9	1	6	29	3	0	4	3	15	1	37	3	2	7	.257	.380	.305	27	189	3.79	.425	2
*Grubb	78	155	19	38	62	7	1	5	25	2	0	4	1	24	0	25	0	1	5	.245	.400	.342	22	127	4.65	.527	3
*Bergman	69	140	8	25	36	2	0	3	7	2	1	2	0	14	0	15	0	0	6	.179	.257	.250	9	124	1.89	.155	1
Sanchez	71	133	19	33	61	6	2	6	12	2	0	0	0	0	0	39	2	2	4	.248	.459	.248	13	106	3.21	.347	1
Castillo	57	84	4	10	18	2	0	2	5	0	0	1	0	2	0	19	0	2	1	.119	.214	.138	2	78	0.68	.023	1
Melvin	41	82	10	18	24	4	1	0	4	0	2	0	0	3	0	21	0	0	1	.220	.293	.247	6	67	2.39	.228	0
†Pittaro	28	62	10	15	20	3	1	0	7	1	1	0	0	5	0	13	1	1	0	.242	.323	.299	6	49	3.44	.379	0
Flynn	32	51	2	13	17	2	1	0	2	0	3	1	0	0	0	3	0	0	1	.255	.333	.250	4	43	2.61	.261	1
*Laga	9	36	3	6	13	1	0	2	6	0	0	0	0	0	0	9	0	0	1	.167	.361	.167	2	31	1.57	.113	0
†Baker	15	27	4	5	6	1	0	0	1	0	0	0	0	0	0	9	0	0	0	.185	.222	.185	1	22	1.36	.088	0
†Madison	6	11	0	0	0	0	0	0	1	0	0	1	0	2	0	0	0	0	0	.000	.000	.143	0	12	0.33	.006	0
*Weaver	12	7	2	1	2	1	0	0	0	0	0	0	0	1	0	4	0	1	0	.143	.286	.250	0	7	1.09	.058	0
Kuntz	5	5	0	0	0	0	0	0	0	0	0	0	0	2	0	2	0	1	0	.000	.000	.286	0	6	0.16	.003	0
*Hernandez	74	1	0	0	0	0	0	0	0	0	0	0	0	0	0	0	0	0	0	.000	.000	.000	0	1	0.00	.000	0
Morris	36	0	0	0	0	0	0	0	0	0	0	0	0	0	0	0	0	0	0	.000	.000	.000	0	0	0.00	.000	0

*left-handed hitter, †switch hitter

DEFENSIVE STATISTICS

FIRST	G	PO	A	Er	TC	DP	PCT.
Evans	113	827	114	15	956	80	.984
Bergman	44	306	25	3	334	25	.991
Garbey	37	190	20	2	212	24	.991
Laga	4	33	5	1	39	4	.974
Kuntz	1	0	0	1	1	0	.000
TEAM:	199	1356	164	22	1542	133	.986
AVG:	180	1440	123	14	1577	141	.991

SECOND	G	PO	A	Er	TC	DP	PCT.
Whitaker	150	314	414	11	739	101	.985
Flynn	20	31	32	1	64	14	.984
Pittaro	4	5	9	1	15	4	.933
Brookens	3	2	6	0	8	1	1.000
Baker	1	0	0	0	0	0	.000
TEAM:	178	352	461	13	826	120	.984
AVG:	189	347	501	15	863	114	.982

THIRD	G	PO	A	Er	TC	DP	PCT.
Brookens	151	123	261	23	407	26	.943
Castillo	25	6	19	1	26	1	.962
Pittaro	22	10	27	5	42	1	.881
Evans	7	4	11	5	20	1	.750
Flynn	4	0	1	0	1	0	1.000
Garbey	1	0	0	0	0	0	.000
TEAM:	210	143	319	34	496	29	.931
AVG:	192	129	327	23	479	32	.953

SHORTSTOP	G	PO	A	Er	TC	DP	PCT.
Trammell	149	225	400	15	640	89	.977
Baker	12	12	12	1	25	2	.960
Brookens	8	3	9	1	13	1	.923
Flynn	8	8	11	0	19	3	1.000
TEAM:	177	248	432	17	697	95	.976
AVG:	189	269	474	28	771	104	.964

CATCHER	G	PO	A	Er	TC	DP	PCT.	PB
Parrish	120	695	53	5	753	9	.993	8
Melvin	41	175	13	2	190	1	.989	1
Castillo	32	117	12	3	132	1	.977	1
Madison	1	1	0	0	1	0	1.000	0
Brookens	1	7	1	0	8	0	1.000	2
TEAM:	195	995	79	10	1084	11	.991	12
AVG:	193	895	74	13	982	13	.987	13

OUTFIELD	G	PO	A	Er	TC	DP	PCT.
Gibson	144	286	1	11	298	0	.963
Lemon	144	411	6	4	421	3	.990
Herndon	136	273	7	7	287	4	.976
Simmons	38	67	2	4	73	1	.945
Sanchez	31	35	1	3	39	0	.923
Garbey	24	38	0	1	39	0	.974
Grubb	18	23	0	0	23	0	1.000
Weaver	4	1	0	0	1	0	1.000
Bergman	1	0	0	0	0	0	.000
TEAM:	540	1134	17	30	1181	8	.975
AVG:	559	1141	33	21	1196	8	.982

COMPLETE PITCHERS RECORDS

Pitcher	W	L	Pct	ERA	G	GS	CG	GF	SHO	SV	IP	H	TBF	R	ER	HR	SH	SF	HB	BB	IB	SO	WP	BK	Appr Value
												Starters (One-half of Game Appearances)													
Morris	16	11	.593	3.33	35	35	13	0	4	0	257.0	212	1077	102	95	21	11	7	5	110	7	191	15	3	12
Petry	15	13	.536	3.36	34	34	8	0	0	0	238.2	190	962	98	89	24	0	2	3	81	9	109	6	0	11
Terrell	15	10	.600	3.85	34	34	5	0	3	0	229.0	221	983	107	98	9	11	7	4	95	5	130	5	0	9
Tanana	10	7	.588	3.34	20	20	4	0	0	0	137.1	131	567	59	51	13	3	4	2	34	6	107	2	1	6
Wilcox	1	3	.250	4.85	8	8	0	0	0	0	39.0	51	177	24	21	6	1	0	0	14	2	20	2	0	0
*Mahler	1	2	.333	1.74	3	2	0	0	0	0	20.2	19	84	8	4	2	1	0	0	4	2	14	4	0	0
												Relievers													
*Hernandez	8	10	.444	2.70	74	0	0	64	0	31	106.2	82	415	38	32	13	4	5	1	14	2	76	2	0	13
Berenguer	5	6	.455	5.59	31	13	0	9	0	0	95.0	96	424	67	59	12	1	4	1	48	3	82	4	1	3
O'Neal	5	5	.500	3.24	28	12	1	8	0	1	94.1	82	388	42	34	8	1	7	2	36	3	52	5	0	4
Lopez	3	7	.300	4.80	51	0	0	22	0	5	86.1	82	379	50	46	15	3	6	1	41	9	53	4	0	3
*Scherrer	3	2	.600	4.36	48	0	0	14	0	0	66.0	62	299	35	32	10	5	2	1	41	13	46	5	0	2
Bair	2	0	1.000	6.24	21	3	0	4	0	0	49.0	54	224	38	34	3	2	4	1	25	5	30	6	1	1
*Cary	0	1	.000	3.42	16	0	0	6	0	2	23.2	16	95	9	9	2	0	1	2	8	1	22	0	0	0
Stoddard	0	0	.000	6.75	8	0	0	3	0	1	13.1	15	61	11	10	3	0	0	0	5	0	11	2	0	0

Lance PARRISH, Catcher

	G	AB	Hit	2B	3B	HR	Run	RBI	TBB	SO	SB	CS	Avg
6.51 years		606	160	30	3	29	80	98	45	117	3	5	.263
1985	140	549	150	27	1	28	64	98	41	90	2	6	.273
First Half	78	310	82	13	0	12	29	52	23	49	0	4	.265
Second Half	62	239	68	14	1	16	35	46	18	41	2	2	.285
Vs. RHP		398	104	17	0	19	46	71	23	73	2	3	.261
Vs. LHP		151	46	10	1	9	18	27	18	17	0	3	.305
Home	71	268	75	14	1	11	28	43	26	51	2	2	.280
Road	69	281	75	13	0	17	36	55	15	39	0	4	.267
Grass	117	456	131	25	1	25	59	86	40	73	2	5	.287
Turf	23	93	19	2	0	3	5	12	1	17	0	1	.204

Darrell EVANS, First Base

	G	AB	Hit	2B	3B	HR	Run	RBI	TBB	SO	SB	CS	Avg
13.18 years		550	138	21	3	24	83	81	98	82	7	4	.252
1985	151	505	125	17	0	40	81	94	85	85	0	4	.248
First Half	75	240	59	9	0	17	36	41	40	33	0	2	.246
Second Half	76	265	66	8	0	23	45	53	45	52	0	2	.249
Vs. RHP		384	100	13	0	31	62	73	74	56	0	4	.260
Vs. LHP		121	25	4	0	9	19	21	11	29	0	0	.207
Home	77	242	59	7	0	21	38	46	45	41	0	2	.244
Road	74	263	66	10	0	19	43	48	40	44	0	2	.251
Grass	127	425	104	14	0	31	66	77	75	67	0	4	.245
Turf	24	80	21	3	0	9	15	17	10	18	0	0	.263

Lou WHITAKER, Second Base

	G	AB	Hit	2B	3B	HR	Run	RBI	TBB	SO	SB	CS	Avg
7.03 years		586	165	25	6	10	89	64	73	72	12	7	.282
1985	152	609	170	29	8	21	102	73	80	56	6	4	.279
First Half	76	305	94	13	1	15	60	40	44	28	4	3	.308
Second Half	76	304	76	16	7	6	42	33	36	28	2	1	.250
Vs. RHP		464	137	25	6	19	86	58	60	33	6	4	.295
Vs. LHP		145	33	4	2	2	16	15	20	23	0	0	.228
Home	78	303	81	13	3	11	55	43	42	30	2	0	.267
Road	74	306	89	16	5	10	47	30	38	26	4	4	.291
Grass	129	512	134	20	6	19	85	63	71	48	5	2	.262
Turf	23	97	36	9	2	2	17	10	9	8	1	2	.371

Tom BROOKENS, Third Base

	G	AB	Hit	2B	3B	HR	Run	RBI	TBB	SO	SB	CS	Avg
5.12 years		465	114	22	5	9	55	54	31	73	12	8	.244
1985	156	485	115	34	6	7	54	47	27	78	14	5	.237
First Half	78	223	61	18	5	4	27	25	16	30	6	3	.274
Second Half	78	262	54	16	1	3	27	22	11	48	8	2	.206
Vs. RHP		323	68	21	3	3	36	29	12	57	6	2	.211
Vs. LHP		162	47	13	3	4	18	18	15	21	8	3	.290
Home	76	232	54	17	4	3	33	22	12	40	6	2	.233
Road	80	253	61	17	2	4	21	25	15	38	8	3	.241
Grass	131	407	98	28	4	7	50	43	24	66	9	4	.241
Turf	25	78	17	6	2	0	4	4	3	12	5	1	.218

Alan TRAMMELL, Shortstop

	G	AB	Hit	2B	3B	HR	Run	RBI	TBB	SO	SB	CS	Avg
7.02 years		578	162	26	5	10	85	61	61	66	18	9	.281
1985	149	605	156	21	7	13	79	57	50	71	14	5	.258
First Half	74	313	88	12	4	7	41	28	22	38	9	2	.281
Second Half	75	292	68	9	3	6	38	29	28	33	5	3	.233
Vs. RHP		421	110	16	5	9	59	39	30	56	11	4	.261
Vs. LHP		184	46	5	2	4	20	18	20	15	3	1	.250
Home	76	296	85	10	2	7	47	34	28	32	6	3	.287
Road	73	309	71	11	5	6	32	23	22	39	8	2	.230
Grass	124	500	132	16	6	12	67	50	44	55	11	4	.264
Turf	25	105	24	5	1	1	12	7	6	16	3	1	.229

Larry HERNDON, Left Field

	G	AB	Hit	2B	3B	HR	Run	RBI	TBB	SO	SB	CS	Avg
7.81 years		537	147	20	9	11	67	57	36	87	11	7	.275
1985	137	442	108	12	7	12	45	37	33	79	2	1	.244
First Half	75	265	64	8	4	8	28	20	19	45	0	0	.242
Second Half	62	177	44	4	3	4	17	17	14	34	2	1	.249
Vs. RHP		286	67	9	2	5	24	18	11	55	2	0	.234
Vs. LHP		156	41	3	5	7	21	19	22	24	0	1	.263
Home	67	211	54	7	3	7	23	20	16	28	1	1	.256
Road	70	231	54	5	4	5	22	17	17	51	1	0	.234
Grass	118	379	93	10	5	12	37	35	31	70	2	1	.245
Turf	19	63	15	2	2	0	8	2	2	9	0	0	.238

Chet LEMON, Center Field

	G	AB	Hit	2B	3B	HR	Run	RBI	TBB	SO	SB	CS	Avg
8.28 years		573	160	34	5	19	85	74	59	84	6	8	.280
1985	145	517	137	28	4	18	69	68	45	93	0	2	.265
First Half	69	249	64	15	2	4	25	26	16	39	0	1	.257
Second Half	76	268	73	13	2	14	44	42	29	54	0	1	.272
Vs. RHP		368	89	20	2	10	45	42	31	61	0	1	.242
Vs. LHP		149	48	8	2	8	24	26	14	32	0	1	.322
Home	69	243	70	12	3	9	35	37	20	41	0	0	.288
Road	76	274	67	16	1	9	34	31	25	52	0	2	.245
Grass	121	433	113	21	3	14	55	54	36	76	0	2	.261
Turf	24	84	24	7	1	4	14	14	9	17	0	0	.286

Kirk GIBSON, Right Field

	G	AB	Hit	2B	3B	HR	Run	RBI	TBB	SO	SB	CS	Avg
3.99 years		572	158	26	8	25	88	84	60	123	27	10	.277
1985	154	581	167	37	5	29	96	97	71	137	30	4	.287
First Half	77	296	86	18	3	17	46	58	35	67	11	2	.291
Second Half	77	285	81	19	2	12	50	39	36	70	19	2	.284
Vs. RHP		411	129	28	3	22	68	76	54	85	24	4	.314
Vs. LHP		170	38	9	2	7	28	21	17	52	6	0	.224
Home	76	286	89	21	1	18	53	53	35	58	10	1	.311
Road	78	295	78	16	4	11	43	44	36	79	20	3	.264
Grass	129	487	152	33	4	26	86	82	63	102	27	4	.312
Turf	25	94	15	4	1	3	10	15	8	35	3	0	.160

Nelson SIMMONS, Designated Hitter

	G	AB	Hit	2B	3B	HR	Run	RBI	TBB	SO	SB	CS	Avg
0.52 years		542	141	25	0	19	68	69	54	89	4	0	.260
1985	75	251	60	11	0	10	31	33	26	41	1	0	.239
First Half	30	96	23	6	0	3	11	11	9	16	0	0	.240
Second Half	45	155	37	5	0	7	20	22	17	25	1	0	.239
Vs. RHP		203	48	10	0	7	24	22	21	34	1	0	.236
Vs. LHP		48	12	1	0	3	7	11	5	7	0	0	.250
Home	43	133	36	3	0	7	18	22	15	20	1	0	.271
Road	32	118	24	8	0	3	13	11	11	21	0	0	.203
Grass	64	213	52	7	0	9	27	30	24	31	1	0	.244
Turf	11	38	8	4	0	1	4	3	2	10	0	0	.211

Barbaro GARBEY, Designated Hitter

	G	AB	Hit	2B	3B	HR	Run	RBI	TBB	SO	SB	CS	Avg
1.21 years		466	128	21	2	9	60	67	26	60	7	7	.275
1985	86	237	61	9	1	6	27	29	15	37	3	2	.257
First Half	38	81	22	5	0	3	10	10	8	14	2	0	.272
Second Half	48	156	39	4	1	3	17	19	7	23	1	2	.250
Vs. RHP		99	24	2	0	2	11	14	6	17	2	2	.242
Vs. LHP		138	37	7	1	4	16	15	9	20	1	0	.268
Home	48	134	32	4	1	4	15	19	9	19	3	0	.239
Road	38	103	29	5	0	2	12	10	6	18	0	2	.282
Grass	74	194	51	7	1	5	25	24	15	31	3	1	.263
Turf	12	43	10	2	0	1	2	5	0	6	0	1	.233

JACK MORRIS

	(W–L)	GS	Run	Avg	DP	Avg	SB	Avg
1984	(19-11)	35	173	4.94	24	.69	24	.69
1985	(16-11)	35	162	4.63	32	.91	23	.66
1977-1985		245	1150	4.69	234	.96	153	.62

	G	IP	W	L	Pct	ER	BB	SO	ERA
1984 Home	20	139.3	11	7	.611	59	52	73	3.81
1985 Home	16	106.3	5	5	.500	53	48	80	4.49
1984 Road	15	101.0	8	4	.667	37	35	75	3.30
1985 Road	19	150.7	11	6	.647	42	62	111	2.51
1984 Grass	28	193.0	16	9	.640	78	79	114	3.64
1985 Grass	30	212.7	13	9	.591	88	93	154	3.72
1984 Turf	7	47.3	3	2	.600	18	8	34	3.42
1985 Turf	5	44.3	3	2	.600	7	17	37	1.42
1985 Total	35	257.0	16	11	.593	95	110	191	3.33

DAN PETRY

	(W–L)	GS	Run	Avg	DP	Avg	SB	Avg
1984	(18-8)	35	184	5.26	31	.89	10	.29
1985	(15-13)	34	136	4.00	33	.97	22	.65
1979-1985		204	957	4.69	228	1.12	104	.51

	G	IP	W	L	Pct	ER	BB	SO	ERA
1984 Home	17	121.3	10	4	.714	37	31	83	2.74
1985 Home	19	132.3	7	9	.438	53	52	58	3.60
1984 Road	18	112.0	8	4	.667	47	35	61	3.78
1985 Road	15	106.3	8	4	.667	36	29	51	3.05
1984 Grass	28	192.0	16	5	.762	65	54	123	3.05
1985 Grass	30	210.0	14	11	.560	81	72	96	3.47
1984 Turf	7	41.3	2	3	.400	19	12	21	4.14
1985 Turf	4	28.7	1	2	.333	8	9	13	2.51
1985 Total	34	238.7	15	13	.536	89	81	109	3.36

FRANK TANANA

	(W–L)	GS	Run	Avg	DP	Avg	SB	Avg
1984	(15-15)	35	155	4.43	27	.77	20	.57
1985	(12-14)	33	139	4.21	26	.79	16	.48
1976-1985		289	1237	4.28	228	.79	193	.67

	G	IP	W	L	Pct	ER	BB	SO	ERA
1984 Home	17	112.7	6	8	.429	47	39	62	3.75
1985 Home	18	109.7	8	8	.500	59	33	64	4.84
1984 Road	18	133.7	9	7	.562	42	42	79	2.83
1985 Road	15	105.3	4	6	.400	43	24	95	3.67
1984 Grass	31	220.7	14	13	.519	77	72	125	3.14
1985 Grass	29	189.0	11	11	.500	88	49	138	4.19
1984 Turf	4	25.7	1	2	.333	12	9	16	4.21
1985 Turf	4	26.0	1	3	.250	14	8	21	4.85
1985 Total	33	215.0	12	14	.462	102	57	159	4.27

WALT TERRELL

	(W–L)	GS	Run	Avg	DP	Avg	SB	Avg
1984	(11-12)	33	142	4.30	51	1.55	12	.36
1985	(15-10)	34	156	4.59	34	1.00	16	.47
1982-1985		90	366	4.07	108	1.20	55	.61

	G	IP	W	L	Pct	ER	BB	SO	ERA
1984 Home	17	102.0	3	7	.300	47	40	58	4.15
1985 Home	17	119.7	9	2	.818	38	45	63	2.86
1984 Road	16	113.0	8	5	.615	37	40	56	2.95
1985 Road	17	109.3	6	8	.429	60	50	67	4.94
1984 Grass	23	143.3	5	9	.357	65	52	80	4.08
1985 Grass	28	191.3	13	7	.650	72	81	97	3.39
1984 Turf	10	71.7	6	3	.667	19	28	34	2.39
1985 Turf	6	37.7	2	3	.400	26	14	33	6.21
1985 Total	34	229.0	15	10	.600	98	95	130	3.85

OTHERS

	(W–L)	GS	Run	Avg	DP	Avg	SB	Avg
Berenguer	(5-6)	13	65	5.00	7	.54	10	.77
O'Neal	(5-5)	12	50	4.17	14	1.17	6	.50
Wilcox	(1-3)	8	36	4.50	7	.88	3	.38
Bair	(2-0)	3	23	7.67	4	1.33	2	.67
Mahler	(1-2)	2	7	3.50	3	1.50	1	.50

BALTIMORE ORIOLES

"If the Baltimore Orioles had done it . . . by the numbers, Storm Davis would have been a spectator rather than a participant on opening day . . .

But Altobelli and Miller had a plan . . . and they were determined to follow it. It is their contention that hard throwers fare better in cold weather than do finesse pitchers such as Boddicker and McGregor. Since Davis is the hardest thrower among the starters, the idea was to get him as many starts as possible before warm weather arrived."

That comes from *The Sporting News* of April 22, 1985, under the headline of "Stormy Strategy Pays off Quickly." There should have been a headline the next week entitled "Storm Blows Over in No Time," because after Storm Davis pitched well in the opening-day game against the Rangers, he couldn't get anybody out the rest of the month; his ERA by the end of April was up to 7.23, and it took him most of the year to get it down below 5.00. Davis, the hardest thrower among the starters, was also the least effective of the starters in the cold weather of April, and had by far his own worst month.

You can probably imagine what this did to my predictable little brain. Storm Davis aside, what about this notion that hard throwers are most effective in the cold weather?

I decided to study this by "matching" pitchers with identical won/lost records, one a group of hard throwers, the other a group of finesse pitchers with the same won/lost records. I began by drawing up a list of pitchers who

throw or threw extremely hard, guys like Jim Maloney, Bob Gibson, Bob Veale, Sam McDowell, Earl Wilson, Vida Blue, Nolan Ryan, Frank Tanana when he was young, Mario Soto, Tom Seaver when he was younger . . . you get the idea. I included on the list Sandy Koufax and Dwight Gooden, although, for reasons that will become apparent shortly, they didn't make it into the final study. Then I drew up a list of dedicated finesse pitchers, guys like Mike Caldwell, Scott McGregor, Doyle Alexander, Bill Lee, Larry Jackson, Rick Waits, Tommy John, Randy Jones, etc.

Then I wrote down won/lost records of seasons for the pitchers in each group, following these rules so as to avoid biases from pitchers who might, for example, have not been in the rotation in April:

1) No rookie seasons.

2) No seasons in which the pitcher missed a significant amount of time with an injury.

3) No seasons of less than 25 decisions.

4) No seasons prior to 1963, so that I could figure won/lost records by months using the *Sporting News Guides*.

Then I started "matching" won/lost records on the two lists . . . one guy from each list who went 21-9, one who went 17-13, etc. Sandy Koufax and Dwight Gooden dropped out of the study because of a critical shortage of finesse pitchers who post records like 24-4, 26-8 or 27-9.

I suppose this is obvious, but for the sake of clarity, I

reckoned that if there was any validity at all to the idea of a hard thrower being extra-effective early in the season, then guys like Nolan Ryan, Sam McDowell, etc. should have good records in April—that they should have *better* records in April than would a group of finesse pitchers whose overall records were the same. It's a way of holding the quality constant so that the particular effect under study can be isolated—like the similarity scores except not so much work.

Sometimes pitchers were in one class or another only for part of their careers—that is, a pitcher might be considered a hard thrower only in the early part of his career, or a finesse pitcher only in the late part. I avoided anybody who was hard to classify, like Dan Petry or Don Sutton, or else restricted their inclusion in the study to that part of their careers in which the classification was pretty obvious. I included no knuckleball pitchers.

In this way, I identified 30 sets of matched won/lost records, with it being clear in every case that one of the pitchers threw much harder than the other. For the benefit of anyone who might want to double-check or extend the study further, I'll list the matched sets that I identified, with the hard thrower listed first:

Jim Maloney, 1963, and Warren Spahn, 1963, 23–7; Camilo Pascual, 1963, and Tommy John, 1979, 21–9; Bob Gibson, 1964, and Rick Wise, 1975, 19–12; Bob Veale, 1964, and Rick Reuschel, 1979, 18–12; Dean Chance, 1964, and Mel Stottlemyre, 1965, 20–9; Sam McDowell, 1965, and Doyle Alexander, 1977, 17–11; Earl Wilson, 1965, and Randy Jones, 1978, 13–14; Bob Veale, 1965, and Steve Comer, 1979, 17–12; Tony Cloninger, 1965, and Larry Jackson, 1964, 24–11; Bob Gibson, 1965, and Randy Jones, 1975, 20–12; Jim Lonborg, 1967, and Tommy John, 1980, 22–9; Sam McDowell, 1967, and Rick Waits, 1978, 13–15; Bill Singer, 1968, and George Brunet, 1968, 13–17; Steve Carlton, 1975, and Lary Sorensen, 1979, 15–14; Tom Seaver, 1975, and Mike Caldwell, 1978, 22–9; Bob Gibson, 1966, and Luis Tiant, 1976, 21–12; Vida Blue, 1976, and Ross Grimsley, 1974, 18–13; Frank Tanana, 1976, and Burt Hooton, 1978, 19–10; Denny LeMaster, 1964, and Dick Drago, 1971, 17–11; Dennis Leonard, 1977, and Jim Colborn, 1973, 20–12; Sam McDowell, 1969, and Jim Colborn, 1977, 18–14; Steve Carlton, 1969, and Jim Slaton, 1978, 17–11; Steve Carlton, 1978, and Rick Waits, 1979, 16–13; Steve Carlton, 1979, and Jerry Reuss, 1982, 18–11; Nolan Ryan, 1982, and Bob Stanley, 1979, 16–12; Mario Soto, 1983, and Mike Caldwell, 1982, 17–13; Dave Stieb, 1983, and Bud Black, 1984, 17–12; Mario Soto, 1984, and Scott McGregor, 1983, 18–7; Floyd Bannister, 1984, and Doyle Alexander, 1980, 14–11; Floyd Bannister, 1983, and Bill Lee, 1979, 16–10.

The 30 sets identified in no way represent a comprehensive list; I could probably have identified a few hundred comparisons which were just as legitimate. The pitchers in each group had a composite record of 539 wins, 345 losses, for a winning percentage of .610.

Altobelli was dead wrong.

He couldn't have been more wrong.

As Storm Davis did in 1985, hard throwers throughout the study struggled in April. The overall winning percent-

age was .610; the lowest winning percentage for either group in any month was .580—except for the hard throwers in April. There it was .490. Here's the full data:

	HARD THROWERS		FINESSE PITCHERS	
APRIL	49–51	.490	63–37	.630
MAY	102–57	.642	87–57	.604
JUNE	80–58	.580	91–64	.587
JULY	90–62	.592	94–61	.606
AUGUST	104–56	.650	109–58	.653
SEPTEMBER	106–56	.654	91–66	.580
OCTOBER	8–5	.615	4–2	.667
TOTAL	539–345	.610	539–345	.610

From June 1 through August 31, there was no appreciable difference in the won/lost records of the two groups. The power pitchers were markedly more effective in May (7½ games better) and September (12½ games)—both of which are relatively cold months, thus suggesting that there was a kernel of original truth in Altobelli's design. But the power pitchers were 14 games worse off in April, powerfully suggesting that the specific application of the design was not appropriate.

Below are the lists of power pitchers and finesse pitchers who won three or more games in April in the seasons in which they were part of the study:

POWER PITCHERS		FINESSE PITCHERS	
Gibson, 1965	3–0	Spahn, 1963	4–1
Seaver, 1975	3–2	John, 1979	4–0
Soto, 1983	3–2	Alexander, 1977	3–1
Stieb, 1983	3–2	John, 1980	3–0
		Sorensen, 1979	3–2
		Tiant, 1976	3–0
		Grimsley, 1974	3–1
		Drago, 1971	3–1
		Colborn, 1977	4–1
		Black, 1984	3–1
		McGregor, 1983	3–0

And if you throw all of these pitchers out of the study, the finesse pitchers *still* had a better record in April than did the power pitchers.

The random chance that a .610 pitcher would go 49–51 or worse in 100 decisions is .00573—slightly over one-half of one percent. It is also interesting to note that, while Dwight Gooden didn't make it into the study, over his two-year major league career his record in April is 4–2 with a 1.96 ERA, whereas in September he is 8–1 with an 0.63 ERA in 86 innings—consistent with the pattern of the power pitchers in this study.

In April of 1985, Storm Davis walked 13 men in 23 and ⅔ innings. The rest of the year his control was quite good. April is cold, compared to the other baseball months, but that is not the only identifying characteristic of the game at that time. Baseball in April fights its way through an uncertain, on-again, off-again playing schedule in which many pitchers have trouble getting enough work. Apparently, it takes the power pitchers longer than it does the finesse pitchers to hit their stride and refine their mechanics under these conditions. It would be more work to do this, but I'd bet that if you checked you'd find that the control record of the power pitchers was the source of the problem.

There remains a separate, and probably more important, question of whether it would have been wise for Altobelli to act as he did even if his belief that a power pitcher would be effective in April had been based on fact. Altobelli designed this strategy, one supposes, as a response to a problem: the Orioles have, for many years, played poorly in April. Their April record over the last ten years is 90–97, this for an organization which in all other months has been among the four best in baseball. They were 10–13 in April of 1984, and owner Edward Bennett Williams is on record as expressing his frustration at these repeated slow getaways.

The weather in Baltimore does not tend to be the best at that time of the year—the Orioles lose as many games to weather as anybody—and this may contribute to the problem. But Earl Weaver has always been noted for his determination in staying with the pitchers that he thinks are the best he has, even when they pitch poorly in the first few weeks. What he has essentially tried to do in April is to get as many innings as he can for his four or five best starting pitchers, hoping that, when the weather finally allows them to settle down and start playing regularly, the rotation will be set and ready to run. While many organizations will jocky their rotation in April so that their best pitchers will get the most work, Weaver tries instead to shepherd the staff through the rocky part of the season with a minimum of disruption.

What Altobelli did was more or less the opposite; he based his decisions for April not on what was best for the staff in the long run, but on what should produce the best results in April. One can't help noticing that, when the mid-summer crunch came, the Oriole staff wasn't in any kind of shape to get the job done.

I'm quite certain that what Earl Weaver will do in 1986 will be to select in spring training the four or five pitchers that he thinks have the best chance to win the pennant for him—let's guess it will be Flanagan, McGregor, Davis, Dixon and Snell. What he will do in the early part of the year will be to try to get those four or five pitchers ready to roll. And let's guess that, by the time the season's over, the Orioles will *not* have a staff ERA of 4.38.

COMPLETE BATTING RECORDS

Player	G	AB	R	H	TB	2B	3B	HR	RBI	GW	SH	SF	HB	BB	IB	SO	SB	CS	GI DP	Avg	Slug	OBP	Runs	Outs Made	Runs/ 27 Outs	OW%	Appr Value
Dempsey	132	362	54	92	147	19	0	12	52	4	5	2	1	50	0	87	0	1	2	.254	.406	.345	55	280	5.27	.535	8
†Murray	156	583	111	173	305	37	1	31	124	15	0	8	2	84	12	68	5	2	8	.297	.523	.383	122	428	7.68	.710	13
†Wiggins	76	298	43	85	104	11	4	0	21	0	6	0	2	29	0	16	30	13	2	.285	.349	.353	39	234	4.55	.462	5
Rayford	105	359	55	110	187	21	1	18	48	3	2	1	0	10	0	69	3	1	10	.306	.521	.324	56	263	5.80	.582	8
Ripken	161	642	116	181	301	32	5	26	110	15	0	8	1	67	1	68	2	3	32	.282	.469	.347	96	504	5.17	.525	16
†Young	139	450	72	123	231	22	1	28	81	9	1	1	4	48	5	104	1	5	9	.273	.513	.348	78	343	6.16	.611	11
*Lynn	124	448	59	118	201	12	1	23	68	8	0	6	1	53	6	100	7	3	7	.263	.449	.339	70	346	5.48	.554	10
Lacy	121	492	69	144	201	22	4	9	48	5	1	6	2	39	0	95	10	3	10	.293	.409	.343	70	368	5.15	.524	9
*Sheets	113	328	43	86	145	8	0	17	50	4	1	1	2	28	2	52	0	1	15	.262	.442	.323	43	260	4.42	.448	5
*Dwyer	101	233	35	58	93	8	3	7	36	3	2	1	1	37	2	31	0	3	5	.249	.399	.353	33	186	4.84	.493	3
Roenicke	113	225	36	49	103	9	0	15	43	5	2	3	0	44	1	36	2	2	5	.218	.458	.342	37	188	5.31	.539	5
*Gross	103	217	31	51	92	8	0	11	18	1	1	0	0	46	0	48	1	1	3	.235	.424	.369	37	171	5.84	.586	5
Dauer	85	208	25	42	55	7	0	2	14	2	5	0	1	20	0	7	0	1	9	.202	.264	.275	14	181	2.13	.158	2
†Shelby	69	205	28	58	89	6	2	7	27	4	2	0	0	7	0	44	5	1	4	.283	.434	.307	26	154	4.64	.472	4
Connally	50	112	16	26	39	4	0	3	15	0	2	1	1	19	0	21	0	0	1	.232	.348	.346	15	90	4.58	.465	2
Sakata	55	97	15	22	34	3	0	3	6	1	1	0	1	6	0	15	3	2	3	.227	.351	.279	9	81	2.89	.257	1
Ford	28	75	4	14	19	2	0	1	1	0	0	0	0	7	0	17	0	1	3	.187	.253	.256	4	65	1.79	.118	0
†Pardo	34	75	3	10	11	1	0	0	1	0	0	0	0	3	0	15	0	0	0	.133	.147	.167	2	65	0.82	.027	0
*Nolan	31	38	1	5	7	2	0	0	6	0	0	1	0	5	1	5	0	0	1	.132	.184	.227	2	35	1.35	.070	0
*Lowenstein	12	26	0	2	2	0	0	0	2	1	0	1	0	2	0	3	0	0	0	.077	.077	.138	0	25	0.45	.008	0
Hernandez	12	21	0	1	1	0	0	0	0	0	0	0	0	0	0	4	0	0	2	.048	.048	.048	0	22	0.06	.000	0
*O'Malley	8	14	1	1	4	0	0	1	2	0	0	0	0	0	0	2	0	0	1	.071	.286	.071	0	14	0.00	.000	0
Paris	5	9	0	0	0	0	0	0	0	0	0	0	0	0	0	0	0	0	0	.000	.000	.000	0	9	0.00	.000	0
Dixon	37	0	0	0	0	0	0	0	0	0	0	0	0	0	0	0	0	0	0	.000	.000	.000	0	0	0.00	.000	0
Boddicker	34	0	1	0	0	0	0	0	0	0	0	0	0	0	0	0	0	0	0	.000	.000	.000	0	0	0.00	.000	0

*left-handed hitter, †switch hitter

DEFENSIVE STATISTICS

FIRST	G	PO	A	Er	TC	DP	PCT.
Murray	154	1338	152	19	1509	154	.987
Gross	9	40	4	0	44	1	1.000
Connally	2	16	0	0	16	1	1.000
Dauer	1	2	0	0	2	0	1.000
Hernandez	1	2	0	0	2	0	1.000
Sheets	1	5	1	0	6	1	1.000
TEAM:	168	1403	157	19	1579	157	.988
AVG:	180	1440	123	14	1577	141	.991

SECOND	G	PO	A	Er	TC	DP	PCT.
Wiggins	76	148	186	14	348	58	.960
Dauer	73	117	181	3	301	44	.990
Sakata	50	58	87	6	151	18	.960
Paris	2	3	3	1	7	0	.857
Shelby	1	0	1	0	1	0	1.000
TEAM:	202	326	458	24	808	120	.970
AVG:	189	347	501	15	863	114	.982

THIRD	G	PO	A	Er	TC	DP	PCT.
Rayford	78	62	145	6	213	13	.972
Gross	67	41	98	10	149	14	.933
Connally	46	23	57	2	82	3	.976
Dauer	17	7	21	1	29	0	.966
O'Malley	3	2	3	1	6	0	.833
TEAM:	211	135	324	20	479	30	.958
AVG:	192	129	327	23	479	32	.953

SHORTSTOP	G	PO	A	Er	TC	DP	PCT.
Ripken	161	286	474	26	786	123	.967
TEAM:	161	286	474	26	786	123	.967
AVG:	189	269	474	28	771	104	.964

CATCHER	G	PO	A	Er	TC	DP	PCT.	PB
Dempsey	131	575	49	8	632	5	.987	2
Pardo	29	131	7	3	141	0	.979	0
Rayford	29	114	7	1	122	0	.992	2
Nolan	5	22	2	0	24	0	1.000	0
TEAM:	194	842	65	12	919	5	.987	4
AVG:	193	895	74	13	982	13	.987	13

OUTFIELD	G	PO	A	Er	TC	DP	PCT.
Lynn	123	314	6	2	322	2	.994
Lacy	115	231	9	4	244	0	.984
Young	90	190	6	5	201	0	.975
Roenicke	88	134	6	1	141	0	.993
Dwyer	78	131	4	1	136	0	.993
Shelby	59	148	3	3	154	0	.981
Sheets	9	7	0	1	8	0	.875
Lowenstein	4	7	0	0	7	0	1.000
Hernandez	1	0	0	0	0	0	.000
TEAM:	567	1162	34	17	1213	2	.986
AVG:	559	1141	33	21	1196	8	.982

COMPLETE PITCHERS RECORDS

Pitcher	W	L	Pct	ERA	G	GS	CG	GF	SHO	SV	IP	H	TBF	R	ER	HR	SH	SF	HB	BB	IB	SO	WP	BK	Appr Value
									Starters (One-half of Game Appearances)																
*McGregor	14	14	.500	4.81	35	34	8	0	1	0	204.0	226	884	118	109	34	10	8	1	65	2	86	2	1	8
Boddicker	12	17	.414	4.07	32	32	9	0	2	0	203.1	227	899	104	92	13	9	2	5	89	7	135	5	0	8
D. Martinez	13	11	.542	5.15	33	31	3	1	1	0	180.0	203	789	110	103	29	0	11	9	63	3	68	4	1	6
Davis	10	8	.556	4.53	31	28	8	0	1	0	175.0	172	750	92	88	11	3	3	1	70	5	93	2	1	6
Dixon	8	4	.667	3.67	34	18	3	7	1	1	162.0	144	683	68	66	20	8	2	2	64	7	108	5	2	7
*Flanagan	4	5	.444	5.13	15	15	1	0	0	0	86.0	101	379	49	49	14	7	2	2	28	0	42	3	0	1
Huffman	0	0	.000	15.43	2	1	0	0	0	0	4.2	7	26	8	8	1	1	0	0	5	1	2	0	0	0
									Relievers																
Stewart	5	7	.417	3.61	56	1	0	36	0	9	129.2	117	557	60	52	15	9	5	1	66	10	77	5	1	7
Snell	3	2	.600	2.69	43	0	0	15	0	5	100.1	100	421	44	30	4	4	1	1	30	5	41	1	0	6
Aase	10	6	.625	3.78	54	0	0	43	0	14	88.0	83	366	44	37	6	5	3	1	35	7	67	0	1	9
*T. Martinez	3	3	.500	5.40	49	0	0	20	0	4	70.0	70	312	48	42	8	3	4	0	37	8	47	5	0	3
*Havens	0	1	.000	8.79	8	1	0	3	0	0	14.1	20	70	14	14	4	0	0	0	10	1	19	0	0	0
*Bell	0	0	.000	4.76	4	0	0	3	0	0	5.2	4	24	3	3	1	0	0	0	4	0	4	0	0	0
Habyan	1	0	1.000	.00	2	0	0	1	0	0	2.2	3	12	1	0	0	0	0	0	0	0	2	0	0	0
Swaggerty	0	0	.000	5.40	1	0	0	0	0	0	1.2	3	10	1	1	0	0	0	0	2	1	2	0	0	0

Rick DEMPSEY, Catcher

	G	AB	Hit	2B	3B	HR	Run	RBI	TBB	SO	SB	CS	Avg
8.01 years		452	109	21	1	8	49	44	53	62	2	2	.240
1985	132	362	92	19	0	12	54	52	50	87	0	1	.254
First Half	66	199	48	12	0	5	25	27	29	49	0	1	.241
Second Half	66	163	44	7	0	7	29	25	21	38	0	0	.270
Vs. RHP		206	42	8	0	5	27	19	29	46	0	1	.204
Vs. LHP		156	50	11	0	7	27	33	21	41	0	0	.321
Home	66	179	42	10	0	4	27	26	30	50	0	0	.235
Road	66	183	50	9	0	8	27	26	20	37	0	1	.273
Grass	114	311	80	15	0	11	49	48	45	78	0	0	.257
Turf	18	51	12	4	0	1	5	4	5	9	0	1	.235

Eddie MURRAY, First Base

	G	AB	Hit	2B	3B	HR	Run	RBI	TBB	SO	SB	CS	Avg
8.41 years		610	182	32	2	31	98	111	75	86	6	2	.298
1985	156	583	173	37	1	31	111	124	84	68	5	2	.297
First Half	75	285	79	17	1	13	51	57	34	34	2	1	.277
Second Half	81	298	94	20	0	18	60	67	50	34	3	1	.315
Vs. RHP		384	117	23	1	21	71	84	53	39	4	2	.305
Vs. LHP		199	56	14	0	10	40	40	31	29	1	0	.281
Home	81	291	86	19	0	15	60	63	49	29	2	1	.296
Road	75	292	87	18	1	16	51	61	35	39	3	1	.298
Grass	136	506	149	34	0	27	96	107	74	61	5	2	.294
Turf	20	77	24	3	1	4	15	17	10	7	0	0	.312

Cal RIPKEN, Shortstop

	G	AB	Hit	2B	3B	HR	Run	RBI	TBB	SO	SB	CS	Avg
4.12 years		626	182	36	5	26	105	95	59	87	2	3	.290
1985	161	642	181	32	5	26	116	110	67	68	2	3	.282
First Half	80	321	89	15	2	13	61	54	33	35	1	1	.277
Second Half	81	321	92	17	3	13	55	56	34	33	1	2	.287
Vs. RHP		441	126	19	4	20	78	82	44	55	1	2	.286
Vs. LHP		201	55	13	1	6	38	28	23	13	1	1	.274
Home	81	311	90	13	1	15	68	53	41	33	2	2	.289
Road	80	331	91	19	4	11	48	57	26	35	0	1	.275
Grass	138	545	156	25	4	21	102	90	64	59	2	3	.286
Turf	23	97	25	7	1	5	14	20	3	9	0	0	.258

Wayne GROSS, Third Base

	G	AB	Hit	2B	3B	HR	Run	RBI	TBB	SO	SB	CS	Avg
6.81 years		459	107	19	1	18	55	58	71	73	4	3	.233
1985	103	217	51	8	0	11	31	18	46	48	1	1	.235
First Half	63	154	40	8	0	8	23	15	37	33	0	1	.260
Second Half	40	63	11	0	0	3	8	3	9	15	1	0	.175
Vs. RHP		213	50	8	0	10	30	15	43	48	1	1	.235
Vs. LHP		4	1	0	0	1	1	3	3	0	0	0	.250
Home	52	102	23	2	0	9	20	11	28	24	0	0	.225
Road	51	115	28	6	0	2	11	7	18	24	1	1	.243
Grass	86	176	44	6	0	10	27	13	38	40	1	1	.250
Turf	17	41	7	2	0	1	4	5	8	8	0	0	.171

Mike YOUNG, Left/Right Field

	G	AB	Hit	2B	3B	HR	Run	RBI	TBB	SO	SB	CS	Avg
1.81 years		492	127	23	2	25	76	75	60	123	4	4	.259
1985	139	450	123	22	1	28	72	81	48	104	1	5	.273
First Half	59	155	39	10	1	6	20	20	16	41	1	2	.252
Second Half	80	295	84	12	0	22	52	61	32	63	0	3	.285
Vs. RHP		269	70	14	0	16	37	51	36	70	1	2	.260
Vs. LHP		181	53	8	1	12	35	30	12	34	0	3	.293
Home	72	216	60	9	1	15	38	42	33	49	0	2	.278
Road	67	234	63	13	0	13	34	39	15	55	1	3	.269
Grass	119	378	108	16	1	26	64	72	44	83	1	4	.286
Turf	20	72	15	6	0	2	8	9	4	21	0	1	.208

Alan WIGGINS, Second Base

	G	AB	Hit	2B	3B	HR	Run	RBI	TBB	SO	SB	CS	Avg
2.93 years		580	153	18	5	1	95	31	63	47	69	18	.264
1985	86	335	87	12	4	0	46	21	31	20	30	14	.260
First Half	15	59	9	2	0	0	5	5	3	6	6	2	.153
Second Half	71	276	78	10	4	0	41	16	28	14	24	12	.283
Vs. RHP													
Vs. LHP													
Home	46	183	39	7	1	0	22	12	17	12	10	7	.213
Road	40	152	48	5	3	0	24	9	14	8	20	7	.316
Grass	75	296	76	10	4	0	40	20	27	16	23	13	.257
Turf	11	39	11	2	0	0	6	1	4	4	7	1	.282

Fred LYNN, Center Field

	G	AB	Hit	2B	3B	HR	Run	RBI	TBB	SO	SB	CS	Avg
8.80 years		590	173	37	4	25	95	98	75	90	7	5	.292
1985	124	448	118	12	1	23	59	68	53	100	7	3	.263
First Half	75	280	75	6	1	14	36	46	28	56	5	2	.268
Second Half	49	168	43	6	0	9	23	22	25	44	2	1	.256
Vs. RHP		295	81	5	0	19	42	49	37	58	5	2	.275
Vs. LHP		153	37	7·	1	4	17	19	16	42	2	1	.242
Home	59	217	59	8	0	14	27	38	24	49	1	2	.272
Road	65	231	59	4	1	9	32	30	29	51	6	1	.255
Grass	101	364	98	9	0	20	48	56	41	82	3	3	.269
Turf	23	84	20	3	1	3	11	12	12	18	4	0	.238

Floyd RAYFORD, Third Base

	G	AB	Hit	2B	3B	HR	Run	RBI	TBB	SO	SB	CS	Avg
1.78 years		439	116	22	1	16	52	53	21	93	2	3	.264
1985	105	359	110	21	1	18	55	48	10	69	3	1	.306
First Half	25	66	24	6	0	3	12	9	1	16	0	0	.364
Second Half	80	293	86	15	1	15	43	39	9	53	3	1	.294
Vs. RHP	56	218	63	13	1	6	28	26	5	45	1	1	.289
Vs. LHP	49	141	47	8	0	12	27	22	5	24	2	0	.333
Home	52	177	57	9	1	6	24	21	4	33	1	0	.322
Road	53	182	53	12	0	12	31	27	6	36	2	1	.291
Grass	91	321	98	19	1	17	51	44	10	61	3	1	.305
Turf	14	38	12	2	0	1	4	4	0	8	0	0	.316

Lee LACY, Right Field

	G	AB	Hit	2B	3B	HR	Run	RBI	TBB	SO	SB	CS	Avg
8.06 years		471	136	22	5	9	67	48	38	67	22	10	.289
1985	121	492	144	22	4	9	69	48	39	95	10	3	.293
First Half	50	222	68	9	1	4	34	20	11	42	5	1	.306
Second Half	71	270	76	13	3	5	35	28	28	53	5	2	.281
Vs. RHP		326	92	13	3	4	49	32	24	66	8	1	.282
Vs. LHP		166	52	9	1	5	20	16	15	29	2	2	.313
Home	61	250	77	13	0	3	33	21	20	55	9	1	.308
Road	60	242	67	9	4	6	36	27	19	40	1	2	.277
Grass	107	436	129	22	2	9	59	41	36	91	10	2	.296
Turf	14	56	15	0	2	0	10	7	3	4	0	1	.268

Larry SHEETS, Designated Hitter

	G	AB	Hit	2B	3B	HR	Run	RBI	TBB	SO	SB	CS	Avg
0.75 years		461	125	12	0	24	62	70	39	74	0	1	.270
1985	113	328	86	8	0	17	43	50	28	52	0	1	.262
First Half	64	193	50	6	0	9	27	30	16	29	0	0	.259
Second Half	49	135	36	2	0	8	16	20	12	23	0	1	.267
Vs. RHP		311	84	7	0	17	41	46	24	47	0	1	.270
Vs. LHP		17	2	1	0	0	2	4	4	5	0	0	.118
Home	59	170	47	5	0	5	20	25	16	27	0	1	.276
Road	54	158	39	3	0	12	23	25	12	25	0	0	.247
Grass	94	283	72	6	0	12	35	42	23	46	0	1	.254
Turf	19	45	14	2	0	5	8	8	5	6	0	0	.311

SCOTT McGREGOR

	(W–L)	GS	Run	Avg	DP	Avg	SB	Avg
1984	(15-12)	30	128	4.27	34	1.13	13	.43
1985	(14-14)	34	167	4.91	38	1.12	21	.62
1977-1985		255	1105	4.33	254	1.00	111	.44

	G	IP	W	L	Pct	ER	BB	SO	ERA
1984 Home	17	124.0	11	4	.733	40	33	43	2.90
1985 Home	17	100.0	8	6	.571	46	24	48	4.14
1984 Road	13	72.3	4	8	.333	46	21	24	5.72
1985 Road	18	104.0	6	8	.429	63	41	38	5.45
1984 Grass	29	200.3	11	7	.611	84	46	67	3.77
1985 Grass	29	173.0	13	10	.565	83	52	74	4.32
1984 Turf	4	27.3	1	3	.250	19	19	19	6.26
1985 Turf	6	31.0	1	4	.200	26	13	12	7.55
1985 Total	35	204.0	14	14	.500	109	65	86	4.81

MIKE BODDICKER

	(W–L)	GS	Run	Avg	DP	Avg	SB	Avg
1984	(20-11)	34	148	4.35	33	.97	25	.74
1985	(12-17)	32	142	4.44	40	1.25	39	1.22
1980-1985		93	413	4.44	93	1.00	86	.92

	G	IP	W	L	Pct	ER	BB	SO	ERA
1984 Home	16	120.3	8	6	.571	29	38	56	2.17
1985 Home	15	103.3	5	9	.357	39	48	69	3.40
1984 Road	18	141.0	12	5	.706	52	43	72	3.32
1985 Road	17	100.0	7	8	.467	53	41	66	4.77
1984 Grass	30	232.7	18	10	.643	73	72	110	2.82
1985 Grass	27	175.7	9	16	.360	76	80	113	3.89
1984 Turf	4	28.7	2	1	.667	8	9	18	2.51
1985 Turf	5	27.7	3	1	.750	16	9	22	5.20
1985 Total	32	203.3	12	17	.414	92	89	135	4.07

STORM DAVIS

	(W–L)	GS	Run	Avg	DP	Avg	SB	Avg
1984	(14-9)	31	132	4.26	28	.90	21	.68
1985	(10-8)	28	151	5.39	24	.86	24	.86
1982-1985		96	480	5.00	85	.89	62	.65

	G	IP	W	L	Pct	ER	BB	SO	ERA
1984 Home	18	119.3	8	6	.571	42	34	57	3.17
1985 Home	15	89.3	5	5	.500	45	37	51	4.53
1984 Road	17	105.7	6	3	.667	36	36	36	3.07
1985 Road	16	85.7	5	3	.625	43	33	42	4.52
1984 Grass	30	194.0	12	8	.600	70	62	85	3.25
1985 Grass	26	153.0	10	6	.625	74	53	87	4.35
1984 Turf	5	31.0	2	1	.667	8	8	8	2.32
1985 Turf	5	22.0	0	2	0.000	14	17	6	5.73
1985 Total	31	175.0	10	8	.556	88	70	93	4.53

DENNIS MARTINEZ

	(W–L)	GS	Run	Avg	DP	Avg	SB	Avg
1984	(6-9)	20	78	3.90	23	1.15	14	.70
1985	(13-11)	31	191	6.16	29	.94	21	.68
1977-1985		241	1121	4.65	238	.99	196	.81

	G	IP	W	L	Pct	ER	BB	SO	ERA
1984 Home	17	75.0	3	6	.333	42	18	41	5.04
1985 Home	15	73.7	5	6	.455	50	22	35	6.11
1984 Road	17	66.7	3	3	.500	37	37	37	4.99
1985 Road	18	106.3	8	5	.615	53	41	33	4.49
1984 Grass	28	112.7	5	8	.385	65	49	54	5.19
1985 Grass	28	149.7	9	10	.474	88	57	53	5.29
1984 Turf	6	29.0	1	1	.500	14	14	14	4.34
1985 Turf	5	30.3	4	1	.800	15	6	15	4.45
1985 Total	33	180.0	13	11	.542	103	63	68	5.15

OTHERS

	(W–L)	GS	Run	Avg	DP	Avg	SB	Avg
Dixon	(8-4)	18	94	5.22	17	.94	10	.56
Flanagan	(4-5)	15	60	4.00	18	1.20	11	.73
Havens	(0-1)	1	2	2.00	0	0.00	2	2.00
Huffman	(0-0)	1	9	9.00	0	0.00	0	0.00
Stewart	(5-7)	1	2	2.00	1	1.00	1	1.00

BOSTON RED SOX

The ripping debate in the Boston area has to do with what is called the "chemistry" of the Red Sox team, and with how this relates to their fabled ballpark. In recent years, as the team has slid toward mediocrity (they were declared safe under the tag last August) critics have charged the Red Sox with building too much to suit their park, thus leaving themselves unable to win on the road, or with building incorrectly for the park, concentrating on right-handed power to the exclusion of other factors which might also be favored by Fenway and more valuable on the road. Because of these things the time has come, many have argued, to tear the Red Sox apart and rebuild the team. The Red Sox have become pitiably slow, so let's trade Tony Armas or Mike Easler. Let's entertain offers for Jim Rice. The Red Sox lack pitching, others have added; maybe we should see if we can't trade Wade Boggs and get a faster player—maybe a centerfielder, someone like Willie McGee or Tony Gwynn—or a starting pitcher.

The Red Sox management has replied, in essence, that they have built the kind of team that they think that they have to have to win in Fenway Park, and it would be a mistake to tear that nucleus apart and try to reconstruct it.

To figure out what kind of team should do well in Fenway Park (or any other park) is a more difficult logical problem than most of us will give it credit for being. It's easy to say that Fenway Park helps right-handers and hurts left-handers and is a good park for a power hitter, so what the team needs is right-handed power hitters. But first, we're not all that sure that it is the right-handers who are helped most by the park—all the people who win batting titles here seem to be left-handed—nor are we all that sure that the park helps *power* more than it helps *sequential*

offense. We know that it helps all of these things, but we don't have precise enough information to do a good job of balancing the advantages.

Second, even if we did possess some certain knowledge about these issues, it would still not be clear how a team should interpret them in practice. Take the Ferguson Jenkins problem. Many pitchers feel that, with Fenway Park offering such an inviting home-run target in left field, it is imperative to pitch carefully to the power hitters, not to challenge them and get beaten by the home run. For this reason, many people felt that Ferguson Jenkins, who always challenged hitters and consequently gave up many home runs, would have trouble in Fenway. Other people, including Jenkins, have argued that with home runs coming as frequently as they do in Fenway Park, it is more important than ever to avoid walks, since two walks and Fenway can turn a high fly to left into three runs.

In fact, Jenkins did pitch extremely well in Fenway Park, but who's right? How do the percentages on the risks involved change? The God's truth is that nobody knows, and it would be a Ph.D. math problem to figure it out. Even given a lot of precise data which doesn't exist.

What we can do, however, is look carefully at history. In view of this controversy, it seemed to me that it might be a contribution to the discussion to look carefully at the post-war Red Sox teams which have been successful, the championship and near-championship teams. What *are* the characteristics of the successful Red Sox teams? Did they hit a million homers? Did they hit for exorbitant averages? Did they lead the league in ERA? Did they have large home-field advantages? Did they have good team speed? How many left-handed batters did they have in the lineup? Did they use many left-handed pitchers?

You're going to know the answers to all of those questions in a few minutes. Using the method discussed in the Minnesota comment to formalize something which is fairly obvious anyway, I identified the seven most successful Red Sox teams since 1945 as:

The Red Sox of 1946, 1967 and 1975, who won the American League championship.

The Red Sox of 1948 and 1978, who had records of 96–58 and 99–63 before losing one-game playoffs.

The Red Sox of 1949 and 1977, who had records of 96–58 and 97–64 but missed titles by one game and 2 and a half games.

What did these teams have in common, and what can be learn from that?

1) *Almost all led the league in runs scored.* Actually, five of the teams led the league in runs scored, and the Red Sox of '77 and '78, who narrowly missed the pennant, also narrowly missed leading the league in runs scored, finishing second by margins of 8 runs each year.

2) *All seven teams had earned run averages which were essentially the league average.* The average ERA for the seven teams was 3.80; the average ERA for the leagues they were in was 3.84. No team deviated from the league average by more than 0.23 (in 1985, only 9 of the 26 teams had ERAs which were that close to the league average). None of the teams led the league in ERA or was close to so doing. The highest finish of any of the seven was fourth in ERA; the lowest was ninth, and that was done twice.

3) *Six of the seven teams led the league in runs scored in their home park by very wide margins.* The seventh team, the 1978 team, missed by one of leading the league in runs scored at home. By contrast, *none of the successful Red Sox teams led the league in runs scored in neutral parks,* and none was close to so doing.

The lesson of this seems clear: The Red Sox, to win, have to expect to score at least 450 runs in Fenway Park, and have to lead the league in runs scored. It is not enough for them to have *one* of the best offenses, as they did in 1985; they have to have the best, or very close to it. Conversely, it is not reasonable to expect them to lead the league in ERA, inasmuch as this would be a remarkable accomplishment for a team in Fenway Park, and has not been accomplished or approached even by the most successful Red Sox teams.

4) *All hit above average numbers of home runs, but most were not great home-run hitting teams.* Of the seven teams, three led the league in home runs and one—the 1977 team—hit oodles and scads of home runs, 213 of them. However, four of the successful Red Sox teams did not lead the league in homers. The 1946 Red Sox hit just 109 home runs, 27 fewer than the Yankees. The 1948 Red Sox hit just 121 homers, 34 fewer than the Indians, with whom they wound up in a tie. The 1949 and 1967 Red sox did lead the league in home runs, but in both cases with unusually low league-leading totals. The 1949 team led with 131 homers, one of the lowest American League leading figures since 1930, and the 1967 team led with 158 homers, the lowest A.L.-leading total between 1954 and 1972. The 1975 league champions hit just 134 home runs, tying the Texas Rangers for fourth in the American League. By contrast, any number of Red Sox teams which

were *not* successful, including the inept Sox teams of the early sixties, have hit many more home runs.

I was on a talk show last summer, and somebody asked me whether I thought the Red Sox concentrated too much on getting power in the lineup. I said that I thought if you checked the history of the Red Sox, you'd find that when they win, they lead the league in home runs. Then I realized that I shouldn't have said that without checking it out, and that was what started me thinking about doing this.

One can make a pretty good argument, I think, that Red Sox history shows that when they have concentrated too much on getting *power* in the lineup at the expense of all-around skills, the performance of the team has suffered. There are three times within the era examined when the Red Sox had a championship team, and *all three times,* the championship team has been retooled into a team which would hit more home runs—but not win as many games. The 1946 team, which won 104 games, hit only 109 home runs. They had an off year in 1947, and tried to compensate by adding power to the lineup. By 1949 the Red Sox, having added Vern Stephens at short, were up to 131 home runs—but down to second place. In 1950, adding Walt Dropo, they were up to 161 home runs—but down to third place. After that, the aging team began to drop off in the power categories as well, and fell out of contention.

Following the 1967 championship, essentially the same thing happened. the 1967 team hit 158 home runs—but won the pennant. They had a disappointing year in 1968, and tried to compensate by adding power to the lineup, shifting George Scott to third base and Yastrzemski in from left field to get another outfielder's bat in the lineup. By 1969 they were up to 197 home runs—but in third place. In 1970 they went up to 203 home runs—but held third. After that, the team began to drop off in the power categories, and fell out of contention.

And following the 1975 championship, what happened? The pennant-winning team, remember, hit only 134 home runs. They had a disappointing year in 1976, and tried to compensate by adding power to the lineup, exchanging the young line drive hitter, Cecil Cooper, for the aging power hitter, George Scott. In 1977 they were one of the greatest slugging teams of all time, hitting 213 home runs—but they finished in a tie for second. After contending for two more years they began to drop off in the power categories, and fell out of contention.

5) *All seven of the pitching staffs of the successful teams featured good control relative to league norms, while none of the seven featured outstanding strikeout totals.* All seven teams finished higher in the league in (fewest) walks allowed than they did in (most) strikeouts. The Red Sox in 1975 and 1977 issued the fewest walks in the league, but were tenth in strikeouts; in 1946 and 1948 they missed leading the league in fewest walks allowed by only four (1946) and three (1948). The 1977 team issued only 378 walks, which I believe is the lowest total in the American League since 1920 (excepting the strike-shortened 1981 season).

The comparatively low strikeout totals of successful Boston pitching staffs might be a park illusion created by the excellent visibility of Fenway Park . . . no, (checking sources) that doesn't appear to be the case. In 1985 Red Sox pitchers and hitters both registered strikeouts more often in Fenway Park than on the road. The 1984 data is split but still suggests that Fenway somewhat increases, rather than decreases, strikeouts.

Anyway, this appears to support Ferguson Jenkins' position in the don't walk 'em/don't challenge the hitters debate. The successful Red Sox pitching staffs were all in the "don't walk 'em" camp.

6) In a perhaps related point, *none of the successful Red Sox pitching staffs allowed a particularly low number of home runs, even in their road games*. One might think that a successful Boston pitching staff would be one which could stay away from the home run, but this has not been so. The 1946 Red Sox staff allowed 45 home runs in road games, whereas the league average was 43. The 1975 staff allowed 145 home runs, most in the league, and allowed 62 home runs in road games, 4th-highest total in the league. The 1977 and 1978 home runs allowed data is very similar. Though we cannot assert this with unlimited confidence, it seems to be that the type of pitcher who succeeds in Fenway Park is not the one who avoids the homer, but the one who avoids the walk which multiplies the value of the homer.

7) *The seven teams had, as a group, a larger-than-normal home field advantage*. A normal home-park advantage for a good team would be 9 or 10 games; the Red Sox of the late forties had enormous edges of 18, 13½ and 26 games, and the 1978 team was 18 and a half games better in Fenway than on the road. However, the 1967 and 1977 teams had relatively small improvements in their record at home, and the 1975 team actually played better on the road. The seven teams as a group were 85 and a half games better in Fenway than on the road, an average of better than twelve games. A comparison group of seven average teams which played in Fenway had a home field advantage of only 54 games.

8) *Of the seven successful teams, five led the league in doubles*. However, this could be misleading, inasmuch as even Red Sox teams which are just average will usually lead the league in doubles, as they did in 1985.

9) *Of the seven successful teams, four led the league in batting average, and the other three were fairly close*. No Red Sox team was successful unless its team batting average was far above the league average. On the other hand, several Red Sox teams, like that in 1985, were not successful even though they led the league in batting average.

10) *Six of the seven successful Red Sox teams had at least three left-handed hitters in the regular lineup*. The only successful Red Sox team which was imbalanced with right-handed hitters was the 1967 club. In most cases, the team's Most Valuable Player was a left-handed power hitter (Williams, Yastrzemski or Lynn).

As a group, 24 of 59 regulars on the seven successful teams were either left-handed hitters or switch hitters; that's 41%. The comparison group of seven average teams had 19 of 60 regulars who were left-handed hitters or switch hitters, or 32%.

11) *Five of the seven successful Red Sox teams had at least one successful left-handed starting pitcher*. The 1967 and 1977 teams did not:

	RECORD OF RIGHT-HANDED PITCHERS			RECORD OF LEFT-HANDED PITCHERS	
1946	78-36	.684		26-14	.650
1948	64-36	.640		32-23	.582
1949	51-32	.608		45-26	.635
1967	84-62	.575		8-8	.500
1975	63-50	.558		32-15	.681
1977	87-57	.604		10-7	.588
1978	85-50	.630		14-14	.500

12) *The most difficult aspect of the successful teams to evaluate is their team speed*. None of the seven teams was a base stealing team, and none hit many triples, although one was second in the league in the latter category. However, both of these things are heavily influenced by park effects, and so we must look further, at things like stolen base percentages, double play balls and subjective judgments.

Even so doing, one must reach the conclusion that the team speed of all seven successful Red Sox teams was below average, and far below average for successful teams. Four of the teams (1946, 1967, 1975 and 1978) had poor or very poor stolen base percentages; the stolen base percentage of the 1977 team was not very good (58%). The 1948 and 1949 teams had good stolen base percentage in very limited trials, the 1948 team going 38 for 55 in base stealing efforts.

GIDP (Grounded into double play) data is not available prior to 1954; three of the four teams since grounded into above-average numbers of double plays, and the fourth was barely under the league average.

None of the seven teams possessed a single regular of truly exceptional speed. All had center fielders with good speed (Dom DiMaggio, Reggie Smith and Fred Lynn), but if we look at the other positions where speed often is utilized, such as shortshop, second base, left field and right field, we find a collection of players who were certainly *mobile*, but not really *fast*. Prominent among these are Bobby Doerr, Vern Stephens, Johnny Pesky, Rico Petrocelli, Mike Andrews, Rick Burleson and Denny Doyle. The only base stealer in the group was Jerry Remy, for one season.

However, if none of these teams was fast, none was exceptionally slow, either. The really lumbering Red Sox that you may remember—Dropo, Gernet, Stuart, etc.—all missed the championship teams.

IT TRIVIALIZES HISTORY to imagine that we can reduce it to a few simple lessons that will guide us through our own times. I think that one can accurately generalize this far about the successful Red Sox teams: that they have had a good mix of left-handed and right-handed hitters, that they have probably had less power than most people imagine, that they have scored a great many runs by hitting for average, hitting a lot of doubles and their share of home runs, that their pitching staffs have had good to exceptional control but (because of the park) have had only average earned run averages, that they have had some speed in center field but little otherwise, that they have had some left-handed pitching but not a lot.

How does that jibe with the current edition of the Boston Red Sox? It seems to me that it in essence defends the position of the Red Sox management—that is, that the problem with the team is *not* in the chemistry of park and team, *not* in any supposed mismatch between the two, but simply in the talent and execution of the ballclub. If you look at this club, what do you see? As have the successful teams which have played here, they led the league in doubles and batting average and hit an above-average number of home runs. As have the successful teams which have played here, they have several left-handed hitters in the lineup.

In certain respects, the team differs from the successful seven. The successful Sox had a player with some speed in center field; this team, in recent years, has not had that. They certainly need to add some speed somewhere. The Red Sox in recent years have had more left-handed pitching than their successful teams, and probably more than is advisable for Fenway Park. The 1985 Red Sox were well above average in strikeouts (third in the league) but had below-average control. This may be the most important respect in which they differ from their successful history.

OK, so some changes need to be made. But I am no advocate of tearing apart a team and starting over. To tear apart the center of a team, to deal from the nucleus of the roster—I think this is largely a frustration reaction, and I think it is easy to underestimate how dangerous it is, how easy it is, in doing this, to wind up with a team which is 15 or 20 games worse than what you started with. The Red Sox haven't had a really *bad* team in twenty years; they've forgotten that you can do a whole lot worse than 81–81. I would call to your attention two examples—the Pittsburgh Pirates of 1984, and the Texas Rangers of 1982. The Pirates in 1984 were frustrated. After winning the Worlds' Championship in 1979, they had slipped to third place in 1980 (83–79), fourth in 1981 (46–56), fourth in 1982 (84–78) and second in 1983 (84–78). They were, in short, about where the Red Sox are now.

In frustration, they began to make moves involving the core of the roster. They traded Mike Easler. They traded Dale Berra. They traded Kent Tekulve. They let Dave Parker go because he wasn't doing anything for them anyway. And before you could say Jack Spratt could eat no fat, they had lost 100 games.

After winning 94 games in 1977, the Texas Rangers encountered a run of frustrating seasons. They finished second in 1978 (87–75), third in 1979 (83–79), fourth in 1980 (76–85) and failed to win either half of the split season in 1981 despite a good overall record (57–48). In frustration, they traded Al Oliver that spring, Al Oliver and their second baseman (Bump Wills) and a pitcher.

They lost 98 games in 1982. They have never gotten back on their feet.

You never know, but it is easy for me to see the same thing happening to the Red Sox should they decide to start reconstructing the team. A team newly assembled doesn't know whether they can win or not. Sometimes they decide they can. Sometimes they decide they can't. I don't think that Jim Rice has been a great player over the last two seasons, but I think that Jim Rice is very close to the center of this team. I would not consider trading him.

Even without making those moves, the Red Sox *could* collapse in 1986. They've got a few old guys that I'm not crazy about—Buckner, Armas, Easler. If the Red Sox get disappointing seasons from their crowd of 33-and-up veterans, which includes Rice and Evans, they could be in serious trouble.

Short of that, I am optimistic about their prospects for the immediate future. In looking at the 1986 season, I see five positive question marks. If Roger Clemens is healthy, and I assume he is, he'll improve the team by two to five games, which is a great many. Jim Rice in September of 1985 hit .525 (32/61) with a .951 slugging percentage. If Rice were to snap back to top form, the Red Sox would gain a couple more games.

There are two technical factors which indicate that improvement by the Red Sox is likely. Number one, they scored 44 runs fewer than predicted by the runs created formula. Number two, that they won 8 games fewer than predicted by the pythagorean formula, even given the number of runs that they did score. (Both factors, which have been shown to be valid indicators of future performance, tell us that the talent on the team is better than is reflected in the won/lost column, hence that the team, given the same performance by the individuals, is likely to post a better record in the following season.)

And I love their trades. I love their trades because they bring the team closer to the image suggested by past Red Sox successes, and I love their trades because I like the talent. The argument about the Ojeda trade is that Ojeda might pull a John Tudor, out of Fenway park, and post a 1.90-something ERA with the Mets. That would make the Red Sox look bad—but it really has nothing to do with the Red Sox. The only value that Ojeda had to the Sox was what he was going to do for the Sox, which is alright but not anything sensational.

In exchange for Ojeda and a couple of young pitchers they got a couple of young pitchers and LaSchelle Tarver, who might well develop into the center fielder with speed that they have been looking for. I think it has a chance to be an excellent trade for them. They got Jackie Gutierrez off the roster, entrusting the shortstop position to Glenn Hoffman. I see that as positive both ways. They picked up Mike Stenhouse cheap, and you know I like Stenhouse, while of course his chance of making it big in the big leagues now isn't half what it was a couple of years ago.

Either the Red Sox will fall apart, or they'll come together; there is too much talent here to play .500 ball, and there are plenty of problems to sink them if they start to take on water. But I don't think they will.

I think the Red Sox have made the moves that they needed to make to move back into contention in 1986.

COMPLETE BATTING RECORDS

Player	G	AB	R	H	TB	2B	3B	HR	RBI	GW	SH	SF	HB	BB	IB	SO	SB	CS	GI DP	Avg	Slug	OBP	Runs	Outs Made	Runs/ 27 Outs	OW%	Appr Value
*Gedman	144	498	66	147	241	30	5	18	80	10	3	2	3	50	11	79	2	0	12	.295	.484	.362	86	368	6.34	.649	13
*Buckner	162	673	89	201	301	46	3	16	110	11	2	11	2	30	5	36	18	4	16	.299	.447	.325	96	505	5.14	.549	12
Barrett	156	534	59	142	183	26	0	5	56	3	12	4	2	56	3	50	7	5	14	.266	.343	.336	62	427	3.94	.416	11
*Boggs	161	653	107	240	312	42	3	8	78	5	3	2	4	96	5	61	2	1	20	.368	.478	.450	143	439	8.81	.781	15
Hoffman	96	279	40	77	116	17	2	6	34	3	9	3	5	25	0	40	2	2	6	.276	.416	.343	40	222	4.92	.527	5
Rice	140	546	85	159	266	20	3	27	103	9	0	9	2	51	5	75	2	0	35	.291	.487	.349	83	431	5.18	.553	9
Armas	103	385	50	102	198	17	5	23	64	10	0	5	2	18	4	90	0	0	14	.265	.514	.298	54	302	4.82	.517	8
Evans	159	617	110	162	280	29	1	29	78	13	1	7	5	114	4	105	7	2	16	.263	.454	.378	112	481	6.30	.646	10
*Easler	155	568	71	149	234	29	4	16	74	7	0	7	3	53	1	129	0	1	15	.262	.412	.325	75	442	4.61	.494	8
*Lyons	133	371	52	98	133	14	3	5	30	3	2	3	1	32	0	64	12	9	2	.264	.358	.322	44	289	4.12	.439	5
Gutierrez	103	275	33	60	75	5	2	2	21	2	9	1	0	12	0	37	10	2	9	.218	.273	.250	18	236	2.08	.166	3
Sullivan	32	69	10	12	20	2	0	2	3	0	2	0	0	6	0	15	0	0	1	.174	.290	.240	5	59	2.42	.212	1
Stapleton	30	66	4	15	21	6	0	0	2	0	1	0	0	4	0	11	0	0	1	.227	.318	.271	6	53	2.91	.281	1
*Miller	41	45	5	15	17	2	0	0	9	0	0	1	0	5	0	6	1	0	1	.333	.378	.392	7	32	6.08	.630	1
Sax	22	36	2	11	14	3	0	0	6	0	3	1	0	3	0	3	0	1	0	.306	.389	.350	5	30	4.59	.492	0
Nichols	21	32	3	6	10	1	0	1	3	2	1	1	1	2	0	4	1	0	1	.188	.313	.250	3	29	2.48	.221	0
*Greenwell	17	31	7	10	23	1	0	4	8	2	0	0	3	1	1	4	1	0	1	.323	.742	.382	9	21	11.82	.865	1
Romine	24	28	3	6	8	2	0	0	1	0	2	0	0	1	0	4	0	0	1	.214	.286	.241	2	25	2.05	.162	0
Jurak	26	13	4	3	3	0	0	0	0	0	0	0	0	1	0	3	0	0	1	.231	.231	.286	1	11	1.71	.119	0
*Lollar	17	1	0	0	0	0	0	0	0	0	0	0	0	0	0	0	0	0	0	.000	.000	.000	0	1	0	0	0

*left-handed hitter

DEFENSIVE STATISTICS

FIRST

FIRST	G	PO	A	Er	TC	DP	PCT.
Buckner	162	1384	184	12	1580	140	.992
Stapleton	8	12	1	1	14	3	.929
Jurak	1	0	0	0	0	0	.000
TEAM:	171	1396	185	13	1594	143	.992
AVG:	180	1440	123	14	1577	141	.991

SECOND

SECOND	G	PO	A	Er	TC	DP	PCT.
Barrett	155	355	479	11	845	110	.987
Stapleton	14	29	35	0	64	8	1.000
Nichols	3	1	1	0	2	1	1.000
Hoffman	3	2	0	0	2	0	1.000
TEAM:	175	387	515	11	913	119	.996
AVG:	189	347	501	15	863	114	.982

THIRD

THIRD	G	PO	A	Er	TC	DP	PCT.
Boggs	161	134	335	17	486	30	.965
Jurak	7	3	7	2	12	0	.833
Hoffman	3	0	1	1	2	0	.500
Lyons	1	0	2	0	2	0	1.000
TEAM:	172	137	345	20	502	30	.960
AVG:	192	129	327	23	479	32	.953

SHORTSTOP

SHORTSTOP	G	PO	A	Er	TC	DP	PCT.
Gutierrez	99	143	238	23	404	47	.943
Hoffman	93	155	231	10	396	61	.975
Jurak	3	2	3	0	5	0	1.000
Lyons	1	0	0	0	0	0	.000
TEAM:	196	300	472	33	805	108	.959
AVG:	189	269	474	28	771	104	.964

CATCHER

CATCHER	G	PO	A	Er	TC	DP	PCT.	PB
Gedman	139	768	78	15	861	13	.983	11
Sullivan	32	129	8	1	138	1	.993	3
Sax	16	66	0	1	67	0	.985	0
TEAM:	187	963	86	17	1066	14	.984	14
AVG:	193	895	74	13	982	13	.987	13

OUTFIELD

OUTFIELD	G	PO	A	Er	TC	DP	PCT.
Evans	152	291	9	3	303	1	.990
Rice	130	236	8	9	253	1	.964
Lyons	114	253	4	7	264	0	.973
Armas	79	173	3	3	179	1	.983
Romine	23	20	1	0	21	0	1.000
Easler	20	32	0	3	35	0	.914
Greenwell	17	14	0	0	14	0	1.000
Nichols	10	14	0	1	15	0	.933
Miller	8	9	0	0	9	0	1.000
Sax	4	0	0	0	0	0	.000
Jurak	1	0	0	0	0	0	.000
TEAM:	558	1042	25	26	1093	3	.976
AVG:	559	1141	33	21	1196	8	.982

COMPLETE PITCHERS RECORDS

Pitcher	W	L	Pct	ERA	G	GS	CG	GF	SHO	SV	IP	H	TBF	R	ER	HR	SH	SF	HB	BB	IB	SO	WP	BK	Appr Value
											Starters (One-half of Game Appearances)														
Boyd	15	13	.536	3.70	35	35	13	0	3	0	272.1	273	1132	117	112	26	9	7	4	67	3	154	1	1	11
*Hurst	11	13	.458	4.51	35	31	6	0	1	0	229.1	243	973	123	115	31	6	4	3	70	4	189	3	4	7
Nipper	9	12	.429	4.06	25	25	5	0	0	0	162.0	157	713	83	73	14	4	4	9	82	3	85	3	1	6
*Ojeda	9	11	.450	4.00	39	22	5	0	10	1	157.2	166	671	74	70	11	10	3	2	48	9	102	3	3	7
Clemens	7	5	.583	3.29	15	15	3	0	1	0	98.1	83	407	38	36	5	1	2	3	37	0	74	1	3	5
*Lollar	5	5	.500	4.57	16	10	1	4	0	1	67.0	57	291	37	34	9	1	1	1	40	0	44	5	0	2
Sellers	2	0	1.000	3.63	4	4	1	0	0	0	22.1	24	97	10	9	1	1	1	0	7	1	6	1	0	0
Dorsey	0	1	.000	20.25	2	1	0	0	0	0	5.1	12	37	12	12	2	0	0	0	10	1	2	0	0	0
Brown	0	0	.000	21.60	2	1	0	0	0	0	3.1	9	22	8	8	0	0	0	1	3	0	3	0	1	0
											Relievers														
Kison	5	3	.625	4.11	22	9	0	5	0	1	92.0	98	398	43	42	9	4	3	1	32	4	56	1	0	4
Crawford	6	5	.545	3.76	44	1	0	26	0	12	91.0	103	394	47	38	5	6	3	0	28	8	58	5	0	7
Trujillo	4	4	.500	4.82	27	7	1	7	0	1	84.0	112	379	55	45	7	1	2	3	23	1	19	1	0	2
Clear	1	3	.250	3.72	41	0	0	30	0	3	55.2	45	259	26	23	1	2	2	5	50	10	55	8	0	2
Stanley	6	6	.500	2.87	48	0	0	41	0	10	87.2	76	360	30	28	7	3	4	2	30	10	46	1	0	7
Woodward	1	0	1.000	1.69	5	2	0	3	0	0	26.2	17	113	8	5	0	1	0	0	9	0	16	0	0	0
McCarthy	0	0	.000	10.80	3	0	0	0	0	0	5.0	7	25	6	6	1	0	1	0	4	0	2	1	0	0
Mitchell	0	0	.000	16.20	2	0	0	0	0	0	1.2	5	10	3	3	1	0	0	0	0	0	2	0	0	0

Rich GEDMAN, Catcher

	G	AB	Hit	2B	3B	HR	Run	RBI	TBB	SO	SB	CS	Avg
3.22 years		519	144	32	4	16	61	69	35	81	1	1	.278
1985	144	498	147	30	5	18	66	80	50	79	2	0	.295
First Half	75	252	74	19	3	5	35	36	24	46	1	0	.294
Second Half	69	246	73	11	2	13	31	44	26	33	1	0	.297
Vs. RHP		363	114	24	4	16	51	51	40	52	1	0	.314
Vs. LHP		135	33	6	1	2	15	29	10	27	1	0	.244
Home	73	248	83	16	4	9	41	51	21	33	2	0	.335
Road	71	250	64	14	1	9	25	29	29	46	0	0	.256
Grass	124	429	132	28	4	15	59	75	42	64	2	0	.308
Turf	20	69	15	2	1	3	7	5	8	15	0	0	.217

Jim RICE, Left Field

	G	AB	Hit	2B	3B	HR	Run	RBI	TBB	SO	SB	CS	Avg
10.08 years		646	195	29	7	33	100	117	50	113	5	3	.302
1985	140	546	159	20	3	27	85	103	51	75	2	0	.291
First Half	82	330	91	10	1	16	51	53	26	44	1	0	.276
Second Half	58	216	68	10	2	11	34	50	25	31	1	0	.315
Vs. RHP		397	120	11	2	20	63	85	26	59	2	0	.302
Vs. LHP		149	39	9	1	7	22	18	25	16	0	0	.262
Home	69	274	96	13	3	11	44	64	20	44	2	0	.350
Road	71	272	63	7	0	16	41	39	31	31	0	0	.232
Grass	118	461	140	17	3	24	72	93	39	64	2	0	.304
Turf	22	85	19	3	0	3	13	10	12	11	0	0	.224

Bill BUCKNER, First Base

	G	AB	Hit	2B	3B	HR	Run	RBI	TBB	SO	SB	CS	Avg
12.49 years		624	184	34	4	12	75	78	29	30	14	5	.295
1985	162	673	201	46	3	16	89	110	30	36	18	4	.299
First Half	82	328	94	21	0	8	37	44	16	16	9	2	.287
Second Half	80	345	107	25	3	8	52	66	14	20	9	2	.310
Vs. RHP		443	134	36	1	12	69	72	22	24	12	2	.302
Vs. LHP		230	67	10	2	4	20	38	8	12	6	2	.291
Home	80	328	98	22	2	6	46	52	12	22	7	1	.299
Road	82	345	103	24	1	10	43	58	18	14	11	3	.299
Grass	136	563	170	41	3	13	78	88	26	30	14	4	.302
Turf	26	110	31	5	0	3	11	22	4	6	4	0	.282

Tony ARMAS, Center Field

	G	AB	Hit	2B	3B	HR	Run	RBI	TBB	SO	SB	CS	Avg
6.81 years		600	150	22	5	31	74	98	30	144	2	2	.250
1985	103	385	102	17	5	23	50	64	18	90	0	0	.265
First Half	48	192	47	8	1	14	25	30	5	41	0	0	.245
Second Half	55	193	55	9	4	9	25	34	13	49	0	0	.285
Vs. RHP		245	55	8	2	14	27	41	8	66	0	0	.224
Vs. LHP		140	47	9	3	9	23	23	10	24	0	0	.336
Home	50	173	50	7	3	11	26	30	11	26	0	0	.289
Road	53	212	52	10	2	12	24	34	7	64	0	0	.245
Grass	87	316	85	14	5	20	44	56	16	74	0	0	.269
Turf	16	69	17	3	0	3	6	8	2	16	0	0	.246

Marty BARRETT, Second Base

	G	AB	Hit	2B	3B	HR	Run	RBI	TBB	SO	SB	CS	Avg
2.07 years		516	143	24	2	4	59	50	49	37	5	4	.277
1985	156	534	142	26	0	5	59	56	56	50	7	5	.266
First Half	81	253	73	12	0	2	32	31	32	19	3	2	.289
Second Half	75	281	69	14	0	3	27	25	24	31	4	3	.246
Vs. RHP		370	97	15	0	5	47	38	34	43	4	3	.262
Vs. LHP		164	45	11	0	0	12	18	22	7	3	2	.274
Home	78	265	73	15	0	3	33	26	27	35	4	4	.275
Road	78	269	69	11	0	2	26	30	29	15	3	1	.257
Grass	132	450	125	23	0	4	55	49	50	45	6	5	.278
Turf	24	84	17	3	0	1	4	7	6	5	1	0	.202

Dwight EVANS, Right Field

	G	AB	Hit	2B	3B	HR	Run	RBI	TBB	SO	SB	CS	Avg
10.99 years		558	150	30	5	24	91	77	81	107	5	4	.269
1985	159	617	162	29	1	29	110	78	114	105	7	2	.263
First Half	80	294	68	12	0	9	42	27	67	52	1	2	.231
Second Half	79	323	94	17	1	20	68	51	47	53	6	0	.291
Vs. RHP		449	119	23	1	19	83	53	72	80	4	2	.265
Vs. LHP		168	43	6	0	10	27	25	42	25	3	0	.256
Home	77	292	81	18	0	14	58	34	49	49	4	2	.277
Road	82	325	81	11	1	15	52	44	65	56	3	0	.249
Grass	133	513	137	27	1	23	96	63	94	86	7	2	.267
Turf	26	104	25	2	0	6	14	15	20	19	0	0	.240

Wade BOGGS, Third Base

	G	AB	Hit	2B	3B	HR	Run	RBI	TBB	SO	SB	CS	Avg
3.56 years		618	217	37	4	7	103	71	88	46	3	2	.351
1985	161	653	240	42	3	8	107	78	96	61	2	1	.368
First Half	81	320	107	21	1	2	44	35	54	28	1	1	.334
Second Half	80	333	133	21	2	6	63	43	42	33	1	0	.399
Vs. RHP		440	166	30	2	6	84	50	72	40	2	0	.377
Vs. LHP		213	74	12	1	2	23	28	24	21	0	1	.347
Home	80	311	130	24	2	6	60	39	51	38	1	1	.418
Road	81	342	110	18	1	2	47	39	45	23	1	0	.322
Grass	135	545	198	33	2	7	89	67	81	51	2	1	.363
Turf	26	108	42	9	1	1	18	11	15	10	0	0	.389

Mike EASLER, Designated Hitter

	G	AB	Hit	2B	3B	HR	Run	RBI	TBB	SO	SB	CS	Avg
5.60 years		520	152	27	4	18	68	74	45	99	3	4	.293
1985	155	568	149	29	4	16	71	74	53	129	0	1	.262
First Half	80	304	83	16	2	9	42	39	28	68	0	1	.273
Second Half	75	264	66	13	2	7	29	35	25	61	0	0	.250
Vs. RHP		395	101	20	4	14	52	57	36	77	0	1	.256
Vs. LHP		173	48	9	0	2	19	17	17	52	0	0	.277
Home	75	273	68	17	3	4	30	31	24	75	0	1	.249
Road	80	295	81	12	1	12	41	43	29	54	0	0	.275
Grass	130	478	124	26	4	14	59	67	44	117	0	1	.259
Turf	25	90	25	3	0	2	12	7	9	12	0	0	.278

Glenn HOFFMAN, Shortstop

	G	AB	Hit	2B	3B	HR	Run	RBI	TBB	SO	SB	CS	Avg
3.98 years		464	115	23	2	6	56	48	30	69	1	3	.247
1985	96	279	77	17	2	6	40	34	25	40	2	0	.276
First Half	57	157	43	11	2	2	18	18	11	21	2	0	.274
Second Half	39	122	34	6	0	4	22	16	14	19	0	2	.279
Vs. RHP		199	52	11	2	2	32	20	19	30	2	2	.261
Vs. LHP		80	25	6	0	4	8	14	6	10	0	0	.313
Home	48	129	33	9	1	2	18	17	17	20	1	2	.256
Road	48	150	44	8	1	4	22	17	8	20	1	0	.293
Grass	82	236	67	15	2	5	37	26	22	32	1	2	.284
Turf	14	43	10	2	0	1	3	8	3	8	1	0	.233

Steve LYONS, Center Field

	G	AB	Hit	2B	3B	HR	Run	RBI	TBB	SO	SB	CS	Avg
0.82 years		452	119	17	4	6	63	37	39	78	15	11	.264
1985	133	371	98	14	3	5	52	30	32	64	12	9	.264
First Half	55	144	38	4	0	2	22	12	12	14	4	5	.264
Second Half	78	227	60	10	3	3	30	18	20	50	8	4	.264
Vs. RHP		304	80	13	2	4	44	24	25	50	8	9	.263
Vs. LHP		67	18	1	1	1	8	6	7	14	4	0	.269
Home	69	193	51	8	1	4	25	19	17	35	2	6	.264
Road	64	178	47	6	2	1	27	11	15	29	10	3	.264
Grass	114	318	85	11	2	4	43	27	24	57	9	9	.267
Turf	19	53	13	3	1	1	9	3	8	7	3	0	.245

OIL CAN BOYD

	(W–L)	GS	Run	Avg	DP	Avg	SB	Avg
1984	(12-12)	26	131	5.04	22	.85	13	.50
1985	(15-13)	35	178	5.09	27	.77	18	.51
1983-1985		74	360	4.86	62	.84	41	.55

	G	IP	W	L	Pct	ER	BB	SO	ERA
1984 Home	16	115.7	6	8	.429	50	24	71	3.89
1985 Home	20	158.0	11	8	.579	66	45	94	3.76
1984 Road	13	82.0	6	4	.600	46	29	63	5.05
1985 Road	15	114.3	4	5	.444	46	22	60	3.62
1984 Grass	25	174.0	10	11	.476	83	43	121	4.29
1985 Grass	31	242.7	14	13	.519	100	63	140	3.71
1984 Turf	4	23.7	2	1	.667	13	10	13	4.94
1985 Turf	4	29.7	1	0	1.000	12	4	14	3.64
1985 Total	35	272.3	15	13	.536	112	67	154	3.70

TIM LOLLAR

	(W–L)	GS	Run	Avg	DP	Avg	SB	Avg
1984	(11-13)	31	120	3.87	24	.77	26	.84
1985	(8-10)	23	108	4.70	29	1.26	15	.65
1980-1985		99	408	4.12	81	.82	66	.67

	G	IP	W	L	Pct	ER	BB	SO	ERA
1984 Home	15	103.0	5	6	.455	31	51	74	2.71
1985 Home	15	77.3	5	2	.714	31	50	57	3.61
1984 Road	16	92.7	6	7	.462	54	54	57	5.24
1985 Road	19	71.3	3	8	.273	46	48	48	5.80
1984 Grass	22	140.3	8	8	.500	56	70	100	3.59
1985 Grass	31	140.0	7	10	.412	76	93	99	4.89
1984 Turf	9	55.3	3	5	.375	29	35	31	4.72
1985 Turf	3	10.0	1	0	1.000	1	5	6	.90
1985 Total	34	150.0	8	10	.444	77	98	105	4.62

BRUCE HURST

	(W–L)	GS	Run	Avg	DP	Avg	SB	Avg
1984	(12-12)	33	160	4.85	20	.61	16	.48
1985	(11-13)	31	186	6.00	28	.90	17	.55
1980-1985		127	649	5.11	122	.96	80	.63

	G	IP	W	L	Pct	ER	BB	SO	ERA
1984 Home	17	108.0	6	6	.500	56	47	69	4.67
1985 Home	16	106.3	6	8	.429	55	28	81	4.66
1984 Road	16	110.0	6	6	.500	39	41	67	3.19
1985 Road	19	123.0	5	5	.500	60	42	108	4.39
1984 Grass	29	192.0	11	10	.524	86	78	118	4.03
1985 Grass	30	197.3	11	12	.478	98	58	162	4.47
1984 Turf	4	26.0	1	2	.333	9	10	18	3.12
1985 Turf	5	32.0	0	1	0.000	17	12	27	4.78
1985 Total	35	229.3	11	13	.458	115	70	189	4.51

BOB OJEDA

	(W–L)	GS	Run	Avg	DP	Avg	SB	Avg
1984	(12-12)	32	149	4.66	31	.97	18	.56
1985	(9-11)	22	84	3.82	23	1.05	8	.36
1980-1985		113	526	4.65	121	1.07	70	.62

	G	IP	W	L	Pct	ER	BB	SO	ERA
1984 Home	15	92.0	4	5	.444	51	42	57	4.99
1985 Home	21	97.7	4	7	.364	36	27	74	3.32
1984 Road	18	124.7	8	7	.533	45	54	80	3.25
1985 Road	18	60.0	5	4	.556	34	21	28	5.10
1984 Grass	28	185.0	12	8	.600	77	78	122	3.75
1985 Grass	33	139.0	7	11	.389	62	43	95	4.01
1984 Turf	5	31.7	0	4	0.000	19	18	15	5.40
1985 Turf	6	18.7	2	0	1.000	8	5	7	3.86
1985 Total	39	157.7	9	11	.450	70	48	102	4.00

AL NIPPER

	(W–L)	GS	Run	Avg	DP	Avg	SB	Avg
1984	(11-6)	24	125	5.21	16	.67	16	.67
1985	(9-12)	25	102	4.08	29	1.16	8	.32
1983-1985		51	231	4.53	48	.94	27	.53

	G	IP	W	L	Pct	ER	BB	SO	ERA
1984 Home	14	93.0	5	2	.714	33	25	38	3.19
1985 Home	13	94.3	5	6	.455	35	35	51	3.34
1984 Road	15	89.7	6	4	.600	46	27	46	4.62
1985 Road	12	67.7	4	6	.400	38	47	34	5.05
1984 Grass	24	147.3	8	6	.571	70	43	69	4.28
1985 Grass	18	125.0	7	8	.467	56	52	65	4.03
1984 Turf	5	35.3	3	0	1.000	9	9	15	2.29
1985 Turf	7	37.0	2	4	.333	17	30	20	4.14
1985 Total	25	162.0	9	12	.429	73	82	85	4.06

OTHERS

	(W–L)	GS	Run	Avg	DP	Avg	SB	Avg
Clemens	(7-5)	15	61	4.07	13	.87	24	1.60
Kison	(5-3)	9	48	5.33	7	.78	4	.44
Trujillo	(4-4)	7	40	5.71	10	1.43	4	.57
Sellers	(2-0)	4	23	5.75	5	1.25	1	.25
Woodward	(1-0)	2	15	7.50	2	1.00	0	0.00
Crawford	(6-5)	1	5	5.00	2	2.00	0	0.00
Brown	(0-0)	1	6	6.00	0	0.00	2	2.00
Dorsey	(0-1)	1	3	3.00	0	0.00	1	1.00

MILWAUKEE BREWERS

BREAKDOWNS FOR THE LAST TEN SEASONS

Won-Lost Record: 789-774, .505 (5th in the Division, 12th in the Majors)
Runs Scored: 7,110 (4th in the Division, 6th in Majors)
Runs Allowed: 6,894 (4th highest in the Division, 10th in Majors)
Home Runs Hit: 1,415 (5th in the Division, also 5th in the Majors)
Home Runs Allowed: 1,312 (4th highest in the Division, 7th in the Majors)

RECORD IN:
April: 95-82, .537 (2nd in the Division, 6th in Majors)
May: 135–138, .495 (5th in the Division, 14th in Majors)
June: 135-124, .521 (5th in the Division, 10th in Majors)
July: 135-123, .523 (4th in the Division, 8th in the Majors)
August: 152-148, .507 (5th in the Division, 11th in the Majors)
September: 125-147, .460 (5th in the Division, 19th in Majors)
October: 12-12, .500 (4th in the Division, 14th in the Majors)

Won-Lost Record in Road Games: 364-420, .464 (5th in the Division, 12th in Majors)
Won-Lost Record at Home: 425-354, .546 (5th in the Division, 11th in Majors)
Home Field Advantage: 63½ Games
Runs Scored on the Road: 3,654 (2nd Highest in the Division and 2nd highest in Baseball)
Runs Scored at Home: 3,456 (6th in the Division, 14th in the Majors)
Runs Allowed on the Road: 3,605 (2nd in the Division, 5th in Majors)
Runs Allowed at Home: 3,289 (5th in the Division, 12th in Majors)

Home Runs Hit on the Road: 768 (2nd Highest total in the Division, also 2nd in Majors)
Home Runs Hit at Home: 647 (6th in the Division, 15th in the Majors)
Home Runs Allowed on the Road: 715 (Highest total in the Division, 2nd Highest in Majors)
Home Runs Allowed at Home: 597 (6th highest in the Division, 15th in the Majors)

RECORD FOR LAST THREE SEASONS: 225-259, .465 (6th in the Division, 21st in Majors)

THE BALLPARK

The 1985 season was the best hitter's year in the 32-year history of Milwaukee County Stadium. Although there were more home runs hit in their road games, the Brewers in 1985 scored and allowed 784 runs in Milwaukee, only 708 on the road. Perhaps in response to this, I got a letter last summer from a reader wanting to know why I didn't do a thorough, once-and-for-all examination of the park effects in Milwaukee County Stadium, and put to a permanent rest the dispute about whether it is a hitter's or a pitcher's park. The answer to that is simple: because there is no conflict of evidence. With the exception of an occasional abberation in data such as happened in 1985, Milwaukee County Stadium is (and has always been) a pitcher's park (and a poor home run park) and it would be silly to do an in-depth study of the issue because there is no evidence which would show anything else.

Baseball men have arrived at the belief that County Stadium is a hitter's park through a kind of intuitive logic which goes:

1) The teams which have played here, both the Braves and the Brewers, have hit a lot of home runs and scored a lot of runs.

2) Generally, when a team over a period of years hits a lot of home runs and scores a lot of runs, they do so in part because they play in a hitter's park.

3) The dimensions in County Stadium are fairly short, 315 down the lines, so

4) It's got to be a hitter's park.

All three points are correct as stated, but it just happens to be a kind of flukey thing, that despite the short dimensions down the lines the overall home run charac-teristics of the park are poor, and that while it is *generally* true that teams which hit a lot of home runs do so in part because of their parks, in this *specific* case the Braves and Brewers have hit a lot of home runs *despite* the park, not because of the park. There might also be a self-sustaining illusion involved, in that if the people who run the team *believe* it to be a home run park, then they would tend to acquire home run hitters (as opposed to other types of players), so that the teams which play here would continue to hit lots of home runs.

Anyway, the "dispute" isn't a disagreement about the evidence, but a disagreement between people who are looking at the evidence and people who aren't. It's like asking a naturalist why he doesn't do a complete, once-and-for-all study of the evidence on evolution and crea-tionism. The evidence is already conclusive; it's just that there are people who don't intend to accept it unless the hand of God appears in the sky one afternoon and writes "ALL RIGHT! I CONFESS! I DID IT BY EVOLUTION! IT TOOK ME YEARS! I'SE JUST KIDDING ABOUT THE SEVEN DAYS! AND BY THE WAY, MILWAUKEE COUNTY STADIUM IS A PITCHER'S PARK . . . BE BACK NEXT MILLENNIUM. LOVE, GOD. P.S. IF YOU DO ANY MORE MOVIES I'D PREFER DEBRA WINGER TO GEORGE BURNS."

PIVOT POINT

On receiving the letter, I wandered from checking the dimensions in County Stadium now to checking what they were a few years ago to checking what they were in 1953, to the realization that with one minor exception (the left field line until 1981 was listed as 320, instead of 315—if memory serves me, the one change was a remeasuring, rather than a remodeling) they had never changed, to the realization that this information was potentially valuable to us.

In this way. The number of runs scored in baseball changes a great deal from decade to decade. There are many dynamics of that change—changing rules, changing social and economic structures within the game and without, changing ethics, strategies and customs, changing equipment. It has been my belief that the one largest dynamic of change within the game is the ballparks. Still, baseball from 1930 to 1968 evolved from a game which produced an average of over eleven runs a game to one which produced about seven, and nobody really can explain why with any great confidence. Since 1968 the American League ERA has gone from under 3.00 to 4.15, some of which is caused by the DH rule, some by a redefinition of the strike zone, and some by the ballparks. A very interesting question, to me, is how much is caused by the parks.

One of the complicating factors of studying this issue is that the ballparks themselves change. Some of them change more than others, but if you study, let's say, Candlestick Park, you've got a couple or three changes in the field dimensions, plus you've got a remodeling in the early seventies which cut off a good part of the wind, plus at one time they put in artificial turf and then tore it out again. Usually, it is hard to distinguish the changes in the park from the changes in the game. But in the middle of these changes *and in both leagues, no less* sits County Stadium, more or less immutable over a 32-year span.

We can use County Stadium, then, as a sort of "surveying instrument" to evaluate the other ballparks. If the number of runs scored in County Stadium rises relative to the number of runs scored by the Brewers/Braves in road games, then, since this park is the same, the movement must be due to the changes in the other parks. As the *league* moves relative to *the park,* then, the park is a fixed point from which to study those changes in offensive levels which are *not* caused by the park. If the runs scored in Milwaukee (relative to the team's road games) move up and down with the league averages, then those changes are caused by internal factors of the game. If the movements of the league are independent, and are not reflected in the games played here, then those changes are probably caused by changes in the ballparks.

To do this, we have to begin by looking at the number of runs scored and allowed by the Braves/Brewers in their home games and their road games since 1953. This material is available to us in the new *Macmillan Encyclopedia* (which, if I haven't mentioned this anywhere else here, is tremendous. The 1985 Big Mac is the first edition since the original in 1969 to include a significant amount of important new information that you don't already have in your library. Included in this is runs scored and allowed at home and on the road for every team since 1900). In the Braves first years in Milwaukee, the "park factor," as Pete Palmer calls it, was very low (that is, the Braves scored and allowed many, many more runs on the road than they did in Milwaukee):

	GAMES PLAYED IN MILWAUKEE			GAMES PLAYED ON THE ROAD		
YEAR	G	HR	Runs	G	HR	Runs
1953	79	95	592	78	168	735
1954	77	72	536	77	173	690
1955	77	126	639	77	194	772
1956	77	130	609	78	180	669
1957	78	126	601	77	197	784
1958	77	120	498	77	172	718
1959	79	147	624	78	168	723
1960	77	146	612	77	154	770
1961	77	156	604	78	185	764
1962	81	167	681	81	165	714
1963	82	149	648	81	139	632
1964	81	167	761	81	152	786
1965	81	173	697	81	146	644
1970	81	140	675	82	132	689
1971	82	110	601	79	124	542
1972	79	81	529	77	123	559
1973	81	125	692	81	139	747
1974	81	127	671	81	119	636
1975	81	137	746	81	144	721
1976	81	88	613	80	99	612
1977	81	103	670	81	158	734
1978	81	144	764	81	138	690
1979	81	172	763	80	175	766
1980	82	155	704	80	185	789
1981	49	62	406	60	106	546
1982	82	153	750	81	215	858
1983	81	121	761	81	144	811
1984	81	110	730	80	123	745
1985	80	136	784	81	140	708
	2287	3738	18961	2287	4457	20554

As you can see, in the years that the stadium has been occupied, the Milwaukee teams have hit and allowed more than 800 more home runs on the road than in Milwaukee, and have scored and allowed about 1600 more runs on the road. The number of home runs hit in Milwaukee has been lower than in Brewer road games every year since 1978.

In the first three years that Milwaukee was in the National League (1953–1955), the average National League game had 9.24 runs. In ten years (1963–1965) this had dropped to 7.90 runs. *On the basis of a comparison to County Stadium, it appears that virtually 100% of this difference was caused by changes in the other ballparks.* Between 1953 and 1965, four ballparks came into the National League which might have contributed to this:

1) The Brooklyn Dodgers moved from Ebbets Field, one of the better hitter's parks, to Dodger Stadium, one of the worst hitter's parks of all time.

2) The New York Giants moved from the Polo Grounds, a home run park with decent overall offensive characteristics, into Candlestick Park.

3) The Astros, and the Astrodome, came into the National League.

4) The Mets, and Shea Stadium, came into the National League.

All of those things favored the pitcher, and made it easier for the pitcher to dominate the game.

Between the first period (1953–55) and second (1963–65), while the number of runs scored in the National League as a whole was declining dramatically, the number of runs scored in games played in Milwaukee actually *increased*—presumably due primarily to changes in the composition of the Milwaukee roster, but also perhaps due in part to other changes in the game.

The conclusion that the change in the level of runs throughout the league results almost 100% from the parks is based on this mathematical inference: The ratio between runs scored in Milwaukee and those in Milwaukee road games in 1953–55 was 1:1.23. In 1963–65 it was 1:.98. This would imply that, given no other changes in the game other than the parks, the number of runs scored throughout the National League *in games not involving the Braves* should have declined between 1953–55 and 1963–65 by about 19%. In fact, it declined by almost exactly that much—hence the difference was probably 100% explained by the changes in parks.

In 1985 the American League ERA was 4.15, while the NL ERA was 3.59. While most of this difference is no doubt attributable to the designated hitter rule, it has also been widely speculated that some of it is due to the fact that the American League has more of the older, home-run hitters type of parks. Since County Stadium has been used in both leagues, we also have here a rare opportunity to compare the park characteristics of the two leagues—albeit a rather dated comparison, between the National League in the 1963–65 period and the American League in the years 1970–73.

The N.L. in the years 1963–65 averaged, as we mentioned, 7.90 runs per game. The A.L. average in the years 1970–73 was exactly the same, 7.90. Comparing the ratios of runs scored in Milwaukee and on the road, it appears that the American League parks at that time were very slightly better hitter's parks than were the National League parks, but that this difference did not manifest itself at that time because of other differences between the leagues.

Since then, American League runs per game have gone from 7.9 to over 9.0. Several things have contributed to this, including the DH rule, and the new parks in Seattle, Toronto and Minnesota, all of which tend to be hitter's parks, as well as a new park in Kansas City (neutral park), and a remodeling of the Anaheim and New York Stadiums which probably tended to improve the hitting characteristics of each.

Despite these changes, this study suggests that over 90% of the difference between the American League offensive levels then and those of now is caused by factors other than the parks. Over the last years, the ratio of runs scored and allowed by the Brewers at home and on the road has changed only a tiny bit, from 1:1.03 to 1:1.04. In other words, most of the difference is not the parks, but is probably due to the DH rule.

The left field line in Milwaukee used to be listed as 320; now it is 315. If that was really changed in 1981, then that would throw the study off a little—that is, we might find that the increase in offense was created 15% by changes in the parks, rather than 9½% as estimated here.

Still, if the American League parks were a little bit better hitter's parks in 1970, and if they have gotten better since, then that might well lead us to conclude, pending further study, that a small but measurable portion of the difference between the 4.15 ERA in the A.L. and the 3.59 in the N.L. is due to the difference in parks. If you're wondering why anybody cares, the answer is that this type of knowledge is necessary to projecting performance when a player changes leagues. Remember when Dave Kingman came over to the A.L. and started busting home runs all over the place, and people said that one reason for it was because the American League had so many good home run parks? If you're an American League general manager and you're considering trading for a National League player, it makes a little bit of difference whether he will or will not be coming into a better set of hitter's parks.

Anyway, County Stadium is still a pitcher's park, as it always has been. I didn't mean to say that baseball men refuse to look at the evidence on parks, as the biblical literalists refuse to look at the evidence on evolution, but rather that the types of information that are available now are outside the realm of the things that baseball men grew up reading. That is changing. The *Abstract* helps to change it; the *Historical Abstract,* which contains home and road home run totals for players like Aaron and Mathews, will do more to change it. The new Macmillan will help to change it. Pete Palmer's *The Hidden Game,* which presented park factors for each time each year, will help to change it. It just takes time.

SPLINTERS

Milwaukee pinch hitters in 1985 hit .115 (7/61), with no doubles, no triples and no home runs. They drew 4 walks, struck out 19 times and drove in 3 runs. This was the worst performance by any team's pinch hitters in at least 25 years. The 1972 Texas Ranger pinch hitters hit only .135, but drove in 17 runs; the 1971 Cubs pinch hitters also hit .135, but hit 3 homers and drove in 13. These were the lowest averages of the previous 24 years.

Leading Milwaukee pinch hitters included Rick Manning (0 for 9, no walks either), Mark Brouchard (0 for 7, no walks, five strikeouts), and Ben Oglivie (1 for 9, no walks).

COMPLETE BATTING RECORDS

Player	G	AB	R	H	TB	2B	3B	HR	RBI	GW	SH	SF	HB	BB	IB	SO	SB	CS	GIDP	Avg	Slug	OBP	Runs	Outs Made	Runs/27 Outs	OW%	Appr Value
Moore	105	349	35	81	102	13	4	0	31	8	8	1	1	27	0	53	4	0	12	.232	.292	.288	29	289	2.72	.257	4
*Cooper	154	631	82	185	288	39	8	16	99	10	1	10	2	30	3	77	10	3	24	.293	.456	.322	86	484	4.82	.520	10
*Gantner	143	523	63	133	171	15	4	5	44	5	10	4	3	33	7	42	11	8	13	.254	.327	.300	49	425	3.14	.315	9
Molitor	140	576	93	171	235	28	3	10	48	2	7	4	1	54	6	80	21	7	12	.297	.408	.356	85	435	5.29	.566	11
*Riles	116	448	54	128	169	12	7	5	45	3	6	3	2	36	0	54	2	2	16	.286	.377	.339	55	347	4.29	.462	7
*Oglivie	101	341	40	99	150	17	2	10	61	7	4	10	2	37	3	51	0	2	8	.290	.440	.354	54	266	5.50	.584	7
†Yount	122	466	76	129	206	26	3	15	68	3	1	9	2	49	3	56	10	4	8	.277	.442	.342	73	359	5.49	.584	10
†Householder	95	299	41	77	125	15	0	11	34	0	1	1	1	27	0	60	1	2	5	.258	.418	.320	40	231	4.66	.503	5
†Simmons	143	528	60	144	212	28	2	12	76	13	1	5	1	57	9	32	1	1	17	.273	.402	.342	71	408	4.70	.507	9
Romero	88	251	24	63	76	11	1	0	21	1	5	0	0	26	0	20	1	1	3	.251	.303	.321	26	197	3.55	.370	4
*Manning	79	216	19	47	64	9	1	2	18	3	1	0	0	14	0	19	1	0	2	.218	.296	.265	18	172	2.75	.261	1
Schroeder	53	194	18	47	79	8	0	8	25	1	0	2	2	12	1	61	0	1	5	.242	.407	.290	22	155	3.81	.403	3
Ready	48	181	29	48	70	9	5	1	21	3	2	2	1	14	0	23	0	0	6	.265	.387	.318	22	143	4.09	.438	1
Brouhard	37	108	11	28	42	7	2	1	13	1	1	0	1	5	1	26	1	1	3	.259	.389	.298	12	83	3.97	.423	1
Clark	29	93	6	21	24	3	0	0	8	1	0	1	0	7	0	19	1	0	3	.226	.258	.277	6	77	2.24	.189	1
*Loman	24	66	10	14	21	3	2	0	7	0	2	1	0	1	0	12	0	0	4	.212	.318	.221	5	59	2.40	.212	0
Ponce	21	62	4	10	15	2	0	1	5	0	1	2	0	1	0	9	0	0	0	.161	.242	.169	2	55	0.82	.030	0
Giles	34	58	6	10	14	1	0	1	1	0	0	0	0	7	0	16	2	1	2	.172	.241	.262	4	50	2.10	.171	0
†Felder	15	56	8	11	12	1	0	0	0	0	1	0	0	5	0	6	4	1	0	.196	.214	.262	3	49	1.84	.136	0
*Robidoux	18	51	5	9	20	2	0	3	8	3	0	0	0	12	0	16	0	0	1	.176	.392	.333	7	43	4.61	.497	1
*James	18	49	5	11	12	1	0	0	3	0	0	0	0	6	0	6	0	0	0	.224	.245	.309	4	38	2.98	.292	0
Huppert	15	21	1	1	1	0	0	0	0	0	0	2	0	2	0	7	0	0	1	.048	.048	.130	0	23	0.37	.014	0
Waits	24	1	0	0	0	0	0	0	0	0	0	0	0	0	0	1	0	0	0	.000	.000	.000	0	1	0.00	.000	0

*left-handed hitter, †switch hitter

DEFENSIVE STATISTICS

FIRST

	G	PO	A	Er	TC	DP	PCT.
Cooper	123	1087	94	17	1198	101	.986
Simmons	28	226	17	2	245	22	.992
Ponce	10	54	3	0	57	7	1.000
Robidoux	6	49	5	0	54	6	1.000
Yount	2	9	1	0	10	0	1.000
Schroeder	1	5	0	0	5	1	1.000
TEAM:	170	1430	120	19	1569	137	.988
AVG:	180	1440	123	14	1577	141	.991

SECOND

	G	PO	A	Er	TC	DP	PCT.
Gantner	124	262	402	8	672	89	.988
Romero	31	80	104	4	188	26	.979
Giles	13	27	27	0	54	5	1.000
Ready	3	4	2	0	6	0	1.000
TEAM:	171	373	535	12	920	120	.987
AVG:	189	347	501	15	863	114	.982

THIRD

	G	PO	A	Er	TC	DP	PCT.
Molitor	135	126	263	19	408	30	.953
Gantner	24	16	34	3	53	5	.943
Ready	7	4	7	0	11	0	1.000
Simmons	2	0	5	0	5	0	1.000
Romero	1	1	0	0	1	0	1.000
TEAM:	169	147	309	22	478	35	.954
AVG:	192	129	327	23	479	32	.953

SHORTSTOP

	G	PO	A	Er	TC	DP	PCT.
Riles	115	183	310	22	515	62	.957
Romero	43	57	115	4	176	27	.977
Giles	20	21	31	2	54	5	.963
Gantner	1	0	0	0	0	0	.000
TEAM:	179	261	456	28	745	94	.962
AVG:	189	269	474	28	771	104	.964

CATCHER

	G	PO	A	Er	TC	DP	PCT.	PB
Moore	102	504	54	13	571	7	.977	10
Schroeder	48	211	23	3	237	4	.987	0
Simmons	15	65	4	1	70	1	.986	1
Huppert	15	45	3	2	50	2	.960	1
TEAM:	180	825	84	19	928	14	.980	12
AVG:	193	895	74	13	982	13	.987	13

OUTFIELD

	G	PO	A	Er	TC	DP	PCT.
Yount	108	258	4	8	270	2	.970
Householder	91	202	5	3	210	0	.986
Oglivie	91	190	4	7	201	0	.965
Manning	74	160	2	4	166	0	.976
Ready	37	85	5	1	91	1	.989
Brouhard	29	53	0	2	55	0	.964
Clark	27	72	1	0	73	0	1.000
Loman	20	41	4	0	45	2	1.000
Felder	14	32	1	0	33	0	1.000
Romero	14	19	0	0	19	0	1.000
James	11	20	0	0	20	0	1.000
Robidoux	11	15	1	0	16	0	1.000
Ponce	6	13	0	0	13	0	1.000
Moore	3	7	0	0	7	0	1.000
TEAM:	536	1167	27	25	1219	5	.979
AVG:	559	1141	33	21	1196	8	.982

COMPLETE PITCHERS RECORDS

Pitcher	W	L	Pct	ERA	G	GS	CG	GF	SHO	SV	IP	H	TBF	R	ER	HR	SH	SF	HB	BB	IB	SO	WP	BK	Appr Value
								Starters (One-half of Game Appearances)																	
Darwin	8	18	.308	3.80	39	29	11	8	1	2	217.2	212	919	112	92	34	7	9	4	65	4	125	6	0	8
*Higuera	15	8	.652	3.90	32	30	7	2	2	0	212.1	186	874	105	92	22	5	10	3	63	0	127	4	3	9
Burris	9	13	.409	4.81	29	28	6	0	0	0	170.1	182	738	95	91	25	6	6	3	53	0	81	7	0	4
Haas	8	8	.500	3.84	27	26	6	0	1	0	161.2	165	666	85	69	21	1	5	1	25	3	78	2	0	6
Cocanower	6	8	.429	4.33	24	15	3	2	1	0	116.1	122	534	72	56	6	4	4	8	73	2	44	13	0	3
Vuckovich	6	10	.375	5.51	22	22	1	0	0	0	112.2	134	511	74	69	16	5	1	7	48	2	55	3	0	2
Leary	1	4	.200	4.05	5	5	0	0	0	0	33.1	40	146	18	15	5	2	0	1	8	0	29	1	0	0
Wegman	2	0	1.000	3.57	3	3	0	0	0	0	17.2	17	73	8	7	3	0	1	0	3	0	6	0	1	0
								Relievers																	
Gibson	6	7	.462	3.90	41	1	0	25	0	11	92.1	86	392	44	40	10	7	4	1	49	3	53	4	0	7
*McClure	4	1	.800	4.31	38	1	0	12	0	3	85.2	91	370	43	41	10	3	2	3	30	2	57	5	0	3
Fingers	1	6	.143	5.04	47	0	0	37	0	17	55.1	59	241	33	31	9	4	1	0	19	5	24	1	0	5
*Waits	3	2	.600	6.51	24	0	0	8	0	1	47.0	67	220	37	34	3	2	1	0	20	5	24	1	0	1
Ladd	0	0	.000	4.53	29	0	0	13	0	2	45.2	58	202	26	23	5	0	6	2	10	0	22	1	0	1
*Searage	1	4	.200	5.92	33	0	0	18	0	1	38.0	54	189	27	25	2	4	1	0	24	4	36	0	0	1
Porter	0	0	.000	1.98	6	1	0	1	0	0	13.2	15	58	8	3	1	1	0	0	2	0	8	0	0	1
Kern	0	1	.000	6.55	5	0	0	1	0	0	11.0	14	50	8	8	1	1	0	0	5	1	3	3	0	0
Lesley	1	0	1.000	9.95	5	0	0	0	0	0	6.1	8	29	7	7	2	0	0	0	2	0	5	0	0	0

Charlie MOORE, Catcher

	G	AB	Hit	2B	3B	HR	Run	RBI	TBB	SO	SB	CS	Avg
7.43 years		497	130	22	5	4	56	49	42	57	6	7	.262
1985	105	349	81	13	4	0	35	31	27	53	4	0	.232
First Half	53	193	45	9	2	0	20	17	16	34	2	0	.233
Second Half	52	156	36	4	2	0	15	14	11	19	2	0	.231
Vs. RHP		226	46	7	2	0	20	16	12	39	2	0	.204
Vs. LHP		123	35	6	2	0	15	15	15	14	2	0	.285
Home	48	169	43	8	4	0	19	16	9	29	0	0	.254
Road	57	180	38	5	0	0	16	15	18	24	4	0	.211
Grass	82	279	66	12	4	0	29	25	19	44	4	0	.237
Turf	23	70	15	1	0	0	6	6	8	9	0	0	.214

Paul MOLITOR, Third Base

	G	AB	Hit	2B	3B	HR	Run	RBI	TBB	SO	SB	CS	Avg
5.59 years		663	193	32	7	13	110	60	58	78	38	11	.292
1985	140	576	171	28	3	10	93	48	54	80	21	7	.297
First Half	77	306	97	17	2	7	58	30	36	44	17	6	.317
Second Half	63	270	74	11	1	3	35	18	18	36	4	1	.274
Vs. RHP		393	112	20	2	5	58	29	37	61	13	3	.285
Vs. LHP		183	59	8	1	5	35	19	17	19	8	4	.322
Home	64	257	83	15	2	6	46	31	25	31	9	4	.323
Road	76	319	88	13	1	4	47	17	29	49	12	3	.276
Grass	114	471	144	25	2	7	77	41	44	61	17	7	.306
Turf	26	105	27	3	1	3	16	7	10	19	4	0	.257

Cecil COOPER, First Base

	G	AB	Hit	2B	3B	HR	Run	RBI	TBB	SO	SB	CS	Avg
10.49 years		625	190	36	4	21	90	97	37	74	8	4	.303
1985	154	631	185	39	8	16	82	99	30	77	10	3	.293
First Half	75	304	96	21	8	5	38	50	13	31	9	2	.316
Second Half	79	327	89	18	0	11	44	49	17	46	1	1	.272
Vs. RHP		419	117	26	5	10	52	50	17	51	8	3	.279
Vs. LHP		212	68	13	3	6	30	49	13	26	2	0	.321
Home	77	309	88	19	4	6	38	52	17	36	2	3	.285
Road	77	322	97	20	4	10	44	47	13	41	8	0	.301
Grass	128	521	154	31	6	13	69	82	23	63	8	3	.296
Turf	26	110	31	8	2	3	13	17	7	14	2	0	.282

Earnest RILES, Shortstop

	G	AB	Hit	2B	3B	HR	Run	RBI	TBB	SO	SB	CS	Avg
0.72 years		626	179	17	10	7	75	63	50	75	3	3	.286
1985	116	448	128	12	7	5	54	45	36	54	2	2	.286
First Half	40	152	40	3	4	2	21	19	11	18	1	1	.263
Second Half	76	296	88	9	3	3	33	26	25	36	1	1	.297
Vs. RHP		302	94	10	4	5	38	34	23	30	2	2	.311
Vs. LHP		146	34	2	3	0	16	11	13	24	0	0	.233
Home	60	226	75	9	3	2	27	24	18	29	1	1	.332
Road	56	222	53	3	4	3	27	21	18	25	1	1	.239
Grass	96	367	109	10	6	4	43	37	28	49	2	1	.297
Turf	20	81	19	2	1	1	11	8	8	5	0	1	.235

Jim GANTNER, Second Base

	G	AB	Hit	2B	3B	HR	Run	RBI	TBB	SO	SB	CS	Avg
6.06 years		557	154	21	4	4	65	54	36	46	8	7	.276
1985	143	523	133	15	4	5	63	44	33	42	11	8	.254
First Half	74	270	72	9	2	3	30	29	19	19	4	4	.267
Second Half	69	253	61	6	2	2	33	15	14	23	7	4	.241
Vs. RHP		359	79	10	3	5	35	29	24	31	9	5	.220
Vs. LHP		164	54	5	1	0	28	15	9	11	2	3	.329
Home	72	261	62	6	2	4	35	25	14	23	4	3	.238
Road	71	262	71	9	2	1	28	19	19	19	7	5	.271
Grass	118	425	105	12	4	5	52	39	28	36	7	7	.247
Turf	25	98	28	3	0	0	11	5	5	6	4	1	.286

Ben OGLIVIE, Left Field

	G	AB	Hit	2B	3B	HR	Run	RBI	TBB	SO	SB	CS	Avg
10.19 years		546	149	25	3	23	74	83	52	80	8	7	.272
1985	101	341	99	17	2	10	40	60	37	51	0	2	.290
First Half	61	197	51	7	0	5	20	25	23	35	0	2	.259
Second Half	40	144	48	10	2	5	20	36	14	16	0	0	.333
Vs. RHP		268	83	12	1	8	33	48	35	39	0	2	.310
Vs. LHP		73	16	5	1	2	7	13	2	12	0	0	.219
Home	47	160	51	11	2	4	24	33	12	23	0	2	.319
Road	54	181	48	6	0	6	16	28	25	28	0	0	.265
Grass	89	304	89	17	2	9	38	56	31	45	0	2	.293
Turf	12	37	10	0	0	1	2	5	6	6	0	0	.270

Robin YOUNT, Center Field

	G	AB	Hit	2B	3B	HR	Run	RBI	TBB	SO	SB	CS	Avg
10.31 years		632	180	34	7	14	93	76	46	69	15	6	.285
1985	122	466	129	26	3	15	76	68	49	56	10	4	.277
First Half	75	287	79	14	2	6	38	36	26	41	6	3	.275
Second Half	47	179	50	12	1	9	38	32	23	15	4	1	.279
Vs. RHP		316	84	19	1	11	49	47	34	37	8	3	.266
Vs. LHP		150	45	7	2	4	27	21	15	19	2	1	.300
Home	65	243	75	17	1	11	47	46	30	25	6	1	.309
Road	57	223	54	9	2	4	29	22	19	31	4	3	.242
Grass	108	410	117	23	2	15	68	62	46	48	8	4	.285
Turf	14	56	12	3	1	0	8	6	3	8	2	0	.214

TEDDY HIGUERA

	(W–L)	GS	Run	Avg	DP	Avg	SB	Avg
1985	(15-8)	30	133	4.43	24	.80	16	.53

	G	IP	W	L	Pct	ER	BB	SO	ERA
1985 Home	15	89.3	7	4	.636	54	29	53	5.44
1985 Road	17	123.0	8	4	.667	38	34	74	2.78
1985 Grass	26	166.3	11	7	.611	80	46	102	4.33
1985 Turf	6	46.0	4	1	.800	12	17	25	2.35
1985 Total	32	212.3	15	8	.652	92	63	127	3.90

Paul HOUSEHOLDER, Right Field

	G	AB	Hit	2B	3B	HR	Run	RBI	TBB	SO	SB	CS	Avg
2.63 years		470	112	21	4	11	53	48	44	88	13	10	.239
1985	95	299	77	15	0	11	41	34	27	60	1	2	.258
First Half	33	94	22	5	0	1	16	7	12	24	0	0	.234
Second Half	62	205	55	10	0	10	25	27	15	36	1	2	.268
Vs. RHP		178	41	8	0	6	21	20	17	37	1	2	.230
Vs. LHP		121	36	7	0	5	20	14	10	23	0	0	.298
Home	48	134	32	8	0	3	18	14	16	24	0	0	.239
Road	47	165	45	7	0	8	23	20	11	36	1	2	.273
Grass	82	250	62	14	0	9	35	28	26	50	1	2	.248
Turf	13	49	15	1	0	2	6	6	1	10	0	0	.306

DANNY DARWIN

	(W–L)	GS	Run	Avg	DP	Avg	SB	Avg
1984	(8-12)	32	132	4.12	29	.91	22	.69
1985	(8-18)	29	98	3.38	23	.79	21	.72
1978-1985		119	492	4.13	91	.76	83	.70

	G	IP	W	L	Pct	ER	BB	SO	ERA
1984 Home	17	104.0	4	6	.400	45	32	51	3.89
1985 Home	16	94.7	2	10	.167	30	29	62	2.85
1984 Road	18	119.7	4	6	.400	53	22	72	3.99
1985 Road	23	123.0	6	8	.429	62	36	63	4.54
1984 Grass	29	179.3	6	9	.400	80	44	97	4.01
1985 Grass	35	197.0	7	16	.304	78	64	111	3.56
1984 Turf	6	44.3	2	3	.400	18	10	26	3.65
1985 Turf	4	20.7	1	2	.333	14	1	14	6.10
1985 Total	39	217.7	8	18	.308	92	65	125	3.80

Ted SIMMONS, Designated Hitter

	G	AB	Hit	2B	3B	HR	Run	RBI	TBB	SO	SB	CS	Avg
13.76 years		601	172	34	3	17	75	96	59	47	1	2	.287
1985	143	528	144	28	2	12	60	76	57	32	1	1	.273
First Half	73	265	70	17	1	5	30	41	25	16	1	0	.264
Second Half	70	263	74	11	1	7	30	35	32	16	0	1	.281
Vs. RHP		365	94	18	2	5	38	46	37	21	1	1	.258
Vs. LHP		163	50	10	0	7	22	30	20	11	0	0	.307
Home	70	251	71	13	1	8	30	40	24	19	0	0	.283
Road	73	277	73	15	1	4	30	36	33	13	1	1	.264
Grass	119	437	122	25	1	9	50	61	47	28	1	1	.279
Turf	24	91	22	3	1	3	10	15	10	4	0	0	.242

RAY BURRIS

	(W–L)	GS	Run	Avg	DP	Avg	SB	Avg
1984	(13-10)	28	124	4.43	23	.82	12	.43
1985	(9-13)	28	127	4.54	25	.89	18	.64
1976-1985		249	1024	4.11	180	.72	158	.63

	G	IP	W	L	Pct	ER	BB	SO	ERA
1984 Home	19	129.0	9	4	.692	37	43	55	2.58
1985 Home	18	105.0	7	7	.500	52	31	54	4.46
1984 Road	15	82.7	4	6	.400	37	47	38	4.03
1985 Road	11	65.3	2	6	.250	39	22	27	5.37
1984 Grass	28	177.7	12	6	.667	60	67	75	3.04
1985 Grass	26	160.3	9	11	.450	79	49	78	4.43
1984 Turf	6	34.0	1	4	.200	14	23	18	3.71
1985 Turf	3	10.0	0	2	0.000	12	4	3	10.80
1985 Total	29	170.3	9	13	.409	91	53	81	4.81

Ed ROMERO, Infield

	G	AB	Hit	2B	3B	HR	Run	RBI	TBB	SO	SB	CS	Avg
2.54 years		440	113	19	0	2	49	39	35	36	3	2	.257
1985	88	251	63	11	1	0	24	21	26	20	1	1	.251
First Half	36	89	18	3	0	0	4	9	11	7	0	1	.202
Second Half	52	162	45	8	1	0	20	12	15	13	1	0	.278
Vs. RHP		148	42	6	1	0	16	15	16	15	0	1	.284
Vs. LHP		103	21	5	0	0	8	6	10	5	1	0	.204
Home	44	128	33	5	1	0	15	8	11	13	1	0	.258
Road	44	123	30	6	0	0	9	13	15	7	0	1	.244
Grass	75	214	56	9	1	0	21	21	22	20	1	0	.262
Turf	13	37	7	2	0	0	3	0	4	0	0	1	.189

MOOSE HAAS

	(W–L)	GS	Run	Avg	DP	Avg	SB	Avg
1984	(9-11)	30	111	3.70	27	.90	11	.37
1985	(8-8)	26	114	4.38	34	1.31	12	.46
1977-1985		229	1036	4.52	236	1.03	159	.69

	G	IP	W	L	Pct	ER	BB	SO	ERA
1984 Home	15	101.3	7	3	.700	33	22	52	2.93
1985 Home	17	102.7	6	3	.667	39	15	59	3.42
1984 Road	16	88.0	2	8	.200	51	21	32	5.22
1985 Road	10	59.0	2	5	.286	30	10	19	4.58
1984 Grass	26	155.7	9	8	.529	67	36	76	3.87
1985 Grass	23	138.7	8	6	.571	59	24	69	3.83
1984 Turf	5	33.7	0	3	0.000	17	7	8	4.54
1985 Turf	4	23.0	0	2	0.000	10	1	9	3.91
1985 Total	27	161.7	8	8	.500	69	25	78	3.84

PETE VUCKOVICH

	(W–L)	GS	Run	Avg	DP	Avg	SB	Avg
1985	(6-10)	22	101	4.59	20	.91	21	.95
1977-1985		171	780	4.56	166	.97	136	.80

	G	IP	W	L	Pct	ER	BB	SO	ERA
1985 Home	10	56.7	4	4	.500	26	23	28	4.13
1985 Road	12	56.0	2	6	.250	43	25	27	6.91
1985 Grass	17	88.0	6	8	.429	47	39	42	4.81
1985 Turf	5	24.7	0	2	0.000	22	9	13	8.03
1985 Total	22	112.7	6	10	.375	69	48	55	5.51

OTHERS

	(W–L)	GS	Run	Avg	DP	Avg	SB	Avg
Cocanower	(6-8)	15	67	4.47	17	1.13	15	1.00
Leary	(1-4)	5	10	2.00	4	.80	5	1.00
Wegman	(2-0)	3	23	7.67	5	1.67	2	.67
Gibson	(6-7)	1	2	2.00	4	4.00	1	1.00
McClure	(4-1)	1	4	4.00	0	0.00	0	0.00
Porter	(0-0)	1	9	9.00	1	1.00	0	0.00

CLEVELAND INDIANS

BREAKDOWNS FOR THE LAST TEN SEASONS

Won-Lost Record: 716-835, .462 (6th in the Division, 21st in the Majors)
Runs Scored: 6,807 (6th in the Division, 11th in Majors)
Runs Allowed: 7,298 (Highest total in the Division, 2nd highest in Majors)
Home Runs Hit: 991 (Lowest in the Division, 22nd in the Majors)
Home Runs Allowed: 1,211 (6th highest in the Division, 12th in the Majors)

RECORD IN:
April:74-99, .428 (Worst in the Division, 24th in Majors)
May: 129-141, .478 (6th in the Division, 18th in Majors)
June: 121-136, .471 (6th in the Division, 20th in Majors)
July: 112-143, .439 (Last in the Division, 24th in the Majors)
August: 146-155, .485 (6th in the Division, 14th in the Majors)
September: 124-146, .459 (6th in the Division, 20th in Majors)
October: 10-15, .400 (Last in the Division, 21st in the Majors)

Won-Lost Record in Road Games: 321-455, .414 (6th in the Division, 22nd in Majors)
Won-Lost Record at Home: 395-380, .510 (6th in the Division, 22nd in Majors)
Home Field Advantage: 74½ Games
Runs Scored on the Road: 3,300 (6th in the Division, 11th in Majors)
Runs Scored at Home: 3,507 (4th in the Division, 9th in Majors)
Runs Allowed on the Road: 3,766 (Highest in the Division, 3rd in Majors)
Runs Allowed at Home: 3,532 (3rd highest in the Division, 7th in Majors)

• Home Runs Hit on the Road: 472 (Lowest in the Division, 22nd in Majors)
Home Runs Hit at Home: 519 (Lowest in the Division, 19th in the Majors)
Home Runs Allowed on the Road: 610 (6th highest in the Division, 13th in Majors)
Home Runs Allowed at Home: 601 (5th highest in the Division, 13th in Majors)

RECORD FOR LAST THREE SEASONS: 205-281, .422 (Worst in Baseball)

I don't suppose that too many people are going to step forward and admit this, either, but I talked to a number of people last spring who thought that the Indians would contend in 1985, and to at least two people who thought they would win. They had won 75 games in 1984 and finished strong—they were over .500 the last two months—and they didn't look all that bad, what with four to six good young players in the lineup, an excellent rotation anchor in Blyleven, and a relief ace (Camacho) coming off a fine season. The figuring was that if they could come up with a third starting pitcher behind Blyleven and Neal Heaton, their pitching would be about as good as anybody else's, and with the young hitters gaining a year of experience . . . well, you never know.

You sure don't. Once the season began, the Indians started out fairly well, for the Indians, if a little disappointing to those who expected a contender; they were 10–13 in early May. At this point, some bright boy in the Cleveland front office—we will discuss who in a moment—decided to solve the shortstop "problem" with Johnnie LeMaster, heh? Let's make a record of this for posterity. The Cleveland Indians already had an outstanding young shortstop, in Julio Franco. They already had a second baseman named Tony Bernazard, who was trying to get his game back together and was hitting .318 through May 7, when the Indians decided to move Franco to second, and acquire Johnnie LeMaster from San Francisco to play shortstop.

A few details of this story may help you to understand the reasoning behind the move. It was especially recommended by the facts that:

1) Franco was 23 years old, an established star and leading the league in hitting at the time in question.

2) Julio Franco had never played second base in his life, and was thoroughly P.O.'d about being assigned to learn the position in mid-season,

3) Johnnie LeMaster, affectionately known to the masses as Johnnie Disaster, was a 31-year-old lifetime .226 hitter who has avoided leading the National League in errors several times only by virtue of the fact that he couldn't hit well enough to stay in the lineup, and

4) LeMaster had made himself extra expendable to the worst team in the National League by becoming involved in conflicts with his managers.

I thought Tony Bernazard summed it up well. "I don't mean to be rude," he said, "but who the hell is Johnnie LeMaster?" Franco, despite being assigned to the second base position for eight games, managed to keep alive his record of never having played the position. Following this move, the Indians dropped out of contention in twelve minutes and seventeen seconds, and LeMaster was sent on his way in a few days, as soon as the Indians had a firm grip on last place.

It was the strangest, most incomprehensible organizational strategem in many years, and in view of this I was wondering who should be given the credit for it. It seemed to me that this decision ought to have been one of those things like a terrorist attack that somebody should have called a radio station in Madrid afterward and tried to claim responsibility for, but the people who like to do that missed the opportunity. Of course, it goes without saying that if the Cleveland Indians had a manager who was worthy of the title he would have laughed and told the front office to go sleep it off. Since he didn't do this and no one else has come forward to take responsibility, the horrible suspicion persists that it may have been Corrales himself who initiated the move.

May have been, but not necessarily, for the Cleveland Indians front office is sort of like an All-Star roster composed of the General Managers who have been fired by all of the worst teams in baseball for pulling crap like this. The Indians are the only team in baseball history which has more General Managers on their payroll than outfielders.

The Head GM is Peter Bavasi, who earned the position by having the worst record of all. At the time that he "resigned" from the Toronto czarship, Bavasi said that he was doing so to pursue other interests. I recommended that he sell shoes. Don't you always love that . . . college football coaches are particularly good at it. Two weeks after they are fired they always pop up on the radio and report that they have received a number of attractive offers and are weighing their options. Seventy-three percent of the time they opt to sell life insurance.

Anyway, it should be pointed out in restrospect that during the years Bavasi was running the Toronto organization, the Blue Jays acquired nine of the players who played key roles on the 1985 American League East champions—Ernie Whitt and Garth Iorg (1976), Jesse Barfield and Willie Upshaw (1977), Dave Stieb and Lloyd Moseby (1978), Damaso Garcia and Tony Fernandez (1979), and George Bell (1980). If Bavasi can repeat that performance in accumulating talent, then with the young players the Indians already have this team is shortly going to be formidable. It should also be pointed out that Bavasi has now been a General Manager for six years with two organizations, and the best record by any Bavasi-led team was 67–95. While I haven't actually checked, this is a distinction which I am certain must be appalling.

Actually, before that Peter was listed for four years as the General Manager of the San Diego Padres, although at the time it was generally thought that it was his father Buzzie who made the tough decisions. But, not to be cheap about it, Peter can claim credit for them, too, if he wants it. They stunk, too.

The Cleveland Indians remind you of one of those movies that is supposed to be a metaphor for Life, and the only thing you can think of while watching it is that if this is life I'm sure glad it isn't mine. In Life, as in the Indians, we seem to waste so much of our talent, we seem to spend so much of our time bashing ourselves against entrenched and immovable forces. We make blind decisions about our lives and look back on them in awe of our own stupidity. They should call themselves the Cleveland Metaphor, or simply the Cleveland Life. I spent many years rooting for a terrible team, and I watch this team with a certain sympathy. But I'm sure glad it isn't mine.

WE'RE NOT ALL SO LUCKY

Last summer and fall I received two pieces of mail from Indians fans, which I thought I might reprint here. The first (as it appears here) was a 25-page article on the team by Geoff Beckman, *Project Scoresheet* team captain for the Indians. It appears here in a heavily edited form—actually, only a few selected comments from it are retained. The opinions expressed here are Geoff's, and not mine, but I did want to say that I agree with him almost entirely. Geoff isn't crazy about Bavasi, but holds Pat Corrales essentially responsible for the Tribe disaster of 1985. The second was an exceptionally fine letter about the team written by George Zeller, which is printed here almost exactly as received. George isn't crazy about Corrales, but holds Bavasi to be the major culprit. I'll let you make up your own mind:

ON RE-HIRING CORRALES

STRANGE BUT TRUE: There have been 105 100-loss seasons since 1901, and the manager kept his job in 55 of them. It supports a pet theory of mine—people will forgive a bad manager, but they won't forgive a mediocre one. If a team goes 72–90, any fan can find 9 games that good managing would have won, so they scream for blood. 100 losses means that you must find 19 of those games before you can call for the ax. It's harder to do, so people fall into the trap of saying "you can't win without the players."

When Cleveland rehired Corrales, the media, front office and most of the fans defended the move, using the same tired excuses that everyone offers when a team stinks out the league:

1) "The team isn't good enough to do any better."
2) "Pitching is 90% of the game and the Indians' pitching was awful."
3) "What would Billy Martin or Earl Weaver have done that Corrales didn't?"

Those arguments stink on ice for two reasons. First, they suggest that a manager is an innocent victim of circumstance; that he can't fix a problem area. That simply isn't true. No manager has ever had a problem-free season—somebody is going to get injured, somebody is going to have a bad year. Good managers find solutions; bad ones sit there and lose. Bobby Cox won the AL East despite off seasons from Upshaw, Moseby, Clancy, Caudill and Lavelle. Herzog had a bad catcher and a bad third baseman, and he lost his 1984 relief ace too. Dick Howser went all the way with no shortstop, no right fielder, and one player who batted .250 while hitting 10 homers. The Mets had a horrible infield, all three outfielders were injured, and both their relievers had off-seasons. The Indians weren't very lucky, but they didn't have half the problems the four division winners did.

OK, that's philosophy—let's argue facts. There are three reasons that the Indians lost 102 games—they didn't hit for half the year, they had a bad starting rotation, and a bad bullpen. If we are going to forgive Corrales for the team's records, then we must be able to show two things:

1) That he recognized each of the problems and dealt with them in a reasonable way, and
2) That none of his solutions worked.

There is no proof that Corrales did either. I scored 148 games, and all I can see is that he mishandled everything he possibly could have. If you don't believe me, let's look at the records. Look at the Batting Disorder.

Cleveland was 28–58 at the All-Star break. The pitchers were giving up 4.96 runs (earned and otherwise) a game (13th in the A.L.), and taking most of the blame for the record, but the 1984 staff had given up 4.73 runs a game, only 37 runs less over a full season. The offense was the problem—it was scoring 3.90 runs a game (down from 4.70 in 1984), or 130 runs over a full season.

Corrales blamed injuries. Cleveland was 10–16 (despite losing Andre Thornton for the first 14 games) when Mel Hall was lost for the season on May 9th. He noted that the team had gone 18–42 since the injury, and said (I am not making this up) "If Mel Hall were healthy, we'd have won half of those games."

Suggesting that Hall could have won 12 games of the 60 is dumb—Babe Ruth didn't win 20% of his team's games. It's even sillier when you remember that Hall couldn't crack the lineup in spring training. The problem with the offense was the lineup that Corrales was using. Look at the stats for every Indians batter over those 60 games:

PLAYER	AB	R	H	2B	3B	HR	RBI	BB	Avg	OBP	Slug
Butler	263	44	85	17	4	2	27	21	.323	.373	.441
Franco	250	29	67	13	1	2	25	12	.268	.301	.352
Jacoby	246	31	67	9	0	7	36	23	.272	.334	.435
Carter	207	19	50	9	0	5	20	14	.242	.290	.357
Tabler	208	29	41	5	2	3	31	11	.197	.237	.284
Bernazard	193	24	51	11	1	4	25	24	.264	.346	.394
Thornton	174	13	32	2	0	7	26	19	.184	.264	.316
Vukovich	178	15	41	8	0	2	4	10	.230	.271	.309
Willard	98	10	26	8	0	1	14	12	.265	.345	.378
Hargrove	87	10	23	4	0	0	5	14	.264	.366	.310
Bando	63	1	5	1	0	0	5	15	.079	.147	.095
Castillo	41	7	14	1	0	3	6	1	.341	.357	.585
Ayala	42	7	9	2	0	1	5	0	.214	.214	.333
Benton	31	4	5	1	0	0	3	1	.161	.188	.194
Nixon	29	5	3	0	0	0	2	0	.103	.103	.103
Fischlin	29	7	7	0	1	0	1	2	.241	.310	.310
LeMaster	18	0	3	0	0	0	2	0	.167	.167	.167

Now look at where they batted:

Leadoff: Butler–58 Nixon–2

Second: Franco–54 Bernazard–4 Butler–2

Third: Jacoby–38 Bernazard–7 Hargrove–8 Franco–3 Carter–2 Tabler–1 Vukovich–1

Cleanup: Thornton–38 Tabler–11 Jacoby–10 Vukovich–1

Fifth: Tabler–18 Vukovich–10 Ayala–10 Jacoby–10 Thornton–7 Hargrove–4 Bernazard–1

Sixth: Tabler–19 Vukovich–12 Carter–10 Bernazard–9 Hargrove–5 Castillo–2 Jacoby–1 Ayala–1 Willard–1

Seventh: Carter–28 Vukovich–16 Bernazard–7 Castillo–3 Willard–2 Hargrove–2 Tabler–1 Jacoby–1

Eighth: Bernazard–16 Carter–12 Castillo–8 Benton–8 Willard–8 Bando–4 Hargrove–2 Vukovich–1 Fischlin–1

Ninth: Willard–17 Bando–14 Benton–7 LeMaster–7 Fischlin–7 Nixon–4 Bernazard–3

Could he have done better? How could he have done worse? It doesn't take a Billy Martin to see what would

help—get the guy with the .301 OBP out of the #2 spot, find a cleanup hitter who could hit .200, give the only catcher who was hitting more playing time and let Carmen Castillo (.585 slugging) play until he stopped hitting.

THE PITCHING CHAFF

Pat Corrales used a lot of clichés when he talked about his 1985 staff—he kept saying that he was "letting them get their feet wet," and "kids need time and suffering." The translation (according to *Webster's Sabermetric*) is "I have a very young pitching staff. I'm doing my best to help them out, but they need time, and they're going to pitch badly until they learn how to pitch."

Uh-huh . . . Gooden and Saberhagen win the Cy Young Awards, Browning, Darling, Hesketh, Cox and Key have great years and the Indians lose because their staff is too young. Let's look at his "kids" and how he broke them in, shall we?

The best way to find the age of a starting rotation is to multiply every pitcher's starts by his 7/1/85 age, add them up and divide the total by 162. Here are the figures for the Indians over the last four years:

1982:	27.0
1983:	27.4
1984:	27.4
1985:	27.2

The 1985 Indians gave 81 starts to young (21–25) pitchers, 35 starts to prime (26–29) pitchers, 7 starts to past prime (30–33) pitchers and 39 starts to old (34+) ones. Both the Royals (26.1) and Mets (24.5) were younger in 1984, and if I used 1985 data (which I don't have), they'd be even younger in 1985. The future for these guys is right now.

A FEW WORDS FROM OUR SPONSOR

I hoped that Project Scoresheet would give me a steady flow of data about the 1985 season. I didn't expect the flood I got. Scoring 148 games made me think about what the team was doing game in and game out and it gave me the tools I needed to study the problems and see if there were answers. I'd have known that the staff was in turmoil and that the hitters weren't from the papers, but I wouldn't have known how bad things truly were, and how many things could be done. Project Scoresheet was the most intense and rewarding chance to learn about the mechanics of baseball that I can imagine. Theories I had read crystallized into hard truth, and most of the opinions and ideas I now have came out of the hours I spent this year. If you have any interest in learning about how teams win and lose, I strongly advise you to join up in 1986.

ON THE MORONAGER

The other thing that Project Scoresheet did was turn my opinion of Corrales around 180 degrees. I was a big fan of his at the beginning of the season—he seemed like a sound baseball man, a decent in-game manager and a fair judge of talent. I was defending him as late as June, until the amount of evidence against him became over-whelming.

In April, I felt that the Indians could win 85 games. I still believe that the right manager would have. Earl Weaver would have stayed with Chris Bando. Dave Johnson would have let his young starters pitch. Dick Howser would have had everyone working on 4 days rest. Billy Martin would have had the lineup producing. Gene Mauch would have turned Jeff Barkley into Rollie Fingers. Dick Williams would have done wonders with the lefties. Whitey Herzog would have had everyone throwing strikes. These men have a history of working miracles—each has done them for every team that they managed. They have always taken clubs that were not expected to win and gotten them to do just that. If a team has talent, they use it—when it doesn't, they find some.

When I counted the teams that lost 100 games, I kept looking at their rosters. Most of them were collections of 20 awful players—guys like Mike Parrott, Mario Mendoza and Ted Cox. Do the Indians have 20 awful players? No, they don't. If the Indians had a first baseman who could hit, they'd have a better team of regulars than the Royals do. Pat Corrales did an atrocious job with the talent he had. He deserved to be fired for losing 100 games and, if the front office had one iota of common sense, they would have sent him packing.

THE SALVATION ARMY

The 1984 *Abstract* (p. 150) asked the question, "What do bad general managers do when they get fired?" Why, they come to Cleveland to run the Indians. I didn't know much about Peter Bavasi when Cleveland hired him. I hoped that he could field a winning team. I thought that he couldn't be worse than Gabe Paul. Until I looked at his record:

Bavasi has run two clubs (San Diego and Toronto) who claimed to play major league baseball for 13 years. Eleven of his thirteen teams finished last. Eleven of his 13 teams lost 90+ games (one lost 89 games, the other was thwarted by the strike). Seven have lost 100+ games. He has rehired a manager who lost 100 games four times. The man is a force of nature; baseball's answer to Nero, Joe Blfsptk, Typhoid Mary or Curly.

Given yet another team to run, a team that had 756 points of trade value (1985 *Abstract*, p. 101), a team that both the *Baseball Abstract* and the *Elias Baseball Analyst* had agreed would improve in 1985 (did they agree on anything else?) Peter Bavasi managed to tie the team record for losses in a season in his first year. They're going to lose 100 games this year, and every year until either somebody rides Bavasi out of town on a rail, or the team leaves Cleveland. If you're reading this, Gabe Paul, please come home—all is forgiven.

ON PAT CORRALES' STRONGEST POINT AS A MANAGER

If he thinks that he can do something that will give him a better chance to win, he'll do it. He is not timid—if he tries something unpopular that doesn't work, he won't bow to public pressure until he convinces himself that his idea won't help him win.

ON PAT CORRALES' WEAKEST POINTS AS A MANAGER

Pat Corrales has been a difficult man to judge fairly. It's always been clear that he would sacrifice a team's future for short-term gains. Until 1985, he always had good reason to do so. Relying on veterans when you are managing a team that wants a winner *right away* is self preservation. If he had tried to rebuild the Rangers or Phillies with rookies, he would have been fired long before his projects bore fruit. It becomes inexcusable when you have a long term contract to manage a perennial doormat.

But Pat Corrales in 1985 was not a product of his environment. He chose to lose 100 games using players like Hargrove, Ayala, Clark and Creel when he had younger players who can do the same things on the bench or in the minors. Last year, it would have been unfair to write this. After the 1985 season, it is not:

He mistrusts any talent from his own farm system. He won't stick with slumping players. He rides a hot hand incessantly. He costs himself games by trying to force a big inning. He does not stabilize his rotation. He won't let young pitchers get out of their own jams. He has no patience with young players. Given a choice between giving unproven talent a chance (and maybe losing games in the process) and winning a few more games with a mediocre veteran (and crushing the prospect's confidence) he will play the veteran. He has arguably mishandled a number of young players, and made trades that have inarguably damaged his team's future. If he'd gone to the "Joe Torre School of Baseball Management," he'd have graduated with honors.

—Geoff Beckman

DEAR BILL

July 21, 1985
George Zeller
Cleveland, Ohio

Mr. Bill James
Winchester, Kansas

Dear Bill:

I have at last decided to take pen in hand and send some random musings off to you. I thought that an unsolicited viewpoint from Cleveland might give you some insight into our local situation as you prepare the next issue of the *Baseball Abstract*. The Indians are stretching the credulity of baseball fans even more than usual this year, and it may be of some use to you if you receive some observations from the center of the garbage dump here as you evaluate the continued festering of the boil in this beleaguered franchise.

Let me briefly introduce myself and attempt to establish a thimblefull of credibility. I have been a lifelong and diehard Indians fan for most of my 35 years, although my conscious memory does not go back far enough to remember the last Indians' pennant. I have attended well over 300 Indians games at Municipal Stadium. Professionally I am a Sociologist; while unpublished, I have dabbled in the statistical analysis of baseball for many years. My most ambitious effort was a factor analysis/path analysis exploration of the effect of numerous independent variables on team wins, the findings of which Gabe Paul refused to discuss with me in 1978, despite making several appointments to do so.

In Cleveland this year we have an unusual opportunity to study a truly bankrupt and retrograde franchise. Although the Mets' record for modern ineptitude seems out of reach, the Indians' club record for worst winning percentage at .333 is well within sight. If one looks at the club as a whole, a case study presents itself. Except for Bert Blyleven (who we have been vigorously trying to trade all year), the Indians present the first historical example of a major league franchise that has gone through an entire season with a minor league pitching staff. A major front office shift has resulted incredibly in backward movement. Attendance runs last in the majors. Perhaps my rambling analysis will shed some light on this for you, although this letter will consist more of qualitative than quantitative analysis.

The principal facts must have filtered out to you in Kansas. The front office of the Indians was finally cleaned out with the exile of Gabe Paul and Phil Seghi. The replacements have been worse. Bavasi, O'Brien and Klein represent a unique management team with the all-time record of the worst credentials ever assembled. Their collective prior record at Toronto, Texas, and Seattle sets some sort of record for most previous last place finishes on a resume. Their performance here is following the linear trend.

Given normal statistical inference standards, it is perhaps a little early to make definitive judgments on the Indians' current trend. But, let us try anyway. Their only major player move, aside from the active shuttle of personnel from Maine to Cleveland, was the acquisition of Johnnie LeMaster from the Giants to replace Julio Franco at shortstop, a genuinely insane move. This diminished Franco's confidence, installed an extremely marginal player at short, and benched the team leader at the time (Tony Bernazard) in home runs. This was done while Franco was in a fielding slump with an unusually high error rate, showing no regard for the long run at all.

Franco, with the possible exception of Brett Butler, is the Indians' best player. The only consolation in this bizarre deal was that the Indians bailed out of the disaster by quickly trading LeMaster to Pittsburgh. Wags in San Francisco said that it took the Giants 10 years to figure out that LeMaster was not a major league baseball player, while the Indians discovered this in 10 days. Do not be deceived by this joke; it overestimates the Indians' wisdom.

Let me stick in another Indians' joke floating around. A judge in a divorce custody hearing is questioning the child involved about his future residence. Judge: Do you want to live with your mother? Child: No, she beats me all the time. Judge: Well then, do you want to live with your father? Child: No, he beats me even more than she does. Judge (exasperated): Where *do* you want to live? Child: I want to live with the Cleveland Indians. They never beat anybody.

The major factors behind the Indians' current difficulties have probably not yet filtered out to a national audience. Let me try to summarize the major ones as quickly as possible:

1) Underfinanced organization for 25 years.

2) Exceptionally inept front office in the Paul/Seghi/Bavasi regal line.

3) A revolving door trading philosophy. (e.g. Dade for Hargrove, Orta for Sutcliffe, McDowell for Gaylord Perry, Alexander/Cruz for Blyleven, and Barker for Butler/Jacoby have brought in top notch talent for hamburger. However, Denny for Garbage, Sutcliffe/Hassey for Carter/Hall, Perry for Barker, Whitson for Eichelberger, etc, send the talent right back out for more hamburger again. Bert Blyleven will be next; just wait and see.

4) An undercapitalized minor league system that has been unusually unproductive. The talent that it does occasionally produce is quickly traded.

5) A succession of youth movements and five year plans, abruptly aborted by quick fixes of over the hill Robinsons, Powells, Pinsons, McBrides, Cartys, etc., that are subsequently replaced by yet another youth movement and five year plans. The club never sticks with a fixed talent base for a long-run shot at contention. (The last Indian to retire with the club of any note, with the unusual exception of Frank Robinson, was Ken Harrelson in 1971.)

The local bumper sticker of "Save the Tribe, Fire the Chief" was finally consummated this year. Things then took a turn for the worse. The Bavasi regime has been an unparalleled fiasco and a horrible disaster. Bavasi came in as an unproven quantity with a supposed strength in marketing. Here is a reasonably comprehensive list of his achievements so far, if you want to call them that:

1. Bavasi hired Klein and O'Brien to run player personnel. They came with strikingly bad previous records in Texas and Seattle.

2. Bavasi has repeatedly failed to hire a scouting director. He publicly offered the job to several candidates, who all declined.

3. Bavasi's first act was to close the Municipal Stadium bleachers, as an economy move. A vigorous protest by fans led him to compromise by reopening them only for day games, a small fraction of the total schedule.

4. Bavasi also eliminated well over 50% of the General Admission stadium seats, turning them into empty and higher priced Box and Reserved seats.

5. Bavasi eliminated all discount fan promotions, some with a local history of 40 years, including Ladies' Day, Senior Citizens' Day, Sandlot Little League Day, Cleveland Plain Dealer Grandstand Managers' Day, and so forth.

6. Bavasi ordered that my banner "Bavasi Must Go" be taken down from Municipal Stadium, citing an American League rule banning "derogatory signs." Bob Fishel, Executive Vice President of the American League, denied that there was any such league rule after being contacted by the Cleveland media.

7. Bavasi has essentially broken the stadium employee's union, much to the disgruntlement of ushers, police, groundskeepers, concessionaires, ticket sellers/takers, etc.

8. At most home games, the only full service conces-

sion stands open in Cleveland Stadium are at Gate A, directly behind home plate. All the others are closed.

I could go on much further, but I'm tired of writing and my pen's ink supply is diminishing. Clearly the Indians are being operated as though they were being liquidated, perhaps to be sold out of town. The dismal team record and fascist management policies have resulted in an average attendance around 8000, well below even the Pirates. We have an unusually grim situation even for a town that is used to a long history of grim baseball situations.

Do not blame this on the stadium itself. Municipal Stadium is a vastly overcriticized park. I speak from experience, having been to 26 different major league parks (some defunct, such as Crosley and Forbes Fields, D.C. and Yankee (original) stadiums, etc.). Cleveland, even on days of rare big crowds, has the easiest access and egress, the most good unobstructed seats, the lowest ticket prices, and the best sight lines of any big league park. This is a largely unknown and overlooked fact. Its huge size also totally eliminates sellouts, which are a serious nuisance in smaller parks with good teams. The coma that the Indians are in is not the fault of the ballpark—local management must shoulder this blame.

After the All-Star game I did a quick study by assembling the 1985 records of ex-Indians now on major league rosters of other teams. Creating a 25 man roster from these players, with all positions covered, this phantom team had a .273 team average with 84 home runs and a 3.66 ERA. Projecting wins from runs scored vs. runs allowed, this team would be 5 games out of first in the AL East, a full 20 games better than the current Indians. The study has limitations, as do all statistical analyses, but this is a highly significant difference that tells you something.

I hope that there may be a few kernels of information or insight in this letter that may be useful to you.

Sincerely yours,
George Zeller

More than a few, George, and thanks. I will close on a mildly positive note. The talent that made the Indians' expectations higher a year ago is, for the most part, still there. Few teams in baseball have four good young players to match Franco, Butler, Carter and Jacoby. The road back to respectability may be miles long, or surprisingly short.

Bill James

COMPLETE BATTING RECORDS

Player	G	AB	R	H	TB	2B	3B	HR	RBI	GW	SH	SF	HB	BB	IB	SO	SB	CS	GI DP	Avg	Slug	OBP	Runs	Outs Made	Runs/ 27 Outs	OW%	Appr Value
*Willard	104	300	39	81	115	13	0	7	36	6	4	1	1	28	1	59	0	0	3	.270	.383	.333	40	227	4.76	.485	4
Tabler	117	404	47	111	150	18	3	5	59	5	2	3	2	27	2	55	0	6	15	.275	.371	.321	43	319	3.67	.359	6
†Bernazard	153	500	73	137	202	26	3	11	59	5	5	4	1	69	2	72	17	9	11	.274	.404	.361	75	392	5.19	.528	9
Jacoby	161	606	72	166	258	26	3	20	87	4	1	7	0	48	3	120	2	3	17	.274	.426	.324	81	468	4.65	.473	10
Franco	160	636	97	183	242	33	4	6	90	9	0	9	4	54	2	74	13	9	26	.288	.381	.343	79	497	4.27	.430	11
Carter	143	489	64	128	200	27	0	15	59	7	3	4	2	25	2	74	24	6	9	.262	.409	.298	60	383	4.20	.423	12
*Butler	152	591	106	184	255	28	14	5	50	6	8	3	1	63	2	42	47	20	8	.311	.431	.377	100	446	6.02	.601	15
*Vukovich	149	434	43	106	152	22	0	8	45	4	1	4	1	30	6	75	2	2	9	.244	.350	.292	43	344	3.41	.326	6
Thornton	124	461	49	109	188	13	0	22	88	6	0	6	0	47	1	75	3	2	14	.236	.408	.304	56	374	4.02	.402	6
*Hargrove	107	284	31	81	100	14	1	1	27	0	2	1	0	39	2	29	1	0	8	.285	.352	.370	38	214	4.84	.493	5
Castillo	67	184	27	45	85	5	1	11	25	1	0	0	3	11	0	40	3	0	6	.245	.462	.298	24	145	4.50	.456	2
†Bando	73	173	11	24	30	4	1	0	13	1	2	2	0	22	0	21	0	1	6	.139	.173	.234	7	160	1.25	.061	1
†Nixon	104	162	34	38	51	4	0	3	9	1	4	0	0	8	0	27	20	11	2	.235	.315	.271	12	141	2.38	.191	1
Ayala	46	76	10	19	32	7	0	2	15	2	0	1	0	4	1	17	0	0	2	.250	.421	.284	9	60	3.88	.385	1
Benton	31	67	5	12	16	4	0	0	7	0	1	2	0	3	2	9	0	0	1	.179	.239	.208	3	59	1.56	.092	1
*Hall	23	66	7	21	27	6	0	0	12	0	0	1	0	8	0	12	0	1	2	.318	.409	.387	10	49	5.65	.570	1
Fischlin	73	60	12	12	18	4	1	0	2	0	4	0	0	5	0	7	0	1	0	.200	.300	.262	5	53	2.53	.209	0
LeMaster	11	20	0	3	3	0	0	0	2	0	1	0	0	0	0	6	0	1	0	.150	.150	.150	0	19	0.48	.009	0
Wilson	4	14	2	5	5	0	0	0	4	1	0	0	0	1	0	3	0	0	0	.357	.357	.400	2	9	6.31	.623	0

*left-handed hitter, †switch hitter

FIRST	G	PO	A	Er	TC	DP	PCT.
Tabler	92	739	72	14	825	77	.983
Hargrove	84	595	66	6	667	66	.991
Carter	11	33	5	1	39	2	.974
Fischlin	6	8	0	0	8	0	1.000
Wilson	2	23	0	0	23	1	1.000
TEAM:	195	1398	143	21	1562	146	.987
AVG:	180	1440	123	14	1577	141	.991

SECOND	G	PO	A	Er	TC	DP	PCT.
Bernazard	147	311	399	16	726	86	.978
Fischlin	31	44	59	1	104	15	.990
Franco	8	14	18	1	33	4	.970
Jacoby	1	0	0	0	0	0	.000
Carter	1	0	1	0	1	0	1.000
Tabler	1	1	2	0	3	1	1.000
TEAM:	189	370	479	18	867	106	.979
AVG:	189	347	501	15	863	114	.982

THIRD	G	PO	A	Er	TC	DP	PCT.
Jacoby	163	114	319	19	452	26	.958
Tabler	4	4	3	0	7	0	1.000
Fischlin	3	1	2	0	3	0	1.000
Carter	1	0	0	0	0	0	.000
TEAM:	171	119	324	19	462	26	.959
AVG:	192	129	327	23	479	32	.953

SHORTSTOP	G	PO	A	Er	TC	DP	PCT.
Franco	151	238	419	35	692	95	.949
Fischlin	22	20	28	3	51	5	.941
LeMaster	10	19	18	2	39	7	.949
Bernazard	1	2	0	0	2	1	1.000
TEAM:	184	279	465	40	784	108	.949
AVG:	189	269	474	28	771	104	.964

CATCHER	G	PO	A	Er	TC	DP	PCT.	PB
Willard	96	427	52	5	484	11	.990	5
Bando	67	251	28	4	283	3	.986	3
Benton	26	75	13	4	92	1	.957	5
TEAM:	189	753	93	13	859	15	.985	13
AVG:	193	895	74	13	982	13	.987	13

OUTFIELD	G	PO	A	Er	TC	DP	PCT.
Butler	150	437	19	1	457	5	.998
Vukovich	137	250	4	3	257	0	.988
Carter	135	278	11	5	294	2	.983
Nixon	80	129	5	4	138	1	.971
Castillo	51	101	0	5	106	0	.953
Ayala	20	21	1	2	24	0	.917
Hall	15	18	0	0	18	0	1.000
Hargrove	1	4	0	0	4	0	1.000
TEAM:	589	1238	40	20	1298	8	.985
AVG:	559	1141	33	21	1196	8	.982

COMPLETE PITCHERS RECORDS

Pitcher	W	L	Pct	ERA	G	GS	CG	GF	SHO	SV	IP	H	TBF	R	ER	HR	SH	SF	HB	BB	IB	SO	WP	BK	Appr Value
											Starters (One-half of Game Appearances)														
*Heaton	9	17	.346	4.90	36	33	5	2	1	0	207.2	244	921	119	113	19	7	8	7	80	2	82	2	2	6
Blyleven	9	11	.450	3.26	23	23	15	4	0	0	179.2	163	743	76	65	14	4	4	7	49	1	129	1	1	7
Schulze	4	10	.286	6.01	19	18	1	0	0	0	94.1	128	429	75	63	10	6	3	4	19	2	37	3	0	1
*Romero	2	3	.400	6.58	19	10	0	5	0	0	64.1	69	295	48	47	13	1	1	5	38	0	38	6	0	0
Smith	1	4	.200	5.34	12	11	1	0	0	0	62.1	84	285	40	37	8	1	4	1	17	0	28	1	0	1
Creel	2	5	.286	4.79	15	8	0	5	0	0	62.0	73	277	35	33	7	0	5	2	23	2	31	1	0	1
Behenna	0	2	.000	7.78	4	4	0	0	0	0	19.2	29	91	17	17	3	0	1	0	8	0	4	1	0	0
Roman	0	4	.000	6.61	5	3	0	1	0	0	16.1	13	79	17	12	3	0	0	0	14	0	12	1	1	0
											Relievers														
Ruhle	2	10	.167	4.32	42	16	1	7	0	3	125.0	139	532	65	60	16	4	4	2	30	6	54	2	0	4
Waddell	8	6	.571	4.87	49	9	1	28	0	9	112.2	104	471	61	61	20	5	4	1	39	8	53	1	0	6
*Easterly	4	1	.800	3.92	50	7	0	18	0	0	98.2	96	435	52	43	9	5	9	4	53	4	58	7	0	4
Thompson	3	8	.273	6.30	57	0	0	24	0	5	80.0	95	379	63	56	8	5	6	6	48	6	30	6	2	3
Reed	3	5	.375	4.11	33	5	0	19	0	8	72.1	67	301	41	33	12	2	4	3	19	2	37	4	0	5
*Wardle	7	6	.538	6.68	15	12	0	0	0	0	66.0	78	305	51	49	11	2	5	1	34	0	37	2	0	0
*Clark	3	4	.429	6.32	31	3	0	10	0	2	62.2	78	290	47	44	8	3	2	0	32	2	24	5	0	2
*Von Ohlen	3	2	.600	2.91	26	0	0	9	0	0	43.1	47	196	20	14	3	9	4	0	20	6	12	0	0	2
Barkley	0	3	.000	5.27	21	0	0	6	0	1	41.0	37	174	26	24	5	5	2	0	15	3	30	2	1	1
*Jeffcoat	0	0	.000	2.79	9	0	0	3	0	0	9.2	8	44	5	3	1	2	0	0	6	1	4	0	0	0
Camacho	0	1	.000	8.10	2	0	0	1	0	0	3.1	4	15	3	3	0	0	2	0	1	0	2	1	0	0

Jerry WILLARD, Catcher

	G	AB	Hit	2B	3B	HR	Run	RBI	TBB	SO	SB	CS	Avg
1.18 years		463	115	18	1	14	51	62	46	97	1	0	.249
1985	104	300	81	13	0	7	39	36	28	59	0	0	.270
First Half	36	109	27	9	0	1	15	10	15	16	0	0	.248
Second Half	68	191	54	4	0	6	24	26	13	43	0	0	.283
Vs. RHP		252	74	11	0	7	34	33	24	39	0	0	.294
Vs. LHP		48	7	2	0	0	5	3	4	20	0	0	.146
Home	51	136	37	4	0	4	16	21	10	30	0	0	.272
Road	53	164	44	9	0	3	23	15	18	29	0	0	.268
Grass	85	239	65	8	0	6	34	28	23	48	0	0	.272
Turf	19	61	16	5	0	1	5	8	5	11	0	0	.262

Pat TABLER, First Base

	G	AB	Hit	2B	3B	HR	Run	RBI	TBB	SO	SB	CS	Avg
2.75 years		544	150	25	5	8	69	74	54	82	2	4	.276
1985	117	404	111	18	3	5	47	59	27	55	0	6	.275
First Half	77	274	74	7	3	2	30	38	16	33	0	4	.270
Second Half	40	130	37	11	0	3	17	21	11	22	0	2	.285
Vs. RHP		255	65	11	3	2	27	38	16	38	0	4	.255
Vs. LHP		149	46	7	0	3	20	21	11	17	0	2	.309
Home	62	218	71	11	0	5	33	36	13	25	0	3	.326
Road	55	186	40	7	3	0	14	23	14	30	0	3	.215
Grass	103	364	105	18	3	5	43	54	22	45	0	6	.288
Turf	14	40	6	0	0	0	4	5	5	10	0	0	.150

Tony BERNAZARD, Second Base

	G	AB	Hit	2B	3B	HR	Run	RBI	TBB	SO	SB	CS	Avg
4.81 years		545	140	26	5	9	75	56	67	93	18	8	.257
1985	153	500	137	26	3	11	73	59	69	72	17	9	.274
First Half	73	222	65	14	2	7	32	32	29	36	6	7	.293
Second Half	80	278	72	12	1	4	41	27	40	36	11	2	.259
Vs. RHP		372	104	19	3	11	55	49	47	58	9	8	.280
Vs. LHP		128	33	7	0	0	18	10	22	14	8	1	.258
Home	76	246	74	16	2	4	43	27	34	35	12	4	.301
Road	77	254	63	10	1	7	30	32	35	37	5	5	.248
Grass	129	412	120	25	2	10	66	51	59	58	15	6	.291
Turf	24	88	17	1	1	1	7	8	10	14	2	3	.193

Brett BUTLER, Center Field

	G	AB	Hit	2B	3B	HR	Run	RBI	TBB	SO	SB	CS	Avg
3.65 years		578	160	21	11	4	96	40	68	58	46	20	.277
1985	152	591	184	28	14	5	106	50	63	42	47	20	.311
First Half	81	325	97	20	7	2	52	28	26	23	26	11	.298
Second Half	71	266	87	8	7	3	54	22	37	19	21	9	.327
Vs. RHP		404	122	21	10	4	72	34	47	27	35	11	.302
Vs. LHP		187	62	7	4	1	34	16	16	15	12	9	.332
Home	73	289	95	12	7	1	53	25	26	14	26	11	.329
Road	79	302	89	16	7	4	53	25	37	28	21	9	.295
Grass	128	494	151	22	11	5	88	46	50	36	40	14	.306
Turf	24	97	33	6	3	0	18	4	13	6	7	6	.340

Brook JACOBY, Third Base

	G	AB	Hit	2B	3B	HR	Run	RBI	TBB	SO	SB	CS	Avg
1.86 years		570	152	24	3	14	73	69	43	106	3	3	.267
1985	161	606	166	26	3	20	72	87	48	120	2	3	.274
First Half	81	303	87	12	0	10	37	46	28	57	2	2	.287
Second Half	80	303	79	14	3	10	35	41	20	63	0	1	.261
Vs. RHP		424	118	19	3	12	53	61	32	83	2	3	.278
Vs. LHP		182	48	7	0	8	19	26	16	37	0	0	.264
Home	81	303	82	14	3	9	29	45	25	58	1	2	.271
Road	80	303	84	12	0	11	43	42	23	62	1	1	.277
Grass	137	515	132	22	3	16	55	74	42	104	1	3	.256
Turf	24	91	34	4	0	4	17	13	6	16	1	0	.374

George VUKOVICH, Right Field

	G	AB	Hit	2B	3B	HR	Run	RBI	TBB	SO	SB	CS	Avg
3.88 years		413	111	20	3	7	42	52	33	59	2	5	.268
1985	149	434	106	22	0	8	43	45	30	75	2	2	.244
First Half	76	230	57	9	0	2	19	20	15	32	1	1	.248
Second Half	73	204	49	13	0	6	24	25	15	43	1	1	.240
Vs. RHP		392	100	20	0	8	42	44	28	63	2	2	.255
Vs. LHP		42	6	2	0	0	1	1	2	12	0	0	.143
Home	74	212	49	7	0	4	23	23	12	36	1	2	.231
Road	75	222	57	15	0	4	20	22	18	39	1	0	.257
Grass	125	373	92	20	0	6	37	35	24	66	2	2	.247
Turf	24	61	14	2	0	2	6	10	6	9	0	0	.230

Julio FRANCO, Shortstop

	G	AB	Hit	2B	3B	HR	Run	RBI	TBB	SO	SB	CS	Avg
2.99 years		629	178	27	6	6	84	84	42	65	21	11	.283
1985	160	636	183	33	4	6	97	90	54	74	13	9	.288
First Half	79	304	88	19	1	2	44	36	31	33	3	4	.289
Second Half	81	332	95	14	3	4	53	54	23	41	10	5	.286
Vs. RHP		441	127	21	4	2	63	68	40	47	10	6	.288
Vs. LHP		195	56	12	0	4	34	22	14	27	3	3	.287
Home	80	307	94	16	1	3	54	49	22	32	9	3	.306
Road	80	329	89	17	3	3	43	41	32	42	4	6	.271
Grass	136	533	163	28	4	6	89	84	48	62	13	7	.306
Turf	24	103	20	5	0	0	8	6	6	12	0	2	.194

Andre THORNTON, Designated Hitter

	G	AB	Hit	2B	3B	HR	Run	RBI	TBB	SO	SB	CS	Avg
8.70 years		552	143	26	3	27	85	95	92	87	5	4	.258
1985	124	461	109	13	0	22	49	88	47	75	3	2	.236
First Half	51	189	34	2	0	5	12	27	16	35	2	1	.180
Second Half	73	272	75	11	0	17	37	61	31	40	1	1	.276
Vs. RHP		308	68	9	0	14	29	58	24	54	1	2	.221
Vs. LHP		153	41	4	0	8	20	30	23	21	2	0	.268
Home	61	221	51	6	0	12	24	48	24	32	2	0	.231
Road	63	240	58	7	0	10	25	40	23	43	1	2	.242
Grass	106	392	90	8	0	22	44	81	39	67	2	1	.230
Turf	18	69	19	5	0	0	5	7	8	8	1	1	.275

Joe CARTER, Left Field

	G	AB	Hit	2B	3B	HR	Run	RBI	TBB	SO	SB	CS	Avg
1.43 years		547	142	24	1	20	71	71	25	100	19	7	.260
1985	143	489	128	27	0	15	64	59	25	74	24	6	.262
First Half	69	240	57	11	0	6	30	27	15	45	10	1	.238
Second Half	74	249	71	16	0	9	34	32	10	29	14	5	.285
Vs. RHP		334	89	19	0	10	41	47	14	46	19	3	.266
Vs. LHP		155	39	8	0	5	23	12	11	28	5	3	.252
Home	73	247	66	15	0	5	34	25	18	39	13	3	.267
Road	70	242	62	12	0	10	30	34	7	35	11	3	.256
Grass	122	412	110	24	0	13	58	52	22	63	21	6	.267
Turf	21	77	18	3	0	2	6	7	3	11	3	0	.234

Mike HARGROVE, First Base

	G	AB	Hit	2B	3B	HR	Run	RBI	TBB	SO	SB	CS	Avg
10.28 years		541	157	26	3	8	76	67	94	53	2	4	.290
1985	107	284	81	14	1	1	31	27	39	29	1	0	.285
First Half	41	100	22	5	0	0	9	3	16	12	0	0	.220
Second Half	66	184	59	9	1	1	22	24	23	17	1	0	.321
Vs. RHP		264	79	14	1	1	30	23	32	28	1	0	.299
Vs. LHP		20	2	0	0	0	1	4	7	1	0	0	.100
Home	55	139	42	7	1	0	17	15	19	14	1	0	.302
Road	52	145	39	7	0	1	14	12	20	15	0	0	.269
Grass	90	234	71	13	1	1	28	24	34	22	1	0	.303
Turf	17	50	10	1	0	0	3	3	5	7	0	0	.200

NEAL HEATON

	(W–L)	GS	Run	Avg	DP	Avg	SB	Avg
1984	(12-15)	34	169	4.97	39	1.15	21	.62
1985	(9-17)	33	129	3.91	40	1.21	28	.85
1982-1985		87	382	4.39	96	1.10	63	.72

	G	IP	W	L	Pct	ER	BB	SO	ERA
1984 Home	18	105.7	6	7	.462	56	31	35	4.77
1985 Home	18	116.7	7	5	.583	46	38	49	3.55
1984 Road	20	93.0	6	8	.429	59	44	40	5.71
1985 Road	18	91.0	2	12	.143	67	42	33	6.63
1984 Grass	33	171.3	10	13	.435	99	65	67	5.20
1985 Grass	31	173.7	8	15	.348	92	67	76	4.77
1984 Turf	5	27.3	2	2	.500	16	25	32	5.27
1985 Turf	5	34.0	1	2	.333	21	13	6	5.56
1985 Total	36	207.7	9	17	.346	113	80	82	4.90

OTHERS

	(W–L)	GS	Run	Avg	DP	Avg	SB	Avg
Schulze	(4-10)	18	80	4.44	15	.83	12	.67
Ruhle	(2-10)	16	52	3.25	18	1.12	13	.81
Wardle	(8-9)	12	74	6.17	10	.83	5	.42
Smith	(1-4)	11	62	5.64	14	1.27	11	1.00
Romero	(2-3)	10	39	3.90	11	1.10	12	1.20
Waddell	(8-6)	9	55	6.11	8	.89	10	1.11
Creel	(2-5)	8	40	5.00	7	.88	5	.62
Easterly	(4-1)	7	51	7.29	5	.71	2	.29
Reed	(3-5)	5	18	3.60	3	.60	3	.60
Behenna	(0-2)	4	17	4.25	4	1.00	6	1.50
Clark	(3-4)	3	11	3.67	3	1.00	4	1.33
Roman	(0-4)	3	4	1.33	2	.67	2	.67

NATIONAL LEAGUE EAST
DIVISION SHEET

Club	1st	2nd	vRHP	vLHP	Home	Road	Grass	Turf	Day	Night	Total	Pct
St. Louis	52-33	49-28	71-35	30-26	54-27	47-34	27-15	74-46	35-28	66-33	101-61	.623
New York	50-36	48-28	55-40	43-24	51-30	47-34	73-41	25-23	36-25	62-39	98-64	.605
Montreal	49-39	35-38	58-55	26-22	44-37	40-40	23-19	61-58	38-24	46-53	84-77	.522
Chicago	45-41	32-43	58-65	19-19	41-39	36-45	55-58	22-26	48-57	29-27	77-84	.478
Philadelphia	37-49	38-38	52-60	23-27	41-40	34-47	14-28	61-59	26-26	49-61	75-87	.463
Pittsburgh	29-56	28-48	43-72	14-32	35-45	22-59	11-31	46-73	14-41	43-63	57-104	.354

COME FROM BEHIND WINS

Club	1	2	3	4	5	6	7	Total	Points
St. Louis	19	10	3	0	2	1		35	99
New York	17	13	2					32	81
Montreal	14	11	2	1	1			29	80
Chicago	18	10	5	3	2			38	113
Philadelphia	15	11	5	3	2			33	94
Pittsburgh	12	9	3	1				25	68

BLOWN LEADS

Club	1	2	3	4	5	6	7	Total	Points
St. Louis	19	6	0	0	0	1		26	63
New York	10	10	4	2				26	76
Montreal	13	8	4	2	2			29	88
Chicago	15	10	6	2	0	1		34	101
Philadelphia	17	12	5	1				35	95
Pittsburgh	24	16	3	3				46	123

RECORDS WHEN AHEAD, TIED, BEHIND AFTER SEVEN

Club	Ahead	Tied	Behind
St. Louis	83-1	11- 7	7-53
New York	82-4	13-13	3-47
Montreal	68-7	13- 8	3-62
Chicago	62-3	11- 7	4-74
Philadelphia	60-6	9-10	6-71
Pittsburgh	47-10	7-13	3-81

CLUB BATTING

Club	G	AB	R	H	TB	2B	3B	HR	RBI	GW	SH	SF	HP	BB	IB	SO	SB	CS	GIDP	LOB	SHO	Avg	Slug	OBP
St. Louis	162	5467	747	1446	2070	245	59	87	687	94	70	41	18	586	61	853	314	96	91	1105	8	.264	.379	.355
New York	162	5549	695	1425	2136	239	35	134	651	90	89	44	20	546	88	872	117	53	131	1149	11	.257	.385	.323
Montreal	161	5429	633	1342	2036	242	49	118	593	76	61	45	26	492	73	880	169	77	112	1061	13	.247	.375	.310
Chicago	162	5492	686	1397	2142	239	28	150	640	72	66	39	18	562	62	937	182	49	119	1147	14	.254	.390	.324
Philadelphia	162	5477	667	1343	2098	238	47	141	628	71	49	44	25	527	51	1095	122	51	124	1099	13	.245	.383	.312
Pittsburgh	161	5436	568	1340	1887	251	28	80	535	56	91	44	14	514	64	842	110	60	131	1132	19	.247	.347	.311

OPPOSITION BATTING

Club	G	AB	R	H	TB	2B	3B	HR	RBI	GW	SH	SF	HP	BB	IB	SO	SB	CS	GIDP	LOB	SHO	Avg	Slug	OBP
St. Louis	162		572	1343				98			60	39	28	453	80	798	102				20			
New York	162	5520	568	1306	1921	232	25	111	539	62	66	27	18	515	36	1039	122	66	111		19	.237	.348	.302
Montreal	161	5456	636	1346	1932	229	30	99	595	73	87	35	21	509	70	870	189	46	121		13	.247	.354	.312
Chicago	162	5513	729	1492	2318	264	47	156	694	84	95	45	23	519	83	820	137	82	126		8	.271	.420	.333
Philadelphia	162	5506	673	1424	2116	235	56	115	626	81	66	47	26	596	63	899	164	57	140		9	.259	.384	.331
Pittsburgh	161	5504	708	1406	2077	266	42	107	660	96	57	28	32	584	72	962	105	69	104		6	.255	.377	.329

CLUB PITCHING

Club	W	L	ERA	G	CG	SHO	SV	IP	H	TBF	R	ER	HR	SH	SF	HB	TB	IB	SO	WP	BK
St. Louis	101	61	3.10	162	37	20	44	1464.0	1343	6048	572	505	98	60	39	28	453	80	798	35	6
New York	98	64	3.11	162	32	19	37	1488.0	1306	6146	568	514	111	66	27	18	515	36	1039	41	14
Montreal	84	77	3.55	161	13	13	54	1457.0	1346	6109	636	574	99	87	35	21	509	70	870	46	12
Chicago	77	84	4.16	162	20	8	42	1442.1	1492	6195	729	666	156	95	45	23	519	83	820	31	11
Philadelphia	75	87	3.68	162	24	9	30	1447.0	1424	6241	673	592	115	66	47	26	596	63	899	34	9
Pittsburgh	57	104	3.97	161	15	6	29	1445.1	1406	6205	708	638	107	57	28	32	584	72	962	48	11

OPPOSITION PITCHING

Club	W	L	ERA	G	CG	SHO	SV	IP	H	TBF	R	ER	HR	SH	SF	HB	TB	IB	SO	WP	BK
St. Louis	61	101		162		8			1446	6182	747		87	70	41	18	586	61	853		
New York	64	98	3.61	162	18	11	31	1468.0	1425	6248	695	589	134	89	44	20	546	88	872	53	10
Montreal	77	84	3.44	161	22	13	35	1453.0	1342	6053	633	556	118	61	45	26	492	73	880	41	8
Chicago	84	77	3.80	162	23	14	38	1448.0	1397	6177	686	611	150	66	39	18	562	62	937	46	6
Philadelphia	87	75	3.69	162	18	13	47	1452.0	1343	6122	667	595	141	49	44	25	527	51	1095	42	8
Pittsburgh	104	57	3.10	161	25	19	51	1466.1	1340	6099	568	505	80	91	44	14	514	64	842	40	8

CLUB FIELDING

Club	G	PO	A	E	TC	DP	TP	PB	OSB	OCS	OSB%	OA/SFA	Pct	DER	OR
St. Louis	162	4392	1859	108	6359	166	0	15	102			44/39	.983	716	572
New York	162	4464	1696	115	6275	138	0	9	122	66	.649	22/27	.982	714	568
Montreal	161	4371	1856	121	6348	152	0	16	189	46	.804	31/35	.981	711	636
Chicago	162	4327	1934	134	6395	150	1	17	137	82	.626	26/45	.979	694	729
Philadelphia	162	4341	1777	139	6257	142	0	15	164	57	.742	43/47	.978	694	673
Pittsburgh	161	4336	1799	133	6268	127	0	6	105	69	.603	32/28	.979	692	708

ST. LOUIS CARDINALS

FOR WANT OF A LOGICAL SHOENAIL

The St. Louis Cardinals in 1985 were a study in sequential misinterpretation of reality, with one misunderstanding rolling gracefully into the next. The initial misunderstanding had to do with the impact that one player, and in particular a relief ace, has on the performance of an entire team. Most analysts of the Cardinal team a year ago began their analysis by fastening on a factor which, in truth, had absolutely nothing to do with how the 1985 Cardinals would perform: the fact that Bruce Sutter was no longer there. The Cardinals had won 84 games in 1984, and many people began by subtracting about ten or twelve games for the loss of Sutter, coupling this with the possible psychic devastation of the team, and penciled in figures of 68, 70 wins for the 1985 Cardinals.

Now this was a completely unreasonable assessment, both of the impact that the loss of Sutter would have (see Atlanta comment) and of the talent remaining on the Cardinal roster. I mean, if you looked at the team in St. Louis, rather than the pitcher in Atlanta, you had to see the names Jack Clark, Ozzie Smith, Joacquin Andujar and Willie McGee, and behind them some more names like Andy Van Slyke, Tommie Herr, Darrell Porter and John Tudor. It is hard to see how anyone could have thought that the Cardinals were a last-place team—but, focusing on the void in the bullpen to the exclusion of all else, many people did.

When the season began and the Cardinals started winning, these same people felt the need to figure out what the difference was. In so doing, they focused on the most obvious late change to the Cardinal roster, the record-setting rookie Vince Coleman.

And so it was, in the 1985 season, that Vince Coleman wound up with his share of the credit for the Cardinal pennant—his share, and also most of Tommie Herr's, and Ozzie Smith's, and Terry Pendleton's, and Andy Van Slyke's. Now in reality, there is virtually no difference between the Vince Coleman of 1985 and the Lonnie Smith of 1985 as offensive players. Their batting averages were almost the same (.267, .257). Their on-base percentages were almost the same (.320, .335). Their stolen-base percentages were almost the same (82%, 80%). The frequency with which they scored runs was almost the same (156/1000 plate appearances, and 152/1000; in all cases Coleman's stat is listed first). Their double play frequencies were almost the same. The frequency with which they could have been expected to score runs, figured by the lead-off man formula, is identical—both players could be expected to score 146 runs/1000 plate appearances if batting leadoff for an average team. Coleman runs twice as often as Smith, but Smith has more power and gets on base a few extra times, so that in reality he was, even in 1985 (a poor year for him) a better offensive player than was Coleman.

More relevant than the comparison of Coleman to Smith was the comparison of Coleman to his teammates like Ozzie Smith, Tommie Herr and Andy Van Slyke. All

165

of those players (as well as, of course, Clark and McGee) were superior to Coleman by any reasonable measure of offensive performance—on base percentage, slugging percentage, runs created (per opportunity) or runs actually scored and driven in per opportunity. But not only is this true, it is also obvious; I need point it out only because so many people have written the opposite. It is obvious to anybody who watches the whole team and looks over the whole scoresheet, rather than reacting on a "Gee-isn't-that-Coleman-FAST level." Coleman *is* fast, and he's also got a loop in his swing the size of a freeway cutoff. If he wasn't fast, he'd hit .184. The addition of Vince to the outfield had value in that, and only in that, it improved the Cardinals defensively.

Anyway, the public was led from

a) The loss of Sutter is going to cost the Cardinals ten or fifteen games, to

b) The Cardinals have become a lousy team, to

c) Vince Coleman has turned the Cardinal offense around.

Congratulate yourself if you didn't buy it.

None of which is intended to deny that base stealing in general, and Vince Coleman in particular, played a valuable role in the Cardinal offense in 1985. On radio talk shows this winter I was asked a lot whether, in view of the superlative showing of the Cardinal base-stealing force, I had reconsidered my reservations about the impact of the stolen base. The answer is that prior to 1985 I had 85 seasons of modern baseball history to study and draw conclusions from, and after 1985 I had 86 seasons. It would be foolish to let the 86th reverse the conclusion of the other 85, even if there were no other way to explain the success of this fine team.

Which is hardly the case. As I have written God knows how many times over the last ten years, the one most universal truth about good offenses is that they get lots of people on base. If there is one thing that separates a good team from a bad team, it is the ability to get runners on base—as well as, defensively, the ability to keep runners off the bases.

If you look at the 1985 Cardinals, what do you see?

1) They led the National League in batting average, at .264.

2) They led the National League in the number of walks drawn, with 586.

Combining those, the Cardinals had a team on-base percentage of .335, easily the best in the National League (the second-best was .328, by the Dodgers, champions of the other division). That, and not the base stealing, is the essential reason that the Cardinals led the National League in runs scored.

There were many examples of base-stealing teams being successful teams prior to 1985. There is one more now. There were many examples of base-stealing teams being unsuccessful teams. There still are. The ratio has changed by one, that's all.

But while anyone who really studies baseball has to reach the conclusion that base stealing, in general, adds very few runs to a team's offense, it is also true that 1) the Cardinals of 1985 were hardly a "general" team, but one of the greatest base-stealing forces of all time, and 2) even

if the runs added by base stealing are relatively few compared to those that can be added by hitting home runs or other offensive methods, it is still true that those runs can, in a close race, be a decisive factor, making the four-game difference between finishing three games ahead and finishing second.

It becomes a question, then, of exactly how many runs the Cardinals' base stealers did add to the St. Louis offense in 1985. This can be estimated in many different ways, of which I will try a few, but first of all it is necessary to establish a frame of reference for the information. The Cardinals in 1985 scored 747 runs, which was the highest total in the National League by a margin of 41 runs. It is not in any sense a historic figure, as five American League teams scored more runs, but it's a normal N.L.–leading type figure. Now the estimates:

The Palmer Approach: Pete Palmer has estimated that the incremental value of a stolen base is about 3/10 of a run, while the cost of a runner caught stealing is around 6/10 of a run. Since the Cardinals in 1985 stole 314 bases and had 96 runners caught stealing, this would imply a net gain on stolen base attempts of slightly less than 37 runs.

The Palmer "linear weights" method is the most direct analytical approach to this question.

The Runs Created Method: There exist a number of formulas, known as the runs created formulas, which can be used to predict with a high degree of accuracy how many runs a team will score, and thus can be used to predict how many runs a team would be likely to score given certain altered assumptions, such as "no base stealing."

The technical version of the runs created formula estimates that the Cardinals should have scored 733 runs, close (14 too low) to the number they actually scored. The formula estimates that without stealing any bases, they would have scored about 719 runs. However, this version of the formula also considers the number of double plays grounded into, and there is an adjustment needed for the fact that, not attempting to steal any bases, the Cardinals would likely have grounded into about 40 more double plays, which would reduce their runs created estimate to 704. So, depending on whether you compare to the expected runs scored (733) or the actual (747), the Cardinals' base-stealing efforts probably produced about 29 to 43 runs.

There are many other options in interpreting the data from the runs created formulas, some of which would even suggest that the Cardinals would have scored more runs than they did without stealing any bases, and others of which would place the estimate as high as 52 runs.

Comparison by selecting comparable teams which did not steal bases: This is the new option made possible this year by the development of similarity scores.

What I did in this case was to figure similarity scores for a large number of teams as compared to the 1985 Cardinals, but *with the sign reversed for a difference in the stolen base column* so that the similarity comparison system identified teams which were *like* the Cardinals in all other respects, but *different* from them in regard to stealing bases. Among teams of recent years, the 1985 Cards are a pretty unique outfit; it is unusual in our time for a good ballclub, with outstanding doubles and triples totals and a good average, to hit so few home runs. Such similar teams as there would be in recent years would be, for the most part, other base-stealing teams.

But the history of baseball is, fortunately, quite long, and over time almost all combinations, including that represented by a .264 batting average and 87 home runs but with little base stealing, have been common in one era or another. The era in which this particular combination would have been typical can easily by seen by looking at the ten offenses that we identified:

TEAM	AVG	2B	3B	HR	TBB	SB
1939 Dodgers	.265	265	57	78	564	59
1939 Browns	.268	242	50	91	559	48
1940 Dodgers	.260	256	70	93	522	56
1941 Tigers	.263	247	55	81	637	43
1941 A's	.268	240	69	85	588	27
1946 Cards	.265	265	56	81	530	58
1948 Dodgers	.261	256	54	91	601	114
1951 Cards	.264	230	57	95	569	30
1978 Twins	.267	259	47	82	604	99
1983 Indians	.265	249	31	86	605	109
AVERAGES	.265	251	55	86	577	64
1985 CARDS	.264	245	59	87	586	314

These ten teams are, as you can see, *extremely* comparable to the 1985 Cardinals in terms of batting average (.2647 as opposed to .2645), doubles, triples, and home runs hit, and walks drawn—but they stole an average of only 64 bases. The aggregate slugging percentage and on-base percentage of the comparison group were identical to the Cardinals figures of .379 and .335. As such, they give us a good indication of how many runs the Cardinals would likely have scored had they had the same statistics in all other respects, but not been a base-stealing team.

These ten comparison teams scored an average of 705 runs, with six of the ten teams scoring between 700 and 718. The most runs scored by any of them was by the 1948 Dodgers—also the best base-stealing team of the comparison group—which scored 744 runs, only four fewer than the Cardinals scored in seven more games. The difference between the Cardinals and the comparison teams is 42 runs; however, the comparison teams played an average of only 157 games, five fewer than the '85 Cards. An adjustment for this would eliminate approximately one-half of the Cardinals' 42-run advantage.

So the indications are that the 1985 Cardinals, had they hit as they did and not stolen many bases, would likely have scored somewhere between 25 and 40 runs fewer than they actually did. That being the case, they would probably have led the National League in runs scored anyway, but there is a very good chance that they would not have won the National League East. They would have won 95–98 games; that probably would not have been enough.

It could also be explained in this way: that offense is accomplished in two parts, the first being to get runners on base, and the second being to score those runners who succeed in reaching base. The stolen-base offense contributes only to the second goal, not the first—yet the 1985 Cardinals were probably a more outstanding team with re-

gard to the first goal than with regard to the second. Many teams which get as many people on base as the 1985 Cardinals did will score *more* runs—for example, the 1978 Milwaukee Brewers had almost exactly the same number of runners on base as the Cardinals did, yet scored 57 more runs (804–747). This is because power is a much more effective way of increasing the percentage of runners who score than is speed. But the Cardinals compensated for their lack of power (and the difficulty of hitting a home run in Busch Stadium) with base stealing, and they did a good job of it.

The argument that I haven't dealt with, of course, is the argument that the running attack has side-benefits in the distraction of the pitcher, the pressure on the defense, etc. Whenever a stolen base is accompanied by any other offensive accomplishment, the announcer can usually be counted on to attribute the latter to the distraction of the pitcher. Carrying this to its ultimate logical extension, there was an occasion during the playoffs (Game 3, 2nd inning) in which a Cardinal was caught stealing and the next man hit a home run, and the announcer actually suggested that the player might have hit the home run because the pitcher's concentration had been broken by the stolen base attempt.

If you attribute every positive thing that happens in a game to the running offense, then of course the running game must be seen as being enormously valuable. The problem is that there is no reasonable basis for making such an attribution. What I must point out with regard to this argument is that the running game has negative as well as positive secondary consequences, as witness:

1) Joe Morgan never liked to have the man on first base break with the pitch when he was hitting, because he found it distracting to him as a hitter. In other words, it is not only the pitcher who can be distracted by this side-game, but also the hitter.

2) When Maury Wills stole 104 bases in 1962, a National League umpire said after the season that Wills had cost the Dodgers the pennant with his running. He said that he had seen Junior Gilliam take too many pitches that he knew Gilliam could have hit, getting behind in the count, just to allow Wills to steal. Several of the games greatest pitchers, including Tom Seaver, Nolan Ryan and Jim Palmer, have chosen not to worry about the bases stolen against them for essentially that reason—that if the batter at the plate wants to take pitches in order to let the man on base try to steal, great. Let him. If you get the guy at the plate, you'll get out of it.

3) Many managers, including Earl Weaver, do not like to steal second with a left-handed batter at the plate. With a runner on first, the first baseman has to hold the runner on, creating a hole for the left-handed hitter; the stolen base attempt releases the fielder to cover the hole.

Of course, there are real positive side-benefits. Although Willie is tired of hearing about this, I think it is certainly true that Willie McGee had an outstanding year in 1985 in part because he was able to take advantage of the tendency of pitchers to throw fastballs with Coleman on first. My point is not that such side-benefits do not exist, but that there is no reasonable basis for the assumption that the sum of them is significantly positive. If it *were* significantly positive, one would expect that base-stealing teams would consistently be winning teams, and that simply isn't true; many of them are losers. You may suspect that the sum of these secondary consequences is strongly positive; I suspect that it is, on balance, negative.

Neither of us really knows. But absent compelling evidence to the contrary, one must attribute Tommie Herr's home run to Tommie Herr's ability to hit, and not to Willie McGee's ability to be caught stealing in front of him.

One final pair of charts, and then I'll shut up about it. The most essential offensive abilities are measured in two categories: slugging percentage, and on base percentage. Here is the data for the eight Cardinal regulars in 1985:

SLUGGING PCT.		ON BASE PCT.	
McGee	.503	Clark	.393
Clark	.502	McGee	.384
Van Slyke	.439	Herr	.379
Herr	.416	Ozzie	.355
Porter	.413	Porter	.335
Ozzie	.361	Van Slyke	.335
COLEMAN	.335	COLEMAN	.320
Pendleton	.306	Pendleton	.285

COMPLETE BATTING RECORDS

Player	G	AB	R	H	TB	2B	3B	HR	RBI	GW	SH	SF	HB	BB	IB	SO	SB	CS	GI DP	Avg	Slug	OBP	Runs Created	Outs Made	Runs/ 27 Outs	OW%	Appr Value
Nieto	95	253	15	57	71	10	2	0	34	5	6	0	3	26	8	37	0	2	9	.225	.281	.305	21	213	2.63	.294	2
Clark	126	442	71	124	222	26	3	22	87	7	0	5	2	83	14	88	1	4	10	.281	.502	.393	89	337	7.15	.755	10
†Herr	159	596	97	180	248	38	3	8	110	14	5	13	2	80	5	55	31	3	6	.302	.416	.379	107	443	6.50	.718	17
†Pendleton	149	559	56	134	171	16	3	5	69	12	3	3	0	37	4	75	17	12	18	.240	.306	.285	45	461	2.63	.294	8
†O. Smith	158	537	70	148	194	22	3	6	54	5	9	2	2	65	11	27	31	8	13	.276	.361	.355	73	421	4.66	.567	14
†Coleman	151	636	107	170	213	20	10	1	40	3	5	1	0	50	1	115	110	25	3	.267	.335	.320	79	500	4.29	.526	11
†McGee	152	612	114	216	308	26	18	10	82	17	1	5	0	34	2	86	56	16	3	.353	.503	.384	123	421	7.92	.791	17
*Van Slyke	146	424	61	110	186	25	6	13	55	7	1	1	2	47	6	54	34	6	7	.259	.439	.335	66	329	5.45	.642	10
*Porter	84	240	30	53	99	12	2	10	36	6	0	2	1	41	6	48	6	1	3	.221	.413	.335	36	193	5.04	.606	5
Landrum	85	161	21	45	69	8	2	4	21	3	1	0	0	19	1	30	1	4	3	.280	.429	.356	24	124	5.12	.613	3
*Jorgensen	72	112	14	22	28	6	0	0	11	2	2	0	1	31	0	27	2	1	3	.196	.250	.375	13	96	3.70	.452	1
L. Smith	28	96	15	25	31	2	2	0	7	1	1	0	3	15	0	20	12	6	2	.260	.323	.377	13	80	4.36	.534	1
*Tudor	37	94	9	13	20	3	2	0	2	1	7	0	0	5	0	25	0	1	1	.138	.213	.182	4	90	1.13	.071	0
†Andujar	38	94	2	10	12	2	0	0	8	0	7	0	0	5	0	50	3	1	2	.106	.128	.152	2	94	0.60	.021	0
Cox	35	79	3	12	13	1	0	0	6	0	8	1	1	4	0	24	0	0	1	.152	.165	.200	3	77	1.15	.073	0
DeJesus	59	72	11	16	21	5	0	0	7	0	1	1	0	4	0	16	2	2	0	.222	.292	.260	6	60	2.50	.275	1
Cedeño	28	76	14	33	57	4	1	6	19	4	0	1	0	5	2	7	5	1	2	.434	.750	.463	26	47	14.93	.931	3
*Braun	64	67	7	16	23	4	0	1	6	2	0	1	1	10	1	9	0	0	0	.239	.343	.342	9	52	4.64	.565	1
Lawless	47	58	8	12	17	3	1	0	8	2	1	0	0	4	2	1	0	2	0	.207	.293	.270	5	48	2.79	.320	0
Harper	43	52	5	13	17	4	0	0	8	1	0	1	0	2	0	3	0	0	2	.250	.327	.273	4	42	2.74	.312	1
*Kepshire	32	51	6	6	9	3	0	0	2	0	7	1	0	1	0	18	0	0	0	.118	.176	.132	2	53	0.80	.037	0
Forsch	34	45	3	11	18	2	1	1	4	1	2	0	0	0	0	10	0	0	2	.244	.400	.244	4	36	3.34	.403	0
*Lavalliere	12	34	2	5	6	1	0	0	6	0	0	3	0	7	0	3	0	0	2	.147	.176	.273	4	34	1.69	.147	0
Hunt	14	19	1	3	3	0	0	0	1	0	1	0	0	0	0	5	0	1	0	.158	.158	.158	0	18	0.53	.017	0
*Horton	49	16	1	1	1	0	0	0	0	0	2	0	0	3	0	5	0	0	0	.063	.063	.211	1	17	0.85	.042	0
*Ford	11	12	2	6	8	2	0	0	3	1	0	0	0	4	0	1	1	0	0	.500	.667	.625	6	6	26.89	.978	0
Lahti	52	9	0	0	0	0	0	0	0	0	0	0	0	0	0	5	0	0	0	.000	.000	.000	0	9	0.00	.000	0
Campbell	50	6	2	2	2	0	0	0	1	0	0	0	0	3	0	2	0	1	0	.333	.333	.556	1	5	6.67	.729	0
*Dayley	57	5	0	2	2	0	0	0	0	0	0	0	0	1	0	1	0	0	0	.400	.400	.400	1	3	7.20	.758	0
Howe	4	3	0	0	0	0	0	0	0	0	0	0	0	0	0	0	0	0	0	.000	.000	.000	0	3	0.00	.000	0
Keough	4	2	0	0	0	0	0	0	0	0	0	0	0	0	0	0	0	0	1	.000	.000	.000	0	3	0.00	.000	0
*Perry	6	2	0	1	1	0	0	0	0	0	0	0	0	0	0	0	0	0	0	.500	.500	.500	1	1	13.50	.917	0
Allen	23	2	0	0	0	0	0	0	0	0	0	0	0	0	0	2	0	0	0	.000	.000	.000	0	2	0.00	.000	0
Worrell	17	1	0	0	0	0	0	0	0	0	0	0	0	1	0	0	0	0	0	.000	.000	.000	0	1	0.00	.000	0
*Hassler	10	0	0	0	0	0	0	0	0	0	0	0	0	0	0	0	0	0	0	.000	.000	.000	0	0	0.00	.000	0
Bair	2	0	0	0	0	0	0	0	0	0	0	0	0	0	0	0	0	0	0	.000	.000	.000	0	0	0.00	.000	0
Boever	13	0	0	0	0	0	0	0	0	0	0	0	0	0	0	0	0	0	0	.000	.000	.000	0	0	0.00	.000	0

*left-handed hitter, †switch hitter

FIRST	G	PO	A	Er	TC	DP	PCT.
Clark	121	1116	66	14	1196	102	.988
Jorgensen	49	318	17	2	337	32	.994
Cedeño	23	145	5	1	151	16	.993
Van Slyke	2	3	0	0	3	2	1.000
Howe	1	4	0	0	4	1	1.000
Harper	1	2	0	0	2	0	1.000
TEAM:	197	1588	88	17	1693	153	.990
AVG:	191	1513	114	12	1639	136	.993

SECOND	G	PO	A	Er	TC	DP	PCT.
Herr	158	337	448	12	797	120	.985
Lawless	11	10	20	0	30	2	1.000
TEAM:	169	347	468	12	827	122	.985
AVG:	184	384	502	16	901	110	.982

THIRD	G	PO	A	Er	TC	DP	PCT.
Pendleton	149	129	361	18	508	26	.965
DeJesus	20	7	24	0	31	2	1.000
Lawless	13	9	24	1	34	2	.971
Harper	6	5	5	0	10	0	1.000
Howe	1	1	1	0	2	0	1.000
TEAM:	189	151	415	19	585	30	.968
AVG:	189	125	341	25	492	29	.948

SHORTSTOP	G	PO	A	Er	TC	DP	PCT.
O. Smith	158	264	549	14	827	111	.983
DeJesus	13	8	16	2	26	1	.923
TEAM:	171	272	565	16	853	112	.981
AVG:	185	268	521	30	819	99	.963

CATCHER	G	PO	A	Er	TC	DP	PCT.	PB
Nieto	95	384	28	4	416	3	.990	10
Porter	82	386	26	4	416	4	.990	5
Hunt	13	33	1	0	34	0	1.000	0
Lavalliere	12	48	5	0	53	3	1.000	0
Harper	2	0	0	0	0	0	.000	0
TEAM:	204	851	60	8	919	10	.991	15
AVG:	191	952	87	14	1053	11	.987	14

OUTFIELD	G	PO	A	Er	TC	DP	PCT.
Coleman	150	305	16	7	328	1	.979
McGee	149	382	11	9	402	2	.978
Van Slyke	142	234	13	1	248	4	.996
Landrum	73	91	2	0	93	1	1.000
L. Smith	28	43	1	0	44	1	1.000
Braun	14	14	1	0	15	0	1.000
Harper	13	8	0	0	8	0	1.000
Clark	12	12	0	0	12	0	1.000
Ford	4	3	0	1	4	0	.750
Jorgensen	2	0	0	0	0	0	.000
Cedeño	2	0	0	0	0	0	.000
TEAM:	589	1092	44	18	1154	9	.984
AVG:	569	1036	34	23	1093	6	.979

COMPLETE PITCHERS RECORDS

Pitcher	W	L	Pct	ERA	G	GS	CG	GF	SHO	SV	IP	H	TBF	R	ER	HR	SH	SF	HB	BB	IB	SO	WP	BK	Appr Value
							Starters (One-half of Game Appearances)																		
*Tudor	21	8	.724	1.93	36	36	14	0	10	0	275.0	209	1062	68	59	14	4	3	5	49	4	169	4	0	16
Andujar	21	12	.636	3.40	38	38	10	0	2	0	269.2	265	1127	113	102	15	11	4	11	82	12	112	2	0	13
Cox	18	9	.667	2.88	35	35	10	0	4	0	241.0	226	989	91	77	19	12	9	3	64	5	131	3	1	13
Kepshire	10	9	.526	4.75	32	29	0	0	0	0	153.1	155	671	89	81	16	5	7	0	71	3	67	6	2	5
Forsch	9	6	.600	3.90	34	19	3	4	1	2	136.0	132	567	63	59	11	5	1	2	47	4	48	4	0	6
							Relievers																		
*Horton	3	2	.600	2.91	49	3	0	10	0	1	89.2	84	382	30	29	5	8	3	3	34	13	59	3	2	4
Lahti	5	2	.714	1.84	52	0	0	31	0	19	68.1	63	279	15	14	3	2	0	0	26	10	41	1	0	7
*Dayley	4	4	.500	2.76	57	0	0	27	0	11	65.1	65	271	24	20	2	4	2	0	18	9	62	4	0	7
Campbell	5	3	.625	3.50	50	0	0	18	0	4	64.1	55	270	32	25	5	5	3	2	21	9	41	1	0	5
Allen	1	4	.200	5.59	23	1	0	13	0	2	29.0	32	135	22	18	3	1	3	1	17	6	10	1	1	0
Worrell	3	0	1.000	2.91	17	0	0	11	0	5	21.2	17	88	7	7	2	0	2	0	7	2	17	2	0	2
Boever	0	0	.000	4.41	13	0	0	5	0	0	16.1	17	69	8	8	3	1	1	0	4	1	20	1	0	0
*Perry	1	0	1.000	0.00	6	0	0	1	0	0	12.1	3	42	0	0	0	0	0	0	3	1	6	1	0	0
*Hassler	0	1	.000	1.80	10	0	0	4	0	0	10.0	9	45	5	2	0	0	1	0	4	0	5	0	0	0
Keough	0	1	.000	4.50	4	1	0	0	0	0	10.0	10	43	5	5	2	0	1	0	4	1	10	0	0	0
Bair	0	0	.000	0.00	2	0	0	1	0	0	2.0	1	8	0	0	0	0	0	0	2	0	0	0	0	0

*left-handed

Tom NIETO, Catcher

	G	AB	Hit	2B	3B	HR	Run	RBI	TBB	SO	SB	CS	Avg
0.79 years		429	119	18	3	4	28	58	39	70	0	3	.277
1985	95	253	57	10	2	0	15	34	26	37	0	2	.225
First Half	59	173	42	5	1	0	11	29	16		0		.243
Second Half	36	80	15	5	1	0	4	5	10		0		.188
Vs. RHP		129	31			0		20					.240
Vs. LHP		125*	26			0		14					.208
Home	48	128	31	6	1	0	6	19			0		.242
Road	47	125	26	4	1	0	9	15			0		.208
Grass	24	61	12	2	1	0	4	8			0		.197
Turf	71	192	45	8	1	0	11	26			0		.234

*Data supplied by team.

Jack CLARK, First Base

	G	AB	Hit	2B	3B	HR	Run	RBI	TBB	SO	SB	CS	Avg
7.22 years		578	160	31	5	26	92	94	80	89	8	7	.278
1985	126	442	124	26	3	22	71	87	83	88	1	4	.281
First Half	85	306	88	21	2	17	47	63	55		1		.288
Second Half	41	136	36	5	1	5	24	24	28		0		.265
Vs. RHP		300	77			13		54					.257
Vs. LHP		142	47			9		33					.331
Home	64	225	52	14	1	8	27	34			0		.231
Road	62	217	72	12	2	14	44	53			1		.332
Grass	34	120	47	4	2	9	28	35			1		.392
Turf	92	322	77	22	1	13	43	52			0		.239

Tommy HERR, Second Base

	G	AB	Hit	2B	3B	HR	Run	RBI	TBB	SO	SB	CS	Avg
4.45 years		585	165	27	6	3	84	65	64	56	24	9	.282
1985	159	596	180	38	3	8	97	110	80	55	31	3	.302
First Half	84	317	106	23	1	3	51	68	37		17		.334
Second Half	75	279	74	15	2	5	46	42	43		14		.265
Vs. RHP		383	120			5		82					.313
Vs. LHP		213	60			3		28					.282
Home	79	277	87	21	2	4	41	55			17		.314
Road	80	319	93	17	1	4	56	55			14		.292
Grass	42	182	52	9	1	3	30	30			6		.286
Turf	117	414	128	29	2	5	67	80			25		.309

Andy VAN SLYKE, Right Field

	G	AB	Hit	2B	3B	HR	Run	RBI	TBB	SO	SB	CS	Avg
2.37 years		462	118	24	6	12	66	60	66	80	35	8	.255
1985	146	424	110	25	6	13	61	55	47	54	34	6	.259
First Half	74	217	58	16	4	6	33	29	26		16		.267
Second Half	72	207	52	9	2	7	28	26	21		18		.251
Vs. RHP		369	104			13		52					.282
Vs. LHP		55	6			0		3					.109
Home	69	193	58	15	4	5	32	23			20		.301
Road	77	231	52	10	2	8	29	32			14		.225
Grass	41	119	28	7	0	5	14	16			7		.235
Turf	105	305	82	18	6	8	47	39			27		.269

Terry PENDLETON, Third Base

	G	AB	Hit	2B	3B	HR	Run	RBI	TBB	SO	SB	CS	Avg
1.33 years		616	164	24	5	5	70	77	40	80	28	13	.267
1985	149	559	134	16	3	5	56	69	37	75	17	12	.240
First Half	72	281	64	8	0	3	31	36	14		9		.228
Second Half	77	278	70	8	3	2	25	33	23		8		.252
Vs. RHP		389	95			3		48					.244
Vs. LHP		170	39			2		21					.229
Home	73	272	62	8	3	3	27	32			9		.228
Road	76	287	72	8	0	2	29	37			8		.251
Grass	40	153	39	4	0	1	17	22			4		.255
Turf	109	406	95	12	3	4	39	47			13		.234

Cesar CEDEÑO, First Base

	G	AB	Hit	2B	3B	HR	Run	RBI	TBB	SO	SB	CS	Avg
12.15 years		595	170	36	5	16	89	80	54	76	45	15	.286
1985	111	296	86	16	1	9	38	49	24	42	14	6	.291
First Half	60	176	43	10	0	3	20	22	16		7		.244
Second Half	51	120	43	6	1	6	18	27	8		7		.358
Vs. RHP		156	42			4		23					.269
Vs. LHP		140	44			5		26					.314
Home	57	138	49	9	1	5	22	29			6		.355
Road	54	158	37	7	0	4	16	20			8		.234
Grass	30	83	25	6	0	2	11	13			4		.301
Turf	81	213	61	10	1	7	27	36			10		.286

Ozzie SMITH, Shortstop

	G	AB	Hit	2B	3B	HR	Run	RBI	TBB	SO	SB	CS	Avg
7.19 years		588	143	22	5	2	72	45	62	39	38	10	.243
1985	158	537	148	22	3	6	70	54	65	27	31	8	.276
First Half	85	290	82	13	2	4	37	24	27		11		.283
Second Half	73	247	66	9	1	2	33	30	38		20		.267
Vs. RHP		375	99			0		34					.264
Vs. LHP		162	49			6		20					.302
Home	80	258	79	14	2	2	41	26			16		.306
Road	78	279	69	8	1	4	29	28			15		.247
Grass	40	145	36	5	0	1	14	14			6		.248
Turf	118	392	112	17	3	5	56	40			25		.286

Vince COLEMAN, Left Field

	G	AB	Hit	2B	3B	HR	Run	RBI	TBB	SO	SB	CS	Avg
0.93 years		682	182	21	11	1	115	43	54	123	118	27	.267
1985	151	636	170	20	10	1	107	40	50	115	110	25	.267
First Half	74	309	86	11	6	1	64	16	29		63		.278
Second Half	77	327	84	9	4	0	43	24	21		47		.257
Vs. RHP		425	120			1		27					.282
Vs. LHP		211	50			0		13					.237
Home	67	325	96	11	6	1	58	22			59		.295
Road	84	311	74	9	4	0	49	18			51		.238
Grass	38	164	45	5	4	0	25	12			24		.274
Turf	113	472	125	15	6	1	82	28			86		.265

Darrell PORTER, Catcher

	G	AB	Hit	2B	3B	HR	Run	RBI	TBB	SO	SB	CS	Avg
10.06 years		522	129	23	5	17	72	77	85	93	4	4	.247
1985	84	240	53	12	2	10	30	36	41	48	6	1	.221
First Half	21	64	8	1	1	2	6	6	11		0		.125
Second Half	63	176	45	11	1	8	24	30	30		6		.256
Vs. RHP		197	45			9		31					.228
Vs. LHP		43	8			1		5					.186
Home	38	101	25	6	2	4	14	18			4		.248
Road	46	139	28	6	0	6	16	18			2		.201
Grass	27	80	13	5	0	3	7	8			1		.163
Turf	57	160	40	7	2	7	23	28			5		.250

Willie McGEE, Center Field

	G	AB	Hit	2B	3B	HR	Run	RBI	TBB	SO	SB	CS	Avg
3.50 years		630	194	23	13	7	90	75	29	92	46	13	.308
1985	152	612	216	26	18	10	114	82	34	86	56	16	.353
First Half	79	306	104	12	10	3	55	39	17		36		.340
Second Half	73	306	112	14	8	7	59	43	17		20		.366
Vs. RHP		402	143			3		48					.356
Vs. LHP		210	73			7		34					.348
Home	72	283	101	11	7	3	52	32			28		.357
Road	80	329	115	15	11	7	62	50			28		.350
Grass	42	171	58	10	4	3	32	23			12		.339
Turf	110	441	158	16	14	7	82	59			44		.358

JOAQUIN ANDUJAR

	(W–L)	GS	Run	Avg	DP	Avg	SB	Avg
1984	(20-14)	36	158	4.39	33	.92	32	.89
1985	(21-12)	38	186	4.89	48	1.26	36	.95
1976-1985		256	1027	4.01	235	.92	226	.88

	G	IP	W	L	Pct	ER	BB	SO	ERA
1984 Home	19	138.7	8	11	.421	57	35	89	3.70
1985 Home	20	145.7	9	9	.500	55	44	55	3.40
1984 Road	17	122.7	12	3	.800	40	35	58	2.93
1985 Road	18	124.0	12	3	.800	47	38	57	3.41
1984 Grass	9	60.0	6	1	.857	16	20	34	2.40
1985 Grass	11	73.0	8	1	.889	28	23	30	3.45
1984 Turf	27	201.3	14	13	.519	81	50	113	3.62
1985 Turf	27	196.7	13	11	.542	74	59	82	3.39
1985 Total	38	269.7	21	12	.636	102	82	112	3.40

JOHN TUDOR

	(W–L)	GS	Run	Avg	DP	Avg	SB	Avg
1984	(12-11)	32	108	3.38	22	.69	21	.66
1985	(21-8)	36	160	4.44	25	.69	16	.44
1979-1985		162	683	4.22	146	.90	95	.59

	G	IP	W	L	Pct	ER	BB	SO	ERA
1984 Home	14	102.3	6	5	.545	31	27	47	2.73
1985 Home	20	161.3	15	2	.882	25	21	102	1.39
1984 Road	18	109.7	6	6	.500	46	29	70	3.78
1985 Road	16	113.7	6	6	.500	34	28	67	2.69
1984 Grass	9	57.7	4	3	.571	19	14	40	2.97
1985 Grass	8	57.3	3	4	.429	15	11	37	2.35
1984 Turf	23	154.3	8	8	.500	58	42	77	3.38
1985 Turf	28	217.7	18	4	.818	44	38	132	1.82
1985 Total	36	275.0	21	8	.724	59	49	169	1.93

KURT KEPSHIRE

	(W–L)	GS	Run	Avg	DP	Avg	SB	Avg
1984	(6-5)	16	69	4.31	19	1.19	23	1.44
1985	(10-9)	29	142	4.90	36	1.24	28	.97
1984-1985		45	211	4.69	55	1.22	51	1.13

	G	IP	W	L	Pct	ER	BB	SO	ERA
1984 Home	10	56.3	3	2	.600	24	25	29	3.83
1985 Home	16	70.3	6	5	.545	41	33	24	5.25
1984 Road	7	52.7	3	3	.500	16	19	42	2.73
1985 Road	16	83.0	4	4	.500	40	38	43	4.34
1984 Grass	3	16.0	1	1	.500	8	20	37	4.50
1985 Grass	9	52.7	3	0	1.000	18	21	26	3.08
1984 Turf	14	93.0	5	4	.556	32	24	34	3.10
1985 Turf	23	100.7	7	9	.438	63	50	41	5.63
1985 Total	32	153.3	10	9	.526	81	71	67	4.75

DANNY COX

	(W–L)	GS	Run	Avg	DP	Avg	SB	Avg
1984	(9-11)	27	103	3.81	39	1.44	14	.52
1985	(18-9)	35	150	4.29	30	.86	13	.37
1983-1985		74	287	3.88	87	1.18	35	.47

	G	IP	W	L	Pct	ER	BB	SO	ERA
1984 Home	14	76.7	5	6	.455	34	26	35	3.99
1985 Home	19	133.0	10	5	.667	38	28	72	2.57
1984 Road	15	79.7	4	5	.444	36	28	35	4.07
1985 Road	16	108.0	8	4	.667	39	36	59	3.25
1984 Grass	8	34.7	1	4	.200	26	16	10	6.75
1985 Grass	7	46.7	4	2	.667	17	16	23	3.28
1984 Turf	21	121.7	8	7	.533	44	38	60	3.25
1985 Turf	28	194.3	14	7	.667	60	48	108	2.78
1985 Total	35	241.0	18	9	.667	77	64	131	2.88

OTHERS

	(W–L)	GS	Run	Avg	DP	Avg	SB	Avg
Forsch	(9-6)	19	90	4.74	25	1.32	10	.53
Horton	(3-2)	3	13	4.33	2	.67	1	.33
Keough	(0-1)	1	3	3.00	0	0.00	1	1.00
Allen	(1-4)	1	2	2.00	0	0.00	0	0.00

NEW YORK METS

DEAR BILL

Steven Goldleaf
DeWitt, New York

Bill James
Winchester, Kansas

Dear Bill:

With the Mets finishing in second place for two years in a row, despairing thoughts of their '86 prospects filled my mind recently. How have other teams done after finishing second for two straight years?

From 1901–1980, there are 48 instances of a team finishing second two years in a row. Slightly more than half of those teams (25/48) finished first or second in the third year, and most of those (15/25) finished first. So my despair was inappropriate. Met prospects, on this basis, look good for 1986.

Of the teams which declined in the third year, 22% (5/23) have had losing records, but most of those just barely. The only two which lost big in the third year were the 1943 Red Sox and the 1918 Phillies, both war-time teams. But both of those teams were past their prime, whereas the 1985 Mets would appear to be a tad under-prime.

Incidentally, I stopped the study in 1980 to avoid having to figure out who finished second in 1981, but the '84 Royals also won the division after finishing second in 1982 and 1983. And the study also lost a third big flop, as the 1985 Braves, after finishing second in 1983 and 1984, did a collective double-gainer, in full uniform, into a cesspool.

Cheers,
Steven Goldleaf

ON DECK

As an afterward to Mr. Goldleaf's comment, I wanted to note that, during the last four years in which the division champions have not been repeating, as is much commented upon, what has generally happened is that the second-place teams have been moving up. In the American League East, for example:

In 1981 the Yankees won the division with the Brewers finishing second. In 1982 the Brewers won with the Orioles finishing second. In 1983 the Orioles won with the Detroit Tigers in second place. In 1984 the Tigers won and the Blue Jays finished second. In 1985 the Blue Jays won the division.

In the other divisions it has been less regular, but the Phillies in 1983, the Royals in 1984, and the Dodgers in 1983 all finished second in the previous year. A few other teams moved up after just missing second place, such as the 1985 Dodgers, who finished one game away from a second-place tie in 1984. And there is an excellent chance that the two New York teams could join the list in 1986.

RUNS AND WINS

One of the basic principles of sabermetrics is that offense is measured in terms of runs scored. The purpose of an offense, as I write annually, is not to compile a high batting average, not to hit as many home runs as possible, not to steal as many bases as possible, but to score as many runs as possible.

However, like most other things, this turns out not to be an absolute truth. Suppose that two offenses score 16 runs each in four games, but one of the teams scores four runs in each game (4,4,4,4), and the other scores 16 in one shot (16,0,0,0). The two offenses obviously are not equivalent, since the first team would expect to win two of the four games, and the second could not possibly win more than once.

I've always known that this was true, but before now I've never been in a position to do anything about it. But last fall I was sent a fascinating study of run patterns, done by Jeffrey Eby of San Diego. Folks, we are coming to one of those articles that you're going to have to study in order to understand; this isn't one of the easy ones. One feature of Eby's report was each team's record with each number of runs scored and runs allowed. For example, the Mets:

Were shut out eleven times (0–11).

Scored one run in a game 22 times, and lost 16 of those games (6–16).

Scored two runs in a game 23 times, and won ten of those (10–13).

Scored three runs in a game 21 times, and won eleven of those 21 games (11–10).

Won 15 of 23 games in which they scored four runs (15–8).

Won 14 of 15 games in which they scored five runs (14–1).

Won 10 of 13 games in which they scored six runs (10–3).

Won 11 of 13 games in which they scored seven runs (11–2).

Won all four games in which they scored eight runs (4–0), all six games in which they scored nine runs (6–0), three games in which they scored ten runs (3–0), won one game in which they scored eleven (1–0), two in which they scored twelve (2–0), one in which they scored fourteen (1–0), one with fifteen (1–0) and three with sixteen (3–0).

I could play around with this kind of data all summer, but it's hard to know what to select to give you a frame of reference. I guess I could give you the National League totals . . . there were 149 shutouts in the N.L. last year, and obviously all 149 teams which were shut out lost. N.L. teams were 33–202 (.140) when they scored one run (the Mets did much better than that), 79–197 (.286) when they scored two runs (the Mets, again, were much better than that), 119–172 (.409) when they scored three runs (again, the Mets were much better, 11–10), 139–111 (.556) when they scored four runs (again, the Mets were far better than that, winning 65% of the time when they scored four runs), and 146–64 (.695) when they scored five runs (the Mets were a terrific 14–1, best in the league except for the Expos' 15–1, whereas the Braves actually lost most of the time, ten of seventeen games, when they scored five runs).

One thing that this shows, which I've always been curious about, is that each of the first five runs that a team scores in a game has almost equal "win value"—that is, each of the first five runs that a team scores, given the offensive levels in the National League in 1985, has a value of about 14/100 of a win. It's a good approximation of the data to say that a team wins 0% of the time when they are shut out, 14% of the time when they score one run, 28% of the time when they score two runs, 42% of the time when they score three runs, 56% of the time when they score four runs, and 70% of the time when they score five runs. Actually, if you want to get technical, the least valuable run is the third (win value of .123) and the most valuable is the second (.146), but those are probably just random fluctuations, and I wouldn't attribute any significance to them.

This was a surprise to me. My first guess would have been that the most valuable run that a team scored in a game was the first one, the one which would give them a theoretical chance to win.

My second guess would have been that the incremental value of a run increased up to three runs a game, and then declined. In the American League this was sort of true; in the American League the value of the first run was almost zilch, since there were only eleven games in which an American League team scored one run and still won (eleven 1–0 games). The winning percentage of A.L. teams scoring one run was .047, so that would also be the win value of the first run. But after that, runs two through five were of almost equal value, each being worth 15/100 of a run. As in the National League, the value of each run declined sharply after more than five runs had been scored in the game (that is, the twelfth run that a team scores in any game has virtually no value, since teams almost always win when they score eleven anyway). Another thing that this means is that five runs a game is the most efficient number; that is, a team scoring exactly five runs in every game would score 810 runs a year (not an unusual total in the American League). But the team scoring exactly five runs in every game would win more often than a team scoring 810 runs a season in any other distribution or pattern.

Teams which scored six runs were 134–36, .788. The incremental value of the sixth run that a team scores in a game was .093.

Teams which scored seven runs in a game were 112–22, .836. The incremental value of the seventh run was .048 wins.

Teams which scored eight runs were 66–4, .943. After this the data samples are so small that the incremental value calculations become erratic and meaningless; however, it is obvious that the incremental value of each run after eight is very small.

Teams which scored nine runs were 53–7, .883.

Teams which scored ten runs were 35–3, .921.

Teams which scored eleven runs were 19–1, .950.

Teams which scored twelve or more runs in a game were 35–2, a winning percentage of .946.

If you want to, you can also turn these around and use them for pitching standards; that is, since teams which *scored* one run in a game were 33–202, those which *allowed* one run in a game had to be 202–33.

Anyway, this information can be used to evaluate the performance of an offense (or a pitching staff) even more accurately than is reflected in the runs scored and runs allowed category. What this analysis will show is that the Met offense in 1985 was not as good as is reflected in their runs scored total, whereas the Met pitching staff is better than is reflected in theirs. We'll use the Dodgers as a comparison. In 1985, although the two teams are extremely close in both areas, the Mets scored a few more runs than the Dodgers (695–682) and allowed a few less (568–579). Both teams play in similar parks, fair home run parks with runs scored totals reduced by visibility and other factors so that they tend to be pitchers' parks.

But the Met offense, in fact, was not as good as the Dodgers', while the Met pitching and defense was better than the Dodger pitching and defense by a larger margin than is reflected in the eleven-run difference. The Met offense was not as good because they had many more games in which they failed to move up through those first five runs which ordinarily separate victory from defeat. The Mets were shut out more times, 11–6, meaning five extra certain defeats. The Mets were held to just one run more times, 22 to 17. The Dodgers scored five runs in a game, the most efficient number, many more times (25–15).

Conversely, the Mets had more games in which they scored large numbers of superfluous runs. The Dodgers had two games in which they scored 12 or more runs; the Mets had seven. While there are a couple of games in which those big-run explosions paid off (the Mets were the only N.L. team to win two games in which they allowed ten or more runs), those runs still were not equivalent, on a one-to-one basis, to the essential first few runs of the game.

One way to formalize this approach would be to add up the "win expectations" for each game. That is, since teams which score one run will win 14.0% of the time, then for any game in which a team scores exactly one run, we can consider them to have an "offensive winning percentage" for that game of .140. For any game in which the team scores five runs, they have an offensive winning percentage of .695. Their offensive winning percentage for the season is the average of their offensive wining percentages for all the games.

For the Mets in 1985, their offensive winning percentage was .506. For the Dodgers, it was .524.

Offensive winning percentages, as you know, can also be calculated by use of the Pythagorean method, comparing runs scored and runs allowed to the league averages. If calculated in that way, the Mets' offensive winning percentage is .527, and the Dodgers' .518. In other words, the Mets' offensive winning percentage drops by .021 in a game-by-game calculation. Although this is a very small movement relative to the best and worst teams in the league, it is the largest movement for any major league team except the Giants, whose offensive winning percentage improves from .416 to .443.

If the offensive and defensive winning percentages of each major league team are figured in this way and combined, they do predict wins and losses with an accuracy which exceeds that of the pythagorean method—barely. For the 26 teams, the gross error of estimated wins by the Pythagorean method is 82.0 games. By this method, it is 79.7 games. But, to be honest, it's a hundred times more work and 3% more accurate, and that isn't any great bargain. I think it's something which is interesting to do once in awhile, and it could be used to analyze a specific anomaly—that is, a team which wins more often or less often

than one might expect. But I don't think I'm likely to incorporate it as a standard part of the methodology.

Another way to look at an offense is to look not at the number of times that they score each number of runs, but at the number of times that they *win* when they *allow* each number of runs. In other words, one could well say that "the test of an offense is not the frequency with which they score four runs, but the frequency with which they *win* when they allow three runs."

This shows the same thing; although the Mets offense scored more runs than the Dodgers, they were less able to win when allowing a given number of runs. When allowing one run the Mets were 22–6, whereas the Dodgers were 21–1. When allowing two runs, the Mets were 18–7 (.720), but the Dodgers were 19–6 (.760). When allowing three runs, the Mets were 17–7 (.708), whereas the Dodgers were 16–5 (.762). While the Mets did hold the advantage when allowing four or more runs, on balance the edge goes to the Dodger offense, inasmuch as both teams accounted for about 80% of their victories in games in which they allowed three runs or less.

Focusing on the pitchers, we get the opposite picture; the Mets are far better. When the Dodgers scored only one run, the LA pitchers were able to make it stand up only three times (3–14, .176), while the Met pitchers did it six times (6–16, .273). Given two runs, the Dodger pitchers were .333 (10–20), whereas the Mets were .435 (10–13). Although they had a one-game edge when working with three runs (12–9 vs 11–10), the Dodger pitchers didn't approach the Mets' ability to make four or five runs stand up (Dodgers 12–9 and 18–7; Mets 15–8 and 14–1).

To structure this knowledge is somewhat more complicated than with the other option. It requires that we overlay the winning percentages of the team with each level of support and the expected frequencies with which that support is obtained. Let's do the offensive. We can calculate the "expected offensive wins"—we're going to get back to offensive winning percentage again here—in this way: Take the frequency with which the team won the game given each level of runs allowed, and multiply that by the frequency with which an average N.L. team would have provided them with that level of support. Since the Mets had a winning percentage of .786 when they allowed one run, and since an average N.L. team allows one run 12.2% of the time, the Mets expected wins with one run allowed is .122 times .786. Do this for every level of runs allowed, add up the total and you'll have yet another offensive winning percentage.

Just think; Davey Johnson probably understands all this crap. Anyway, if you do this, you do reduce the error of the win projections to almost nothing. The problem with it is that a critic could argue that it introduces a tautology—that is, that if you measure a team's ability to win in terms of the frequency with which they actually do win, then of course your measurements will be accurate. I think that's right; I think it's an invalid method, producing statements which are true by definition (e.g ., the team which wins most often will win the most games).

To return to the earlier analysis, the most important consequence of the work might be in its potential use in strategy analysis. We can show by other methods that if a team steals bases 64% of the time, then they will score fewer runs over the course of a season than if they didn't steal at all. However, it is not *absolutely* true that if you reduce the number of runs you score, you hurt the team; it could be that you would reduce the number of times that you score ten runs rather than eight, but increase the number of times that you score four runs rather than three. One of the criticisms of Tommy Lasorda is that he tends to be a one-run manager—but the sabermetric defense for one-run baseball is that it produces efficient offense, and the Dodgers did have an efficient offense.

By using the methods introduced here, one could study whether first-run strategies tend to produce significantly more efficient offenses. Looking at the issue very quickly, I note that the St. Louis Cardinals' offensive winning percentage does improve from .563 to .570 if figured by the method introduced here, but the California Angels' does not; it is .497 if figured by either method. That's about all the figuring I want to do right now.

COMPLETE BATTING RECORDS

Player	G	AB	R	H	TB	2B	3B	HR	RBI	GW	SH	SF	HB	BB	IB	SO	SB	CS	GI DP	Avg	Slug	OBP	Runs Created	Outs Made	Runs/ 27 Outs	OW%	Appr Value
Carter	149	555	83	156	271	17	1	32	100	18	0	3	6	69	16	46	1	1	18	.281	.488	.365	97	421	6.19	.717	16
*Hernandez	158	593	87	183	255	34	4	10	91	24	0	10	2	77	15	59	3	3	14	.309	.430	.384	100	437	6.18	.716	12
†Backman	145	520	77	142	179	24	5	1	38	3	14	3	1	36	1	72	30	12	3	.273	.344	.320	61	410	4.00	.514	9
†Johnson	126	389	38	94	153	18	4	11	46	8	1	4	0	34	10	78	6	4	6	.242	.393	.300	45	310	3.96	.509	4
Santana	154	529	41	136	160	19	1	1	29	6	4	2	0	29	12	54	1	0	14	.257	.302	.295	45	413	2.94	.364	9
Foster	129	452	57	119	208	24	1	21	77	10	0	4	2	46	5	87	0	1	8	.263	.460	.331	69	346	5.41	.659	7
†Wilson	93	337	56	93	143	16	8	6	26	1	1	1	0	28	6	52	24	9	9	.276	.424	.331	46	264	4.66	.589	5
*Strawberry	111	393	78	109	219	15	4	29	79	8	0	3	1	73	13	96	26	11	9	.277	.557	.389	87	307	7.62	.793	11
*Heep	95	271	26	76	114	17	0	7	42	3	0	6	1	27	1	27	2	2	12	.280	.421	.341	37	215	4.64	.586	4
Knight	90	271	22	59	89	12	0	6	36	2	0	5	1	13	1	32	1	1	17	.218	.328	.252	18	235	2.08	.222	4
*Dykstra	83	236	40	60	78	9	3	1	19	3	4	2	1	30	0	24	15	2	4	.254	.331	.338	30	188	4.34	.553	3
Chapman	62	144	16	25	28	3	0	0	7	1	3	1	2	9	0	15	5	4	2	.174	.194	.231	7	129	1.40	.115	1
Paciorek	46	116	14	33	41	3	1	1	11	1	1	0	1	6	1	14	1	0	2	.284	.353	.325	13	86	4.19	.537	1
Christensen	51	113	10	21	36	4	1	3	13	0	1	0	0	19	1	23	1	2	3	.186	.319	.303	11	98	3.02	.376	1
Gooden	35	93	11	21	26	2	0	1	9	0	9	0	0	5	0	15	0	0	1	.226	.280	.265	7	82	2.46	.285	0
*Hurdle	43	82	7	16	29	4	0	3	7	1	1	0	1	13	3	20	0	1	1	.195	.354	.313	9	69	3.66	.468	1
Darling	42	76	9	13	17	4	0	0	0	0	13	0	0	4	0	25	1	0	0	.171	.224	.213	5	76	1.64	.151	0
*Fernandez	26	52	2	11	13	0	1	0	1	0	7	0	0	0	0	26	0	0	1	.212	.250	.212	3	49	1.55	.137	0
Lynch	31	52	1	4	4	0	0	0	0	0	9	0	0	3	0	30	0	0	1	.077	.077	.127	1	58	0.41	.011	0
*Staub	54	45	2	12	18	3	0	1	8	0	0	0	0	10	3	4	0	0	1	.267	.400	.400	8	34	6.01	.704	1
Reynolds	28	43	4	9	11	2	0	0	1	0	2	0	1	0	0	18	0	0	1	.209	.256	.227	2	37	1.76	.169	0
Gardenhire	26	39	5	7	11	2	1	0	2	0	2	0	0	8	0	11	0	0	2	.179	.282	.319	4	36	2.81	.342	0
Aguilera	22	36	1	10	12	2	0	0	2	0	7	0	0	1	0	5	0	0	1	.278	.333	.297	4	34	2.87	.351	0
McDowell	62	19	1	3	4	1	0	0	1	0	2	0	0	1	0	7	0	0	0	.158	.211	.200	1	18	1.45	.121	0
Bowa	14	19	2	2	3	1	0	0	2	1	1	0	0	2	0	2	0	0	0	.105	.158	.190	1	18	1.10	.074	0
*Blocker	18	15	1	1	1	0	0	0	0	0	0	0	0	1	0	2	0	0	0	.067	.067	.125	0	14	0.30	.006	0
Sisk	42	12	1	0	0	0	0	0	0	0	0	0	0	0	0	7	0	0	0	.000	.000	.000	0	12	0.00	.000	0
Leach	22	12	1	2	3	1	0	0	0	0	1	0	0	1	0	8	0	0	0	.167	.250	.231	1	11	1.99	.206	0
Schiraldi	10	8	0	1	1	0	0	0	0	0	0	0	0	0	0	4	0	0	1	.125	.125	.125	0	8	0.00	.000	0
Beane	8	8	0	2	3	1	0	0	1	0	0	0	0	0	0	3	0	0	0	.250	.375	.250	1	6	3.38	.428	0
Orosco	54	7	0	3	3	0	0	0	0	0	2	0	0	0	0	1	0	0	0	.429	.429	.429	1	6	6.06	.689	0
*Gorman	34	5	0	0	0	0	0	0	0	0	1	0	0	0	0	3	0	0	0	.000	.000	.000	0	6	0.00	.000	0
Berenyi	3	4	1	1	2	1	0	0	0	0	2	0	0	0	0	2	0	0	0	.250	.500	.250	1	5	2.74	.311	0
*Latham	7	3	1	1	1	0	0	0	1	0	1	0	0	1	0	0	0	0	0	.333	.333	.500	1	3	6.41	.712	0
Gardner	9	0	0	0	0	0	0	0	0	0	0	0	0	0	0	0	0	0	0	.000	.000	.000	0	0	0.00	.000	0
*Myers	1	0	0	0	0	0	0	0	0	0	0	0	0	0	0	0	0	0	0	.000	.000	.000	0	0	0.00	.000	0
*Niemann	4	0	0	0	0	0	0	0	0	0	0	0	0	0	0	0	0	0	0	.000	.000	.000	0	0	0.00	.000	0
*Sambito	8	0	0	0	0	0	0	0	0	0	0	0	0	0	0	0	0	0	0	.000	.000	.000	0	0	0.00	.000	0

*left-handed hitter, †switch hitter

DEFENSIVE STATISTICS

FIRST

FIRST	G	PO	A	Er	TC	DP	PCT.
Hernandez	157	1310	139	4	1453	113	.997
Paciorek	8	41	3	0	44	3	1.000
Carter	6	31	3	0	34	2	1.000
Heep	4	28	4	1	33	3	.970
Knight	1	2	1	0	3	0	1.000
TEAM:	176	1412	150	5	1567	121	.997
AVG:	191	1513	114	12	1639	136	.993

SECOND

SECOND	G	PO	A	Er	TC	DP	PCT.
Backman	140	272	370	7	649	76	.989
Chapman	48	70	89	5	164	17	.970
Gardenhire	5	5	5	0	10	0	1.000
Bowa	4	9	7	0	16	2	1.000
Knight	2	2	3	0	5	0	1.000
TEAM:	199	358	474	12	844	95	.986
AVG:	184	384	502	16	901	110	.982

THIRD

THIRD	G	PO	A	Er	TC	DP	PCT.
Johnson	113	67	171	15	253	21	.941
Knight	73	52	109	7	168	5	.958
Gardenhire	2	1	1	0	2	0	1.000
Chapman	1	0	0	0	0	0	.000
TEAM:	189	120	281	22	423	26	.948
AVG:	189	125	341	25	492	29	.948

SHORTSTOP

SHORTSTOP	G	PO	A	Er	TC	DP	PCT.
Santana	153	301	396	25	722	81	.965
Gardenhire	13	15	26	4	45	3	.911
Bowa	9	9	6	2	17	3	.882
Johnson	7	11	19	3	33	6	.909
Backman	1	1	0	0	1	0	1.000
TEAM:	183	337	447	34	818	93	.958
AVG:	185	268	521	30	819	99	.963

CATCHER

CATCHER	G	PO	A	Er	TC	DP	PCT.	PB
Carter	143	956	67	8	1031	11	.992	5
Reynolds	25	86	9	1	96	2	.990	1
Hurdle	17	79	6	0	85	0	1.000	5
TEAM:	185	1121	82	9	1212	13	.993	11
AVG:	191	952	87	14	1053	11	.987	14

OUTFIELD

OUTFIELD	G	PO	A	Er	TC	DP	PCT.
Foster	123	198	7	5	210	2	.976
Strawberry	110	211	5	2	218	2	.991
Wilson	83	216	0	8	224	0	.964
Heep	78	126	1	3	130	0	.977
Dykstra	74	165	6	1	172	2	.994
Christensen	38	41	2	2	45	0	.956
Paciorek	29	35	0	0	35	0	1.000
Hurdle	10	10	1	1	12	0	.917
Blocker	5	4	0	0	4	0	1.000
Beane	2	1	0	0	1	0	1.000
Carter	1	0	0	0	0	0	.000
Johnson	1	0	0	0	0	0	.000
Staub	1	1	0	0	1	0	1.000
TEAM:	555	1008	22	22	1052	6	.979
AVG:	569	1036	34	23	1093	6	.979

COMPLETE PITCHERS RECORDS

Pitcher	W	L	Pct	ERA	G	GS	CG	GF	SHO	SV	IP	H	TBF	R	ER	HR	SH	SF	HB	BB	IB	SO	WP	BK	Appr Value
									Starters (One-half of Game Appearances)																
Gooden	24	4	.857	1.53	35	35	16	0	8	0	276.2	198	1065	51	47	13	6	2	2	69	4	268	6	2	19
Darling	16	6	.727	2.90	36	35	4	1	2	0	248.0	214	1043	93	80	21	13	4	3	114	1	167	7	1	12
Lynch	10	8	.556	3.44	31	29	6	1	1	0	191.0	188	777	76	73	19	9	5	1	27	1	65	0	0	8
*Fernandez	9	9	.500	2.80	26	26	3	0	0	0	170.1	108	685	56	53	14	4	3	2	80	3	180	3	2	6
Aguilera	10	7	.588	3.24	21	19	2	1	0	0	122.1	118	507	49	44	8	7	4	2	37	2	74	5	2	5
Berenyi	1	0	1.000	2.63	3	3	0	0	0	0	13.2	8	58	6	4	0	0	0	1	10	0	13	3	0	0
									Relievers																
McDowell	6	5	.545	2.83	62	2	0	36	0	17	127.1	108	516	43	40	9	6	2	1	37	8	70	6	2	9
*Orosco	8	6	.571	2.73	54	0	0	39	0	17	79.0	66	331	26	24	6	1	1	0	34	7	68	4	0	8
Sisk	4	5	.444	5.30	42	0	0	22	0	2	73.0	86	341	48	43	3	3	0	2	40	2	26	1	1	3
Leach	3	4	.429	2.91	22	4	1	4	1	1	55.2	48	226	19	18	3	5	2	1	14	3	30	0	0	2
*Gorman	4	4	.500	5.13	34	2	0	12	0	0	52.2	56	227	32	30	8	6	1	0	18	2	32	2	2	2
Schiraldi	2	1	.667	8.89	10	4	0	2	0	0	26.1	43	131	27	26	4	0	0	3	11	0	21	2	1	0
*Latham	1	3	.250	3.97	7	3	0	1	0	0	22.2	21	93	10	10	1	1	1	0	7	1	10	1	1	0
Gardner	0	2	.000	5.25	9	0	0	8	0	0	12.0	18	61	14	7	1	4	1	0	8	2	11	1	0	0
*Sambito	0	0	.000	12.66	8	0	0	2	0	0	10.2	21	60	18	15	1	1	1	0	8	0	3	0	0	0
*Niemann	0	0	.000	0.00	4	0	0	0	0	0	4.2	5	18	0	0	0	0	0	0	0	0	2	0	0	0
*Myers	0	0	.000	0.00	1	0	0	1	0	0	2.0	0	7	0	0	0	0	0	0	1	0	2	0	0	0

*left-handed

Gary CARTER, Catcher

	G	AB	Hit	2B	3B	HR	Run	RBI	TBB	SO	SB	CS	Avg
9.61 years		580	158	28	2	26	80	93	64	73	4	3	.273
1985	149	555	156	17	1	32	83	100	69	46	1	1	.281
First Half	81	298	79	9	1	11	37	40	42		1		.265
Second Half	68	257	77	8	0	21	46	60	27		0		.300
Vs. RHP		336	84			19		64					.250
Vs. LHP		219	72			13		36					.329
Home	75	263	70	9	0	12	35	42			0		.266
Road	74	292	86	8	1	20	48	58			1		.295
Grass	106	389	114	11	1	25	60	76			0		.293
Turf	43	166	42	6	0	7	23	24			1		.253

Keith HERNANDEZ, First Base

	G	AB	Hit	2B	3B	HR	Run	RBI	TBB	SO	SB	CS	Avg
9.70 years		571	172	35	6	12	90	84	85	75	10	6	.301
1985	158	593	183	34	4	10	87	91	77	59	3	3	.309
First Half	85	312	87	17	2	7	43	43	50		2		.279
Second Half	73	281	96	17	2	3	44	48	27		1		.342
Vs. RHP		333	101			7		51					.303
Vs. LHP		260	82			3		40					.315
Home	78	285	81	12	1	4	39	44			2		.284
Road	80	308	102	22	3	6	48	47			1		.331
Grass	110	406	115	20	2	7	60	63			3		.283
Turf	48	187	68	14	2	3	27	28			0		.364

Wally BACKMAN, Second Base

	G	AB	Hit	2B	3B	HR	Run	RBI	TBB	SO	SB	CS	Avg
2.77 years		502	138	21	4	2	74	35	57	76	26	11	.275
1985	145	520	142	24	5	1	77	38	36	72	30	12	.273
First Half	71	228	61	6	2	1	28	13	22		12		.268
Second Half	74	292	81	18	3	0	49	25	14		18		.277
Vs. RHP		389	126			1		31					.324
Vs. LHP		131	16			0		7					.122
Home	72	251	65	13	3	0	42	17			13		.259
Road	73	269	77	11	2	1	35	21			17		.286
Grass	103	378	104	18	3	1	59	28			24		.275
Turf	42	142	38	6	2	0	18	10			6		.268

Howard JOHNSON, Third Base

	G	AB	Hit	2B	3B	HR	Run	RBI	TBB	SO	SB	CS	Avg
1.99 years		484	123	19	3	15	58	58	49	93	12	7	.254
1985	126	389	94	18	4	11	38	46	34	78	6	4	.242
First Half	67	205	45	6	1	4	13	18	16		3		.220
Second Half	59	184	49	12	3	7	25	28	18		3		.266
Vs. RHP		312	82			8		40					.263
Vs. LHP		77	12			3		6					.156
Home	62	188	43	7	2	5	21	25			4		.229
Road	64	201	51	11	2	6	17	21			2		.254
Grass	86	264	59	10	4	8	31	32			4		.223
Turf	40	125	35	8	0	3	7	14			2		.280

Rafael SANTANA, Shortstop

	G	AB	Hit	2B	3B	HR	Run	RBI	TBB	SO	SB	CS	Avg
1.43 years		485	126	21	1	1	39	30	28	51	1	3	.260
1985	154	529	136	19	1	1	41	29	29	54	1	0	.257
First Half	84	280	71	9	0	1	22	18	14		1		.254
Second Half	70	249	65	10	1	0	19	11	15		0		.261
Vs. RHP		333	84			1		24					.252
Vs. LHP		196	52			0		5					.265
Home	76	264	62	8	0	0	16	13			1		.235
Road	78	265	74	11	1	1	25	16			0		.279
Grass	107	366	87	12	0	0	22	17			1		.238
Turf	47	163	49	7	1	1	19	12			0		.301

George FOSTER, Left Field

	G	AB	Hit	2B	3B	HR	Run	RBI	TBB	SO	SB	CS	Avg
11.67 years		578	160	26	4	29	82	103	55	116	4	3	.276
1985	129	452	119	24	1	21	57	77	46	87	0	1	.263
First Half	69	244	61	14	0	14	31	46	23		0		.250
Second Half	60	208	58	10	1	7	26	31	23		0		.279
Vs. RHP		264	68			12		41					.258
Vs. LHP		188	51			9		36					.271
Home	67	225	59	12	1	9	29	41			0		.262
Road	62	227	60	12	0	12	28	36			0		.264
Grass	89	308	78	16	1	12	35	51			0		.253
Turf	40	144	41	8	0	9	22	26			0		.285

Mookie WILSON, Center Field

	G	AB	Hit	2B	3B	HR	Run	RBI	TBB	SO	SB	CS	Avg
4.18 years		630	173	26	11	7	93	49	33	102	51	17	.275
1985	93	337	93	16	8	6	56	26	28	52	24	9	.276
First Half	62	223	58	11	4	3	32	17	14		17		.260
Second Half	31	114	35	5	4	3	24	9	14		7		.307
Vs. RHP		188	49			4		13					.261
Vs. LHP		149	44			2		13					.295
Home	45	152	50	7	2	2	29	14			13		.329
Road	48	185	43	9	6	4	27	12			11		.232
Grass	62	216	62	9	2	4	41	18			17		.287
Turf	31	121	31	7	6	2	15	8			7		.256

Darryl STRAWBERRY, Right Field

	G	AB	Hit	2B	3B	HR	Run	RBI	TBB	SO	SB	CS	Avg
2.35 years		569	148	24	6	35	92	107	83	151	31	11	.261
1985	111	393	109	15	4	29	78	79	73	96	26	11	.277
First Half	40	144	33	4	1	8	26	19	29		11		.229
Second Half	71	249	76	11	3	21	52	60	44		15		.305
Vs. RHP		237	69			18		53					.291
Vs. LHP		156	40			11		26					.256
Home	56	188	56	10	1	14	42	45			16		.298
Road	55	205	53	5	3	15	36	34			10		.259
Grass	75	265	81	12	3	19	53	61			22		.306
Turf	36	128	28	3	1	10	25	18			4		.219

Danny HEEP, Outfield

	G	AB	Hit	2B	3B	HR	Run	RBI	TBB	SO	SB	CS	Avg
2.93 years		382	97	22	1	7	41	40	42	49	3	3	.253
1985	95	271	76	17	0	7	26	42	27	27	2	2	.280
First Half	59	186	48	11	0	5	15	28	19		2		.258
Second Half	36	85	28	6	0	2	11	14	8		0		.329
Vs. RHP		222	63			7		31					.284
Vs. LHP		49	13			0		11					.265
Home	42	120	34	5	0	2	8	13			0		.283
Road	53	151	42	12	0	5	18	29			2		.278
Grass	68	192	53	12	0	4	17	25			0		.276
Turf	27	79	23	5	0	3	9	17			2		.291

Ray KNIGHT, Third Base

	G	AB	Hit	2B	3B	HR	Run	RBI	TBB	SO	SB	CS	Avg
6.81 years		511	141	30	3	8	53	62	36	58	2	3	.275
1985	90	271	59	12	0	6	22	36	13	32	1	1	.218
First Half	51	155	32	9	0	3	16	18	8		0		.206
Second Half	39	116	27	3	0	3	6	18	5		1		.233
Vs. RHP		101	15			0		10					.149
Vs. LHP		170	44			6		26					.259
Home	43	127	25	6	0	4	10	23			0		.197
Road	47	144	34	6	0	2	12	13			1		.236
Grass	63	206	44	9	0	6	18	33			1		.214
Turf	27	65	15	3	0	0	4	3			0		.231

Lenny DYKSTRA, Center Field

	G	AB	Hit	2B	3B	HR	Run	RBI	TBB	SO	SB	CS	Avg
0.51 years		461	117	18	6	2	78	37	59	47	29	4	.254
1985	83	236	60	9	3	1	40	19	30	24	15	2	.254
First Half	23	86	22	2	1	1	13	11	11		7		.256
Second Half	60	150	38	7	2	0	27	8	19		8		.253
Vs. RHP		180	45			1		14					.250
Vs. LHP		56	15			0		5					.268
Home	41	109	26	4	1	0	23	8			6		.239
Road	42	127	34	5	2	1	17	11			9		.268
Grass	61	169	41	6	3	0	32	13			11		.243
Turf	22	67	19	3	0	1	8	6			4		.284

DWIGHT GOODEN

	(W–L)	GS	Run	Avg	DP	Avg	SB	Avg
1984	(17-9)	31	115	3.71	12	.39	54	1.74
1985	(24-4)	35	171	4.89	33	.94	25	.71
1984-1985		66	286	4.33	45	.68	79	1.20

	G	IP	W	L	Pct	ER	BB	SO	ERA
1984 Home	16	118.3	12	2	.857	25	41	155	1.90
1985 Home	18	144.0	13	2	.867	24	31	143	1.50
1984 Road	15	99.7	5	7	.417	38	32	121	3.43
1985 Road	17	132.7	11	2	.846	23	38	125	1.56
1984 Grass	23	164.3	15	6	.714	47	58	215	2.57
1985 Grass	26	206.3	18	3	.857	32	47	208	1.40
1984 Turf	8	53.7	2	3	.400	16	15	61	2.68
1985 Turf	9	70.3	6	1	.857	15	22	60	1.92
1985 Total	35	276.7	24	4	.857	47	69	268	1.53

ED LYNCH

	(W–L)	GS	Run	Avg	DP	Avg	SB	Avg
1984	(9-8)	13	46	3.54	17	1.31	3	.23
1985	(10-8)	29	118	4.07	16	.55	12	.41
1980-1985		98	382	3.90	97	.99	40	.41

	G	IP	W	L	Pct	ER	BB	SO	ERA
1984 Home	21	63.3	7	4	.636	31	9	32	4.41
1985 Home	15	103.3	5	4	.556	31	12	38	2.70
1984 Road	19	60.7	2	4	.333	31	15	30	4.60
1985 Road	16	87.7	5	4	.556	42	15	27	4.31
1984 Grass	28	92.7	8	7	.533	48	16	46	4.66
1985 Grass	21	142.0	7	5	.583	45	17	48	2.85
1984 Turf	12	31.3	1	1	.500	14	8	16	4.02
1985 Turf	10	49.0	3	3	.500	28	10	17	5.14
1985 Total	31	191.0	10	8	.556	73	27	65	3.44

RON DARLING

	(W–L)	GS	Run	Avg	DP	Avg	SB	Avg
1984	(12-9)	33	146	4.42	20	.61	26	.79
1985	(16-6)	35	144	4.11	34	.97	26	.74
1983-1985		73	303	4.15	65	.89	59	.81

	G	IP	W	L	Pct	ER	BB	SO	ERA
1984 Home	15	101.7	7	2	.778	34	46	78	3.01
1985 Home	21	148.3	9	5	.643	51	56	107	3.09
1984 Road	18	104.0	5	7	.417	53	58	58	4.59
1985 Road	15	99.7	7	1	.875	29	58	60	2.62
1984 Grass	21	132.0	7	4	.636	55	65	99	3.75
1985 Grass	29	196.7	13	6	.684	67	88	139	3.07
1984 Turf	12	73.7	5	5	.500	32	39	37	3.91
1985 Turf	7	51.3	3	0	1.000	13	26	28	2.28
1985 Total	36	248.0	16	6	.727	80	114	167	2.90

SID FERNANDEZ

	(W–L)	GS	Run	Avg	DP	Avg	SB	Avg
1984	(6-6)	15	66	4.40	14	.93	21	1.40
1985	(9-9)	26	105	4.04	23	.88	31	1.19
1984-1985		41	171	4.17	37	.90	52	1.27

	G	IP	W	L	Pct	ER	BB	SO	ERA
1984 Home	7	40.3	3	3	.500	16	15	30	3.57
1985 Home	11	70.7	5	4	.556	21	34	90	2.67
1984 Road	8	49.7	3	3	.500	19	19	32	3.44
1985 Road	15	99.7	4	5	.444	32	46	90	2.89
1984 Grass	10	57.7	4	5	.444	24	23	40	3.75
1985 Grass	18	115.3	7	5	.583	34	60	127	2.65
1984 Turf	5	32.3	2	1	.667	11	11	22	3.06
1985 Turf	8	55.0	2	4	.333	19	20	53	3.11
1985 Total	26	170.3	9	9	.500	53	80	180	2.80

OTHERS

	(W–L)	GS	Run	Avg	DP	Avg	SB	Avg
Aguilera	(10-7)	19	66	3.47	13	.68	10	.53
Leach	(3-4)	4	32	8.00	4	1.00	5	1.25
Schiraldi	(2-1)	4	19	4.75	3	.75	4	1.00
Berenyi	(1-0)	3	14	4.67	4	1.33	6	2.00
Latham	(1-3)	3	9	3.00	2	.67	1	.33
McDowell	(6-5)	2	7	3.50	5	2.50	0	0.00
Gorman	(4-4)	2	10	5.00	3	1.50	3	1.50

MONTREAL EXPOS

Brett is convinced, as are many other players, that the turf shortens careers. "It's taken its toll," he says. "It's hard out there, and . . . you hurt all over. Playing on grass is like a paid vacation." The Royals' second baseman, Frank White (says) "I think it shortens careers, and if it doesn't do that, it certainly shortens productivity."

Sports Illustrated
August 12, 1985

When artificial turf was hot, back about 1970, one of its selling points was supposed to be that it would help avoid injuries. "A team has a big investment in its players," a rug salesman would argue, "Shouldn't they do everything they can to keep them playing as long as possible?" It comes a generation later, and we find out that it ain't necessarily so; the players of today, or at least some of them, claim that the turf is actually shortening their careers.

Ballplayers, like other people, tend to focus on factors in the outside world which are working against them, while ignoring things outside of their own personal qualities which might be helping them. Pitchers who play in Fenway Park or Wrigley Field have been known to explain carefully that this has an impact on their ERA—but how many times did you ever hear a batting champion attribute his success to playing in Fenway, or an ERA champion expounding upon the virtues of pitching in Dodger Stadium? Artificial turf has negative qualities with respect to career length, but it also has positive qualities, in that it reduces a number of things, like drainage ditches, sudden soft spots and bad hops, which have, at times, been associated with major injuries.

It's an important issue, of course, for if there is a significant negative effect on career length, then teams which have artifical turf, such as Montreal, are carrying a ball and chain. Andre Dawson, three years ago regarded by many as the best player in baseball, has been reduced to half the player he was by aching knees. Larry Parrish, once regarded as a potential superstar, developed a bad back midway through his career. Brett specifically cited knee and lower back trouble among his litany of turf aches and pains.

I designed a study to evaluate the effect of artificial turf on career length. I based the study on the 1973 season, a season which comes at the end of the period of enthusiastic ballpark building, and which has some other advantages for this particular study. For each regular player (other than designated hitters) who played on one of the six artificial-turf teams of that time, I identified the one most similar player who played for a team with a grass field. These selections were made, of course, with the use of individual similarity scores. Since I was studying durability, I modified the system to include a huge penalty for a difference in age, 45 points off for each one year of difference in age, so that in all cases players would be selected who were of about the same age, and also included a 13-point difference for each point of difference in the "position value," so that a shortstop would not ordinarily be matched with an outfielder who had similar batting statistics (unless no infielder was available in the same age range).

This study strongly suggests that if artificial turf has important durability effects, then those effects tend on balance to make careers longer. In other words, it appears to help more than it hurts.

The study yields 48 sets of "matches." In 30 of the 48 cases, the player who played on artificial turf played (or has played) longer in the major leagues than the most similar player who played for a team playing on a grass field.

The 48 players who played on artificial turf have played a total of 45,922 major league games between 1974 and 1985, an average of 957 apiece.

The 48 very similar players who played on grass fields have played a total of 33,174 games, an average of only 691 apiece.

The 1973 totals of the two groups of players, taken as a whole, are extremely similar in every respect—age, games played, hits, home runs, etc. The players on turf teams total 1,313 years of age (average age: 27.35); those on grass fields total 1,316 years (average age: 27.42). These are the group totals:

	G	AB	R	H	2B	3B	HR	RBI	TBB	SO	SB	AVG.
Turf	6574	22973	3072	6177	1037	150	620	2916	2322	3158	441	.269
Grass	6439	22358	2823	6021	908	140	600	2740	2275	3319	360	.269

The turf players have a slugging percentage of .408 and an on-base percentage of .336; the grass players have a slugging percentage of .403 and an on base percentage of .337. I'll translate the totals into per-player averages so they'll make more sense:

	G	AB	R	H	2B	3B	HR	RBI	TBB	SO	SB	AVG.
Turf	137	479	64	129	22	3	13	61	48	66	9	.269
Grass	134	466	59	125	19	3	13	57	47	69	8	.269

The players on turf teams hit quite a few more doubles and struck out a little less, but the differences are very minor. The position spectrum—number of catchers, first basemen, etc.—show no appreciable distinctions.

Since we have these two extraordinarily similar groups of players, then, why did the players who played on turf teams go on to play almost 40% more games in the 1974–1985 period?

It may have been luck; it may have been due to some differences between the two groups of players which we failed to control. I didn't control, for example, the performance of the players in previous years. I didn't control defensive *skills* apart from defensive position. I didn't control career statistics or minor league performance as an indicator of potential. Not all of the players selected as similar are truly similar; sometimes *most similar* doesn't mean *truly similar,* but merely the best you can do. To give you a few examples:

The most similar player to Mike Schmidt (23 years old, 132 games, 18 home runs, 52 RBI, .196) was Mike Jorgensen (24 years old, 138 games, 9 home runs, 47 RBI, .230). Although this comparison is reasonable based on all information which was available at that time, it is not a good comparison, and it is unlikely that the subsequent differences between them (Schmidt has played 1,802 games since, Jorgensen 1,253) result in any part from the fact that Schmidt played for a turf team. Schmidt was a unique player; Jorgensen was just less unlike him than everybody else.

The most similar player to Cookie Rojas (34 years old, 139 games, 6 homers, .276) was Matty Alou (34 years old, 134 games, 2 homers, .295). While their batting stats are similar, it is obvious that the fact that Rojas played in 391 more games, while Alou played in only 48 more, is due to the differences between them (Rojas was a second baseman, Alou an outfielder) and not to the turf/grass distinction.

The most similar player to Lou Brock (.297, 7 homers, 63 RBI, 70 stolen bases) was Tommy Harper (2 years younger, .281, 17 homers, 71 RBI, 54 stolen bases). The most similar player to Pete Rose was Willie Davis. The most similar player to Cesar Cedeño (22 years old, 25 homers, .320) was Dave Roberts (22 years old, 21 homers, .286). Again, obviously, Brock, Rose and Cedeño were unique performers, and the most similar turf players were not really similar enough.

Although there are important *individual* differences, there are no important *collective* differences between the groups of players. The degree to which Cedeño (turf) is faster than Roberts (grass) tends to be offset, in the aggregate, by the degree to which Davis (grass) is faster than Rose (turf). However, such individual variations are still distracting and perhaps damaging to the study.

Suppose, then, that we throw out of the study all cases in which the "similarity" of the players selected scores below 775, which eliminates all of these cases and nine more. While I was at it, I also removed from the study any cases in which a player was traded off of (or onto) turf, so that he did not spend most of the rest of his career on the surface with which he was identified. Does that change the result of the study?

It does, but not much. Now there are 34 matched pairs of players. The player who played on artificial turf played longer in 20 of the 34 cases. The 34 players who played on artificial turf played an average of 941 games in the remainder of their careers (seven are still active). The 34 players who played on grass fields played an average of only 738 games (seven are also still active).

Most of the remaining matchups are excellent, though none are perfect; there are no similarity scores of 1000. A few examples, with the turf player in every case listed first: Greg Luzinski (22 years old, 29 homers, 97 RBI, .285, slow) and Jeff Burroughs (22 years old, 30 homers, 85 RBI, .279, slow); Dave Cash (25-year-old second baseman, 116 games, 2 homers, 31 RBI, .271) and Doug Griffin (26-year-old second baseman, 113 games, 1 homer, 33 RBI, .255); Al Oliver (26-year-old center fielder, 20 homers, 99 RBI, .292) and Bobby Murcer (27-year-old center fielder, 22 homers, 95 RBI, .304); Johnny Bench (25, 104, .253) and Carlton Fisk (26, 71, .246, same age and position); Doug Rader (21, 89, .254) and Graig Nettles (22, 81, .234, same age and position). Actually, Rader is three weeks older than Nettles, and Rader in 1973 won his fourth of five Gold Gloves—while Nettles did not win one until four years later. Amos Otis (26 homers, 93 RBI, .300) was matched with Ken Singleton (23, 103, .302, same age). Turf catcher Bob Boone (10, 61, .261) was matched with grass catcher Ray Fosse (7, 52, .256, same age), and turf catcher Skip Jutze (90 games, .223 average) with grass catcher Johnny Oates (93 games, .248, same age).

In several of those cases, such as Bench, Rader and Otis, there is good reason to think that the artificial turf may have shortened the career of the player who was subjected to it. I am not able to recall any specific injuries to the "grass" group which might not have happened had the player played on artificial turf—yet here we have two very meticulously matched groups of players, and those who played on artificial turf played almost 7000 games more in the remainder of their careers.

If there is an important uncontrolled factor in the study, it might be this: that while we are dealing with 48 players, we are dealing with only six teams (since I didn't use the two who put in turf temporarily) and thus only six organizations, for whom those turf players played. Three of those organizations—the Royals, Phillies and Reds—have had relatively stable personnel over the period in question. I don't really buy it, but one could certainly argue that these organizations' tradition of commitment to their players biases the study in favor of the turf teams, and that the results would be different if the Texas Rangers and Cleveland Indians had artificial turf.

That is certainly possible.

One more note on this, and then I'll close the subject. In the generation of artificial turf, there has been a tremendous upswing in the number of players who are able to remain in the game until they are well up in years. Here, I'll draw up a list of the players (excluding pitchers) who were still playing in 1985 who were born in 1948 or earlier, and a comparative list of players who played in 1970 who were born in 1933 or earlier:

1970	1985
Johnny Roseboro	Darrell Evans
Minnie Mendoza	Johnny Grubb
Tito Francona	Cliff Johnson
Ernie Banks	Buck Martinez
Maury Wills	Toby Harrah
Willie Mays	Rick Miller
Al Spangler	Al Bumbry
Jim Davenport	John Lowenstein
	Hal McRae
	Rod Carew
	Bob Boone
	Reggie Jackson
	Dave Kingman
	Davey Lopes
	Carlton Fisk
	Tom Paciorek
	Bill Stein
	Larry Bowa
	Ron Cey
	Jay Johnstone
	Richie Hebner
	George Foster
	Rusty Staub
	Art Howe
	Steve Braun
	Mike Jorgensen
	Al Oliver
	Pete Rose
	Lee Lacy

1985

Steve Garvey	Bill Russell
Graig Nettles	Steve Yeager
Kurt Bevacqua	Dave Concepcion
Chris Chambliss	Tony Perez
Jose Cruz	

In 1970, at the time that artificial turf was just getting a toe-hold (sorry) in the game, there were eight major league players born in 1933 or earlier. In 1985 there were 38 comparable players—essentially a five-fold increase in the number of older players still active. Whereas there were two 37-year-olds (or older) playing regularly in 1970, there were ten in 1985. Of the 38 players and ten regulars, about half are players who have played most of their careers on artificial turf, and about the same number are playing on turf fields now.

I just thought I would mention it. It seems to me that if, in fact, artificial turf is depressing career length, then it would be powerful strange that, in the era in which artificial turf has become common, career length has shown exponential growth. Of course, there are many factors which have an impact on how long a player remains active, and it is quite possible that there could be one negative factor, or even a powerful negative factor, hidden amongst a complex of positives.

But is also seems to me to be strange that, if artificial turf is reducing career length to any significant degree, it failed to show up in my study.

So I don't think it is. I think that, if anything, artificial turf has reduced injuries in baseball, and tends to make careers longer.

BETTER LIVING WITHOUT CHEMISTRY

The Brett quote at the head of the article is from an article by Ron Fimrite attacking artificial turf with every weapon handy. I should say, to begin with, that a) Fimrite is a terrific writer, and I enjoy his work a great deal, usually, and b) I agree with him completely about the general idea that it would be best if artificial turf would pack up and move to South Yemen. I think, however, that a good cause is best served by the truth, and that in this particular case Fimrite has enlisted in the service of a good king a number of bad soldiers. The article also quoted George Brett as saying that "The turf helped me when I was young and just learning to hit . . . but I'm a different hitter now—a line-drive hitter—and the turf just doesn't make that much difference." In 1984 George Brett hit .314 on the turf in Kansas City and .318 on the turf in other parks—but .242 on grass fields. In 1985 he hit .352 on turf and .306 on grass fields.

On the more substantial disagreement, Fimrite denies that artificial turf has made the game more exciting, and complains about cheap inside-the-park home runs and "a whole generation of mediocre and overrated fielders," whatever that means. At one moment, he complains about a ball that bounces away from Harold Baines, making a "laughable" hit—but in the next, argues that bad hops are a sacred part of the game. "The true hop is a sop to the mediocre, the unimaginative, the unresourceful." Apparently, they are a sacred part of the game only as long as they occur on grass fields, proving again that if you start with the assumption that the world was perfect twenty years ago, one can easily prove any change to be a change for the worse.

I think it is better not to deny that artificial turf has made baseball faster, more aggressive and more exciting. I think it is better not to deny that artificial turf has given us some of the most exciting defensive play that we could ever hope to see. Artificial turf has made fielders confident enough to try some wonderful and innovative things; it's ludicrous to say that "On turf all you have to do is get your glove down." Artificial turf has helped immensely to open up a game that had become slow and methodical; I think we should acknowledge our gratitude for this.

But the fact that it was turf which brought the speed back into the game doesn't mean we have to keep the damn stuff. We can keep the speed in the game by doing a few simple things that ought to be done anyway, like limiting the number of times a pitcher can throw to first base to two (runner goes to second on third unsuccessful try to pick runner off first).

I don't believe George Brett when he says that artificial turf has made careers shorter—but I do believe him, of course, when he says that it hurts his legs, and his ankles, and his back. To me, that's enough. It is not necessary that it shorten his career; it is enough that it makes a game painful, which is meant to be played in a kind of controlled joy. Baseball is not football, which is supposed to hurt. George Brett and Frank White are among my heroes; I don't like to go to the game and see them ache and broil in insufferable heat. I think it is appalling to ask people to play football on artificial turf, but that's another story.

But when I think about artificial turf, I am most struck by this: that it has made so little progress in so much time. You know, I don't think that any successful innovation in baseball history has ever been adopted so slowly. Shin guards, face masks, the hit and run, the spitball . . . they all received intense criticism from the moment of their invention—but within a few years, all were in universal service throughout the game. The players of the dead-ball era had not a good word to say about Babe Ruth's bringing the home run back into baseball—but within eight years, every team in baseball had adapted its offense to the new reality. When lights came in there was intense controversy surrounding them—yet within a few years, every park except one had night ball, and within twenty years fixed lights had worked their way even into small towns in Kansas.

Yet here we are, more than twenty years after Astro-Turf, fifteen years after there seemed to be no doubt that the future of the game lay on artificial fields—and *most* major league teams still do not use it, the fans still have not accepted it, and the companies which pimp for it have long since given up trying to talk the caretakers of the older stadiums into converting. They are on the defensive; John Schuerholz is constantly forced to defend his decision not to convert Royals Stadium into a grass park. I wonder if the human body of baseball has not already rejected this foreign tissue, and if the transplant has not already failed?

What I think is that our values have changed. It's hard to remember this now, but in the sixties women who nursed their own babies were regarded as odd-balls; it was so easy to buy formula, you know. That seems so stupid to us now; we don't think that way anymore. We are so much more suspicious of artificial things than we used to be, so much more protective of things which are natural. We don't buy aero-dynamic shaped toasters anymore. In the fifties and sixties we tore down shrines like Ebbetts Field, Forbes Field and Sportsman's Park with hardly a thought. Artificial turf, it survives from that time like a purple plastic dodo bird.

COMPLETE BATTING RECORDS

Player	G	AB	R	H	TB	2B	3B	HR	RBI	GW	SH	SF	HB	BB	IB	SO	SB	CS	GI DP	Avg	Slug	OBP	Runs Created	Outs Made	Runs/ 27 Outs	OW%	Appr Value
Fitzgerald	108	295	25	61	85	7	1	5	34	6	1	5	2	38	12	55	5	3	8	.207	.288	.297	26	251	2.78	.333	4
*Francona	107	281	19	75	98	15	1	2	31	4	2	0	1	12	4	12	5	5	1	.267	.349	.299	29	214	3.63	.460	3
Law	147	519	75	138	210	30	6	10	52	5	8	6	2	86	0	96	6	5	11	.266	.405	.369	82	411	5.40	.653	11
Wallach	155	569	70	148	256	36	3	22	81	8	0	5	5	38	8	79	9	9	17	.260	.450	.310	73	452	4.35	.549	11
Brooks	156	605	67	163	250	34	7	13	100	13	0	8	5	34	6	79	6	9	20	.269	.413	.310	73	479	3.98	.504	10
†Raines	150	575	115	184	273	30	13	11	41	4	3	3	3	81	13	60	70	9	9	.320	.475	.405	119	425	7.59	.788	14
*Winningham	125	312	30	74	99	6	5	3	21	3	1	4	0	28	3	72	20	9	1	.237	.317	.297	33	168	5.27	.641	4
Dawson	139	529	65	135	235	27	2	23	91	12	1	7	4	29	8	92	13	4	12	.255	.444	.295	67	418	4.35	.549	8
Driessen	91	312	31	78	114	18	0	6	25	5	1	2	2	33	9	29	2	2	8	.250	.365	.324	36	247	3.97	.503	3
†Webster	74	212	32	58	103	8	2	11	30	2	1	1	0	20	3	33	15	9	3	.274	.486	.335	33	168	5.27	.641	4
†Washington	68	193	24	48	68	9	4	1	17	1	0	1	0	15	1	33	6	3	2	.249	.352	.301	21	151	3.74	.473	1
Wohlford	70	125	7	24	34	5	1	1	15	6	1	0	0	16	5	18	0	2	1	.192	.272	.284	10	105	2.50	.288	1
Butera	67	120	11	24	34	1	0	3	12	0	3	1	1	13	1	12	0	0	1	.200	.283	.281	11	101	2.83	.340	1
Dilone	51	84	10	16	20	0	2	0	6	1	0	1	0	6	0	11	7	3	4	.190	.238	.242	4	76	1.51	.127	0
Galarraga	24	75	9	14	21	1	0	2	4	1	0	0	1	3	0	18	1	2	0	.187	.280	.228	5	63	1.96	.198	0
Smith	32	72	6	14	18	1	0	1	4	0	11	0	0	3	0	24	0	0	1	.194	.250	.227	5	70	1.76	.166	0
Nicosia	42	71	4	12	14	2	0	0	1	0	1	0	0	7	0	11	1	0	2	.169	.197	.244	4	62	1.58	.138	0
Gullickson	29	64	2	12	16	4	0	0	6	0	4	0	0	4	0	17	0	0	1	.188	.250	.188	3	57	1.39	.110	0
†Shines	47	50	6	6	6	0	0	0	3	1	0	0	0	4	0	9	0	1	2	.120	.120	.185	1	47	0.52	.017	0
*Hesketh	26	44	0	4	4	0	0	0	1	0	5	0	0	4	0	30	0	0	1	.091	.091	.167	1	46	0.59	.022	0
Palmer	24	36	1	4	5	1	0	0	0	0	5	0	0	0	0	10	0	0	2	.111	.139	.111	0	39	0.26	.004	0
Thompson	34	32	2	9	10	1	0	0	4	2	0	1	0	3	0	7	0	1	1	.281	.313	.333	3	25	3.73	.472	0
*Schatzeder	24	31	4	6	13	1	0	2	5	1	1	0	0	1	0	10	0	0	1	.194	.419	.219	3	27	2.51	.288	0
†Newman	25	29	7	5	6	1	0	0	1	1	0	0	0	3	0	4	2	1	0	.172	.207	.250	2	25	1.85	.180	0
Barnes	19	26	0	4	5	1	0	0	0	0	0	0	0	2	0	1	1	1	1	.154	.192	.154	0	24	0.43	.012	0
Frobel	12	23	3	3	7	1	0	1	4	0	1	0	0	2	0	6	0	0	2	.130	.304	.200	1	23	1.09	.071	0
O'Berry	20	21	2	4	4	0	0	0	0	0	1	0	0	4	0	3	1	0	0	.190	.190	.320	2	18	2.81	.336	0
Youmans	14	19	1	1	1	0	0	0	0	0	3	0	0	3	0	10	0	0	0	.053	.053	.182	1	21	0.69	.029	0
Manrique	9	13	5	4	10	1	1	1	1	0	0	0	0	1	0	3	0	0	0	.308	.769	.357	4	9	10.99	.886	0
Yost	5	11	1	2	2	0	0	0	0	0	0	0	0	0	0	2	0	0	0	.182	.182	.182	0	9	1.09	.071	0
Burke	78	10	0	1	1	0	0	0	0	0	0	0	0	1	0	5	0	0	0	.100	.100	.182	0	9	0.69	.030	0
Laskey	11	7	1	1	1	0	0	0	1	0	3	0	0	0	0	4	0	0	0	.143	.143	.143	0	9	0.77	.037	0
Reardon	63	7	0	2	2	0	0	0	1	0	2	0	0	0	0	4	0	0	0	.286	.286	.286	1	7	2.61	.304	0
Flynn	9	6	0	1	1	0	0	0	0	0	0	0	0	0	0	0	0	0	0	.167	.167	.167	0	5	0.90	.050	0
*Johnson	3	5	0	0	0	0	0	0	0	0	0	0	0	0	0	3	0	0	0	.000	.000	.000	0	5	0.00	.000	0
St. Claire	42	5	1	1	1	0	0	0	0	0	1	0	0	2	0	3	0	0	0	.200	.200	.429	1	5	4.13	.524	0
*Lucas	49	5	0	0	0	0	0	0	0	0	0	0	0	0	0	4	0	0	0	.000	.000	.000	0	5	0.00	.000	0
*Dopson	4	4	0	0	0	0	0	0	0	0	0	0	0	2	0	3	0	0	0	.000	.000	.333	0	4	1.17	.076	0
Roberge	42	1	0	0	0	0	0	0	0	0	0	0	0	0	0	1	0	0	0	.000	.000	.000	0	1	0.00	.000	0
*O'Connor	20	0	0	0	0	0	0	0	0	0	0	0	0	0	0	0	0	0	0	.000	.000	.000	0	0	0.00	.000	0

*left-handed hitter, †switch hitter

DEFENSIVE STATISTICS

FIRST

	G	PO	A	Er	TC	DP	PCT.
Driessen	88	804	64	3	871	79	.997
Francona	57	382	35	5	422	32	.988
Galarraga	23	173	22	1	196	14	.995
Law	20	136	12	1	149	10	.993
Shines	5	34	4	2	40	1	.950
Thompson	3	11	1	0	12	1	1.000
Nicosia	2	6	0	0	6	0	1.000
Barnes	1	4	0	0	4	0	1.000
TEAM:	199	1550	138	12	1700	137	.993
AVG:	191	1513	114	12	1639	136	.993

SECOND

	G	PO	A	Er	TC	DP	PCT.
Law	126	276	367	10	653	86	.985
Washington	43	70	104	4	178	22	.978
Newman	15	18	33	0	51	6	1.000
Flynn	6	3	2	0	5	0	1.000
Manrique	2	2	4	0	6	0	1.000
TEAM:	192	369	510	14	893	114	.984
AVG:	184	384	502	16	901	110	.982

THIRD

	G	PO	A	Er	TC	DP	PCT.
Wallach	154	148	383	18	549	34	.967
Law	11	8	23	1	32	2	.969
Barnes	4	4	6	0	10	1	1.000
Washington	3	1	1	2	4	0	.500
Francona	1	0	3	0	3	0	1.000
Manrique	1	1	3	0	4	1	1.000
TEAM:	174	162	419	21	602	38	.965
AVG:	189	125	341	25	492	29	.948

SHORTSTOP

	G	PO	A	Er	TC	DP	PCT.
Brooks	155	203	441	28	672	81	.958
Washington	9	5	25	1	31	7	.968
Manrique	2	2	3	0	5	0	1.000
Newman	2	1	3	0	4	1	1.000
Flynn	1	0	0	0	0	0	.000
TEAM:	169	211	472	29	712	89	.959
AVG:	185	268	521	30	819	99	.963

CATCHER

	G	PO	A	Er	TC	DP	PCT.	PB
Fitzgerald	108	542	46	8	596	7	.987	9
Butera	66	227	20	4	251	5	.984	3
Nicosia	23	80	5	1	86	1	.988	0
O'Berry	20	53	6	0	59	2	1.000	2
Yost	5	24	1	1	26	0	.962	2
TEAM:	222	926	78	14	1018	15	.986	16
AVG:	191	952	87	14	1053	11	.987	14

OUTFIELD

	G	PO	A	Er	TC	DP	PCT.
Raines	146	284	8	2	294	4	.993
Dawson	131	248	9	7	264	1	.973
Winningham	116	229	6	4	239	2	.983
Webster	64	133	3	1	137	0	.993
Wohlford	43	58	1	0	59	1	1.000
Francona	28	49	2	1	52	0	.981
Dilone	22	36	1	1	38	0	.974
Frobel	6	12	0	1	13	0	.923
Johnson	3	0	0	0	0	0	.000
Barnes	3	5	0	0	5	0	1.000
Thompson	3	1	1	0	2	0	1.000
Law	1	0	0	0	0	0	.000
TEAM:	566	1055	31	17	1103	7	.985
AVG:	569	1036	34	23	1093	6	.979

COMPLETE PITCHERS RECORDS

Pitcher	W	L	Pct	ERA	G	GS	CG	GF	SHO	SV	IP	H	TBF	R	ER	HR	SH	SF	HB	BB	IB	SO	WP	BK	Appr Value
							Starters (One-half of Game Appearances)																		
Smith	18	5	.783	2.91	32	32	4	0	2	0	222.1	193	890	85	72	12	13	4	1	41	3	127	1	1	11
Gullickson	14	12	.538	3.52	29	29	4	0	1	0	181.1	187	759	78	71	8	12	8	1	47	9	68	1	1	7
*Hesketh	10	5	.667	2.49	25	25	2	0	1	0	155.1	125	618	52	43	10	8	2	0	45	2	113	3	3	7
Palmer	7	10	.412	3.71	24	23	0	0	0	0	135.2	128	588	60	56	5	5	2	3	67	5	106	9	0	3
*Schatzeder	3	5	.375	3.80	24	15	1	2	0	0	104.1	101	431	52	44	13	7	3	0	31	0	64	4	0	2
Youmans	4	3	.571	2.45	14	12	0	2	0	0	77.0	57	331	27	21	3	2	2	1	49	1	54	5	0	2
*Mahler	1	4	.200	3.54	9	7	1	2	1	1	48.1	40	203	22	19	3	2	1	1	24	1	32	3	0	1
Rogers	2	4	.333	5.68	8	7	1	1	0	0	38.0	51	179	25	24	1	2	2	0	20	1	18	0	1	0
Laskey	0	5	.000	9.44	11	7	0	3	0	0	34.1	55	171	36	36	9	2	1	2	14	1	18	1	0	0
Dopson	0	2	.000	11.08	4	3	0	0	0	0	13.0	25	70	17	16	4	0	0	0	4	0	4	2	0	0
							Relievers																		
Burke	9	4	.692	2.39	78	0	0	31	0	8	120.1	86	483	32	32	9	8	3	7	44	14	87	7	0	9
Reardon	2	8	.200	3.18	63	0	0	50	0	41	87.2	68	356	31	31	7	3	1	1	26	4	67	2	0	10
St. Claire	5	3	.625	3.93	42	0	0	14	0	0	68.2	69	294	32	30	3	6	1	1	26	7	25	1	0	3
Roberge	3	3	.500	3.44	42	0	0	15	0	2	68.0	58	280	28	26	5	6	0	2	22	5	34	1	5	4
*Lucas	6	2	.750	3.19	49	0	0	18	0	1	67.2	63	284	29	24	6	7	2	0	24	8	31	5	0	5
*O'Connor	0	2	.000	4.94	20	1	0	7	0	0	23.2	21	106	14	13	1	3	2	0	13	7	16	1	1	0
Grapenthin	0	0	.000	14.14	5	0	0	1	0	0	7.0	13	43	11	11	0	0	1	1	8	2	4	0	0	0
*Glynn	0	0	.000	19.29	3	0	0	1	0	0	2.1	5	16	5	5	0	1	0	0	4	0	2	0	0	0
Butera	0	0	.000	0.00	1	0	0	1	0	0	1.0	0	3	0	0	0	0	0	0	0	0	0	0	0	0
Shines	0	0	.000	0.00	1	0	0	1	0	0	1.0	1	4	0	0	0	0	0	0	0	0	0	0	0	0

*left-handed

Mike FITZGERALD, Catcher

	G	AB	Hit	2B	3B	HR	Run	RBI	TBB	SO	SB	CS	Avg
1.41 years		480	107	16	1	6	33	49	46	94	4	2	.222
1985	108	295	61	7	1	5	25	34	38	55	5	3	.207
First Half	73	208	43	4	0	5	19	23	29		4		.207
Second Half	35	87	18	3	1	0	6	11	9		1		.207
Vs. RHP													
Vs. LHP													
Home	57	163	27	2	1	3	12	14			0		.166
Road	51	132	34	5	0	2	13	20			5		.258
Grass	23	55	16	1	0	2	9	11			3		.291
Turf	85	240	45	6	1	3	16	23			2		.188

Tim WALLACH, Third Base

	G	AB	Hit	2B	3B	HR	Run	RBI	TBB	SO	SB	CS	Avg
4.35 years		586	151	31	3	21	66	77	45	92	4	6	.258
1985	155	569	148	36	3	22	70	81	38	79	9	9	.260
First Half	83	300	83	23	3	7	30	39	24		4		.277
Second Half	72	269	65	13	0	15	40	42	14		5		.242
Vs. RHP													
Vs. LHP													
Home	79	272	70	18	1	12	30	45			2		.257
Road	76	297	78	18	2	10	40	36			7		.263
Grass	41	161	43	11	1	8	24	19			2		.267
Turf	114	408	105	25	2	14	46	62			7		.257

Terry FRANCONA, First Base

	G	AB	Hit	2B	3B	HR	Run	RBI	TBB	SO	SB	CS	Avg
2.25 years		422	122	21	2	3	37	39	16	27	4	4	.290
1985	107	281	75	15	1	2	19	31	12	12	5	5	.267
First Half	52	113	29	4	1	0	2	13	7		3		.257
Second Half	55	168	46	11	0	2	17	18	5		2		.274
Vs. RHP													
Vs. LHP													
Home	48	122	34	6	1	0	12	13			2		.279
Road	59	159	41	9	0	2	7	18			3		.258
Grass	29	71	18	5	0	2	5	11			1		.254
Turf	78	210	57	10	1	0	14	20			4		.271

Hubie BROOKS, Shortstop

	G	AB	Hit	2B	3B	HR	Run	RBI	TBB	SO	SB	CS	Avg
4.36 years		607	165	27	4	9	60	73	37	93	8	6	.271
1985	156	605	163	34	7	13	67	100	34	79	6	9	.269
First Half	85	331	87	16	2	6	29	48	16		5		.263
Second Half	71	274	76	18	5	7	38	52	18		1		.277
Vs. RHP													
Vs. LHP													
Home	80	308	85	16	5	3	27	64			3		.276
Road	76	297	78	18	2	10	40	36			3		.263
Grass	41	161	43	11	1	8	24	19			2		.267
Turf	115	444	120	23	6	5	43	81			4		.270

Vance LAW, Second Base

	G	AB	Hit	2B	3B	HR	Run	RBI	TBB	SO	SB	CS	Avg
3.78 years		505	128	24	5	10	64	56	55	78	5	3	.254
1985	147	519	138	30	6	10	75	52	86	96	6	5	.266
First Half	82	283	70	17	4	4	40	26	43		4		.247
Second Half	65	236	68	13	2	6	35	26	43		2		.288
Vs. RHP													
Vs. LHP													
Home	75	247	65	17	2	5	31	26			2		.263
Road	72	272	73	13	4	5	44	26			4		.268
Grass	36	137	35	6	1	5	20	17			3		.255
Turf	111	382	103	24	5	5	55	35			3		.270

Tim RAINES, Left Field

	G	AB	Hit	2B	3B	HR	Run	RBI	TBB	SO	SB	CS	Avg
4.51 years		619	185	32	10	9	114	56	87	70	87	13	.299
1985	150	575	184	30	13	11	115	41	81	60	70	9	.320
First Half	82	319	94	12	8	4	60	18	33		28		.295
Second Half	68	256	90	18	5	7	55	23	48		42		.352
Vs. RHP		397	135	25	10	5		24	60	45			.340
Vs. LHP		178	49	5	3	6		17	21	15			.275
Home	79	280	97	17	11	4	62	18			40		.346
Road	71	295	87	13	2	7	53	23			30		.295
Grass	39	161	49	8	1	5	31	18			9		.304
Turf	111	414	135	22	12	6	84	23			61		.326

Herm WINNINGHAM, Center Field

	G	AB	Hit	2B	3B	HR	Run	RBI	TBB	SO	SB	CS	Avg
0.86 years		395	99	8	7	3	41	30	34	92	26	12	.251
1985	125	312	74	6	5	3	30	21	28	72	20	9	.237
First Half	60	159	42	2	2	3	19	12	17		12		.264
Second Half	65	153	32	4	3	0	11	9	11		8		.209
Vs. RHP													
Vs. LHP													
Home	66	162	31	1	4	0	16	10			8		.191
Road	59	150	43	5	1	3	14	11			12		.287
Grass	33	87	22	1	1	2	8	5			5		.253
Turf	92	225	52	5	4	1	22	16			15		.231

Andre DAWSON, Right Field

	G	AB	Hit	2B	3B	HR	Run	RBI	TBB	SO	SB	CS	Avg
8.10 years		633	177	32	8	25	94	94	39	101	29	9	.279
1985	139	529	135	27	2	23	65	91	29	92	13	4	.255
First Half	71	267	70	16	0	9	32	41	13		6		.262
Second Half	68	262	65	11	2	14	33	50	16		7		.248
Vs. RHP													
Vs. LHP													
Home	69	253	63	8	1	11	32	40			9		.249
Road	70	276	72	19	1	12	33	51			4		.261
Grass	39	155	44	11	1	8	20	36			3		.284
Turf	100	374	91	16	1	15	45	55			10		.243

Mitch WEBSTER, Center Field

	G	AB	Hit	2B	3B	HR	Run	RBI	TBB	SO	SB	CS	Avg
0.69 years		358	95	15	4	16	63	50	32	60	22	13	.265
1985	74	212	58	8	2	11	32	30	20	33	15	9	.274
First Half	20	73	15	4	1	3	5	5	3		3		.205
Second Half	54	139	43	4	1	8	27	25	17		12		.309
Vs. RHP		124	31	5	1	5		12	16	19			.250
Vs. LHP		88	27	3	1	6		18	4	14			.307
Home	30	85	21	3	2	3	8	12			7		.247
Road	44	127	37	5	0	8	24	18			8		.291
Grass	20	60	20	2	0	4	16	11			4		.333
Turf	54	152	38	6	2	7	16	19			11		.250

U. L. WASHINGTON, Infield

	G	AB	Hit	2B	3B	HR	Run	RBI	TBB	SO	SB	CS	Avg
5.09 years		521	132	20	6	5	67	48	48	74	25	10	.254
1985	68	193	48	9	4	1	24	17	15	33	6	3	.249
First Half	35	114	38	6	4	0	17	14	7		6		.333
Second Half	33	79	10	3	0	1	7	3	8		0		.127
Vs. RHP		115	33	4	3	0		11	9	16			.287
Vs. LHP		78	15	5	1	1		6	6	17			.192
Home	28	79	15	3	0	1	8	7			2		.190
Road	40	114	33	6	4	0	16	10			4		.289
Grass	25	74	23	4	3	0	12	10			2		.311
Turf	43	119	25	5	1	1	12	7			4		.210

BRYN SMITH

	(W–L)	GS	Run	Avg	DP	Avg	SB	Avg
1984	(12-13)	28	103	3.68	23	.82	23	.82
1985	(18-5)	32	174	5.44	32	1.00	28	.88
1979-1985		72	318	4.42	73	1.01	54	.75

	G	IP	W	L	Pct	ER	BB	SO	ERA
1984 Home	15	94.0	4	8	.333	32	28	67	3.06
1985 Home	15	112.3	11	2	.846	29	25	62	2.32
1984 Road	13	85.0	8	5	.615	34	23	34	3.60
1985 Road	17	110.0	7	3	.700	43	16	65	3.52
1984 Grass	7	47.3	4	3	.571	17	12	17	3.23
1985 Grass	12	78.0	6	3	.667	28	13	46	3.23
1984 Turf	21	131.7	8	10	.444	49	39	84	3.35
1985 Turf	20	144.3	12	2	.857	44	28	81	2.74
1985 Total	32	222.3	18	5	.783	72	41	127	2.91

BILL GULLICKSON

	(W–L)	GS	Run	Avg	DP	Avg	SB	Avg
1984	(12-9)	32	132	4.12	25	.78	14	.44
1985	(14-12)	29	103	3.55	26	.90	37	1.28
1980-1985		170	709	4.17	128	.75	130	.76

	G	IP	W	L	Pct	ER	BB	SO	ERA
1984 Home	16	123.0	7	3	.700	43	17	53	3.15
1985 Home	14	98.3	10	2	.833	18	22	40	1.65
1984 Road	16	103.7	5	6	.455	48	20	47	4.17
1985 Road	15	83.0	4	10	.286	53	25	28	5.75
1984 Grass	9	57.3	3	2	.600	25	9	31	3.92
1985 Grass	8	45.0	2	6	.250	29	12	13	5.80
1984 Turf	23	169.3	9	7	.562	66	28	69	3.51
1985 Turf	21	136.3	12	6	.667	42	35	55	2.77
1985 Total	29	181.3	14	12	.538	71	47	68	3.52

JOE HESKETH

	(W–L)	GS	Run	Avg	DP	Avg	SB	Avg
1984	(2-2)	5	19	3.80	6	1.20	3	.60
1985	(10-5)	25	92	3.68	19	.76	16	.64
1984-1985		30	111	3.70	25	.83	19	.63

	G	IP	W	L	Pct	ER	BB	SO	ERA
1984 Home	5	23.3	1	1	.500	5	7	16	1.93
1985 Home	12	76.3	6	2	.750	14	22	63	1.65
1984 Road	6	21.7	1	1	.500	4	8	16	1.66
1985 Road	13	79.0	4	3	.571	29	23	50	3.30
1984 Grass	2	11.7	1	1	.500	2	5	7	1.54
1985 Grass	5	31.0	2	1	.667	11	7	18	3.19
1984 Turf	9	33.3	1	1	.500	7	10	25	1.89
1985 Turf	20	124.3	8	4	.667	32	38	95	2.32
1985 Total	25	155.3	10	5	.667	43	45	113	2.49

DAVE PALMER

	(W–L)	GS	Run	Avg	DP	Avg	SB	Avg
1984	(7-3)	19	73	3.84	14	.74	17	.89
1985	(7-10)	23	77	3.35	27	1.17	33	1.43
1984-1985		86	355	4.13	77	.90	88	1.02

	G	IP	W	L	Pct	ER	BB	SO	ERA
1984 Home	9	48.0	2	1	.667	15	19	34	2.81
1985 Home	15	79.7	4	9	.308	37	40	62	4.18
1984 Road	11	57.3	5	2	.714	30	25	32	4.71
1985 Road	9	56.0	3	1	.750	19	27	44	3.05
1984 Grass	5	28.3	2	0	1.000	10	14	20	3.18
1985 Grass	4	26.7	0	1	0.000	8	16	23	2.70
1984 Turf	15	77.0	5	3	.625	35	30	46	4.09
1985 Turf	20	109.0	7	9	.438	48	51	83	3.96
1985 Total	24	135.7	7	10	.412	56	67	106	3.71

BILL LASKEY

	(W–L)	GS	Run	Avg	DP	Avg	SB	Avg
1984	(9-14)	34	127	3.74	22	.65	33	.97
1985	(5-16)	26	82	3.15	21	.81	29	1.12
1982-1985		116	452	3.90	86	.74	121	1.04

	G	IP	W	L	Pct	ER	BB	SO	ERA
1984 Home	19	107.3	3	9	.250	50	27	36	4.19
1985 Home	13	67.7	2	8	.200	42	21	30	5.59
1984 Road	16	100.3	6	5	.545	50	23	35	4.49
1985 Road	17	80.7	3	8	.273	39	32	30	4.35
1984 Grass	26	153.0	6	11	.353	71	31	54	4.18
1985 Grass	15	79.7	3	7	.300	30	31	30	3.39
1984 Turf	9	54.7	3	3	.500	29	19	17	4.77
1985 Turf	15	68.7	2	9	.182	51	22	30	6.68
1985 Total	30	148.3	5	16	.238	81	53	60	4.91

OTHERS

	(W–L)	GS	Run	Avg	DP	Avg	SB	Avg
Schatzeder	(3-5)	15	56	3.73	19	1.27	18	1.20
Youmans	(4-3)	12	50	4.17	9	.75	27	2.25
Mahler	(1-4)	7	26	3.71	8	1.14	4	.57
Rogers	(2-4)	7	24	3.43	6	.86	10	1.43
Dopson	(0-2)	3	6	2.00	1	.33	1	.33
O'Connor	(0-2)	1	2	2.00	1	1.00	0	0.00

CHICAGO CUBS

BREAKDOWNS FOR THE LAST TEN SEASONS

Won-Lost Record: 734-825, .471 (5th in division, 18th in the majors)
Runs Scored: 6,482 (4th in the division)
Runs Allowed: 6,861 (Most in the division)
Home Runs Hit: 1,115 (3rd in the division)
Home Runs Allowed: 1,168 (Most in the division)

RECORD IN:
April: 83-98, .459 (Worst in the division)
May: 130-134, .492 (4th in the division)
June: 128-133, .490 (3rd best in division)
July: 122-138, .469 (Worst in the division)
August: 142-145, .495 (4th in the division)
September: 120-162, .426 (Worst in the division, second-worst in the majors)
October: 9-15, .375 (Worst in the division)

Won-Lost Record in Road Games: 320-454, .413 (Worst in the division)
Won-Lost Record at Home: 414-371, .527 (5th in the division)
Home Field Advantage: 88½ games (tied with Philadelphia for the largest home-field advantage in the N.L. East)
Runs Scored on the Road: 2,774 (Fewest of any major league team)
Runs Scored at Home: 3,782 (Most in the National League)
Runs Allowed on the Road: 3,246 (2nd-highest in the division)
Runs Allowed at Home: 3,678 (Most in the division)

Home Runs Hit on the Road: 452 (Fewest in the major leagues)
Home Runs Hit at Home: 663 (Second-most in the division)
Home Runs Allowed on the Road: 449 (Fewest in the division)
Home Runs Allowed at Home: 719 (Most in the division)

RECORD FOR LAST THREE SEASONS: 244-240, .504 (Fourth in the division)

ZMINDA

A Chicago fellow by the name of Don Zminda, who I guess is actually a White Sox fan, has a fine analytical mind and a dogged determination to root out the necessary facts, and has done a number of intriguing studies about the Cubs. A few notes from his work, which is published in John Dewan's *Chicago Baseball Report*:

1) It's no surprise, but Zminda documents the Cubs late-season frustrations over a long period of time. From 1969–1984 (except 1981), the Cubs' winning percentage was .499 from opening day through August 31, but .439 in September, a change in performance which has basically no likelihood of resulting from simple chance. The only comparable September movements in baseball have been that the Orioles have improved by .060 in September (from .482 to .642), the Tigers have declined in September by almost as much as the Cubs (from .524 to .466), and the Expos have done extremely well in the month (up from .460 to .511). Going back even further, from 1946 through 1984 the Cubs' winning percentage in other months was .466, as opposed to .438 in September.

Incidentally, the 1985 data was almost the same as the 1969–1984 average. The Cubs played .487 ball through August, .441 in September.

2) From 1969 through 1984 the Cubs played .475 baseball on the road in day games (188–208), but dropped to .425 in night baseball (347–469). No other team in the National League shows any similar decline.

3) Reacting to a couple of comments from Cubs old-timers about having trouble picking up the ball in night games, Zminda actually looked up all the box scores for the Cubs' first games of road trips from 1960 through 1971. He found that Ron Santo, one of those quoted, did indeed have trouble hitting in the first game of a road trip, hitting .245 with comparatively little power in those games. So did Ernie Banks (.220) and Billy Williams (.277. .277 is trouble for Billy Williams). Each player had about 400 at bats in first games of road trips. However, oddly, the Cubs had played fairly well in these games despite the struggles of their big stars.

DEAR BILL

June 1, 1985
Steven Carter
Des Plaines, Illinois

Bill James
Winchester, Ks

Dear Bill:

This is to shed some light regarding your comment . . . that the (1984) Cubs won only three games that they had fallen behind in by three runs or more.

Although it would be very difficult to verify, the reason I believe this happened was Wrigley Field. In 1984, for the first time in (many years) they scheduled 18 games starting at 3:05. The scoring was very minimal in these games after the first four to five innings. Basically it was a five-inning game.

With the normal starting time of 1:20, the shadows start to fall in the last two innings or even earlier, which also tends to shorten a game, making comebacks difficult.

Sincerely,
Steven Carter

Let's see, what can I check here . . . the effect did not repeat in 1985. The Cubs won ten games in 1985 in which they trailed by three or more, second-highest total in the league (the Reds won eleven). The Cubs in 1985 scored 51% of their runs in the first five innings, their opponents 53%; the National League average was 55%. So I guess we'd have to go back to 1984 to figure it out.

DEAR BILL

Al Yellon
Chicago

Bill James
Winchester, Ks

Dear Bill:

Did you notice the Cubs did not play a single double-header in 1985? They were the only team not to play at least two. Is that the first time that has happened since double-headers became common?

The five dumbest reasons why the Cubs didn't repeat in 1985:

1) They fired Milo.

2) On opening day '84, I flung my umbrella over the Wrigley Field Bleacher fence onto the street. This year, I sat somewhere else in the park and couldn't.

3) Leon Durham got a short haircut (the Michael Jordan look).

4) The Cubs were being punished for Harry's Bud Man/Cub Fan commercial.

5) And most important, 15 of us bought season tickets with a playoff seat guaranteed.

Sincerely,
Al Yellon

I like the Bud Man commercial, but I guess I'm the only one. Seattle played no double headers in 1983, and California none in 1982; I don't know how many teams there have been which have done this. Double headers were very common in 19th century baseball, and I would guess have declined regularly throughout this century, probably declining most rapidly in periods of attendance increase.

A LATE NOTE

When the Cubs won their division in 1984, they allowed only 29 home runs in road games (70 in Wrigley Field). The 29 in road games is the lowest total by any major league team since Detroit allowed 29 in road games in 1946.

A year ago I wouldn't have had any way to know this; the comparison is made possible by the publication of the new *Macmillan Encyclopedia*. It does seem clear that teams which play in home run parks usually lead the league in fewest road home runs allowed, as you might expect since these teams would need to collect pitchers who could avoid the home run.

NEWS HEAH!

Two newsletters about the Cubs commenced in 1985, both done by people who are more interested, I think, in furthering fanaticism than producing a profit. One, *The Scoreboard News,* is done by Jerry and Karen Johnson. It has unusually good graphics for a small newsletter, and each issue includes a few articles doing things like picking Cubs All-Star teams of the last 30 years (with letters arguing about the selections), reviewing the current fortunes of the Cubs and their history or looking at the prospects in the Cub farm system, plus a few pages of graphs charting the progress of the race and the accomplishments of the players. They're good people, and if you're a Cub fan you might enjoy the effort.

The other, which will be quoted here at more length, is the Cub version of John and Sue Dewan's *Chicago Baseball Report.* John's effort contains some similar articles on the current Cubs, plus Zminda's reports on his research, all of which are very well written. Reading the last issue of the *Chicago Baseball Report,* I learn:

• Keith Moreland hit .414 in 35 games from September 1 to the end of the season, and drove in 36 runs in those 35 games.

• In those same 35 games, the great Ryne Sandberg scored 27 runs and drove in 27 more.

• And Shawon Dunston hit .328 and scored 28 runs.

The Cubs scored 5.2 runs a game after September 1, but lost during that period because their pitchers were getting hammered. The Cubs allowed only 2.6 runs per game in April, 3.9 in May, 3.5 in June, 4.9 in July, 5.6 in August and 5.4 in September-October. This reminds me that I have never checked to see whether the Cubs late-season failures were of more offensive or defensive origin, something which obviously ought to be done if one were trying to develop a strategy to avoid future collapses.

• Ryne Sandberg hit .370 in the late innings of close games, with a .617 slugging percentage.

• Keith Moreland, who also led the team in batting with runners in scoring position (.335), drove in 21 runs in the late innings of close games, most on the team.

• Jody Davis was just awful in both situations, hitting .159 with runners in scoring position and .114 (9/79) in the late innings of close games. All but one of the nine hits were singles.

• Ray Fontenot limited opposition left-handed hitters to a .174 batting average with almost no power (.058 isolated power), but was murthered by right-handers, who hit .310 and slugged .492 (.182 isolated power) against him. Obviously, Fontenot might have been a more effective pitcher in the days before platooning enabled opposition managers to get 88% right-handed hitters to the plate against him.

• Dennis Eckersley was the most effective Cub pitcher against right-handers, limiting them to a .208 average.

• Rick Sutcliffe picked five runners off base in 1985; Dennis Eckersley three and Ray Fontenot four. Fontenot, Trout and Sanderson were extremely tough to run on; runners were 15/27 against Fontenot, which becomes a ruinous 15/31 if you include the four pickoffs. They were even worse against Trout (7/19) and Sanderson (4/12). On the whole the Cubs were excellent against the running game. If you count their 16 baserunners picked off by pitchers and four picked off by catchers, they caught 87 runners while giving up 131 stolen bases.

Lake, although he can't hit a lick, truly is terrific

against base stealers, limiting opponents to a 41% success rate (62% against Davis).

• Although Thad Bosley didn't play a great deal in the outfield, he showed exceptional range. In left field he played 219 and 2/3 innings, and made 60 plays for a 2.46 range factor; no other Cub left fielder, and they used eight of them, was above 1.94. In 18 innings in center field he had eight putouts, or 4.0 per game, which again is far higher than anyone else on the team, although it's just two games. In 48 innings in right field, he made even more plays than he did in left, 2.63 per nine innings.

• Davey Lopes also played all three positions, and displayed poor range at all three. In 304 innings in left his range factor was 1.69 (per nine innings), almost the lowest on the team. He played 172 innings in center field, and made only 1.99 plays per nine innings there, fewest on the team. In 102 and a third innings in right field, he made only 18 plays, 1.59 per nine innings—again the lowest figure on the team. (In addition to the eight players in left, the Cubs used six players in center and six in right, with Hatcher and Woods also playing all three positions.)

There's also an article that looks interesting comparing Guillen to Dunston, but I'm not going to read it because I don't want to be influenced by it if I do the same comparison. I recommend the *Chicago Baseball Reports* very highly, and John's address again is P.O. Box 46074, Chicago, Illinois 60646.

THE DEVIL'S THEORY OF PARK EFFECTS

I have speculated for several years upon what I call the devil's theory of ballpark effects. The devil's theory of ballpark effects is that *baseball teams tend to develop those characteristics which are least favored by the park in which they play.* Despite their protestations to the contrary, baseball teams tend to evaluate their personnel essentially by their statistical accomplishments, without making adequate adjustments for the illusions in the statistics created by the parks in which they play. Basing personnel judgments upon those illusions, a team will tend to identify as its weakness that which is in reality its strength, and vice versa. Thus a team will tend to ignore its weakness and concentrate on improving what is already it's strong area.

In specifics, a team which plays in a pitcher's park will usually have a good team earned run average, even if their pitching staff is just mediocre. On the other hand, it will be difficult for them to score very many runs, to hit very many home runs or hit for a high team average, even if they have a decent offense. For that reason, that team will usually tend to concentrate on acquiring better hitters, while assuming that their pitching staff is good enough. Thus, in the end, teams which play in great pitchers' parks tend to develop mediocre pitching staffs.

In the same way, a team which plays in Wrigley Field, a great hitter's park, will always score runs, regardless of how good their offense is. For that reason, over a period of years, they will tend not to address the offensive problems, and will tend to develop a mediocre offense. On the other hand, a mediocre pitcher, who might have ERAs of 4.00 to 4.75 in another park, will tend to have ERAs of 4.50 to 5.50 in Wrigley Field, and thus will quickly be identified as inadequate, and quickly replaced. *Park illusions create unequal and misplaced pressures upon teams and players, which in the long run yield results which are precisely opposed to the characteristics of the park.*

Until this year, I have always labelled this as speculation. No more; it is true. The statistics that I have compiled this year, showing runs scored and home runs at home and on the road over a period of years, leave no doubt that the devil's theory of ballparks does operate, and does play a very important role in the shaping of team characteristics. The illustrations of this are abundant and dramatic:

The Chicago Cubs, playing in the best hitter's park in the National League, have developed good pitching staffs but inept offenses. Over the last ten years, the Cubs have scored 3,708 runs in Wrigley Field, more than any other National League team has scored in its home park. Because of this, they have tended to assume that their offense was doing well—and have scored only 2,774 runs when not in their home park, the fewest of any major league team. They have hit 663 home runs at home, which is well above average, but only 452 home runs when they were not in Wrigley Field—again, the fewest of any major league team. Of course, the performance in road games is a much truer measure of the team's nature than is the performance in their own park.

On the other hand, the Cubs pitching staff, while on the road, hasn't been half bad. They have allowed, in those ten years, 3,678 runs in Wrigley Field, more than any other team in the division has allowed in its home park. They have allowed 719 home runs at home, the most of any team in the division. But on the road, they have allowed only 449 home runs, the *fewest* of any team in the division. They have allowed 3,246 runs on the road, which is 1% above the division average (3,216).

The Atlanta Braves, playing in the National League's second-best hitter's park, have shown exactly the same effect. The Braves offense in their home park has been so strong—3,457 runs, 700 home runs—that they have tended to assume that their offense (led by Murphy and Horner) was good enough. The 700 home runs in their home park is the highest total in the National League. But on the road, the Braves offense has been the weakest in the National League except for the Cubs, scoring only 2,884 runs and hitting only 491 home runs.

On the other hand the Braves' pitching staffs, *because they always think that their pitching staff is weak,* have been pretty decent over the last years. When not in Fulton County Stadium, they have allowed only 3,235 runs in ten years—the second-lowest total in their division. In Atlanta, they have allowed 3,727—most in the N.L. They have allowed only 461 home runs on the road, a very low total—but 765 home runs in Atlanta, by far the highest total in the National League.

The Boston Red Sox, playing in the best hitter's park in the American League, have shown the same tendency at a different performance level. The Red Sox, unlike the two N.L. teams which play in hitters' havens, have been a consistently good organization over the ten-year period. However, while fans almost always think of the Red Sox as being a good-hitting team which lacks pitching, their performance in the league's other 13 parks shows that exactly the opposite is true. While the Red Sox have scored far more runs than any other major league team while in their home park and overall, their offense has been very mediocre in road games, 5th in their seven-team division. Granted, it's been a hell of a division. But their *pitchers* have carried the team, allowing only 3,313 runs in road games, the fewest of any American League team.

If you think about this a while, the name "John Tudor" may come to mind.

The Houston Astros, playing in the best pitcher's park in baseball, have developed better offenses than pitching staffs. The Astros, allowing only 280 home runs at home—(the fewest in the division—have allowed 588 at home—the second highest total in their division. Although the effect is not extreme, their road offense has fared better than their road defense.

The San Diego Padres, playing in the second-best pitcher's park in baseball, have developed decent offenses but very poor pitching staffs. Because of the perception that pitchers like Randy Jones, Gaylord Perry, Rollie Fingers and Goose Gossage were heading up outstanding pitching staffs, the Padres have allowed their pitching to be consistently weak over the ten-year period, allowing 3,527 runs and 615 home runs in road games—both figures the highest of any National League team.

The New York Mets, playing in a pitcher's park and consequently inclined to believe that their pitching is good, have allowed more runs in road games than any other team in the division over the ten-year period.

The Oakland A's, playing in an outstanding pitcher's park, have 3,878 runs to score in road games over the last ten years—the most of any American league team.

What it all has to do with is *standards*. We interpret statistical evidence by the relationship to standards. If a hitter hits .290, he's doing alright because he is close to the .300 standard. If a pitcher posts a 3.50 ERA, he's OK because that is better than the league average.

But when parks change performance, they must also change standards—and for many people, this doesn't happen. It would be easy if there was one player that you could focus on, and say here's the man, here's the guy who is actually bad although people think that he is good. It isn't that simple; it is more a matter of everybody on a team not being as good as you think he is. If you look at the Cubs' home/road breakdowns, you've got to see that none of those guys—Moreland, Sandberg, Dernier—are really doing quite what people think they are doing. It is a matter of superstars who are really only stars, stars who are really only solid players, solid players who are really below-average, and fill-in type players who should have been replaced three years ago. You just have to make adjustments, to try to remember that the player who hits .300 with 25 home runs here is really more like a .280 hitter with 20 homers, that the player who hits .290 with 16 homers might really be more equivalent to .270 and 13.

There are a few teams which haven't fallen into the trap. The most prominent example would be the Dodgers. Playing in a pitcher's park, the Dodgers might have tended to think that a pitcher with a 3.80 ERA for them was alright. In fact, they have adjusted their standards in an appropriate fashion, and thus have developed a truly outstanding pitching staff, allowing fewer runs than any other major league team on the road as well as the second-lowest total in their home park. The Phillies, Yankees, and Orioles have also made appropriate adaptations to their parks.

To join that club, the Cubs have to remember one thing. If they finish second in the league in runs scored, they're not going to win the pennant. They have to lead the league in runs scored to have a realistic chance to win the pennant.

COMPLETE BATTING RECORDS

Player	G	AB	R	H	TB	2B	3B	HR	RBI	GW	SH	SF	HP	BB	IB	SO	SB	CS	GI DP	Avg	Slug	OBP	Runs Created	Outs Made	Runs/ 27 Outs	OW%	Appr Value
Davis	142	482	47	112	193	30	0	17	58	8	2	4	0	48	5	83	1	0	14	.232	.400	.300	57	390	3.92	.446	11
*Durham	153	542	58	153	252	32	2	21	75	6	0	1	0	64	24	99	7	6	5	.282	.465	.357	90	401	6.09	.660	12
Sandberg	153	609	113	186	307	31	6	26	83	10	2	4	1	57	5	97	54	11	10	.305	.504	.364	117	450	7.00	.720	17
Cey	145	500	64	116	204	18	2	22	63	4	0	2	4	58	9	106	1	1	10	.232	.408	.316	65	397	4.42	.506	9
Dunston	74	250	65	65	97	12	4	4	18	2	1	2	0	19	3	42	11	3	3	.260	.388	.310	31	194	4.33	.495	4
Matthews	97	298	45	70	121	12	0	13	40	3	0	3	2	64	2	64	2	0	8	.235	.406	.362	47	239	5.33	.599	4
Dernier	121	469	63	119	148	20	3	1	21	3	7	2	3	40	1	44	31	8	7	.254	.316	.315	51	374	3.66	.413	8
Moreland	161	587	74	180	258	30	3	14	106	12	2	9	1	68	7	58	12	3	14	.307	.440	.374	100	435	6.18	.667	12
Lopes	99	275	52	78	122	11	0	11	44	6	1	3	0	46	1	37	47	4	14	.284	.444	.383	52	219	6.44	.715	6
Speier	106	218	16	53	76	11	0	4	24	6	3	2	0	17	0	34	1	3	7	.243	.349	.295	21	180	3.13	.340	3
†Bowa	72	195	13	48	62	6	4	0	13	3	5	1	0	11	2	20	5	1	3	.246	.318	.285	18	157	3.13	.339	2
*Bosley	108	180	25	59	92	6	3	7	27	3	0	2	0	20	1	29	5	1	3	.328	.511	.391	37	127	7.94	.768	5
Hatcher	53	163	24	40	60	12	1	2	10	1	2	2	3	8	0	12	2	4	9	.245	.368	.290	14	140	2.72	.280	1
Hebner	83	120	10	26	37	2	0	3	22	3	0	0	1	7	1	15	0	1	2	.217	.308	.266	9	97	2.62	.265	1
Lake	58	119	5	18	23	2	0	1	11	1	4	1	1	3	1	21	1	0	1	.151	.193	.177	4	109	0.99	.049	1
Woods	81	82	11	20	23	3	0	0	4	0	1	0	0	14	0	18	0	1	2	.244	.280	.354	9	66	3.55	.399	1
Eckersley	26	56	1	7	10	0	0	1	1	0	2	0	0	7	0	25	0	0	0	.125	.179	.222	3	51	1.47	.102	0
*Trout	24	46	2	5	6	1	0	0	2	0	9	0	0	2	0	13	0	0	0	.109	.130	.146	1	50	0.74	.028	0
*Sutcliffe	20	43	4	10	13	0	0	1	3	0	2	1	0	2	0	10	0	0	1	.233	.302	.261	3	37	2.52	.251	0
*Fontenot	38	41	2	2	2	0	0	0	0	0	4	0	0	0	0	18	0	0	1	.049	.049	.049	0	44	0.06	.000	0
Sanderson	19	31	1	2	2	0	0	0	1	0	6	0	1	1	0	17	0	0	0	.065	.065	.121	1	35	0.45	.010	0
Dayett	22	26	1	6	9	0	0	1	4	1	0	0	1	0	0	6	0	0	1	.231	.346	.259	2	21	2.65	.269	0
Ruthven	20	24	1	5	5	0	0	0	1	0	6	0	0	0	0	7	0	1	1	.208	.208	.208	1	27	0.81	.034	0
†Owen	22	19	6	7	7	0	0	0	4	0	0	0	0	1	0	5	1	1	0	.368	.368	.400	3	13	5.66	.627	0
Engel	11	16	1	3	6	0	0	1	4	0	0	0	0	3	0	7	0	0	0	.188	.375	.316	2	13	4.45	.510	0
Botelho	11	14	2	2	2	0	0	0	0	0	0	0	0	1	0	5	0	0	0	.143	.143	.200	0	12	1.02	.052	0
†Walker	21	12	3	1	1	0	0	0	0	0	0	0	0	0	0	5	1	0	0	.083	.083	.083	0	11	0.31	.005	0
Jackson	5	11	0	1	1	0	0	0	0	0	0	0	0	0	0	3	0	0	0	.091	.091	.091	0	10	0.25	.003	0
Patterson	8	10	1	1	1	0	0	0	0	0	0	0	2	1	0	4	0	0	0	.100	.100	.182	0	11	0.87	.038	0
Abrego	6	9	0	0	0	0	0	0	1	0	0	0	0	0	0	2	0	0	0	.000	.000	.000	0	9	0.00	.000	0
Baller	20	8	0	0	0	0	0	0	0	0	1	0	0	0	0	6	0	0	0	.000	.000	.000	0	9	0.00	.000	0
Brusstar	51	7	0	1	1	0	0	0	0	0	0	0	0	0	0	5	0	0	0	.143	.143	.250	0	6	1.42	.108	0
Smith	65	6	0	0	0	0	0	0	0	0	0	0	0	1	0	5	0	0	0	.000	.000	.143	0	6	0.17	.002	0
Frazier	51	6	0	0	0	0	0	0	0	0	0	0	0	0	0	6	0	0	0	.000	.000	.000	0	6	0.00	.000	0
Sorensen	45	6	1	0	0	0	0	0	4	0	0	0	0	1	0	4	0	0	1	.000	.000	.143	0	7	0.00	.000	0
*Gura	5	6	0	0	0	0	0	0	0	0	0	0	0	1	0	4	0	0	0	.000	.000	.143	0	6	0.17	.002	0
Meredith	32	4	0	1	1	0	0	0	0	0	0	0	0	1	0	1	0	0	0	.250	.250	.400	1	3	4.54	.554	0
Gumpert	9	1	0	0	0	0	0	0	0	0	0	0	0	0	0	1	0	0	0	.000	.000	.000	0	1	0.00	.000	0
*Perlman	6	1	0	0	0	0	0	0	0	0	0	0	0	0	0	1	0	0	0	.000	.000	.000	0	1	0.00	.000	0

*left-handed hitter, †switch hitter

DEFENSIVE STATISTICS

FIRST	G	PO	A	Er	TC	DP	PCT.
Durham	151	1421	107	7	1535	121	.995
Hebner	12	108	6	1	115	15	.991
Moreland	12	70	6	3	79	4	.962
TEAM:	175	1599	119	11	1729	140	.994
AVG:	191	1513	114	12	1639	136	.993

SECOND	G	PO	A	Er	TC	DP	PCT.
Sandberg	153	353	500	12	865	99	.986
Speier	13	21	28	2	51	9	.961
Owen	4	1	1	0	2	0	1.000
Walker	2	1	0	0	1	0	1.000
Lopes	1	1	2	0	3	1	1.000
TEAM:	173	377	531	14	922	109	.985
AVG:	184	384	502	16	901	110	.982

THIRD	G	PO	A	Er	TC	DP	PCT.
Cey	140	75	273	21	369	21	.943
Speier	31	5	24	2	31	1	.935
Moreland	11	8	13	4	25	1	.840
Hebner	7	2	18	3	23	0	.870
Owen	7	2	5	1	8	0	.875
Lopes	4	1	2	0	3	0	1.000
TEAM:	200	93	335	31	459	23	.932
AVG:	189	125	341	25	492	29	.948

SHORTSTOP	G	PO	A	Er	TC	DP	PCT.
Dunston	73	144	248	17	409	39	.958
Bowa	66	91	197	9	297	34	.970
Speier	58	61	125	7	193	33	.964
Owen	7	3	8	1	12	2	.917
Sandberg	1	0	1	0	1	0	1.000
TEAM:	205	299	579	34	912	108	.963
AVG:	185	268	521	30	819	99	.963

CATCHER	G	PO	A	Er	TC	DP	PCT.	PB
Davis	138	694	84	8	786	7	.990	14
Lake	55	182	25	1	208	1	.995	3
Moreland	2	2	0	0	2	0	1.000	0
TEAM:	195	878	109	9	996	8	.991	17
AVG:	191	952	87	14	1053	11	.987	14

OUTFIELD	G	PO	A	Er	TC	DP	PCT.
Moreland	148	233	10	6	249	2	.976
Dernier	116	310	4	9	323	1	.972
Matthews	85	119	7	3	129	2	.977
Lopes	79	113	2	1	116	0	.991
Woods	56	42	1	0	43	0	1.000
Bosley	55	84	0	1	85	0	.988
Hatcher	44	77	2	1	80	0	.987
Dayett	10	8	0	0	8	0	1.000
Walker	6	3	0	0	3	0	1.000
Jackson	4	7	0	0	7	0	1.000
Hebner	1	0	0	0	0	0	.000
TEAM:	604	996	26	21	1043	5	.980
AVG:	569	1036	34	23	1093	6	.979

COMPLETE PITCHERS RECORDS

Pitcher	W	L	Pct	ERA	G	GS	CG	GF	SHO	SV	IP	H	TBF	R	ER	HR	SH	SF	HB	BB	IB	SO	WP	BK	Appr Value
							Starters (One-half of Game Appearances)																		
Eckersley	11	7	.611	3.08	25	25	6	0	2	0	169.1	145	664	61	58	15	6	2	3	19	4	117	0	3	7
*Fontenot	6	10	.375	4.36	38	23	0	5	0	0	154.2	177	661	86	75	23	12	2	0	45	4	70	3	2	4
*Trout	9	7	.563	3.39	24	24	3	0	1	0	140.2	142	601	57	53	8	7	5	1	63	7	44	2	1	5
Sutcliffe	8	8	.500	3.18	20	20	6	0	3	0	130.0	119	549	51	46	12	3	4	3	44	3	102	6	0	5
Sanderson	5	6	.455	3.12	19	19	2	0	0	0	121.0	100	480	49	42	13	7	7	0	27	4	80	1	0	3
Ruthven	4	7	.364	4.53	20	15	0	3	0	0	87.1	103	392	49	44	6	5	6	0	37	3	26	0	0	1
*Engel	1	5	.167	5.57	11	8	1	1	0	1	51.2	61	237	36	32	10	5	1	0	26	1	29	2	1	1
Botelho	1	3	.250	5.32	11	7	1	0	0	0	44.0	52	203	27	26	8	4	0	2	23	1	23	2	0	1
*Patterson	3	0	1.000	3.00	8	5	1	0	0	0	39.0	36	157	13	13	2	2	1	0	10	1	17	1	0	1
Abrego	1	1	.500	6.38	6	5	0	0	0	0	24.0	32	109	18	17	3	5	1	0	12	1	13	0	0	0
*Gura	0	3	.000	8.41	5	4	0	0	0	0	20.1	34	102	19	19	4	3	0	1	6	0	7	0	0	0
							Relievers																		
Smith	7	4	.636	3.04	65	0	0	57	0	33	97.2	87	397	35	33	9	3	1	1	32	6	112	4	0	11
Sorensen	3	7	.300	4.26	45	3	0	18	0	0	82.1	86	355	44	39	8	11	2	4	24	10	34	0	2	2
Frazier	7	8	.467	6.39	51	0	0	17	0	2	76.0	88	357	57	54	11	7	1	3	52	9	46	4	2	1
Brusstar	4	3	.571	6.05	51	0	0	20	0	4	74.1	87	346	55	50	8	4	5	3	36	11	34	3	0	2
Baller	2	3	.400	3.46	20	4	0	4	0	1	52.0	52	223	21	20	8	4	1	1	17	7	31	2	0	1
*Meredith	3	2	.600	4.47	32	0	0	8	0	1	46.1	53	209	24	23	3	5	3	1	24	6	23	0	0	3
Beard	0	0	.000	6.39	9	0	0	5	0	0	12.2	16	59	9	9	2	1	0	0	7	2	4	0	0	0
Gumpert	1	0	1.000	3.48	9	0	0	3	0	0	10.1	12	52	7	4	0	0	2	0	7	1	4	0	0	0
Perlman	1	0	1.000	11.42	6	0	0	1	0	0	8.2	10	42	11	11	3	1	1	0	8	2	4	1	0	0

*left-handed

Jody DAVIS, Catcher

	G	AB	Hit	2B	3B	HR	Run	RBI	TBB	SO	SB	CS	Avg
3.88 years		544	139	28	2	20	55	80	48	102	2	3	.255
1985	142	482	112	30	0	17	47	58	48	83	1	0	.232
First Half	71	248	63	15	0	8	24	39	22		0		.254
Second Half	71	234	49	15	0	9	23	19	26		1		.209
Vs. RHP		363	87			13		48					.240
Vs. LHP		119	25			4		10					.210
Home	74	259	66	15	0	10	29	36			0		.255
Road	68	223	46	15	0	7	18	22			1		.206
Grass	104	364	87	21	0	13	38	42			0		.239
Turf	38	118	25	9	0	4	9	16			1		.212

Ron CEY, Third Base

	G	AB	Hit	2B	3B	HR	Run	RBI	TBB	SO	SB	CS	Avg
11.92 years		571	149	25	2	25	77	92	79	95	2	2	.261
1985	145	500	116	18	2	22	64	63	58	106	1	1	.232
First Half	78	266	56	7	1	12	32	27	40		1		.211
Second Half	67	234	60	11	1	10	32	36	18		0		.256
Vs. RHP		376	88			16		50					.234
Vs. LHP		124	28			6		13					.226
Home	71	238	62	6	1	15	37	45			1		.261
Road	74	262	54	12	1	7	27	18			0		.206
Grass	103	355	88	11	1	18	48	50			1		.248
Turf	42	145	28	7	1	4	16	13			0		.193

Leon DURHAM, First Base

	G	AB	Hit	2B	3B	HR	Run	RBI	TBB	SO	SB	CS	Avg
4.45 years		567	161	32	7	22	83	88	70	102	22	11	.284
1985	153	542	153	32	2	21	58	75	64	99	7	6	.282
First Half	84	294	85	18	1	11	33	39	34		4		.289
Second Half	69	248	68	14	1	10	25	36	30		3		.274
Vs. RHP		411	116			17		51					.282
Vs. LHP		131	37			4		24					.282
Home	75	257	85	21	1	15	36	50			6		.331
Road	78	285	68	11	1	6	22	25			1		.239
Grass	108	378	116	26	1	16	42	56			6		.307
Turf	45	164	37	6	1	5	16	19			1		.226

Shawon DUNSTON, Shortstop

	G	AB	Hit	2B	3B	HR	Run	RBI	TBB	SO	SB	CS	Avg
0.46 years		547	142	26	9	9	88	39	42	92	24	7	.260
1985	74	250	65	12	4	4	40	18	19	42	11	3	.260
First Half	23	72	14	4	1	1	9	4	7		5		.194
Second Half	51	178	51	8	3	3	31	14	12		6		.287
Vs. RHP		205	54			3		14					.263
Vs. LHP		45	11			1		4					.244
Home	43	147	44	7	3	3	29	8			8		.299
Road	31	103	21	5	1	1	11	10			3		.204
Grass	50	165	45	8	3	3	30	8			8		.273
Turf	24	85	20	4	1	1	10	10			3		.235

Ryne SANDBERG, Second Base

	G	AB	Hit	2B	3B	HR	Run	RBI	TBB	SO	SB	CS	Avg
3.93 years		642	184	32	9	15	109	69	50	94	39	10	.287
1985	153	609	186	31	6	26	113	83	57	97	54	11	.305
First Half	79	320	93	16	2	14	60	31	28		25		.291
Second Half	74	289	93	15	4	12	53	52	29		29		.322
Vs. RHP		451	144			21		70					.319
Vs. LHP		158	42			5		13					.266
Home	74	293	89	17	3	17	67	41			29		.304
Road	79	316	97	14	3	9	46	42			25		.307
Grass	107	427	136	25	5	23	86	61			36		.319
Turf	46	182	50	6	1	3	27	22			18		.275

Gary MATTHEWS, Left Field

	G	AB	Hit	2B	3B	HR	Run	RBI	TBB	SO	SB	CS	Avg
11.24 years		589	167	27	4	19	91	81	77	92	16	6	.284
1985	97	298	70	12	0	13	45	40	59	64	2	0	.235
First Half	39	119	26	3	0	4	16	14	27		1		.218
Second Half	58	179	44	9	0	9	29	26	32		1		.246
Vs. RHP		217	48			9		31					.221
Vs. LHP		81	22			4		9					.272
Home	43	125	33	6	0	8	23	23			1		.264
Road	54	173	37	6	0	5	22	17			1		.214
Grass	65	195	51	8	0	13	34	34			1		.262
Turf	32	103	19	4	0	0	11	6			1		.184

Bob DERNIER, Center Field

	G	AB	Hit	2B	3B	HR	Run	RBI	TBB	SO	SB	CS	Avg
3.26 years		493	128	20	3	3	79	28	48	60	48	14	.260
1985	121	469	119	20	3	1	63	21	40	44	31	8	.254
First Half	51	196	51	7	2	0	21	10	17		18		.260
Second Half	70	273	68	13	1	1	42	11	23		13		.249
Vs. RHP		351	85			1		11					.242
Vs. LHP		118	34			0		10					.288
Home	59	230	64	12	1	1	34	10			18		.278
Road	62	239	55	8	2	0	29	11			13		.230
Grass	87	345	86	18	1	1	47	17			22		.249
Turf	34	124	33	2	2	0	16	4			9		.266

Keith MORELAND, Right Field

	G	AB	Hit	2B	3B	HR	Run	RBI	TBB	SO	SB	CS	Avg
4.51 years		553	160	25	3	16	64	88	54	68	4	4	.289
1985	161	587	180	30	3	14	74	106	68	58	12	3	.307
First Half	85	302	91	17	1	8	38	55	42		7		.301
Second Half	76	285	89	13	2	6	36	51	26		5		.312
Vs. RHP		457	141			12		88					.309
Vs. LHP		130	39			2		18					.300
Home	81	300	102	16	2	11	47	63			6		.340
Road	80	287	78	14	1	3	27	43			6		.272
Grass	114	412	132	20	2	12	56	75			7		.320
Turf	47	175	48	10	1	2	18	31			5		.274

Thad BOSLEY, Outfield-Pinch Hitter

	G	AB	Hit	2B	3B	HR	Run	RBI	TBB	SO	SB	CS	Avg
3.09 years		375	104	11	3	5	44	36	33	61	13	7	.277
1985	108	180	59	6	3	7	25	27	20	29	5	1	.328
First Half	48	85	23	5	1	2	12	8	10		3		.271
Second Half	60	95	36	1	2	5	13	19	10		2		.379
Vs. RHP		165	54			6		24					.327
Vs. LHP		15	5			1		3					.333
Home	54	97	35	5	0	5	14	18			2		.361
Road	54	83	24	1	3	2	11	9			3		.289
Grass	80	130	42	5	1	6	18	20			3		.323
Turf	28	50	17	1	2	1	7	7			2		.340

Davey LOPES, Outfield

	G	AB	Hit	2B	3B	HR	Run	RBI	TBB	SO	SB	CS	Avg
10.30 years		588	154	21	5	14	94	56	75	79	51	10	.263
1985	99	275	78	11	0	11	52	44	46	37	47	4	.284
First Half	65	182	55	5	0	8	34	30	36		33		.302
Second Half	34	93	23	6	0	3	18	14	10		14		.247
Vs. RHP		178	54			6		27					.303
Vs. LHP		97	24			5		17					.247
Home	50	131	37	6	0	6	28	21			26		.282
Road	49	144	41	5	0	5	24	23			21		.285
Grass	67	180	48	9	0	8	35	31			32		.267
Turf	32	95	30	2	0	3	17	13			15		.316

DENNIS ECKERSLEY

	(W–L)	GS	Run	Avg	DP	Avg	SB	Avg
1984	(14-12)	33	159	4.82	23	.70	48	1.45
1985	(11-7)	25	101	4.04	11	.44	19	.76
1976-1985		303	1314	4.34	208	.69	324	1.07

	G	IP	W	L	Pct	ER	BB	SO	ERA
1984 Home	17	110.7	9	7	.562	48	19	51	3.90
1985 Home	10	70.3	5	2	.714	27	7	64	3.45
1984 Road	16	114.3	5	5	.500	42	17	30	3.31
1985 Road	15	99.0	6	5	.545	31	12	53	2.82
1984 Grass	25	171.7	12	9	.571	71	23	62	3.72
1985 Grass	14	94.3	5	4	.556	34	11	76	3.24
1984 Turf	8	56.3	2	3	.400	19	13	19	3.04
1985 Turf	11	75.0	6	3	.667	24	8	41	2.88
1985 Total	25	169.3	11	7	.611	58	19	117	3.08

STEVE TROUT

	(W–L)	GS	Run	Avg	DP	Avg	SB	Avg
1984	(13-7)	31	159	5.13	37	1.19	24	.77
1985	(9-7)	24	115	4.79	29	1.21	16	.67
1978-1985		156	710	4.55	180	1.15	100	.64

	G	IP	W	L	Pct	ER	BB	SO	ERA
1984 Home	18	105.7	5	5	.500	46	41	49	3.92
1985 Home	13	79.7	6	2	.750	30	38	24	3.39
1984 Road	14	84.3	8	2	.800	26	18	32	2.77
1985 Road	11	61.0	3	5	.375	23	25	20	3.39
1984 Grass	24	145.3	9	6	.600	57	50	66	3.53
1985 Grass	18	106.0	7	4	.636	42	48	29	3.57
1984 Turf	8	44.7	4	1	.800	15	9	15	3.02
1985 Turf	6	34.7	2	3	.400	11	15	15	2.86
1985 Total	24	140.7	9	7	.562	53	63	44	3.39

RAY FONTENOT

	(W–L)	GS	Run	Avg	DP	Avg	SB	Avg
1984	(8-9)	24	102	4.25	38	1.58	16	.67
1985	(6-10)	23	96	4.17	22	.96	21	.91
1983-1985		62	284	4.58	76	1.23	49	.79

	G	IP	W	L	Pct	ER	BB	SO	ERA
1984 Home	15	82.0	4	5	.444	27	28	40	2.96
1985 Home	22	90.3	2	6	.250	52	28	37	5.18
1984 Road	20	87.3	4	4	.500	41	30	45	4.23
1985 Road	16	64.3	4	4	.500	23	17	33	3.22
1984 Grass	31	152.0	7	8	.467	60	50	75	3.55
1985 Grass	30	124.3	3	10	.231	66	38	55	4.78
1984 Turf	4	17.3	1	1	.500	8	8	10	4.15
1985 Turf	8	30.3	3	0	1.000	9	7	15	2.67
1985 Total	38	154.7	6	10	.375	75	45	70	4.36

RICK SUTCLIFFE

	(W–L)	GS	Run	Avg	DP	Avg	SB	Avg
1984	(20-6)	35	190	5.43	28	.80	21	.60
1985	(8-8)	20	74	3.70	20	1.00	20	1.00
1976-1985		164	787	4.80	139	.85	141	.86

	G	IP	W	L	Pct	ER	BB	SO	ERA
1984 Home	15	109.0	10	2	.833	41	16	65	3.39
1985 Home	8	55.0	4	2	.667	21	21	37	3.44
1984 Road	20	135.7	10	4	.714	58	23	90	3.85
1985 Road	12	75.0	4	6	.400	25	23	65	3.00
1984 Grass	27	186.0	15	5	.750	75	26	95	3.63
1985 Grass	14	89.7	7	4	.636	31	34	65	3.11
1984 Turf	8	58.7	5	1	.833	24	13	60	3.68
1985 Turf	6	40.3	1	4	.200	15	10	37	3.35
1985 Total	20	130.0	8	8	.500	46	44	102	3.18

OTHERS

	(W–L)	GS	Run	Avg	DP	Avg	SB	Avg
Sanderson	(5-6)	19	83	4.37	13	.68	14	.74
Ruthven	(4-7)	15	51	3.40	21	1.40	14	.93
Engel	(1-5)	8	33	4.12	7	.88	8	1.00
Botelho	(1-3)	7	37	5.29	4	.57	2	.29
Patterson	(3-0)	5	25	5.00	4	.80	5	1.00
Abrego	(1-1)	5	30	6.00	7	1.40	5	1.00
Baller	(2-3)	4	9	2.25	3	.75	3	.75
Gura	(0-3)	4	16	4.00	2	.50	7	1.75
Sorensen	(3-7)	3	16	5.33	2	.67	3	1.00

PHILADELPHIA PHILLIES

BREAKDOWNS FOR THE LAST TEN SEASONS

Won-Lost Record: 861-704, .550 (Best in the division, 5th-best in baseball)
Runs Scored: 6,977 (Most of any National League team)
Runs Allowed: 6,292 (4th-most in the division)
Home Runs Hit: 1,259 (Best in the division)
Home Runs Allowed: 1,057 (2nd-Fewest in the division)

RECORD IN:
April: 93-82, .531 (2nd in the division)
May: 150-114, .568 (Best in the division, 3rd in majors)
June: 147-118, .555 (Best in the division, 3rd in majors)
July: 141-113, .555 (2nd in the division)
August: 152-140, .521 (2nd in the division)
September: 161-126, .561 (Best in the division, 4th in majors)
October: 17-11, .607 (Best in the division, 2nd in majors)

Won-Lost Record in Road Games: 385-395, .494 (Best in the division)
Won-Lost Record at Home: 476-309, .606 (Best in the division, 3rd in baseball)
Home Field Advantage: 88½ games (Tied with Chicago for largest home-field advantage in the division)
Runs Scored on the Road: 3,302 (Most in the division)
Runs Scored at Home: 3,675 (2nd Best in division)
Runs Allowed on the Road: 3,177 (2nd-best [lowest] in division)
Runs Allowed at Home: 3,115 (3rd-best in division)

Home Runs Hit on the Road: 589 (2nd in division)
Home Runs Hit at Home: 670 (Best in the division)
Home Runs Allowed on the Road: 511 (2nd fewest in the division)
Home Runs Allowed at Home: 546 (3rd fewest in the division)

RECORD FOR LAST THREE SEASONS: 246-240, .506 (3rd in the division)

The player who has a secondary average similar to Rickey Henderson's is one of the new Phillies, Gary Redus. You remember I asked you to think about it, in the Yankees' comment? It's Redus. In 1985 he batted just 246 times, but had 40 bases on extra base hits, drew 44 walks and stole 48 bases, a total of 132 secondary bases for a secondary average of .537. His career secondary average is a still-remarkable .429.

You might expect that I would now argue that Redus was, despite his comparatively low batting average, an extremely valuable offensive player, and that the Reds, failing to look at the full spectrum of his offensive contribution, let one of the best offensive players in the league get away from them without ever giving him a chance to play. If you expected that, you're right, because that's exactly what I think. I mean, the man scored 51 runs last year while playing less than half the time. What more does he have to do? Throughout his career he has scored runs at a similar rate.

Sure, there is a difference between doing this half-time and doing it full-time. Maybe Redus will lose his concentration, playing everyday. Granted, the 1985 figures for runs scored and secondary average are slightly polluted because Redus pinch-ran quite a few times, thus giving him a chance to score runs and steal bases without having an at bat. Still, that's a very minor influence; his secondary average would have been at least .500 anyway. If the Phillies do what they say they intend to do—put Redus in left field and let him lead off—he'll score 115 runs.

Incidentally, Redus was 6-for-17 (.353) as a pinch hitter last year, and is now 11-for-31 (.355) lifetime while wearing his pinch-hitter suit.

Two years ago, in the Phillie comment for the *1984 Abstract,* I raised a question about the validity of our common concept of what makes a good artificial-turf team. The issue arose in view of the fact that in the previous season (that woud be 1983, I think) the Phillies had had the *best* record in the National League on artificial turf, but the *worst* record in the league on grass fields. This is an odd occurrence anyway—what would more commonly happen, as happened in 1985, is that the same teams would be strong on either surface—but what made it stranger is the fact that the Phillies were playing a bunch of lamed-up old guys like Joe Morgan, Pete Rose, Gary Matthews and Sixto Lezcano, and didn't look like they should be able to do anything on a fast surface.

And it wasn't just the Phillies. If you looked over the whole league, it looked like all the wrong teams had played well on artificial turf. The power-hitting, error-prone Dodgers had the second-best turf record in the league, and the plodding, brutish Braves were third. In view of this, I suggested that perhaps we should reexamine whether our idea of what makes a good turf team had a solid basis in fact. What do we really know about successful turf teams, anyway? Aren't we just sort of riding along, thinking we know more about it than we really do? I concluded with this paragraph:

Artificial turf sprang onto the scene in our lifetime; there is no traditional, inherited wisdom here for us to be guided by. It is up to our generation, you and me, to figure it out. Apart from discovering the increased value of speed on the turf, I don't think we've done a very good job of it yet.

Well, the gentlemen from the Elias Bureau did not take kindly to this supplication. In their comment on the

Phillies in the *1985 Elias Baseball Analyst,* they cited my article and responded that "we don't care to spend too much time on that issue because, the author's invitation notwithstanding, we think we've built up a pretty accurate profile already. . . . If we are to rethink our attitudes with such regularity, there will be little time to think about anything else."

Well, I guess that puts me in my place. This is, in a nutshell, the difference between the *Abstract* and the *Elias Analyst.* The Elias Bureau sees itself as being a part of the baseball establishment, and as such is likely to defend all of baseball's traditional wisdom. The *Baseball Abstract* is, if not quite anti-establishment, at least determinedly non-establishment. I *like* to reexamine my attitudes; I think it's fun, and occasionally I learn something. The essential work of the *Abstract* is to challenge traditional wisdom about baseball, to try to identify and help to reexamine the basis of our assumptions. The *Elias Analyst,* should it survive over a period of years, would systematically refuse to reexamine those assumptions, but would concentrate instead on building the case in defense of the old-school line of thought. *Of course* clutch hitters exist, they argue. *Of course* defensive statistics are meaningless; everybody knows that. It's a pain in the ass, but what the hell; if I'm going to play Galileo, somebody's got to play the Pope, right?

Anyway, to get back to the issue at hand . . . Elias concluded their comment on the Phillies by pointing out that in 1984 "things were back to normal." The Phillies' record on artificial turf declined dramatically (from 74–46 to 56–64) while their winning percentage on grass fields improved from .381 to almost .600 (16–26 to 25–17).

What they didn't point out was that between 1983 and 1984, the Phillies radically changed their personnel, dumping the old slow guys and bringing in a cartload of speed merchants. Joe Morgan at second base was replaced by Juan Samuel, who stole 72 bases and hit 19 triples. Gary Matthews was dismissed from left field, and the playing time was given first to Glenn Wilson, then to Jeff Stone, who stole 27 bases in 51 games. Von Hayes was promoted to full-time status in center, and moved from 20 stolen bases to 48. Pete Rose was removed from his first-base slot, and replaced by a couple of younger men, one of whom (Corcoran) was reasonably mobile.

So what happened in 1984 was that the Phillies fielded a much younger, faster team, got 18 games worse on artificial turf and 9 games better on grass. If the traditional view of what makes a good turf team is correct, does this make any sense? In truth, the mystery of the 1984 Phillies playing *badly* on turf and *well* on grass fields simply compounds the argument: if the traditional view of what makes a team succeed on artificial turf is valid, this shouldn't happen.

Suppose that we study the issue systematically. The Elias article insists that "We think we've built up a pretty accurate profile already," and summarizes the elements of that profile as "good team speed, high-average line-drive hitters." Well, suppose we state that profile in a statistical image, and in that way define groups of very good and very bad artificial-turf type teams. Then we can check to see how those teams actually performed on artificial turf,

and how they performed on grass fields. We can select the teams by the use of similarity scores.

I defined the ultimate artificial-turf team as one which meets the following standards:
1) a team batting average of .300,
2) a team total of 320 doubles,
3) a team total of 115 triples,
4) a team total of 350 stolen bases,
5) with only 60 runners caught stealing,
6) a team with only 70 double plays grounded into,
7) and only 600 (batting) strikeouts.

The .300 batting average was entered as 1680/5600; the other elements of the comparison were blocked out, so that they were considered neither positively nor negatively—that is, hitting home runs is not to be considered a disadvantage on artificial turf, but hitting lots of home runs does not make you into the kind of team that is usually thought of as doing especially well on artificial turf.

Every major league team since 1977 was compared to this profile of a turf super-team, deriving a "similarity score" for each. The ten teams selected as the most-similar to the turf profile were these:

1985 St. Louis Cardinals
1983 St. Louis Cardinals
1979 St. Louis Cardinals
1979 Pittsburgh Pirates
    We are Fam-i-lee
1984 Toronto Blue Jays
1983 Toronto Blue Jays
1982 Kansas City Royals
1980 Kansas City Royals
1979 Kansas City Royals
1978 Kansas City Royals

These were all good teams; we were selecting the best turf teams, as opposed to selecting average teams with turf-type characteristics, which would have been an alternative. All except the '83 Cardinals had winning records.

At this point, we've got no problems; I think no one will question that those ten teams are exactly the types of teams that we think of as being in their natural element when inhaling the aroma of the plastic. All ten played on artificial turf in their home parks. It's kind of an irritant that we selected six American League teams, while there is more turf in the National League, and that we selected teams from only four organizations; later on in the study I'll make some adjustments for that, but at this point I wanted to follow through on the stated premises of the exercise. I'm certain that anyone, selecting a group of the best turf-type teams by any method (assuming that the traditional image is a valid one) would have to wind up with most of the same bunch.

For those ten teams, I looked up their records on artificial turf and their records on grass fields. I then calculated their expected wins and losses on grass fields, and their expected wins and losses on artificial turf, making adjustments for a) the normal home-park advantage, and b) the calibre of the opponents they faced when playing on grass and turf for road games. I figured this in three different ways, using slightly different assumptions about home-park advantages, etc.

Using the most conservative of the calculations, the ten artificial-turf type teams won seven games *fewer* than could have been expected while playing on artificial turf. That is, they won seven games fewer than could have been expected *if they were not particularly well suited to win on artificial turf*. In other words, the finding that they won no more games than could have been expected would, by itself, have been evidence that they were not particularly good artificial turf teams. I found them to fall seven games below that level.

The normal home-park advantage is about eight games. If these ten teams were especially good turf-type teams, then (since they were playing on turf) at home, one might expect them to have larger-than-average home-park advantages.

They don't.

When they went on the road, one might have expected them to play better on turf than on grass fields.

They didn't.

They had relatively small home-park advantages, and they played better on the road when they were on grass.

Let's look at them case by case:

The 1985 St. Louis Cardinals had a home-park advantage of a normal seven games. But on the road, their record on artificial turf was 20–19. Their record on grass fields was six games better, 27–15.

This was despite the fact that the quality of the opposition on grass fields was better than the opposition which played on turf. The two best opponents in the league were the Mets and Dodgers, both playing on grass. The worst team in the league was the Pirates, which played on turf.

The 1983 Cardinals had a normal home-park advantage (nine games), and similar records on the road on either suface (17–22, 18–24).

The 1979 Pirates, Worlds Champions with Omar Moreno and Dave Parker leading the most successful of Chuck Tanner's aggressive base-running outfits, actually played better on the road (50–31) than on the Three Rivers carpet (48–33). And when they went on the road, they played far better on grass (29–13) than on turf (21–18), although in 1979 the strongest teams in the National League were predominantly turf teams, so that the calibre of the competition was better on road turf.

The 1979 Cardinals, a team which won 86 games for Ken Boyer in Lou Brock's memorable final season, led the National League in doubles, triples and batting average. They, too, played better on the road (44–37) than in Busch Stadium (42–39) and better on road grass (25–17) than road turf (19–20).

The Toronto Blue Jays in 1983 and 1984 had a normal home-park advantage (16 games over the two years) and were 22–14 on road turf, but against generally poor road/turf competition (Seattle, Minnesota, and Kansas City in a down phase. KC was 163–161 over those two years; the others were far worse). On the whole, Toronto's turf record over the two seasons (119–79) is exactly what could have been expected with no special turf advantage for them.

The Kansas City Royals of 1980, a team which lost the World Series by 11 innings, had a home-park advantage of only one game. On the road they were just 6–6 on turf (42–27 on grass), despite the fact that the two turf opponents at the time (Toronto and Seattle) were both awful teams, losing almost 200 games between them.

The Royals of 1979 had a normal home-park advantage (seven games) and were 8–5 on road turf, facing the same two wretched opponents.

The Royals of 1978 and 1982 did, in fact, play very well on artificial turf. Both teams had very large home-field advantages (20 and 22 games). The 1982 team played badly on road turf (7–12 against three losing teams); the 1978 team played as well as expected (8–4) on the road against the two expansion opponents. On the whole, these two teams won ten games more on artificial turf than could have been expected in the absence of a special preference for turf.

But the other 8 teams won 17 fewer turf games (and 17 more grass games) than could have been expected.

Because of the problem mentioned before, I decided to amend the study by including the three National League teams with the highest "Turf Scores" who were not in the original study. This added to the study the Houston Astros of 1980 (the team which beat the Dodgers in a playoff, then played that thrilling championship series with the Phillies), the Pittsburgh Pirates of 1980 (the Family, one year later) and the Philadelphia Phillies of 1979. As before, all three had artificial turf in their home parks.

The three fail to alter the conclusion of the study; they won one game fewer than should have been expected on artificial turf, dropping the 13 teams to −8 on turf (+8 on grass). The 1979 Phillies had a home-field advantage of only two games, plus they were just 16–23 on road turf, 25–17 on grass. The 1980 Astros did have a large home-park advantage (17½ games), but they had a dismal 14–19 record on artificial turf away from Houston. The 1980 Pirates did play well on artificial turf.

What about the teams which were *least* similar to the turf profile? Here the result of the study is different; the ten teams which should have played poorly on artificial turf, did. The names of the teams won't mean as much to you as the names of the best turf-type teams because these were, generally, not good teams. Whereas you may remember almost every regular from the 1979 Pirates, most of you probably wouldn't have much notion who played shortstop for the 1979 Oakland A'S:

1985 Atlanta Braves
1985 San Francisco Giants
1984 Los Angeles Dodgers
1984 Baltimore Orioles
1983 New York Mets
1983 Cincinnati Reds
1983 Seattle Mariners
1982 Texas Rangers
1979 Oakland A's
1979 Atlanta Braves

Although some of these teams had good power and good pitching, they were teams which hit for low averages, didn't hit many doubles or triples or steal many bases. They grounded into lots of double plays. All except one (the 1984 Orioles) had losing records. Eight of the ten played on natural grass in their home parks.

As a group, they had a won/lost record on artificial turf of 189–311 (.378). Even though they were bad teams and (for the most part) on the road in these games, this record is 17 games worse than should have been expected. They did, in fact, play poorly on artificial turf.

The two teams which were at home on artificial turf (the Reds and Mariners) both had poor home-park records, the Mariners having no home-park advantage, and the Reds having a home-park record that was two games worse than their road record.

Three of the teams did play fairly well on artificial turf, but most did not. The worst of them was the Atlanta Braves of 1978, a team which had a respectable record both at home (40–41) and on road grass (20–19), but which was 9–33 on artificial turf. The key features of this team included catcher Biff Pocoroba, center fielder Barry Bonnell and left fielder Jeff Burroughs. Rookie third baseman Bob Horner also hit 23 home runs that year—19 of them in County Stadium in Atlanta.

As to what this all means, I would suggest this: Clearly, the notion that a good artificial turf team is a team with high-average hitters, line-drive power and outstanding team speed is inadequate. Teams such as the 1976–1980 Royals, the 1982–1985 Cardinals, the Pirates of the late seventies and the Blue Jays of today succeed not because they are able to take advantage of the artificial turf, but because they are simply good ballclubs, and they would win anywhere.

We get back to the general theory of ballparks. One of the recurring lessons of sabermetrics is arrived at by this three-step walkway:

1) The way in which people think about baseball players is essentially formed by their statistics;

2) Those statistics are heavily influenced by the park in which the player performs;

3) The image of the park tends to become confused with the image of the player.

Many people continue to think of the Boston Red Sox as a traditional offensive powerhouse which can never come up with the pitching, even though over the last ten years they have allowed fewer runs (when not in Fenway Park) than any other American League team, while their offense (when not in Fenway Park) has been just fair. The park draws out the elements of power, hitting for average, accentuates them and makes them the identity of the team.

In the same way, Busch Stadium creates triples. With the home run rare and players able to run faster because of the turf, it makes more sense to steal bases, and so more bases are stolen. These elements become the identity of the team—but the fact is that it is simply a good team, and would be no matter where it played. If the Blue Jays played in Tiger Stadium in Detroit, how many home runs would they hit? Plenty. The turf creates doubles and triples; it emphasizes these elements in the statistics, and the statistics form the images of the players.

But, the Elias Bureau aside, images are not ideas, and assumptions are not thought. There are so many things that go into making up a ballclub, and they are all altered in one way or another by turf, but what do we really *know* about any of them? What type of *pitcher* does best on artificial turf? Craig Wright has done some work on that, but it's something that's got a long way to go. What about the double play—is it a larger factor or a smaller factor on turf? Are the defensive costs of immobility different? Might it not be that many third basemen who would be considered adequate on grass might be considered inadequate on turf? Does anybody really *know*? What are the key defensive elements of a good turf team?

I think that when we talk about what makes a team successful on artificial turf, we should be thinking about these questions. Another way to approach these questions would be not to ask "Does a team with these characteristics tend to do well on artificial turf?" but "What are the characteristics of those teams which do well on artificial turf?" For now, though, I come back to where I started: it is time for us all to face up to the fact that we simply do not know what it is that makes a team successful on artificial turf.

COMPLETE BATTING RECORDS

Player	G	AB	R	H	TB	2B	3B	HR	RBI	GW	SH	SF	HB	BB	IB	SO	SB	CS	GI DP	Avg	Slug	OBP	Runs Created	Outs Made	Runs/27 Outs	OW%	Appr Value
Virgil	131	426	47	105	184	16	3	19	55	7	1	2	5	49	6	85	0	0	14	.246	.432	.330	59	338	4.75	.569	9
Schmidt	158	549	89	152	292	31	5	33	93	8	0	6	3	87	8	117	1	3	10	.277	.532	.375	113	416	7.30	.757	13
Samuel	161	663	101	175	289	31	13	19	74	13	2	5	6	33	2	141	53	19	8	.264	.436	.303	87	522	4.50	.542	13
Schu	112	416	54	105	155	21	4	7	24	2	1	0	2	38	3	78	6	6	7	.252	.373	.318	49	325	4.06	.491	5
Foley	46	158	17	42	59	8	0	3	17	3	0	0	0	13	7	18	1	3	2	.266	.373	.322	24	195	3.35	.396	2
*Stone	88	264	36	70	89	4	3	3	11	1	2	0	1	15	0	50	15	5	3	.265	.337	.307	28	204	3.73	.449	2
*Hayes	152	570	76	150	227	30	4	13	70	9	2	4	0	61	6	99	21	8	6	.263	.398	.332	79	440	4.85	.579	11
Wilson	161	608	73	167	258	39	5	14	102	12	0	7	0	35	1	117	7	4	24	.275	.424	.311	73	476	4.16	.503	11
Russell	81	216	22	47	86	12	0	9	23	1	0	0	0	18	0	72	2	0	5	.218	.398	.278	24	174	3.65	.438	2
Jeltz	89	196	17	37	43	4	1	0	12	1	5	1	0	26	4	55	1	1	6	.189	.219	.283	13	172	2.02	.192	2
Maddox	105	218	22	52	74	8	1	4	23	3	1	3	1	13	2	26	4	2	4	.239	.339	.281	21	176	3.17	.370	3
*Corcoran	103	182	11	39	47	6	1	0	22	2	1	7	0	29	1	20	0	0	6	.214	.258	.312	16	157	2.81	.315	2
*G. Gross	93	169	21	44	53	5	2	0	14	1	2	2	0	32	1	9	1	0	5	.260	.314	.374	22	134	4.44	.536	2
Aguayo	91	165	27	46	77	7	3	6	21	4	4	3	6	22	5	26	1	0	7	.279	.467	.378	29	133	5.93	.672	3
*Daulton	36	103	14	21	38	3	1	4	11	0	0	0	0	16	0	37	3	0	1	.204	.369	.311	13	83	4.30	.520	1
†Thomas	63	92	16	19	33	2	0	4	12	2	0	0	0	11	1	14	2	0	3	.207	.359	.291	10	76	3.41	.405	1
Denny	33	81	2	10	11	1	0	0	4	0	3	0	0	4	0	19	2	0	0	.123	.136	.165	2	74	0.85	.041	0
Diaz	26	76	9	16	29	5	1	2	16	0	0	0	0	6	0	7	0	0	5	.211	.382	.268	6	65	2.63	.288	1
K. Gross	39	65	1	9	14	2	0	1	6	1	8	0	0	2	0	23	0	0	1	.138	.215	.164	2	65	1.03	.059	0
Rawley	36	58	3	8	9	1	0	0	6	0	7	2	0	5	0	21	0	0	0	.138	.155	.200	3	59	1.24	.082	0
†Hudson	38	57	2	8	8	0	0	0	3	0	3	0	1	1	0	18	0	0	1	.140	.140	.169	1	53	0.75	.031	0
Wockenfuss	32	37	1	6	6	0	0	0	2	0	0	0	0	8	1	7	0	0	3	.162	.162	.311	2	34	1.52	.119	0
Koosman	19	34	1	3	3	0	0	0	4	1	1	1	0	1	0	9	0	0	2	.088	.088	.111	0	35	0.18	.002	0
*Carlton	16	28	2	5	6	1	0	0	3	0	1	1	0	1	0	8	0	0	1	.179	.214	.200	1	26	1.22	.080	0
*Rucker	41	12	2	4	5	1	0	0	0	0	1	0	0	1	0	5	0	0	0	.333	.417	.385	2	9	6.19	.692	0
Knicely	7	7	0	0	0	0	0	0	0	0	0	0	0	0	0	4	0	0	0	.000	.000	.000	0	7	0.00	.000	0
Childress	16	6	0	1	1	0	0	0	0	0	2	0	0	0	0	2	0	0	0	.167	.167	.167	0	7	0.98	.054	0
Anderson	57	4	1	0	0	0	0	0	0	0	0	1	0	0	0	0	0	0	0	.000	.000	.000	0	5	0.00	.000	0
Toliver	11	4	0	2	2	0	0	0	0	0	0	0	0	0	0	1	0	0	0	.500	.500	.500	1	2	13.50	.914	0
Garcia	4	3	0	0	0	0	0	0	0	0	0	0	0	0	0	0	0	0	0	.000	.000	.000	0	3	0.00	.000	0
*Carman	71	3	0	0	0	0	0	0	0	0	1	0	0	0	0	1	0	0	0	.000	.000	.000	0	4	0.00	.000	0
Shipanoff	26	3	0	0	0	0	0	0	0	0	0	0	0	0	0	3	0	0	0	.000	.000	.000	0	3	0.00	.000	0
Tekulve	58	3	0	0	0	0	0	0	0	0	0	0	0	0	0	1	0	0	0	.000	.000	.000	0	3	0.00	.000	0
Zachry	10	1	0	0	0	0	0	0	0	0	0	0	0	0	0	1	0	0	0	.000	.000	.000	0	1	0.00	.000	0
Holland	3	0	0	0	0	0	0	0	0	0	0	0	0	0	0	0	0	0	0	.000	.000	.000	0	0	0.00	.000	0
Stewart	4	0	0	0	0	0	0	0	0	0	0	0	0	0	0	0	0	0	0	.000	.000	.000	0	0	0.00	.000	0
Surhoff	2	0	0	0	0	0	0	0	0	0	0	0	0	0	0	0	0	0	0	.000	.000	.000	0	0	0.00	.000	0

*left-handed hitter, †switch hitter

DEFENSIVE STATISTICS

FIRST	G	PO	A	Er	TC	DP	PCT.
Schmidt	106	880	83	7	970	89	.993
Corcoran	59	386	25	3	414	27	.993
Russell	18	114	5	4	123	6	.967
Gross	8	18	4	0	22	1	1.000
Wockenfuss	7	39	1	0	40	5	1.000
Knicely	1	4	0	0	4	1	1.000
TEAM:	199	1441	118	14	1573	129	.991
AVG:	191	1513	114	12	1639	136	.993

SECOND	G	PO	A	Er	TC	DP	PCT.
Samuel	159	389	463	15	867	88	.983
Aguayo	17	27	25	1	53	5	.981
Thomas	1	0	0	1	1	0	.000
TEAM:	177	416	488	17	921	93	.982
AVG:	184	384	502	16	901	110	.982

THIRD	G	PO	A	Er	TC	DP	PCT.
Schu	111	86	191	20	297	19	.933
Schmidt	54	31	109	11	151	8	.927
Aguayo	7	4	16	0	20	1	1.000
Garcia	1	0	0	0	0	0	.000
Thomas	1	0	0	0	0	0	.000
TEAM:	174	121	316	31	468	28	.934
AVG:	189	125	341	25	492	29	.948

SHORTSTOP	G	PO	A	Er	TC	DP	PCT.
Jeltz	86	106	215	14	335	38	.958
Aguayo	60	61	117	8	186	21	.957
Foley	45	75	128	4	207	26	.981
Thomas	21	21	37	6	64	4	.906
Garcia	3	0	2	0	2	0	1.000
Schmidt	1	0	1	0	1	0	1.000
TEAM:	216	263	500	32	795	89	.960
AVG:	185	268	521	30	819	99	.963

CATCHER	G	PO	A	Er	TC	DP	PCT.	PB
Virgil	120	667	52	4	723	11	.994	12
Daulton	28	160	15	1	176	3	.994	3
Diaz	24	127	10	4	141	2	.972	0
Wockenfuss	2	5	0	0	5	0	1.000	0
Thomas	1	3	0	0	3	0	1.000	0
TEAM:	175	962	77	9	1048	14	.991	15
AVG:	191	952	87	14	1053	11	.987	14

OUTFIELD	G	PO	A	Er	TC	DP	PCT.
Wilson	158	343	18	12	373	4	.968
Hayes	146	368	9	6	383	1	.984
Maddox	94	143	3	3	149	0	.980
Stone	69	82	4	3	89	0	.966
Gross	52	48	4	0	52	0	1.000
Russell	49	56	4	0	60	1	1.000
Thomas	7	7	1	0	8	0	1.000
Corcoran	3	3	0	0	3	0	1.000
TEAM:	578	1050	43	24	1117	6	.979
AVG:	569	1036	34	23	1093	6	.979

COMPLETE PITCHERS RECORDS

Pitcher	W	L	Pct	ERA	G	GS	CG	GF	SHO	SV	IP	H	TBF	R	ER	HR	SH	SF	HB	BB	IB	SO	WP	BK	Appr Value
Starters (One-half of Game Appearances)																									
Denny	11	14	.440	3.82	33	33	6	0	2	0	230.2	252	998	112	98	15	11	8	3	83	5	123	8	0	7
Gross	15	13	.536	3.41	38	31	6	0	2	0	205.2	194	873	86	78	11	7	5	7	81	6	151	2	0	10
*Rawley	13	8	.619	3.31	36	31	6	1	2	0	198.2	188	849	82	73	16	6	5	2	81	6	106	7	0	9
Hudson	8	13	.381	3.78	38	26	3	7	0	0	193.0	188	833	92	81	23	8	4	1	74	7	122	4	3	6
*Koosman	6	4	.600	4.62	19	18	3	0	0	1	99.1	107	433	56	51	14	5	4	3	34	3	60	2	2	3
*Carlton	1	8	.111	3.33	16	16	0	0	0	0	92.0	84	401	43	34	6	9	1	0	53	4	48	3	2	3
Relievers																									
*Carman	9	4	.692	2.08	71	0	0	33	0	7	86.1	52	342	25	20	6	5	5	2	38	3	87	1	0	9
*Rucker	3	2	.600	4.31	39	3	0	11	0	1	79.1	83	350	42	38	6	4	6	2	40	6	41	2	0	3
Anderson	3	3	.500	4.32	57	0	0	19	0	3	73.0	78	318	41	35	5	3	1	3	26	4	50	1	1	4
Tekulve	4	10	.286	2.99	58	0	0	41	0	14	72.1	67	306	28	24	4	5	2	2	25	9	36	0	0	0
Shipanoff	1	2	.333	3.22	26	0	0	12	0	3	36.1	33	162	15	13	3	0	2	1	16	3	26	0	1	1
Childress	0	1	.000	6.21	16	1	0	3	0	0	33.1	45	151	23	23	3	2	2	0	9	3	14	1	0	0
Toliver	0	4	.000	4.68	11	3	0	4	0	1	25.0	27	117	15	13	2	0	1	0	17	1	23	0	0	0
Zachry	0	0	.000	4.26	10	0	0	1	0	0	12.2	14	61	7	6	1	0	0	0	11	1	8	1	0	0
Stewart	0	0	.000	6.23	4	0	0	3	0	0	4.1	5	22	4	3	0	0	0	0	4	0	2	2	0	0
*Holland	0	1	.000	4.50	3	0	0	3	0	1	4.0	5	21	2	2	0	1	1	0	4	2	1	0	0	0
Surhoff	1	0	1.000	0.00	2	0	0	0	0	0	1.0	2	4	0	0	0	0	0	0	0	0	1	0	0	0

*left-handed

Ozzie VIRGIL, Catcher

	G	AB	Hit	2B	3B	HR	Run	RBI	TBB	SO	SB	CS	Avg
2.36 years		480	118	22	2	19	55	65	47	101	0	2	.246
1985	131	426	105	16	3	19	47	55	49	85	0	0	.246
First Half	74	242	69	9	0	11	27	33	26				.285
Second Half	57	184	36	7	3	8	20	22	23				.196
Vs. RHP		304	76			15		41					.250
Vs. LHP		122	29			4		14					.238
Home	69	214	54	10	3	7	26	23			0		.252
Road	62	212	51	6	0	12	21	32			0		.241
Grass	33	110	18	1	0	8	10	20			0		.164
Turf	98	316	87	15	3	11	37	35			0		.275

Rick SCHU, Third Base

	G	AB	Hit	2B	3B	HR	Run	RBI	TBB	SO	SB	CS	Avg
0.80 years		559	142	29	6	11	83	36	55	105	10	8	.254
1985	112	416	105	21	4	7	54	24	38	78	8	6	.252
First Half	39	140	37	8	2	0	15	4	8		3		.264
Second Half	73	276	68	13	2	7	39	20	30		5		.246
Vs. RHP		284	68			3		15					.239
Vs. LHP		132	37			4		9					.280
Home	49	175	47	9	2	2	19	11			4		.269
Road	63	241	58	12	2	5	35	13			4		.241
Grass	32	118	23	3	1	4	18	5			1		.195
Turf	80	298	82	18	3	3	36	19			7		.275

Mike SCHMIDT, First Base

	G	AB	Hit	2B	3B	HR	Run	RBI	TBB	SO	SB	CS	Avg
12.02 years		561	149	27	5	38	104	106	105	138	14	7	.266
1985	158	549	152	31	5	33	89	93	87	117	1	3	.277
First Half	85	298	72	17	2	11	41	38	37		1		.242
Second Half	73	251	80	14	3	22	48	55	50		0		.319
Vs. RHP		394	108			27		76					.274
Vs. LHP		155	44			6		17					.284
Home	78	265	74	18	1	14	47	41			1		.279
Road	80	284	78	13	4	19	42	52			0		.275
Grass	41	149	42	8	3	10	20	26			0		.282
Turf	117	400	110	23	2	23	69	67			1		.275

Tom FOLEY, Shortstop

	G	AB	Hit	2B	3B	HR	Run	RBI	TBB	SO	SB	CS	Avg
1.62 years		385	92	15	3	5	35	36	34	54	4	3	.240
1985	89	250	60	13	1	3	24	23	19	34	2	3	.240
First Half	36	86	16	3	1	0	6	6	3		1		.186
Second Half	53	164	44	10	0	3	18	17	16		1		.268
Vs. RHP		130	38			3		16					.292
Vs. LHP		120	22			0		7					.183
Home	45	115	34	11	0	2	11	15			1		.296
Road	44	135	26	2	1	1	13	8			1		.193
Grass	28	86	13	0	0	1	8	5			1		.151
Turf	61	164	47	13	1	2	16	18			1		.287

Juan SAMUEL, Second Base

	G	AB	Hit	2B	3B	HR	Run	RBI	TBB	SO	SB	CS	Avg
2.09 years		683	184	32	16	17	105	71	31	155	61	17	.269
1985	161	663	175	31	13	19	101	74	33	141	53	19	.264
First Half	86	363	94	17	6	8	55	32	16		30		.259
Second Half	75	300	81	14	7	11	46	42	17		23		.270
Vs. RHP		467	129			15		55					.276
Vs. LHP		196	46			4		19					.235
Home	80	327	81	12	6	8	52	32			30		.248
Road	81	336	94	19	7	11	49	42			23		.280
Grass	42	172	45	6	4	8	24	18			10		.262
Turf	119	491	130	25	9	11	77	56			43		.265

Jeff STONE, Left Field

	G	AB	Hit	2B	3B	HR	Run	RBI	TBB	SO	SB	CS	Avg
1.02 years		471	140	14	10	6	63	37	30	83	36	10	.296
1985	88	264	70	4	3	3	36	11	15	50	15	5	.265
First Half	51	161	40	1	2	2	24	7	11		10		.248
Second Half	37	103	30	3	1	1	12	4	4		5		.291
Vs. RHP		230	60			3		9					.261
Vs. LHP		34	10			0		2					.294
Home	47	143	40	2	2	2	20	9			8		.280
Road	41	121	30	2	1	1	16	2			7		.248
Grass	28	82	19	1	0	0	9	1			3		.232
Turf	60	182	51	3	3	3	27	10			12		.280

Von HAYES, Center Field

	G	AB	Hit	2B	3B	HR	Run	RBI	TBB	SO	SB	CS	Avg
3.83 years		553	148	26	5	13	76	70	55	81	34	12	.268
1985	152	570	150	30	4	13	76	70	61	99	21	8	.263
First Half	80	277	77	16	2	8	42	40	39		12		.278
Second Half	72	293	73	14	2	5	34	30	22		9		.249
Vs. RHP		413	114			9		51					.276
Vs. LHP		157	36			4		19					.229
Home	75	278	80	13	4	12	47	43			10		.288
Road	77	292	70	17	0	1	29	27			11		.240
Grass	40	150	34	10	0	0	14	8			6		.227
Turf	112	420	116	20	4	13	62	62			15		.276

JOHN DENNY

	(W–L)	GS	Run	Avg	DP	Avg	SB	Avg
1984	(7-7)	22	94	4.27	17	.77	14	.64
1985	(11-14)	33	149	4.52	38	1.15	38	1.15
1976-1985		271	1219	4.50	289	1.07	179	.66

	G	IP	W	L	Pct	ER	BB	SO	ERA
1984 Home	12	88.0	3	5	.375	24	15	53	2.45
1985 Home	18	123.0	4	10	.286	55	42	59	4.02
1984 Road	10	66.3	4	2	.667	18	14	41	2.44
1985 Road	15	107.7	7	4	.636	43	41	64	3.59
1984 Grass	8	54.3	4	1	.800	15	12	30	2.48
1985 Grass	9	65.3	4	2	.667	22	22	40	3.03
1984 Turf	14	100.0	3	6	.333	27	17	64	2.43
1985 Turf	24	165.3	7	12	.368	76	61	83	4.14
1985 Total	33	230.7	11	14	.440	98	83	123	3.82

Glenn WILSON, Right Field

	G	AB	Hit	2B	3B	HR	Run	RBI	TBB	SO	SB	CS	Avg
3.22 years		552	149	31	5	13	61	72	29	94	5	3	.269
1985	161	608	167	39	5	14	73	102	35	117	7	4	.275
First Half	86	316	84	19	5	8	38	61	16		3		.266
Second Half	75	292	83	20	0	6	35	41	19		4		.284
Vs. RHP		437	118			8		71					.270
Vs. LHP		171	4			6		31					.287
Home	80	301	88	19	4	7	39	61			3		.292
Road	81	307	79	20	1	7	34	41			4		.257
Grass	42	161	43	10	0	5	17	20			2		.267
Turf	119	447	124	29	5	9	56	82			5		.277

SHANE RAWLEY

	(W–L)	GS	Run	Avg	DP	Avg	SB	Avg
1984	(12-9)	28	108	3.86	27	.96	15	.54
1985	(13-8)	31	142	4.58	30	.97	32	1.03
1978-1985		114	489	4.29	110	.96	71	.62

	G	IP	W	L	Pct	ER	BB	SO	ERA
1984 Home	19	102.0	6	6	.500	45	39	60	3.97
1985 Home	18	99.3	6	6	.500	38	46	51	3.44
1984 Road	10	60.3	6	3	.667	35	15	22	5.22
1985 Road	18	99.3	7	2	.778	35	35	55	3.17
1984 Grass	12	54.7	3	2	.600	30	28	31	4.94
1985 Grass	10	58.0	2	2	.500	23	20	32	3.57
1984 Turf	17	107.7	9	7	.562	50	26	51	4.18
1985 Turf	26	140.7	11	6	.647	50	61	74	3.20
1985 Total	36	198.7	13	8	.619	73	81	106	3.31

Steve JELTZ, Shortstop

	G	AB	Hit	2B	3B	HR	Run	RBI	TBB	SO	SB	CS	Avg
0.80 years		339	65	5	4	1	30	25	42	85	4	2	.191
1985	89	196	37	4	1	0	17	12	26	55	1	1	.189
First Half	69	159	30	3	1	0	10	11	17		0		.189
Second Half	20	37	7	1	0	0	7	1	9		1		.189
Vs. RHP		134	25			0		6					.187
Vs. LHP		62	12			0		6					.194
Home	49	99	20	4	1	0	9	8			0		.202
Road	40	97	17	0	0	0	8	4			1		.175
Grass	16	38	3	0	0	0	0	2			0		.079
Turf	73	158	34	4	1	0	17	10			1		.215

KEVIN GROSS

	(W–L)	GS	Run	Avg	DP	Avg	SB	Avg
1984	(8-5)	14	53	3.79	12	.86	17	1.21
1985	(15-13)	31	104	3.35	25	.81	35	1.13
1983-1985		62	225	3.63	53	.85	78	1.26

	G	IP	W	L	Pct	ER	BB	SO	ERA
1984 Home	24	71.3	5	4	.556	34	23	49	4.29
1985 Home	18	96.3	8	4	.667	32	33	79	2.99
1984 Road	20	57.7	3	1	.750	25	21	35	3.90
1985 Road	20	109.3	7	9	.438	46	48	72	3.79
1984 Grass	10	25.3	2	1	.667	14	11	20	4.97
1985 Grass	10	49.3	3	6	.333	31	22	39	5.66
1984 Turf	34	103.7	6	4	.600	45	33	64	3.91
1985 Turf	28	156.3	12	7	.632	47	59	112	2.71
1985 Total	38	205.7	15	13	.536	78	81	151	3.41

John RUSSELL, First Base

	G	AB	Hit	2B	3B	HR	Run	RBI	TBB	SO	SB	CS	Avg
0.74 years		425	101	27	1	15	45	46	41	142	3	1	.238
1985	81	216	47	12	0	9	22	23	18	72	2	0	.218
First Half	37	78	15	5	0	2	7	6	14		1		.192
Second Half	44	138	32	7	0	7	15	17	4		1		.232
Vs. RHP		121	26			5		12					.215
Vs. LHP		95	21			4		11					.221
Home	45	117	31	8	0	7	15	18			1		.265
Road	36	99	16	4	0	2	7	5			1		.162
Grass	17	44	8	2	0	1	4	2			0		.182
Turf	64	172	39	10	0	8	18	21			2		.227

CHARLES HUDSON

	(W–L)	GS	Run	Avg	DP	Avg	SB	Avg
1984	(9-11)	30	120	4.00	18	.60	34	1.13
1985	(8-13)	26	127	4.88	13	.50	25	.96
1983-1985		82	379	4.62	47	.57	92	1.12

	G	IP	W	L	Pct	ER	BB	SO	ERA
1984 Home	14	73.0	3	7	.300	41	22	51	5.05
1985 Home	18	93.3	3	5	.375	40	28	56	3.86
1984 Road	16	100.7	6	4	.600	37	30	43	3.31
1985 Road	20	99.7	5	8	.385	41	46	66	3.70
1984 Grass	8	53.7	4	2	.667	19	17	18	3.19
1985 Grass	10	46.0	1	4	.200	24	21	25	4.70
1984 Turf	22	120.0	5	9	.357	59	35	76	4.42
1985 Turf	28	147.0	7	9	.438	57	53	97	3.49
1985 Total	38	193.0	8	13	.381	81	74	122	3.78

OTHERS

	(W–L)	GS	Run	Avg	DP	Avg	SB	Avg
Koosman	(6-4)	18	92	5.11	14	.78	15	.83
Carlton	(1-8)	16	39	2.44	14	.88	15	.94
Rucker	(3-2)	3	15	5.00	4	1.33	4	1.33
Toliver	(0-4)	3	5	1.67	0	0.00	6	2.00
Childress	(0-1)	1	0	0.00	0	0.00	2	2.00

PITTSBURGH PIRATES

BREAKDOWNS FOR THE LAST TEN SEASONS

Won-Lost Record: 803-755, .515 (2nd in the division, 9th in majors)
Runs Scored: 6,540 (3rd-best in division)
Runs Allowed: 6,264 (2nd-best in division)
Home Runs Hit: 1,110 (4th in division)
Home Runs Allowed: 1,078 (3rd in division)

RECORD IN:
April: 82-90, .477 (5th in the division)
May: 129-136, .487 (5th in the division)
June: 125-134, .483 (5th in the division)
July: 149-114, .567 (Best in the division, 4th in baseball)
August: 146-143, .505 (3rd in the division)
September: 156-127, .551 (2nd in the division)
October: 16-11, .593 (2nd in the division)

Won-Lost Record in Road Games: 367-413, .471 (3rd in the division)
Won-Lost Record at Home: 436-342, .460 (2nd in the division)
Home Field Advantage: 70 Games
Runs Scored on the Road: 3,124 (4th in the division)
Runs Scored at Home: 3,416 (3rd-most in the division)
Runs Allowed on the Road: 3,130 (Fewest in the division)
Runs Allowed at Home: 3,134 (3rd-most in the division)

Home Runs Hit on the Road: 545 (3rd-most in the division)
Home Runs Hit at Home: 565 (3rd-most in the division)
Home Runs Allowed on the Road: 513 (4th in the division)
Home Runs Allowed at Home: 565 (3rd-most in the division)

RECORD FOR LAST THREE SEASONS: 216-269, .445 (Worst in the division, 22nd in baseball)

TANNER'S SPRING

In his first managerial role, Chuck Tanner's team blasted its way out of mediocrity, moving into contention in two seasons after losing 106 games in 1970. The key to this accomplishment was the acquisition of Dick Allen, a man of considerable intelligence and charm and a truly great ballplayer, who was available cheap at that time because he was a manager's Excedrin headache #1—insubordinate, irresponsible and injury-prone. The three eyes; everything a manager wants in a superstar. To give Tanner due credit, this was not the *only* key to the 1972 season; Tanner moved Wilbur Wood out of the bullpen into the starting rotation, saving the team a woodpile of runs—maybe as many as forty or fifty—and helping cut the staff ERA from 4.54 to 3.12.

Tanner was the baseball manager for the seventies; his approach to "handling" Richie Allen was just not to worry about Richie's little eccentricities. He had seen Gene Mauch and several other managers, challenging Allen on some minor point, find themselves locked in tooth-and-nail ego battles that divided their teams. If Richie wanted to spend spring training at Hialeah and batting practice at Arlington Park, Tanner just wasn't going to worry about it. If it feels good, Richie, have at it. Allen responded to this revolution in managerial morality with his best season, and the White Sox won 87 games to challenge the formidable A's in 1972.

Chuck Tanner received, and deserved, great praise for the progress of the Chicago team. It developed in time that the White Sox castle was built on sand; Allen signed a record-breaking contract early in the 1973 season, and sat out most of the season with a nagging ankle injury. The nagging part was wondering whether Richie really wanted to play the game, and Allen answered this question by "retiring" in September of the next year, having already hit enough home runs by early August to lead the American League for the year. Worse, several of the White Sox' young players, notably Carlos May, began to emulate Dick Allen's casual attitude toward the game of baseball. Tanner's other key pitcher in 1972 had been Stan Bahnsen, who over a two-season period (1972–73) made 83 starts with a 39–37 won lost record (21–16, 18–21); his arm proved incapable of sustaining this workload. Wilbur Wood worked even harder, but, being a knuckleballer, wasn't destroyed by it; however, Wood became champion of the White Sox' fat brigade—excess flab was another thing that Chuck had decided it didn't pay to nag about—and his effectiveness also declined rapidly.

In three more seasons under Tanner the White Sox never beat .500 again—yet the press never reneged on its praise of Tanner. Chuck Tanner, it turned out, was a heck of a nice guy, many say the nicest in baseball. His reputation survived the poor years in Chicago. Everybody who interviewed him came away from it finding something NICE to say about such a NICE manager. Tanner managed one year in Oakland, and the A's failed to win the division for the first time in six years and had their poorest record in eight years. In truth, it was an extremely difficult summer in Oakland, yet Tanner's reputation survived this.

Tanner was traded to Pittsburgh in 1977. The Pirates had been a very successful team, and they remained one for three years, winning the World's Championship (again) in 1979. Since then, lacking any sense of discipline or direction, the Pirates have unravelled, and Chuck Tanner has become Exhibit A in Leo Durocher's brief, a walking lecture on why nice guys finish last, how nice guys finish last, and how long it takes them to reach last if they start out with a good team. Nice guys finish last because nice guys don't go up to their players and tell them that they're going to lose 15 pounds or 15 hundred dollars. Nice guys finish last because nice guys don't tell the clowns on the bench to shut up and pay attention to the game. Nice guys finish last because nice guys don't go up to their players and tell them to keep their shabby friends out of the clubhouse.

Every good manager effectively threatens his players with professional extermination if they don't give him the best effort that they are capable of giving; Casey Stengel, Billy Martin, Whitey Herzog and Earl Weaver are masters at it, as was Durocher. They are *not* nice people; they are manipulative, cunning SOBs, hard and crass and they drink too much. Nice guys finish last because a nice guy is not going to coldly exploit the insecurities of his players. Nice guys finish last because a nice guy is not going to kick an old friend out of his comfortable sinecure the minute that old friend becomes a millisecond too slow on the fastball.

Of course the generalization contains as much falsehood as truth; the point here is only that it does contain much truth. For if you believe in sports, then you must believe in stretching abilities to the limit. What is the sporting arena, but a world in which the best is demanded from each and every one; what else? If you believe in sports, you must believe in using the best players that you can find and demanding from each of them all that he can give, because without that sports would have no interest and no meaning. The sporting world is a refuge in a world of laziness and sloth, indecision and lack of commitment, hedged values and shortcuts, a corner in which individuals are commanded to reach down inside and find the best that's in there, and apply it to . . . this nothing, these games, these silly rules that tell them where to run and when to run there. Athletes are heroes; that is their job.

TANNER'S FALL

We come then to the summer of 1985, and to the bizarre confluence of news stories which joined at the Allegheny and the Monongahela. On the one hand, there was the story of the on-going drug investigation centering on Pirates and former Pirates; on the other, a steady stream of stories about what a hell of a job Chuck Tanner was doing of managing the Pittsburgh Pirates through their nightmare. The theme of these stories was "He's just the same. I interviewed him in '79, when the Pirates were in their glory days, and I interviewed him in '85, and he's the same now as he was then."

The logic of this argument misses me. Would you defend the pilot of a crashed jet-liner by saying that he flew the plane just the same through a thunderstorm as he had on a sunny day? Would you defend the general of a slaughtered infantry by saying that he marched his men into a hail of bullets just as if they were marching in a Fourth of July parade? Would you defend a doctor by saying that he treated you the same when you were healthy

as when you were ill? What kind of moron is going to manage a team like this just the same as he managed a World Champion?

I know I write too much about Whitey Herzog, but what I am struck by is the extreme similarity (to Tanner's) of the challenges that Herzog faced after having successful teams in Kansas City and St. Louis, and the 180-degree difference of his reaction to it. After winning three divisional titles in Kansas City, Herzog began to have drug problems with the team, as well as having players who put on weight. The record of the Pirates in 1980 (83–79) is almost the same as the record of the Royals in 1979 (85–77) and the Cardinals in 1983 (79–83).

In response to potential weight problems, Whitey adopted, and enforced, weight limits for all players, a practice which I think he continues in St. Louis. As the Pirates began to degenerate into a collection of fat and lazy players, the Pirate front office got involved in a couple of nasty hassles when, burned by big contracts given to Dave Parker, Jason Thompson and Bill Madlock, they tried to include weight clauses in new contracts. But every time I heard about the Pirates trying to put a weight clause in somebody's contract, I kept wondering where Chuck Tanner was.

A few years ago, writing about Dave Parker, I came to the defense of weight clauses in contracts, describing them as "an intelligent attempt to deal with a problem that major league teams have been attempting to deal with from day one." (Page 223, 1984 *Baseball Abstract*) In retrospect, I'm not so sure. One of the problems with a weight clause is that it sets the price of being overweight. If a player has, let us say, an $800,000 contract with a $15,000 weight clause, it is difficult for the team to take any further action against the player on this account. Suppose, if push came to shove, that the team released the player and refused to pay the balance due him, arguing that the player had violated the contract by being out of shape. The team would be quite within their rights to do this, but *if the contract contained a weight clause*, they would almost certainly lose the case in front of an arbitrator. The arbitrator would almost certainly rule that by agreeing to pay the player $800,000 plus $15,000 for meeting his weight, the team had in effect agreed to pay the player $800,000 even if he failed to meet the weight. The weight clause effectively sets the price of being overweight at $15,000, which would amount to about $2.56 to the player once the lawyers, the bankers, the agents and the government get done with it.

In retrospect, I would still defend the Pirate front office for attempting to deal with the problem—but confronting the player about conditioning is something which has traditionally been the province of the manager. In this case, Tanner was conspicuously absent from the debate.

As I see it, there's just a whole lot of people around this year who owe Whitey Herzog an apology. With the revelations in Pittsburgh, we are in a position to see some things that we couldn't have seen clearly before. We can start with the Kansas City front office. When the KC players began to experiment with chemicals, Herzog confronted the problem—just as he later would in St. Louis. First there was John Mayberry; then there was Keith Hernandez. In actions speaking much louder than words, Herzog sent a clear message to everyone in his organization: Stay away from drugs, or *Get Out Of My Life!* He didn't say "I wish you would clean up your act." He didn't say "John, I'm concerned about your health." He said "Look, you mess with drugs and I'm going to ruin your career. I don't care how good a player you are. I don't give a damn how much money the front office is paying you. I don't care what the public, which doesn't know what you're putting up your nose, says about it. I don't care what your friends tell you about it not affecting your game. I don't care what the press says. I don't care if I have to give you away in a trade. I don't care if I have to play some kid out of AAA ball in your place. I don't care what the front office says. I don't care if they fired me once before over this issue. I don't care if they fire me again. If you take drugs there is no place on this ballclub for you."

Sometimes in my profession we make the things that managers do sound easy—but certainly, it was not easy for Whitey Herzog to do this. The Royals fired him for it. The press in St. Louis and New York, who regard Keith Hernandez as an icon, broiled him for it. The fans, both in KC and St. Louis, were incensed that he would get rid of star players and put unproven rookies in their place. Even I second-guessed the Hernandez trade, and I'm Whitey Herzog's biggest fan. His own players, his own peers must have questioned his fanaticism on this issue— yet he was to this crisis what Christy Mathewson was to the game-fixing scandal: the only man in baseball who stood up to the problem before it reached epidemic proportions.

So Hernandez got his act together. Great. The point was still made. No doubt all managers say their piece about drugs in spring training, or some time during the year. Uniquely among major league managers, Whitey could say his piece, and there couldn't be any doubt that he meant precisely what he said. Suppose that you were a young player on one of Whitey Herzog's teams, or perhaps that you were an established regular trying to hold onto your job, and somebody offered you a little help. What's going to go through your head? "If Whitey did *that* to John Mayberry, what's he going to do to me? If Whitey told *Keith Hernandez* that his services would not be required in the future, what's he going to do to me if he finds out I'm using stuff?"

The Royals' organization decided, in 1979, that they didn't want to bite the bullet; they replaced Whitey with a much nicer man, Jim Frey. The forces that were trying to introduce drugs onto the roster had a heyday then; they fed the nice guy to the sharks. It didn't hurt the team for a year or so.

In the weight debate, Tanner stayed at home; when it came to drugs, Tanner stayed at home and hid under the bed. To hear Tanner tell it, he had never heard of cocaine until it came out in the papers that his players were using it. Of course, the pretense that Chuck Tanner didn't know that there were drug problems on his team is ludicrous; his press being so forgiving, it remained for the judge hearing the pandering trial to tear into Tanner in strong language for adopting this pose. I know a few people in baseball, but not very many or very well—yet *I* knew that the Pirate roster was riddled with drug problems. Didn't you? I remember in the summer of 1983 I almost got in trouble

when I let it slip on KMOX radio, and somebody had to remind me off the air that it wasn't technically public. Everybody remotely connected with baseball knew that Rod Scurry had a serious problem; it understates the case to say that this was common knowledge. Anybody with an ounce of horse sense had to know that Dave Parker wasn't losing his batting eye by playing too much Trivial Pursuit. Tanner may claim he was unaware, but we all know that it is not physically possible to get your head stuck that far up your rectum.

I realized after the Pittsburgh drug trial was over that for the first time in years I was not aware of any major league player who had been involved with drugs whose name had not now become public. It has been my observation, about insider information, that it exists only in passing. I remember one time about six years ago, when I first started dealing with player agents, I learned through one of them that a trade had been made a couple of hours earlier that had not yet been announced. The trade was announced about an hour later, but in that hour, as stupid as it sounds, I felt like such an important person, that I knew something which ordinary fans did not know.

Whereas fans tend to imagine that there is a standard type of information, insider information, which players and writers and a few others share about the game, I have learned that in fact insider status is just a stage that information goes through on its way to becoming public, that if the knowledge is of any interest it cannot help but escape. It may take an hour; it may take years, but the circle inside of which information is held grows inevitably larger and larger; it cannot grow smaller, and the boundaries of the circle are not firm enough to hold it in. Insiders use inside information to buy respect from those that they deal with, thus blurring to indefinable the line of the privy circle.

With something like the use of illegal drugs, the line is clearer—but the forces which draw it out are stronger, and its escape, while slower, is no less inevitable. By the use of hints and code words ("motivational problem," "lifestyle," "getting his act together," "getting straightened out," etc.) the information will get into the press. In time, the hints will become broader and the codewords more obvious, until the line altogether disappears. The steps by which the background of the Hernandez trade gradually seeped out to the public, I think, is an excellent study in the process.

For this reason and others, journalism tends to have a lag time of about three years with respect to certain issues. Gary Gaetti, who emerged as an outstanding defensive player in 1983, should begin to receive credit for it in 1986 or 1987. And baseball's drug problem, which was quite serious from 1981 to 1983 but, I think, isn't anything like as serious now, has finally become the property of the public press. But unless I'm badly mistaken, we have seen the worst of it. If I think about it I guess I can recall a few people who got involved with drugs and got out clean, but for the most part, all the names are out now.

Incidentally, I remember writing an article about managers in 1983 in which I wrote that "A manager's job isn't to know when to hit and run. A manager's job is to know who is taking drugs so he can get rid of him before the rent on the habit comes due." The magazine wouldn't use the comment; they changed it to something more innocuous about knowing whether a player was over the hill or just in a slump. But think about that, and then think about the pathetic defense of Chuck Tanner: I didn't know what was going on.

I'm not pretending to be shocked about drug usage. I have friends who used cocaine a few years ago; I don't think any less of them. Most of you do, too, and most of you know that you do. Many people truly, sincerely believed a few years ago that cocaine usage was really no big deal, that it was on its way toward becoming the social norm. Possibly Chuck Tanner is one of those people. That was *many people*, I said—but it wasn't most of us. It's kind of like the sexual revolution; I'm not the kind of person who has a strong desire to share my body with the masses, but I'm not going to pass judgment on those who do, or did. But the seventies are over, folks.

Comparisons are drawn between "Baseball's" drug problem and the gambling scandals of 1918–1920, remembered now as the Black Sox scandal. There have been calls for players to be banned from baseball, as about two dozen players were then. Somehow the managers always get off clean. Black Sox manager Kid Gleason continued to work in baseball for several years, but doesn't it occur to anyone to ask what he was doing when the gamblers came into his clubhouse and seduced his players? According to the sworn testimony in a Federal court, Tanner knowingly let the drug traffickers into his clubhouse. According to the sworn testimony, he tried to warn his players that Curtis Strong was being watched, that they should avoid him for a while. Do we go that far in forgiving the excesses of an innocent, indulgent era?

Ueberroth didn't even choose to talk to him about it. There was a shocking psychological study a few years ago which showed that if the researchers created a moral climate in which torture was acceptable, most people would be willing to torture another human being. Who is more culpable: the man who commits a crime, or the man who creates the moral climate in which the crime is acceptable? An impossible dilemma, I suppose. But I cannot understand how anyone can say, in essence, "Sure, he let the drug trade destroy his team, but he's a nice guy."

Sometimes I think that Chuck Tanner should be hung in effigy in every sporting place in the country. Other times, I think that his only offense was the cowardice of being nice. I think it is a sick, twisted mind which places congeniality so high in the hierarchy of values.

What is rarely mentioned about the Black Sox scandal is that it was merely an act of its own time, a time in which corruption was gaining rapidly in American society; it is so odd that this is remembered now not as the period when governors took bribes to free criminals, but as the time when a few baseball players threw the big game.

In society at large we use sports to express and defend our values, as well as to teach them. Strange as it seems, the reaction of the public in the period after the War to End All Wars was, in essence, that it was one thing when the police were corrupt, that it was one thing when juries were bribed and judges kept on retainer, that it was one thing when elections were rigged and politicians let contracts go to the highest briber, but when *baseball players* started fixing games, well that was just too much; something had to be done about it. And it was; the expulsion of the crooked players was a symbolic purging and cleansing of society which set the stage for the many other purgings and cleansings which are remembered now as the Teapot Dome scandal.

And in our time, what have we done? We have said that it is one thing when doctors and lawyers use illegal drugs. It is one thing when policemen and politicians use illegal drugs. It is one thing when talk show hosts use drugs, and actors and actresses and our musicians and our children, and drugs may run rampant in the military and who really cares but when *baseball players* use drugs . . . well, gentlemen, something has got to be done. In time, will the 1980s be remembered as the period when *baseball* had a drug problem? And will it be forgotten that baseball shared this problem with the rest of the nation?

Very likely, yes. People say that it is hypocritical to judge baseball players more harshly than we judge others in society, that if school teachers and airline pilots and architects and engineers use drugs, that that is a lot more serious than a few baseball players. I say that it is not hypocritical in the least. We judge athletes more harshly even than we judge our friends, more harshly than we judge ourselves. Athletes are heroes. That is their job.

COMPLETE BATTING RECORDS

Player	G	AB	R	H	TB	2B	3B	HR	RBI	GW	SH	SF	HB	BB	IB	SO	SB	CS	GIDP	Avg	Slug	OBP	Runs Created	Outs Made	Runs/27 Outs	OW%	Appr Value
Pena	147	546	53	136	197	27	2	10	59	7	7	5	0	29	4	67	12	8	19	.249	.361	.284	51	449	3.05	.373	9
*Thompson	123	402	42	97	152	17	1	12	61	6	0	4	0	84	10	58	0	0	8	.241	.378	.369	61	317	5.21	.634	7
†Ray	154	594	67	163	223	33	3	7	70	5	5	6	1	46	10	24	13	9	11	.274	.375	.325	71	462	4.17	.526	9
Madlock	110	399	49	100	155	23	1	10	41	4	3	3	5	39	2	42	3	3	12	.251	.388	.323	49	320	4.14	.508	6
Khalifa	95	320	30	76	102	14	3	2	31	3	9	4	0	34	8	56	5	2	9	.238	.319	.307	32	268	3.22	.398	3
Reynolds	31	130	22	40	60	5	3	3	17	6	2	0	1	9	1	18	12	2	3	.308	.462	.357	45	263	4.59	.573	2
Orsulak	121	397	54	119	145	14	6	0	21	0	9	3	1	26	3	27	24	11	5	.300	.365	.342	51	306	4.47	.560	7
Brown	57	205	29	68	105	18	2	5	33	2	3	3	0	22	4	27	2	2	7	.332	.512	.391	40	152	7.03	.759	4
*Wynne	103	337	21	69	87	6	3	2	18	2	7	0	1	18	2	48	10	5	8	.205	.258	.247	21	288	1.94	.194	3
Hendrick	69	256	23	59	80	15	0	2	25	4	0	3	0	18	1	42	1	0	11	.230	.313	.278	21	211	2.64	.307	2
Morrison	92	244	17	62	84	10	0	4	22	0	1	3	0	8	1	44	3	0	6	.254	.344	.277	23	190	3.32	.413	3
Almon	88	244	33	66	101	17	0	6	29	1	4	3	1	22	0	61	10	7	6	.270	.414	.330	32	198	4.38	.550	4
*Kemp	92	236	19	59	82	13	2	2	21	3	1	4	0	25	1	54	1	0	5	.250	.347	.317	27	187	3.92	.494	3
Gonzalez	35	124	11	28	44	4	0	4	12	2	1	0	0	13	2	27	2	4	1	.226	.355	.299	13	102	3.34	.416	1
†Mazzilli	92	117	20	33	44	8	0	1	9	1	1	0	0	29	1	17	4	1	3	.282	.376	.425	21	89	6.45	.726	2
Lezcano	72	116	16	24	35	2	0	3	9	0	0	1	1	35	3	17	0	0	3	.207	.302	.392	16	96	4.62	.576	2
Frobel	53	109	14	22	27	5	0	0	7	2	2	0	0	19	5	24	4	3	2	.202	.248	.320	9	94	2.69	.315	1
Bream	26	95	14	27	43	7	0	3	15	3	1	1	0	11	2	14	0	2	4	.284	.453	.355	14	76	4.88	.603	2
Rhoden	37	74	2	14	17	3	0	0	6	3	2	0	0	2	0	7	0	0	2	.189	.230	.211	3	64	1.41	.112	0
Ortiz	23	72	4	21	26	2	0	1	5	1	1	0	0	3	1	17	1	0	1	.292	.361	.320	8	53	4.25	.535	1
Reuschel	31	59	8	10	15	2	0	1	7	1	6	0	0	3	0	17	1	0	0	.169	.254	.210	4	55	1.82	.175	0
LeMaster	22	58	4	9	12	0	0	1	6	0	2	0	0	5	2	12	1	0	1	.155	.207	.222	3	52	1.49	.124	0
Tunnell	24	47	2	4	6	0	1	0	1	0	0	1	0	1	0	20	0	1	0	.085	.128	.102	1	45	0.33	.007	0
*McWilliams	32	40	2	5	6	1	0	0	2	0	4	0	0	1	0	19	0	0	1	.125	.150	.146	1	40	0.63	.024	0
Foli	19	37	1	7	7	0	0	0	2	0	0	0	0	4	1	2	0	0	4	.189	.189	.268	1	34	1.05	.066	0
DeLeon	31	36	1	2	2	0	0	0	0	0	7	0	0	3	0	19	0	0	0	.056	.056	.128	1	41	0.46	.013	0
Robinson	44	21	2	5	10	2	0	1	4	0	0	0	1	0	0	11	0	0	0	.238	.476	.273	3	16	4.72	.587	0
Belliard	17	20	1	4	4	0	0	0	1	0	0	0	0	0	0	5	0	0	0	.200	.200	.200	1	16	1.35	.104	0
Winn	30	18	2	2	3	1	0	0	0	0	2	0	0	1	0	8	0	0	0	.111	.167	.158	1	18	0.92	.051	0
Walk	9	17	0	0	0	0	0	0	0	0	4	0	1	0	0	9	0	0	0	.000	.000	.056	0	21	0.14	.001	0
Guante	63	17	0	1	1	0	0	0	0	0	0	0	0	0	0	12	0	0	0	.059	.059	.059	0	16	0.10	.001	0
Bielecki	13	10	1	0	0	0	0	0	0	0	0	0	1	0	0	5	0	0	0	.000	.000	.091	0	11	0.16	.002	0
Kipper	5	8	1	2	2	0	0	0	0	0	2	0	0	0	0	3	0	0	0	.250	.250	.250	1	8	2.05	.203	0
*Davis	2	7	1	1	1	0	0	0	0	0	0	0	0	0	0	0	1	0	1	.143	.143	.143	0	6	0.98	.054	0
Loucks	4	7	1	2	4	2	0	0	0	0	0	0	0	2	0	2	0	0	0	.286	.571	.444	2	5	10.85	.877	0
Holland	38	5	1	2	4	0	1	0	0	0	1	0	0	1	0	0	0	0	0	.400	.800	.500	2	4	13.83	.920	0
Dybzinski	5	4	0	0	0	0	0	0	0	0	0	0	0	0	0	0	0	0	0	.000	.000	.000	0	4	0.00	.000	0
*Scurry	30	4	0	0	0	0	0	0	0	0	0	0	0	0	0	2	0	0	0	.000	.000	.000	0	4	0.00	.000	0
Clements	27	3	0	1	1	0	0	0	0	0	1	0	0	0	0	2	0	0	0	.333	.333	.333	0	3	3.42	.414	0
†Candelaria	37	1	0	0	0	0	0	0	0	0	2	0	0	1	0	0	0	0	0	.000	.000	.000	0	3	0.00	.000	0
Krawczyk	8	0	0	0	0	0	0	0	0	0	0	0	0	0	0	0	0	0	0	.000	.000	.000	0	0	0.00	.000	0
Tekulve	3	0	0	0	0	0	0	0	0	0	0	0	0	0	0	0	0	0	0	.000	.000	.000	0	0	0.00	.000	0
Tomlin	1	0	0	0	0	0	0	0	0	0	0	0	0	0	0	0	0	0	0	.000	.000	.000	0	0	0.00	.000	0

*left-handed hitter, †switch hitter

DEFENSIVE STATISTICS

FIRST

	G	PO	A	Er	TC	DP	PCT.
Thompson	114	995	82	9	1086	69	.992
Bream	25	219	21	2	242	21	.992
Mazzilli	19	139	6	2	147	15	.986
Madlock	12	81	5	0	86	3	1.000
Almon	7	25	1	2	28	3	.929
Pena	1	3	2	0	5	0	1.000
TEAM:	178	1462	117	15	1594	111	.991
AVG:	191	1513	114	12	1639	136	.993

SECOND

	G	PO	A	Er	TC	DP	PCT.
Ray	151	305	423	18	746	89	.976
Morrison	15	34	37	0	71	5	1.000
Gonzalez	6	9	14	0	23	2	1.000
TEAM:	172	348	474	18	840	96	.979
AVG:	184	384	502	16	901	110	.982

THIRD

	G	PO	A	Er	TC	DP	PCT.
Madlock	98	46	175	14	235	10	.940
Morrison	59	39	84	5	128	9	.961
Gonzalez	21	14	28	5	47	3	.894
Almon	7	2	4	1	7	0	.857
TEAM:	185	101	291	25	417	22	.940
AVG:	189	125	341	25	492	29	.948

SHORTSTOP

	G	PO	A	Er	TC	DP	PCT.
Khalifa	95	156	316	16	488	45	.967
Almon	43	50	101	2	153	19	.987
LeMaster	21	43	71	2	116	12	.983
Foli	13	16	34	1	51	6	.980
Belliard	12	13	23	2	38	3	.947
Dybzinski	5	4	5	1	10	0	.900
TEAM:	189	282	550	24	856	85	.972
AVG:	185	268	521	30	819	99	.963

CATCHER

	G	PO	A	Er	TC	DP	PCT.	PB
Pena	146	922	100	12	1034	9	.988	6
Ortiz	23	115	14	2	131	3	.985	0
TEAM:	169	1037	114	14	1165	12	.988	6
AVG:	191	952	87	14	1053	11	.987	14

OUTFIELD

	G	PO	A	Er	TC	DP	PCT.
Orsulak	115	229	10	6	245	1	.976
Wynne	99	229	7	3	239	1	.987
Hendrick	65	133	2	4	139	0	.971
Kemp	63	105	1	0	106	0	1.000
Brown	56	87	3	6	96	1	.937
Lezcano	40	57	2	2	61	0	.967
Frobel	36	46	2	3	51	1	.941
Almon	32	27	2	0	29	0	1.000
Reynolds	31	65	3	3	71	0	.958
Gonzalez	13	21	0	3	24	0	.875
Mazzilli	5	13	0	1	14	0	.929
Loucks	4	2	0	0	2	0	1.000
Davis	2	2	0	1	3	0	.667
Morrison	1	0	0	0	0	0	.000
TEAM:	562	1016	32	32	1080	4	.970
AVG:	569	1036	34	23	1093	6	.979

Pitcher	W	L	Pct	ERA	G	GS	CG	GF	SHO	SV	IP	H	TBF	R	ER	HR	SH	SF	HB	BB	IB	SO	WP	BK	Appr Value
							Starters (One-half of Game Appearances)																		
Rhoden	10	15	.400	4.47	35	35	2	0	0	0	213.1	254	944	119	106	18	10	0	6	69	3	128	8	3	5
Reuschel	14	8	.636	2.27	31	26	9	4	1	1	194.0	153	773	58	49	7	5	3	3	52	10	138	4	0	11
DeLeon	2	19	.095	4.70	31	25	1	5	0	3	162.2	138	700	93	85	15	7	4	3	89	3	149	7	1	4
Tunnell	4	10	.286	4.01	24	23	0	1	0	0	132.1	126	565	70	59	11	3	2	1	57	4	74	3	0	3
*McWilliams	7	9	.438	4.70	30	19	2	2	0	0	126.1	139	568	70	66	9	4	3	7	62	11	52	4	0	3
Walk	2	3	.400	3.68	9	9	1	0	1	0	58.2	60	248	27	24	3	3	1	0	18	2	40	2	3	1
Bielecki	2	3	.400	4.53	12	7	0	1	0	0	45.2	45	211	26	23	5	4	0	1	31	1	22	1	1	1
*Kipper	1	2	.333	5.11	5	4	0	1	0	0	24.2	21	104	16	14	4	1	1	0	7	0	13	0	0	0
							Relievers																		
Guante	4	6	.400	2.72	63	0	0	31	0	5	109.0	84	445	34	33	5	4	3	5	40	9	92	5	0	6
Robinson	5	11	.313	3.87	44	6	0	22	0	3	95.1	95	418	49	41	6	2	0	2	42	11	65	2	0	4
Winn	3	6	.333	5.23	30	7	0	10	0	0	75.2	77	326	45	44	4	2	1	2	31	2	22	5	2	2
Holland	1	3	.250	3.38	38	0	0	19	0	4	58.2	48	235	22	22	5	4	3	0	17	6	47	0	1	3
*Candelaria	2	4	.333	3.64	37	0	0	26	0	9	54.1	57	229	23	22	7	3	4	1	14	2	47	0	0	4
*Scurry	0	1	.000	3.21	30	0	0	13	0	2	47.2	42	210	17	17	4	2	2	0	28	1	43	3	0	2
*Clements	0	2	.000	3.67	27	0	0	7	0	2	34.1	39	153	14	14	2	2	1	0	15	3	17	2	0	0
Krawczyk	0	2	.000	14.04	8	0	0	3	0	0	8.1	20	51	13	13	1	0	0	1	6	3	9	1	0	0
Tekulve	0	0	.000	16.20	3	0	0	1	0	0	3.1	7	21	7	6	1	1	0	0	5	1	4	0	0	0
*Tomlin	0	0	.000	0.00	1	0	0	0	0	0	1.0	1	4	0	0	0	0	0	0	1	0	1	0	1	0

Tony PENA, Catcher

	G	AB	Hit	2B	3B	HR	Run	RBI	TBB	SO	SB	CS	Avg
4.06 years		582	166	28	3	13	62	71	30	75	8	8	.285
1985	147	546	136	27	2	10	53	59	29	67	12	8	.249
First Half	80	306	82	14	1	6	32	31	17		4		.268
Second Half	67	240	54	13	1	4	21	28	12		8		.225
Vs. RHP		395	97			8		50					.246
Vs. LHP		151	39			2		9					.258
Home	77	280	69	15	2	2	32	32			3		.246
Road	70	266	67	12	0	8	21	27			9		.252
Grass	36	137	29	4	0	4	9	8			4		.212
Turf	111	409	107	23	2	6	44	51			8		.262

Sam KHALIFA, Shortstop

	G	AB	Hit	2B	3B	HR	Run	RBI	TBB	SO	SB	CS	Avg
0.59 years		544	130	24	5	3	51	53	58	95	9	3	.238
1985	95	320	76	14	3	2	30	31	34	56	5	2	.238
First Half	20	70	21	5	0	0	7	3	8		0		.300
Second Half	75	249	55	9	3	2	23	28	26		5		.221
Vs. RHP		233	53			2		24					.227
Vs. LHP		86	23			0		7					.267
Home	49	165	42	12	0	1	17	14			1		.255
Road	46	154	34	2	3	1	13	17			4		.221
Grass	23	80	14	2	0	1	4	10			1		.175
Turf	72	239	62	12	3	1	26	21			4		.259

Jason THOMPSON, First Base

	G	AB	Hit	2B	3B	HR	Run	RBI	TBB	SO	SB	CS	Avg
8.57 years		555	145	23	1	24	74	91	93	99	1	1	.262
1985	123	402	97	17	1	12	42	61	84	58	0	0	.241
First Half	73	245	58	11	1	10	25	42	43		0		.237
Second Half	50	157	39	6	0	2	17	19	41		0		.248
Vs. RHP		281	65			9		42					.231
Vs. LHP		121	32			3		19					.264
Home	65	215	43	10	0	9	26	39			0		.200
Road	58	187	54	7	1	3	16	22			0		.289
Grass	33	106	37	6	0	3	8	17			0		.349
Turf	90	296	60	11	1	9	34	44			0		.203

R. J. REYNOLDS, Left Field

	G	AB	Hit	2B	3B	HR	Run	RBI	TBB	SO	SB	CS	Avg
1.24 years		509	137	22	7	6	58	62	31	79	24	8	.269
1985	104	337	95	15	7	3	44	42	22	49	18	5	.282
First Half	57	177	47	10	3	0	16	23	11		6		.266
Second Half	47	160	48	5	4	3	28	19	11		12		.300
Vs. RHP		226	66	9	4	3		29	18	40			.292
Vs. LHP		111	29	6	3	0		13	4	9			.261
Home	48	150	45	10	3	1	20	18			8		.300
Road	56	187	50	5	4	2	24	24			10		.267
Grass	53	160	45	8	1	0	19	20			7		.281
Turf	51	177	50	7	6	3	25	22			11		.282

Johnny RAY, Second Base

	G	AB	Hit	2B	3B	HR	Run	RBI	TBB	SO	SB	CS	Avg
4.03 years		614	175	37	6	6	74	64	40	31	14	8	.285
1985	154	594	163	33	3	7	67	70	46	24	13	9	.274
First Half	82	331	87	20	1	5	34	35	11		5		.263
Second Half	72	263	76	13	2	2	33	35	35		8		.289
Vs. RHP		424	120	24	2	6		57	36	7			.283
Vs. LHP		170	43	9	1	1		13	10	17			.253
Home	76	283	81	21	2	3	36	37			10		.286
Road	78	311	82	12	1	4	31	33			3		.264
Grass	41	161	40	6	1	2	12	14			0		.248
Turf	113	433	123	27	2	5	55	56			13		.284

Joe ORSULAK, Center Field

	G	AB	Hit	2B	3B	HR	Run	RBI	TBB	SO	SB	CS	Avg
0.99 years		481	140	15	8	0	67	25	27	36	27	13	.291
1985	121	397	119	14	6	0	54	21	26	27	24	11	.300
First Half	54	162	47	6	2	0	14	7	12		5		.290
Second Half	67	235	72	8	4	0	40	14	14		19		.306
Vs. RHP		332	105			0		17					.316
Vs. LHP		65	14			0		4					.215
Home	58	184	68	5	5	0	28	12			12		.370
Road	63	213	51	9	1	0	26	9			12		.239
Grass	29	93	21	5	0	0	9	2			5		.226
Turf	92	304	98	9	6	0	45	19			19		.322

Mike BROWN, Right Field

	G	AB	Hit	2B	3B	HR	Run	RBI	TBB	SO	SB	CS	Avg
1.30 years		471	135	31	5	15	64	65	38	70	2	5	.287
1985	117	358	109	27	3	9	52	53	29	48	2	3	.304
First Half	47	122	31	8	1	3	17	17	5		0		.254
Second Half	70	236	78	19	2	6	35	36	24		2		.331
Vs. RHP		223	62			4		25					.278
Vs. LHP		135	47			5		28					.348
Home	53	163	44	14	0	4	25	24			2		.270
Road	64	195	65	13	3	5	27	29			0		.333
Grass	58	156	44	8	1	6	24	24			0		.282
Turf	59	202	65	19	2	3	28	29			2		.322

RICK RHODEN

	(W–L)	GS	Run	Avg	DP	Avg	SB	Avg
1984	(14-9)	33	123	3.73	33	1.00	19	.58
1985	(10-15)	35	128	3.66	19	.54	23	.66
1976-1985		259	1084	4.19	232	.90	168	.65

	G	IP	W	L	Pct	ER	BB	SO	ERA
1984 Home	17	129.3	8	3	.727	27	32	70	1.88
1985 Home	19	118.0	7	9	.438	58	38	66	4.42
1984 Road	16	109.0	6	6	.500	45	30	66	3.72
1985 Road	16	95.3	3	6	.333	48	31	62	4.53
1984 Grass	9	58.7	3	5	.375	30	19	44	4.60
1985 Grass	9	58.0	2	4	.333	25	17	35	3.88
1984 Turf	24	179.7	11	4	.733	42	43	92	2.10
1985 Turf	26	155.3	8	11	.421	81	52	93	4.69
1985 Total	35	213.3	10	15	.400	106	69	128	4.47

Marvell WYNNE, Center Field

	G	AB	Hit	2B	3B	HR	Run	RBI	TBB	SO	SB	CS	Avg
2.22 years		610	149	21	7	4	74	37	44	81	21	15	.245
1985	103	337	69	6	3	2	21	18	18	48	10	5	.205
First Half	58	213	51	5	3	1	14	13	11		9		.239
Second Half	45	124	18	1	0	1	7	5	7		1		.145
Vs. RHP		226	42			1		9					.186
Vs. LHP		111	27			1		9					.243
Home	52	158	37	3	2	1	11	11			5		.234
Road	51	179	32	3	1	1	10	7			5		.179
Grass	28	97	15	3	0	0	3	4			2		.155
Turf	75	240	54	3	3	2	18	14			8		.225

RICK REUSCHEL

	(W–L)	GS	Run	Avg	DP	Avg	SB	Avg
1984	(5-5)	14	67	4.79	18	1.29	9	.64
1985	(14-8)	26	96	3.69	25	.96	14	.54
1977-1985		240	954	3.98	195	.81	149	.62

	G	IP	W	L	Pct	ER	BB	SO	ERA
1984 Home	11	54.0	4	1	.800	34	13	25	5.67
1985 Home	16	104.3	12	3	.800	26	25	76	2.24
1984 Road	8	38.3	1	4	.200	19	10	18	4.46
1985 Road	15	89.7	2	5	.286	23	27	62	2.31
1984 Grass	15	67.7	4	3	.571	40	17	31	5.32
1985 Grass	8	52.0	1	2	.333	14	15	41	2.42
1984 Turf	4	24.7	1	2	.333	13	6	12	4.74
1985 Turf	23	142.0	13	6	.684	35	37	97	2.22
1985 Total	31	194.0	14	8	.636	49	52	138	2.27

Jim MORRISON, Infield

	G	AB	Hit	2B	3B	HR	Run	RBI	TBB	SO	SB	CS	Avg
4.51 years		490	129	24	2	16	54	58	28	72	7	4	.264
1985	92	244	62	10	0	4	17	22	8	44	3	0	.254
First Half	55	140	36	6	0	0	10	8	5		1		.257
Second Half	37	104	26	4	0	4	7	14	3		2		.250
Vs. RHP		135	33			3		13					.244
Vs. LHP		109	29			1		9					.266
Home	51	132	34	5	0	4	9	9			2		.258
Road	41	112	28	5	0	0	8	13			1		.250
Grass	17	42	11	3	0	0	3	3			0		.262
Turf	75	202	51	7	0	4	14	19			3		.252

Bill ALMON, Utility

	G	AB	Hit	2B	3B	HR	Run	RBI	TBB	SO	SB	CS	Avg
6.46 years		470	121	19	4	4	54	41	32	88	18	9	.258
1985	88	244	66	17	0	6	33	29	22	61	10	7	.270
First Half	57	170	48	10	0	4	22	22	16		6		.282
Second Half	31	74	18	7	0	2	11	7	6		4		.243
Vs. RHP		108	28			3		18					.259
Vs. LHP		136	38			3		11					.279
Home	46	113	39	11	0	3	21	16			6		.345
Road	42	131	27	6	0	3	12	13			4		.206
Grass	24	77	16	5	0	2	8	9			2		.208
Turf	64	167	50	12	0	4	25	20			8		.299

JOSE DeLEON

	(W–L)	GS	Run	Avg	DP	Avg	SB	Avg
1984	(7-13)	28	93	3.32	21	.75	41	1.46
1985	(2-19)	25	58	2.32	11	.44	24	.96
1983-1985		68	216	3.18	47	.69	86	1.26

	G	IP	W	L	Pct	ER	BB	SO	ERA
1984 Home	15	112.7	6	8	.429	39	39	100	3.12
1985 Home	15	88.0	2	9	.182	38	45	94	3.89
1984 Road	15	79.7	1	5	.167	41	53	53	4.63
1985 Road	16	74.7	0	10	0.000	47	44	55	5.67
1984 Grass	7	37.0	1	1	.500	21	23	27	5.11
1985 Grass	8	37.3	0	5	0.000	20	19	35	4.82
1984 Turf	23	155.3	6	12	.333	59	69	126	3.42
1985 Turf	23	125.3	2	14	.125	65	70	114	4.67
1985 Total	31	162.7	2	19	.095	85	89	149	4.70

LEE TUNNELL

	(W–L)	GS	Run	Avg	DP	Avg	SB	Avg
1984	(1-7)	6	23	3.83	4	.67	5	.83
1985	(4-10)	23	89	3.87	22	.96	17	.74
1983-1985		57	230	4.04	61	1.07	36	.63

	G	IP	W	L	Pct	ER	BB	SO	ERA
1984 Home	9	30.0	1	4	.200	19	23	22	5.70
1985 Home	12	68.3	2	4	.333	36	30	35	4.74
1984 Road	17	38.3	0	3	0.000	21	17	29	4.93
1985 Road	12	64.0	2	6	.250	23	27	39	3.23
1984 Grass	8	25.0	0	1	0.000	11	10	14	3.96
1985 Grass	5	23.3	1	3	.250	10	6	13	3.86
1984 Turf	18	43.3	1	6	.143	29	30	37	6.02
1985 Turf	19	109.0	3	7	.300	49	51	61	4.05
1985 Total	24	132.3	4	10	.286	59	57	74	4.01

OTHERS

	(W–L)	GS	Run	Avg	DP	Avg	SB	Avg
McWilliams	(7-9)	19	87	4.58	21	1.11	5	.26
Walk	(2-3)	9	42	4.67	5	.56	8	.89
Winn	(3-6)	7	19	2.71	6	.86	7	1.00
Bielecki	(2-3)	7	18	2.57	5	.71	1	.14
Robinson	(5-11)	6	18	3.00	6	1.00	3	.50
Kipper	(1-2)	4	15	3.75	3	.75	4	1.00

NATIONAL LEAGUE WEST
DIVISION SHEET

Club	1st	2nd	v RHP	v LHP	Home	Road	Grass	Turf	Day	Night	Total	Pct
Los Angeles	48-37	47-30	65-49	30-18	48-33	47-34	71-49	24-18	28-24	67-43	95-67	.586
Cincinnati	44-41	45-31	67-55	22-17	47-34	42-38	22-25	67-47	32-24	57-48	89-72	.553
Houston	43-45	40-34	44-50	39-29	44-37	39-42	28-20	55-59	23-13	60-66	83-79	.512
San Diego	49-39	34-40	57-51	26-28	44-37	39-42	64-56	19-23	26-29	57-50	83-79	.512
Atlanta	39-47	27-49	53-68	13-28	32-49	34-47	46-74	20-22	24-26	42-70	66-96	.407
San Francisco	33-55	29-45	47-72	15-28	38-43	24-57	51-69	11-31	39-52	23-48	62-100	.383

COME FROM BEHIND WINS

Club	1	2	3	4	5	6	7	Total	Points
Los Angeles	21	12	7	2				42	116
Cincinnati	19	14	6	2	1	2		44	134
Houston	21	10	4	1	1			37	99
San Diego	17	8	2	3				30	81
Atlanta	17	9	4	1	1			32	88
San Francisco	16	9	1	1	1			28	74

BLOWN LEADS

Club	1	2	3	4	5	6	7	Total	Points
Los Angeles	14	7	4	1	2			28	82
Cincinnati	13	9	1	0	2			25	69
Houston	15	11	3	2	2			33	97
San Diego	21	11	3	3	1	1		40	115
Atlanta	19	7	6	1				33	88
San Francisco	26	19	4	1				50	130

RECORDS WHEN AHEAD, TIED, BEHIND, AFTER SEVEN

Club	Ahead	Tied	Behind
Los Angeles	78-5	8-13	9-49
Cincinnati	66-2	13- 7	10-63
Houston	66-8	9-13	6-58
San Diego	70-3	8-17	5-59
Atlanta	48-9	12- 8	6-79
San Francisco	42-11	13-11	7-78

CLUB BATTING

Club	G	AB	R	H	TB	2B	3B	HR	RBI	GW	SH	SF	HP	BB	IB	SO	SB	CS	GI DP	LOB	SHO	Avg	Slug	OBP
Los Angeles	162	5502	682	1434	2103	226	28	129	632	87	104	46	31	539	69	846	136	58	108	1187	6	.261	.382	.328
Cincinnati	162	5431	677	1385	2044	249	34	114	634	84	72	41	23	576	72	856	159	70	136	1134	16	.255	.376	.327
Houston	162	5582	706	1457	2165	261	42	121	666	77	66	44	23	477	63	873	96	56	127	1117	10	.261	.388	.319
San Diego	162	5507	650	1405	2029	241	28	109	611	81	75	32	23	513	68	809	60	39	128	1156	7	.255	.368	.320
Atlanta	162	5526	632	1359	2006	213	28	126	598	58	65	41	22	553	56	849	72	52	154	1163	18	.246	.363	.315
San Francisco	162	5420	556	1263	1887	217	31	115	517	58	93	25	37	488	53	962	99	55	121	1090	14	.233	.348	.299

OPPOSITION BATTING

Club	G	AB	R	H	TB	2B	3B	HR	RBI	GW	SH	SF	HP	BB	IB	SO	SB	CS	GI DP	LOB	SHO	Avg	Slug	OBP
Los Angeles	162	5465	579	1280	1862	218	29	102	534	60	57	38	21	462	56	979	99	65	108		21	.234	.341	
Cincinnati	162	5426	666	1347	2039	223	38	131	622	63	74	51	14	535	61	910	133	58	118		11	.248	.376	.315
Houston	162		691	1393				119			72	58	25	543	50	909	143				9			
San Diego	162	5447	622	1399	2069	221	34	127	589	76	91	43	25	443	50	727	138	65	125		19	.257	.380	.313
Atlanta	162	5579	781	1512	2246	262	35	134	737	90	88	35	28	642	83	776	158	60	169		9	.271	.403	.347
San Francisco	162	5448	674	1348	2035	242	35	125	628	90	88	40	19	572	76	985	143	54	109		5	.247	.374	.319

CLUB PITCHING

Club	W	L	ERA	G	CG	SHO	SV	IP	H	TBF	R	ER	HR	SH	SF	HB	TB	IB	SO	WP	BK
Los Angeles	95	67	2.96	162	37	21	36	1465.0	1280	6043	579	482	102	57	38	21	462	56	979	42	10
Cincinnati	89	72	3.71	162	24	11	45	1451.1	1347	6100	666	598	131	74	51	14	535	61	910	42	5
Houston	83	79	3.66	162	17	9	42	1458.0	1393	6185	691	593	119	72	58	25	543	50	909	69	8
San Diego	83	79	3.40	162	26	19	44	1451.1	1399	6049	622	549	127	91	43	25	443	50	727	23	14
Atlanta	66	96	4.19	162	9	9	29	1457.1	1512	6374	781	679	134	88	35	28	642	83	776	35	4
San Francisco	62	100	3.61	162	13	5	24	1448.0	1348	6168	674	581	125	88	40	19	572	76	985	57	16

OPPOSITION PITCHING

Club	W	L	ERA	G	CG	SHO	SV	IP	H	TBF	R	ER	HR	SH	SF	HB	TB	IB	SO	WP	BK
Los Angeles	67	95	3.75	162	23	6	29	1451.2	1434	6222	682	605	129	10	46	31	539	69	846	49	7
Cincinnati	72	89	3.73	162	24	16	28	1444.2	1385	6143	677	598	114	72	41	23	576	72	856	34	11
Houston	79	83		162		10			1457	6192	706		121	66	44	23	477	63	873		
San Diego	79	73	3.62	162	15	7	40	1448.0	1405	6150	650	582	109	75	32	23	513	68	809	44	8
Atlanta	96	66	3.37	162	25	18	44	1471.0	1359	6207	632	550	126	65	41	22	553	56	849	39	7
San Francisco	100	62	2.96	162	35	14	48	1472.1	1263	6063	556	485	115	93	25	37	488	53	962	37	9

CLUB FIELDING

Club	G	PO	A	E	TC	DP	TP	PB	OSB	OCS	OSB%	OA/SFA	Pct	DER	OR
Los Angeles	162	4395	1903	166	6464	131	0	7	99	65	.604	34/38	.974	711	579
Cincinnati	162	4354	1679	122	6155	142	0	10	133	58	.686	39/51	.980	711	666
Houston	162	4374	1789	152	6315	159	0	36	143			33/58	.976	698	691
San Diego	162	4354	1730	124	6208	158	0	6	138	65	.680	44/43	.980	712	622
Atlanta	162	4372	2028	159	6559	197	0	8	158	60	.725	27/35	.976	689	781
San Francisco	162	4344	1773	148	6265	134	0	20	143	54	.726	28/40	.976	703	674

LOS ANGELES DODGERS

BREAKDOWNS FOR THE LAST TEN SEASONS

Won-Lost Record: 872-697, .556 (Best in the division, 3rd-best in the majors)
Runs Scored: 6,563 (2nd-best in the division)
Runs Allowed: 5,762 (Fewest of any major league team)
Home Runs Hit: 1,359 (Most of any National League team)
Home Runs Allowed: 939 (2nd-fewest in the division)

RECORD IN:
April: 129-80, .617 (Best in baseball)
May: 154-118, .566 (Best in the division, 4th in baseball)
June: 130-131, .498 (5th in the division)
July: 127-117, .520 (Best in the division, 9th in baseball)
August: 164-114, .590 (Best in the division, 2nd best in the majors)
September: 155-123, .558 (2nd in the division)
October: 13-14, .481 (4th in the division)

Won-Lost Record in Road Games: 405-379, .517 (Best in the division, 3rd in the majors)
Won-Lost Record at Home: 467-318, .595 (Best in the division, 5th in baseball)
Home Field Advantage: 61½ games
Runs Scored on the Road: 3,349 (Best in the division)
Runs Scored at Home: 3,214 (3rd in the division)
Runs Allowed on the Road: 3,010 (Fewest of any major league team)
Runs Allowed at Home: 2,752 (2nd-fewest of any major league team)

Home Runs Hit on the Road: 691 (Most in the National League)
Home Runs Hit at Home: 668 (2nd-best in the division)
Home Runs Allowed on the Road: 442 (Fewest of any major league team)
Home Runs Allowed at Home: 497 (3rd-fewest in the division)

RECORD FOR LAST THREE SEASONS: 265-221, .545 (Best in the division, 5th-best in the major leagues)

It's always easy to take the test after you know the answer. After the 1985 N.L. Playoff, Tommy Lasorda was very widely second-guessed for making a decision which is obviously correct. I refer, of course, to the decision to pitch to Jack Clark in the ninth inning of the fifth game of the N.L. Playoffs. The game situation was:

- Dodgers leading 5–4,
- runners on second and third,
- first base open,
- two out,
- Clark batting,
- Van Slyke on deck,
- right-hander (Niedenfuer) on the mound.
- Niedenfuer had struck out Clark in the seventh.

Clark is a great hitter, and Van Slyke is not. When Clark hit a home run many people were inevitably going to argue that he should have been walked. Mike Downey in *The Sporting News,* still kinder than many, wrote that "I would have cut Clark's bat in half with a Texas chainsaw before I'd let him swing at a pitch." Whitey Herzog got in the act, solidifying his reputation as baseball's lowest-ranking diplomat, by being quoted as saying that "I've always figured that if I can pitch to a guy making $1.3 million a year or a guy making $100,000 a year, I pitch to the guy making $100,000."

Not in this case, you wouldn't. The first thing to look at is batting average, the chance that the batter will get the hit that will score the two runs. With a right-hander on the mound, the left-handed Van Slyke had a much better batting average than the right-handed Clark (.282 to .257). What makes Clark a great hitter and Van Slyke a platoon player is that Clark destroys left-handers (.331 in 1985) while Van Slyke doesn't hit them (.109)—an irrelevant difference with a right-hander on the mound.

But had the difference been reversed—even if Clark were a .282 hitter against a right-hander, and Van Slyke .257—it still would not make sense to walk Clark, since, if you walk Clark, then another walk scores the tying run. The other comparison that has to be made is between Clark's *batting average* (.257) and Van Slyke's *on base percentage* (probably about .370 against a right-hander). Of course, the .370 on-base percentage would go down with the pitcher aware that he couldn't give up the walk—but the batting average and (worse yet) the slugging percentage would go up. Van Slyke is a very disciplined hitter, and thus would have maximum ability to take advantage of the bases loaded situation. With the pitcher forced to come in to him, his batting average probably would have been in the neighborhood of .320.

The batting average is the key to this situation because it covers both of the major possibilities, the one- and two-run possibilities. But what happened, as it turns out, was three runs. If you focus not on the outcome, which we can see now but Lasorda could not have seen at the time, but on the possibilities, well . . . With a right-hander on the mound, Clark *doesn't* have significantly more power. These are their batting stats against a right-hander:

	AB	H	HR	RBI	AVG.
Clark	300	77	13	54	.257
Van Slyke	369	104	13	52	.282

Clark hits home runs a little more often, but since Van Slyke hits doubles and triples more frequently than Clark overall, against any type of pitcher, then facing a right-hander it is likely that he would more than off-set this difference by his added doubles and triples.

But to put the Dodgers two runs behind, Clark has to hit a home run; Van Slyke could do it with a home run, a double or a triple. Clark's chance of hitting a home run is 4.3%; guessing that probably no more than one of Van Slyke's six hits against lefties was a double or triple, Van Slyke's chance of putting the Dodgers two runs behind would be 11.7%—almost three times as great.

So if you walk Clark:

1) You're bringing a *better* hitter to the plate facing a right-hander,

2) You're allowing the Cardinals to tie the game with a walk,

3) You're using up the margin of error for the pitcher, and

4) You're making an extra-base hit as damaging as a home run.

Against this you have one advantage—the fact that the veteran Clark has a well-deserved reputation as a clutch terror, while the young Van Slyke does not.

That's a lunatic trade.

Even giving Clark enormous credit for his clutch ability, you can't believe that Clark is as likely to hit a home run as Van Slyke is to hit a double.

The other option which has been discussed would have been to walk Clark, bring in Jerry Reuss out of the bullpen, and force Herzog to pinch-hit Brian Harper for Van Slyke. Harper is even more unproven than Van Slyke—but Reuss also gives up nine hits per nine innings, whereas Niedenfuer gives up seven, plus, again, you're letting the Cardinals tie it up with a walk, etc., plus, again, you're giving up the platoon advantage. You're trading a deterioration in the game situation, a platoon advantage and the use of your best available pitcher to get rid of one outstanding hitter. And Brian Harper, who can't throw, run, or field, is on a major league roster *only* because he can hit. Again, that's no trade in my book.

Lasorda made the only reasonable move in the circumstances. It just didn't work.

DEAR BILL

Steven Goldleaf
DeWitt, N.Y.

Bill James
Winchester, Ks

Dear Bill,

On page 245 of the '85 *Abstract,* you asked why someone doesn't do a study of "these" outfield-to-third-base conversions to see if more than 5% of them work. I just did one.

"These" conversions take in a lot of room, so I stuck close to instances most like Pedro Guerrero, whose career you were talking about. I looked for people who:

a) had played at least 150 outfield games (Pedro had 264 outfield games before the 1983 season);

b) had played no more than 100 games at third (Pedro had 51 at third before the 1983 season);

c) and then proceeded to play at least 100 career games at third, with at least one year as their team's regular (defined as half the team's games) at third base.

I found twenty such players. (Actually, I found closer to thirty, but the others brought complicating extraneous problems, which don't exist in Guerrero's case, mostly by dint of having played another position in addition to outfield before the switch.) Excluded are such players as Pete Rose (2b), Dan Meyer (1b), Deron Johnson (1b), Bobby Lowe (2b), Buck Ewing (c-1b) and Jackie Robinson (1b-2b).

Immediate disasters at third base have also excluded some notable experiments—Yastrzemski is the most well-known, but the Reds in '58 seem to have toyed briefly with Frank Robinson at third base, and I can recall the '63 Mets trying Jim Hickman at third base for 59 games. Also excluded from my survey were such disasters as Tommy Davis (147 games lifetime at third, but no season as the regular) and Dave Kingman (154 games, and likewise). But lest you think that all marginal non-qualifiers are disasters, let me bring forth such examples as Graig Nettles (70 outfield games, with 26 third base games in 1968–1969), Buddy Bell (123 outfield games his rookie year, 1972) and Enos Cabell (67 outfield games in 1975, then 143 third base games in 1976). These might suggest that those transplants marginally excluded from my survey succeeded on occasion. (Bell, I think, did play third in the minors and was in a holding pattern his rookie year, but still . . . .)

Of the twenty players who qualified, 13 were failures at third base by anyone's standards. They are Don Demeter, Sid Gordon, Tommy Harper, Peanuts Lowrey, Mel Ott, Andy Pafko, Joe Sommer, Bobby Thomson, Possum Whitted, Dick Williams, Chuck Workman and Joel Youngblood. Of these 13, 10 were returned to an easier position after a year at third, and the other three were returned after another season. The only room for argument here would concern those players who were shifted back despite what seem to be adequate defensive statistics—Ott, Pafko—accompanied by an increase in offensive ability, but since their managers obviously thought otherwise, I will accept their judgment for the nonce.

Two transplants decidedly took: Bob Elliot followed his first three outfield years with twelve solid seasons, including an MVP year, at third base, and George Davis. Entirely anomalously, Davis's career took the opposite shape from that ordained in the 1981 *Abstract,* p. 169: "all players, virtually without exception, move *downward* and *leftward* over time." Davis, however, moved rightward; his first three years were as an outfielder, his next five as a third baseman, then for his last thirteen years in the bigs Davis played well over 90% of his games at shortstop. Better change that "virtually" to an "almost."

The other six cases are less clear. Three of them are outfielders shifted to third base who then retired after neither distinguishing nor disgracing themselves: Frenchy Bordagaray played parts of nine seasons (for six teams) mostly at outfield, then was put at third, where he played one season as regular in 1944 and one part-time in 1945, and then he retired in 1946. The return of players from World War II and Bordagaray's age (34) suggest that the shift in position didn't play much of a role in Bordagaray's retirement.

Paul Dade also retired soon after switching. He had been a Cleveland outfielder (224 outfield games, 30 at third base) when he was traded in mid-year, 1979, to San Diego, where he put in two years at third. The first year he hit .276 with some speed and no power, with average fielding stats (2.94 range factor and .949 fielding percentage). Then he batted (and slugged) .189, and he was history. His inability to hit seems more relevant than his adaption to third base.

Elliot Maddox played third in 1980, his final year, for the Mets, after which he, too, fell off the earth's edge, again more for offensive than defensive reasons.

The fourth unclear case is Frank Thomas, who played 394 games lifetime at third, and seems like another attempt to force an extra bat into the lineup, à la Tommy Davis, Dave Kingman, Carl Yastrzemski. (Cincinnati, the year before trying Thomas at third for 64 games, had tried Frank Robinson there.) Of this "unclear" group, Thomas seems to have been the weakest third baseman; the only reason he got 394 games in (with two seasons as a regular) seems to have been the desperation of the teams that he played for. In both of those seasons, he was far and away the worst third baseman in captivity.

The best of the problem cases, probably, is Mike Shannon. Finishing his career (with three and a half years at third base) prematurely for health reasons, Shannon was a good player and a good third baseman, though his credentials are inflated to my mind in the '85 *Abstract,* where you say he was "just becoming a top-flight third baseman." Top-flight? Nah. But he was OK.

Finally, we have Pepper Martin, who was repotted to third for three full seasons for the Gas House Gang. Martin's defensive stats were only slightly below average for two years, but his third year, 1935, he fielded a Hobsonian .904 (with a low range factor) and spent the rest of his career in the outfield. Since Martin never recovered offensively either, and mostly played part-time for the six years he was returned to the outfield, his downslide probably wasn't affected by playing third base as much as by old age (Martin was 31 the last year he played third regularly).

So, counting three of this problem group as successes at handling the switch to third (Shannon, Martin, and either Bordagaray, Dade, or Maddox), and adding our two clear successes, I count about five out of twenty of "these" outfield-to-third-base conversions that work. The odds, then, may be closer to 3-to-1 than to 20-to-1 that you surmised, but your point is well taken—turning an outfielder into a third baseman is a risky proposition and likely to flop.

Cheers,
Steven Goldleaf

DEAR STEVEN

Bill James

Steven Goldleaf

Dear Steven:

Terrific letter. A few reactions to your fine study (which I will print in the '86 *Abstract* if you will give permission).

1) While obviously I can see why you did it, it seems clear to me that the 100-games and one-season-as-the-regular requirements exclude from the study the most apparent failures, and thus bias the study toward a higher percentage of successes than really occurs.

2) Your comment to the contrary is that this also excludes such "positive" examples as Graig Nettles, Buddy Bell and Enos Cabell, but in truth Bell and Nettles were both accomplished third basemen who had to play a year in the outfield before their position became open; they did *not* attempt to convert to it at the major league level, like Tommy Davis and Pedro Guerrero. Cabell had also played the position in the minors, although it was not his primary position.

3) Bob Elliot is the strongest case. I checked out his minor league career, and he apparently had never played third base before his switch there in 1942; if he had, at least not in his last three sessions in the minors. But he turned into a good one.

4) If you have to go back to 1897 and George Davis to find an exception, I'll stick with "virtually without exception."

5) Paul Dade, Elliot Maddox and Frank Thomas, I think, are clear failures. I mean, when a guy gets released after two years of trying to convert to third base, you can hardly call that a success, can you?

6) I can think of a whole lot more experiments that I would have to consider failures, including Clint Hurdle, Roy Sievers (yes, they did), Orlando Cepeda (they *really* did) and Manny Mota. In fact, it is generally true that between 1958 and 1975 the Giants tried to make a third baseman out of every outfielder in their system except Willie Mays.

7) But Mike Shannon, I think, was an unqualified success, and I can't share your reservations about him. I mean, look at the MVP voting in 1968. Shannon finished seventh, behind five sure Hall of Famers (Bob Gibson, Pete Rose, Willie McCovey, Juan Marichal, and Lou Brock) and Curt Flood. Behind him were Billy Williams, Glenn Beckert, the Alou brothers, Hank Aaron, Willie Mays, Ernie Banks, Jerry Koosman and Johnny Bench. Either he was doing the job pretty well, or he sure fooled the people who saw him play. He was listed on 11 of 20 MVP votes that year.

8) Pepper Martin was an infielder prior to 1927, converted to the outfield by Houston. I'll give you Pepper. That leaves 4 out of 20 by your count, which I think should be more like 4 out of 40. So at one out of 20, I was probably a little low; it's probably more like one out of ten.

Best,
Bill James

DEAR BILL

Steven Goldleaf

Bill James

Dear Bill,

Sure. I'd be delighted to be quoted in the 1986 *Abstract.* (If you could change the title, though—maybe to the *1986 Abstract of Applied Physics as Interfaced with 19th and 20th Century Americanist Folklore?*—it would do more for my tenure chances). Glad you liked it. A few quibbles and retorts:

Points 1), 2) and 3): Absolutely, yup, and uh-huh.

Point 4), Cryptic, but OK.

Pount 5) With Thomas, as I said, I'm inclined to agree. With Dade and Maddox, we've got differences. No one could defend their performances at bat during their final year (1980 for both). They were lousy hitters, but as far as I can tell, not bad third basemen. I was trying to measure, in part, the effect that switching positions has on players. Third base from the outfield is an interesting choice in this regard because third base fits in between center and the other outfield spots on your defensive spectrum, so center fielders like Maddox would move leftward while left fielders like Thomas would move right—and to the same (controlled) position, so this is the position to look at if you are interested in the effect that defensive switches bear on offensive. My study only covers a corner of that issue. Bearing Guerrero in mind as my model, though, I was looking to see if the defensive strain of playing third could be at fault (and, if so, how much), or if failures at third could be judged more by the failure to field the position. Maddox and Dade, obviously, lost the battle not because of their fielding, but because of their bats.

I'd be interested in a more systematic study of defensive switching of positions affecting hitting. Was that what stopped Santo, as you've suggested, or was it his age, the switch of leagues, the switch of parks from Wrigley to Comiskey. Harrah seems to be coping well with many of the same conditions.

With respect to Shannon, there's not much point in quibbling over adjectives. I have to wonder how important minor league positions are to this argument. I'd guess there are very few players who *hadn't,* for a protracted period in the minors, played a more demanding position than the one they ended up playing in the majors, as an organization tested the limits of their skills. Except for the rare times when a team has a glut of talent at one position, as in Bell and Nettles, or thinks they do, then the fact that a minor-league infielder was switched to an easier position in the majors is a pretty damning appraisal of his ability at the minor-league position.

Best,
Steven Goldleaf

P.S. Do you know why Dick Stuart had such an ungodly assists record?

DEAR STEVEN

Bill James
Steven Goldleaf

Dear Steven:

I dunno, maybe his pitchers figured he needed a lot of help.

The argument about Dade and Maddox is kind of a "the operation was a success but the patient died" argument. Regardless of your theoretical interests in the issue, which I can share, it seems to me that the basic question of interest to Dodger fans and others in a similar position is whether such a move has a reasonable chance to help the team. As such, I am interested in *whether* the move succeeded, and not *why* it failed.

While it is true that most players attempt a more difficult position in the minor leagues, I do not think that the case of a team coming up with a surplus of talent at one position is in any sense rare; after all, probably 70% of positions in baseball are solidly occupied at any moment, so it seems to me that *most* players, in coming to the majors, are likely to encounter an entrenched player. I think that most of the time, when a player is shifted to another position *on coming to the major leagues,* as opposed to being shifted in the low minors like Guerrero, it is a response to talent surpluses, and not a reflection on the player's defensive skills.

The fact is that, studying the issue reasonably comprehensibly, the study reports only four clear-cut cases of outfielders successfully converting to third base—while there must be almost that many failures every year, although most of those failures are with marginal players trying to save their careers, and not with Pedro Guerrero. It seems to me that, unless someone can point out a half-dozen examples that were missed (not infielders being reconverted after a stay in the outfield), that we must conclude that, in considering such shifts, major league organizations have tended to overestimate the chances of success. Teams have focused on the physical skills demanded by the position—Pedro Guerrero has the arm, the agility and the reflexes required to play third base—and have underestimated the difficulty of developing the refined skills which the position requires.

COMPLETE BATTING RECORDS

Player	G	AB	R	H	TB	2B	3B	HR	RBI	GW	SH	SF	HB	BB	IB	SO	SB	CS	GI DP	Avg	Slug	OBP	Runs Created	Outs Made	Runs/ 27 Outs	OW%	Appr Value
*Scioscia	141	429	47	127	180	26	3	7	53	4	11	3	5	77	9	21	3	3	10	.296	.420	.407	78	329	6.37	.728	11
*Brock	129	438	64	110	192	19	0	21	66	4	2	2	0	54	4	72	4	2	9	.251	.438	.332	65	343	5.08	.630	8
Sax	136	488	62	136	155	8	4	1	42	6	3	3	3	54	12	43	27	11	15	.279	.318	.352	56	384	3.92	.503	11
Madlock	34	114	20	41	51	4	0	2	15	2	0	1	3	10	0	11	7	1	3	.360	.447	.422	23	78	7.92	.805	2
†Duncan	142	562	74	137	191	24	6	6	39	5	13	4	3	38	4	113	38	8	9	.244	.340	.293	60	459	3.50	.447	8
Guerrero	137	487	99	156	281	22	2	33	87	16	0	5	6	83	14	68	12	4	13	.320	.577	.422	121	353	9.29	.851	13
*Landreaux	147	482	70	129	195	26	2	12	50	10	3	8	1	33	2	37	15	5	9	.268	.405	.311	61	378	4.38	.559	8
Marshall	135	518	72	152	267	27	2	28	95	12	2	4	3	37	6	137	3	10	8	.293	.515	.342	87	390	5.99	.703	12
Anderson	77	221	24	44	62	6	0	4	18	4	4	1	1	35	3	42	5	4	4	.199	.281	.310	21	190	2.96	.346	2
Maldonado	121	213	20	48	72	7	1	5	19	2	2	1	0	19	4	40	1	1	3	.225	.338	.288	21	172	3.28	.416	2
Reynolds	73	207	22	55	73	10	4	0	25	2	5	3	1	13	0	31	6	3	3	.266	.353	.308	23	166	3.76	.482	2
Cabell	57	192	20	56	67	11	0	0	22	5	2	0	0	14	1	21	6	2	0	.292	.349	.340	24	140	4.70	.593	2
Russell	76	169	19	44	52	6	1	0	13	2	3	1	1	18	1	9	4	0	2	.260	.308	.333	19	131	3.98	.512	3
Yeager	53	121	4	25	31	4	1	0	9	2	1	2	0	7	2	24	0	1	3	.207	.256	.246	7	103	1.90	.192	1
Bailor	74	118	8	29	34	3	1	0	7	1	8	0	1	3	0	5	1	0	3	.246	.288	.270	9	100	2.47	.288	1
*Whitfield	79	104	8	27	43	7	0	3	16	2	0	0	0	6	1	27	0	0	2	.260	.413	.300	12	79	4.27	.546	1
*Valenzuela	35	97	7	21	26	2	0	1	7	0	5	1	0	0	0	9	0	1	3	.216	.268	.214	5	86	1.51	.131	0
*Oliver	35	79	1	20	25	5	0	0	8	2	0	1	0	5	0	11	1	0	3	.253	.316	.294	7	63	3.03	.378	0
Hershiser	37	76	5	15	16	1	0	0	4	0	10	0	1	4	0	20	1	0	0	.197	.211	.247	5	71	1.92	.196	0
*Reuss	34	74	1	10	10	0	0	0	7	2	6	1	0	2	0	28	0	0	1	.135	.135	.156	2	72	0.70	.032	0
*Matuszek	43	63	10	14	27	2	1	3	13	2	1	3	1	8	2	14	0	1	0	.222	.429	.307	9	54	4.47	.569	1
Bream	24	53	4	7	16	0	0	3	6	0	2	1	0	7	3	10	0	0	1	.132	.302	.230	4	49	2.28	.255	1
Welch	25	50	4	9	10	1	0	0	4	0	7	0	0	3	0	13	0	0	1	.180	.200	.226	3	49	1.46	.123	0
*Honeycutt	32	38	5	5	6	1	0	0	1	1	8	0	0	3	0	6	0	0	1	.132	.158	.195	2	42	1.00	.062	0
Johnstone	17	15	0	2	3	1	0	0	2	1	0	0	0	1	1	2	0	0	0	.133	.200	.188	0	15	0.34	.007	0
†Ramsey	9	15	1	2	3	1	0	0	0	0	0	0	0	2	0	4	0	0	0	.133	.200	.235	1	13	1.72	.163	0
Gonzalez	23	11	6	3	5	2	0	0	0	0	0	0	0	1	0	3	1	1	1	.273	.455	.333	1	10	2.60	.309	0
Castillo	36	10	0	1	1	0	0	0	0	0	0	2	0	0	0	4	0	0	0	.100	.100	.182	0	11	0.87	.047	0
Niedenfuer	64	9	0	1	1	0	0	0	0	0	0	0	0	0	0	3	0	0	0	.111	.111	.111	0	9	0.46	.014	0
Williams	22	9	4	3	3	0	0	0	0	0	0	0	0	4	1	0	0	0	0	.333	.333	.333	1	6	5.28	.648	0
*Stubbs	10	9	0	2	2	0	0	0	2	0	0	0	0	0	0	3	0	0	0	.222	.222	.222	0	7	1.71	.162	0
Brennan	12	8	0	1	1	0	0	0	0	0	0	0	0	0	0	2	0	0	0	.125	.125	.125	0	8	0.57	.019	0
*Bryant	6	6	0	2	2	0	0	0	1	0	0	0	0	0	0	2	0	0	0	.333	.333	.333	1	4	4.50	.550	0
Howell	56	4	0	0	0	0	0	0	0	0	0	0	0	0	0	2	0	0	0	.000	.000	.000	0	4	0.00	.000	0
Diaz	46	4	0	0	0	0	0	0	0	0	0	0	0	0	0	2	0	0	0	.000	.000	.000	0	4	0.00	.000	0
*Pederson	8	4	1	0	0	0	0	0	0	0	0	1	0	0	0	2	0	0	0	.000	.000	.000	0	5	0.00	.000	0
Powell	16	3	0	0	0	0	0	0	0	0	2	0	0	0	0	2	0	0	0	.000	.000	.000	0	5	0.00	.000	0
Pena	2	1	0	0	0	0	0	0	0	0	0	0	0	0	0	0	0	0	0	.000	.000	.000	0	1	0.00	.000	0
Reyes	6	1	0	0	0	0	0	0	0	0	0	0	1	1	0	0	0	0	0	.000	.000	.667	0	1	9.36	.841	0
Holton	3	0	0	0	0	0	0	0	0	0	0	0	0	0	0	0	0	0	0	.000	.000	.000	0	0	0.00	.000	0
*Howe	19	0	0	0	0	0	0	0	0	0	0	0	0	0	0	0	0	0	0	.000	.000	.000	0	0	0.00	.000	0

*left-handed hitter, †switch hitter

DEFENSIVE STATISTICS

FIRST

	G	PO	A	Er	TC	DP	PCT.
Brock	122	1113	84	7	1204	86	.994
Cabell	21	119	4	1	124	5	.992
Bream	16	148	14	1	163	8	.994
Guerrero	12	89	5	0	94	7	1.000
Matuszek	10	23	1	0	24	2	1.000
Marshall	7	59	3	2	64	7	.969
Stubbs	4	11	0	0	11	1	1.000
TEAM:	192	1562	111	11	1684	116	.993
AVG:	191	1513	114	12	1639	136	.993

SECOND

	G	PO	A	Er	TC	DP	PCT.
Sax	135	330	357	22	709	84	.969
Duncan	19	50	44	3	97	7	.969
Bailor	16	18	30	0	48	5	1.000
Russell	8	10	17	1	28	0	.964
Anderson	2	4	2	0	6	1	1.000
Ramsey	2	1	3	1	5	0	.800
TEAM:	182	413	453	27	893	97	.970
AVG:	184	384	502	16	901	110	.982

THIRD

	G	PO	A	Er	TC	DP	PCT.
Anderson	51	28	107	6	141	10	.957
Bailor	45	14	63	3	80	6	.962
Guerrero	44	21	111	9	141	9	.936
Cabell	32	21	71	8	100	6	.920
Madlock	32	28	63	5	96	7	.948
Russell	5	0	1	0	1	0	1.000
Matuszek	1	0	1	0	1	0	1.000
Sax	1	0	1	0	1	0	1.000
TEAM:	211	112	418	31	561	38	.945
AVG:	189	125	341	25	492	29	.948

SHORTSTOP

	G	PO	A	Er	TC	DP	PCT.
Duncan	123	174	386	27	587	57	.954
Anderson	25	29	78	3	110	9	.973
Russell	23	27	64	8	99	11	.919
Bailor	5	3	10	0	13	1	1.000
Ramsey	4	4	8	1	13	1	.923
TEAM:	180	237	546	39	822	79	.953
AVG:	185	268	521	30	819	99	.963

CATCHER

	G	PO	A	Er	TC	DP	PCT.	PB
Scioscia	139	818	66	13	897	8	.986	5
Yeager	48	212	28	2	242	2	.992	2
Reyes	6	6	4	0	10	0	1.000	0
TEAM:	193	1036	98	15	1149	10	.987	7
AVG:	191	952	87	14	1053	11	.987	14

OUTFIELD

	G	PO	A	Er	TC	DP	PCT.
Landreaux	140	267	4	7	278	1	.975
Marshall	125	206	9	2	217	2	.991
Maldonado	113	121	6	2	129	0	.984
Guerrero	81	141	7	4	152	2	.974
Reynolds	54	94	3	3	100	0	.970
Whitfield	28	23	2	2	27	0	.926
Russell	21	23	0	1	24	0	.958
Gonzales	18	10	0	0	10	0	1.000
Matuszek	17	24	0	0	24	0	1.000
Oliver	17	13	2	2	17	0	.882
Williams	15	8	1	1	10	0	.900
Pederson	5	2	0	0	2	0	1.000
Cabell	4	5	0	0	5	0	1.000
Bryant	3	0	0	0	0	0	.000
Bailor	1	0	0	0	0	0	.000
TEAM:	642	937	34	24	995	5	.976
AVG:	569	1036	34	23	1093	6	.979

COMPLETE PITCHERS RECORDS

Pitcher	W	L	Pct	ERA	G	GS	CG	GF	SHO	SV	IP	H	TBF	R	ER	HR	SH	SF	HB	BB	IB	SO	WP	BK	Appr Value
								Starters (One-half of Game Appearances)																	
*Valenzuela	17	10	.630	2.45	35	35	14	0	5	0	272.1	211	1109	92	74	14	13	8	1	101	5	208	10	1	13
Hershiser	19	3	.864	2.03	36	34	9	1	5	0	239.2	179	953	72	54	8	5	4	6	68	5	157	5	0	16
*Reuss	14	10	.583	2.92	34	33	5	0	3	0	212.2	210	883	78	69	13	8	6	3	58	7	84	5	0	10
Welch	14	4	.778	2.31	23	23	8	0	3	0	167.1	141	675	49	43	16	6	2	6	35	2	96	7	4	9
*Honeycutt	8	12	.400	3.42	31	25	1	2	0	1	142.0	141	600	71	54	9	5	4	1	49	7	67	2	0	7
Pena	0	1	.000	8.31	2	1	0	0	0	0	4.1	7	23	5	4	1	0	0	0	3	1	2	0	0	0
								Relievers																	
Niedenfuer	7	9	.438	2.71	64	0	0	43	0	19	106.1	86	415	32	32	6	1	3	1	24	5	102	0	0	10
Howell	4	7	.364	3.77	56	0	0	31	0	12	86.0	66	356	41	36	8	4	0	0	35	3	85	4	2	7
*Diaz	6	3	.667	2.61	46	0	0	21	0	0	79.1	70	326	28	23	7	3	1	0	18	6	73	1	0	4
Castillo	2	2	.500	5.43	35	5	0	5	0	0	68.0	59	301	42	41	9	1	2	1	41	6	57	2	0	2
Brennan	1	3	.250	7.39	12	4	0	2	0	0	31.2	41	144	26	26	2	5	5	0	11	4	17	0	3	0
Powell	1	1	.500	5.22	16	2	0	6	0	1	29.1	30	133	19	17	7	4	1	1	13	3	19	3	0	0
*Howe	1	1	.500	4.91	19	0	0	14	0	3	22.0	30	104	17	12	2	2	2	1	5	2	11	2	0	1
Holton	1	1	.500	9.00	3	0	0	0	0	0	4.0	9	21	7	4	0	0	0	0	1	0	1	1	0	0

*left-handed

Mike SCIOSCIA, Catcher

	G	AB	Hit	2B	3B	HR	Run	RBI	TBB	SO	SB	CS	Avg
3.35 years		476	127	22	1	6	43	52	67	32	2	2	.267
1985	141	429	127	26	3	7	47	53	77	21	3	3	.296
First Half	71	223	60	11	2	3	17	32	36		0		.269
Second Half	70	206	67	15	1	4	30	21	41		3		.325
Vs. RHP		342	105			6		44					.307
Vs. LHP		87	22			1		9					.253
Home	70	202	60	11	0	1	19	27			1		.297
Road	71	227	67	15	3	6	28	26			2		.295
Grass	105	313	101	19	2	6	35	40			2		.323
Turf	36	116	26	7	1	1	12	13			1		.224

Bill MADLOCK, Third Base

	G	AB	Hit	2B	3B	HR	Run	RBI	TBB	SO	SB	CS	Avg
9.80 years		595	184	32	3	14	84	76	55	43	17	9	.309
1985	144	513	141	27	1	14	69	56	49	53	10	4	.275
First Half	73	279	71	21	1	4	33	18	25		3		.254
Second Half	71	234	70	6	0	10	36	38	24		7		.299
Vs. RHP		355	97			8		34					.273
Vs. LHP		158	44			4		22					.278
Home	73	250	73	15	0	8	36	32			6		.292
Road	71	263	68	12	1	6	33	24			4		.259
Grass	62	220	65	8	0	6	30	22			6		.295
Turf	82	293	76	19	1	8	39	34			4		.259

Greg BROCK, First Base

	G	AB	Hit	2B	3B	HR	Run	RBI	TBB	SO	SB	CS	Avg
2.35 years		502	117	17	1	23	69	71	75	83	7	1	.233
1985	129	438	110	19	0	21	64	66	54	72	4	2	.251
First Half	62	230	60	9	0	14	37	33	25		3		.261
Second Half	67	208	50	10	0	7	27	33	29		1		.240
Vs. RHP		337	92			19		55					.273
Vs. LHP		101	18			2		11					.178
Home	65	219	55	9	0	7	26	32			4		.251
Road	64	219	55	10	0	14	38	34			0		.251
Grass	95	333	83	14	0	17	44	55			4		.249
Turf	34	105	27	5	0	4	20	11			0		.257

Mariano DUNCAN, Shortstop

	G	AB	Hit	2B	3B	HR	Run	RBI	TBB	SO	SB	CS	Avg
0.88 years		641	156	27	7	7	84	44	43	128	43	9	.244
1985	142	562	137	24	6	6	74	39	38	113	38	8	.244
First Half	68	261	63	14	0	3	23	10	17		14		.241
Second Half	74	301	74	10	6	3	51	29	21		24		.246
Vs. RHP		380	85	14	4	2		24	26	78			.224
Vs. LHP		182	52	10	2	4		15	12	35			.286
Home	72	275	66	13	2	1	37	14			22		.240
Road	70	287	71	11	4	5	37	25			16		.247
Grass	106	417	100	17	4	4	52	29			30		.240
Turf	36	145	37	7	2	2	22	10			8		.255

Steve SAX, Second Base

	G	AB	Hit	2B	3B	HR	Run	RBI	TBB	SO	SB	CS	Avg
3.81 years		640	174	20	5	3	86	46	56	62	45	15	.272
1985	136	488	136	8	4	1	62	42	54	43	27	11	.279
First Half	61	227	61	2	1	0	33	14	26		19		.269
Second Half	75	261	75	6	3	1	29	28	28		8		.287
Vs. RHP		348	107			0		30					.307
Vs. LHP		140	29			1		12					.207
Home	69	239	54	4	0	1	27	16			16		.226
Road	67	249	82	4	4	0	35	26			11		.329
Grass	100	350	90	5	1	1	46	29			25		.257
Turf	36	138	46	3	3	0	16	13			2		.333

Pedro GUERRERO, Left Field, finally

	G	AB	Hit	2B	3B	HR	Run	RBI	TBB	SO	SB	CS	Avg
4.90 years		567	173	27	4	27	90	92	64	97	15	7	.306
1985	137	487	156	22	2	33	99	87	83	68	12	4	.320
First Half	81	292	91	12	2	21	56	48	45		8		.312
Second Half	56	195	65	10	0	12	43	39	38		4		.333
Vs. RHP		349	114			24		65					.327
Vs. LHP		138	42			9		22					.304
Home	74	257	80	9	0	14	50	41			9		.311
Road	63	230	76	13	2	19	49	46			3		.330
Grass	99	342	104	12	0	17	62	53			9		.304
Turf	38	145	52	10	2	16	37	34			3		.359

Ken LANDREAUX, Center Field

	G	AB	Hit	2B	3B	HR	Run	RBI	TBB	SO	SB	CS	Avg
6.46 years		563	153	25	7	13	73	66	40	55	20	8	.272
1985	147	482	129	26	2	12	70	50	33	37	15	5	.268
First Half	79	246	61	13	1	6	29	23	13		7		.248
Second Half	68	236	68	13	1	6	41	27	20		8		.288
Vs. RHP		423	118			10		45					.279
Vs. LHP		59	11			2		5					.186
Home	71	223	55	10	0	2	31	19			13		.247
Road	76	259	74	16	2	10	39	31			2		.286
Grass	109	349	99	17	0	8	54	32			14		.284
Turf	38	133	30	9	2	4	16	18			1		.226

FERNANDO VALENZUELA

	(W–L)	GS	Run	Avg	DP	Avg	SB	Avg
1984	(12-17)	34	107	3.15	31	.91	38	1.12
1985	(17-10)	35	147	4.20	24	.69	19	.54
1981-1985		166	658	3.96	129	.78	140	.84

	G	IP	W	L	Pct	ER	BB	SO	ERA
1984 Home	17	134.7	6	8	.429	44	43	115	2.94
1985 Home	17	133.7	7	5	.583	31	49	108	2.09
1984 Road	17	126.3	6	9	.400	44	63	125	3.13
1985 Road	18	138.7	10	5	.667	43	52	100	2.79
1984 Grass	25	192.3	9	13	.409	64	68	180	2.99
1985 Grass	26	201.3	12	8	.600	48	79	159	2.15
1984 Turf	8	68.7	3	4	.429	24	38	60	3.15
1985 Turf	9	71.0	5	2	.714	26	22	49	3.30
1985 Total	35	272.3	17	10	.630	74	101	208	2.45

Mike MARSHALL, Right Field

	G	AB	Hit	2B	3B	HR	Run	RBI	TBB	SO	SB	CS	Avg
2.91 years		548	151	26	1	24	69	81	46	132	5	5	.275
1985	135	518	152	27	2	28	72	95	37	137	3	10	.293
First Half	60	218	57	9	0	10	29	32	21		1		.261
Second Half	75	300	95	18	2	18	43	63	16		2		.317
Vs. RHP		316	107			20		65					.339
Vs. LHP		202	45			8		30					.223
Home	70	261	79	14	1	14	31	48			1		.303
Road	65	257	73	13	1	14	41	47			2		.284
Grass	101	389	116	16	1	19	50	69			3		.298
Turf	34	129	36	11	1	9	22	26			0		.279

OREL HERSHISER

	(W–L)	GS	Run	Avg	DP	Avg	SB	Avg
1984	(11-8)	20	74	3.70	19	.95	12	.60
1985	(19-3)	34	153	4.50	33	.97	36	1.06
1984-1985		54	227	4.20	52	.96	48	.89

	G	IP	W	L	Pct	ER	BB	SO	ERA
1984 Home	24	100.7	6	5	.545	38	29	78	3.40
1985 Home	19	133.3	11	0	1.000	16	39	96	1.08
1984 Road	21	89.0	5	3	.625	18	21	72	1.82
1985 Road	17	106.3	8	3	.727	38	29	61	3.22
1984 Grass	31	132.7	8	6	.571	44	38	108	2.98
1985 Grass	28	188.7	15	2	.882	38	52	134	1.81
1984 Turf	14	57.0	3	2	.600	12	12	42	1.89
1985 Turf	8	51.0	4	1	.800	16	16	23	2.82
1985 Total	36	239.7	19	3	.864	54	68	157	2.03

Enos CABELL, First Base-Third Base

	G	AB	Hit	2B	3B	HR	Run	RBI	TBB	SO	SB	CS	Avg
9.76 years		581	161	26	6	6	74	58	25	68	23	12	.278
1985	117	335	91	19	1	2	40	36	30	36	9	3	.272
First Half	65	161	42	9	1	2	23	16	17		3		.261
Second Half	52	174	49	10	0	0	17	20	13		6		.282
Vs. RHP		159	39			1		18					.245
Vs. LHP		176	52			1		18					.295
Home	62	182	49	12	0	1	16	19			5		.269
Road	55	153	42	7	1	1	24	17			4		.275
Grass	64	137	34	8	1	1	22	15			4		.248
Turf	53	198	57	11	0	1	18	21			5		.288

JERRY REUSS

	(W–L)	GS	Run	Avg	DP	Avg	SB	Avg
1984	(5-7)	15	56	3.73	14	.93	10	.67
1985	(14-10)	33	133	4.03	28	.85	10	.30
1976-1985		262	1114	4.25	259	.99	143	.55

	G	IP	W	L	Pct	ER	BB	SO	ERA
1984 Home	14	59.3	3	4	.429	23	12	27	3.49
1985 Home	14	93.3	6	4	.600	25	23	30	2.41
1984 Road	16	39.7	2	3	.400	19	19	17	4.31
1985 Road	20	119.3	8	6	.571	44	35	54	3.32
1984 Grass	20	70.0	3	4	.429	27	18	29	3.47
1985 Grass	25	151.0	10	7	.588	48	41	53	2.86
1984 Turf	10	29.0	2	3	.400	15	13	15	4.66
1985 Turf	9	61.7	4	3	.571	21	17	31	3.06
1985 Total	34	212.7	14	10	.583	69	58	84	2.92

Dave ANDERSON, Infield

	G	AB	Hit	2B	3B	HR	Run	RBI	TBB	SO	SB	CS	Avg
1.60 years		444	98	16	3	5	54	34	58	70	16	8	.221
1985	77	221	44	6	0	4	24	18	35	42	5	4	.199
First Half	51	171	35	5	0	4	19	13	30		4		.205
Second Half	26	50	9	1	0	0	5	5	5		1		.180
Vs. RHP		154	31			2		13					.201
Vs. LHP		67	13			2		5					.194
Home	40	106	20	1	0	1	12	6			2		.189
Road	37	115	24	5	0	3	12	12			3		.209
Grass	59	171	34	3	0	4	19	13			4		.199
Turf	18	50	10	3	0	0	5	5			1		.200

RICK HONEYCUTT

	(W–L)	GS	Run	Avg	DP	Avg	SB	Avg
1984	(10-9)	28	99	3.54	31	1.11	20	.71
1985	(8-12)	25	93	3.72	24	.96	14	.56
1981-1985		217	836	3.85	252	1.16	112	.52

	G	IP	W	L	Pct	ER	BB	SO	ERA
1984 Home	14	96.3	6	2	.750	24	21	37	2.24
1985 Home	17	80.0	5	6	.455	24	22	43	2.70
1984 Road	15	87.3	4	7	.364	34	30	38	3.50
1985 Road	14	62.0	3	6	.333	30	27	24	4.35
1984 Grass	22	140.0	8	6	.571	35	36	55	2.25
1985 Grass	22	103.0	6	8	.429	32	31	54	2.80
1984 Turf	7	43.7	2	3	.400	23	15	20	4.74
1985 Turf	9	39.0	2	4	.333	22	18	13	5.08
1985 Total	31	142.0	8	12	.400	54	49	67	3.42

BOB WELCH

	(W–L)	GS	Run	Avg	DP	Avg	SB	Avg
1984	(13-13)	29	109	3.76	26	.90	24	.83
1985	(14-4)	23	107	4.65	13	.57	13	.57
1979-1985		199	808	4.06	140	.70	125	.63

	G	IP	W	L	Pct	ER	BB	SO	ERA
1984 Home	14	88.3	6	6	.500	36	23	65	3.67
1985 Home	13	96.7	9	3	.750	29	21	64	2.70
1984 Road	17	90.3	7	7	.500	39	35	61	3.89
1985 Road	10	70.7	5	1	.833	14	14	32	1.78
1984 Grass	22	136.0	11	8	.579	53	40	97	3.51
1985 Grass	17	121.3	10	3	.769	34	26	75	2.52
1984 Turf	9	42.7	2	5	.286	22	18	29	4.64
1985 Turf	6	46.0	4	1	.800	9	9	21	1.76
1985 Total	21	167.3	14	4	.778	43	35	96	2.31

OTHERS

	(W–L)	GS	Run	Avg	DP	Avg	SB	Avg
Castillo	(2-2)	5	26	5.20	5	1.00	2	.40
Brennan	(1-3)	4	9	2.25	2	.50	3	.75
Powell	(1-1)	2	7	3.50	1	.50	1	.50
Pena	(0-1)	1	5	5.00	0	0.00	2	2.00

CINCINNATI REDS

In the last few years, you have begun to see breakdowns of team records. *USA Today,* the national newspaper with the fine sports section, presents weekly breakdowns of how each team is doing against right-handed and left-handed pitching, at home and on the road, on grass fields and artificial turf, in day games and night games, against the Eastern division and Western division, and what their record is in one-run games, double headers and extra-inning games. It is good to see this kind of stuff getting out; five years ago, if you wanted to know what a team's record was against right-handed and left-handed pitchers, you were out of luck.

But now that this information is out there, it occurs to me to ask a basic question: does it mean anything? Which breakdowns are the most significant, the most meaningful? To which categories should we pay the most careful attention?

If the rest of you will excuse me for a second, I'm going to write a little lecture for the benefit of amateur sabermetricians on the misuse of the concept of statistical significance. This is a related but distinct problem from that discussed in the Twins comment, where I spoke of the problem of people thinking that they have shown that A and B are not related merely because A and B fail to show a correlation.

Let's assume that we are using a 99.5% significance level. To say that a split in performance is statistically significant would mean, precisely, that the frequency with which simple chance would produce such a split given the same conditions is less than one-half of one percent. But what this does not mean is that if we show that a split in

the category *could* result from chance, then we have shown that that split does not result from a very real difference in performance quality. If a .500 team wins seven out of ten games, then one can accurately say that there is a 17% probability that chance alone could create such a record—but one absolutely *cannot* say that there is a 17% chance that this record results from luck, nor even that there is any likelihood at all that it does result from luck. We know that this record *could* result from chance, but we have not the slightest clue as to whether or not it *does*. It only shows that *if* there were no cause for it, IF there were no cause for it, this split might still occur.

This distinction may not be meaningful to you if you don't do research, but I get many, many letters from people who fail to understand this, and who make very important misinterpretations of their data because of it.

To put this in a specific context which is difficult to misunderstand, suppose that the Yankees beat the Cleveland Indians in a single ballgame. This does not prove that the Yankees are a better team than the Cleveland Indians; obviously, there is a 50% chance that the Yankees would beat the Cleveland Indians in a given game even if the two teams were of equal quality. The Yankees *could* beat the Indians by dumb luck—nonetheless, it is extremely likely that they beat them in a given game not because they are lucky, but because they are a better team. A demonstration that a performance split could result from chance is completely silent on the issue of whether or not it does. *Many distinctions in data are meaningful even though we cannot infer that they are meaningful given the limitations of the data which is available to us.* It is quite true that I don't always respect this fine difference in my own phrasing of a statement.

End of lecture.

Among the splits in team records in 1985—home/road, right/left, that sort of thing—there is none which is statistically significant at the 99% level. Any one of the breakdowns in these records would occur more than one percent of the time, even given that there were no valid differences to be measured in these categories. I have figured the chance likelihood of all standard splits occuring in team breakdowns in 1985. (Two notes for the sake of that 1% of you to whom they will be meaningful. There is a common method which is used to estimate chance frequencies. I did not use that method; I calculated exactly what the chance was of each record that could occur. Also, in figuring, for example, the chance that the Cincinnati Reds would go 12–3 in one-run games, one can figure either the chance that a .553 team would go 12–3 in fifteen games, or the chance that an 89–72 team would go 12–3 in fifteen games. The latter option would be infinitessimally more accurate, but the former is much simpler, and I chose the former. The method that I used is also more conservative; it is possible, but I think not likely, that some of the breakdowns might have cleared a higher significance hurdle had I used the other method.)

Anyway, to get to the meat . . . below are the eleven breakdowns in major league records in 1985 which would be the least likely to result from simple chance:

1) **The New York Yankees at home were 58–22; on the road they were 39–42.** The chance that such a split (or a worse one) would result from random chance is 1.5%, making this the one split of the 1985 season which would be least likely to result from chance.

The major reasons for the split are fairly obvious, and they mostly have to do with left-handed pitching. In Yankee Stadium, Ron Guidry was 13–2 with a 2.87 ERA; on the road he was 9–4 with a 3.77 ERA. In Yankee Stadium, Dave Righetti was 9–1 with a 2.24 ERA; on the road he was 3–6 with a 3.38 ERA. In Yankee Stadium Bob Shirley was 5–1 with a 1.86 ERA; on the road he was 0–4 with a 3.92 ERA.

In Yankee Stadium Don Mattingly hit .336 with 22 homers and 87 RBI; in road games he hit .311 with 13 homers and 58 RBI. However, the Yankees actually scored more runs on the road (428–411) than they did in New York.

2) **The Minnesota Twins were 49–35 at home, 28–50 on the road.** This split would have only a 2.5% probability of occuring in the absence of cause.

Most responsible for this split were Kent Hrbek, who hit .312 and drove in 60 runs in his home town, but .240 with 33 RBI on the road, Kirby Puckett, who hit .324 in Minnesota but .251 on the road, and Tim Teufel, who hit .276 and scored 38 runs in Minnesota, but .244 with 20 runs scored on the road.

The Twins scored 407 runs in Minnesota as opposed to 298 on the road, but it should be noted that home runs were not the cause of this; they hit 71 home runs in Minnesota, 70 on the road. Their batting average was .281 in Minnesota, .246 on the road. They hit 166 doubles in Minnesota, 116 on the road.

They also had a 4.21 ERA in Minnesota, as opposed to 4.79 on the road.

3) **The Oakland A's were 37–24 in day games, but 40–61 in the dark.** Such a split would have only a 2.7% likelihood of occurring by chance.

This is one of the more intriguing additions to the list; we ordinarily don't pay much attention to day/night splits except in the case of the Chicago Cubs, whereas we tend to focus on stuff like left/right tendencies and turf/grass biases. But in the list of the eleven least-probable splits, there is only one left/right split, whereas there are three pronounced day/night tendencies.

The problem was both offensive and defensive. The A's in day games hit .283 and scored 347 runs in 65 games (5.34 per games), whereas at night they hit .252 and scored 410 runs in 97 games (4.24 per game. You will note that the game totals are inconsistent, probably because the Sports Information Center and the Elias Bureau use different definitions of what makes a night game. The 37–24 record in day games comes from the breakdowns in *USA Today,* which are compiled by the Elias Bureau. The other information quoted here comes from the Sports Information Center, which compiles the official American League stats. Official A.L. stats show the A's as 39–26 in day games. In any case, since both figures show the same effect, no problem).

I see no obvious reason why this should occur; the A's simply had a number of individual players who played much better in daylight ball. Alfredo Griffin hit .306 in day games, .247 in night games. Donnie Hill hit .322 in day games, .262 at night. Dave Kingman hit .283 in day games, .208 at night. Carney Lansford hit .337 in day games, .229 at night. Dwayne Murphy hit .290 in day games, .195 at night.

Chris Codiroli was 9–1 with a 3.77 ERA in day games, but 5–13 with a 4.81 ERA at night. Jay Howell was 3–1 with a 1.59 ERA in day games, but 6–7 with a 3.52 ERA at night. Bill Krueger was 6–5 with a 3.79 ERA in day games, but 3–5 with a 5.35 ERA at night. Don Sutton, while with the A's, was 8–1 with a 3.28 ERA in day games, but 5–7 with a 4.32 ERA at night.

4) **The Cincinnati Reds were 39–18 in one-run games, whereas they were 50–54 in all other contests.** The random probability that a .553 team would win 39 (or more) of 57 contests is 3.0%.

In sabermetrics we generally regard one-run records as being heavily subject to luck, and I'm certainly not going to back away from that. However, this is the one National League breakdown which has the highest level of statistical significance, and there are several features of the team which are traditionally associated with a strong performance in one-run games. The most obvious is a strong bullpen. The Reds' bullpen was excellent, headed by Franco (12–3, 2.18 ERA, 12 saves), Power (2.70 ERA, 27 saves) and Hume (3.26 ERA). Certainly, the Reds' bullpen was much stronger than their starting rotation.

The next most obvious is a strong bench; the Reds' bench was excellent. Perez, Venable, Krenchicki and Redus had fine seasons, plus Rose used enough players in rotating combinations that there were always a couple of near-regulars on the bench, such as himself, Esasky, Milner and Cedeño. Cincinnati pinch hitters hit .246, 25 points over the league average (but nowhere near the lead. Remarkably, Pittsburgh Pirate pinch hitters hit .286 on the season, 25 points higher than the pinch hitters for any other team).

Third, the Reds, with the additions of Rose, Bell, Parker and Diaz and the resurrection of Dave Concepcion, have become very much a veteran team, and thus a team which might be expected to do well in close games.

Rose as a manager invested an above-average number of outs (142) in first-run strategies.

The Reds were 66–2 in games in which they held a lead after seven innings, whereas they won *ten* games in which they were behind after seven (10–63). The Reds after seven innings were ahead in 68 games, behind in 74 and tied in 20; they improved their performance after that by eleven and a half games, the best performance of any major league team. (The Cardinals were second, improving their position by eight games after the seventh inning.)

5) **The Toronto Blue Jays were 75–36 against right-handed pitchers, whereas they were only 24–26 against left-handers.** The random chance that a .615 team would go 24–26 (or worse) in 50 games is 3.6%.

The obvious reason for this one is that the Blue Jay platoon combinations were much stronger from the left side than the right. Left-handers Whitt, Mulliniks and Oliver were stronger than their right-handed counterparts.

6) **The Cleveland Indians were 38–43 at home, 22–59 on the road.** Random probability: 4.0%.

This was mostly a defensive distinction; although the Indians did hit .279 at home, .252 on the road, with Bernazard and Tabler showing the largest differences. The big problem was that the staff ERA ballooned from 4.17 to 5.72 on the road. Young Neal Heaton was actually quite effective in Cleveland (7–5, 3.55 ERA) but 2–12 with a 6.63 ERA on the road. Curt Wardle was 5–1 with a 4.54 ERA in Cleveland, but 2–5 with a 9.20 ERA on the road. Other Indian ERAs in road games: Jeff Barkley, 7.64; Rick Behenna, 11.00; Ernie Camacho, 8.10; Bryan Clark, 7.11; Jose Roman, 8.76; Ramon Romero, 8.91; Don Schulze, 9.12; and Roy Smith, 7.92. (Nice staff, huh? Ramon Romero has taken it upon himself to prove that not *everybody* from San Pedro de Macoris can play baseball. A beautiful, four-color map of the Dominican Republic, suitable for giving your mother-in-law on Arbor Day, is available to any baseball fan who can pick Jose Roman and Ramon Romero out of a police lineup and tell which one is which in less than three guesses. Look for details of contest on the left sleeve of the Indians road uniform, or write Peter Bavasi in person at Peter's Pitchers on Parade, P.O. Box 8.76, Outback, Egypt, Dominican Republic. A stamped, self-addressed envelope will be a waste of your money.)

7) **The California Angels were 30–13 in one-run games, 60–59 otherwise.** We talked about this; it would have a 4.1% probability of occurring by simple chance.

8) **The Kansas City Royals were 73–46 in night baseball, but just 18–25 in day games.** The chance frequency of such an event would be 4.2%.

An incidental observation is that all seven World Series games were played at night, when the Royals were far

more effective than in day ball. The Cardinals, however, were not at a disadvantage, as they also were far better at night (66–33, .667) than in day games (35–28, .556). However, if the breakdowns represent true levels, then the Cardinals could have been expected to win 55.1% of night games, but 63.5% of day games—so it would have been more difficult for the Royals to win had the series been played in the day.

There were large differences in both the offensive and defensive performance of the Royals in day and night games. The Royals hit only .239 in day games, .257 at night; they scored 179 runs in day games (3.98 per games), but 508 at night (4.34). George Brett hit .278 in day games, .358 at night.

The pitching difference was larger; the pitchers had a 4.27 ERA in day games, 3.18 at night. All of the Royals' key pitchers, all five starters and Quisenberry, were more effective at night than in day games, with the largest difference belonging to Saberhagen, who was 1–2 with a 5.06 ERA in day games, but 19–4 with a 2.50 ERA at night.

9) **The Milwaukee Brewers were 55–55 in night games, but 16–35 in the daylight.** The random probability that a .441 team would go 16–35 (or worse) in 51 games is 4.4%.

The American League source has this one even worse, the Brewers being 16–38 in day games, 55–52 at night, which would move it several notches up the list. Again, the team was better both offensively and defensively at night, with the key figures being Higuera, Burris, Cooper, Yount, and Danny Darwin. Darwin lost *ten* day games—remarkable when you remember that the team only played 54 day games.

10) **The Cincinnati Reds were 12–3 in extra-inning games, 77–69 in other games.** This also would have a 4.4% chance of occurring without a true split in the performance.

The Reds are the only team to appear on the list twice, but obviously it's loaded, since many of the extra-inning games were also one-run games, and the two effects probably have the same cause.

11) **The Houston Astros were just 2–8 in double header games, whereas they were 81–71 in other games.** The chance that this would happen at random is 4.7%.

I would assume this one was just dumb luck, but there may be a reason for it. You can take a look at the double headers and try to see if there's anything unusual if you want to.

In a larger sense, what have we learned from doing this? We have learned that few breakdowns in team performance can be proven to be significant over a period as short as one season. Any of these breakdowns *could* occur by chance.

We have seen that the difference between being at home and being on the road is probably the one largest reliable "edge" in team performances. One might also note this: that while even the most extreme home/road distinctions for each team do not cross the 99% confidence threshold if studied over a season, if studied over a period of seasons it is likely that even the smallest home/road distinctions would be statistically significant. In 1985 the New York Yankees had the largest home-field advantage in baseball, nineteen and a half games (as noted above). But over the last ten seasons, the Cincinnati Reds have the *smallest* home-field advantage in baseball—twenty-nine and a half games. So if studied over a longer period of time, all home-field advantages would become statistically significant.

One cannot say this about any of the other distinctions here. If studied over a period of years, differences in how a team plays against right-handed and left-handed pitching will tend to disappear. Differences between records in one-run games and other games will disappear in no time. One would guess that differences in play between day and night baseball probably would not be consistent over a period of years. The home-field advantage is the largest consistent bias that one can focus on in analyzing performance.

We have learned that, at least in the 1985 season, the differences between how a team played in day ball and in night ball were sometimes surprisingly large. We have seen that differences between how teams played against right-handed and left-handed pitching in the 1985 season did not have the same level of statistical significance, either because they were truly not as significant or for some other reason, perhaps related to the size of the groups in which they were studied.

But at least one of the left/right splits does make our list. Interestingly, *not one of the splits between how teams play on grass and how they play on artificial turf was significant enough to make this list.* The most significant breakdown in that category was for the Milwaukee Brewers, who were 64–71 on grass fields, but 7–19 on artificial turf (5.6%); most significant in the National League was that for the Philadelphia Phillies, who were 61–59 on artificial turf, 14–28 on grass (would happen at random 6.2% of the time). Perhaps the reason we have so much trouble identifying what type of team should play well on artificial turf (see Phillies) is that the differences here just aren't as large as we think they are.

Less surprisingly, no breakdown between performance against Eastern and Western division teams was significant enough to make the list. The split having the smallest random probability is that for the Baltimore Orioles, who battered the West for a 50–34 record, but were 33–44 against the foes of their own division (7.9%). A little more surprisingly than that, the second-largest distinction in East/West performance was for the Detroit Tigers, who almost reversed that, beating their own kind (46–31), but having trouble out West (38–46).

What *I* learned from doing this is that I needed to look at the breakdowns over a longer period of time, and that's why I did the ten-year breakdowns for each team which appear at the top of the team comment. Maybe next year I'll break down day/night and left/right performances over a three- or four-year period, and see whether they glide over the 99% standard.

COMPLETE BATTING RECORDS

Player	G	AB	R	H	TB	2B	3B	HR	RBI	GW	SH	SF	HB	BB	IB	SO	SB	CS	GI DP	Avg	Slug	OBP	Runs Created	Outs Made	Runs/ 27 Outs	OW%	Appr Value
Diaz	51	161	12	42	59	8	0	3	15	1	2	2	1	15	0	18	0	0	6	.261	.366	.324	25	194	3.50	.416	2
†Rose	119	405	60	107	129	12	2	2	46	6	1	4	4	86	5	35	8	1	10	.264	.319	.395	59	314	5.05	.597	7
†Oester	152	526	59	155	190	26	3	1	34	4	2	5	0	51	17	65	5	0	13	.295	.361	.354	68	391	4.68	.560	11
Bell	67	247	28	54	91	15	2	6	36	4	1	2	0	34	2	27	0	1	10	.219	.368	.311	27	207	3.57	.426	3
Concepcion	155	560	59	141	185	19	2	7	48	7	3	4	3	50	3	67	16	12	23	.252	.330	.314	54	461	3.15	.367	9
Redus	101	246	51	62	102	14	4	6	28	4	2	1	1	44	2	52	48	12	0	.252	.415	.366	63	324	5.22	.613	5
Milner	145	453	82	115	157	19	7	3	33	4	2	3	1	61	3	31	35	13	3	.254	.347	.342	60	359	4.50	.541	10
Parker	160	635	88	198	350	42	4	34	125	18	0	4	3	52	24	80	5	13	26	.312	.551	.365	112	480	6.29	.697	14
Esasky	125	413	61	108	192	21	0	21	66	9	3	3	4	41	3	102	3	4	9	.262	.465	.332	63	324	5.22	.622	7
Cedeño	83	220	24	53	74	12	0	3	30	4	1	2	3	19	1	35	9	5	5	.241	.336	.307	23	180	3.41	.404	2
Perez	72	183	25	60	86	8	0	6	33	4	0	2	0	22	1	22	0	2	2	.328	.470	.396	35	129	7.30	.762	4
*Krenchicki	90	173	16	47	68	9	0	4	25	1	2	2	0	28	4	20	0	0	3	.272	.393	.369	27	133	5.44	.633	6
Knicely	48	158	17	40	64	9	0	5	26	2	1	2	1	16	2	34	0	0	0	.253	.405	.322	20	127	4.23	.510	2
Van Gorder	73	151	12	36	49	7	0	2	24	3	2	3	1	9	2	19	0	0	6	.238	.325	.280	13	126	2.77	.309	2
*Venable	77	135	21	39	57	12	3	0	10	3	3	2	0	6	0	17	11	3	2	.289	.422	.315	18	106	4.67	.559	2
Davis	56	122	26	30	63	3	3	8	18	4	2	0	0	7	0	39	16	3	1	.246	.516	.287	19	98	5.15	.607	2
Bilardello	42	102	6	17	20	0	0	1	9	2	1	0	1	4	1	15	0	0	5	.167	.196	.206	3	91	1.01	.056	0
Foley	43	92	7	18	25	5	1	0	6	1	0	0	0	6	1	16	1	0	0	.196	.272	.245	7	74	2.40	.251	1
Browning	39	88	4	17	21	2	1	0	2	0	9	0	0	4	0	29	0	0	2	.193	.239	.228	5	82	1.66	.138	0
Soto	37	83	3	11	13	0	1	0	4	1	6	0	0	1	0	24	0	0	1	.133	.157	.143	2	79	0.68	.027	0
Tibbs	36	65	3	6	6	0	0	0	3	0	6	0	0	2	0	33	0	0	1	.092	.092	.119	1	66	0.38	.008	0
*Walker	37	48	5	8	18	2	1	2	6	0	0	0	0	6	1	18	1	0	1	.167	.375	.259	5	41	3.14	.365	0
†Runnells	28	35	3	7	8	1	0	0	0	0	4	0	0	1	0	4	0	0	1	.200	.229	.263	2	33	1.90	.174	0
McGaffigan	15	29	0	1	2	1	0	0	1	1	1	0	0	1	0	18	0	0	0	.034	.069	.067	0	29	0.17	.002	0
Robinson	33	22	0	2	2	0	0	0	1	0	5	0	0	0	0	8	0	0	0	.091	.091	.091	0	25	0.37	.008	0
Stuper	33	17	0	1	1	0	0	0	1	1	7	0	0	3	0	10	1	1	0	.059	.059	.200	1	24	0.74	.031	0
Price	26	14	0	0	0	0	0	0	0	0	1	0	0	1	0	7	0	0	0	.000	.000	.067	0	15	0.09	.000	0
Pastore	17	14	1	2	3	1	0	0	0	0	2	0	0	0	0	6	0	0	1	.143	.214	.143	1	14	0.97	.052	0
O'Neill	5	12	1	4	5	1	0	0	1	0	0	0	0	1	0	3	0	0	0	.333	.417	.333	2	8	5.62	.648	0
Rowdon	5	9	2	2	2	0	0	0	2	0	0	0	0	2	0	1	0	0	0	.222	.222	.364	1	7	3.53	.421	0
Franco	67	6	1	2	2	0	0	0	1	0	2	0	0	0	0	0	0	0	0	.333	.333	.333	1	6	3.42	.405	0
Hume	56	5	0	0	0	0	0	0	0	0	0	0	0	2	0	0	0	0	0	.000	.000	.000	0	5	0.00	.000	0
*Buchanan	14	1	0	0	0	0	0	0	0	0	0	0	0	0	0	0	0	0	0	.000	.000	.000	0	1	0.00	.000	0
*Willis	11	0	0	0	0	0	0	0	0	0	1	0	0	1	0	1	0	0	0	.000	.000	.500	0	2	3.51	.426	0
Power	64	0	0	0	0	0	0	0	0	0	0	0	0	0	0	1	0	0	0	.000	.000	1.000	0	0	0.00	.000	0
*Murphy	2	0	0	0	0	0	0	0	0	0	0	0	0	0	0	0	0	0	0	.000	.000	.000	0	0	0.00	.000	0
Smith	2	0	0	0	0	0	0	0	0	0	0	0	0	0	0	0	0	0	0	.000	.000	.000	0	0	0.00	.000	0

*left-handed hitter, †switch hitter

DEFENSIVE STATISTICS

FIRST	G	PO	A	Er	TC	DP	PCT.
Rose	110	870	73	5	948	80	.995
Perez	50	340	22	2	364	34	.995
Cedeño	34	110	8	1	119	11	.992
Esasky	12	37	3	0	40	3	1.000
TEAM:	206	1357	106	8	1471	128	.995
AVG:	191	1513	114	12	1639	136	.993

SECOND	G	PO	A	Er	TC	DP	PCT.
Oester	149	366	457	9	832	100	.989
Foley	18	23	36	1	60	10	.983
Krenchicki	3	1	3	0	4	0	1.000
Runnels	1	2	2	0	4	0	1.000
TEAM:	171	392	498	10	900	110	.989
AVG:	184	384	502	16	901	110	.982

THIRD	G	PO	A	Er	TC	DP	PCT.
Bell	67	54	105	9	168	13	.946
Esasky	62	41	99	8	148	13	.946
Krenchicki	52	34	84	4	122	9	.967
Concepcion	5	2	1	0	3	0	1.000
Rowdon	4	1	3	2	6	0	.667
Foley	1	0	0	0	0	0	.000
TEAM:	191	132	292	23	447	35	.949
AVG:	189	125	341	25	492	29	.948

SHORTSTOP	G	PO	A	Er	TC	DP	PCT.
Concepcion	151	212	404	24	640	64	.962
Foley	15	29	38	2	69	11	.971
Runnells	11	8	20	0	28	4	1.000
TEAM:	177	249	462	26	737	79	.965
AVG:	185	268	521	30	819	99	.963

CATCHER	G	PO	A	Er	TC	DP	PCT.	PB
Van Gorder	70	255	11	3	269	2	.989	1
Diaz	51	301	32	4	337	8	.988	3
Knicely	46	231	13	8	252	1	.968	4
Bilardello	42	198	20	3	221	1	.986	2
TEAM:	209	985	76	18	1079	12	.983	10
AVG:	191	952	87	14	1053	11	.987	14

OUTFIELD	G	PO	A	Er	TC	DP	PCT.
Parker	159	329	12	10	351	1	.972
Milner	135	340	12	6	358	3	.983
Redus	85	140	3	2	145	0	.986
Esasky	54	91	4	0	95	0	1.000
Cedeno	53	96	1	1	98	0	.990
Davis	47	75	3	1	79	1	.987
Venable	39	60	3	0	63	0	1.000
Walker	10	15	0	2	17	0	.882
O'Neill	2	3	1	0	4	0	1.000
TEAM:	584	1149	39	22	1210	5	.982
AVG:	569	1036	34	23	1093	6	.979

COMPLETE PITCHERS RECORDS

Pitcher	W	L	Pct	ERA	G	GS	CG	GF	SHO	SV	IP	H	TBF	R	ER	HR	SH	SF	HB	BB	IB	SO	WP	BK	Appr Value
Starters (One-half of Game Appearances)																									
*Browning	20	9	.690	3.55	38	38	6	0	4	0	261.1	242	1083	111	103	29	13	7	3	73	8	155	2	0	11
Soto	12	15	.444	3.58	36	36	9	0	1	0	256.2	196	1055	109	102	30	13	9	2	104	3	214	8	2	9
Tibbs	10	16	.385	3.92	35	34	5	0	2	0	218.0	216	938	111	95	14	11	8	0	83	10	98	12	1	6
McGaffigan	3	3	.500	3.72	15	15	2	0	0	0	94.1	88	392	40	39	4	4	0	2	30	4	83	2	0	2
Relievers																									
Robinson	7	7	.500	3.99	33	12	0	9	0	1	108.1	107	453	53	48	11	3	4	1	32	3	76	3	0	5
Stuper	8	5	.615	4.55	33	13	1	11	0	0	99.0	116	432	60	50	8	5	7	0	37	3	38	1	1	4
*Franco	12	3	.800	2.18	67	0	0	33	0	12	99.0	83	407	27	24	5	11	1	1	40	8	61	4	0	11
Power	8	6	.571	2.70	64	0	0	50	0	27	80.0	65	342	27	24	2	6	4	1	45	8	42	1	0	10
Hume	3	5	.375	3.26	56	0	0	15	0	3	80.0	65	331	33	29	7	2	1	3	35	5	50	3	1	5
Price	2	2	.500	3.90	26	8	0	5	0	1	64.2	59	274	35	28	10	2	5	0	23	7	52	2	0	1
Pastore	2	1	.667	3.83	17	6	1	3	0	0	54.0	60	232	23	23	1	3	3	1	16	1	29	2	0	1
*Buchanan	1	0	1.000	8.44	14	0	0	3	0	0	16.0	25	77	15	15	4	0	0	0	9	1	3	1	0	0
Willis	1	0	1.000	9.22	11	0	0	6	0	1	13.2	21	69	18	14	3	1	2	0	5	0	6	1	0	0
Smith	0	0	.000	5.40	2	0	0	1	0	0	3.1	2	13	2	2	2	0	0	0	1	0	2	0	0	0
*Murphy	0	0	.000	6.00	2	0	0	2	0	0	3.0	2	12	2	2	1	0	0	0	2	0	1	0	0	0

*left-handed

Bo DIAZ, Catcher	G	AB	Hit	2B	3B	HR	Run	RBI	TBB	SO	SB	CS	Avg
3.60 years		515	132	27	1	14	54	75	35	71	2	3	.256
1985	77	237	58	13	1	5	21	31	21	25	0	0	.245
First Half	21	57	11	4	0	0	5	11	5				.193
Second Half	56	180	47	9	1	5	16	20	16				.261
Vs. RHP		175	43			5		21					.246
Vs. LHP		62	15			0		10					.242
Home	36	103	31	7	0	4	12	19			0		.301
Road	41	134	27	6	1	9	12				0		.201
Grass	20	66	18	4	0	1	5	7			0		.273
Turf	57	171	40	9	1	4	16	24			0		.234

Pete ROSE, First Base	G	AB	Hit	2B	3B	HR	Run	RBI	TBB	SO	SB	CS	Avg
21.54 years		641	195	34	6	7	100	60	71	52	9	7	.304
1985	119	405	107	12	2	2	60	46	86	35	8	1	.264
First Half	70	229	60	9	1	1	33	25	49		5		.262
Second Half	49	176	47	3	1	1	27	21	37		3		.267
Vs. RHP		357	90	9	2	2		41	74	32			.252
Vs. LHP		48	17	3	0	0		5	12	3			.354
Home	60	196	50	5	2	0	27	23			2		.255
Road	59	209	57	7	0	2	33	23			6		.273
Grass	30	114	30	1	0	3	14	11			3		.263
Turf	89	291	77	11	2	0	46	35			5		.265

Ron OESTER, Second Base

	G	AB	Hit	2B	3B	HR	Run	RBI	TBB	SO	SB	CS	Avg
5.10 years		557	149	25	5	6	64	47	48	87	5	3	.267
1985	152	526	155	26	3	1	59	34	51	65	5	0	.295
First Half	76	259	74	18	2	0	28	18	21			2	.286
Second Half	76	267	81	8	1	1	31	16	30			3	.303
Vs. RHP		378	113	19	2	1		27	43	40			.299
Vs. LHP		148	42	7	1	0		7	8	25			.284
Home	80	270	82	16	2	0	30	15				3	.304
Road	72	256	73	10	1	1	29	19				2	.285
Grass	43	151	34	5	0	1	15	14				1	.225
Turf	109	375	121	21	3	0	44	20				4	.323

Buddy BELL, Third Base

	G	AB	Hit	2B	3B	HR	Run	RBI	TBB	SO	SB	CS	Avg
12.21 years		614	173	30	4	13	78	75	54	53	4	6	.282
1985	151	560	128	28	5	10	61	68	67	48	3	3	.229
First Half	79	298	73	13	3	4	31	30	31	21	3	2	.245
Second Half	72	262	55	15	2	6	30	38	36	27	0	1	.210
Vs. RHP		412	88			9		49					.214
Vs. LHP		148	40			1		19					.270
Home	75	273	64	17	3	6	34	39				1	.234
Road	76	287	64	11	2	4	27	29				2	.223
Grass	92	343	78	13	3	5	37	37				2	.227
Turf	59	217	50	15	2	5	24	31				1	.230

Dave CONCEPCION, Shortstop

	G	AB	Hit	2B	3B	HR	Run	RBI	TBB	SO	SB	CS	Avg
13.64 years		582	155	26	3	7	67	64	49	80	22	7	.267
1985	155	560	141	19	2	7	59	48	50	67	16	12	.252
First Half	81	292	76	14	1	5	42	25	26			13	.260
Second Half	74	268	65	5	1	2	17	23	24			3	.243
Vs. RHP		404	103			3		39					.255
Vs. LHP		156	38			4		9					.244
Home	78	273	74	11	2	1	32	22				8	.271
Road	77	287	67	8	0	6	27	26				8	.233
Grass	46	176	43	4	0	3	17	8				5	.244
Turf	109	384	98	15	2	4	42	40				11	.255

Gary REDUS, Left Field

	G	AB	Hit	2B	3B	HR	Run	RBI	TBB	SO	SB	CS	Avg
2.28 years		516	128	25	8	14	97	47	76	112	64	17	.248
1985	101	246	62	14	4	6	51	28	44	52	48	12	.252
First Half	58	174	44	10	3	4	31	22	29	31			.253
Second Half	43	72	18	4	1	2	20	6	15	17			.250
Vs. RHP		115	32			4		16					.278
Vs. LHP		131	30			2		12					.229
Home	55	138	40	10	2	4	34	15			29		.290
Road	46	108	22	4	2	2	17	13			19		.204
Grass	29	73	15	3	1	2	9	11			13		.205
Turf	72	173	47	11	3	4	42	17			35		.272

Eddie MILNER, Center Field

	G	AB	Hit	2B	3B	HR	Run	RBI	TBB	SO	SB	CS	Avg
3.30 years		517	131	22	7	7	80	38	67	55	35	12	.254
1985	145	453	115	19	7	3	82	33	61	31	35	13	.254
First Half	76	231	54	7	2	0	40	15	30	18			.234
Second Half	69	222	61	12	5	3	42	18	31	17			.275
Vs. RHP		406	105			3		32					.259
Vs. LHP		47	10			0		1					.213
Home	77	223	55	12	4	1	43	12			18		.247
Road	68	230	60	7	3	2	39	21			17		.261
Grass	36	116	29	3	2	1	17	11			10		.250
Turf	109	337	86	16	5	2	65	22			25		.255

Dave PARKER, Right Field

	G	AB	Hit	2B	3B	HR	Run	RBI	TBB	SO	SB	CS	Avg
9.98 years		610	185	37	7	22	89	98	44	95	14	9	.304
1985	160	635	198	42	4	34	88	125	52	80	5	13	.312
First Half	85	335	102	21	3	16	44	62	31			3	.304
Second Half	75	300	96	21	1	18	44	63	21			2	.320
Vs. RHP		434	142			27		86					.327
Vs. LHP		201	56			7		39					.279
Home	80	312	96	21	1	16	45	65			1		.308
Road	80	323	102	21	3	18	43	60			4		.316
Grass	48	193	58	11	0	12	24	31			3		.301
Turf	112	442	140	31	4	22	64	94			2		.317

Nick ESASKY, Outfield-First Base

	G	AB	Hit	2B	3B	HR	Run	RBI	TBB	SO	SB	CS	Avg
1.99 years		520	125	21	5	22	66	79	60	152	5	4	.241
1985	125	413	108	21	0	21	61	66	41	102	3	4	.262
First Half	63	187	47	12	0	6	28	30	28			3	.251
Second Half	62	226	61	9	0	15	33	36	13			0	.270
Vs. RHP		273	66			14		47					.242
Vs. LHP		140	42			7		19					.300
Home	58	192	45	13	0	7	20	27			1		.234
Road	67	221	63	8	0	14	41	39			2		.285
Grass	42	138	41	6	0	9	28	27			1		.297
Turf	83	275	67	15	0	12	33	39			2		.244

Tony PEREZ, Pinch Hitter-First Base

	G	AB	Hit	2B	3B	HR	Run	RBI	TBB	SO	SB	CS	Avg
16.67 years		575	161	30	5	23	75	97	54	111	3	2	.280
1985	72	183	60	8	0	6	25	33	22	22	0	2	.328
First Half	35	81	25	3	0	4	10	18	9			0	.309
Second Half	37	102	35	5	0	2	15	15	13			0	.343
Vs. RHP		59	18			0		8					.305
Vs. LHP		124	42			6		25					.339
Home	41	103	38	6	0	4	15	26			0		.369
Road	31	80	22	2	0	2	10	7			0		.275
Grass	20	60	16	1	0	2	6	4			0		.267
Turf	52	123	44	7	0	4	19	29			0		.358

TOM BROWNING

	(W–L)	GS	Run	Avg	DP	Avg	SB	Avg
1984	(1-0)	3	9	3.00	3	1.00	1	.33
1985	(20-9)	38	182	4.79	35	.92	20	.53
1984-1985		41	191	4.66	38	.93	21	.51

	G	IP	W	L	Pct	ER	BB	SO	ERA
1984 Home	1	8.0	0	0	0.000	2	0	3	2.25
1985 Home	19	131.3	10	6	.625	60	38	70	4.11
1984 Road	2	15.3	1	0	1.000	2	5	11	1.17
1985 Road	19	130.0	10	3	.769	43	35	85	2.98
1984 Grass	1	8.3	1	0	1.000	1	2	4	1.08
1985 Grass	12	80.7	4	2	.667	29	26	53	3.24
1984 Turf	2	15.0	0	0	0.000	3	3	10	1.80
1985 Turf	26	180.7	16	7	.696	74	47	102	3.69
1985 Total	38	261.3	20	9	.690	103	73	155	3.55

MARIO SOTO

	(W–L)	GS	Run	Avg	DP	Avg	SB	Avg
1984	(18-7)	33	150	4.55	14	.42	39	1.18
1985	(12-15)	36	133	3.69	22	.61	47	1.31
1977-1985		185	739	3.99	107	.58	192	1.04

	G	IP	W	L	Pct	ER	BB	SO	ERA
1984 Home	17	132.3	11	2	.846	55	55	120	3.74
1985 Home	18	125.7	6	8	.429	59	59	109	4.23
1984 Road	16	105.0	7	5	.583	38	32	65	3.26
1985 Road	18	131.0	6	7	.462	43	45	105	2.95
1984 Grass	10	62.7	5	2	.714	21	19	38	3.02
1985 Grass	11	82.0	3	5	.375	28	25	66	3.07
1984 Turf	23	174.7	13	5	.722	72	68	147	3.71
1985 Turf	25	174.7	9	10	.474	74	79	148	3.81
1985 Total	36	256.7	12	15	.444	102	104	214	3.58

JAY TIBBS

	(W–L)	GS	Run	Avg	DP	Avg	SB	Avg
1984	(6-2)	14	61	4.36	20	1.43	11	.79
1985	(10-16)	34	140	4.12	38	1.12	16	.47
1984-1985		48	201	4.19	58	1.21	27	.56

	G	IP	W	L	Pct	ER	BB	SO	ERA
1984 Home	8	60.0	4	1	.800	17	19	23	2.55
1985 Home	17	108.3	5	7	.417	44	3	51	3.66
1984 Road	6	40.7	2	1	.667	15	14	17	3.32
1985 Road	18	109.7	5	9	.357	51	46	47	4.19
1984 Grass	3	19.0	1	0	1.000	9	8	5	4.26
1985 Grass	10	59.0	0	7	0.000	33	24	26	5.03
1984 Turf	11	81.7	5	2	.714	23	25	35	2.53
1985 Turf	25	159.0	10	9	.526	62	59	72	3.51
1985 Total	35	218.0	10	16	.385	95	83	98	3.92

OTHERS

	(W–L)	GS	Run	Avg	DP	Avg	SB	Avg
McGaffigan	(3-3)	15	56	3.73	9	.60	19	1.27
Stuper	(8-5)	13	67	5.15	15	1.15	13	1.00
Robinson	(7-7)	12	38	3.17	11	.92	6	.50
Price	(2-2)	8	36	4.50	5	.62	1	.12
Pastore	(2-1)	6	25	4.17	6	1.00	12	2.00

HOUSTON ASTROS

BREAKDOWNS FOR THE LAST TEN SEASONS

Won-Lost Record: 803-766, .512 (3rd in the division, 11th in the majors)
Runs Scored: 6,135 (5th in the division)
Runs Allowed: 6,030 (2nd-fewest in the division, 2nd-fewest in the majors)
Home Runs Hit: 790 (Fewest of any major league team)
Home Runs Allowed: 868 (Fewest of any major league team)

RECORD IN:
April: 100-108, .481 (3rd in the division)
May: 126-143, .468 (5th in the division)
June: 137-121, .531 (Best in the division)
July: 126-130, .492 (3rd in the division)
August: 156-121, .563 (2nd in the division)
September: 141-134, .513 (3rd in the division)
October: 17-9, .654 (Best in the major leagues)

Won-Lost Record in Road Games: 347-440, .441 (3rd in the division)
Won-Lost Record at Home: 456-326, .583 (2nd in the division)
Home Field Advantage: 111½ games (Largest in the major leagues)
Runs Scored on the Road: 3,232 (3rd in the division)
Runs Scored at Home: 2,903 (Fewest in the major leagues)
Runs Allowed on the Road: 3,424 (3rd-highest in the division)
Runs Allowed at Home: 2,606 (Fewest in the major leagues)

Home Runs Hit on the Road: 507 (4th in the division)
Home Runs Hit at Home: 283 (Fewest of any major league team)
Home Runs Allowed on the Road: 588 (2nd-most in the division)
Home Runs Allowed at Home: 280 (Fewest of any major league team)

RECORD FOR LAST THREE SEASONS: 248-238, .510 (3rd in the division)

IS STEVE SAX AVAILABLE?

The Houston Astros, I have decided, must be an acquired taste. You know what an acquired taste is, something like French cooking, modern sculpture, jazz, fat women, ballet, Scotch, Russian films . . . it's hard to define. An acquired taste is a fondness for something the advantages of which are not immediately apparent. An acquired taste in my part of the country is painted saw blades. Do they have those where you are? You go to somebody's house and you discover that above their fireplace they've got a bunch of old, rusty saw blades with farm scenes painted on them, look like a hybrid of Currier and Ives and Norman Rockwell. I don't really understand what the advantages are of having them around, but I figure that they must be an acquired taste. Or like Charlie Chaplin. I mean, W.C. Fields is *funny*. The Marx Brothers are *funny*. Charlie Chaplin is an acquired taste.

We all acquire a certain number of inexplicable attachments; mine include Bob Newhart, Jethro Tull albums, sabermetrics and Pringles potato chips. I am assured by other people in my life that all of these can be hard to get into if you have no history with them. If taken literally, everything in life is an acquired taste with the exception of a few basic staples like salt, sugar, sex and slapstick comedy, which we all share an enjoyment of; however, the term is not usually applied to things which make an obvious display of their attractions—in the case of a baseball team, by doing things like winning lots of games, playing interesting baseball or developing exciting young players. One would never describe the New York Mets, for example, as an acquired taste. Acquired tastes have very subtle advantages. The expression "this must be

an acquired taste" is quite useful, inasmuch as it can be adapted to hundreds of situations, meaning something a little different each time:

• If you hear the expression "Must be an acquired taste," on leaving a French restaurant or any other restaurant in which the food costs more than $20 a pound and tastes as if the oregano was left out, what it means is "I suppose you'd rather have stopped at Kentucky Fried Chicken, wouldn't you?"

• On a date, if you hear the expression "Must be an acquired taste," what it means is "This is the last time I'm going out with this bozo."

• In an art gallery, if you hear the expression "I guess it's an acquired taste," what it probably means is "What the hell are we doing here?"

• If you're discussing a fondness for some particular poet, painter, playwright or breed of dog with someone you are close to, and he or she says "I guess it's just an acquired taste," what that means is "I don't want to talk about it right now."

"It's an acquired taste" means either that I'm in the know and you're not, or that this is a particular type of sophistication to which the speaker does not aspire. I do not aspire to be an Astros fan. The Astros are to baseball what jazz is to music. Think about it:

1) Jazz is improvisational. Jazz musicians, uniquely among musicians I hope, sometimes string the elements of their music together as they go, with no particular plan or outline. Do you think the Astros know where they're going? Do you think there's a score for this?

2) Jazz ambles along without crescendos or refrains,

going neither andante or allegro and without reaching either fortissimo or pianissimo. A good piece of jazz only uses about half an octave. The ultimate jazz tune is a saxophone player undulating slowly between D flat and middle C.

Similarly, the Houston Astros amble along at 80, 82 wins a year; in the last four years they've been 77–85, 85–77, 80–82 and 83–79. Since 1969 the Oakland A's have finished a total of 216 games over .500 in their good seasons, and 169 games under .500 in their bad seasons. The Houston Astros have finished 70 games over .500 in their good seasons, and 67 under in their bad seasons. The ultimate Houston Astros season is one in which they lose on opening day, then win, lose, win, lose, win, etc. until they reach 81–81.

3) Jazz is usually played indoors.

4) Jazz uses comparatively few instruments. Jazz ensembles are rarely enlivened with sousaphones, steel guitars, oboes, bassoons, or any other instrument which might tend to break up the monotony. Similarly, the Houston Astros use comparatively few weapons, relying heavily on the stolen base and the starting pitcher, but with no power hitters, no batting champions, no Ozzie Smiths or Jack Clarks. Both jazz and the Houston Astros, in short, are boring.

5) All jazz music sounds pretty much alike to the uninitiated, that 99.97% of us who haven't acquired the taste; it's repetitious, depressing, ugly and inclined to bestow a headache upon the recipient. Much the same can be said of the Houston Astros, well known for wearing baseball's ugliest home and road uniforms. Similarly, one Houston Astros season, one Astros game and one Astros player looks pretty much like the next one.

No, I'm kidding, of course; the Astros have been a little boring in recent years, but they'll get over it, and I'm sure jazz is as beautiful, varied and enjoyable as real music if you happen to have a taste for it. It's just that . . . well, I'm a night person. During the *Abstract* crunch (a fifth season, unique to Winchester, Kansas) I start to work about 4:00 P. M. and I work until daybreak. About ten years ago we went through a period when the only thing on the radio between one and four A. M. was country music. I've never understood this . . . I mean, if you don't like C & W in the middle of the afternoon, why do radio executives think you're suddenly going to be struck with a yen to hear some Merle Haggard at 12:59 A. M.? Now it's jazz; I listen to a mixture of classical music, rock music and talk shows as I work, and at seven o'clock every evening they all decide that I'd like to hear Count Basie. Public radio stations, usually a reliable port in a storm, have for some unfathomable reason decided that jazz is socially and morally uplifting, and that they have a responsibility to impose it on us. But if I want to listen to Mozart in the afternoon, why does anybody think I'd want to listen to Miles Davis all night?

Ah well, I've got my Jethro Tull and a stereo, and baseball season's coming . . . what I should do is get a VCR and record a couple hundred baseball games, and play them back while I'm working. I might even acquire a taste for the Astros. Let's report on a couple of pieces of research here . . .

LATE SEASON SUCCESS

The Houston Astros finished the season well in 1985. After dropping to 46–55 by the end of July, the Astros won 14 of 26 games in August, 18 of 29 in September and 5 of 6 in October to finish four games over .500. Although the Astros have generally played well late in the season—their problems are in April and May—this was the best finish to a season that they have had in many years; the 37–24 record after August 1 is their best in the last ten years, except for the 33–20 mark in the second part of the 1981 tumor.

But does that mean anything for 1986? Anytime a team plays particularly well or particularly badly in the latter part of the season, it becomes one of the themes of the winter. It works both ways; the team which finishes strong says, "Yeah, we were just 83–79, but we played well the last two months, and we're ready to go in 1986," while the team which played poorly late in the year says, "Yeah, we finished at 83–79, but we were fourteen games over .500 until we had some injuries in early August, and we feel that we've arrived as a legitimate contender for 1986." But where does the edge really lie—with the team which finishes strong, or with the other? A year ago the Cleveland Indians were talking about how well they had played after the All-Star break.

I decided to study this by matching teams with identical overall records, but very different records over the last two months of the year, and comparing the performance of the two in the following season. At each "integer" between 90–72 and 72–90, I matched the four teams with the best and worst records over the last two months of the season (that is, the two best and two worst late-season records). The study covers 1968–1984, excepting of course the 1981 out-take. For example, the 1983 Philadelphia Phillies, the 1971 St. Louis Cardinals, the 1977 Chicago White Sox and the 1971 San Francisco Giants all finished with records of 90–72, but the Phillies and the Cardinals finished strong (39–24 and 32–23, respectively, from August 1 to the end of the season), while the White Sox and Giants finished poorly (28–34 and 25–29). Does that distinction have any "carryover" value for the next season? Are the Cardinals and Phillies likely to do better in the following seasons?

They did do better in this case; although all four teams had disappointing seasons following the 90–72 year, the White Sox and Giants were even more disappointing (71–90 and 69–86) than the Phillies and Cardinals (81–81 and 75–81):

90–72	1983 Philadelphia	39–24 81–81	
	1971 St. Louis	32–23 75–81	156–162
	1977 Chicago (A)	28–34 71–90	
	1971 San Francisco	25–29 69–86	140–176

A fifteen-game advantage for the two teams which finished well.

On the whole, there is an unmistakable advantage to the teams which finished well. The difference is not enormous, but it is significant; it is meaningful, for the Houston Astros, that they finished well. There were 72 teams in the study, 36 which finished well and 36 which had the same overall record but finished poorly. In the subsequent seasons, the 36 teams which finished well had a composite record of 2,941 wins, 2,751 losses. The 36 teams which finished poorly had a composite record of 2,809 wins, 2,829 losses—105 games worse.

Virtually all of the separation occurred in teams which finished at .500 or above, as the Astros did; for teams which won 72–80 games there was only a miniscule advantage for the teams which had finished well. But for teams winning 81–90 games, the teams which had finished well won an average of about five additional games in the following season.

Seven of the teams which finished well, but only two of the teams which finished poorly, won division championships in the following season.

Standard scientific procedure compels me to list the teams involved in this study for the benefit of those who might wish to reexamine the work, but to save space I will do so in a code which you can easily decipher; in all cases the two teams listed first finished well (they had the best records over the last two months of any teams in the 1968–1984 period with this overall record) and those listed third and fourth finished poorly (having the worst records of any eligible team over the last two months). The teams are: 89–73, 80 Cin, 74 NYA, 82 Atl, 78 SF; 88–74, 77 Cin, 74 Pit, 83 Atl, 69 Oak; 87–75, 78 Tex, 82 SF, 83 Mil, 69 Bos; 86–76, 70 SF, 69 Wash, 80 Mil, 75 Phi; 85–77, 76 Min, 79 KC, 71 Bos, 70 Bal; 84–78, 84 KC, 84 StL, 80 Det, 74 Bos; 83–79, 76 Bos, 80 Oak, 70 NYN, 80 Pit; 82–80, 74 Min, 71 NYA, 75 NYN, 79 Min; 81–81, 83 SD, 77 Hou, 84 Phi, 77 Chi; 80–82, 84 Hou, 76 Hou, 79 Chi N, 73 NYA; 79–83, 71 Cin, 79 LA, 70 Det, 83 StL; 77–85, 82 Hou, 84 Oak, 74 KC, 74 Cle; 76–86, 70 StL, 76 Cal, 70 Atl, 74 Mil; 75–87, 76 Chi N, 84 Pit, 77 Mon, 75 Chi N; 74–88, 76 SF, 83 Cin, 77 Det, 73 Mil; 73–89, 70 Mon, 82 Chi N, 76 SD, 78 Mon; 72–90, 68 Hou, 76 StL, 74 Det, 74 SF.

The 78–84 record had to be left out because of an odd lack of teams; I think there was only one team in that period which finished 78–84, whereas there were at least six at all the other stations.

HOT STREAKS

One of the major essays that I am going to write in each year's book, which somehow never seems to get done, has to do with the way in which the nature of the baseball profession—and, in a way, the nature of the world—predisposes baseball players and others who follow the game to believe in "hot streaks" and "slumps," and to invest in these concepts a faith and interest which they do not deserve. To state a 6000-word argument in 60 words, it is difficult for a man whose whole life has turned sour because he has only one hit in his last 26 at bats to believe that there is no reason why he isn't hitting—but it is difficult for an analyst to believe that batting skills change dramatically from week to week when they usually do not change dramatically over a period of years.

It has been common in recent years to hear breakdowns of how a player has done in his last five games, over the last ten games, last week, etc.—but it is very much an open question as to whether or not this type of information means anything. Is a .300 hitter any more likely to get a hit today, in this at bat, if he is "on a hot streak"—let's say 9 for his last 20—than if he is in a slump? If so, how much more likely?

If Mike Schmidt is in a hot streak, having homered in three of his last four at bats, then any baseball manager would treat him differently than if he was perceived to be slumping—but despite this, sabermetricians are extremely skeptical about whether Schmidt is actually any more likely to get a hit in the one case than he is in the other.

I've commissioned one study to deal with that issue (recognizing that it will take many studies to deal with it adequately). The study was done by Steven Copley of Tracy, California, a life-long Astros fan (how he feels about jazz, I don't know). Steven studied the 1985 seasons of seven Astros players (Cruz, Reynolds, Davis, Bass, Garner, Bailey, and Doran) in great detail, focusing on the question of whether each player hit any better in a given game when he was coming off a good game as opposed to a poor game, or when he came into the game perceived as being in a slump as opposed to when he would have been perceived as being hot. Since the 1985 material on Doran was most interesting, he also went back and included Doran's 1984 season in the study.

With regard to the player's performance in the one previous game, Steven did find a very small carryover effect from day to day. He defined a "poor" game as 0 for 3 or worse, a good day as 2 for 6 or better (that is 2 for 5, 2 for 4, or 3 for anything) and other days as in-between. Following poor games, the eight players (considering Doran two players) hit .268 as a group (250/933). Following good games, they hit .280 (274/977). Following in-between games, they hit .270 (503/1823). To the very questionable extent to which this shows any correlation between performance in one game and performance in the next, that effect could probably be explained by ballpark biases (that is, when you were playing in Wrigley Field yesterday, there is a good chance you are also playing in Wrigley Field today).

Neither does any individual player show any dramatic performance fluctuations in this regard. The most improved hitter when coming off a good game was Jose Cruz, who hit .337 (62/184) following good games, but only .270 following games in which he had worn the collar. On the other hand, Craig Reynolds hit only .231 (18/78) in games following a good game, and hit .304 (21/69) in the games which followed his worst games. These effects are certainly not statistically significant (while of course they might result from a real cause).

Steven also studied how four of the players performed as a function of how they had hit in the Astros' previous ten games. One intriguing result of this study is that Bill Doran, in 1985, hit much better when he came into the game in a slump than when he came into the game on a hot streak. Steven found:

Following ten-game periods in which Doran's batting average was below .200, Doran hit .311 (14/45).

Following ten-game periods in which Doran's batting average was .200 to .224, Doran hit .302 (13/43).

Following ten-game periods in which Doran's batting average was .225 to .249, Doran hit .353 (18/51).

However, following ten-game periods in which Doran had hit .350 to .369, Doran hit .154 (6/39).

And following ten-game periods in which Doran had hit .370 or better, he hit just .194 (12/62).

One can certainly relate this pattern to Doran's very consistent performance during the 1985 season; obviously, if you hit .300 in games following ten-game stretches in which you have hit below .200, then you're not going to get into any prolonged slump. It is quite possible that there is a psychological compensation which takes place here, that Doran really hunkers down when he starts to go into a tailspin, and thus avoids that fate.

However, when the 1984 season was examined, this pattern largely disappeared; Doran in 1984 hit no better or no worse following ten-game stretches in which he had hit poorly than he did following periods in which he had hit well. Further, when the 1985 season is analyzed by comparing Doran's games to his performance in the previous five games, the pattern again is not evident.

So, again, it is very questionable that any real tendency is observed here. There is an apparent pattern, yet that pattern would disappear if less than ten hits were moved from one game to another—not much of a body of evidence to base a conclusion on. There is a little more data on this, which we get to later.

Steven found no absolute reason to believe that any other Astros player was a better or worse hitter when he had hit well in the previous ten games than when he had not. Consider this chart for Jose Cruz:

Batting Average In Previous 10 Games	Performance	
Less than .200	14/50	.280
.200–.249	20/55	.364
.250–.279	13/48	.271
.280–.289	17/58	.293
.290–.314	19/59	.322
.315–.329	21/44	.477
.330–.349	11/44	.250
.350–.389	12/56	.214
.390 and up	15/52	.288

How Cruz hits bears no obvious relationship to how he has performed over the previous ten games. However, breaking it down into three groups of three areas, this data can be seen as showing a Doran-like relationship, in which Cruz hits better following periods in which his average is low. In fact, all four of the players studied hit *better* following ten-game periods in which their average was low than following ten-game periods in which it is high. Adding together the top three into a "top third," Cruz hit .250 (38/152) in the following games. He hit .307 in the bottom third (47/153). In addition:

• Glenn Davis hit .297 in the one-third of his games which followed periods in which his average was lowest, and .278 following periods in which it was highest.

• Kevin Bass hit .312 in the games which followed periods in which his average was low, and .257 following periods in which it was high.

As Steven concluded from this, "These tables indicate a moderately strong inverse relationship between a player's average in his last ten games and his likely performance 'today' . . . I think this is a tactical corollary to Bill's Plexiglass principle. When a player has hit poorly over a ten-game period, he has extra incentive to do whatever he can to maximize his hit chances."

In other words, when you hear that a player is hot, he may well be *less* likely, not more likely, to get a hit.

This pattern might also suggest that batting performance levels are psychologically fixed—that is, that .300 hitters are .300 hitters because they demand that of themselves, because they start to take extra work as soon as they reach .299.

Steven's study also found that the batting average of all players dropped following ten-game periods in which they had fewer than 24 at bats (that is, had been out of the lineup).

Obviously, these studies must be repeated many times and in many different ways before any general or safe conclusions can be drawn from them.

COMPLETE BATTING RECORDS

Player	G	AB	R	H	TB	2B	3B	HR	RBI	GW	SH	SF	HB	BB	IB	SO	SB	CS	GI DP	Avg	Slug	OBP	Runs Created	Outs Made	Runs/ 27 Outs	OW%	Appr Value
†Bailey	114	332	47	88	132	14	0	10	45	4	1	1	1	67	13	70	0	2	16	.265	.398	.389	51	264	5.17	.590	8
Davis	100	350	51	95	166	11	0	20	64	7	2	4	7	27	6	68	0	0	12	.271	.474	.332	53	273	5.23	.596	6
†Doran	148	578	84	166	251	31	6	14	59	6	3	5	0	69	6	69	23	15	10	.287	.434	.362	92	445	5.56	.625	14
Garner	135	463	65	124	185	23	10	6	51	9	1	5	2	34	3	72	4	4	12	.268	.400	.317	57	361	4.24	.492	7
*Reynolds	107	379	43	103	149	18	8	4	32	7	3	2	0	12	2	30	4	4	4	.272	.393	.293	42	289	3.95	.456	6
*Cruz	141	544	69	163	232	34	4	9	79	9	0	3	0	43	10	74	16	5	11	.300	.426	.349	81	400	5.44	.615	10
†Bass	150	539	72	145	230	27	5	16	68	6	4	2	6	31	1	63	19	8	10	.269	.427	.315	71	418	4.59	.532	11
†Mumphrey	130	444	52	123	176	25	2	8	61	3	1	6	0	37	8	57	6	7	9	.277	.396	.329	56	344	4.41	.511	7
*Walling	119	345	44	93	136	20	1	7	45	4	0	4	0	25	2	26	5	2	8	.270	.394	.316	42	266	4.30	.493	4
Thon	84	251	26	63	89	6	1	6	29	5	1	2	0	18	4	50	8	3	2	.251	.355	.299	27	196	3.79	.430	4
*Puhl	57	194	34	55	81	14	3	2	23	1	4	3	1	18	4	23	6	2	0	.284	.418	.343	30	148	5.47	.612	3
†Ashby	65	189	20	53	85	8	0	8	25	4	1	1	1	24	1	27	0	0	9	.280	.450	.363	29	147	5.40	.605	4
Pankovits	75	172	24	42	57	3	0	4	14	2	1	0	1	17	1	29	1	0	3	.244	.331	.316	19	134	3.76	.426	1
*Knepper	38	78	5	11	15	1	0	1	5	0	8	0	0	2	0	38	0	0	0	.141	.192	.163	3	75	1.05	.054	0
Scott	36	72	7	11	17	3	0	1	11	1	3	2	0	4	0	24	1	0	2	.153	.236	.192	3	68	1.35	.087	0
Niekro	32	68	6	17	18	1	0	0	6	1	10	1	0	1	0	16	0	0	4	.250	.265	.257	4	66	1.72	.134	0
*Spilman	44	66	3	9	13	1	0	1	4	0	0	0	0	3	0	7	0	0	2	.136	.197	.174	2	59	0.91	.042	0
Ryan	35	63	2	7	9	2	0	0	4	0	14	1	0	1	0	21	0	1	1	.111	.143	.162	2	73	0.72	.027	0
Tolman	31	43	4	6	13	1	0	2	8	2	1	0	1	1	0	10	0	1	0	.140	.302	.178	2	39	1.48	.103	0
*Mizerock	15	38	6	9	13	4	0	0	6	2	0	0	1	2	0	8	0	0	4	.237	.342	.293	3	33	2.20	.203	0
*Gainey	13	37	5	6	6	0	0	0	0	0	1	0	2	2	0	9	0	0	0	.162	.162	.244	2	32	1.52	.108	0
Rivera	13	36	3	7	11	2	1	0	2	0	1	0	0	4	1	8	0	0	2	.194	.306	.275	3	32	2.28	.214	0
Pena	20	29	7	8	10	2	0	0	4	1	1	1	0	1	0	6	0	0	1	.276	.345	.290	3	24	3.18	.347	0
*Jones	31	25	0	5	5	0	0	0	1	0	0	0	0	3	0	7	0	0	0	.200	.200	.286	2	20	2.23	.207	0
*Bullock	18	25	3	7	9	2	0	0	2	1	0	0	0	1	0	3	0	1	0	.280	.360	.308	2	19	3.54	.398	0
Heathcock	14	16	1	1	1	0	0	0	0	0	0	0	0	4	0	11	0	0	0	.063	.063	.250	1	15	0.92	.042	0
Mathis	23	14	0	1	1	0	0	0	0	0	2	0	0	1	0	6	0	0	0	.071	.071	.133	0	15	0.49	.012	0
Kerfeld	11	14	0	0	0	0	0	0	0	0	0	2	0	0	0	9	0	0	0	.000	.000	.000	0	16	0.00	.000	0
*DiPino	54	12	1	2	2	0	0	0	0	1	0	0	0	0	0	7	0	0	0	.167	.167	.167	0	10	0.90	.041	0
Dawley	49	10	1	2	2	0	0	0	0	0	0	0	0	1	0	3	0	0	0	.200	.200	.273	1	8	2.08	.185	0
*Calhoun	44	5	0	0	0	0	0	1	0	0	1	0	1	1	0	2	0	0	0	.000	.000	.143	0	6	0.50	.015	0
Smith	64	3	1	0	0	0	0	0	1	0	1	0	0	1	0	2	0	0	0	.000	.000	.250	0	4	1.05	.063	0
Solano	20	2	0	0	0	0	0	0	0	0	0	0	0	0	0	1	0	0	0	.000	.000	.000	0	2	0.00	.000	0
Knudson	2	2	0	0	0	0	0	0	0	0	0	0	0	1	0	2	0	0	0	.000	.000	.333	0	2	1.17	.076	0
Ross	8	1	0	0	0	0	0	0	0	0	0	0	0	0	0	0	0	0	0	.000	.000	.000	0	1	0.00	.000	0
*Madden	13	0	0	0	0	0	0	0	0	0	0	0	0	0	0	0	0	0	0	.000	.000	.000	0	0	0.00	.000	0
*Deshaies	2	0	0	0	0	0	0	0	0	0	0	0	0	0	0	0	0	0	0	.000	.000	.000	0	0	0.00	.000	0

*left-handed hitter, †switch hitter

DEFENSIVE STATISTICS

FIRST

	G	PO	A	Er	TC	DP	PCT.
Davis	89	749	57	12	818	76	.985
Cabell	49	311	22	2	335	30	.994
Walling	46	283	20	2	305	22	.993
Spilman	19	131	4	0	135	15	1.000
Tolman	6	12	2	0	14	1	1.000
Bailey	2	1	1	0	2	0	1.000
TEAM:	211	1487	106	16	1609	144	.990
AVG:	191	1513	114	12	1639	136	.993

SECOND

	G	PO	A	Er	TC	DP	PCT.
Doran	147	345	440	16	801	108	.980
Pankovits	21	24	35	0	59	7	1.000
Garner	15	26	32	1	59	10	.983
Pena	2	1	0	0	1	0	1.000
Reynolds	1	1	1	0	2	0	1.000
TEAM:	186	397	508	17	922	125	.982
AVG:	184	384	502	16	901	110	.982

THIRD

	G	PO	A	Er	TC	DP	PCT.
Garner	123	75	197	20	292	14	.932
Walling	51	31	104	9	144	9	.937
Rivera	11	7	25	2	34	3	.941
Pena	7	3	7	0	10	0	1.000
Pankovits	1	0	0	0	0	0	.000
TEAM:	193	116	333	31	480	26	.935
AVG:	189	125	341	25	492	29	.948

SHORTSTOP

	G	PO	A	Er	TC	DP	PCT.
Reynolds	102	158	318	11	487	65	.977
Thon	79	106	218	11	335	48	.967
Pena	6	5	8	1	14	2	.929
Pankovits	1	1	1	1	3	0	.667
TEAM:	188	270	545	24	839	115	.971
AVG:	185	268	521	30	819	99	.963

CATCHER

	G	PO	A	Er	TC	DP	PCT.	PB
Bailey	110	565	51	13	629	6	.979	19
Ashby	60	312	37	8	357	1	.978	14
Mizerock	15	77	8	3	88	1	.966	3
Spilman	2	3	0	0	3	0	1.000	0
TEAM:	187	957	96	24	1077	8	.978	36
AVG:	191	952	87	14	1053	11	.987	14

OUTFIELD

	G	PO	A	Er	TC	DP	PCT.
Bass	141	328	10	1	339	1	.997
Cruz	137	257	12	8	277	3	.971
Mumphrey	126	248	6	8	262	1	.969
Puhl	53	92	3	0	95	1	1.000
Pankovits	33	56	2	1	59	1	.983
Jones	15	15	0	0	15	0	1.000
Walling	13	12	0	1	13	0	.923
Davis	9	17	0	0	17	0	1.000
Gainey	9	21	0	2	23	0	.913
Tolman	9	12	0	0	12	0	1.000
Bullock	7	6	0	2	8	0	.750
TEAM:	552	1064	33	23	1120	7	.979
AVG:	569	1036	34	23	1093	6	.979

COMPLETE PITCHERS RECORDS

Pitcher	W	L	Pct	ERA	G	GS	CG	GF	SHO	SV	IP	H	TBF	R	ER	HR	SH	SF	HB	BB	IB	SO	WP	BK	Appr Value
										Starters (One-half of Game Appearances)														
*Knepper	15	13	.536	3.55	37	37	4	0	0	0	241.0	253	1016	119	95	21	15	9	3	54	5	131	4	0	10
Ryan	10	12	.455	3.80	35	35	4	0	0	0	232.0	205	983	108	98	12	11	12	9	95	8	209	14	2	7
Scott	18	8	.692	3.29	36	35	4	1	2	0	221.2	194	922	91	81	20	6	6	3	80	4	137	7	2	11
Niekro	9	12	.429	3.72	32	32	4	0	1	0	213.0	197	925	100	88	21	10	12	5	99	6	117	21	1	7
Heathcock	3	1	.750	3.36	14	7	1	5	0	1	56.1	50	226	25	21	9	2	1	1	13	0	25	2	0	2
Kerfeld	4	2	.667	4.06	11	6	0	2	0	0	44.1	44	193	22	20	2	1	3	0	25	2	30	1	0	2
Knudson	0	2	.000	9.00	2	2	0	0	0	0	11.0	21	53	11	11	0	1	0	0	3	0	4	0	0	0
										Relievers														
Dawley	5	3	.625	3.56	49	0	0	19	0	2	81.0	76	347	35	32	7	12	4	0	37	7	48	2	0	4
Smith	9	5	.643	2.27	64	0	0	46	0	27	79.1	69	315	26	20	3	3	1	1	17	5	40	4	1	11
DiPino	3	7	.300	4.03	54	0	0	29	0	6	76.0	69	329	44	34	7	3	3	2	43	6	49	4	1	3
Mathis	3	5	.375	6.04	23	8	0	5	0	1	70.0	83	319	54	47	7	4	4	1	27	1	34	1	0	0
Calhoun	2	5	.286	2.54	44	0	0	21	0	4	63.2	56	259	21	18	2	3	2	0	24	4	47	4	1	4
Solano	2	2	.500	3.48	20	0	0	9	0	0	33.2	34	144	13	13	5	1	0	0	13	2	17	2	0	0
*Madden	0	0	.000	4.26	13	0	0	4	0	0	19.0	29	92	15	9	1	0	1	0	11	0	16	1	0	0
Ross	0	2	.000	4.85	8	0	0	4	0	1	13.0	12	52	7	7	2	0	0	0	2	0	3	2	0	0
*Deshaies	0	0	.000	0.00	2	0	0	0	0	0	3.0	1	10	0	0	0	0	0	0	0	0	2	0	0	0

*left-handed

Mark BAILEY, Catcher

	G	AB	Hit	2B	3B	HR	Run	RBI	TBB	SO	SB	CS	Avg
1.37 years		493	117	22	1	14	62	58	88	103	0	2	.238
1985	114	332	88	14	0	10	47	45	67	70	0	2	.265
First Half	55	165	42	7	0	5	22	24	30			0	.255
Second Half	59	167	46	7	0	5	25	21	37			0	.275
Vs. RHP		209	52			6		24					.249
Vs. LHP		123	36			4		21					.293
Home	62	171	45	8	0	4	22	24				0	.263
Road	52	161	43	6	0	6	25	21				0	.267
Grass	29	88	28	4	0	3	17	12				0	.318
Turf	85	244	60	10	0	7	30	33				0	.246

Phil GARNER, Third Base

	G	AB	Hit	2B	3B	HR	Run	RBI	TBB	SO	SB	CS	Avg
10.03 years		555	146	28	8	9	71	67	50	75	21	9	.262
1985	135	463	124	23	10	6	65	51	34	72	4	4	.268
First Half	75	268	64	12	5	4	35	30	23		2		.239
Second Half	60	195	60	11	5	2	30	21	11		2		.308
Vs. RHP		244				1		32					.246
Vs. LHP		219				5		19					.274
Home	71	235	63	13	2	2	28	21				3	.268
Road	64	228	61	10	8	4	37	30				1	.268
Grass	36	135	40	9	7	4	29	21				1	.296
Turf	99	328	84	14	3	2	36	30				3	.256

Glenn DAVIS, First Base

	G	AB	Hit	2B	3B	HR	Run	RBI	TBB	SO	SB	CS	Avg
0.73 years		564	148	22	0	30	78	99	43	110	0	0	.263
1985	100	350	95	11	0	20	51	64	27	68	0	0	.271
First Half	28	86	20	1	0	2	9	8	5			0	.233
Second Half	72	264	75	10	0	18	42	56	22			0	.284
Vs. RHP		211	55			8		33					.261
Vs. LHP		139	40			12		31					.288
Home	46	164	52	5	0	8	22	31				0	.317
Road	54	186	43	6	0	12	29	33				0	.231
Grass	37	126	27	4	0	6	20	19				0	.214
Turf	63	224	68	7	0	14	31	45				0	.304

Craig REYNOLDS, Shortstop

	G	AB	Hit	2B	3B	HR	Run	RBI	TBB	SO	SB	CS	Avg
6.56 years		523	136	16	9	4	57	43	24	44	7	5	.260
1985	107	379	103	18	8	4	43	32	12	30	4	4	.272
First Half	64	217	59	8	4	3	20	22	11		1		.272
Second Half	43	162	44	10	4	1	23	10	1		3		.272
Vs. RHP		325	86			4		29					.265
Vs. LHP		54	17			0		3					.315
Home	57	191	44	8	3	1	16	16				0	.230
Road	50	188	59	10	5	3	27	16				4	.314
Grass	26	95	31	5	2	2	14	11				1	.326
Turf	81	284	72	13	6	2	29	21				3	.254

Bill DORAN, Second Base

	G	AB	Hit	2B	3B	HR	Run	RBI	TBB	SO	SB	CS	Avg
2.93 years		600	164	22	8	9	88	49	77	74	21	13	.274
1985	148	578	166	31	6	14	84	59	69	69	23	15	.287
First Half	83	329	95	19	1	7	45	30	40		16		.289
Second Half	65	249	71	12	5	7	39	29	31		7		.285
Vs. RHP		363	102			9		37					.281
Vs. LHP		215	64			5		22					.298
Home	70	269	76	20	5	5	40	28				7	.283
Road	78	309	90	11	1	9	44	31				16	.291
Grass	47	183	60	7	1	6	35	24				12	.328
Turf	101	395	106	24	5	8	49	35				11	.268

Jose CRUZ, Left Field

	G	AB	Hit	2B	3B	HR	Run	RBI	TBB	SO	SB	CS	Avg
12.64 years		553	159	28	7	11	74	76	63	69	25	10	.288
1985	141	544	163	34	4	9	69	79	43	74	16	5	.300
First Half	75	291	87	13	3	5	31	39	19		8		.299
Second Half	66	253	76	21	1	4	38	40	24		8		.300
Vs. RHP		323	101			4		35					.313
Vs. LHP		221	62			5		44					.281
Home	67	255	79	15	2	1	31	35				8	.310
Road	74	289	84	19	2	8	38	44				8	.291
Grass	43	173	46	11	1	5	24	30				5	.266
Turf	98	371	117	23	3	4	45	49				11	.315

Kevin BASS, Center Field

	G	AB	Hit	2B	3B	HR	Run	RBI	TBB	SO	SB	CS	Avg
2.40 years		457	116	21	5	8	57	48	18	65	11	6	.253
1985	150	539	145	27	5	16	72	68	31	63	19	8	.269
First Half	77	268	66	11	0	10	34	33	10		11		.246
Second Half	73	271	79	16	5	6	38	35	21		8		.292
Vs. RHP		320	77			6		36					.241
Vs. LHP		219	68			10		32					.311
Home	76	264	66	11	1	9	34	37			9		.250
Road	74	275	79	16	4	7	38	31			10		.287
Grass	46	178	50	12	2	4	26	18			7		.281
Turf	104	361	95	15	3	12	46	50			12		.263

Jerry MUMPHREY, Right Field

	G	AB	Hit	2B	3B	HR	Run	RBI	TBB	SO	SB	CS	Avg
7.98 years		540	155	23	6	7	73	61	51	73	21	10	.287
1985	130	444	123	25	2	8	52	61	37	57	6	7	.277
First Half	64	220	61	10	2	4	23	32	18		3		.277
Second Half	66	224	62	15	0	4	29	29	19		3		.277
Vs. RHP		311	91			8		48					.293
Vs. LHP		133	32			0		13					.241
Home	62	199	61	14	1	4	27	27			3		.307
Road	68	245	62	11	1	4	25	34			3		.253
Grass	39	140	41	4	1	4	20	24			2		.293
Turf	91	304	82	21	1	4	32	37			4		.270

Denny WALLING, First Base

	G	AB	Hit	2B	3B	HR	Run	RBI	TBB	SO	SB	CS	Avg
4.77 years		367	100	15	5	6	49	49	40	39	8	1	.271
1985	119	345	93	20	1	7	44	45	25	26	5	2	.270
First Half	76	238	63	14	0	4	27	27	15		4		.265
Second Half	43	107	30	6	1	3	17	18	10		1		.280
Vs. RHP		300	81			7		40					.270
Vs. LHP		45	12			0		5					.267
Home	65	181	47	12	1	2	20	20			2		.260
Road	54	164	46	8	0	5	24	25			3		.280
Grass	36	103	33	4	0	4	14	19			1		.320
Turf	83	242	60	16	1	3	30	26			4		.248

Dickie THON, Shortstop

	G	AB	Hit	2B	3B	HR	Run	RBI	TBB	SO	SB	CS	Avg
3.35 years		537	148	26	7	9	70	51	40	67	27	10	.275
1985	84	251	63	6	1	6	26	29	18	50	8	3	.251
First Half	40	119	25	4	0	1	10	6	5		1		.210
Second Half	44	132	38	2	1	5	16	23	13		7		.288
Vs. RHP		89	20			2		11					.225
Vs. LHP		162	43			4		18					.265
Home	44	121	23	2	1	3	14	12			3		.190
Road	40	130	40	4	0	3	12	17			5		.308
Grass	26	88	27	3	0	1	8	13			4		.307
Turf	58	163	36	3	1	5	18	16			4		.221

BOB KNEPPER

	(W–L)	GS	Run	Avg	DP	Avg	SB	Avg
1984	(15-10)	34	162	4.76	41	1.21	17	.50
1985	(15-13)	37	150	4.05	44	1.19	15	.41
1977-1985		280	1101	3.93	276	.99	244	.87

	G	IP	W	L	Pct	ER	BB	SO	ERA
1984 Home	19	138.7	10	4	.714	40	26	82	2.60
1985 Home	19	123.0	5	8	.385	48	22	64	3.51
1984 Road	16	95.0	5	6	.455	43	29	58	4.07
1985 Road	18	118.0	10	5	.667	47	32	67	3.58
1984 Grass	9	57.7	3	4	.429	25	13	31	3.90
1985 Grass	9	61.7	6	1	.857	19	16	33	2.77
1984 Turf	26	176.0	12	6	.667	58	42	109	2.97
1985 Turf	28	179.3	9	12	.429	76	38	98	3.81
1985 Total	37	241.0	15	13	.536	95	54	131	3.55

MIKE SCOTT

	(W–L)	GS	Run	Avg	DP	Avg	SB	Avg
1984	(5-11)	29	118	4.07	28	.97	42	1.45
1985	(18-8)	35	176	5.03	38	1.09	24	.69
1979-1985		148	638	4.31	144	.97	135	.91

	G	IP	W	L	Pct	ER	BB	SO	ERA
1984 Home	14	78.7	4	5	.444	34	16	49	3.89
1985 Home	17	120.0	11	2	.846	29	35	74	2.17
1984 Road	17	75.3	1	6	.143	46	27	34	5.50
1985 Road	19	101.7	7	6	.538	52	45	63	4.60
1984 Grass	12	49.0	0	6	0.000	35	19	21	6.43
1985 Grass	11	65.0	4	3	.571	25	25	41	3.46
1984 Turf	19	105.0	5	5	.500	45	24	62	3.86
1985 Turf	25	156.7	14	5	.737	56	55	96	3.22
1985 Total	36	221.7	18	8	.692	81	80	137	3.29

NOLAN RYAN

	(W–L)	GS	Run	Avg	DP	Avg	SB	Avg
1984	(16-12)	30	120	4.00	16	.53	41	1.37
1985	(10-12)	35	135	3.86	29	.83	36	1.03
1977-1985		326	1258	3.86	260	.80	380	1.17

	G	IP	W	L	Pct	ER	BB	SO	ERA
1984 Home	13	79.0	5	5	.500	19	32	80	2.16
1985 Home	19	134.7	7	3	.700	47	43	118	3.14
1984 Road	17	104.7	7	6	.538	43	37	117	3.70
1985 Road	16	97.3	3	9	.250	51	52	91	4.72
1984 Grass	9	59.0	4	3	.571	21	12	57	3.20
1985 Grass	9	52.0	3	4	.429	32	24	45	5.54
1984 Turf	21	124.7	8	8	.500	41	57	140	2.96
1985 Turf	26	180.0	7	8	.467	66	71	164	3.30
1985 Total	35	232.0	10	12	.455	98	95	209	3.80

JOE NIEKRO

	(W–L)	GS	Run	Avg	DP	Avg	SB	Avg
1984	(16-12)	38	182	4.79	39	1.03	46	1.21
1985	(11-13)	35	144	4.11	35	1.00	53	1.51
1977-1985		287	1184	4.13	264	.92	347	1.21

	G	IP	W	L	Pct	ER	BB	SO	ERA
1984 Home	21	136.0	6	8	.429	41	61	71	2.71
1985 Home	16	99.7	4	5	.444	43	51	57	3.88
1984 Road	17	112.3	10	4	.714	43	28	56	3.45
1985 Road	19	125.7	7	8	.467	53	58	64	3.80
1984 Grass	8	55.0	7	0	1.000	19	10	30	3.11
1985 Grass	14	92.7	8	4	.667	33	41	41	3.21
1984 Turf	30	193.3	9	12	.429	65	79	97	3.03
1985 Turf	21	132.7	3	9	.250	63	66	80	4.27
1985 Total	35	225.3	11	13	.458	96	107	121	3.83

OTHERS

	(W–L)	GS	Run	Avg	DP	Avg	SB	Avg
Mathis	(3-5)	8	36	4.50	5	.62	7	.88
Heathcock	(3-1)	7	53	7.57	7	1.00	3	.43
Kerfeld	(4-2)	6	26	4.33	8	1.33	6	1.00
Knudson	(0-2)	2	5	2.50	3	1.50	2	1.00

SAN DIEGO PADRES

BREAKDOWNS FOR THE LAST TEN SEASONS

Won-Lost Record: 745-822, .475 (4th in the division, 17th in the major leagues)
Runs Scored: 6,093 (Fewest in the division)
Runs Allowed: 6,451 (3rd-Most in the division)
Home Runs Hit: 843 (5th in the division)
Home Runs Allowed: 1,122 (3rd-Most in the division)

RECORD IN:
April: 94-111, .459 (5th in the division)
May: 139-103, .517 (3rd in the division)
June: 134-131, .506 (4th in the division)
July: 120-136, .469 (Poorest in the division)
August: 125-147, .443 (5th in the division)
September: 119-146, .449 (5th in the division)
October: 14-11, .560 (2nd in the division)

Won-Lost Record in Road Games: 332-452, .423 (Worst in the division)
Won-Lost Record at Home: 413-370, .527 (4th in the division)
Home Field Advantage: 81½ games
Runs Scored on the Road: 3,168 (4th in the division)
Runs Scored at Home: 2,925 (2nd-fewest in the division)
Runs Allowed on the Road: 3,527 (Most of any National League team)
Runs Allowed at Home: 2,924 (3rd-fewest in the division)

Home Runs Hit on the Road: 464 (Fewest in the division)
Home Runs Hit at Home: 379 (Second-fewest in the division)
Home Runs Allowed on the Road: 615 (Most in the National League)
Home Runs Allowed at Home: 507 (3rd in the division)

RECORD FOR LAST THREE SEASONS: 256-230, .527 (2nd in the division)

Alan Wiggins was one of the key success stories for the San Diego Padres in 1984. Making the very difficult move from the outfield to second base, he had gotten along well defensively and contributed steadily on offense, enabling the Padres to get an extra bat in the lineup. In spring training of 1985 Wiggins confessed that he had developed a dependence on drugs, and needed to fight his way clear of it. The Padres were understanding about this, up to a point, but in the second week of the season Wiggins had a relapse, and had to seek further treatment.

It was late June when he was ready to return to the team, but by this time the Padres were playing real well, and they had reached the conclusion that they didn't really need Alan Wiggins—not only that they didn't need him, but that he did not deserve to walk among them any more; yessir, they took a vote on it, and they decided that they just didn't want any of his kind around. The owner of the team took the same position, and took it with such determination that it was clear she would, if need be, fight in court for the right to throw Alan Wiggins away like a lump of rotten cheese.

Now that was, to tell the truth, a right arrogant, self-righteous attitude, and as I think I mentioned earlier in the book, it has been my experience that the Lord rarely wastes much time in punishing this particular failing in us. I mean, I've found that a lot of times it is just damned difficult to figure out what the Old Bugger is up to; I don't know too much about it, but I was raised to believe in God, and there are a number of areas which I was led to believe were his assignments to which it seems to me he doesn't pay as much attention as he might. He is, however, quite alert to punishing arrogance and reinstructing us in humility; in fact, I think this is only one among his deific

duties that he really enjoys, and I've found that he can be tremendously creative in accomplishing this task swiftly.

This was, by the way, about the eleventh consecutive season for which the story of the year for Dick Williams' team has revolved around the weird comings and goings of his second basemen. Some of Williams' actions there, such as the 1984 decisions to release Juan Bonilla and shift Alan Wiggins in from left field, have been courageous and brilliant. Some, such as the time he tried rotating four men at the position and pinch-hitting for them whenever they were due at the plate, have been funny. Some, such as his 1973 decision to resign as manager of the A's over the shabby treatment of Mike Andrews, have been courageous and sad. Some, such as his dogged determination to play Rodney Scott in Montreal *and* San Diego, carried to the extent of claiming that Rodney was the best player on his Montreal team and pouting publicly when he couldn't have him for the Padres, have been courageous and stupid.

The 1985 decision was in the stupid category; courageous, but stupid. Now, it is important to note, lest I be accused of contradicting what I wrote about Chuck Tanner and Whitey Herzog, that Alan Wiggins had come to the Padres, had apologized for letting the team down and had asked for forgiveness. Darrell Porter got ahold of his problems, and Whitey Herzog was happy to have him on his team; Lonnie Smith faced up to his problem, and Whitey stuck by him until he was back on his feet. But the trouble with Wiggins was, as the Padres saw it at the time, that they had already forgiven him once. As I understand it, the team held a special meeting of their John Birch Society chapter, and they prayed for guidance and asked how many times they should forgive their brother, and the answer came to them that the appropriate number was seven times seven, unless you had a platoon combination that could do his job just as well, in which case once ought to do it. I mean, this is God's own team, right? You can't have a doper on the same team with God and Steve Garvey.

Well, you see, the Lord was giving the Padres a little pop quiz, and that wasn't the right answer. It wasn't even close. Speaking of quizzes, you may have heard the story that when Alan Wiggins tried to demonstrate to the team the depth of his reformation they asked him to identify from photographs some of the nations most respected religious leaders, but when Wiggins mixed up Oral Roberts and Pat Robertson they realized he was a hopeless miscreant; however, I count this an idle rumor, and doubt that there is more than a kernel of truth to it.

Anyway, the Padres had no sooner voted to drive Wiggins from their doorway than they realized that they had been struck slow. God-awful slow. Slow in the infield. Slow in the outfield. Catcher was a guy named Terry Kennedy, slower'n the fat girl chasing her chihuahua up the staircase. All of a sudden they couldn't buy a win. They looked around one day and said "Hey, you know, we ain't got no lead-off man." Tony Gwynn, who in 1984 had hit .406 with runners on base, suddenly lost about 50 points off his batting average. The team didn't have a bench; Wiggins, who would have been an invaluable bench man with his speed, switch hitting, ability to get on base and experience both in the infield and outfield, wasn't around. I'll get to more of the details in the next article, but in sum the Padres, who were 35–22 on or about the day they voted on Wiggins' right to return, went 48–57 the rest of the way. They were out of contention within 45 days.

Well, I think you can safely infer from this that the Lord was not pleased with his Padres, and that's about all I had to say about it. At least Dick Williams had the guts to face up to it. He stated bluntly late in the season that the loss of Wiggins was the largest factor leading to the decline of the Padres. In other words, "We blew it, guys." I apologize if I offended anyone along the way, but for those of you who weren't offended, did you ever think that maybe we should form an entire league of teams with ecclesiastical monikers? I figure you could make up a good league with the Padres, the San Francisco Missionaries, the Atlanta TV Evangelists, the Houston Pastors, the St. Louis Cardinals, the California Angels and the Pittsburgh Men of the Cloth. I figure it would be a lot of fun drawing up the logos and all; for example, I reckon the symbol for the New England Deacons should be Fire and Brimstone, while the Cincinnati Clerics could be represented by a hand clutching a rosary or something. Any further ideas along these lines should be directed to the Commissioner's office.

THE PADRE LEAD-OFF PROBLEM

San Diego lead-off men in 1985 scored only 83 runs, the lowest total in the National League, and very probably the lowest total in baseball. The Padres tried quite a number of people in the lead-off role (eight, actually) but since they have one lead-off man, Tim Flannery, who had an excellent .386 on-base percentage, it seemed to me that he should have been leading off whenever he was in the lineup, and that the late-season decision to start leading off Garry Templeton (on base percentage: .332) was more of a frustration reaction than something which logically had a good chance to solve the problem.

I studied the Padres' offensive patterns with various lead-off men, and it doesn't exactly show that. With Tim Flannery leading off, the Padres *lead-off position* did score more runs than with the other players. Flannery led off in 60 games, in which the lead-off spot produced 35 runs, the best rate on the team:

Player	Lead-off Games	Lead-Off	Runs
Flannery	60	35	(.58)
Templeton	36	19	(.53)
Royster	35	16	(.46)
Others	31	13	(.42)

The "others" include Wiggins for nine games, Dilone for nine games, Bumbry for eight, Gerald Davis for four and Bobby Brown for one (referring, of course, to the starting leadoff hitter.)

But while Flannery did score more often, the whole team did not:

Player	Lead-off Games	Team	Runs
Flannery	60	224	3.80
Templeton	36	143	3.97
Royster	35	159	4.68
Others	31	120	3.87

It probably is not fair to attribute the failures of the players who followed him to Flannery; it probably is not fair, but it's probably inevitable. What I think happened was that . . . well, here, I'll present the entire run spectrum for the four groups:

RUNS SCORED BY BATTERS IN POSITION

Lead-off Hitter	Games									
	1	2	3	4	5	6	7	8	9	
Flannery	60	35	33	27	31	25	24	19	22	8
Templeton	36	19	23	17	13	16	20	11	13	11
Royster	35	16	22	24	22	17	14	22	18	8
Others	31	13	17	20	22	9	17	16	8	2
TEAM TOTAL	162	83	96	89	82	67	75	68	61	29

The number of runs scored by the #2 spot was higher with Templeton and Royster batting second than with Flannery, supporting the notion (for which there is considerable independent evidence) that Gwynn hits better with a fast man on first base. This, then, is a legitimate consequence of Flannery's lack of speed, and a legitimate reason not to bat him lead-off. The extremely low number of runs scored by #9 hitters with Flannery leading off probably reflects two things (beyond random chance)—the Padres virtually nonexistent left-handed bench, and Flannery's very low isolated power (hence little ability to drive a runner home from first).

However, Royster isn't *that* much faster than Flannery, and the vastly improved performance of the #3 spot with Royster leading off rather than Flannery is almost certainly due to the fact that Royster led off against left-handers, and Steve Garvey hits left-handers much better than right-handers—a fact which really shouldn't be held against Flannery.

In addition to having the fewest runs scored by lead-off men, the Padres missed by only one of having the fewest runs scored by #9 hitters, obviously reflecting the poor quality of the bench. The Padre offense was a funny one; the middle of the offense (spots 3–5) was also very weak, scoring only 238 runs (9th in the league, and 71 runs behind the division-champion Dodgers, who outscored the Padres overall by only 32 runs). Yet the 6–8 spots for the Padres were nearly the strongest in the league, often including a number of players with very good on-base percentages (Martinez, .362, Nettles, .363, and Flannery, .386), and consequently scoring more runs than any other offense in the league except Houston's. A slot-by-slot comparison of the San Diego and Los Angeles offenses shows just how radical the differences were:

RUNS SCORED BY POSITION

	1	2	3	4	5	6	7	8	9
San Diego	83	96	89	82	67	75	68	61	29
Los Angeles	100	72	101	109	99	69	46	50	36
Difference:	−17	+24	−12	−27	−32	+6	+22	+11	−7

The San Diego offense was far stronger at the "off-spots"—second, sixth, seventh and eighth—while the Dodger offense was much stronger at the traditional pivot points of an offense—leadoff, and the heart of the order.

Much more material of this type is discussed in the San Francisco team comment.

A LEAGUE FULL OF GOODENS

Garry Templeton was quoted as saying last summer that one of the reasons the Padres had struggled was that the other teams had stacked their rotations against the defending champions, so that the Padres were facing nothing except front-line pitchers. This statement, if true, would be a matter of considerable interest, inasmuch as it might help to explain one of the most-commented upon features of baseball in the eighties, the difficulty that championship teams have had in repeating. So I thought, "Well, that's something I can check out." Naturally I did.

Templeton's description obviously is not intended to apply to only the half-dozen best pitchers in the league, the Goodens and Valenzuelas, since it would be impossible to face nothing but these types of pitchers for any period of time. I used, then, a more liberal definition of a quality pitcher, that being any pitcher who pitches 162 innings and has 1) a winning record or 2) an ERA better than league.

As it turns out, this definition may not be liberal enough yet; it excludes pitchers such as Nolan Ryan, Joe Niekro and John Denny, who have big names but had losing records and above-league ERAs in 1985. I don't think that this really affects the validity of the study, because if you can't beat the pitchers that other people are beating, then I don't think you can use that as an explanation for why you didn't win; nonetheless, Garry Templeton and the Padres probably don't feel like they're catching any

breaks when they have to face Nolan Ryan, and it might have been better to have written a definition that would have included more pitchers in the "front-line" category.

Anyway, with that reservation, it turns out that the San Diego Padres faced *fewer* front-line pitchers, both in 1984 and 1985, than any other team in the National League West. One factor that contributed to this was that the Padres starting pitching in 1985 was excellent, with Dravecky, Show, Hawkins and Hoyt all qualifying as front-line, so that when, let us say, Atlanta is facing San Diego, the chance that Atlanta will be facing a front-line pitcher is much greater than the chance that San Diego will be. This, however, is a minor problem; it certainly wouldn't explain why the Padres faced fewer front-line pitchers than the Dodgers.

The data from the 1984 season first, since it is much more interesting than that for 1985:

TEAM	Front-Line Starters Faced	Second-Line Starters Faced
Cincinnati	94	68
Atlanta	88	74
Los Angeles	87	75
San Francisco	82	80
Houston	75	87
San Diego	74	88

I was quite surprised to find that the difference between the number of front-line pitchers faced by different teams was so large—20 games—but there is no particular reason why opposition managers should have been gunning for the Cincinnati Reds, a 70–92 team, and one must suppose that this was essentially luck. A quick mathematical assessment says that this difference should have given the Padres about a two and one half game advantage (as compared to the Reds) over the course of the season, since the "front-line" pitchers had an overall winning percentage in 1984 of .575, and the rest of the league had a winning percentage of .452 (.575−.452 equals .123; .123 times 20 equals 2½ games). One's gut instinct is that the difference might have been larger than that.

In 1985, the luck was much more even:

TEAM	Front-Line Starters Faced	Second-Line Starters Faces
San Francisco	78	84
Cincinnati	77	85
Atlanta	76	86
Los Angeles	76	86
Houston	75	87
San Diego	72	90

Using the most liberal possible interpretation of the data, we might figure that the average pitcher faced by the Padres in 1985 *was* tougher than in 1984 (relative to the league)—but it was not that they faced particularly *tough* pitchers in 1985, but that they were very fortunate in this regard in 1984. Which I think helps to explain, in retrospect, why that essentially unremarkable team was able to win the National League pennant.

Other notes of interest:

In July, 1985, when the Dodgers had their famous hot streak, they faced only seven front-line starting pitchers in 27 games. This was the poorest quality of opposition pitching faced by any team in the division in any month over the two seasons. Which takes nothing away from them; when they got to a soft spot in their schedule, they took advantage of it, but it helps to explain why they did so well at that particular time, rather than before or after. In a sense, the Dodgers may have performed every bit as well in April, when they faced front-line starters in 14 of 21 games, but still finished at 11–10.

In July and August, 1985, the Astros faced 30 front-line starting pitchers in 52 games; their record was the inverse, 22–30. In September, they faced only 9 front-line starters in 29 games, and went 18–11—lending support to the supposition that their late-season improvement was fueled largely by the fact that they were out of the race.

In 1984, the Atlanta Braves' record (with the exception of the month of May) reflects almost perfectly the quality of the pitching that they faced. In April they faced 12 front-line starters in 21 games and were 9–12. In June

they faced only 12 front-line starters in 29 games, and jumped to 17–12. In July they faced 17 quality starters in 28 games, and fell to 12–16. In August they faced another 18 good ones in 28 games, and limped along at 11–17. In September they faced only 13 in 28 games, and improved to 14–14. This pattern is not apparent to the same degree for any other team.

Although the Padres got off easy, on balance, in 1984, in July of that month they faced 20 front-line starters in 30 games, which was the toughest month that any team had over the two seasons. They responded to this magnificently, beating eight front-line pitchers during the month, and winning 19 of 30.

But with respect to the original issue here, one must conclude that either

a) Templeton's statement was inadequately represented in the study, which would mean that the Padres faced an inordinate number of front-line pitchers who just happened to have losing records and high ERAs, or

b) Templeton's statement is false.

COMPLETE BATTING RECORDS

Player	G	AB	R	H	TB	2B	3B	HR	RBI	GW	SH	SF	HB	BB	IB	SO	SB	CS	GI DP	Avg	Slug	OBP	Runs Created	Outs Made	Runs/ 27 Outs	OW%	Appr Value
*Kennedy	143	532	54	139	198	27	1	10	74	9	0	2	0	31	10	102	0	0	19	.261	.372	.301	55	414	3.56	.452	9
Garvey	162	654	80	184	281	34	6	17	81	11	1	6	3	35	7	67	0	0	25	.281	.430	.318	82	502	4.44	.561	10
*Flannery	126	384	50	108	131	14	3	1	40	6	3	2	9	58	1	39	2	5	4	.281	.341	.386	55	290	5.14	.632	7
*Nettles	137	440	66	115	185	23	1	15	61	4	0	3	0	72	5	59	0	0	10	.261	.420	.363	70	338	5.60	.670	9
†Templeton	148	546	63	154	206	30	2	6	55	5	5	3	1	41	24	88	16	6	5	.282	.377	.332	69	411	4.55	.573	12
Martinez	150	514	64	130	223	28	1	21	72	13	2	4	3	87	4	82	0	4	10	.253	.434	.362	84	404	5.61	.671	10
McReynolds	152	564	61	132	209	24	4	15	75	12	2	4	3	43	6	81	4	0	17	.234	.371	.290	59	455	3.48	.440	10
*Gwynn	154	622	90	197	254	29	5	6	46	8	1	1	2	45	4	33	14	11	17	.317	.408	.364	88	455	5.22	.639	12
Royster	90	249	31	70	102	13	2	5	31	4	3	2	1	32	1	31	6	5	6	.281	.410	.363	37	195	5.15	.632	4
Bevacqua	71	138	17	33	48	6	0	3	25	3	1	3	0	25	5	17	0	0	3	.239	.348	.349	18	112	4.39	.556	2
Bochy	48	112	16	30	50	2	0	6	13	1	2	0	0	6	1	30	0	0	1	.268	.446	.305	15	85	4.85	.604	2
*Bumbry	68	95	6	19	25	3	0	1	10	1	1	0	0	7	0	9	2	0	4	.200	.263	.255	6	81	2.02	.209	0
†Brown	79	84	8	13	16	3	0	0	6	0	1	1	0	5	0	20	6	4	2	.155	.190	.200	3	79	0.97	.057	1
Show	35	79	3	10	13	0	0	1	6	0	7	0	1	0	0	30	0	0	1	.127	.165	.138	2	76	0.76	.036	0
Hawkins	33	77	1	6	6	0	0	0	3	1	13	0	0	3	0	16	0	0	1	.078	.078	.113	1	85	0.37	.009	0
Dravecky	34	69	5	8	11	1	1	0	1	0	6	0	0	4	0	20	0	0	0	.116	.159	.164	2	67	0.93	.053	0
Hoyt	31	64	4	4	4	0	0	0	2	0	12	0	0	1	0	21	0	0	1	.063	.063	.077	1	73	0.20	.003	0
Ramirez	37	60	6	17	23	0	0	2	5	0	0	0	0	3	0	11	0	0	0	.283	.383	.317	8	43	4.74	.593	1
Davis	44	58	10	17	22	3	1	0	2	1	1	0	0	5	0	7	0	0	2	.293	.379	.349	7	44	4.57	.575	1
Dilone	27	46	8	10	12	0	1	0	1	1	0	0	0	4	0	8	10	3	0	.217	.261	.280	4	39	2.78	.334	0
†Wiggins	10	37	3	2	3	1	0	0	0	0	0	1	0	2	0	4	0	1	1	.054	.081	.103	0	38	0.14	.001	0
*Thurmond	36	34	2	3	3	0	0	0	2	1	9	1	0	1	0	10	0	0	0	.088	.088	.111	1	41	0.50	.016	0
Wojna	15	12	0	2	2	0	0	0	0	0	0	0	0	0	0	8	0	0	0	.167	.167	.167	0	10	0.90	.050	0
Gossage	50	11	1	0	0	0	0	0	0	0	0	0	0	0	2	5	0	0	0	.000	.000	.154	0	11	0.20	.002	0
DeLeon	29	5	1	1	1	0	0	0	0	0	0	0	0	0	0	1	0	0	0	.200	.200	.200	0	4	1.35	.106	0
Jackson	22	5	0	0	0	0	0	0	0	0	1	0	0	0	0	3	0	0	0	.000	.000	.000	0	6	0.00	.000	0
Stoddard	44	5	0	0	0	0	0	0	0	0	1	0	0	0	0	1	0	0	0	.000	.000	.000	0	6	0.00	.000	0
*Lefferts	60	4	0	1	1	0	0	0	0	0	0	0	0	0	0	2	0	0	0	.250	.250	.250	0	3	2.25	.247	0
†McCullers	21	4	0	0	0	0	0	0	0	0	0	0	0	0	0	0	0	0	0	.000	.000	.000	0	4	0.00	.000	0
*Walter	15	1	0	0	0	0	0	0	0	0	0	0	0	1	0	0	0	0	0	.000	.000	.500	0	1	3.51	.444	0
Booker	17	1	0	0	0	0	0	0	0	0	0	0	0	0	0	0	0	0	0	.000	.000	.000	0	1	0.00	.000	0
Rodriguez	1	1	0	0	0	0	0	0	0	0	0	0	0	0	0	0	0	0	0	.000	.000	.000	0	1	0.00	.000	0
Patterson	3	0	0	0	0	0	0	0	0	0	0	0	0	0	0	0	0	0	0	.000	.000	.000	0	0	0.00	.000	0

*left-handed hitter, †switch hitter

FIRST	G	PO	A	Er	TC	DP	PCT.
Garvey	162	1442	92	5	1539	138	.997
Bevaqua	9	16	4	2	22	1	.909
Kennedy	5	8	1	0	9	0	1.000
Martinez	3	4	1	0	5	2	1.000
TEAM:	179	1470	98	7	1575	141	.996
AVG:	191	1513	114	12	1639	136	.993

SECOND	G	PO	A	Er	TC	DP	PCT.
Flannery	121	261	287	13	561	72	.977
Royster	58	112	165	7	284	33	.975
Wiggins	9	22	21	0	43	4	1.000
Ramirez	7	3	4	0	7	0	1.000
TEAM:	195	398	477	20	895	109	.978
AVG:	184	384	502	16	901	110	.982

THIRD	G	PO	A	Er	TC	DP	PCT.
Nettles	130	122	229	15	366	16	.959
Bevaqua	130	122	229	15	366	16	.959
Royster	29	13	24	1	38	1	.974
Flannery	1	0	0	0	0	0	.000
TEAM:	290	257	482	31	770	33	.960
AVG:	189	125	341	25	492	29	.948

SHORTSTOP	G	PO	A	Er	TC	DP	PCT.
Templeton	148	245	460	23	728	96	.968
Ramirez	27	22	34	5	61	9	.918
Royster	7	4	25	0	29	3	1.000
TEAM:	182	271	519	28	818	108	.966
AVG:	185	268	521	30	819	99	.963

CATCHER	G	PO	A	Er	TC	DP	PCT.	PB
Kennedy	140	654	67	10	731	12	.986	4
Bochy	46	148	11	2	161	2	.988	2
TEAM:	186	802	78	12	892	14	.987	6
AVG:	191	952	87	14	1053	11	.987	14

OUTFIELD	G	PO	A	Er	TC	DP	PCT.
Gwynn	152	337	14	4	355	2	.989
Martinez	150	298	13	7	318	3	.978
McReynolds	150	430	12	3	445	3	.993
Brown	28	20	2	0	22	2	1.000
Davis	23	18	2	1	21	0	.952
Bumbry	17	31	0	2	33	0	.939
Dilone	14	21	1	2	24	0	.917
Royster	2	1	0	0	1	0	1.000
Bevacqua	1	1	0	0	1	0	1.000
TEAM:	537	1157	44	19	1220	10	.984
AVG:	569	1036	34	23	1093	6	.979

COMPLETE PITCHERS RECORDS

Pitcher	W	L	Pct	ERA	G	GS	CG	GF	SHO	SV	IP	H	TBF	R	ER	HR	SH	SF	HB	BB	IB	SO	WP	BK	Appr Value
								Starters (One-half of Game Appearances)																	
Show	12	11	.522	3.09	35	35	5	0	2	0	233.0	212	977	95	80	27	9	5	5	87	7	141	4	0	9
Hawkins	18	8	.692	3.15	33	33	5	0	2	0	228.2	229	953	88	80	18	13	12	4	65	8	69	3	3	11
*Dravecky	13	11	.542	2.93	34	31	7	1	2	0	214.2	200	876	79	70	18	13	3	1	57	5	105	2	2	10
Hoyt	16	8	.667	3.47	31	31	8	0	3	0	210.1	210	839	85	81	20	9	3	2	20	2	83	0	4	10
*Thurmond	7	11	.389	3.97	36	23	1	4	1	2	138.1	154	592	70	61	9	12	4	3	44	5	57	0	0	5
								Relievers																	
Lefferts	7	6	.538	3.35	60	0	0	24	0	2	83.1	75	345	34	31	7	7	1	0	30	4	48	2	0	5
Gossage	5	3	.625	1.82	50	0	0	38	0	26	79.0	64	308	21	16	1	3	4	1	17	1	52	0	0	8
Stoddard	1	6	.143	4.65	44	0	0	20	0	1	60.0	63	279	35	31	3	6	2	0	37	7	42	5	0	2
Wojna	2	4	.333	5.79	15	7	0	1	0	0	42.0	53	198	35	27	6	3	3	3	19	0	18	1	2	0
Jackson	2	3	.400	2.70	22	2	0	6	0	2	40.0	32	163	13	12	4	4	2	1	13	1	28	0	1	2
DeLeon	0	3	.000	4.19	29	0	0	13	0	3	38.2	39	163	18	18	6	3	1	3	10	4	31	1	0	0
McCullers	0	2	.000	2.31	21	0	0	11	0	5	35.0	23	142	15	9	3	7	0	1	16	3	27	0	1	1
Booker	0	1	.000	6.85	17	0	0	9	0	0	22.1	20	102	17	17	3	1	2	1	17	2	7	5	0	0
*Walter	0	2	.000	2.05	15	0	0	7	0	3	22.0	12	86	6	5	0	1	1	0	8	1	18	0	0	0
*Patterson	0	0	.000	24.75	3	0	0	2	0	0	4.0	13	26	11	11	2	0	0	0	3	0	1	0	1	0

*left-handed

Terry KENNEDY, Catcher

	G	AB	Hit	2B	3B	HR	Run	RBI	TBB	SO	SB	CS	Avg
5.07 years		580	158	31	2	14	59	83	40	97	1	1	.273
1985	143	532	139	27	1	10	54	74	31	102	0	0	.261
First Half	80	297	79	16	1	7	32	47	16				.266
Second Half	63	235	60	11	0	3	22	27	15				.255
Vs. RHP													
Vs. LHP													
Home	76	279	65	12	1	7	27	39					.233
Road	67	253	74	15	0	3	27	35					.292
Grass	108	379	95	20	1	9	35	54					.251
Turf	35	153	44	7	0	1	19	20					.288

Steve GARVEY, First Base

	G	AB	Hit	2B	3B	HR	Run	RBI	TBB	SO	SB	CS	Avg
13.27 years		618	184	31	3	19	81	92	34	69	6	5	.298
1985	162	654	184	34	6	17	80	81	35	67	0	0	.281
First Half	88	364	95	17	2	13	45	45	12				.261
Second Half	74	290	89	17	4	4	35	36	23				.307
Vs. RHP													
Vs. LHP													
Home	81	313	89	17	3	10	44	40					.284
Road	81	341	95	17	3	7	36	41					.279
Grass	120	485	142	26	5	17	66	64					.293
Turf	42	169	42	8	1	0	14	17					.249

Tim FLANNERY, Second Base

	G	AB	Hit	2B	3B	HR	Run	RBI	TBB	SO	SB	CS	Avg
3.58 years		427	109	14	5	2	44	37	40	42	3	3	.255
1985	126	384	108	14	3	1	50	40	58	39	2	5	.281
First Half	64	202	55	11	3	1	26	21	28		1		.272
Second Half	62	182	53	3	0	0	24	19	30		1		.291
Vs. RHP													
Vs. LHP													
Home	60	165	45	5	1	1	24	17			1		.273
Road	66	219	63	9	2	0	26	23			1		.288
Grass	91	263	76	8	2	1	36	26			2		.289
Turf	35	121	32	6	1	0	14	14			0		.264

Graig NETTLES, Third Base

	G	AB	Hit	2B	3B	HR	Run	RBI	TBB	SO	SB	CS	Avg
14.70 years		569	142	21	2	25	77	82	69	75	2	2	.251
1985	137	440	115	23	1	15	66	61	72	59	0	0	.261
First Half	73	220	55	8	1	8	43	27	52		0		.250
Second Half	64	220	60	15	0	7	23	34	20		0		.273
Vs. RHP													
Vs. LHP													
Home	70	217	56	10	0	6	27	34			0		.258
Road	67	223	59	13	1	9	39	27			0		.265
Grass	102	311	76	14	0	12	45	43			0		.244
Turf	35	129	39	9	1	3	21	18			0		.302

Garry TEMPLETON, Shortstop

	G	AB	Hit	2B	3B	HR	Run	RBI	TBB	SO	SB	CS	Avg
7.88 years		641	184	28	11	5	84	60	28	87	26	14	.287
1985	148	546	154	30	2	6	63	55	41	88	16	6	.282
First Half	84	291	85	18	2	3	35	35	24		7		.292
Second Half	64	255	69	12	0	3	28	20	17		9		.271
Vs. RHP													
Vs. LHP													
Home	72	257	75	14	2	4	29	24			8		.292
Road	76	289	79	16	0	2	34	31			8		.273
Grass	109	403	110	21	2	6	44	39			10		.273
Turf	39	143	44	9	0	0	19	16			6		.308

Carmelo MARTINEZ, Left Field

	G	AB	Hit	2B	3B	HR	Run	RBI	TBB	SO	SB	CS	Avg
2.02 years		539	136	29	1	20	67	76	79	90	0	3	.252
1985	150	514	130	28	1	21	64	72	87	82	0	4	.253
First Half	79	276	70	17	1	11	36	38	37		0		.254
Second Half	71	238	60	11	0	10	28	34	50		0		.252
Vs. RHP													
Vs. LHP													
Home	79	256	70	10	1	16	34	45			0		.273
Road	71	258	60	18	0	5	30	27			0		.233
Grass	113	382	103	19	1	19	49	60			0		.270
Turf	37	132	27	9	0	2	15	12			0		.205

Kevin McREYNOLDS, Center Field

	G	AB	Hit	2B	3B	HR	Run	RBI	TBB	SO	SB	CS	Avg
2.09 years		589	148	25	5	19	69	79	43	86	4	3	.251
1985	152	564	132	24	4	15	61	75	43	81	4	0	.234
First Half	86	326	82	13	3	10	41	54	26		3		.252
Second Half	66	238	50	11	1	5	20	21	17		1		.210
Vs. RHP													
Vs. LHP													
Home	74	264	62	9	3	6	28	34			1		.235
Road	78	300	70	15	1	9	33	41			3		.233
Grass	112	414	91	13	4	12	43	53			2		.220
Turf	40	150	41	11	0	3	18	22			2		.273

Tony GWYNN, Right Field

	G	AB	Hit	2B	3B	HR	Run	RBI	TBB	SO	SB	CS	Avg
2.79 years		617	200	27	7	5	88	61	51	33	22	13	.325
1985	154	622	197	29	5	6	90	46	45	33	14	11	.317
First Half	83	341	103	20	4	4	48	25	19		8		.302
Second Half	71	281	94	9	1	2	42	21	26		6		.335
Vs. RHP													
Vs. LHP													
Home	80	316	103	14	4	3	50	23			8		.326
Road	74	306	94	15	1	3	40	23			6		.307
Grass	114	462	149	21	4	5	68	33			12		.323
Turf	40	160	48	8	1	1	22	13			2		.300

Jerry ROYSTER, Second Base

	G	AB	Hit	2B	3B	HR	Run	RBI	TBB	SO	SB	CS	Avg
7.22 years		506	127	19	5	4	67	41	49	61	25	12	.250
1985	90	249	70	13	2	5	31	31	32	31	6	5	.281
First Half	49	137	40	11	1	1	17	17	18		5		.292
Second Half	41	112	30	2	1	4	14	14	14		1		.268
Vs. RHP													
Vs. LHP													
Home	50	118	34	7	1	4	17	16			3		.288
Road	40	131	36	6	1	1	14	15			3		.275
Grass	73	195	50	8	1	4	25	23			4		.256
Turf	17	54	20	5	1	1	6	8			2		.370

Kurt BEVAQUA, Utility

	G	AB	Hit	2B	3B	HR	Run	RBI	TBB	SO	SB	CS	Avg
5.99 years		354	83	15	2	5	36	46	37	55	2	3	.236
1985	71	138	33	6	0	3	17	25	25	17	0	0	.239
First Half	35	62	16	4	0	2	11	15	15		0		.258
Second Half	36	76	17	2	0	1	6	10	10		0		.224
Vs. RHP													
Vs. LHP													
Home	39	65	16	2	0	2	9	11			0		.246
Road	32	73	17	4	0	1	8	14			0		.233
Grass	56	103	25	4	0	2	12	17			0		.243
Turf	15	35	8	2	0	1	5	8			0		.229

ERIC SHOW

	(W–L)	GS	Run	Avg	DP	Avg	SB	Avg
1984	(15-9)	32	117	3.66	26	.81	24	.75
1985	(12-11)	35	134	3.83	29	.83	30	.86
1982-1985		114	438	3.84	90	.79	94	.82

	G	IP	W	L	Pct	ER	BB	SO	ERA
1984 Home	15	90.7	6	5	.545	38	40	54	3.77
1985 Home	17	107.3	6	5	.545	42	42	69	3.52
1984 Road	17	116.0	9	4	.692	40	48	50	3.10
1985 Road	18	125.7	6	6	.500	38	45	72	2.72
1984 Grass	23	141.7	12	7	.632	63	63	80	4.00
1985 Grass	25	160.0	9	8	.529	63	61	104	3.54
1984 Turf	9	65.0	3	2	.600	15	25	24	2.08
1985 Turf	10	73.0	3	3	.500	17	26	37	2.10
1985 Total	35	233.0	12	11	.522	80	87	141	3.09

ANDY HAWKINS

	(W–L)	GS	Run	Avg	DP	Avg	SB	Avg
1984	(8-9)	22	109	4.95	20	.91	12	.55
1985	(18-8)	33	149	4.52	41	1.24	18	.55
1983-1985		74	323	4.36	81	1.09	49	.66

	G	IP	W	L	Pct	ER	BB	SO	ERA
1984 Home	21	92.7	5	5	.500	41	37	44	3.98
1985 Home	18	126.0	10	6	.625	44	35	35	3.14
1984 Road	15	53.3	3	4	.429	35	35	33	5.91
1985 Road	15	102.7	8	2	.800	36	30	34	3.16
1984 Grass	28	116.3	6	8	.429	59	54	61	4.56
1985 Grass	25	174.7	14	7	.667	61	45	49	3.14
1984 Turf	8	29.7	2	1	.667	17	18	16	5.16
1985 Turf	8	54.0	4	1	.800	19	20	20	3.17
1985 Total	33	228.7	18	8	.692	80	65	69	3.15

LaMARR HOYT

	(W–L)	GS	Run	Avg	DP	Avg	SB	Avg
1984	(13-18)	34	133	3.91	25	.74	14	.41
1985	(16-8)	31	110	3.55	33	1.06	28	.90
1980-1985		146	657	4.50	136	.93	86	.59

	G	IP	W	L	Pct	ER	BB	SO	ERA
1984 Home	18	122.3	9	9	.500	67	23	65	4.93
1985 Home	17	117.0	9	5	.643	53	12	56	4.08
1984 Road	16	113.3	4	9	.308	50	20	61	3.97
1985 Road	14	93.3	7	3	.700	28	8	27	2.70
1984 Grass	28	197.7	11	15	.423	93	35	108	4.23
1985 Grass	23	158.0	11	6	.647	64	16	71	3.65
1984 Turf	6	38.0	2	3	.400	24	8	18	5.68
1985 Turf	8	52.3	5	2	.714	17	4	12	2.92
1985 Total	31	210.3	16	8	.667	81	20	83	3.47

DAVE DRAVECKY

	(W–L)	GS	Run	Avg	DP	Avg	SB	Avg
1984	(9-8)	14	69	4.93	11	.79	10	.71
1985	(13-11)	31	110	3.55	33	1.06	29	.94
1982-1985		83	326	3.93	83	1.00	75	.90

	G	IP	W	L	Pct	ER	BB	SO	ERA
1984 Home	27	78.7	5	4	.556	28	23	37	3.20
1985 Home	14	97.0	6	3	.667	32	25	54	2.97
1984 Road	23	78.0	4	4	.500	23	28	34	2.65
1985 Road	20	117.7	7	8	.467	38	32	51	2.91
1984 Grass	39	110.0	5	7	.417	38	37	49	3.11
1985 Grass	24	156.0	9	7	.562	53	40	73	3.06
1984 Turf	11	46.7	4	1	.800	13	14	22	2.51
1985 Turf	10	58.7	4	4	.500	17	17	32	2.61
1985 Total	34	214.7	13	11	.542	70	57	105	2.93

MARK THURMOND

	(W–L)	GS	Run	Avg	DP	Avg	SB	Avg
1984	(14-8)	29	123	4.24	27	.93	23	.79
1985	(7-11)	23	82	3.57	21	.91	29	1.26
1983-1985		70	286	4.09	66	.94	74	1.06

	G	IP	W	L	Pct	ER	BB	SO	ERA
1984 Home	18	86.3	5	6	.455	36	26	33	3.75
1985 Home	18	69.3	3	5	.375	23	17	30	2.99
1984 Road	14	92.3	9	2	.818	23	29	24	2.24
1985 Road	18	69.0	4	6	.400	38	27	27	4.96
1984 Grass	24	126.3	10	6	.625	44	42	42	3.13
1985 Grass	27	103.3	5	8	.385	39	30	39	3.40
1984 Turf	8	52.3	4	2	.667	15	13	15	2.58
1985 Turf	9	35.0	2	3	.400	22	14	18	5.66
1985 Total	36	138.3	7	11	.389	61	44	57	3.97

OTHERS

	(W–L)	GS	Run	Avg	DP	Avg	SB	Avg
Wojna	(2-4)	7	31	4.43	10	1.43	9	1.29
Jackson	(2-3)	2	5	2.50	1	.50	1	.50

ATLANTA BRAVES

THE END OF THE FREE AGENT BOOM
AN OVERVIEW

Andy Messersmith will be remembered as the pitcher who opened the era of the megabucks free agents in 1976. Bruce Sutter may be remembered as the pitcher who brought it to a close. In 1984 the St. Louis Cardinals had Bruce Sutter, baseball's relief ace, and the Atlanta Braves did not; the two teams were almost even, the Braves winning 80 games and the Cardinals 84. In 1985 the Braves had Bruce Sutter and the Cardinals had 35 extra wins; on the basis of this sample one would have to fix the value of Bruce Sutter at -31 games.

This is probably not a reasonable estimate, but it certainly had an effect. Since the beginning of the Peter Seitz era, the owners had been trying to organize resistance to the escalating expectations of free agents. Prior to the 1985 season, these efforts had never met with much success. It was different in 1985. The key difference was the death of the belief that a free agent could turn a team around. It was a slow death and had been a long time coming, but Bruce Sutter provided the final bullet.

To go back in time to about 1978, when the free agent era was beginning and I was trying to establish myself in this field, I wrote at that time a series of articles for the *Baseball Bulletin* which argued that the value of an individual player in terms of wins was being enormously overstated. Those articles were probably the best that I had written at that time, and I am tempted to reconstruct the argument here, but will restrain myself and instead merely outline the series. The argument went: Baseball men are saying now (citing specific quotes) that this player or that player is worth ten or fifteen or twenty games to his team,

while in fact one can show by a variety of methods that the difference between a superstar and an average player at his position is in the range of three to five games a year, not fifteen or twenty. Among the ways in which one can show this are:

1) By studying what happens to teams which suddenly lose superstar players to injuries or other unexpected causes. Yes, they do sometimes decline dramatically, as the Dodgers did when Koufax retired, but more often they decline by a small amount, as the Tigers did in 1936 when they lost both Greenberg and Cochrane to injuries, or even show improvement, as the Yankees did in 1939 when they lost Gehrig.

2) By studying what happens to teams when superstars are suddenly neutralized by injuries or other causes, and have seasons which make them quite ordinary players for a year.

3) By studying what happens to teams on those relatively rare, once-in-a-decade type occasions when a rookie comes up and has a true superstar type season, as Tony Oliva did in 1964 or Fred Lynn did in 1975.

4) By studying what happens to teams subsequent to player sales (many of the best players in baseball history have been sold for cash in mid-career, including Babe Ruth, the game's greatest player, and Lefty Grove, the game's greatest pitcher).

5) By statistical inference. Measuring the runs created by a superstar, let's say Dale Murphy, and those created by an ordinary player and switching the two around, one can conclude that the substitution of an ordinary player for

the great Dale Murphy would probably cost the Atlanta Braves three to five games a year.

I could add now a sixth and perhaps most technically persuasive argument. If you play around with a statistical model of a team, it becomes quickly obvious that if a superstar had a potential impact of 15 or 20 games a year, then the standard deviation of team wins would have to be much larger than it is (around nine games). Given that teams consist of 15 to 18 "roles," it is irrational to suggest that the impact of a player playing one of those roles could be twice the standard deviation of the whole.

Anyway, I won't repeat those analyses, each of which could run the length of a team comment, but I will say this: that if you just think about, if you just reflect on the cases that you can remember, you might well think that the change which occurs with the sudden, unexpected loss or gain of a superstar is large. This is because when such a loss or gain is accompanied by a dramatic change in the performance of the team, sportswriters will always ascribe the change in the team to the player, and so those cases will stick out and will be remembered. The Vince Coleman phenomenon in 1985 is an excellent study in the matter—I mean, here's a guy who's not even real good, and the press thinks he single-handedly won the Cardinals the pennant. But if you actually do it, if you actually study the question—identify the greatest rookies, identify the greatest sudden losses to teams through injury—you'll find the same thing that I found: that the average concurrent change in the performance of the teams is three to five games. While the value of an MVP season might go somewhat larger than that, the expected performance of a superstar is worth three to five games as measured by any method.

What I did *not* foresee at that time was the full economic consequences of the misperception. One of the unwritten laws of economics is that it is impossible, truly impossible, to prevent the values of the society from manifesting themselves in dollars and cents. This is, ultimately, the reason why we pay athletes so much money: that it is very important to us to be represented by winning teams. The standard example is cancer research; letters pop up all the time saying that it is absurd for baseball players to make twenty times as much money as cancer researchers. But the hard, unavoidable fact is that we are, as a nation, far more interested in having good baseball teams than we are in finding a cure for cancer.

Now look, both of my parents died of cancer, and I fully expect that it's going to get me, too, in time. It would be very easy for me to say that cancer research is more important to me than baseball—but I must admit that I don't do anything which would be consistent with such a belief. I think about cancer research a few times a month; I think about baseball virtually every waking hour of my life. I spend many times as much money on baseball in a year as I give to cancer research—and so do you, and so does almost every goddamned one of those guys who writes the letters saying that it is ridiculous for baseball players to make more money than cancer researchers. You write it down on paper, the money you spend going to baseball games, the money you spend willingly on transportation to and from sporting events, the money you spend on over-priced beer and hot dogs at baseball games,

and in buying books and magazines about baseball, and on baseball cards or other collectibles—and on the other hand, how much you spend on cancer research.

That pool of money which we pour into athletics makes it inevitable that athletes are going to be better paid than cancer researchers. *Dollars and cents are an incarnation of our values. Economic realities represent not what we should believe, not what we like to say that we believe, not what we might choose to believe in a more perfect world, but what our beliefs really are.* However much we complain about it, nobody can stop that truth from manifesting itself.

The internal economic structures of baseball determine only one thing: how much of that money will go to the players, and how much the owners will get to keep. Owners, from 1978 through 1983, tried mightily to slow down the amount of money that was going to the players—but they truly believed that a star player could win them an extra ten or twenty games a year. The salaries of players rose to a level that was commensurate with that belief.

But in this way, economics ultimately correct the belief. Baseball men could *say* that a player was worth ten or fifteen or twenty games a year, and they could go on believing that—as long as they didn't have to pay for it. But when they had to begin putting the dollars out to back that up, they were forced to reexamine their belief, and to realize that it was false. If it were true, the Atlanta Braves, enriched by so many free agents, would long since have pulled away from the National League.

Because of the time at which his dramatic failure occurred, Bruce Sutter played a very important role in the reevaluation. Because of earlier failures, major league owners prior to 1984 had begun to have serious doubts about whether the "game impact" of a star player was as large as they used to think it was. In 1985 those doubts got a gigantic boost, not only from Sutter but from the entire free agent crop.

All of the teams which "won" the free agent wars a year ago came out of it worse than they went in. Fred Lynn, the best everyday player who jumped teams a year ago, moved from California to Baltimore—yet in spite of this, the Angels had their best season in several years, and the Orioles had their worst. The Chicago Cubs retained Rick Sutcliffe, the other number one pitching ace of the 1985 free agent crop—yet they, too, had a miserable year.

And the owners finally accepted this fact: that the addition of one player, even a star player, even a great player, does not substantially alter the outlook for that team.

THE END OF THE FREE AGENT BOOM
A STUDY

The new free-agent lockout was initiated last fall when a number of the best organizations in baseball announced that they were withdrawing from future free-agent negotiations. The Kansas City Royals, on making their announcement, cited research showing that of 98 free-agent signings over the last three years, 61 players experienced significantly sub-par seasons on joining their new teams. Of the 98 players, 56 joined new teams, and of those 56, only 9 played better than they had before—

seven of those nine being players who signed for less money than they had been getting. Royals owner Ewing Kauffman was quoted as saying that "Last September we kept hearing that if we just got Sutcliffe, we could solve all of our pitching problems. Several years ago we heard that if we just signed Pete Rose, we would win for the foreseeable future. . . . There has been no collusion. We have just seen too many free agents who haven't produced. There's a 50–50 chance they will hurt the team."

This announcement elicited a predictable reaction both from a segment of the Kansas City fans, who were busy lusting after Kirk Gibson and felt that the withdrawal would hurt the team, and from the players, who felt that the Royals were acting in concert with other teams. For what it is worth, I believe that what Kauffman said is literally true: that the Royals studied the issue, on their own, and concluded that their attempts to sign free agents had not contributed toward the success of the organization in the past and were not likely to contribute toward the success of the organization in the future. I do not believe that Kauffman would have taken the action that he took had he not sincerely believed that it was in the best interests of the Royals organization to do so, even if no other team took any similar stand. "Look at what we've done," he was saying. "We've contributed to the salary inflation in baseball, which hurts us as much as it hurts anyone. We've made good offers to players, yet we have gotten nothing from it—and maybe we're better off that way. If you look at what the Royals have done, and then you look at the performance of the teams which *have* signed free agents, like Atlanta, California and Houston, you've got to conclude that we're lucky we missed out on most of these people. So what's the point of continuing to do it?"

Anyway, I thought that I might try to repeat some of the research which the Royals cited—not by doing exactly the same things, of course, but study the same issue in my own way.

I decided to focus only on the best of the free agents. The Royals study apparently includes all free agents, regardless of ability. But obviously, only a fool would conclude that since Kirk Gibson and Steve Nicosia were both free agents, he could study the impact of signing Kirk Gibson by studying what happened to Steve Nicosia. I drew up a list of the 45 top free agents from Catfish Hunter through Bruce Sutter, determined by a complicated method that I'm not about to recount here. The 45 players will be listed later.

The Royals study apparently focused on the *players*; I decided to focus on what happened to the *teams* which signed the players. For each major free agent, I "tracked" what happened to four teams over a five-year period:
1) The team which signed him:
2) The team whose record over the previous two seasons had been most similar to that of the team which signed him, but which neither signed nor lost a free agent over the winter:
3) The team which lost him:
4) The team whose record over the previous two seasons had been most similar to that of the team which lost him, but which was bypassed by the free agent wars for that winter.

For Catfish Hunter, this meant that I studied what hap-

pened to the New York Yankees in the five years 1975–1979. The Yankees in the two years prior to signing Catfish had had records of 80–82 and 89–73; the most similar team was the Pittsburgh Pirates, who had gone 80–82 and 88–74. As a control, I also looked at what happened to them over the next five seasons. I followed the Oakland A's (94–68 and 90–72); as a control, I also followed the Baltimore Orioles (97–65 and 91–71).

The 45 players involved in the study could generally be classed as stars and superstars; some were just good players. The players are given below with their stats in the season prior to entering the free agent market (if not specified, stats given are home runs, RBI and batting averages for everyday players, wins, losses and ERA for pitchers):

1974 Catfish Hunter (25–12, 2.49); 1975 Andy Messersmith (19–14, 2.29); 1976 Reggie Jackson (27, 91, .277, 28 SB); 1976 Bobby Grich (13, 54, .266, Gold Glove); 1976 Wayne Garland (20–7, 2.68); 1976 Joe Rudi (13, 94, .270); 1976 Sal Bando (27, 84, .240); 1976 Don Baylor (15, 68, .247, 52 SB); 1976 Rollie Fingers (13–11, 2.47, 20 Saves); 1976 Bert Campaneris (1, 52, .256, 54 SB); 1976 Dave Cash (1, 56, .284); 1976 Gary Matthews (20, 84, .279); 1976 Bill Campbell (17–5, 3.00, 20 Saves); 1977 Richie Zisk (30, 101, .290); 1977 Lyman Bostock (14, 90, .336); 1977 Oscar Gamble (31, 83, .297); 1977 Larry Hisle (28, 119, .302); 1977 Goose Gossage (11–9, 1.62, 26 Saves); 1977 Ross Grimsley (14–10, 3.96); 1977 Mike Torrez (17–13, 3.89); 1978 Pete Rose (7, 52, .302, 51 doubles); 1978 Tommy John (17–10, 3.30); 1978 Jim Slaton (17–11, 4.12); 1978 Elias Sosa (8–2, 2.64, 14 Saves); 1979 Dave Goltz (14–13, 4.16); 1979 Nolan Ryan (16–14, 3.59); 1979 Don Stanhouse (7–3, 2.84, 21 Saves); 1979 Bob Watson (16, 71, .303); 1979 Joe Morgan (9, 32, .250, 28 SB and 93 Walks); 1980 Dave Winfield (20, 87, .276, 23 SB); 1980 Don Sutton (13–5, 2.21); 1980 Darrell Porter (7, 51, .249); 1981 Reggie Jackson (15, 54, .237); 1981 Dave Collins (3, 23, .272, 26 SB); 1982 Steve Garvey (16, 86, .282); 1982 Floyd Bannister (12–13, 3.43, 209 Strikeouts); 1982 Steve Kemp (19, 98, .286); 1982 Don Baylor (24, 93, .263); 1982 Omar Moreno (3, 44, .245, 60 SB); 1983 Goose Gossage (13–5, 2.27, 22 saves); 1983 Dave Parker (12, 69, .279); 1983 Phil Niekro (11–10, 3.97); 1983 Darrell Evans (30, 82, .277); 1984 Bruce Sutter (5–7, 1.54, 45 Saves); and 1984 Fred Lynn (23, 79, .271).

There are others who could be added or subtracted from the list—but obviously, one could not draw up any independent list, a list not using most of these same players, which was of comparable quality. These are the best of the free agents. You might also notice that the number of high-quality free agents changing teams has declined with almost perfect consistency since 1977—indicating a gradual realization.

The study shows that the teams signing these players did gain a small advantage over a period of years. The "signing" teams improved in the first season by almost exactly the same amount as the control group; however, in subsequent years they did show an advantage.

The teams which signed these free agents had a combined winning percentage of .501 in the year prior to signing the star. In the season prior to that they had a .494 percentage.

The control group, the comparable teams, had winning percentages over those two seasons of .503 and .500.

The teams signing the free agents improved in the first year to a winning percentage of .530. The control group, composed of teams which neither signed nor lost a free agent, showed an identical improvement, to .530.

However, in subsequent seasons the teams which had added the free agents were better able to maintain this improvement, with percentages of .533, .519, .522 and .529 in the following years, as opposed to a fall-off to .521, .510, .489 and .493 for the control group. These are the full records:

	Teams Signing Free Agents		Control Group	
Second Year Prior:	2720–2782	.494	2765–2731	.503
Year Prior to Signing:	2814–2798	.501	2804–2806	.500
YEAR AFTER SIGNING:	2911–2586	.530	2907–2583	.530
Two years after:	2759–2419	.533	2692–2476	.521
Three years after:	2400–2227	.519	2333–2246	.510
Four years after:	2110–1935	.522	2008–2096	.489
Five years after:	1994–1781	.528	1850–1901	.493

To clear up a few technical points, lest they puzzle you to death, the number of *teams* was less than 45 because multiple free agents joined some teams, and the number decreases as time passes because we can only study one year in the case of players like Bruce Sutter and Fred Lynn. Also, teams which both signed and lost a major free agent (there were four such teams) were excluded from the calculations. One reason for the improvement of both groups of teams was the large number of free agents in 1976, the year before the American League expansion. The losses of the Mariners and Blue Jays upped the winning percentage around the rest of the American League, where most of the free agents and most of the control teams were located.

However, as you can likely figure out, if both the teams which signed free agents and their control group improved in the first year, then those teams which lost free agents must have suffered. This is true; they did. You will note that those teams which lost free agents were generally of excellent quality, (an overall .534 winning percentage, meaning that the average of them won about 86 games). This tends to support the idea that free agency has contributed to competitive balance in baseball, causing fewer repeating champions, as opposed to the original fear that free agency would help the rich grow richer while the poor grew poorer.

This is the data for the teams which lost free agents:

	Teams Losing Free Agents		Control Group	
Second Year Prior:	2635–2481	.515	2643–2467	.517
Year Prior to Loss:	2815–2461	.534	2826–2462	.534
YEAR AFTER LOSS:	2594–2575	.502	2682–2492	.518
Two years after:	2405–2391	.501	2446–2342	.511
Three years after:	2217–2097	.514	2236–2078	.518
Four years after:	1801–1856	.492	1926–1743	.525
Five years after:	1735–1664	.510	1706–1670	.505

Despite frequent counter-examples such as the 1985 Cardinals, in the first year after the loss the teams losing free agents finished about two and one-half games behind their control group; it would be closer to two on a per-player basis (remembering that some of these teams lost multiple free agents).

The one thing in the study which stands out most clearly is that a team cannot sustain heavy free agent losses without suffering an almost inevitable breakdown. The teams which lost heavily in the free agent market—the A's, the Twins, the Reds—paid a heavy price in the won/lost column. Only one team, the Orioles, was able to sustain heavy free agent losses and continue to compete.

The other thing which stands out is that, with that exception, the movement of major, high-quality free agents is barely traceable in the won and lost column. Even teams which signed a number of free agents, like the Atlanta Braves and the Texas Rangers, did not necessarily improve as a consequence of this.

What happened in 1985 with respect to Sutter and Lynn—that is, the "losing" team improving while the "gaining" team declined—has happened many times.

It happened in the first case. The A's and Yankees were almost even in 1974, when Hunter was in Oakland; in 1975, when Hunter won 23 games for the Yankees, the A's won 98 games to the Yankees' 83.

It happened again in the second case. The Dodgers went 88–74 in 1975 with Andy Messersmith and his 2.29 ERA; in 1976 they improved to 92–70 and in 1977 to 98–64—while the Braves, adding Messersmith and then Gary Matthews, dropped from 67–94 to 61–101.

There are, of course, other cases in which the free agent acquisition was accompanied by an improvement in the team's performance. But it is quite clear that Ewing Kauffman was right: free agents have hurt their new teams almost as often as they have helped them. The gain clearly does not justify the expense.

I'm not saying that there was no collusion on the part of the owners. I am saying this: *collusion only works when the owners believe it is in the individual, selfish interest of each ballclub to make it work*. Early in the free agent era, the owners *said* that the salaries were too high—but they truly *believed* that they could help their teams by signing players at the prices being asked. Following the fiasco of the 1984 free agent crop, they no longer believe that. Now they actually *believe* that the free agent outlays are not justified by the probable return. That is the difference.

COMPLETE BATTING RECORDS

Player	G	AB	R	H	TB	2B	3B	HR	RBI	GW	SH	SF	HP	BB	IB	SO	SB	CS	GI DP	Avg	Slug	OBP	Runs Created	Outs Made	Runs/ 27 Outs	OW%	Appr Value
Cerone	96	282	15	61	79	9	0	3	25	2	0	4	1	29	1	25	0	3	15	.216	.280	.288	20	243	2.27	.214	3
Horner	130	483	61	129	241	25	3	27	89	6	0	6	1	50	4	57	1	1	18	.267	.499	.333	77	379	5.46	.610	11
Hubbard	142	439	51	102	138	21	0	5	39	5	7	6	4	56	2	54	4	3	11	.232	.314	.321	47	364	3.47	.388	7
*Oberkfell	134	412	30	112	148	19	4	3	35	2	1	2	6	51	6	38	1	2	10	.272	.359	.359	54	315	4.66	.533	7
Ramirez	138	568	54	141	189	25	4	5	58	5	2	5	0	20	1	63	2	6	21	.248	.333	.272	45	461	2.62	.265	9
Harper	138	492	58	130	200	15	2	17	72	7	1	2	3	44	4	76	9	9	13	.264	.407	.327	62	387	4.34	.497	8
Murphy	162	616	118	185	332	32	2	37	111	14	0	5	1	90	15	141	10	3	14	.300	.539	.388	131	453	7.80	.762	16
*Washington	122	398	62	110	181	14	6	15	43	2	0	2	1	40	11	66	14	4	11	.276	.455	.342	61	305	5.38	.604	7
Komminsk	106	300	52	68	98	12	3	4	21	2	2	2	1	38	1	71	10	8	4	.227	.327	.314	32	248	3.47	.388	3
*Perry	110	238	22	51	65	5	0	3	13	3	0	1	0	23	1	28	9	5	7	.214	.273	.282	18	200	2.43	.236	2
Benedict	70	208	12	42	48	6	0	0	20	1	4	2	1	22	1	12	0	1	8	.202	.231	.279	13	181	2.00	.174	2
Zuvella	81	190	16	48	58	8	1	0	4	0	4	0	0	16	1	14	2	0	3	.253	.305	.311	19	149	3.42	.381	2
*Thompson	73	182	17	55	66	7	2	0	6	1	1	0	3	7	0	36	9	4	1	.302	.363	.339	23	133	4.66	.533	1
*Chambliss	101	170	16	40	56	7	0	3	21	2	0	1	0	18	4	22	0	0	5	.235	.329	.307	17	136	3.35	.371	2
Mahler	39	90	9	14	15	1	0	0	8	3	11	1	0	3	0	18	0	0	2	.156	.167	.181	3	90	0.94	.045	0
Runge	50	87	15	19	25	3	0	1	5	0	4	1	0	18	0	18	1	0	3	.218	.287	.349	10	77	3.40	.377	1
Owen	26	71	7	17	26	3	0	2	12	0	2	1	0	8	3	17	0	0	2	.239	.366	.313	8	59	3.70	.419	1
Bedrosian	37	64	3	5	5	0	0	0	1	0	6	0	0	1	0	22	0	0	0	.078	.078	.092	1	65	0.29	.005	0
†Hall	54	47	5	7	9	0	1	0	3	1	1	0	0	9	1	12	1	1	3	.149	.191	.286	3	45	1.53	.110	0
*Smith	43	37	1	6	6	0	0	0	3	1	6	0	0	1	0	5	0	0	1	.162	.162	.184	1	38	0.91	.042	0
Perez	22	25	0	3	3	0	0	0	1	1	4	0	0	3	0	13	0	0	0	.120	.120	.214	1	26	1.14	.064	0
Johnson	15	23	0	1	2	1	0	0	2	0	3	0	0	3	0	8	0	0	0	.043	.087	.154	1	25	0.65	.022	0
Shields	23	18	0	2	2	0	0	0	0	0	0	0	0	1	0	6	0	0	0	.111	.111	.158	0	16	0.60	.019	0
Thomas	15	18	6	5	5	0	0	0	2	0	1	0	0	0	0	2	0	0	1	.278	.278	.278	1	15	2.09	.187	0
Barker	20	17	0	0	0	0	0	0	0	0	0	0	0	7	0	1	0	1	0	.000	.000	.000	0	18	0.00	.000	0
McMurtry	17	14	0	1	1	0	0	0	0	0	1	0	0	7	0	1	0	1	0	.071	.071	.071	0	15	0.00	.000	0
Camp	66	13	1	3	6	0	0	1	2	0	1	0	0	1	0	5	0	0	0	.231	.462	.286	2	11	4.44	.509	0
*Dedmon	60	9	0	1	1	0	0	0	1	0	1	0	0	1	0	3	0	0	0	.111	.111	.200	0	9	0.97	.047	0
Garber	59	5	1	1	1	0	0	0	1	0	1	0	0	0	0	1	0	0	0	.200	.200	.200	0	5	1.37	.090	0
*Forster	46	4	0	0	0	0	0	0	0	0	1	0	0	0	0	0	0	0	0	.000	.000	.000	0	5	0.00	.000	0
Sutter	58	4	0	0	0	0	0	0	0	0	0	0	0	0	0	1	0	0	0	.000	.000	.000	0	4	0.00	.000	0
Rabb	3	2	0	0	0	0	0	0	0	0	0	0	0	0	0	1	0	0	0	.000	.000	.000	0	2	0.00	.000	0
Schuler	9	0	0	0	0	0	0	0	0	0	0	0	0	0	0	0	0	0	0	.000	.000	.000	0	0	0.00	.000	0

*left-handed hitter, †switch hitter

DEFENSIVE STATISTICS

FIRST

	G	PO	A	Er	TC	DP	PCT.
Horner	87	892	58	0	950	105	1.000
Perry	55	541	37	9	587	48	.985
Chambliss	39	299	25	1	325	31	.997
TEAM:	181	1732	120	10	1862	184	.995
AVG:	191	1513	114	12	1639	136	.993

SECOND

	G	PO	A	Er	TC	DP	PCT.
Hubbard	140	339	539	10	888	127	.989
Zuvella	42	55	88	2	145	15	.986
Oberkfell	16	18	37	1	56	7	.982
Runge	2	0	0	0	0	0	.000
TEAM:	200	412	664	13	1089	149	.988
AVG:	184	384	502	16	901	110	.982

THIRD

	G	PO	A	Er	TC	DP	PCT.
Oberkfell	117	70	220	11	301	19	.963
Horner	40	25	61	11	97	6	.887
Runge	28	10	55	5	70	3	.929
Zuvella	5	0	4	0	4	1	1.000
TEAM:	190	105	340	27	472	29	.943
AVG:	189	125	341	25	492	29	.948

SHORTSTOP

	G	PO	A	Er	TC	DP	PCT.
Ramirez	133	214	451	32	697	115	.954
Zuvella	33	57	81	6	144	23	.958
Thomas	10	6	17	2	25	2	.920
Runge	5	5	11	2	18	2	.889
TEAM:	181	282	560	42	884	142	.952
AVG:	185	268	521	30	819	99	.963

CATCHER

	G	PO	A	Er	TC	DP	PCT.	PB
Cerone	91	384	48	6	438	4	.986	6
Benedict	70	314	35	4	353	1	.989	1
Owen	25	129	11	5	145	1	.966	1
TEAM:	186	827	94	15	936	6	.984	8
AVG:	191	952	87	14	1053	11	.987	14

OUTFIELD

	G	PO	A	Er	TC	DP	PCT.
Murphy	161	334	8	7	349	4	.980
Harper	131	215	10	5	230	0	.978
Washington	99	122	3	5	130	1	.962
Komminsk	92	161	2	7	170	0	.959
Thompson	49	78	2	3	83	0	.964
Hall	13	7	2	1	10	0	.900
Perry	1	0	0	0	0	0	.000
Rabb	1	0	0	0	0	0	.000
TEAM:	547	917	27	28	972	5	.971
AVG:	569	1036	34	23	1093	6	.979

COMPLETE PITCHERS RECORDS

Pitcher	W	L	Pct	ERA	G	GS	CG	GF	SHO	SV	IP	H	TBF	R	ER	HR	SH	SF	HB	BB	IB	SO	WP	BK	Appr Value
								Starters (One-half of Game Appearances)																	
Mahler	17	15	.531	3.48	39	39	6	0	1	0	266.2	272	1110	116	103	24	10	5	2	79	8	107	3	1	11
Bedrosian	7	15	.318	3.83	37	37	0	0	0	0	206.2	198	907	101	88	17	6	7	5	111	6	134	6	0	6
Perez	1	13	.071	6.14	22	22	0	0	0	0	95.1	115	453	72	65	10	5	3	1	57	10	57	2	2	0
Johnson	4	4	.500	4.10	15	14	1	0	0	0	85.2	95	367	44	39	9	4	3	3	24	5	34	2	0	1
Barker	2	9	.182	6.35	20	18	0	1	0	0	73.2	84	335	55	52	10	4	1	1	37	1	47	3	0	0
								Relievers																	
*Smith	9	10	.474	3.80	42	18	2	3	2	0	147.0	135	631	70	62	4	16	1	3	80	5	85	2	0	6
Camp	4	6	.400	3.95	66	2	0	23	0	3	127.2	130	569	72	56	8	4	4	5	61	11	49	4	0	5
Garber	6	6	.500	3.61	59	0	0	31	0	1	97.1	98	409	41	39	8	9	1	2	25	8	66	1	0	6
Sutter	7	7	.500	4.48	58	0	0	50	0	23	88.1	91	382	46	44	13	7	2	3	29	4	52	0	0	8
Dedmon	6	3	.667	4.08	60	0	0	15	0	0	86.0	84	377	52	39	5	8	1	1	49	14	41	2	1	4
Shields	1	2	.333	5.16	23	6	0	3	0	0	68.0	86	311	46	39	9	6	3	1	32	6	29	6	0	1
*Forster	2	3	.400	2.28	46	0	0	19	0	1	59.1	49	253	22	15	7	2	2	0	28	4	37	1	0	4
McMurtry	0	3	.000	6.60	17	6	0	3	0	1	45.0	56	220	36	33	6	7	2	1	27	1	28	3	0	1
*Schuler	0	0	.000	6.75	9	0	0	5	0	0	10.2	19	50	8	8	4	0	0	0	3	0	10	0	0	0

*left-handed

Rick CERONE, Catcher

	G	AB	Hit	2B	3B	HR	Run	RBI	TBB	SO	SB	CS	Avg
4.88 years		529	125	23	2	8	50	59	38	54	1	3	.236
1985	96	282	61	9	0	3	15	25	29	25	0	3	.216
First Half	42	146	33	3	0	2	10	13	11		0		.226
Second Half	54	136	28	6	0	1	5	12	18		0		.206
Vs. RHP		194	44			2		16			0		.227
Vs. LHP		88	17			1		9			0		.193
Home	51	151	33	6	0	3	5	18			0		.219
Road	45	131	28	3	0	0	10	7			0		.214
Grass	74	215	49	8	0	3	11	22			0		.228
Turf	22	67	12	1	0	0	4	3			0		.179

Ken OBERKFELL, Third Base

	G	AB	Hit	2B	3B	HR	Run	RBI	TBB	SO	SB	CS	Avg
5.60 years		521	149	26	6	3	62	45	59	38	8	6	.286
1985	134	412	112	19	4	3	30	35	51	38	1	2	.272
First Half	76	225	65	11	4	1	21	22	26		0		.289
Second Half	58	187	47	8	0	2	9	13	25		1		.251
Vs. RHP		299	84			3		27			0		.281
Vs. LHP		113	28			0		8			0		.248
Home	72	209	63	9	2	2	30	20			1		.301
Road	62	203	49	10	2	1	0	15			0		.241
Grass	100	308	91	15	4	3	30	31			1		.295
Turf	34	104	21	4	0	0	0	4			0		.202

Bob HORNER, First Base

	G	AB	Hit	2B	3B	HR	Run	RBI	TBB	SO	SB	CS	Avg
5.06 years		604	169	27	1	37	94	112	56	82	3	3	.279
1985	130	483	129	25	3	27	61	89	50	57	1	1	.267
First Half	67	249	67	17	2	15	36	47	25		0		.269
Second Half	63	234	62	8	1	12	25	42	25		1		.265
Vs. RHP		324	82			17		56			0		.253
Vs. LHP		159	47			10		33			1		.296
Home	58	219	59	19	2	13	32	50					.269
Road	72	264	70	6	1	14	29	39					.265
Grass	90	333	91	22	2	17	46	62			0		.273
Turf	40	150	38	3	1	10	15	27			1		.253

Rafael RAMIREZ, Shortstop

	G	AB	Hit	2B	3B	HR	Run	RBI	TBB	SO	SB	CS	Avg
4.55 years		629	168	23	4	6	68	54	32	68	15	12	.267
1985	138	568	141	25	4	5	54	58	20	63	2	6	.248
First Half	78	336	96	15	3	4	37	34	12		2		.286
Second Half	60	232	45	10	1	1	17	24	8		0		.194
Vs. RHP		379	96			5		31					.253
Vs. LHP		189	45			0		27					.238
Home	68	272	80	13	2	4	31	32			0		.294
Road	70	296	61	12	2	1	23	26			2		.206
Grass	102	415	110	19	2	4	42	42			0		.265
Turf	36	153	31	6	2	1	12	16			2		.203

Glenn HUBBARD, Second Base

	G	AB	Hit	2B	3B	HR	Run	RBI	TBB	SO	SB	CS	Avg
5.63 years		562	137	26	3	10	69	58	61	78	5	5	.244
1985	142	439	102	21	0	5	51	39	56	54	4	3	.232
First Half	72	221	51	10	0	3	21	27	33		1		.231
Second Half	70	218	51	11	0	2	30	12	23		3		.234
Vs. RHP		296	69			4		29					.233
Vs. LHP		143	33			1		10					.231
Home	75	232	58	9	0	3	26	23			2		.250
Road	67	207	44	12	0	2	25	16			2		.213
Grass	107	334	82	14	0	5	40	37			3		.246
Turf	35	105	20	7	0	0	11	2			1		.190

Terry HARPER, Left Field

	G	AB	Hit	2B	3B	HR	Run	RBI	TBB	SO	SB	CS	Avg
2.27 years		473	120	16	2	11	48	59	44	84	15	9	.253
1985	138	492	130	15	2	17	58	72	44	76	9	9	.264
First Half	72	260	67	8	2	8	26	41	26		5		.258
Second Half	66	232	63	7	0	9	32	31	18		4		.272
Vs. RHP		321	92			9		44					.287
Vs. LHP		171	38			8		28					.222
Home	68	248	71	9	0	9	33	50			4		.286
Road	70	244	59	6	2	8	25	22			5		.242
Grass	101	365	100	11	2	13	46	60			5		.274
Turf	37	127	30	4	0	4	12	12			4		.236

Dale MURPHY, Center Field

	G	AB	Hit	2B	3B	HR	Run	RBI	TBB	SO	SB	CS	Avg
7.41 years		588	165	25	3	32	98	100	73	129	16	6	.281
1985	162	616	185	32	2	37	118	111	90	141	10	3	.300
First Half	86	328	95	17	1	23	65	69	51		4		.290
Second Half	76	288	90	15	1	14	53	42	39		6		.313
Vs. RHP		434	124			27		80					.286
Vs. LHP		182	61			10		31					.335
Home	81	308	92	15	1	20	63	59			5		.299
Road	81	308	93	17	1	17	55	52			5		.302
Grass	120	462	138	22	1	32	96	88			7		.299
Turf	42	154	47	10	1	5	22	23			3		.305

Claudell WASHINGTON, Right Field

	G	AB	Hit	2B	3B	HR	Run	RBI	TBB	SO	SB	CS	Avg
8.86 years		589	164	29	7	13	82	72	41	110	29	13	.279
1985	122	398	110	14	6	15	62	43	40	66	14	4	.276
First Half	66	250	70	9	4	9	37	25	20		8		.280
Second Half	56	148	40	5	2	6	25	18	20		6		.270
Vs. RHP		335	97			14		35					.290
Vs. LHP		63	13			1		8					.206
Home	59	191	53	7	2	4	31	18			3		.277
Road	63	207	57	7	4	11	31	25			11		.275
Grass	88	286	83	12	4	8	45	31			8		.290
Turf	34	112	27	2	2	7	17	12			6		.241

Gerald PERRY, First Base

	G	AB	Hit	2B	3B	HR	Run	RBI	TBB	SO	SB	CS	Avg
1.60 years		390	98	12	1	7	49	41	56	44	15	11	.252
1985	110	238	51	5	0	3	22	13	23	28	9	5	.214
First Half	63	153	29	3	0	1	12	6	17		6		.190
Second Half	47	85	22	2	0	2	10	7	6		3		.259
Vs. RHP		197	44			2		10					.223
Vs. LHP		41	7			1		3					.171
Home	56	141	31	4	0	3	15	12			3		.220
Road	54	97	20	1	0	0	7	1			6		.206
Grass	79	176	40	5	0	3	19	13			6		.227
Turf	31	62	11	0	0	0	3	0			3		.177

Brad KOMMINSK, Outfield

	G	AB	Hit	2B	3B	HR	Run	RBI	TBB	SO	SB	CS	Avg
1.33 years		480	103	18	2	9	69	46	54	117	21	12	.215
1985	106	300	68	12	3	4	52	21	38	71	10	8	.227
First Half	63	189	41	4	2	0	33	10	23		8		.217
Second Half	43	111	27	8	1	4	19	11	15		2		.243
Vs. RHP		119	29			1		11					.244
Vs. LHP		181	39			3		10					.215
Home	60	163	33	9	3	1	26	11			4		.202
Road	46	137	35	3	0	3	26	10			6		.255
Grass	83	234	54	10	3	4	40	20			6		.231
Turf	23	66	14	2	0	0	12	1			4		.212

RICK MAHLER

	(W–L)	GS	Run	Avg	DP	Avg	SB	Avg
1984	(13-10)	29	103	3.55	24	.83	27	.93
1985	(17-15)	39	184	4.72	50	1.28	14	.36
1981-1985		115	471	4.10	120	1.04	80	.70

	G	IP	W	L	Pct	ER	BB	SO	ERA
1984 Home	18	94.0	5	6	.455	42	28	43	4.02
1985 Home	19	135.0	8	5	.615	49	38	57	3.27
1984 Road	20	128.0	8	4	.667	35	34	63	2.46
1985 Road	20	131.7	9	10	.474	54	41	50	3.69
1984 Grass	27	159.3	9	8	.529	58	47	72	3.28
1985 Grass	28	193.3	11	11	.500	67	60	81	3.12
1984 Turf	11	62.7	4	2	.667	19	15	34	2.73
1985 Turf	11	73.3	6	4	.600	36	19	26	4.42
1985 Total	39	266.7	17	15	.531	103	79	107	3.48

STEVE BEDROSIAN

	(W–L)	GS	Run	Avg	DP	Avg	SB	Avg
1984	(9-6)	4	19	4.75	4	1.00	2	.50
1985	(7-15)	37	138	3.73	42	1.14	47	1.27
1981-1985		46	172	3.74	53	1.15	58	1.26

	G	IP	W	L	Pct	ER	BB	SO	ERA
1984 Home	18	46.0	3	3	.500	15	25	38	2.93
1985 Home	17	96.3	4	5	.444	37	41	66	3.46
1984 Road	22	37.7	6	3	.667	7	8	43	1.67
1985 Road	20	110.3	3	10	.231	51	70	68	4.16
1984 Grass	30	65.3	6	6	.500	22	15	38	3.03
1985 Grass	27	149.0	5	9	.357	64	67	95	3.87
1984 Turf	10	18.3	3	0	1.000	0	18	43	0.00
1985 Turf	10	57.7	2	6	.250	24	44	39	3.75
1985 Total	37	206.7	7	15	.318	88	111	134	3.83

PASCUAL PEREZ

	(W–L)	GS	Run	Avg	DP	Avg	SB	Avg
1984	(14-8)	30	130	4.33	30	1.00	27	.90
1985	(1-13)	22	84	3.82	25	1.14	19	.86
1982-1985		96	407	4.24	100	1.04	86	.90

	G	IP	W	L	Pct	ER	BB	SO	ERA
1984 Home	13	94.7	6	4	.600	38	28	60	3.61
1985 Home	11	46.3	1	8	.111	36	28	30	6.99
1984 Road	17	117.0	8	4	.667	50	23	85	3.85
1985 Road	11	49.0	0	5	0.000	29	29	27	5.33
1984 Grass	21	145.7	9	6	.600	65	21	54	4.02
1985 Grass	15	66.7	1	11	.083	50	37	41	6.75
1984 Turf	11	62.7	4	2	.667	19	30	91	2.73
1985 Turf	7	28.7	0	2	0.000	15	20	16	4.71
1985 Total	22	95.3	1	13	.071	65	57	57	6.14

OTHERS

	(W–L)	GS	Run	Avg	DP	Avg	SB	Avg
Smith	(9-10)	18	66	3.67	26	1.44	17	.94
Barker	(2-9)	18	52	2.89	13	.72	26	1.44
Johnson	(4-4)	14	60	4.29	20	1.43	11	.79
Shields	(1-2)	6	24	4.00	11	1.83	10	1.67
McMurtry	(0-3)	6	16	2.67	8	1.33	11	1.83
Camp	(4-6)	2	8	4.00	2	1.00	4	2.00

SAN FRANCISCO GIANTS

BREAKDOWNS FOR THE LAST TEN SEASONS

Won-Lost Record: 734-834, .468 (5th in the division, 19th in the majors)
Runs Scored: 6,151 (4th in the division)
Runs Allowed: 6,655 (2nd-highest in the division)
Home Runs Hit: 1,106 (4th in the division)
Home Runs Allowed: 1,044 (4th-highest in the division)

RECORD IN:
April: 79-124, .389 (Worst in the division, 2nd-worst in baseball)
May: 139-134, .509 (4th in the division)
June: 122-144, .463 (Worst in the division)
July: 123-126, .494 (2nd-best in the division)
August: 131-144, .476 (4th in the division)
September: 128-147, .465 (4th in the division)
October: 10-15, .400 (5th in the division)

Won-Lost Record in Road Games: 334–452, .425 (5th in the division)
Won-Lost Record at Home: 400-382, .512 (5th in the division)
Home Field Advantage: 68 games
Runs Scored on the Road: 3,124 (5th in the division)
Runs Scored at Home: 3,027 (5th in the division)
Runs Allowed on the Road: 3,462 (Second-highest in the division)
Runs Allowed at Home: 3,124 (Third-highest in the division)

Home Runs Hit on the Road: 614 (2nd in the division)
Home Runs Hit at Home: 492 (4th in the division)
Home Runs Allowed on the Road: 563 (3rd-most in the division)
Home Runs Allowed at Home: 481 (2nd-lowest in the division)

RECORD FOR LAST THREE SEASONS: 207-279, .426 (Worst in the division, 2nd-worst in the major leagues)

I promised earlier that in the San Francisco comment I would pass on some information about offensive configurations. The chart below gives the number of runs scored by each batting order position in the National League (that is, Cardinal leadoff men scored 119 runs. Houston ninth hitters scored 44, etc.):

Team	1	2	3	4	5	6	7	8	9	Total
St. Louis	119	116	99	92	88	66	59	58	50	747
Houston	102	90	93	88	73	89	56	71	44	706
New York	102	94	90	90	105	70	49	54	41	695
Chicago	96	111	111	85	74	68	50	46	45	686
Los Angeles	100	72	101	109	99	69	46	50	36	682
Cincinnati	108	101	81	89	81	63	59	57	38	677
Philadelphia	97	91	99	87	75	63	70	57	28	667
San Diego	83	96	89	82	67	75	68	61	29	650
Montreal	127	88	80	73	56	68	54	50	37	633
Atlanta	84	75	114	95	80	47	53	49	35	632
Pittsburgh	87	73	76	69	68	55	52	47	41	568
San Francisco	96	56	61	73	68	49	68	44	41	556
Totals	1201	1063	1094	1032	934	782	684	644	465	7899
Averages	100	89	91	86	78	65	57	54	39	658

There are many points to be made with respect to this information, only some of which have to do with the Giants, so I'll just string them along at random . . .

• The St. Louis Cardinals' offense worked in perfect declining order from one through nine. No other offense did this, and only three other offenses (Cincinnati, Montreal and Pittsburgh) were close to it.

• If you break down offenses into three groups (1–2 spots, middle of the order [3–5], and back of order [6–8]) the Cardinals got the most runs out of their top two hitters,

the Dodgers got the most out of the middle of their order, and the Astros had the strongest 6–8 spots.

When a team is notably weak at the top or middle of the order, but strong at the end of it, I think it is fair to wonder whether that offense has been properly constructed. The Giants number seven hitter, for example, scored more runs than their number two or three hitters (with, obviously, fewer plate appearances). Cris Brown usually hit seventh, along with Brenly, with Manny Trillo the one most guilty in the second spot and Chili Davis and Jeff Leonard sharing credit for third. I'm sure that Jim Davenport would say that if he knew Brown was going to hit so well and Leonard so poorly, he would have done things differently. The Giants were last in the league in runs scored by the 1–2 spots (152), last in runs scored by the middle of the order (202), but tenth in runs scored by the 6–8 spots.

• The position scoring the most runs in the National League was the Montreal lead-off spot, where Tim Raines (mostly) scored 127 runs (the Expos were ninth overall in the league in runs scored). As a percentage of team's runs, the National League leaders were:

1. Montreal Leadoff (Tim Raines). . . 20.1%
2. Atlanta Third (Dale Murphy) . . . 18.0%
3. San Francisco Leadoff (Gladden) . . 17.3%
4. (tie) Chicago Second and Third
   Sandberg and Several others . . 16.2%
6. Cincinnati Leadoff (Mixed) 16.0%
7. Los Angeles Fourth (Guerrero). . . 16.0%

• Several years ago I wrote an article for *Inside Sports* on batting order positioning. One of the main points of that article was that many managers tend to waste the second spot in the order by putting somebody there who isn't one of the better hitters on the team. The idea was that there are two principles guiding offensive selection—one, the desire to get all of the best hitters together, and two, the desire to get the best hitters up the most often, hence at the top of the order. Too many managers will say "bat control" as if these words were a magic wand, and place some .260 hitter with a secondary average of .150 batting second, thus violating both principles.

When I did this new study, I found several things that one can use to support the old thesis, particularly if one is determined to support the position already taken. The standard deviation of runs scored in the second spot is easily the highest of any position (that is, there is more difference there than anywhere else). The Giants' second-place hitters scored only 56 runs, whereas the Cardinals' second-place hitters (Willie McGee) scored 116—a difference of 60, and a ratio of more than 2–1. No other two teams in the National League have slots separated by either 60 runs or a 2–1 margin.

Also, the correlation of runs scored in the number two slot to the total runs scored by the team is closer than for any other position—that is, the teams which got a lot of runs out of their number two hitters, also got a lot of runs period.

This could also be taken to reflect the marginal nature of the position. Everybody has at least one good hitter to hit third, so that doesn't tell you that much about the offense, but the only teams which have good hitters hitting second are those which have five good hitters, hence score lots of runs. I don't buy this argument, but it's as good as you can do in Davenport's defense.

• The smallest standard deviations were for the eighth spot and for the cleanup spot.

• The Giants' odd 1–2 split—96 runs by leadoff hitters, but only 56 by number two hitters—is partially created by Davenport's fondness for the bunt. The three National League teams laying down the most sacrifice bunts were San Francisco, Los Angeles and Pittsburgh; the three National League teams scoring the fewest runs in the second spot were also San Francisco, Los Angeles and Pittsburgh. Those three managers (Lasorda, Tanner and Davenport) like the bunt enough that they will on occasion bunt with the number two hitter when the leadoff man gets on, which is a pretty rare play for most of the league.

• All N.L. teams were led in runs scored by their first, second or third spots except the Dodgers, who were led by their cleanup hitters (Guerrero) and the Mets, who were led by their #5 hitters (the magnificent Darryl Strawberry).

• Only three National League spots were more than 18 runs below the league average for the position. Those three are the Montreal number five spot (−22), and the Giants number two and three spots, which were 33 and 30 runs below average.

Enough; you can work that data even harder if you want to. I think it is safe to say that it was generally felt, in the Bay Area, that Jim Davenport was a good baseball man but not a particularly good baseball manager. Specifically, many people felt that Davenport had more than the usual amount of trouble with such things as selecting the right lineup, knowing when to bunt, when to pinch hit, when to send runners and where to put the infield. Davenport had limited managerial experience—three years in the minors, a long time ago—and it is not especially surprising that he should have some trouble here.

I thought, in connection with this, how odd it is that a baseball manager should be at a disadvantage to his fans on issues such as these, how completely unnecessary it is for a manager to arrive at the major league level unprepared in this respect, when there is available such a perfect tool to educate a manager in these things. I refer, of course, to table games like APBA and Strat-O-Matic. In many other professions, simulations are much prized as educational tools; a major airline would never think of sending a pilot up with lives in his hands unless he had pulled a few dozen planes out of simulated crashes. And what is an APBA game, anyway? Why, it is a simulation of a manager's job, nothing more nor less.

And from playing one of these games, any competent table manager would know that if you bat a guy with a .287 on-base percentage in the second slot, you're going to lose runs; there is no way in hell you can add enough runs by moving the other guy along to compensate for the ones the #2 hitter himself doesn't score. Any table game manager could make a good instinctive guess about when to issue an intentional walk, how likely it is to blow up on you.

Why is it, then, that an inexperienced manager is not simply instructed to manage his team through a thousand or so games of table baseball before he really takes the field, just to get a feel for what works and what doesn't?

Because those games are for *fans,* that's why. We're *professionals,* you know; we don't have anything to learn from these *fans.*

In *Good Enough to Dream,* Roger Kahn reports on his minor-league manager who says, whenever confronted with the notion that there may be better ways to do things, "You always think you know baseball. *I* know baseball. *I'm* the manager." Baseball is something that everybody has an opinion about, and so it develops that to baseball men, the distinction between professional and fan is blinding, obliterating all other distinctions. Professionalism is the sun around which all baseball knowledge must revolve.

I know that if I proposed this table-game theory to any general manager in baseball, I would probably get a lecture on the differences between managing the table game and managing the real team. In the table game, players' levels are fixed; they don't fall into slumps. They don't have pitchers who have the whammy on them, or pitchers that they can tear apart. Pitchers in table games lose their stuff at known and predictable stages of the game; in the real game they may lose it gradually or suddenly. In the table game pitchers can be brought into the game without being warmed up. In the table game, players are not going to quit on you if they don't like the way they're being used.

Of course, all of that is true and much more. The table game teaches only the percentages, not the individual case. But is it an argument against using the table game to teach those things which it can teach? Isn't it a better argument that a major league manager should be so thoroughly grilled in the percentages that he is able to move past that stage, and use his mind to concentrate on the other factors which complicate the real game? Couldn't a general manager say, "Look, I don't want my manager sitting there trying to figure out what the percentages are. I want him to *know* what the percentages are like he was born with them. Then he'll be able to clean his mind out and work on those subtler things that complicate the game on the field."

Of course, you wouldn't ask Earl Weaver, who managed in the minor leagues for twelve years, to go play a few hundred games of APBA. Maybe Jim Davenport didn't need the help, either, I don't know; maybe my friends in the Bay Area had a less than accurate view of him. Maybe, if he did need the help, he wouldn't have benefited from it anyway.

But I know that I've seen major league managers who would finish sixth in a good table league. Jim Frey is one of them—a good man, in many ways, but an atrocious chess player. It seems to me an unnecessary price to pay for defending one's professional status. A command of the percentages is not the whole job—but one would think it was one of the prerequisites.

COMPLETE BATTING RECORDS

Player	G	AB	R	H	TB	2B	3B	HR	RBI	GW	SH	SF	HP	BB	IB	SO	SB	CS	GI DP	Avg	Slug	OBP	Runs Created	Outs Made	Runs/ 27 Outs	OW%	Appr Value
Brenly	133	440	41	97	172	16	1	19	56	5	4	2	2	57	5	62	1	4	6	.220	.391	.311	55	359	4.12	.541	9
Driessen	54	181	22	42	59	8	0	3	22	1	0	3	1	17	3	22	0	0	2	.232	.326	.297	55	391	3.78	.498	1
Trillo	125	451	36	101	130	16	2	3	25	4	11	2	1	40	0	44	2	0	6	.224	.288	.287	40	369	2.95	.376	5
Brown	131	432	50	117	191	20	3	16	61	10	1	0	11	38	4	78	2	3	19	.271	.442	.345	61	338	4.87	.622	9
†Uribe	147	476	46	113	150	20	4	3	26	3	5	0	2	30	8	57	8	2	5	.237	.315	.285	44	375	3.16	.409	7
Leonard	133	507	49	122	199	20	3	17	62	7	1	1	1	21	5	107	11	6	19	.241	.393	.272	47	412	3.09	.398	6
Gladden	142	502	64	122	174	15	8	7	41	6	10	2	7	40	1	78	32	15	10	.243	.347	.307	54	417	3.47	.455	7
†Davis	136	481	53	130	198	25	2	13	56	3	1	7	0	62	12	74	15	7	16	.270	.412	.349	68	382	4.83	.618	11
Green	106	294	36	73	102	10	2	5	20	7	2	2	1	22	3	58	6	5	12	.248	.347	.301	28	242	3.09	.398	2
Youngblood	95	230	24	62	80	6	0	4	24	1	1	1	1	30	1	37	3	2	6	.270	.348	.355	29	178	4.43	.577	2
Wellman	71	174	16	41	54	11	1	0	16	2	5	1	4	4	1	33	5	2	3	.236	.310	.268	14	144	2.70	.336	1
Deer	78	162	22	30	61	5	1	8	20	2	0	2	0	23	0	71	0	1	0	.185	.377	.283	19	135	3.78	.498	0
Trevino	57	157	17	34	64	10	1	6	19	0	1	1	0	20	0	24	0	0	5	.217	.408	.303	19	130	3.99	.525	3
†Roenicke	65	133	23	34	54	9	1	3	13	1	1	1	0	35	3	27	6	2	1	.256	.406	.408	26	104	6.70	.757	2
Adams	54	121	12	23	34	3	1	2	10	2	3	0	1	5	3	23	1	1	2	.190	.281	.228	7	104	1.91	.203	1
Thompson	64	111	8	23	28	5	0	0	6	1	1	0	0	2	0	10	0	0	5	.207	.252	.221	5	94	1.46	.129	0
*Rajsich	51	91	5	15	21	6	0	0	10	2	2	0	0	17	4	22	0	1	0	.165	.231	.296	7	79	2.45	.294	0
*Woodard	24	82	12	20	21	1	0	0	9	0	1	0	0	5	0	3	6	1	0	.244	.256	.287	7	64	2.98	.382	0
*LaPoint	31	60	4	10	11	1	0	0	6	1	5	0	0	6	0	11	0	0	0	.167	.183	.242	3	55	1.68	.163	0
Krukow	28	55	2	12	19	4	0	1	3	0	8	0	2	1	0	15	1	1	0	.218	.345	.259	5	52	2.69	.335	0
*Nokes	19	53	3	11	19	2	0	2	5	0	0	0	1	1	0	9	0	0	2	.208	.358	.236	4	44	2.40	.285	0
Gott	26	51	6	10	21	2	0	3	3	0	4	0	0	1	0	30	0	1	0	.196	.412	.212	4	46	2.45	.293	0
†Hammaker	29	47	0	4	4	0	0	0	0	0	6	0	0	0	0	17	0	0	0	.085	.085	.085	1	49	0.30	.006	0
†Blue	33	30	0	4	5	1	0	0	0	0	8	0	0	3	0	12	0	0	0	.133	.167	.212	2	34	1.35	.112	0
Laskey	19	30	1	4	4	0	0	0	1	0	5	0	1	3	0	12	0	0	0	.133	.133	.235	2	31	1.36	.114	0
LeMaster	12	16	1	0	0	0	0	0	0	0	1	0	0	0	0	5	0	0	0	.000	.000	.000	0	16	0.03	.000	
*M. Davis	77	12	0	3	5	0	1	0	0	0	0	0	0	4	0	5	0	1	0	.250	.417	.250	1	14	1.71	.168	0
Mason	5	11	1	1	1	0	0	0	0	0	0	0	1	0	0	5	0	0	1	.091	.091	.167	0	11	0.26	.005	0
Garrelts	74	9	1	2	3	1	0	0	2	0	0	0	0	1	0	4	0	0	0	.222	.333	.300	1	7	3.77	.497	0
†Minton	68	8	1	0	0	0	0	0	1	0	0	0	0	1	0	6	0	0	0	.000	.000	.111	0	8	0.10	.001	0
*Kuiper	9	5	0	3	3	0	0	0	0	0	0	2	0	1	0	0	0	0	0	.600	.600	.667	2	4	11.14	.882	0
Williams	49	3	0	0	0	0	0	0	0	0	1	0	0	0	0	0	0	0	0	.000	.000	.000	0	4	0.00	.000	0
Moore	11	2	0	0	0	0	0	0	0	0	0	0	0	0	0	0	0	0	0	.000	.000	.000	0	2	0.00	.000	0
*Ward	6	2	0	0	0	0	0	0	0	0	0	0	0	0	0	1	0	0	0	.000	.000	.000	0	2	0.00	.000	0
Jeffcoat	19	1	0	0	0	0	0	0	0	0	0	0	0	1	0	0	0	0	0	.000	.000	.500	0	1	0.00	.000	0
Robinson	8	0	0	0	0	0	0	0	0	0	0	0	0	0	0	0	0	0	0	.000	.000	.000	0	0	0.00	.000	0

*left-handed hitter, †switch hitter

DEFENSIVE STATISTICS

FIRST	G	PO	A	Er	TC	DP	PCT.
Green	78	628	42	9	679	54	.987
Driessen	49	399	27	1	427	32	.998
Thompson	24	168	16	1	185	13	.995
Rajsich	23	185	11	2	198	17	.990
Brenly	10	42	3	1	46	4	.978
Deer	10	73	1	1	75	4	.987
TEAM:	194	1495	100	15	1610	124	.991
AVG:	191	1513	114	12	1639	136	.993

SECOND	G	PO	A	Er	TC	DP	PCT.
Trillo	120	262	357	12	631	73	.981
Wellman	36	55	60	2	117	11	.983
Woodard	23	49	46	1	96	14	.990
Adams	6	9	13	1	23	1	.957
Uribe	1	0	0	0	0	0	.000
TEAM:	186	375	476	16	867	99	.982
AVG:	184	384	502	16	901	110	.982

THIRD	G	PO	A	Er	TC	DP	PCT.
Brown	120	94	243	10	347	15	.971
Wellman	25	10	45	6	61	2	.902
Brenly	17	15	20	4	39	4	.897
Adams	16	2	31	1	34	3	.971
Trevino	1	0	0	0	0	0	.000
Trillo	1	1	4	1	6	0	.833
Youngblood	1	0	2	1	3	0	.667
TEAM:	181	122	345	23	490	24	.953
AVG:	189	125	341	25	492	29	.948

SHORTSTOP	G	PO	A	Er	TC	DP	PCT.
Uribe	145	209	438	26	673	77	.961
Adams	25	24	57	3	84	9	.964
LeMaster	10	12	9	1	22	1	.955
Wellman	3	1	2	1	4	2	.750
TEAM:	183	246	506	31	783	89	.960
AVG:	185	268	521	30	819	99	.963

CATCHER	G	PO	A	Er	TC	DP	PCT.	PB
Brenly	110	662	62	12	736	8	.984	16
Trevino	55	299	19	7	325	1	.978	4
Nokes	14	84	2	2	88	0	.977	0
TEAM:	179	1045	83	21	1149	9	.982	20
AVG:	191	952	87	14	1053	11	.987	14

OUTFIELD	G	PO	A	Er	TC	DP	PCT.
C. Davis	126	279	10	6	295	2	.980
Leonard	126	203	10	5	218	0	.977
Gladden	124	273	3	7	283	0	.975
Youngblood	56	103	4	5	112	0	.955
Deer	37	54	1	1	56	0	.982
Roenicke	35	63	0	1	64	0	.984
Green	12	17	0	1	18	0	.944
TEAM:	516	992	28	26	1046	2	.975
AVG:	569	1036	34	23	1093	6	.979

COMPLETE PITCHERS RECORDS

Pitcher	W	L	Pct	ERA	G	GS	CG	GF	SHO	SV	IP	H	TBF	R	ER	HR	SH	SF	HB	BB	IB	SO	WP	BK	Appr Value
							Starters (One-half of Game Appearances)																		
*LaPoint	7	17	.292	3.57	31	31	2	0	1	0	206.2	215	886	99	82	18	7	5	0	74	6	122	10	0	7
Krukow	8	11	.421	3.38	28	28	6	0	1	0	194.2	176	804	80	73	19	10	3	3	49	10	150	10	3	6
*Hammaker	5	12	.294	3.74	29	29	1	0	1	0	170.2	161	713	81	71	17	8	6	0	47	5	100	4	4	4
Gott	7	10	.412	3.88	26	26	2	0	0	0	148.1	144	629	73	64	10	6	4	1	51	3	78	3	2	4
*Blue	8	8	.500	4.47	33	20	1	5	0	0	131.0	115	574	70	65	17	11	3	1	80	1	103	8	2	4
Laskey	5	11	.313	3.55	19	19	0	0	0	0	114.0	110	485	55	45	10	11	4	0	39	0	42	2	1	3
Mason	1	3	.250	2.12	5	5	1	0	1	0	29.2	28	128	13	7	1	2	0	0	11	1	26	0	0	0
							Relievers																		
*Davis	5	12	.294	3.54	77	1	0	38	0	7	114.1	89	465	49	45	13	13	1	3	41	7	131	6	1	6
Garrelts	9	6	.600	2.30	74	0	0	44	0	13	105.2	76	454	37	27	2	6	3	3	58	12	106	7	1	11
Minton	5	4	.556	3.54	68	0	0	36	0	4	96.2	98	424	42	38	6	6	4	0	54	18	37	2	0	7
Williams	2	4	.333	4.19	49	0	0	15	0	0	73.0	65	318	39	34	5	4	4	6	35	7	54	3	1	2
*Jeffcoat	0	2	.000	5.32	19	1	0	7	0	0	22.0	27	99	13	13	4	2	1	2	6	3	10	1	0	0
Moore	0	0	.000	3.24	11	0	0	4	0	0	16.2	18	78	6	6	1	1	0	0	10	2	10	0	1	0
Robinson	0	0	.000	5.11	8	0	0	0	0	0	12.1	16	59	11	7	2	0	1	0	10	1	8	1	0	0
*Ward	0	0	.000	4.38	6	2	0	0	0	0	12.1	10	52	6	6	0	1	1	0	7	0	8	0	0	0

*left-handed

Bob BRENLY, Catcher

	G	AB	Hit	2B	3B	HR	Run	RBI	TBB	SO	SB	CS	Avg
2.88 years		505	130	22	2	18	63	66	58	67	8	8	.257
1985	133	440	97	16	1	19	41	56	57	62	1	4	.220
First Half	73	244	56	11	1	12	24	33	31		1		.230
Second Half	60	196	41	5	0	7	17	23	26		0		.209
Vs. RHP		328	75			13		43					.229
Vs. LHP		112	22			6		13					.196
Home	70	225	51	10	1	10	20	26			0		.227
Road	63	215	46	6	0	9	21	30			1		.214
Grass	101	339	74	13	1	15	31	42			1		.218
Turf	32	101	23	3	0	4	10	14			0		.228

Dan DRIESSEN, First Base

	G	AB	Hit	2B	3B	HR	Run	RBI	TBB	SO	SB	CS	Avg
10.35 years		520	139	27	2	15	71	72	72	68	15	6	.268
1985	145	493	120	26	0	9	53	47	50	51	2	2	.243
First Half	78	275	73	17	0	6	27	25	30		2		.265
Second Half	67	218	47	9	0	3	26	22	20		0		.216
Vs. RHP		401	93			7		39					.232
Vs. LHP		92	27			2		8					.293
Home	81	262	61	14	0	5	30	28			2		.233
Road	64	231	59	12	0	4	23	19			0		.255
Grass	63	214	56	11	0	6	26	22			0		.262
Turf	82	279	64	15	0	3	27	25			2		.229

Manny TRILLO, Second Base

	G	AB	Hit	2B	3B	HR	Run	RBI	TBB	SO	SB	CS	Avg
9.25 years		582	152	23	4	6	57	55	43	70	6	6	.261
1985	125	451	101	16	2	3	36	25	40	44	2	0	.224
First Half	77	289	69	10	1	3	19	19	25		0		.239
Second Half	48	162	32	6	1	0	17	6	15		2		.198
Vs. RHP		320	71			2		19					.222
Vs. LHP		131	30			1		6					.229
Home	67	230	46	9	0	1	17	12			0		.200
Road	58	221	55	7	2	2	19	13			2		.249
Grass	99	351	77	13	0	3	27	21			2		.219
Turf	26	100	24	3	2	0	9	4			0		.240

Chris BROWN, Third Base

	G	AB	Hit	2B	3B	HR	Run	RBI	TBB	SO	SB	CS	Avg
0.95 years		543	148	28	3	18	59	76	49	102	4	4	.273
1985	131	432	117	20	3	16	50	61	38	78	2	3	.271
First Half	70	244	66	12	3	8	27	31	19		2		.270
Second Half	61	188	51	8	0	8	23	30	19		0		.271
Vs. RHP		324	95			11		52					.293
Vs. LHP		108	22			5		9					.204
Home	62	203	54	14	1	5	20	29			0		.266
Road	69	229	63	6	2	11	30	32			2		.275
Grass	98	318	88	18	1	10	35	47			2		.277
Turf	33	114	29	2	2	6	15	14			0		.254

Jose URIBE, Shortstop

	G	AB	Hit	2B	3B	HR	Run	RBI	TBB	SO	SB	CS	Avg
0.96 years		517	122	21	4	3	52	30	31	62	9	2	.236
1985	147	476	113	20	4	3	46	26	30	57	8	2	.237
First Half	83	261	60	15	4	1	22	16	14		3		.230
Second Half	64	215	53	5	0	2	24	10	16		5		.247
Vs. RHP		351	86	13	4	2		16	23	38			.245
Vs. LHP		125	27	7	0	1		10	7	19			.216
Home	80	248	53	13	2	2	28	10			5		.214
Road	67	228	60	7	2	1	18	16			3		.263
Grass	115	366	86	18	3	2	35	19			5		.235
Turf	32	110	27	2	1	1	11	7			3		.245

Jeff LEONARD, Left Field

	G	AB	Hit	2B	3B	HR	Run	RBI	TBB	SO	SB	CS	Avg
4.77 years		550	149	24	6	16	69	81	42	117	22	8	.272
1985	133	507	122	20	3	17	49	62	21	107	11	6	.241
First Half	85	335	78	11	3	9	30	32	17		10		.233
Second Half	48	172	44	9	0	8	19	30	4		1		.256
Vs. RHP		366	86			10		48					.235
Vs. LHP		141	36			7		14					.255
Home	67	238	57	5	1	8	25	24			6		.239
Road	66	269	65	15	2	9	24	38			5		.242
Grass	103	388	93	10	1	16	42	53			9		.240
Turf	30	119	29	10	2	1	7	9			2		.244

Dan GLADDEN, Center Field

	G	AB	Hit	2B	3B	HR	Run	RBI	TBB	SO	SB	CS	Avg
1.52 years		597	169	22	7	8	93	53	51	83	44	22	.282
1985	142	502	122	15	8	7	64	41	40	78	32	15	.243
First Half	78	295	67	8	5	2	37	20	23		22		.227
Second Half	64	207	55	7	3	5	27	21	17		10		.266
Vs. RHP		355	84			6		35					.237
Vs. LHP		147	38			1		6					.259
Home	70	254	59	8	4	6	34	24			18		.232
Road	72	248	63	7	4	1	30	17			14		.254
Grass	104	371	88	12	4	6	46	33			23		.237
Turf	38	131	34	3	4	1	18	8			9		.260

Chili DAVIS, Right Field

	G	AB	Hit	2B	3B	HR	Run	RBI	TBB	SO	SB	CS	Avg
3.53 years		601	161	27	5	18	80	77	58	106	18	11	.268
1985	136	481	130	25	2	13	53	56	62	74	15	7	.270
First Half	83	297	79	17	2	8	32	36	32		9		.266
Second Half	53	184	51	8	0	5	21	20	30		6		.277
Vs. RHP		376	104	21	2	12		45	54	55			.277
Vs. LHP		105	26	4	0	1		11	8	19			.248
Home	65	234	62	12	0	7	26	31			6		.265
Road	71	247	68	13	2	6	27	25			9		.275
Grass	96	350	92	14	1	11	40	43			10		.263
Turf	40	131	38	11	1	2	13	13			5		.290

David GREEN, First Base

	G	AB	Hit	2B	3B	HR	Run	RBI	TBB	SO	SB	CS	Avg
2.93 years		467	125	16	6	10	56	61	28	93	23	12	.268
1985	106	294	73	10	2	5	36	20	22	58	6	5	.248
First Half	59	164	36	6	1	2	22	7	13		4		.220
Second Half	47	130	37	4	1	3	14	13	9		2		.285
Vs. RHP		188	51			4		16					.271
Vs. LHP		106	22			1		4					.208
Home	50	135	28	4	1	3	17	10			3		.207
Road	56	159	45	6	1	2	19	10			3		.283
Grass	79	223	52	6	2	4	27	15			5		.233
Turf	27	71	21	4	0	1	9	5			1		.296

Joel YOUNGBLOOD, Utility

	G	AB	Hit	2B	3B	HR	Run	RBI	TBB	SO	SB	CS	Avg
6.69 years		470	126	23	3	10	60	53	43	75	9	8	.268
1985	95	230	62	6	0	4	24	24	30	37	3	2	.270
First Half	47	104	23	2	0	0	10	2	13		1		.221
Second Half	48	126	39	4	0	4	14	22	17		2		.310
Vs. RHP		154	38			3		21					.247
Vs. LHP		76	24			1		3					.316
Home	45	107	29	4	0	1	5	13			2		.271
Road	50	123	33	2	0	3	19	11			1		.268
Grass	67	157	43	6	0	2	12	16			3		.274
Turf	28	73	19	0	0	2	12	8			0		.260

DAVE LAPOINT

	(W–L)	GS	Run	Avg	DP	Avg	SB	Avg
1984	(12-10)	33	130	3.94	49	1.48	27	.82
1985	(7-17)	31	94	3.03	32	1.03	27	.87
1980-1985		119	498	4.18	155	1.30	107	.90

	G	IP	W	L	Pct	ER	BB	SO	ERA
1984 Home	15	95.0	8	2	.800	40	40	60	3.79
1985 Home	16	110.7	2	10	.167	38	41	74	3.09
1984 Road	18	98.0	4	8	.333	45	37	70	4.13
1985 Road	15	96.0	5	7	.417	44	33	48	4.12
1984 Grass	9	45.0	2	4	.333	25	17	28	5.00
1985 Grass	22	146.7	3	13	.188	55	52	90	3.38
1984 Turf	24	148.0	10	6	.625	60	60	102	3.65
1985 Turf	9	60.0	4	4	.500	27	22	32	4.05
1985 Total	31	206.7	7	17	.292	82	74	122	3.57

ATLEE HAMMAKER

	(W–L)	GS	Run	Avg	DP	Avg	SB	Avg
1984	(2-0)	6	27	4.50	4	.67	4	.67
1985	(5-12)	29	98	3.38	30	1.03	29	1.00
1981-1985		85	307	3.61	75	.88	81	.95

	G	IP	W	L	Pct	ER	BB	SO	ERA
1984 Home	3	17.0	1	0	1.000	4	5	12	2.12
1985 Home	15	90.3	2	3	.400	34	19	64	3.39
1984 Road	3	16.0	1	0	1.000	4	4	12	2.25
1985 Road	14	80.3	3	9	.250	37	28	36	4.15
1984 Grass	3	17.0	1	0	1.000	4	5	12	2.12
1985 Grass	21	126.3	3	6	.333	51	33	77	3.63
1984 Turf	3	16.0	1	0	1.000	4	4	12	2.25
1985 Turf	8	44.3	2	6	.250	20	14	23	4.06
1985 Total	29	170.7	5	12	.294	71	47	100	3.74

JIM GOTT

	(W–L)	GS	Run	Avg	DP	Avg	SB	Avg
1984	(7-6)	12	53	4.42	13	1.08	6	.50
1985	(7-10)	26	99	3.81	18	.69	16	.62
1982-1985		91	365	4.01	77	.85	60	.66

	G	IP	W	L	Pct	ER	BB	SO	ERA
1984 Home	21	70.7	5	3	.625	29	26	52	3.69
1985 Home	12	77.7	4	4	.500	20	22	49	2.32
1984 Road	14	39.0	2	3	.400	20	23	21	4.62
1985 Road	14	70.7	3	6	.333	44	29	29	5.60
1984 Grass	12	33.0	2	1	.667	12	20	19	3.27
1985 Grass	18	105.7	5	6	.455	36	32	57	3.07
1984 Turf	23	76.7	5	5	.500	37	29	54	4.34
1985 Turf	8	42.7	2	4	.333	28	19	21	5.91
1985 Total	26	148.3	7	10	.412	64	51	78	3.88

VIDA BLUE

	(W–L)	GS	Run	Avg	DP	Avg	SB	Avg
1985	(7-11)	20	96	4.80	14	.70	15	.75
1976-1985		258	1015	3.93	178	.69	163	.63

	G	IP	W	L	Pct	ER	BB	SO	ERA
1985 Home	19	79.0	6	2	.750	39	44	56	4.44
1985 Road	14	52.0	2	6	.250	26	3	47	4.50
1985 Grass	29	119.7	8	6	.571	58	71	97	4.36
1985 Turf	4	11.3	0	2	0.000	7	9	6	5.56
1985 Total	33	131.0	8	8	.500	65	80	103	4.47

MIKE KRUKOW

	(W–L)	GS	Run	Avg	DP	Avg	SB	Avg
1984	(11-12)	32	165	5.16	21	.66	37	1.16
1985	(8-11)	28	81	2.89	18	.64	29	1.04
1976-1985		264	1129	4.28	208	.79	298	1.13

	G	IP	W	L	Pct	ER	BB	SO	ERA
1984 Home	18	103.7	6	4	.600	42	40	69	3.65
1985 Home	15	116.3	6	5	.545	29	29	98	2.24
1984 Road	15	95.7	5	8	.385	59	38	72	5.55
1985 Road	13	78.3	2	6	.250	44	20	52	5.06
1984 Grass	28	162.0	8	9	.471	78	66	113	4.33
1985 Grass	20	148.0	8	5	.615	46	36	115	2.80
1984 Turf	7	37.3	3	3	.500	23	12	28	5.54
1985 Turf	8	46.7	0	6	0.000	27	13	35	5.21
1985 Total	28	194.7	8	11	.421	73	49	150	3.38

OTHERS

	(W–L)	GS	Run	Avg	DP	Avg	SB	Avg
Mason	(1-3)	5	13	2.60	3	.60	5	1.00
Ward	(0-0)	2	9	4.50	2	1.00	1	.50
Davis	(5-12)	1	2	2.00	1	1.00	1	1.00
Jeffcoat	(0-2)	1	9	9.00	0	0.00	0	0.00

PLAYER COMMENTS

INTRODUCTION TO PLAYER RATINGS

In the 1986 *Baseball Abstract,* the players have been rated by a poll of the scorers who participated in *Project Scoresheet*. Here's the way it worked:

Each person who scored a number of games for the project during the 1985 season was extended the opportunity to participate in the balloting for the player ratings which appear here. Ballots were distributed with the names of the people to be rated, and the voters were instructed to rate the players one through fourteen in the American League or one through twelve in the National. An attached information sheet included the runs created, outs made and offensive winning percentages for each player, along with a little other information (opposition stolen bases), and a copy of my ballot.

The voters were asked to consider *any information that they possessed which was relevant to the* current *abilities of the players.* In other words, I made it clear that I wasn't interested in either how good a player used to be, or how good he was going to be; it was how good he is now that counts. But what information was considered relevant to that issue—the last two years, the last three years, the last one year—was up to the individual voter. And he could consider any information that was relevant to that issue, from statistics to leadership to clutch performance to defense; whatever he believed to be true and germane.

Voters only voted in the league for which they had scored games. Cincinnati voters were not extended a vote that would cover the Boston players, whom they had not seen and were not necessarily familiar with.

Each league was divided into a number of "precincts"—one for each team in the league, plus one at-large precinct.

Each ballot within that precinct was "weighted" according to the instructions of the local captain for *Project Scoresheet*. Some gave equal weight to each ballot within their precinct; most weighted the ballots according to the number of games scored by the voter, so that the ballot of a person who had scored 30 games would count three times as much as the vote of a person who had scored ten games.

The voting within each precinct was then compiled, just as one would compile an MVP vote except for the weighting of ballots, into one ballot representing the precinct. Each precinct was given equal weight, and the precinct ratings were combined into one in the same way.

In this way, we incorporated the basic virtues of the Most Valuable Player vote—control of the ballots to insure that the people voting have some idea of what they are doing, equal representation for each team—into a system which allows the fans to vote.

I believe in fan voting. The fans have been excluded from too many things. There is no reason in the world that the fans shouldn't get to vote on who gets into the Hall of Fame, but they don't. They don't get to vote on MVPs, Rookie of the Years, Gold Gloves, anything but the All-Star game and then there are so many ballots in such a crazy system that it hardly seems worthwhile. Fans should get to vote on proposed rule changes. Instead, all we get to do is sound off after the fact.

Anyway, here's something, however small, that the fans can participate in. I was, on the whole, quite satisfied with how the voting turned out. I thought the voting was thoughtful, intelligent, and resulted in player rankings which are, while only arguable, as good as any I could have hoped for.

There were some problems with the voting. I should have gotten the ballots out in September, rather than sending them out a few days before I needed them back. Some people, not thinking through the process, amended their ballots to include people who weren't being rated. Those portions of those ballots, obviously, had to be thrown out. Some people returned unidentified ballots, and we were left to puzzle out who they were from and what weight they should be given in which precinct. This left some precincts nearly empty; we filled in the missing portion with the at-large ballot.

There were a couple of portions of ballots which had to be thrown out for idiot votes or votes that were obviously designed to try to create a disproportionate weight to one's own opinion. Let us say, for example, that a Baltimore voter had placed Don Mattingly thirteenth among American League first basemen, obviously trying to knock Mattingly down far enough to enable Murray to squeeze by him. This portion of that ballot would have been stricken. That only happened a couple of times. Some people complained about the inclusion of the runs created and other information and my own ballot along with the voting. Tough; I'm going to do it that way, anyway. *The most essential goal is not to create an open, unfettered democratic election. The most essential goal is to produce intelligent, informed rankings.* If somebody places Don Mattingly thirteenth among American League first basemen, then either he doesn't know what the hell he's doing, or he's trying to influence the vote beyond his prerogative. In either case, that vote is not going to count. But a reasonable argument can be made both ways about most issues. Some people rated Gary Pettis first among American League center fielders, and some people rated him last. They're both reasonable arguments.

My vote may have influenced some other people's ballots—if they didn't really know how they wanted to vote, anyway. But I had Keith Hernandez third on my ballot, and he won easily. I had Murray over Mattingly; it turned out the other way. I had Saberhagen third among A.L. right handers; he finished first in the voting. If people thought I was wrong, they ignored me.

There were two basic reasons for turning the vote over to *Project Scoresheet*. One was to reward, and thus encourage, participation in the project. The other is that I sincerely believe that it's the best way that I can devise to rate the players. I know that I will get letters saying that I shouldn't turn the ratings into a popularity contest, and the players should be rated by formal analysis, by scientifically verifiable assumptions and methods.

Well, I don't buy it. There's a lot to be said for consensus wisdom. If you ask a dozen sportswriters to pick a dozen football games, the odds are great that the consensus picks will beat any individual sportswriter. This is a very similar sort of problem.

In fact, I've *always* said that the best evaluation of players is subjective judgment; this is just the first time I have acted in a way that is consistent with what I have written. I've always railed against "great statistics," arguing that it is inappropriate to try to summarize everything a player can do in one number unless or until you can actually measure everything that he does. The problem with formal rating structures is that there are simply too many things that we don't know. To rate players by strictly objective methods, we have to construct a model of the baseball world. The real baseball world is inevitably going to be hundreds of times more complicated than the model that we construct, and therefore we are going to have to

a) leave out many factors, factors which are very real and very important even though we can't measure them, and b) make assumptions about things that we don't really know.

When we do that, we are, in effect, pretending to know things that we don't know. And that is the most damaging thing that an infant science can do to itself—to pretend to know things that it doesn't know. We must not pretend that the baseball world is simpler than it is. We must not pretend to know more than we know; it will only draw to us disrespect. As I wrote in 1984, "The search for a great statistic is not and can never be a scientific undertaking."

The consensus, on the other hand, can contain and reflect a much broader spectrum of information. The consensus contains not one set of assumptions, but many different sets of assumptions, in each of which there is much truth. So that's what I'm going to try to do. I'm going to try to see what the informed consensus is.

The parenthetical numbers after the top players at each position represent the number of precincts in which the player finished first in the voting.

RECORDS WITH DIFFERENT STARTING CATCHERS

AMERICAN LEAGUE

Baltimore	Inn	Runs	W-L	ERA
Rick Dempsey	985.8	498	56-55	4.55
Al Pardo	205.2	105	12-11	4.61
Floyd Rayford	201.1	76	12-11	3.40
Joe Nolan	35.0	12	3- 1	3.09

Boston	Inn	Runs	W-L	ERA
Rich Gedman	1153.1	505	67-62	3.94
Marc Sullivan	211.2	113	9-13	4.82
Dave Sax	96.1	41	5- 6	3.84

California	Inn	Runs	W-L	ERA
Bob Boone	1230.1	534	75-61	3.91
Jerry Narron	227.0	99	15-11	3.93

Chicago	Inn	Runs	W-L	ERA
Carlton Fisk	1064.1	459	63-53	3.88
Marc Hill	255.0	138	12-17	4.87
Joel Skinner	132.1	59	8- 7	4.02

Cleveland	Inn	Runs	W-L	ERA
Jerry Willard	733.2	403	36-47	4.95
Chris Bando	495.1	297	15-42	5.40
Butch Benton	192.0	76	9-13	3.56

Detroit	Inn	Runs	W-L	ERA
Lance Parrish	1071.2	465	66-52	3.91
Bob Melvin	226.1	83	12-13	3.30
Marty Castillo	158.0	66	6-12	3.76

Kansas City	Inn	Runs	W-L	ERA
Jim Sundberg	969.1	372	61-46	3.45
John Wathan	357.2	142	21-19	3.58
Jamie Quirk	134.0	52	9- 6	3.49

Milwaukee	Inn	Runs	W-L	ERA
Charlie Moore	861.0	413	43-53	4.32
Bill Schroeder	407.0	194	19-27	4.29
Ted Simmons	100.0	57	6- 5	5.13
Dave Huppert	69.0	41	3- 5	5.35

Minnesota	Inn	Runs	W-L	ERA
Mark Salas	839.1	424	48-47	4.55
Tim Laudner	466.0	240	21-32	4.64
Dave Engle	104.0	43	7- 5	3.72
Jeff Reed	17.0	3	1- 1	1.59

New York	Inn	Runs	W-L	ERA
Butch Wynegar	813.1	310	54-36	3.43
Ron Hassey	576.0	260	41-24	4.06
Juan Espino	26.0	9	2- 1	3.12
Scott Bradley	25.0	11	0- 3	3.96

Oakland	Inn	Runs	W-L	ERA
Mike Heath	829.1	470	40-54	5.10
Mickey Tettleton	601.2	236	36-30	3.53
Charlie O'Brien	22.0	6	1- 1	2.45

Seattle	Inn	Runs	W-L	ERA
Bob Kearney	831.0	451	41-53	4.88
Donnie Scott	439.0	193	26-23	3.96
Dave Valle	162.0	100	7-12	5.56

Texas	Inn	Runs	W-L	ERA
Don Slaught	852.1	412	38-59	4.35
Geno Petralli	280.2	177	8-24	5.69
Glenn Brummer	278.2	126	16-16	4.08

Toronto	Inn	Runs	W-L	ERA
Ernie Whitt	1015.2	363	73-40	3.22
Buck Martinez	287.1	123	18-14	3.86
Gary Allenson	101.0	31	7- 4	2.72
Steve Nicosia	27.0	6	1- 2	2.00
Jeff Hearron	17.0	9	0- 2	4.76

NATIONAL LEAGUE

Atlanta	Inn	Runs	W-L	ERA
Rick Cerone	703.0	360	26-52	4.61
Bruce Benedict	572.1	246	28-37	3.87
Larry Owen	182.0	73	12- 7	3.61

Chicago	Inn	Runs	W-L	ERA
Jody Davis	1147.1	544	63-65-1	4.27
Steve Lake	295.0	124	14-19	3.78

Cincinnati	Inn	Runs	W-L	ERA
Bo Diaz	423.0	164	27-20	3.49
Dave Van Gorder	379.2	172	24-18	4.08
Alan Knicely	379.0	166	23-19	3.94
Dann Bilardello	269.2	96	15-15	3.21

Houston	Inn	Runs	W-L	ERA
Mark Bailey	859.0	349	55-41	3.66
Alan Ashby	500.2	191	24-31	3.44
John Mizerock	98.1	54	4- 7	4.95

Los Angeles	Inn	Runs	W-L	ERA
Mike Scioscia	1178.0	380	78-52	2.90
Steve Yeager	287.0	104	17-15	3.26

Montreal	Inn	Runs	W-L	ERA
Mike Fitzgerald	853.1	281	55-38	2.96
Sal Butera	351.2	164	19-21	4.20
Steve Nicosia	130.0	63	6- 9	4.36
Mike O'Berry	87.0	46	3- 6	4.76
Ned Yost	35.0	20	1- 3	5.14

New York	Inn	Runs	W-L	ERA
Gary Carter	1282.0	439	85-54	3.08
Clint Hurdle	104.0	39	6- 6	3.38
Ronn Reynolds	102.0	36	7- 4	3.18

Philadelphia	Inn	Runs	W-L	ERA
Ozzie Virgil	1024.1	397	57-58	3.49
Darren Daulton	238.2	120	11-16	4.53
Bo Diaz	184.0	75	7-13	3.67

Pittsburgh	Inn	Runs	W-L	ERA
Tony Pena	1247.0	510	52-86	3.68
Junior Ortiz	198.1	128	5-18	5.82

San Diego	Inn	Runs	W-L	ERA
Terry Kennedy	1208.0	452	70-65	3.37
Bruce Bochy	244.1	97	13-14	3.58

San Francisco	Inn	Runs	W-L	ERA
Bob Brenly	911.2	354	37-65	3.50
Alejandro Trevino	419.0	170	22-25	3.65
Matt Nokes	117.1	59	4- 9	4.53

St. Louis	Inn	Runs	W-L	ERA
Tom Nieto	751.1	263	53-30	3.15
Darrell Porter	590.2	197	41-24	3.00
Mike Lavalliere	96.0	34	6- 5	3.19
Randy Hunt	26.0	12	1- 2	4.15

OPPOSITION STOLEN BASES
The following are the records of stolen bases against catchers, 1975–1985.

Gary ALLENSON

Year	Team	League	GS	SB	Avg
1979	Bos	A	83	59	.71
1980	Bos	A	19	11	.58
1981	Bos	A	40	36	.90
1982	Bos	A	86	41	.48
1983	Bos	A	78	62	.79
1984	Bos	A	27	20	.74
1985	Tor	A	11	4	.36
7 Years			344	233	.68

Alan ASHBY

Year	Team	League	GS	SB	Avg
1975	Cle	A	82	64	.78
1976	Cle	A	73	75	1.03
1977	Tor	A	121	67	.56
1978	Tor	A	79	51	.65
1979	Hous	N	103	70	.68
1980	Hous	N	105	100	.95
1981	Hous	N	74	59	.80
1982	Hous	N	90	104	1.16
1983	Hous	N	79	82	1.04
1984	Hous	N	54	63	1.17
1985	Hous	N	55	60	1.09
11 Years			915	795	.87

Mark BAILEY

Year	Team	League	GS	SB	Avg
1984	Hous	N	102	112	1.10
1985	Hous	N	96	70	.73
2 Years			198	182	.92

Chris BANDO

Year	Team	League	GS	SB	Avg
1981	Cle	A	8	4	.50
1982	Cle	A	49	24	.49
1983	Cle	A	34	17	.50
1984	Cle	A	59	28	.47
1985	Cle	A	57	53	.93
5 Years			207	126	.61

Bruce BENEDICT

Year	Team	League	GS	SB	Avg
1978	Atl	N	16	15	.94
1979	Atl	N	69	64	.93
1980	Atl	N	111	81	.73
1981	Atl	N	86	83	.97
1982	Atl	N	111	96	.86
1983	Atl	N	129	128	.99
1984	Atl	N	96	84	.88
1985	Atl	N	65	71	1.09
8 Years			683	622	.91

Butch BENTON

Year	Team	League	GS	SB	Avg
1980	N Y	N	5	5	1.00
1982	Chi	N	1	2	2.00
1985	Cle	A	22	14	.64
3 Years			28	21	.75

Dann BILARDELLO

Year	Team	League	GS	SB	Avg
1983	Cin	N	88	70	.80
1984	Cin	N	51	42	.82
1985	Cin	N	30	19	.63
3 Years			169	131	.78

Bruce BOCHY

Year	Team	League	GS	SB	Avg
1978	Hous	N	45	46	1.02
1979	Hous	N	37	40	1.08
1980	Hous	N	2	1	.50
1982	N Y	N	16	16	1.00
1983	S D	N	8	4	.50
1984	S D	N	20	18	.90
1985	S D	N	27	30	1.11
7 Years			155	155	1.00

Bob BOONE

Year	Team	League	GS	SB	Avg
1975	Phil	N	81	31	.38
1976	Phil	N	97	79	.57
1977	Phil	N	119	79	.56
1978	Phil	N	117	68	.58
1979	Phil	N	110	54	.49*
1980	Phil	N	130	123	.95
1981	Phil	N	64	77	1.20
1982	Cal	A	138	48	.35*
1983	Cal	A	135	65	.48
1984	Cal	A	133	54	.41
1985	Cal	A	136	57	.42*
11 Years			1261	711	.56

Scott BRADLEY

Year	Team	League	GS	SB	Avg
1985	N Y	A	3	3	1.00
1 Year			3	3	1.00

Bob BRENLY

Year	Team	League	GS	SB	Avg
1981	S F	N	10	7	.70
1982	S F	N	48	53	1.10
1983	S F	N	75	56	.75
1984	S F	N	114	101	.89
1985	S F	N	102	85	.83
5 Years			349	302	.87

Glenn BRUMMER

Year	Team	League	GS	SB	Avg
1981	StL	N	7	9	1.29
1982	StL	N	15	11	.73
1983	StL	N	25	24	.96
1984	StL	N	16	7	.44
1985	Tex	A	32	31	.97
5 Years			95	82	.86

Sal BUTERA

Year	Team	League	GS	SB	Avg
1980	Minn	A	28	16	.57
1981	Minn	A	51	23	.45
1982	Minn	A	42	29	.69
1983	Det	A	1	1	1.00
1984	Mon	N	1	1	1.00
1985	Mon	N	40	42	1.05
6 Years			163	112	.69

Gary CARTER

Year	Team	League	GS	SB	Avg
1975	Mon	N	55	21	.38
1976	Mon	N	54	27	.50
1977	Mon	N	142	110	.77
1978	Mon	N	147	80	.54*
1979	Mon	N	135	75	.56
1980	Mon	N	146	94	.64*
1981	Mon	N	99	53	.54*
1982	Mon	N	154	106	.69
1983	Mon	N	140	89	.64
1984	Mon	N	135	103	.76
1985	N Y	N	139	100	.72
11 Years			1346	858	.64

Marty CASTILLO

Year	Team	League	GS	SB	Avg
1983	Det	A	4	5	1.25
1984	Det	A	27	16	.59
1985	Det	A	18	13	.72
3 Years			49	34	.69

Rick CERONE

Year	Team	League	GS	SB	Avg
1975	Cle	A	3	2	.67
1976	Cle	A	4	4	1.00
1977	Tor	A	28	10	.36
1978	Tor	A	79	48	.61
1979	Tor	A	133	69	.52
1980	N Y	A	146	56	.38*
1981	N Y	A	65	34	.52
1982	N Y	A	86	55	.64
1983	N Y	A	70	45	.67
1984	N Y	A	36	16	.44
1985	Atl	N	78	64	.82
11 Years			628	403	.64

Darren DAULTON

Year	Team	League	GS	SB	Avg
1983	Phil	N	1	2	2.00
1985	Phil	N	27	25	.93
2 Years			28	27	.96

Jody DAVIS

Year	Team	League	GS	SB	Avg
1981	Chi	N	53	38	.72
1982	Chi	N	120	93	.78
1983	Chi	N	140	129	.92
1984	Chi	N	141	119	.84
1985	Chi	N	129	120	.93
5 Years			583	499	.86

Rick DEMPSEY

Year	Team	League	GS	SB	Avg
1975	NY	A	11	8	.73
1976	NY/Bal	A	59	27	.46
1977	Bal	A	84	30	.36
1978	Bal	A	130	62	.48*
1979	Bal	A	113	47	.42*
1980	Bal	A	95	50	.53
1981	Bal	A	72	32	.44
1982	Bal	A	101	46	.46
1983	Bal	A	109	65	.60
1984	Bal	A	104	57	.55
1985	Bal	A	111	80	.72
11 Years			989	504	.51

Bo DIAZ

Year	Team	League	GS	SB	Avg
1978	Cle	A	39	23	.59
1979	Cle	A	11	11	1.00
1980	Cle	A	52	40	.77
1981	Cle	A	42	20	.48
1982	Phil	N	135	115	.85
1983	Phil	N	127	110	.87
1984	Phil	N	22	20	.91
1985	Phi/Cin	N	67	54	.85
8 Years			515	393	.76

Dave ENGLE

Year	Team	League	GS	SB	Avg
1983	Minn	A	70	43	.61
1984	Minn	A	80	50	.63
1985	Minn	A	12	5	.42
3 Years			162	98	.60

Juan ESPINO

Year	Team	League	GS	SB	Avg
1983	NY	A	8	5	.63
1985	NY	A	3	1	.33
2 Years			11	6	.55

Carlton FISK

Year	Team	League	GS	SB	Avg
1975	Bos	A	68	34	.50
1976	Bos	A	130	89	.68*
1977	Bos	A	149	61	.41
1978	Bos	A	150	102	.68
1979	Bos	A	34	24	.71
1980	Bos	A	112	73	.65
1981	Chi	A	89	64	.72
1982	Chi	A	129	79	.61
1983	Chi	A	123	73	.59
1984	Chi	A	82	50	.61
1985	Chi	A	119	84	.71
11 Years			1185	733	.62

Mike FITZGERALD

Year	Team	League	GS	SB	Avg
1983	NY	N	7	12	1.17
1984	NY	N	101	88	.87
1985	Mon	N	93	107	1.15
3 Years			201	207	1.03

Rich GEDMAN

Year	Team	League	GS	SB	Avg
1980	Bos	A	2	2	1.00
1981	Bos	A	57	51	.89
1982	Bos	A	74	60	.81
1983	Bos	A	52	70	1.35
1984	Bos	A	115	77	.67
1985	Bos	A	129	67	.52
6 Years			429	327	.76

Ron HASSEY

Year	Team	League	GS	SB	Avg
1978	Cle	A	23	18	.78
1979	Cle	A	61	50	.82
1980	Cle	A	103	77	.75
1981	Cle	A	53	23	.43
1982	Cle	A	91	85	.93
1983	Cle	A	96	62	.66
1984	Cle/Chi	A/N	40	29	.73
1985	NY	A	65	51	.78
8 Years			532	395	.74

Jeff HEARRON

Year	Team	League	GS	SB	Avg
1985	Tor	A	2	2	1.00

Mike HEATH

Year	Team	League	GS	SB	Avg
1978	NY	A	23	12	.52
1979	Oak	A	18	13	.72
1980	Oak	A	43	23	.53
1981	Oak	A	76	34	.45
1982	Oak	A	77	37	.48
1983	Oak	A	69	43	.62
1984	Oak	A	95	54	.57
1985	Oak	A	94	44	.47
8 Years			495	260	.53

Marc HILL

Year	Team	League	GS	SB	Avg
1975	SF	N	47	31	.66
1976	SF	N	41	27	.66
1977	SF	N	95	84	.88
1978	SF	N	105	90	.86
1979	SF	N	53	42	.79
1980	SF/Sea	N/A	33	25	.76
1982	Chi	A	26	17	.65
1983	Chi	A	37	24	.65
1984	Chi	A	57	31	.54
1985	Chi	A	29	18	.62
10 Years			523	389	.74

Randy HUNT

Year	Team	League	GS	SB	Avg
1985	StL	N	3	0	.00

Dave HUPPERT

Year	Team	League	GS	SB	Avg
1985	Mil	A	8	5	.63

Clint HURDLE

Year	Team	League	GS	SB	Avg
1985	NY	N	12	14	1.17

Bob KEARNEY

Year	Team	League	GS	SB	Avg
1982	Oak	A	20	12	.60
1983	Oak	A	89	46	.52
1984	Sea	A	127	67	.53
1985	Sea	A	94	54	.57
4 Years			330	179	.54

Terry KENNEDY

Year	Team	League	GS	SB	Avg
1978	StL	N	9	5	.56
1979	StL	N	27	21	.78
1980	StL	N	38	50	1.32
1981	SD	N	97	84	.87
1982	SD	N	133	102	.77
1983	SD	N	141	139	.99
1984	SD	N	141	105	.74
1985	SD	N	135	109	.81
8 Years			721	615	.85

Alan KNICELY

Year	Team	League	GS	SB	Avg
1981	Hous	N	1	0	.00
1982	Hous	N	16	12	.75
1983	Cin	N	16	19	1.19
1984	Cin	N	1	2	2.00
1985	Cin	N	42	52	1.24
5 Years			76	85	1.12

Steve LAKE

Year	Team	League	GS	SB	Avg
1983	Chi	N	22	23	1.05
1984	Chi	N	15	10	.67
1985	Chi	N	33	17	.52
3 Years			70	50	.71

Tim LAUDNER

Year	Team	League	GS	SB	Avg
1981	Minn	A	10	6	.60
1982	Minn	A	89	74	.83
1983	Minn	A	47	53	1.13
1984	Minn	A	75	36	.48
1985	Minn	A	53	34	.64
5 Years			274	203	.74

Mike LAVALLIERE

Year	Team	League	GS	SB	Avg
1984	Phil	N	2	0	.00
1985	StL	N	11	5	.45
2 Years			13	5	.38

Buck MARTINEZ

Year	Team	League	GS	SB	Avg
1975	KC	A	70	66	.94
1976	KC	A	86	77	.90
1977	KC	A	22	14	.64
1978	Mil	A	85	44	.52
1979	Mil	A	67	35	.52
1980	Mil	A	74	37	.50
1981	Tor	A	44	25	.57
1982	Tor	A	80	30	.38
1983	Tor	A	67	31	.46
1984	Tor	A	65	20	.31
1985	Tor	A	32	22	.69
11 Years			692	401	.58

Bob MELVIN

Year	Team	League	GS	SB	Avg
1985	Det	A	25	19	.76

John MIZEROCK

Year	Team	League	GS	SB	Avg
1983	Hous	N	30	26	.87
1985	Hous	N	11	13	1.18
2 Years			41	39	.95

Charlie MOORE

Year	Team	League	GS	SB	Avg
1975	Mil	A	40	29	.72
1976	Mil	A	46	44	.96
1977	Mil	A	118	81	.69
1978	Mil	A	74	36	.49
1979	Mil	A	89	61	.69
1980	Mil	A	78	39	.50
1981	Mil	A	29	18	.62
1982	Mil	A	17	5	.29
1984	Mil	A	4	6	1.50
1985	Mil	A	96	58	.60
10 Years			591	377	.64

Jerry NARRON

Year	Team	League	GS	SB	Avg
1979	NY	A	29	18	.62
1980	Sea	A	29	20	.69
1981	Sea	A	58	45	.78
1983	Cal	A	3	3	1.00
1984	Cal	A	29	17	.59
1985	Cal	A	26	17	.65
6 Years			174	120	.69

Steve NICOSIA

Year	Team	League	GS	SB	Avg
1978	Pitt	N	1	2	2.00
1979	Pitt	N	54	28	.52
1980	Pitt	N	52	36	.69
1981	Pitt	N	49	38	.78
1982	Pitt	N	31	22	.71
1983	Pi/SF	N	20	22	1.10
1984	SF	N	33	42	1.27
1985	Tor/Mon	A/N	18	10	.56
8 Years			258	200	.78

Tom NIETO

Year	Team	League	GS	SB	Avg
1984	StL	N	28	20	.71
1985	StL	N	83	58	.70
2 Years			111	78	.70

Matt NOKES

Year	Team	League	GS	SB	Avg
1985	SF	N	13	21	1.62

Joe NOLAN

Year	Team	League	GS	SB	Avg
1977	Atl	N	13	19	1.46
1978	Atl	N	52	55	1.06
1979	Atl	N	58	78	1.34
1980	Atl/Cin	N	45	71	1.58
1981	Cin	N	63	67	1.06
1982	Bal	A	62	52	.84
1983	Bal	A	52	33	.64
1984	Bal	A	5	3	.60
1985	Bal	A	4	4	1.00
9 Years			354	382	1.08

Mike O'BERRY

Year	Team	League	GS	SB	Avg
1979	Bos	A	19	11	.58
1980	Chi	N	15	15	1.00
1981	Cin	N	38	31	.82
1982	Cin	N	14	8	.57
1983	Cal	A	18	9	.50
1984	NY	A	9	3	.33
1985	Mon	N	9	19	2.11
7 Years			122	96	.79

Charlie O'BRIEN

Year	Team	League	GS	SB	Avg
1985	Oak	A	2	0	.00

Junior ORTIZ

Year	Team	League	GS	SB	Avg
1982	Pitt	N	4	2	.50
1983	Pi/NY	N	58	68	1.17
1984	NY	N	25	26	1.04
1985	Pitt	N	23	19	.83
4 Years			110	115	1.05

Larry OWEN

Year	Team	League	GS	SB	Avg
1981	Atl	N	5	8	1.60
1983	Atl	N	2	1	.50
1985	Atl	N	19	22	1.16
3 Years			26	31	1.19

Al PARDO

Year	Team	League	GS	SB	Avg
1985	Bal	A	23	30	1.30

Lance PARRISH

Year	Team	League	GS	SB	Avg
1978	Det	A	74	31	.42
1979	Det	A	135	71	.53
1980	Det	A	114	56	.49
1981	Det	A	88	44	.50
1982	Det	A	127	51	.40
1983	Det	A	125	56	.45*
1984	Det	A	124	44	.35*
1985	Det	A	118	61	.52
8 Years			905	414	.46

Tony PENA

Year	Team	League	GS	SB	Avg
1980	Pitt	N	5	6	1.20
1981	Pitt	N	54	28	.50
1982	Pitt	N	127	78	.61*
1983	Pitt	N	144	116	.81
1984	Pitt	N	139	97	.70*
1985	Pitt	N	138	86	.62*
6 Years			607	411	.68

Geno PETRALLI

Year	Team	League	GS	SB	Avg
1982	Tor	A	8	6	.75
1985	Tex	A	32	32	1.00
2 Years			40	38	.95

Darrell PORTER

Year	Team	League	GS	SB	Avg
1975	Mil	A	120	86	.72
1976	Mil	A	105	87	.83
1977	KC	A	121	60	.50
1978	KC	A	141	76	.53
1979	KC	A	141	64	.45
1980	KC	A	80	39	.49
1981	StL	N	51	41	.80
1982	StL	N	108	94	.87
1983	StL	N	121	63	.62*
1984	StL	N	116	94	.81
1985	StL	N	65	39	.60
11 Years			1179	743	.63

Jamie QUIRK

Year	Team	League	GS	SB	Avg
1979	KC	A	2	1	.50
1980	KC	A	11	13	1.18
1981	KC	A	15	13	.87
1982	KC	A	14	11	.79
1983	StL	N	16	23	1.44
1985	KC	A	15	11	.73
6 Years			73	72	.99

Floyd RAYFORD

Year	Team	League	GS	SB	Avg
1984	Bal	A	50	35	.70
1985	Bal	A	23	18	.78
2 Years			73	53	.73

Jeff REED

Year	Team	League	GS	SB	Avg
1984	Minn	A	7	6	.86
1985	Minn	A	2	2	1.00
2 Years			9	8	.89

Ronn REYNOLDS

Year	Team	League	GS	SB	Avg
1982	NY	N	2	1	.50
1983	NY	N	23	28	1.22
1985	NY	N	11	8	.73
3 Years			36	37	1.03

Mark SALAS

Year	Team	League	GS	SB	Avg
1984	StL	N	2	4	2.00
1985	Minn	A	95	58	.61
2 Years			97	62	.64

Dave SAX

Year	Team	League	GS	SB	Avg
1983	LA	N	1	4	4.00
1985	Bos	A	11	13	1.18
2 Years			12	17	1.42

Bill SCHROEDER

Year	Team	League	GS	SB	Avg
1983	Mil	A	22	17	.77
1984	Mil	A	58	50	.86
1985	Mil	A	46	39	.85
3 Years			126	106	.84

Mike SCIOSCIA

Year	Team	League	GS	SB	Avg
1980	LA	N	44	49	1.11
1981	LA	N	87	64	.74
1982	LA	N	107	84	.79
1983	LA	N	10	3	.30
1984	LA	N	101	75	.74
1985	LA	N	130	81	.62
6 Years			479	356	.74

Donnie SCOTT

Year	Team	League	GS	SB	Avg
1983	Tex	A	1	0	.00
1984	Tex	A	71	39	.55
1985	Sea	A	49	36	.73
3 Years			121	75	.62

Ted SIMMONS

Year	Team	League	GS	SB	Avg
1975	StL	N	148	99	.67
1976	StL	N	107	62	.58
1977	StL	N	139	96	.69
1978	StL	N	119	120	1.01
1979	StL	N	118	100	.85
1980	StL	N	121	116	.96
1981	Mil	A	73	47	.64
1982	Mil	A	119	94	.79
1983	Mil	A	84	84	1.00
1985	Mil	A	11	8	.73
10 Years			1039	826	.79

Joel SKINNER

Year	Team	League	GS	SB	Avg
1983	Chi	A	2	2	1.00
1984	Chi	A	23	19	.83
1985	Chi	A	15	11	.73
3 Years			40	32	.80

Don SLAUGHT

Year	Team	League	GS	SB	Avg
1982	KC	A	31	12	.39
1983	KC	A	73	48	.66
1984	KC	A	112	65	.58
1985	Tex	A	97	55	.57
4 Years			313	180	.58

Marc SULLIVAN

Year	Team	League	GS	SB	Avg
1984	Bos	A	2	1	.50
1985	Bos	A	23	13	.57
2 Years			25	14	.56

Jim SUNDBERG

Year	Team	League	GS	SB	Avg
1975	Tex	A	149	78	.52
1976	Tex	A	134	98	.73
1977	Tex	A	136	47	.35*
1978	Tex	A	146	74	.51
1979	Tex	A	144	74	.51
1980	Tex	A	147	101	.69
1981	Tex	A	97	40	.41*
1982	Tex	A	129	74	.57
1983	Tex	A	118	78	.66
1984	Mil	A	99	40	.40
1985	KC	A	107	60	.56
11 Years			1406	764	.54

Mickey TETTLETON

Year	Team	League	GS	SB	Avg
1984	Oak	A	22	8	.36
1985	Oak	A	66	60	.91
2 Years			88	68	.77

Alejandro TREVINO

Year	Team	League	GS	SB	Avg
1978	NY	N	3	0	1.86
1979	NY	N	33	22	.67
1980	NY	N	78	58	.74
1981	NY	N	37	17	.46
1982	Cin	N	104	89	.86
1983	Cin	N	51	40	.78
1984	Atl	N	65	68	1.05
1985	SF	N	47	37	.79
8 Years			418	351	.84

Dave VALLE

Year	Team	League	GS	SB	Avg
1984	Sea	A	7	3	.43
1985	Sea	A	19	15	.79
2 Years			26	18	.69

David VAN GORDER

Year	Team	League	GS	SB	Avg
1984	Cin	N	31	29	.94
1985	Cin	N	43	29	.67
2 Years			74	58	.78

Ozzie VIRGIL

Year	Team	League	GS	SB	Avg
1982	Phil	N	26	32	1.23
1983	Phil	N	35	53	1.51
1984	Phil	N	124	105	.85
1985	Phil	N	115	118	1.03
4 Years			300	308	1.03

John WATHAN

Year	Team	League	GS	SB	Avg
1976	KC	A	8	4	.50
1977	KC	A	19	10	.53
1978	KC	A	16	12	.75
1979	KC	A	18	7	.39
1980	KC	A	71	57	.80
1981	KC	A	68	44	.65
1982	KC	A	117	62	.53
1983	KC	A	90	59	.66
1984	KC	A	49	30	.61
1985	KC	A	40	20	.50
10 Years			496	305	.61

Ernie WHITT

Year	Team	League	GS	SB	Avg
1978	Tor	A	1	0	.00
1979	Tor	A	92	73	.79
1981	Tor	A	60	28	.47
1982	Tor	A	74	43	.58
1983	Tor	A	95	51	.54
1984	Tor	A	97	51	.53
1985	Tor	A	113	55	.49
7 Years			532	301	.57

Jerry WILLARD

Year	Team	League	GS	SB	Avg
1984	Cle	A	67	45	.67
1985	Cle	A	83	66	.80
2 Years			150	111	.74

Butch WYNEGAR

Year	Team	League	GS	SB	Avg
1976	Minn	A	133	124	.93
1977	Minn	A	138	80	.58
1978	Minn	A	121	72	.60
1979	Minn	A	141	60	.43
1980	Minn	A	133	60	.45
1981	Minn	A	36	29	.81
1982	Min/NY	A	82	57	.70
1983	NY	A	84	59	.70
1984	NY	A	117	69	.59
1985	NY	A	90	54	.60
10 Years			1075	664	.62

Steve YEAGER

Year	Team	League	GS	SB	Avg
1975	LA	N	131	50	.38
1976	LA	N	108	51	.47*
1977	LA	N	118	70	.59
1978	LA	N	72	39	.54
1979	LA	N	89	54	.61
1980	LA	N	66	57	.86
1981	LA	N	23	14	.61
1982	LA	N	54	37	.69
1983	LA	N	96	67	.70
1984	LA	N	53	48	.91
1985	LA	N	32	16	.50
11 Years			842	503	.60

CATCHERS

American League

1. Lance PARRISH, Detroit (9)

Backup catcher Marty Castillo filed for arbitration after hitting .119, and was released. I don't know whether that qualifies as chutzpa or chutzpidity . . . I think Tiger fans will be amazed to see how good Dave Engle, back-up catcher acquired from Minnesota, is. Sparky should be able to DH Parrish as much as he wants to this year . . .

2. Rich GEDMAN, Boston (4)

Challenging for the number one spot, as you can see. Is only three years younger than Parrish . . . I'm still waiting to hear what Marc Sullivan is doing on a major league roster.

3. Carlton FISK, Chicago (1)

Became the oldest player ever to hit 30 home runs for the first time, according to a reader whose name I have lost . . . the winning percentage of the White Sox dropped from .543 to .417 when Fisk wasn't the starting catcher last year . . . hit a solid .276 in the late innings of close games, according to John Dewan's *Chicago Baseball Report,* including the aforementioned 7-for-13 (.538) record in the late innings of close games with runners in scoring position . . . hit .336 and slugged .641 with men in scoring position . . .

4. Ernie WHITT, Toronto

Batting stats very similar to Mike Pagliarulo's (946 similarity score). Whitt hit .245 with 19 home runs, 64 RBI, Pagliarulo .238 with 19 and 62. Both are left-handed platoon players . . . the major league equivalencies of Ernie Whitt's minor league records are very, very similar to what he actually did in the major leagues in his first two seasons, 1980 and 1981. The break in his record came when he became a platoon regular in 1982 . . . did you notice that three of the top four catchers in the American League are products of the Red Sox farm system?

5. Jim SUNDBERG, Kansas City

He really did help the Royals—not as much as the press said, probably, but he was good with the young pitchers and decent with the bat. Still throws extremely well. Now twelfth on all-time list of games caught, with 1,607; record is 1,918 but Boone might extend it before Sunny gets there . . . I said a year ago that I thought it was 80% certain he would hit below .240. I was wrong but barely; he hit .245 but missed a third of the season with injuries.

6. Rick DEMPSEY, Baltimore

We may have rated him a little too high. The Orioles had the league's worst record against base stealers, catching only 38 of 168. The percentage was the poorest; the 130 SB they allowed was the most in the A.L. except for Cleveland (133). Actually, though, Pardo was mostly responsible for that. Besides hitting .133 with one RBI, Pardo was raked for 30 opposition stolen bases in 23 starts, up toward double the rate against Dempsey or Rayford . . . but it is nice that we now have a major league catcher from Spain as well as one from France . . . Dempsey had excellent year with the bat, with a secondary average close to .300.

7. Don SLAUGHT, Texas

I still love this kid. He's smart, he works hard, he's a good athlete, a good defensive catcher and he improved his secondary average last year from .164 to .216 . . . Rangers had good record and ERAs last year with Brummer starting, terrible with Petralli, but released Brummer anyway. Cardinals also had excellent 2.80 ERA in 1984 with Brummer catching . . . Petralli is legitimate major league hitter, but woeful defensive skills . . . I think Slaught will be the American League's All-Star catcher in three or four years . . .

8. Mark SALAS, Minnesota

Prime candidate for the sophomore jinx. Was inconsistent hitter in the minor leagues, very aggressive hitter with low secondary average . . .

9. Mike HEATH, Oakland

Now with St. Louis. Although Heath throws better, the A's had a far better record and ERA with Tettleton catching than with Heath; I'm sure the A's were aware of this and that it was one of the reasons for the trade, inasmuch as it was in the papers. (Is it immodest to point out that before the *Abstract* no one would have been aware of this?) The ERA difference was enormous (3.53 against 5.10), and such differences *do* tend to be consistent from year to year. The 1984 data was similar (3.91 ERA with Tettleton as starting catcher, 4.77 with Heath). Even so, there's a real risk to it, going with a young catcher who is suspect as a hitter and doesn't throw well. If it works, remember to give credit for a gutsy decision . . .

10. Bob BOONE, California

California catchers had the best record in the league against base stealers, with a league-best 79 Opposition Stolen Bases and 41% throwout rate . . . a characteristic of Gene Mauch teams . . .

11. Butch WYNEGAR, New York

Pretty decent defensively and walks a lot, but has to hit more than .223 to rate high . . . Yankees had 3.43 ERA with Wynegar catching, 4.06 with Hassey. But Hassey was valuable, chipping in a .324 average and slugging percentage near .600 against right-handed pitching. Only 3 of Hassey's 13 home runs were hit in Yankee Stadium . . . Hassey caught only 8 of 58 opposition base stealers in 1985, Wynegar much better.

12. Jerry WILLARD, Cleveland

Seems to have outlasted the competition and wound up with the job. His defense isn't great but he's working on it, and he looks like he can hit some.

13. Bob KEARNEY, Seattle

Strikeout to walk ratio, not much worse than 2–1 in first year as a regular in 1983, deteriorated to 4–1 in 1984 and worse than 5–1 last year . . . had the best fielding percentage of any major league catcher, for what that's worth . . .

14. Charlie MOORE, Milwaukee

B. J. Surhoff will have the job as soon as he shows any sign of being ready.

National League

1. Gary CARTER, New York (12)

Only Met regular with a secondary average over .300 (.333), except Strawberry, who was in the stratosphere at .532 but didn't qualify for the batting title.

2. Mike SCIOSCIA, Los Angeles

Strikeout to walk ratio (21–77) was the best in baseball, which combined with a .296 average in a pitcher's park and good defense fully justifies the rankings . . . again last year, as was mentioned in the 1985 book, the Dodgers' record with Scioscia catching was far better than with Yeager . . . it's too bad the Seattle team didn't keep the "Pilots" nickname. It would be so appropriate, now, what with having Chuck Yeager's nephew on the team . . .

3. Tony PENA, Pittsburgh

I also commented last year that the Pirates' winning percentage went way down with Pena out of the lineup (1982–1984). Last year it was down more than ever. The Pirates were 5–18 without Tony starting . . . toughest N.L. catcher to run on for the third time . . .

4. Ozzie VIRGIL, Philadelphia

Now with Atlanta. It's a risky move, trading two established catchers to play an unproven kid, although Daulton looks very good. His secondary average last year was .350 in 103 at bats . . .

5. Jody DAVIS, Chicago

If it wasn't for Wrigley Field, making his batting stats looks so much better than they really are, I'm not sure this guy would be able to stay in the league. Last year he hit .206 with seven homers, 22 RBI away from Wrigley. In addition to his atrocious clutch statistics last season, his defense has never been anything special. He hustles and you have to like some things about him. If he gets back where he was in '83 and '84 he'll stay around . . .

6. Mark BAILEY, Houston

Becoming one of the league's best; I personally would rate him far above Davis. The Astros in 1984 were 58–44 with Bailey catching, 21–33 with Ashby. Last year was about the same, 55–41 with Bailey, 24–31 with Ashby. Over the two years, that's 28 over .500 with Bailey, 19 under with Ashby. They're both switch hitters and share left/right playing time, but it might be that Ashby catches certain pitchers or something; I don't know. Ashby is a fine hitter.

7. Bob BRENLY, San Francisco

Maintained secondary average of .302, best on the Giants, despite dropoff in batting average.

8. Terry KENNEDY, San Diego

Wonder who will play here? I used to like Kennedy but he just hasn't been consistent with the bat. He might have been better off to take off 35 games a year and let the bruises heal . . . Back-up Bochy is decent fringe player, and AAA catcher is 30 years old.

9. Bo DIAZ, Cincinnati

I like this trade, from Cincinnati's standpoint. Diaz is like Carlton Fisk was for a long time. An accumulation of injuries has caused him to miss a lot of playing time, but that's going to be a big factor in his favor as he gets up in years. Carlton Fisk is the same age as Johnny Bench, but Fisk is still going strong in part because he had enough injuries to keep him from destroying his knees by age 30.

10. Darrell PORTER, St. Louis

I suspect the Cardinals may feel the loss of Porter more than they think they will . . . secondary average remains superb, at .388 . . .

11. Mike FITZGERALD, Montreal

Was intentionally walked 12 times even though most of the Expos' pitchers hit about as well as he did. Fitzgerald hit .207 with seven doubles and five homers on the season. By comparison, Bill Gullickson hit .188 with four doubles, Bryn Smith hit .194 with a double and a homer, Dan Schatzeder hit .194 with a double and two homers (.419 slugging percentage), and even Jeff Reardon hit .286 (2/7).

All of the intentional walks occurred with a runner in scoring position, as is normal. Why walk a .207 hitter and risk setting up a big inning if the pitcher gets a bloop hit and Tim Raines gets to the plate? When you have two chances to get out of an inning cheap, wouldn't it make sense to use both of them?

12. Rick CERONE, Atlanta

Eddie Haas had three things going against him—his personality, his luck and a few of his decisions. His luck with the pitchers, particularly Perez and Sutter, was lousy. But he also made three bad mistakes in the construction of the team. He failed to get Rafael Ramirez, a really awful offensive player, out of the middle of the offense. He kept using Komminsk, rather than trying Milt Thompson or just giving the full-time job back to Washington. Komminsk didn't come through. And, for no apparent reason, he decided to make Rick Cerone his #1 catcher, rather than, say, Bruce Benedict or Art Howe or somebody. Cerone throws better than Benedict—most anybody does—but Benedict overall is a better defensive catcher and has a chance to contribute offensively. The point isn't that Benedict is any good—although he was once he hasn't been for two years—but that almost any decision is preferable to playing a player that you know can't do the job.

FIRST BASEMEN

American League

1. Don MATTINGLY, New York (9)

Besides the RBI, he led the American League in total bases, 370 (most in majors since Rice had 400 in 1978), in doubles, 48, (most in majors since 1980), game-winning RBI (21), and extra base hits (86) . . . career stats projected by BROCK6 show 2,994 Hits, .320 Average, 434 Homers and 641 Doubles. It seems unlikely he'll retire with exactly 2,994 . . .

Mattingly had almost as many home runs (35) as strikeouts (41). Another little study I did compared the career growth and durability of similar players who strike out a lot and strike out less. I selected a high-strikeout group as "all the *young* players from the 1973 season who struck out in at least one sixth of their at bats." There were 26 such players. I selected a "comparison" group of the most-similar players who tended to strike out less; for example, Pedro Garcia (23-year-old second baseman, 32 doubles, 15 homers, 54 RBI, .245 average but 119 strikeouts) was matched with Bobby Grich (24-year-old second baseman, 29 doubles, 12 homers, 50 RBI, .251 average but only 91 strikeouts). Then I checked to see how many games the players in each group played in the rest of their major league careers, or at least have played up to now.

The study suggested that there might be a "survivability" advantage to the player who strikes out less often. In the 26 matches, the player who struck out less often had a longer major league career 16 times. The "high strikeout" group played an average of 866 major league games from 1974 through 1985. The "low strikeout" group played an average of 975. Very far from conclusive, but tends to indicate that low-strikeout players might be better risks for future performance than equally talented high-strikeout players.

2. Eddie MURRAY, Baltimore (5)

Well, I hit it. In the 1982 *Abstract,* after 2 years of GWRBI, I said that in 1986 Eddie Murray would be the first player to get 100 GWRBI. Three more and it's official . . . in 1993 he'll become the first player to get 200 . . . led A.L. in road-game RBI, with 61 . . .

3. Alvin DAVIS, Seattle

Another young player with an old player's skills—superb strike-zone judgment, power, but slow and already lodged at the left end of the defensive spectrum . . . I didn't realize he was quite so slow before reading Jeff Welch's study. He can hit, though . . .

4. Kent HRBEK, Minnesota

Good enough to drive in 93 runs and be thought of as having an off year . . . hit .312 in Minnesota, only .240 on the road. Had a poor first four months, but saved his season by hitting .365 with 17 RBI in August and .303 with 20 RBI after September 1 . . .

5. Darrell EVANS, Detroit

Secondary average was .440; career mark is over .360 . . .

6. Willie UPSHAW, Toronto

Hit .344 after the All-Star break. Hasn't come close to his big 1983 season in last two years, but he plays good D and chips in with the bat . . . Cecil Fielder, trying to move into a platoon role at first base, follows the general rule that players named White are always Black and players named Black are always White. He's a born DH . . .

7. Pete O'BRIEN, Texas

Fine, fine young player. Probably the best glove man in the league at the position, maybe the best in baseball, and has had two straight good years with the bat in difficult circumstances . . .

8. Steve BALBONI, Kansas City

Tied with Darrell Evans for the American League lead in home runs in neutral parks (19) . . . As an offensive player almost identical to Dave Kingman. Balboni's 1984 season (28 HR, 77 RBI, .244) matches Kingman in 1978 (28, 79, .266) and Balboni's 1985 (36, 88, .243) matches Kingman's 1975 (36, 88, .231). Both players have career averages of .238, strike out and walk about the same. Bones is a better defensive player.

9. Cecil COOPER, Milwaukee

Has progressed from having a large platoon differential as a young player to having a small platoon differential (1981–1983) to being a legitimate reverse-platoon player the last two years, hitting .304 and .321 against left-handed pitching, but .260 and .279 against right-handers, and with more power against lefties as well.

10. Greg WALKER, Chicago

Didn't have a particularly good year except for his clutch statistics (see Chicago comment); development as a hitter has been disappointing, although not so disappointing as that of Kittle. The change in fence dimensions might throw him for a loop, but he's more of a line-drive than a power hitter, anyway.

11. Bill BUCKNER, Boston

He now holds the record for assists by a first baseman in both leagues. He set the major league record for assists by a first baseman with 159 in 1982, upped that to 161 in 1982 and then to 184 in 1985. What other records are there which are held by the same person in both leagues? The only ones I know of, not counting Chicago Shirley, are by relief pitcher Mike Marshall (Game Appearances) and Don Money, who holds the record for consecutive errorless chances at third base in both leagues.

12. Bruce BOCHTE, Oakland

Regained his batting eye; may platoon with Dusty Baker this year. They can both hit.

13. Rod CAREW, California

Sconiers' problems have kept him playing beyond his time, and,

like Pete Rose, he can still get on base, which is one of the most important skills in the game.

14. Pat TABLER, Cleveland

Hit .326 in Cleveland but dropped to .215 on the road. 1984 data was similar (.336 in Cleveland,

.248 on the road). Has no power, very low secondary average, grounds into too many double plays and was 0 for 6 as a base stealer. Strikeout to walk ratio skidded badly last year . . . would be valuable as right-handed platoon player if he would accept the role (hit .309 against lefties).

National League

1. Keith HERNANDEZ, New York (6)

Led the N.L. in batting in turf parks, .364 . . .

2. Jack CLARK, St. Louis (4)

Hit .392 with .683 slugging percentages, 35 RBI in 34 games on grass fields in '85. The good hitter's parks in the N.L. are the grass fields, Wrigley and Fulton County Stadium. Awesome hitter, still isn't in a good park for him but I'm sure he doesn't mind . . .

3. Mike SCHMIDT, Philadelphia (2)

Reportedly returning to third base. I ran the Brock6 projections for him from each point of his career, just to see how they had developed. From 1973, his first year up (he hit .196) he still projected as good enough to play for several years, with expected career totals of 273 home runs, 815 RBI and a .216 average. After his first two good years (from 1975) his projections were up to 479 home runs, 1,438 RBI and a .246 average. For three years after that, his projections actually went *down,* as he failed to advance his skills; from 1978 he figured to end up with 344 home runs, 1098 RBI and a .248 average. Turning on the juice in 1979, by 1981 he had lifted his projections in three giant steps, two of them MVP seasons, to .263 with 570 home runs, 1,664 RBI. Since then the projections have essentially not moved; as of now his projected career totals are 577 home runs, 1,663 RBI, 1,623 walks and a .263 average.

4. Leon DURHAM, Chicago

May have the biggest home-field differential in baseball over the last two seasons:

	G	AB	R	H	2B	3B	HR	RBI	Avg
At Home	145	502	90	165	36	4	34	110	.329
On Road	145	513	54	120	26	2	10	60	.234

MVP stats at home, inadequate on the road . . .

5. Bob HORNER, Atlanta

One of the amazing things about the Braves' season is how many things went *right* in the course of a season that was a complete disaster. If they had told you at the end of the 1984 season that 1) The Braves would sign Bruce Sutter, 2) Dale Murphy would have possibly his best season ever in 1985, 3) Bob Horner, his career in jeopardy, would come back to play 130 games and hit like Bob Horner, 4) Terry Harper would take over the left field job and develop into a pretty decent major league hitter, and 5) Rick Mahler would win 17 games, wouldn't you have sworn they would win a hundred games? But all of those things happened, and they won 66.

6. Greg BROCK, Los Angeles

Dodgers had three regulars with secondary averages over .300, in Guerrero (.452), Brock (.320) and Scioscia (.310), plus Mike Marshall at .299.

7. Steve GARVEY, San Diego

There is talk of platooning Kennedy and Garvey at first base. The arrangement would help the team if they could find a catcher.

8. Glen DAVIS, Houston

Had a terrific half a season, hitting .284 with 18 homers, 56 RBI in 72 games after the All-Star break. Hit .317 in Houston, only .231 on the road, but with 12 of the 20 homers on

the road. Not a super prospect; he's pretty one-dimensional and probably isn't going to be a great hitter. But he's one of four promising young players in the Houston lineup, with Bailey, Doran and Bass. If Thon comes back and they pop a third baseman out of their minor league system, they're going to get good in a hurry.

9. Jason THOMPSON, Pittsburgh

There are two things that have killed Thompson's career, besides the fact that he's a little overweight. One is that he's a platoon player, always was, and he should have had some rest against the tough lefties. The other is the turf park. In the last two seasons he has hit .317 and .349 on grass fields, but .232 and .203 on artificial turf. His hitting will recover if he's traded to an appropriate situation.

10. Pete ROSE, Cincinnati

Who?

11. Tony FRANCONA, Montreal

One reason he didn't score any runs (19 in half-time play) is that he hit just .229 when leading off an inning (36/157), whereas he hit .349 with runners on first base only. A good guess would be that he hits through the hole quite a bit . . . credit Brent MacInnes with the information.

12. Dan DRIESSEN, San Francisco

The ultimate San Francisco Giant.

SECOND BASEMEN

American League

1. Lou WHITAKER, Detroit (14)

May have been the only unanimous selection other than Gooden. I don't remember seeing any ballots that didn't have him marked "1." What do you think of him as a Hall of Fame candidate? . . . Has about a 19% chance of getting 3000 hits in his career.

2. Willie RANDOLPH, New York

Best strikeout to walk ratio in the American League (39–85); Brett was second . . . remains very strong on the double play. I don't understand why he didn't bat second, but I suppose Billy must have had a reason for it.

3. Frank WHITE, Kansas City

A.L. leader in assists, total chances . . . exceptional 5.73 adjusted range factor. Really, I can't see that he's lost anything as a second baseman . . . established a new career high in home runs for the sixth time in his career; after hitting none as a rookie he has moved his total to 1, 7, 10, 11, 17 and 22 . . . also established career highs in walks, with 28, and strikeouts, with 86 . . .

4. Bobby GRICH, California

Remarkable defensive season. His .997 fielding percentage is an all-time record for 100 or more games. (If you use a higher standard, like 130 or 150 games, Grich still holds the record with his .995 in 1973). He also holds the lifetime mark, with .984. The Angels also turned 202 double plays, most in the major leagues in five years. And his secondary average is still over .300 . . .

5. Tony BERNAZARD, Cleveland

Somehow, I would imagine that when Tony Bernazard was a young boy growing up in Puerto Rico, he never fantasized about playing for the Cleveland Indians . . . Had a fine season, hitting .274 and contributing in just about every other area—61 walks, 40 extra base hits including 11 homers, 17 stolen bases, decent defensive year. Only major career high was 59 RBI, but it may have been his best season overall.

6. Damaso GARCIA, Toronto

Blue Jay lead-off men in '85 scored only 86 runs, remarkably few for a team which scored 759 runs (or 84 per batting order position). I'll give the full scan of Blue Jays runs by position, and repeat the Cardinals for comparison:

	1	2	3	4	5	6	7	8	9	Total
Toronto	86	93	91	81	82	93	80	85	68	759
St. Louis	119	116	99	92	88	66	59	58	50	747

The bottom of the Blue Jays lineup, with Fernandez and Barfield often hitting 7th and 8th, was remarkably strong, arguably stronger than the top part of the lineup. Fernandez apparently will lead off in '86, which makes sense. Anyway, the Cardinals were a whopping 81 runs better in spots 1–5 of the batting order, but the Blue Jays were 93 runs better in 6–9.

7. Toby HARRAH, Texas

I have a theory that when an older player's walks total suddenly shoots upward, his batting average will decline the next year by at least 20 points—as, for example, Gary Matthews a year ago, or Willie Mays in 1971. One of the reasons that walk totals explode like this is that it is a case of a veteran hitter compensating for slowing reflexes by trying to work the count in his favor. That only works for so long; then the pitchers will start making the hitter hit good pitches. We'll see what happens.

8. Jack PERCONTE, Seattle

Remains an excellent percentage base stealer, as he was in the minor leagues. In AAA ball (1979–1981 and 1983) he was 134/160 as a base stealer (84%); so far in the majors he is 76/89 (86%) . . . may yet prove that the Dodgers chose the wrong one . . .

9. Alan WIGGINS, Baltimore

Adjusted range factor, 4.63, was the lowest in baseball. That's not surprising in view of the fact that he's new to the league and still learning the position . . . gives the Orioles something they needed offensively and will improve with the glove.

10. Marty BARRETT, Boston

Could rate higher. Adjusted range factor is excellent 5.63, can hit a little. I like him, but there are a lot of good second basemen in this league . . . hit only .202 on artificial turf. The entire Boston team, except Boggs and Easler, hits poorly on turf (.251 as opposed to .301 in Fenway and .272 on road grass).

11. Tim TEUFEL, Minnesota

Now with the Mets, which means that he and Jim Gott will get to match up and reenact their periodic pageants for control of the universe (I'll be sure to report on how it goes). Will probably play some third as well as spelling Backman at second. He's a good player, and I think the Twins made a mistake in turning him loose to play Lombardozzi.

12. Jim GANTNER, Milwaukee

A left-handed hitter, had outstanding year against left-handed pitchers (.329) but skidded to .254 against the people he is supposed to be able to hit . . . secondary average of .156 largely explains the rating. Somehow he was left off the "American League Worst" list, for secondary average, but he is one of the lowest.

13. Donnie HILL, Oakland

Hit .300 in road games, but dropped to .268 in Oakland. That's pretty normal in this park . . . just fair defensively and has low secondary average, but he contributes . . .

14. Chicago (Vacant)

National League

1. Ryne SANDBERG, Chicago (12)
Power/Speed number, 35.1, was the highest in the National League, and just missed establishing a record for his age group. He overcame a rocky start to have arguably a better season in '85 than in his MVP year . . . hit .370 (30/81) and slugged .617 in the late innings of close games.

2. Tommie HERR, St. Louis
It was widely noted that he was the first player since George Kell in 1950 to drive in 100 runs with less than ten homers, but did you know there was a team not that long ago that had two players who combined for over 200 RBI with less than 20 homers? The 1970 Dodgers, an offense in many ways similar to this one, had Willie Davis and Wes Parker, who combined for 204 RBI with 18 homers, 10 and 111 for Parker, 8 and 93 for Davis.

3. Bill DORAN, Houston
Secondary average of .310 is one of the best in the league for a middle infielder, second-best on the Astros . . . despite the fences being moved in in Houston, he still hit better on the road (nine homers, .291 on the road, five and .283 at home) . . . in his three years as a regular has hit .291, .304 and .328 on grass fields, as opposed to just .263, .242 and .268 on artificial turf. He might not be quite as good as Whitaker and Sandberg, but if he ain't, he ain't far behind, either.

4. Juan SAMUEL, Philadelphia
I'm much more impressed with him now than I was a year ago. He cut down his strikeouts and increased his walks while increasing his power. As a second baseman he cut his errors from 33 to 15, increased his range and improved somewhat on the double play, although he still has a long way to go in that regard. Most importantly, he didn't get hurt, and he didn't show any signs of the soph-

omore jinx. This kind of broad-based improvement speaks well for him as an athlete.

5. Johnny RAY, Pittsburgh
He didn't have his best year, but he hasn't hung his head; he continues to play despite the performance of his team. He struck out only 24 times, hit 33 doubles and drove in 70 runs. A fine player.

6. Vance LAW, Montreal
Hit .299 with runners on first base, just .224 with runners in scoring position. That's probably the effect of hitting behind Tim Raines . . . Excellent strike zone judgment, medium-range power and solid defense make him a valuable player.

7. Ron OESTER, Cincinnati
Hit .323 on artificial turf, second in the league for a player who played most of his games on turf . . . secondary average remains very low (.173) . . .

8. Wally BACKMAN, New York
Game declined badly when he lost his platoon partner (Kelvin Chapman) to a ruptured bat. He really cannot hit left-handers—he hit .122 against them (16/131) as opposed to .324 against right-handers—and the experience of trying to hit them didn't seem to help his game any. He became more impatient at the plate, and by year's end had all but stopped drawing walks. His on-base percentage dropped from .360 to .320, and his on-base percentage is the reason he's in the lineup. Defensively, he led the league in fielding percentage but the range and double play performance was not what it might have been. He needs help.

9. Steve SAX, Los Angeles
Hit .333 on artificial turf, restored his batting average to his usual .280 range after off year. Actually, Sax out-hit Ron Oester both on artificial turf (.333–.323) and grass

fields (.257–.225), but was 16 points lower overall because of the different balance between the two.

10. Jerry ROYSTER & Tim FLANNERY, San Diego
They did a good job, really; the loss of Wiggins hurt the Padres not because these guys were bad but because it aggravated the problems of lack of speed, a problem that might more naturally be solved in the outfield, rather than at second base, and lack of bench material, a problem which shouldn't be all that hard to correct. The key to a successful 1986 for the Padres isn't replacing these guys—it is 1) facing up to the fact that the highly regarded veterans Garvey and Kennedy aren't getting the job done, and 2) getting Kevin McReynolds lined out and headed in the right direction.

11. Glenn HUBBARD, Atlanta
As Tim Marcou shows in his article in Section IV, Hubbard made an astonishing number of fielding plays per nine innings. He did this because 1) Atlanta has a groundball staff, 2) Hubbard is exceptional at turning the double play, and 3) he knows where to play the hitters. Perhaps the term "range factor" is misleading as applied in this case, but one could make a very good argument that Hubbard deserves to rate higher for this reason. It's hard to rate a guy who loses his job over an entrenched regular, though.

12. Manny TRILLO, San Francisco
Mike Woodard apparently has the job after hitting .316 at Phoenix. Woodard is a very small man, 26 years old, picked up by the Giants as a minor league free agent. He is very unlikely to be a hitting star in the majors; his average will be in the same range as Trillo's. But with luck he will contribute more doubles and triples, more walks and more stolen bases, plus giving the team more mobility at second base. That's the best option they have now.

THIRD BASEMEN

American League

1. George BRETT, Kansas City (12)

One thing you definitely cannot say about the MVP vote is that Mattingly won it because he plays in New York. Since the split into divisions in 1969 New York teams have won six pennants, but (until Mattingly) only one MVP Award (Munson in 1976). Tom Seaver, Dwight Gooden, Ron Guidry and Reggie Jackson are among the New York players who could just as well have won MVP Awards as not . . . Brett is just starting to appear on the lists of active career leaders. He is third in batting (.316), third in triples (108) . . .

2. Wade BOGGS, Boston (2)

Led the A.L. in hitting both on grass (.363) and on artificial turf (.389) . . . hit .418 in Fenway, just .322 on the road . . . according to the Waseleski Baseball Report (10 Newton Street, Millers Falls, Mass. 01349), Boggs hit .402 in the late innings of close games, hit .392 with runners in scoring position, and, amazingly, *hit .390 (39/100) after getting behind in the count, 0–2* . . . you may remember that two years ago I presented Wade Boggs "final" career statistics. In 1984 I was way off, but 1985 was picked to be Boggs' best year, and he was supposed to hit .377 (he actually hit .368) with 8 home runs (he hit 8), 43 doubles (he hit 42), 88 walks (he had 96) and 224 hits (he had 240).

3. Paul MOLITOR, Milwaukee

Hit .453 against the Yankees . . .

4. Rance MULLINIKS & Garth IORG, Toronto

Iorg came back strong, becoming more disciplined at the plate and getting average up to .318. Mulliniks has developed into a fine defensive third baseman, led league in fielding percentage. A few of the outstanding multi-year platoon combinations of all time:

1920–22	Cleveland, Left Field	Charlie Johnson & Joe Evans
1920–23	New York (N), Catcher	Frank Snyder & Earl Smith
1925–26	Pittsburgh, First Base	George Grantham & Stuffy McInnis
1930–32	Cardinals, Right Field	George Watkins & Ray Blades
1933–35	Detroit, Center Field	JoJo White & Gee Walker
1947–48	Boston (N), First Base	Earl Torgeson & Frank McCormick
1956–57	Red Sox, First Base	Mickey Vernon & Dick Gernet
1947–51	Yankees, Third Base	Bobby Brown & Billy Johnson
1956–60	Milwaukee, First Base	Frank Torre & Joe Adcock
1968–70	Mets, Right Field	Art Shamsley & Ron Swoboda
1979–85	Baltimore, Left Field	John Lowenstein & Gary Roenicke
1982–85	Toronto, Third Base	Rance Mulliniks & Garth Iorg

Stengel's platoon systems were too complicated to be listed, and often involved right-handers who were 80% regulars but rested when somebody was shifted from another position to get somebody else off the bench. Another list is great one-year platoon tandems, but that one has to have stats and I haven't gotten to it . . .

5. Jim PRESLEY, Seattle

Established a major league record for fewest putouts by a third baseman, 150 or more games (82). Putout totals for Seattle third basemen before Presley were normal, so it doesn't seem to be a park illusion or anything . . . hit .358 against left-handed pitchers, second in the league.

6. Carney LANSFORD, Oakland

Range factor, which has never been very high, was all the way down to 2.17 last year, lowest in baseball. The Oakland staff doesn't throw a lot of ground balls . . .

7. Brook JACOBY, Cleveland

Hit .374 on artificial turf . . . didn't show the same tendency in '84, hitting just .241 then. Don't you think that you could make an argument that, from the standpoint of the Braves, this might well turn out to be the worst trade ever made?

8. Wayne GROSS & Floyd RAYFORD, Baltimore

Rayford, baseball's answer to William the Refrigerator, hit .306 despite the worst strikeout to walk ratio in baseball (69–10) except for Alejandro Sanchez (39–0 in 133 AB). Gross hit just .235 but had secondary average of .406, second straight year over .400 . . . combined they hit .280 with 29 HR, 93 Runs Created, in 576 at bats. I can't believe anybody would want to bench that production and put Jackie Goddamned Gutierrez in the lineup, not to mention that at shortstop they would lose about 20 double plays and add a dozen errors.

9. Doug DeCINCES, California

Hit seven home runs in September to finish with 20 . . .

10. Mike PAGLIARULO, New York

A year ago I commented that there wasn't much to choose from between Pagliarulo and Jim Presley. Presley went on to have a year that is superficially much more impressive, (28 homers, 84 RBI and .275 against 19 homers, 62 RBI and .239), but atually the statement is as much true now as it was then. If you look closer, you'll note that:

Pagliarulo homered more often than did Presley, 1/20 at bats against 1/20.4.

Pagliarulo drove in more runs per at bat.

Pagliarulo scored more runs per at bat.

Pagliarulo, with 380 at bats, drew more walks than Presley did with 570 (45–44).

Presley grounded into 29 double plays, Pagliarulo only 6.

This last item is the big one, and largely explains why Pagliarulo was creating more runs per 27 outs (5.05–4.74) than was Presley.

11. Gary GAETTI, Minnesota
Could be ready to inherit a Gold Glove here, with Bell out of the league. The nature of the public's perception is that *somebody* in each league has to be recognized as the defensive standout at the position. Brett won't really do, what with being well past 30 and a hitter, so Gaetti figures to be the most qualified.

12. Tim HULETT, Chicago
Probably will return to second base, his native position. Another strong candidate for the sophomore jinx.

13. Tom BROOKENS, Detroit
Darnell Coles may get a shot at the job. I definitely think that Coles is a major league hitter, but his ability to do the job with the glove is questionable. Brookens was the worst regular player in the league last year.

14. Steve BUECHELE, Texas
The opposite of Coles, a sure glove but has to prove he can hit. Has made strong strides as a hitter in the last two years, but still has probably 20–25% chance to make it. Hit five home runs in September, but didn't pick up his average any.

National League

1. Tim WALLACH, Montreal (12)
I had mentioned for two or three years that his defensive statistics were the best in the league, but I really soft-pedaled this because he was never regarded as a defensive stand-out. Last year the recognition caught up with him, though. I notice, in looking back, that it is pretty common for a player to have the best defensive stats at a position for two or three years before he becomes the Gold Glove winner. For example, Ron Santo led the National League in double plays and range factor in 1961, in putouts, assists and range in 1962, in putouts and assists in 1963 and in putouts, assists, double plays and range in 1964 before becoming the annual Gold Glove winner in 1965. Graig Nettles had the best defensive stats in the American League from 1970 on, almost every year, but didn't get the Gold Glove until 1977. Garry Maddox led N.L. outfielders in range factor in 1973, but didn't win the Gold Glove until 1975. Andre Dawson had superb defensive stats from the time he came up in 1977, but didn't get the Gold Glove until 1980; now, although his defensive ability (and statistics) have slipped badly the last two years, he continues to win the Gold Glove. In a lot of areas, it just takes two years or more for the recognition to catch up to the reality . . . Incidentally, Wallach's offensive stats are also very similar to typical years for Brooks Robinson and Graig Nettles. 22 homers, 81 RBI, .260 . . . that could easily be Brooks or Graig.

2. Bill MADLOCK, Los Angeles
What should be kept in mind about his late-season finish is that he has *always* finished strong; it's one of the most consistent individual rhythms in the sport. I really don't think he can hit .300 in Dodger Stadium.

3. Chris BROWN, San Francisco
Odd story, wasn't it . . . rookie hits, rookie fields, rookie can't get along with anybody. Why does this keep happening to the Giants? . . . apart from the alleged attitude problems, I'm not crazy about the player. I think he was hitting over his head last year . . . grounded into 19 double plays.

4. Buddy BELL, Cincinnati
It seems fairly obvious that his range factor was low in the National League because he was just learning the hitters and just learning his own pitchers . . . wonder when the last time a little major league city like Cincinnati had three of their biggest stars home-grown? It would be hell to check . . .

5. Graig NETTLES, San Diego
Had a remarkable season, doing a good job with the glove and the bat while turning 41 in August. It was the best season ever for a 40-year-old third baseman . . .

6. Terry PENDLETON, St. Louis
Terrific defensive player, as you saw during the World Series. His adjusted range factor is 3.46, just missing Wallach's 3.52, the best in baseball. His fielding average and double plays were also good. His offensive stats are impossible to defend, but he did get his share of big hits. He's one of those players that you kinda have to like for a year or two, regardless of what the statistics show.

7. Howard JOHNSON, New York
Maintained a steady .260–.270 pace for the last four months after almost dropping out of sight in April and May . . . hit just .156 against left-handed pitchers, also didn't hit them well (.224) with Detroit in '84 . . . hits very well on artificial turf, .291 in '84 and .280 last year, as opposed to .240 and .223 on grass fields.

8. Ken OBERKFELL, Atlanta
Secondary average of .214, so-so glove make him very marginal regular unless he hits .300 . . .

9. Phil GARNER, Houston
What can you say, Phil Garner is still Phil Garner. He's always been Phil Garner, and he'll always be Phil Garner . . . he hit ten triples last year at the age of 36; that's got to be worth a note.

10. Ron CEY, Chicago
Drove in only 18 runs in 74 games away from Wrigley Field, hit .206 . . . can't really do the job de-

fensively any more, isn't hitting enough to keep his bat in the lineup unless he does.

11. Rich SCHU, Philadelphia

Almost too good to be called a washout; but not quite good enough to keep playing. Stats are similar to Brook Jacoby a year ago, offensively and defensively, similar K/W ratios, except that Schu has that 24-RBI total staring him in the face . . . I think Schu would develop into a decent player if they were patient enough with him, but the Phillies have options; they have other kids they want to try.

12. Denio GONZALEZ, Pittsburgh

Looks like he could be major league hitter, but ability to make it at third is very doubtful. About like Darnell Coles, I guess.

SHORTSTOPS

American League

1. Cal RIPKEN, Baltimore (14)

Performance was off a little bit across the boards, offensive and defensive. He dropped by 109 assists (583–474), for which there has got to be some identifiable reason if you took the trouble to identify it. Runs and RBI were up because the Oriole offense was having such a terrific year, but batting average, doubles, triples, home runs and walks were all down a little . . . hit just .163 against Toronto and just .205 against the Yankees . . . remains a great player.

2. Tony FERNANDEZ, Toronto

Finished second in ten of fourteen precincts . . . awfully impressive player. Defensively, he may not quite match Ozzie, but he is something to watch, bouncing around the infield like a colt, snarfing up balls over half the diamond. With his offensive plusses, which include everything except power, he's as good as Trammell and Franco, and that's real good . . . hit .429 with a .714 slugging percentage in 13 games against Boston . . .

3. Alan TRAMMELL, Detroit

After leading the league in hitting on artificial turf for two straight years, hit just .229 on it last year (.264 on grass) . . . hit only .233 after the All-Star break . . .

4. Julio FRANCO, Cleveland

Strikeout to walk ratio, which was not good when he came up (50/27) has improved to above average (74/54) . . . set career highs in runs (97), RBI (90), average (.288) and doubles (33) . . .

5. Ozzie GUILLEN, Chicago

Set American League record for fewest putouts in a season, 220 (150 or more games). He did miss quite a few innings by being pinch hit for, but then shortstops often do . . .

This is one of those arguments that you have to make, even though you know nobody's going to believe

you. The Hoyt-for-Guillen trade hurt the Sox badly in 1985. In addition to the fact that they gave up a decent pitcher, the effect of which was magnified with the loss of Dotson, Guillen replaced a player, Scott Fletcher, who is offensively and defensively at least even with him. Although Guillen hit .273, he never walks, doesn't hit for power and doesn't steal bases. His secondary average just missed being the lowest in the league. He is not a good offensive player, nor is it likely that he ever will be.

But besides that, Scott Fletcher, though not recognized for it, is one of the most capable defensive shortstops in the league. One professional study a year ago, given good access to game data, concluded that Fletcher may have been the best defensive shortstop in the American League in 1984. Last year, John Dewan's *Chicago Baseball Report* kept track of precise defensive performance. His records show that Scott Fletcher played 248 innings at shortstop last year, as opposed to 1,202 and a third for Guillen. The number of batters per inning and the number of balls in play per inning were almost exactly the same for the two players as shortstops—yet Fletcher made markedly more plays, 4.86 per nine innings as opposed to 4.46 for Guillen. Fletcher handled 16.8% of balls in play while he was the shortstop; Guillen handled 15.7%. Although Guillen led the league in fielding percentage, at .980, Fletcher also beat him in this regard, making only one error for a .993 fielding percentage.

In 1984, Chicago shortstops (primarily Fletcher) had 263 putouts, 540 assists and turned 108 double plays; they fielded .973. In 1985 they were up to 277 putouts, but dropped to 466 assists—down 74—and 99 double plays. They did field .983. Scott Fletcher is simply a better shortstop than Ozzie Guillen at this point.

6. Earnest RILES, Milwaukee

Hit .311 against right-handed pitching, ninth in the league. Riles and Guillen went through the minor leagues together; they were both in the California League in 1982, the Texas League in 1983 and the Pacific Coast League in 1984 before coming to the American League in 1985. Riles' defensive stats have always been better. Guillen led the California League in putouts and the PCL in assists, but Riles led the California League in assists and the PCL in putouts, and the Texas League in both as well as fielding percentage.

7. Spike OWEN, Seattle

I really like him. Adjusted range factor was the best in the American League, plus his offensive contribution was pretty good and he doesn't make errors. Has come a long way in two years, and deserves more respect . . . hit .329 in day games, only .238 at night . . .

8. Alfredo GRIFFIN, Oakland

Finished second in the Oakland precinct, but no higher than seventh anywhere else . . . drew only one walk with 132 at bats after September 1 . . . hit .326 against left-handed pitchers, only .245 against right-handers . . .

One of the amusing sidelights of the post-season circus was watching the Toronto fans, who spent six years trying to convince the world that Alfredo Griffin was really a fine player no matter how bad his record was, scream bloody murder when Alfredo won the Gold Glove Award. Of course Fernandez is three times the shortstop Griffin is, but how can you expect the Gold Glove voters to recognize this right away, when it took the Toronto management two and a half years to figure it out?

9. Bobby MEACHAM, New York

Walks some, good percentage base stealer, led American League in sacrifice hits with 23 . . . hit just .169 in Yankee Stadium, but .264 on the road . . .

10. Dick SCHOFIELD, California

Pretty even with Meacham, decent defensive player, hits about .220 with secondary average about .220 . . . may be gaining a little as a hitter. After hitting .193 as a rookie and .188 the first half last year, he hit .247 in August and .286 in September to lift average to .219 . . . hit .219 in California and .219 on the road . . .

11. Glenn HOFFMAN, Boston

Did you notice that Glenn Hoffman's stats are extremely similar to those of Jerry Willard of Cleveland? Hoffman hit .276 with 6 HR, 34 RBI in 96 games, Willard hit .270 with 7 HR, 36 RBI in 104 games. They are fairly close in all areas . . . a much better hitter than he was a few years ago, more selective, more powerful. I think he'll have his best year this year . . .

12. Curtis WILKERSON & Wayne TOLLESON, Texas

Tolleson, now the Chicago third baseman, hit .333 against right-handed pitching . . . I can't say too much for the trade, in which the Rangers gave up two major leaguers and Sebra, a long-odds pitching prospect, for Fletcher and Correa, a good pitching prospect. I like Fletcher, but they don't seem to realize what they have in him, and apparently plan to use him as a spare infielder (like Tolleson). I can't see too much point in a trade like that . . . Wilkerson, the holdover at short, is a good glove at second base, but hasn't proven himself to be anything else yet.

13. Greg GAGNE, Minnesota

Here's where the Twins have the need and opportunity to improve. Either Gagne has to get better, or they've got to find somebody else . . .

14. Buddy BIANCALANA, Kansas City

Adjusted range factor is quite good, 4.87 . . . the voting for thirteenth/fourteenth was close, but Buddy lost it . . . a classic example of a player who would be replaced if his team hadn't won the pennant, but who might be carried along because he contributed something to the success of the team.

National League

1. Ozzie SMITH, St. Louis (11)

I was surprised and disappointed in the National League MVP vote in 1985. Meaning no disrespect to Willie McGee, to my way of thinking it was obvious that the Most Valuable Player in the N.L. in 1985 was Ozzie Smith.

Before the 1985 season, it was widely written that the Cardinal pitching was weak. With the loss of Bruce Sutter and poor late-season pitching of Joacquin Andujar, many felt that the Cardinals didn't have the pitching to win. I approached the issue a different way. There are three things which beat pitchers: walks, home runs and balls in play. The Cardinal pitchers would be receiving huge breaks on two of the three. Busch Stadium would help control the number of home runs that they allowed. With Ozzie Smith behind them, Ozzie Smith and Willie McGee and Tommie Herr, they would be receiving a huge break on balls in play. Therefore, as long as they didn't walk people, the Cardinal pitchers would be alright. And Whitey won't use a pitcher who walks a lot of people. He'll instruct his pitchers to go after the hitters, and he'll get rid of the ones who don't do it.

Given those advantages, and given the presence on the staff of Andujar, John Tudor, Rickey Horton and Danny Cox, it seemed to me that the Cardinal pitching would be perceived as being outstanding. Ozzie Smith would save the Cardinal pitchers enough runs that they could win—not Ozzie alone, clearly, but Ozzie as the lynchpin of a strong defense. The Cardinals would win, and Ozzie would be the MVP.

But nobody saw it.

If Ozzie Smith wasn't the MVP in 1985, then can any player of his type even be the MVP? It is hard to see how. Ozzie is unquestionably the greatest player of his type, isn't he? He is generally regarded as the greatest defensive shortstop ever to play the game, and he has the best defensive statistics of any shortstop to play the game. Of his species—the light hitting defensive wizzard—he is one of the best offensive players. He isn't a high-average hitter or a power hitter, but he hits for a decent average (second best in the league at the position), his strikeout and walk data is exceptional (the second-best in baseball, exceeded only by Mike Scioscia), and he is a base stealer and a good percentage base stealer. He is not only the best defensive, but also the best offensive shortstop in the league:

	Hits	Bttng Avg	Scndry Bases	Scndry Avg
Templeton	154	.282	109	.200
OZZIE	148	.276	142	.264
Reynolds	103	.272	62	.164
Brooks	163	.269	127	.210
Santana	136	.257	54	.102
Concepcion	141	.252	110	.196
Ramirez	141	.248	70	.123
Duncan	137	.244	130	.231
Uribe	113	.237	75	.158

So what you have is:

1) The greatest defensive player ever;

2) At one of the two most important defensive positions;

3) Who is also the best hitter in the league at his position;

4) Having his best season offensively as well as possibly defensively;

5) Holding together a team expected to collapse;

6) and leading them to the league championship.

That is about as good a definition of an MVP as one can write—yet Ozzie finished eighteenth in the MVP voting! He was mentioned on only two ballots, placing eighth and ninth on those two.

I didn't expect that, I don't understand it, I can't justify it, and I don't think it reflects very well on the award or the men who did the voting.

2. Garry TEMPLETON, San Diego (1)

Drew a career-high 41 walks last year, but most (24 of the 41) were intentional . . .

3. Hubie BROOKS, Montreal

I still don't really believe he can play shortstop. His adjusted range factor was 4.21, the lowest in the National League. He drove in 100 runs largely because he batted third/fourth behind the N.L.'s best lead-off man. He surprised me in that he held the job and fooled most people into thinking he was succeeding. But there are five shortstops in the National League and eleven in the American League that I would rather have.

4. Mariano DUNCAN, Los Angeles

Impressive athlete; impressive season. Just 22 years old, he started the season as a minor league second baseman. He switched to shortstop in an emergency move, and by the end of the year had become the rock around which the shaky Dodger defense had been anchored. For good measure, he made solid, consistent offensive contributions.

5. Dickie THON, Houston

Hit .288 with good power after the All-Star break. Sometimes I don't understand what makes a "story." When Dickie Thon was one of the five best players in baseball in 1983, nobody ever heard of him. When he got hurt in 1984, all of a sudden he was a big story. When he tried to come back early in 1985 and had trouble seeing the ball, that was a big story. But when he started hitting again, all of a sudden everybody forgot about him again. I don't understand this . . . how come he's only a story when he can't play?

6. Shawon DUNSTON, Chicago

I watched him on cable a lot, and I want to tell you, his adjusted range factor (5.85) is no illusion. Particularly on line drives, he's just amazing; if the ball is hit in the air within 20 feet of him, he's going to get it 90% of the time. I like him way, way more than Guillen, particularly as a defensive player.

7. Rafael RAMIREZ, Atlanta

Secondary average of .123, worst in the league except Santana. Led league in errors, 32, despite playing only 133 games at short; it was the fifth straight season of leading in errors. The record at the position is six, by Dick Groat . . . drew only 20 walks, was 2 for 8 as a base stealer and grounded into 21 double plays . . . does that sound like a number two hitter to you?

8. Rafael SANTANA, New York

Lowest secondary average in baseball (.102), with only 24 extra bases on hits, 29 walks and 1 stolen base . . . was quietly efficient on defense and hit .257, but I think it is generally accepted that, like Backman and Hojo, he needs more help in '86 . . .

9. Jose URIBE, San Francisco

Worst secondary average in the league for a player not named "Rafael." At least, not at the moment . . .

10. Dave CONCEPCION, Cincinnati

Three years away from Luis Aparicio's record of 2,581 games played at shortstop, but less than one year away from the #2 spot on that list. If he were to get the record, I would think that would put him in the Hall of Fame . . .

11. Tom FOLEY, Philadelphia

Not too young (he's 26) and a .240 hitter in the minors, he faces a battle to make it in the majors. I'd give him a 30, 35% shot.

12. Sam KHALIFA, Pittsburgh

There was a lot of variation in where he placed in the voting; some people had him as high as third. He's very young—turned 22 in December—but I have trouble seeing the positives. Doesn't look to me like he has a shortstop's arm or mobility; best chance to make it might be to get his average up to .260 and switch to second base . . .

LEFT FIELDERS

American League

1. George BELL, Toronto (5)

Career stats as projected by Brock6: 1,927 games, 312 home runs, 1,110 RBI, .280 average . . . big improvement in K/W ratio, from 86–24 in 1984 to 90–43 in 1985 . . .

2. Phil BRADLEY, Seattle (9)

Finished first in most precincts, but finished 3rd/4th in four precincts to drop him below Bell, who was one or two in all 14 precincts.

His home-run outburst, moving from 0 home runs to 26, is apparently unprecedented. According to Jeff Welch, twelve men have had increases in home runs of 26 or more following a season of 300 or more at bats. Those are:

Dave Johnson, 1973	5 to 43	38
Lou Gehrig, 1927	16 to 47	31
Johnny Mize, 1947	22 to 51	29
Rico Petrocelli, 1969	12 to 40	28
Carl Yastrzemski, 1967	16 to 44	28
Ralph Kiner, 1947	23 to 51	28
Jimmie Foxx, 1932	30 to 58	28
Bob Cerv, 1968	11 to 38	27
PHIL BRADLEY, 1985	0 to 26	26
Dusty Baker, 1977	4 to 30	26
Dick Stuart, 1963	16 to 42	26

Many of these increases were recoveries from abnormally low totals—Dick Stuart, for example, had hit 35 home runs the year before he hit 16, and Dusty Baker, Johnny Mize and others were established power hitters. Bradley had hit *no* previous homers. Welch found that the most home runs hit by a player who had hit no home runs the prior year was 21, by Cap Anson in 1884. That, however, was a fluke, with the Chicago team moving into Lakefront Park and having home run explosions all over the lineup. The largest previous jump from 0 home runs other than that was to 15—barely over half Bradley's total—by Joe Moore in 1934. Dave Philley in 1950 and Dick Bartell in 1935 jumped from 0 to 14; no one else has hit more than ten following a season in which they hit none in 300 or more at bats.

3. Mike YOUNG, Baltimore

Hit 22 home runs, drove in 61 runs after the all-star break . . . hit well against both left-handers and right-handers, at home and on the road . . . how many runs will the Orioles score if he keeps hitting this way? Can you imagine going through Ripken and Murray and then getting to a 40-homer switch hitter?

4. Jim RICE, Boston

As has been true in recent years, Rice hit very well with runners in scoring position (.341), but not very well in the late innings of close games (.257; credit Chuck Waseleski for information) . . . hit .342 in day games with .605 slugging percentage, dropped off in night games to .264 and .424. Over the years he has hit with more power in day games, but day/night averages fluctuate . . . hit only .232 on the road last year, .118 home/road differential was largest among Sox . . . Brock6 projection retires him in just a few more years with totals of 399 home runs, 1,434 RBI and a .298 average, 2,419 hits. That probably is much too conservative . . .

5. Brian DOWNING, California

Started slowly but made it into another solid season, with 20 homers, 85 RBI, secondary average well above .300 . . . as always, hit better on the road (.284) than in California (.241) . . .

6. Gary WARD, Texas

Hit .344 with 50 RBI in Texas, .235 with 20 RBI on the road . . .

7. Joe CARTER, Cleveland

Joe Carter was the second player taken in the 1981 draft, taken out of Wichita State University. In that particular draft, eight of the first ten players were taken out of college. As has been true in almost every draft, the players drafted out of college have proven to be more productive, one for one, than those taken out of high school. All ten players have since played in the major leagues; the best of them are Mike Moore, drafted by Seattle out of Oral Roberts, and Ron Darling, drafted by the Rangers out of Yale. I have written some about this before, but I designed a little study this year to determine whether there might be a "career growth" advantage to players who have a college background.

The study worked this way. Using the 1973 season, again, I identified similar young players who did and did not have a college background. Sets of similar players in this group include Oscar Gamble (23 years old, 113 games, 21 homers, 61 RBI, .268 average) and George Hendrick (23 years old, 113 games, 20 homers, 44 RBI, .267), Don Money (26 years old, 11 homers, 71 RBI, .284) and Larry Hisle (26 years old, 15 homers, 64 RBI, .272), and Wayne Garrett (25 years old, 16 homers, 58 RBI, .256 average) and Ron Cey (25 years old, 15 homers, 80 RBI, .245 average). Hendrick, Hisle and Cey had attended college; Gamble, Money and Garrett did not. By fixing virtually equal groups of players who were unlike in this one respect and figuring what happened to them later in their careers, I hoped to figure out if, other things being equal, a player who has a college education is better able to adapt and grow in his career.

The indication of the study is not strong. There were 40 matched sets of players. The statistics of the two, the average age and position spectrum, are nearly identical. Of the 40 pairs, the less-educated player played more games in the remainder of his career 18 times; the more-educated player played more games 22 times. The players who had been to college have played a total of 41,554 games in the 1974–1985 period, an average of 1,038 apiece. The players who had not been to college played a total of 37,047 games, or 926 apiece. This would suggest that there might be an advantage to the educated player. However, obviously, such a separation could well result from chance.

Another form of this study, using only the best matches, showed a stronger result. Of the 16 educated players in the "best matches" portion of the study, 11 subsequently outperformed their less educated counterparts, and outlasted them by a margin of almost one third 19,368 games against 14,503.

8. Lonnie SMITH, Kansas City

I would try to tell you what a bad outfielder Lonnie is, except that I confess that I would never have believed it myself if somebody had tried to tell me, so why bother. It is generally assumed that the Royals will have to get Lonnie out of the outfield as soon as possible, and make him a DH. I will say, though, that the real cost of Lonnie's defense is not nearly as great as the psychic impact of it. He makes you wail and gnash your teeth a lot, but he doesn't really cost you all that many runs. One reason for that is that he recovers so quickly after he makes a mistake. You have to understand that Lonnie makes defensive mistakes every game; he knows how to handle it. I mean, your average outfielder is inclined to panic when he falls down chasing a ball in the corner; he may just give up and set there a while, trying to figure it out. Lonnie has a pop-up slide perfected for the occasion. Another outfielder might have no idea where the ball was when it bounded off his glove; Lonnie can calculate with the instinctive astrophysics of a veteran tennis player where a ball will land when it skips off the heel of his glove, what the angle of glide will be when he tips it off the webbing, what the spin will be when the ball skids off the thumb of the mitt. Many players can kick a ball behind them without ever knowing it; Lonnie can judge by the pitch of the thud and the subtle pressure through his shoe in which direction and how far he has projected the sphere. He knows exactly what to do when a ball spins out of his hand and flies crazily into a void on the field, when it is appropriate for him to scamper after the ball and when he needs to back up the man who will have to recover it. He has experience in these matters; when he retires he will be hired to come to spring training and coach defensive recovery and cost containment. This is his specialty, and he is good at it.

9. Ken GRIFFEY, New York

Hit just .107 against Toronto . . . hit .335 in day games, .236 at night . . .

10. Dusty BAKER, Oakland

Not really an outfielder, but he saves me from having to rate Dave Collins. Don't take Sparky seriously when he talks about leading off Dave Collins for the Tigers; Sparky's not half as stupid as the things he says. He's just figuring, "Well, maybe it will work out. Maybe he'll come to spring training on fire and have a great year for us. If he doesn't, nobody will remember what I said last winter anyway." Sparky only drives you crazy if you remember that stuff. I would guess Canseco will wind up in left for the A's, but it could be Canseco in right and Davis in left.

11. Ben OGLIVIE, Milwaukee

Hit .310 against right-handers, only .219 against left-handers. He hasn't hit left-handers for years; why he had 73 at bats against them last year I couldn't guess.

12. Mickey HATCHER, Minnesota

Secondary average, .119, was the lowest in the league, and really unacceptable for an outfielder unless he hits .340 or something.

13. Larry HERNDON, Detroit

Probably has played himself out of a job, but could reemerge as platoon player.

14. Chicago (Vacant)

National League

1. Pedro GUERRERO, Los Angeles (11)

Sensational batting stats on artificial turf in '85, hit .359 with 16 homers in 38 games, slugging percentage (on artificial turf) of .733 . . . also slugged almost .600 on artificial turf in 1983 . . . one thing I really need to do is a neutral-park-and-pitchers comparison of Guerrero and Dale Murphy. I think it will show that, facing the same pitchers in the same parks, Dale Murphy isn't even close to Guerrero as a hitter and I'm a great admirer of Murphy's, too, but Pedro is the best hitter God has made in a long time. His stats, for Dodger stadium, are as good as Brett's or Rice's or anybody else's in their own context . . . .839 offensive winning percentage was easily the best in the N.L. . . .

2. Tim RAINES, Montreal (1)

Now clearly the greatest lead-off man in National League history. He hit .326 on artificial turf, the highest turf average of any player who played on turf in his home park. His .788 offensive winning percentage was third in the league, behind Guerrero and Strawberry. As mentioned in the San Diego comment, Montreal lead-off men—Raines, for the most part—scored 128 runs, by far the largest percentage of team runs scored by any batting position in the league. A great, great player.

3. José CRUZ, Houston

Added his third straight .300 season and sixth of his career; crossed 2000 hits late in the season. Went 16/21 as a base stealer . . .

4. Vince COLEMAN, St. Louis

There are rumors that the leg is not healing well following the run-in with the tarp. I sure hope that's not the case. It would be very sad for a player who generates this much excitement to lose his essential skill.

5. Carmello MARTINEZ, San Diego

Secondary average was outstanding, .350 . . . the Padres had six regulars with secondary averages of .220 or below: Kennedy (.169), Garvey

(.202), Flannery (.216), Templeton (.200), McReynolds (.220) and Gwynn (.186). This is not quite as bad as having six regulars with primary batting averages below .220, but it's close . . . the Cardinals had only one regular with a secondary average below .264, and the Reds had only two regulars with secondary averages below .280 . . .

6. Nick ESASKY, Cincinnati

Had a fine second half, hitting 15 homers with .270 average . . . hit only .234 with 7 homers in Cincinnati, .285 with 14 home runs on the road.

One of the things that has made Pete a successful manager to this point, I think, is that he has been smart enough not to ask players to do things that they're not very good at. Esasky can play third base, but he's not very good at it; trying to do it tends to distract from the other parts of his game. The acquisition of Bell, although Bell himself didn't hit well, enabled Esasky to contend with less demanding defensive positions, and he responded by hitting better.

7. George FOSTER, New York

Since 1977 his home run and RBI counts have gone down every single year except 1983, when he went up from 13/70 to 28/90 . . . has 334 career homers, and is likely to hit at least 335 . . .

8. Gary MATTHEWS, Chicago

Hit just .214 with 5 homers away from Wrigley Field.

9. Terry HARPER, Atlanta

Has to do better than what he did last year to have a safe job. 17 homers, 72 RBI are *close* to the levels of job security, but they're not quite there.

10. Jeff LEONARD, San Francisco

Should be a platoon player.

Strikeout/walk ratio started out almost even (68/56) and has deteriorated to 107/21, worse than 5–1. There are very few successful players who have strikeout/walk ratios worse than 5–1.

11. Jeff STONE, Philadelphia

Obviously, having Stone, Thompson and Redus is heavily redundant. The Phillies are talking about moving Von Hayes to first base so that two of them can play, which makes no sense in that it would waste Hayes' speed and arm, but they probably know as well as we do that they'll be lucky if one of those guys pans out as an everyday player.

12. R.J. REYNOLDS, Pittsburgh

Suspect he will hit close to .300 and will steal 30–40 bases. If he can hit with a little power or draw a few walks, that would make him valuable.

CENTER FIELDERS

American League

1. Rickey HENDERSON, New York (14)

Got to see more left-handed pitching, as a Yankee, and pounded lefties for league-leading .359 batting average with .652 slugging percentage (181 at bats). Half his home runs were against lefties, and he scored 58 runs against them . . . set age group record for power/speed number . . .

The American League MVP vote, while not as offensive as the National League's forgetting that Ozzie Smith existed, was no prize either. Baseball writers tend to be fascinated with "pay-off" statistics, statistics like RBI, wins and saves. These are important performance areas, but one must remember that they represent the end products of accomplishments to which others must contribute. A pitcher does not "win" the game by himself; he must receive help from the rest of the team. Pitchers who are the recipients of lots of help, as Bryn Smith was last year or Lamarr Hoyt was in 1983, tend to be credited with the surplus.

So it is with RBI, and so it was with the Henderson/Mattingly combination. What Henderson did was far more unique than what Don Mattingly did—yet Mattingly received the lion's share of the credit for it. Since 1950, 15 men other than Don Mattingly have driven in 140 or more runs. None, other than Rickey Henderson, has scored 140 or more. Henderson scored more runs than any player since 1949, and became the first player since 1939 to score more than one run per game played. Henderson's year was very possibly the greatest season that any lead-off man has ever had—while Mattingly's year, while an exceptional effort, was obviously not the greatest year ever for a number three hitter. Mattingly was outstanding. His offensive winning percentage was .733, which is terrific. Henderson's was .802. Henderson created two more runs and made 76 fewer outs. Henderson

played a more central defensive position.

Another way to put it is this: that if you took away Mattingly and replaced him with Eddie Murray, there would be no significant change in the Yankee offense. If you took away Mattingly and replaced him with Brett, the Yankees would score more runs, not fewer. If you took away Mattingly and replaced him with Dave Parker or Dale Murphy or Pedro Guerrero, the Yankees would still score as many runs as they do. But if you took away Rickey Henderson and replaced him with anybody else at all, even the magnificent Tim Raines, then the Yankees would lose runs. Henderson, and not Mattingly, was the unique and irreplaceable element of the combination. But instead of receiving credit for that, he was subjected to a lot of silly, irresponsible carping about missing a game at the end of the strike and other ridiculous and imaginary failings of his attitude toward the game.

One odd note about this historic duo is that they tended to strike on different sides of the line. Mattingly was much more deadly against right-handed than left-handed pitching; Henderson was tougher on lefties. Mattingly was much better in Yankee Stadium, while Henderson was better on the road. One is tempted to say that God knows how many runs they would have scored had they been in sync, but if you think about it you realize that had they both been right-handed hitters, then the Yankees would never have seen a left-handed pitcher. It was the balance that kept them going from start to finish.

I think in the Yankee comment I wrote that Henderson had to be the best player in baseball in 1985. Now that I think about it, I realize that it has to be Brett. Brett created more runs with a much higher offensive winning percentage, a phenomenal .861. Brett won, and deserved, a Gold Glove. Brett's team won the

pennant. And Brett, with the pennant on the line in the last week of the season, had what may well be as good a week as any player ever had under those conditions, hitting two doubles and driving in two runs on Sunday, homering and driving in two more on Monday, singling to drive in one on Tuesday, hitting a single, a double and a three-run homer on Wednesday, homering again on Thursday, homering again on Friday, adding an RBI single as a bonus, and finishing it off with a 2-run homer on Saturday—seven crucial games, five homers, 3 doubles, 13 RBI, one pennant. Willie Stargell won the MVP award in 1979 for having one hot week, and his week wasn't that good. I didn't see it at first because I was over-compensating for being a Royal's fan, but if you step back and look at it, of course Brett was the MVP.

Dear Bill:

I would like to address a point that has been driven home to me by the play of Rickey Henderson this year—that is, whether actual runs scored should somehow be factored into the runs created formula.

It has become apparent to me Henderson scores more often than the average ballplayer and that stolen bases and the production of the hitters behind him do not fully account for that. He has consistently, as a baserunner, taken extra bases that others do not and scored runs that others do not.

I believe that runs created under-measures the good baserunner—that is, the ability to take extra bases over and above stolen bases. To illustrate the point, a double by Ron Hassey simply does not have the same scoring potential as a double by Henderson, after the fact. Henderson is far more likely to score on a single, far more likely to score given almost any sequence of events. I am not even addressing the psychological pressure or advantage that a Henderson creates. (Editor's note: Thank God for small favors.)

As the purpose of runs created is to best possibly approximate the offensive value or production of a ballplayer, it seems that this should be accounted for. I am aware that the formula has a low variation from total runs scored, but I would presume that it works because most teams have a balance of "good" and "bad" baserunners, thereby averaging out the deviations. I think you should try to account for this factor in future editions.

Thanks,
Jeffrey Loeb
Flushing, New York

Dear Jeffrey:

Well, your argument is intelligent and well thought through, but there just isn't any reason to believe that it is true. Rickey Henderson scores more runs than the average ballplayer for a lot of reasons besides his stolen bases. He hits home runs, he draws lots of walks and he hits over .300, in addition to being the greatest base stealer in the history of the game. The runs created formula is very generous to Rickey Henderson; the formula gives him credit for each of these things, and estimates that he created 138 runs, which is very similar to the number of runs that he actually scored, only eight off. Whereas the consensus, as registered in the MVP vote, is that Mattingly is the key element of the Yankee offense, the runs created formula insists that it is actually Henderson who creates the most runs.

But there is no reason to believe that he creates even more than that, no reason to think that his estimate should be even higher. In fact, if you compare Henderson's runs created to his runs produced, you'll find that Henderson *already* has one of the highest ratios in baseball. He had 138 runs created last year with 194 runs produced, whereas most players with 194 runs produced would have about 110 runs created. His ratio would get even more extreme if you made the adjustments that you request.

You say that a double by Ron Hassey does not have the same value, after the fact, as a double by Rickey Henderson, and this is true, but the key words are after the fact. But *be-fore* the fact, the double by Ron Hassey has much *more* value than the double by Henderson. Hassey has to hit the ball harder or farther or faster to get a double in the first place; any Ron Hassey double will score a runner from first base, while many of Rickey Henderson's doubles, leg doubles, will not. And much of the after-the-fact difference that you refer to can be and is negated by pinch-running.

While it is true, as you say, that *most* teams have a balance of "good" and "bad" baserunners, this is not true of *all* teams, and those teams which are exceptions—those teams which are all slow or all fast—do not lead us to believe that the value of speed is being under-estimated. On the one hand, you have the 1985 Cardinals, the team of seven leadoff hitters and Jack Clark. They deviated from their runs created by only a few, the normal 2% error. At the other end, you have the 1955–1958 Washington Senators, the slowest team that ever was.

The Senators started out with an aging Eddie Yost, who wasn't called the Running Man, and went downhill from there. It's hard to say who the fastest man on this team was, but it seems like a safe guess that whoever he was, he couldn't have beaten Dale Berra in a footrace. This team used Harmon Killebrew a number of times as a pinch runner. The baserunning accomplishments of this team are remarkable and numerous. In 1955 they stole only 25 bases. In 1956 they stole 37 bases. In 1957 they established a major league record, stealing only 13 bases. In 1958 they stole 22 bases.

Their failure to steal bases wasn't by choice; it wasn't from a lack of trying. In 1955, when they stole 25 bases, they were third in the league in caught stealing, with 32. In 1956, when they stole 37 bases, they were caught stealing 34 times. In 1957, when they set the record with 13 stolen bases on the season, the team had 38 runners caught stealing—almost three times as many as were successful. And in 1958, stealing 22 bases, they had 41 runners caught stealing.

There were other unique testimonies to their fleetness afoot. In 1958 they hit only 161 doubles on the year, the fewest of any team of the fifties. As to defensive mobility, they led the league in hits allowed yearly, and in 1956 allowed 1,539 hits, 115 more than any other team in the league.

In spite of those accomplishments, these teams scored *more* runs, over the four-year period and in three of the four seasons, than would be projected by the runs created formula.

It is quite true that baserunning is not very well measured in baseball statistics, and if we had the information that we would like to have, we feel that we could develop runs created formulas which are even more accurate than the ones that we have.

But while the runs created formula doesn't measure baserunning directly, it does measure many related categories, such as stolen bases, caught stealing, double play balls and doubles and triples hit. If the teams which do well in these areas tended to score more runs because of it—and your thesis is that they do—then, since we make empirical, not theoretical, measurements, that would cause the runs created formula to over-state the literal value of these accomplishments, and thus to give credit for baserunning indirectly by over-valuing things like stolen bases and double play avoidance. The runs created formula measures speed in many different ways. But being designed so as to measure actual runs resulting, the formula would not care *why* speed is important; it only cares how important it is. And it measures that, while indirectly, very well.

Brock6 projections for Rickey Henderson show 2,488 career hits, 247 runs, 1,847 runs scored and .288 average. Brock6 doesn't project stolen bases, but 1,300 would be the number that fits in about right.

2. Lloyd MOSEBY, Toronto

According to David Driscoll, Moseby made 68 outs on infield pop-ups in 1985, tying George Bell for the team lead . . . . the number sounds awfully high, and I'm guessing that a lot of line drives and smashes caught by infielders must have been included in a somewhat inapt description there. Anyway, Moseby flied out to the outfield 100 times, fourth on the team (George Bell flied out 137 times), Moseby hit 10 balls caught on the warning track (George Bell again led the team, with 18), and Moseby had a team-leading 8 extra base hits off the wall . . .

3. Brett BUTLER, Cleveland

Left-handed batter but hit .332 against lefty pitching, .302 against right-handers . . . has really developed into a fine, fine player, the league's #2 lead-off man, a .300 hitter, a base stealer, an exceptional outfielder. He led the league in fielding percentage (.998), was second in assists (19) and third in putouts (437) and was among the league leaders in batting both at home and on the road.

4. Willie WILSON, Kansas City

His 21 triples in a season were the most since Dale Mitchell hit 23 in 1949. Kansas City installed a new, springy turf before the season, and 14 of the 21 were hit in Royals Stadium . . . Since Tony Kubek has been telling us for five years that Willie Wilson didn't hit in the 1980 series because Philadelphia had a staff of power pitchers and Willie gets most of his hits off of control pitchers, I decided that a study of this effect was in order. Mike Kopf and I defined two balanced groups of pitchers, one a group of 34 pitchers with outstanding fastballs (Floyd Bannister, Jay Howell, Dennis Rasmussen, Jose Rijo, Roger Clemens, Mike Witt, Jack Morris, Edwin Nunez, Dave Righetti, etc.) and the other a group of 34 pitchers who had the same level of skill—the same record—but without the Grade A Heat. This list included Doyle Alexander, Don Sutton, Ron Romanick, Frank Tanana, people like that. The power pitchers pitched 4,966 innings with a 298–287 record and a 3.86 ERA; the other group pitched 4,914 innings with a 299–285 record and a 3.89 ERA.

For some reason, Willie per-

formed less well against all the pitchers in the study than he did overall. On the whole, we found no particular reason to believe Kubek's thesis. These are his records:

	AB	H	2B	3B	HR	RBI	BB	Avg.
POWER	164	40	6	4	1	16	7	.244
OTHER	146	37	5	5	0	7	7	.523

His performance against the two groups of pitchers was essentially the same.

5. Chet LEMON, Detroit

Has had 400 putouts in a season five times (American League record) . . . 1985 batting stats were very similar to Willie Upshaw's . . .

6. Robin YOUNT, Milwaukee

Hit .214 on turf, .285 on grass fields . . . See article on Hall of Fame progress . . .

7. Fred LYNN, Baltimore

Used to be inconsistent and have big splits in his record; over the last four years he's been as consistent as you can be, and he has hardly any splits left in his record. Last four years has hit 21, 22, 23 and 23 homers; averages have declined from .299 to .272 to .271 to .263 . . . set a career high in strikeouts with 98 in 1984 and upped that to 100 in 1985 . . . used to hit a lot of doubles, dropped all the way down to 12 last year . . .

8. Oddibe McDOWELL, Texas

What an *athlete*. The first time I ever saw Oddibe I was watching a game on TV and he hit a routine ground ball to short, was out at first, and I sat bolt upright in my chair and said "Who was THAT?!" Greatest athlete to come into the American League since Gibson and Wilson in the late seventies . . . Did a fine job

in center field and had secondary average of .335 . . .

9. Dwayne MURPHY, Oakland

Hit just .215 with 5 homers, 18 RBI in Oakland, .249 with 15 and 41 on the road . . .

10. Gary PETTIS, California

Sensational defensive player, best defensive outfielder in baseball. Could be rated higher on that basis.

11. Kirby PUCKETT, Minnesota

Hit .355 against left-handed pitching (.315 as a rookie in '84) . . . He did improve his walk frequency, as I had guessed that he would, taking 41 walks after only 16 as a rookie . . . could well have rated higher. Despite .288 average, he really isn't much of an offensive player, with a .187 secondary average. His defensive stats are terrific, 19 assists, led league in put-outs (465). But there are a lot of good center fielders in this league; the team guys ahead of him can all play.

12. Dave HENDERSON, Seattle

The other Henderson.

13. Steve LYONS, Boston

Armas had big year against left-handers, hitting .339 and slugging .636 . . . Armas also was able to advance a runner from first base with nobody out only 6 times in 32 tries, or 19% . . . It's hard to see any strong positives for Lyons. He doesn't hit real good or hit for power or steal bases or shine real bright at any defensive position.

14. Darryl BOSTON, Chicago

Reportedly looked much improved when he came back up at the end of the year . . . What other major league players have had the names of major league cities? Reggie Cleveland is the only one that comes to mind . . .

National League

1. Dale MURPHY, Atlanta (11)

I know you probably won't believe this, but there are Cardinal fans who believe that Willie McGee is a better player than Dale Murphy. I

hear from them all the time. It's kind of like in the fifties there were Phillies fans who insisted that Richie Ashburn was better than Willie Mays. When you step back from the

issue, little things like 30 home runs a year become pretty obvious.

2. Willie MCGEE, St. Louis (1)

Led N.L. in hitting both at home

(.357) and on the road (.350), with 28 stolen bases each place but far more power on the road, up 21 extra base hits to 33 . . . Ranks fifth among active players in career batting average, .308 . . .

3. Von HAYES, Philadelphia

Reportedly going to play first base. One of the signs that a player has gone as far as he's going to go as a hitter is when his season's record is about the same as his career record in seasonal notation. That arrived last year for Hayes, although he still could do better . . .

4. Eddie MILNER, Cincinnati

Fine defensive player, stole 35 bases and scored 82 runs, grounded into only three double plays . . .

5. Kevin BASS, Houston

Led National League in fielding percentage, .997 . . . Hit for good average with 17.3 power/speed number and good defense, but needs to improve command of strike zone to rate higher . . .

6. Larry DYKSTRA or Mookie WILSON, New York

The Indians have a player in their system named Pookie Bernstein. I can hardly wait 'til he reaches the majors, so he can join the All-Star team with Mookie Wilson, Tookie Gilbert, and Cookie Rojas. They'll be managed by the Wookie from Star Wars, and should have the inside track in the voting for Rookie of the Year.

7. Kevin McREYNOLDS, San Diego

Wonder how he'd like to be called Fookie McReynolds, just to help us out . . . at war with his manager, offensive game fell apart. May be being asked to do more than he's really capable of defensively . . .

8. Ken LANDREAUX, Los Angeles

Keep expecting the Dodgers to come up with a center fielder they like better, but they never have . . . hit .389 in the playoffs last year. Before that his lifetime average in post-season play was .160 in 19 games . . .

9. Joe ORSULAK, Pittsburgh

An unquestioned improvement over Marvell Wynne, but still possibly a platoon player. Hit .316 against right-handers, but .215 against lefties. In the position the Pirates are in, they'll probably give him a couple of years to even that out. Has a chance to be in the top five in a couple of years . . .

10. Bob DERNIER, Chicago

Hit just .205 with runners in scoring position . . .

11. Dan GLADDEN, San Francisco

Probably isn't as good as he looked in 1984, or as bad as he looked in 1985. If he can keep his lifetime average where it is (.282), he'll probably make it into the pension fund . . .

12. Mitch WEBSTER, Montreal

Winner of N.L.'s "If Phil Bradley Can Do It, So Can I" award. Showed completely unexpected power, and must be granted a chance to play if he keeps it up. But he is older than Tim Raines, and the odds are that the pitchers are going to catch up to him pretty quickly in '86.

RIGHT FIELDERS

American League

1. Kirk GIBSON, Detroit (7)

Now very similar to Reggie at his peak, but probably just a hair below him due to less power . . . power/speed number of 29.5, secondary average of .404 are his qualifications as the best of a good lot.

2. Jesse BARFIELD, Toronto (5)

Toronto opponents were last in the American League in both doubles (220) and triples (28)—despite the fact that it's an excellent line-drive hitter's park. That's what having an all-Hourtzer outfield will do for you . . . Barfield, who may have the best outfield arm since Clevents, led the majors in outfield assists, and now has 64 in his brief career . . . among the league leaders in secondary average, power/speed number of 24.2 . . .

3. Harold BAINES, Chicago (2)

Led the American League in batting average on the road, .335 . . . has become super-effective against left-handed pitching (for a lefty). In 418 at bats against southpaws over last two years has hit .311 with 16 homers . . .

4. Dave WINFIELD, New York

Could rate first as well as fourth. Stats very similar to George Bell's (936 similarity score) . . . drove in 50 runs after August 1 . . . a note from Craig Christmann, relating to the changed dimensions of Yankee Stadium:

I (meaning Christmann) kept track of the home runs hit in Yankee Stadium in 1985 and noted those that would not have left the field of play in 1984. Since I scored all of the Yankees' home games I don't think I missed any. There were only nine home runs which cleared the new fences but not the old ones. Six of the nine were hit by the Yankees, three by their opponents, and five of those six by Dave Winfield. The other was by Don Baylor. The really odd thing is that Dave Henderson of Seattle hit

two of the opponents' three, with Jim Rice hitting the other.

Fourteen runs scored on those nine home runs; of those only five would probably have scored with the old dimensions. The results of the games in which these home runs were hit would not have been changed if they had been played with the old dimensions . . .

Craig Christmann

Thank you, Craig. Craig also says that he does not think that the changed dimensions altered positioning in the outfield (hence no secondary effects), and estimates that the net effect of the change was to increase runs scored in Yankee Stadium by 1.3% . . .

5. Dwight EVANS, Boston

Hit just .177 with runners in scoring position . . . had 21 hits off of or over the left field wall in Fenway, most on the team . . . only Boston regular with a secondary average of .300 (.387) . . .

I made note of three occasions last year on which major league hitters were quoted as saying something quite interesting about the way that one hitter supposedly helps the hitters around him. In a March 19, 1985 Kansas City Times article by Tracy Ringolsby, Eddie Murray was quoted upon the effect of Fred Lynn's joining the Orioles, *"Everybody keeps asking me, 'How good is he going to make me and Cal?'"* Murray said. *"I'm not going to see any different pitches. The difference is going to be somebody to drive us (Ripken and Murray) in."*

The second quote was by Dwight Evans on April 17, 1985, during a pre-game interview with Kevin Wall, Kansas City sports broadcaster, who was asked to talk about the "strategic advantages of batting second." *"Well, I've answered a lot of questions about that,"* said Dwight, *"but you know I walk a hundred times a year.*

If they're coming in to me, it sure doesn't show. It's great to have Jim Rice and Easler and Armas behind me, and it's great to have Wade Boggs up ahead of me, but the pitchers are still trying to get ME out."

I didn't make a good note about the third, but it was by Willie McGee in *Sports Illustrated* late in the season. The quote may be a little inexact, but, addressing the impact of batting behind Vince Coleman, Willie said *"Sure, Vince has been getting some fastballs for me, but hey, seeing a lot of fastballs doesn't make you a .350 hitter unless you know what to do with 'em when you see 'em."*

What all three players were saying is exactly what I've been saying for years—that it just doesn't make that much difference who is batting behind you or who is batting ahead of you. Both Evans and Murray are very disciplined hitters, and thus hitters who have the maximum ability to protect their pitch selection by themselves. Other players, less disciplined hitters, might be more inclined to buy the notion that it makes a big difference. All three statements were worded in such a way as to say not only that it wasn't true, but that it's just something we hear way too much about. There is no evidence that it is any easier to hit with a great hitter up behind you than without one. And it is *writers,* not *players,* who have promulgated this myth about it making a big difference.

6. Tom BRUNANSKY, Minnesota

Batting averages for May through August: .329, .320, .213, .190, .181. Recovered a little (.241) in September . . .

7. Mike DAVIS, Oakland

Like Brunansky, started out gangbusters (9 homers in April) . . . Oakland park hurt his statistics, as it usually does . . . 1986 is the pivotal year of his career. If he can repeat his 1985 season, he's going to be a very fine player.

8. Lee LACY, Baltimore

Aged 36, set career highs in at bats (498), walks (39), strikeouts (95); most of other career highs set in 1984, at age 35 . . .

9. Reggie JACKSON, California

His career record for strikeouts (2,385) will not be broken this century . . . secondary average remains high, .407 in '85, although batting average has settled down . . . adjusted range factor was very, very low, 1.63.

10. Al COWENS, Seattle

Didn't steal a base for the first time in his career . . . crossed 100 home runs last year, will move past 1500 hits this year . . .

11. Darryl MOTLEY, Kansas City

Here's a study for you: Do World Series heroes who have struggled during the season tend to get going the next year? Motley looks like a good hitter, is real strong and has a quick bat. He struggled all year but hit .357 (5/14) with two homers in post-season play. Will that give him some confidence, let the season end on a positive note? It seems possible, but who knows?

12. Paul HOUSEHOLDER, Milwaukee

Who was wearing his uniform in September? Didn't do anything all year—went into September hitting .223 with 3 homers, 14 RBI, then hit .321 with 8 homers, 20 RBI, .613 slugging percentage after Robin Yount missed September for an operation . . . if he can have two months a year like that, he's going to be able to hold a job . . .

13. George VUKOVICH & Carmen CASTILLO, Cleveland

Castillo was all right (4.50 runs created per 27 outs), but Vukovich is a glove man at a hitter's position (3.41 runs created per 27 outs) . . .

14. George WRIGHT, Texas

Stats speak for themselves . . .

National League

1. Dave PARKER, Cincinnati (7)

He had a fine season, but I didn't think it was an MVP year. He led the N.L. in grounding into double plays (26) and was 5 for 18 as a base stealer. With the exception of the 24 intentional walks, his strikeout to walk ratio was almost 3–1, and he made ten errors in right field, second in the N.L. . . . despite the drug cloud, he has a chance to go into the Hall of Fame. History forgets an awful lot. Thirty years from now, Dave's stats will still be exactly what they are, but there's a good chance that not one sportswriter in twenty would be able to tell you why he went into a decline phase in the years 1980–1984. On the other hand, as time passes everything else about him might tend to be forgotten *except* the fact that he messed up a super career with drugs. History simplifies, but nobody can get which simplifications time will choose.

2. Darryl STRAWBERRY, New York (5)

Marvelous season, apart from the injury time-out . . . no major leaguer reached 30/30 (30 homers and 30 stolen bases) last year; Strawberry would have passed it easily without the injury. There were eight major leaguers who hit 20 homers and stole 20 bases, the most in several years; there have now been 109 seasons of 20 homers and 20 SB in major league history. There were five such seasons from 1900–1950, and have been 104 since 1950. Bobby Bonds had ten 20/20 seasons; no one else has had more than six. Active leaders are Andre Dawson (five), Reggie Jackson and Don Baylor (four), and Toby Harrah and Cesar Cedeno (three) . . .

3. Mike MARSHALL, Los Angeles

Lost his speed early in his career, went 3/13 as a base stealer . . . Although he hit fairly well in LA, his .295 average with 28 homers, 95 RBI in Dodger Stadium is equivalent to about .310 with 32 homers, 105 RBI in another park. In other words, it's close to being a Dale Murphy season . . . Had exceptional second half . . .

4. Keith MORELAND, Chicago

Again, his stats away from Wrigley Field aren't much—.272 with 3 homers—but he has improved a great deal in the last couple of years. His 12 for 15 performance as a base stealer is remarkable for a player who had 5 stolen bases in seven previous years, and his 68/58 strikeout/walk ratio is a dramatic one-year improvement from the 34/71 of the previous year . . . Turns 32 early in the year . . .

5. Tony GWYNN, San Diego

One of five N.L. players who was among the league leaders in batting both at home (.326) and on the road (.307) . . . the five were McGee, Parker, Raines, Guerrero and Gwynn.

6. Chili DAVIS, San Francisco

Talented player, seems to be sort of biding his time, waiting for San Francisco to get rid of him so he can show people how good he is . . .

7. Andre DAWSON, Montreal

Hit .331 with runners in scoring position, but .227 with the bases empty, even more extreme than his 1984 data (.281 with runners in scoring position, .217 with bases empty, credit Brent MacInnes with 1985 data, Elias with 1984).

8. Glen WILSON, Philadelphia

If it wasn't for the 102 RBI, the season wouldn't impress you. He did hit 39 doubles, second in the league to Parker, but he also grounded into 24 double plays, second in the league to Parker. He committed 12 outfield errors, most in the majors (Parker was second in N.L. here). He also led in outfield assists (18), but his K/W data was awful 117/35. He's all right; he can play a little. But I put the season in a class with Hubie Brooks and Tony Gwynn: the season looks good if you don't look too close . . .

9. Andy VAN SLYKE, St. Louis

Career totals as projected by Brock6 are unimpressive: 1,816 games, 1,299 hits, 143 home runs, .257 average . . . I noted Mike Shannon, Cardinal broadcaster, as saying (August 1) that "one thing that drives Whitey crazy about Andy is all the called strikes that he looks at." One of the odd things about Whitey Herzog is that we hear this often about him, how he likes his hitters to be aggressive, but his taste in players, particularly marginal players, does not reflect this. He always keeps on his bench players like Steve Braun, Mike Jorgensen and Gene Tenace who walk a great deal, and many of his trades, such as the David Green/Jack Clark trade and the Ozzie/Templeton trade, trade out aggressive hitters and trade in selective hitters, among the other things that they accomplish. So Whitey's teams usually walk a lot, as they did last year, and his personnel do not reflect the things that he says.

10. Mike BROWN, Pittsburgh

Waited a long time to get his chance (he is older than Tony Gwynn or Chili Davis), but he's a fine line-drive hitter with power. Definitely expect him to move up in the rankings next season . . .

11. Jerry MUMPHREY, Houston

Doesn't really hit enough to make it as a right fielder. With Bass moving into center, the Astros should be looking for a young Mike Brown, a hitter trapped in the minors or on the bench somewhere.

12. Claudell WASHINGTON & Brad KOMMINSK, Atlanta

Komminsk had decent secondary average, grounded into only four double plays, but just hasn't hit the way his minor league stats show that he is capable of hitting, and the way he will have to hit to play major league ball. Washington hit well in the platoon role, but his defense is pretty awful.

DESIGNATED HITTERS

1. Ruppert JONES, California (6)

First time in his career he has had productive seasons back to back . . . odd thing about designated hitters is that one would think that, with the job being one dimensional, it would be easier to tell the best from the worst, but in fact it is all but impossible. The raw stats of the #14 man (Sheets) don't look all that much worse than those of the #1 man (Jones), and indeed there is probably almost a 50% chance that Sheets will have a better season than Jones does. This happens because, with the prejudice against being a DH, the teams are still reluctant to take young players and make designated hitters out of them, even if it is obvious that that is what their skills dictate, such as with Ron Kittle, Ken Phelps and Mike Stenhouse.

2. Hal McRAE, Kansas City (6)

The only career designated hitters to amount to anything have been these next two men—McRae and Baylor. McRae has 1,346 career games as a designated hitter, hundreds more than anyone else. Baylor has 951 games as a DH—six years' worth—and he is in second place, two hundred ahead of anybody else. Behind Baylor are Willie Horton (753), Rico Carty (653), Cliff Johnson (651) and Andre Thornton (607)—most unimpressive figures after 13 years of designated hitting. McRae and Baylor hold all the DH records, and in view of the fact that there are no bright young talents in the profession, it seems likely that they will hold them all for several years.

3. Don BAYLOR, New York (1)

Holds A.L. record for being hit by pitch, 192 times. His 24 HBP in 1985 also tied the A.L. record for one season . . .

4. Gorman THOMAS, Seattle (1)

Mariner DH's led the league in home runs (39), walks (101), runs scored (94), strikeouts (155) and slugging percentage (.445), but had the worst batting average (.221). But their secondary average was over .400 . . . Thomas' 32 HR was the top figure for one DH . . .

I did a study a few years ago (Rangers comment, 1984) which suggested that right-handed hitters might tend to reach base on errors significantly more often than left-handed hitters. Jeff Welch studied this issue with the Mariner scoresheets, and did not confirm the conclusion. Although Gorman, a right-handed hitter, did lead the team in reaching base on errors (ten times), the team totals were almost the same, with Mariner right-handed hitters reaching base safely on errors once every 64.4 at bats, and left-handed hitters once every 66.2 at bats. Well, the right-handers did reach a little bit more often, but his study found much more of a separation between fast players and slow players. Slow players, like Thomas, reached base on error once every 70.1 at bats; fast players reached once every 60.1.

5. Mike EASLER, Boston

Hit just .208 in the late innings of close games, .208 with 1 home run and 4 RBI in 96 at bats . . . only Sox regular to hit better on the road (.275 with 12 homers, 43 RBI) than in Fenway (.249 with 4 and 31) . . .

6. Dave KINGMAN, Oakland

Hit his career average, .238 . . . struck out 114 times to push his career total to 1,690. With 67 more Ks he will pass Killebrew, Mantle, Brock and Bonds to move into fourth place of all time.

After the development of similarity scores, I spent three or four days trying to design a study that would evaluate the run effect of strikeouts as opposed to other outs. The difference between a strikeout and an ordinary out is difficult to detect in run production, for not only is the difference very small, but it also tends to be cross-correlated with several other features. Strikeouts are inversely related to batting average but directly related to home runs, on balance tending to correlate positively with runs scored (that is, high-strikeout teams tend to score more runs than low-strikeout teams).

I thought that I could isolate the effect of strikeouts from these other features, and I still think I can, by adapting similarity scores. In principle, one can select teams which have similar statistics in all other areas but different strikeout totals, thus creating a separation in strikeouts as we would, for example, in stolen bases. However, this doesn't work with strikeouts because of the strong cross-correlations; the high strikeout teams selected will still tend to hit for a lower average with more home runs. Not many more, but enough to confuse the issue.

I invented a way to get around this by adjusting the similarity selection for the previous error. For illustration, let's start with the 1977 Baltimore Orioles, who struck out a lot. The most-similar team with a low strikeout total was the 1979 Yankees:

	HR	SO	B. Avg.
1977 Orioles	148	945	.261
1979 NYY	150	590	.226
Error	+ 2		+5

Of course, the comparison was not based on two categories, but on the whole light show, but you get the idea. Since we have an error of +2 HR and +5 in batting average, we make counter-adjustments to the next team before we make the selection as most-similar. The next team is the 1977 Boston Red Sox, who hit .281 with 213 home runs—but instead of looking for that, we look for a low-strikeout team which hits .276 with 211 home runs.

This helps—yet even so, it doesn't yield the near-perfect comparison groups that are needed to isolate the small effect of the strikeouts. I made several attempts, and came up with comparison groups ranging from 30 teams each to over 200 teams each. The best effort had 51 teams in each group. These are their totals:

| | Strikeout | |
	Low	High
At Bats	278,211	280,512
Hits	72,035	71,231
Total Bases	107,669	108,086
Doubles	11,762	12,043
Triples	1,901	1,969
Home Runs	6,690	6,958
Walks	27,952	27,442
Strikeouts	36,508	49,482
Stolen Bases	6,092	6,564
Batting Ave.	.259	.254
Slugging %	.387	.385
RUNS	35,489	34,822

There is a separation between the two groups of about 13,000 strikeouts, compared to which the other differences between the groups are minor—but not minor enough, not inconsequential. There is a difference of 531 runs created between the two groups, as well as a separation of 667 actual runs.

However, to the extent that one can draw any conclusions at all, that conclusion would be that the difference between 13,000 strikeouts and 13,000 ordinary outs is about 136 runs—or one run per 100 outs.

The other studies, though equally troubled, tend to lead toward the same conclusion—about one run is lost for each 100 strikeouts (as opposed to other outs).

In the past I have written that, because strikeouts are not double play balls, and because double play balls are so costly, it was likely that a strikeout could actually be considered as preferable to another out. On the basis of the best available evidence now, this does not appear to be the case. It appears that the strikeout does have a true negative value, albeit a very slight one.

Very slight, indeed. Strikeouts account for about 20% of outs for an average non-pitcher; for Dave Kingman, they account for 37%. The difference over the course of Kingman's career is a little less than 800 outs. The cost of that? About 8 runs.

7. Roy SMALLEY & Randy BUSH, Minnesota

Kansas City and Minnesota designated hitters tied in batting average (.286), doubles (39) and home runs (19); Twin DHs were very slightly better in other categories, except RBI . . . Funderburk apparently will do the job against left-handers this year. He reminds me a great deal of Cliff Johnson as a hitter.

8. Larry PARRISH, Texas

Ranger Bill Stein was the A.L.'s best pinch hitter in 1984, going 10 for 24 (.417). No one else was over .300 in 20 or more tries. Since joining the Rangers in 1981 Stein is now 39 for 109 (.358) as a pinch hitter . . . my friend Jim Carothers has an All-Star team of people like Dick Schofield, Sr., Phil Roof and Bill Henry, who managed to stay in the major leagues for a long time despite modest accomplishments. Stein is becoming a candidate for the team; he's now a fourteen-year vet with 751 career hits . . . the two teams with the best pinch hitters in 1985 were Pittsburgh (.286) and Texas (.288 with 31 RBI in 146 AB) . . . Parrish is good hitter when healthy, and may wind up as the Ranger third baseman for a couple of years if he is healthy and Buechele doesn't pan out.

9. Ron KITTLE, Chicago

Hit 16 homers in 191 at bats as a DH in '85 . . . Finally seemed to get his jock put on straight last August, and belted 12 home runs good for 30 RBI after September 1 . . .

10. Andre THORNTON, Cleveland

Also finished the season torrid, driving in even more runs in September (35) than Kittle. Hit .321 after August 1 with 16 homers and 57 RBI in 55 games . . . Indian designated hitters hit just .231 with a .374 slugging percentage (12th in the league) but led the league with 117 RBI . . . more similar stats: Andre Thornton and Don Baylor, 1985 . . .

11. Al OLIVER & Cliff JOHNSON, Toronto

Toronto designated hitters drove in only 78 runs, last in the league . . .

12. Ted SIMMONS, Milwaukee

Had a better year with the bat, had a fine 57–32 strikeout/walk ratio. Still has to hit better than he did last year to be considered quality DH . . .

13. Nelson SIMMONS, Detroit

Just 22 years old, should be an outstanding major league hitter, whether as a DH or outfielder. DH'd 31 games last season (Darrell Evans and John Grubb tied for the team lead, with 33), and didn't hit nearly as well as a DH as he did as an outfielder. Hit .216 as a DH, .259 as an outfielder.

14. Larry SHEETS, Baltimore

Could be a very effective Baltimore platoon player, but will have to become a little more patient. I wouldn't be at all surprised if he was the league's best DH this year . . .

AMERICAN LEAGUE STARTING PITCHERS

Right Handers

1. Bret SABERHAGEN, Kansas City (7)

The Royals won 24 of his 32 starts, the highest percentage in the American League . . . the Yankees scored far more runs with Guidry starting, but won 23 of 33 . . .

2. Dave STIEB, Toronto (5)

Leibrandt and Stieb, who were 1–2 in the league in ERA, were also the league's top two worm-killers, tying for the lead in assists, with 53 apiece.

Chuck Waseleski figured for me the number of "quality starts" for each pitcher. (I guess you know that stat; I'd give you the definition except that I'm not sure of it.) Anyway, he sent these along with the record of the team in games started by each man. It's strange, but the relationship seems very weak; Dave Stieb, for example, had far more quality starts than the other Blue Jays:

	QS/GS	Pct.
Stieb	26/36	.72
Alexander	15/36	.42
Key	12/32	.38
Clancy	8/23	.35

But when you look at team wins and losses, you get exactly the opposite picture:

	W–L	Pct.
Clancy	16–7	.696
Key	20–12	.625
Alexander	22–14	.611
Stieb	17–19	.472

This material is so surprising that I suppose I should mention the possibility of error, but Chuck is very careful and the material agrees with what I've seen printed. Anyway, it seems strange that the more quality starts a pitcher had, the less often his team won. The data around the rest of the league is far better, but there are still a lot of anomalies. For example:

Baltimore starter Mike Boddicker had his team's highest percentage of quality starts (17/32), but the Orioles had a worse record with him pitching (13–19) than with any other starter.

Boston starter Bob Ojeda had his team's highest percentage of quality starts (13/22), but the Red Sox had a worse record with him pitching (9–12, one tie) than with any other starter.

Cleveland only had two pitchers with 20 starters, but of the two, Heaton had a higher percentage of quality starts (16/33) while Blyleven had a higher percentage of wins for the team.

Well, any performance measure has anomalies, I guess; it doesn't invalidate the statistic that it fails to predict wins and losses in all cases. It's just that I would have expected the relationship to be closer. The connection on a team level is tighter.

3. Bert BLYLEVEN, Minnesota (2)

Remains easy to run on . . . 1985 was the fourth time in his career, but the first time since 1974, that he both won and lost 15 or more games.

4. Jack MORRIS, Detroit

See Hall of Fame article.

5. Mike WITT, California

After a slow start was 13–4 over the last four months.

6. Tom SEAVER, Chicago

Had the highest percentage of quality starts in the American League (25/33 or 76%). In comparison with National Leaguers, of course, quality starts discriminate against the American League pitcher at the top end of the scale, inasmuch as there are more hitters, more runs, and fewer games when you can hold the other side to three . . . Seaver was 15–6 in his quality starts, but won just once in

his eight games that weren't quality starts.

7. Mike MOORE, Seattle

Struck out 75 batters in the last two months of the year . . . another study by Jeff Welch shows that Moore retains his effectiveness on repeated trips through the lineup far better than any other Mariner pitcher. Going through the lineup the first time, his ERA in 1985 was 3.31; the second time 4.64. But going through the lineup the third time, it drops to 3.34, and the fourth time, to 2.33. So that shows excellent durability, which is something you've got to see about him anyway. He probably throws harder in the seventh, eighth and ninth than anybody in the American League . . . uses only 14.9 pitches per inning, or 134 a game, on the average, the lowest figure among the Mariner starters . . .

8. Doyle ALEXANDER, Toronto

Now has 149 career wins . . . set a career high for strikeouts in 1984, and broke it last year in his fifteenth season in the major leagues . . .

One interesting thing about quality starts is looking at who had how many wins that *weren't* quality starts. Most major league rotation starters had two or three; Doyle Alexander had the most in the majors, with eight. I don't know how fair that is; it may be that he had some games where he stayed in and allowed the fourth run with a big lead. The Blue Jays were 38–42, almost .500, when their starting pitcher did not have a quality start, the best in the majors except that the Yankees were 39–43. A few pitchers didn't have any wins that were not quality starts, including Dwight Gooden, Walt Terrell and Danny Jackson.

9. Dan PETRY, Detroit

Losing his stuff fast; trying to adapt and become a successful finesse pitcher. He's making it work so far.

10. Charlie HOUGH, Texas

Would have gone about 17–13 with league-average offensive support . . . your basic knuckleballer, never gets hurt, gets better as he goes along . . . why there aren't more of them, I'll never know.

11. Oil Can BOYD, Boston

Did not pick a runner off first base, but only 16 or 35 runners who attempted to steal against him were successful . . .

12. Walt TERRELL, Detroit

Did what the Tigers asked him to do.

13. Don SUTTON, California

Set a major league record with 20 consecutive seasons of 100 or more strikeouts . . .

14. Phil NIEKRO, New York

Holds the major league record for career wild pitches, with 207. I don't know about you, but personally, I'm awfully glad I'm not the one who has to keep track of that stuff . . .

Did you know that Phil Niekro is five years older than Denny McLain? Phil Niekro is older than Ron Santo. Phil Niekro is older than Joe Torre. Phil Niekro is older than Lou Brock or Carl Yastrzemski. Phil Niekro is older than Joe Pepitone. Phil Niekro is older than Richie Allen.

Jeff Torborg was dismissed in his third season as manager of Cleveland; that was seven years ago. Phil Niekro is older than Jeff Torborg, two and a half years older. Phil Niekro is older than Bobby Cox or Pat Corrales.

Do you remember Zoilo Versalles, who was the American League's MVP 21 years ago? Phil Niekro is older than Zoilo Versalles. Do you remember Jose Azcue, the great Azcue? Phil Niekro is older than Joe Azcue. Phil Niekro is older than Bernie Allen, Gene Alley, Mike Shannon, Dave Nicholson or Roger Repoz. Phil Niekro is older than Tony LaRussa, Doug Rader or Ken Harrelson of the White Sox.

We can do this by teams . . . let's do the Cardinals. You probably know all the current Cardinals; Steve Braun is the oldest of them. Mike Torrez, who started with the Cardinals and then pitched for everybody else before dropping out of the game, was older than Steve Braun. Rick Wise, another peripatetic pitcher of similar talent, was older and earlier than Torrez. Steve Carlton is older than Wise, for whom he was once traded. Jose Cardenal, who patrolled the Cardinal outfield behind Carlton, was older than Steve. Tim McCarver, who caught for that team, is older than Jose Cardenal. Ray Sadecki, a teammate of McCarver's in his early days, a twenty-game winner on the 1964 Worlds Champions, was older than McCarver. You may remember Dick Nen, who hit the gigantic home run which buried the Cardinals the year before that, 1963. Nen was older than Sadecki. If you think hard enough, you may remember Julio Gotay, the Cardinal's shortstop before they traded for Dick Groat. Gotay, who was most famous as the man who dropped his mail in a green-painted trash bin for several weeks before Curt Flood discovered it, was older than Dick Nen. Von McDaniel, the Cardinals' pitching sensation of 1957, was older than Julio Gotay. But Phil Niekro is older than Von McDaniel.

Phil Niekro is older than Claude Osteen, the veteran pitching coach, or Milt Pappas. Phil Niekro is older than Sammy Ellis, one of the Yankee pitching coaches, or Dick Ellsworth. Phil Niekro is older than Tommie Aaron, except that Aaron is dead and you can't get any older than dead. I remember a few years ago at spring training, when Tommie was a coach with the Braves, he was hitting fungoes one day, his claim to alphabetical supremacy stretched across his back. Susie and I were sitting and watching him. A little woman about fifty yelled out from behind us, sounding for all the world like a character in the background of an old movie, "Haank. Oh, Haannk." She had a camera. At length, Tommie turned around, and gave a dutiful, patient half-smile. She took a picture and yelled, "Oh, thank you, Hank." Then he died, a year or so later.

You remember Don Kessinger? Phil Niekro is older than Kessinger or Beckert. Glenn Beckert got the job as Cubs' second baseman after Ken Hubbs was killed in a plane crash in the spring of 1964. Phil Niekro is three years older than Ken Hubbs would be. Phil Niekro is older than Felix Millan or Sonny Jackson or Rico Carty. Phil Niekro is older than Martin Luther King or either of the Kennedys were at the time of their assasinations. Phil Niekro is older than Boog Powell. Phil Niekro is more than ten years older than I am.

Funny thing, though. He don't look a day over 60.

15. Mike BODDICKER, Baltimore

For some reason the running game got out of hand against him, 39 OSB in 32 starts (only American League starter allowing more than one stolen base a game) . . .

16. Mark GUBICZA, Kansas City

Had 2–0 record, 0.55 ERA against the Angels. Turn that around and the Angels are division champions . . . was 5–2 with 3.32 ERA on grass fields after poor grass record as a rookie.

17. Ron ROMANICK, California

Don't care much for him as a pitcher. He's a control type pitcher without great control, sort of a groundball pitcher but not really, a right hander with a so-so move to first. I give him almost no chance of winning over a period of years . . . Angels won 20 of his 31 starts, their best percentage with any starter.

18. Mike SMITHSON, Minnesota

Only American League pitcher to hit ten batters with pitches, and he was way up there, with 15. The last pitcher to hit that many batters in a year was Pete Brobey in 1975 . . . incidentally, major league hit batsmen were up 5% last year, with the increase coming in the National League.

19. Joe COWLEY, New York

Gave up 29 home runs in just 160 innings.

20. Jim CLANCY, Toronto

Blue Jays turned only 15 double plays in his 23 starts, lowest ratio in American League.

21. Storm DAVIS, Baltimore

The Orioles won 16 of Storm's 28 starts, their best winning percentage with any pitcher. And therein lies the problem, for it is simply not a matter of finding a replacement for one or two ineffective pitchers, but rather a matter of finding leadership and stability in a rudderless staff. If *somebody* doesn't win you can do something about it, replace him with somebody else. But if everybody wins half the time and loses half the time, then what?

22. Moose HAAS, Milwaukee

Excellent control, good K/W ratios. Now has 91 career wins.

23. Danny DARWIN, Milwaukee

Run support the poorest in the American League, 3.38 runs per start. Allowed 34 opposition home runs, tying Scott McGregor for the most in the majors.

24. Al NIPPER, Boston

Second-toughest pitcher in the American League to run on in 1985, with 8 OSB in 25 starts . . .

25. Chris CODIROLI, Oakland

Has had exactly the same winning percentage (.500) and ERA (4.46) in two of the last three years. Was 12–12 with a 4.46 ERA in '83, 14–14 with a 4.46 ERA last year.

26. Kirk McCASKILL, California

Opposition stole only 8 bases in his 29 starts, making him the toughest major league pitcher to run on in '85 . . .

27. John BUTCHER, Minnesota

Wonder what the announcers say when he faces Dusty Baker? . . . Had 6.49 ERA on artificial turf, 3.42 on grass fields . . .

28. Ed WHITSON, New York

Remarkably, the Yankees won 19 of his 30 starts, 5th best percentage in the league . . .

29. Jim SLATON, California

Angels turned 35 double plays in his 24 starts, highest rate in baseball (1.46 DP per game) . . . very tough to run on, which keeps DP in order . . .

30. Ray BURRIS, Milwaukee

Career record of 102–127 . . . I wonder how many pitchers have won 100 games in their careers with winning percentages below .450? I wouldn't think there were very many.

31. Bill SWIFT, Seattle

Great name for a pitcher, and for once he really is. He and Oddibe are the first players from the 1984 draft to surface in the majors; Swift was the second player taken, behind Shawn Abner. Mariners' top selections in recent years have been excellent—Mike Moore in '82, Spike Owen in '83. Swift looked like a ma-

jor league pitcher at times . . . had seventy 0–2 counts on hitters, but allowed them to hit .271 after being down 0–2. By contrast, Mike Moore had 177 0–2 counts on hitters (by far the most on the Mariners), and held hitters to .153 batting average after having them 0–2 . . .

32. Dennis MARTINEZ, Baltimore

Orioles scored phenomenal 6.16 runs a game for him, best in the major leagues . . . why is Dennis Martinez still in the major leagues?

33. Ken SCHROM, Minnesota

Was 7–5 with decent ERA through June, but 2–7 the rest of the way.

34. Burt HOOTON, Texas

Had 7.89 ERA after the All-Star break.

35. Pete VUKOVICH, Milwaukee

Second-easiest American League pitcher to run on, being hit for 21 OSB in 22 starts. Granted, with a pitcher with a 5.51 ERA, this is sort of like pointing out that a pig doesn't know how to use a napkin properly.

Left Handers

1. Ron GUIDRY, New York (12)

His career winning percentage, .694, is the best ever for a pitcher with 200 or more decisions. It is likely that he will lose that distinction before the end of his career—two losses would do it—but it's still an impressive accomplishment . . . offensive support was outstanding (5.39 runs a game).

2. Charlie LEIBRANDT, Kansas City (2)

Seems to pitch his best ball in cold weather. Posted a 1.69 ERA in April, 1.43 in September, plus of course he has been brilliant in postseason play, although his record to some degree disguises this . . .

3. Jimmy KEY, Toronto

Has some Tommy John characteristics but is missing a few. His DP support was the best of any left-

hander in baseball, his motion is extremely efficient and he doesn't waste pitches—big factors in the ability to win with his kind of stuff. But his ability to cut off the running game is so-so, and he was hit for 22 home runs last year. A ground-ball pitcher can't be a big winner unless he improves in those areas.

4. Danny JACKSON, Kansas City

I wanted to say a couple of things about pitching motions, or Why I Love To Watch Danny Jackson Pitch. Let's start by talking about the trailing leg. When a right-handed pitcher starts toward home plate, he steps out with the left leg, committing the momentum of his whole body forward. Almost all pitchers will plant the lead foot, push off the other foot onto the lead ankle and pivot the entire body off of that ankle, with the lead leg

being stiff. When the pitcher's torso—his main body weight— passes from behind the front leg to ahead of it, the trailing leg has to fly forward to maintain the balance of the whole.

The way in which the trailing leg does this is interesting for many different reasons. It is sort of an "index" to what the pitcher is doing. As a general rule, the faster the torso moves forward, the more violently the trailing leg has to jerk forward to counter-balance it.

Most pitchers—not just some, but most—will kick the leg less energetically when throwing an off-speed pitch than when throwing a fastball. Pitchers have to carefully disguise everything that happens *before* the pitch is thrown, so as to avoid tipping the hitter about the pitch. But after the pitch is thrown it doesn't make any difference, so they don't bother to disguise it. Thus the movement of the trailing leg, the last part of the delivery, is often the only thing that a fan can see which will tell him, even up in the cheap seats, what the pitching patterns are.

The movement of the trailing leg is an indicator of how hard a pitcher throws—not a perfect indicator, but a valuable indicator. A real old guy, like Phil Niekro or Woodie Fryman, may not throw the leg forward at all, but just bend from the waist and step up at the conclusion of the pitch. If you see that, you know the guy isn't throwing 80 miles an hour. When a pitcher is warming up, you can tell how hard he is working by watching the trailing leg. Many relief pitchers will come in and just flip the ball to the plate a few times, not working hard enough to make themselves throw the trailing leg, whereas Lee Smith will come in and throw just as hard as he will throw when the game starts.

Most importantly, *the movement of the trailing leg is often the first indicator of when a pitcher is tired*. When a pitcher gets tired, he'll start to conserve energy by diminishing the force with which he propels himself forward; the end result of this will be a dramatic reduction in the movement of the trailing leg. *Many managers pay no attention to this, and will allow a pitcher to stay in the game, even with men on base and the game on the line, when it is very obvious, from the movement of the trailing leg, that the pitcher is tired*. The pitcher disguises everything he does before the delivery, and after the delivery the manager, like everybody else, moves his eyes to follow the pitch. I don't know how many times I have seen pitchers lose games within three to eight batters after they started dragging the trailing leg, because the manager was waiting for the arm to drop down, or waiting for the pitches to start getting up in the strike zone, or waiting for something else to happen which is a very unreliable indicator of a tired pitcher.

Then, on the other hand, there is Danny Jackson. Danny's delivery is unique; there is no other major league pitcher with a delivery that is even vaguely similar. Danny starts out with a very long stride, and plants his right leg way out in front of him. But as he vaults forward, rather than pivoting the body weight on the right ankle, he bends the right leg at the knee, so that when the arm comes around the leg acts as a "spring" to absorb the shock of the delivery. When the arm comes forward, the force of the delivery hurls his torso downward into his knees, both feet being planted, rather than forward into the ankle. His center of balance never does pass in front of the right leg, thus there is no need to throw the trailing leg forward. He completes his delivery facing directly at the plate, sometimes almost collapsing onto the right knee, but usually springing up off the right knee.

There is nothing like it. At least in the American League; there are a few National League pitchers whose deliveries I'm not familiar with. Sometimes when I describe it people say, "Oh, like Tom Seaver," because Tom Seaver lectures on absorbing the shock of the pitching motion with the knees. But Seaver flies off the mound; Seaver uses the large muscles of the leg to vault forward, thus reducing the strain on the arm. It's not similar at all. The only pitcher I know of who had a somewhat similar delivery was Koufax.

Anyway, because there is no radical alteration in the pitcher's center of balance, there are no sudden movements to adjust and rebalance the body. This makes the delivery, rather than being a series of related jerks and spasms (to overstate the case), into one continuous, fluid, graceful movement. How it will affect him over a period of years, how it will affect his arm and his knees, this I wouldn't pretend to know. But it's gorgeous. I mean, sometimes he winds up a little off-balance and looks like he's going to wrench his knee, but most of the time it's a smooth, beautiful, reliable delivery. Make it a point to watch.

5. Britt BURNS, Chicago

I don't know how seriously to take his comment about not being able to repeat at this level, 18 wins. The 18 wins don't really go with the 3.96 ERA, and he did pick up six wins that weren't quality starts, plus one win in a short relief outing. Still, his strikeouts were way up (172; pre-

vious high was 133). Obviously, the Yankees don't believe his shoulder is hanging by a thread and his back hurts.

6. Frank VIOLA, Minnesota

Opponents stole only 12 bases in his 36 starts, one of the best ratios in baseball . . .

7. Teddy HIGUERA, Milwaukee

Small man with nice, fluid delivery; is going to win a lot of games over the next ten years if he doesn't hurt his arm. He throws hard, he has control, and he knows what he's trying to do. After the All-Star break he was 10–3 . . . could well be a Cy Young candidate.

8. Bud BLACK, Kansas City

Had 52% quality starts, as opposed to American League average of 47%. 52% was still easily the lowest on the Royals, and I'd have to say that most of those were marginal . . .

9. Frank TANANA, Detroit

Pitched terrific after joining home-town Tigers, 3.34 ERA, strikeout-to-walk ratio almost 4–1 not counting intentional walks, had 16 quality starts in 20 outings.

10. Bob OJEDA, Boston

Kept opponents from scoring a runner from third base with less than two out 21 of 35 times, or 60%, best of any Red Sox starter. Boyd was least successful in this respect (15/39, 38%) . . . opposition base stealers last year were just 5 for 15 against Ojeda, including 4 men who were picked off . . . I suppose he replaced Lynch in the Met pitching plans. He's a better pitcher than Lynch . . .

11. Tim BIRTSAS, Oakland

His 10–6 record is a lie: the man was lousy. In 141 innings he walked 91 men and gave up 18 homers. There's no way in hell a pitcher can do that and win with any consistency. He had only 8 quality starts in 25 outings, the lowest percentage in the American League; four of his wins were not. In his last seven starts he never lasted more than 5⅓ innings, but posted a 4–3 record as his team scored 68 runs.

12. Floyd BANNISTER, Chicago

Since joining Chicago in 1983 has always pitched much better in Comiskey than on the road. ERAs in

Chicago are 3.09, 4.47, 3.61; on the road they're 3.67, 5.16 and 5.90 . . . before last season his winning percentage had been better than that of his team for five straight years. Not much better, to be sure, but better.

13. Scott McGREGOR, Baltimore

Was 5–1 with 3.04 ERA in day games, 9–13 with 5.49 at night . . . combining the last two years his record on artificial turf is 2–7 with an ERA of almost 7.00 . . . got hammered last year, but posted his eighth straight season of 13 or more wins and a winning percentage of at least .500 . . .

14. Bruce HURST, Boston

The Sox scored six runs a game for him and he still had a losing record. I'm sure I've never seen that before. Odd thing . . . the four major league pitchers receiving 5.50 runs a game or more (Dennis Martinez, Bruce Hurst, Ed Whitson and Bill Krueger) all got hammered and compiled a sad 43–42 won-lost mark. Usually the top man is a Cy Young candidate . . . Hurst doesn't have control trouble, yet walked the leadoff man 22 times in 1985, most on the Red Sox . . . picked 11 runners off first base . . .

15. Bill KRUEGER, Oakland

Nobody wins with his kind of K/W ratios—56/69 last year (13 more walks than strikeouts) and 175/207 in his career . . . pitched pretty well after the All-Star break (4–2, 3.09), but he's 28 years old, and it's hard to see anything in his resume that reminds you of Steve Carlton.

16. Neal HEATON, Cleveland

The Indians won only 11 of his 33 starts, the lowest percentage in the American League for a pitcher with 20 or more starts. But the Indians did far worse with Schulze (4/18) and Vern Ruhle (4/16) . . .

17. Matt YOUNG, Oakland

Mariner opponents scored 67 runs against Young with two men out in the inning. By contrast, they scored only 39 against Mike Moore with two out in the inning, and he pitched more innings. Two-out runs accounted for 50% of runs scoring against Young, 39% against Moore.

18. Mike MASON, Texas

There is no apparent reason that he shouldn't be able to pitch, but his season was consistently bad. His ERAs were between 4.24 and 5.45 in every month of the season, at home and on the road, on turf and on grass, in day games and night games. He just didn't get people out.

The only speck of light in his record is that he did post a 0.71 ERA in eight relief appearances; tracking that back, I see that in 12 relief appearances in 1984 he was 3–0 with a 0.95 ERA, as opposed to 4.10 as a starter. So he may be just miscast as a starting pitcher, like Goose Gossage in '76 . . .

19. Mark LANGSTON, Seattle

I know this is hard to believe, but do you know that just *one year ago,* many Seattle fans thought that Mark Langston was a better pitcher than Dwight Gooden?

20. Tim LOLLAR, Boston

Stuff is pretty decent, but his command of it is severely limited. Now thirty years old; we might hope we have heard the last about outstanding left-handers not blooming until they are in their late twenties. What he looks like, really, is a kid who needs to spend two or three years in AAA ball. But it's too late for that . . .

NATIONAL LEAGUE STARTING PITCHERS

Right Handers

1. Dwight GOODEN, New York (12)

Was named number one on every ballot . . . offensive support was excellent, 4.89 runs a game. In his case it makes very little difference; he would have gone about 23–5 with average offensive support.

2. Orel HERSHISER, Los Angeles

Established age/record for winning percentage, .864; winning percentage was the ninth highest of this century and the highest since 1978 (Guidry and Stanley) . . . allowed only 8 home runs in 240 innings, lowest rate of any N.L. starting pitcher.

3. Bryn SMITH, Montreal

Received the best offensive support in the National League, 5.44 runs per start. Would have gone about 15–8 with team-average offensive support . . . all the big winners in the N.L. were among the best supported except John Tudor and Orel Hershiser.

4. Bob WELCH, Los Angeles

The Dodgers won 19 of his 23 starts (83%), the highest percentage in baseball. Gooden was second in the league, 28/35 for 80%, and Hershiser third 25/34 for 74%.

5. Ron DARLING, New York

Goes on a team with Rob Deer, John "Honey" Romano, Les "Sugar" Sweetland, and Slim Love (Personal note to Jim Baker: add Slim Love to your Estel Crabtree List; he was from Love, Missouri) . . . led the league in walks with 114, which gives him something to work on if he wants to get even better . . . perhaps because he is a power pitcher and was much more effective in Shea Stadium in 1984, he did 60% of his pitching last year in New York. But he was 7–1 with a 2.62 ERA on the road.

6. Mario SOTO, Cincinnati

Hit hard by base stealers last year (47 in 36 starts) . . . again led N.L. in home runs allowed, with 30 . . .

He pitched just as well as Tom Browning did. The difference in their won-lost records (20–9 against 12–15) is completely a result of the fact that Browning received much better offensive support (49 extra runs in 2 more starts) . . . pitches consistently better in the grass parks than on the turf ones. I would guess his career ERA in Shea Stadium is probably about 2.20 . . .

7. Danny COX, St. Louis

Very tough to run against (13 OSB in 37 starts).

8. Joaquin ANDUJAR, St. Louis

Now with Oakland. I tend to view the trade as more smoke than substance, with the Cardinals fairly certain to come out ahead as to individual performance, but Oakland likely to have a better 1986 season. Heath is nothing great—31 years old and still rough defensively—but he's a pretty good hitter, throws well and hasn't caught too many games, so he should be able to hold a job and contribute for several years. The problem Andujar has is that because of his personality, managers lose confidence in him when he has a few bad games. As such he could provide a test for Jackie Moore that will be instructive for the rest of us. What will Moore do when Joaquin starts acting up? Conroy has 10–15% chance to be a big star, which may make him the most valuable commodity in the trade.

Joaquin never pitched well in Busch Stadium, going 8–11 and 9–9 there the last two years (17–20), as opposed to 12–3 and 12–3 on the road (24–6). Over the last two years he is 14–2 on grass fields, just 27–24 on turf. So that could help him make it with the A's . . . led National League in hit batsmen, with 11 . . .

9. Lamarr HOYT, San Diego

Cruising through an old guide, I happened to notice a player named Dewey Hoyt. Sure enough, the Baseball Register shows that Lamar

Hoyt's father, Dewey, was a minor league pitcher in 1947 and 1948.

I didn't notice him because of his pitching. I noticed him because the man hit .537, with 22 hits in 41 at bats. You might remember that this Dewey has the famous clause in his contract that makes him some money if he wins the silver bat. He wasn't real close last year, hitting .063.

Dewey Hoyt, Sr., pitched that year for Mooresville in the North Carolina State League, where he was a teammate of the other Hoyt, Hoyt Wilhelm. Hoyt Wilhelm is a famous trivia question because he homered in his first major league at bat, played 20 years in the majors and never homered again. But he could hit some, too, in the minors. With Mooresville in '47, Wilhelm hit .299 and drove in 28 runs in 47 games.

10. Rick SUTCLIFFE, Chicago

Do you realize that the last six Cy Young winners have all dropped to .500 or below in the following seasons? 1982 Cy Young winners Steve Carlton and Pete Vukovich dropped to 15–16 and 0–2 in 1983. 1983 Cy Young winners John Denny and Lamarr Hoyt dropped off to 13–18 and 7–7 in 1984. 1984 Cy Young winners Rick Sutcliffe and Willie Hernandez dropped to 8–8 and 8–10 in 1985 . . . somehow, I get the feeling that Dwight Gooden is not going to go 12–17 this year . . .

11. Andy HAWKINS, San Diego

Double play support was way up last year, tough to run on. Showed big improvement in control, but struck out and walked fewer men in 229 innings last year than he had in 146 innings the year before. It would be tough to name a starting pitcher who had been effective over a period of years striking out less than three men per nine innings.

12. Rick REUSCHEL, Pittsburgh

Had 24 quality outings in 26 starts . . . now has 153 career wins.

13. Mike SCOTT, Houston

Terrific offensive support (5.03 per game) was a key factor in his 18-[?] summer, but he also cut his opposition stolen base rate in half . . . over last two seasons is 15–7 (.682) in Houston, but 8–12 (.400) on the road . . .

14. Eric SHOW, San Diego

Has had terrific ERAs last two seasons on artificial turf, 2.08 and 2.10 (4.00 and 3.54 on grass fields). One reason for this might be that he gives up a lot of home runs (27 in 233 innings) and the turf parks in the N.L. are the tough home-run parks, like the Astrodome and Busch Stadium.

15. Dennis ECKERSLEY, Chicago

Last in league in double play support, 11 in 25 starts. He's been there before . . .

16. Rick MAHLER, Atlanta

Mahler led the N.L. in double play support last year, 50 in 39 starts. He was followed by Joaquin Andujar and Andy Hawkins. What do you notice about them? They all started the year like gangbusters, but faded badly. I wonder if there is any pattern of ground-ball pitchers pitching well early in the season? Also second-toughest N.L. pitcher to run on—remarkable for a right-handed pitcher with little defensive help at catcher.

17. Bill GULLICKSON, Montreal

Now with Cincinnati. In his years at Montreal he had a massive home/road differential. Over the last two years he was 17–5 (.773) with a 2.48 ERA at home, but 9–16 (.360) with an ERA just below 5.00 on the road. In the two years prior to that he was 18–8 (.692) at home, but 11–18 (.379) on the road. In his career he is now 46–20 in Montreal (.697), but 26–41 on the road (.388)—probably baseball's biggest home/road split . . . I'd be a little surprised if he were able to win for the Reds . . .

18. Kevin GROSS, Philadelphia

Still has some trouble controlling the running game, but he was 15–13 last year with lousy offensive support (3.35 runs a start) . . .

19. Nolan RYAN, Houston

Nolan has created 74 errors, which is a great many for a pitcher.

I was wondering what the career record is for a pitcher; apparently nobody really knows. The Official Record book lists records for the American League (55, by Ed Walsh) and National League (64, by Hippo Vaughn), but does not list a record-holder for both leagues combined, as is the normal practice. Ryan had 48 in the American League and was closing rapidly on Walsh's American League record when he returned to the N.L.; he now has 26 in the National League, 12 before he left and 14 since he came back.

However, the 74 is not the record. Hippo Vaughn, who holds the National League record with 64, also pitched in the American League from 1910 to 1912, being charged with an additional 16 errors to give him 80. He also appeared in two games in the A.L. in 1908; I was not able to find out whether he committed any errors then. It is very likely that Vaughn holds the modern record with 80 errors; he does unless somebody had 45 in one league and 40 in the other. Unless somebody tells me otherwise, I will assume that Ryan is six away from annexing another record.

20. Mike KRUKOW, San Francisco

Turned in a fine season, with excellent K/W ratio (150–39, not counting intentional walks) and solid 3.38 ERA, 8–11 record despite dismal support. Pitches much better in San Francisco than on the road (road ERAs last three years—4.45, 5.54 and 5.21, home ERAs—3.45, 3.65, and 2.24) and much better on grass fields than on turf.

21. David PALMER, Montreal

Opponents stole 33 bases in his 23 starts, second worst figure in N.L. His OSB records were just so-so when Carter was there to protect him, and went to hell in a hurry without him.

22. Joe NIEKRO, Houston

Re-signed with the Yankees . . . opponents stole 50 bases in his 32 starts, worst OSB ratio in baseball. The man above (Palmer) was second worst . . . Over the last two years is 15–4 (.789) on grass fields, but 12–21 (.364) on artificial turf . . . led majors with 21 wild pitches thrown . . .

23. John DENNY, Philadelphia

Might be helped by trade to grass park (Cincinnati). Over the last three years he is 11–4 with 2.70 ERA on grass fields, as opposed to 26–23 with ERA not 3.20 on turf. And, of course, all the "grass" games have been on the road . . .

24. Ed LYNCH, New York

Consistent (10–10, 9–8, 10–8), never walks anybody. Probably has the best control in the league, other than Hoyt . . .

25. Jay TIBBS, Cincinnati

Was 0–7 with 5.03 ERA on grass fields, 10–9 with 3.51 ERA on turf . . .

26. Rick RHODEN, Pittsburgh

Didn't have much of a year with the bat, by his own standards (he hit .189) but won the Silver Slugger anyway. Actually, no pitcher had much of a year with the bat; probably the best was Bob Forsch, who hit .244 with two doubles, a triple and a homer for a .400 slugging percentage . . .

27. Charlie HUDSON, Philadelphia

Is becoming a challenge to the detective's old saw about quacking like a duck. He looks like a pitcher, walks like a pitcher, talks like a pitcher and throws in the low 90s, but if he don't start winning some games, he's not going to be pitching very long. He had excellent offensive support last year and finished 8–13. That ain't good enough.

28. Steve BEDROSIAN, Atlanta

Back to the bullpen in Philly.

29. Jim GOTT, San Francisco

Hasn't shown anything too good or too bad yet.

30. Jose DeLEON, Pittsburgh

I'm not saying he was great or anything, but there aren't many pitchers who are going to win with 2.32 runs per start to work with. His offensive support was more than half a run a game worse than any other major league pitcher, and was the worst for any major league pitcher since Ross Baumgarten in 1980 received 2.04 runs per game. Baumgarten was 2–12 . . . DeLeon would have been about 7–14 with league-average offensive support . . . He also was tied for last in the majors in double play support, although that is more or less a function of his ability . . . Had eleven quality starts, but took a 1–6 record in those 11 games.

31. Kurt KEPHSIRE, St. Louis

32. Bill LASKEY, San Francisco

33. Lee TUNNELL, Pittsburgh
OK.

34. Pascual PEREZ, Atlanta
Had only 6 quality starts, the lowest percentage in the majors (27%) . . .

Left Handers

1. John TUDOR, St. Louis (8)
Sportswriters insisted on interpreting Tudor's turnaround as being a result of his slider. When Tudor himself was asked about what had made him so effective, he said it was largely due to working in better circumstances—out of Fenway Park, away from the Pirates, on a good team with a great defense behind him. Sportswriters won't buy that because they won't accept that conditions have the massive impact that they actually do on playing statistics; they assume that if a pitcher has a 3.00-something ERA one year and 1.93 the next, the man himself has to have changed. But Tudor was right— he was *always* a good pitcher, but until 1985 he worked in conditions which disguised his skills. Last year he worked in conditions which emphasized his skills. That's the only difference.

2. Fernando VALENZUELA, Los Angeles (4)
Had probably his best season . . . 2.45 ERA was his best, .630 winning percentage was his best except for the .650 in the strike-shortened 1981 . . . has career record of 5–1, 2.00 ERA in post-season play . . .

3. Tom BROWNING, Cincinnati
Won six games which were not quality starts, most in the National League . . . Reds won 26 of his 38 starts. Only other major league pitcher to start 26 victories was Gooden (28) . . .

4. Dave DRAVECKY, San Diego
Very consistent. Has had 2.93 ERAs twice in a row. Has had winning percentage over .500, but not much over .500, all four of his major league seasons. Now 30, he established career highs last year in innings (215) and strikeouts (105) . . . very poor hitter . . .

5. Jerry REUSS, Los Angeles
Toughest N.L. pitcher to run on in 1985, with opponents stealing only 10 bases in his 33 starts. This man has had more comebacks than Rocky, and now is up to 192 career wins.

6. Bob KNEPPER, Houston
Has had two solid seasons in a row for the first time; now has 97 career wins. His control has improved, and he may have benefitted more than the other Houston pitchers by the development of Marc Bailey. He used to get hurt by the stolen base pretty badly, but his opposition stolen bases have dropped sharply in the last two years.

7. Sid FERNANDEZ, New York
His hits per nine innings (5.71) were the best in the major leagues since Nolan Ryan in 1972; he allowed only 108 hits in 170.1 innings . . . was the only major league starter to strike out more than one batter per nine innings . . . these can be taken as obvious, broad hints that he is on the edge of a breakthrough season, like Sam McDowell had in '65, perhaps. If it happens, that's going to be some kind of a 1–2–3 punch, ain't it?

8. Joe HESKETH, Montreal
He's got one of those records, like Ron Guidry or Don Gullett, that you can just look at and you know that he's always going to win if he can pitch. In the minors he spent most of the time on the disabled list, but when he pitched he won 35 of 51 decisions and posted excellent strikeout/walk ratios and low ERAs. He's done the same thing in the majors (10–5, 2.49 ERA, 113/45 K/W ratio) and he probably always will. It's just a question of how much he'll be able to pitch between injuries.

9. Shane RAWLEY, Philadelphia
Needs 10 or 15 wins this year to finish the straight. In his four years as a starter he's won 11, 14, 12 and 13 . . . career record as a starter is solid, if unspectacular, 46–38.

10. Steve TROUT, Chicago
Only major league pitcher to place among his league's best supported in both 1984 and 1985. He's not a hitter, either . . .

11. Dave LaPOINT, San Francisco
Ended a string of ten straight .500 or better winning percentages (majors and minors) with a crash, going 7–17. He'd been awfully lucky, anyway; his ERAs in St. Louis were well above-league, but he got out of it with more wins than losses. Set a career high with 207 innings, had best ERA in three years despite dismal log with Giants . . .

12. Rick HONEYCUTT, Los Angeles
Record would be better if they just wouldn't pitch him on artificial turf. Over the last three years his ERAs on grass fields are 2.15, 2.25 and 2.80, but on turf they're 3.81, 4.74 and 5.08.

13. Atlee HAMMAKER, San Francisco
His terrific control was a little off last year after a season's inactivity, or maybe he just lost the confidence to throw the ball into the strike zone and take his chances with the San Francisco defense. Would win with a good team if healthy.

14. Mark THURMOND, San Diego
Somehow his return to earth was less of a surprise than his 14–8 record of a year ago . . . Has B.S. degree in finance from Texas A & M . . . I've never really seen him pitch well, so it's hard for me to see him as successful.

15. Ray FONTENOT, Chicago
Fontenot, on the other hand, I continue to like despite the fact that

he's never done anything to justify my confidence in him. As mentioned in the Cub comment, there was a huge difference between his effectiveness against left-handed and right-handed hitters, left handers hitting only .174 with 1 home run against him (69 at bats), and right handers hitting .310 with 22 homers (532 at bats). I just have the feeling that in time he might refine his game enough that he'll be able to win.

16. Vida BLUE, San Francisco

Can still throw hard, but it seems to be taking him a mighty long time to regain his command of the strike zone or at least the surrounding neighborhood.

RELIEF ACES

American League

1. Dan QUISENBERRY, Kansas City (10)

The greatest control pitcher of this century was Deacon Phillippe of the Pittsburgh Pirates, retired 1910, who walked only 363 men in 2,607 innings, 1.25 per nine innings. (Actually, Phillippe pitched in 1899; his figure would be even a little better if you limited him to the 2,286 innings that he pitched in this century.) To this point in his career Dan Quisenberry has pitched 764 innings and walked 100 men, or 1.18 per nine innings. However, since Quisenberry is a reliever, a much higher percentage of his walks are intentional. We don't know how many of Phillippe's were intentional (they didn't count them separately), but of the 100 walks issued by Quiz, 41 have been intentional. So Quisenberry has issued 0.69 unintentional walks per nine innings—clearly the best control record of any pitcher since they established the four-ball standard.

2. Willie HERNANDEZ, Detroit (2)

Carried through like a champion for the first half of the 1985 season, posting 1.84 ERA and 18 saves by the All-Star break, then posted 3.98 ERA, 3–6 won/lost record the second half, including five losses and 7.13 ERA in August. The Tigers could use a comeback.

3. Donnie MOORE, California (2)

Posted 1.01 ERA in California, 2.92 on the road. The reason for this was that he allowed nine home runs on the season—all of them on the road. He allowed three homers in Detroit, two in Cleveland, two in Seattle and one each in Boston and Kansas City—but none in his home park.

4. Jay HOWELL, Oakland

Pitched super for first half, but faded badly in second. At the All-Star break he was 8–3 with a 1.96 ERA and 17 saves. The second half he was 1–5 with a 4.23 ERA and 12 saves . . . here's hoping it was just arm fatigue . . .

5. Dave RIGHETTI, New York

Presumably returns to starting rotation, with Brian Fisher taking over the relief ace role . . . has always pitched extremely well in Yankee Stadium . . . in '85 posted ERAs no worse than 3.75 against every American League team except the two the Yankees are most worried about. His ERA in two appearances against Detroit was 15.43, and in 7 appearances against Toronto it was 10.50 . . .

6. Bob JAMES, Chicago

Doesn't have much of a platoon split, actually. Right-handed hitters hit .217 against him, left-handers .235 (credit John Dewan) . . . It took him a long time to turn the corner with his control, but when he turned it, he really turned it. He walked only 19 men last year, plus 4 intentional—an amazing performance from a man who just two years ago walked 25 in 31 innings at Wichita.

7. Tom HENKE, Toronto

Took him a long time to get his chance. He's a year older than Dave Righetti, only a couple of years younger than Willie Hernandez. But he looks ready . . . Toronto lost 13 games last year in which they held a lead through seven innings, the most in baseball. But they *had* the lead through seven 95 times, and that also was the most in baseball . . .

8. Greg HARRIS, Texas

He pitched great, allowing only 74 hits and striking out 111 in 113 innings. There is an understandable reserve about him; a lot of times no-name relievers on bad teams will turn in one big year, like Ernie Camacho a couple of years ago. We'll see.

9. Ron DAVIS, Minnesota

Struck out 72 men in 65 innings, posted 2.20 ERA after the All-Star game. Posted 1.97 ERA in the Metrodome, but was 1–6 with 4.96 ERA on the road.

10. Edwin NUNEZ, Seattle

Two terrific stats on him supplied by Jeff Welch: when he got ahead of hitters 0–2, they hit .074 (6/81), and only 13 runs scored against him with two out in the inning—this in 102 innings (he pitched only 90 total, but remember that as a reliever he often pitches only the final part of an inning). That's one of the best rates of 2-out run allowance on the team—and he probably pitched with more men on in those situations than anyone.

11. Don AASE, Baltimore

Was very effective after the All-Star break, posting 5–2 record, 12 saves and 1.94 ERA . . . but you know what they say, a chicken doesn't change its lips . . . well, something like that . . .

12. Steve CRAWFORD, Boston

Red Sox opponents hit .316 in the late innings of close games with runners in scoring position; the .316 was based on 71/225 and resulted in 96 runs batted in . . . Bob Stanley again was the Red Sox least effective pitcher at keeping a runner on first with nobody out, with 15 of 31 moving up against him. Crawford was good in this respect, with only 11 of 30 moving . . . Crawford posted 2.00 ERA on artificial turf . . .

13. Bob GIBSON, Milwaukee

I know it doesn't make any sense, but every time I see this guy and realize how manifestly unimpressive he is, I get offended that he is using Bob Gibson's name . . . anybody else have that problem?

14. Tom WADDELL, Cleveland

Allowed 20 home runs in 113 innings.

National League

1. Lee SMITH, Chicago (4)

Like James, didn't have big platoon difference. Left-handed batters hit .249 against him, right-handers .236 . . .

2. Jeff REARDON, Montreal (3)

Posted 41 saves but the worst won/lost record (2–8) and worst ERA (3.18) of his career . . . strikeout frequency also was down.

3. Goose GOSSAGE, San Diego (4)

Workload was down to 50 games and he could almost be called a control pitcher—only 52 strikeouts and 17 walks in 79 innings. But great players are great players because they can make use of what they have to work with. Goose's 1.82 ERA was his fourth below 2.00 . . . see Hall of Fame article . . . San Diego had excellent 70–3 record when holding a lead through seven innings . . .

4. Dave SMITH, Houston

Doesn't have the great heat, but how can you argue with ERAs of 2.21 and 2.27? Houston was below average (68–8) at holding a lead after seven innings . . .

5. Jesse OROSCO, New York

Hasn't shown any signs yet of repeating the superb performance of two years ago . . . Roger McDowell might be the number one man in the Met bullpen now . . .

6. Ted POWER, Cincinnati

Stats are suspect. He had 42 strikeouts and 45 walks in 80 innings, which doesn't really sound like a relief ace despite 27 saves and 2.70 ERA . . . but, combined with Franco and the powerful Reds bench, the Rosemen were 66–2 when they held a lead through seven innings, and 13–7 when they were tied.

7. Jeff LAHTI, St. Louis

The one most effective member of a team bullpen; appears Worrell will be the bullpen stopper here in '86 . . . Cardinals, as you probably know, were 83–1 when they held the lead through seven innings, and 87–0 when they led going into the ninth . . .

8. Bruce SUTTER, Atlanta (1)

My guess is he comes back.

9. Scott GARRELTS, San Francisco

Probably rated too low, like Greg Harris, because it is hard to evaluate the performance of a relief ace on a bad team. Had 2.30 ERA and struck out 106 in 106 innings . . . the Giants were just 42–11 when they held a lead after seven innings, the worst record in baseball, and lost 50 games in which they held a lead at some point, most in the National League . . .

10. Tom NIEDENFUER, Los Angeles

Strikeout ratios have been going up the last couple of years, from 66 in 95 innings two years ago to 102 in 106 innings last year . . . you have to wonder how the playoff fiasco will affect him . . .

11. Cecilio GUANTE, Pittsburgh

Pitched well, had only five saves . . . Pirates had poor record (47–10) when they held a lead through seven . . .

12. Kent TEKULVE, Philadelphia

Didn't pitch so well; Bedrosian probably has the job . . . Tekulve in his career has walked over three men per nine innings, so his control has never been comparable to Quisenberry's. That is probably the big difference between them . . .

SECTION
IV

ESSAYS, ETC

AGE AND PERFORMANCE

One of the unique features of the 1985 baseball season was the number of outstanding seasons being turned in by players at odd ages. With Bret Saberhagen being nine months younger than Vida Blue was when he won his Cy Young Award in 1971, and Dwight Gooden being a few days younger than Fernando Valenzuela was in '81, both leagues had their youngest Cy Young cytations ever. On the other slope, the American League's top two power hitters were Carlton Fisk, who went to high school with Norm Cash (Norm, by the way, was also a free agent last winter) and Darrell Evans, who had a 40-home-run fit at the age of 38.

That being the case, I thought it might be kind of fun to look at performance by age, not in a real serious way, as I did back in the first nationally circulated *Abstract* back in '82, but in more of a light-hearted, casual way. What is the greatest performance ever by a 20-year-old kid? What are the greatest offensive seasons at that age—or at any age? How many players have been stars at age 20 or 21? How many players have remained stars at age 38 or 40? What's the most homers ever hit by a fellow that old, or that young? What was Ty Cobb doing at that age, or Willie Mays? How do the active leaders compare with those guys at the same ages?

The charts on the twenty-five following pages examine those questions in reprehensible detail. There are two sort-of-serious purposes to studying these things. One is that it gives us a sense—not precise information, as I tried to do in '82, but an informed intuition—about how performance varies over the course of a spectrum of ages, running 18 to 42. The other is that this is one way to look at the question of what records might be vulnerable, how records are approached, etc. Does any player active have a chance to break Henry's Hammerin' Home Run Haul? If you look at where Henry Aaron was in the HR column at the age of 25, or 29, or whatever, and you look at highest totals posted by active players, you're quickly going to realize that nobody has much of a shot at him. Other records might be more vulnerable—one active player still has quite a few more hits than Petie had at the same age, for

example, and another is virtually certain to erase one major career mark. Which you probably know, anyway.

Mostly, though, this is just for the heck of it . . . something to argue about, something to jog the memory, something to help us realign our perceptions of where players are and where they are heading. A player's "Age" during any season for these purposes is his age as of June 30; I think that's traditional in this area. That is, a player who was born July 1, 1956 would be considered 29 years old in the summer of 1986. To be considered eligible to be the batting leader at any age, a player had to have 200 career at bats for each year of age beginning with 18 (that is, an 18-year-old had to have 200 at bats, a 19-year-old 400, a 20-year-old 600, etc.) You'll notice that Cobb is ahead in batting average all the way from a very young age, and you might get the idea that nobody is close to him. Actually, that's quite untrue. There were several other players who got their career averages over .360 at one time or another, and up to the mid-thirties there's always somebody who is nipping at Cobb's heels—Sisler or Hornsby or Musial or Jackson or Williams or Boggs or Lajoie—but he always manages to stay a point or five ahead of them. Eligibility for the leaderships in career winning percentage is based on 12 decisions per year beginning at age 18; the ERA crown hinges on 100 innings per year beginning at 18.

In 1879 a pitcher named Monte Ward won 47 games for the Providence team in the National League; he was 19 years old at the time. Because of performances like this, it seemed to me to be advisable not to consider 19th-century players eligible for these charts, except that I did count 19th-century career totals for players who established recognized marks, like Cy Young. I hope you enjoy looking over these charts, and seeing who is ahead of who and who was behind who and where and when he caught him, because there's a hell of a lot of work went into them, and that's really all they're there for. I can't guarantee that I got every record correct—I could have missed somebody who had 454 doubles by the age of 29, or something—but I'm sure I got 99% of them right. Have fun.

AGE 18

ALL-TIME ALL-STAR TEAM

POS	Player, Season	G	AB	H	2B	3B	HR	Run	RBI	BB	SO	SB	Avg
C	Eddie Ainsmith, 1910	33	104	20	1	2	0	4	9	6		0	.192
1B	Phil Cavaretta, 1935	146	589	162	28	12	8	85	82	39	61	4	.275
2B	Sibby Sisti, 1939	63	215	49	7	1	1	19	11	12	38	4	.228
3B	Wayne Causey, 1955	68	175	34	2	1	1	14	9	17	25	0	.194
SS	Robin Yount, 1974	107	344	86	14	5	3	48	26	12	46	7	.250
LF	Ed Kranepool, 1963	86	273	57	12	2	2	22	14	18	50	4	.209
CF	Whitey Lockman, 1945	32	129	44	9	0	3	16	18	13	10	1	.341
RF	Johnny Lush, 1906	106	369	102	22	3	2	39	42	27		12	.275

POS	Player, Season	G	IP	W	L	Pct.	SO	BB	ERA	ShO	Sv
RS	Bob Feller, 1937	26	149	9	7	.563	150	106	3.38	0	1
LS	Bill Bailey, 1907	6	48	4	1	.800	17	15	2.44	0	0
3S	Von McDaniel, 1957	17	87	7	5	.583	45	31	3.21	2	0
4S	Larry Dierker, 1965	26	147	7	8	.467	109	37	3.49	0	0
RA	Bob Miller, 1954	32	70	1	1	.500	27	26	2.45	0	1

	RECORD AT AGE 18		CAREER LEADER THROUGH AGE 18		LEADER AMONG ACTIVE PLAYERS		PACE OF RECORD HOLDER	
Games	Phil Cavaretta	146	Phil Cavaretta	152	Robin Yount	107	Rose	0
At Bats	Phil Cavaretta	589	Phil Cavaretta	610	Robin Yount	344	Rose	0
Runs	Phil Cavaretta	85	Phil Cavaretta	90	Robin Yount	48	Cobb	19
Hits	Phil Cavaretta	162	Phil Cavaretta	170	Robin Yount	86	Rose	0
Doubles	Phil Cavaretta	28	Phil Cavaretta	28	Robin Yount	14	Speaker	0
Triples	Phil Cavaretta	12	Phil Cavaretta	13	Robin Yount	5	Crawford	0
Home Runs	Phil Cavaretta	8	Phil Cavaretta	9	Robin Yount	3	Aaron	0
RBI	Phil Cavaretta	82	Phil Cavaretta	88	Robin Yount	26	Aaron	0
Walks	Phil Cavaretta	39	Phil Cavaretta	41	Robin Yount	12	Ruth	0
Strikeouts	Phil Cavaretta	61	Phil Cavaretta	64	Robin Yount	46	Jackson	0
Stolen Bases	Johnny Lush	12	Johnny Lush	12	Robin Yount	7	Brock	0
Average	Phil Cavaretta	.275	Mel Ott	.309	Robin Yount	.250	Cobb	.240
Power/Speed	Phil Cavaretta	5.3	Phil Cavaretta	6.4	Robin Yount	4.2	Mays	0.0
Wins	Bob Feller	9	Bob Feller	14			Young	0
WL %	Von McDaniel	.583	Feller & McDaniel	.583			Ford	.000
Strikeouts	Bob Feller	150	Bob Feller	226			Ryan	0
ERA	Von McDaniel	3.21	Bob Feller	3.37			Walsh	
Shutouts	Von McDaniel	2	Von McDaniel	2			Johnson	0
Saves	Several With	1	Bob Feller	2			Fingers	0

TOP ALTERNATIVE SELECTIONS

POS	Player, Season	G	AB	H	2B	3B	HR	Run	RBI	BB	SO	SB	Avg
OF	Mel Ott, 1927	82	163	46	7	3	1	23	19	13	9	2	.282

	Player, Season	G	IP	W	L	Pct	SO	BB	ERA	ShO	Sv
	Jim Brillheart, 1922	31	120	4	6	.400	47	72	3.60	0	1
	Rick Wise, 1965	25	69	5	3	.625	39	25	4.04	0	0

NOTES: Ed Walsh had no game appearances, and hence no ERA, until age 23. I believe that the only active major league pitchers who appeared in a game at the age of 18 were Mike Morgan and Tim Conroy; however, neither pitcher won or saved a game, struck out a batter or qualified for any percentage leaderships, so that those entries are left blank here.

OTHER PLAYERS WHO COULD HAVE BEEN CHOSEN TO THE 18-YEAR-OLD ALL-STAR TEAM INCLUDE: Catchers Jimmie Foxx (1926; 26 G, .313) and Ed Kirkpatrick (1963), Second Basemen Lew Malone (1915; 76 G, .204) and Fred Lindstrom (1924), Third Baseman Brooks Robinson (1955), Shortstop Stuffy McInnis (1909), Outfielders Ty Cobb (1905; 41 G, .240), Merito Acosta (1914; 38 G, .257) and Al Kaline (1953), and Pitchers Herb Pennock (1912), Randy Gumpert (1936), Rex Barney (1943), Cal McLish (1944), Mike McCormick (1957; 75 Innings, 4.08 ERA, 3-1), Lew Krause (1962) and David Clyde (1973; 4-8).

MOST VALUABLE 18-YEAR-OLD: Phil Cavaretta

AGE 19
ALL-TIME ALL-STAR TEAM

POS	Player, Season	G	AB	H	2B	3B	HR	Run	RBI	BB	SO	SB	Avg
C	Del Crandall, 1949	67	228	60	10	1	4	21	34	9	18	2	.263
1B	Phil Cavaretta, 1936	124	458	125	18	1	9	55	56	17	36	8	.273
2B	Bill Mazeroski, 1956	81	255	62	8	1	3	30	14	18	24	0	.243
3B	Buddy Lewis, 1936	143	601	175	21	13	6	100	67	47	46	6	.291
SS	Robin Yount, 1975	147	558	149	28	2	8	67	52	33	69	12	.267
LF	Tony Conigliaro, 1964	111	404	117	21	2	24	69	52	35	78	2	.290
CF	Cesar Cedeno, 1970	90	355	110	21	4	7	46	42	15	57	17	.310
RF	Mel Ott, 1928	124	435	140	26	4	18	69	77	52	36	3	.322

		G	IP	W	L	Pct.	SO	BB	ERA	ShO	Sv
RS	Wally Bunker, 1964	29	214	19	5	.792	96	62	2.69	1	0
LS	Rube Bressler, 1914	29	148	10	3	.769	96	56	1.76	1	2
3S	Dwight Gooden, 1984	31	218	17	9	.654	276	73	2.60	3	0
4S	Bob Feller, 1938	39	278	17	11	.607	240	208	4.08	2	1
5S	Gary Nolan, 1967	33	227	14	8	.636	206	62	2.58	5	0
RA	Billy McCool, 1964	40	89	6	5	.545	87	29	2.43	0	7

	RECORD AT AGE 19		CAREER LEADER THROUGH AGE 19		LEADER AMONG ACTIVE PLAYERS		PACE OF RECORD HOLDER	
Games	Bob Kennedy	154	Phil Cavaretta	277	Robin Yount	254	Rose	0
At Bats	Buddy Lewis	601	Phil Cavaretta	1068	Robin Yount	902	Rose	0
Runs	Buddy Lewis	100	Phil Cavaretta	145	Robin Yount	115	Cobb	64
Hits	Buddy Lewis	175	Phil Cavaretta	295	Robin Yount	235	Rose	0
Doubles	Robin Yount	28	Phil Cavaretta	46	Robin Yount	42	Speaker	0
Triples	Buddy Lewis	13	Phil Cavaretta	14	Robin Yount	7	Crawford	8
Home Runs	Tony Conigliaro	24	Tony Conigliaro	24	Robin Yount	11	Aaron	0
RBI	Mel Ott	77	Phil Cavaretta	144	Robin Yount	78	Aaron	0
Walks	Rusty Staub	59	Mel Ott	66	Rusty Staub	59	Ruth	0
Strikeouts	Conigliaro	78	Robin Yount	115	Robin Yount	115	Jackson	0
Stolen Bases	Ty Cobb	23	Ty Cobb	25	Robin Yount	19	Brock	0
Average	Mel Ott	.322	Mel Ott	.318	Robin Yount	.261	Cobb	.296
Power/Speed	Mantle & Cedeno	9.9	Phil Cavaretta	15.1	Robin Yount	13.9	Mays	0.0
Wins	Wally Bunker	19	Bob Feller	31	Dwight Gooden	17	Young	0
WL %	Wally Bunker	.792	Wally Bunker	.760	Dwight Gooden	.654	Ford	.000
Strikeouts	Dwight Gooden	276	Bob Feller	466	Dwight Gooden	276	Ryan	6
ERA	Gary Nolan	2.58	Gary Nolan	2.58	Dwight Gooden	2.60	Walsh	
Shutouts	Gary Nolan	5	Gary Nolan	5	Dwight Gooden	3	Johnson	2
Saves	Billy McCool	7	Billy McCool	7	Jose Rijo	2	Fingers	0

TOP ALTERNATIVE SELECTIONS

POS	Player, Season	G	AB	H	2B	3B	HR	Run	RBI	BB	SO	SB	Avg
1B	Ed Kranepool, 1964	119	420	108	19	4	10	47	45	32	50	0	.257
3B	Fred Lindstrom, 1925	104	356	102	15	12	4	43	33	22	20	5	.287
RF	Sherry Magee, 1904	95	364	101	15	12	3	51	57	14		11	.277
CF	Ty Cobb, 1906	98	358	113	13	7	1	45	34	19		23	.316
CF	Mickey Mantle, 1951	95	341	91	11	5	13	61	65	43	74	8	.267

OTHER PLAYERS WHO COULD HAVE BEEN CHOSEN TO THE 19-YEAR-OLD ALL-STAR TEAM INCLUDE: Catcher Frankie Hayes (1926; 92 G, .226), First Basemen Jimmie Foxx (1927; 61 G with .323 average) and Rusty Staub (1963; .257), Third Baseman Bob Kennedy (1940), Shortstop Travis Jackson (1923), Outfielders Al Kaline (1954; 138 G, .276 Average) and Claudell Washington (1974; 73 G, .285), and pitchers Smokey Joe Wood (1909; 11-7, 2.21 ERA), Rube Bressler (1914; 10-3, 1.76 ERA), Chuck Stobbs (1949; 11-6), Milt Pappas (1958; 10-10), Mike McCormick (1958; 11-8), Don Gullett (1970; 5-2, all other stats almost identical to McCool's) and Bert Blyleven (1971; 10-9).

MOST VALUABLE 19-YEAR-OLD: Wally Bunker

AGE 20
ALL-TIME ALL-STAR TEAM

POS	Player, Season	G	AB	H	2B	3B	HR	Run	RBI	BB	SO	SB	Avg
C	Johnny Bench, 1968	154	564	155	40	2	15	67	82	31	96	1	.275
1B	Orlando Cepeda, 1958	148	603	188	38	4	25	88	96	29	84	15	.312
2B	Bill Mazeroski, 1957	148	526	149	27	7	8	59	54	27	49	3	.283
3B	Buddy Lewis, 1937	156	668	210	32	6	10	107	79	52	44	11	.314
SS	Rogers Hornsby, 1916	139	495	155	17	15	6	63	65	40	63	17	.313
LF	Ted Williams, 1939	149	585	185	44	11	31	131	145	107	64	2	.327
CF	Vada Pinson, 1959	154	648	205	47	9	20	131	84	55	98	21	.316
RF	Mel Ott, 1929	150	545	179	37	2	42	138	151	113	38	6	.328
RF	Sherry Magee, 1905	155	603	180	24	17	5	100	98	44		48	.299

POS	Player, Season	G	IP	W	L	Pct.	SO	BB	ERA	ShO	Sv
RS	Dwight Gooden, 1985	35	277	24	4	.857	268	69	1.53	8	0
LS	Babe Ruth, 1915	32	218	18	6	.750	112	85	2.44	1	0
3S	Bob Feller, 1939	39	297	24	9	.727	246	142	2.85	4	1
4S	Paul Dean, 1934	39	233	19	11	.633	150	52	3.44	5	2
RA	Terry Forster, 1972	62	100	6	5	.545	104	44	2.25	0	29

	RECORD AT AGE 20		CAREER LEADER THROUGH AGE 20		LEADER AMONG ACTIVE PLAYERS		PACE OF RECORD HOLDER	
Games	Cedeno & Yount	161	Robin Yount	415	Robin Yount	415	Rose	0
At Bats	Buddy Lewis	668	Robin Yount	1540	Robin Yount	1540	Rose	0
Runs	Mel Ott	138	Mel Ott	237	Robin Yount	174	Cobb	161
Hits	Buddy Lewis	210	Robin Yount	396	Robin Yount	396	Rose	0
Doubles	Vada Pinson	47	Mel Ott	72	Cedeno & Yount	61	Speaker	2
Triples	Cobb & Magee	17	Sherry Magee	29	Claudell Washington	12	Crawford	23
Home Runs	Mel Ott	42	Mel Ott	61	Bob Horner	23	Aaron	13
RBI	Mel Ott	151	Mel Ott	251	Robin Yount	132	Aaron	69
Walks	Mel Ott	113	Mel Ott	179	Robin Yount	83	Ruth	9
Strikeouts	Tony Conigliaro	116	Tony Conigilaro	194	Robin Yount	184	Jackson	0
Stolen Bases	Ty Cobb	49	Ty Cobb	74	Claudell Washington	47	Brock	0
Average	Ty Cobb	.350	Ty Cobb	.326	Claudell Washington	.302	Cobb	.326
Power/Speed	Vada Pinson	20.5	Cesar Cedeno	23.3	Cesar Cedeno	23.3	Mays	10.4
Wins	Dwight Gooden	24	Bob Feller	55	Dwight Gooden	41	Young	0
WL %	Dwight Gooden	.857	Dwight Gooden	.759	Dwight Gooden	.759	Ford	.000
Strikeouts	Dwight Gooden	268	Bob Feller	712	Dwight Gooden	544	Ryan	6
ERA	Dwight Gooden	1.53	Walter Johnson	1.71	Dwight Gooden	2.00	Walsh	
Shutouts	Gooden & Valenzuela	8	Dwight Gooden	11	Dwight Gooden	11	Johnson	8
Saves	Terry Forster	29	Terry Forster	30	Terry Forster	30	Fingers	0

TOP ALTERNATIVE SELECTIONS

POS	Player, Season	G	AB	H	2B	3B	HR	Run	RBI	BB	SO	SB	Avg
LF	Al Kaline, 1955	152	588	200	24	8	27	121	102	82	57	6	.340
CF	Ty Cobb, 1907	144	582	188	34	17	4	102	81	37		49	.350
RF	Frank Robinson, 1956	152	572	166	27	6	38	122	83	64	95	8	.290
SS	Arky Vaughan, 1932	129	497	158	15	10	4	71	61	39	36	10	.318

POS	Player, Season	G	IP	W	L	Pct	SO	BB	ERA	ShO	Sv
4S	Don Drysdale, 1957	34	225	17	9	.654	148	61	2.69	4	0
4S	Walter Johnson, 1908	36	257	14	14	.500	160	53	1.64	6	1
4S	Don Gullett, 1971	35	218	16	6	.727	107	64	2.64	3	0

OUTSTANDING PLAYERS WHO WERE 20 YEARS OLD IN 1985 INCLUDE: Dwight Gooden

OTHER PLAYERS WHO COULD HAVE BEEN CHOSEN TO THE 20-YEAR-OLD ALL-STAR TEAM INCLUDE: First Basemen Dick Hoblitzell (1909; .308) and Stuffy McInnis (1911; .321), Second Basemen Bobby Doerr (1938) and Ken Hubbs (1962), Third Baseman Fred Lindstrom (1926; .302), Shortstops Travis Jackson (1924) and Arky Vaughn (1932; .318), Outfielders Sherry Magee (1905; 100 Runs, 98 RBI, .299), Mickey Mantle (1952; 23 HR, 87 RBI, .311), Tony Conigliaro (1965; 32 home runs) and Claudell Washington (1975) and Pitchers Christy Mathewson (1901; 20-17), Johnny Lush (1906; 18-15), Milt Pappas (1959; 15-9), Billy McCool (1965; 21 Saves, 120 K in 105 innings), Jim Palmer (1966; 15-10), Bert Blyleven (1971; 16-15, 2.82 ERA) and Fernando Valenzuela (1981; 13-7).

MOST VALUABLE 20-YEAR-OLD: Dwight Gooden

AGE 21
ALL-TIME ALL-STAR TEAM

POS	Player, Season	G	AB	H	2B	3B	HR	Run	RBI	BB	SO	SB	Avg
C	Johnny Bench, 1969	148	532	156	23	1	26	83	90	49	86	6	.293
1B	Hal Trosky, 1934	154	625	206	45	9	35	117	142	58	49	2	.330
2B	Joe Morgan, 1965	157	601	163	22	12	14	100	40	97	77	20	.271
3B	Eddie Mathews, 1953	157	579	175	31	8	47	110	135	99	83	1	.302
SS	Garry Templeton, 1977	153	621	200	19	18	8	94	79	15	70	28	.322
LF	Joe Jackson, 1911	147	571	233	45	19	7	126	83	56		41	.408
CF	Cesar Cedeno, 1971	139	559	179	39	8	22	103	82	56	62	55	.320
RF	Joe DiMaggio, 1936	138	637	206	44	15	29	132	125	24	39	4	.323

		G	IP	W	L	Pct.	SO	BB	ERA	ShO	Sv
RS	Bob Feller, 1940	43	320	27	11	.711	261	118	2.62	4	4
LS	Vida Blue, 1971	39	312	24	8	.750	301	88	1.82	8	0
3S	Bret Saberhagen, 1985	32	235	20	6	.769	158	38	2.87	1	0
4S	Babe Ruth, 1916	44	324	23	12	.657	170	118	1.75	9	1
RA	Billy McCool, 1966	57	105	8	8	.500	104	41	2.48	0	18

	RECORD AT AGE 21		CAREER LEADER THROUGH AGE 21		LEADER AMONG ACTIVE PLAYERS		PACE OF RECORD HOLDER	
Games	Eddie Murray	160	Robin Yount	569	Robin Yount	569	Rose	0
At Bats	Buddy Lewis	656	Robin Yount	2145	Robin Yount	2145	Rose	0
Runs	Ted Williams	134	Mel Ott	359	Robin Yount	240	Cobb	249
Hits	Joe Jackson	233	Buddy Lewis	582	Robin Yount	570	Rose	0
Doubles	Jackson & Trosky	45	Mel Ott	106	Cesar Cedeno	100	Speaker	28
Triples	Ty Cobb	20	Ty Cobb	42	Garry Templeton	20	Crawford	39
Home Runs	Eddie Mathews	47	Mel Ott	86	Bob Horner	56	Aaron	40
RBI	Hal Trosky	142	Mel Ott	370	Cesar Cedeno	205	Aaron	175
Walks	Rickey Henderson	117	Mel Ott	282	Rickey Henderson	151	Ruth	19
Strikeouts	Darryl Strawberry	128	Tony Conigliaro	306	Robin Yount	264	Jackson	46
Stolen Bases	Rickey Henderson	100	Rickey Henderson	133	Rickey Henderson	133	Brock	0
Average	Joe Jackson	.408	Jimmie Foxx	.342	Garry Templeton	.314	Cobb	.325
Power/Speed	Cesar Cedeno	31.4	Cesar Cedeno	54.8	Cesar Cedeno	54.8	Mays	15.1
Wins	Bob Feller	27	Bob Feller	82	Bert Blyleven	43	Young	0
WL %	Moose & Simpson	.824	(Dwight Gooden)	.759	(Dwight Gooden)	.759	Ford	.900
Strikeouts	Vida Blue	301	Bob Feller	973	Bert Blyleven	587	Ryan	139
ERA	Harry Krause	1.39	Walter Johnson	1.93	(Dwight Gooden)	2.00	Walsh	
Shutouts	Babe Ruth	9	Christy Mathewson	13	Fernando Valenzuela	12	Johnson	12
Saves	Billy McCool	18	McCool & Forster	46	Terry Forster	46	Fingers	0

TOP ALTERNATIVE SELECTIONS

POS	Player, Season	G	AB	H	2B	3B	HR	Run	RBI	BB	SO	SB	Avg
1B	Jimmie Foxx, 1929	149	517	183	23	9	33	123	117	103	70	9	.354
SS	Rogers Hornsby, 1917	145	523	171	24	17	8	86	66	45	34	17	.327
SS	Arky Vaughan, 1933	152	573	180	29	19	9	85	97	64	23	3	.314
LF	Ted Williams, 1940	144	561	193	43	14	23	134	113	96	54	4	.344
LF	Rickey Henderson, 1980	158	591	179	22	4	9	111	53	117	54	100	.303
CF	Ty Cobb, 1908	150	581	188	36	20	4	88	108	34		39	.324
RF	Hank Aaron, 1955	153	602	189	37	9	27	105	106	49	61	3	.314

NOTES: Joe Jackson's age is subject to some dispute. The Macmillan *Baseball Encyclopedia* says that he was born on July 16, 1887, while *Daguerreotypes*, from *The Sporting News*, says that it was July 16, 1888, and *The Sports Encyclopedia: Baseball* prefers July 16, 1889. I have used the latter as my primary source for this article, and so accepted their date in this and most other cases of such disagreement.

Whitey Ford's winning percentage here and for the next two seasons is based on only ten decisions. He will be shown with a higher winning percentage than the leader through the same age for several years because he did not have enough decisions to be considered the leader.

OUTSTANDING PLAYERS WHO WERE 21 YEARS OLD IN 1985 INCLUDE: Bret Saberhagen

OTHER PLAYERS WHO COULD HAVE BEEN CHOSEN TO THE 21-YEAR-OLD ALL-STAR TEAM INCLUDE: First Basemen Stuffy McInnis (1912; 101 RBI, .327) and Orlando Cepeda (1959; 27 HR, 105 RBI, .317), Second Basemen Bobby Doerr (1939), Bill Mazeroski (1958) and Rod Carew (1967, .292), Third Baseman Buddy Lewis (1938; 122 Runs Scored), Outfielders Lloyd Waner, (1927; 133 runs, 223 Hits), Joe Vosmik (1931; .320, 117 RBI), Joe Medwick (1933; .306, 40 Doubles), Al Kaline (1956; 128 RBI), Tim Raines (1981) and Darryl Strawberry (1983) and Pitchers Nick Maddox (1908; 23-8), Harry Krause (1909; 18-8), Rube Marquard (1911; 24-7), Wes Ferrell (1929; 21-10), Lefty Gomez (21-9, 2.63 ERA), Frank Tanana (1975;16-9; 269 K) and Mark Fidrych (1976; 19-9).

MOST VALUABLE 21-YEAR-OLD: Eddie Mathews

AGE 22

ALL-TIME ALL-STAR TEAM

POS	Player, Season	G	AB	H	2B	3B	HR	Run	RBI	BB	SO	SB	Avg
C	Johnny Bench, 1970	158	605	177	35	4	45	97	148	54	102	5	.293
1B	Jimmie Foxx, 1930	153	562	188	33	13	37	127	156	93	66	7	.335
2B	Eddie Collins, 1909	153	572	198	30	10	3	104	56	62		67	.346
3B	Richie Allen, 1964	162	632	201	38	13	29	125	91	67	138	3	.318
SS	Cal Ripken, 1982	162	663	211	47	2	27	121	102	58	97	0	.318
LF	Ted Williams, 1941	143	456	185	33	3	37	135	120	145	27	2	.406
CF	Joe DiMaggio, 1937	151	621	215	35	15	46	151	167	64	37	3	.346
RF	Ty Cobb, 1909	156	573	216	33	10	9	116	107	48		76	.377

POS	Player, Season	G	IP	W	L	Pct.	SO	BB	ERA	ShO	Sv
RS	Smokey Joe Wood, 1912	43	344	34	5	.872	258	82	1.91	10	1
LS	Rube Marquard, 1912	43	295	26	11	.703	175	80	2.57	1	0
3S	Walter Johnson, 1910	45	374	25	17	.595	313	76	1.35	8	2
4S	Christy Mathewson, 1903	45	366	30	13	.698	267	100	2.26	3	2
RA	Terry Forster, 1974	59	134	7	8	.467	105	48	3.63	0	24

	RECORD AT AGE 22		CAREER LEADER THROUGH AGE 22		LEADER AMONG ACTIVE PLAYERS		PACE OF RECORD HOLDER	
Games	Several with	162	Robin Yount	696	Robin Yount	696	Rose	157
At Bats	Juan Samuel	701	Robin Yount	2647	Robin Yount	2647	Rose	623
Runs	Joe DiMaggio	151	Mel Ott	463	Cesar Cedeno	320	Cobb	365
Hits	Fred Lindstrom	231	Ty Cobb	764	Robin Yount	717	Rose	170
Doubles	Stan Musial	48	Cesar Cedeno	135	Cesar Cedeno	135	Speaker	48
Triples	Joe Jackson	26	Sam Crawford	62	Garry Templeton	33	Crawford	62
Home Runs	Joe DiMaggio	46	Mel Ott	115	Bob Horner	91	Aaron	66
RBI	Joe DiMaggio	167	Mel Ott	485	Cesar Cedeno	275	Aaron	267
Walks	Ted Williams	145	Met Ott	362	Rickey Henderson	215	Ruth	31
Strikeouts	Reggie Jackson	171	Mickey Mantle	382	Claudell Washington	326	Jackson	217
Stolen Bases	Tim Raines	78	Cobb & Henderson	189	Rickey Henderson	189	Brock	0
Average	Ted Williams	.406	Joe Jackson	.394	Cesar Cedeno	.301	Cobb	.338
Power/Speed	Cesar Cedeno	34.6	Cesar Cedeno	89.4	Cesar Cedeno	89.4	Mays	15.1
Wins	Joe Wood	34	Bob Feller	107	Bert Blyleven	63	Young	0
WL %	Joe Wood	.872	Lefty Gomez	.691	Fernando Valenzuela	.620	Ford	.900
Strikeouts	Sam McDowell	325	Bob Feller	1233	Bert Blyleven	845	Ryan	231
ERA	Dutch Leonard	1.01	Walter Johnson	1.72	(Dwight Gooden)	2.00	Walsh	
Shutouts	Joe Wood	10	Walter Johnson	20	Bert Blyleven	18	Johnson	20
Saves	Terry Forster	24	Terry Forster	70	Terry Forster	70	Fingers	12

TOP ALTERNATIVE SELECTIONS

POS	Player, Season	G	AB	H	2B	3B	HR	Run	RBI	BB	SO	SB	Avg
SS	Arky Vaughan, 1934	149	558	186	41	11	12	115	94	94	38	10	.333
LF	Stan Musial, 1943	157	617	220	48	20	13	108	81	72	18	9	.357
RF	Joe Jackson, 1912	152	572	226	44	26	3	121	90	54		35	.395
CF	Pete Reiser, 1941	137	536	184	39	17	14	117	76	46	71	4	.343

POS	Player, Season	G	IP	W	L	Pct	SO	BB	ERA	ShO	Sv
4S	Bill James, 1914	46	332	26	7	.788	156	118	1.90	4	2
4S	Bob Feller, 1941	44	343	25	13	.658	260	194	3.15	5	2
LS	Dutch Leonard, 1914	36	223	19	5	.792	174	60	1.01	7	3
LS	Babe Ruth, 1917	41	326	24	13	.649	128	108	2.02	6	2

OUTSTANDING PLAYERS WHO WERE 22 YEARS OLD IN 1985 INCLUDE: Tony Fernandez

OTHER PLAYERS WHO COULD HAVE BEEN CHOSEN TO THE 22-YEAR-OLD ALL-STAR TEAM INCLUDE: Second Basemen Billy Herman (1932; 206 Hits) and Juan Samuel (1984), Third Basemen Fred Lindstrom (1928), Eddie Mathews (1954; 40 Home Runs) and George Brett (1975), Outfielders Jimmy Sheckard (1901; .353), Ben Chapman (1931; 61 Stolen Bases, 120 Runs Scored, 122 RBI) and Boog Powell (1964; 39 HR), and Pitcher Wes Ferrell (1930; 25-13).

MOST VALUABLE 22-YEAR-OLD: Ted Williams

AGE 23

ALL-TIME ALL-STAR TEAM

POS	Player, Season	G	AB	H	2B	3B	HR	Run	RBI	BB	SO	SB	Avg
C	Joe Torre, 1964	154	601	193	36	5	20	87	109	36	67	2	.321
1B	Orlando Cepeda, 1961	152	585	182	28	4	46	105	142	39	91	12	.311
2B	Eddie Collins, 1910	153	583	188	16	15	3	81	81	49		81	.322
3B	Pie Traynor, 1923	153	616	208	19	19	12	108	101	34	19	28	.338
SS	Arky Vaughan, 1935	137	499	192	34	10	19	108	99	97	18	4	.385
LF	Ty Cobb, 1910	140	508	194	35	13	8	106	91	64		65	.382
CF	Willie Mays, 1954	151	565	195	33	13	41	119	110	66	57	8	.345
RF	Hank Aaron, 1957	151	615	198	27	6	44	118	132	57	58	1	.322

		G	IP	W	L	Pct.	SO	BB	ERA	ShO	Sv
RS	Dizzy Dean, 1934	50	312	30	7	.811	195	75	2.65	7	7
LS	Hal Newhouser, 1944	47	312	29	9	.763	187	102	2.22	6	2
4S	Dean Chance, 1964	46	278	20	9	.690	207	86	1.65	11	4
4S	Christy Mathewson, 1904	48	368	33	12	.733	212	78	2.03	4	0
RA	Goose Gossage, 1975	62	142	9	8	.529	130	70	1.84	0	26

	RECORD AT AGE 23		CAREER LEADER THROUGH AGE 23		LEADER AMONG ACTIVE PLAYERS		PACE OF RECORD HOLDER	
Games	Tommy Davis	163	Robin Yount	845	Robin Yount	845	Rose	293
At Bats	Tony Oliva	672	Robin Yount	3224	Robin Yount	3224	Rose	1139
Runs	Woody English	152	Mel Ott	582	Cesar Cedeno	415	Cobb	471
Hits	Al Simmons	253	Ty Cobb	960	Robin Yount	871	Rose	309
Doubles	Hank Greenberg	63	Cesar Cedeno	164	Cesar Cedeno	164	Speaker	82
Triples	Sam Crawford	25	Sam Crawford	87	Garry Templeton	52	Crawford	87
Home Runs	Reggie Jackson	47	Ott & Mathews	153	Bob Horner	106	Aaron	110
RBI	Hal Trosky	162	Mel Ott	608	Cesar Cedeno	377	Aaron	399
Walks	Ted Williams	145	Ted Williams	493	Rickey Henderson	331	Ruth	88
Strikeouts	Bobby Bonds	187	Mickey Mantle	479	Cesar Cedeno	403	Jackson	359
Stolen Bases	Rickey Henderson	130	Rickey Henderson	319	Rickey Henderson	319	Brock	16
Average	Arky Vaughan	.385	Joe Jackson	.388	George Brett	.306	Cobb	.347
Power/Speed	Bobby Bonds	37.4	Cesar Cedeno	125.1	Cesar Cedeno	125.1	Mays	29.4
Wins	Christy Mathewson	33	Bob Feller	107	Bert Blyleven	80	Young	9
WL %	Bob Stanley	.882	Lefty Gomez	.670	Vida Blue	.654	Ford	.900
Strikeouts	Jim Maloney	265	Bob Feller	1233	Bert Blyleven	1094	Ryan	356
ERA	George McQuillan	1.52	Walter Johnson	1.76	Frank Tanana	2.69	Walsh	2.60
Shutouts	Dean Chance	11	Walter Johnson	26	Bert Blyleven	21	Johnson	26
Saves	Goose Gossage	26	Terry Forster	74	Terry Forster	74	Fingers	14

TOP ALTERNATIVE SELECTIONS

POS	Player, Season	G	AB	H	2B	3B	HR	Run	RBI	BB	SO	SB	Avg
1B	Hal Trosky, 1936	151	629	216	45	9	42	124	162	36	58	6	.343
LF	Ted Williams, 1942	150	522	186	34	5	36	141	137	145	51	3	.356
CF	Al Simmons, 1925	153	658	253	43	12	24	122	129	35	41	7	.384
CF	Joe DiMaggio, 1938	145	599	194	32	13	32	129	140	59	21	6	.324
LF	Stan Musial, 1944	146	568	197	51	14	12	112	94	90	28	7	.347
RF	Tony Oliva, 1964	161	672	217	43	9	32	109	94	34	68	12	.323

OUTSTANDING PLAYERS WHO WERE 23 YEARS OLD IN 1985 INCLUDE: Julio Franco, Jim Presley, Darryl Strawberry

OTHER PLAYERS WHO COULD HAVE BEEN CHOSEN TO THE 23-YEAR-OLD ALL-STAR TEAM INCLUDE: Catchers Rudy York (1937; 35 HR, 103 RBI) and Gary Carter (1977; .284, 31 Homers), First Baseman Hank Greenberg (1934; 63 Doubles), Second Baseman Rod Carew (1969; .332), Third Basemen Rogers Hornsby (1919), Harland Clift (1936; .302, 45 Doubles, 145 Runs Scored), Eddie Mathews (1955; 41 Home Runs) and George Brett (1976; .333, 215 Hits), Outfielders Sam Crawford (1903; .335, 25 Triples), Joe Jackson (1913; .373), Joe Medwick (.353, 126 RBI), Tommy Davis (1962; 230 Hits, .346, 153 RBI), Reggie Jackson (1969; 47 Home Runs), Bobby Bonds (1969), Rickey Henderson (1982; 130 Stolen Bases), and Tim Raines (1983) and Pitchers Ed Reulbach (1903; 19-4), George McQuillan, (1908; 23-17), Walter Johnson (1911; 25-13, 1.89 ERA), Herb Score (1956), and Jim Maloney (1963; 23-7).

MOST VALUABLE 23-YEAR-OLD: Arky Vaughan

AGE 24
ALL-TIME ALL-STAR TEAM

POS	Player, Season	G	AB	H	2B	3B	HR	Run	RBI	BB	SO	SB	Avg
C	Johnny Bench, 1972	147	538	145	22	2	40	87	125	100	84	6	.270
1B	Lou Gehrig, 1927	155	584	218	52	18	47	149	175	109	84	10	.373
2B	Ryne Sandberg, 1984	156	636	200	36	19	19	114	84	52	101	32	.314
3B	Jimmie Foxx, 1932	154	585	213	33	9	58	151	169	116	96	3	.364
SS	Arky Vaughan, 1936	156	568	190	30	11	9	122	78	118	21	6	.335
LF	Mickey Mantle, 1956	150	533	188	22	5	52	132	130	112	99	10	.353
CF	Willie Mays, 1955	152	580	185	18	13	51	123	127	79	60	24	.319
RF	Ty Cobb, 1911	146	591	248	47	24	8	147	127	44		83	.420

POS	Player, Season	G	IP	W	L	Pct.	SO	BB	ERA	ShO	Sv
RS	Denny McLain, 1968	41	336	31	6	.838	280	63	1.96	6	0
LS	Hal Newhouser, 1945	40	313	25	9	.735	212	110	1.81	8	2
3S	Walter Johnson, 1912	50	368	32	12	.727	303	76	1.39	7	3
4S	Christy Mathewson, 1905	43	339	31	8	.795	206	64	1.27	8	2
RA	Bruce Sutter, 1977	62	107	7	3	.700	129	23	1.35	0	31

	RECORD AT AGE 24		CAREER LEADER THROUGH AGE 24		LEADER AMONG ACTIVE PLAYERS		PACE OF RECORD HOLDER	
Games	Brooks Robinson	163	Robin Yount	988	Robin Yount	988	Rose	455
At Bats	Willie Wilson	705	Robin Yount	3835	Robin Yount	3835	Rose	1809
Runs	Jimmie Foxx	151	Mel Ott	680	Cesar Cedeno	508	Cobb	618
Hits	Ty Cobb	248	Ty Cobb	1208	Robin Yount	1050	Rose	518
Doubles	Joe Medwick	64	Joe Medwick	202	Cesar Cedeno	195	Speaker	135
Triples	Larry Doyle	25	Sam Crawford	104	Garry Templeton	61	Crawford	104
Home Runs	Jimmie Foxx	58	Eddie Mathews	190	Bob Horner	138	Aaron	140
RBI	Lou Gehrig	175	Mel Ott	711	Cesar Cedeno	440	Aaron	494
Walks	Ed Yost	126	Mel Ott	537	Rickey Henderson	434	Ruth	189
Strikeouts	Bobby Bonds	189	Mickey Mantle	578	Reggie Jackson	494	Jackson	494
Stolen Bases	Vince Coleman	110	Rickey Henderson	427	Rickey Henderson	427	Brock	40
Average	Ty Cobb	.420	Joe Jackson	.378	Don Mattingly	.323	Cobb	.360
Power/Speed	Bobby Bonds	33.7	Cesar Cedeno	146.7	Cesar Cedeno	146.7	Mays	62.7
Wins	Walter Johnson	32	Christy Mathewson	128	Bert Blyleven	95	Young	36
WL %	Emil Yde	.842	Lefty Gomez	.712	John Candelaria	.659	Ford	.794
Strikeouts	Walter Johnson	303	Bert Blyleven	1327	Bert Blyleven	1327	Ryan	493
ERA	Christy Mathewson	1.27	Ed Reulbach	1.57	Tom Seaver	2.38	Walsh	2.36
Shutouts	Newhouser & Tesreau	8	Walter Johnson	33	Bert Blyleven	24	Johnson	33
Saves	Bruce Sutter	31	Terry Forster	75	Terry Forster	75	Fingers	31

TOP ALTERNATIVE SELECTIONS

POS	Player, Season	G	AB	H	2B	3B	HR	Run	RBI	BB	SO	SB	Avg
1B	Hank Greenberg, 1935	152	619	203	46	16	36	121	170	87	91	4	.328
2B	Billy Herman, 1935	154	606	227	57	6	7	113	83	42	29	6	.341
2B	Rogers Hornsby, 1920	149	589	218	44	20	9	96	94	60	50	12	.370
3B	Ron Santo, 1964	161	592	.185	33	13	30	94	114	86	96	3	.313
LF	Ralph Kiner, 1947	152	565	177	23	4	51	118	127	98	81	1	.313
RF	Chuck Klein, 1929	149	616	219	45	6	43	126	145	54	61	5	.356
CF	Tris Speaker, 1912	153	580	222	53	12	10	136	98	82		52	.383
LF	Joe Medwick, 1936	155	636	223	64	13	18	115	138	34	33	3	.351
CF	Joe DiMaggio, 1939	120	462	176	32	6	30	108	126	52	20	3	.381
RF	Paul Waner, 1927	155	623	237	40	17	9	113	131	60	14	5	.380

POS	Player, Season	G	IP	W	L	Pct	SO	BB	ERA	ShO	Sv
4S	Lefty Gomez, 1934	38	282	26	5	.839	158	96	2.33	6	1
4S	Dizzy Dean, 1935	50	324	28	12	.700	182	82	3.11	3	5
4S	Tom Seaver, 1969	36	273	25	7	.781	208	82	2.21	5	0
RA	Lindy McDaniel, 1960	65	116	12	4	.750	105	24	2.09	0	26

OUTSTANDING PLAYERS WHO WERE 24 YEARS OLD IN 1985 INCLUDE: Tom Brunansky, Ron Darling, Alvin Davis, Don Mattingly, Cal Ripken, Juan Samuel, Fernando Valenzuela, Mike Witt.

OTHER PLAYERS WHO COULD HAVE BEEN CHOSEN TO THE 24-YEAR-OLD ALL-STAR TEAM INCLUDE: First Baseman Don Mattingly (1985), Second Basemen Larry Doyle (1911), Frankie Frisch (1923), Johnny Hodapp (1930; 225 Hits, 51 Doubles) and Pete Rose (1965; 209 Hits), Third Basemen Bill Madlock (1975) and Dick Allen (1966; 40 Homers, .317), Shortstops Joe Cronin (1931; 126 RBI), Arky Vaughan (1936, .335), Ernie Banks (1955; 44 Home Runs), and Robin Yount (1980), Outfielders Babe Ruth (1919) and Al Simmons (.343, 53 Doubles), and Pitchers King Cole (1910; 20-4), Grover Cleveland Alexander (1911; 28-13), Eddie Rommel (1922; 27-13), Ewell Blackwell (1947), Jim Lonborg (1967; 22-9, 246 K) and Steve Busby (1974).

MOST VALUABLE 24-YEAR-OLD: Ty Cobb

AGE 25
ALL-TIME ALL-STAR TEAM

POS	Player, Season	G	AB	H	2B	3B	HR	Run	RBI	BB	SO	SB	Avg
C	Yogi Berra, 1950	151	597	192	30	6	28	116	124	55	12	4	.322
1B	Jimmie Foxx, 1933	149	573	204	37	9	48	125	163	96	93	2	.356
2B	Nap Lajoie, 1901	131	543	229	48	13	14	145	125	24		27	.422
3B	Home Run Baker, 1911	148	592	198	40	14	11	96	115	40		38	.334
SS	Joe Cronin, 1932	143	557	177	43	18	6	95	116	66	45	7	.318
LF	Hank Aaron, 1959	154	629	223	46	7	39	116	123	51	54	8	.355
CF	Ty Cobb, 1912	140	553	227	30	23	7	119	83	43		61	.410
RF	Babe Ruth, 1920	142	458	172	36	9	54	158	137	148	80	14	.376

		G	IP	W	L	Pct.	SO	BB	ERA	ShO	Sv
RS	Robin Roberts, 1952	39	330	28	7	.800	148	45	2.59	3	2
LS	Hal Newhouser, 1946	37	293	26	9	.743	275	98	1.94	6	1
3S	Walter Johnson, 1913	47	346	36	7	.837	243	38	1.14	11	3
4S	Don Drysdale, 1962	43	314	25	9	.735	232	78	2.84	2	1
RA	Goose Gossage, 1977	72	133	11	9	.550	151	49	1.62	0	26

	RECORD AT AGE 25		CAREER LEADER THROUGH AGE 25		LEADER AMONG ACTIVE PLAYERS		PACE OF RECORD HOLDER	
Games	Ron Santo	164	Mel Ott	1136	Robin Yount	1084	Rose	611
At Bats	Omar Moreno	695	Robin Yount	4212	Robin Yount	4212	Rose	2463
Runs	Ruth & Klein	158	Mel Ott	799	Cesar Cedeno	597	Cobb	737
Hits	Chuck Klein	250	Ty Cobb	1435	Robin Yount	1153	Rose	723
Doubles	Chuck Klein	59	Joe Medwick	258	Cesar Cedeno	221	Speaker	170
Triples	Kiki Cuyler	26	Sam Crawford	114	Garry Templeton	69	Crawford	114
Home Runs	Babe Ruth	54	Foxx & Mathews	222	Bob Horner	158	Aaron	179
RBI	Chuck Klein	170	Met Ott	846	Cesar Cedeno	523	Aaron	617
Walks	Babe Ruth	148	Mickey Mantle	670	Rickey Henderson	520	Ruth	337
Strikeouts	Mike Schmidt	180	Reggie Jackson	655	Reggie Jackson	655	Jackson	655
Stolen Bases	Clyde Milan	88	Rickey Henderson	493	Rickey Henderson	493	Brock	83
Average	Nap Lajoie	.422	Ty Cobb	.367	Rod Carew	.307	Cobb	.367
Power/Speed	Willie Mays	37.9	Cesar Cedeno	174.5	Cesar Cedeno	174.5	Mays	107.4
Wins	Walter Johnson	36	Johnson & Mathewson	150	Bert Blyleven	108	Young	72
WL %	Ralph Terry	.842	Ed Reulbach	.736	John Candelaria	.648	Ford	.741
Strikeouts	Nolan Ryan	329	Bert Blyleven	1546	Bert Blyleven	1546	Ryan	822
ERA	Walter Johnson	1.14	Walter Johnson	1.58	Tom Seaver	2.49	Walsh	2.11
Shutouts	Walter Johnson	11	Walter Johnson	44	Bert Blyleven	30	Johnson	44
Saves	Jack Aker	32	Terry Forster	76	Terry Forster	76	Fingers	52

TOP ALTERNATIVE SELECTIONS

POS	Player, Season	G	AB	H	2B	3B	HR	Run	RBI	BB	SO	SB	Avg
1B	Lou Gehrig, 1928	154	562	210	47	13	27	139	142	95	69	4	.374
1B	Stan Musial, 1946	156	624	228	50	20	16	124	103	73	31	7	.365
2B	Rogers Hornsby, 1921	154	592	235	44	18	21	131	126	60	48	13	.397
LF	Joe Medwick, 1937	156	633	237	56	10	31	111	154	41	50	4	.374
LF	Jime Rice, 1978	163	677	213	25	15	46	121	139	58	126	7	.315
CF	Mickey Mantle, 1957	144	474	173	28	6	34	121	94	146	75	16	.365
RF	Chuck Klein, 1930	156	648	250	59	8	40	158	170	54	50	4	.386
RF	Frank Robinson, 1961	153	545	176	32	7	37	117	124	71	64	22	.323

		G	IP	W	L	Pct	SO	BB	ERA	ShO	Sv
4S	Denny McLain, 1969	42	325	24	9	.727	181	67	2.80	9	0
RA	Al Hrabosky, 1975	65	97	13	3	.813	82	33	1.67	0	22

OUTSTANDING PLAYERS WHO WERE 25 YEARS OLD IN 1985 INCLUDE: George Bell, Vince Coleman, Chili Davis, Tony Gwynn, Kent Hrbek, Mike Marshall, Lloyd Moseby, Tim Raines, Ryne Sandberg, Frank Viola.

OTHER PLAYERS WHO COULD HAVE BEEN CHOSEN TO THE 25-YEAR-OLD ALL-STAR TEAM INCLUDE: First Baseman Harmon Killebrew (1961; 46 Homers), Third Basemen Ron Santo (1965) and Bill Madlock (1976), Outfielders Tris Speaker (1913), Goose Goslin (1926), Paul Waner (1928; .370, 50 Doubles, 142 Runs Scored), Joe Vosmik (1935; .348, 47 Doubles, 20 Triples) and Joe DiMaggio (.352, 31 Homers, 133 RBI), and Pitchers Ed Reulbach (1908; 24-7), Claude Hendrix (1914; 29-11), Howie Pollett (1946; 21-10, 2.10 ERA), Dave McNally (1968; 22-10, 1.95), Rollie Fingers (1972, 21 Saves) and Mike Norris (1980; 22-9).

MOST VALUABLE 25-YEAR-OLD: Babe Ruth

AGE 26
ALL-TIME ALL-STAR TEAM

POS	Player, Season	G	AB	H	2B	3B	HR	Run	RBI	BB	SO	SB	Avg
C	Johnny Bench, 1974	160	621	174	38	2	33	108	129	80	90	5	.280
1B	Norm Cash, 1961	159	535	193	22	8	41	119	132	124	85	11	.361
2B	Rogers Hornsby, 1922	154	623	250	46	14	42	141	152	65	50	17	.401
3B	George Brett, 1979	154	645	212	42	20	23	119	107	51	36	17	.329
SS	Honus Wagner, 1900	135	528	201	45	22	4	107	100	41		38	.381
LF	Frank Robinson, 1962	162	609	208	51	2	39	134	136	76	62	18	.342
CF	Rickey Henderson, 1985	143	547	172	28	5	24	146	72	99	65	80	.314
RF	Babe Ruth, 1921	152	540	204	44	16	59	177	171	144	81	17	.378

POS	Player, Season	G	IP	W	L	Pct.	SO	BB	ERA	ShO	Sv
RS	Walter Johnson, 1914	51	372	28	18	.609	225	74	1.72	9	1
LS	Warren Spahn, 1946	40	290	21	10	.677	123	84	2.33	7	3
3S	Tom Seaver, 1971	36	286	20	10	.667	289	61	1.76	4	0
4S	Christy Mathewson, 1907	41	346	24	13	.649	178	53	1.99	8	2
RA	Dick Radatz, 1963	66	132	15	6	.714	162	51	1.97	0	25

	RECORD AT AGE 26		CAREER LEADER THROUGH AGE 26		LEADER AMONG ACTIVE PLAYERS		PACE OF RECORD HOLDER	
Games	Cesar Tovar	164	Mel Ott	1288	Robin Yount	1240	Rose	759
At Bats	Bobby Richardson	692	Robin Yount	4847	Robin Yount	4847	Rose	3048
Runs	Babe Ruth	177	Mel Ott	912	Rickey Henderson	732	Cobb	807
Hits	Rogers Hornsby	250	Ty Cobb	1602	Robin Yount	1363	Rose	899
Doubles	Frank Robinson	51	Joe Medwick	305	Cesar Cedeno	257	Speaker	216
Triples	Wagner & Stirnweiss	22	Sam Crawford	130	Garry Templeton	77	Crawford	130
Home Runs	Roger Maris	61	Jimmie Foxx	266	Jim Rice	172	Aaron	219
RBI	Hank Greenberg	183	Met Ott	960	Cesar Cedeno	594	Aaron	743
Walks	Babe Ruth	144	Mickey Mantle	799	Rickey Henderson	619	Ruth	481
Strikeouts	Dick Allen	161	Reggie Jackson	780	Reggie Jackson	780	Jackson	780
Stolen Bases	Omar Moreno	96	Rickey Henderson	573	Rickey Henderson	573	Brock	146
Average	Rogers Hornsby	.401	Ty Cobb	.369	Dave Parker	.314	Cobb	.369
Power/Speed	Rickey Henderson	36.9	Cesar Cedeno	198.4	Cesar Cedeno	198.4	Mays	146.9
Wins	Walter Johnson	28	Walter Johnson	178	Bert Blyleven	122	Young	104
WL %	Orel Hershiser	.864	Ed Reulbach	.719	Tom Seaver	.638	Ford	.735
Strikeouts	Nolan Ryan	383	Bert Blyleven	1728	Bert Blyleven	1728	Ryan	1205
ERA	Howie Camnitz	1.56	Walter Johnson	1.61	Tom Seaver	2.34	Walsh	1.88
Shutouts	Johnson & Alexander	9	Walter Johnson	53	Bert Blyleven	35	Johnson	53
Saves	Bruce Sutter	37	Bruce Sutter	105	Bruce Sutter	105	Fingers	74

TOP ALTERNATIVE SELECTIONS

POS	Player, Season	G	AB	H	2B	3B	HR	Run	RBI	BB	SO	SB	Avg
1B	Jimmie Foxx, 1934	150	539	180	28	6	44	120	130	111	75	11	.334
1B	Hank Greenberg, 1937	154	594	200	49	14	40	137	183	102	101	8	.337
LF	Harry Heilmann, 1921	149	602	237	43	14	19	114	139	53	37	2	.394
LF	Ralph Kiner, 1949	152	549	170	19	5	54	116	127	117	61	6	.310
CF	Joe DiMaggio, 1941	139	541	193	43	11	30	122	125	76	13	4	.357
CF	Duke Snider, 1953	153	590	198	38	4	42	132	126	82	90	16	.336
RF	Chuck Klein, 1931	148	594	200	34	10	31	121	121	59	49	7	.337

POS	Player, Season	G	IP	W	L	Pct.	SO	BB	ERA	ShO	Sv
3S	Nolan Ryan, 1973	41	326	21	16	.568	383	162	2.87	4	1
4S	Robin Roberts, 1953	44	347	23	16	.590	198	61	2.75	5	2

OUTSTANDING PLAYERS WHO WERE 26 YEARS OLD IN 1985 INCLUDE: Harold Baines, Britt Burns, Rickey Henderson, Orel Hershiser, Willie McGee, Dan Petry, Dave Righetti

OTHER PLAYERS WHO COULD HAVE BEEN CHOSEN TO THE 26-YEAR-OLD ALL-STAR TEAM INCLUDE: Second Baseman Charlie Gehringer (1929; .339, 45 Doubles, 131 Runs Scored), Shortstops Ernie Banks (1957; 43 Homers), Rico Petrocelli (1969; 40 Homers) and Robin Yount (1982), Outfielders Ty Cobb (1913; .390, 122 G), Heine Manush (1928; 241 Hits, 20 Triples), Babe Herman (1929; .381), Jeff Heath (1941; .340, 123 RBI) and Willie McGee (1985) and Pitchers Grover Cleveland Alexander (1913; 22-8), Dick Rudolph (1914; 27-10), Mel Parnell (1947; 25-7), Catfish Hunter (1972), Jim Palmer (1972; 21-10, 2.07), Rollie Fingers (1973; 1.92 ERA, 22 Saves) and Bruce Sutter (1979).

MOST VALUABLE 26-YEAR-OLD: Babe Ruth

AGE 27
ALL-TIME ALL-STAR TEAM

POS	Player, Season	G	AB	H	2B	3B	HR	Run	RBI	BB	SO	SB	Avg
C	Mickey Cochrane, 1930	130	487	174	42	5	10	110	85	55	18	5	.357
1B	George Sisler, 1920	154	631	257	49	18	19	137	122	46	19	42	.407
2B	Charlie Gehringer, 1930	154	610	201	47	15	16	144	98	69	17	19	.330
3B	George Brett, 1980	117	449	175	33	9	24	87	118	58	22	15	.390
SS	Ernie Banks, 1958	154	617	193	23	11	47	119	129	52	87	4	.313
LF	Stan Musial, 1948	155	611	230	46	18	39	135	131	79	34	7	.376
CF	Duke Snider, 1954	149	584	199	39	10	40	120	130	84	96	6	.341
RF	Carl Yastrzemski, 1967	161	579	189	31	4	44	112	121	91	69	10	.326

POS	Player, Season	G	IP	W	L	Pct.	SO	BB	ERA	ShO	Sv
RS	Ed Walsh, 1908	66	464	40	15	.727	269	56	1.42	11	6
LS	Ron Guidry, 1978	35	274	25	3	.893	248	72	1.74	9	0
3S	Christy Mathewson, 1908	56	391	37	11	.771	259	42	1.43	12	5
4S	Steve Carlton, 1972	41	346	27	10	.730	310	87	1.98	8	0
RA	Ron Perranoski, 1963	69	129	16	3	.842	75	43	1.67	0	21

	RECORD AT AGE 27		CAREER LEADER THROUGH AGE 27		LEADER AMONG ACTIVE PLAYERS		PACE OF RECORD HOLDER	
Games	B. Williams & Pagan	164	Mel Ott	1438	Robin Yount	1389	Rose	908
At Bats	Dave Cash	699	Robin Yount	5425	Robin Yount	5425	Rose	3674
Runs	Chuck Klein	152	Mel Ott	1032	Robin Yount	780	Cobb	876
Hits	George Sisler	257	Ty Cobb	1729	Robin Yount	1541	Rose	1109
Doubles	George Kell	56	Joe Medwick	353	Robin Yount	296	Speaker	241
Triples	Dale Mitchell	23	Sam Crawford	147	George Brett	82	Crawford	147
Home Runs	Hank Greenberg	58	Jimmie Foxx	302	Eddie Murray	198	Aaron	253
RBI	Lou Gehrig	174	Mel Ott	1095	Eddie Murray	697	Aaron	863
Walks	Ted Williams	156	Mickey Mantle	893	Henderson & Staub	619	Ruth	565
Strikeouts	Tommy Agee	156	Mickey Mantle	899	Reggie Jackson	891	Jackson	891
Stolen Bases	Bob Bescher	81	(Rickey Henderson)	573	(Rickey Henderson)	573	Brock	220
Average	George Sisler	.407	Ty Cobb	.369	Wade Boggs	.351	Cobb	.369
Power/Speed	Bobby Bonds	40.9	Cesar Cedeno	209.2	Cesar Cedeno	209.2	Mays	178.4
Wins	Ed Walsh	40	Christy Mathewson	211	Bert Blyleven	136	Young	129
WL %	Ron Guidry	.893	Ed Reulbach	.703	Tom Seaver	.637	Ford	.741
Strikeouts	Nolan Ryan	367	Sam McDowell	1967	Bert Blyleven	1910	Ryan	1572
ERA	Carl Lundgren	1.17	Walter Johnson	1.60	Tom Seaver	2.43	Walsh	1.73
Shutouts	Jack Coombs	13	Walter Johnson	60	Bert Blyleven	39	Johnson	60
Saves	Bill Caudill	36	Bruce Sutter	133	Bruce Sutter	133	Fingers	92

TOP ALTERNATIVE SELECTIONS

POS	Player, Season	G	AB	H	2B	3B	HR	Run	RBI	BB	SO	SB	Avg
1B	Hank Greenberg, 1938	155	556	175	23	4	58	144	146	119	92	7	.315
1B	Lou Gehrig, 1930	154	581	220	42	17	41	143	174	101	63	12	.379
3B	Brooks Robinson, 1964	163	612	194	35	3	28	82	118	51	64	1	.317
LF	Ted Williams, 1946	150	514	176	37	8	38	142	123	156	44	0	.342
CF	Al Simmons, 1929	143	581	212	41	9	34	114	157	31	38	4	.365
RF	Babe Herman, 1930	153	614	241	48	11	35	143	130	66	56	18	.393
RF	Chuck Klein, 1932	154	650	226	50	15	38	152	137	60	49	20	.348
RF	Bobby Bonds, 1973	160	643	182	34	4	39	131	96	87	148	43	.283

POS	Player, Season	G	IP	W	L	Pct	SO	BB	ERA	ShO	Sv
RS	Jack Coombs, 1910	45	353	31	9	.775	224	115	1.30	13	1
RS	Bob Feller, 1946	48	371	25	13	.634	348	153	2.18	10	4
4S	Sandy Koufax, 1963	40	311	25	5	.833	306	58	1.88	11	0
RA	Sparky Lyle, 1972	59	108	9	5	.643	75	29	1.91	0	35

OUTSTANDING PLAYERS WHO WERE 27 YEARS OLD IN 1985 INCLUDE: Wade Boggs, Bob Horner, Dave Stieb, Tim Wallach
OTHER PLAYERS WHO COULD HAVE BEEN CHOSEN TO THE 27-YEAR-OLD ALL-STAR TEAM INCLUDE: Catcher Darrell Porter (1979), First Basemen Johnny Mize (1940; 43 HR, 137 RBI) and Jim Gentile (1961; 141 RBI), Second Basemen Rogers Hornsby (1923; .384, 107 G) and Rod Carew (1973; .350, 41 SB), Third Basemen George Kell, (1950; .340) and Wade Boggs (1985), Shortstop Honus Wagner (1901; .353, 126 RBI), Outfielders Goose Goslin (1928; .379), Ralph Kiner (1950; 47 Home Runs, 122 Walks) and Rocky Colavito (1961; 45 HR, 140 RBI), and Pitchers Pete Alexander (1914; 27-15), Walter Johnson (1915; 27-13, 1.55 ERA), Waite Hoyt (1927; 22-7, 2.63), Dave McNally (1970; 24-9), Ferguson Jenkins (1971; 24-13), Catfish Hunter (1973; 21-5), Jim Palmer (1973; 22-9, 2.40 ERA) and Nolan Ryan (1974; 22-16, 367 K).
MOST VALUABLE 27-YEAR-OLD: Ed Walsh

AGE 28
ALL-TIME ALL-STAR TEAM

POS	Player, Season	G	AB	H	2B	3B	HR	Run	RBI	BB	SO	SB	Avg
C	Mickey Cochrane, 1931	122	459	160	31	6	17	87	89	56	21	2	.349
1B	Lou Gehrig, 1931	155	619	211	31	15	46	163	184	117	56	17	.341
2B	Rogers Hornsby, 1924	143	536	227	43	14	25	121	94	89	32	5	.424
3B	Tony Perez, 1970	158	587	186	28	6	40	107	129	83	134	8	.317
SS	Ernie Banks, 1959	155	589	179	25	6	45	97	143	64	72	2	.304
LF	George Foster, 1977	158	615	197	31	2	52	124	149	61	107	6	.320
CF	Al Simmons, 1930	138	554	211	41	16	36	152	165	39	34	9	.381
RF	Babe Ruth, 1923	152	522	205	45	13	41	151	131	170	93	17	.393

POS	Player, Season	G	IP	W	L	Pct.	SO	BB	ERA	ShO	Sv
RS	Pete Alexander, 1915	49	376	31	10	.756	241	64	1.22	12	3
LS	Lefty Grove, 1928	39	262	24	8	.750	183	64	2.58	1	9
4S	Christy Mathewson, 1909	37	275	25	6	.806	149	36	1.14	8	2
4S	George Mullin, 1909	40	304	29	8	.784	124	78	2.22	3	1
RA	Willie Hernandez, 1984	80	140	9	3	.750	112	36	1.92	0	32

	RECORD AT AGE 28		CAREER LEADER THROUGH AGE 28		LEADER AMONG ACTIVE PLAYERS		PACE OF RECORD HOLDER	
Games	Frank Taveras	164	Mel Ott	1589	Robin Yount	1549	Rose	1064
At Bats	Woodie Jensen	696	Robin Yount	6049	Robin Yount	6049	Rose	4301
Runs	Lou Gehrig	163	Met Ott	1131	Robin Yount	885	Cobb	1020
Hits	Rogers Hornsby	227	Ty Cobb	1937	Robin Yount	1727	Rose	1327
Doubles	Gee Walker	55	Joe Medwick	383	Robin Yount	323	Speaker	282
Triples	Owen Wilson	36	Sam Crawford	163	George Brett	89	Crawford	163
Home Runs	George Foster	52	Jimmie Foxx	343	Eddie Murray	227	Aaron	298
RBI	Lou Gehrig	184	Jimmie Foxx	1217	Eddie Murray	807	Aaron	991
Walks	Babe Ruth	170	Mickey Mantle	1004	Rusty Staub	650	Ruth	735
Strikeouts	Gorman Thomas	175	Mickey Mantle	1024	Reggie Jackson	996	Jackson	996
Stolen Bases	Ty Cobb	96	Billy Hamilton	648	(Rickey Henderson)	573	Brock	272
Average	Rogers Hornsby	.424	Ty Cobb	.369	Rod Carew	.323	Cobb	.369
Power/Speed	Willie Mays	30.1	Cesar Cedeno	219.8	Cesar Cedeno	219.8	Mays	208.6
Wins	Pete Alexander	31	Christy Mathewson	236	Bert Blyleven	148	Young	164
WL %	Hoyt Wilhelm	.833	Ed Reulbach	.694	Tom Seaver	.640	Ford	.734
Strikeouts	J. R. Richard	303	Sam McDowell	2159	Bert Blyleven	2082	Ryan	1758
ERA	Christy Mathewson	1.14	Walter Johnson	1.63	Tom Seaver	2.38	Walsh	1.68
Shutouts	Pete Alexander	12	Walter Johnson	63	Bert Blyleven	39	Johnson	63
Saves	Gossage & Stanley	33	Bruce Sutter	158	Bruce Sutter	158	Fingers	116

TOP ALTERNATIVE SELECTIONS

POS	Player, Season	G	AB	H	2B	3B	HR	Run	RBI	BB	SO	SB	Avg
1B	Jimmie Foxx, 1936	155	585	198	32	8	41	130	143	105	119	13	.338
SS	Vern Stephens, 1949	155	610	177	31	2	39	113	159	101	73	2	.290
LF	Ted Williams, 1947	156	528	181	40	9	32	125	114	162	47	0	.343
LF	Stan Musial, 1949	157	612	207	41	13	36	128	123	107	38	3	.338
RF	Harry Heilmann, 1923	144	524	211	44	11	18	121	115	74	40	8	.403
RF	Chuck Klein, 1933	152	606	223	44	7	28	101	120	56	36	15	.368
RF	Tommy Holmes, 1945	154	636	224	47	6	28	125	117	70	9	15	.352
RF	Hank Aaron, 1962	156	592	191	28	6	45	127	128	66	73	15	.323

POS	Player, Season	G	IP	W	L	Pct	SO	BB	ERA	ShO	Sv
RS	Jack Chesbro, 1902	35	286	28	6	.824	136	62	2.17	8	1
RA	Hoyt Wilhelm, 1952	71	159	15	3	.833	108	57	2.43	0	11

OUTSTANDING PLAYERS WHO WERE 28 YEARS OLD IN 1985 INCLUDE: Brett Butler, Kirk Gibson, Tony Pena, Mario Soto, Lou Whitaker

OTHER PLAYERS WHO COULD HAVE BEEN CHOSEN TO THE 28-YEAR-OLD ALL-STAR TEAM INCLUDE: Second Basemen Nap Lajoie (1904, .381) and Joe Morgan (1972; 16 Homers, 58 Stolen Bases), Shortstops Honus Wagner (1902) and Arky Vaughan (1940; .300, 115 Runs), Outfielders Ty Cobb (1915; .369, 144 Runs Scored, 96 Steals), Tris Speaker (1916; .386), Gee Walker (1936; .353, 55 Doubles), Duke Snider (1955; 42 HR, 138 RBI), Lou Brock (1967; 206 Hits, 52 Steals) and Pete Rose (1969; .348, 120 Runs), and Pitchers Rube Waddell (1905; 26-11, 1.48 ERA, 287 K), Jack Coombs (1911; 28-12), Waite Hoyt (1928; 23-7), Luis Tiant (1968; 21-9, 1.60 ERA), Dave McNally (1971; 21-5), Catfish Hunter (1974; 25-12) and Rick Sutcliffe (1984).

MOST VALUABLE 28-YEAR-OLD: Ernie Banks

AGE 29

ALL-TIME ALL-STAR TEAM

POS	Player, Season	G	AB	H	2B	3B	HR	Run	RBI	BB	SO	SB	Avg
C	Yogi Berra, 1954	151	584	179	28	6	22	88	125	56	29	0	.307
1B	George Sisler, 1922	142	586	246	42	18	8	134	105	49	14	51	.420
2B	Rogers Hornsby, 1925	138	504	203	41	10	39	133	143	83	39	5	.403
3B	Al Rosen, 1953	155	599	201	27	5	43	115	145	85	48	8	.336
SS	Luke Appling, 1936	138	526	204	31	7	6	111	128	85	25	10	.388
LF	Hank Greenberg, 1940	148	573	195	50	8	41	129	150	93	75	6	.340
CF	Mickey Mantle, 1961	153	514	163	16	6	54	132	128	126	112	12	.317
RF	Babe Ruth, 1924	153	529	200	39	7	46	143	121	142	81	9	.378

		G	IP	W	L	Pct.	SO	BB	ERA	ShO	Sv
RS	Pete Alexander, 1916	48	389	33	12	.733	167	50	1.55	16	3
LS	Sandy Koufax, 1965	43	336	26	8	.765	382	71	2.04	8	0
3S	Three Finger Brown, 1906	36	277	26	6	.813	144	61	1.04	10	3
4S	Juan Marichal, 1968	38	353	26	9	.743	218	46	2.43	5	0
RA	Phil Regan, 1966	65	117	14	1	.933	88	24	1.62	0	21

	RECORD AT AGE 29		CAREER LEADER THROUGH AGE 29		LEADER AMONG ACTIVE PLAYERS		PACE OF RECORD HOLDER	
Games	Maury Wills	165	Mel Ott	1741	Robin Yount	1671	Rose	1223
At Bats	Maury Wills	695	Robin Yount	6515	Robin Yount	6515	Rose	4950
Runs	Babe Ruth	143	Mel Ott	1247	Robin Yount	961	Cobb	1133
Hits	George Sisler	246	Ty Cobb	2138	Robin Yount	1856	Rose	1532
Doubles	Paul Waner	62	Joe Medwick	416	Robin Yount	349	Speaker	324
Triples	W. Wilson & Combs	21	Sam Crawford	177	George Brett	98	Crawford	177
Home Runs	Mickey Mantle	54	Jimmie Foxx	379	Eddie Murray	258	Aaron	342
RBI	Hack Wilson	159	Jimmie Foxx	1344	Eddie Murray	931	Aaron	991
Walks	Ed Yost	151	Mickey Mantle	1130	Rusty Staub	724	Ruth	877
Strikeouts	Gorman Thomas	170	Bobby Bonds	1153	Reggie Jackson	1129	Jackson	1129
Stolen Bases	Maury Wills	104	Billy Hamilton	741	(Rickey Henderson)	573	Brock	334
Average	George Sisler	.420	Ty Cobb	.369	Rod Carew	.328	Cobb	.369
Power/Speed	Joe Morgan	37.5	Bobby Bonds	250.0	Cesar Cedeno	237.1	Mays	235.7
Wins	Pete Alexander	33	Christy Mathewson	263	Blyleven & Blue	156	Young	193
WL %	Phil Regan	.933	Whitey Ford	.724	Tom Seaver	.627	Ford	.724
Strikeouts	Sandy Koufax	382	Walter Johnson	2304	Bert Blyleven	2250	Ryan	2085
ERA	Three Finger Brown	1.04	Ed Walsh	1.61	Tom Seaver	2.47	Walsh	1.61
Shutouts	Pete Alexander	16	Walter Johnson	71	Bert Blyleven	41	Johnson	71
Saves	Jeff Reardon	41	Bruce Sutter	194	Bruce Sutter	194	Fingers	136

TOP ALTERNATIVE SELECTIONS

POS	Player, Season	G	AB	H	2B	3B	HR	Run	RBI	BB	SO	SB	Avg
C	Gabby Hartnett, 1930	141	508	172	31	3	37	84	122	55	62	0	.339
C	Roy Campanella, 1951	143	505	164	33	1	33	90	108	53	51	1	.325
C	Bill Dickey, 1936	112	423	153	26	8	22	99	107	46	16	0	.362
C	Mickey Cochrane, 1932	130	429	138	30	4	15	104	60	106	22	8	.322
1B	Ted Kluszewski, 1954	149	573	187	28	3	49	104	141	78	35	0	.326
2B	Joe Morgan, 1973	157	576	167	35	2	26	116	82	111	61	67	.290
LF	Hack Wilson, 1929	150	574	198	30	5	39	135	159	78	83	3	.345
CF	Al Simmons, 1931	128	513	200	37	13	22	105	128	47	45	3	.390
RF	Hank Aaron, 1963	161	631	201	29	4	44	121	130	78	94	31	.319

OUTSTANDING PLAYERS WHO WERE 29 YEARS OLD IN 1985 INCLUDE: Pedro Guerrero, Willie Hernandez, Tommy Herr, Dale Murphy, Eddie Murray, Lance Parrish, Jeff Reardon, Rick Sutcliffe, Willie Wilson, Robin Yount

OTHER PLAYERS WHO COULD HAVE BEEN CHOSEN TO THE 29-YEAR-OLD ALL-STAR TEAM INCLUDE: Third Baseman Tony Perez (1970), Shortstops Ernie Banks (1960) and Maury Wills (1962), Outfielders Ty Cobb (1916; .371), Joe Jackson (1919), Baby Doll Jacobson (1920; .355, 122 RBI), Wally Berger (1935; 130 RBI), Beau Bell (1937; 218 Hits, 51 Doubles), Ted Williams (1948; .369) and Duke Snider (1956; 43 Homers), and Pitchers Joe McGinnity (1900; 29-9), Christy Mathewson (1910; 27-9), Ed Walsh (1910; 1.27 ERA), Walter Johnson (1917; 23-16), Carl Mays (1921; 27-9), Dizzy Trout (1944; 27-14), Catfish Hunter (1975; 23-14) and Jim Palmer (1975; 23-11, 2.09 ERA).

MOST VALUABLE 29-YEAR-OLD: Al Rosen

AGE 30
ALL-TIME ALL-STAR TEAM

POS	Player, Season	G	AB	H	2B	3B	HR	Run	RBI	BB	SO	SB	Avg
C	Bill Dickey, 1937	140	530	176	35	2	29	87	133	73	22	3	.332
1B	Jimmie Foxx, 1938	149	565	197	33	9	50	139	175	119	76	5	.349
2B	Jackie Robinson, 1949	156	593	203	38	12	16	122	124	86	27	37	.342
3B	Mike Schmidt, 1980	150	548	157	25	8	48	104	121	89	119	12	.286
SS	Honus Wagner, 1904	132	490	171	44	14	4	97	75	59		53	.349
LF	Ted Williams, 1949	155	566	194	39	3	43	150	159	162	98	1	.343
CF	Hack Wilson, 1930	155	585	208	35	6	56	146	190	105	84	3	.356
RF	Frank Robinson, 1966	155	576	182	34	2	49	122	122	87	90	8	.316

		G	IP	W	L	Pct.	SO	BB	ERA	ShO	Sv
RS	Jack Chesbro, 1904	55	455	41	12	.774	239	88	1.82	6	0
LS	Lefty Grove, 1930	50	291	28	5	.848	209	60	2.54	2	9
3S	Sandy Koufax, 1966	41	323	27	9	.750	317	77	1.73	5	0
4S	Pete Alexander, 1911	45	388	30	13	.698	201	58	1.86	8	0
RA	John Hiller, 1973	65	125	10	5	.667	124	39	1.44	0	38

	RECORD AT AGE 30		CAREER LEADER THROUGH AGE 30		LEADER AMONG ACTIVE PLAYERS		PACE OF RECORD HOLDER	
Games	Mazeroski & Williams	163	Mel Ott	1866	Rusty Staub	1682	Rose	1383
At Bats	Matty Alou	698	Vada Pinson	6830	(Robin Yount)	6515	Rose	5582
Runs	Kiki Cuyler	155	Jimmie Foxx	1355	(Robin Yount)	961	Cobb	1240
Hits	Matty Alou	231	Ty Cobb	2363	(Robin Yount)	1856	Rose	1724
Doubles	Hal McRae	54	Joe Medwick	453	(Robin Yount)	349	Speaker	357
Triples	Ty Cobb	24	Sam Crawford	196	George Brett	100	Crawford	196
Home Runs	Hack Wilson	56	Jimmie Foxx	429	Mike Schmidt	283	Aaron	366
RBI	Hack Wilson	190	Jimmie Foxx	1519	Jim Rice	954	Aaron	1216
Walks	Ted Williams	162	Mickey Mantle	1252	Rusty Staub	801	Ruth	936
Strikeouts	Frank Howard	155	Bobby Bonds	1243	Reggie Jackson	1237	Jackson	1237
Stolen Bases	Ron LeFlore	68	Billy Hamilton	811	(Rickey Henderson)	573	Brock	387
Average	Harry Heilmann	.393	Ty Cobb	.370	Rod Carew	.329	Cobb	.370
Power/Speed	Joe Morgan	31.9	Bobby Bonds	267.3	Cesar Cedeno	244.2	Mays	261.8
Wins	Jack Chesbro	41	Christy Mathewson	289	Vida Blue	170	Young	214
WL %	Wild Bill Donovan	.862	Whitey Ford	.708	Tom Seaver	.636	Ford	.708
Strikeouts	Nolan Ryan	341	Walter Johnson	2466	Nolan Ryan	2426	Ryan	2426
ERA	Walter Johnson	1.27	Walter Johnson	1.66	Tom Seaver	2.46	Walsh	1.70
Shutouts	Carl Hubbell	10	Walter Johnson	79	Bert Blyleven	42	Johnson	79
Saves	Dan Quisenberry	45	Bruce Sutter	215	Bruce Sutter	215	Fingers	171

TOP ALTERNATIVE SELECTIONS

POS	Player, Season	G	AB	H	2B	3B	HR	Run	RBI	BB	SO	SB	Avg
2B	Joe Morgan, 1974	149	512	150	31	3	22	107	67	120	69	58	.293
3B	Joe Torre, 1971	161	634	230	34	8	24	97	137	63	70	4	.363
LF	Stan Musial, 1951	152	578	205	30	12	32	124	108	98	40	4	.355
LF	Carl Yastrzemski, 1970	161	566	186	29	0	40	125	102	128	66	23	.329
CF	Ty Cobb, 1917	152	588	225	44	24	6	107	102	61	34	55	.383
CF	Al Simmons, 1932	154	670	216	28	9	35	144	151	47	76	4	.322
CF	Earl Averill, 1933	153	631	198	37	14	32	116	124	75	40	5	.314

		G	IP	W	L	Pct	SO	BB	ERA	ShO	Sv
4S	Jim Bagby, 1920	48	340	31	12	.721	73	79	2.89	3	0
4S	Bucky Walters, 1939	39	319	27	11	.711	137	109	2.29	2	0
LS	Carl Hubbell, 1933	45	309	23	12	.657	156	47	1.66	10	5
RA	Dan Quisenberry, 1982	69	139	5	3	.625	48	11	1.94	0	45

OUTSTANDING PLAYERS WHO WERE 30 YEARS OLD IN 1985 INCLUDE: Jack Morris, Ozzie Smith

OTHER PLAYERS WHO COULD HAVE BEEN CHOSEN TO THE 30-YEAR-OLD ALL-STAR TEAM INCLUDE: First Basemen Bill Terry (1929; .372), Lou Gehrig (1933; .334, 139 RBI) and Ted Kluszewski (1955; 47 Home Runs), Second Basemen Nap Lajoie (1906; .355, 49 Doubles), Red Schoendienst (1953; 15 HR, .342) and Dave Johnson (1973; 43 Home Runs), Shortstop Joe Cronin (1937; 110 RBI), Outfielders Joe Jackson (1920; .382), Harry Heilmann (1925; .393), Willie Mays (1961; 40 Home Runs), Jim Rice (1983; 39 HR, 126 RBI, .305), Designated Hitter Don Baylor (1979; 139 RBI), and Pitchers Christy Mathewson (1911; 26-13, 1.99 ERA), Walter Johnson (1918; 23-13, 1.27 ERA), Hoyt Wilhelm (1954; 12-4, 2.10 ERA), Don Newcombe (1956; 27-7), Bob Gibson (1966; 21-12), Mickey Lolich (1971; 25-14, 308 K), Mike Marshall (1973; 31 Saves), Ferguson Jenkins (1974; 25-12), Tom Seaver (1975; 22-9, 2.38 ERA, 243 K) and Jim Palmer (1975; 22-13).

MOST VALUABLE 30-YEAR-OLD: Jackie Robinson

AGE 31
ALL-TIME ALL-STAR TEAM

POS	Player, Season	G	AB	H	2B	3B	HR	Run	RBI	BB	SO	SB	Avg
C	Roy Campanella, 1953	144	519	162	26	3	41	103	142	67	58	4	.312
1B	Lou Gehrig, 1934	154	579	210	40	6	49	128	165	109	31	9	.363
2B	Joe Morgan, 1975	146	498	163	27	6	17	107	94	132	52	67	.327
3B	Mike Schmidt, 1981	102	354	112	19	2	31	78	91	73	71	12	.316
SS	Phil Rizutto, 1950	155	617	200	36	7	7	125	66	91	38	12	.324
LF	Willie Stargell, 1971	141	511	151	26	0	48	104	125	83	154	0	.295
CF	Willie Mays, 1962	162	621	189	36	5	49	130	141	78	85	18	.304
RF	Babe Ruth, 1926	152	495	184	30	5	47	139	145	144	76	11	.372

		G	IP	W	L	Pct.	SO	BB	ERA	ShO	Sv
4S	Three Finger Brown, 1912	44	312	29	9	.763	123	49	1.47	9	5
LS	Lefty Grove, 1931	41	289	31	4	.886	175	62	2.05	4	5
RS	Ed Walsh, 1912	62	393	27	17	.614	254	94	2.15	6	10
4S	Walter Johnson, 1919	39	290	20	14	.588	147	51	1.49	7	2
RA	Bruce Sutter, 1984	71	123	5	7	.417	77	23	1.54	0	45

	RECORD AT AGE 31		CAREER LEADER THROUGH AGE 31		LEADER AMONG ACTIVE PLAYERS		PACE OF RECORD HOLDER	
Games	Several with	163	Mel Ott	2017	Rusty Staub	1837	Rose	1537
At Bats	Dick Groat	678	Vada Pinson	7404	Rusty Staub	6582	Rose	6227
Runs	Ruth & Terry	139	Jimmie Foxx	1485	Pete Rose	992	Cobb	1323
Hits	Bill Terry	254	Ty Cobb	2524	Pete Rose	1922	Rose	1922
Doubles	Joe Cronin	51	Joe Medwick	483	Cesar Cedeno	378	Speaker	395
Triples	4 Players with	22	Sam Crawford	210	George Brett	103	Crawford	210
Home Runs	Gehrig & Mays	49	Jimmie Foxx	464	Mike Schmidt	314	Aaron	398
RBI	Lou Gehrig	165	Jimmie Foxx	1624	Jim Rice	1076	Aaron	1305
Walks	Babe Ruth	144	Mickey Mantle	1292	Rusty Staub	878	Ruth	1080
Strikeouts	Tony Armas	156	Bobby Bonds	1384	Reggie Jackson	1366	Jackson	1366
Stolen Bases	Ron LeFlore	78	Billy Hamilton	870	(Rickey Henderson)	573	Brock	438
Average	Bill Terry	.401	Ty Cobb	.371	Rod Carew	.328	Cobb	.371
Power/Speed	Bobby Bonds	38.9	Bobby Bonds	306.7	Cesar Cedeno	244.2	Mays	290.5
Wins	Lefty Grove	31	Christy Mathewson	312	Tom Seaver	182	Young	239
WL %	Elroy Face	.947	Lefty Grove	.705	Tom Seaver	.630	Ford	.693
Strikeouts	Nolan Ryan	260	Nolan Ryan	2686	Nolan Ryan	2686	Ryan	2686
ERA	Mordecai Brown	1.47	Walter Johnson	1.65	Tom Seaver	2.47	Walsh	1.77
Shutouts	Mordecai Brown	9	Walter Johnson	86	Don Sutton	44	Johnson	86
Saves	Bruce Sutter	45	Bruce Sutter	260	Bruce Sutter	260	Fingers	208

TOP ALTERNATIVE SELECTIONS

POS	Player, Season	G	AB	H	2B	3B	HR	Run	RBI	BB	SO	SB	Avg
1B	Bill Terry, 1930	154	633	254	39	15	23	139	129	57	33	8	.401
1B	Rod Carew, 1977	155	616	239	38	16	14	128	100	69	55	23	.388
1B	Willie McCovey, 1969	149	491	157	26	2	45	101	126	121	66	0	.320
3B	Ken Keltner, 1948	153	558	166	24	4	31	91	119	89	52	2	.297
2B	Rogers Hornsby, 1927	155	568	205	32	9	26	133	125	86	38	9	.361
RF	Sam Crawford, 1911	146	574	217	36	14	7	109	115	61		37	.378
SS	Honus Wagner, 1905	147	548	199	32	14	6	114	101	54		57	.363

OUTSTANDING PLAYERS WHO WERE 31 YEARS OLD IN 1985 INCLUDE: Gary Carter, Keith Hernandez, John Tudor

OTHER PLAYERS WHO COULD HAVE BEEN CHOSEN TO THE 31-YEAR-OLD ALL-STAR TEAM INCLUDE: Second Baseman Charlie Gehringer (1934; 134 Runs, 127 RBI), Shortstops Dave Bancroft (1922; Stats quite similar to Rizutto's), Joe Cronin (1938; .325, 51 Doubles), Arky Vaughan (1943; 112 Runs Scored) and Alvin Dark (1953), Outfielders Ty Cobb (1918; .382), Heine Manush (1933), Paul Waner (1934; .362, 122 Runs Scored), Minnie Minoso (1954; .320, 116 RBI, 18 Triples), Richie Ashburn (1958; .350, 97 Walks), Dave Kingman (1979; 48 Homers, .288) and Ben Oglivie (1980; 41 Home Runs, .304), and Pitchers Christy Mathewson (1912; 23-12, 2.12 ERA), Elroy Face (1959; 18-1), Mickey Lolich (1972; 22-14), Mike Marshall (1974; 106 Appearances), Don Sutton (1976; 21-10), Rollie Fingers (1978; 37 Saves) and John Tudor (1985).

MOST VALUABLE 31-YEAR-OLD: Joe Morgan

AGE 32

ALL-TIME ALL-STAR TEAM

POS	Player, Season	G	AB	H	2B	3B	HR	Run	RBI	BB	SO	SB	Avg
C	Walker Cooper, 1947	140	515	157	24	8	35	79	122	24	43	2	.305
1B	Johnny Mize, 1947	154	586	177	26	2	51	137	138	74	72	2	.302
2B	Joe Morgan, 1976	141	472	151	30	5	27	113	111	114	41	60	.320
3B	George Brett, 1985	155	550	184	38	5	30	108	112	103	49	9	.335
SS	Joe Cronin, 1939	143	520	160	33	3	19	97	107	87	48	6	.308
LF	Billy Williams, 1937	161	636	205	34	4	42	137	129	72	65	7	.322
CF	Jesse Burkett, 1901	142	597	228	21	17	10	139	75	59		27	.382
RF	Babe Ruth, 1927	154	540	192	29	8	60	158	164	138	89	7	.356

POS	Player, Season	G	IP	W	L	Pct.	SO	BB	ERA	ShO	Sv
RS	Dolf Luque, 1923	41	322	27	8	.771	151	88	1.93	6	2
LS	Whitey Ford, 1961	39	283	25	4	.862	209	92	3.21	3	0
3S	Bob Gibson, 1968	34	305	22	9	.710	268	62	1.12	13	0
4S	Warren Spahn, 1953	35	266	23	7	.767	148	70	2.10	5	3
RA	Dan Quisenberry, 1985	84	129	8	9	.471	54	16	2.37	0	37

	RECORD AT AGE 32		CAREER LEADER THROUGH AGE 32		LEADER AMONG ACTIVE PLAYERS		PACE OF RECORD HOLDER	
Games	Dwight Evans	162	Mel Ott	2165	Rusty Staub	1998	Rose	1697
At Bats	Pete Rose	680	Vada Pinson	7970	Rusty Staub	7171	Rose	6907
Runs	Babe Ruth	158	Jimmie Foxx	1591	Pete Rose	1107	Cobb	1415
Hits	Lefty O'Doul	254	Ty Cobb	2715	Pete Rose	2152	Rose	2152
Doubles	Earl Webb	67	Joe Medwick	507	George Brett	400	Speaker	445
Triples	Crawford & Seymour	21	Sam Crawford	231	George Brett	108	Crawford	231
Home Runs	Babe Ruth	60	Jimmie Foxx	500	Mike Schmidt	349	Aaron	442
RBI	Babe Ruth	164	Jimmie Foxx	1743	Jim Rice	1179	Aaron	1432
Walks	Jimmy Sheckard	147	Eddie Yost	1409	Rusty Staub	961	Ruth	1218
Strikeouts	Donn Clendenon	163	Bobby Bonds	1504	Reggie Jackson	1499	Jackson	1499
Stolen Bases	Ron LeFlore	97	Billy Hamilton	889	(Rickey Henderson)	573	Brock	502
Average	O'Doul & Heilmann	.398	Ty Cobb	.372	Rod Carew	.334	Cobb	.372
Power/Speed	Ken Williams	37.9	Bobby Bonds	342.7	Cesar Cedeno	266.9	Mays	307.9
Wins	McGinnity & Bagby	31	Christy Mathewson	337	Tom Seaver	203	Young	266
WL %	Whitey Ford	.862	Whitey Ford	.715	Tom Seaver	.642	Ford	.715
Strikeouts	Bob Gibson	268	Nolan Ryan	2909	Nolan Ryan	2909	Ryan	2909
ERA	Bob Gibson	1.12	Mordecai Brown	1.63	Tom Seaver	2.48	Walsh	1.79
Shutouts	Bob Gibson	13	Walter Johnson	90	Don Sutton	47	Johnson	90
Saves	Dan Quisenberry	37	Bruce Sutter	283	Bruce Sutter	283	Fingers	221

TOP ALTERNATIVE SELECTIONS

POS	Player, Season	G	AB	H	2B	3B	HR	Run	RBI	BB	SO	SB	Avg
C	Bill Dickey, 1939	128	480	145	23	3	24	98	105	77	37	5	.302
LF	Lefty O'Doul, 1929	154	638	254	35	6	32	152	122	76	19	2	.398
RF	Harry Heilmann, 1927	141	505	201	50	9	14	106	120	72	16	11	.398
CF	Tris Speaker, 1920	150	552	214	50	11	8	137	107	97	13	10	.388
CF	Cy Seymour, 1905	149	581	219	40	21	8	95	121	51		21	.377
LF	Ken Williams, 1922	153	585	194	34	11	39	128	155	74	31	37	.332
RF	Roberto Clemente, 1967	147	585	209	26	10	23	103	110	41	103	9	.357

POS	Player, Season	G	IP	W	L	Pct	SO	BB	ERA	ShO	Sv
4S	Mordecai Brown, 1909	50	343	27	9	.750	172	53	1.31	8	7
4S	Joe McGinnity, 1903	55	434	31	20	.608	171	109	2.43	3	2
4S	Jim Bagby, 1920	48	340	31	12	.721	73	79	2.89	3	0

OUTSTANDING PLAYERS WHO WERE 32 YEARS OLD IN 1985 INCLUDE: George Brett, Dan Quisenberry, Jim Rice, Bruce Sutter

OTHER PLAYERS WHO COULD HAVE BEEN CHOSEN TO THE 32-YEAR-OLD ALL-STAR TEAM INCLUDE: First Basemen George Sisler (1925) and Bill Terry (1931; .349, 20 Triples), Second Baseman Rogers Hornsby (1928; .387), Shortstops Honus Wagner (1906; .339, 53 Stolen Bases) and Luke Appling (1939; .314), Outfielders Gavvy Cravath (1913; .341, 128 RBI), Stan Musial (1953; .337, 53 Doubles, 30 Home Runs), Henry Aaron (1966; 44 Home Runs, 127 RBI), Frank Howard (1969; 48 Home Runs), Jim Wynn (1974) and Dwight Evans (1984), and Pitchers Christy Mathewson (1913; 25-11), Herb Pennock (1926; 23-11), Lefty Grove (1932; 25-10), Bob Feller (1951; 22-8), Bob Purkey (1962; 23-5), Mike Cuellar (1969; 23-11, 2.38 ERA), Steve Carlton (1977; 23-10), Jim Palmer (1978; 21-12) and Sparky Lyle (1977; 13-5, 26 Saves).

MOST VALUABLE 32-YEAR-OLD: Babe Ruth

AGE 33
ALL-TIME ALL-STAR TEAM

POS	Player, Season	G	AB	H	2B	3B	HR	Run	RBI	BB	SO	SB	Avg
C	Roy Campanella, 1955	123	446	142	20	1	32	81	107	56	41	2	.318
1B	Lou Gehrig, 1936	155	579	205	37	7	49	167	152	130	46	3	.354
2B	Rogers Hornsby, 1929	156	602	229	47	8	39	156	149	87	65	2	.380
3B	Harmon Killebrew, 1969	162	555	153	20	2	49	106	140	145	84	8	.276
SS	Honus Wagner, 1907	142	515	180	42	14	6	98	82	46		61	.350
LF	Paul Waner, 1936	148	585	218	53	9	5	107	94	74	29	7	.373
CF	Joe DiMaggio, 1948	153	594	190	26	11	39	110	155	67	30	1	.320
RF	Babe Ruth, 1928	154	536	173	29	8	54	163	142	135	87	4	.323

POS	Player, Season	G	IP	W	L	Pct.	SO	BB	ERA	ShO	Sv
RS	Dazzy Vance, 1924	35	309	28	6	.824	262	77	2.16	3	0
LS	Carl Hubbell, 1936	42	304	26	6	.813	123	57	2.31	3	0
3S	Joe McGinnity, 1904	51	408	35	8	.814	144	86	1.61	9	5
4S	Lefty Grove, 1933	45	275	24	8	.750	114	83	3.20	2	6
RA	Jim Konstanty, 1950	74	152	16	7	.696	56	50	2.60	0	22

	RECORD AT AGE 33		CAREER LEADER THROUGH AGE 33		LEADER AMONG ACTIVE PLAYERS		PACE OF RECORD HOLDER	
Games	Rose & Oliver	163	Mel Ott	2317	Rusty Staub	2156	Rose	1860
At Bats	Felipe Alou	662	Vada Pinson	8454	Rusty Staub	7794	Rose	7759
Runs	Lou Gehrig	163	Jimmie Foxx	1678	Pete Rose	1217	Aaron	1501
Hits	Rogers Hornsby	229	Ty Cobb	2858	Pete Rose	2337	Rose	2337
Doubles	George Burns	64	Joe Medwick	524	Cesar Cedeno	418	Speaker	497
Triples	Sam Crawford	23	Sam Crawford	254	(George Brett)	108	Crawford	254
Home Runs	Babe Ruth	54	Jimmie Foxx	519	Mike Schmidt	389	Aaron	481
RBI	Lou Gehrig	152	Jimmie Foxx	1848	Ted Simmons	1195	Aaron	1541
Walks	Eddie Joost	149	Eddie Yost	1534	Mike Schmidt	1086	Ruth	1353
Strikeouts	Dave Kingman	156	Bobby Bonds	1639	Reggie Jackson	1606	Jackson	1606
Stolen Bases	Lou Brock	63	Billy Hamilton	918	(Rickey Henderson)	573	Brock	565
Average	Lefty O'Doul	.383	Ty Cobb	.370	Rod Carew	.333	Cobb	.370
Power/Speed	Bobby Bonds	36.0	Bobby Bonds	371.6	Cesar Cedeno	280.4	Mays	336.0
Wins	Joe McGinnity	35	Christy Mathewson	361	Tom Seaver	219	Young	285
WL %	Sandy Consuegra	.842	Lefty Grove	.712	Ron Guidry	.680	Ford	.709
Strikeouts	Bob Gibson	269	Nolan Ryan	3109	Nolan Ryan	3109	Ryan	3109
ERA	Eddie Cicotte	1.53	Mordecai Brown	1.66	Tom Seaver	2.51	Walsh	1.81
Shutouts	Joe McGinnity	9	Walter Johnson	91	Don Sutton	49	Johnson	91
Saves	Ron Perranoski	31	(Bruce Sutter)	283	(Bruce Sutter)	283	Fingers	244

TOP ALTERNATIVE SELECTIONS

POS	Player, Season	G	AB	H	2B	3B	HR	Run	RBI	BB	SO	SB	Avg
1B	Bill Terry, 1932	154	613	225	42	11	28	124	117	32	23	4	.350
1B	Stan Musial, 1954	153	591	195	41	9	35	120	126	103	39	1	.330
2B	Charlie Gehringer, 1936	154	641	227	60	12	15	144	116	83	13	4	.354

POS	Player, Season	G	IP	W	L	Pct	SO	BB	ERA	ShO	Sv
4S	Eddie Cicotte, 1917	49	347	28	12	.700	150	70	1.53	7	4
RA	Ron Perranoski, 1969	75	120	9	10	.474	62	52	2.11	0	31

OUTSTANDING PLAYERS WHO WERE 33 YEARS OLD IN 1985 INCLUDE: Buddy Bell, Dwight Evans, Goose Gossage, Dave Winfield

OTHER PLAYERS WHO COULD HAVE BEEN CHOSEN TO THE 33-YEAR-OLD ALL-STAR TEAM INCLUDE: First Baseman George Burns (1921; .358, 64 Doubles), Second Baseman Joe Gordon (1948; 32 Homers, 124 RBI), Third Basemen Ken Boyer (1964; 119 RBI) and Mike Schmidt (1982; 40 Home Runs, 128 Walks), Shortstops Luke Appling (1940; .348) and Eddie Joost (1949; 149 Walks, 128 Runs Scored), Outfielders Sam Crawford (1913; .316, 23 Triples), Tris Speaker (1921; .362, 52 Doubles), Lefty O'Doul (1930; .383), Dixie Walker (1944; .357), Willie Mays (1964; 47 Home Runs), Frank Howard (1970; 44 Homers, 126 RBI, 132 Walks) and Willie Stargell (1973; 44 Homers, 43 Doubles), and Pitchers Grover Cleveland Alexander (1920; 27-14), Bob Lemon (1954; 23-7), Warren Spahn (1954; 21-12), Larry Jackson (1964; 24-11), Mike Cuellar (1970; 23-8), Gaylord Perry (1972; 24-16, 1.92 ERA), Luis Tiant (1974; 22-13) and Tom Seaver (1977; 21-6).

MOST VALUABLE 33-YEAR-OLD: Lou Gehrig

AGE 34
ALL-TIME ALL-STAR TEAM

POS	Player, Season	G	AB	H	2B	3B	HR	Run	RBI	BB	SO	SB	Avg
C	Elston Howard, 1963	135	487	140	21	6	28	75	85	35	68	0	.287
1B	Lou Gehrig, 1937	157	569	200	37	9	37	138	159	127	49	4	.351
2B	Charlie Gehringer, 1937	144	564	209	40	1	14	133	96	90	25	11	.371
3B	Peter Rose, 1975	162	662	210	47	4	7	112	74	89	50	0	.317
SS	Honus Wagner, 1908	151	568	201	39	19	10	100	109	54		53	.354
LF	Earl Averill, 1936	152	614	232	39	15	28	136	126	65	35	3	.378
CF	Willie Mays, 1965	157	558	177	21	3	52	118	112	76	71	9	.317
RF	Babe Ruth, 1929	135	499	172	26	6	46	121	154	72	60	5	.345

		G	IP	W	L	Pct.	SO	BB	ERA	ShO	Sv
RS	Cy Young, 1901	43	371	33	10	.767	158	37	1.62	5	0
LS	Ron Guidry, 1985	34	259	22	6	.786	143	42	3.27	2	0
3S	Sal Maglie, 1951	42	298	23	6	.793	146	86	2.93	3	4
4S	Dazzy Vance, 1925	31	265	22	9	.710	221	66	3.53	4	0
RA	Rollie Fingers, 1981	47	78	6	3	.667	61	13	1.04	0	28

	RECORD AT AGE 34		CAREER LEADER THROUGH AGE 34		LEADER AMONG ACTIVE PLAYERS		PACE OF RECORD HOLDER	
Games	Ernie Banks	163	Mel Ott	2442	Rusty Staub	2318	Rose	2022
At Bats	Pete Rose	662	Vada Pinson	8920	Rusty Staub	8436	Rose	8221
Runs	Lou Gehrig	138	Lou Gehrig	1771	Pete Rose	1329	Cobb	1625
Hits	Earl Averill	232	Ty Cobb	3055	Pete Rose	2547	Rose	2547
Doubles	Lajoie & Burns	51	Tris Speaker	545	Pete Rose	441	Speaker	545
Triples	Sam Crawford	26	Sam Crawford	280	(George Brett)	108	Crawford	280
Home Runs	Willie Mays	52	Jimmie Foxx	527	Mike Schmidt	425	Aaron	510
RBI	Lou Gehrig	159	Jimmie Foxx	1881	Rusty Staub	1255	Aaron	1627
Walks	Harmon Killebrew	128	Eddie Yost	1584	Mike Schmidt	1178	Ruth	1425
Strikeouts	Thomas & D. Johnson	126	Reggie Jackson	1728	Reggie Jackson	1728	Jackson	1728
Stolen Bases	Lou Brock	118	Billy Hamilton	937	(Rickey Henderson)	573	Brock	635
Average	Ty Cobb	.389	Ty Cobb	.371	Rod Carew	.333	Cobb	.371
Power/Speed	Henry Aaron	28.5	Bobby Bonds	380.2	Cesar Cedeno	292.1	Mays	356.9
Wins	Cy Young	33	Christy Mathewson	369	Tom Seaver	235	Young	318
WL %	Sal Maglie	.793	Whitey Ford	.718	Ron Guidry	.694	Ford	.718
Strikeouts	Bob Gibson	274	Nolan Ryan	3249	Nolan Ryan	3249	Ryan	3249
ERA	Cy Young	1.62	Mordecai Brown	1.79	Tom Seaver	2.55	Walsh	1.81
Shutouts	Gaylord Perry	7	Walter Johnson	95	Tom Seaver	52	Johnson	95
Saves	Ron Perranoski	34	(Bruce Sutter)	283	(Bruce Sutter)	283	Fingers	272

TOP ALTERNATIVE SELECTIONS

POS	Player, Season	G	AB	H	2B	3B	HR	Run	RBI	BB	SO	SB	Avg
2B	Nap Lajoie, 1910	159	591	227	51	7	4	92	76	60		26	.384
SS	Joe Cronin, 1941	143	518	161	38	8	16	98	95	82	55	1	.311
LF	Ed Delahanty, 1902	123	473	178	43	14	10	103	93	62		16	.376
CF	Ty Cobb, 1921	128	507	197	37	16	12	124	101	56	19	22	.389
LF	Billy Williams, 1972	150	574	191	34	6	37	95	122	62	59	3	.333
LF	Lou Brock, 1974	153	635	194	25	7	3	105	48	61	88	118	.306
LF	Reggie Jackson, 1980	143	514	154	22	4	41	94	111	83	122	1	.300

		G	IP	W	L	Pct	SO	BB	ERA	ShO	Sv
4S	Carl Hubbell, 1937	39	262	22	8	.733	159	55	3.20	4	4
4S	Bob Gibson, 1970	34	294	23	7	.767	274	88	3.12	3	0

OUTSTANDING PLAYERS WHO WERE 34 YEARS OLD IN 1985 INCLUDE: Doyle Alexander, Bert Blyleven, Ron Guidry, Bill Madlock, Dave Parker

OTHER PLAYERS WHO COULD HAVE BEEN CHOSEN TO THE 34-YEAR-OLD ALL-STAR TEAM INCLUDE: Second Baseman Red Schoendienst (1957; 200 hits, 15 HR), Third Basemen Harmon Killebrew (1970; 41 HR, 128 Walks) and Mike Schmidt (1984), Shortstop Luke Appling (1941), Outfielders Zack Wheat (1920), Tris Speaker (1922; .378),Paul Waner (1937), Harry Heilmann (1929), Dave Parker (1985), and Pitchers Three Finger Brown (1911; 21-11, 13 Saves), Burleigh Grimes (1928; 25-14), Red Ruffing (1938; 21-7), Virgil Trucks (1973; 20-10) and Early Wynn (1954; 23-11, 2.73 ERA).

MOST VALUABLE 34-YEAR-OLD: Cy Young

AGE 35
ALL-TIME ALL-STAR TEAM

POS	Player, Season	G	AB	H	2B	3B	HR	Run	RBI	BB	SO	SB	Avg
C	Elston Howard, 1964	150	550	172	27	3	15	63	84	48	73	4	.313
1B	Mickey Vernon, 1953	152	608	205	43	11	15	101	115	63	57	4	.337
2B	Charlie Gehringer, 1938	152	568	174	32	5	20	133	107	112	21	14	.306
3B	Pete Rose, 1976	162	665	215	42	6	10	130	63	86	54	9	.323
SS	Honus Wagner, 1910	137	495	168	39	10	5	92	100	66		35	.339
LF	Ty Cobb, 1922	137	526	211	42	16	4	99	99	55	24	9	.401
CF	Tris Speaker, 1923	150	574	218	59	11	17	133	130	93	15	10	.380
RF	Babe Ruth, 1930	145	518	186	28	9	49	150	153	136	61	10	.359
DH	Hal McRae, 1982	159	613	189	46	8	27	91	133	55	61	4	.308

		G	IP	W	L	Pct.	SO	BB	ERA	ShO	Sv
RS	Spud Chandler, 1943	30	253	20	4	.833	134	54	1.64	5	0
LS	Steve Carlton, 1980	38	304	24	9	.727	286	90	2.34	3	0
3S	Cy Young, 1902	45	385	32	11	.744	160	53	2.15	3	0
4S	Bucky Walters, 1944	34	285	23	8	.741	77	87	2.40	6	1
RA	Tug McGraw, 1980	57	92	5	4	.556	75	23	1.47	0	20

	RECORD AT AGE 35		CAREER LEADER THROUGH AGE 35		LEADER AMONG ACTIVE PLAYERS		PACE OF RECORD HOLDER	
Games	Rose & Buckner	162	Mel Ott	2561	Rusty Staub	2424	Rose	2184
At Bats	Bill Buckner	673	Henry Aaron	9436	Pete Rose	8886	Rose	8886
Runs	Babe Ruth	150	Lou Gehrig	1886	Pete Rose	1459	Cobb	1724
Hits	Sam Rice	227	Ty Cobb	3266	Pete Rose	2762	Rose	2762
Doubles	Tris Speaker	59	Tris Speaker	604	Pete Rose	483	Speaker	604
Triples	Sam Crawford	19	Sam Crawford	299	(George Brett)	108	Crawford	299
Home Runs	Babe Ruth	49	Babe Ruth	565	Mike Schmidt	458	Aaron	554
RBI	Babe Ruth	136	Lou Gehrig	1989	Ted Simmons	1323	Aaron	1724
Walks	Ruth & Williams	136	Mel Ott	1629	Mike Schmidt	1265	Ruth	1561
Strikeouts	Dave Kingman	119	Reggie Jackson	1810	Reggie Jackson	1810	Jackson	1810
Stolen Bases	Lou Brock	56	Billy Hamilton	937	(Rickey Henderson)	573	Brock	753
Average	Ty Cobb	.401	Ty Cobb	.373	Rod Carew	.332	Cobb	.373
Power/Speed	Bill Bruton	19.2	Bobby Bonds	386.0	(Cesar Cedeno)	292.1	Mays	370.1
Wins	Cy Young	32	Christy Mathewson	373	Steve Carlton	249	Young	350
WL %	Spud Chandler	.833	Whitey Ford	.720	(Ron Guidry)	.694	Ford	.720
Strikeouts	Steve Carlton	286	Nolan Ryan	3494	Nolan Ryan	3494	Ryan	3494
ERA	Spud Chandler	1.64	Ed Walsh	1.81	Tom Seaver	2.60	Walsh	1.81
Shutouts	Walters & Bunning	6	Walter Johnson	98	Tom Seaver	53	Johnson	98
Saves	Rollie Fingers	29	Rollie Fingers	301	Rollie Fingers	301	Fingers	301

TOP ALTERNATIVE SELECTIONS

POS	Player, Season	G	AB	H	2B	3B	HR	Run	RBI	BB	SO	SB	Avg
C	Carlton Fisk, 1983	138	488	141	26	4	26	85	86	46	88	9	.289
LF	Hank Aaron, 1969	147	547	164	30	3	44	100	97	87	47	9	.300
CF	Cy Williams, 1923	136	535	157	22	3	41	98	114	59	57	11	.293
CF	Joe DiMaggio, 1950	139	525	158	33	10	32	114	122	80	33	0	.301
RF	Tommy Henrich, 1948	146	588	181	42	14	25	138	100	76	42	2	.308

		G	IP	W	L	Pct	SO	BB	ERA	ShO	Sv
4S	Joe McGinnity, 1906	45	340	27	12	.692	105	71	2.25	3	2
4S	Eddie Cicotte, 1919	40	307	29	7	.806	110	49	1.82	5	1
RA	Stu Miller, 1963	71	112	5	8	.385	114	53	2.24	0	27

OUTSTANDING PLAYERS WHO WERE 35 YEARS OLD IN 1985 INCLUDE: Cecil Cooper, Mike Schmidt, Ted Simmons

OTHER PLAYERS WHO COULD HAVE BEEN CHOSEN TO THE 35-YEAR-OLD ALL-STAR TEAM INCLUDE: First Basemen Bill Terry (1934; .354), Hank Greenberg (1946; 44 HR, 127 RBI), Johnny Mize (1948; 40 HR, 125 RBI) and Al Oliver (1982; 22 HR, 109 RBI, .331), Second Basemen Larry Gardner (1921; .319, 115 RBI) and Rogers Hornsby (1931; .331, 100 G), Shortstop Eddie Joost (1951), Outfielders Zack Wheat (1921; .320), Lefty O'Doul (1932; .368), Goose Goslin (1936; 125 RBI), Hank Sauer (1954; 41 Homers), Ted Williams (1954; .345, 136 Walks) and Stan Musial (1956; 27 Homers, 109 RBI, .310), and Pitchers Lefty Grove (1935; 20-12), Red Ruffing (1939; 21-7), Warren Spahn (1956; 20-11), Luis Tiant (1976; 21-12) and Rollie Fingers (1982).

MOST VALUABLE 35-YEAR-OLD: Tris Speaker

AGE 36
ALL-TIME ALL-STAR TEAM

POS	Player, Season	G	AB	H	2B	3B	HR	Run	RBI	BB	SO	SB	Avg
C	Gabby Hartnett, 1937	110	356	126	21	6	12	47	82	43	19	0	.354
1B	Stan Musial, 1957	134	502	176	38	3	29	82	102	66	34	1	.351
2B	Eddie Collins, 1923	145	505	182	22	5	5	89	67	84	8	47	.360
3B	Lave Cross, 1902	137	559	191	39	8	0	90	108	27		25	.342
SS	Luke Appling, 1943	155	585	192	33	2	3	63	80	90	29	27	.328
LF	Zack Wheat, 1922	152	600	201	29	12	16	92	112	45	22	9	.335
CF	Sam Rice, 1926	152	641	216	32	14	3	98	76	42	20	25	.337
RF	Babe Ruth, 1931	145	534	199	31	3	46	149	163	128	51	5	.373

		G	IP	W	L	Pct.	SO	BB	ERA	ShO	Sv
RS	Cy Young, 1903	40	342	28	9	.757	176	37	2.08	7	2
LS	Eddie Plank, 1912	37	260	26	6	.813	110	83	2.21	3	2
3S	Walter Johnson, 1924	38	278	23	7	.767	158	77	2.72	6	0
4S	Preacher Roe, 1951	34	258	22	3	.880	113	64	3.03	2	0
RA	Mike Marshall, 1979	90	143	10	15	.400	81	48	2.64	0	32

	RECORD AT AGE 36		CAREER LEADER THROUGH AGE 36		LEADER AMONG ACTIVE PLAYERS		PACE OF RECORD HOLDER	
Games	Several with	162	Mel Ott	2697	Rusty Staub	2533	Rose	2346
At Bats	Pete Rose	655	Hank Aaron	9952	Pete Rose	9541	Rose	9541
Runs	Babe Ruth	149	Lou Gehrig	1888	Pete Rose	1554	Cobb	1827
Hits	Sam Rice	216	Ty Cobb	3455	Pete Rose	2966	Rose	2966
Doubles	Hal McRae	41	Tris Speaker	640	Pete Rose	521	Speaker	640
Triples	Earl Averill	15	Sam Crawford	312	Rose & Brett	108	Crawford	312
Home Runs	Babe Ruth	46	Babe Ruth	611	Reggie Jackson	464	Aaron	592
RBI	Babe Ruth	163	Lou Gehrig	1990	Reggie Jackson	1386	Aaron	1842
Walks	Babe Ruth	128	Mickey Mantle	1734	(Mike Schmidt)	1265	Ruth	1689
Strikeouts	Reggie Jackson	156	Reggie Jackson	1966	Reggie Jackson	1966	Jackson	1966
Stolen Bases	Lou Brock	56	Billy Hamilton	937	(Rickey Henderson)	573	Brock	809
Average	Babe Ruth	.373	Ty Cobb	.371	Rod Carew	.331	Cobb	.371
Power/Speed	Dave Lopes	15.8	Bobby Bonds	386.0	Reggie Jackson	294.8	Mays	380.4
Wins	Cy Young	28	Cy Young	378	Steve Carlton	262	Young	378
WL %	Preacher Roe	.880	Whitey Ford	.705	Tom Seaver	.644	Ford	.705
Strikeouts	Gaylord Perry	233	Nolan Ryan	3677	Nolan Ryan	3677	Ryan	3677
ERA	Cy Young	2.08	Ed Walsh	1.82	Tom Seaver	2.60	Walsh	1.82
Shutouts	Cy Young	7	Walter Johnson	104	Don Sutton	55	Johnson	104
Saves	Mike Marshall	32	Rollie Fingers	301	Rollie Fingers	301	Fingers	301

TOP ALTERNATIVE SELECTIONS

POS	Player, Season	G	AB	H	2B	3B	HR	Run	RBI	BB	SO	SB	Avg
3B	Pete Rose, 1977	162	655	204	38	7	9	95	64	66	42	16	.311
SS	Luis Aparicio, 1970	146	552	173	29	3	5	86	43	53	34	8	.313
CF	Ty Cobb, 1923	145	556	189	40	7	6	103	88	66	14	9	.340
CF	Tris Speaker, 1924	135	486	167	36	9	9	94	65	72	13	5	.344
RF	Roberto Clemente, 1971	132	522	178	29	8	13	82	86	26	65	1	.341
SS	Honus Wagner, 1910	150	556	178	34	8	4	90	81	59	47	24	.320
RF	Henry Aaron, 1970	150	516	154	26	1	38	103	118	74	63	9	.298
LF	Jose Cruz, 1984	160	600	187	28	13	12	96	95	73	68	22	.312

OUTSTANDING PLAYERS WHO WERE 36 YEARS OLD IN 1985 INCLUDE: George Foster, Steve Garvey, Bobby Grich, Dave Kingman

OTHER PLAYERS WHO COULD HAVE BEEN CHOSEN TO THE 36-YEAR-OLD ALL-STAR TEAM INCLUDE: First Baseman Jake Beckley (1904; .325), Second Basemen Nap Lajoie (1912) and Charlie Gehringer (1939), Outfielders Earl Averill (1938; .330), Bob Johnson (1944), Dixie Walker (1947), Enos Slaughter (1952) and Minnie Minoso (1959; .302, 21 HR, 92 RBI), Designated Hitters Reggie Jackson (1982; 39 Homers, 101 RBI) and Hal McRae (1982; .311, 41 Doubles) and Pitchers Eddie Cicotte (1920; 21-10), Pete Alexander (1923; 22-12), Stan Coveleski (1925; 20-5), Early Wynn (1956; 20-9), Warren Spahn (1957; 21-11), Bob Gibson (1972; 19-11) and Tommy John (1979; 21-9).

MOST VALUABLE 36-YEAR-OLD: Babe Ruth

AGE 37

ALL-TIME ALL-STAR TEAM

POS	Player, Season	G	AB	H	2B	3B	HR	Run	RBI	BB	SO	SB	Avg
C	Carlton Fisk, 1985	153	543	129	23	1	37	85	107	52	81	17	.238
1B	Carl Yastrzemski, 1977	150	558	165	27	3	28	99	102	73	40	11	.296
2B	Charlie Gehringer, 1940	139	515	161	33	3	10	108	81	101	17	10	.313
3B	Pete Rose, 1978	159	655	198	51	3	7	103	52	62	30	13	.302
SS	Honus Wagner, 1911	130	473	158	23	16	9	87	89	67	34	20	.334
LF	Babe Ruth, 1932	133	457	156	13	5	41	120	137	130	62	2	.341
CF	Tris Speaker, 1925	117	429	167	35	5	12	79	87	70	12	5	.389
RF	Hank Aaron, 1971	139	495	162	22	3	47	95	118	71	58	1	.327

POS	Player, Season	G	IP	W	L	Pct.	SO	BB	ERA	ShO	Sv
RS	Dazzy Vance, 1928	38	280	22	10	.688	200	72	2.09	4	2
LS	Steve Carlton, 1982	38	296	23	11	.676	286	86	3.10	6	0
3S	Cy Young, 1904	43	380	26	16	.619	203	29	1.97	10	1
4S	Allie Reynolds, 1952	35	244	20	8	.714	160	97	2.06	6	6
RA	Stu Miller, 1965	67	119	14	7	.667	104	32	1.89	0	24

	RECORD AT AGE 37		CAREER LEADER THROUGH AGE 37		LEADER AMONG ACTIVE PLAYERS		PACE OF RECORD HOLDER	
Games	Pete Rose	159	Mel Ott	2728	Rusty Staub	2603	Rose	2505
At Bats	Pete Rose	655	Henry Aaron	10447	Pete Rose	10196	Rose	10196
Runs	Babe Ruth	120	Babe Ruth	1986	Pete Rose	1657	Cobb	1942
Hits	Ty Cobb	211	Ty Cobb	3666	Pete Rose	3164	Rose	3164
Doubles	Pete Rose	51	Tris Speaker	675	Pete Rose	572	Speaker	675
Triples	Honus Wagner	16	Sam Crawford	312	Pete Rose	111	Crawford	312
Home Runs	Hank Aaron	47	Babe Ruth	652	Reggie Jackson	478	Aaron	639
RBI	Babe Ruth	137	Babe Ruth	2012	Reggie Jackson	1435	Aaron	1960
Walks	Babe Ruth	130	Babe Ruth	1819	(Mike Schmidt)	1265	Ruth	1819
Strikeouts	Reggie Jackson	140	Reggie Jackson	2106	Reggie Jackson	2106	Jackson	2106
Stolen Bases	Lou Brock	56	Billy Hamilton	937	(Rickey Henderson)	573	Brock	865
Average	Tris Speaker	.389	Ty Cobb	.369	Rod Carew	.331	Cobb	.369
Power/Speed	Carlton Fisk	23.3	Willie Mays	396.2	Reggie Jackson	297.5	Mays	396.2
Wins	Cy Young	26	Cy Young	404	Steve Carlton	285	Young	404
WL %	Walter Johnson	.741	Whitey Ford	.696	Tom Seaver	.629	Ford	.696
Strikeouts	Steve Carlton	286	Nolan Ryan	3874	Nolan Ryan	3874	Ryan	3874
ERA	Cy Young	1.97	Ed Walsh	1.82	Tom Seaver	2.68	Walsh	1.82
Shutouts	Cy Young	10	Walter Johnson	107	Don Sutton	56	Johnson	107
Saves	Stu Miller	24	Rollie Fingers	324	Rollie Fingers	324	Fingers	324

TOP ALTERNATIVE SELECTIONS

POS	Player, Season	G	AB	H	2B	3B	HR	Run	RBI	BB	SO	SB	Avg
CF	Ty Cobb, 1924	155	625	211	38	10	4	115	74	85	18	23	.338
LF	Minnie Minoso, 1960	154	591	184	32	4	20	89	105	52	63	17	.311
LF	Ted Williams, 1956	136	400	138	28	2	24	71	82	102	39	0	.345

POS	Player, Season	G	IP	W	L	Pct	SO	BB	ERA	ShO	Sv
LS	Tommy John, 1980	36	265	22	9	.710	78	56	3.43	6	0
LS	Warren Spahn, 1958	38	290	22	11	.667	150	76	3.07	2	1
4S	Walter Johnson, 1925	30	229	20	7	.741	108	78	3.07	3	0
RA	Hoyt Wilhelm, 1961	51	110	9	7	.563	87	41	2.30	0	18
RA	Don McMahon, 1967	63	109	6	2	.750	84	40	1.98	0	5

OUTSTANDING PLAYERS WHO WERE 37 YEARS OLD IN 1985 INCLUDE: Jose Cruz, Carlton Fisk

OTHER PLAYERS WHO COULD HAVE BEEN CHOSEN TO THE 37-YEAR-OLD ALL-STAR TEAM INCLUDE: First Basemen Stan Musial (1957; .337), Mickey Vernon (1955; .301, 85 RBI), Ernie Banks (1968; 32 Home Runs) and Rod Carew (1983; .339), Second Baseman Nap Lajoie (1913; .335), Designated Hitter Frank Robinson (1973; 30 HR, 97 RBI), and Pitchers George McConnell (1914; 25-10), Ray Kremer (1930; 20-12) and Mike Cuellar (1974; 22-10).

MOST VALUABLE 37-YEAR-OLD: Henry Aaron

AGE 38
ALL-TIME ALL-STAR TEAM

POS	Player, Season	G	AB	H	2B	3B	HR	Run	RBI	BB	SO	SB	Avg
C	Gabby Hartnett, 1939	97	306	85	18	2	12	36	59	37	32	0	.278
1B	Jake Daubert, 1922	156	610	205	15	22	12	114	66	56	21	14	.336
2B	Joe Morgan, 1982	134	463	134	19	4	14	68	61	85	60	24	.289
3B	Lave Cross, 1904	155	607	176	31	10	1	73	71	13		10	.290
SS	Honus Wagner, 1912	145	558	181	35	20	7	91	102	59	38	26	.324
LF	Ted Williams, 1957	132	420	163	28	1	38	96	87	119	43	0	.388
CF	Ty Cobb, 1925	121	415	157	31	12	12	97	102	65	12	13	.378
RF	Zack Wheat, 1924	141	566	212	41	8	14	92	97	49	18	3	.375

		G	IP	W	L	Pct.	SO	BB	ERA	ShO	Sv
RS	Spud Chandler, 1946	34	257	20	8	.714	138	90	2.10	6	2
LS	Warren Spahn, 1959	40	292	21	15	.583	143	70	2.96	4	0
3S	Three Finger Brown, 1915	35	236	17	8	.680	95	64	2.09	3	3
4S	Dutch Leonard, 1947	32	235	17	12	.586	103	57	2.68	3	0
5S	Fred Fitzsimmons, 1940	20	134	16	2	.889	35	25	2.82	4	1
RA	Gerry Staley, 1959	67	116	8	5	.615	54	25	2.25	0	14

	RECORD AT AGE 38		CAREER LEADER THROUGH AGE 38		LEADER AMONG ACTIVE PLAYERS		PACE OF RECORD HOLDER	
Games	Pete Rose	163	Henry Aaron	2844	Rusty Staub	2715	Rose	2668
At Bats	Pete Rose	628	Henry Aaron	10896	Pete Rose	10824	Rose	10824
Runs	Jake Daubert	114	Babe Ruth	2083	Pete Rose	1747	Cobb	2039
Hits	Zack Wheat	212	Ty Cobb	3823	Pete Rose	3372	Rose	3372
Doubles	Tris Speaker	52	Tris Speaker	727	Pete Rose	612	Speaker	727
Triples	Jake Daubert	22	Sam Crawford	312	Pete Rose	116	Crawford	312
Home Runs	Darrell Evans	40	Babe Ruth	686	Reggie Jackson	503	Aaron	673
RBI	Ernie Banks	106	Babe Ruth	2115	Reggie Jackson	1516	Aaron	2037
Walks	Ted Williams	119	Babe Ruth	1933	Darrell Evans	1289	Ruth	1933
Strikeouts	Reggie Jackson	141	Reggie Jackson	2247	Reggie Jackson	2247	Jackson	2247
Stolen Bases	Lou Brock	35	Lou Brock	938	(Rickey Henderson)	573	Brock	900
Average	Ted Williams	.388	Ty Cobb	.369	Rod Carew	.330	Cobb	.369
Power/Speed	Joe Morgan	17.7	Willie Mays	404.4	Reggie Jackson	310.0	Mays	404.4
Wins	Warren Spahn	21	Cy Young	422	Steve Carlton	300	Young	422
WL %	Fred Fitzsimmons	.889	Whitey Ford	.690	Tom Seaver	.616	Ford	.690
Strikeouts	Steve Carlton	275	Nolan Ryan	4083	Nolan Ryan	4083	Ryan	4083
ERA	Cy Young	1.82	Ed Walsh	1.82	Tom Seaver	2.73	Walsh	1.82
Shutouts	Babe Adams	8	Walter Johnson	109	Sutton & Seaver	56	Johnson	109
Saves	Stu Miller	18	Rollie Fingers	341	Rollie Fingers	341	Fingers	341

TOP ALTERNATIVE SELECTIONS

POS	Player, Season	G	AB	H	2B	3B	HR	Run	RBI	BB	SO	SB	Avg
1B	Pete Rose, 1979	163	628	208	40	5	4	90	59	95	32	20	.331
1B	Darrell Evans, 1985	151	505	125	17	0	40	81	94	85		0	.248
1B	Ernie Banks, 1969	155	565	143	19	2	23	60	106	42	101	0	.253
LF	Minnie Minoso, 1961	152	540	151	28	3	14	91	82	67	46	9	.280
RF	Sam Rice, 1928	148	616	202	32	15	2	95	55	49	15	16	.328
RF	Babe Ruth, 1928	137	459	138	21	3	34	97	103	114	90	4	.301

		G	IP	W	L	Pct	SO	BB	ERA	ShO	Sv
5S	Babe Adams, 1920	35	263	17	13	.567	84	18	2.16	8	2
5S	Lefty Grove, 1938	24	164	14	4	.778	99	52	3.08	1	1
RA	Hoyt Wilhelm, 1962	52	93	7	10	.412	90	34	1.94	0	15

OUTSTANDING PLAYERS WHO WERE 38 YEARS OLD IN 1985 INCLUDE: Rollie Fingers, Al Oliver, Nolan Ryan

OTHER PLAYERS WHO COULD HAVE BEEN CHOSEN TO THE 38-YEAR-OLD ALL-STAR TEAM INCLUDE: Catchers Wally Schang (1928), Ernie Lombardi (1946) and Bob Boone (1985), First Baseman Tony Perez (1980; 105 RBI), Designated Hitter Frank Robinson (1974; 22 HR, 81 RBI), Outfielder Tris Speaker (1926; .304, 52 Doubles, 96 Runs) and Pitchers Cy Young (1905; 18-19), Pete Alexander (1925; 15-11) and Stu Miller (1966; 9-4, 2.25 ERA, 18 Saves).

MOST VALUABLE 38-YEAR-OLD: Ted Williams

AGE 39
ALL-TIME ALL-STAR TEAM

POS	Player, Season	G	AB	H	2B	3B	HR	Run	RBI	BB	SO	SB	Avg
C	Wilbert Robinson, 1903	91	335	98	16	7	1	39	57	12		11	.293
1B	Willie Stargell, 1979	126	424	119	19	0	32	60	82	47	105	0	.281
2B	Nap Lajoie, 1915	129	490	137	24	5	1	40	61	11	16	10	.280
3B	Lave Cross, 1905	147	583	155	29	5	0	68	77	26		8	.266
SS	Luke Appling, 1946	149	582	180	27	5	1	59	55	71	41	6	.309
LF	Zack Wheat, 1925	150	616	221	42	14	14	125	103	45	22	3	.359
CF	Willie Mays, 1970	139	478	139	15	2	28	94	83	79	90	5	.291
RF	Hank Aaron, 1973	120	392	118	12	1	40	84	96	68	51	1	.301

		G	IP	W	L	Pct.	SO	BB	ERA	ShO	Sv
RS	Gaylord Perry, 1978	37	261	21	6	.778	154	66	2.72	2	0
LS	Eddie Plank, 1915	42	268	21	11	.656	147	54	2.08	6	3
3S	Early Wynn, 1959	37	256	22	10	.688	179	119	3.16	5	0
4S	Warren Spahn, 1960	40	268	21	13	.618	154	74	3.49	4	0
RA	Joe Berry, 1944	53	111	10	8	.556	44	23	1.95	0	12

	RECORD AT AGE 39		CAREER LEADER THROUGH AGE 39		LEADER AMONG ACTIVE PLAYERS		PACE OF RECORD HOLDER	
Games	Pete Rose	162	Henry Aaron	2964	Pete Rose	2830	Rose	2830
At Bats	Pete Rose	655	Pete Rose	11479	Pete Rose	11479	Rose	11479
Runs	Zack Wheat	125	Babe Ruth	2161	Pete Rose	1842	Cobb	2087
Hits	Zack Wheat	221	Ty Cobb	3902	Pete Rose	3557	Rose	3557
Doubles	Tris Speaker	43	Tris Speaker	770	Pete Rose	654	Speaker	770
Triples	Zack Wheat	14	Sam Crawford	312	Pete Rose	117	Crawford	312
Home Runs	Hank Aaron	40	Henry Aaron	713	Reggie Jackson	530	Aaron	713
RBI	Zack Wheat	103	Babe Ruth	2199	Reggie Jackson	1601	Aaron	2133
Walks	Babe Ruth	103	Babe Ruth	2036	(Darrell Evans)	1289	Ruth	2036
Strikeouts	Reggie Jackson	138	Reggie Jackson	2385	Reggie Jackson	2385	Jackson	2385
Stolen Bases	Dave Lopes	47	Lou Brock	938	(Rickey Henderson)	573	Brock	917
Average	Zack Wheat	.359	Ty Cobb	.369	Rod Carew	.328	Cobb	.369
Power/Speed	Dave Lopes	17.9	Willie Mays	415.1	Reggie Jackson	315.9	Mays	415.1
Wins	Early Wynn	22	Steve Carlton	313	Steve Carlton	313	Young	435
WL %	Lefty Grove	.789	Tom Seaver	.614	Tom Seaver	.614	Ford	.690
Strikeouts	Phil Niekro	248	(Nolan Ryan)	4083	(Nolan Ryan)	4083	Ryan	4083
ERA	Lefty Grove	2.54	Tom Seaver	2.80	Tom Seaver	2.80	Walsh	1.82
Shutouts	Eddie Plank	6	Tom Seaver	60	Tom Seaver	60	Johnson	110
Saves	Ted Abernathy	23	(Rollie Fingers)	341	(Rollie Fingers)	341	Fingers	341

TOP ALTERNATIVE SELECTIONS

POS	Player, Season	G	AB	H	2B	3B	HR	Run	RBI	BB	SO	SB	Avg
1B	Willie McCovey, 1977	141	478	134	21	0	28	54	86	67	106	3	.280
LF	Ted Williams, 1958	129	411	135	23	2	26	81	85	98	49	1	.328
CF	Tris Speaker, 1927	141	523	171	43	6	2	71	73	55	8	9	.327
RF	Sam Rice, 1929	150	616	199	39	10	1	119	62	55	9	16	.323
RF	Reggie Jackson, 1985	143	460	116	27	0	27	64	85	78	138	1	.252

		G	IP	W	L	Pct	SO	BB	ERA	ShO	Sv
3S	Dazzy Vance, 1930	35	259	17	15	.531	173	55	2.61	4	0
4S	Lefty Grove, 1939	23	191	15	4	.789	81	58	2.54	2	0
RA	Hoyt Wilhelm, 1963	55	136	5	8	.385	111	30	2.64	0	21

OUTSTANDING PLAYERS WHO WERE 39 YEARS OLD IN 1985 INCLUDE: Rod Carew, Reggie Jackson

OTHER PLAYERS WHO COULD HAVE BEEN CHOSEN TO THE 39-YEAR-OLD ALL-STAR TEAM INCLUDE: Catchers Chief Zimmer (1900), Wally Schang (1929) and Walker Cooper (1954), First Basemen Jake Daubert (1923; .292) and Pete Rose (1980; 162 G, 42 Doubles), Second Basemen Eddie Collins (1926; .344, 106 G) and Joe Morgan (1983), Outfielders Ty Cobb (1926; .339, 79 G), Cy Williams (1927; 30 Home Runs), Babe Ruth (1934; 22 HR), Enos Slaughter (1955; .315; 118 G), Stan Musial (1960) and Dave Lopes (1985), Designated Hitter Carl Yastrzemski (1979), and Pitcher Phil Niekro (1978; 19-18, 248 K).

MOST VALUABLE 39-YEAR-OLD: Zack Wheat

AGE 40

ALL-TIME ALL-STAR TEAM

POS	Player, Season	G	AB	H	2B	3B	HR	Run	RBI	BB	SO	SB	Avg
C	Gabby Hartnett, 1941	64	150	45	5	0	5	20	26	12	14	0	.300
1B	Pete Rose, 1981	107	431	140	18	5	0	73	33	46	26	4	.325
2B	Dave Shean, 1918	115	425	112	16	3	0	58	34	40	25	11	.264
3B	Graig Nettles, 1985	134	440	115	23	1	15	66	61	72		0	.261
SS	Luke Appling, 1947	139	503	154	29	0	8	67	49	64	28	8	.306
LF	Willie Mays, 1971	136	417	113	24	5	18	82	61	112	123	23	.271
CF	Ty Cobb, 1927	134	490	175	32	7	5	104	94	67	12	22	.357
RF	Sam Rice, 1930	147	593	207	35	13	1	121	73	55	14	13	.349

POS	Player, Season	G	IP	W	L	Pct.	SO	BB	ERA	ShO	Sv
RS	Pete Alexander, 1927	37	268	21	10	.677	48	38	2.52	2	3
LS	Warren Spahn, 1961	38	263	21	13	.618	115	64	3.01	4	0
4S	Phil Niekro, 1979	44	342	21	20	.512	208	113	3.39	1	0
4S	Tom Seaver, 1985	35	239	16	11	.593	134	69	3.17	1	0
RA	Hoyt Wilhelm, 1964	73	131	12	9	.571	95	30	1.99	0	27

	RECORD AT AGE 40		CAREER LEADER THROUGH AGE 40		LEADER AMONG ACTIVE PLAYERS		PACE OF RECORD HOLDER	
Games	Honus Wagner	150	Henry Aaron	3076	Pete Rose	2937	Rose	2937
At Bats	Sam Rice	593	Pete Rose	11910	Pete Rose	11910	Rose	11910
Runs	Sam Rice	121	Ty Cobb	2191	Pete Rose	1915	Cobb	2191
Hits	Sam Rice	207	Ty Cobb	4077	Pete Rose	3697	Rose	3697
Doubles	Sam Rice	35	Tris Speaker	793	Pete Rose	672	Speaker	793
Triples	Sam Rice	13	Sam Crawford	312	Pete Rose	122	Crawford	312
Home Runs	Hank Aaron	20	Hank Aaron	733	(Reggie Jackson)	530	Aaron	733
RBI	Ty Cobb	94	Babe Ruth	2211	(Reggie Jackson)	1601	Aaron	2202
Walks	Willie Mays	112	Babe Ruth	2056	Pete Rose	1292	Ruth	2056
Strikeouts	Willie Mays	123	Reggie Jackson	2385	(Reggie Jackson)	2385	Jackson	2385
Stolen Bases	Wagner & Mays	23	Lou Brock	938	(Rickey Henderson)	573	Brock	938
Average	Ty Cobb	.357	Ty Cobb	.368	(Rod Carew)	.328	Cobb	.368
Power/Speed	Willie Mays	20.2	Willie Mays	439.5	(Reggie Jackson)	315.9	Mays	439.5
Wins	Cy Young	22	Cy Young	457	Steve Carlton	314	Young	457
WL %	Pete Alexander	.677	Whitey Ford	.690	Tom Seaver	.613	Ford	.690
Strikeouts	Phil Niekro	208	(Nolan Ryan)	4083	(Nolan Ryan)	4083	Ryan	4083
ERA	Cy Young	1.99	Ed Walsh	1.82	Tom Seaver	2.82	Walsh	1.82
Shutouts	Cy Young	6	Walter Johnson	110	Tom Seaver	61	Johnson	110
Saves	Hoyt Wilhelm	27	(Rollie Fingers)	341	(Rollie Fingers)	341	Fingers	341

TOP ALTERNATIVE SELECTIONS

POS	Player, Season	G	AB	H	2B	3B	HR	Run	RBI	BB	SO	SB	Avg
1B	Mickey Vernon, 1958	119	355	104	22	3	8	49	55	44	56	0	.293
SS	Honus Wagner, 1914	150	552	139	15	9	1	60	50	51	51	23	.252
LF	Stan Musial, 1961	123	372	107	22	4	15	46	70	52	35	0	.288
LF	Lou Brock, 1979	120	405	123	15	4	5	56	38	23	43	21	.304
RF	Henry Aaron, 1974	112	340	91	16	0	20	47	69	39	29	1	.268

POS	Player, Season	G	IP	W	L	Pct	SO	BB	ERA	ShO	Sv
3S	Cy Young, 1907	43	343	22	15	.595	147	51	1.99	6	3

OUTSTANDING PLAYERS WHO WERE 40 YEARS OLD IN 1985 INCLUDE: Steve Carlton, Graig Nettles, Tom Seaver, Don Sutton

OTHER PLAYERS WHO COULD HAVE BEEN CHOSEN TO THE 40-YEAR-OLD ALL-STAR TEAM INCLUDE: Catchers Chief Zimmer (1901), Deacon McGuire (1906) and Walker Cooper (1955), Second Basemen Eddie Collins (1927; .338, 95 G) and Rabbit Maranville (1932), Third Baseman Lave Cross (1906; .263, 130 G), Outfielders Dummy Hoy (1902; .294, 72 G), Zack Wheat (1926; .290, 111 G) and Johnny Cooney (1941; 123 G, .319), and Pitchers Eddie Plank (1916; 15-15, 2.33 ERA) and Don Sutton (1985; 15-10).

MOST VALUABLE 40-YEAR-OLD: Willie Mays

AGE 41

ALL-TIME ALL-STAR TEAM

POS	Player, Season	G	AB	H	2B	3B	HR	Run	RBI	BB	SO	SB	Avg
C	Chief Zimmer, 1902	42	142	38	4	2	0	13	17	11		4	.268
1B	Pete Rose, 1982	162	634	172	25	4	3	80	54	66	32	8	.271
2B	Honus Wagner, 1915	156	566	155	32	17	6	68	78	39	64	22	.274
3B	Bert Campaneris, 1983	60	143	46	5	0	0	19	11	8	9	6	.322
SS	Luke Appling, 1948	129	497	156	16	2	0	63	47	94	35	10	.314
LF	Ted Williams, 1960	113	310	98	15	0	29	56	72	75	41	1	.316
CF	Ty Cobb, 1928	95	353	114	27	4	1	54	40	34	16	5	.323
RF	Stan Musial, 1962	135	433	143	18	1	19	57	82	64	46	3	.330

		G	IP	W	L	Pct.	SO	BB	ERA	ShO	Sv
RS	Cy Young, 1908	36	299	21	11	.656	150	37	1.26	3	2
LS	Warren Spahn, 1962	34	269	18	14	.563	118	55	3.04	0	0
3S	Ted Lyons, 1941	20	180	14	6	.700	50	26	2.10	0	0
4S	Pete Alexander, 1928	34	244	16	9	.640	59	37	3.36	1	2
5S	Rip Sewell, 1948	21	122	13	3	.813	36	37	3.47	0	0
RA	Hoyt Wilhelm, 1965	66	144	7	7	.500	106	32	1.81	0	20

	RECORD AT AGE 41		CAREER LEADER THROUGH AGE 41		LEADER AMONG ACTIVE PLAYERS		PACE OF RECORD HOLDER	
Games	Pete Rose	162	Henry Aaron	3213	Pete Rose	3099	Rose	3099
At Bats	Pete Rose	634	Pete Rose	12544	Pete Rose	12544	Rose	12544
Runs	Sam Rice	81	Ty Cobb	2245	Pete Rose	1995	Cobb	2245
Hits	Pete Rose	172	Ty Cobb	4191	Pete Rose	3869	Rose	3869
Doubles	Honus Wagner	32	Tris Speaker	793	Pete Rose	697	Speaker	793
Triples	Honus Wagner	17	Sam Crawford	312	Pete Rose	126	Crawford	312
Home Runs	Ted Williams	29	Hank Aaron	745	(Reggie Jackson)	530	Aaron	745
RBI	Stan Musial	82	Hank Aaron	2262	(Reggie Jackson)	1601	Aaron	2262
Walks	Luke Appling	94	Babe Ruth	2056	Pete Rose	1358	Ruth	2056
Strikeouts	Willie McCovey	70	Reggie Jackson	2385	(Reggie Jackson)	2385	Jackson	2385
Stolen Bases	Honus Wagner	22	Lou Brock	938	(Rickey Henderson)	573	Brock	938
Average	Stan Musial	.330	Ty Cobb	.367	(Rod Carew)	.328	Cobb	.367
Power/Speed	Honus Wagner	9.4	Willie Mays	444.8	(Reggie Jackson)	315.9	Mays	444.8
Wins	Cy Young	21	Cy Young	478	(Steve Carlton)	314	Young	478
WL %	Rip Sewell	.813	Whitey Ford	.690	(Tom Seaver)	.613	Ford	.690
Strikeouts	Phil Niekro	176	(Nolan Ryan)	4083	(Nolan Ryan)	4083	Ryan	4083
ERA	Cy Young	1.26	Ed Walsh	1.82	(Tom Seaver)	2.82	Walsh	1.82
Shutouts	Cy Young	3	Walter Johnson	110	(Tom Seaver)	61	Johnson	110
Saves	Hoyt Wilhelm	20	(Rollie Fingers)	341	(Rollie Fingers)	341	Fingers	341

TOP ALTERNATIVE SELECTIONS

POS	Player, Season	G	AB	H	2B	3B	HR	Run	RBI	BB	SO	SB	Avg
RF	Sam Rice, 1931	120	413	128	21	8	0	81	42	35	11	6	.310
LF	Zack Wheat, 1927	88	247	80	12	1	1	34	38	18	5	2	.324

		G	IP	W	L	Pct	SO	BB	ERA	ShO	Sv
5S	Jack Quinn, 1925	37	205	13	11	.542	43	42	4.13	0	0
5S	Phil Niekro, 1980	40	275	15	18	.455	176	85	3.63	3	1
5S	Red Ruffing, 1945	11	87	7	3	.700	24	20	2.89	1	0
RA	Earl Caldwell, 1946	39	91	13	4	.765	42	29	2.08	0	8

OTHER PLAYERS WHO COULD HAVE BEEN CHOSEN TO THE 41-YEAR-OLD ALL-STAR TEAM INCLUDE: Catcher Rick Ferrell (1947; 37 G, .303), Second Baseman Rogers Hornsby (1937), Third Baseman Lave Cross (1907), and Pitchers Babe Adams (1923; 13-7), Mike Ryba (1944; 12-7) and Connie Marerro (1952; 11-8, 2.89 ERA).

MOST VALUABLE 41-YEAR-OLD: Honus Wagner

AGE 42

ALL-TIME ALL-STAR TEAM

POS	Player, Season	G	AB	H	2B	3B	HR	Run	RBI	BB	SO	SB	Avg
C	Walker Cooper, 1957	48	78	21	5	1	3	7	10	5	18	0	.269
1B	Pete Rose, 1983	151	493	121	14	3	0	52	45	52	28	7	.245
2B	Honus Wagner, 1916	123	432	124	15	9	1	45	39	34	36	11	.287
3B	Jimmy Austin, 1922	15	31	9	3	1	0	6	1	3	2	0	.290
SS	Luke Appling, 1949	142	492	148	21	5	5	82	58	121	24	7	.301
LF	Stan Musial, 1963	124	337	86	10	2	12	34	58	35	43	2	.255
CF	Enos Slaughter, 1958	77	138	42	4	1	4	21	19	21	16	2	.304
RF	Sam Rice, 1932	106	288	93	16	7	1	58	34	32	6	7	.323
DH	Carl Yastrzemski, 1982	131	459	126	22	1	16	53	72	59	50	0	.275

		G	IP	W	L	Pct.	SO	BB	ERA	ShO	Sv
RS	Cy Young, 1909	35	295	19	15	.559	109	59	2.26	3	0
LS	Warren Spahn, 1963	33	260	23	7	.767	102	49	2.60	7	0
3S	Murry Dickson, 1958	33	119	10	7	.588	55	43	3.70	0	2
4S	Eppa Rixey, 1933	16	94	6	3	.667	10	12	3.15	1	0
5S	Jack Quinn, 1926	31	164	10	11	.476	58	36	3.41	3	1
RA	Hoyt Wilhelm, 1966	46	81	5	2	.714	61	17	1.66	0	6

	RECORD AT AGE 42		CAREER LEADER THROUGH AGE 42		LEADER AMONG ACTIVE PLAYERS		PACE OF RECORD HOLDER	
Games	Pete Rose	151	Henry Aaron	3298	Pete Rose	3250	Rose	3250
At Bats	Pete Rose	493	Pete Rose	13037	Pete Rose	13037	Rose	13037
Runs	Luke Appling	82	Ty Cobb	2245	Pete Rose	2047	Cobb	2245
Hits	Luke Appling	148	Ty Cobb	4191	Pete Rose	3990	Rose	3990
Doubles	Carl Yastrzemski	22	Tris Speaker	793	Pete Rose	711	Speaker	793
Triples	Honus Wagner	9	Sam Crawford	312	Pete Rose	129	Crawford	312
Home Runs	Carl Yastrzemski	16	Henry Aaron	755	(Reggie Jackson)	530	Aaron	755
RBI	Carl Yastrzemski	72	Henry Aaron	2297	(Reggie Jackson)	1601	Aaron	2297
Walks	Luke Appling	121	Babe Ruth	2056	Pete Rose	1410	Ruth	2056
Strikeouts	Carl Yastrzemski	50	Reggie Jackson	2385	(Reggie Jackson)	2385	Jackson	2385
Stolen Bases	Honus Wagner	11	Lou Brock	938	(Rickey Henderson)	573	Brock	938
Average	Luke Appling	.301	Ty Cobb	.367	(Rod Carew)	.328	Cobb	.367
Power/Speed	Luke Appling	5.8	Willie Mays	447.1	(Reggie Jackson)	315.9	Mays	447.1
Wins	Warren Spahn	23	Cy Young	497	(Steve Carlton)	314	Young	497
WL %	Warren Spahn	.767	Whitey Ford	.690	(Tom Seaver)	.613	Ford	.690
Strikeouts	Cy Young	109	(Nolan Ryan)	4083	(Nolan Ryan)	4083	Ryan	4083
ERA	Cy Young	2.26	Ed Walsh	1.82	(Tom Seaver)	2.82	Walsh	1.82
Shutouts	Warren Spahn	7	Walter Johnson	110	(Tom Seaver)	61	Johnson	110
Saves	Joe Heving	9	(Rollie Fingers)	341	(Rollie Fingers)	341	Fingers	341

TOP ALTERNATIVE SELECTIONS

POS	Player, Season	G	AB	H	2B	3B	HR	Run	RBI	BB	SO	SB	Avg
OF	Willie Mays, 1973	66	209	44	10	0	6	24	25	27	47	1	.211
DH	Henry Aaron, 1976	85	271	62	8	0	10	22	35	35	38	0	.229

		G	IP	W	L	Pct	SO	BB	ERA	ShO	Sv
5S	Red Ruffing, 1946	8	61	5	1	.833	19	23	1.77	2	0

OUTSTANDING PLAYERS WHO WERE 42 YEARS OLD IN 1985 INCLUDE: Tommy John

OTHER PLAYERS WHO COULD HAVE BEEN CHOSEN TO THE 42-YEAR-OLD ALL-STAR TEAM INCLUDE: Catcher Chief Zimmer (1903), First Baseman Tony Perez (1984) and Pitchers Grover Cleveland Alexander (1929; 9-8), Red Faber (1931; 10-14), Dazzy Vance (1933; 6-2), Dolph Luque (1933; 8-2) and Dutch Leonard (1951; 10-6, 2.63).

MOST VALUABLE 42-YEAR-OLD: Warren Spahn

LOOKING BACKWARD AT TEN

By Susan McCarthy

In the midst of all this serious baseball business, the following would appear to be a rather sentimental interlude. Forgive me for interrupting, but you see this edition of the *Baseball Abstract* is the tenth of the series. Ten years is a sizeable chunk of one's life and for most businesses or marriages or publications that have weathered a decade of ups and downs, the tenth anniversary usually merits some type of special celebration. So I thought maybe we could plan to take you all out to dinner and then to a movie . . . no, wait a minute. I don't think there is a ballpark in the country, let alone a restaurant that could accommodate you all. Well, maybe we can't reward you loyal and faithful readers directly (any interest in a special two for the price of one sale on outdated issues of the Newsletter?), but we can at the very least acknowledge your importance to the growth and endurance of the *Abstract* and thank you for your support.

The audience is of course an integral part of a writer's work. After sampling Bill's mail over the years—mostly I like to go through and read some of the personal tidbits—it seems that many readers feel a personal connection with Bill and his work. Whether this is due to a shared interest in and love for the game or stems more from jealousy because he gets to do this for his living and you don't, is open for question. The *Abstract* doesn't appeal to all baseball fans though. Its following is composed largely of the hard-core nuts, those who take their baseball seriously with every meal and who, if they have not actually done sabermetrical research, have at least thought analytically about these issues.

The personal connection between reader and author might be engendered further by the informal style of the *Abstract*. Bill encourages, even demands, readers think along with him and participate actively in the exploration of long held assumptions and in the development of new knowledge. His mail suggests that, if nothing else, he does a good job at provocation. People write in to agree or disagree with his views, to argue a specific point, to suggest changes, to share information. Particularly this past year, he has received a number of unsolicited studies and articles, a gratifying sign to Bill that people are taking it upon themselves to investigate the records on points of specific interest to them. Before you take pen in hand, however, I feel it my duty to warn you, your letter may get buried . . . in any one of about five or six boxes. Bill feels badly about not answering each letter but at least you can rest assured that he does eventually read most of it and in his own good-hearted way, still expects one day to plow through the stacks. Just sit loose.

Probably most of you have read something somewhere about the beginnings of the *Abstract* and you are indignantly wondering what this little tribute is doing here. Well, Bill has vetoed all my other ideas for articles

. . ."How to get and keep your wife interested in Baseball," "Good Snacks to Pack for an Afternoon at the Ballpark," "How to Get the Most Out of Your Ballpark $," and "Learning to Crack a Baseball Nut," *so what was I left with?* Besides, I figure if I can get this little piece past a man who is repulsed by any sort of horn tooting, except after winning the World Series, then maybe there is a place for it.

Care to take a quick look back? The first edition, the 1977 *Baseball Abstract,* sold only about 75 copies. This initial, almost primitive effort truly was a stab in the dark and might have been laid to rest after one edition if Bill had had any other sort of viable outlet. During the gestation period of this first edition, we were not married. I was only just beginning to understand the extent of his obsession with baseball and certainly didn't have a clue about the scope or focus of his work. Bill was working a dead-end job, tolerable to him only because it allowed him time, after doing his hourly security checks around the plant, to pore over the *Macmillan* for hours on end filling up notebook after notebook with pages and pages of numbers. When he settled in his own mind to do what was to become the *Abstract,* it was known to me for months only as the "secret project." He didn't show it to me until the book was about done and then only to get my ideas about a title for it. I quickly seconded the motion for "Abstract," some of the other alternatives being "Baseball Almanac" and "Baseball Analyst."

One of the all time favorite questions asked by interviewers of Bill concerns his expectations when the *Abstract* was first conceived . . . how large did he think the market would be, how long was he willing to wait for recognition, how did he plan for its growth. Quite simply, I don't think he had any realistic or unrealistic notions about the market for the type of analysis he wanted to do. He felt there was a need for something different among the annual spring baseball publications which always left him frustrated by not offering enough after a long cold winter, but didn't know how many people there were out there whose interests traveled along the same tracks as his. He never would have thought of testing the market or in some way (who understands these things?) trying to gauge whether his project was feasible. It would have been totally out of character for him to even seek advice from others who had launched their own publications. He's basically just not one for planning, finding it easier in a way, to just do something rather than worrying about its chances to succeed or fail. So the *Abstract* came to life one day in a quiet, rather unpretentious way. No fanfare. No complimentary copies mailed to journalists or baseball people.

You can't say 75 orders was exactly an overwhelming mandate but he went ahead with a second edition mostly because the form was now there to do the sort of work he wanted to do. He didn't have to put up with "writer's pain" of finding some place that would accept his work. He didn't have to adapt his work and style to a form mandated by magazine editors nor deal with topics editors tried to steer him toward because of their established public appeal. But most importantly, the work he would have done anyway for his own edification and amusement now found a home in a cohesive and unified form. Instead of one page of a stolen base study lying on top of a couple pages of pitcher data in the dungeon of a cardboard Stokley Van Camps box for years and years, ideas and questions about issues he had been chewing on for a long time took up residence in a climate that allowed for growth and maturation.

In the 1977 edition, the ratio of numbers to words is about five to one. Featured are monthly records for batters, teams and pitchers. Stolen base statistics, stolen bases against catchers and pitchers, are introduced along with the concepts of range factor and seasonal notation. The first edition also included a table baseball game. At a photocopying business in downtown, Lawrence, Kansas, called "The House of Usher," the manuscript was simply photocopied, collated, sandwiched between two pieces of blue cover stock and side stapled. I believe it sold for $5, including cost of mailing, and was advertised by a small ad in *The Sporting News*.

The second edition looks much the same; the table of contents appears on the cover, pages are printed on one side only and the book is still stapled on the side. The 1978 *Abstract* expanded to 115 pages and featured the team by team format you are all familiar with, only the team notes are sort of combined with rambling player notes. Month by month batting stats are again featured along with various pitcher stats, now obsolete, such as home and road attendance during each pitcher's starts, his ability to hold baserunners and an assessment of his working speed. There are several major essays; one explaining formulas and methods used and the other dealing with ratings and records and the distinction between the two.

The form of the 1979 edition doesn't really break much new ground but solidifies the leap forward from the first to the second edition, including more essay-like team comments. The Account Form Box Score is introduced. The book is skinnier than the previous two editions because the typewritten copy is printed front and back— every little inch of space is filled.

With the 1980 and 1981 editions, we're getting close to the present form of the *Abstract* today. Both editions are bound like real books and more attention was invested in the graphics, particularly in the '81 edition which proudly displays player comments set in type. That was a major step forward; who knows what the *Abstract* would have looked like if we had actually thought of hiring a professional to do the lay-out, design and all that good stuff. Not that we could have afforded it anyway.

That's about where Ballantine Books enters upon the scene and most of you are familiar with the development since then so I won't keep you any longer. Thanks for bearing with me. And thanks for your part in making the *Baseball Abstract* what it is today.

In the 1985 *Baseball Abstract* there is an article entitled *Range Factor: Revisited* which is about the number of plays made per defensive *inning* played. Because of an error in the preparation of the manuscript, the book gives the appearance that I had written that article. This is very unfortunate, because I didn't; the article was written by Tim Marcou of Brookfield, Wisconsin. What Tim has done, estimating defensive innings for each player, is a great deal of work, and is much appreciated. Tim has returned this year, with another article on the same issue.

RANGE FACTOR: REVISITED AGAIN

By Tim Marcou

I look forward to the time each year. The early December mail with its first Christmas cards, those once a year greetings from many far away friends. And always buried in the blue, red, green envelopes is a chilled copy of the *Sporting News* containing the first published fielding averages.

Later in the evening I always make time to renew acquaintance with the quiet, unassuming, but friendly baseball stat, the range factor. After all, the range factor did receive mention in a few other publications during the year.

An article I wrote in the *1985 Bill James Baseball Abstract* entitled "Range Factor: Revisited" describes its good qualities. Range Factor is a measure of the number of defensive plays made per game, and thus a measure of the amount of territory—the "range" covered by each fielder. Easy to figure with just pencil and calculator; putouts plus assists divided by games played at the respective position. Always interesting, each calculation a never before seen number. And good conversation for hot stove league sessions.

The article also mentions the limitations of the range factor. Well, we all have limitations. It's main flaw is that it is based on successfully fielded chances per *Game*. A game for some fielders consists of seven, eight, or nine innings. But for some defensive specialists like Gary Maddox, a game lasts one, two, or three innings. As mentioned last year, the range factor should be based on innings by position and recited, like the ERA, in plays per nine innings.

I decided this season to tabulate approximate innings by position to better adjust the range factor, to better welcome its visit this year.

My method was simple. I just dissected each and every *Sporting News* boxscore, 2106 to be exact, and charted the innings each fielder in both leagues played at each position, including breakdowns in left, center, and right field.

It is not impossible to puzzle out this information. Most National League replacements occur with the flip-flop removal of the pitchers. The line score also provides numerous clues, especially when pinch hitters/runners create runs.

What the project requires is time, many hours, with game-by-game notations on what players participated in what contests and for what duration. But as the project unfolded, I discovered I had created a season scorecard for myself and other baseball friends.

The following numbers show range factor by itself and on a per 9 inning basis. For infielders, I present a seven-column chart. The seven columns show:

1) G (Games). The official total of "games" at the position.

2) SCh (Successful Chances). The official total of putouts plus assists.

3) RF (Range Factor). The range factor, or successful plays per game, as calculated from the official stats.

4) EstIn (Estimated Innings). My estimate of exactly how many defensive innings the player has played at the position.

5) As9 (Assists/9 Innings). The number of assists made by the player per nine innings, as best we can calculate it.

6) %TC (Percentage of Team Chances). The player's putouts and assists per estimated nine innings, expressed as a percentage of the team's putouts and assists minus strikeouts per nine innings. For example, Spike Owen's .159 represents his 5.27 plays per 9 innings divided by Seattle's 33.06, which information is found on the team chart.

7) RF9 (Range Factor per 9 innings). The number of plays made by the player per nine estimated innings, which is also called Adjusted Range Factor.

These charts will be found at the conclusion of the article.

Range is not necessarily the ability to scoot faster to the left or right than the next guy, but rather is the ability to make the play. Maybe Frank White has lost a step heading for the hole, but his positioning and guile maintain the excellent range numbers of his youth. Marty Barrett hardly moved at all on a pair of hidden ball tricks in 1985, yet he made a couple of plays few others made. Tag plays, over-the-shoulder grabs, and even acrobatic force-out putouts require skill. I like to count them all.

For outfielders, I show breakdowns for innings in left, center and right. I list outfielders by position most often played. Robin Yount played a lot of center field in 1985, and is considered the Brewer center fielder in 1986, but played more left field last season.

Yount's left field range factor is probably inflated because of play in center. Conversely, Tony Armas' center field range factor deflates because of his play in left. Then again, better left/right fielders will get time in center field while lesser center fielders will occasionally step aside to left or right.

For outfielders, I also include another homemade number which I call "percentage of flyout chances" or %FC. It's merely the outfielder's range factor per nine innings divided by an approximate number of plays which did not require an assist—hopefully, these plays mainly being fly balls per nine innings. For example, Vince Coleman's .206 represents his 2.20 chances per nine innings divided by the Cardinals' supposed 10.66 "fly ball" outs per nine innings. I realize that not even "Vincent Van Go" can catch up to some pop-ups over the mound, but I think this ratio has some relative worth.

I present the team charts in an attempt to show the characteristics of pitching staffs. The three columns in the middle show outs per nine innings in strikeouts, assists, and putouts which do not require an assist—hopefully a crude approximation of strikeout, ground ball, and fly/pop/line outs. The far right column is the total number of fielded chances per nine innings.

With this chart in mind, I'll say I did rank each fielder in his respective position by successful chances (putouts and assists) per estimated nine innings. I do so, however, without making a value judgment as to the actual skill of the fielder. Because of these pitching staff characteristics, adjustments need to be made in some situations. I am not saying that Bobby Meacham is seventeenth most skillful as in the A.L. in 1985, just that his numbers place him in that spot. The Yankee hurlers strike out a lot of hitters, allowing fewer opportunities for chances for its fielder, and also give up many fly ball outs. Possibly the "death valley" park effect at work. The New York infielders seemingly are not involved in as many plays as their other A.L. counterparts.

How about Glenn Hubbard! I have rechecked his numbers a half dozen times and he still outdistances Sandberg by a chance per nine innings and Herr by almost two. Atlanta pitchers do induce the ground ball. The Braves led the N.L. in fielding assists, but this fact does not diminish Hubbard's fine ratio.

Maybe someone can explain to me why Buddy Bell ranks on the top for his A.L. play, but near the bottom for N.L. innings?

The Gold Glove selections are always open to dispute, the stuff of the hot stove league. It is common knowledge that a fielder's hitting prowess may influence his fielding reputation (don't get me wrong—I like the George Brett selection) and it's difficult to unseat an incumbent. But I'd like to give an honorable mention to Eddie Milner, Kevin McReynolds, Glenn Wilson, Jessie Barfield, Tony Fernandez, Gary Gaetti, Spike Owen and Glenn Hubbard, just to mention a few.

Again, I hope the reader enjoys this study. I present it not so much to show my results, but more to share the results and ask the powers-that-be to present such numbers and ratios for the fan's enjoyment. If I error egregiously in any tabulation, I apologize, but then let the real numbers appear. Only a half dozen fielding categories exist in comparison to the score or more for hitting and pitching. Why not add the following?

1) innings by position;
2) successful chances/assists per nine innings side by side with the fielding averages;
3) a separate breakdown of left, center and right field categories;
4) fielded putouts for first basemen as opposed to those received from tosses from other infielders (also force out putouts by other infielders);
5) fielded chances by catchers, separating out strikeout, putouts and caught stealing assists.

I also wanted to demonstrate that it is not impossible to uncover innings by position from those seasons when such numbers were not counted. Of course, this project would require several armies of sabermetricians. But I, for one, found the work to be fun and rewarding.

Again, the numbers are approximations. I'm rechecking the numbers through official TSN boxscores and will share final tallies for the asking: A SASE to Tim Marcou, 2890 Monterey Blvd., Brookfield WI 53005. And, hopefully, I did not cause the mathematicians amongst you to cringe with my homemade range factor adjustments. These numbers are more a calculator gone mad than an attempt to outdo multi-variable regressions and the like.

What then does the future hold for the range factor? Hopefully more recognition, more defensive categories like the above mentioned, better formulas to adjust it by, and more credit to the unsung defensive specialist.

AMERICAN LEAGUE SECONDBASEMEN

Player, Team	G	SCh	RF	EstIn	As9	%TC	RF9
1. White, KC	149	832	5.38	1307.0	3.37	.171	5.73
2. Grich, CAL	116	604	5.21	965.0	3.54	.167	5.63
3. Barrett, BOS	155	834	5.38	1332.2	3.23	.172	5.63
4. Gantner, MIL	124	664	5.35	1084.2	3.34	.169	5.51
5. Perconte, SEA	125	625	5.00	1031.0	3.33	.165	5.46
6. Cruz, CHI	87	378	4.34	648.0	3.05	.169	5.25
7. Bernazard, CL	147	710	4.83	1219.1	2.95	.157	5.24
8. Randolph, NY	143	728	5.09	1258.0	3.04	.168	5.21
9. Garcia, TOR	143	673	4.71	1212.0	2.75	.153	5.00
10. Harrah, TX	122	563	4.61	1014.0	3.12	.155	5.00
11. Whitaker, DET	150	728	4.85	1312.2	2.83	.158	4.99
12. Hill, OAK	122	548	4.49	1012.1	2.85	.153	4.87
13. Teufel, MIN	137	589	4.29	1120.1	2.83	.143	4.73
14. Wiggins, BAL	76	334	4.39	649.0	2.58	.141	4.63

NATIONAL LEAGUE SECONDBASEMEN

Player, Team	G	SCh	RF	EstIn	As9	%TC	RF9
1. Hubbard, ATL	140	878	6.27	1155.0	4.20	.197	6.84
2. Sandberg, CHI	153	853	5.58	1329.2	3.38	.169	5.73
3. Oester, CIN	149	823	5.52	1324.2	3.10	.176	5.59
4. Doran, HOU	147	785	5.34	1267.1	3.12	.172	5.57
5. Law, MON	126	643	5.10	1047.1	3.15	.167	5.53
6. Samuel, PHI	159	852	5.36	1394.0	2.99	.169	5.50
7. Trillo, SF	120	619	5.16	1017.0	3.15	.172	5.47
8. Flannery, SD	121	548	4.53	923.2	2.80	.161	5.34
9. Sax, LA	135	687	5.09	1169.1	2.75	.162	5.29
10. Backman, NY	140	642	4.59	1131.1	2.94	.165	5.10
11. Ray, PITT	151	728	4.82	1303.2	2.92	.156	5.03
12. Herr, STL	158	785	4.97	1411.0	2.86	.149	5.01

AMERICAN LEAGUE THIRDBASEMEN

Player, Team	G	SCh	RF	Estin	As9	%TC	RF9
1. Bell, TX	83	262	3.16	725.0	2.38	.101	3.25
2. Gaetti, Min	156	452	2.90	1269.1	2.24	.096	3.20
3. Rayford, BAL	78	207	2.65	612.1	2.13	.093	3.04
4. Brookens, DET	151	384	2.54	1156.1	2.03	.095	2.99
5. Brett, KC	152	446	2.93	1345.2	2.27	.088	2.98
6. Molitor, MIL	135	389	2.88	1174.0	2.03	.091	2.98
7. Boggs, BOS	161	469	2.91	1419.1	2.12	.091	2.97
8. Hullett, CHI	115	279	2.43	850.0	2.22	.095	2.95
9. Buechele, TX	69	189	2.74	580.0	2.13	.091	2.93
10. Jacoby, CLE	161	433	2.69	1389.2	2.07	.083	2.80
11. Presley, SEA	154	417	2.71	1348.0	2.24	.084	2.78
12. DeCinces, CAL	111	297	2.68	973.1	1.87	.084	2.75
13. Iorg, TOR	104	172	1.65	563.2	2.18	.084	2.74
14. Gross, BAL	67	139	2.07	456.0	1.93	.084	2.74
15. Mulliniks, TOR	119	237	1.99	846.2	1.72	.077	2.52
16. Pagliarulo, NY	134	254	1.89	941.0	1.79	.078	2.43
17. Lansford, OAK	97	204	2.10	844.2	1.27	.068	2.17

NATIONAL LEAGUE THIRDBASEMEN

Player, Team	G	SCh	RF	Estin	As9	%TC	RF9
1. Wallach, MON	154	531	3.45	1357.1	2.54	.107	3.52
2. Pendleton, STL	149	490	3.28	1273.2	2.55	.103	3.46
3. Nettles, SD	130	351	2.70	1072.2	1.92	.089	2.94
4. Brown, SF	120	337	2.81	1035.0	2.11	.092	2.93
5. Schmidt, PHI	54	140	2.59	434.1	2.26	.089	2.90
6. Morrison, PIT	59	123	2.08	383.1	1.97	.090	2.89
7. Oberkfell, ATL	117	290	2.48	922.0	2.15	.081	2.83
8. Esasky, CIN	62	140	2.26	459.2	1.94	.086	2.74
9. Cey, CHI	140	348	2.49	1181.2	2.08	.078	2.65
10. Garner, HOU	123	272	2.21	942.0	1.88	.080	2.60
11. Schu, PHI	111	277	2.50	969.2	1.77	.079	2.57
12. Madlock, PI-LA	130	312	2.40	1110.2	1.93	.078	2.53
13. Johnson, NY	113	238	2.11	870.0	1.77	.079	2.46
14. Bell, CIN	67	159	2.37	585.1	1.61	.076	2.44
15. Knight, NY	73	161	2.21	605.0	1.62	.077	2.40

AMERICAN LEAGUE SHORTSTOPS

Player, Team	G	SCh	RF	Estin	As9	%TC	RF9
1. Owen, SEA	117	557	4.76	951.0	3.41	.159	5.27
2. Hoffman, BOS	93	386	4.15	709.0	2.93	.149	4.89
3. Biancalana, KC	74	248	3.35	458.1	3.30	.145	4.87
4. Fernandez, TOR	160	761	4.76	1415.0	3.04	.148	4.84
5. Schofield, CAL	147	658	4.48	1225.2	2.91	.144	4.83
6. Gagne, MIN	106	418	3.94	778.0	3.14	.146	4.83
7. Ripken, BAL	161	760	4.72	1427.1	2.99	.146	4.79
8. Concepcion, KC	128	494	3.86	939.2	3.51	.141	4.73
9. Griffin, OAK	162	718	4.43	1392.1	2.84	.146	4.64
10. Gutierrez, BOS	99	381	3.85	744.1	2.87	.140	4.60
11. Franco, CLE	151	657	4.35	1297.0	2.91	.138	4.59
12. Guillen, CHI	150	602	4.01	1205.1	2.85	.145	4.50
13. Wilkerson, TX	110	399	3.63	815.1	3.02	.136	4.40
14. Riles, MIL	115	493	4.29	1009.2	2.76	.134	4.39
15. Tolleson, TX	81	278	3.43	584.1	2.80	.132	4.28
16. Trammell, DET	149	625	4.19	1327.2	2.71	.134	4.23
17. Meacham, NY	155	626	4.04	1347.2	2.60	.134	4.18

NATIONAL LEAGUE SHORTSTOPS

Player, Team	G	SCh	RF	Estin	As9	%TC	RF9
1. Dunston, CHI	73	392	5.36	603.0	3.70	.172	5.85
2. Reynolds, HOU	102	476	4.67	816.0	3.51	.162	5.25
3. Smith, STL	158	813	5.15	1407.0	3.51	.155	5.20
4. Ramirez, ATL	133	665	5.00	1155.1	3.51	.149	5.18
5. Foley, CIN-PHI	60	270	4.50	468.2	3.18	.161	5.18
6. Khalifa, PIT	95	472	4.97	832.0	3.41	.158	5.10
7. Templeton, SD	148	705	4.76	1278.1	3.24	.149	4.96
8. Jeltz, PHI	86	321	3.73	596.2	3.24	.149	4.84
9. Thon, HOU	79	324	4.10	605.0	3.24	.148	4.81
10. Santana, NY	153	697	4.56	1320.1	2.69	.153	4.75
11. Duncan, LA	123	560	4.55	1061.1	3.27	.145	4.74
12. Uribe, SF	145	647	4.46	1241.0	3.17	.147	4.68
13. Concepcion, CIN	151	616	4.08	1300.1	2.80	.134	4.26
14. Brooks, MON	155	644	4.15	1376.1	2.88	.136	4.21

AMERICAN LEAGUE LEFTFIELDERS

Player, Team	G	SCh	RF	Estin	%FC	L	C	R	RF9
1. Roenicke, BAL	88	140	1.59	490.2	.229	405.2	35	50	2.57
2. Collins, OAK	91	222	2.43	781.1	.206	781.1			2.56
3. Yount, MIL	108	262	2.43	937.2	.217	593.1	344		2.51
4. Carter, CLE	135	289	2.14	1036.2	.213	920.1	10	106.1	2.51
5. Hatcher, MIN	97	221	2.28	794.1	.223	794.1			2.50
6. Griffey, NY	110	230	2.09	869.0	.206	831.0	30	8	2.38
7. Young, BAL	90	196	2.17	742.1	.213	653.1		89	2.38
8. Law, CHI	120	226	1.86	857.2	.228	620.2	237		2.34
9. Herndon, DET	136	280	2.06	1088.2	.213	1084.2		4	2.31
10. Bradley, SEA	159	346	2.18	1410.0	.221	1104.0	232	74	2.21
11. Ward, TX	153	315	2.05	1298.0	.205	1145.0	153		2.18
12. Downing, CAL	121	249	2.06	1037.2	.198	1037.2			2.16
13. Bell, TOR	157	333	2.12	1382.0	.194	1382.0			2.16
14. Rice, BOS	130	244	1.87	1137.1	.193	1137.1			1.93
15. Smith, KC	119	205	1.72	976.1	.188	976.1			1.89

NATIONAL LEAGUE LEFTFIELDERS

Player, Team	G	SCh	RF	Estin	%FC	L	C	R	RF9
1. Redus, CIN	85	140	1.68	555.2	.215	324.2	231		2.36
2. Coleman, STL	150	321	2.14	1315.2	.206	1171.2	65	79	2.20
3. Martinez, SD	150	311	2.07	1318	.187	1318.0			2.12
4. Raines, MON	146	292	2.00	1301.0	.199	1301			2.02
5. Cruz, HOU	137	269	1.96	1203.0	.194	1203			2.01
6. Kemp, PIT	63	106	1.68	492.1	.198	492.1			1.94
7. Guerrero, LA	81	148	1.83	693.0	.206	611.0	83		1.92
8. Harper, ATL	131	225	1.71	1090.2	.192	1079.2	2	9	1.86
9. Lopes, CHI	79	115	1.46	572.0	.184	302.0	165	105	1.81
10. Foster, NY	123	205	1.67	1064.0	.166	1064			1.73
11. Leonard, SF	126	213	1.69	1124.0	.175	1107.0	17		1.72
12. Matthews, CHI	85	126	1.48	659.0	.175	659			1.72
13. Stone, PHI	69	86	1.25	514.0	.146	514			1.51

Outfield categories also include: %PC = percentage of "Flyout" plays (PO + A) divided by team's putout chances (those not requiring an assist—Team POs – Assists – strikeouts), L = estimated innings in left field, C = center field, R = right field

AMERICAN LEAGUE CENTERFIELDERS

Player, Team	G	SCh	RF	Estin	%FC	L	C	R	RF9
1. Pettis, CAL	122	381	3.12	1040.0	.303		1040.0		3.30
2. Henderson, NY	141	446	3.16	1222.1	.283	24	1198.2		3.28
3. Butler, CLE	150	456	3.04	1269.0	.275		1269.0		3.23
4. Puckett, MIN	161	484	3.01	1408.1	.275		1408.1		3.09
5. McDowell, TEX	103	291	2.83	856.1	.288		856.1		3.06
6. Murphy, OAK	150	438	2.92	1292.0	.245		1292.0		3.05
7. Lemon, DET	144	417	2.90	1273.1	.272		1273.1		2.95
8. Manning, MIL	74	162	2.19	525.1	.240	2	415.1	108	2.78
9. Boston, CHI	93	186	2.00	601.2	.271		601.2		2.78
10. Wilson, KC	140	382	2.72	1254.0	.273		1254.0		2.74
11. Lynn, CAL	123	320	2.60	1050.1	.245		1050.1		2.74
12. Lyons, BOS	114	257	2.25	847.2	.272	4	839.2	4	2.73
13. Moseby, TOR	152	401	2.63	1335.1	.242		1335.3		2.70
14. Henderson, SEA	138	343	2.49	1174.0	.263		1044.0	130	2.63
15. Armas, BOS	79	176	2.23	649.1	.243	79.2	569.2		2.44

NATIONAL LEAGUE CENTERFIELDERS

Player, Team	G	SCh	RF	Estin	%FC	L	C	R	RF9
1. Milner, CIN	135	352	2.61	993.0	.291		993.0		3.19
2. McReynolds, SD	150	442	2.94	1318.2	.257		1318.2		3.02
3. Dykstra, NY	74	171	2.31	509.1	.289		509.1		3.02
4. Dernier, CHI	116	314	2.70	985.1	.291		985.1		2.86
5. Maddox, PHI	94	146	1.55	461.1	.274		461.1		2.84
6. Wynne, PIT	99	229	2.38	772.0	.280		772.0		2.75
7. Wilson, NY	83	216	2.60	705.1	.263	13	692.1		2.75
8. McGee, STL	149	393	2.63	1295.1	.256	4	1291.1		2.73
9. Winningham, NY	116	235	2.03	775.0	.269	1	773.0	1	2.73
10. Hayes, PHI	146	377	2.59	1295.2	.278	277	983.2	35	2.62
11. Bass, HOU	141	338	2.40	1184.0	.257	56	891.0	237	2.57
12. Orsulak, PIT	115	239	2.08	874.0	.251	179	566.0	129	2.46
13. Gladden, SF	124	276	2.23	1059.0	.238	107	952		2.34
14. Landreaux, LA	140	271	1.94	1060.1	.248	32	988.1	40	2.30
15. Murphy, ATL	161	342	2.12	1434.1	.221		1434.1		2.14

AMERICAN LEAGUE RIGHTFIELDERS

Player, Team	G	SCh	RF	Estin	%FC	L	C	R	RF9
1. Davis, OAK	151	376	2.49	1292.0	.210		158.0	1134.0	2.62
2. Householder, MIL	91	209	2.27	711.2	.226	16	259.2	436.0	2.62
3. Barfield, TOR	154	371	2.41	1350.1	.221		58.2	1291.2	2.47
4. Wright, TEX	102	221	2.17	828.2	.226		381.1	447.1	2.40
5. Vukovich, CLE	137	254	1.85	983.2	.197	39		944.1	2.32
6. Oglivie, MIL	91	194	2.13	775.0	.194	339.1		436.1	2.25
7. Winfield, NY	152	329	2.16	1353.1	.189			1353.1	2.19
8. Lacy, BAL	115	240	2.09	992.0	.194		1.0	991.0	2.17
9. Motley, KC	114	202	1.77	848.1	.213	293.0	1.0	554.1	2.14
10. Brunansky, MIN	155	314	2.03	1331.1	.189		6.0	1325.1	2.12
11. Baines, CHI	159	326	2.05	1398.0	.205			1398.0	2.10
12. Gibson, DET	144	287	1.99	1254.0	.190		167.2	1086.1	2.06
13. Evans, BOS	152	300	1.97	1335.1	.201			1335.1	2.02
14. Cowens, SEA	110	208	1.89	956.0	.196			956.0	1.96
15. Jackson, CAL	81	112	1.46	651.2	.149			651.2	1.63

NATIONAL LEAGUE RIGHTFIELDERS

Player, Team	G	SCh	RF	Estin	%FC	L	C	R	RF9
1. Wilson, PHI	158	361	2.28	1365.2	.230	4		1365.2	2.38
2. Gwynn, SD	152	351	2.31	1339.2	.201			1339.2	2.35
3. Davis, SF	126	289	2.29	1106.2	.239		309.0	797.2	2.35
4. Mumphrey, HOU	126	254	2.02	1011.1	.219		478.0	533.1	2.26
5. Parker, CIN	159	341	2.14	1411.1	.198			1411.2	2.17
6. Van Slyke, STL	142	247	1.74	1039.1	.200	5	107.1	927.0	2.14
7. Dawson, MON	131	257	1.96	1126.2	.202		169.2	957.0	2.05
8. Strawberry, NY	110	216	1.96	977.2	.189		218.0	759.2	1.98
9. Moreland, CHI	148	243	1.64	1228.2	.181			1228.1	1.78
10. Marshall, LA	125	215	1.72	1111.1	.187			1111.1	1.87
11. Brown, PIT	56	87	1.61	487.2	.169			487.2	1.66
12. Washington, ATL	99	122	1.26	838.2	.138			838.2	

AMERICAN LEAGUE

Team	F. AVG	SO9	As9	PO9	SCh9
California	.982	4.73	11.36	10.89	33.61
Chicago	.982	6.34	10.40	10.26	33.06
Seattle	.980	5.45	11.53	10.00	33.06
Minnestoa	.980	4.83	10.92	11.23	33.07
Kansas City	.980	5.21	11.75	10.04	33.54
Texas	.980	5.50	10.85	10.64	32.34
Toronto	.980	5.11	10.75	11.14	32.64
New York	.979	5.67	9.76	11.56	31.08
Baltimore	.979	4.99	10.80	11.20	32.80
Boston	.977	5.62	11.37	10.01	32.75
Oakland	.977	4.86	9.70	12.44	31.84
Cleveland	.977	4.45	10.78	11.76	33.32
Milwaukee	.977	4.87	10.55	11.57	32.67
Detroit	.977	5.82	10.33	10.84	31.50

NATIONAL LEAGUE

Team	F. AVG	SO9	As9	PO9	SCh9
St. Louis	.983	4.91	11.43	10.66	33.52
New York	.982	6.28	10.26	10.45	30.97
Montreal	.981	5.37	11.46	10.16	33.08
Cincinnati	.980	5.64	10.41	10.95	31.77
San Diego	.980	4.51	10.73	11.76	33.22
Chicago	.979	5.12	12.07	9.82	33.96
Pittsburgh	.979	5.99	11.20	9.81	32.21
Philadelphia	.978	5.59	11.05	10.36	32.46
San Francisco	.976	6.12	11.02	9.85	31.89
Houston	.976	5.61	11.04	10.34	32.42
Atlanta	.976	4.79	12.52	9.68	34.72
Los Angeles	.974	6.01	11.69	9.29	32.67

SO9 = strikeouts per 9 innings
As9 = assists per 9 innings
PO9 = putouts per 9 innings—plays in which only fielded putout is recorded. PO minus assists minus strikeouts
SCh9 = successful team chances per 9 innings. PO + A − K.

STARTING PITCHERS RECEIVING BEST OFFENSIVE SUPPORT
(Based on the number of runs scored in games the pitcher has started.)

AMERICAN LEAGUE

Pitcher, Team	Starts	Runs	Runs Per Start
Dennis Martinez, Baltimore	31	191	6.16
Bruce Hurst, Boston	31	186	6.00
Ed Whitson, New York	30	178	5.93
Bill Krueger, Oakland	23	127	5.52
Ron Guidry, New York	33	178	5.39
Storm Davis, Baltimore	28	151	5.39
Jim Clancy, Toronto	23	120	5.22
Joe Cowley, New York	26	134	5.15
Britt Burns, Chicago	34	175	5.15
Oil Can Boyd, Boston	35	178	5.09

NATIONAL LEAGUE

Pitcher, Team	Starts	Runs	Runs Per Start
Bryn Smith, Montreal	32	174	5.44
Mike Scott, Houston	35	176	5.03
Kurt Kepshire, St. Louis	29	142	4.90
Joaquin Andujar, St. Louis	38	186	4.89
Dwight Gooden, New York	35	171	4.89
Charles Hudson, Philadelphia	26	127	4.88
Vida Blue, San Francisco	20	96	4.80
Steve Trout, Chicago	24	115	4.79
Tom Browning, Cincinnati	38	182	4.79
Rick Mahler, Atlanta	39	184	4.72

STARTING PITCHERS RECEIVING WORST OFFENSIVE SUPPORT

AMERICAN LEAGUE

Pitcher, Team	Starts	Runs	Runs Per Start
Danny Darwin, Milwaukee	29	98	3.38
Charlie Hough, Texas	34	123	3.62
Danny Jackson, Kansas City	32	121	3.78
Bob Ojeda, Boston	22	84	3.82
Bud Black, Kansas City	33	127	3.85
Neal Heaton, Cleveland	33	129	3.91
Scott Langston, Seattle	24	95	3.96
Jim Slaton, California	24	95	3.96
Burt Hooton, Texas	20	80	4.00
Ken Schrom, Minnesota	26	104	4.00
Dan Petry, Detroit	34	136	4.00

NATIONAL LEAGUE

Pitcher, Team	Starts	Runs	Runs Per Start
Jose DeLeon, Pittsburgh	25	58	2.32
Mike Krukow, San Francisco	28	81	2.89
Dave LaPoint, San Francisco	31	94	3.03
Bill Laskey, San Fran/Montreal	26	82	3.15
David Palmer, Montreal	23	77	3.35
Kevin Gross, Philadelphia	31	104	3.35
Atlee Hammaker, San Francisco	29	98	3.38
Dave Dravecky, San Diego	31	110	3.55
Bill Gullickson, Montreal	29	103	3.55
Mark Thurmond, San Diego	23	82	3.57

HIGHEST DOUBLE PLAY SUPPORT

AMERICAN LEAGUE

Pitcher, Team	Starts	DPs	DPs Per Start
Jim Slaton, California	24	35	1.46
Ron Romanick, California	31	42	1.35
Jimmy Key, Toronto	32	43	1.34
Moose Haas, Milwaukee	26	34	1.31
Mike Witt, California	35	44	1.26
Mike Boddicker, Baltimore	32	40	1.25
Neal Heaton, Cleveland	33	40	1.21
Danny Jackson, Kansas City	32	38	1.19
Phil Niekro, New York	33	39	1.18
Al Nipper, Boston	25	29	1.16

NATIONAL LEAGUE

Pitcher, Team	Starts	DPs	DPs Per Start
Rick Mahler, Atlanta	39	50	1.28
Joaquin Andujar, St. Louis	38	48	1.26
Andy Hawkins, San Diego	33	41	1.24
Kurt Kepshire, St. Louis	29	36	1.24
Steve Trout, Chicago	24	29	1.21
Bob Knepper, Houston	37	44	1.19
David Palmer, Montreal	23	27	1.17
John Denny, Philadelphia	33	38	1.15
Pascual Perez, Atlanta	22	25	1.14
Steve Bedrosian, Atlanta	37	42	1.14

LEAST DOUBLE PLAY SUPPORT

AMERICAN LEAGUE

Pitcher, Team	Starts	DPs	DPs Per Start
Jim Clancy, Toronto	23	15	.65
Don Sutton, Oakland/California	34	24	.71
Frank Tanana, Texas/Detroit	33	26	.76
Joe Cowley, New York	26	20	.77
Oil Can Boyd, Boston	35	27	.77
Burt Blyleven, Cincinnati/Minn.	37	29	.78
Chris Codiroli, Oakland	37	29	.78
Danny Darwin, Milwaukee	29	23	.79
Teddy Higuera, Milwaukee	30	24	.80
John Butcher, Minnesota	33	27	.82
Charlie Hough, Texas	34	28	.82

NATIONAL LEAGUE

Pitcher, Team	Starts	DPs	DPs Per Start
Jose DeLeon, Pittsburgh	25	11	.44
Dennis Eckersley, Chicago	25	11	.44
Charles Hudson, Philadelphia	26	13	.50
Rick Rhoden, Pittsburgh	35	19	.54
Ed Lynch, New York	29	16	.55
Bob Welch, Los Angeles	23	13	.57
Mario Soto, Cincinnati	36	22	.61
Mike Krukow, San Francisco	28	18	.64
Fernando Valenzuela, Los Angeles	35	24	.69
Jim Gott, San Francisco	26	18	.69
John Tudor, St. Louis	36	25	.69

TOUGHEST STARTING PITCHERS TO RUN ON

(Based on the number of bases stolen by the opposition in this pitcher's starts.)

AMERICAN LEAGUE

Pitcher, Team	Starts	OSB	OSB Per Start
Kirk McCaskill, California	29	8	.28
Al Nipper, Boston	25	8	.32
Jim Slaton, California	24	8	.33
Frank Viola, Minnesota	36	12	.33
Mike Moore, Seattle	34	12	.35
Bob Ojeda, Boston	22	8	.36
Danny Jackson, Kansas City	32	12	.38
Dave Stieb, Toronto	36	14	.39
Ron Guidry, New York	33	13	.39
Bret Saberhagen, Kansas City	32	14	.44

NATIONAL LEAGUE

Pitcher, Team	Starts	OSB	OSB Per Start
Jerry Reuss, Los Angeles	33	10	.30
Rick Mahler, Atlanta	39	14	.36
Danny Cox, St. Louis	35	13	.37
Bob Knepper, Houston	37	15	.41
Ed Lynch, New York	29	12	.41
John Tudor, St. Louis	36	16	.44
Jay Tibbs, Cincinnati	34	16	.47
Tom Browning, Cincinnati	38	20	.53
Rick Reuschel, Pittsburgh	26	14	.54
Fernando Valenzuela, Los Angeles	35	19	.54

EASIEST STARTING PITCHERS TO RUN ON

AMERICAN LEAGUE

Pitcher, Team	Starts	OSB	OSB Per Start
Mike Boddicker, Baltimore	32	39	1.22
Pete Vukovich, Milwukee	22	21	.95
Burt Blyleven, Cleveland/Minnesota	37	35	.95
Tom Seaver, Chicago	33	31	.94
Storm Davis, Baltimore	28	24	.86
Neal Heaton, Cleveland	33	28	.85
Mark Gubicza, Kansas City	28	23	.82
Phil Niekro, New York	33	27	.82
Mike Smithson, Minnesota	37	30	.81
Mark Langston, Seattle	24	19	.79

NATIONAL LEAGUE

Pitcher, Team	Starts	OSB	OSB Per Start
Joe Niekro, Houston	32	50	1.56
David Palmer, Montreal	23	33	1.43
Mario Soto, Cincinnati	36	47	1.31
Bill Gullickson, Montreal	29	37	1.28
Steve Bedrosian, Atlanta	37	47	1.27
Mark Thurmond, San Diego	23	29	1.26
Sid Fernandez, New York	26	31	1.19
Kevin Gross, Philadelphia	31	35	1.13
Bill Laskey, San Francisco/Montreal	26	29	1.12
John Denny, Philadelphia	33	36	1.09

LEADING HITTERS AT HOME
(Minimum 200 At-Bats)

AMERICAN LEAGUE

Player, Team	G	AB	Run	Hit	2B	3B	HR	RBI	SB	Avg
Boggs, Boston	80	311	60	130	24	2	6	39	1	.418
Brett, Kansas City	81	285	64	105	21	4	15	66	7	.368
Rice, Boston	69	274	44	96	13	3	11	64	2	.350
Ward, Texas	74	282	48	97	15	5	10	50	15	.344
Mattingly, New York	80	318	56	107	21	1	22	87	1	.336
Gedman, Boston	73	248	41	83	16	4	9	51	2	.335
Riles, Milwaukee	60	226	27	75	9	3	2	24	1	.332
Butler, Cleveland	73	289	53	95	12	7	1	25	26	.329
Beniquez, California	70	214	31	70	6	3	6	28	2	.327
Tabler, Cleveland	62	218	33	71	11	0	5	36	0	.326

NATIONAL LEAGUE

Player, Team	G	AB	Run	Hit	2B	3B	HR	RBI	SB	Avg
McGee, St. Louis	72	283	52	101	11	7	3	32	28	.357
Raines, Montreal	79	280	62	97	17	11	4	18	40	.346
Moreland, Chicago	81	300	47	102	16	2	11	63	6	.340
Durham, Chicago	75	257	36	85	21	1	15	50	6	.331
Gwynn, San Diego	80	316	50	103	14	4	3	23	8	.326
Herr, St. Louis	79	277	41	87	21	2	4	55	17	.314
Guerrero, Los Angeles	74	257	50	80	9	0	14	41	9	.311
J. Cruz, Houston	67	255	31	79	15	2	1	35	8	.310
Parker, Cincinnati	80	312	45	96	21	1	16	65	1	.308
Smith, St. Louis	80	258	41	79	14	2	2	26	16	.306

LEADING HITTERS ON NATURAL GRASS
(Minimum 100 At-Bats)

AMERICAN LEAGUE

Player, Team	G	AB	Run	Hit	2B	3B	HR	RBI	SB	Avg
Boggs, Boston	135	545	89	198	33	2	7	67	2	.363
Mattingly, New York	135	548	92	180	40	2	29	126	2	.328
Tolleson, Texas	102	275	41	89	8	4	1	17	19	.324
Beniquez, California	109	342	46	110	13	5	7	38	3	.322
Hassey, New York	77	225	29	72	14	1	13	39	0	.320
Bradley, Seattle	59	244	41	78	11	3	9	37	9	.320
Baines, Chicago	138	554	79	177	28	3	18	99	1	.319
Henderson, New York	119	456	130	144	25	4	21	60	74	.316
Gibson, Detroit	129	487	86	152	33	4	26	82	27	.312
Bochte, Oakland	114	350	38	108	17	1	11	49	3	.309

NATIONAL LEAGUE

Player, Team	G	AB	Run	Hit	2B	3B	HR	RBI	SB	Avg
Clark, St. Louis	34	120	28	47	4	2	9	35	1	.392
Thompson, Pittsburgh	33	106	8	37	6	0	3	17	0	.349
McGee, St. Louis	42	171	32	58	10	4	3	23	12	.339
Doran, Houston	47	183	35	60	7	1	6	24	12	.328
Gwynn, San Diego	114	462	68	149	21	4	5	33	12	.323
Bosley, Chicago	80	130	18	42	5	1	6	20	3	.323
Scioscia, Los Angeles	105	313	35	101	19	2	6	40	2	.323
Moreland, Chicago	114	412	56	132	20	2	12	75	7	.320
Walling, Houston	36	103	14	33	4	0	4	19	1	.320
Sandberg, Chicago	107	427	86	136	25	5	23	61	36	.319

LEADING HITTERS ON THE ROAD
(Minimum 200 At-Bats)

AMERICAN LEAGUE

Player, Team	G	AB	Run	Hit	2B	3B	HR	RBI	SB	Avg
Baines, Chicago	80	325	46	109	13	2	9	53	0	.335
Boggs, Boston	81	342	47	110	18	1	2	47	1	.322
Henderson, New York	75	301	71	97	16	4	16	50	43	.322
Mattingly, New York	79	334	51	104	27	2	13	58	1	.311
Cooper, Milwaukee	77	322	44	97	20	4	10	47	8	.301
Hill, Oakland	61	203	28	61	7	0	3	30	3	.300
Buckner, Boston	82	345	43	103	24	1	10	58	11	.299
Murray, Baltimore	75	292	51	87	18	1	16	61	3	.298
Davis, Oakland	80	301	54	89	19	0	12	43	15	.296
Butler, Cleveland	79	302	53	89	16	7	4	25	21	.295

NATIONAL LEAGUE

Player, Team	G	AB	Run	Hit	2B	3B	HR	RBI	SB	Avg
McGee, St. Louis	80	329	62	115	15	11	7	50	28	.350
Clark, St. Louis	62	217	44	72	12	2	14	53	1	.332
Hernandez, New York	80	308	48	102	22	3	6	47	1	.331
Guerrero, Los Angeles	63	230	49	76	13	2	19	46	3	.330
Sax, Los Angeles	67	249	35	82	4	4	0	26	11	.329
Parker, Cincinnati	80	323	43	102	21	3	18	60	4	.316
Sandberg, Chicago	79	316	46	97	14	3	9	42	25	.307
Gwynn, San Diego	74	306	40	94	15	1	3	23	6	.307
Murphy, Atlanta	81	308	55	93	17	1	17	52	5	.302
Carter, New York	74	292	48	86	8	1	20	58	1	.295
Raines, Montreal	71	295	53	87	13	2	7	23	30	.295
Scioscia, Los Angeles	71	227	28	67	15	3	6	26	2	.295

LEADING HITTERS ON ARTIFICIAL TURF
(Minimum 70 At-Bats)

AMERICAN LEAGUE

Player, Team	G	AB	Run	Hit	2B	3B	HR	RBI	SB	Avg
Boggs, Boston	26	108	18	42	9	1	1	11	0	.389
Jacoby, Cleveland	24	91	17	34	4	0	4	13	1	.374
Hill, Oakland	24	79	12	28	5	0	3	14	0	.354
Brett, Kansas City	98	344	70	121	28	4	15	75	7	.352
Butler, Cleveland	24	97	18	33	6	3	0	4	7	.340
Mulliniks, Toronto	73	198	34	63	16	1	5	28	1	.318
Downing, California	27	101	12	32	4	1	3	17	1	.317
Randolph, New York	24	83	13	26	2	1	0	5	2	.313
Murray, Baltimore	20	77	15	24	3	1	4	17	0	.312
Henderson, New York	24	91	16	28	3	1	3	12	6	.308

NATIONAL LEAGUE

Player, Team	G	AB	Run	Hit	2B	3B	HR	RBI	SB	Avg
Hernandez, New York	48	187	27	68	14	2	3	28	0	.364
Guerrero, Los Angeles	38	145	37	52	10	2	16	34	3	.359
Perez, Cincinnati	52	123	19	44	7	0	4	29	0	.358
Sax, Los Angeles	36	138	16	46	3	3	0	13	2	.333
Raines, Montreal	111	414	84	135	22	12	6	23	61	.326
Oester, Cincinnati	109	375	44	121	21	3	0	20	4	.323
Orsulak, Pittsburgh	92	304	45	98	9	6	0	19	19	.322
Brown, Pittsburgh	59	202	28	65	19	2	3	29	2	.322
Parker, Cincinnati	112	442	64	140	31	4	22	94	2	.317
Lopes, Chicago	32	95	17	30	2	0	3	13	15	.316

335

LEADING HITTERS AGAINST
RIGHT-HANDED PITCHING
(Minimum 200 At Bats)

AMERICAN LEAGUE

Player, Team	AB	Run	Hit	2B	3B	HR	RBI	SB	Avg
Boggs, Boston	440	84	166	30	2	6	50	2	.377
Mattingly, New York	388	65	135	28	3	17	78	1	.348
Brett, Kansas City	360	78	121	28	4	20	73	8	.336
Tolleson, Texas	234	36	78	4	3	1	12	14	.333
Hassey, New York	219	31	71	15	1	13	41	0	.324
Gedman, Boston	363	51	114	24	4	16	51	1	.314
Gibson, Detroit	411	68	129	28	3	22	68	24	.314
Bradley, Seattle	463	66	145	26	6	17	64	17	.313
Riles, Milwaukee	302	38	94	10	4	5	34	2	.311
Oglivie, Milwaukee	268	33	83	12	1	8	48	0	.310

NATIONAL LEAGUE

Player, Team	AB	Hit	HR	RBI	Avg
McGee, St. Louis	402	143	3	48	.356
Parker, Cincinnati	434	142	27	86	.327
Sandberg, Chicago	451	144	21	70	.319
Herr, St. Louis	383	120	5	82	.313
J. Cruz, Houston	323	101	4	35	.313
Moreland, Chicago	457	141	12	88	.309
Sax, Los Angeles	348	107	0	30	.307
Scioscia, Los Angeles	342	105	6	44	.307
C. Brown, San Francisco	324	95	11	52	.293
Mumphrey, Houston	311	91	8	48	.293

NOTE: The Montreal Expos and the San Diego Padres did not send us the Right/Left breakdowns in time for players on those two teams to be included in this chart.

LEADING HITTERS AGAINST
LEFT-HANDED PITCHING
(Minimum 100 At Bats)

AMERICAN LEAGUE

Player, Team	AB	Run	Hit	2B	3B	HR	RBI	SB	Avg
Henderson, New York	181	58	65	13	2	12	25	27	.359
Presley, Seattle	151	25	54	10	1	8	26	0	.358
Puckett, Minnesota	220	27	78	11	7	4	34	5	.355
Beniquez, California	169	31	60	6	4	6	20	1	.355
Boggs, Boston	213	23	74	12	1	2	28	0	.347
Armas, Boston	140	23	47	9	3	9	23	0	.336
Baines, Chicago	220	29	74	7	1	6	29	0	.336
Brett, Kansas City	190	30	63	10	1	10	30	1	.332
Butler, Cleveland	187	34	62	7	4	1	16	12	.332
Gantner, Milwaukee	164	28	54	5	1	0	15	2	.329

NATIONAL LEAGUE

Player, Team	AB	Hit	HR	RBI	Avg
McGee, St. Louis	210	73	7	34	.348
Brown, Pittsburgh	135	47	5	28	.348
Perez, Cincinnati	124	42	6	25	.339
Murphy, Atlanta	182	61	10	31	.335
Clark, St. Louis	142	47	9	33	.331
Cedeno, St. Louis	140	44	5	26	.314
Bass, Houston	219	68	10	32	.311
Guerrero, Los Angeles	138	42	9	22	.304
O. Smith, St. Louis	162	49	6	20	.302
Moreland, Chicago	130	39	2	18	.300

NOTE: The Montreal Expos and the San Diego Padres did not send us the Right/Left breakdowns in time for players on those two teams to be included in this chart.

A GLOSSARY OF TERMS IN USE IN SABERMETRICS

Adjusted Range Factor

The number of plays made by a player per estimated nine innings of defensive play.

Approximate Value

A crude integer estimate of the value of a given season, ranging from 0 for ineffective, part-time play up to an average of 9 or 10 for a regular player, 16 to 20 for an MVP-type season.

Award Share

The total MVP Award vote drawn by a player over the course of his career, stated in constant terms with 1.00 representing the potential vote for one season. (Award Shares could also be calculated for a few other awards, such as the Cy Young.)

Base-Out Percentage

A method developed by Barry Codell for the evaluation of offensive statistics; quite similar to total average.

Brock6 System

A complex set of several hundred interlocking formulas, designed to project a player's final career totals on the basis of his performance up to a given point in time. An earlier form was Brock2.

Career Value

The value of a player to his team over the course of his entire career.

Defensive Efficiency Record

A mathematical attempt to answer this question: Of all balls put into play against this team, what percentage did the defense succeed in turning into outs?

Defensive Spectrum

An arrangement of defensive positions according to raw abilities needed to learn to play each. The spectrum has shifted at times throughout history, but generally reads "designated hitter, first base, left field, right field, third base, center field, second base, shortstop." Catcher is not a part of the spectrum.

Defensive Winning Percentage

A technique of evaluation of defensive statistics by a series of charts, resulting in a two-digit percentage estimate. An average defensive player should have a defensive winning percentage of .50.

Estimated Runs Produced

A method developed by Paul Johnson to estimate the number of runs resulting from any combination of offensive incidents. Closely parallels runs created.

Expected Remaining Future Value

Also called "Trade Value."

The Favorite Toy

A method used to estimate the chance that a player, at a given point in his career, will reach some standard of career excellence (such as 3000 hits, 500 home runs).

Hall of Fame Assessment System

A method used to evaluate whether a player is doing or has done the things which characterize Hall of Famers.

Isadora

One of Bill and Susie's dogs.

Isolated Power

The difference between batting average and slugging percentage.

Johnson Effect

The tendency of teams which exceed their Pythagorean projection for wins in one season to relapse in the following season. Parallel effects have also been established for the tendency of teams which violate the normal relationship between offensive incidents and runs resulting; these are also sometimes referred to as Johnson Effects.

Linear Weights

A common mathematical tool used to derive the value of each element within a data set, and thus produce formulas that can combine those values. Commonly used by Pete Palmer in analyzing baseball.

Major League Equivalency

The major league performance that is equivalent to a given performance in the minor leagues.

Offensive Earned Run Average

A method developed by Thomas Cover to estimate the number of earned runs created by each player per 27 outs.

Offensive Losses

An estimate of the number of team losses that would result from a player's offensive production.

Offensive Winning Percentage

A mathematical answer to this question: If every player on a team hit the same way that this player hits, and the team allowed an average number of runs to score, what would the team's winning percentage be?

Offensive Wins

An estimate of the number of team wins that would result from a player's offensive production.

On Base Percentage

If you don't know what on base percentage is you shouldn't be reading this book.

Overall Winning Percentage

A combination of offensive and defensive winning percentages.

Palmer Method

The collective analytical procedures developed by Pete Palmer.

Park Adjustment

Any of a number of methods used to adjust offensive or defensive statistics for park illusions.

Park Illusion

The distortion of offensive or defensive abilities as reflected in statistics due to the characteristics of a given park.

Peak Value

The value of a player to his team at his highest clearly established level of performance.

Project Scoresheet

A volunteer effort currently in progress to make scoresheets of all major league games available to the public.

Pythagorean Method

The practical application of the Pythagorean theory to derive conclusions or state relationships.

Pythagorean Theory

The name given to a known property of any baseball team, that being that the ratio between their wins and their losses will be similar to the relationship between the square of their runs scored and the square of their runs allowed.

Quality Starts

The number of starts in which a pitcher pitches six innings or more and gives up three runs or less.

Range Factor

The average number of plays per game successfully made by a fielder (that is, total chances per game minus errors per game).

RBI Importance

That portion of a player's runs batted which are counted as victory-important.

RBI Value

A method of assessing the value of each run batted in, developed by Tim Mulligan.

Reservoir Estimation Technique

The process of comparing a team's talent resources by figuring the "trade value" of all players on the roster.

Runs Created

An estimate of the number of team runs that would result from a player's offensive statistics; can be derived by any of a number of formulas.

Sabermetrics

The search for objective knowledge about baseball.

SABR

The Society For American Baseball Research.

Secondary Average

The sum of a player's extra bases on hits, walks and stolen bases, expressed as a percentage of at bats.

Signature Significance

The existence, rare but occasionally seen, of significant evidence about the ability of a player that can be seen in a very small sample of his work.

Similarity Scores

A method used for evaluating the "degree of resemblance" between two players or two teams.

Stokely

Bill and Susie's other dog.

Total Average

A method developed by Thomas Boswell for the evaluation of offensive statistics.

Trade Value

An estimate of the approximate value that a player will have in the rest of his career.

Victory-Important RBI (VI-RBI)

An attempt to measure the number of a player's runs batted in which are contributions to eventual victory.

APPENDIX

APPROXIMATE VALUE AND THE VALUE APPROXIMATION METHOD

The Value Approximation Method has 13 rules for non-pitchers, 5 rules for pitchers. These are:

NON-PITCHERS:

1) Award 1 point if the player has played at least 10 games, 2 if 50 games, 3 if 100 games, 4 if 130 games or more.

2) Award 1 point if the player has hit .250 or better, 2 if .275, 3 if .300 . . . 7 if .400 or better.

3) Award 1 point if the player's slugging percentage is above .300, 2 if above .400 . . . 6 if above .800.

4) Award 1 point if the player has a home run percentage (home runs divided by at bats) of 2.5 or more, two if 5.0 or more, three if 7.5 or more, 4 if 10.0 or more.

5) Award 1 point if the player walks one time for each 10 official at bats, 2 if twice for each 10 at bats, 3 if three times for each ten at bats.

6) Award 1 point if the player steals 20 bases, 2 if 50 bases, 3 if 80 bases.

7) Award 1 point if the player drives in 70 runs while slugging less than .400, 1 point if he drives in 100 runs while slugging less than .500, or 1 if he drives in 130 while slugging less than .600.

8) Award 1 point if the player's primary defensive position (the position at which he plays the most games) is second base, third base or center field, 2 if it is shortstop. For catchers, award 1 point if the player catches 10 games, 2 if he catches 80, 3 if he catches 150.

9) Award 1 point if the player's range factor is above the league average at his position. Catchers and first basemen have no range factors; first basemen get 1 point if they have 100 assists.

10) Award 1 point if the player's fielding average is above the league average at his position.

On rules nine and ten, if you are figuring a player over the course of his career, you will probably want to establish period norms for fielding average and range at the position, rather than trying to figure the league average for each season separately.

11) Award 1 point to a shortstop or second baseman who participates in 90 or more double plays, 2 for 120 or more, 3 for 150

or more. Award 1 point to an outfielder who has 12 or more assists plus double plays. Award 1 to a catcher who is better than the league average in opposition stolen bases per game.

12) Award 1 point if the player has 200 hits. Award 1 point if the player leads the league in RBI.

13) Reduce all points awarded on rules one through twelve for players who have less than 500 at bats and less than 550 plate appearances. Reduce by at bats divided by 500 or plate appearances divided by 550, whichever is better for the player.

PITCHERS:

1) Award 1 point if the pitcher has pitched in 30 or more games, 2 if 55 or more, 3 if 80 or more.

2) Award 1 point if the pitcher has pitched 40 innings, 2 if 90 innings, 3 if 140 innings . . . 7 if 340 innings.

3) Figure for the pitcher his total of 2 (wins + saves) minus losses. Award 1 point if the pitcher's total is 6 or more, 2 if 14 or more, 3 if 24 or more, 4 if 36 or more, 5 if 50 or more, 6 if 66 or more, and 7 if 84 or more.

4) Award 1 point if the pitcher has won 18 or more games. Award 1 point if the pitcher led the league in ERA. Award one point if the pitcher led the league in saves.

5) Establish a mark 1.00 run above the league ERA. Subtract the pitcher's ERA from this, and multiply that by the number of decisions that the pitcher has had. Divide by 13. (What you are doing here is giving credit for a low ERA. If the pitcher's ERA is more than a run above the league average, this will result in a negative figure, a subtraction. A pitcher's approximate value can be reduced by this factor, but no player's approximate value can be reduced below zero.)

The outcome of this point-count system is called approximate value.

BROCK2 SYSTEM

A full account of the Brock2 system can be found on pages 301–305 of the 1985 *Baseball Abstract*.

DEFENSIVE EFFICIENCY RECORD

A Defensive Efficiency Record is a *team* statistic, intended to estimate the percentage of all balls in play that a team has turned into outs.

To figure DER, you begin by making two estimates of the number of times that a team's defense has turned a batted ball into an out. The first is:

$$PO - K - DP - 2(TP) - OCS - A \text{ (of)}$$

This assumes that a batted ball has been turned into an out every time a putout is recorded unless (1) the putout was a strikeout, (2) two or three putouts were recorded on the same play, or (3) a runner has been thrown out on the bases. OCS is opponents caught stealing, and A (of) is outfielder's assists, both of which can be found on the division sheets.

The second estimate is:

$$TBF - K - H - W - HBP - .71 \text{ Errors}$$

This assumes that every batter facing the team's pitchers has been put out by the fielders unless 1) he strikes out, 2) he gets a hit, 3) he walks, 4) he is hit by the pitch, or 5) he reaches base on an error.

These two estimates will almost always be within 1% of one another, usually within one-half or one percent. You then take the average of the two, which is called Plays Made (PM).

DER is Plays Made divided by Plays Made Plus Plays NOT Made:

$$\frac{PM}{PM + H - HR + .71 \text{ Errors}}$$

An average defensive efficiency record is about .695. Almost all successful teams will be above average.

DEFENSIVE WINNING PERCENTAGE

The exact method for deriving a defensive winning percentage is explained in the appendix to the 1983 and 1984 *Baseball Abstracts*. It has not been changed.

EXPECTED REMAINING APPROXIMATE VALUE

Also known as

TRADE VALUE

Trade Value is used to assess the size of a team's talent pool, by comparing the "apparent futures" that a team has (see Minnesota comment).

The formula for this has two stages. First of all, you find the player's "Y Score" by the formula $24 - .6$ (Age):

$$Y = 24 - .6 \text{ (Age)}$$

The Y score and the player's approximate value are then put together by the following formula:

$$(AV - Y) \times \frac{(Y + 1) \times AV}{190} + \frac{AV \, (Y)}{13}$$

This formula was rendered incoherent in the 1984 edition of the book due to a production error; I apologize for that. Let's work through this a sample player—say, a 24-year-old player with an approximate value of 9.

The player's Y score would be:

$$24 - .6 \, (24)$$

or 9.6. His trade value would then be:

$$(9.6 - 9) \times \frac{(9.6 + 1) \times 9}{190} + \frac{9 \, (9.6)}{13}$$

Which would be:

$$(.6) \times \frac{(10.6) \times 9}{190} + \frac{9 \, (92.16)}{13}$$

Which would be:

$$.36 \times \frac{(95.4)}{190} + \frac{(829.44)}{13}$$

Which would be:

$$.36 \times .502 + 63.8$$

Which would be 64.

If the player was a pitcher we would reduce that by 30%, to 45. This formula makes more sense than you can see right off the top of your head. Basically the right end of it carries most of the freight, and increases the player's trade value proportional to his youth—his Y score—and his current value. The first two parts of the equation are sort of for special situations when you have an unusual player, such as a 37-year-old player with an approximate value of 14 or something. The closer together the player's AV and Y score are, the less the first two parts of the equation yield; as they move apart, the first part of the equation becomes more meaningful.

THE FAVORITE TOY

The Favorite Toy is a method that is used to estimate a player's chance of getting to a specific goal—let us say, 3000 hits.

Four things are considered in this matter. Those are:

1) The Need Hits—the number of hits needed to reach the goal. (This, of course, could also be "Need Home Runs" or "Need Doubles"—whatever.)

2) The Years Remaining. The number of years remaining to reach the goal is estimated by the formula $24 - .6(age)$. This formula assigns a 20-year-old player 12.0 remaining seasons, a 25-year-old player 9.0 remaining seasons, a 30-year-old player 6.0 remaining seasons, and a 35-year-old player 3.0 remaining seasons. Any player who is still playing regularly is assumed to have at least 1.5 seasons remaining, regardless of his age.

3) The Established Hit Level. For 1984, the established hit level would be found by adding 1982 hits, two times 1983 hits, and three times 1984 hits, and dividing by six. However, a player cannot have an established performance level that is less than ¾ of his most recent performance—that is, a player who had 200 hits in 1984 cannot have an established hit level below 150.00.

4) The Projected Remaining Hits. This is found by multiplying the second number, the years remaining, by the third, the established hit level.

Once you get the projected remaining hits, the chance of getting to the goal is figured by:

$$\frac{\text{Projected Remaining Hits} - .5 \text{ (Need Hits)}}{\text{Need Hits}}$$

By this method, if your "need hits" and your "projected remaining hits" are the same, your chance of reaching the goal is 50%.

Two special rules:

1) A player's chances of continuing to progress toward a goal cannot exceed .97 per year. (This rule prevents a player from figuring to have a 148% chance of reaching a goal.)

2) If a player's offensive winning percentage is below .500, his chance of reaching the goal cannot exceed .75 per season. (That is, if a below-average hitter is two years away from reaching a goal, his chance of reaching that goal cannot be shown as better than 9/16 (three-fourths times three-fourths) regardless of his age.)

I hate to confess this, but I must. I had carried this explanation in the appendix with the elements of the numerator reversed for several years before a high school student called it to my attention last summer. That is, I had been running it Need Hits − .5 (Projected Remaining Hits), rather than the other way around. I was amazed, and obviously embarrassed; the only thing I can say is that this particular method is so ingrained in me that the words that are used to explain it don't mean much to me; I don't think of it that way. I apologize to anyone who has been confused by this error.

RUNS CREATED

There are three forms of the runs created formula. All three have an A factor, a B factor, and a C factor; in all cases the formula is assembled by (A times B) divided by C. These are the three versions:

1. Basic Runs Created

  A   Hits Plus Walks
      (H + W)
  B   Total Bases
      (TB)
  C   At Bats Plus Walks
      (AB + W)

2. Stolen Base Version

  A   Hits Plus Walks Minus Caught Stealing
      (H + W − CS)
  B   Total Bases Plus (.55 times Stolen Bases)
      (TB + .55 SB)
  C   At Bats Plus Walks
      (AB + W)

3. Technical Version

  A   Hits Plus Walks and Hit Batsmen Minus Caught Stealing and Grounded Into Double Plays
      (H + W + HBP − CS − GIDP)
  B   Total Bases Plus .26 Times Hit Batsmen and Unintentional Walks Plus .52 Times Sacrifice Hits, Sacrifice Flies, And Stolen Bases
      (TB + .26 (TBB − IBB + HBP) + .52 (SH + SF + SB))
  C   At Bats Plus Walks Plus Hit Batsmen Plus Sacrifice Hits Plus Sacrifice Flies
      (AB + TBB + HBP + SH + SF)

OFFENSIVE WINNING PERCENTAGE

To figure a player's offensive winning percentage, start with three things: his runs created, the number of outs that he has made (at bats minus hits, plus sacrifice hits and flies, caught stealing and grounded into double plays), and the number of runs per game scored and allowed by his team (if his team has scored 750 runs and allowed 600 runs in 150 games, that would be 1,350/300, or 4.50 runs per team game).

Figure the number of runs the player has created per 27 outs (let's say that in this case it is 5.00). Divide this by the offensive context, the runs scored and allowed per game by his team (4.50; 5.00 divided by 4.50 would be 1.1111).

Square this figure to obtain the Pythagorean relationship (1.1111 squared is 1.2345). Divide this figure by itself plus one to obtain the offensive winning percentage. (The Pythagorean relationship would be 1.2345 − 1, so the offensive winning percentage would be 1.2345/2.2345, which would be .556).

VICTORY-IMPORTANT RBI

VI-RBI are an attempt to measure the extent to which a player's Runs Batted In are contributions to victory. Only runs batted in in wins are counted as victory-important. The importance of each RBI in a victory is measured by:

$$\frac{\text{Opposition Runs} + 1.00}{\text{Runs Scored}}$$

That is, if the team wins by one run (4–3, 7–6, 1–0), then each RBI is essential to the win, and each RBI has an "RBI importance" of 1.00. But if you win 10–3, then the importance of each RBI is only .40:

$$\frac{3 + 1}{10} = .40$$

And if the team wins 16–1, then the importance of each RBI is only .125:

$$\frac{1 + 1}{16} = .125$$

Victory-Important RBI are an attempt to mitigate a blind spot in the records. There is no suggestion that they provide a clear view of the subject.